The Raiders
Encyclopedia

The Raiders Encyclopedia

*All Players, Coaches, Games
and More through 2009–2010*

RICHARD J. SHMELTER

McFarland & Company, Inc., Publishers
Jefferson, North Carolina, and London

LIBRARY OF CONGRESS CATALOGUING-IN-PUBLICATION DATA

Shmelter, Richard J., 1959–
The Raiders encyclopedia : all players, coaches, games and more through
2009-2010 / Richard J. Shmelter.
p. cm.
Includes bibliographical references and index.

ISBN 978-0-7864-4834-0
softcover : 50# alkaline paper ∞

1. Los Angeles Raiders (Football team)— History — Encyclopedias.
I. Title.
GV956.L59S46 2011   796.332'640979466 — dc22   2010054419

BRITISH LIBRARY CATALOGUING DATA ARE AVAILABLE

On the cover: Oakland Raiders quarterback Ken Stabler (12) hands off
the ball in Super Bowl XI in Pasadena, California, on January 9, 1977
(Associated Press); (inset) Al Davis, owner, general manager and former
head coach of the Raiders

Manufactured in the United States of America

*McFarland & Company, Inc., Publishers
Box 611, Jefferson, North Carolina 28640
www.mcfarlandpub.com*

To every player and coach who had the great honor of taking the field as a Raider.

To every Raiderette, "Football's Fabulous Females," who cheered for the team through their years in both Oakland and Los Angeles.

To Raiders fans all over the world who have shared in all the trials and tribulations.

And as always, to my little angel, who watches over me from above. You allowed me the greatest honor in being called a daddy.

ACKNOWLEDGMENTS

In preparing a project of this magnitude, there are many people who touch you, some in significant ways, and others with just a kind or encouraging word and helpful advice. In whatever way an individual participated while I was working on this book, I say thank you, one and all. Your input was greatly appreciated and will never be forgotten.

To my wife Helen (Molly). Despite your being a die-hard Cleveland sports fanatic, I am, as usual, extremely grateful for all the time and energy you put forth to work your magic in helping me make this something I can be proud of.

To my parents, Arlene and the late Joseph, who always allowed me to dream.

To John Mitchell, a former editor who told me to have fun with writing. Your advice proved to be priceless, and for that I thank you, my friend.

To Chad Reese of the Pro Football Hall of Fame, who provided incredible assistance to me at the beginning of this project.

To Kevin O'Sullivan of the Associated Press, who came through in a swift, professional manner when supplying photographs.

To the people who run the Pro Football Reference website. This site proved invaluable to whatever a researcher/writer needs, and is truly the best of the best.

To the many people at Cleveland Electric Labs who encourage me on a daily basis, with special thanks going to the following: Matt Victor, who, like my wife, is a die-hard Cleveland fan. However, he still took the time to encourage me and taught me how to work smarter and not harder on this project. Bob Martin, an honorary Raiders fan at heart, who took the time to proofread portions of this project. Don Lieske, whose devotion for the Cleveland Browns never got in the way of his taking the time to listen to my ideas despite our friendly battles over each other's team affiliations. And to John "Pappy" Shoby, whose love of the Pittsburgh Steelers still allowed him to be my sounding board. And remember, Pappy, dinner will still be my treat at Gladstone's in Malibu.

To Jessica Fejes, Meghan Fowler, Patty O'Connell, and Vicky Salsbury, for their continued assistance in enlightening our fellow co-workers about the greatness that is the Raiders.

TABLE OF CONTENTS

Acknowledgments — vi

Preface — 1

Introduction: The Founding of the Team — 3

Part I. The Games

Season-by-Season Reviews — 5

Part II. The Team

All-Time Roster — 205

All-Time Head Coaches — 227

All-Time Schedules and Results — 250

All-Time Draft Picks — 261

Individual Records — 266

Awards and Honors — 269

Part III. Bad Boys, Legends, and Raiders Vignettes

Players of Yore — 273

Executives, Stadiums, Uniforms, Cheerleaders, Nicknames — 303

Notes — 311

Bibliography — 319

Index — 321

PREFACE

The Oakland Raiders have been called misfits, mavericks, renegades, and, above all, champions. This juggernaut, donning the silver and black, blazed a path of destruction through virtually every gridiron cathedral they invaded. Along the way, these marauders earned a lasting legacy as one of the most successful professional sports franchises for more than half of their existence.

This proud organization has achieved countless milestones for more than fifty years, played in some of the greatest games, and had some of the best and most colorful athletes wear its colors. Amidst all the accolades bestowed upon this incredible franchise, one presence stands tall, patriarch Al Davis. Davis made the team a winner, first as a coach and later as majority owner. He took control of a doomed franchise on the verge of collapse in 1963, and immediately instilled the mantra "Commitment to Excellence," which will forever permeate throughout the Raiders organization and its rabid legion of fans around the world.

Al Davis also unleashed what he termed "Raider Mystique" on the pro football world, and it left countless opponents battered and forlorn. The philosophy behind the mystique was based on power and intimidation, with emphasis on relentless assault on both sides of the ball. Davis also coined the term "Pride and Poise" which constitutes a belief in what you're doing, and doing it with total control and confidence.

Words can motivate individuals, but backing them up with action is another beast altogether. However, Davis not only got his teams to believe in his statements, but also to follow through on them as well. In the process, Davis quickly turned a dismal team into one of the greatest professional sports organizations in history. No other team so dominated the violent confines of the professional gridiron circuit on such a consistent basis, like the Silver & Black did from 1963 to 2002.

Davis also had a keen eye for talent, regardless of a player's reputation. If someone could play, Davis brought him into the silver and black fold and allowed him the opportunity to reinvent himself. Most of these athletes were cast-offs from other teams who became burdens on their previous employers. However, with the Raiders, these misfits found a home and a new lease on their football careers. In no time, with an "us against the world" mentality, many rose to the summit of their profession, giving everything they had to the man who believed in them when others did not.

Throughout the decades, the Raiders employed men with colorful pseudonyms such as Mad Bomber, Snake, Kick 'Em, Tooz, Assassin, Killer, Dr. Death, and Hit Man. These unique individuals, along with their fellow renegades, inflicted mental and physical abuse on opponents from coast to coast on a ruthless quest for supremacy. They also performed in some of the greatest games such as the Heidi Game, Sea of Hands, Ghost-to-the-Post, Holy Roller, and three convincing Super Bowl victories. As a lasting tribute to those championships, these men helped earn the organization lasting immortality in the form of three Vince Lombardi trophies, symbolic proof of a world champion. Those trophies shine like beacons into magnificent moments captured forever in a sterling silver statue 20 inches high and seven pounds in weight, and serve as the holy grail in the world of controlled violence that is professional football, and are true testaments to the Raiders long-standing "Commitment to Excellence."

Hall of Fame coach John Madden led the Raiders to 100 victories in ten seasons from 1969 to 1978. While serving as mentor to this collection of marauders, he had only three simple rules. Show up on time, pay attention, and play like hell on game days. In regard to the latter, this wrecking machine clad in silver and black uniforms showed no mercy and took no prisoners on a path of destruction that would have made even Lucifer himself cower.

As proof of utter domination, this great franchise has produced 33 seasons at .500 or better, 17 divisional titles, 21 playoff seasons, 43 post-season games, 14 conference title games, an AFL championship, and four AFC titles. The Raiders are the only team in history to appear in the Super Bowl in four different decades.

Part I is a season-by-season review, covering each game and player from every campaign. Part II includes a complete all-time roster with vital information on every player who had the ultimate privilege to don the silver and black from the dawn of the 1960s through the first decade of the millennium. The head coaches then get their moment in the spotlight with a section detailing the lives of the mentors who guided the team from the sidelines. The next sections include schedules, all-time draft picks, individual records, and awards and honors. The book then moves on to Part III, which looks at the heroes, bad boys, and players of yore that made this incredible team both glorious and infamous. Raiders vignettes feature other integral people, including "Football's Fabulous Females," the Oakland Raiderettes cheerleading squad, and team executives that helped lead the team from behind the scenes. It also details the uniforms through the years; the various nicknames associated with the teams; and the stadiums that the Raiders called home over the decades.

As Al Davis stood on a podium following the Raiders Super Bowl XVIII blowout victory over the Washington Redskins on

January 22, 1984, the maverick owner looked at his players, flashed the smile of a champion, and said, "Just win, baby." Those words are forever remembered and linked to this incredible moment in time. I now convey those words to Raider Nation, and believe that this comprehensive encyclopedia dedicated to the greatness that is the Silver & Black will "just win" with all those who read it. I hope you enjoy my labor of love as much as I enjoyed writing it. LONG LIVE THE SILVER & BLACK!!!

INTRODUCTION:
THE FOUNDING OF THE TEAM

For forty seasons of their fifty-year existence, the silver and black-clad menace known as the Raiders cast an ominous aura across the pro football landscape. Their mere presence instilled both fear and respect, and they left many opponents crawling away demoralized and defeated in their wake. Their throne resided on the summit of the gridiron world multiple times, and the Raiders legacy filled with rogue warriors will forever be revered throughout the history of professional football.

The Raiders were indeed the bullies of the street. However, in the beginning, they could best be compared to unwanted urchins selected last for a neighborhood pickup game only to even out the sides. And when the game was through, they were the ones crawling away filled with despair, but dreaming of one day rising up through hard work and perseverance to conquer all detractors to become the ultimate alpha dog.

The concept that eventually led to the existence of the Oakland Raiders originated in Chicago, circa 1959, and involved two young men from extremely wealthy Texas oil families. Lamar Hunt and Bud Adams were interested in purchasing an NFL franchise. They heard that the Chicago Cardinals were for sale and looking to relocate.[1] The Cardinals were one of the original teams from the NFL's first season in 1920, and were a part of the Windy City's sports culture for twenty years prior to that. Despite their deep roots in Chicago, they always played second fiddle to the Second City's much-beloved Chicago Bears.

Lamar Hunt inquired about purchasing the Cardinals then moving them to his native Texas to give the football-ravenous people of Dallas a pro team to follow. At the same time, another Texan, Bud Adams, in addition to Bob Howsam and Max Winter, were also expressing interest. After all parties were denied the chance to gain controlling interest in the floundering Cardinals, Hunt took it upon himself to remain steadfast in the quest to own a piece of the gridiron world.[2]

Hunt, Adams, and Howsam next took their case to the top of the National Football League, Commissioner Bert Bell. Their mission was to convince the gridiron czar to add expansion franchises to the 12-team league. Pro football was just beginning to capture the public's attention from coast to coast, thanks to the medium of television. With both forms of entertainment merging into such a successful union, it seemed like an excellent time to expand the league. Unfortunately, Mr. Bell did not embrace the concept, and declined the young millionaires' proposal. Hunt,

still undaunted even though it appeared his options with the NFL were eradicated, decided on another path toward pro football ownership.[3]

Once back in his native Lone Star State, Hunt contacted Bud Adams and arranged to have dinner at the latter's Charcoal Inn. Ironically, the dinner conversation never included anything to do with football. Hunt eventually turned to the topic on the way to the airport. It was then that Hunt proposed the idea of starting a new football league. Adams liked the idea, and they agreed to talk more about it in the near future.[4]

Moving ahead five months to August of 1959, Hunt had six other very wealthy colleagues sold on the same idea, and the eight-team American Football League was ready to make its maiden voyage into shaky waters that no other league was able to stay afloat in against the powerful monopoly known as the National Football League. Besides Hunt in Dallas and Adams in Houston, the rest of the owners were from New York, Buffalo, Boston, Denver, Los Angeles, and Minneapolis. They were dubbed "the Foolish Club" by many throughout the pro football community, who felt they were not going to succeed, and would lose a small fortune in the process. Regardless, the league was set to begin in 1960, with Lamar Hunt as president, and World War II Medal of Honor winner and former South Dakota governor Joe Foss as commissioner.[5]

With everything looking to be going full speed ahead, a roadblock was thrown in the new league's path. In November of 1959, Max Winter, the owner of the Minneapolis franchise, was enticed by the NFL to join their established league.[6] It seemed strange that just months after negating any thoughts of expansion, the NFL suddenly embraced the idea when a new league comprised of owners with deep pockets and a lucrative television deal in the works arrived on the scene. Maybe the old guard became a touch leery of the upcoming competition from the young turks after all. Winter's franchise became the Minnesota Vikings and began play in 1961.

Upon hearing of Winter's exodus, the AFL's powers-that-be were faced with a serious dilemma. Left with only seven teams, the league would be unbalanced with four in the Eastern Division and now only three out west. The Eastern Division was represented by cold weather cities, while the Western Division, with the exception of Denver, had the warm climates covered.

With this in mind, the AFL sought a city with tranquil

weather conditions to even out the divisions. Oakland, Atlanta and Miami were brought to the forefront of discussions, with the delegates apparently leaning toward placing a team in the south, which would eliminate Oakland. However, all that changed when Los Angeles Chargers owner Barron Hilton, who was a hotel tycoon, showed his displeasure with the league's proposal of bringing in a team from the south. He was looking to land a team in California to establish a territorial rivalry with his Chargers, and he threatened to pull out of the league if his demand was not met. Unwilling to see another franchise drop out, which would have placed a major strain on the AFL's structure, the other owners decided to go along with Hilton.[7]

Because of Hilton's appeal, the Raiders were born and announced to the world on January 30, 1960. The original ownership group consisted of Robert Osborne, Chet Soda, Charles Harney, Wayne Valley, Harvey Binns, Art Beckett, Ed McGah, and Don Blessing. A deal was struck with the San Francisco Park and Recreation District that said the new team could use either Kezar Stadium or Candlestick Park as their home field.[8]

On February 9, 1960, the owners hired former Navy head coach Eddie Erdelatz to coach the team, and one month later, the AFL conducted a meeting about stocking the Oakland franchise with players. It was decided to make up the first Oakland roster with the 52 players selected by Minneapolis, of which 13 chose to latch on with the team instead of explore other options from the NFL or in Canada. The rest of the roster was supplied by a twelfth man draft that saw the other seven AFL franchises make available a list of their players that Oakland could pick from over the course of five rounds. From this the Oakland entry was able to obtain 35 more players to go to training camp. In a hurry to put together the team, uniforms were rushed to Oakland from the College of the Pacific, and the colors of the new franchise would consist of black and gold.[9]

The *Oakland Tribune* conducted a contest among its readership to name the team, with the winner getting a week's vacation in Acapulco, Mexico. On March 24, 1960, the winner was announced, and with it the team was christened the Oakland Señors in honor of California's strong Spanish heritage. The Señors had a quick and rocky history that ran a whole eight days. The masses of Oakland did not seem taken by the name, and on April 1, the team was renamed the Raiders.[10] The new name gave the team a more rough and tumble sound, with the underlying meaning of invading and devouring the opposition.

On July 10, the Raiders assembled for their first training camp at Santa Cruz High School in Santa Cruz, California, and established headquarters at the nearby Hotel Palomar. The team was then officially unleashed upon the football world in September of 1960, and its impact on the sports world might not have been immediate, but their days of glory would come eventually.

Part I. The Games

SEASON-BY-SEASON REVIEWS

Each season includes a capsule description of each game. A roster of players and individual statistics follow; the bold print in these sections denotes a player who led the league in that category.

1960 Season Review

1. Sept. 11: In the first half of their inaugural regular season game, the Raiders held their own against the powerful Houston Oilers, who went on to win the first AFL championship a few months later. Down 7–0, the Raiders evened the score when rookie quarterback Tom Flores connected with Tony Teresa from 13 yards out for Oakland's first-ever regular season touchdown in front of 13,000 new Raiders fans. The Raiders managed to forge ahead against the elite Oilers after cornerback Ed Macon returned an interception 42 yards to give Oakland a 14–7 lead in the third quarter. Houston quarterback George Blanda was a crafty pro in his eleventh season, and looked to redeem himself after Macon's theft. Throughout the remainder of this contest, Blanda tore the Oakland defense apart with his passes and kicking abilities. The young upstarts from the Bay Area quickly learned from the old master, as Blanda threw four touchdown passes, kicked four conversions, and added a field goal just for good measure in a 37–22 Houston win at Kezar Stadium. Oakland's other touchdown came on a 46-yard pass from Flores to Jack Larscheid.[1]

2. Sept. 16: Just like in their first game, the Raiders played tough throughout the first half only to succumb in the latter stages of the contest. Another opponent from the Lone Star state invaded Kezar Stadium, this time in the likes of the Dallas Texans. After spotting the Texans an early 10–0 lead, Oakland came back to close the gap to 17–10 at the half on a 26-yard pass from Babe Parilli to Tony Teresa, and a 33-yard field goal by Larry Barnes. The second half was a different story. The Texans completely shut the Oakland offense down, victimizing them with five interceptions, and rolled to an easy 34–16 win in front of a scarce crowd of only 8,021. Two Johnny Robinson touchdowns allowed the Texans to expand their lead. The Raiders received their final points with 1:47 remaining in the game on a 12-yard pass from Parilli to J.D. Smith. Despite throwing two of his team's five interceptions,

veteran signal caller Babe Parilli performed admirably by completing 16 out of 28 pass attempts for 174 yards and two touchdowns. Halfback Tony Teresa also had a fine showing despite the mauling. The second-year pro led the team with five receptions for 94 yards and one six-pointer.[2]

3. Sept. 25: Prior to this game, head coach Eddie Erdelatz came down with a case of laryngitis and broke a toe. A more severe incident occurred when assistant coach Ernie Jorge suffered a heart attack just before the team was ready to fly to Houston. Erdelatz gathered the team together and asked that they play hard for Jorge. In response to their coach's plea, the Raiders registered their first-ever regular season win in exciting fashion on a sweltering day by beating the Houston Oilers, 14–13. An Eddie Macon interception was turned into a 3-yard run by J.D. Smith to open the scoring. The Oilers battled back to take a 13–7 lead into the fourth quarter before the Raiders came back to secure the win. Tom Flores showed no signs of rookie jitters as he took the team 52 yards on seven plays to paydirt. He capped the winning drive off with a 14-yard pass to end Gene Prebola to tie the game. Larry Barnes then added the go-ahead conversion kick. The Oilers almost spoiled Oakland's victory party after recovering a fumble on the Raiders' 28 with less than one minute left in the game. With time nearly expired, Houston lined up for a field goal attempt on third down from the Oakland 28-yard line. The ever-reliable George Blanda booted the ball toward the uprights, but the football gods decided to shine on the Raiders this time, as Blanda's kick went wide.[3]

4. Oct. 2: Oakland took the momentum from their first win to Denver, but they left the Mile High City on the short end of a 31–14 beat down. The Raiders seemed to do everything wrong, and the Broncos capitalized on each of their errors, converting two fumbles and two interceptions into touchdowns. Just like in the previous game, J.D. Smith put the Raiders in the lead early with a 1-yard run against the league's top-rated defense. The Broncos then jumped out to a 24–7 halftime lead before Billy Lott scored Oakland's other six-pointer on a 2-yard run in the third quarter.[4]

5. Oct. 9: After trailing 7–0 at the half against Dallas, the Raiders exploded for twenty points in the third quarter to win, 20–19. Dallas scored the first half's only points when Dave Webster snagged a tipped pass from Tom Flores and raced 80 yards to paydirt. During the halftime intermission, Eddie Erdelatz tore into his team for not playing tough. Oakland responded to the tongue lashing right at the start of the second half when James

Smith returned a kickoff 98 yards. Alan Goldstein added touchdown runs from eight and 16 yards to help the Raiders squeak out their second win of the season. The Texans scored with two minutes left in the game, and went for a two-point conversion, but Oakland's defense stopped Bo Dickinson two feet shy of the goal line.[5]

6. Oct. 16: Oakland evened their record at 3–3 with a 27–14 home win over the Boston Patriots. The Raiders jumped out to an early lead when Jack Larscheid broke loose for an 87-yard touchdown run on the game's second play. Tom Flores tossed scoring strikes to Gene Prebola (36 yards) and Al Hoisington (9 yards), and Billy Lott finished Oakland's scoring with a 40-yard run early in the fourth quarter. The Raiders pounded out 225 yards on the ground and forced seven Boston turnovers.[6]

7. Oct. 23: The Raiders looked to extend their winning streak, but the Buffalo Bills had other ideas. Buffalo quarterback Johnny Green dismantled the Oakland defense on four scoring passes in the first half, with three going to Wray Carlton. The Bills added 10 second-half points to their tally, and won their first-ever home game in convincing fashion, 38–9. The Raiders suffered five turnovers in the mud and rain, and this proved to be the team's worst defeat in their early history. Oakland received their lone touchdown on a 1-yard run from J.D. Smith after being down, 21–0, in the second quarter. They added a safety in the fourth quarter to complete the game's scoring.[7]

8. Oct. 28: A trip to the Big Apple provided the Raiders with possibly the best performance of their early existence. On a cold, rainy day at New York's famed Polo Grounds, the Titans had everything go their way throughout most of the game. Led by quarterback Al Dorow and receivers Don Maynard and Art Powell, New York had a 24–14 advantage. Leon Burton also helped pad New York's lead by returning a kickoff 101 yards. The Raiders received their first half points on two Tom Flores scoring strikes to Billy Lott (25 yards), and Al Hoisington (61 yards). In the fourth quarter, Oakland's fortunes took a turn upward when cornerback Eddie Macon intercepted a pass at his own nine-yard line. Veteran quarterback Babe Parilli took over the offensive controls and led the Raiders 91 yards. Rookie James "Jetstream" Smith from Compton Junior College finished the drive off by running three yards into the end zone. After Larry Barnes' conversion, the Raiders trailed, 24–21. A Bill Shockley field goal extended New York's lead to 27–21 with five minutes left to play. It was now up to the Parilli-led Oakland offense to pull out a victory from the jaws of defeat. The old pro decided to place the outcome of this game on his ground attack of Tony Teresa and "Jetstream" Smith. With Teresa sweeping to the outside and Smith pounding the ball between the tackles, the Raiders ate up 62 yards on eight plays. With the ball now resting at the New York nine, Smith got the call, and barreled his way off left tackle across soggy turf and landed in the end zone for the tying score. Larry Barnes added the conversion to send Oakland back to the west coast with a well-earned 28–27 victory earned with a well-balanced offensive attack consisting of 175 rushing yards and 231 through the air.[8]

9. Nov. 4: Led by the passing of Butch Songin and the running of Dick Christy, the Boston Patriots ran up a 34–14 lead on Oakland in the fourth quarter. The Raiders refused to die, and with Tony Teresa adding two late touchdown runs from three

and 20 yards out, Oakland rallied to within six points. Teresa accounted for Oakland's first points as well, with a 1-yard run in the second quarter. Tom Flores added the team's other touchdown with an 8-yard run. However, unlike in the previous game, Oakland's hope of a comeback fell short after a Boston interception killed their momentum and preserved a 34–28 Patriot win.[9]

10. Nov. 13: In a battle of last place teams, the Raiders emerged victorious over the Buffalo Bills, 20–7. After suffering through a 38–9 slaughter at the hands of Buffalo a month earlier, Oakland never let the Bills get in this game. The Bills had the league's top-rated defense despite a 3–6 record, but it was Oakland's defensive unit that rose up on this day. They kept Buffalo pinned between the 30's throughout the game until the later stages when they scored their only points after being down, 20–0. Tony Teresa provided the most excitement by breaking loose for an 83-yard touchdown run on the final play of the third quarter. Teresa finished the game with 141 rushing yards, and became the first Raider to break the century mark for a single game. Billy Lott added a 1-yard scoring run, and Larry Barnes connected on two field goals (20 and 40 yards), to give the Raiders their other points on this day that allowed them to even their record at 5–5.[10]

11. Nov. 27: On the final weekend of November, the Raiders traveled south to Los Angeles to do battle with the Western Division–leading Chargers. This game proved to be no contest, as Los Angeles pounded Oakland, 52–28. The Raiders were outclassed in every category, especially in the rushing department, where they were outgained 232 yards to 92. Leading the ground assault for the Chargers was superstar running back Paul Lowe, who gained 149 yards and scored two touchdowns. The Raiders kept the game interesting in the early stages when a Tom Louderback interception on the Los Angeles 13 led to a J.D. Smith 1-yard run that tied things up at 7–7 in the first quarter. Los Angeles then ran off 31 straight points to put the game out of reach in the third quarter. Tony Teresa caught an 11-yard pass from Tom Flores, and Billy Lott ran for a 4-yard score to close to within 16 points in the fourth. The Chargers added two more six-pointers before Babe Parilli and Doug Asad teamed up for Oakland's final touchdown.[11]

12. Sept. 4: The Chargers enjoyed beating up on the Raiders so much that they did it again seven days later in Oakland's Candlestick Park debut. However, this time the Raiders kept it close for three quarters. They went into the fourth quarter trailing by only three, but Los Angeles then exploded for 27 points to make it a 41–17 final. Quarterback Jack Kemp was the main weapon for Los Angeles. He passed for three touchdowns and ran for two more. The Raiders scored on a Billy Lott 2-yard run, an 11-yard pass from Tom Flores to Charlie Hardy, and on a 25-yard field from Larry Barnes. Despite the loss, Hardy had a great day receiving, with four catches for 123 yards. With this win, the Chargers became the first team to sweep Oakland in a season series. This loss also eliminated Oakland from the divisional race.[12]

13. Dec. 11: The Raiders suffered their third straight loss after a seesaw battle with the New York Titans. With a chance to stay in the Eastern Division race, the Titans rolled up 471 total yards, and rallied in the final minutes on an Al Dorow to Dewey Bohling 20-yard touchdown pass. Tom Flores kept the Raiders in the game until the end by throwing for three touchdowns in a 34–28 defeat. On the receiving end of Flores' scoring strikes were

Nyle McFarlane (14 yards), Charlie Hardy (19 yards), and Tony Teresa (3 yards). Teresa also ran for a 1-yard touchdown.[13]

14. Dec. 18: San Francisco's Candlestick Park was the setting for the Raiders final game of their inaugural season. With a small crowd of 5,159 on hand, the 5–8 Raiders played host to the 4-8-1 Denver Broncos in a game that would determine who finished in the cellar of the Western Division. Going into the fourth quarter, Oakland held a close 17–10 advantage on 1-yard touchdown runs by Tom Flores and Tony Teresa, and a Larry Barnes field goal from 18 yards out. The Raiders then quickly pulled away by lighting up the scoreboard for 31 points in the final fifteen minutes to maul the Broncos, 48–10. This game produced Oakland's finest offensive performance of the season. Flores ran for another six-pointer (7 yards), Barnes added a 28-yard field goal, and Babe Parilli ran for a 1-yard touchdown, and passed for two more, with Nyle McFarlane (49 yards) and Charlie Hardy (20 yards), accounting for the tallies. Billy Lott gained 87 yards on nine carries, and Tony Teresa added 75 more on a day that saw the Raiders explode for 532 offensive yards. The defense also played a great game. Led by linebackers Riley Morris and Tom Louderback, the Raiders held the hapless Broncos to a mere five rushing yards and 206 total yards.[14]

Individual Statistics and Roster

Head Coach: Eddie Erdelatz
Assistant Coaches: Ed Cody, Marty Feldman, Ernie George, Tom Kalminar
1960 Regular Season Record: 6–8
3rd Place in AFL Western Division
Scored 319 points to rank 5th out of 8 teams
Allowed 388 points to rank 6th
Led the league in rushing yards (2,056)

STARTERS — OFFENSE

QB — Tom Flores: Active for 14 games and started in 12. The 1960 AFL passing leader completed 136 out of 252 attempts for 1,738 yards, 12 TD and 12 INT. Rushed for 123 yards on 19 carries and scored 3 TD. **Led the AFL in passing rating (71.8 percent) and pass completion percentage (54.0).**

QB — Babe Parilli: Active for 14 games and started in 2. Shared quarterback duties with Flores. Had 87 completions out of 187 attempts for 1,003 yards, 5 TD and 11 INT. Rushed for 131 yards on 21 carries and 1 TD.

HB — Tony Teresa: Active for 14 games, Teresa was the first-ever featured running back in Raiders history. Rushed for a team-high 608 yards on 139 carries and 6 TD. Had 35 receptions for 393 yards and 4 TD. Completed 9 passes in 18 attempts for 111 yards and 1 TD, returned 5 punts for 12 yards, and 4 kickoffs for 61 yards.

HB — Jack Larscheid: Active for 14 games. Rushed for 397 yards on 94 carries and 1 TD. Had 22 receptions for 187 yards and 1 TD, and completed 3 of 6 pass attempts for 71 yards. Returned **30** kickoffs for 852 yards and 12 punts for 106 yards. **Also led the AFL in combined kickoff and punt return yardage with 958 yards.**

FB — Billy Lott: Active for 14 games. Rushed for 520 yards on 99 carries and 5 TD. Had 49 receptions for 524 yards and 1 TD.

WR — Alan Goldstein: Active for 14 games, and had 27 receptions for 354 yards and 1 TD.

WR — Charlie Hardy: Active for 14 games, and had 24 receptions for 423 yards and 3 TD.

TE — Gene Prebola: Active for 14 games, and had 33 receptions for 404 yards and 2 TD.

LT — Ron Sabal: Active for 14 games.
LG — Don Manoukian: Active for 14 games.
C — Jim Otto: Active for 14 games.
RG — Wayne Hawkins: Active for 14 games.
RG — John Dittrich: Active for 11 games while sharing time with Hawkins.
RT — Paul Oglesby: Active for 14 games.

RESERVE OFFENSIVE PLAYERS

Doug Asad (TE): Active for 13 games, and had 14 receptions for 197 yards and 1 TD.
Al Hoisington (WR): Active for 9 games.
L.C. Joyner (RB): Active for 2 games.
Bob Keyes (RB): Active for 4 games, rushed for 7 yards on 1 carry, had 1 reception for 19 yards, and 1 punt return for 5 yards.
Paul Larson (QB): Active for 1 game.
Nyle McFarlane (RB): Active for 13 games, rushed for 52 yards on 4 carries, had 5 receptions for 89 yards and 2 TDs, and returned 5 kickoffs for 71 yards.
Billy Reynolds (RB): Active for 6 games. Rushed for 6 yards on 1 carry, had 3 receptions for 43 yards, and returned 7 punts for 24 yards.
J.D. Smith (RB): Active for 14 games. Rushed for 214 yards on 63 carries and 6 TD. Had 17 receptions for 194 yards and 1 TD, and returned 14 kickoffs for 373 yards and 1 TD.
Dalton Truax (T): Active for 14 games.

STARTERS — DEFENSE

DE — Carmen Cavalli: Active for 14 games.
DE — Charley Powell: Active for 14 games.
DT — George Fields: Active for 14 games and had 2 INT.
DT — Don Deskins: Active for 14 games and returned 1 kickoff 15 yards.
LLB — Bob Dougherty: Active for 14 games.
MLB — Tom Louderback: Active for 14 games and had 2 INT.
RLB — Riley Morris: Active for 14 games and returned 1 kickoff 3 yards.
CB — Eddie Macon: Active for 14 games and had 9 INT and 1 TD.
CB — Joe Cannavino: Active for 14 games, had 4 INT, and returned 1 punt for 4 yards.
S — Alex Bravo: Active for 14 games and had 4 INT.
S — Wayne Crow: Active in 14 games and had 4 INT.

RESERVE DEFENSIVE PLAYERS

Ray Armstrong (DT): Active for 14 games.
Joe Barbee (DT): Active for 1 game.
Don Churchwell (DT): Active for 1 game.
John Harris (DB): Active for 14 games.
Billy Locklin (LB): Active for 2 games.
Bill Striegel (LB): Active for 1 game.
Ron Warzeka (DT): Active for 14 games.

KICKING/PUNTING

K — Larry Barnes: Active for 14 games. Made 6 of 25 field goal attempts, and 37 of 39 extra point attempts for 55 points.
P — Wayne Crow: Active for 14 games. Punted 76 times for a 38.9 average.

1961 Season Review

1. Sept. 9: The Houston Oilers were the reigning AFL champions, and made a bold statement to the rest of the league that they were not going to rest on their laurels after a 55–0 season opening blowout over the hapless Raiders. Houston held Tom

Flores to only seven completions out of 21 pass attempts, and the entire Oakland offense to only 59 total yards. With this mauling, the Oilers set an AFL record for most points scored in a game. It also proved to be the worst defeat in Raiders history. The Houston defense helped set up three of the Oilers seven touchdowns with fumble recoveries. Quarterback George Blanda led the assault by throwing for three touchdowns and added two field goals.[1]

2. Sept. 17: Oakland's woes continued, with the San Diego Chargers doing the damage this time, 44–0. Prior to the season, the Chargers relocated to San Diego from Los Angeles. The defending Western Division champions totally outclassed the Raiders in every department, with the greatest being 188 passing yards to a mere 21. The Raiders also had five passes intercepted. This game marked the end of Eddie Erdelatz's coaching tenure in Oakland. After losing the first two games of the season in such convincing fashion, Oakland's front office personnel decided to make a coaching change and appointed assistant coach Marty Feldman to succeed Erdelatz.[2]

3. Sept. 24: In Feldman's first game at the helm, the Raiders showed signs of improvement in their home opener against the Dallas Texans with a crowd of only 6,737 on hand. Feldman attempted to help the lethargic offense by adding 13 new plays to give them 25 to choose from. Something must have worked, because late in the game, the Raiders clung to a one-point lead at 35–34. They received their slim advantage on touchdown runs by Wayne Crow (4 yards) and Tom Flores (1 yard). Flores also threw for two scores, with Charlie Hardy (8 yards) and Bob Coolbaugh (28 yards) on the receiving end of the six-pointers. George Fleming chipped in with field goals from 45 and 24 yards, and the offense churned out 307 yards for a vast improvement over the two previous games. Unfortunately, Oakland's defense could not hold off the Dallas offense despite coming at the Texans throughout the game with a good pass rush. With 1:55 remaining in the fourth quarter, the Texans scored on a Johnny Robinson 13-yard run, and with the two-point conversion, Dallas left Oakland with a 42–35 win. The Raiders tried in vain to pull out the win, but two dropped passes in the time remaining sealed their fate.[3]

4. Oct. 1: After three failed attempts, the Raiders got their first win of the season, 33–19, over the Denver Broncos. In their first three games, Oakland gave up an average of 47 points a game, but in this one, they managed to keep the Broncos out of the end zone until the fourth quarter. In addition to fine performances by Tom Flores and Wayne Crow, kicker George Fleming set a new AFL record by hitting on a 54-yard field goal. Flores hit on 10 out of 19 pass attempts for 121 yards, and Crow rushed for 107 yards on 16 carries. A Bob Garner interception gave the Raiders the ball on the Denver 21 in the first quarter, and six plays later, Crow scored on a 1-yard run. Oakland never looked back after that. Tom Flores threw two touchdown passes, with Alan Miller (18 yards) and Bob Coolbaugh (27 yards) getting the honors. Miller also ran for a 1-yard touchdown, and the defense recorded a safety.[4]

5. Oct. 15: Denver got even with the Raiders by handing them a heart-breaking 27–24 defeat. After giving up a ten-point lead, Oakland watched a Jack Hill 27-yard field goal split the uprights with eight seconds remaining in the game to seal a Denver win. This loss gave the Raiders sole possession of last place in the

Western Division with a 1–4 record. George Fleming provided the Raiders with a 13-yard scoring run, and a 15-yard field goal. Alan Miller ran for a 1-yard touchdown, and Tom Flores teamed up with Charlie Hardy from 34-yards out to account for the remainder of Oakland's point production.[5]

6. Oct. 22: Throughout the city of Oakland, a "Beat the Chargers" campaign gripped the town, and drummed up interest in the Raiders. The hype worked great at the gate, as a then-record home crowd of 12,014 turned out. Despite all the fanfare surrounding this game, the Raiders still lost to AFL powerhouse San Diego, 41–10. On the way to a 7–0 record, the Chargers were led by All-Pro running back Paul Lowe, who helped San Diego amass 218 yards on the ground to just two for the hapless Raiders. A 28-yard pass from Tom Flores to Bob Coolbaugh gave the fans reason to be optimistic early, as the Raiders jumped out to a first quarter lead before San Diego stormed back to open a 34–7 lead. George Fleming added a 44-yard field goal for Oakland in the third quarter to close out the team's scoring against one of the league's elite.[6]

7. Oct. 29: After playing host to the Western Division leaders the previous week, Oakland received no letup, as they hosted the Eastern Division–leading New York Titans. This time the Raiders fought the good fight, but still lost the battle. New York running back Bill Mathis provided the needed points with two short yardage touchdown runs in a 14–6 victory. Wedged between Mathis' scores were two George Fleming field goals from 30 and 33 yards out that provided the Raiders with their points. This game also saw Wayne Crow set a team record with a 77-yard punt that still ranks first in the Raiders' record book as of 2010.[7]

8. Nov. 5: Quarterback Tom Flores showed his toughness by taking a fierce beating served up by the Buffalo Bills' defense, and came out the victor. In a passing duel with Buffalo's Johnny Green, Flores overcame an incredible pass rush to complete 14 of 24 passes for 271 yards and three touchdowns in a 31–22 Oakland win. On the first play from scrimmage, Flores connected with Charley Fuller for an 85-yard touchdown, and threw his other two scoring strikes to Doug Asad (30 yards) and Alan Miller (55 yards). Miller also ran for a 1-yard touchdown, and George Fleming drilled a 45-yard field goal to help the Oakland cause.[8]

9. Nov. 11: In a poorly played game that saw both teams turn the ball over six times, the New York Titans beat the Raiders, 23–12. Oakland slipped to 2–7 with this defeat, which gave them the league's worst record. The Raiders drew first blood in the second quarter when Charlie Hardy caught a 55-yard touchdown pass from Tom Flores. They did not score again until the fourth quarter when Nick Papac connected with Charley Fuller from 43 yards out.[9]

10. Nov. 17: Throughout the 1961 season, the Raiders found many ways to lose games, and a trip to Boston showed them another one. In the fourth quarter, the Raiders were up, 17–13, thanks to two touchdown passes by Tom Flores and a George Fleming field goal (16 yards). Charley Hardy (31 yards) and Doug Asad (5 yards), caught Flores' touchdown tosses. It was then that the demons got them. After taking a bad snap from center, Oakland punter Wayne Crow tried to get the kick off from deep in the end zone. Crow got the kick off, but it hit the goal post and bounced back into the end zone. Boston's Leroy Moore reacted

quickly by jumping on the ball for the go-ahead touchdown. With only seconds remaining in the game, George Fleming tried to tie the game with a 61-yard field goal, but it fell short by quite a distance, and the Raiders succumbed to the Patriots, 20–17.[10]

11. Nov. 26: Running back Abner Haynes was the man of the hour for the Dallas Texans in a 43–11 romp over the Raiders. Haynes rushed for 158 yards, caught two passes for 84 yards, scored five touchdowns, and helped Dallas gain an incredible 284 yards on the ground against a pathetic Oakland defense. The win helped Dallas snap a six-game losing streak, while the Raiders lost their ninth game of the year. Getting Oakland their points on this day were George Fleming (45-yard field goal) and Nick Papac (1-yard run).[11]

12. Dec. 3: The Raiders took an early 7–6 lead over the Buffalo Bills on a 15-yard pass from Nick Papac to Alan Miller, but could not hold it and lost, 26–21. Miller caught a second 15-yard touchdown pass in the fourth quarter, this time from Tom Flores. Clem Daniels provided the other Oakland six-pointer with a 39-yard run in the third stanza. The Bills were sparked by running back Art Baker's game-leading 97 rushing yards. His touchdown run in the second quarter gave Buffalo the lead, and he added another six-pointer in the fourth quarter for good measure. The Raiders had a chance to win down the stretch, but two sacks ended their hopes.[12]

13. Dec. 9: The Boston Patriots kept their quest for the Eastern Division title alive with a 35–21 win over the hapless Raiders. Boston's victory was aided by two ex–Raiders, Billy Lott and Babe Parilli. Lott scored three touchdowns, and Parilli threw for three, with one of them going to Lott. The Boston defense did their part by totally shutting down Oakland's running game, holding it to a minuscule 27 yards. Oakland's scoring came on two Tom Flores touchdown passes and a Riley Morris interception return that covered 35 yards. Hauling in Flores' scoring tosses were Bob Coolbaugh (36 yards) and Jerry Burch (54 yards).[13]

14. Dec. 17: The nightmare the Raiders called the 1961 season finally ended with their sixth straight loss. The Houston Oilers mauled the Raiders, 47–16, to clinch their second consecutive Eastern Division title. In doing so, Houston sent Oakland home with an AFL-worst 2–12 record. Quarterback George Blanda led the way for the Oilers, passing for four touchdowns, and helped Houston amass 350 yards through the air. Helping the Oilers put on an offensive clinic were Billy Cannon (145 rushing yards), Charley Hennigan (5 receptions for 123 yards), and Willard Dewveall (3 receptions for 108 yards). Capping off Oakland's second season of operation in the scoring department on this day were George Fleming (26-yard field goal), Clem Daniels (10-yard run), and Tom Louderback (46-yard interception return).[14]

Individual Statistics and Roster

Head Coach: Eddie Erdelatz (2 games), Marty Feldman (12 games)
Assistant Coaches: George Dickson, Marty Feldman, Tom Kalminar
1961 Regular Season Record: 2–12
4th Place in AFL Western Division
Scored 237 points to rank 8th out of 8 teams
Allowed 458 points to rank 8th

STARTERS — OFFENSE

QB — Tom Flores: Started in 14 games. Completed 190 of 366 pass attempts for 2,176 yards, 15 TD and 19 INT. Rushed for 36 yards on 23 carries and 1 TD.

HB — Wayne Crow: Active for 14 games — Rushed for 490 yards on 119 carries and 2 TD. Had 23 receptions for 196 yards, and completed 6 of 10 pass attempts for 165 yards.

FB — Alan Miller: Active for 14 games.— Rushed for 255 yards on 85 carries and 3 TD. Had 36 receptions for 315 yards and 4 TD. Had 6 kickoff returns for 66 yards.

WR — Bob Coolbaugh: Active for 14 games. Had 32 receptions for 435 yards and 4 TD, and 1 kickoff return for 15 yards.

WR — Charlie Hardy: Active for 14 games. Had 24 receptions for 337 yards and 4 TD.

TE — Doug Asad: Active for 14 games. Had 36 receptions for 501 yards and 2 TD, and 1 kickoff return for 10 yards.

LT — Ron Sabal: Active for 14 games.

LG — Willie Smith: Active for 14 games.

C — Jim Otto: Active for 14 games.

RG — Wayne Hawkins: Active for 14 games.

RT — Jack Stone: Active for 14 games.

RESERVE OFFENSIVE PLAYERS

Jim Brewington (T): Active for 14 games.

Jerry Burch (WR): Active for 14 games, had 18 receptions for 235 yards and 1 TD, and punted 11 times for a 28.6 average.

Clem Daniels (RB): Active for 8 games, rushed for 154 yards on 31 carries and 2 TD, had 13 receptions for 150 yards, 5 punt returns for 34 yards, and 13 kickoff returns for 276 yards.

Charley Fuller (RB): Active for 14 games, rushed for 134 yards on 38 carries, had 12 receptions for 277 yards and 2 TD, 4 punt returns for 52 yards, 8 kickoff returns for 155 yards, and 1 pass attempt for 0 yards.

Walt Kowalczyk (RB): Active for 4 games, rushed for 28 yards on 10 carries, had 3 receptions for 8 yards, and 1 kickoff return for 19 yards.

Jack Larscheid (RB): Active for 2 games, rushed for 3 yards on 6 carries, had 2 receptions for 11 yards, 9 kickoff returns for 254 yards, and 1 pass attempt for 0 yards.

Nick Papac (QB): Active for 14 games, completed 13 of 44 pass attempts for 173 yards and 2 TD, and rushed for 28 yards on 6 carries and 1 TD.

Cliff Roberts (T): Active for 10 games.

Herb Roedel (G): Active for 14 games.

STARTERS — DEFENSE

DE — Gary Finneran: Active for 13 games.

DE — Charley Powell: Active for 14 games.

DT — Bob Voight (14 games) & Volney Peters (12 games): Shared time at left tackle

DT — Hal Smith (8 games) & Harry Jagielski (8 games): Shared time at right tackle. Jagielski had 1 INT, and Smith had 1 punt return for 2 yards

LLB — Bob Dougherty: Active for 14 games and had 2 INT.

MLB — Tom Louderback: Active for 14 games, had 1 INT and 1 TD.

RLB — Riley Morris: Active for 14 games, had 3 INT and 1 TD.

CB — Fred Williamson: Active for 14 games and had 5 INT.

CB — Bob Garner: Active for 13 games, had 2 INT, and 2 punt returns for 5 yards.

S — Joe Cannavino: Active for 14 games and had 5 INT.

S — Alex Bravo: Active for 14 games and had 2 INT.

RESERVE DEFENSIVE PLAYERS

Al Bansavage (LB): Active for 14 games.

George Fields (T/E): Active for 1 game.

John Harris (DB): Active for 14 games and had 2 INT.

Jon Jelacic (DE): Active for 4 games.

Jim R. Jones (DB): Active for 1 game.

KICKING/PUNTING

K — George Fleming: Active for 14 games. Made 11 out of 26 field goals and 24 out of 25 extra point kicks for 57 points. Rushed for 112 yards on 31 carries and 1 TD, had 10 receptions for 49 yards, 3 punt returns for 24 yards, **29** kickoff returns for 588 yards, and 1 pass attempt for 0 yards.

P — Wayne Crow: Active for 14 games. Punted 61 times for a 42.8 average.

1962 Season Review

1. Sept. 9: The previous season's misfortunes seemed to follow the Raiders into the 1962 campaign. The New York Titans came into Oakland, and immediately established momentum by scoring touchdowns on their first two possessions. Quarterback Lee Grosscup threw three touchdown passes, and running back Dick Christy ran for 106 yards on 10 carries in a 28–17 win. One bright spot for the Raiders was the fine running of Clem Daniels, who totaled 101 yards on 10 carries. Jackie Simpson opened the Raiders' third season with a 31-yard field goal to give them a 3–0 lead in the second quarter. Gene White caught a 21-yard pass from Don Heinrich, and Alan Miller ran for a 1-yard score to give Oakland their six-pointers.[1]

2. Sept. 23: Once again an opposing quarterback filled the air with touchdown passes against the Raiders. This time it was Len Dawson of the Dallas Texans who did the damage in a 26–16 win. All three of Dawson's scoring strikes went to Chris Burford. Cotton Davidson came to Oakland in a trade with the Texans, and repaid his old teammates by passing for 248 yards and scored on a 10-yard run. He also threw four interceptions, which hurt the Raiders. Adding to Oakland's point production were Jackie Simpson (16-yard field goal), and Clem Daniels (2-yard run).[2]

3. Sept. 30: Opposing quarterbacks were having career days against the Oakland defense in the early stages of the '62 season. San Diego's rookie signal caller, John Hadl, was the next one to shine, as he led the Chargers to a 42–33 win. Within six minutes of the second quarter, Hadl ripped the Oakland secondary for three touchdown passes, each going to a different receiver. The Raiders did come to life in the fourth quarter, and scored 16 points on two touchdown passes from Chan Gallegos, but the game was pretty much out of reach by that time. Dobie Craig (35 yards) and Roberson (32 yards) were on the receiving end of Gallegos' touchdown tosses. Jackie Simpson rounded out Oakland's scoring with a 25-yard field goal. Despite being set down for the third straight week, the Raiders got some exciting moments in this one. Bo Roberson returned a kickoff 87 yards to help tie the game at 7–7, and then Fred "the Hammer" Williamson gave the Raiders a quick lead by running an interception back 91 yards to paydirt.[3]

4. Oct. 5: The Denver Broncos improved to 4–1 by crushing the AFL doormat Oakland Raiders, 44–7. The star of the game for Denver was running back Gene Mingo, who ran for over 100 yards, scored two touchdowns, kicked a field goal, and added four extra point kicks. The Denver defense also came up with three interceptions and just as many fumble recoveries to help in their quest. A Jon Jelasic interception deep in Denver territory helped Oakland get their only points of the game when Cotton Davidson ran for a 1-yard score after the Raiders were already down, 21–0, in the fourth quarter.[4]

5. Oct. 14: In a rematch with Denver, the result was the same, with the Broncos winning this time, 23–6, on a muddy field in Oakland. Despite the poor conditions, it was once again Gene Mingo who came up big for Denver. This time he scored 17 of Denver's points on three field goals, two conversions, and one touchdown. With this win, the Broncos took over first place in the Western Division. Clem Daniels prevented the Raiders from being shut out when he scored on a 1-yard run in the fourth quarter. The hapless Raiders, however, fell to 0–5, and were losers of 11 straight games over the course of two seasons. This game proved to be the last for head coach Marty Feldman, who was fired after compiling a 2–15 record since taking over in 1961. His replacement was William "Red" Conkright, the defensive line coach and head scout.[5]

6. Oct. 20: With new coach Red Conkright on the sideline, the Raiders were still lousy, but managed to out gain the Bills in total yards 290 to 252. The coaching change did little to spark the dismal atmosphere, as Oakland lost to Buffalo, 14–6. The Bills won their second straight game with the aid of powerful fullback Cookie Gilchrist. The 240-pound Gilchrist smashed his way across a muddy War Memorial Stadium field for 144 yards on 19 carries and one touchdown on a day where passing the ball proved to be very difficult. The Raiders threw for 143 yards, while the Bills could only muster 51. Bo Roberson scored Oakland's lone touchdown on a 14-yard run to close the Buffalo advantage to one point in the third quarter.[6]

7. Oct. 26: For the third straight week, the Raiders played in the mud, and just like in previous encounters, they suffered a defeat. With an offensive attack called the "Runnin' Gun," which focused on the power running of Clem Daniels and the speed of Bo Roberson, Oakland held a 13–6 halftime lead thanks to a 34-yard pass from Cotton Davidson to Dobie Craig, and a 63-yard run by Roberson. All the Raiders offense could muster up in the second half was a 19-yard field goal by Davidson, while the defense gave up twenty points in a 26–16 lose to the Boston Patriots. Gino Cappelletti led Boston by kicking four field goals, two conversions, and caught a touchdown pass from former Raider Babe Parilli.[7]

8. Nov. 4: It officially became one full year since the Raiders last victory, a 31–22 win over Buffalo on November 5, 1961. One year later, Oakland was still looking for their first win of the '62 season. They almost had it against New York, but the Titans rallied with four touchdowns in the second half to win, 31–21. Clem Daniels ran for touchdowns from two and three yards out to give the Raiders a 14–3 advantage before the defense fell apart in the third quarter. Quarterback Johnny Green provided much of the momentum for the Titans by hitting on key passes to keep drives alive. Green threw for one score and ran for another. Running backs Dick Christy and Bill Mathis also chipped in with solid performances to give New York a well-balanced offensive attack. Oakland added a touchdown in the fourth quarter on a 72-yard pass from Cotton Davidson to Bo Roberson.[8]

9. Nov. 11: The Raiders were looking like giant killers by holding a 20–7 lead in the third quarter against the two-time AFL champion Houston Oilers. They took an early 7–0 lead on a 36-yard sweep around the right end by Bo Roberson. Roberson also scored on a 67-yard reception from Cotton Davidson in the third quarter. Wedged between Roberson's two scores, Dobie Craig chipped in with a 46-yard touchdown grab from Davidson.

The Oilers eventually came to life, and scored three touchdowns to pull out a hard-fought 28–20 win. Their last two scoring drives came just 45 seconds apart, as George Blanda threw to Charley Tolar for the go-ahead points, then Gene Babb returned an interception 31 yards for an insurance touchdown.[9]

10. Nov. 18: The term "sweet sixteen" was anything but that for the Oakland Raiders, as they fell for the sixteenth straight time. For the third time in as many weeks, the Raiders had a lead late in the game, but failed to put it away when they had the chance. In this game against the Buffalo Bills, Oakland led, 6–3, in the third quarter until Bob Garner fumbled a punt return. Ben Agajanian accounted for Oakland's point production with field goals from 49 and 36 yards. The Bills struck quickly after Monte Crockett pounced on the fumble at the Oakland 33 when Jack Kemp threw a touchdown pass to Wayne Crow from 16 yards out. That proved to be all the Bills needed to snatch a 10–6 victory away from the Raiders.[10]

11. Nov. 25: After two close games, the winless Raiders were blown out, 35–7, by the Dallas Texans. The lopsided win allowed the Texans to clinch a tie for the Western Division title. The running tandem of Abner Haynes and Curtis McClinton provided most of the offensive punch. Haynes ran for 112 yards and two scores, which enabled him to tie a then-single season professional record of 18 rushing touchdowns. McClinton added 109 yards to Dallas' offensive output. Dobie Craig caught a 17-yard pass from Hunter Enis in the second quarter to close the gap to 14–7 before Dallas added three straight touchdowns to put the game out of reach.[11]

12. Dec. 2: A losing streak was finally snapped with a 31–21 win, but unfortunately, it was a six-game slide by the San Diego Chargers. Despite going down for the eighteenth straight time, Oakland got a huge performance from offensive end Dick Dorsey. With the Chargers leading, 28–7, Dorsey teamed up with quarterback Cotton Davidson on two long scoring strikes that covered 65 and 90 yards respectively. Clem Daniels scored on a 2-yard run in the third quarter to account for Oakland's other six-pointer.[12]

13. Dec. 9: The Houston Oilers clinched their third straight Eastern Division title with a 32–17 thumping over the Raiders. Besides the passing and kicking of George Blanda, Houston scored touchdowns on defense and special teams when Bobby Jancik returned an interception and Tony Banfield scored on a blocked field goal attempt. Clem Daniels showed his worth to the Raiders despite another loss by rushing for a then-team record 187 yards. With head coach Red Conkright and assistant Ollie Spencer on a scouting trip, the team was left to defensive back coach Walt Michaels for this game. Down 20–0 in the second quarter, the Raiders rallied back to close to within three points by halftime. Oakland achieved this on the strength of touchdown runs from Daniels (72 yards) and Cotton Davidson (1 yard), and on a 27-yard field goal by Ben Agajanian. Houston then shut out the Raiders in the second half, and scored three times by the only ways a team can in football, with those being on a touchdown, a field goal, and a safety.[13]

14. Dec. 16: Finally after nineteen straight beatings, the Oakland Raiders got one in the win column. With a constant rain making the field a mud bath, the Raiders dominated the Boston Patriots, 20–0, in front of 8,000 wet but loyal Oakland fans. The Raiders took advantage of eight turnovers, and Cotton Davidson threw for 230 yards. The biggest offensive spark of the day came on a 74-yard pass from Davidson to Clem Daniels that went for a touchdown. Daniels added a 7-yard touchdown run to the festivities, and Ben Agajanian kicked two field goals from 19 and 21 yards to help the Raiders record their first shutout victory in team history. Even though the Raiders finished the season 1–13, they ended it on a positive note, and looked to the future with a glimmer of hope. This also proved to be the final game in which the Raiders wore black and gold, turning that combination in for the colors silver and black at the beginning of their fourth season.[14]

Individual Statistics and Roster

Head Coach: Marty Feldman (5 games), Red Conkright (9 games)
Assistant Coaches: Red Conkright, Tom Kalminar, Walt Michaels, Ollie Spencer
1962 Regular Season Record: 1–13
4th Place in AFL Western Division
Scored 213 points to rank 8th out of 8 teams
Allowed 370 points to rank 6th

Starters — Offense

QB — Cotton Davidson: Active for 13 games, and started in 12. Completed 119 of 321 pass attempts for 1,977 yards, 7 TD and 23 INT. **Led AFL with a 16.6 yards per completion average.** Rushed for 54 yards on 25 carries and 3 TD. Also punted 40 times for 39.2 average, and made 4 of 5 extra point kicks and 1 of 2 field goal attempts.

HB — Clem Daniels: Active for 14 games. Rushed for 766 yards on 161 carries and 7 TD. Had 24 receptions for 318 yards and 1 TD, 24 kickoff returns for 530 yards, and 1 pass attempt for 0 yards.

FB — Alan Miller: Active for 14 games. Rushed for 182 yards on 65 carries and 1 TD. Had 20 receptions for 259 yards, and 6 kickoff returns for 45 yards.

WR — Dobie Craig: Active for 14 games, and started in 11. Had 27 receptions for 492 yards and 4 TD, and rushed for 8 yards on 1 carry.

WR — Dick Dorsey: Active for 11 games, and had 21 receptions for 344 yards and 2 TD.

TE — Max Boydston: Active for 14 games, and had 30 receptions for 374 yards.

LT — Charles Brown: Active for 14 games.

LG — Stan Campbell: Active for 14 games.

C — Jim Otto: Active for 14 games.

RG — Wayne Hawkins: Active for 14 games.

RT — Jack Stone: Active for 14 games.

Reserve Offensive Players

Hunter Enis (QB): Active for 7 games, and started in 1. Completed 27 of 51 pass attempts for 225 yards, 1 TD and 1 INT. Rushed for 24 yards on 2 carries.

Dan Ficca (G): Active for 14 games.

Charley Fuller (RB): Active for 3 games, and had 5 receptions for 67 yards.

Chon Gallegos (QB): Active for 6 games, completed 18 out of 35 pass attempts for 298 yards, 2 TD and 3 INT. Rushed for 25 yards on 3 carries.

Charlie Hardy (WR): Active for 5 games, and had 6 receptions for 80 yards.

Don Heinrich (QB): Active for and started in 1 game. Completed 10 of 29 pass attempts for 156 yards, 1 TD and 2 INT. Rushed for 4 yards on 1 carry.

Hal Lewis (RB): Active for 11 games. Rushed for 18 yards on 9 carries, had 7 receptions for 53 yards, 9 punt returns for 65 yards, and 3 kickoff returns for 65 yards.

Pete Nicklas (T): Active for 14 games.

M.C. Reynolds (QB): Active for 1 game, completed 2 of 5 pass attempts for 23 yards, and rushed for 9 yards on 1 carry.

Bo Roberson (WR/RB): Active for 14 games. Rushed for 270 yards on 89 carries and 3 TD, had 29 receptions for 583 yards and 3 TD, 27 kickoff returns for 748 yards and 1 TD, and attempted 6 passes for 0 yards.

Willie Simpson (RB): Active for 10 games, rushed for 32 yards on 10 carries, and had 1 kickoff return for 7 yards.

Gene White (RB): Active for 7 games, and had 6 receptions for 101 yards and 1 TD.

STARTERS — DEFENSE

DE — Jon Jelacic: Active for 14 games and had 1 INT.

DE — Dalva Allen: Active for 14 games.

DT — Orville Trask: Active for 7 games.

DT — Chuck McMurtry: Active for 11 games.

LLB — Bob Dougherty: Active roster for 14 games, and had 1 kickoff return for 20 yards.

MLB — Jackie Simpson: Active for 14 games and had 3 INT. Kicked 6 of 6 extra point attempts, and connected on 3 of 10 field goals attempts.

RLB — Charlie Rieves: Active for 14 games.

CB — Fred Williamson: Active for 14 games. Had 8 INT, 1 TD, **and led the AFL with 151 return yards on his interceptions**. Had 1 punt return for 3 yards.

CB — Bob Garner: Active for 14 games. Had 3 INT, 20 punt returns for 162 yards, and 1 kickoff return for 8 yards.

S — Vern Valdez: Active for 10 games. Had 4 INT and 2 punt returns for 14 yards.

S — Tommy Morrow: Active for 14 games. Had 10 INT and 2 punt returns for 13 yards.

RESERVE DEFENSIVE PLAYERS

Dan Birdwell (T/E): Active for 14 games and attempted 1 field goal.

George Boynton (DB): Active for 3 games.

Mel Montalbo (DB): Active for 2 games.

Riley Morris (LB/E): Active for 4 games.

Rich Mostardi (DB): Active for 5 games.

Jim Norris (T): Active for 7 games, and had 1 kickoff return for 2 yards.

Joe Novsek (DE): Active for 14 games, and had 1 kickoff return for 0 yards.

Hank Rivera (DB): Active for 9 games.

George Shirkey (T): Active for 14 games.

KICKING/PUNTING

K — Ben Agajanian: Active for 6 games. Made 5 of 14 field goals and 10 of 11 extra points for 25 points.

P — Tommy Morrow: Active for 14 games. Punted 45 times for a 36.8 average.

1963 Season Review

1. Sept. 7: With head coach Al Davis at the helm, the Raiders were given a new attitude. Tom Flores returned at quarterback after missing the previous season due to tuberculosis, threw for 217 yards, and rallied Oakland to a 24–13 win over perennial AFL powerhouse Houston. With the Oilers holding a slim 6–0 lead in the third quarter, Flores came off the bench and took Oakland 56 yards in seven plays for the go-ahead touchdown. Clem Daniels capped the drive off with a 3-yard

touchdown run that started a 24-point Oakland scoring barrage. Flores added an 85-yard scoring toss to Art Powell later in the fourth quarter to cap off a fine performance by the receiver, who had seven receptions for 181 yards. The Oakland defense did their part by picking off six Houston passes, with three from defensive back Tommy Morrow. Rookie linebacker Ken Herlock returned a fumble recovery 15 yards for a touchdown, and Mike Mercer added an 11-yard field goal to finish off Oakland's great day. This marked the first time in their young history that the Raiders won their opening game and that they wore the new team colors of silver and black.[1]

2. Sept. 15: The Raiders made it two in a row by crushing Buffalo in Oakland's home opener, 35–17, in front of a then-record crowd of 17,568. This was also the first time since 1960 that the Raiders had a winning streak. Cotton Davidson was back at quarterback for Oakland, and responded with a spectacular performance. He completed 14 of 29 passes for 315 yards and two touchdowns, and ran another one in from five yards out. On the receiving end of Davidson's touchdown tosses were Art Powell from five yards and Clem Daniels from 73 yards. Daniels ran for 76 yards, gathered in three receptions for a whopping 172 yards, and Powell gained 91 yards on eight catches. Capping off Oakland's scoring were Alan Miller (2-yard run) and Jon Jelacic (1-yard interception).[2]

3. Sept. 22: It was the Boston Patriots who helped break Oakland's 19-game losing streak in the previous season's finale. This same Boston team came into Oakland to spoil the Raiders' three-game winning streak by a 20–14 count. Tom Flores did help Oakland close to within six points thanks to two touchdown passes in the fourth quarter, but they came too late to make a difference. Art Powell, who had a tremendous game with eight receptions for 150 yards, snagged one of Flores' scoring strikes from 33 yards, and Bo Roberson caught the other from 53 yards.[3]

4. Sept. 28: For the sixth straight time since 1960, the New York Jets (formally the Titans from 1960–62), beat the Raiders, this time, 10–7. A 35-yard Dick Guesman field goal in the third quarter proved to be the game winner. Cotton Davidson scored Oakland's lone touchdown on a 2-yard run in the first quarter to give the Raiders an early lead.[4]

5. Oct. 5: After such a fantastic start, the Raiders now saw themselves slip below .500, thanks to a 12–0 loss to the Buffalo Bills. Buffalo won the game by scoring in every way possible. They first scored on a Mack Yoho field goal, then added a touchdown, and capped the day by sacking Cotton Davidson in the end zone for a safety.[5]

6. Oct. 11: With the same final score from three weeks earlier, the Boston Patriots knocked off Oakland, 20–14, despite suffering four sacks and 11 penalties. Ex-Raiders quarterback Babe Parilli came back to haunt his old teammates by throwing a game winning touchdown pass in the fourth quarter. The loss was Oakland's fourth straight, aided by two fumbles and three interceptions, and dropped them to 2–4 on the season. Oakland looked to be in good shape to stop their current losing streak when Jim McMillin returned an interception 47 yards to open the scoring. Coton Davidson then ran for an 11-yard touchdown to extend the Oakland advantage to 14–3.[6]

7. Oct. 20: Two streaks were ended at the conclusion of this game, and both were good for the Oakland Raiders. After losing

six straight to the New York Jets, the Raiders finally broke through against their nemesis for a 49–26 win. They also snapped their four-game losing streak of this season. Leading the charge was running back Clem Daniels with 200 yards rushing on 27 carries. He also scored two rushing touchdowns from eight and 74 yards, and caught a third six-pointer from Cotton Davidson that covered 56 yards. His rushing total broke a team record that he set himself the previous season. Tom Flores suffered a concussion after he led the Raiders to three of their seven touchdowns, and accounted for one with a 93-yard pass to Dobie Craig in the first quarter. Cotton Davidson took over at quarterback, and threw three touchdowns on a day that saw the Raiders compile an incredible 523 yards of total offense. Besides his touchdown toss to Daniels, Davidson teamed up with Ken Herock on a 49-yarder and Alan Miller from eight yards out. Miller also ran for a 3-yard score in the first quarter to open Oakland's productive day.[7]

8. Oct. 27: The Raiders evened their record at 4–4 with an exciting 34–33 win over the San Diego Chargers that produced eight lead changes. Cotton Davidson was once again called on to quarterback the team after Tom Flores went down in the second quarter with a head injury. Before he left the game, Flores threw two touchdowns to Art Powell (20 yards) and Alan Miller (5 yards). Davidson added three of his own, with the final one to fullback Glen Shaw providing the game winner from nine yards out. Dobie Craig (39 yards) and Powell (46 yards) were on the receiving end of Davidson's other six-pointers. Clem Daniels gave the Raiders a solid ground attack with 125 yards on 19 carries, and the defense came up with five interceptions. Fred "the Hammer" Williamson led the defense with two picks, while Claude Gibson, Joe Krakoski, and Archie Matsos each intercepted one New York pass. This win broke an 11-game losing streak to the Chargers.[8]

9. Nov. 3: Claude Gibson was the man of the hour in Oakland's 10–7 win over the Kansas City Chiefs (formally the Dallas Texans and defending AFL champions). He returned a punt 85 yards for the deciding touchdown in the fourth quarter, and Oakland improved to 5–4 and was in second place in the Western Division behind San Diego. Mike Mercer opened the scoring in the second quarter with a 10-yard field goal before Kansas City came back to take a 7–3 lead. Alan Miller helped the Silver and Black cause with six receptions for 96 yards.[9]

10. Nov. 8: The Raiders kept their longest winning streak of four games alive with a 22–7 victory in a rematch with the Chiefs. Oakland used a balanced offensive attack on the arm of Tom Flores, who threw two touchdown passes to Art Powell (24 and 34 yards), and the running of Clem Daniels, who churned out 122 yards on 31 carries. Mike Mercer added field goals from 14 and 41 yards, and the Raiders also recorded a safety to produce their points by scoring every way a team can. The defense played a magnificent game, allowing only 61 yards of total offense, recorded six sacks, and held the Chiefs out of the end zone until the contest was out of reach. The win put Oakland one game out of first place in the division.[10]

11. Nov. 28: After a twenty-day layoff, the well-rested Raiders traveled to Denver, and handed the Broncos a 26–10 defeat. The Raiders once again scored in all the ways a team can. They started out by tackling fullback Billy Joe in the end zone for a safety. After trailing by a baseball-like score of 3–2 at the

half, Oakland added touchdowns by Bo Roberson on a 39-yard pass from Cotton Davidson, a Jon Jelacic 19-yard fumble recovery, a Glenn Shaw 1-yard run, and wedged in between the six-pointers, Mike Mercer booted a 16-yard field goal. Clem Daniels tripled Denver's rushing total as a team with 90 yards on 16 carries, and the defense came through with five sacks and three interceptions. This win guaranteed Oakland of their best season to date, and their 7–4 record kept them in the hunt for a division title.[11]

12. Dec. 8: In a bid to clinch their third Western Division title in four seasons, the San Diego Chargers held a 17-point lead over the Raiders in the fourth quarter. Possibly looking ahead to a victory party, the Chargers got sloppy and Oakland took advantage of each San Diego mistake. In a 31-point fourth quarter barrage, the Raiders turned two fumbles, a lousy punt, and a personal foul into scores. With Cotton Davidson running for a 9-yard touchdown, and throwing to Art Powell for two more scores (10 and 41 yards), Oakland rallied to pull out a 41–27 stunner to sweep the season series from their interstate rivals for the first time in team history. Also scoring for Oakland during this point explosion were Alan Miller (2-yard run), and Mike Mercer (30-yard field goal). The Raiders received their first half points on a 44-yard pass from Tom Flores to Powell and on a 37-yard Mercer field goal. Clem Daniels once again led all ball carriers, this time doubling San Diego's entire rushing output with 90 yards on 17 attempts. Art Powell smoked the enemy secondary for 132 yards on six receptions, and the Silver and Black rolled up 406 total offensive yards.[12]

13. Dec. 15: Tom Flores passed for 272 yards, and five touchdowns in a 35–31 win over Denver. His first scoring pass came on the game's opening play, going to Bo Roberson from 32 yards out. His other touchdown tosses went to Art Powell (18 and 3 yards) and Clem Daniels (26 and 43 yards). Daniels proved to be the total offensive weapon during this campaign. In addition to being one of the best running back in the league, he also showed his pass catching abilities by hauling in five receptions for a game-high 127 yards. The win put Oakland at 9–4, while San Diego clinched at least a tie for the division title with a 10–3 record.[13]

14. Dec. 22: A year earlier the Raiders were down in the basement of the AFL. However, by the end of the 1963 season, they were perched among the league elite. With their eighth consecutive win, a 52–49 shootout with the Houston Oilers, the Raiders finished the regular season with a sterling 10–4 record. Unfortunately, the San Diego Chargers also won their finale, and in doing so, clinched their third Western Division crown with an 11–3 mark. They eventually went on to win the AFL championship two weeks later over the Boston Patriots. Even though Oakland came up short in the division race, their incredible turnaround left the Raiders with the prospect of a very bright future. The Raiders rang up 540 offensive yards, and Tom Flores played brilliantly in the finale by completing 17 of 29 passes for a then-team record 407 yards and six touchdowns. Art Powell caught four of Flores' scoring strikes from 81, 20, 45, and 23 yards out, and established a team record 247 receiving yards in the process. Clem Daniels placed his name in the team and league record books by rushing for a season total of 1,098 yards, and also caught a 56-yard scoring strike from Flores. Ken Herock was on the receiving end of Flores' other six-point toss, that one coming from seven yards out. Claude Gibson returned a punt 69 yards,

and Mike Mercer added a 39-yard field goal to complete the scoring in Oakland's explosive '63 finale.[14]

Individual Statistics and Roster

Head Coach: Al Davis

Assistant Coaches: Tom Dahms, Bob Maddock, John Rauch, Ollie Spencer, Charles Sumner

1963 Regular Season Record: 10–4

2nd Place in AFL Western Division

Scored 363 points to rank 2nd out of 8 teams

Allowed 282 points to rank 4th

Led league in touchdowns passing (31), fewest passing yards allowed (2,557), and turnovers caused by a defense (52)

STARTERS — OFFENSE

QB — Tom Flores: Active for 14 games, and started in 9. Completed 113 of 247 pass attempts for 2,101 yards, 20 TD and 13 INT. **Led the AFL with an 18.6 yards per completion average**. Rushed for 2 yards on 11 carries.

HB — Clem Daniels: Active for 14 games. Rushed for **1,099** yards on 215 carries and 3 TD. **His 78.5 yards per game rushing average led the AFL**. Had 30 receptions for 685 yards and 5 TD, and **his 22.8 yards per reception led the AFL**. Threw 1 pass for 10 yards, and **led the AFL with 1,784 yards from scrimmage**.

FB — Alan Miller: Active for 14 games. Rushed for 270 yards on 62 carries and 3 TD. Had 34 receptions for 404 yards and 2 TD.

WR — Bo Roberson: Active for 14 games. Had 25 receptions for 407 yards and 3 TD, rushed for 47 yards on 19 carries, had 2 punt returns for 34 yards and 38 kickoff returns for 809 yards.

WR — Art Powell: Active for 14 games. Had 73 receptions for **1,304** yards and **16 TD**. **Also led the AFL with a 93.1 yards per game receiving average**.

TE — Ken Herock: Active for 14 games. Had 15 receptions for 269 yards, and 2 TD, and 1 kickoff return for 3 yards.

LT — Proverb Jacobs: Active for 14 games.

LG — Wayne Hawkins: Active for 14 games.

C — Jim Otto: Active for 14 games.

RG — Sonny Bishop: Active for 14 games.

RT — Dick Klein: Active for 14 games and had 1 kickoff return for 7 yards.

RESERVE OFFENSIVE PLAYERS

Jan Barrett (E): Active for 3 games, and had 1 reception for 9 yards.

Dobie Craig (WR/HB): Active for 12 games, and had 7 receptions for 196 yards and 2 TD.

Cotton Davidson (QB): Active for 14 games, and started in 5. Completed 77 of 194 pass attempts for 1,276 yards, 11 TD and 10 INT. Rushed for 115 yards on 26 carries and 4 TD.

Doug Mayberry (FB): Active for 2 games.

Bob Mischak (G/TE): Active for 14 games, and had 2 receptions for 25 yards.

Jesse Murdock (HB): Active for 1 game.

Glenn Shaw (FB): Active for 12 games, rushed for 46 yards on 20 carries and 1 TD, had 2 receptions for 64 yards and 1 TD, and 2 kickoff returns for 19 yards.

Mike Sommer (HB/DB): Active for 4 games. Rushed for 21 yards on 5 carries, had 1 reception for 24 yards, 4 punt returns for 44 yards, and 5 kickoff returns for 102 yards.

Ollie Spencer (T/G/C): Active for 14 games.

Frank Youso (T/DT): Active for 4 games.

STARTERS — DEFENSE

DE — Dalva Allen: Active for 14 games.

DE — Jon Jelacic: Active for 14 games, had 1 INT and 1 TD.

DT — Chuck McMurtry: Active for 14 games.

DT — Dave Costa: Active for 14 games.

LLB — Jackie Simpson: Active for 14 games, had 2 INT and 1 kickoff return for 11 yards.

MLB — Archie Matsos: Active for 14 games and had 4 INT.

RLB — Clancy Osborne: Active for 14 games and had 2 INT.

CB — Fred Williamson: Active for 14 games and had 6 INT.

CB — Claude Gibson: Active for 14 games, had 3 INT, **26** punt returns for **307** yards and **2** TD, and 2 kickoff returns for 10 yards. **His 11.8 average per punt return led the AFL**.

S — Joe Krakoski: Active for 14 games, had 4 INT and 4 punt returns for 10 yards.

S — Tommy Morrow: Active for 14 games and had 9 INT.

RESERVE DEFENSIVE PLAYERS

Dan Birdwell (T/E): Active for 10 games and had 1 kickoff return for 7 yards.

Bob Dougherty (LB): Active for 5 games.

Jim McMillin (DB): Active for 14 games, had 4 INT, 1 TD, and 1 kickoff return for 23 yards.

Jim Norris (T): Active for 14 games.

Warren Powers (DB): Active for 5 games.

Charlie Rieves (LB): Active for 9 games.

Herman Urenda (E/DB): Active for 2 games.

KICKING/PUNTING

K & P — Mike Mercer: Active for 14 games. Made 8 out of 19 field goal attempts and 47 out of 47 extra point kicks for 71 points and rushed for -5 yards on 1 carry. Punted 75 times for a 40.0 average.

1964 Season Review

1. Sept. 13: The Boston Patriots loved to help the Raiders start and end streaks. In 1962 it was against the Patriots that Oakland snapped a 19-game losing streak, and in 1963, Boston was responsible for halting a three-game winning one. The 1964 season opener proved to be no different. Coming into the new season, the Raiders sported an eight-game winning streak, but after the defending Eastern Division champions left Oakland, the sensational run was over for the Raiders. A 48-yard field goal by Gino Cappelletti in the fourth quarter provided the clincher in a 17–14 Boston win. The Raiders, who were hit hard by injuries coming into the new campaign, got another great performance from Art Powell. The gifted receiver caught seven passes for 135 yards, and scored on a 33-yard strike from Tom Flores. Glenn Shaw produced Oakland's touchdown with a 1-yard run.[1]

2. Sept. 19: Three touchdowns by Clem Daniels just wasn't enough, as the Houston Oilers beat Oakland, 42–28. Daniels scored on an 8-yard run and on two receptions from Cotton Davidson that covered 19 and 22 yards. Tom Flores also quarterbacked in this one, but only completed six of 22 attempts for 136 yards and suffered four interceptions. Glenn Shaw provided the other six-pointer on a 2-yard run. Houston's defense came up big with five interceptions, two of which were returned for touchdowns.[2]

3. Sept. 27: Mike Mercer kicked three field goals (32, 19, and 28 yards) to give Oakland a 9–7 lead going in to the fourth quarter. It was then that quarterback Len Dawson and running back Abner Haynes took control of the Kansas City offense. Dawson threw for two scores, and Haynes ran for over 100 yards. He

also caught the go-ahead touchdown from 56 yards out in a 21–9 win.[3]

4. Oct. 3: For the third straight week, Buffalo back-up quarterback Daryle Lamonica came off the bench to help the Bills win, 23–20, and in doing so, dropped the Raiders to 0–4. Lamonica came into the game with Buffalo trailing, 10–7, midway through the third quarter. He then proceeded to score from the 1-yard line to put the Bills up, 14–10. Lamonica then threw what turned out to be the winning touchdown to Elbert Dubenion from 44 yards out. In the short time he was in, Lamonica completed seven of 10 passes for 164 yards. Despite Oakland's unfortunate beginning, Art Powell once again played well, catching six passes for 98 yards to led both teams. Cotton Davidson accounted for two of Oakland's scores by first running for a 6-yard touchdown, and then throwing a 4-yarder to Ken Herock. Mike Mercer added Oakland's other points with field goals from 25 and 19 yards away.[4]

5. Oct. 10: The 1964 season began with high expectations for Oakland, but was quickly turning into a major disaster. Adding to the Raiders woes was a 35–13 beating handed to them by the New York Jets. The key to the New York attack was rookie running back Matt Snell, who battered the Oakland defense for 168 yards on 26 carries and two touchdowns. Cotton Davidson, Billy Cannon, and Art Powell provided the only positive offensive showings in this game. Davidson threw for 282 yards and one touchdown that Clem Daniels hauled in from 12 yards out. Powell caught six passes for 141 yards, and Cannon also snagged six for 110 yards, and scored on a 1-yard run to give the Raiders their first points after being down, 35–0, in the fourth quarter.[5]

6. Oct. 16: It wasn't a win, but a 43–43 tie with Boston was close enough for the faltering Raiders, who rolled up 431 offensive yards and Boston 495. Oakland had a 34–21 lead in the fourth quarter, but a 22-point assault by the Patriots put them up, 43–40, late in the game. Mike Mercer stepped up to get Oakland out of Boston with a tie by kicking a 38-yard field goal with five seconds left. He also opened the game's scoring with a 42-yard three-pointer in the first quarter, and added a 37-yarder in the third stanza. Billy Cannon flashed some of his old Heisman Trophy–winning skills by leading all ball carriers in the game with 90 yards on 13 attempts, with one of them going for a 34-yard touchdown. Quarterback Cotton Davidson turned in a great performance with 337 yards through the air and four touchdown passes. Art Powell was on the receiving end of two of them from 39 and nine yards, while Bo Roberson (50 yards) and Clem Daniels (26 yards) accounted for the others. Powell as usual was brilliant, catching seven passes for 121 yards, and Roberson also went over the century mark with three receptions for 115 yards. Despite giving up 22 points in the final quarter, the defense recorded three sacks and intercepted four Boston passes, with Archie Matsos leading the charge with two.[6]

7. Oct. 25: Cotton Davidson continued to impress. This time he threw for a team record 419 yards on 23 completions out of 36 attempts and five touchdowns in a 40–7 blowout victory over the Denver Broncos. Art Powell was once again his go-to guy, catching two of Davidson's touchdown tosses from 20 and four yards on a day that saw him haul in nine receptions for 152 yards. Billy Cannon had five catches for 111 yards, and was on the receiving end of two scoring strikes from 23 and 11 yards. Jan Bar-

rett added his name to the scoring column with an 11-yard catch. Mike Mercer kicked a 20-yard field goal, and the defense recorded a safety when Denver's Mickey Slaughter stepped out of the end zone. Clem Daniels added to the offensive fireworks by running for 167 yards. This first win put the Raiders at 1-5-1 going into the second half of the season.[7]

8. Nov. 1: Over the course of three games, Cotton Davidson threw 11 touchdown passes, but his two against the mighty San Diego Chargers were not enough in a 31–17 loss. He also tossed six interceptions despite throwing for 317 yards. Art Powell (14 yards) and Jan Barrett (41 yards) were on the receiving end of Davidson's six-point throws, and Mike Mercer booted a 33-yard field goal in the first quarter to give the Raiders their only lead of the game. Providing the offensive punch for San Diego was their All-Pro receiver Lance Alworth. The talented receiver caught eight catches for 203 yards and had two long touchdown receptions. As a team, the Chargers had 430 yards of total offense.[8]

9. Nov. 8: The Kansas City Chiefs turned two fumbles and an interception into touchdowns in a 42–7 rout of the Raiders. The Chiefs dominated so much that they opened up a 21-point lead in the second quarter before Oakland could muster a single first down. They recorded seven sacks, and held Oakland to 169 yards of total offense. Meanwhile, Kansas City signal caller Len Dawson needed to complete only eight of 17 pass attempts in the mauling, with four of his tosses going for touchdowns. Avoiding a shutout for Oakland came compliments of Ken Herock, who caught a 6-yard pass from Cotton Davidson after the Chiefs were well in control of the game.[9]

10. Nov. 15: The Raiders finally found a team in worse shape. Taking advantage of numerous errors by Houston quarterback George Blanda, the Raiders handed the two-win Oilers their seventh straight loss, 20–10. Cotton Davidson threw for two scores to Art Powell covering 26 and 20 yards, Mike Mercer kicked two field goals (32 and 12 yards), and Clem Daniels rushed for 104 yards on 16 carries to help Oakland improve to 2-7-1.[10]

11. Nov. 22: The New York Jets had trouble scoring in the second half of games throughout the season, and the Cotton Davidson–led Raiders seized the opportunity. Davidson threw for 358 yards and three touchdowns, ran for another, and Oakland won their second in a row, 35–26. Billy Cannon helped the cause by catching two touchdown passes from 10 and nine yards out and running for a third (1-yard). Davidson ran for a 6-yard score, and threw his other scoring strike to Clem Daniels (60 yards).[11]

12. Nov. 29: A trip to Denver produced a 20–20 tie after Oakland rallied despite being penalized 10 times for 111 yards throughout the game and turning the ball over six times. Down, 20–10, in the fourth quarter, the Raiders first scored on a Tom Flores to Art Powell 34-yard pass. Mike Mercer then added a 40-yard field goal to tie the game with less than four minutes remaining. Mercer kicked an earlier three-pointer from 29 yards. Flores passed for 270 yards despite being sacked nine times and tossing three interceptions. Powell had five receptions for 143 yards, and Clem Daniels ran for 94 yards and opened the scoring with a 25-yard run in the first quarter.[12]

13. Dec. 6: The Raiders continued on their four-game unbeaten streak with a 16–13 win over the Eastern Division–leading

10–2 Buffalo Bills. Cotton Davidson was injured right before half-time, and Tom Flores relieved him. Flores wasted little time in getting Oakland on the board. He connected with Clem Daniels from 35 yards out to give the Raiders a 7–0 lead at the intermission. Oakland extended their lead to 10–0 on a 40-yard field goal from Mike Mercer before losing their advantage. Buffalo's backup quarterback Daryle Lamonica threw a touchdown pass, and Pete Gogolak kicked two field goals to put the Bills out in front, 13–10, late in the game. The Raiders did not rattle, as Flores guided the offense to the winning points by finding Art Powell in the end zone from one yard out with just four seconds left. Powell's catch caused such hysteria that Oakland fans rushed the field, and the conversion was not attempted. Flores passed for 244 yards, and Powell rolled up 106 receiving yards on nine catches. The defense did their part by recording five sacks, and Warren Powers had two interceptions.[13]

14. Dec. 20: The Raiders were once again giant killers. This time they beat the Western Division champion San Diego Chargers, 21–20, for their fourth win in the final five games to end the year at 5-7-2. Tom Flores and Clem Daniels took the Raiders into the off-season on a high note by passing and running around the Chargers when it counted the most. Flores threw touchdown passes to Art Powell (26 yards) and Gene Mingo (10 yards) to give Oakland a 14–10 lead at the half. His third and final scoring strike of the afternoon was the game winner, going to Billy Cannon from 13 yards out in the fourth quarter. On the day, Flores hit on 21 of 39 pass attempts for 242 yards, and helped the offense roll up 421 total yards. Clem Daniels exploded for 144 rushing yards on 16 carries to power the Oakland ground attack. Over on defense, Warren Powers intercepted two passes for the second straight game.[14]

Individual Statistics and Roster

Head Coach: Al Davis
Assistant Coaches: Tom Dahms, John Rauch, Ollie Spencer, Charles Sumner
1964 Regular Season Record: 5-7-2
3rd Place in AFL Western Division
Scored 303 points to rank 6th out of 8 teams
Allowed 350 points to rank 6th
Led the league in fewest passing touchdowns allowed by a defense (21)

STARTERS — OFFENSE

QB — Tom Flores: Active for 14 games, and started in 7. Completed 98 of 200 pass attempts for 1,389 yards, 7 TD and 14 INT. Rushed for 64 yards on 11 carries.

HB — Clem Daniels: Active for 14 games. Rushed for 824 yards on 173 carries and 2 TD. Had 42 receptions for 696 yards and 6 TD. Threw 1 incomplete pass, and had 1 kickoff return for 32 yards.

FB — Billy Cannon: Active for 14 games. Rushed for 338 yards on 89 carries and 3 TD. Had 37 receptions for 454 yards and 5 TD, and 21 kickoff returns for 518 yards.

WR — Bo Roberson: Active for 14 games. Had 44 receptions for 624 yards and 1 TD, rushed for -4 yards on 1 carry, had 1 punt return for 20 yards and 36 kickoff returns for 975 yards. **Led the AFL with 1,615 all-purpose yards and a 27.1 yards per kickoff return average.**

WR — Art Powell: Active for 14 games. Had 76 receptions for 1,361 yards and 11 TD.

TE — Ken Herock: Active for 14 games. Had 23 receptions for 360 yards and 2 TD.

LT — Ken Rice: Active for 14 games.

LG — Bob Mischak: Active for 13 games.
C — Jim Otto: Active for 14 games.
RG — Wayne Hawkins: Active for 14 games.
RT — Dick Klein: Active for 14 games and had 1 kickoff return for 0 yards.

RESERVE OFFENSIVE PLAYERS

Jan Barrett (E): Active for 14 games. Had 12 receptions for 212 yards and 2 TD.

Cotton Davidson (QB): Active for 14 games, and started in 7. Completed 155 of 320 pass attempts for 2,497 yards, 21 TD and 19 INT. Rushed for 167 yards on 29 carries and 2 TD.

Bo Dickinson (RB): Active for 7 games. Rushed for 8 yards on 3 carries, had 3 receptions for 28 yards, and 1 kickoff return for 0 yards.

Fred Gillett (C/G/LB): Active for 3 games.

Bobby Jackson (RB): Active for 8 games. Rushed for 64 yards on 23 carries and 3 TD, had 10 receptions for 81 yards, and 2 kickoff returns for 32 yards.

Proverb Jacobs (T): Active for 6 games.

Bill Miller (WR): Active for 12 games. Had 2 receptions for 29 yards.

Gene Mingo (RB/K): Active for 7 games.

Glenn Shaw (RB): Active for 2 games. Rushed 9 for 26 yards on 9 carries and 2 TD, and had 3 receptions for 31 yards.

Frank Youso (T): Active for 14 games.

STARTERS — DEFENSE

DE — Dalva Allen: Active for 14 games.
DE — Dan Birdwell: Active for 14 games.
DT — Rex Mirich: Active for 14 games.
DT — Dave Costa: Active for 14 games.
LLB — Bill Budness: Active for 9 games and had 2 INT.
MLB — Archie Matsos: Active for 14 games and had 2 INT.
RLB — Clancy Osborne: Active for 14 games.
CB — Fred Williamson: Active for 14 games and had 6 INT.
CB — Howie Williams: Active for 12 games and had 1 INT.
S — Joe Krakoski: Active for 14 games and had 1 punt return for 8 yards.
S — Tommy Morrow: Active for 14 games, had 4 INT and 1 punt return for 0 yards.

RESERVE DEFENSIVE PLAYERS

Doug Brown (T): Active for 12 games.

Dan Conners (LB): Active for 5 games and had 1 kickoff return for 0 yards.

Ben Davidson (DE/T): Active for 12 games.

Claude Gibson (DB): Active for 14 games, had 2 INT and 29 punt returns for **419 yards and a 14.4 yards per punt return average.**

Louis Guy (DB): Active for 6 games.
Jon Jelacic (DE): Active for 3 games.
Mark Johnston (DB): Active for 1 game.
Jim McMillin (DB): Active for 1 game.
Jim Norris (T): Active for 1 game.
Warren Powers (DB): Active for 10 games and had 5 INT.
Jackie Simpson (LB/K): Active for 2 games.
J.R. Williamson (LB/C): Active for 14 games.

KICKING/PUNTING

K & P — Mike Mercer: Active for 14 games. Made 15 of 24 field goal attempts and 34 out of 34 extra point kicks for 79 points. Punted 58 times for a 42.1 average.

1965 Season Review

1. Sept. 12: The Raiders kept the momentum going from the previous season's final five games while sporting the youngest

team in professional football with the average age being 26.3 years. With the offense sputtering early, Dick Wood replaced Tom Flores after he was blasted hard on the third play of the game and was extremely woozy during his time running the offense. Davis took his veteran field general out, and Wood responded to the challenge. He connected on 12 of 25 pass attempts for 196 yards and ignited the Silver & Black with two touchdown passes to Art Powell (14 and 5 yards), and ran for a 3-yard score in a 37–10 romp over the Kansas City Chiefs. Gene Mingo kicked three field goals, two from 28 yards and the other from 40, and Claude Gibson rounded out the scoring fest with a 58-yard punt return in the fourth quarter to add the final touches to this opening day rout. The defense also played a great game, allowing Kansas City a mere 154 yards of total offense.[1]

2. Sept. 19: In front of their largest home crowd up to this time (21,000), the Raiders fell, 17–6, to the San Diego Chargers. Defensive back Ken Graham picked off a Dick Wood pass and returned it 25 yards into Oakland territory to give the Chargers a little breathing room in an otherwise tight game. Graham's interception came with the Raiders driving, and San Diego clinging to a slim 10–6 lead. Two plays after the interception, John Hadl threw a 25-yard pass to Lance Alworth that broke the game open for the Chargers. Gene Mingo supplied the Raiders with their points on two field goals from 48 and 35 yards.[2]

3. Sept. 26: With less than one minute left in the game, Tom Flores threw a 5-yard touchdown pass to Alan Miller that pulled out a 21–17 come-from-behind win over the Houston Oilers. The Oilers came into this game riding a four-game winning streak carried over from the previous season, and looked good in continuing it by jumping out to an early 7–0 lead. Undaunted by Houston's impressive start, Tom Flores came right back to tie the game within 56 seconds on a 69-yard pass to Clem Daniels. On the day, Daniels ignited the offense with 115 yards rushing on 20 carries and had 88 yards on four receptions. Houston took a 10–7 lead into the half, but a 43-yard pass from Flores to Art Powell on the second half's opening possession regained the lead for Oakland. Houston took over control of the scoreboard with 4:06 left in the fourth quarter, and led, 17–14, as the clock ticked closer to 0:00. Then came Flores' scoring strike to Miller with 56 seconds left to earn the Raiders their second win of the campaign.[3]

4. Oct. 3: The defending AFL-champion Buffalo Bills remained undefeated with a 17–12 win in Oakland's first road game of the season. Buffalo quarterback Jack Kemp broke a 10–10 tie in the third quarter by connecting with Ernie Warlick for what turned out to be the winning points. Alan Miller accounted for Oakland's only touchdown on a 5-yard pass from Tom Flores. Gene Mingo added a 33-yard field goal and Ike Lassiter forced Kemp out of the end zone for a safety for Oakland's other points.[4]

5. Oct. 8: Art Powell was a one man wrecking machine in a 24–10 victory over the Boston Patriots. Even though Powell was double and triple teamed for most of the game, he still managed to catch a then-team record 11 passes for 206 yards and two touchdowns from Tom Flores that covered 47 and two yards. Roger Hagberg ran for a 1-yard touchdown, and Gene Mingo kicked a 38-yard field goal for the rest of Oakland's point production. Flores had a great game with 261 yards passing on 20 of 34 attempts, and Clem Daniels ran for 113 yards on 20 carries. The win pushed Oakland over the .500 mark with a 3–2 record while

Boston remained winless. This also was the first time that the Raiders won in Boston.[5]

6. Oct. 16: The Raiders had to settle for a 24–24 tie with the New York Jets after Gene Mingo missed two field goal attempts from 28 and 42 yards late in the game. The Jets came into this game winless, and led by rookie sensation Joe Namath. The star signal caller was unable to produce much, as Oakland's front four pressured him throughout the game. Namath was only able to complete five of 21 passes for 126 yards, and even though he connected on a touchdown toss, he also threw an interception that Dave Grayson returned 79 yards to open the scoring in the first quarter. His counterpart, Tom Flores, threw for 207 yards and threw scoring strikes to Art Powell (31 yards) and Clem Daniels (11 yards), and Mingo connected on a 38-yard three-pointer for Oakland's tallies.[6]

7. Oct. 24: A 30–21 win gave the Raiders a season sweep over the Boston Patriots. This win was sealed when linebacker Gus Otto returned an interception 34 yards for a score with just 46 seconds left. The Raiders moved to 4-2-1, while Boston was still looking for their first win. Mike Mercer replaced Gene Mingo as kicker after the latter struggled by connecting on only eight of 19 field goal attempts. Mercer responded to the promotion in fine fashion by giving the Raiders their first nine points of the game on field goals from 22, 19, and nine yards. Dick Wood replaced Tom Flores after he was blasted by defensive end Larry Eisenhauer and would be out of action for one month. Wood did well in place of "the Iceman," hitting on 13 of 33 pass attempts for 213 yards and two touchdown tosses to Art Powell (15 and 22 yards). Rookie receiver Fred Biletnikoff started off his Hall of Fame career with fantastic numbers, catching seven passes for 118 yards.[7]

8. Oct. 31: Len Dawson took Kansas City 80 yards in the final minutes to give the Chiefs a 14–7 win. He capped the winning drive off himself with a 1-yard run. With two minutes left in the game, the Raiders had the opportunity to at least force a tie, but two bad calls nullified any chances they might have had. Quarterback Dick Wood and Art Powell were so infuriated with the officials that they lost their tempers and were ejected. When Al Davis and the rest of the team protested even more, the Raiders were penalized twenty yards. Clem Daniels gave the Raiders a first quarter lead with a 1-yard run, and rookie Fred Biletnikoff continued to impress by catching three passes for 82 yards to lead all receivers in the game. This win allowed the Chiefs to tie the Raiders for second place in the Western Division at 4-3-1.[8]

9. Nov. 7: Clem Daniels caught three passes for 109 yards and two of Dick Wood's three touchdown passes from 34 and 67 yards out in a 33–21 Oakland win on the road in Houston. Alan Miller caught Wood's other scoring toss from nine yards and Mike Mercer added four field goals (41, 17, 29, and 45 yards) to Oakland's total.[9]

10. Nov. 14: Despite two Clem Daniels touchdowns, the Raiders fell short to the Eastern Division–leading Buffalo Bills, 17–14. The Bills won the game in the final seven seconds on a Billy Joe 1-yard touchdown run. The heart-breaking loss kept the Raiders from getting within a half game of the Western Division lead. Clem Daniels provided the Raiders with both their six-pointers on a 41-yard run and a 25-yard pass from Dick Wood. Daniels led all ball carriers in the game with 91 yards on 14 carries.[10]

11.   Nov. 21: With the score tied at 14-all in the fourth quarter, linebacker Gus Otto intercepted a pass and went 68 yards for an Oakland touchdown. After the ensuing kickoff, defensive back Dave Grayson picked off another pass, returning this one 42 yards for a score. Tom Flores returned to the starting lineup, passed for two touchdowns, and Oakland won, 28–20, over Denver. Clem Daniels (34 yards) and Art Powell (3 yards) were on the receiving end of Flores' end zone strikes.[11]

12.   Dec. 5: Tom Flores once again threw touchdown passes to Clem Daniels (40 yards) and Art Powell (3 yards) against Denver, and the Raiders once again topped the Broncos, this time by a 24–13 tally. Alan Miller (2-yard run) and Mike Mercer (33-yard field goal) gave Oakland their other points. Daniels displayed his versatility by leading all ball carriers with 103 rushing yards, and added 94 more yards on two receptions. The win put Oakland at 7-4-1, giving them slim hopes of still beating out the 7-2-3 San Diego Chargers for the division title.[12]

13.   Dec. 12: Two Clem Daniels touchdown runs from one and 30 yards provided the edge in a 24–13 win over the New York Jets. Daniels once again led the game in rushing with 110 yards on 23 carries. A Tom Flores to Art Powell 26-yard scoring pass, and a Mike Mercer 22-yard field goal helped the Oakland cause. Powell led the Raiders' air attack with four receptions for 116 yards. The defensive backfield cooled down a hot Joe Namath with three interceptions despite the strong-armed rookie throwing for 280 yards. Warren Powers led the way with two thefts. Coming up with their third straight win, the Raiders improved to 8-4-1. Despite the win, Oakland's hopes of a division title were taken away after San Diego clinched the division with a win over Houston.[13]

14.   Dec. 19: In Al Davis' final game as Oakland's head coach, his Raiders lost to San Diego, 24–14, but finished the campaign with a very respectable 8-5-1 record. With the score tied at 14-all in the fourth quarter, San Diego's Lance Alworth sparked the home crowd by taking a Don Breaux pass 66 yards for the go-ahead touchdown. Alworth played a great game, catching five passes for 160 yards. The Raiders held a 14-0 advantage in the second quarter on a 4-yard pass from Tom Flores to Art Powell, and on a Clem Daniels 1-yard run before the bottom fell out on the Silver and Black. Daniels was the offensive spark in Oakland's arsenal, as he led the game in rushing with 85 yards, and led the team with seven receptions for 61 yards.[14]

Individual Statistics and Roster

Head Coach: Al Davis
Assistant Coaches: Tom Dahms, John Rauch, Ollie Spencer, Charles Sumner
1965 Regular Season Record: 8-5-1
2nd Place in AFL Western Division
Scored 298 points to rank 5th out of 8 teams
Allowed 239 points to rank 3rd

STARTERS — OFFENSE

QB — Tom Flores: Active for 14 games, and started in 11. Completed 122 of 269 pass attempts for 1,593 yards, 14 TD and 11 INT. Rushed for 32 yards on 11 carries.
HB — Clem Daniels: Active for 14 games. Rushed for 884 yards on 219 carries and 5 TD. Had 36 receptions for 568 yards and 7 TD, and completed 2 of 2 pass attempts for 95 yards.
FB — Alan Miller: Active for 14 games. Rushed for 272 yards on 73 carries and 1 TD. Had 21 receptions for 208 yards and 3 TD.
WR — Fred Biletnikoff: Active for 14 games, and started in 7. Had 24 receptions for 331 yards.
WR — Art Powell: Active for 14 games. Had 52 receptions for 800 yards and 12 TD.
TE — Billy Cannon: Active for 10 games. Had 7 receptions for 127 yards.
LT — Bob Svihus: Active for 14 games.
LG — Ken Rice: Active for 14 games.
C — Jim Otto: Active for 14 games.
RG — Wayne Hawkins: Active for 14 games.
RT — Harry Schuh: Active for 14 games.

RESERVE OFFENSIVE PLAYERS

Pervis Atkins (WR/RB): Active for 5 games and had 1 reception for 6 yards.
Cotton Davidson (QB): Active for 2 games and had 1 completion in 1 pass attempt for 8 yards.
Roger Hagberg (RB/WR): Active for 14 games. Rushed for 171 yards on 48 carries and 1 TD. Had 12 receptions for 121 yards, 1 punt return for 3 yards, and 3 kickoff returns for 50 yards.
Ken Herock (TE/LB): Active for 14 games and had 18 receptions for 221 yards.
Marv Marinovich (G): Active for 1 game.
Gene Mingo (RB/K): Active for 14 games. Had 1 reception for 5 yards, and made 8 of 19 field goal attempts.
Bob Mischak (G/TE): Active for 8 games.
Bo Roberson (WR/RB): Active for 6 games.
Larry Todd (RB): Active for 14 games. Rushed for 183 yards on 32 carries, had 8 receptions for 106 yards, 20 kickoff returns for 461 yards, and threw 1 incomplete pass.
Dick Wood (QB): Active for 14 games, and started in 3. Completed 69 of 157 pass attempts for 1,003 yards, 8 TD and 6 INT. Rushed for 16 yards on 4 carries and 1 TD.
Frank Youso (T): Active for 11 games.

STARTERS — DEFENSE

DE — Ike Lassiter: Active for 14 games.
DE — Ben Davidson: Active for 14 games.
DT — Rex Mirich: Active for 14 games.
DT — Dave Costa: Active for 14 games.
LLB — J.R. Williamson: Active for 14 games.
MLB — Archie Matsos: Active for 12 games and had 3 INT.
RLB — Gus Otto: Active for 14 games, had 3 INT and **2 TD**.
CB — Kent McCloughan: Active for 14 games and had 3 INT.
CB — Dave Grayson: Active for 14 games, had 3 INT, 2 TD, and 1 kickoff return for 34 yards.
S — Joe Krakoski: Active for 12 games and had 2 punt returns for 5 yards.
S — Howie Williams: Active for 14 games and had 2 INT.

RESERVE DEFENSIVE PLAYERS

Dan Birdwell (T/E): Active for 14 games.
Bill Budness (LB): Active for 14 games and had 1 INT.
Dan Conners (LB): Active for 14 games.
John Diehl (T): Active for 8 games.
Claude Gibson (DB): Active for 14 games, had 4 INT, 1 TD, **31** punt returns for 357 yards and 1 TD, and 9 kickoff returns for 186 yards.
Dick Hermann (LB): Active for 14 games and had 1 kickoff return for 0 yards.
Carleton Oats (T/E): Active for 14 games.
Warren Powers (DB): Active for 12 games and had 5 INT.
Rich Zecher (T): Active for 14 games.

KICKING/PUNTING

K & P — Mike Mercer: Active in 14 games. Made 9 of 15 field goal attempts and 35 of 35 extra point kicks for 62 points. Punted 75 times for a 41.1 average, threw 1 pass for 14 yards, and ran the ball once for -1 yard.

AFL-NFL Merger

When the American Football League first started, the old guard NFL did not take it seriously. The NFL felt the AFL was a collection of castoffs that did not have the talent to play in the established National Football League. However, unlike other leagues that attempted to compete with the NFL, the American Football league managed to survive and prosper thanks to the magic of television and a wide-open offensive attack that ran up points at a steady clip. The fans loved it, and before too long, the AFL gained a lot of national attention.

In 1965, the NBC Television Network paid the AFL $36 million for the right to broadcast their games. This alone secured a bright future, and with this vast fortune, the AFL was able to go after many big-name NFL stars, with the main focus on quarterbacks. The battle for top talent was getting ugly, and the AFL had the NFL on the ropes, and something had to be done to resolve this bitter tussle.[1]

After years of bidding wars between the two leagues, talks got underway for a solution. On June 8, 1966, an agreement was reached that transformed pro football into what we know of it today. On that June day, both leagues officially merged. It was agreed upon that the leagues would become one at the start of the 1970 season with NFL commissioner Pete Rozelle in control, and would still be called the National Football League and divided into two conferences.[2]

All the old AFL teams became known as the American Football Conference, and the old NFL teams were grouped together into the National Football Conference. To make both conferences even at 13 teams apiece, the Cleveland Browns, Pittsburgh Steelers, and Baltimore Colts shifted over to the AFC. The winners of each conference would then play for the NFL championship in what came to be known as the Super Bowl.

Before 1970, the leagues remained the NFL and AFL with one common draft, but with the exception of pre-season, not a common schedule until 1970. Even though they would not play a common schedule from 1966 through 1969, both leagues agreed upon staging a championship game between their respective champions. After each league crowned its champion, they would then play in a neutral, warm weather site in January. For the first three encounters, the game was called the AFL-NFL World Championship Game. By the 1970 contest, it was already being called the Super Bowl.[3]

1966 Season Review

1. Sept. 2: The Raiders helped the Miami Dolphins kick of their inaugural season. Joe Auer got the Dolphins off to a tremendous start when he returned the opening kickoff 95 yards for Miami's first-ever regular season touchdown. Auer's return provided the only points until the second quarter. Defensive backs Howie Williams and Dave Grayson gave Oakland some much-needed momentum with interceptions thrown by ex–Raiders quarterback Dick Wood. The offense took advantage of the thefts in the form of a Mike Mercer field goal (16 yards) and a 2-yard run by fullback Hewritt Dixon. Tom Flores passed for two touchdowns in the second half to Art Powell (16 yards) and Tom Mitchell (16 yards), and the Raiders left Miami with a 23–14 win for new head coach John Rauch. Powell led the offensive attack with eight receptions for 104 yards, and the Oakland held the Dolphins under the century mark in both rushing and passing.[1]

2. Sept. 10: After scoring points in 37 straight games, the Raiders ran into a strong Houston defense and fell, 31–0. Ageless 39-year-old wonder George Blanda threw for two scores and added a 47-yard field goal. Oakland only had two legitimate scoring opportunities, but both were ended by interceptions. In all the Raiders suffered seven turnovers on four interceptions and three fumbles.[2]

3. Sept. 18: The Oakland-Kansas City rivalry is one of pro football's most heated, and what better way to add fuel to an already out-of-control fire than to beat your nemesis in their new stadium. The Raiders christened their new Oakland Alameda Coliseum on this date, but the festivities were spoiled by a 32–10 loss. The Raiders' first-ever points scored in the Oakland Coliseum were provided by Clem Daniels on a 22-yard pass from Cotton Davidson in the first quarter that gave the Silver and Black their only lead of the game. Mike Eischeid added a 31-yard field goal in the second quarter to tie the score at 10-all. Even in defeat, Art Powell was his stellar self, catching nine passes for 133 yards. Kansas City quarterback Len Dawson threw for three touchdowns, and the special teams chipped in with two blocked punts that were turned into scores. With this win, the Chiefs remained undefeated while Oakland fell to 1–2, and were outscored 63–10 in their two previous outings.[3]

4. Sept. 25: One of the premier AFL teams in the early to mid–1960's were the San Diego Chargers, and they lived up to their reputation with a 29–20 win over Oakland. With the win, the Chargers were tied with Kansas City for the Western Division lead. On offense, quarterback John Hadl ran for a touchdown, threw for one, and set up another with a long pass to receiver Lance Alworth. On defense defensive back Speedy Duncan provided thrills with three interceptions. Scoring for the Raiders in their third straight loss were Clem Daniels (1-yard run), Fred Biletnikoff (8-yard pass from Tom Flores), and Mike Eischeid (49 and 33 yard field goals).[4]

5. Oct. 9: The Raiders remained perfect against the Miami Dolphins with a 21–10 win. Thanks to the expansion Dolphins, Oakland had their second win of the year, with both coming against Miami. This was also the first win for the Raiders in their new stadium. Tom Flores threw for 261 yards and three touchdowns. His first one went to Art Powell from 25 yards out, his second to Roger Hagberg (24 yards), and the third went to Fred Biletnikoff from the Miami 4-yard line, which broke open a close game with two minutes remaining to be played. Oakland's defense did a great job against the upstart Dolphins by recording four sacks, allowing only 77 rushing yards, and 115 through the air.[5]

6. Oct. 16: After spoiling the dedication of Oakland Alameda Coliseum one month earlier, the Chiefs were paid back at their stadium in a 34–13 upset loss. Tom Flores threw for 301 yards, and tossed three touchdown passes in the second quarter,

and the Chiefs never recovered. Fullback Hewritt Dixon was on the receiving end of two Flores' touchdown passes from 10 and 76 yards out, and ran for a 1-yard score, also in the second quarter. For the game, Dixon caught five passes for 129 yards. Billy Cannon caught Flores' first scoring strike from 75 yards to put the Raiders in the lead for good. Mike Eischeid added two second half field goals from 37 and 22 yards to complete Oakland's scoring. Defensive lineman Tom Keating played a fantastic game, recording 15 tackles and recovering two fumbles. The loss stopped Kansas City from taking over the top spot in the Western Division, while the Raiders were able to even their record at 3–3.[6]

7. Oct. 23: Oakland recorded their third straight win thanks to a Hewritt Dixon 1-yard run with two seconds remaining in the game. Dixon's late score finished off an 83-yard drive, and gave the Raiders a 24–21 victory over the Eastern Division–leading New York Jets. Art Powell caught five passes for 109 yards that included a 31-yard touchdown from Tom Flores in the second quarter to open Oakland's scoring and tie the game at 7–7. Flores added an 8-yard run to once again tie the game at 14–14 in the fourth quarter. Mike Eischeid gave the Raiders their first lead of the game with a 32-yard field goal before New York fullback Matt Snell put the Jets up, 21–17, with a 1-yard run. Dixon then provided the winning score to get Oakland out of the Big Apple with another one in the win column. Clem Daniels did not score for Oakland, but provided the team with a steady ground attack, rushing for a game-high 104 yards on 15 carries.[7]

8. Oct. 30: The Boston Patriots snapped Oakland's three-game winning streak, 24–21, with the brunt on the damage being done by powerhouse fullback Jim Nance. Nance set a single-game AFL record with 28 rushing attempts. He gained a whopping 208 yards, and scored two short yardage touchdowns. The win helped the Patriots move into first place in the Eastern Division. Clem Daniels carried the load for the Oakland offense, with 112 yards receiving on five catches and 52 yards on the ground. He scored all of Oakland's six-pointers, with the first coming on a 50-yard reception from Cotton Davidson, and runs for 22 and one yard in the fourth quarter after the Raiders were down by 17 points. Davidson replaced Tom Flores at quarterback in the first quarter after Flores was knocked unconscious by linemen Larry Eisenhauer and Jim Hunt.[8]

9. Nov. 6: One week earlier, Tom Flores was knocked out early in the first quarter and missed the rest of the game. In this game against the Houston Oilers, Flores was back under center, and responded by throwing for 269 yards and two scores in a 38–23 win. Fred Biletnikoff (78 yards) and Art Powell (46 yards) were on the receiving end of Flores' six-point tosses. Clem Daniels was also responsible for Oakland's success by running for three short yardage touchdowns from six, four, and nine yards out. Daniels proved to be the complete offensive weapon by running for 63 yards and catching four passes for 97 more. Mike Eischeid added to Oakland's tally with a 24-yard field goal.[9]

10. Nov. 13: Oakland jumped out to an 18-point halftime lead and never looked back in a 41–19 blow out victory over San Diego. Art Powell caught two short yardage touchdown passes from Tom Flores that covered eight and one yard, and Clem Daniels snagged another from two yards. Daniels also led Oakland's backfield with 104 rushing yards on 11 carries. Hewritt Dixon chipped in with two touchdown runs from three and two

yards out, and rushed for 90 yards on 16 carries. Mike Eischeid kicked two field goals (22 and 23 yards), and Flores passed for 279 yards to help put Oakland at 6–4, two games behind first place Kansas City. With this loss, the Chargers were eliminated from the division race. It was the end of an incredible run for the Chargers, who had won five of the first six Western Division titles since 1960.[10]

11. Nov. 20: Two long passes from Tom Flores to Billy Cannon that gained 109 yards helped set the Raiders up for both of their touchdowns in a 17–3 win over the Denver Broncos. Flores capped off both drives with touchdown passes. Art Powell scored on an 18-yarder to give Oakland their go-ahead points in the second quarter, and Larry Todd caught Flores' second scoring strike from two yards out. Mike Eischeid closed out the scoring with a 12-yard field goal. The defense did their part by allowing Denver a mere 31 yards passing, recorded six sacks, and got two interceptions from Kent McCloughan and one from Dave Grayson. Oakland improved to 7–4, which enabled them to stay alive in the division race.[11]

12. Nov. 24: Oakland's three-game winning streak ended with a 31–10 romp at the hands of the Eastern Division–leading Buffalo Bills. The defending two-time AFL champion Bills were led by quarterback Jack Kemp's arm and legs. Kemp's ball handling allowed Buffalo to produce a well-balanced offensive attack. He threw for 241 yards and ran for an additional 45. Wray Carlton ran for a game-high 97 yards and scored on two short yardage runs to help the Bills roll up 24 points while holding the Raiders to none. Tom Flores and Art Powell provided big numbers in defeat. Flores passed for 286 yards, and Powell had four receptions for 116 yards. With this loss, the Raiders were officially eliminated from the Western Division race. Billy Cannon gave the Raiders a first quarter lead on a 16-yard reception from Flores, and Mike Eischeid kicked an 8-yard field goal to give the Silver and Black their last advantage of the game in the second quarter.[12]

13. Dec. 3: Within a span of 43 seconds, the Raiders scored twice to take a 28–20 fourth quarter lead over the New York Jets. The quick scores came on a 31-yard pass from Tom Flores to Art Powell and a 28-yard interception return by linebacker Dan Conners. The Raiders got their other points on touchdown passes from Flores, with Powell (32 yards) and Hewritt Dixon (5 yards) hauling them in. On the day, Flores threw for 282 yards to help the Raiders compile 415 yards of total offense. Oakland's defense stayed busy picking off Joe Namath passes, as they gathered in five. Conners added another theft to his day's work, Rodger Bird also came up with two, and Warren Powers had one. Just when things looked bleak for the Jets, a bad punt by Mike Eischeid gave them a break. Halfback Emerson Boozer quickly seized the opportunity given the New Yorkers by running for a 47-yard touchdown on the first play following the punt. Quarterback Joe Namath then connected with George Sauer for the two-point conversion to end the game in a 28–28 tie. When not throwing interceptions, Namath managed to hook up with his own receivers for 327 yards and two six-pointers that helped the Jets finish with 489 yards of offensive production.[13]

14. Dec. 11: The Raiders finished the 1966 campaign with an 8-5-1 record, which was good enough for a second place finish in the division behind rival Kansas City. Oakland obtained their

runner-up status by defeating the Denver Broncos, 28–10. Art Powell set two AFL records in this game when he registered his fifth season of topping the 1,000-yard receiving barrier, and the fifth time he caught at least 10 touchdown passes in a season. This game was the last that Powell played in an Oakland uniform, and he left on a high note by hauling in two of Tom Flores' three touchdown passes from 46 and 45 yards out. The "Iceman" also connected with Hewritt Dixon on a 2-yard pass for Oakland's other six-pointer through the air. For the game, Flores completed 17 of 28 pass attempts for 236 yards. This game also marked the final time that Flores wore the silver and black as a player. Powell topped the century mark with four receptions for 109 yards, and Clem Daniels rushed for a game-high 88 yards, and scored Oakland's other touchdown on a 3-yard run.[14]

Individual Statistics and Roster

Head Coach: John Rauch

Assistant Coaches: Tom Dahms, Ollie Spencer, Charles Sumner, Bill Walsh

1966 Regular Season Record: 8-5-1

2nd Place in AFL Western Division

Scored 315 points to rank 6th out of 9 teams

Allowed 288 points to rank 5th

Led the league in least amount of offensive yards allowed by a defense (4,571), and least amount of passing yards allowed by a defense (2,118)

STARTERS — OFFENSE

QB — Tom Flores: Active for 14 games, and started in 10. Completed 151 of 306 pass attempts for 2,638 yards, 24 TD and 14 INT. **His 17.5 yards per completion average led the AFL.** Rushed for 50 yards on 5 carries and 1 TD.

HB — Clem Daniels: Active for 14 games. Rushed for 801 yards on 204 carries and 7 TD. Had 40 receptions for 652 yards and 3 TD, and threw 3 passes for 0 yards and 1 INT.

FB — Roger Hagberg: Active for 14 games. Rushed for 282 yards on 62 carries, had 21 catches for 248 yards and 1 TD, and 1 kickoff return for 13 yards.

WR — Fred Biletnikoff: Active for 10 games. Had 17 receptions for 272 yards and 3 TD.

WR — Art Powell: Active for 14 games. Had 53 receptions for 1,026 yards and 11 TD.

TE — Billy Cannon: Active for 14 games. Had 14 receptions for 436 yards and 2 TD, and 1 punt return for 12 yards.

LT — Bob Svihus: Active for 14 games.

LG — Wayne Hawkins: Active for 14 games.

C — Jim Otto: Active for 14 games.

RG — Jim Harvey: Active for 14 games.

RT — Harry Schuh: Active for 14 games.

RESERVE OFFENSIVE PLAYERS

Pervis Atkins (WR/RB): Active for 14 games. Rushed for 10 yards on 143 carries, had 1 punt return for 13 yards and 29 kickoff returns for 608 yards.

Pete Banaszak (RB): Active for 14 games. Rushed 4 for 18 yards on 4 carries, and had 1 reception for 11 yards.

Cotton Davidson (QB): Active for 14 games, and started in 4. Completed 59 of 139 pass attempts for 770 yards, 2 TD and 11 INT. Rushed for -11 yards on 6 carries.

Hewritt Dixon (RB): Active for 14 games. Rushed for 277 yards on 68 carries and 5 TD. Had 29 receptions for 345 yards and 4 TD.

Charlie Green (QB): Active for 14 games, and completed 2 of 2 pass attempts for 17 yards.

Greg Kent (T/E): Active for 7 games.

Mike Mercer (K): Active for 2 games.

Bill Miller (WR): Active for 5 games.

Tom Mitchell (TE/WR): Active for 14 games and had 23 receptions for 301 yards and 1 TD.

Palmer Pyle (G): Active for 13 games.

Larry Todd (RB): Active for 14 games, and had 14 receptions for 134 yards and 1 TD.

Dick Tyson (G): Active for 3 games.

STARTERS — DEFENSE

DE — Ike Lassiter: Active for 14 games and had 1 INT.

DE — Ben Davidson: Active for 14 games.

DT — Dan Birdwell: Active for 14 games and had 1 INT.

DT — Tom Keating: Active for 14 games.

LLB — J.R. Williamson: Active for 13 games.

MLB — Bill Budness: Active for 14 games.

RLB — Gus Otto: Active for 14 games.

CB — Kent McCloughan: Active for 14 games and had 4 INT.

CB — Dave Grayson: Active for 14 games, had 3 INT and 6 kickoff returns for 128 yards.

S — Warren Powers: Active for 14 games, had 5 INT and 1 kickoff return for 0 yards.

S — Howie Williams: Active for 14 games and had 3 INT.

RESERVE DEFENSIVE PLAYERS

Rodger Bird (DB): Active for 14 games, had 4 INT, **37** punt returns for **323** yards, and 19 kickoff returns for 390 yards. **His total of 56 punt and kickoff returns also led the AFL.**

Dan Conners (LB): Active for 14 games, had 2 INT and 1 TD.

Dave Daniels (T): Active for 14 games.

Rich Jackson (E/LB): Active for 5 games.

Joe Krakoski (DB): Active for 11 games, and had 2 punt returns for 19 yards.

Bill Laskey (LB): Active for 14 games.

Rex Mirich (T): Active for 14 games, and had 2 kickoff returns for 0 yards.

Carleton Oats (T/E): Active for 14 games.

Ray Schmautz (LB): Active for 10 games.

Willie Williams (DB): Active for 6 games, and had 2 kickoff returns for 52 yards.

KICKING/PUNTING

K &P — Mike Eischeid: Active for 12 games. Made 11 of 26 field goal attempts and 37 out of 37 extra point kicks for 70 points. Punted 64 times for a 42.3 average.

1967 Season Review

1. Sept. 10: Oakland started off their new season with a 51–0 slaughter over the Denver Broncos for their best opening day victory ever. Oakland so dominated Denver that the Broncos could only achieve two first downs throughout the entire game. This was also the first time in 76 games that Denver was held scoreless. Daryle Lamonica and George Blanda quickly fit into their new surroundings. Lamonica guided Oakland to their first five touchdowns. Of the five, he scored one himself on a 4-yard run, and passed for a 10-yarder to Hewritt Dixon for another. Dixon also scored on a 3-yard run for Oakland's first points of the new campaign in the first quarter. The 40-year-old Blanda took over at quarterback once the game was out of reach, and

produced a 50-yard touchdown pass to receiver Warren Wells. Blanda also kicked a 23-yard field goal and six conversions. Joining in the scoring fest were Clem Daniels (6-yard run), Rod Sherman (13-yard run), and Warren Powers (36-yard interception return). Rodger Bird stood out on special teams by setting Oakland up with excellent field position after two long punt returns. The offense took advantage of Bird's efforts by scoring quickly after each return. The Oakland defense, also known as "The 11 Angry Men," was also outstanding, allowing Denver two first downs, 48 rushing yards, and a mere 53 yards through the air. This game was the best total team effort up to this time in Raiders history, and they looked to keep the momentum from it going throughout the season.[1]

2. Sept. 17: Showing that their opening day rout of Denver was no fluke, the Raiders continued on a path of destruction by whipping the Boston Patriots, 35–7. Daryle Lamonica led the offense charge by throwing for 251 yards and tossing touchdowns to three different receivers. In the first quarter, "the Mad Bomber" connected with Fred Biletnikoff from 32 yards out. He then threw a 17-yarder to Hewritt Dixon, and finished up with a 9-yard toss to Bill Miller. Lamonica also added a 21-yard scoring run to his day's total. Clem Daniels ran for a score from three yards out to account for Oakland's other touchdown. Even though he did not score, Billy Cannon led the receiving corps with 114 yards on four receptions. Once again, the defense did their part with a dominating effort. The unit forced two fumbles, intercepted three passes, allowed only 65 yards rushing, and kept constant pressure on Boston quarterback Babe Parilli.[2]

3. Oct. 1: After outscoring their first two opponents by a combined 86–7 margin, the Raiders played a close one against the defending AFL champion Kansas City Chiefs. Despite a close game, Oakland prevailed, 23–21. The defense stuffed the Chiefs throughout the first three quarters, and held the powerful Kansas City running attack to 93 yards. This was the third straight week that Oakland's defense kept an opponent from topping the century mark on the ground. Daryle Lamonica threw for 236 yards, and connected on touchdown passes to Clem Daniels (1 yard) and Billy Cannon (29 yards). George Blanda added field goals from 31, 33, and 42 yards to help provide the offensive punch for the undefeated Raiders.[3]

4. Oct. 7: The two division leaders met on this date with Oakland traveling to Shea Stadium to do battle with Joe Namath and the New York Jets. The Jets had the league's top offense, and used it to jump out to a 20–0 lead over the AFL's top defense. The Jets held on to win, 27–14, and put the Raiders in the loss column for the first time in 1967. Despite being under a heavy blitz throughout the game, quarterback Joe Namath managed to keep the Jets moving with his strong arm. The Oakland defense held Namath to only 166 yards through the air after he exploded for 399 and 415 yards in his two previous games. They also prevented Namath from throwing for a touchdown. Defensive back Willie Brown came up big despite the loss by intercepting two passes. The Raiders received their points on touchdown passes from Daryle Lamonica to Bill Miller (5 yards) and Warren Wells (25 yards). The loss knocked Oakland out of first place. The San Diego Chargers assumed the Western Division lead with a 3-0-1 record.[4]

5. Oct. 15: Oakland rebounded nicely from their first loss

by beating the Buffalo Bills, 24–20. In his first game against his old team, Daryle Lamonica was intercepted four times, and only completed nine out of 23 pass attempts. However, two of his completions went for touchdowns, with Fred Biletnikoff hauling in one from 41 yards, and Billy Cannon the other from three yards out. Linebacker Dan Conners raced 30 yards with an interception to produce Oakland's other touchdown, and George Blanda topped the scoring off with a 31-yard field goal. Oakland's defensive unit once again played tough, recording 11 sacks and holding Buffalo's running attack to 38 yards.[5]

6. Oct. 22: Four Daryle Lamonica touchdown passes, and a punishing defensive effort, allowed Oakland to manhandle the Boston Patriots, 48–14. The Raiders allowed Boston only 74 yards of total offense, and Lamonica threw at will against a beleaguered defense. Bill Miller (8 yards), Roger Hagberg (12 yards), Billy Cannon (4 yards), and Warren Wells (24 yards) were all on the receiving end of scoring tosses from "the Mad Bomber." Fred Biletnikoff led the game with 109 receiving yards on just three receptions. Hagberg added a 1-yard run to his day's work to open the scoring in the first quarter. Wells also scored on a 52-yard reception later in the game from George Blanda, who added field goals from 12 and 24 yards.[6]

7. Oct. 29: Oakland's domination of the 1967 Western Division race was finally in place after the 5–1 Raiders blasted the 5-0-1 Chargers, 51–10. Daryle Lamonica continued to ring up points for the explosive Oakland offense. This time he did it by throwing for 316 yards and two long scoring strikes, plus running for two himself (1 and 3 yards). Fred Biletnikoff caught a Lamonica touchdown pass from 70 yards out, and Clem Daniels hauled in the other from 40 yards away to finish the game with four receptions for 101 yards. Daniels also ran for a 1-yard touchdown, and with his 94 rushing yards, he became the first running back in AFL history to break the 5,000-yard barrier. Oakland's other six-pointers came compliments of Warren Wells on a 14-yard pass from George Blanda, and Hewritt Dixon on a 7-yard run. The punishing Oakland defense picked off 4 passes, with David Grayson leading the way with 3, and recorded a safety to open the scoring in the first quarter. The Raiders were now firmly entrenched in the Western Division's top spot, and dared anyone to come and knock them out of it.[7]

8. Nov. 5: George Blanda kicked two field goals (46 and 43 yards) to give him 100 in his AFL career. Daryle Lamonica threw two touchdown passes to Bill Miller (7 and 2 yards), and the Oakland defense recorded 11 sacks, allowed a mere six yards rushing, and 52 through the air in a 21–17 victory over the winless Denver Broncos.[8]

9. Nov. 19: Billy Cannon was a standout running back for the Houston Oilers, and after coming to Oakland, he became just as impressive at tight end. In a 31–17 win over Miami, Cannon caught six passes for 99 yards, and hit paydirt on three of them. Daryle Lamonica, who threw for 292 yards, connected with Cannon on touchdown strikes from eight, nine, and 46 yards. Clem Daniels added a 1-yard run, and George Blanda kicked a field goal (11 yards) to round out Oakland's point production in a game that saw the Silver and Black roll up 396 yards of offense.[9]

10. Nov. 23: With Clem Daniels injured, second-year man Pete Banaszak filled in brilliantly in a 44–22 rout of Kansas City. He carried the ball 13 times for 81 yards, scored a touchdown (1-

yard run), and caught four passes for an additional 27 yards. Daryle Lamonica threw for 281 yards and one touchdown. Fred Biletnikoff was on the receiving end of Lamonica's scoring toss from five yards out. For the game, Biletnikoff hauled in six passes for 158 yards. The Oakland defense was exceptional as ever. They picked off four passes, returning two for scores, and held the Kansas City backfield to 56 yards, and recorded six sacks. Returning interceptions for touchdowns were Willie Brown (25 yards), and Warren Powers (33 yards). Larry Todd scored Oakland's final points on a 4-yard run, and George Blanda added three field goals (10, 18, and 43 yards). With this ninth win of the season, the Raiders swept the season series from the defending AFL champs for the second time in team history.[10]

11. Dec. 3: The "Mad Bomber" was on top of his game in a 41–21 win over the second place San Diego Chargers. This game marked the 50th regular season victory in Raiders' history. Lamonica hit on 21 of 34 pass attempts for 349 yards and four touchdowns, as Oakland compiled 460 yards of offensive production. His scoring passes went to Fred Biletnikoff (18 yards), Billy Cannon (64 and 1 yard), and Bill Miller (29 yards). Larry Todd added a 2-yard scoring run, and George Blanda hit on two field goals (24 and 21 yards). The win improved the Raiders to 10–1, and moved them closer to their first-ever division title.[11]

12. Dec. 10: With a hard-fought 19–7 win over the Houston Oilers, the Raiders clinched their first Western Division championship. With the honor, the Raiders became the first team other than San Diego or Kansas City to win the division crown since 1960. This victory did not come easy, as Oakland trailed, 7–3, going into the fourth quarter. Houston's defense dominated the first half, never allowing the Raiders to get any farther than the Oilers' 38-yard line. Willie Brown ignited Oakland with an interception that produced their first points of the day, which was a George Blanda 12-yard field goal. After that, Daryle Lamonica got untracked, finished the game with 286 yards passing, and the Raiders added sixteen more points to their total. Blanda added three more field goals (32, 31, and 45 yards), and Hewritt Dixon ran for a 27-yard touchdown to help him finish with a game-high 96 rushing yards. This win also gave the Raiders their most wins in a single season.[12]

13. Dec. 17: Even though they clinched the division, the Raiders refused to rest on their laurels. Getting revenge on the only team to beat them during the season was what they had on their minds. In the end, revenge was sweet, as the Raiders rallied for 28 points in the second half to beat the New York Jets, 38–29. In an incredible passing show, both Daryle Lamonica and New York's Joe Namath shined. The "Mad Bomber" threw for 336 yards and three touchdowns, while Broadway Joe accounted for 370 yards and three scores as well. Namath also set a new AFL record for most yards passing in a single season with 3,664. He would go on to finish the 1967 season with 4,007 yards, becoming the first pro quarterback to ever reach that mark. Warren Wells (18 yards), Pete Banaszak (4 yards), and Billy Cannon (47 yards) were on the receiving end of Lamonica's touchdown passes. Banaszak also led all ball carriers with 68 yards rushing. Roger Hagberg (6 yards) and Hewritt Dixon (3 yards) added touchdown runs for Oakland, and George Blanda kicked a 36-yard field goal.[13]

14. Dec. 24: On Christmas Eve, the Oakland Raiders wrapped up their magnificent season with a 28–21 win over the

Buffalo Bills. This marked Oakland's tenth straight win, and they finished at a near flawless 13–1. This turned out to be the most wins by a team during a regular season in the history of the AFL. Throughout the year, the Oakland defense was exceptional, and in this game they accounted for two touchdowns on fumble recoveries. Middle linebacker Dan Conners raced 21 yards with one, and defensive tackle Carlton Oats took the other one in from 11 yards. The team's other scores came on a 23-yard pass from Daryle Lamonica to Billy Cannon, and a 1-yard run by Hewritt Dixon. With the spectacular regular season now behind them, the Silver and Black geared up for their first run at the playoffs. Standing in the way of Oakland's quest for a league championship were the Houston Oilers, who would be making their fourth trip to an AFL title contest.[14]

AFL Championship Game, December 31, 1967

Magnificent. This one word can best sum up the Raiders' first exposure to championship play. On the final day of the year, Oakland hosted the Houston Oilers to see who would wear the crown of AFL champions and represent the league in Super Bowl II. It is hard to even call this a game, due to the fact that the Raiders seemed to use it as a scrimmage. In the end, the Silver and Black mauled a well-respected defensive Houston team, 40–7.

This game started out as a close contest, but Oakland then exploded thanks to big plays. George Blanda opened the scoring with a 37-yard field goal in the first quarter. Hewritt Dixon was up next to put his name in the scoring summary. Following great blocking from an offensive line led by rookie guard Gene Upshaw, Dixon ran through a solid defensive unit like it was not even there for a 69-yard touchdown. For the day, Dixon led all ball carriers with 144 yards on 21 attempts, while his running mate Pete Banaszak carried 15 times for 116 yards. With the running game performing so well, Daryle Lamonica did not have to live up to his moniker "the Mad Bomber" on this day. He only threw 24 times, completing 10 passes for 111 yards.

With the first half winding down, the Raiders were driving, but stalled at the Houston 17. With eighteen seconds left before the halftime festivities, the Raiders lined up for a chip shot Blanda field goal attempt. Instead of three points, however, Lamonica decided to take the snap and throw. This caught Houston completely off guard, and Lamonica threw to Dave Kocourek for a 17-yard touchdown pass that proved to be the major turning point of this game. From then on, the Oilers never recovered, and the Silver and Black steamroller continued its onslaught for the final thirty minutes.

The second half started off with Houston's Zeke Moore fumbling the kickoff. Oakland recovered deep in Oiler territory, and this mishap resulted in a 1-yard quarterback sneak by Lamonica to up the Oakland advantage to 24–0. Blanda added three field goals in the second half from 40, 42, and 36 yards to increase the Raiders lead to 30–7. Houston scored in between Blanda's trio of three-pointers on a Charley Frazier 5-yard reception. Bill Miller ended the barrage by catching a 12-yard pass from Lamonica to finish the day off, as well as the Houston Oilers.

George Blanda ended the game with 16 points, which set an AFL Championship Game record for most points scored in a game, and his 31 career championship game points established an all-time point production mark. The Oakland defense of "11 Angry Men" proved that their nickname was no joke. Their aggression hounded and pounded the life out of the Oilers. The linebackers plugged up the running lanes to stop Houston's hard-charging runner Hoyle Granger from going nowhere. Over the season, Granger gained 1,194 yards for the second best total in the league. However, thanks to a great Raiders defense, Granger was limited to only 19 yards on 14 carries. When quarterback Pete Beathard attempted to pass, he was pressured constantly by Oakland's front four. This was a true team effort brought forth by the Raiders, and it earned them the right to be called champions for the first of many times throughout their existence.[15]

Super Bowl II

January 14, 1968; Played in the Orange Bowl, Miami, Florida

The Green Bay Packers of the 1960's were inVINCEable, as in Vince Lombardi, their legendary head coach. Lombardi transformed a pathetic group into a powerhouse that dominated the NFL landscape throughout the 1960's, and the Packers of this time will forever be studied, written about, and revered.

Under Lombardi, the Packers won five NFL championships in the decade, and finished second in their division the other years. Coming into this game against the Raiders, Green Bay just won an unprecedented third straight NFL title, and the inaugural Super Bowl the previous year. However, age, injuries, and the loss of Hall of Fame running backs Jim Taylor and Paul Hornung put a dent in their armor.

Quarterback Bart Starr, at age 33, missed four games with injuries, and running backs Elijah Pitts and Jim Grabowski were also sent to the sideline for the same reason. The saving grace was the aging but still outstanding wall of protection up front anchored by Jerry Kramer, Fuzzy Thurston, and Forrest Gregg. These trench warriors provided holes for backs to run through, regardless of their inexperience, and allowed Starr enough time to find veteran receivers Carroll Dale and Boyd Dowler.

Defenses win championships is an old adage that the '67 Packers held true to. The unit ranked third in the NFL, and despite age also creeping up on it, they remained a devastating force led by perennial All-Pro middle linebacker Ray Nitschke, linemen Willie Davis and Henry Jordan, and defensive backs Willie Wood and Herb Adderley, all of whom are enshrined in the Pro Football Hall of Fame. These men played together throughout the decade, and despite the presence of Father Time, they were all set to go out for one final run at gridiron glory.

After finishing the regular season at 9-4-1, the Packers easily disposed of the Los Angeles Rams, 28–7, in the Western Conference Playoff Game. The following week they had to earn their third straight NFL championship. With brutal, frigid weather conditions dipping well below zero, the Packers won, 21–17, in the final seconds against the Dallas Cowboys in what will forever be remembered as "The Ice Bowl." A trip to the balmy climes of Miami, Florida, awaited the seasoned group of men set out for one last quest to sit on top of pro football's summit.

The Packers came into their clash with the Raiders as 13 point favorites on an 86-degree afternoon inside Miami's famed Orange Bowl. The CBS Television Network had the rights to broadcast the game, with announcers Ray Scott, Jack Kemp, and Pat Summerall calling the action. The Grambling State University Marching Band provided the viewing audience with the national anthem, and then it was time to begin the second AFL-NFL Championship Game, soon to be called Super Bowl II.[16]

The Raiders won the coin toss and elected to receive. Referee Jack Vest gave the signal to Green Bay kicker Don Chandler to kickoff, and the veteran sent the ball on its way toward the Oakland end zone. Larry Todd received the ball on the five, and he got an excellent return of 23 yards before Tommy Crutcher brought him down.

Hewritt Dixon took a handoff from Daryle Lamonica on the first play from scrimmage, and looked to get to the outside on a sweep to the left. Immediately, Dixon had no where to run, as a wall of Packers converged on him, and Ray Nitschke registered the defense's initial tackle by dropping Oakland's battering ram back for no gain. Lamonica then looked to do what earned him the moniker of "the Mad Bomber." He took to the air on second and third downs, but pass attempts to Fred Biletnikoff and Dixon fell incomplete to bring up a punting situation. The Oakland offense made an early exit from

Daryle "the Mad Bomber" Lamonica taking aim against the Green Bay Packers in Super Bowl II, January 14, 1968, at the Orange Bowl in Miami, Florida. Despite going down in a 33–14 defeat on this day, the strong-armed Lamonica won far more than he lost in a Raiders uniform from 1967 to 1974 (AP Photo/NFL Photos).

the playing field, and handed things over to kicker Mike Eischeid, who got off a 38-yard punt that Willie Wood received on the Green Bay 34 and did not attempt a return on.

The Packers opened their defense of the world championship with Donny Anderson running to the right side for five yards. Ben Wilson added three on a sweep to left before Anderson picked up a first down with a gain of four. Bart Starr threw his first pass on first down, and Carroll Dale caught it for nine yards to move the Packers into Oakland territory at the 46. Wilson ran for one, and then was stopped for no gain on second down, but the Raiders were penalized five yards for being offsides, which took the Packers to the 39. Starr connected with tight end Marv Fleming for eight yards and another first down. He then missed on a pass to Dale, which was followed by Anderson getting dumped by Dan Birdwell for a loss of one yard to bring up a third-and-11 situation. Starr attempted a pass to Fleming under a rush of black-clad Raiders, and the ball missed its mark. Don Chandler entered the game, and put the defending champs on the board first with a 39-yard field goal to complete the nine-play, 34-yard drive with 9:53 left in the opening quarter.

Chandler kicked off to Dave Kocourek on the Oakland 14. He then lateraled to David Grayson, who advanced the ball to the 25. Pete Banaszak opened Oakland's second series with a 4-yard gain on a sweep to the left side. Lamonica teamed up with Bill Miller on a pass of nine yards that got the Raiders their initial first down. Dixon struck for four yards on a run to the right side of the line, but was stopped for no gain on a sweep to the left on the following play. To make matters worse for the Raiders, they were penalized 16 yards for clipping. Green Bay decided to return some of those yards back to Oakland on the next play when Nitschke was called for pass interference on Miller. The penalty gave the Raiders a new set of downs and the ball on their own 38. After the two straight penalties, Dixon got off a 3-yard run off right tackle without a flag hitting the ground. Lamonica got the ball near midfield with a 13-yard pickup to Miller, but then the Raiders stalled. A sweep by Dixon loss two yards, and two Lamonica pass attempts missed their targets. Eischeid then did a spectacular job pinning Green Bay deep with a punt of 45 yards that went out of bounds on the 3-yard line.

This was nothing that Bart Starr had not seen during his stellar career, and he looked to get the Packers out of the hole. He started off with two straight running plays that moved the chains. Wilson ran for seven, and Anderson got a first down with a pickup of four. With some room to work, Starr went to the air, connecting with Dale for a gain of 17. It was then back to Wilson for five and Anderson for five and a new set of downs. Defensive back Warren Powers stopped Green Bay's momentum for a brief second by breaking up a Starr pass intended for Fleming. The Raiders looked to converge on Starr on the next play, but he avoided the pass rush, and turned up field for a 14-yard gain. Wilson then ran up the gut for six, Anderson off right tackle for three, and he was stopped attempting to get a first down by Dan Conners on third down. The Packers were clicking very well, and decided to go for it on fourth-and-one from the Oakland 36. On the final play of the opening stanza, Wilson got the first down on a sweep around the left end that picked up five yards.

The second quarter opened with Starr hitting Anderson out of the backfield for a gain of six. Wilson hit off left tackle for 12

yards to get to the Oakland 13. Anderson dropped a pass on first down, and Starr was then sacked by Tom Keating and Dan Birdwell for an 11-yard loss. On third down, Starr got the lost yardage back on a pass to Fleming, but it brought up a fourth-and-10 situation. Don Chandler came on and sent his second three-pointer of the game through the uprights from 20 yards out to give the Packers a 6–0 lead. Despite the advantage, the Packers came off the field not pleased with their performance. Guard Jerry Kramer felt that stupid mistakes like missed blocks had prevented the Packers from being up 14–0 instead of just by six.

David Grayson received Chandler's kickoff on the Oakland two, and advanced the ball 25 yards. Green Bay's defense was continuing to stymie Oakland's explosive offensive attack. Pete Banaszak was stopped after one yard on a sweep around the right end. Fred Biletnikoff then did a rare thing, dropping a pass. A sack by Willie Davis on Lamonica that lost nine yards brought the quick three-and-out series to a climax with a Mike Eischeid 47-yard punt to Willie Wood that was returned four yards to the Green Bay 38.

On Green Bay's first play of this possession, the Raiders felt that Starr was going to call a running play, and defensive back Rodger Bird moved up closer to the line of scrimmage to stop the apparent run. At the snap, Bird committed to coming up close, but Starr had called a pass play in an attempt to catch Oakland off guard. It worked perfectly. With one defensive back now out of the picture, Starr looked to take advantage of this. Defensive back Kent McCloughan tried to slow wide receiver Boyd Dowler with a blast at the line of scrimmage to throw off the receiver's timing. At 6–5,224 pounds, Dowler was able to shake off the bump-and-run attempt, and was all by himself at midfield. Starr sent the ball sailing toward Dowler, who caught it without ever slowing down at the 40 and took it all the way to complete the one-play, 62-yard drive in 11 seconds. Chandler added the extra point, and with 10:50 left in the first half, the Packers were up, 13–0.

Larry Todd took Chandler's kickoff from the goal line to the Oakland 22 to give Lamonica and company some room to work. The Raiders tried hard to establish runs to the outside, but were met with strong opposition up to this stage. Lamonica decided to shy away from that plan of attack for now, and pound between the tackles instead. Banaszak started the series off with a run off right tackle for a gain of five, and followed that with a pickup of four straight up the gut. Dixon got a first down with a nine-yard run off left tackle, and it appeared that Oakland's new plan of attack was working.

After pounded the defense with a ground assault, Lamonica decided to mix things up with the passing game. He teamed up with Biletnikoff for four yards, and to Bill Miller for 16 on a pass across the middle that got Oakland into Green Bay territory at the 40. Dixon dropped a pass, but Banaszak kept the momentum going with a 15-yard reception along the left sideline. He then hit off left tackle for a two-yard gain on the following play. On second-and-eight, Lamonica found Bill Miller along the right sideline at the Green Bay five with linebacker Dave Robinson slightly behind him. Lamonica's pass went over the head of Robinson and into the hands of Miller for the touchdown. The drive took nine plays, and covered 78 yards in four-and-a-half minutes. George Blanda's conversion made it a 13–7 ballgame with 6:15 left in the half.

Tommy Crutcher took the ensuing kickoff from Eischeid, and returned it seven yards to the Green Bay 15. An inspired Oakland defense came out and stopped the Packers cold. Dan Conners dropped Wilson for a loss of one on a run to the left side. Tom Keating then was responsible for preventing the Packers from getting anywhere on the next two plays. He first sacked Starr for eight yards, and then tackled Wilson after a gain of one yard. Anderson got off a 45-yard punt that Rodger Bird returned 12 yards to the Green Bay 40.

Oakland made a quick exit from this possession after Nitschke stopped Banaszak for no gain, Dixon gained a yard, and then was the intended target on a Lamonica pass that was overthrown. Blanda came on in an attempt to salvage some points, but a 47-yard field goal fell short. The ball was picked up by Willie Wood on the two and returned eight yards to the Green Bay 10.

Rookie Travis Williams got his chance on the sport's grandest stage with three straight runs that netted nine yards. On fourth down, Anderson sent a 36-yard punt in the direction of Bird, who awaited the ball near midfield. Bird got underneath it, caught it, but could not hold on. Dick Capp was there to recover the ball for Green Bay on the Oakland 45 to snap the Silver and Black's momentum.

Starr looked to take advantage of this golden opportunity, but Oakland did not want to give up much at first. Starr's pass to Max McGee on first down was broken up by Howie Williams, and his next attempt, intended for Dowler, fell incomplete. With time quickly ticking away in the first half, Starr got the Packers a little closer with a nine-yard pass to Dowler along the right sideline. On third-and-one, Chandler sent his third three-pointer of the day through the uprights from 43 yards away to give the Packers a 16–7 lead with one second left in the half. Chandler's kickoff was fielded by Wayne Hawkins on the Oakland 47 and returned three yards to officially bring the first thirty minutes of Super Bowl II to a close.

It was rumored that this was going to be Vince Lombardi's final game coaching the Packers after nine seasons. Many of the players knew it to be more than speculation, and felt that they wanted to send their legendary mentor, who allowed them the opportunity to succeed on the field, out of the Orange Bowl in fine fashion. Guard Jerry Kramer gathered up a group of the men who were with Lombardi throughout all or most of his reign. He simply stated that he wanted to play the last thirty minutes for Lombardi. It was short, and got the message across.

Travis Williams went back to his end zone ready to receive the second half kickoff from Eischeid. He received the kick on the Green Bay nine, and brought it back 18 yards to the 27. Despite Kramer's request, the Packers' first series did go as planned. A 2-yard run by Wilson, and a pass from Starr to Fleming got the Packers one yard shy of a first down. On third-and-one, Wilson tried to move the chains with a run off left tackle, but was met and dropped for no gain by Willie Brown to force a punting situation. Another Anderson punt was caught and dropped, this time by Warren Wells, but teammate J.R. Williamson pounced on the loose pigskin at the Oakland 32 to save a sure disaster.

Lamonica sent Dixon on a run off left tackle that provided the Raiders with a 14-yard pickup and a new set of downs to work with. Feeling that the left side might be the place to attack once

again, Dixon attempted a sweep, but this time defensive back Bob Jeter knocked him back for a loss of two. Jeter then broke up a pass intended for tight end Billy Cannon, and fellow defensive back Tom Brown chipped in on third down by also breaking up a pass, this one intended for Banaszak. Eischeid sent a 38-yard punt to Willie Wood, who caught it, but did not attempt a return on the Green Bay 18.

With 10:35 left in the third quarter, Starr led the Packers on to the field, and looked to increase the point difference between his team and the silver and black-clad opponents he had to get through to accomplish the task at hand. Wilson started the drive off successfully with a 13-yard gain on a draw play up the middle. Anderson swept the left side for eight, and Wilson added one yard off right tackle to bring up a third-and-one situation.

The Packers under Lombardi had gained a reputation over the decade as a team that liked to mix things up on third-and-short. With the defense looking for the run, Starr would fake one, and then quickly retreat into the pocket looking to hit on a big pass play after sucking the defenders in. Throughout the week leading up to this clash, Oakland's head coach John Rauch had preached to his defense to be aware of this ploy. During this contest, the right situation never presented itself until now. Starr and veteran Max McGee, who was playing in his final game after 13 pro seasons, decided to go for it. The 35-year-old McGee dug deep for one final big burst, and at the snap, he took off down the middle as Starr first faked a handoff to Wilson, and then went looking to see McGee's progress. Thinking the ball was going to Wilson, Rodger Bird came up to defend against the run, and McGee bolted past him. Starr calmly and quickly saw his intended target free for a second, and sent the ball into the Miami sky. McGee hauled in the pass and looked to get his aging wheels across the goal line. Bird recovered from the fake, and took off in pursuit. He managed to catch up with McGee after the veteran receiver covered 35 yards of Orange Bowl real estate, and brought him down on the Oakland 25.

With a new set of downs, Starr once again tried the pass lanes, but this time he overthrew Dowler. After a draw play up the middle by Wilson gained one yard, Starr connected with Dale for 11 yards and a first down at the Oakland 13. An attempt to Anderson missed its mark, but on the next play, Starr rolled out to his right and found his running back for a pickup of 12 across the middle. On first and goal from the one, Anderson tried to hit off the left side, but big Ben Davidson was there to meet him and drive him into the turf for a loss of one yard. Undaunted, Starr called Anderson's number on the next play, and this time the third-year pro went off right tackle from two yards out to cap the 11-play, 82-yard drive with a six-pointer. Chandler added the conversion kick, and the Packers were now in control with a 23–7 lead as the clock showed 5:54 remaining in the third quarter.

The Packers were now feeling that this game was theirs, and looked to pound that point home to the Raiders. Chandler's kickoff sailed into the end zone and was not returned. Lamonica needed to generate something on this next drive if Oakland was going to have any chance at all of making things interesting down the stretch. However, Green Bay's defensive unit did not want things interesting, and clipped "the Mad Bomber's" wings on three straight downs. An overthrown pass to Miller started the quick three-and-out series. Lamonica then connected with Banaszak on a screen pass, but the tough Oakland back was no match for Dave Robinson, who dropped him for no gain. Another attempted pass to Banaszak went for an incompletion, and the Packers got the ball back when Eischeid sent a 41-yard punt to Wood on the Green Bay 39 that was not returned.

A Starr to Dale pass was incomplete, but the Raiders were penalized five yards for holding, which gave Green Bay an automatic first down on their own 44. Starr went back to Dale, this time for a gain of six. Anderson ran twice for a combined 11 yards before Willie Brown broke up a Starr pass intended for Dale. A nine-yard connection to Fleming gave the Packers a new set of downs to work with starting at the Oakland 30. Wilson gained three, Anderson four, but then Wilson was tackled for a loss of one by Dan Birdwell to bring up fourth down. Don Chandler came on and knocked his fourth field goal of the game through the uprights, this time from 31 yards out with two seconds left in the quarter to give the Packers a 26–7 bulge. The quarter ended on Chandler's kickoff to David Grayson, who received the ball on the Oakland 15 and advanced it 25 yards before Willie Wood brought him down.

The final fifteen minutes began badly for the Raiders. On the first play, Lamonica connected with Banaszak on a 13-yard pass only to have the running back fumble. Dave Robinson recovered for Green Bay, and returned the ball 16 yards to the Oakland 37 before Harry Schuh brought him down.

Ben Davidson sacked Starr on first down, and Travis Williams was stopped for no gain on a run to the right side. However, the Packers advanced the ball five yards on the play due to the Raiders being offside. Two incomplete pass attempts by Starr to Fleming and Williams brought up fourth down. Donny Anderson then sent a 27-yard punt into Oakland territory where it was downed on the 16.

Down by 19 points made the Raiders very predictable, as Lamonica went immediately to the air. Billy Cannon dropped a pass on first down, but made up for his error with a 15-yard pickup on the next play. Surprisingly, the Raiders shifted back to the run with Dixon gaining 15 off right tackle and two on a sweep to the left. Another dropped pass by Cannon brought up third down. Lamonica, looking for Fred Biletnikoff, unleashed the ball from his own 48 to the right side of the field at the Green Bay 40. Defensive back par-excellence Herb Adderley read the play, stepped up and intercepted the "Mad Bomber's" pass and then delivered the final evidence that the Packers were going to reign supreme on this day. He raced 60 yards for Green Bay's final touchdown of the day, and Chandler's extra point made it 33–7 with 11:03 left in the fourth quarter.

Chandler's kickoff was received on the Oakland eight by Larry Todd, and returned 18 yards to begin the final stages of the Raiders' beatdown. This also proved to be a successful series for the Raiders. Dixon ran for eight to the right, and then hit the left side for two. On first down, Lamonica connected with Biletnikoff for 41 yards on a deep pass to the left side. On Green Bay's 23, Lamonica found Bill Miller with a deep pass down the middle for his second touchdown of the game. With 9:13 left, Blanda connected on the extra point attempt to make it a 33–14 Green Bay advantage.

Mike Eischeid's kickoff went to Herb Adderley on the Green Bay two and returned 24 yards. Two Travis Williams' runs netted

three yards, and following a gain of four by Wilson up the middle that brought up a fourth down. Anderson's punt travelled 46 yards and Rodger Bird signaled for a fair catch on the Oakland 21.

With 7:01 to go, Larry Todd ran for a gain of five to the right side. Ray Nitschke swatted a Lamonica pass attempt away on second down, but Cannon managed to move the chains with a 10-yard reception on the next play. Biletnikoff caught a pass for six yards, but two incompletions to Todd and Cannon brought up fourth down. Eischeid got off a whopping 55-yard punt to Willie Wood that was returned 31 yards to the Green Bay 34.

Just looking to run out the final 4:34, the Packers stayed on the ground. Williams ran for five off right tackle, Anderson added four off left tackle, and Williams busted loose for 18 off the left side to give the Packers another set of downs. A gain of one by Williams brought the game to the two-minute warning. Chuck Mercein attempted to run to the left, but was stopped for no gain by Tom Keating. Backup quarterback Zeke Bratkowski was then sacked for a 10-yard loss by Keating on the final offensive play of the Vince Lombardi era in Green Bay. Anderson's punt went 48 yards into the end zone for a touchback with 1:07 remaining.

Willie Davis sacked Lamonica for a loss of nine on first down. Todd then broke free around the right end for 32 yards down to the Oakland 43. Lamonica hooked up with Dixon on a pass of three yards, and he attempted to go back to Dixon on the next play, but the ball was batted away by Davis. Lamonica connected with Warren Wells for 17, and was then sacked once again by Davis for a loss of four yards. The final play of Super Bowl II followed with a Lamonica pass attempt to Wells from the Green Bay 41 falling incomplete.[17]

At 6:06 Eastern Standard Time, Vince Lombardi was hoisted up on the shoulders of Jerry Kramer and Forrest Gregg for his final victory ride as Green Bay's mentor, thus climaxing one of the most illustrious coaching reigns in the history of professional football. This was the last golden moment for the Packers for many years. Despite the mauling at the hands of the legendary team of the 60's, the Raiders were on the opposite side of the spectrum. As Green Bay's star was fading, the Silver and Black only began their glorious ride toward professional football dominance as the sun set over Miami's Orange Bowl on that January day in 1968.

Starting Lineup for Super Bowl II

OFFENSE

QB — Daryle Lamonica	LT — Bob Svihus
RB — Pete Banaszak	LG — Gene Upshaw
FB — Hewritt Dixon	C — Jim Otto
WR — Fred Biletnikoff	RG — Wayne Hawkins
WR — Bill Miller	RT — Harry Schuh
TE — Billy Cannon	

DEFENSE

DE — Ike Lassiter	RLB — Gus Otto
DE — Ben Davidson	CB — Kent McCloughan
DT — Dan Birdwell	CB — Willie Brown
DT — Tom Keating	SS — Howie Williams
LLB — Bill Laskey	FS — Warren Powers
MLB — Dan Conners	

KICKING/PUNTING

K — George Blanda   P — Mike Eischeid

Individual Statistics from Super Bowl II

OFFENSE

Daryle Lamonica: 15 completions out of 34 pass attempts for 208 yards, 2 TD and 1 INT.

Pete Banaszak: Rushed for 16 yards on 6 carries and had 4 receptions for 69 yards.

Hewritt Dixon: Rushed for 54 yards on 12 carries and had 1 reception for 3 yards.

Larry Todd: Rushed for 37 yards on 2 carries, and returned 3 kickoffs for 63 yards.

Bill Miller: Had 5 receptions for 84 yards and 2 TD.

Billy Cannon: Had 2 receptions for 25 yards.

Warren Wells: Had 1 reception for 17 yards, and returned 1 punt for 0 yards.

Fred Biletnikoff: Had 2 receptions for 10 yards.

Dave Kocourek: Returned 1 kickoff for 0 yards.

Wayne Hawkins: Returned 1 kickoff for 3 yards.

Dave Grayson: Returned 2 kickoffs for 61 yards.

Rodger Bird: Had 2 punt returns for 12 yards.

George Blanda: Had 2 extra point kicks.

DEFENSE

Dan Birdwell: Had sack.

Ben Davidson: Had 1 sack.

Tom Keating: Had 2 sacks.

Individual Statistics and Roster

Head Coach: John Rauch

Assistant Coaches: Tom Dahms, John Madden, John Polonchek, Ollie Spencer, Charles Sumner

1967 Regular Season Record: 13–1

1st Place in AFL Western Division

Scored 468 points to rank 1st out of 9 teams

Allowed 233 points to rank 2nd

Led the league in points scored (468), touchdown passes (33), rushing touchdowns (19), fewest yards allowed (3,294), fewest first downs allowed (182), and fewest rushing yards allowed (1,129)

STARTERS — OFFENSE

QB — Daryle Lamonica: Started in 14 games. Completed 220 of 425 pass attempts for 3,228 yards, 30 TD and 20 INT. Rushed for 110 yards on 22 carries and 4 TD.

HB — Clem Daniels: Active for 9 games. Rushed for 575 yards on 130 carries and 4 TD. Had 16 receptions for 222 yards and 2 TD, and threw 1 pass for 28 yards.

FB — Hewritt Dixon: Active for 13 games. Rushed for 559 yards on 153 carries and 5 TD. Had 59 receptions for 563 yards and 2 TD.

WR — Fred Biletnikoff: Active for 14 games. Had 40 receptions for 876 yards and 5 TD. **His 21.9 yards per reception average led the AFL.**

WR — Bill Miller: Active for 12 games. Had 38 receptions for 537 yards and 6 TD.

TE — Billy Cannon: Active for 14 games. Had 32 receptions for 629 yards and 10 TD.

LT — Bob Svihus: Active for 14 games.

LG — Gene Upshaw: Active for 14 games.

C — Jim Otto: Active for 14 games.

RG — Wayne Hawkins: Active for 14 games.

RT — Harry Schuh: Active for 14 games.

RESERVE OFFENSIVE PLAYERS

Dan Archer (G/T): Active for 14 games.

Pete Banaszak (RB): Active for 10 games. Rushed for 376 yards on 68 carries and 1 TD. Had 16 receptions for 192 yards and 1 TD.

Estes Banks (RB): Active for 9 games. Rushed for 26 yards on 10 carries.

Roger Hagberg (RB/WR): Active for 12 games. Rushed for 146 yards on 44 carries and 2 TD. Had 11 receptions for 114 yards and 1 TD, and 2 kickoff returns for 12 yards.

Jim Harvey (G/T): Active for 10 games.

Ken Herock (TE/LB): Active for 12 games. Had 1 reception for -1 yard.

Dave Kocourek (TE/WR): Active for 10 games. Had 1 reception for 4 yards.

Bob Kruse (G/T): Active for 13 games.

Rod Sherman (WR): Active for 13 games. Rushed for 13 yards on 1 carry and 1 TD. Had 5 receptions for 61 yards, and 12 kickoff returns for 279 yards.

Larry Todd (RB): Active for 5 games. Rushed for 116 yards on 29 carries and 2 TD. Had 4 receptions for 42 yards, and 5 kickoff returns for 123 yards.

Warren Wells (WR): Active for 14 games. Rushed for 7 yards on 1 carry, and 13 receptions for 302 yards and 6 TD.

STARTERS — DEFENSE

DE — Ike Lassiter: Active for 14 games.

DE — Ben Davidson: Active for 14 games.

DT — Dan Birdwell: Active for 14 games and had 1 INT, and had 1 safety.

DT — Tom Keating: Active for 14 games.

LLB — Bill Laskey: Active for 13 games and had 3 fumble recoveries.

MLB — Dan Conners: Active for 14 games. Had 3 INT and 2 TD, and 4 fumbles recoveries and 1 TD. **His 73 yards on fumble recoveries led the AFL.**

RLB — Gus Otto: Active for 14 games, had 1 INT and 3 fumble recoveries.

CB — Kent McCloughan: Active for 14 games and had 2 INT.

CB — Willie Brown: Active for 14 games and had 7 INT and 1 TD.

S — Howie Williams: Active for 13 games and had 4 INT.

S — Rodger Bird: Active for 14 games. Had **46** punt returns for **612** yards, and 6 kickoff returns for 143 yards.

RESERVE DEFENSIVE PLAYERS

Duane Benson (LB): Active for 8 games and had 1 kickoff return for 0 yards.

Bill Budness (LB): Active for 13 games.

Bill Fairband (LB): Active for 7 games.

Dave Grayson (DB): Active for 14 games. Had 4 INT, 3 punt returns for 11 yards, and 19 kickoff returns for 405 yards.

Carleton Oats (T/E): Active for 9 games, and had 2 fumble recoveries and 1 TD.

Warren Powers (DB): Active for 14 games. Had 6 INT and 2 TD, and 2 punt returns for 19 yards.

Richard Sligh (T): Active for 8 games.

J.R. Williamson (LB/C): Active for 13 games and had 2 INT.

KICKING/PUNTING

K — George Blanda: Active for 14 games. Made 20 of 30 field goals and 56 of 57 extra point kicks for **116** points.

P — Mike Eischeid: Active for 14 games. Punted 76 times for a 44.3 average.

1968 Season Review

1. Sept. 15: The defending AFL champs opened the new season in excellent fashion. They achieved this by handing the

Buffalo Bills their worst defeat up to this time. The 48–6 blowout caused Buffalo head coach Joe Collier to lose his job. Oakland rookie George Atkinson had one of the greatest pro debuts of all time. He started out by scoring Oakland's first points of the 1968 season on an 86-yard punt return. By the end of the day, Atkinson gained an AFL record 205 yards on punt returns. He almost took another in for a score, but was stopped on the Buffalo nine after going 52 yards. The Raiders quickly capitalized on the great effort when Pete Banaszak took the ball in for on a 9-yard touchdown run on the next play. Oakland's other points came on a 57-yard pass from Daryle Lamonica to Warren Wells, a Hewritt Dixon 17-yard run, two Larry Todd runs (11 and 31 yards), and six conversion kicks plus two field goals (22 and 9 yards) from George Blanda. Dixon rushed for a game-high 104 yards on 16 carries, and the defense chipped in with an outstanding effort. They recorded eight sacks, and allowed the Bills a -19 net yards passing.[1]

2. Sept. 21: Daryle Lamonica threw for 344 yards and touchdown passes to four different receivers in the first half of a 47–21 rout of the Miami Dolphins. This game was basically over by halftime, with the Raiders sporting a nineteen-point lead. Lamonica's scoring tosses went to Warren Wells (73 yards), who finished with 106 yards on three receptions, Billy Cannon (3 yards), Bill Miller (11 yards), and Pete Banaszak (49 yards), who also added a 43-yard touchdown run to his credit. Defensive back Willie Brown chipped in with a 27-yard interception return to finish off the Silver and Black's scoring barrage. George Blanda added a 12-yard field goal, and the defense got a safety when Miami running back Jim Kiick was tackled in the end zone to give the Raiders their other five points.[2]

3. Sept. 29: The Raiders registered their thirteenth straight regular season win, 24–15, over the Houston Oilers. They suffered early in this one from fumbles and the inability to move the ball against a tough Houston defense. Once the Raiders started holding onto the ball, and finding dents in the defense, things got much better. Daryle Lamonica capped off two long second half drives with short touchdown passes to Warren Wells and Billy Cannon, with each coming from nine yards out. Defensive back David Grayson had two interceptions, and returned one 25 yards for Oakland's first touchdown that tied the game at 7–7 in the second quarter. George Blanda added a 34-yard field goal to round out Oakland's point production. Powerful fullback Hewritt Dixon supplied the Raiders with a devastating ground attack by tearing through the Houston defense for 187 yards on 28 carries.[3]

4. Oct. 6: After trailing the Boston Patriots by three points in the third quarter, Warren Wells started Oakland on a scoring spree that enabled them to register a 41–10 victory. After taking a pitchout from Daryle Lamonica, Wells swept to the right side and went 41 yards for the go-ahead touchdown. Wells also scored Oakland's first touchdown in the second quarter on a 9-yard pass from Lamonica. After Wells' touchdown run, Hewritt Dixon teamed up with Lamonica from 17 yards out for another score. Fred Biletnikoff added Oakland's fourth six-pointer of the game after recovering a fumble and running seven yards. Biletnikoff also had a game-high 107 yards on six receptions. George Blanda kicked two field goals (19 and 33 yards) and threw a 14-yard touchdown pass to Dave Kocourek, all in the fourth quarter to complete the Boston massacre. The defense dished out their usual

brand of punishment by recording five sacks, allowing 48 yards rushing, and 98 net yards through the air. This was Oakland's fourteenth straight regular season win, and it put them one victory shy of the AFL record held by the 1960-61 San Diego Chargers, who were next on the schedule.[4]

5. Oct. 13: With a chance to tie the consecutive AFL winning streak, the Raiders played host to San Diego. Not ready to relinquish the record, especially to a hated rival, the Chargers flexed their defensive muscle in the second half to beat Oakland, 23–14. In front of a sellout crowd of 53,257, the Raiders came from ten points down to take a 14–10 lead into the half. George Atkinson's 82-yard punt return, and a 7-yard pass from Daryle Lamonica to Warren Wells, gave the Silver and Black their brief advantage. The second half saw the Raiders stymied by a fired up defense that only allowed Lamonica three completions.[5]

6. Oct. 20: With Mike Garrett, Robert Holmes, and Wendell Hayes tearing off power runs against the Oakland defense, the Kansas City Chiefs built a huge 24–0 lead, and held on for a 24–10 win. Oakland's points came on a 45-yard pass from Daryle Lamonica to Billy Cannon, and a 28-yard George Blanda field goal. With this win, the 6–1 Chiefs took over sole possession of first place in the Western Division. The Raiders fell to 4–2, and this marked the first time in two years that they lost back-to-back games.[6]

7. Oct. 27: The Raiders got back to their winning ways by beating up on the expansion Cincinnati Bengals, 31–10. Daryle Lamonica threw three touchdown passes, with two going to Fred Biletnikoff (14 and 12 yards), and the other to Roger Hagberg (7 yards). Hagberg also ran seven yards for another touchdown, George Blanda kicked a 48-yard field goal, and the Raiders rolled up 439 yards of offense. Warren Wells was his stellar self, as the gifted speedster led all receivers in the game with 118 yards on five receptions. The defense was relentless on the infant Bengals, as they rang up seven sacks, and held the air attack to a mere 59 net yards. The only Cincinnati player that seemed to flourish against this tough defense was running back Paul Robinson, who ran for 159 yards on 17 carries and scored his team's only six-pointer on a long 87-yard jaunt.[7]

8. Nov. 3: Oakland broke loose for a 24-point halftime lead, and eventually cruised to a 38–21 win over the division-leading Kansas City Chiefs. Daryle Lamonica left the game with a twisted knee in the third quarter. Prior to the injury, he ripped through the defense for 352 passing yards and two touchdowns. He also scored on a 4-yard run. Warren Wells (29 yards) and Billy Cannon (17 yards) were on the receiving end of Lamonica's touchdown passes. Pete Banaszak added two short scoring runs, each coming from one yard out, and George Blanda connected on a 9-yard field goal to finish Oakland's point production for the afternoon. With this win, the Silver and Black improved to 6–2, and moved to within a half game of the division lead. This game also saw the Raiders penalized 11 times for 103 yards, and the Chiefs 10 times for 91 yards.[8]

9. Nov. 10: With superstar quarterback Daryle Lamonica sidelined with an injury, the Raiders at first appeared vulnerable, but were in good hands with George Blanda as their backup signal caller. The 40-year-old Blanda seemed a lot younger in a 43–7 demolition of the Denver Broncos by throwing four scoring strikes, kicking two field goals (42 and 27 yards), and hitting on

five conversions on a day that saw the Oakland offense finish with 487 yards. Blanda silenced the hot Broncos, who were winners in four of their pervious five games, with two touchdown passes to both Warren Wells (17 and 94 yards), and Fred Biletnikoff (22 and 16 yards). Wells set a then-team record for longest touchdown reception with his 94-yard catch in a game where he produced 127 receiving yards on three receptions. Rookie running back Charlie Smith, who ran for a game-high 96 yards, also enjoyed a moment in the spotlight by rambling 64 yards down the sideline untouched for a score, and the defense got two points on the board by tackling running back Floyd Little in the end zone for a safety. Oakland improved to 7–2, and was still in a second place tie with San Diego.[9]

10. Nov. 17: The Heidi Game. It wasn't the Super Bowl, but this game between the Oakland Raiders and New York Jets might just be remembered more vividly than many of those played for a championship. What puts this game up there with some of the most memorable pro football games of all time is the fact that the NBC network switched to the children's film classic Heidi instead of broadcasting the ending of the game. In some cases this wouldn't have mattered, but this was not one of those times. What makes it so memorable was that while the game was playing, its climax turned out to be one of the greatest finishes of all time.

The Jets and Raiders were two of the AFL's top teams in 1968, and when they met, exciting action was a given. Oakland needed a win to stay in contention for the Western Division crown. If New York won, they would assure themselves at least a tie for the Eastern Division title.

As expected, the game was close and very exciting, with the Raiders getting 437 yards of offensive production, and the Jets 413. This contest also featured two of pro football's premier passers in Daryle Lamonica and Joe Namath, who both lived up to their star billing. Lamonica connected on 21 of 34 passes for 311 yards and four touchdowns while Namath lit up the skies for 381 yards on 19 out of 37 attempts. In the first half, Lamonica threw two of his four touchdown passes to give the Raiders a 14–12 lead. Warren Wells (9 yards) and Billy Cannon (48 yards) were the recipients of "the Mad Bomber's" first half scoring tosses. The game also started to run behind schedule due to numerous penalties and injury time outs throughout the first half.

The Jets took a 19–14 lead on a Bill Mathis 4-yard run in the second half. Undaunted, the Raiders answered with an 80-yard drive capped by running back Charlie Smith's 3-yard run. The Raiders opted to go for the two-point conversion, were successful, and now up, 22–19. Oakland looked to expand their lead early in the fourth quarter. However, after driving to the New York five, Smith fumbled and linebacker Gerry Philbin recovered for the Jets.

Namath immediately took advantage of the costly turnover. He first connected with receiver Don Maynard at midfield, and then once again on the following play for a touchdown. Maynard had a career day with 10 catches for 228 yards. Kicker Jim Turner extended the New York lead to 29–22 a short time later with a 22-yard field goal. Lamonica brought Oakland back quickly with a 22-yard touchdown strike to Fred Biletnikoff, who finished the game with seven receptions for 120 yards. George Blanda's extra point then made it a 29–29 affair. With one minute left in the game, the Jets went back on top, 32–29, on Turner's fourth field

goal of the day. This was also Turner's 28th three-pointer of the season, which tied an AFL record.

A few plays after the ensuing kickoff, the Raiders made their way to the New York 43 with momentum on their side. At this time, with Oakland driving for a possible tie or win in such a critical game, the NBC network went to a break. After coming back from the commercial break, it was 7:00pm EST. Instead of going back to the Oakland Coliseum and informing the viewing audience that there would be a delay in the evening programming schedule, due to the game running longer than expected, the network started showing the movie Heidi, which was set to begin at 7:00 P.M.

Within minutes of seeing Heidi on their screens, the football viewing public from coast to coast bolted to their phones and flooded the NBC studios with complaint calls. Unfortunately, by the time the network got the game back on the air, it was over. To make matters even worse was the fact that the Raiders rallied to win.

When NBC switched over to Heidi, the Raiders were at the New York 43. After the movie came on, Lamonica threw his fourth touchdown pass, this time to Charlie Smith (43 yards). Blanda's extra point kick then gave Oakland a 36–32 lead with 42 seconds remaining. On the ensuing kickoff, New York's Earl Christy fumbled on his own 12-yard line after being hit by Bill Budness, and Preston Ridlehuber recovered the ball for another Oakland touchdown. Blanda's conversion made it 43–32, and that was how the "Heidi Game" ended.[10]

11. Nov. 24: Setting an AFL record with 33 first downs, the Raiders dominated the last place Cincinnati Bengals, 34–0. In doing so, Oakland improved to 9–2, and moved into a first place tie with the Kansas City Chiefs in the Western Division. The Bengals were completely stymied offensively, gaining 148 yards as a team, and only came close to scoring twice. The Raiders, however, scored almost at will, and amassed an incredible 604 yards of total offense. Rookie Charlie Smith ran for two scores (7 and 9 yards), and finished the day with a game-high 118 rushing yards on 16 carries. Fred Biletnikoff caught eight passes for 137 yards, and Warren Wells had seven receptions for 133 yards. Daryle Lamonica threw for 368 yards, connected on scoring strikes to Hewritt Dixon (5 yards) and Billy Cannon (12 yards), and George Blanda added two field goals (43 and 27 yards).[11]

12. Nov. 28: Defensive back George "the Hit Man" Atkinson sparked the Raiders to a 13–10 win over the Buffalo Bills with two third quarter interceptions. Despite coming into this game with the AFL's worst record, the 1-10-1 Bills played tough. Atkinson's interceptions helped Oakland get ten quick points to break open a 3–3 third quarter deadlock. The "Hit Man's" first theft allowed the Raiders offense to begin just across midfield. The drive eventually ended with a George Blanda 33-yard field goal giving Oakland the lead. Blanda also opened the game's scoring with a 39-yard three-pointer in the second quarter. Atkinson's second theft came with under one minute remaining in the third quarter, and he accounted for the touchdown himself by returning the interception 33 yards. The win was Oakland's sixth straight, and allowed them to remain tied with Kansas City atop the Western Division with a 10–2 record.[12]

13. Dec. 8: Charlie Smith started things off with a huge bang by going 65 yards for a touchdown on the third play of the

game. The Denver Broncos did not crumble after Smith's jaunt, and proceeded to go up, 17–7, on the Raiders in the second quarter. With the help of a Hewritt Dixon 1-yard run, a Daryle Lamonica to Warren Wells 6-yard pass, and three George Blanda field goals (26, 20, and 33 yards), Oakland clawed their way back in front, 30–20, in the fourth quarter. After Denver closed the gap to three points, linebacker Dan Conners and defensive back David Grayson shut the Broncos down for good with interceptions. Conner's interception led to a 21-yard Blanda field goal, and Grayson's came with 20 seconds left to seal a 33–27 road win for the Silver and Black. Lamonica finished with 354 yards through the air, and Warren Wells proved to be "the Mad Bomber's" favorite target on this day by catching 10 passes for 163 yards. The Western Division race still remained deadlocked between Oakland and Kansas City going into the regular season finale.[13]

14. Dec. 15: The good news was that the Raiders won their eighth straight, 34–27, over San Diego, to finish the 1968 AFL campaign at 12–2. The bad news was that Kansas City also won, and due to this, a special playoff game the following week was scheduled to decide the Western Division winner. In their game against the Chargers, Oakland had a lethargic first half. The AFL's best offense then woke up in the second half, exploding for 24 points to pull out the victory. Free safety Rodger Bird jump-started the Silver and Black in the third quarter with a 22-yard interception return for a touchdown. Daryle Lamonica, who lit up the airways for 275 yards, threw to Warren Wells (55 yards), Charlie Smith (40 yards), and Fred Biletnikoff (13 yards) for touchdowns. Wells once again was the top receiver with 113 yards on four catches. George Blanda added a short-range field goal from 18 yards to cap Oakland's second half surge, and also kicked a 28-yarder in the first quarter to tie the game at 3–3.[14]

Western Division Playoff, December 22, 1968

After battling fierce rival Kansas City all season long, the Raiders made easy work of the Chiefs when it counted most, winning their second straight division title in convincing fashion, 41–6, at home. They also rang up 454 yards of total offense in the process. Daryle Lamonica wasted little time establishing the tempo, as he threw for 347 yards and five touchdowns. Three of his strikes went to Fred Biletnikoff (24, 44, and 54 yards), who led all receivers with seven catches for 180 yards. Warren Wells caught Lamonica's other two touchdown passes from 23 and 35 yards out. George Blanda finished the scoring with two fourth quarter field goals from 41 and 40 yards away. The defense came up big with four interceptions, as Willie Brown, Dan Conners, Jerry Hopkins, and Nemiah Wilson, all stole passes. This win earned the defending AFL champion Raiders a trip to New York City to do battle with Joe Namath and his Jets for the league title and a trip to Super Bowl III.[15]

AFL Championship Game, December 29, 1968

In a rematch of the Heidi Game, the Raiders and New York Jets squared off to decide who would represent the American Foot-

ball League in Super Bowl III. Unlike in the previous meeting one month earlier, the title game was played on the opposite coast amidst very cold and blustery conditions inside a sold out Shea Stadium.

The '68 Jets under quarterback Joe Namath's leadership had a swagger to them, and Broadway Joe looked to continue that moxie against the tough Oakland defense. Despite the wind whipping around the stadium, Namath refused to allow it to hamper the passing game. He came out throwing, and his strong right arm sent 49 passes into the frosty atmosphere for 266 yards. After just 3:39 of the first quarter expired, Namath's right arm and receiver Don Maynard's great hands collaborated on the game's initial score when the two future Hall of Famers hooked up on a 14-yard pass. Kicker Jim Turner later added a 33-yard field goal to give New York a 10–0 lead after the opening quarter.

The old saying that you can't keep a good man down held true, as the Raiders refused to relinquish their AFL championship without a fight. Fred Biletnikoff began to shake off New York defenders in the second quarter, and Daryle Lamonica capitalized on it by connecting with his star receiver from 29 yards out for a touchdown early in the quarter. Biletnikoff went on to have a career day against the Jets by catching seven passes for 190 yards. From that point on in the quarter, the teams exchanged field goals, with George Blanda hitting from 29 yards away, and Turner from 36, to make it a close 13–10 New York advantage at the half. Early in the second half, the Mad Bomber earned his moniker by heaving long aerials to Biletnikoff and Warren Wells, giving the Silver and Black a first down on the New York six. Three plays later, the Raiders stalled on the one, and Blanda come on to kick a 9-yard field goal to tie things up at 13–13. It was now Namath's turn to refuse defeatism.

Late in the third quarter, Broadway Joe conducted an 80-yard balanced attack that was climaxed by Namath throwing a scoring strike to tight end Pete Lammons from 20 yards out. Turner added the extra point, and the Jets led, 20–13, going into the final stanza.

Oakland looked to get even, and attacked the New York defense early in the fourth quarter. However, after getting deep into Jets' territory, the Raiders stalled and had to settle for a 20-yard Blanda field goal that cut New York's lead to 20–16. The Raiders then got a huge break when rookie defensive back George Atkinson intercepted a Namath pass and returned it 32 yards to the New York four. On the following play, Pete Banaszak ran for a touchdown and Blanda's conversion put Oakland ahead, 23–20, for the first time in the game.

Namath looked to redeem himself for his turnover, and answered the challenge less than one minute later when he completed a 52-yard pass to Maynard on the Oakland ten. Maynard had a step of Atkinson when he caught the bomb, and was dragged down by the rookie defender on the Oakland six. On the next play, Namath rolled out to his left looking to pass to halfback Bill Mathis. The Raiders applied a heavy pass rush on Namath, who quickly stopped rolling and looked to throw the ball as soon as possible. His first two choices, Pete Lammons and George Sauer, were well covered by the Oakland linebackers and secondary. Maynard, however, was able to get a slight crease between himself and Atkinson. Namath saw Maynard and sent a hard throw toward him in the end zone. Maynard hung on to the rocket shot for the go-ahead touchdown, and with eight minutes remaining, the Jets led, 27–23.

Oakland came back in this game before, and looked to do it once again. Their first attempt at regaining the lead was halted at the New York 26 when Lamonica was sacked on fourth down. On their next possession, Oakland drove to the New York 24. Lamonica then looked to connect with Charlie Smith on a swing pass, but the throw was behind the line of scrimmage, which is considered a lateral and not a forward pass. When the ball slid off of Smith's fingertips, it was still a live ball, and linebacker Ralph Baker reacted quickly by jumping on the football at the New York 30 to kill another deep threat by the Raiders. Namath and the rest of the New York offense were unable to move the chains long enough to run out the clock, as Oakland's defense held to allow Lamonica one final shot at victory.

After New York was forced to punt on fourth down, the Raiders took over possession on their own 22 with 42 ticks left on the clock. Lamonica found tight end Billy Cannon for 16 yards to get the ball to the Oakland 38. Two incomplete passes followed to Hewritt Dixon and Warren Wells. Lamonica then was chased out of bounds on third down. Any hopes of defending their AFL championship all rested on a fourth down play. Lamonica, who lit up the frosty New York air for 401 yards, dropped back and threw a screen pass to Dixon, but he was stopped shy of a first down, and the Silver and Black's dreams of another championship ended on the cold turf of Shea Stadium.[16]

Individual Statistics and Roster

Head Coach: John Rauch
Assistant Coaches: Tom Dahms, Buggsy Engleberg, John Madden, Marv Marinovich, John Polonchek, Ollie Spencer, Charles Sumner
1968 Regular Season Record: 12–2
1st Place in AFL Western Division
Scored 453 points to rank 1st out of 10 teams
Allowed 233 points to rank 2nd
Led the league in points scored (453), offensive yards (5,696), first downs (287), touchdown passes (31), fewest touchdowns allowed passing (13)

STARTERS — OFFENSE

QB — Daryle Lamonica: Active for and started in 13 games. Completed 206 of 416 pass attempts for 3,245 yards, 25 TD and 15 INT. Rushed for 98 yards on 19 carries and 1 TD. **He led the AFL in passes completed per game average (15.8) and passing yardage per game average (249.6).**
HB — Pete Banaszak: Active for 13 games, and started in 11. Rushed for 362 yards on 91 carries for 4 TD. Had 15 receptions for 182 yards and 1 TD, and threw 1 pass that was intercepted.
FB — Hewritt Dixon: Active for 14 games, and started in 13. Rushed for 865 yards on 206 carries and 2 TD, and had 38 receptions for 360 yards and 2 TD.
WR — Fred Biletnikoff: Started in 14 games. Had 61 receptions for 1,037 yards and 6 TD.
WR — Warren Wells: Active for 14 games, and started in 12. Had 53 receptions for 1,137 yards and 11 TD, and rushed for 38 yards on 2 carries and 1 TD. **His 12 total TD's led the AFL.**
TE — Billy Cannon: Active for 14 games, and started in 13. Had 23 receptions for 360 yards and 6 TD.
LT — Bob Svihus: Started in 14 games.
LG — Gene Upshaw: Started in 14 games.
C — Jim Otto: Started in 14 games.

RG — Jim Harvey: Active for 14 games, and started in 11.
RT — Harry Schuh: Started in 14 games.

RESERVE OFFENSIVE PLAYERS

Cotton Davidson (QB): Active for 1 game. Had 1 completion out of 2 pass attempts for 4 yards.
Eldridge Dickey (WR): Active for 11 games. Had 1 reception for 34 yards, 6 punt returns for 48 yards, and 1 kickoff return for 17 yards.
John Eason (WR): Active for 3 games.
Roger Hagberg (RB/WR): Active for 14 games, and started in 1. Rushed for 164 yards on 39 carries and 1 TD, had 8 receptions for 78 yards and 1 TD, and 1 kickoff return for 21 yards.
Wayne Hawkins (G): Active for 10 games, and started in 3.
Dave Kocourek (TE/WR): Active for 7 games, and started in 1. Had 3 receptions for 46 yards and 1 TD.
Bob Kruse (G/T): Active for 12 games. Had 1 kickoff return for 1 yard.
Bill Miller (WR): Active for 9 games and started in 2. Had 9 receptions for 176 yards and 1 TD.
Preston Ridlehuber (RB): Active for 10 games. Rushed for 7 yards on 4 carries.
John Roderick (WR): Active for 11 games.
Art Shell (T): Active for 14 games, and had 1 punt return for 0 yards.
Charlie Smith (RB): Active for 14 games, and started in 3. Rushed for 504 yards on 95 carries and 5 TD. **His 5.3 yards per carry average led the AFL.** Had 22 receptions for 321 yards and 2 TD, and 8 kickoff returns for 167 yards.
Larry Todd (RB): Active for 3 games. Rushed for 89 yards on 13 carries and 2 TD, and had 4 receptions for 40 yards.

STARTERS — DEFENSE

DE — Ike Lassiter: Started in 14 games.
DE — Ben Davidson: Started in 14 games and had 1 fumble recovery.
DT — Dan Birdwell: Started in 14 games and had 2 fumble recoveries.
DT — Carleton Oats: Started in 14 games.
LLB — Chip Oliver: Active for 14 games, and started in 10.
MLB — Dan Conners: Started in 14 games, had 2 INT and 1 fumble recovery.
RLB — Gus Otto: Active for 13 games, and started in 12, and had 1 kickoff return for 0 yards.
CB — Kent McCloughan: Active for and started in 8 games, and had 1 INT.
CB — Willie Brown: Started in 14 games, had 2 INT and 1 TD.
S — Rodger Bird: Active for 10 games, and started in 8. Had 3 INT, 1 TD, 1 fumble recovery, and 11 punt returns for 128 yards.
S — Dave Grayson: Started in 14 games. Had **10 INT**, 1 TD, and 1 fumble recovery.

RESERVE DEFENSIVE PLAYERS

George Atkinson (DB): Active for 14 games, and started in 6. Had 4 INT, 3 TD, 3 fumble recoveries, **36 punt returns and 490 yards and 2 TD**, and 32 kickoff returns for 802 yards. **Also led the AFL in yards per kickoff return average (25.1), combined punt and kickoff returns (68), combined yardage on kick and punt returns (1,292), and most non-offensive TD (3).**
Duane Benson (LB): Active for 12 games, started in 6, and had 1 fumble recovery.
Bill Budness (LB): Active for 14 games.
Al Dotson (T): Active for 13 games, and started in 1.
Bill Fairband (LB): Active for 2 games.
Jerry Hopkins (LB): Active for 5 games, had 2 fumble recoveries and 1 kickoff return for 0 yards.
Dave Ogas (LB): Active for 6 games.
Warren Powers (DB): Active for 8 games, started in 4, had 1 INT and 1 fumble recovery.
Karl Rubke (LB/T/E/C): Active for 4 games.

Howie Williams (DB): Active for 13 games, started in 2, and had 2 INT.
Nemiah Wilson (DB): Active for 1 game, had 1 punt return for 0 yards and 4 kickoff returns for 84 yards.

KICKING/PUNTING

K — George Blanda: Active for 14 games. Made 21 of 34 field goal attempts and **54** of **54** extra point kicks for 117 points. Completed 30 of 49 pass attempts for 522 yards, 6 TD and 2 INT.
P — Mike Eischeid: Active for 14 games. Punted 64 times for a 43.6 average, and rushed for 41 yards on 2 carries, and had 1 fumble recovery.

1969 Season Review

1. Sept. 14: Two David Grayson first quarter interceptions set up two 5-yard touchdown runs by Charlie Smith to give the Raiders an early 14–0 lead over the Houston Oilers. Oakland had trouble finding the end zone after that, and with six minutes remaining in the game, they were down, 17–14. It was then that Daryle Lamonica and Warren Wells worked their magic like so many times before. Two plays after Houston scored their go-ahead points, "the Mad Bomber" threw to a wide-open Wells for a 64-yard touchdown to give Oakland a 21–17 win in their home opener, and the first victory for rookie head coach John Madden.[1]

2. Sept. 20: David Grayson once again came through with an early interception to get the Raiders going, this time against the Miami Dolphins. He picked off a pass on the Oakland 24 then went 76 yards to give Oakland a 7–0 lead. The Silver and Black increased their lead to 17–7 in the second quarter on a 13-yard pass from Daryle Lamonica to Fred Biletnikoff and a 37-yard George Blanda field goal. Biletnikoff had a great game with nine receptions for 132 yards, and Willie Brown helped out on the defensive side with two interceptions. The game remained scoreless throughout the second half until Blanda added another three-pointer, this time from 47 yards out with eleven seconds left in the game, to give Oakland a 20–17 win.[2]

3. Sept. 28: After two hard-fought games, the Raiders had little trouble in a 38–23 win over the Boston Patriots. Daryle Lamonica threw four touchdown passes to help keep Oakland undefeated, while Boston remained winless. On the receiving end of Lamonica's scoring tosses were Warren Wells (28 and 55 yards), Fred Biletnikoff (5 yards), and Hewritt Dixon (31 yards). Larry Todd scored on a 1-yard run, and George Blanda kicked a 25-yard field goal to round out Oakland's point production. The Oakland defense, despite giving up 23 points, intercepted two passes and held Boston's running game to a mere 52 yards. The rowdy Raiders were also dominant when it came to infractions, as they were penalized 13 times for 176 yards.[3]

4. Oct. 4: Two weeks prior to this game, George Blanda beat Miami with a last second field goal. This time around it was Miami's Karl Kremser who returned the favor by kicking a 39-yard field goal in the fourth quarter to give the Dolphins a 20–20 tie. This game was a moral victory for Miami, who was still looking for their first win of the year. George Blanda set an AFL record in the first quarter by kicking his 46th straight field goal, which came from 24 yards out. He also added a 37-yarder in the

fourth stanza. Daryle Lamonica threw two scoring strikes, teaming up with Warren Wells from 15 yards, and Fred Biletnikoff from seven, for Oakland's other points. Biletnikoff ran away with game-high honors by catching nine passes for 119 yards. The defense helped in the cause with six sacks and two interceptions. Even with this tie, the Raiders ran their regular season unbeaten streak to 12 games.[4]

5. Oct. 12: Under terrible weather conditions, the Raiders still prevailed over the Denver Broncos, 24–14. Snow, mud, and temperatures of 20 degrees, greeted the Raiders in Denver, Colorado. Despite nature's obstacles, Daryle Lamonica managed to shine. With the running game bogged down, "the Mad Bomber" lived up to his moniker. With his talented right arm and gifted receiving corps, he threw for 253 yards and three touchdowns. Pete Banaszak (4 yards), Fred Biletnikoff (19 yards), and Billy Cannon (2 yards), were on the receiving ends of the scoring strikes, and George Blanda kicked a 24-yard field goal. Biletnikoff had seven receptions for 92 yards, and Warren Wells four for 82 yards on the dismal Denver day.[5]

6. Oct. 19: Daryle Lamonica is mentioned quite a bit when talk about the Oakland Raiders of the late 1960's comes up in conversation. And there is good reason for it. Lamonica was one of the top quarterbacks in all of pro football during this time, and a 50–21 blowout over the Buffalo Bills solidified his place among the elite. He threw for 313 yards and an incredible six touchdowns. With this fantastic performance, Lamonica had 17 touchdown passes in just six games. Pete Banaszak (10 and 1 yard) and Fred Biletnikoff (16 and 23 yards) each caught two scoring passes, while Billy Cannon (53 yards) and Warren Wells (13 yards) hauled in the others. Wells once again turned in a great performance by catching five receptions for 101 yards. George Blanda added two field goals (20 and 36 yards), and the defense tackled Jack Kemp in the end zone for a safety. With this win, Oakland improved to 5-0-1, and held a slim Western Division lead over the 5–1 Kansas City Chiefs.[6]

7. Oct. 26: Oakland continued to be the best team in the AFL, and Daryle Lamonica was once again at his best in a 24–12 win over San Diego. Lamonica ran his season touchdown total to 20 with scoring tosses to Larry Todd (48 yards), Warren Wells (16 yards), and Roger Hagberg (15 yards). George Blanda chipped in with a 28-yard field goal to finish out the scoring, and Pete Banaszak ran for a game-high 123 yards on 25 carries. Even with 180 yards marked off against them on 12 penalties, the rough and tough Raiders were still in control of this game throughout. David Grayson performed brilliantly on defense, as he shut down the San Diego attack with three interceptions.[7]

8. Nov. 2: After a 15-game unbeaten streak, the Raiders fell for the first time in an upset to the Cincinnati Bengals, 31–17. Daryle Lamonica threw for two scores, but was also picked off five times. George Blanda finally got the Raiders on the board in the third quarter with a 27-yard field goal after they were down by a 24–0 count. Lamonica then threw his two six-pointers with the game out of reach in the fourth quarter. His scoring strikes went to Fred Biletnikoff (9 yards) and Warren Wells (43 yards). Despite the upset loss, Wells played up to All-Pro status by catching five passes for 136 yards. This loss knocked Oakland out of first place, as the 7–1 Kansas City Chiefs assumed the top spot in the Western Division.[8]

9. Nov. 9: Oakland rebounded from their first loss with a vengeance. The Denver Broncos took the brunt of Oakland's furry in a 41–10 trouncing. The Oakland defensive line of Tom Keating, Ike Lassiter, Ben Davidson, and Carleton Oats, plowed through Denver's offensive line almost at will, forcing quarterback Steve Tensi to run for his life on virtually every passing down. When he did manage to get a pass off, Tensi was throwing into the league's toughest secondary. Linebacker Ralph Oliver started Tensi's day of horror off by intercepting one of his passes on the Denver 29 and returning it for a score. On offense, Fred Biletnikoff was the star. He caught four passes for 110 yards and three touchdowns (53, 28, and 15 yards) from Daryle Lamonica, who got roughed up a bit and had to leave the game for a while. George Blanda came on in relief, and found Charlie Smith in the end zone from 11 yards out for another Oakland touchdown. Blanda also added two field goals from 45 and 18 yards.[9]

10. Nov. 16: Facing a tough San Diego defense throughout the game, Daryle Lamonica suffered three interceptions, but still managed to complete 15 of 29 passes for 235 yards and two touchdowns in a 21–16 win. His first scoring pass went to Fred Biletnikoff (19 yards), which tied the game. Warren Wells was on the receiving end of Lamonica's other touchdown toss, which covered 80 yards with the Raiders down 16–14 in the fourth quarter. Lamonica had 27 touchdown passes after this game, which was the best in all of pro football. Dan Conners got six points on the board for the defense by returning a fumble 25 yards to paydirt. At 8-1-1, the Raiders were still a half game behind the 9–1 Chiefs.[10]

11. Nov. 23: The Raiders seized the summit of the Western Division once again by ending Kansas City's seven-game winning streak, 27–24. Oakland capitalized on five interceptions and two fumbles, converting them into 17 points. Two of the interceptions were returned for touchdowns, with George Atkinson (22 yards) and Dan Conners (75 yards) getting the honors. David Grayson became the AFL career interception leader with his two thefts, and Gus Otto was credited with the other one. Fullback Hewritt Dixon sparked the offense by leading all ball carriers with 82 yards. Warren Wells caught a 22-yard scoring strike from Daryle Lamonica, and George Blanda kicked two field goals (10 and 14 yards) to help put Oakland over the top against their fierce rival.[11]

12. Nov. 30: In a brutal game that saw 18 penalties marked off, with 10 going against Oakland, the renegade Raiders pulled out their tenth win of the season with a 27–14 win over the defending Super Bowl champion New York Jets. This was the third straight season in which the Raiders won ten or more games. Despite a fierce pounding by the New York defense, Daryle Lamonica still found a way to turn in a stellar performance, completing 19 of 28 pass attempts for 333 yards and two touchdowns. He also ran for a 1-yard score. Both of Lamonica's scoring tosses went to Warren Wells (34 and 20 yards), who was his brilliant self with five receptions for 152 yards. George Blanda kicked two field goals (23 and 37 yards) to provide the Raiders with their other points.[12]

13. Dec. 7: Avenging their only loss of the season, the Raiders beat the Cincinnati Bengals, 37–17. Daryle Lamonica passed to Warren Wells for two scores (51 and 16 yards), and Fred Biletnikoff for another (16 yards). Wells, who finished with four receptions for 102 yards, also caught a 16-yard touchdown pass from George Blanda in the fourth quarter after the old veteran replaced Lamonica once the game was out of reach. Blanda also

kicked three field goals (17, 28, and 31 yards) in a game that saw the Raiders produce 544 yards of offense.[13]

14. Dec. 13: The 11-1-1 Raiders faced the 11–2 Chiefs in Oakland for the right to be crowned Western Division champions. In a defensive battle between these two hated rivals, the Silver and Black earned their third straight division title, 10–6, and the first for head coach John Madden. The Oakland defense limited the Kansas City passing game to a meager 29 yards. Standing out on this great defensive unit were tackles Tom Keating and Carleton Oats, who both came up with big plays all day long. The Raiders held a slim 3–0 lead through three quarters on a 30-yard George Blanda field goal until Daryle Lamonica gave Oakland a little more breathing room with an 8-yard scoring toss to Charlie Smith. This pass to Smith was "the Mad Bomber's" 34th of the season, and it fell two short of the all-time record of 36 shared by Blanda in 1961 while with the Houston Oilers, and Y.A. Tittle in 1963 while playing for the New York Giants.[14]

AFL Divisional Playoff Game, December 21, 1969

In an attempt to extend the post season, the AFL's powers-that-be decided to allow the second place finishers from each division into the playoffs. The Raiders could not hide their displeasure with this setup, feeling that it was a waste of time. Their complaints naturally fell on deaf ears, and the playoff matchups were set. The New York Jets would host Western Division runner-up Kansas City, while the Raiders would entertain the 6-6-2 Houston Oilers.

The Raiders decided to show what a waste of time this extra round was by taking out their displeasure on the Oilers. In the end, the Raiders handed Houston their worst AFL defeat to the tune of a 56–7 dismantling.

Daryle Lamonica lit up the Oakland sky for 276 yards on 13 of 17 completions and an incredible six touchdown passes. Lamonica opened the scoring on what would soon become a gridiron carnage with a 13-yard pass to Fred Biletnikoff, who made the catch with one hand being held back by defender Miller Farr. George "the Hit Man" Atkinson brought one home for the defense when he picked off a Pete Beathard third down pass, and with great blocking from linebacker Dan Conners and fellow defensive back Nemiah Wilson, Atkinson went 57 yards for a touchdown to make it 14–0. Following a Hoyle Granger fumble that Gus Otto recovered on the Houston 24, Rod Sherman caught a 24-yard Lamonica pass and scored after dragging two defensive backs with him before breaking free. The Raiders were now up, 21–0, and produced all these points in a mere 1:59 of the first quarter.

However, the Raiders were still not done ringing up the scoreboard. Another fumble, this time by Beathard, resulted in a 31-yard Lamonica to Biletnikoff touchdown to make it a 28–0 affair with 4:05 still remaining in the opening stanza. Oakland slowed down a bit in the second quarter, as they only added one touchdown, but it was a good, quality effort. Lamonica threw to Charlie Smith at the Oakland 40. Smith was covered by a linebacker, which proved to be a major mismatch. Smith hauled in the pass, and then ran the distance to complete a 60-yard catch and run to make it 35–0 at the half. Smith finished this post-season mauling with a game-high 103 receiving yards on four catches.

Sherman added his second touchdown grab of the day from 23 yards, and Billy Cannon added a 3-yard touchdown reception to up the bulge to 49–0 after three quarters. In the fourth quarter, Oakland sent in the reserves and still managed one final tally. Rookie fullback Marv Hubbard got into the scoring summary on a 4-yard run, and the Raiders were on their way to a third straight AFL Championship Game.[15]

AFL Championship Game, January 4, 1970

After a two-week layoff, the Raiders were ready to return to the Super Bowl. The only obstacle standing in their way was a matchup with bitter rival Kansas City, who beat the defending Super Bowl champion New York Jets in their divisional playoff game, 13–6.

A sellout crowd of 54,544 turned out at Oakland-Alameda Coliseum to witness the final AFL game not counting the All-Star game. The Raiders gave the hometown faithful something to cheer about with 36 seconds left in the first quarter when Charlie Smith ran for a 3-yard touchdown that finished off a 10-play, 66-yard drive. The big play of the drive came on a 24-yard pass from Daryle Lamonica to Warren Wells that set up Smith's jaunt.

Kansas City's defensive unit of the 1960's was considered one of the all-time best, and this tough band of 11 men rose up and prevented Oakland's high-powered offense from entering their territory throughout the second quarter. The Chiefs, meanwhile, were able to get their offense going after struggling for the first 27 minutes of the first half. A Len Dawson to Frank Pitts pass gained 41 yards, and set up the Chiefs on the Oakland one. Wendall Hayes ran it in from there to send the game into halftime knotted at seven points apiece.

Lamonica was sent to the sidelines for eight minutes of the third quarter with an injured hand following a hit from massive 265-pound defensive lineman Aaron Brown. George Blanda came in to replace Lamonica with the score still tied. Blanda was driving the Raiders until an Emmitt Thomas interception in the end zone killed the opportunity. Thomas returned the ball to the six to give Kansas City possession deep in their own territory. Blanda had a rough time in relief of Lamonica, as the Chiefs applied heavy pressure to the aging warrior. He also missed on three field goal attempts.

On first down, Dawson threw an incomplete pass, and Robert Holmes avoided getting tackled in the end zone on second down. Facing a third-and-14 situation, Dawson took to the air with a pass down the right sideline to Otis Taylor, who made a great catch at the 37. Two plays later, Dawson went to the opposite sideline, and connected with Holmes for 23 yards. The Raiders were no strangers to penalties called against them, and this game proved to be no exception. However, this time it proved to be a game-changing one. Dawson went back to Taylor along the right sideline, but the ball sailed over his head. The officials quickly threw a flag, calling pass interference on Nemiah Wilson against Taylor on the Oakland 7-yard line. Holmes then broke the tie with a 5-yard run to cap the 94-yard drive.

The Chiefs intercepted three Lamonica passes in the fourth quarter, as the "the Mad Bomber" was trying to fight off the effects of his injured hand. In an attempt to rally the Raiders, Lamonica, starting from his own six, connected on some passes to get the Raiders to the Kansas City 39. Safety Jim Kearney then intercepted a pass at the 20 and returned it to the 25.

A few minutes later, confusion in the Kansas City backfield caused a fumble that was recovered by Carleton Oats at the 25 to give the Raiders renewed hope. However, the Chiefs did not like giving the ball back to their rivals, and got it back on the following play when rookie cornerback Jim Marsalis picked off Lamonica and returned the ball to the 33. The turnover seesaw once again gave possession back to Oakland when the Robert Holmes fumbled and Dan Conners recovered at the 31.

It is said that the third time is the charm, but not for the Silver and Black on this day. Emmitt Thomas came up with his second interception of the game at the Kansas City 20, and returned the ball 62 yards to the Oakland 18. Jan Stenerud then added a 22-yard field goal to give the Chiefs a 17–7 lead with 4:48 remaining in the game. That was how the final AFL championship game ended, with the Chiefs earning the right to represent the league in Super Bowl IV, which they won in convincing fashion over the Minnesota Vikings, 23–7.[16]

Individual Statistics and Roster

Head Coach: John Madden
Assistant Coaches: Tom Dahms, Sid Hall, Marv Marinovich, Richard Mccabe, John Polonchek, Ollie Spencer, Dick Wood
1969 Regular Season Record: 12-1-1
1st Place in AFL Western Division
Scored 377 points to rank 1st out of 10 teams
Allowed 242 points to rank 2nd
Led the league in points (377), offensive yards (5,036), passing yards (3,271), and touchdown passes (36)

STARTERS — OFFENSE

QB — Daryle Lamonica: Started in 14 games. Completed **221** of **426** pass attempts for **3,302** yards, 34 TD and 25 INT. Rushed for 36 yards on 13 carries and 1 TD. **Also led the AFL in pass completion per game average (15.8) and passing yardage per game average (235.9).**

HB—Charlie Smith: Started in 14 games. Rushed for 600 yards on 177 carries and 2 TD. Had 30 receptions for 322 yards and 2 TD, and 10 kickoff returns for 247 yards.

FB — Hewritt Dixon: Active for 11 games, and started in 10. Rushed for 398 yards on 107 carries, and had 33 receptions for 275 yards and 1 TD.

WR — Fred Biletnikoff: Started in 14 games. Had 54 receptions for 837 yards and 12 TD.

WR — Warren Wells: Started in 14 games. Had 47 receptions for **1,260** yards and 14 TD. Rushed for 24 yards on 2 carries. **Also led the AFL in total yards from scrimmage (1,284), yards per reception average (26.8), and yards receiving per game average (90.0).**

TE — Billy Cannon: Active for 13 games, and started in 11. Had 21 receptions for 262 yards and 1 TD.

LT — Bob Svihus: Active for and started in 13 games.
LG — Gene Upshaw: Started in 14 games.
C — Jim Otto: Started in 14 games.
RG — Jim Harvey: Started in 14 games.
RT — Harry Schuh: Started in 14 games.
Reserve Offensive Players:
Pete Banaszak (RB): Active for 12 games, and started in 4. Rushed for 377 yards on 88 carries, and had 17 receptions for 119 yards and 3 TD.

George Buehler (G): Active for 2 games.

Drew Buie (WR): Active for 14 games. Had 1 reception for 37 yards.

Lloyd Edwards (TE): Active for 14 games.

Roger Hagberg (RB/WR): Active for 14 games, and started in 3. Rushed for 3 yards on 1 carry, and had 6 receptions for 84 yards and 1 TD.

Wayne Hawkins (G): Active for 14 games.

Marv Hubbard (RB): Active for 14 games. Rushed for 119 yards on 21 carries, and had 2 receptions for 30 yards.

Art Shell (T): Active for 14 games, and started in 1.

Rod Sherman (WR): Active for 14 games. Had 9 punt returns for 46 yards and 12 kickoff returns for 300 yards.

Larry Todd (RB): Active for 11 games. Rushed for 198 yards on 47 carries and 1 TD, and had 16 receptions for 149 yards and 1 TD.

STARTERS — DEFENSE

DE — Ike Lassiter: Started in 14 games and had 2 fumble recoveries.

DE — Ben Davidson: Started in 14 games.

DT — Carleton Oats: Active for and started in 13 games. Had 1 fumble recovery.

DT — Tom Keating: Active for 14 games, and started in 13. Had 1 fumble recovery.

LLB — Bill Laskey: Active for 12 games, and started in 8. Had 3 INT.

MLB — Dan Conners: Started in 14 games. Had 1 INT and 1 TD, 3 fumble recoveries and 1 TD.

RLB — Gus Otto: Started in 14 games and had 2 INT.

CB — Nemiah Wilson: Active for 14 games, and started in 12. Had 2 INT and 1 fumble recovery.

CB — Willie Brown: Started in 14 games and had 5 INT.

S — George Atkinson: Active for 14 games, and started in 12. Had 2 INT and 1 TD, 25 punt returns for 153 yards and 16 kickoff returns for 382 yards.

S — Dave Grayson: Started in 14 games. Had 8 INT and 1 TD, 1 fumble recovery, and 4 punt returns for 28 yards.

RESERVE DEFENSIVE PLAYERS

Jackie Allen (DB): Active for 5 games. Had 1 punt return for -2 yards and 3 kickoff returns for 67 yards.

Duane Benson (LB): Active for 14 games. Had 1 fumble recovery, 1 kickoff return for 0 yards.

Dan Birdwell (T/E): Active for 2 games.

Bill Budness (LB): Active for 14 games.

Al Dotson (T): Active for 13 games, and started in 1.

Kent McCloughan (DB): Active for 4 games.

Ralph "Chip" Oliver (LB): Active for 14 games, and started in 6. Had 1 INT, 1 TD, and 2 fumble recoveries.

Art Thoms (T): Active in 12 games, and started in 1.

Howie Williams (DB): Active in 14 games, and started in 4. Had 2 INT and 1 fumble recovery.

KICKING/PUNTING

K — George Blanda: Active for 14 games. Made 20 of 37 field goals and 45 of 45 extra point kicks for 105 points. Had 6 pass completions out of 13 attempts for 73 yards, 2 TD, and 1 INT and 1 rush for 0 yards.

P — Mike Eischeid: Active for 14 games. Punted 69 times for a 42.7 average, and 1 rush for 10 yards.

1970 Season Review

1. Sept. 20: In their inaugural NFL game, the Raiders suffered a 31–21 loss to the Cincinnati Bengals, who were quickly becoming a major thorn in Oakland's side. They handed the Raiders their only loss in 1969, and gave them their first opening day defeat since 1964. Running back Jess Phillips was the main weapon for Cincinnati. He ran for 130 yards on 14 carries, and his 76-yard touchdown run in the third quarter broke a 21–21 tie. Along with Phillips, Essex Johnson helped the Bengals ground attack set a then-team record of 247 yards rushing. Before Phillips go-ahead score, the Raiders battled back from a 21–7 deficit to tie the game on two Daryle Lamonica touchdown passes to Fred Biletnikoff covering 20 and 18 yards. Alvin Wyatt provided Oakland with their other touchdown on a 63-yard punt return.[1]

2. Sept. 27: Oakland was having trouble getting their first NFL win, but they got closer this time with a 27–27 tie against the San Diego Chargers. The Raiders were up, 27–13, thanks to two Pete Banaszak 1-yard touchdown runs, a 23-yard pass from Daryle Lamonica to Fred Biletnikoff, George Blanda field goals from 28 and 13 yards. Lamonica had a good day with 2667 yards passing on 23 of 38 attempts. George Atkinson helped out on the defensive side with two interceptions. San Diego refused to break in front of their home crowd, and they tied the game on two John Hadl scoring tosses. Oakland had a chance to win the game with nine seconds remaining, but a 32-yard Blanda field goal attempt fell short of its mark.[2]

3. Oct. 3: After being in the top spot of the Western Division for three straight seasons, the Raiders were now tied for last place at 0-2-1 with San Diego. Keeping Oakland out of the win column were the Miami Dolphins, who won, 20–13, with the help of Bob Griese's two touchdown passes to Paul Warfield. The game was played in a heavy rainstorm in front of a then-record Miami crowd of 57,140. Oakland's scoring came on two George Blanda field goals from 12 and 17 yards, and a 36-yard pass from Daryle Lamonica to Warren Wells.[3]

4. Oct. 11: Four Daryle Lamonica touchdown passes helped lift the Raiders over the Denver Broncos, 35–23, for their first NFL win. This was a hard-fought contest, as Oakland had to battle back three times. Warren Wells did his part with seven receptions for 198 yards and three touchdown receptions covering 32, 60, and 20 yards. Raymond Chester caught Lamonica's other touchdown pass from 24 yards out for Oakland's first points of the game in the first quarter. Lamonica's brilliant day consisted of 364 yards through the air on 20 of 37 attempts. Charlie Smith ran five yards for the team's fifth six-pointer of the day.[4]

5. Oct. 19: In their Monday Night Football debut, the Silver and Black made it two in a row with a 34–20 victory over the Washington Redskins. This was also Oakland's first regular season game against a pre-merger NFL team. Fullback Hewritt Dixon got the prime time festivities going with a 39-yard touchdown run on the first play from scrimmage. He continued to torment the Redskins throughout this game, finishing with 164 rushing yards. The Raiders never relinquished the lead, and Daryle Lamonica threw three scoring strikes to give him eleven in just five games. Warren Wells was on the receiving end of two touchdown passes from 28 and 24 yards and Charlie Smith had one from 16 yards. George Blanda added two field goals from 35 and 21 yards to complete Oakland's scoring.[5]

6. Oct. 25: The Oakland Raiders and Pittsburgh Steelers waged some classic battles against one another throughout the 1970's. However, their initial meeting was anything but memorable. This was a time before the Steelers were the wrecking machine that dominated opponents in the mid to latter part of the decade, and the Raiders devoured them, 31–14, for their third

straight win. The 43-year-old George Blanda ripped through Pittsburgh's secondary for three touchdown passes, and added a 27-yard field goal to his productive day. The ageless wonder was called into quarterbacking duty after Daryle Lamonica suffered a back injury in the first quarter. Before he exited, Lamonica threw his twelfth touchdown pass of the season. His receiver on the 37-yard play was rookie tight end Raymond Chester. Chester added two more six-pointers from George Blanda covering 19 and 43 yards. Warren Wells also caught a touchdown pass (44 yards), which was Blanda's first of the game, and it broke a 7–7 tie in the second quarter. That touchdown toss proved to be the 225th of Blanda's amazing career.[6]

7. Nov. 1: The Raiders scratched and clawed their way back up the AFC Western Division ladder, and within one month, went from worst to first. They achieved this by tying the defending Super Bowl champion Kansas City Chiefs, 17–17. Oakland was now on top of the division with a 3-2-2 record. George Blanda came through once again, this time with his right foot doing the damage. In a game that saw fists fly among these hated rivals, Blanda kicked a 48-yard field goal with three seconds left to force a tie. Daryle Lamonica was back in action, and threw two touchdown passes to rookie sensation, tight end Raymond Chester from three and eight yards out. Big Ben Davidson caused possibly the biggest altercation of this heated series when he speared quarterback Len Dawson in the back right by the Kansas City sideline. A massive brawl then took place that stopped play for 15 minutes.[7]

8. Nov. 8: George Blanda once again pulled another one out for the Silver and Black. With four minutes left in this game, the Cleveland Browns were up, 20–13. Daryle Lamonica was forced to the sidelines with a shoulder injury, and Blanda came in and quickly tied things up with a 14-yard touchdown pass to Warren Wells. The Raiders got the ball back with 43 seconds left deep in their own territory. Six plays later, Blanda lined up for a 52-yard field goal attempt. It appeared like this game was also going to end in a tie, but Blanda's right foot was too powerful. His long distance attempt split the uprights to give Oakland a 23–20 victory in what was their 16th straight home win. Blanda added two other three-pointers, one from 43 yards to open the scoring, and a 9-yarder to increase Oakland's lead to 13–0 in the second quarter. Charlie Smith chipped in with a 27-yard touchdown grab from Lamonica, and also led the team's ground assault with 73 yards on 16 carries.[8]

9. Nov. 15: After winning Oakland's last two games with his kicking, George Blanda decided to pull out a 24–19 win over the Denver Broncos with his passing. After Daryle Lamonica became woozy following a hard hit, Blanda replaced him. Before he left, however, Lamonica threw two touchdown passes to Warren Wells (36 yards) and Hewritt Dixon (46 yards). In between those touchdowns, Blanda added a 32-yard field goal. The Broncos took a 19–17 lead with four minutes left in the game when Blanda took over. From the Oakland 18, Blanda passed the Raiders downfield and into the end zone within three plays. His final toss of the drive went to Fred Biletnikoff for twenty yards and the winning points. Thanks once again to Blanda's heroics, the Silver and Black remained in first place with a 5-2-2 record.[9]

10. Nov. 22: George Blanda solidified his place in Raiders lore by once again pulling a game out in the closing seconds. This time he did it by hitting a 16-yard field goal with seven seconds left to beat San Diego, 20–17. In the opening minutes of the fourth quarter, Blanda kicked his first three-pointer (18 yards) to put Oakland on top. The Chargers then came back to tie with almost five minutes left in the game. With Daryle Lamonica passing and Charlie Smith running, the Raiders got close enough for Blanda to work his magic. Smith led all ball carriers in this game with 84 yards, and scored on runs of three and one yard. Also helping Oakland's cause were defensive back David Grayson and linebacker Bill Laskey, who each came up with an interception that killed San Diego threats.[10]

11. Nov. 26: Oakland struck quickly in their Thanksgiving Day affair with the Detroit Lions. On the first play from scrimmage, Daryle Lamonica threw a 23-yard touchdown pass to Fred Biletnikoff. This duo also teamed up later in the first quarter on a 21-yarder to give the Raiders a 14–0 advantage. The Lions finally woke up after that. An interception and a blocked punt set Detroit up for two touchdowns, and gave them a huge dose of momentum. The Lions added two more touchdowns, and nailed down a 28–14 victory. In the process, the Lions snapped Oakland's seven-game unbeaten streak.[11]

12. Dec. 6: The George Blanda Show took its act to the Big Apple, and came away with a 14–13 nail-biting victory. Trailing the Jets, 13–7 with seconds remaining, Daryle Lamonica threw a desperation pass in the direction of Warren Wells. A New York defender tipped the ball, and Wells came up with the ball in the end zone for a 33-yard game-tying touchdown. Wells caught an earlier touchdown pass from Blanda covering 13 yards that gave the Raiders their first points of the game in the third quarter. With one tick left on the clock, Blanda came on and drilled home the winning conversion kick. The Raiders were now at 7-3-2, and tied with long-time rival Kansas City for the division lead.[12]

13. Dec. 12: For the first time in many weeks, George Blanda got some time off from his fantastic finishes. Instead of Blanda, Oakland's hero in this Western Division showdown with Kansas City was second-year fullback Marv Hubbard. The battering ram fullback bulled his way to 93 yards on 16 carries and scored on a 6-yard run in a 20–6 win. With Hubbard pounding out yardage, along with Hewritt Dixon and Charlie Smith, the Raiders logged 204 yards on the ground. Blanda added field goals from 23 and 35 yards, and Fred Biletnikoff caught a 36-yard pass from Daryle Lamonica to round out Oakland's point production. The defense completely shut down one of the league's best offenses, as they limited the Chiefs to only seven first downs and a mere 62 rushing yards and 59 through the air.[13]

14. Dec. 20: With the AFC Western Division crown already in their possession, the Raiders had little to play for in this regular season finale against the San Francisco 49ers. After taking a 7–3 first quarter lead on a Daryle Lamonica to Raymond Chester 29-yard pass, Oakland came apart. Led by the league's top passer John Brodie, the 49ers mauled the Raiders, 38–7. Brodie threw three touchdown passes, and helped guide San Francisco into the playoffs for the first time since 1957. The Raiders finished the regular season at 8-4-2, and were headed to the playoffs for the fourth consecutive year.[14]

AFC Divisional Playoff Game,
December 27, 1970

The Miami Dolphins earned a first-ever trip to the post-season in only their fifth campaign. After a successful seven-season run as coach of the Baltimore Colts, Don Shula took over the reins in Miami. His impact was immediate, as the Dolphins posted a 10–4 record, and headed to Oakland for a divisional playoff against the post-season veteran Raiders, who came into this contest as a one touchdown favorite. In muddy conditions, the teams felt each other out during a scoreless first quarter.

Early in the second quarter, running back Charlie Smith fumbled after losing a handoff from Daryle Lamonica. Defensive end Bill Stanfill recovered for Miami on the Oakland 19 to give the underdog Dolphins a big break. In Oakland's regular season finale, they lost four fumbles and got mauled in the process. It seemed that the problem carried into this game, with the stakes being even higher. Miami quarterback Bob Griese wasted little time taking advantage of the mishap, and he connected with Paul Warfield for the game's first points on a 16-yard pass. Garo Yepremian's conversion gave the Dolphins a 7–0 lead.

Near the end of the first half, the Raiders engineered a 62-yard drive kept alive with key third down passes to Raymond Chester and Fred Biletnikoff. Lamonica then finished the drive off with a 22-yard strike to Biletnikoff. With George Blanda's extra point, the teams went into the locker rooms at halftime knotted at seven apiece.

Another fumble by Oakland killed a drive that reached the Miami two in the third quarter. Later, Bob Griese successfully moved the Dolphins downfield to the Oakland 35. A few plays later, Willie Brown quickly shifted the momentum over to the Raiders when he picked off a Griese pass and ran down the sideline for a 50-yard touchdown, which proved to be the turning point of the game. Blanda's conversion extended Oakland's lead to 14–7 going into the final 15 minutes. With the Raiders only up by seven, Pete Banaszak had a near disaster aborted after he fumbled on his own 18. Thankfully, tackle Harry Schuh pounced on the loose pigskin to allow the Raiders to keep possession. They did not need much more time to capitalize on Schuh's recovery. On the next play, Lamonica threw to Rod Sherman at the Miami 45. Sherman then outran defensive back Curtis Johnson on the race to the end zone to complete an 82-yard scoring trek untouched down the right sideline. With Blanda's extra point, the Raiders now had a little more breathing room with a 21–7 lead.

Miami attempted to fight to the end, and completed a 69-yard drive with a pass from Griese to Willie Richardson that covered seven yards. Yepremian added the extra point, and Oakland's lead was cut to 21–14 with 4:28 left to play. The Dolphins then attempted an onside kick, but the ball rolled out of bounds at the Oakland 39. They had one final shot to send the game into overtime, but they ran out of downs on their own 17 with under two minutes remaining.[15]

AFC Championship Game,
January 3, 1971

In their first season as a representative of the American Football Conference mixed in with AFL teams upon the merger, the Baltimore Colts were ready to host the Oakland Raiders for the right to play in Super Bowl V. The Raiders came into this game after defeating Don Shula and his upstart Miami Dolphins. They looked to beat Shula's old team next in what would be their fourth straight attempt at gaining entry into the Super Bowl.

After coming up one game short the past two seasons, Oakland hoped that the third time would be the charm in the new decade. Baltimore's Memorial Stadium was the site of the first-ever AFC Championship Game, and matched up two of the game's top signal callers in legendary Johnny Unitas and Daryle Lamonica. After traded punts following the opening kickoff, the Colts took possession on the Oakland 47 after a short, high punt by Mike Eischeid. Eleven plays later, Baltimore lit the scoreboard up with a 16-yard field goal from Jim O'Brien to give the home team an early 3–0 advantage. That was all the scoring for the first stanza, but Baltimore began mounting a drive as the game progressed into the next fifteen minutes of play. The Raiders caught a break when a dropped pass in the end zone and a missed field goal ended Baltimore's hopes of extending their slim lead. Lamonica looked to capitalize on his opponent's blown opportunities. He guided the Raiders down to the Baltimore 36, mostly with a solid ground attack midway through the quarter. After two incomplete passes, Lamonica dropped back yet again, but was sacked by big Bubba Smith for a 13-yard loss. On the play, "the Mad Bomber" injured a hamstring muscle, and would prove to be a non-factor from this point on.

However, the Raiders had the NFL's miracle man of 1970 in George Blanda, waiting to slip his parka off and come in to possibly work more of the magic that he used to pull out some fantastic finishes throughout the season. With the 43-year-old miracle man perched to take over at quarterback, this contest became the battle of old veteran signal callers with Blanda against 37-year-old Unitas. Following Smith's sack on Lamonica and the punt on fourth down, the Colts took over on their own 10 but could not get anything going. On fourth down, they looked to return possession back over to the Raiders. The Colts got a big break when George Atkinson fumbled the punt and Baltimore's Sam Havrilak recovered on the Oakland 45. Unitas struck with a big pass play to Eddie Hinton that got the ball down to the Oakland two. Bulldozer-like running back Norm Bulaich powered into the end zone for the game's first six-pointer, and following O'Brien's conversion, Baltimore was up, 10–0.

Following the ensuing kickoff, Blanda made his way into Oakland's huddle in an attempt to get his team back on track. He moved Oakland into Baltimore territory, but stalled just across midfield and was forced to punt. It was Oakland's turn to catch a break on a punt return when Baltimore was penalized for roughing the kicker. The Raiders kept possession on the Baltimore 40, but failed to move the ball. Blanda managed to get a solid connection on the ball, and nailed a 48-yard field goal to make the halftime score 10–3. It looked like Blanda was once again on the verge of bringing Oakland back, with this comeback earning them a trip to the Super Bowl. He connected with Fred Biletnikoff on a 38-yard touchdown strike, and his extra point kick knotted the proceedings at ten points apiece in the third quarter.

Undaunted by the turn of events that saw their ten point cut down, the Colts refused to become a footnote in another Blanda miracle. They first broke the tie with a 23-yard O'Brien field goal, and followed that up with Bulaich's second touchdown run of the day, this time from 11 yards. O'Brien added the extra point, and Baltimore led, 20–10, after three quarters.

With fifteen minutes standing between going home or a trip to the Super Bowl, Blanda opted for the latter, and his competitive fire refused to be put out just yet. The crafty old veteran took the Raiders 80 yards, with the final 15 going for a touchdown from Blanda to Warren Wells. Blanda's conversion brought Oakland back to only a three-point deficit at 20–17.

With momentum slightly creeping over to Oakland's side, the Colts had a plan to curb it. The Colts knew that Blanda would be forced to pass if Oakland was going to have any hopes of a comeback. They sent all out rushes at Blanda, which forced him to hurry his passes. On two occasions, Blanda managed to get Oakland close enough to scoring range, but the onslaught thrust at him caused two interceptions in the end zone. The Colts then delivered the coup de grace on a third-and-11 situation from their own 32. Baltimore decided to use four receivers on this play, with Ray Perkins lined up in the tight end spot. At the snap, Perkins shot downfield and was wide open. Unitas connected and the result was a 68-yard touchdown that put Baltimore up, 27–17, following O'Brien's extra point kick. And that was how it ended.

The well went dry on Blanda's miracles, and the Raiders fell one game shy of the ultimate gridiron spectacle for the third straight year. On the day, Blanda hit on 17 of 32 passes for 271 yards and two touchdowns, but suffered three crucial interceptions. In addition to rushing Blanda with reckless abandon, the Baltimore defense also stuffed Oakland's mighty running game, allowing it a combined 107 yards. The Colts, meanwhile, used their rookie power runner Norm Bulaich to control the ground attack and eat time off the clock. He carried the ball on 22 of Baltimore's 38 total running plays for 71 yards and two six-pointers.[16]

Individual Statistics and Roster

Head Coach: John Madden
Assistant Coaches: Tom Dahms, Sid Hall, Marv Marinovich, Richard Mccabe, John Polonchek, Ollie Spencer, Dick Wood
1970 Regular Season Record: 8-4-2
1st Place in AFC Western Division
Scored 300 points to rank 9th out of 26 teams
Allowed 293 points to rank 19th
Led the league in offensive yards (4,829), first downs (270), and touchdowns (28)

STARTERS — OFFENSE

QB — Daryle Lamonica: Started in 14 games. Completed 179 of 356 pass attempts for 2,516 yards, 22 TD and 15 INT. Rushed for 24 yards on 8 carries.
HB — Charlie Smith: Started in 14 games. Rushed for 681 yards on 168 carries and 3 TD. Had 23 receptions for 173 yards and 2 TD.
FB — Hewritt Dixon: Started in 14 games. Rushed for 861 yards on 197 carries and 1 TD. Had 31 receptions for 207 yards and 1 TD.
WR — Fred Biletnikoff: Started in 14 games, and had 45 receptions for 768 yards and 7 TD.
WR — Warren Wells: Active for 14 games, and started in 13. Had 43 receptions for 935 yards and 11 TD. Rushed for 34 yards on 3 carries.
TE — Raymond Chester: Active for 14 games, and started in 13. Had 42 receptions for 556 yards and 7 TD.

LT — Art Shell: Started in 14 games.
LG — Gene Upshaw: Started in 14 games.
C — Jim Otto: Started in 14 games.
RG — Jim Harvey: Started in 14 games.
RT — Harry Schuh: Active for 14 games, and started in 13.

RESERVE OFFENSIVE PLAYERS

Pete Banaszak (RB): Active for 10 games. Rushed for 75 yards on 21 carries and 2 TD. Had 1 reception for 2 yards.
George Buehler (G): Active for 14 games.
Drew Buie (WR): Active for 14 games, and had 2 receptions for 52 yards.
Don Highsmith (RB): Active for 13 games, and rushed for 2 yards on 2 carries.
Marv Hubbard (RB): Active for 13 games. Rushed for 246 yards on 51 carries and 1 TD. Had 2 kickoff returns for 41 yards.
Ted Koy (TE/RB/LB): Active for 14 games.
Jacque MacKinnon (TE/RB): Active for 4 games, and started in 1.
Rod Sherman (WR): Active for 14 games, and started in 1. Had 18 receptions for 285 yards, rushed for 2 yards on 1 carry, had 8 punt returns for 65 yards, and 2 kickoff returns for 39 yards.
Ken Stabler (QB): Active for 3 games, had 2 completions out of 7 pass attempts for 52 yards and 1 INT. Rushed for -4 yards on 1 carry.
Bob Svihus (T): Active for 13 games, and started in 1.
Larry Todd (RB): Active for 10 games, rushed for 39 yards on 17 carries, and had 5 receptions for 51 yards.

STARTERS — DEFENSE

DE — Tony Cline: Active for 14 games, and started in 12. Had 1 INT.
DE — Ben Davidson: Started in 14 games.
DT — Carleton Oats: Active for and started in 13 games.
DT — Tom Keating: Active for 13 games, and started in 12.
LLB — Bill Laskey: Started in 14 games, had 1 INT and 2 fumble recoveries.
MLB — Dan Conners: Active for 10 games, started in 9, and had 2 fumble recoveries.
RLB — Gus Otto: Started in 14 games and had 1 fumble recovery.
CB — Kent McCloughan: Active for 13 games, started in 10, and had 5 INT.
CB — Nemiah Wilson: Active for 14 games, started in 11, and had 2 INT.
SS — George Atkinson: Started in 14 games, had 3 INT, 1 fumble recovery, 4 punt returns for 12 yards and 23 kickoff returns for 574 yards.
FS — Dave Grayson: Started in 14 games and had 1 INT.

RESERVE DEFENSIVE PLAYERS

Duane Benson (LB): Active for 14 games, had 1 INT and 1 fumble recovery.
Willie Brown (DB): Active for 8 games, started in 7, and had 3 INT.
Bill Budness (LB): Active for 14 games, and started in 5.
Al Dotson (T): Active for 11 games, and started in 2.
Gerald Irons (LB): Active for 14 games.
Art Thoms (T): Active for 6 games, started in 3, and had 2 kickoff returns for 30 yards.
Jimmy Warren (DB): Active for 10 games. Had 2 INT and 2 kickoff returns for 47 yards.
Carl Weathers (LB): Active for 7 games.
Alvin Wyatt (DB): Active for 11 games, had 1 fumble recovery, 25 punt returns for 231 yards and 1 TD, and 13 kickoff returns for 286 yards.

KICKING/PUNTING

K — George Blanda: Active for 14 games. Made 16 of 29 field goal attempts, and 36 of 36 extra point kicks for 84 points. Completed 29 of 55 pass attempts for 461 yards, 6 TD and 5 INT. Rushed for 4 yards on 2 carries.
P — Mike Eischeid: Active for 14 games. Punted 79 times for a 39.5 average.

1971 Season Review

1. Sept. 19: After winning the Heisman Trophy the previous year, Jim Plunkett carried his success from the college ranks over to the NFL by having a tremendous pro debut against the Raiders. The rookie signal caller from Stanford led the New England Patriots to a stunning 20–6 upset. The Patriots were the NFL's doormat the previous season, finishing a dismal 2–12. Plunkett fired two touchdown passes, and Charlie Gogolak kicked a pair of field goals in the stunner. Oakland's lone points came on a 4-yard run in the second quarter by Pete Banaszak to give them a 6–0 lead at the half.[1]

2. Sept. 26: Oakland took out their anger of losing on the San Diego Chargers, thrashing them, 34–0. The Oakland offense had a tough time getting started, clinging to a slim 6–0 lead at the half on a pair of George Blanda field goals (37 and 42 yards). Daryle Lamonica got the offense in gear with a 28-point second half bombardment. For the game, the Mad Bomber hit on 11 of 17 passes for 162 yards and two touchdowns, with both going to Fred Biletnikoff from 36 and 13 yards. Running back Clarence Davis scored on a 5-yard run, and back up quarterback Ken Stabler snuck over from the one for the Raiders' final score of the blowout. Dan Conners led the tough Oakland defense with two interceptions. As a unit, the Raiders held the hapless Chargers to 73 rushing yards and intercepted five passes.[2]

3. Oct. 4: In front of 84,285 Cleveland fans, the Raiders handed the Browns their first loss of the season, 34–20, on a Monday Night Football telecast. Cleveland jumped out to an early 14–0 lead, but Oakland chipped the lead down, and then struck for 24 points in the fourth quarter to nail down the win. The barrage was started with a Daryle Lamonica to Raymond Chester 13-yard touchdown pass. This duo teamed up in the second quarter as well from 20 yards out. Clarence Davis ran for a 5-yard touchdown, Pete Banaszak for a 1-yarder, and George Blanda added two field goals from 20 and 26 yards to cap off the point explosion. Fullback Marv Hubbard did his share of the work by pounding away at the Cleveland defense for a game-high 103 rushing yards.[3]

4. Oct. 10: With Daryle Lamonica injuring a hamstring muscle in the first quarter, the fate of the Raiders rested on the passing arm of second-year pro Ken "the Snake" Stabler. The Alabama product rose to the challenge, sparking the offense in the second half with Oakland down, 9–6, against the Denver Broncos. In the third quarter, Stabler ran for a go-ahead touchdown from two yards out, and then teamed up with Raymond Chester on a 9-yard pass for another six-pointer. For the game, Stabler completed 10 of 23 passes for 136 yards. Defensive back Jimmy Warren returned an interception 55 yards for a score,

and George Blanda kicked field goals from 38 and 24 yards in a 27–16 win. This third straight victory helped earn Oakland a share of the Western Division lead with Kansas City.[4]

5. Oct. 17: This time, Daryle Lamonica came off the bench to rally the troops despite a sore hamstring. He was called into action after Ken Stabler could not move the offense against the winless Philadelphia Eagles. In front of a then-record home crowd of 54,615, Lamonica connected on seven of 15 attempts for 133 yards in the second half to help erase a 10–0 deficit. He threw touchdown passes to Eldridge Dickey (27 yards) and Fred Biletnikoff (35 yards), who provided the bulk of offensive production with eight catches for 148 yards. Pete Banaszak (2 yards) and Don Highsmith (14 yards) each ran for scores, George Atkinson returned a fumble 26 yards for another touchdown, and the Silver and Black recorded their fourth straight W, 34–10.[5]

6. Oct. 24: After jumping out to a 17–0 halftime lead, the Raiders saw themselves in a battle with the Cincinnati Bengals, who fought their way back to tie the game in the fourth quarter. Oakland received their first half points on a George Blanda field goal (22 yards), a Daryle Lamonica to Raymond Chester pass (19 yards), and a Marv Hubbard run (7 yards). The Bengals moved out to a three-point lead, and then George Blanda came on to lead Oakland to a 31–27 win. Blanda assumed the quarterback duties in the third quarter after Daryle Lamonica injured his throwing hand. With pinpoint accuracy, Blanda guided the Raiders downfield on a drive capped off with a Marv Hubbard

Big Ben Davidson, one of the original Raiders renegades. A fierce pass rusher, defensive end Davidson made life miserable for opposing quarterbacks on Sunday afternoons. Seen here in 1971 (AP Photo/NFL Photos).

1-yard run. Hubbard consistently ran over and through Cincinnati's defense, running for 96 yards on 20 carries, and scoring three touchdowns in the process. In addition to his game-winning 1-yard plunge, Hubbard broke a 17–17 deadlock early in the fourth quarter by catching a Blanda pass from 17 yards out. With their fifth straight win, the Silver and Black still shared the division lead with Kansas City.[6]

7. Oct. 31: In a Western Division show down with the Kansas City Chiefs, the Raiders battled their hated rivals to a 20–20 tie. Ageless wonder George Blanda once again rallied Oakland after they were down by ten points in the fourth quarter after relieving Daryle Lamonica. Blanda threw a 24-yard touchdown pass to Fred Biletnikoff, who caught seven passes for 128 yards. Blanda then tied the game with an 8-yard field goal with two minutes left. On his game tying three-pointer, Blanda surpassed Lou Groza to become pro football's all-time leading scorer with 1,609 points. He also added a 17-yard field goal in the first quarter, and Marv Hubbard scored on a 1-yard run. With the tie, the Raiders and Chiefs remained deadlocked atop the division with 5-1-1 records.[7]

8. Nov. 7: Another tie gave the 5-1-2 Raiders sole possession of first place in the division. With eight seconds remaining in the game, New Orleans quarterback Edd Hargett threw to Dave Parks for a touchdown, and Charlie Durkee's conversion allowed the Saints to tie the game at 21–21. The Raiders scored their three touchdowns on two Daryle Lamonica to Fred Biletnikoff passes (42 and 20 yards) and a 4-yard run by Pete Banaszak that gave the Raiders a 21–7 lead before New Orleans rallied.[8]

9. Nov. 14: The Raiders exploded for 41 points in the first three quarters, and then coasted to an easy 41–21 victory over the Houston Oilers. Daryle Lamonica completed seven of 12 pass attempts in the first half for 157 yards and two touchdowns, with both going to Drew Buie from 63 and 25 yards. Pete Banaszak scored twice on 1-yard runs, Jimmy Warren returned an interception 59 yards, and George Blanda added two field goals (10 and 33 yards) in the rout. This was Oakland's eighth straight game without a loss.[9]

10. Nov. 21: The Silver and Black rallied from fourteen points down on the arm of the Mad Bomber to produce a 34–33 win over the San Diego Chargers. Daryle Lamonica threw for three touchdowns to help the Raiders improve to 7-1-2 and hold onto a half-game lead over Kansas City in the tight Western Division race. Raymond Chester caught two of Lamonica's scoring strikes (16 and 13 yards), and Rod Sherman hauled one in from 32 yards to give the Raiders a 34–24 lead in the fourth quarter. Pete Banaszak scored on a 2-yard run, and George Blanda added two field goals (34 and 40 yards) to round out Oakland's point production. The Chargers almost pulled the game out in the final minute, but a Dan Conners interception in the end zone sealed the win.[10]

11. Nov. 28: After a nine game unbeaten streak, the Raiders fell to the defending Super Bowl champion Baltimore Colts, 37–14. The Baltimore defense held the NFL's most potent offense at bay. The Colts allowed only 65 rushing yards, and intercepted Daryle Lamonica four times and George Blanda twice. The Raiders were down, 30–0, when they finally erased the goose egg off the scoreboard on two Blanda to Fred Biletnikoff passes covering 18 and four yards. Even with this loss, the 7-2-2 Raiders still held a slim division lead over the 7-3-1 Chiefs.[11]

12. Dec. 5: Two interceptions and three fumbles did not help Oakland, as they suffered a second straight loss, 24–13, to the Atlanta Falcons on the road. The interceptions came deep in Atlanta territory, and a Marv Hubbard fumble was returned 60 yards by Tom Hayes for a touchdown in the first quarter. The usually sure-handed Raymond Chester added to Oakland's woes by dropping a few easy passes that could have gone for six points. The one bright spot for the Raiders on this cold and rainy day was the running of Hubbard. Despite his costly fumble, the battering-ram fullback ran for 143 yards on 26 carries. A pair of George Blanda field goals (27 and 12 yards), and a 31-yard pass from Daryle Lamonica to Fred Biletnikoff accounted for Oakland's scoring. This loss, coupled with a Kansas City win, knocked Oakland out of first place for the first time since the season opener.[12]

13. Dec. 12: Things continued to fall apart for Oakland, as they lost out on a bid for their fourth straight division title. To make matters worse was the fact that their biggest nemesis did them in. Kicker Jan Stenerud hit on a 10-yard field goal with 1:34 remaining in the game to give the Chiefs a 16–14 win. The future Hall of Famer's kick also earned Kansas City the AFC Western Division championship. As usual, this game was a brutal, hard-hitting affair that became customary whenever these teams collided. Throughout his career, Marv Hubbard saved his best for games against the Chiefs. This clash proved to be no exception, as the big fullback scored both Oakland touchdowns, each from one-yard out.[13]

14. Dec. 19: For the first time since 1967, the Raiders failed to make the playoffs despite a 21–13 win in the season finale against the Denver Broncos. Daryle Lamonica threw a touchdown pass to Raymond Chester (67 yards), and finished the game with 182 yards through the air. He also threw three interceptions. Charlie Smith (1 yard) and Pete Banaszak (2 yards) scored Oakland's other touchdowns on the ground.[14]

Individual Statistics and Roster

Head Coach: John Madden
Assistant Coaches: Tom Dahms, Mike Holovak, Ray Malavasi, John Polonchek, Ollie Spencer, Bob Zeman
1971 Regular Season Record: 8-4-2
2nd Place in AFC Western Division
Scored 344 points to rank 2nd out of 26 teams
Allowed 278 points to rank 14th

STARTERS — OFFENSE

QB — Daryle Lamonica: Active for 14 games, and started in 13. Completed 118 of 242 pass attempts for 1,717 yards, 16 TD and 16 INT. Rushed for 16 yards on 4 carries.

HB — Pete Banaszak: Started in 14 games. Rushed for 563 yards on 137 carries and 8 TD. Had 13 receptions for 128 yards, and 1 kickoff return for 0 yards.

FB — Marv Hubbard: Active for 14 games, and started in 11. Rushed for 867 yards on 181 carries and 5 TD. Had 22 receptions for 167 yards and 1 TD, and 3 kickoff returns for 46 yards.

WR — Fred Biletnikoff: Started in 14 games, and had **61** receptions for 929 yards and 9 TD.

WR — Rod Sherman: Active for 12 games, and started in 5. Had 12 receptions for 187 yards and 1 TD. Returned 2 punts for 2 yards.

TE — Raymond Chester: Started in 14 games. Had 28 receptions for 442 yards and 7 TD. Rushed for 5 yards on 3 carries.

LT — Art Shell: Started in 14 games.
LG — Gene Upshaw: Started in 14 games.
C — Jim Otto: Started in 14 games.
RG — George Buehler: Started in 14 games.
RT — Bob Brown: Active for and started in 10 games.

RESERVE OFFENSIVE PLAYERS

Drew Buie (WR): Active for 14 games, and started in 6. Had 5 receptions for 133 yards and 2 TD. Rushed for 32 yards on 2 carries.

Clarence Davis (RB): Active for 14 games. Rushed for 321 yards on 54 carries and 2 TD. Had 15 receptions for 97 yards, and 27 kickoff returns for 734 yards.

Eldridge Dickey (WR): Active for 7 games, and started in 2. Had 4 receptions for 78 yards and 1 TD.

Mike Eischeid (K): Active for 2 games, and punted 11 times for a 41.9 average.

Glenn Ellison (RB): Active for 1 game.

Bill Enyart (RB/LB): Active for 1 game.

Jim Harvey (G/T): Active for 12 games.

Don Highsmith (RB): Active for 14 games, and started in 3. Rushed for 307 yards on 76 carries and 1 TD, had 10 receptions for 109 yards, 1 punt return for 0 yards, and 21 kickoff returns for 454 yards.

Warren Koegel (C): Active for 14 games.

Ron Mix (T/G): Active for 12 games, and started in 4.

Bob Moore (TE): Active for 14 games, and started in 1. Had 2 receptions for 26 yards.

Paul Seiler (C/T): Active for 8 games, and had 1 kickoff return for 0 yards.

Charlie Smith (RB): Active for 8 games. Rushed for 4 yards on 11 carries and 1 TD, had 2 receptions for 67 yards, and 1 kickoff return for 0 yards.

Ken Stabler (QB): Active for 14 games, and started in 1. Completed 24 of 48 pass attempts for 268 yards, 1 TD and 4 INT. Rushed for 29 yards 4 carries and 2 TD.

STARTERS — DEFENSE

DE — Horace Jones: Active for 14 games, and started in 12.
DE — Ben Davidson: Started in 14 games and had 1 fumble recovery.
DT — Art Thoms: Active for 14 games and started in 11. Had 2 fumble recoveries.
DT — Carleton Oats: Active for 12 games, and started in 8.
LLB — Phil Villapiano: Started in 14 games, had 2 INT and 2 fumble recoveries.
MLB — Dan Conners: Started in 14 games, had 3 INT and 2 fumble recoveries.
RLB — Gus Otto: Active for and started in 8 games.
CB — Nemiah Wilson: Active for and started in 13 games. Had 5 INT.
CB — Willie Brown: Started in 14 games and had 2 INT.
SS — George Atkinson: Started in 14 games, had 4 INT, 2 fumble recoveries, returned 1 for a TD, and returned 20 punts for 159 yards.
FS — Jack Tatum: Started in 14 games, had 4 INT and 2 fumble recoveries.

RESERVE DEFENSIVE PLAYERS

Duane Benson (LB): Active for 14 games, and started in 5.
Tony Cline (E): Active for 13 games, started in 6, and 1 fumble recovery.
Thomas Gipson (T): Active for 4 games.
Gerald Irons (LB): Active for 7 games.
Tom Keating (T): Active for 7 games.
Tommy Maxwell (DB): Active for 13 games. Had 2 fumble recoveries, and 6 punt returns for 21 yards.
Terry Mendenhall (LB): Active for 14 games and had 1 fumble recovery.
Harold Rice (E): Active for 12 games and had 1 fumble recovery.
Greg Slough (LB): Active for 13 games and had 1 fumble recovery.

Jimmy Warren (DB): Active for 14 games, started in 1, had 2 INT, and returned both for TD's.
Carl Weathers (LB): Active for 1 game.

KICKING/PUNTING

K — George Blanda: Active for 14 games. Made 15 of 22 field goal attempts, and 41 of 42 extra point kicks for 86 points. Completed 32 of 58 pass attempts for 378 yards, 4 TDs and 6 INT.
P — Jerry DePoyster: Active for 12 games. Punted 51 times for a 39.5 average, and rushed for -14 yards on 1 carry.

1972 Season Review

1. Sept. 17: Helped by a dominating defense, the Pittsburgh Steelers handed the Raiders their third consecutive opening day defeat, 34–28. During the pre-season, third-year pro Ken Stabler beat out Daryle Lamonica for the starting quarterback job, but had a terrible debut. He threw three interceptions and fumbled once. Stabler was eventually replaced by George Blanda right before the half and trailing, 17–0. The 45-year-old Blanda quickly got Oakland on the board with a three-play drive capped off with Raymond Chester scoring on a 26-yard pass. Pittsburgh increased their advantage to 27–7 in the third quarter. Lamonica then came on and threw two touchdown passes to wide receiver Mike Siani that covered 24 and 70 yards. The Steelers also added two touchdowns and a field goal in the second half, and their defense clamped down to stymie Oakland's late surge that saw the Silver and Black close to within six on a Don Highsmith 1-yard run and Siani's second touchdown reception.[1]

2. Sept. 24: The Raiders evened their record with a 20–14 win over the Green Bay Packers. The highlight of this game was a record setting 104-yard fumble recovery by defensive back Jack "the Assassin" Tatum. Two George Blanda field goals (43 and 14 yards) and a Charlie Smith 1-yard run provided Oakland with their other points. Marv Hubbard provided a solid ground attack by churning out 125 yards on 24 carries.[2]

3. Oct. 1: Oakland jumped out to a 14–0 first quarter lead, but lost it and had to settle for a 17–17 deadlock with the San Diego Chargers. The Raiders scored on a Daryle Lamonica to Raymond Chester 23-yard pass, and a Marv Hubbard 1-yard run. The Chargers then came back to take a 17–14 lead on the talents of running back Cid Edwards, who combined for almost 200 yards rushing and receiving. A George Blanda field goal from 40 yards tied the game with 4:28 left. He then missed on a 37-yarder with one minute remaining, which could have given Oakland the win.[3]

4. Oct. 9: The Raiders moved into a second place tie in the AFC West with a 34–0 Monday Night Football shellacking of the Houston Oilers. Three interceptions were turned in to touchdowns, and the hapless Oilers never had a chance at any stage of the game despite sloppy play from the Raiders early on. Interceptions by Phil Villapiano, Otis Sistrunk, and Nemiah Wilson were all turned into touchdowns. Daryle Lamonica threw scoring strikes to Fred Biletnikoff (16 yards) and rookie Mike Siani (27 yards), while tight end Bob Moore teamed up with Ken Stabler for another six-pointer from one yard out. Clarence Davis had a 14-yard run, and George Blanda added two field goals (46 and 35 yards) to complete the primetime rout.[4]

5. Oct. 15: The Silver and Black were back in a position they were accustomed to, first place in the division. Thanks to touchdown runs by Clarence Davis and Marv Hubbard, the Raiders were able to overcome a nine-point deficit to beat the Buffalo Bills, 28–16. Down, 16–7, at the start of the fourth quarter, Oakland capped a six-play, 80-yard drive with Hubbard plowing over the goal line from the one. On the day, Hubbard hammered out 122 yards on 20 carries. The Raiders then took their first lead of the game when Davis scored from seven yards out. After the Bills missed on a fourth down attempt, Davis ran 20 yards for a score two plays later. Raymond Chester provided Oakland with their first points of the game on a 55-yard pass from Daryle Lamonica. With the win, the Raiders were 3-1-1.[5]

6. Oct. 22: The last place Denver Broncos shocked the Raiders, 30–23. In Charley Johnson's first start at quarterback in 1972, he riddled the Oakland defense for 361 passing yards and two touchdowns. The Raiders still had a hold on the Western Division leadership at 3-2-1 despite the loss. George Blanda led the Raiders with nine points coming on three field goals from 32, 35, and 40 yards. Charlie Smith ran for a 1-yard score, and Ken Stabler connected with Mike Siani on a 4-yard pass to give Oakland their other points in this shocker.[6]

7. Oct. 29: A fumbled kickoff and three interceptions cost the Los Angeles Rams dearly. The Raiders took advantage of these errors, and hammered the Rams, 45–17. By the middle of the second quarter, the Raiders had run up a 35–0 lead on three Daryle Lamonica touchdown passes to Fred Biletnikoff (30 yards) Raymond Chester (27 yards), and Mike Siani (31 yards). Scoring on the ground during this point barrage were Charlie Smith (4 yards), and Clarence Davis (8 yards). Linebacker Phil Villapiano added to the rout in fine fashion by returning an interception 82 yards for a score. George Blanda also chipped in with a 30-yard field goal to finish off the scoring.[7]

8. Nov. 5: Despite rumors that his skills were diminished, 37-year-old Kansas City quarterback Len Dawson silenced his critics with a 27–14 win over Oakland. Dawson played brilliantly, throwing for three scores, which enabled the Chiefs to overtake the Raiders for the Western Division lead. Kansas City stood at 5–3, while Oakland slipped to 4-3-1. The Raiders got their points on a Marv Hubbard 4-yard run, and on a 13-yard pass from Ken Stabler to Raymond Chester.[8]

9. Nov. 12: Both the Raiders and the Chiefs did battle against Central Division foes on this date. When it was all over, the Raiders were back on top of their division following a 20–14 win against the Cincinnati Bengals. The Pittsburgh Steelers helped Oakland out by beating Kansas City, 16–7. Running back Charlie Smith had the greatest rushing day of his five-year career with 146 yards, and scored the go-ahead touchdown in the third quarter from eight yards out. Smith's running mate, Clarence Davis, scored on a 1-yard run, and George Blanda kicked two field goals from 24 and 22 yards. Oakland's defense shut the Bengals down almost completely in the second half, holding them to no first downs until late in the fourth quarter.[9]

10. Nov. 19: The running duo of Marv Hubbard and Charlie Smith were a huge reason why the Raiders easily overcame the Denver Broncos, 37–20. Hubbard bulldozed his way for 84 yards and a 3-yard touchdown, while Smith topped the century mark with 101 yards and a 5-yard touchdown. George Blanda also

stood out like so many times throughout his long and illustrious career, this time by kicking three field goals (38, 23, and 44 yards) and four extra points. His four conversion kicks allowed him to become the all-time leader in that category with 812, moving past Lou Groza. Daryle Lamonica threw two touchdown passes to Fred Biletnikoff from 27 and seven yards to round out Oakland's scoring. With this win and a Kansas City loss, the Silver and Black held a game-and-a-half lead in the Western Division.[10]

11. Nov. 26: The Raiders moved one step closer to their fifth division crown with a 26–3 win over Kansas City, which also proved to be the 100th regular season victory in team history. Daryle Lamonica threw touchdown passes to Fred Biletnikoff (14 yards) and Raymond Chester (19 yards) to help the 7-3-1 Raiders gain a two-and-half game lead in the AFC West. Charlie Smith opened the scoring with a 2-yard run, and George Blanda kicked two field goals from 27 and 25 yards.[11]

12. Dec. 3: Oakland made it official by clinching their fifth division title with a 21–19 victory over San Diego. The Chargers did not make it easy on the Raiders, however, as they held a five-point lead with two minutes remaining. It was then that Daryle Lamonica got a hot hand, and led Oakland downfield. Hitting on key passes to Fred Biletnikoff, and rookie receivers Mike Siani and Cliff Branch, he got the offense inside the San Diego 10-yard line. With 1:10 left on the game clock, Charlie Smith scored the go-ahead touchdown from the nine behind incredible blocking from pro football's best offensive line. The Chargers made one final attempt at victory, but a long-range field goal try was short as time expired. Also scoring for the Silver and Black were Raymond Chester and Biletnikoff, who each hauled in a Lamonica pass. Chester's came from 16 yards, and Biletnikoff's from 36.[12]

13. Dec. 11: On a Monday Night Football appearance, the Raiders won their fifth straight, 24–16, over old AFL rivals, the New York Jets. Marv Hubbard dominated all ground gainers with 118 yards on 28 carries. Daryle Lamonica completed 10 of 17 pass attempts for 202 yards and two long scoring strikes. On the receiving end of his touchdown passes were Fred Biletnikoff (40 yards), and Raymond Chester (68 yards). Charlie Smith scored on a 1-yard run, and George Blanda hit on a long 47-yard field goal for Oakland's other points.[13]

14. Dec. 17: Oakland achieved their sixth straight win of the season, 28–21, over the Chicago Bears. Daryle Lamonica and Ken Stabler each threw a touchdown pass to Charlie Smith, with Lamonica's coming from 14 yards and Stabler's from 19. On the ground, the Raiders received six-pointers from Pete Banaszak (1 yard) and Clarence Davis (45 yards). Davis led the Oakland ground attack with 82 yards on only six carries.[14]

AFC Divisional Playoff Game, December 23, 1972

The Oakland Raiders and Pittsburgh Steelers slugged it out throughout the 1970's in the greatest rivalry of the decade, and it all started two days before Christmas in 1972. The Steelers were about to embark on their first playoff experience after forty seasons of existence. Once the league's official doormats season after season, Pittsburgh finally broke free from the loser label attached to them throughout their dismal history thanks to a great head coach in Chuck Noll, a solid offense, and a dominant defense that came to be known and feared as "the Steel Curtain."

In front of 50,327 ravenous Pittsburgh fans rocking Three Rivers Stadium, the heavily favored Raiders squared off against the upstart Steelers. It seemed that this game might go on for a long time, as neither team could penetrate the opposing goal line throughout the first half. It was establishing itself as a classic defensive slugfest that would become the norm when these two teams collided in future encounters. Not helping the Raiders was the fact that Daryle Lamonica was ill, and he could not muster up his usual "Mad Bomber" type of performance. His timing was off, and his passes arrived with little pop in them. He would eventually give way to Ken Stabler in the fourth quarter.

The second half finally saw the scoreboard show signs of life. Three Terry Bradshaw passes got the Steelers to Oakland's 11-yard line, and Roy Gerela gave Pittsburgh their first-ever post-season points with an 18-yard field goal to give the Steel City a 3–0 third quarter lead.

In the fourth quarter, Stabler replaced Lamonica, and it looked like he was not going to fare any better. A hit by defensive end L.C. Greenwood caused Stabler to fumble, and it was later turned into a 29-yard Gerela field goal that gave Pittsburgh a 6–0 advantage with 3:50 left to play. With time running out on Oakland's season, Stabler was facing a fourth-and-one situation against a very tenacious defensive unit. With the '72 campaign hanging in the balance, Stabler handed off to Charlie Smith, who extended Oakland's hopes for at least another series by gaining four yards and a new set of downs. After a completion to rookie Mike Siani got the ball to the Pittsburgh 30, Stabler dropped back to pass, and the Steelers sent a safety blitz at him. With a tackle also coming at him fast and hard, Stabler noticed an open field to the outside. With nothing in front of him, the left-handed signal caller from Alabama seized the opportunity given him and ran all the way for the game's first touchdown to tie it at 6–6. George Blanda added the go-ahead point with his conversion kick, and Oakland clung to a 7–6 advantage with only 1:13 showing on the clock.

Blanda's ensuing kickoff hit the goal posts and no return was tried. Starting from the Pittsburgh 20, Bradshaw threw two passes for a gain of twenty yards. His next two attempts were swatted down by safety Jack Tatum. Staring at a fourth-and-10 situation with 22 seconds remaining, the mood inside Three Rivers Stadium was bleak, as the Raiders were getting ready to advance to the AFC Championship Game.

Bradshaw faded into the pocket for what might have been the last time of the season. He focused his attention on Barry Pearson across the middle. Just then, the play began to quickly crumble when Tony Cline and Horace Jones shot through Bradshaw's wall of protection and were in a position to make the quarterback a part of the turf. Bradshaw reacted quickly as the two white-jersey clad Raiders were on each side of him about to inflict massive force on his body. He ducked to avoid the sack, and then scrambled around to give his receivers a chance to get open. This play was designed to have rookie running back Franco Harris stay in the backfield to help block. However, when Harris witnessed helter skelter all about, he decided to exit the backfield and signaled to Bradshaw to throw him the ball. With the seconds ticking away, Bradshaw threw instead to running back John

"Frenchy" Fuqua at about the Oakland 31. At that moment, linebacker Phil Villapiano, who was covering Harris out of the backfield, broke toward Fuqua to protect that area. As Bradshaw's pass grew close to Fuqua, Jack "the Assassin" Tatum earned his moniker by blasting him with a powerful jolt. The pigskin ricocheted off either Fuqua or Tatum, shot over Villapiano's head, and landed right in the hands of Harris inches away from hitting the ground and ending the game. Harris never broke stride, and ran 60 yards for the touchdown.

Time had expired and the referee still did not signal a touchdown. The indecision on the ref's part was due to the fact if the ball last touched Fuqua or Tatum. At the time, the rule was that the ball could not consecutively touch two players from the same team. Seeing that Tatum and Fuqua were so close to the ball at the time of impact, no one of authority could legitimately make the call. This was also before instant replay, so the officials had to gather themselves up and make a call either way. The stadium that was seconds before a frenzied throng, suddenly felt that the incredible situation they just witnessed was going to fall by the wayside.

As fans of each team held their collective breaths across the American landscape, the officials attempted to sort out the madness cast before them, and send one of these teams on their way to the AFC Championship Game. After much pondering, the officials broke free from their huddle and shared their findings with the world. It was ruled that the ball last went off Tatum before Harris touched it, and the play was ruled a touchdown to give Pittsburgh their first playoff victory by a 13–7 count. Three Rivers Stadium then erupted, as the long-suffering Pittsburgh gridiron faithful rejoiced over the amazing win that was brought to them in what will forever be remembered as "The Immaculate Reception."

On the other side, this proved to be the darkest moment game-wise in the history of the Raiders. There is an old adage that states to the victor goes the spoils. However, did the spoils really go to the right team on this December afternoon in the Steel City? This is one of the greatest questions to be pondered over as long as the sport of pro football is discussed.[15]

Individual Statistics and Roster

Head Coach: John Madden
Assistant Coaches: Tom Dahms, Tom Flores, Ray Malavasi, Paul Roach, Joe Scannella, Ollie Spencer, Bob Zeman
1972 Regular Season Record: 10-3-1
1st Place AFC Western Division
Scored 365 points to rank 3rd out of 26 teams
Allowed 248 to rank 8th
Led the league in first downs (297)

STARTERS — OFFENSE

QB — Daryle Lamonica: Active for 14 games, and started in 13. Completed 149 of 281 pass attempts for 1,998 yards, 18 TD and 12 INT. Rushed for 33 yards on 10 carries.

HB — Charlie Smith: Active for 14 games, and started in 13. Rushed for 686 yards on 170 carries and 8 TD, had 28 receptions for 353 yards and 2 TD, and 1 kickoff return for 0 yards.

FB — Marv Hubbard: Started in 14 games. Rushed for 1,100 yards on 219 carries and 4 TD, and had 22 receptions for 103 yards.

WR — Fred Biletnikoff: Started in 14 games, and had 58 receptions for 802 yards and 7 TD.

WR — Mike Siani: Active for 14 games, and started in 13. Had 28 receptions for 496 yards and 5 TD.

TE — Raymond Chester: Active for 13 games, and started in 10. Had 4 receptions for 576 yards and 8 TD, and rushed for 3 yards on 1 carry.

LT — Art Shell: Started in 14 games.

LG — Gene Upshaw: Started in 14 games.

C — Jim Otto: Started in 14 games.

RG — George Buehler: Started in 14 games.

RT — Bob Brown: Started in 14 games.

RESERVE OFFENSIVE PLAYERS

Pete Banaszak (RB): Active for 14 games, rushed for 138 yards on 30 carries and 1 TD, and had 9 receptions for 63 yards.

Cliff Branch (WR): Active for 14 games, and started in 1. Had 3 receptions for 41 yards, rushed for 5 yards on 1 carry, had 12 punt returns for 21 yards, and 9 kickoff returns for 191 yards.

Dave Dalby (C): Active for 14 games.

Clarence Davis (RB): Active for 11 games. Rushed for 71 rushes for 363 yards and 6 TD. Had 8 receptions for 82 yards, and 18 kickoff returns for 464 yards.

Don Highsmith (RB): Active for 8 games, and started in 1. Rushed for 11 yards on 9 carries and 1 TD, and had 2 receptions for 34 yards.

Bob Moore (TE): Active for 14 games, and started in 3. Had 6 receptions for 49 yards and 1 TD.

Jeff Queen (RB/TE): Active for 14 games, and rushed for 10 yards on 4 carries.

Paul Seiler (C/T): Active for 14 games, and had 1 kickoff return for 0 yards.

Ken Stabler (QB): Active for 14 games, and started in 1. Completed 44 of 74 pass attempts for 524 yards, 4 TD and 3 INT. Rushed for 27 yards on 6 carries.

John Vella (T): Active for 14 games.

STARTERS — DEFENSE

DE — Tony Cline: Started in 14 games, had 1 INT and 1 fumble recovery.

DE — Horace Jones: Started in 14 games and had 1 fumble recovery.

DT — Otis Sistrunk: Started in 14 games, had 1 INT and 1 fumble recovery.

DT — Art Thoms: Started in 14 games, had 1 INT and 1 fumble recovery.

LLB — Phil Villapiano: Started in 14 games, had 3 INT, returned 1 for a TD, and 2 fumble recoveries.

MLB — Dan Conners: Active for 14 games, and started in 9. Had 1 INT and 3 fumble recoveries.

RLB — Gerald Irons: Started in 14 games and had 2 INT.

CB — Nemiah Wilson: Started in 14 games and had 4 INT.

CB — Willie Brown: Started in 14 games, had 4 INT and 2 fumble recoveries.

SS — George Atkinson: Started in 14 games, had 4 INT, 10 punt returns for 33 yards, and 3 kickoff returns for 75 yards.

FS — Jack Tatum: Started in 14 games, had 4 INT, 2 fumble recoveries, and returned 1 for a TD. **Led the NFL with 104 yards on fumble returns.**

RESERVE DEFENSIVE PLAYERS

Joe Carroll (LB): Active for 13 games and had 1 fumble recovery.

Tom Keating (T): Active for 8 games.

Tommy Maxwell (DB): Active for 7 games, had 2 punt returns for 12 yards, and 1 kickoff return for 26 yards.

Terry Mendenhall (LB): Active for 3 games.

Carleton Oats (T/E): Active for 14 games.

Gus Otto (LB): Active for 11 games, and started in 5.

Greg Slough (LB): Active for 9 games and had 1 kickoff return for 0 yards.

Skip Thomas (DB): Active for 14 games and had 1 fumble recovery.

Jimmy Warren (DB): Active for 7 games and had 4 kickoff returns for 57 yards.

KICKING/PUNTING

K — George Blanda: Active for 14 games. Made 17 of 26 field goal attempts, and 44 of 44 extra point kicks for 95 points. Had 5 pass completions in 15 attempts for 77 yards and 1 TD.

P — Jerry DePoyster: Active for 14 games. Punted 55 times for a 36.9 average.

1973 Season Review

1. Sept. 16: The Raiders overcame a ten-point deficit to take a 16–10 third quarter lead on the Minnesota Vikings. Three George Blanda field goals (16, 25, and 9 yards), and a 63-yard punt return by George Atkinson, helped Oakland fight their way back. Unfortunately, the Vikings did not go down easy. Led by quarterback Fran Tarkenton's go-ahead touchdown pass to Chuck Foreman, a Bill Brown 6-yard insurance touchdown run, and a tough defense, the Vikings rallied back to win, 24–16. This was the fourth straight year in which the Raiders lost their season opener. Minnesota's famed "Purple People Eaters" defense ate up Oakland's ground game when it counted most. With the Raiders on the Minnesota 3-yard line, Clarence Davis was sent into the line three times and stopped cold in the third quarter. It was the last time Oakland was able to get close to the goal line.[1]

2. Sept. 23: After losing their opener, the Raiders came back in fine fashion. The defending Super Bowl champion Miami Dolphins came out to play the Silver and Black at the University of California's field due to a scheduling problem that had the Oakland A's baseball team playing in the Oakland Coliseum. Despite the scheduling problem, the Raiders still managed to win, 12–7. In the process, the Raiders ended Miami's 18-game winning streak with a dominant ground attack and a crushing defense. In one of the franchise's most satisfying victories, the Silver and Black rushed for 181 yards on 48 carries, and got the ball close enough for George Blanda to connect on four field goal attempts, with one coming in each quarter. Oakland's ground attack was led by Marv Hubbard (88 yards) and Charlie Smith (80 yards). Blanda's three-pointers were from 12, 46, 19, and 10 yards. The rough and tumble defense held Miami scoreless until the final two minutes.[2]

3. Sept. 30: Oakland slumped to 1–2 with a 16–3 loss to the hated Kansas City Chiefs. In a brutal contest, Jan Stenerud kicked three field goals and linebacker Willie Lanier returned a Ken Stabler interception 17 yards for the game's only touchdown. Kansas City's defensive unit completely smothered Oakland's offensive attack. They held the Raiders to 77 rushing yards, 96 through the air, recorded four sacks, and intercepted Daryle Lamonica once and Stabler twice. Oakland's lone points came on a 21-yard field goal from George Blanda, who provided the team with all their scoring for the second game in a row.[3]

4. Oct. 7: With Ken Stabler passing for 207 yards, and the running game smashing their way for 247 more yards, the Raiders topped the St. Louis Cardinals, 17–10. Charlie Smith scored Oakland's first offensive touchdown of the season on a 2-yard run. After the Cardinals tied the game at 10–10, Marv Hubbard

clinched the win in the fourth quarter with a 1-yard run. George Blanda also added a 17-yard field goal to Oakland's tally. This victory gave the Raiders a record of 2–2 and sole possession of second place in the AFC West.[4]

5. Oct. 14: Oakland went over the .500 mark after coming back from a four-point deficit to beat San Diego, 27–17. After an interference penalty on receiver Cliff Branch put the Raiders on the one, Marv Hubbard scored the go-ahead touchdown two plays later. The Chargers fumbled the ensuing kickoff, and Pete Banaszak recovered for Oakland. Two plays later, Ken Stabler found tight end Bob Moore from 26 yards out for an insurance touchdown. Stabler also teamed up with Cliff Branch earlier on a 54-yard scoring strike. George Blanda provided two field goals from 18 and 15 yards to complete the team's scoring.[5]

6. Oct. 22: Oakland climbed into a first place tie with Kansas City at 3-2-1 despite a 23–23 tie against the Denver Broncos in front of a Monday Night Football audience. Defensive back Bill Thompson returned a Clarence Davis fumble eight yards for an early Denver lead. George Blanda closed the gap to 7–3 in the second quarter with a 35-yard field goal that was the 300th three-pointer of his incredible career. He added two more in this game from 13 and 49 yards. His 49-yarder broke a 20–20 tie in the fourth quarter. Denver's Jim Turner then knotted it up once again, this time for good, with a 35-yard field goal. Oakland went on top, 10–7, on a Ken Stabler to Mike Siani 80-yard pass that the receiver caught at midfield and took it the distance. Stabler added another touchdown pass to Cliff Branch from 16 yards out in the second half. Fred Biletnikoff hit a career-receiving milestone in this prime time affair by going over the 6,000-yard plateau.[6]

7. Oct. 28: Ken Stabler completed 25 passes for 2 touchdowns, while the running game produced 182 yards in a 34–21 win over the Baltimore Colts. With a well-balanced offensive attack, the Raiders scored on Stabler passes to Mike Siani (27 yards), and Bob Moore (9 yards), two Clarence Davis runs (9 and 32 yards), and George Blanda field goals from 27 and 30 yards. This win, coupled with a Kansas City loss, allowed Oakland to gain a hold on 1st place in the AFC West with a 4-2-1 mark.[7]

8. Nov. 4: From the opening kickoff to the final gun, the Raiders completely dominated the New York Giants, 42–0. Oakland did whatever they wanted against one of the league's worst teams. They ran for 211 yards as a team, with Marv Hubbard scoring twice from eight and nine yards away, and Clarence Davis from five. When Ken Stabler wanted to throw, he had all day to find a receiver behind incredible blocking. He threw scoring strikes to Charlie Smith (18 yards) and Bob Moore (21 yards), and Daryle Lamonica came in late and connected with receiver Steve Sweeney for another six-pointer from 34 yards out. The defense ate up the New York offense by allowing a scant 57 yards rushing and 128 through the air.[8]

9. Nov. 11: A five-game unbeaten streak came to an end with a 17–9 loss to the Pittsburgh Steelers. Pittsburgh's "Steel Curtain" defense smothered Oakland with a tremendous pass rush, and sent Ken Stabler to the sideline with a leg injury. They continued their relentless assault on Oakland quarterbacks by battering Daryle Lamonica and intercepting four of his passes. Lamonica did manage to produce Oakland's only touchdown by connecting with Fred Biletnikoff from 27 yards out in the fourth quarter. George Blanda provided the Raiders with their other points on a 40-yard field goal.[9]

10. Nov. 18: The Raiders and Cleveland Browns each brought 5-3-1 records into this game. In a nail-biting, defensive struggle, the Browns got out of Oakland with a slim 7–3 win. Cleveland shut down the AFC's top passer, allowing Ken Stabler only 75 yards through the air. The Browns scored on a Mike Phipps to Fair Hooker pass in the second quarter, and turned the game over to the defense. Oakland was completely smothered, but George Blanda managed to spare the Raiders their first shutout in 105 games with a 23-yard field goal in the fourth quarter. With this second straight loss, Oakland fell to 5-4-1 and into third place in the division.[10]

11. Nov. 25: On a wet afternoon in Oakland, the Raiders got back to their winning ways with a 31–3 blowout

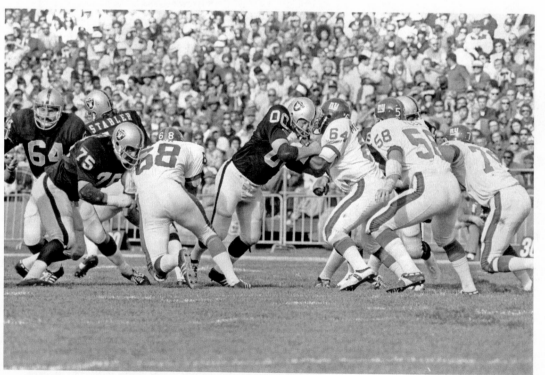

"Mr. Raider." The great Jim Otto (#00) doing what he did better than anyone to ever play the center position. Seen here in action against the New York Giants on November 4, 1973, at Oakland-Alameda Coliseum, Oakland, California (AP Photo).

over San Diego. Defensive back George Atkinson got things going for the Raiders when he returned a fumble 59 yards for the game's first points. Ken Stabler added two touchdown passes, a 16-yarder to Fred Biletnikoff, and a 1-yard toss to Bob Moore. Charlie Smith ran for a 7-yard touchdown, and George Blanda kicked a 34-yard field goal to keep Oakland in the division race at 6-4-1.[11]

12. Dec. 2: The Houston Oilers had the worst record in the league at 1–11, but still held the Raiders scoreless until the third quarter after intercepting Ken Stabler three times and recovering a fumble. The second half was different story. George Blanda got things going for Oakland with a 9-yard chip shot field goal. Stabler then teamed up with Fred Biletnikoff for a 21-yard touchdown to break a 3–3 tie, and Marv Hubbard scored from the two to allow the Silver and Black to get out of Houston with a 17–6 victory.[12]

13. Dec. 8: Fullback Marv Hubbard dominated Oakland's offensive attack in a 37–7 blowout over Kansas City by outrushing the entire Chiefs backfield 115 yards to 33. His touchdown run of 31 yards alone almost outgained the Chiefs on this day. With Hubbard being the main weapon, Ken Stabler's golden arm was not needed much, but when it was, he produced. He hit on 10 of 19 passes for 88 yards, with two going for touchdowns. On the receiving end of the "Snake's" scoring strikes were Fred Biletnikoff (9 yards), and Cliff Branch (3 yards). Charlie Smith ran for 71 yards, including a 10-yard scoring jaunt, and 46-year-old George Blanda enjoyed his best season as a field goal kicker in 1973. His three field goals in this game gave him 23 on the year, which was a single-season high for the ageless wonder. His kicks came from 20, 28, and 27 yards out.[13]

14. Dec. 16: The Western Division crown was Oakland's for the sixth time in seven seasons thanks to a 21–17 win over the Denver Broncos. Denver came into this game hoping to make the playoffs for the first time in their history, but never came close in this contest despite the close final score. The Raiders jumped out to a 14–0 lead on two touchdown runs by Charlie Smith (1 yard) and Clarence Davis (8 yards). The Broncos closed to within four points in the third quarter, but a Ken Stabler to Mike Siani 31-yard touchdown expanded the lead to 21–10. The Broncos got a late touchdown, but a Skip Thomas interception on the final play of the game killed any hopes for the Mile High City. Willie Brown also helped in the defensive cause with two interceptions.[14]

AFC Divisional Playoff Game, December 22, 1973

The Pittsburgh Steelers had beaten the Raiders with the heart-breaking "Immaculate Reception" affair coming 364 days prior to this clash. The Raiders looked for revenge at home, while the Steelers looked to continue being an albatross for the Silver and Black. One team would be right in this post-season contest.

Oakland took a step in the right direction by opening the scoring with an 82-yard drive in the first quarter capped off on a Marv Hubbard 1-yard run. George Blanda added the conversion, and the Raiders gave the hometown crowd reason to be optimistic with an early 7–0 lead. Phil Villapiano got the ball back into the capable hands of quarterback Ken Stabler and the rest of the

offense by intercepting a pass near the end of the first quarter. With the ball on the Oakland 40, Stabler threw to Mike Siani for 21 yards on third down to keep the drive alive. Pete Banaszak ran for 12 yards on two carries, and Oakland got close enough for Blanda to hit on a 25-yard field goal to extend the Oakland bulge to 10–0. Terry Bradshaw got the Steelers on the board with 1:56 left in the first half with a 4-yard pass to Barry Pearson to close the gap to 10–7.

This game saw numerous fights break out, which came as no surprise, seeing that these two teams did not like each other at all. On one occasion, a roughing penalty against Pittsburgh helped Oakland move ahead, 13–7, on a 22-yard Blanda field goal early in the third quarter. He added another three-pointer from 31 yards out to give the Raiders a 16–7 lead. Willie Brown then put a stake in the hearts of Pittsburgh faithful everywhere after intercepting a pass intended for Barry Pearson. Brown took the ball on a 54-yard jaunt right down the middle of the field and into the end zone. Blanda kicked the extra point, and the Raiders were up by a convincing 23–7 score at the end of three quarters.

Early in the fourth, Charlie Smith ran for 40 yards. Later in the drive, he caught a 6-yard pass from Stabler on third down to set up Blanda's fourth field goal of the game, this time from 10 yards to give Oakland a 26–7 lead. Bradshaw led the Steelers on a 68-yard drive that ended on a 26-yard pass to Frank Lewis to narrow the Oakland lead to 26–14 with 9:12 left on the clock. Pittsburgh's slim hopes of a comeback were thwarted with an exceptional ball-controlled attack led by Stabler to virtually eat up every remaining tick off the clock. With 19 seconds left, Hubbard delivered the exclamation mark on this day by blasting over from one yard out for his second touchdown of the game. Blanda then added his 15th point of the game, and the Raiders won convincingly, 33–14. In doing so, the Silver and Black made sure that no miracle finish would take away another shot of advancing in the playoffs. Their 33 points were the most given up by one of the greatest defensive units of all-time during the '73 season. Marv Hubbard pounded out 91 yards on 20 carries to lead the ground attack, and Charlie Smith rang up another 73 to give the Raiders 232 rushing yards on the day.[15]

AFC Championship Game, December 30, 1973

The Raiders next travelled to Miami in an attempt to prevent the Dolphins from repeating as Super Bowl champions. With sunny skies and the temperature in the high 70's, a crowd of 75,105 was on hand waving white handkerchiefs in the Orange Bowl as Oakland kicked off to start another Super Bowl quest. Don Nottingham returned the opening kickoff 19 yards to the Miami 36.

The Dolphins were a run-oriented team. With 6-2, 235-pound battering ram fullback Larry Csonka pounding the ball between the tackles and the swift Mercury Morris getting around the ends, Miami was a devastating force to contain. It came as no surprise that the Dolphins began with four running plays that earned them two first downs. Quarterback Bob Griese then looked to mix things up a bit, and tried a pass to Marlin Briscoe, but it was incomplete. However, the Dolphins caught a break after defensive back Nemiah Wilson was called for holding. This gave Miami another first down. After the Raiders were able to stop the running attack on two downs, Griese went back to the air. Despite a rush by Horace Jones, Griese got away and took off himself, covering 27 yards before Phil Villapiano stopped him on the Oakland 11. Csonka then ended Miami's initial drive with a touchdown run from that spot. Garo Yepremian's extra point kick gave the Dolphins an early 7–0 lead.

Marv Hubbard opened Oakland's first offensive series with a 14-yard run, and got the Raiders two first downs. Ken Stabler added another first down with a pass to Mike Siani at the Miami 36, but a holding penalty wiped the play out and the Raiders were forced to punt. Oakland managed to move again near the end of the first quarter, getting to the Miami 34, but George Blanda missed on a 41-yard field goal try. A 27-yard pass to Paul Warfield got the Dolphins into Oakland territory at the 47. Griese looked to capitalize through the air once again, but Willie Brown came up with an interception and was downed on the Oakland 2-yard line. Oakland could not generate anything after Brown's theft, and they were forced to punt from deep in their own territory.

Rookie punter Ray Guy showed why the Raiders made him their number one draft pick by sending a booming kick 63 yards to get Oakland out of the hole. Miami responded by returning to their famed running attack. With Csonka working the middle, and Morris scooting around the ends, the Dolphins moved the chains all the way to the Oakland one. Csonka then ran for his second touchdown on third down with 17 seconds left in the half. Yepremian's conversion sent the Dolphins into the intermission up, 14–0.

The Raiders took the second half kickoff and got deep into Miami territory, but could not punch it in. Blanda came on and got the Raiders on the scoreboard with a 21-yard field goal. The Dolphins answered with a three-pointer of their own, a 42-yarder from Yepremian to lead, 17–3. Stabler then rang up six points on a 21-yard pass to Mike Siani, and with Blanda's conversion, the Raiders only trailed, 17–10, going into the fourth quarter.

Unfortunately, Oakland never got closer. Yepremian added a 20-yard field goal to extend Miami's lead to 20–10. Oakland got to their own 45, and Stabler handed off to Marv Hubbard on fourth down, but a fumble ended the drive with six minutes left. The Dolphins marched down the field with their devastating running tandem, and Csonka secured the win with a 2-yard run. The running attack was so dominant on this day that it produced 18 of Miami's 21 first downs, and gained 266 yards on 53 attempts, with Csonka leading the charge with 117 yards on 29 carries. Yepremian's extra point kick made the final 27–10, and Miami captured their third straight AFC championship, and two weeks later, their second Super Bowl title. As for the Raiders, this was the fourth time in six seasons that they came up one game shy of the Super Bowl.[16]

Individual Statistics and Roster

Head Coach: John Madden
Assistant Coaches: Tom Dahms, Tom Flores, Bob Mischak, Paul Roach, Joe Scannella, Don Shinnick, Ollie Spencer, Bob Zeman
1973 Regular Season Record: 9-4-1

1st Place AFC Western Division
Scored 292 points to rank 10th out of 26 teams
Allowed 175 points to rank 3rd
Led the league in fewest touchdowns rushing with five.

STARTERS — OFFENSE

QB — Ken Stabler: Active for 14 games, and started in 11. Completed 163 of 260 pass attempts for 1,997 yards, 14 TD and 10 INT. **Led the NFL in pass completion percentage (62.7).** Rushed for 101 yards on 21 carries.
HB — Charlie Smith: Started in 14 games. Rushed for 682 yards on 173 carries and 4 TD. Had 28 receptions for 260 yards and 1 TD, and 2 kickoff returns for 23 yards.
FB — Marv Hubbard: Started in 14 games, rushed for 903 yards on 193 carries and 6 TD. Had 15 receptions for 116 yards.
WR — Fred Biletnikoff: Started in 14 games, and had 48 receptions for 660 yards and 4 TD.
WR — Mike Siani: Started in 14 games, and had 45 receptions for 742 yards and 3 TD.
TE — Bob Moore: Started in 14 games, and had 34 receptions for 375 yards and 4 TD.
LT — Art Shell: Started in 14 games.
LG — Gene Upshaw: Started in 14 games.
C — Jim Otto: Started in 14 games.
RG — George Buehler: Started in 14 games.
RT — Bob Brown: Active for 10 games, and started in 8.

RESERVE OFFENSIVE PLAYERS

Pete Banaszak (RB): Active for 14 games, rushed for 198 yards on 34 carries, had 6 receptions for 31 yards, and 3 kickoff returns for 48 yards.
Warren Bankston (RB/TE): Active for 11 games, and had 1 kickoff return for 12 yards.
Cliff Branch (WR): Active for 13 games, and had 19 receptions for 290 yards and 3 TD.
Dave Dalby (C): Active for 14 games.
Clarence Davis (RB): Active for 13 games. Rushed for 609 yards on 116 carries and 4 TD, had 7 receptions for 76 yards, and 19 kickoff returns for 504 yards.
Bob Hudson (RB): Active for 14 games. Rushed for 3 yards on 4 carries, had 1 reception for 9 yards, and 14 kickoff returns for 350 yards.
Daryle Lamonica (QB): Active for 8 games, and started in 3. Completed 42 of 93 pass attempts for 614 yards, 2 TD and 8 INT. Rushed for -7 yards on 5 carries.
Jeff Queen (RB/TE): Active for 9 games.
Paul Seiler (C/T): Active for 4 games, and started in 1.
Steve Sweeney (WR): Active for 14 games, and had 2 receptions for 52 yards and 1 TD.
John Vella (T): Active for 14 games, and started in 4.

STARTERS — DEFENSE

DE — Bubba Smith: Active for and started in 12 games.
DE — Tony Cline: Active for 14 games, started in 11.
DT — Otis Sistrunk: Started in 14 games and had 1 fumble recovery.
DT — Art Thoms: Active for and started in 13 games. Had 1 fumble recovery.
LLB — Phil Villapiano: Started in 14 games, had 1 INT and 3 fumble recoveries.
MLB — Dan Conners: Started in 14 games and had 1 fumble recovery.
RLB — Gerald Irons: Started in 14 games, had 2 INT and 1 fumble recovery.
CB — Nemiah Wilson: Active for 13 games, and started in 12. Had 3 INT.
CB — Willie Brown: Started in 14 games and had 3 INT.
SS — George Atkinson: Active for 14 games, and started in 13. Had 3 INT, returned 1 for a TD, 2 fumble recoveries, returned 1 for a TD, and 41 punt returns for 336 yards and 1 TD.

FS — Jack Tatum: Active for and started in 13 games. Had 1 INT and 2 fumble recoveries.

RESERVE DEFENSIVE PLAYERS

Joe Carroll (LB): Active for 9 games.
Monte Johnson (LB): active for 13 games.
Horace Jones (E): Active for 14 games, and started in 5.
Kelvin Korver (T): Active for 14 games, had 1 INT and 1 fumble recovery.
Tommy Maxwell (DB): Active for 8 games, had 1 fumble recovery and 3 punt returns for 8 yards.
Skip Thomas (DB): Active for 14 games, and started in 3. Had 2 INT.
Jimmy Warren (DB): Active for 10 games, and started in 1. Had1 INT and 1 punt return for 0 yards.
Gary Weaver (LB): Active for 10 games and had 2 fumble recoveries.

KICKING/PUNTING

K — George Blanda: Active for 14 games. Made 23 of 33 field goal attempts, and 31 of 31 extra point kicks for 100 points.
P — Ray Guy: Active for 14 games. Punted 69 times for a 45.3 average, and rushed for 21 yards on 1 carry.

1974 Season Review

1. Sept. 16: The Raiders and Buffalo Bills opened the Monday Night Football schedule with a thrilling 21–20 Buffalo win. Despite all of their success over the last seven seasons, the Raiders dropped their fifth straight opener. Playing without the NFL's top runner, O.J. Simpson, who left the game before halftime with a sprained ankle, the Bills rallied on the arm of quarterback Joe Ferguson and the pass catching abilities of Ahmad Rashad. The Ferguson to Rashad combination teamed up on two touchdowns, with the second proving to be the game winner with 1:56 left to play. Oakland got to midfield with six seconds remaining, but George Blanda missed on a long field goal attempt. Blanda did connect on two three-pointers early (34 and 41 yards), Clarence Davis ran for a 6-yard touchdown, and Defensive tackle Art Thoms returned a fumble 29 yards to provide the Silver and Black their scoring for the evening.[1]

2. Sept. 22: The Raiders and Chiefs staged another brutal game that saw Kansas City lose quarterback Len Dawson and running Ed Podolak due to injuries. Fred Biletnikoff had his nose broken in the first half, but returned to action later. In the end, Oakland once again dominated the Chiefs, 27–7. The Oakland defense completely smothered the Kansas City offense with five sacks, five interceptions, and allowed only 48 yards through the air. For the Silver and Black, however, Ken Stabler did just about anything he wanted to do. He threw for three touchdowns, with two going to tight end Dave Casper (5 and 2 yards), and Mike Siani (9 yards). Pete Banaszak added a 20-yard scoring dash to complete Oakland's point production.[2]

3. Sept. 29: Oakland's defense continued to shine in a 17–0 shutout victory over Pittsburgh. The Raiders held quarterback Joe Gilliam to only 106 passing yards, and intercepted him twice by the NFL's top-rated defense. This marked the first time since 1964 that the Steelers failed to score. Two punt returns by Ron Smith, and a George Atkinson interception, helped lead to Oakland's points. Smith's returns led to a Ken Stabler 1-yard run, and

a George Blanda 25-yard field goal. Atkinson's theft was quickly turned into a Stabler to Cliff Branch 19-yard touchdown. The Silver and Black were also helped by a steady running attack that churned out 177 yards.[3]

4. Oct. 6: Oakland was establishing themselves as one of the league's dominant teams, and lived up to that reputation by rolling over the Cleveland Browns, 40–24. After spotting the Browns an early 10–0 lead, the Raiders quickly took total control of the game, and could have scored more points than they did. Ken Stabler was the NFL's top rated passer in only his second full season as a starter, and humbled the Browns with 19 completions in 33 attempts for 237 yards and three touchdowns. Fred Biletnikoff (11 yards), Cliff Branch (10 yards), and Clarence Davis (45 yards), were on the receiving end of Stabler's touchdown tosses. Davis added a 1-yard touchdown run, and Pete Banaszak a 3-yarder to a ground attack that registered 222 total yards, with Davis leading the way with 116. George Blanda had a 30-yard field, and Otis Sistrunk tackled running back Ken Brown in the end zone for a safety, for the remainder of Oakland's point explosion against the sub-par Browns. Defensive back George Atkinson led the defense with three interceptions. Willie Brown and Jack Tatum also had one theft apiece for the tough Oakland secondary.[4]

5. Oct. 13: Ken Stabler threw for two touchdowns, with the second one proving to be the game-winner in a 14–10 clash with San Diego. Stabler's first touchdown went to Cliff Branch from 46 yards, and the clincher was placed into Bob Moore's hands from four yards out. The running tandem of Marv Hubbard (94 yards), and Clarence Davis (83 yards), provided Oakland with a well-balanced offensive attack. The win gave the Raiders a 4–1 record, and a two game bulge in the AFC West.[5]

6. Oct. 20: Oakland continued on their roll by beating the Central Division–leading Cincinnati Bengals, 30–27, in the final eight seconds. The game was close throughout, with the lead changing hands six times. It looked like the Bengals were in control when Isaac Curtis caught a Ken Anderson touchdown pass with six minutes left to give Cincinnati a 27–23 lead. Ken Stabler was one of the greatest come-from-behind quarterback in NFL history, and this game helped to build that reputation. Stabler and the offense got one final shot at victory with 1:36 left, and 52 yards to go. The "Snake" took over with his usual calm demeanor, and began the winning drive with a 42-yard completion to Fred Biletnikoff. Two passes to Bob Moore, and one to Mike Siani, got the Raiders to the 2-yard line with 20 seconds remaining. Two plays later, Stabler handed off to Charlie Smith, who swept to the right, jumped over a defender, and landed in the end zone to give the Oakland juggernaut their fifth straight win. Also scoring for the Raiders was George Blanda on three field goals (49, 31, and 18 yards), Marv Hubbard (2-yard run), and Pete Banaszak (1-yard run).[6]

7. Oct. 27: At the halfway point of the season, there already was talk of the Raiders going to the Super Bowl, and for good reason. For the sixth straight week, the Raiders entered the win column, this time as 35–24 victors over San Francisco. Oakland was down by ten in the third quarter before exploding for 21 points while holding the 49ers scoreless. Prior to their second half barrage, the Raiders scored on a 17-yard run by Marv Hubbard, who ran for game-high 117 yards, and on a 64-yard pass from Ken

Stabler to Cliff Branch. After a 1-yard scoring run by Pete Banaszak closed the gap to three points, Dave Casper caught a 2-yard pass from Stabler for the go-ahead touchdown. The Raiders added an insurance touchdown by rookie running back Harold Hart that covered 40 yards following a San Francisco fumble. The Raiders now stood at 6–1 in the Western Division, well ahead of the 3–3–1 Denver Broncos.[7]

8. Nov. 3: Oakland expanded their division lead with a 28–17 win over Denver. The Raiders were in complete control throughout this game thanks in large part to the field leadership of Ken Stabler. The left-handing signal caller completed 12 of 19 passes for 217 yards and four touchdowns, with both his wide receivers accounting for the six-pointers. Fred Biletnikoff caught scoring strikes from 23 and 19 yards, while Cliff Branch covered nine and 61 yards on his touchdown treks. Marv Hubbard chipped in with his second straight game of breaking the century mark, this time rambling for 107 yards on 22 carries.[8]

9. Nov. 10: With a 35–13 win over the Detroit Lions, the Raiders were 8–1, and owners of the best record in the league. They stopped a four-game winning streak by Detroit on Ken Stabler's passing and Marv Hubbard's running. Stabler was near perfect with 20 completions out of 24 attempts for 228 yards and two touchdowns, with both going to Cliff Branch (15 and 36 yards). Hubbard's power runs helped Oakland achieve a balanced offensive attack that kept the Detroit defense guessing throughout the game. He ran for over one hundred yards for he third straight game (111 yards on 16 carries), and scored twice on runs of five and 20 yards. Harold Hart scored Oakland's other touchdown on a 25-yard run. This victory allowed the Silver and Black to achieve a commanding three-and-a-half game lead in the division.[9]

10. Nov. 17: Oakland clinched their seventh division title on this date with a 17–10 win over San Diego. Ken Stabler threw for 240 yards, and fired his 18th touchdown pass of the year, a 60-yarder to Cliff Branch, who had seven receptions for 125 yards. Pete Banaszak scored on a 1-yard run, and George Blanda kicked a 28-yard field goal to round out the Western Division champs scoring.[10]

11. Nov. 24: With the division already wrapped up, the Raiders might have eased up a bit. Whatever the reason, Oakland was upset by the Denver Broncos, 20–17, ending their winning streak at nine games. Led by an incredible running attack of Jon Keyworth and Otis Armstrong, the Broncos ran for 292 yards. Despite the loss, Ken Stabler still shined, throwing for 234 yards on 22 out of 34 attempts. He also accounted for both Oakland touchdowns along with Fred Biletnikoff, who caught the "Snake's" scoring strikes from 34 and seven yards.[11]

12. Dec. 1: The New England Patriots were one of the top teams in the AFC during the early stages of the season, but they fell apart as the schedule progressed. A trip to Oakland did nothing for their playoff hopes, as the Raiders rolled to a 41–26 victory. Ken Stabler continued to stand out as one of the league's elite quarterbacks by hitting on 16 of 21 pass attempts for 251 yards. His four touchdown passes on the day gave him a league-leading 24. Two of his scoring tosses went to the NFL's top receiver, Cliff Branch (67 and 19 yards), while the "Snake's" other touchdown passes went to Fred Biletnikoff (12 yards) and Bob Moore (5 yards). Branch's reputation as an offensive weapon was

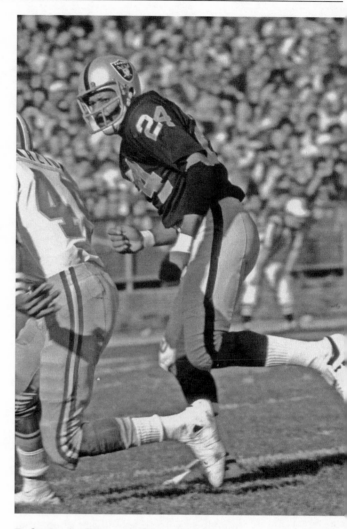

Defensive back par excellence and Hall of Famer Willie Brown, the master of the bump and run, sticks to a Detroit Lions receiver in a 35–13 Raiders win on November 10, 1974, in Oakland, California (AP Photo/NFL Photos).

helped by his 138 yards on six receptions. Adding to Oakland's point barrage were Skip Thomas, who returned an interception 22 yards, and rookie Harold Hart's 7-yard run.[12]

13. Dec. 8: Head coach John Madden decided to give Ken Stabler the afternoon off against Kansas City. With the playoffs just two away, there was no point in risking injury to the NFL's top quarterback. Rookie Larry Lawrence assumed the signal calling duties, but was forced from the game early. Old hero Daryle Lamonica came in to replace the rookie, and just like in the past, the "Mad Bomber" came through for the Silver and Black. In a tough defensive battle, the Chiefs clung to a slim 6–0 advantage in the fourth quarter. It was then that Lamonica returned to his past glory by finding Cliff Branch from 10 yards out for the game's lone touchdown. George Blanda added the go-ahead extra point, and Oakland won with a baseball-like final of 7–6.[13]

14. Dec. 14: The Raiders clinched home field advantage throughout the AFC playoffs by posting a league-best 12–2 record with a 27–23 win over the Dallas Cowboys. Ken Stabler returned to action, but only briefly in the first half. He still managed to

complete 11 of 17 pass attempts for 131 yards and two touchdowns. Fred Biletnikoff (9 yards), and Clarence Davis (14 yards), had the honors of catching the "Snake's" scoring tosses on this day. George Blanda replaced Stabler in the second half, and the 47-year-old wonder threw his first touchdown pass in three seasons, a 28-yarder to Cliff Branch. Blanda also kicked a 35-yard field goal to finish out Oakland's regular season scoring.[14]

AFC Divisional Playoff Game, December 21, 1974

Four days before Christmas, the Miami Dolphins came out to Oakland to begin their quest for an unprecedented fourth straight AFC championship and third consecutive Super Bowl title. What transpired over sixty minutes of football gave all who witnessed it, either in person or via media outlets, an early Christmas gift.

The atmosphere in the Oakland Coliseum was electric and ear piercing, as 52,817 waved black pennants, and some of the female persuasion waved black bras in the air. It was Raider Nation at its finest as Miami received the opening kickoff amidst the frenzy. However, the Dolphins were focused on making history, and 15 seconds after the ball left the tee, the crowd fell silent when Nat Moore returned the opening kickoff 89 yards for a touchdown. The Raiders looked to even the score with their famed air attack, but Stabler and the offense had trouble at first getting things going. The defense helped the cause by keeping Miami's powerful ground attack under control. The score remained 7–0 at the end of the first quarter, and Oakland seemed ready to get their offensive scheme in gear.

On their second possession of the second quarter, Stabler started things off with a completion of nine yards to Fred Biletnikoff. Marv Hubbard powered his way for a gain of five between the tackles. The great offensive line of the Raiders was beginning to wear down the Dolphins at this point, and Stabler took advantage of his stellar wall of protection. He connected with Hubbard on a 9-yard pass, and returned to the run, with Clarence Davis going over left tackle for a ten-yard gain. Three plays later, Stabler decided to strike for paydirt. The swift Charlie Smith broke loose down the middle out of the backfield, and with a linebacker covering him man-for-man, Smith was an easy winner in this foot race. Stabler threaded the needle with a perfect pass that Smith hauled in and registered a 31-yard touchdown for the Silver and Black. George Blanda knotted the game at 7–7 with the extra point kick, and the Coliseum once again was shaking off its foundation.

The Dolphins were able to get their famed ground game churning in the second quarter, and utilized it to the fullest. Mixing things up with Larry Csonka, Jim Kiick, and Benny Malone as the ball carriers, the world champs ate up enough Oakland real estate to allow Garo Yepremian the opportunity to attempt a close-range field goal try with 1:01 left in the first half. Yepremian was true on a 33-yard three-pointer, and the champions from the Sunshine State took a 10–7 advantage into the locker rooms after thirty minutes of play.

Early in the third quarter, Stabler and Biletnikoff teamed up like so many times throughout their playing days together.

The "Snake" connected with Biletnikoff for 20 yards, and then went right back to him. The great receiver made a tremendous leaping catch along the right sideline close to the end zone. However, the official did not see it that way, and ruled Biletnikoff was out of bounds when he made the grab.

After getting to the Miami 13-yard line, Stabler went to Biletnikoff again on a sideline route. Miami defensive back Tim Foley was glued to Biletnikoff, but it did not matter who was covering him or how close. Old number 25 reached up with one hand while shaking off Foley and brought the ball into his body for one of the greatest post-season catches ever. This time there was no doubt about Biletnikoff going out of bounds, and the official signaled touchdown, and with Blanda's extra point kick, the Raiders were back on top by a 14–10 score.

Miami came back to score on a Paul Warfield 16-yard reception from Bob Griese to put the Dolphins up by two points. The Dolphins were helped in this drive by a 29-yard pass interference call on third down. Bubba Smith got one of his big hands on Yepremian's extra point try, and the Raiders went into the final fifteen minutes down by two. The Dolphins were looking to separate themselves from the Raiders, and gained a little extra breathing room when Yepremian kicked a 46-yard field goal to extend the Miami advantage to 19–14.

The game clock now showed 4:54 remaining with the Raiders down by five and pinned deep in their territory at the 17. Stabler connected with Biletnikoff for 11, and then unleashed Oakland's speed demon, Cliff Branch, to attack the secondary. The "Snake" hit Branch with a pass on the left side of the field down at the Miami 27 where he fell to the ground. Reacting quickly, Branch realized that no Dolphin had touched him, so he was still able to get up and run, and that he did. The former sprinter with world-class speed, sprung to his feet and motored his high octane wheels the rest of the way to the end zone to complete a 72-yard scoring play. Blanda's extra point kick sailed through the uprights to give the Raiders a 21–19 lead with 4:37 left after an 83-yard drive ate up a mere 17 seconds.

Undaunted by the quick-hitting play, and the frenzy within the confines of the Oakland Coliseum, Miami signal caller Bob Griese brought the Dolphins back with 2:08 left. Griese led the Dolphins deep into Oakland territory, and then let running back Benny Malone do the rest. From the Oakland 23, Malone took Griese's handoff, ran to the outside, shook off a few tackle attempts, and crossed the goal line to put Miami back on top once again. With Yepremian's conversion, the Dolphins looked to be closing in on their fourth straight trip to the AFC Championship Game.

Ron Smith returned the ensuing kickoff to the Oakland 32 with time not on the side of the Raiders. What they did have on their side was one of the calmest quarterbacks to ever take a snap. Cool Kenny Stabler swaggered into the huddle after conferring with head coach John Madden during the two-minute warning, and looked to give himself, the team, and all of Raider Nation something to cheer about during the holiday season. The only option for the Silver and Black was a six-pointer. Nothing else would do, and Stabler began on a quest to get Oakland what they needed to make the trip back to Florida an unpleasant one for the Dolphins.

With 68 yards of Oakland real estate in front of him, and 11 fierce members of Miami's much acclaimed "No Name Defense" standing in his way, Stabler dropped back to pass as the game clock started ticking down. All eyes were switching from the action on the field to the clock as the "Snake" connected with tight end Bob Moore for a six yard pickup. After a running play on second down mixed things up a bit, Stabler went to the airways again, connecting with Biletnikoff first for 18, and then 20 across the middle. Sixty seconds were all that was left. Stabler connected with Branch next on a quick hitter that gained four yards. Frank Pitts then caught a pass for a first down on the Miami 14 after adding some dramatics. At first, Pitts could not get a handle on the ball, and juggled with it before securing it while the Coliseum faithful held their collective breaths. After Clarence Davis ran behind the right side of his linemen for six yards, the Raiders called their final timeout.

After conferring on the sideline while the heartbeat of Raider Nation was thumping off the charts, Stabler and the Raiders were faced with a first-and-goal from the eight with inside of forty seconds left. At the snap, Stabler dropped back with Biletnikoff as his primary target, but he was locked down tight by the defense. Stabler's wall of protection began to give way to Miami's pass rush, with defensive end Vern Den Herder coming in fast. Den Herder grabbed at Stabler's legs, and as the quarterback was clamped down and falling, he threw into the end zone toward Clarence Davis, who was surrounded by nothing but the white jerseys of Miami defenders.

Stabler's pass had the makings of either something wonderful or tragic. Davis made sure it was the former that occurred by fighting off enemy hands simultaneously reaching for the ball. He gathered the valuable commodity in, pressed it against his chest and fell to the ground as the touchdown signal made it official. The ironic thing was that Davis was never known for his pass catching abilities, yet his incredible effort forever earned the former USC Trojan everlasting fame in what went down in history as the "Sea of Hands" game.

Needless to say, the Oakland Coliseum was rocking off its foundation, thanks to what just happened. Blanda's extra point kick gave the Raiders a 28–26 lead with 24 seconds remaining. On the second play following the ensuing kickoff, linebacker Phil Villapiano delivered the Silver and Black dagger through the Dolphins when he intercepted a Griese pass on the Oakland 45. Marv Hubbard smashed into the line twice before the clock hit 0:00, and the Raiders were one step closer to pro football's grandest stage.[15]

AFC Championship Game, December 29, 1974

After squishing the fish a week earlier, the Raiders were now looked at as the bona fide front runners to advance to and win Super Bowl IX. It appeared to be their right of passage after eliminating the two-time defending champions, not to mention so many close encounters that came up short of the ultimate prize over the previous six years.

The AFC Championship Game meeting with the Pittsburgh Steelers seemed a mere formality, as the men from the Steel City would be nothing more than fodder, or a tune up, on the road to

Silver and Black domination in 1974. It seemed obvious to the majority of the masses that the game's outcome was already decided prior to kickoff. However, the Steelers were not convinced of their opponent's invincibility.

The Raiders drew first blood after rookie Lynn Swann fumbled a punt, and Harold Hart recovered for Oakland on the Pittsburgh 41. Unable to move the ball much farther, the Raiders settled for a 40-yard George Blanda field goal that gave the Silver and Black a 3–0 lead with less than five minutes expired in the first quarter. Pittsburgh came back to tie things up at 3–3 when Roy Gerela kicked a 23-yard three-pointer with 5:26 taken off the clock in the second quarter. That was the way it stayed going into the half.

With Pittsburgh's "Steel Curtain" defense smothering Oakland's running attack, which saw them gain only 29 yards throughout the game, Ken Stabler took to the air early in the third quarter. He connected on four straight passes, with two each going to Fred Biletnikoff and Cliff Branch. Branch ended the drive with a 38-yard touchdown reception that put the Raiders back on top for the first time since the opening quarter. Branch had a magnificent game by catching a conference title game record nine passes, which he turned into 186 yards. With Blanda's extra point, Oakland led, 10–3.

All the Raiders had to do was hold on for another 15 minutes of football and their tickets would be punched for their first Super Bowl appearance in seven years. However, it seemed a lot easier than it looked. Pittsburgh's ground attack of Franco Harris and Rocky Bleier got the Steelers to the Oakland eight at the end of the third quarter. This Steel Town duo hammered away at Oakland all day, with Harris finishing with 111 yards and Bleier 98. On the first play of the fourth quarter, the game was once again knotted up after Harris capped off an eight-play, 61-yard drive with an 8-yard jaunt through 11 black jersey-clad Raiders and Gerela added the extra point.

Stabler quickly looked to return control of the momentum back over to his Raiders. However, Pittsburgh linebacker Jack Ham had other ideas. In man-to-man coverage on Charlie Smith coming out of the backfield, Ham picked off a dump pass intended for him at the Oakland 34, and returned it to the nine. Three plays later, Terry Bradshaw dropped back from the six and connected with a wide-open Lynn Swann in the middle of the end zone for the go-ahead score. Following Gerela's conversion, Pittsburgh was up for the first time by a 17–10 count.

The Raiders came right back on a 42-yard pass from Stabler to Branch that helped Oakland in a drive that started on their own 15 and ended on Pittsburgh's six. The Steelers flexed their defensive muscle, and after failing to pierce the goal line, Oakland got a 24-yard three-pointer off Blanda's right foot to close to within four at 17–13.

Oakland had one more chance to secure victory with time running out. Stabler looked to pass as the game clock showed one minute left, but his attempt was intercepted by defensive back J.T. Thomas. The Steelers quickly ended any doubts to those in attendance or viewing across the country as to who was going to represent the AFC in Super Bowl IX. Franco Harris nailed the coffin shut on Raider Nation's hopes of being crowned 1974 world champions when he ran 21 yards for a touchdown. With Gerela's extra point kick, the Steelers prevailed, 24–13, en route to their first NFL title, which they won against the Minnesota Vikings two weeks later. As for the Raiders, another bitter climax engulfed the team after so much promise.[16]

Individual Statistics and Roster

Head Coach: John Madden
Assistant Coaches: Tom Dahms, Tom Flores, Bob Mischak, Paul Roach, Joe Scannella, Don Shinnick, Ollie Spencer, Bob Zeman
1974 Regular Season Record: 12–2
1st Place AFC Western Division
Scored 355 points to rank 1st out of 26 teams
Allowed 228 points to rank 9th
Led the league in points scored (355), touchdowns passing (28), and net yard average (6.6)

STARTERS — OFFENSE

QB — Ken Stabler: Active for 14 games, and started in 13. Completed 178 of 310 pass attempts for 2,469 yards, **26** TD and 12 INT. Rushed for -2 yards on 12 carries and 1 TD.
HB — Clarence Davis: Active for 11 games, and started in 7. Rushed for 554 yards on 129 carries and 2 TD. Had 11 receptions for 145 yards and 1 TD, and 3 kickoff returns for 107 yards.
FB — Marv Hubbard: Active for 14 games, and started in 13. Rushed for 865 yards on 188 carries and 4 TD, and had 11 receptions for 95 yards.
WR — Fred Biletnikoff: Started in 14 games, and had 42 receptions for 593 yards and 7 TD.
WR — Cliff Branch: Started in 14 games, had 60 receptions for **1,092** yards and **13** TD, **and also led the NFL with a 78.0 yards receiving per game average.**
TE — Bob Moore: Started in 14 games, and had 30 receptions for 356 yards, and 2 TD.
LT — Art Shell: Started in 14 games.
LG — Gene Upshaw: Started in 14 games.
C — Jim Otto: Started in 14 games.
RG — George Buehler: Started in 14 games.
RT — John Vella: Active for and started in 13 games.

RESERVE OFFENSIVE PLAYERS

Pete Banaszak (RB): Active for 14 games, and started in 1. Rushed for 272 yards on 80 carries and 5 TD. Had 9 receptions for 64 yards, and 8 kickoff returns for 137 yards.
Warren Bankston (RB/TE): Active for 16 games, rushed for 6 yards on 1 carry, and had 1 kickoff return for 10 yards.
Morris Bradshaw (WR): Active for 12 games, and had 1 kickoff return for 0 yards.
Dave Casper (TE): Active for 14 games, and had 4 receptions for 26 yards and 3 TD.
Dave Dalby (C): Active for 14 games.
Harold Hart (RB): Active for 13 games, rushed for 268 yards on 51 carries and 2 TD. Had 1 reception for 4 yards, and 18 kickoff returns for 466 yards.
Bob Hudson (RB): Active for 14 games, and rushed for 12 yards on 1 carry.
George Jakowenko (K): Active for 6 games.
Daryle Lamonica (QB): Active for 4 games. Completed 3 of 9 pass attempts for 35 yards, 1 TD and 4 INT, and rushed for -3 yards on 2 carries.
Henry Lawrence (T/G): Active for 14 games, and started in 1.
Larry Lawrence (QB): Active for 7 games, and started in 1. Completed 4 of 11 pass attempts for 29 yards and 1 INT. Rushed for 39 yards on 4 carries.
Dan Medlin (G): Active for 6 games.

Frank Pitts (WR): Active for 13 games, rushed for -10 yards on 1 carry, and had 3 receptions for 23 yards.
Mike Siani (WR): Active for 6 games, and had 3 receptions for 30 yards and 1 TD.
Charlie Smith (RB): Active for 13 games, and started in 7. Rushed for 194 yards on 64 carries and 1 TD. Had 8 receptions for 100 yards and 1 TD.
Mark van Eeghen (RB): Active for 14 games, rushed for 139 yards on 28 carries, and had 4 receptions for 33 yards.

STARTERS — DEFENSE

DE — Bubba Smith: Active for 14 games, and started in 13. Had 1 fumble recovery.
DE — Horace Jones: Started in 14 games, and had 3 fumble recoveries.
DT — Otis Sistrunk: Started in 14 games, had 1 INT, 3 fumble recoveries, and recorded 1 safety.
DT — Art Thoms: Started in 14 games, and had 1 fumble recovery and 1 TD.
LLB — Phil Villapiano: Started in 14 games, and had 1 fumble recovery.
MLB — Dan Conners: Started in 14 games, and had 3 INT.
RLB — Gerald Irons: Started in 14 games, and had 2 INT.
CB — Skip Thomas: Started in 14 games, had 6 INT and 1 TD.
CB — Willie Brown: Active for and started in 9 games, and had 1 INT.
SS — George Atkinson: Started in 14 games, had 4 INT, and 4 punt returns for 31 yards.
FS — Jack Tatum: Active for and started in 10 games, and had 4 INT.

RESERVE DEFENSIVE PLAYERS

Tony Cline (E): Active for 5 games, and started in 1.
Mike Dennery (LB): Active for 14 games.
Monte Johnson (LB): Active for 14 games, had 1 INT, and 1 fumble recovery.
Kelvin Korver (T): Active for 9 games.
Bob Prout (DB): Active for 2 games.
Ron Smith (DB/WR): Active for 14 games, had 2 fumble recoveries, 41 punt returns for 486 yards and 19 kickoff returns for 420 yards.
Jimmy Warren (DB): Active for 14 games, started in 4, and had 2 INT.
Gary Weaver (LB): Active for 14 games.
Nemiah Wilson (DB): Active for 12 games, started in 5, and had 3 INT.

KICKING/PUNTING

K — George Blanda: Active for 14 games. Made 11 out of 17 field goal attempts, and **44** out of **46** extra point kicks for 77 points. Had 1 pass completion in 4 attempts for 28 yards and 1 TD.
P — Ray Guy: Active for 14 games. Punted 74 times for a **42.2** average, and had 1 pass attempt for zero yards.

1975 Season Review

1. Sept. 22: After ending Miami's two-year reign as world champions 11 months earlier, the Raiders once again tormented the Dolphins. In the 1975 Monday Night Football opener, Oakland started Miami's new season off in the loss column, 31–21. This was also the Raiders first opening day victory of the decade. Ken Stabler picked up where he left off after a brilliant 1974

campaign. Almost at will, the NFL's top quarterback found his receivers with ease against Miami's defense. The "Snake" did not throw for any touchdowns, but his pinpoint passes helped set up all of Oakland's offensive scores. After getting deep into Miami territory, Pete Banaszak scored Oakland's first two touchdowns from one and two yards. Mark van Eeghen scored from the one, George Blanda kicked a 25-yard field goal, and Harold Hart scored Oakland's final touchdown on a 102-yard kickoff return.[1]

2. Sept. 28: The Baltimore Colts were looking for their first home victory in two years coming into their game with Oakland. However, things did not go as planned for the Colts. The Raiders kept Baltimore's streak alive with a 31–20 win. Rookie Neal Colzie proved to be the main weapon for Oakland, as he set up three touchdowns with tremendous punt returns. Oakland was down, 13–10, at the half, but a Ken Stabler to Dave Casper 4-yard scoring pass put the Raiders up for good. A 43-yard Colzie punt return helped the Silver and Black extend their advantage. It set the Raiders up with great field position, and Jess Phillips scored from six yards out soon after. Baltimore closed to within four points later, and was driving when Colzie once again provided the heroics with an interception deep in Oakland territory. Providing the Raiders with their other points were Harold Hart (11-yard run), George Blanda (29-yard field goal), and Pete Banaszak (1-yard run).[2]

3. Oct. 5: The grand old man of the Raiders came through once again. The 48-year-old George Blanda accounted for all of Oakland's points in a hard fought defensive struggle against San Diego. The Raiders got close enough for Blanda to connect on field goals from 35 and 29 yards in a 6–0 victory. Both defenses were so stingy that they each held the opposition under 100 yards passing.[3]

4. Oct. 12: When old rivals meet, records do not matter. Such was the case when Kansas City and Oakland took the field. The Chiefs came into this game winless, while the Raiders were a perfect 3–0. On paper, Oakland was set to roll, but when it was all over, it was the Raiders that got rolled. After taking a 3–0 lead on a George Blanda 23-yard field goal, Oakland got hit with a Kansas City barrage that gave the Silver and Black their worst defeat since 1961. Led by a 100-yard rushing performance by Woody Green, three touchdown passes by Mike Livingston, and three interceptions, the Chiefs romped, 42–10. A fourth quarter pass from David Humm to Cliff Branch covering nine yards gave the Raiders their lone six-pointer.[4]

5. Oct. 19: The Raiders were still reeling from their previous beat down when they traveled to Cincinnati in week five. The undefeated Bengals showed no mercy on Oakland, and sent the Raiders down in defeat, 14–10. Quarterbacks Ken Stabler and Cincinnati's Ken Anderson were regarded as two of the premier signal callers. However, this game saw both suffer one of the worst days of their careers. In the first half, Stabler netted no passing yards, and finished the game with only eight completions in 24 attempts for 113 yards. He also threw four interceptions. Anderson only completed four of 19 attempts for 75 yards and also threw four interceptions. Even though the offense had hit a snag as of late, Oakland still got some good performances from receiver Cliff Branch, who caught five passes for 63 yards, and running back Mark van Eeghen's game-leading 69 yards rushing. Clarence

Davis scored Oakland's only touchdown on a 1-yard run, and George Blanda added a 30-yard field goal.[5]

6. Oct. 26: The Raiders finally rebounded from their doldrums against the winless San Diego Chargers. For the second time this season, the Raiders held San Diego scoreless, this time by a 25–0 final. Pete Banaszak scored on two short-yardage touchdown runs from one and two yards, and Cliff Branch hauled in a 45-yard scoring toss from Ken Stabler to give the 4–2 Raiders sole possession of first place in the AFC West. The Raiders also had two safeties. Mike Dennery opened the scoring by tackling punter Dennis Partee in the end zone, and Ted Hendricks closed the events by dropping quarterback Jesse Freitas for the other two-pointer.[6]

7. Nov. 2: The Oakland seemed to definitely be back on the right track as a 42–17 win over Denver would testify to. After trailing, 10–7, at the half, Oakland exploded on two Ken Stabler touchdown passes, two Pete Banaszak scoring runs (1 and 2 yards), and one each from Marv Hubbard (7 yards) and Mark van Eeghen (2 yards). Banaszak also led all ball carriers with 62 yards. Stabler seemed to be back in his groove by hitting on 11 of 15 pass attempts for 166 yards. His scoring strikes went to Fred Biletnikoff (21 yards) and Cliff Branch (16 Yards). The Oakland defense did their part by recording five sacks and three interceptions by George Atkinson, Ted Hendricks, and Phil Villapiano.[7]

8. Nov. 9: Another blowout was recorded, this time against the New Orleans Saints by a score of 48–10. The 2–6 Saints were one of pro football's worst teams, and it showed against the powerful Raiders. The Oakland defense brutalized the opposition, allowing them only 140 total yards, recording four sacks and three interceptions by George Atkinson, Willie Brown, and Skip Thomas. Meanwhile, the Oakland offense could not be stopped. The running game ran for 260 yards, and got touchdowns from Marv Hubbard (6 yards), Pete Banaszak (1-yard), and Clarence Davis (5 and 13 yards). The passing game struck for 263 yards and three touchdowns. Ken Stabler threw for two long touchdowns to Morris Bradshaw (36 and 48 yards), and Warren Bankston caught an 8-yard touchdown pass from David Humm. With this third straight win, the Raiders were 6–2, and two full games ahead of second place Kansas City.[8]

9. Nov. 16: Oakland faced another easy opponent in the winless Cleveland Browns, and dismantled them, 38–17. Ken Stabler was finally healthy after suffering from a strained knee since week three. He completed 16 of 25 attempts for 220 yards and four touchdowns. The first two scoring tosses went to Cliff Branch (22 and 21 yards) in the first half. Stabler followed those up with a 15-yarder to Fred Biletnikoff, and one to Clarence Davis that covered 31 yards of turf. Davis added a 26-yard touchdown run on a day that saw him gain a game-high 120 yards on the ground. George Blanda booted a 28-yard field goal to round out Oakland's scoring. This win now saw the Raiders pulling away from the pack in the AFC West. At 7–2, the closest challenge to their top spot in the division came from the 4–5 Chiefs.[9]

10. Nov. 23: The Raiders continued on their winning ways, but this time they had to work a little harder to achieve victory. After building up a 20–9 halftime lead on three Pete Banaszak touchdown runs (1, 27, and 7 yards), the Silver and Black were held to only a George Blanda 22-yard field goal in the second half. The Washington Redskins, however, found their way over

and around the Oakland defense, and tied the game at 23–23 with 2:30 left in the game. Blanda had a chance to win it in the final eight seconds of regulation, but the kick missed it mark. In 1974, the overtime rule was added to the NFL, and the Raiders and Redskins were ready to test each other's wills for an extra quarter. Washington won the coin toss in the overtime period, and elected to receive the ball. Eight plays later the Redskins were on the Oakland 42. The Oakland defense then stiffened, and they sacked quarterback Billy Kilmer on third down. A bad punt on fourth down gave the Raiders excellent field position on their own 42. Behind protection from the best offensive line in football, Ken Stabler was able to take his time and wait for his receivers to get open. First he found Fred Biletnikoff for 26 yards, and then followed that up with a pass to Cliff Branch, which got the Raiders down inside the Washington 10-yard line. Blanda was called upon two plays later, and the ageless wonder sent a 27-yard field goal through the uprights for a 26–23 Oakland win. Leading the way for the Raiders were Ken Stabler, who hit on 20 of 32 pass attempts for 243 yards. Marv Hubbard rushed for 81 yards on only nine carries, and Biletnikoff led all receivers with nine receptions for 113 yards. With their fifth straight win, the Raiders led the AFC West by three games with four to go.[10]

11. Nov. 30: George Blanda once again saved the day, this time with a 36-yard field in overtime that beat the Atlanta Falcons, 37–34. Blanda's kick also allowed the Silver and Black to clinch their eighth division title in nine years. The Raiders seemed to be in the driver's seat with a 31–20 advantage in the fourth quarter. However, Atlanta's rookie quarterback Steve Bartkowski calmly rallied his team by first scoring himself from the 1-yard line, and then put the Falcons in the lead with a 7-yard pass to Wallace Francis. Oakland also had a calm signal caller in Ken Stabler, and the brilliant field general drove the Raiders down to the Atlanta eight with three seconds left. Blanda then sent the game into overtime with an 18-yard field goal. He also kicked an earlier three-pointer from 37 yards. With 11 seconds left in the extra period, Blanda sent his game winner through the uprights. Other heroes for the Raiders were Cliff Branch, who caught seven passes for 155 yards and three touchdowns (40, 27, and 11 yards), Pete Banaszak's 116 rushing yards led all ball carriers, Mark van Eeghen ran for 82 yards and caught an 18-yard touchdown pass from Stabler, and Clarence Davis ran for 79 yards.[11]

12. Dec. 8: Oakland's offense struggled, but they still went on to win their seventh straight game, 17–10, over the Denver Broncos. Ken Stabler had a bad day passing, as he completed only seven passes for 85 yards and suffered two interceptions. He did manage to come alive when it counted most, however. Two key passes to Fred Biletnikoff got Oakland close enough for Harold Hart and Pete Banaszak to score on short yardage runs. Hart's 2-yard run put the Raiders on top, 7–3, at the half, and Banaszak's 1-yarder extended the Oakland advantage to 14–3 in the third. George Blanda concluded Oakland's point production with an 18-yard field in the fourth quarter. The tough Oakland defense stole the headlines on this day by intercepting four passes, with rookie safety Charles Phillips snagged three of them and Skip Thomas the other. The unit also recorded 10 sacks.[12]

13. Dec. 14: All good things must end, and on this day, Oakland's seven-game winning streak ended at the hands of the Houston Oilers, 27–26. Houston quarterback Dan Pastorini

threw to Mack Alston from two yards out on the last play of the game to tie the score. Skip Butler then gave the Oilers their ninth win of the season by hitting on the extra point kick. Oakland received their points on a 13-yard pass from Ken Stabler to Cliff Branch, a pair of 3-yard runs from Pete Banaszak and Harold Hart, and a 13-yard pass from David Humm to Morris Bradshaw that gave the Raiders what appeared to be a convincing 26–17 third quarter advantage.[13]

14. Dec. 21: George Blanda's long and illustrious career was filled with many outstanding moments, some of them record-setting. The final regular season game of 1975 saw another milestone for Blanda. In a 28–20 win over Kansas City, Blanda kicked four conversions to get him over the 2,000-point mark. Helping to get Blanda over 2,000 points were three Pete Banaszak touchdown runs (1, 3, and 5 yards), and a Ken Stabler to Morris Bradshaw 16-yard pass. Oakland finished at 11–3 to give them the second best record in the AFC behind the 12–2 Pittsburgh Steelers.[14]

AFC Divisional Playoff Game, December 28, 1975

The Cincinnati Bengals finished at 11–3, and clinched a wild card berth on the final weekend of the regular season. Cincinnati was making their third playoff appearance of the 1970's, and was coached by the legendary Paul Brown, who was in the final season of his illustrious career. They also had the NFL's passing leader Ken Anderson running the offense.

The Raiders struck first in front of their home crowd in the opening quarter on a George Blanda field goal from 27 yards that was set up by a 36-yard pass from Ken Stabler to Cliff Branch. Oakland extended their lead to 10–0 in the second quarter when Stabler connected with Mike Siani on a 9-yard pass, and Blanda added the extra point. Siani was filling in for Fred Biletnikoff, who was not completely recovered from a knee injury sustained two weeks earlier. The Bengals finally got on the board with a 65-yard drive that was helped along by two big pass completions of 28 and 26 yards. Stan Fritts finished off the drive with a 1-yard run. Dave Green's conversion allowed the Bengals to close the gap to 10–7.

The Raiders came back to once again give themselves a 10-point bulge at the half when Stabler connected on his second touchdown pass of the game, this time with tight end Bob Moore on the receiving end of an 8-yard pass and Blanda added the conversion. An interesting footnote was that both Siani and Moore did not catch a touchdown pass the entire season, but more than made up for it when it counted most. The Oakland defense was keeping Ken Anderson in check throughout the first half, sacking him three times, and applying a heavy pass rush led by linebacker Ted Hendricks out of a 3–4 alignment where the extra linebacker was capable of causing a lot of problems for an opposing signal caller.

The Raiders increased their lead to 24–7 in the third quarter. Rookie Neal Colzie set the Raiders up nicely with a 20-yard punt return. Stabler and the offense then went 35 yards for the score. Clarence Davis first ran for 16 yards, and two plays later, Pete Banaszak scored on a 6-yard run up the middle. Blanda's conversion then gave Oakland its 24th point. The Bengals were not going away quietly, and they mounted a 91-yard drive that ended on a Lenvil Elliott 6-yard run. Green's extra point then made it a 24–14 affair at the end of three.

Stabler connected with tight end Dave Casper from two yards out, and Blanda's conversion then gave Oakland what seemed to be a comfortable 31–14 lead. Defensive back Ken Riley gave Cincinnati a glimmer of hope when he picked off a Stabler pass and returned it 34 yards to the Oakland 34. Two plays later, Anderson found Charlie Joiner for a 25-yard touchdown, and Green's extra point made it a 31–21 ballgame.

The Raiders had been able to contain the Bengals top receiver Isaac Curtis without a catch until the fourth quarter. He caught three on the day for 20 yards, with one covering 14 yards and a score that brought Cincinnati to within three points of a tie following Green's extra point.

Oakland was now trying to stop Cincinnati's momentum from overtaking them. However, they took a step backwards when Banaszak fumbled a Stabler handoff on the Cincinnati 37 and defensive tackle Ron Carpenter recovered for the Bengals. Ted Hendricks recorded a sack on Anderson at the 43, and Cincinnati gave up the ball later on the 38 after Anderson threw two incomplete passes. The Raiders then began running time off the clock. Stabler found Moore for six yards on third down to keep possession at midfield. They eventually stalled, and Ray Guy came in to punt with 59 seconds remaining. The Bengals were called for roughing the kicker, and Oakland kept the ball and ran the clock out. In doing so, they advanced to their third straight AFC Championship Game.

Ken Stabler connected on 17 of 23 attempts for 199 yards mostly on short passes. He ran a well-balanced ball-controlled game plan that saw Clarence Davis and Pete Banaszak run well, and with almost identical statistics. Davis carried 16 times for 63 yards, and Banaszak 17 times for 62. Bob Moore led the receiving corps with six catches for 57 yards.[15]

AFC Championship Game, January 4, 1976

A return to the scene of their most demoralizing playoff defeat awaited the Raiders on the fourth day of 1976. Standing in the way of a Super Bowl would once again be the Pittsburgh Steelers, who were sixty minutes away from an opportunity to defend their Super Bowl title.

The weather conditions were not congenial, as Mother Nature decided to be a tad bit ornery in the Steel City. Brutal, bone chilling, and snowy were the order of the day as the teams took the field.

This game turned out to be an extremely hard-hitting, violent affair, which was not uncommon when these two teams squared off against each other. Jack Tatum put such a violent hit on receiver Lynn Swann that he had to spend the night in the hospital after receiving a concussion. Quarterback Terry Bradshaw also had to be helped off the field in the final minutes after taking a hard hit to the head. The field resembled an ice rink, and each time a player hit the hard turf, it took something out of him.

There was no doubt that players from both teams were moving a little slower the next day.

The Raiders were able to move the ball well throughout the first half, but came away with no points. Pittsburgh's defensive back Mike Wagner ended one Oakland scoring threat with an interception, and a George Blanda 38-yard field goal attempt went wide. Roy Gerela finally broke the scoreless event with a 36-yard field goal in the second quarter, and that was the way it stood going into the fourth quarter.

Like most players on this day, Pittsburgh's big fullback Franco Harris had his problems throughout the game. He was finally able to get enough footing to make his way around the left end for the game's first score. Harris' 25-yard scoring run was followed by Gerela's conversion, and the Steelers were up, 10–0. Harris finished with 79 yards on 27 carries to lead both teams.

It took the Raiders less than two minutes to get on the board following Harris' touchdown. Ken Stabler hit on three completions to tight end Dave Casper, and finished the drive with a 14-yard scoring strike to Mike Siani. Blanda's extra point cut the Pittsburgh advantage to 10–7.

The Steelers came right back after a hit by defensive end L.C. Greenwood caused Marv Hubbard to fumble. Middle linebacker Jack Lambert recovered on the Oakland 25 to give Pittsburgh excellent field position. Harris gained five yards on two carries, and then Terry Bradshaw, behind excellent protection, found John Stallworth, who had to jump high to get his hands on the ball, in the end zone from 20 yards out. On the extra point try, the snap was bad, and Gerela could not get a solid attempt off.

The Raiders closed to within six on a 41-yard field goal by George Blanda to make it a 16–10 game with 17 seconds left. This proved to be the final points of Blanda's long and incredible career. Marv Hubbard recovered John Stallworth's fumble on the onside kick following Blanda's field goal, and this gave the Raiders seven seconds to pull out a miracle. Stabler connected with Cliff Branch, but the receiver was dragged down on the Pittsburgh 15 as time expired on another Oakland Super Bowl dream. Even though the Raiders were coming up short of the Super Bowl, they appeared to be good luck charms for the teams that beat them in league or conference title games. The New York Jets (1968), Kansas City Chiefs (1969), Baltimore Colts (1970), Miami (1973), and Pittsburgh (1974-75), all went on to win the Super Bowl following their victory over the Raiders.[16]

Individual Statistics and Roster

Head Coach: John Madden
Assistant Coaches: Tom Dahms, Tom Flores, John Robinson, Joe Scannella, Don Shinnick, Ollie Spencer, Bob Zeman
1975 Regular Season Record: 11–3
1st Place AFC Western Division
Scored 375 points to rank 4t out of 26 teams
Allowed 255 points to rank 7th
Led the league in rushing attempts (643), rushing touchdowns (28), and defensive interceptions (35)

STARTERS — OFFENSE

QB — Ken Stabler: Active for 14 games, and started in 13. Completed 171 of 293 pass attempts for 2,296 yards 16 TD and 24 INT. Rushed for -5 yards on 6 carries.

HB — Clarence Davis: Active for 11 games, and started in 8. Rushed for 486 yards on 112 carries and 4 TD, had 11 receptions for 126 yards and 1 TD, and 9 kickoff returns for 268 yards.

FB — Mark van Eeghen: Active for 14 games, and started in 8. Rushed for 597 yards on 136 carries and 2 TD, had 12 receptions for 42 yards and 1 TD, and 7 kickoff returns for 112 yards.

WR — Fred Biletnikoff: Active for 11 games, and started in 10. Had 43 receptions for 587 yards and 2 TD.

WR — Cliff Branch: Started in 14 games. Had 51 receptions for 893 yards and 9 TD. Rushed for 18 yards on 2 carries.

TE — Bob Moore: Started in 14 games, and had 19 receptions for 175 yards.

LT — Art Shell: Started in 14 games.

LG — Gene Upshaw: Started in 14 games.

C — Dave Dalby: Started in 14 games.

RG — George Buehler: Started in 14 games.

RT — John Vella: Active for and started in 13 games.

RESERVE OFFENSIVE PLAYERS

Pete Banaszak (RB): Active for 14 games, rushed for 672 yards on 187 carries and 16 TD, had 10 receptions for 64 yards, and 2 kickoff returns for 24 yards.

Warren Bankston (RB/TE): Active for 14 games, had 2 receptions for 21 yards and 1 TD, and 1 kickoff return for 19 yards.

Morris Bradshaw (WR): Active for 14 games, rushed for -5 yards on 1 carry, and had 7 receptions for 180 yards and 4 TD.

Louis Carter (RB): Active for 8 games, rushed for 27 yards on 11 carries, had 2 receptions for 39 yards, and 1 kickoff return for 13 yards.

Dave Casper (TE): Active for 14 games, and had 5 receptions for 71 yards and 1 TD.

Harold Hart (RB): Active for 9 games, and started in 4. Rushed for 173 yards on 56 carries and 3 TD, had 6 receptions for 27 yards, and 17 kickoff returns for 518 yards and 1 TD.

Marv Hubbard (RB): Active for 7 games, and started in 6. Rushed for 294 yards on 60 carries and 2 TD, and had 7 receptions for 81 yards.

David Humm (QB): Active for 7 games. Completed 18 of 38 pass attempts for 246 yards, 3 TD, 2 INT, and rushed for 21 yards on 7 carries.

Ted Kwalick (TE): Active for 6 games.

Henry Lawrence (T/G): Active for 14 games, and started in 1.

Larry Lawrence (QB): Active for and started in 1 game. Completed 5 of 15 pass attempts for 50 yards and 1 INT. Rushed for -3 yards on 2 carries.

Dan Medlin (G): Active for 14 games.

Jess Phillips (RB/DB): Active for 14 games, and started in 2. Rushed for 298 yards on 63 carries and 1 TD, had 4 receptions for 25 yards, 2 punt returns for 0 yards, and 12 kickoff returns for 310 yards.

Mike Siani (WR): Active for 14 games, and started in 4. Had 17 receptions for 294 yards.

Steve Sylvester (C/G/T): Active for 11 games.

STARTERS — DEFENSE

DE — Tony Cline: Active for and started in 12 games, and had 1 fumble recovery.

DE — Horace Jones: Started in 14 games.

DT — Otis Sistrunk: Started in 14 games.

DT — Art Thoms: Active for 13 games, and started in 11. Had 1 INT and 1 fumble recovery.

LLB — Phil Villapiano: Active for 14 games, and started in 13. Had 2 INT and 2 fumble recoveries.

MLB — Monte Johnson: Active for 14 games, and started in 13. Had 1 INT.

RLB — Gerald Irons: Started in 14 games and had 1 INT.

CB — Skip Thomas: Started in 14 games and had 6 INT.

CB — Willie Brown: Active for and started in 12 games. Had 4 INT.

SS — George Atkinson: Started in 14 games, had 4 INT, 3 fumble recoveries, 8 punt returns for 33 yards, and 2 kickoff returns for 60 yards.

FS — Jack Tatum: Active for and started in 13 games. Had 4 INT.

RESERVE DEFENSIVE PLAYERS

Neal Colzie (DB): Active for 13 games, and started in 2. Had 4 INT, and 48 punt returns for 655 yards.

Mike Dennery (LB): Active for 14 games and recorded 1 safety.

Willie Hall (LB): Active for 7 games.

Ted Hendricks (LB): Active for 14 games, and started in 5. Had 2 INT and recorded 1 safety.

Kelvin Korver (T): Active for and started in 1 game.

Charlie Phillips (DB): Active for 14 games, and started in 1. Had 6 INT and 2 fumble recoveries.

Dave Rowe (T): Active for 10 games, and started in 1.

KICKING/PUNTING

K — George Blanda: Active for 14 games. Made 13 of 21 field goal attempts, and 44 of 48 extra point kicks for 83 points. Completed 1 of 3 pass attempts for 11 yards and 1 INT.

P — Ray Guy: Active for 14 games. Punted 68 times for a 43.8 average, and completed 1 pass in 1 attempt for 22 yards.

1976 Season Review

1. Sept. 12: The schedule makers were brilliant when they decided to open the 1976 campaign with a revival of the Pittsburgh-Oakland blood fest. Simply put, the Raiders and Steelers hated each other in the mid-to-late 70's. Their clashes were the most intense rivalry pro football offered at the time. Both teams were at the top of the pro football world, and usually their games against each other had championship implications attached to them. The hitting and hate was real, and the animosity gained momentum with each meeting. This game helped to add gasoline to an already burning inferno between these two teams. During the game, George Atkinson lived up to his "Hit Man" style of play when he blasted Pittsburgh's Lynn Swann with a blind-side clothes-line hit that knocked Swann unconscious. Pittsburgh head coach Chuck Noll then referred to Atkinson as part of a criminal element within the league. The hit and the attention it brought quickly made its way to NFL commissioner Pete Rozelle, who fined Atkinson $1,500. Within a few months, Atkinson sued Noll for slander with a cash amount of two million dollars attached to it. In July of 1977, the case went before a jury, and they eventually ruled in Noll's favor.

In the fourth quarter, the defending Super Bowl champion Steelers were in front, 21–7. The Raiders only score up to this time was a 30-yard pass from Ken Stabler to Dave Casper in the second quarter. Fred Biletnikoff then closed the gap to 21–14 when he made a diving catch of a 21-yard pass from Stabler. The Steelers came right back with a Franco Harris 6-yard run to make it 28–14 with six minutes left. At this point, Pittsburgh appeared to be in complete control in front of 52,718 Raiders fans. It became more apparent that the Steelers were going to put one in the win column after Stabler was intercepted, and Pittsburgh took over on the Oakland 19.

However, momentum took a turn in Oakland's direction, and resulted in a fantastic finish for the Silver and Black. On the next play, Harris fumbled and linebacker Monte Johnson recovered on the Oakland 25. Stabler quickly rebounded from his previous interception by taking the Raiders 75 yards in five plays that resulted in a touchdown. In this quick drive, Stabler hit on four passes that covered 72 yards, with the last one going to Casper for a 10-yard touchdown. Rookie Fred Steinfort's conversion brought Oakland to within seven points with three minutes remaining.

Warren Bankston was the next to play a pivotal role, as he partially blocked a punt, which Oakland recovered on the Pittsburgh 29 with 1:47 left. After three Stabler passes failed to advance the ball, the Raiders were facing a do-or-die fourth and ten situation. Stabler once again dropped back to pass, and managed to get away from Pittsburgh's fierce Mean Joe Greene. Still upright, the "Snake" found Cliff Branch at the 11, and the gifted speedster ran it down to the two with 1:09 to go. With extra blocking from three tight ends, Stabler ran a bootleg to the left. With a solid wall of protection in front of him, he scored with ease. Steinfort did not rattle, and his conversion split the uprights to tie the game at 28–28 with one minute showing on the clock.

On Pittsburgh's first play following the kickoff, quarterback Terry Bradshaw received heavy pressure from Oakland's defensive line. His pass was deflected by tackle Dave Rowe, and intercepted by linebacker Willie Hall. With fifty seconds left, the Raiders were on Pittsburgh's 12-yard line. Two carries by Pete Banaszak moved the ball eight yards. With 21 seconds to go, Steinfort kicked the winning field goal from 21 yards out to make it a 31–28 final. Even though Steinfort was a rookie, he got heavy exposure to pressure kicking early in the season and came through like a champion.

Also coming through for the Silver and Black was Ken Stabler, who threw for a career-high 342 yards on 21 of 38 attempts and three touchdowns. This was a great moral victory for the Raiders as well. After being snuffed out of the playoffs three of the previous four seasons by the Steelers, the Raiders rallied against their nemesis and looked to build on the momentum from one of the greatest victories in the history of the franchise.[1]

2. Sept. 20: Ken Stabler continued to work brilliantly against enemy defenses. This time he directed his Raiders to a 24–21 victory over Kansas City on Monday Night Football. Stabler was forced to leave the game in the fourth quarter with pulled ligaments in his knee, and the Raiders up, 24–7. Until the injury, the "Snake" hit on 22 of 28 pass attempts for 224 yards and threw touchdown strikes to Dave Casper (15 yards), Cliff Branch (10-yards), and Mike Siani (14 yards). Fred Steinfort added a 37-yard field goal in between Stabler's scoring strikes. The Chiefs rallied late, and came to within three points with 2:50 left to play. An onside kick failed, and Oakland ran out the clock.[2]

3. Sept. 26: With Ken Stabler resting his knee, Oakland's offense was turned over to Mike Rae, who was in his first NFL season after three years in the Canadian Football League. In a tight defensive battle, the Houston Oilers jumped out to a 6–0 first quarter lead. Rae then settled down, and threw two touch-

down passes to Cliff Branch (9 and 33 yards), which was all the Silver and Black needed in a 14–13 win.[3]

4. Oct. 3: A trip to Foxboro, Massachusetts, was next for the Raiders in a game against the red hot New England Patriots, who beat the Pittsburgh Steelers and Miami Dolphins on consecutive weekends. The Patriots did not seem impressed with the NFL's elite, and mauled the Raiders, 48–17. They never trailed in this game thanks to a stellar performance by quarterback Steve Grogan, and the running of Andy Johnson and Sam "the Bam" Cunningham. Grogan threw for three touchdowns, and ran for two more, while the backfield rolled up a then team record 296 rushing yards. Ironically, the Patriots old rushing record was also set against the Raiders ten years earlier. Oakland's points came on a Ken Stabler to Fred Biletnikoff 14-yard pass, a 1-yard run by Mike Rae, and a 44-yard field goal by Fred Steinfort.[4]

5. Oct. 10: The Raiders came into week five in a three-way tie for first place in the AFC West with San Diego and Denver. Oakland did their part to break up the jam with a 27–17 win over the Chargers. The Broncos also lost to give Oakland sole possession of first place. Despite a lot of injuries on defense, Ken Stabler and the offensive unit carried the load. The "Snake" was near perfect with 20 completions in 26 pass attempts for 339 yards and three touchdowns. Cliff Branch caught two of Stabler's touchdown passes from 74 and 41 yards, and led all receivers with 167 yards on just five receptions. Dave Casper also caught a touchdown pass (4 yards), and had seven receptions for 104 yards. Pete Banaszak ended the day's scoring with a 4-yard run.[5]

6. Oct. 17: The Raiders could only muster a 34-yard field goal from Fred Steinfort in the opening thirty minutes, and were down at the half, 10–3, to Denver. A 46-yard Ken Stabler to Cliff Branch touchdown connection tied the game in the third quarter, and then Pete Banaszak put Oakland out in front with a 1-yard run to make the final score 17–10. The defense held off a late Denver rally in the closing seconds, and the special teams came up big by containing the NFL's top kick returner, Rick Upchurch, throughout the entire game.[6]

7. Oct. 24: With Ken Stabler hitting on 11 of 14 first half pass attempts, the Raiders scored all their points in the second quarter in an 18–14 win over the Green Bay Packers. Stabler connected on three scoring passes to Dave Casper (27 yards), Cliff Branch (88 yards), and Fred Biletnikoff (10-yards). In a rare instance for the pros, all of Oakland's extra point attempts were missed. The offense began to sputter throughout the second half, as Stabler was only able to complete two of seven pass attempts. The Silver and Black managed to avert a late Green Bay rally thanks to a Skip "Doctor Death" Thomas interception. This win gave the Raiders a 6–1 record at mid-season, which placed them two games ahead of San Diego in the division.[7]

8. Oct. 31: The Raiders continued to have offensive woes against Denver. Through three quarters, the score was 6–6 on field goals by Denver's Jim Turner and Oakland's Errol Mann (23 and 36 yards). This game marked the Oakland debut of Mann, who was brought in to replace the injured Fred Steinfort. The Raiders defense kept Oakland in this game by pounding away at Denver quarterback Steve Ramsey and sacking him 10 times. Cliff Branch then ignited the offense by hooking up with Ken Stabler on two long receptions of 43 and 52 yards, and finished the game

with three receptions for 103 yards. Stabler later found Fred Bilet-nikoff for the go-ahead touchdown from 31 yards out. Clarence Davis added a 7-yard insurance touchdown run, and Oakland won, 19–6. The 7–1 Raiders now had a whopping three game division lead on second place Denver and San Diego.[8]

9. Nov. 7: Despite three sacks, windy conditions, and a woozy feeling, Ken Stabler carried on in a 28–27 come-from-behind victory over the Chicago Bears. On one of the sacks inflicted on him by the tough Chicago defense, Stabler hit his head hard on the turf. This occurred in the third quarter, and he spent the remainder of the game in a fog. Stabler completed 11 of 17 pass attempts for 234 yards and three touchdowns. The winning score came on Cliff Branch's second six-pointer of the game. His first was a 75-yarder in the second quarter. On the game winner that covered 49 yards with four minutes left to play, Branch caught the ball after it was tipped into his hands by a defender. Errol Mann's conversion then gave Oakland the lead. Branch finished the day with an incredible 163 receiving yards on only five catches. Dave Casper was on the receiving end of Stabler's other scoring toss (17 yards), and Clarence Davis supplied the ground forces with a 2-yard scoring run. The defense did its part by holding the NFL's top runner, Walter Payton, to 97 yards despite a team record 36 carries. Even though Payton led all ball carriers and scored three touchdowns, holding him to under 100 yards after all those carries proved to be a monumental achievement by the rough and tumble Raiders defense.[9]

10. Nov. 14: In a 21–10 win over Kansas City, Fred Biletnikoff and Dave Casper each caught a touchdown pass from Ken Stabler to give him a league-leading 20 scoring strikes. Biletnikoff hauled in a 32-yarder, and Casper's covered 22 yards. Oakland's other touchdown came on a 1-yard run by Pete Banaszak. Despite Stabler's key passes for scores, the Raiders relied on a tough running game that produced 211 yards on 40 carries, with Mark van Eeghen's 95 yards leading the way.[10]

11. Nov. 21: The Raiders became the first team of the season to reach ten wins, and they also clinched a playoff spot with a 26–7 win over the Philadelphia Eagles. Running back Mark van Eeghen stood out in Oakland's lopsided win by rushing for 133 yards that included a 1-yard touchdown. Fred Biletnikoff caught a 16-yard touchdown pass from Ken Stabler, and Clarence Davis ran one in from eight yards out for the other touchdowns. A 32-yard Errol Mann field goal and a safety rounded out Oakland's scoring. Ted Hendricks was responsible for the safety when he blocked a punt in the end zone.[11]

12. Nov. 28: Three things that could be counted on for the most part in the late 60's and 70's were death, taxes, and a division title for the Oakland Raiders. For the eighth time in nine seasons, the Silver and Black wrapped up another Western Division championship. This time the clincher came with their biggest margin of victory during the season, which was a 49–16 blowout over the expansion and winless Tampa Bay Buccaneers. Ken Stabler threw for 245 yards and two touchdowns on 15 out of 23 attempts. Warren Bankston (9 yards) and Cliff Branch (25 yards) were on the receiving end of Stabler's scoring aerials. Mark van Eeghen added two short yardage touchdown runs, each from one yard out, Pete Banaszak a 2-yarder, and Carl Garrett a 1-yard burst. Mike Siani closed out the scoring by catching a 37-yard strike from Mike Rae.[12]

13. Dec. 6: The Raiders clinched home field advantage throughout the AFC playoffs with a 35–20 win over Cincinnati on a Monday Night Football telecast. Ken Stabler was near perfect, connecting on 16 out of 20 pass attempts for 217 yards and four touchdowns. Dave Casper caught two of the "Snake's" touchdown tosses from 24 and three yards out, while Cliff Branch (42 yards) and Fred Biletnikoff (7 yards) scored the others. For the game, Branch had six receptions for 112 yards. Pete Banaszak got Oakland's other touchdown on a 1-yard run. It seemed to appear that the Oakland offense was firmly back on track and hitting their peak at the right time.[13]

14. Dec. 12: Since 1968, the San Diego Chargers were unable to beat the Raiders. That streak remained intact thanks to a 24–0 romp in their season finale. Their 13 wins allowed them to tie the '67 Raiders for the most regular season wins in team history. Head coach John Madden rested some of his starters in preparation for the playoffs, but the Silver and Black still dominated. Mike Rae played in place of Ken Stabler, and produced three touchdown passes to Cliff Branch (5 yards), Dave Casper (6 yards), and Morris Bradshaw (25 yards). An Errol Mann field goal from 42 yards gave the Raiders their other points. Mark van Eeghen, one of the starters who did not rest up, became the third running back in team history to break the 1,000-yard barrier. His 95 yards in this game gave him 1,012 for the season.[14]

AFC Divisional Playoff Game, December 18, 1976

With the offense jelling, and the defense pounding away, the Raiders came into the playoffs hitting on all cylinders. The only blemish on the '76 Raiders was their lone loss to the New England Patriots. Now, two months after that one-sided defeat, they were ready for their first post-season hurdle.

In Oakland's race to the Super Bowl would be the 11–3 Patriots. New England came out to Oakland for their first playoff appearance in 13 years, and like the Raiders, they were clicking very well, riding on the heels of a six-game winning streak.

The Patriots showed that they were not going to be intimidated by the playoff-veteran Raiders by taking an early lead. In the first quarter, quarterback Steve Grogan took the Patriots 86 yards, with the big play coming on a pass to tight end Russ Francis, who made a great one-handed catch that picked up 40 yards. Running back Andy Johnson ended the drive successfully with a 1-yard run. John Smith added the extra point, and the Patriots were in control, 7–0. Late in the quarter, Errol Mann kicked a 40-yard field goal to end the first fifteen minutes with Oakland trailing, 7–3.

That score stayed the same until the final minute of the first half. Fred Biletnikoff was locked in a struggle against cornerback Bob Howard in the end zone. Ken Stabler knew that his great receiver could more likely than not make something happen regardless. For this reason, the "Snake" let the ball go in Biletnikoff's direction. Stabler's assessment of the situation proved to be correct, as Biletnikoff leaped for, and hauled in a beautiful one-handed grab from 31 yards out with 39 seconds left in the half. For the game, Biletnikoff caught nine passes for 137 yards. Mann's extra point extended Oakland's halftime advantage to 10–7.

Things started to look bleak for the Silver and Black throughout the third quarter. New England came back to take a 21–10 lead going into the final fifteen minutes, and possibly the final quarter of play for the Raiders this season. With the help of two Oakland penalties assessed on fourth down punts, the Patriots completed scoring drive of 80 and 55 yards with Russ Francis catching a 26-yard pass from Grogan, and former Raider Jess Phillips running for a 3-yarder. Smith added both extra points, and the Raiders had some serious catching up to do in the fourth quarter.

Oakland closed the gap with four minutes expired in the final stanza by going 70 yards to paydirt. On the drive, Stabler connected with Biletnikoff on two passes totaling 38 yards. Full-back Mark van Eeghen then punched it over for a 1-yard touchdown, and with Mann's conversion, Oakland was within four points of the lead, trailing, 21–17.

The Patriots were looking to put the Raiders away, and got to the Oakland 38 with five minutes remaining. On third-and-one, an offside penalty moved the Patriots back, and the drive stalled when a Grogan pass fell incomplete. Smith attempted a 50-yard field goal, but it missed the mark.

With time running out, Stabler began a drive from the Oakland 32. With the clock down to 52 seconds left, Stabler threw an incomplete pass on third-and-21. However, a penalty flag hit the ground immediately. Middle guard Ray Hamilton hit Stabler after he released the ball, and a roughing the passer call was given. Oakland now had the ball on the New England 13. Stabler threw to Dave Casper for five yards on first down, and then runs by Clarence Davis and Pete Banaszak got the ball down to the 1-yard line. On the following play, Stabler rolled out to his left and dove into the end zone with 10 seconds left for the winning touchdown. Mann added the final point of the game, and Oakland pulled out a 24–21 heart pounding victory that earned them their fourth straight trip to the AFC Championship Game.[15]

AFC Championship Game, December 26, 1976

For the third consecutive time, the Pittsburgh Steelers stood between the Raiders and a much-sought after Super Bowl berth. The Steelers started the defense of their second straight Super Bowl title by winning only one of their first five games. The season looked to be on the verge of total collapse, but the Steelers proved that they were still a force to be reckoned with. They ran off nine straight wins to finish at 10–4, which was good enough to win another AFC Central Division title, and then made it ten in a row by defeating the Baltimore Colts, 40–14, in their divisional playoff encounter.

Despite their great winning streak, the Steelers came into the AFC Championship Game matchup extremely banged up. Kicker Roy Gerela suffered from a groin pull, and both starting running backs were sidelined and would not play against the Raiders. Franco Harris and Rocky Bleier both ran for over 1,000 yards during the regular season, but were now only spectators, as Bleier was out with a sprained toe and Harris bruised ribs.

By kickoff, a 52 degree day with hazy skies greeted 53,739 Raiders fans in the Oakland Coliseum hoping to see their beloved Silver and Black finally break through the AFC Championship Game barrier that plagued them so many times before. Hubie Ginn did his part to help Oakland by deflecting a Bobby Walden punt in the first quarter that led to a 39-yard field goal by Errol Mann to give the Raiders a 3–0 lead at the end of the opening quarter.

Linebacker Willie Hall was next to assist his fellow Raiders by picking off a Terry Bradshaw pass intended for John "Frenchy" Fuqua. The ball bounced off Fuqua's extended hands and into Hall's at the Pittsburgh 23, and he returned it to the 1-yard line. After Mark van Eeghen and Pete Banaszak could not punch it in for six, Clarence Davis accomplished the task, and with Mann's extra point, the Raiders were up 10–0.

With less than six minutes to get before the half, the Steelers mounted a serious drive. Bradshaw finally got settled in after missing on his first six pass attempts by connecting with Frank Lewis for 11 yards on the Pittsburgh 41. He then found John Stallworth on the Oakland 37, and a completion to Lynn Swann added thirty more yards. A facemask penalty against Phil Villapiano got the ball closer, and Reggie Harrison finished off the drive with a 3-yard run. Center Ray Mansfield was called in to handle the kicking chores with Gerela hurting, and he was good on the extra point attempt to close to within three of the Raiders.

The Raiders were not looking to let Pittsburgh get back into this game. Ken Stabler and the offense put together a 13-play, 69-yard drive that extended the Oakland lead to 17–7 at the half. The "Snake" began this scoring jaunt with an 8-yard pass to Cliff Branch. Clarence Davis followed with a run that netted 16 more. A crucial holding penalty on third-and-goal against defensive back J.T. Thomas gave the Raiders a first down on the Pittsburgh 4. Stabler then connected with a wide-open Warren Bankston in the end zone for Oakland's second touchdown of the game, and Mann added the conversion to once again make it a ten-point bulge in favor of the Silver and Black with 19 seconds left before the half.

The Raiders finally had the Steelers on the ropes with a Super Bowl berth only thirty minutes away, and wanted to deliver the knockout blow as soon as possible. In the third quarter, Stabler and Branch teamed up for a 28-yard pickup that got the ball to the Pittsburgh 33. On the big gainer, Stabler saw the Steelers were going to come at him with a safety blitz, and seized the opportunity of catching the secondary one man short. The accurate arm of Stabler coupled with the speed and talent of Branch left no doubt that the result would be a success. After three plays failed following that, Stabler connected with tight end Warren Bankston on fourth down for a gain of seven. Five plays later, Stabler and company were nestled on the Pittsburgh five and looking to put the Steel City's defending champions one step closer to being called ex-champions. Stabler dropped back as Pete Banaszak went toward the left side of the field, got past linebacker Andy Russell, and was headed for the end zone. The "Snake" zeroed in on his long-time teammate, let the ball go, and allowed Banaszak's hands to do the rest. The merger between Banaszak and the pigskin was a success, and the Raiders were up, 24–7, after Mann's extra point. On the play, Stabler took one for the team, as linebacker Jack Ham drilled him with a blindside hit that bruised his ribs and sent a cap off his tooth flying onto the Coliseum turf. The injury hampered Stabler after that, and he was taken out of the game in favor of Mike Rae. At this stage, the Raiders knew they were closing in on the Super Bowl and did not want to risk Stabler aggravating his injured area any more than it already was.

With fifteen minutes left, the Raiders turned the game over to the defense, and that unit stopped the Steelers every time. With his backfield depleted, quarterback Terry Bradshaw had to go to the air repeatedly, which made Pittsburgh one-dimensional and highly predictable. Oakland simply waited for the snap, and reacted quickly and efficiently to dispose of any threat Bradshaw had in mind. The Oakland offense just looked to play it safe without Stabler at the helm, and Rae just handed the ball off without once throwing a pass to eat up the remaining time on the clock.

As the game clock ticked closer to 0:00, the reality became abundantly clear to everyone within the Raiders organization, the 53,739 in attendance, and the television viewers across the American landscape. After nine years of being on the doorstep of the Super Bowl, they were finally going back to the big dance. With the sweet smell of victory hovering all around Raider Nation, an interesting footnote occurred. For the Raiders became the only team in history to end two opponents' hopes of playing for a third Super Bowl title. They ended Miami's two-year run in 1974, and now they sent the Steelers home in '76. It was now time for the Silver and Black to make their mark on the Holy Grail of the American sports scene, and they would be more than ready to seize the moment after so many failed rehearsals.[16]

Super Bowl XI

Jan. 9, 1977; Played at the Rose Bowl in Pasadena, California

The Raiders had finally broken through and reached pro football's ultimate showdown after nine seasons of heartbreaking near misses. So as game day grew near, the Silver and Black were involved in an intense contest of softball with a rolled up wad of adhesive tape on the same field they would be playing on the following day. Some might look at this display as a team not focused, while those close to the pulse of this incredible collections of renegades saw it as being ready after hard work at practice and film studies, extremely prepared, loose, and confident, that the task at hand would just be a sixty minute formality that at its end, would crown them supreme rulers over all comers throughout America's bicentennial year.

Oakland's opponents for the eleventh edition of Super Sunday were the Minnesota Vikings, who like the Raiders, were plagued by much heartache in post-season encounters. This proved to be Minnesota's fourth trip to the Super Bowl in eight seasons, and third in the last four. Each of their previous visits to the big show ended in disaster, with the Vikings totally outclassed and demoralized. However, like an aging pugilist refusing to stay down on the canvas after a beating, the Vikings returned on January 9, 1977, in an attempt to finally be called champions.

The 1976 Minnesota Vikings were an aging team with many key personnel well into their thirties, and were all veterans of the team's past failures in the Super Bowl. They banded together to dispel all the talk of them being over-the-hill by winning the NFC Central Division for the eighth time in nine years with an 11-2-1 record. One month shy of his 37th birthday, Pro Bowl quarterback Fran Tarkenton led a good offensive attack that scored a league-ranked ninth place with 305 points. Tarkenton helped Minnesota rank fourth overall in passing yards with 2,961 through the air, threw 17 touchdown passes against only eight interceptions for a 61.9 percent completion rate. Helping to make Minnesota a well-balanced offensive machine was fourth-year pro running back Chuck Foreman. Foreman was a multi-threat back who could run and catch with the best of them. He finished with 1,155 rushing yards and 13 six-pointers. He also added a team-leading 55 receptions for 567 yards and one touchdown to his illustrious pro resume. Veteran Ahmad Rashad and rookie sensation Sammie White led the wide receivers with 104 catches between them. Rashad caught 53 for 671 yards and three touchdowns, while White hauled in 51, and led the league in receiving yards (906) and touchdowns (10).[17]

Over on the defensive side of things, the Vikings and their feared and highly respected "Purple People Eaters" ate up opposing ball carriers and quarterbacks for many years together, spitting out the battered carcasses at a steady pace. This season was no exception, as the aged by still highly effective unit led the NFC in fewest points allowed with 176, and posted an overall league ranking of second in that category. They led the league in fewest yards allowed passing and for touchdowns through the air.

Mother Nature decided to be kind to the football world on Super Sunday, as the temperature in beautiful California was 74 degrees and sunny as the 3:30 EST/12:30 PST kickoff approached with 103,438 in attendance. Sitting high atop the Rose Bowl to call the action to millions of television viewers on the NBC network were one of the medium's most highly-respected play-by-play announcers of all time, Curt Gowdy, and former Dallas Cowboys quarterback and colorful color commentator, Jeff and Hazel's baby boy himself, Dandy Don Meredith. There was no singing of the National anthem prior to kickoff. Instead, recording artist Vikki Carr sang "America the Beautiful." Jim Tunney was the referee, and his officiating crew was made up of umpire Lou Palazzi, head linesman Ed Marion, line judge Bill Swanson, field judge Armen Terzian, and back judge Tom Kelleher. Tunney met with team captains for the coin toss, and the Raiders made their first successful decision by winning the toss. They elected to receive the opening kickoff, and all that stood in the way of the Silver and Black hoisting the Lombardi Trophy were sixty minutes of controlled violence staged against their adversaries from The North Star State.[18]

Kicker Fred Cox led the Minnesota special teams unit onto the field and placed the ball on the tee while Oakland's white-jerseyed Raiders awaited his boot to officially begin Super Bowl XI. Cox's right foot met the ball and sent it airborne into the California sky. It came down seconds later into the awaiting arms of Carl Garrett on the Oakland 11, and was returned 23 yards to give the Raiders good field position to begin this championship affair.

Ken Stabler led the offense onto the field with at least three plays in mind for the opening series. By the time he entered the huddle, Stabler decided on a simple, straight ahead running play to get the first contact out of the way. Stabler sent Clarence Davis off left tackle for a gain of one, and followed that with a call for Mark van Eeghen off the same spot that picked up four yards. On third down, the Vikings brought in an extra defensive back in anticipation of a pass play. Once Stabler saw this, he knew that his All-Pro tight end Dave Casper would be covered by linebacker Matt Blair in man-to-man coverage while the extra defensive back would be busy watching for speedster Cliff Branch and the crafty Fred Biletnikoff. Stabler took advantage of Blair covering Casper in a mismatch, and hit the tight end for a gain of 25 yards that got the ball into Minnesota territory at the 38. Stabler returned to the running attack, as Davis picked up four yards on first down. The "Snake" then decided to run Davis behind the great wall of protection to the left created by Gene Upshaw, Art Shell, and Dave Casper. Shell and Casper took out Minnesota's stellar defensive end Jim Marshall, van Eeghen led Davis through the hole, keying on any linebacker that came up, and right guard George Buehler pulled in front of Davis to pick up any other opposition. The result was a great gain of 20 yards that got the Raiders to the Minnesota 12. The Vikings then stiffened. Carl Garrett was dropped for a loss of one, and a pass intended for Casper fell incomplete to bring up third-and-11. With everyone across the world expecting a pass, Stabler went for the opposite in an attempt to catch Minnesota off guard. It did not work, as Pete Banaszak was stopped after gaining two yards off the left side by Wally Hilgenberg to bring up fourth down. Errol Mann came on to attempt what looked to be a chip shot field goal attempt from 29 yards out, but his kick went wide to keep the game scoreless with just under 12 minutes left in the opening quarter.[19]

The Oakland defense made quick work of the Minnesota offense on their first possession. The main offensive weapon for the Vikings, Chuck Foreman, was the focal point in Minnesota's first attempt at moving the ball on this Super Sunday. Fran Tarkenton started things off with a five-yard pass to Foreman, which was followed by the multi-threat running back gaining one yard up the middle. Tarkenton went back to the air on third down, but a pass intended for Foreman fell incomplete with George "Hitman" Atkinson on the coverage. Neil Clabo sent a 46-yard punt to Neal Colzie, who returned it six yards to the Oakland 19.

Stabler went the conservative route on Oakland's next possession. Three straight running plays gained 12 yards, with Davis getting four, van Eeghen five, and Banaszak three. With a new set of downs, Stabler went to the air, and connected with the legendary Fred Biletnikoff for the first time for a gain of nine yards. Banaszak was then stopped for no gain in an attempt to pick up a first down, and Davis then lost a yard on third down. Ray Guy came on to punt the Raiders out of trouble by getting off a whopping 51-yard boot that Leonard Willis returned six yards before Hubie Ginn brought him down at the Minnesota 16.

For the fourth straight offensive play, the Vikings went to Foreman, who caught a 16-yard pass from Tarkenton on first down. Minnesota only was able to muster three more yards on this drive, thanks to tackles made by Phil Villapiano on Brent McClanahan after a gain of two, and on Foreman after a 1-yard pickup. Clabo got off a 39-yard punt that Colzie did not return.

From the Oakland 26, Stabler sent van Eeghen up the middle on a carry that gained three yards. A pass attempt to Biletnikoff fell incomplete, and Davis was stopped after a gain of five yards off the left side in an attempt to pick up a first down. Guy came on for the second time to punt on fourth-and-two from the Oakland 34. At the snap, Minnesota's Fred McNeill jumped to the outside of the man set to block him. This allowed him a clear

trek to Guy from the left side. He then had the honor of becoming the first player to ever block a Ray Guy punt in the pro ranks. The ball shot up into the air, landed on the Oakland seven as Bobby Bryant attempted to get his hands on it. McNeill then came on the scene and pounced on the ball at the 3-yard line. After the past few possessions by both teams feeling out the other, the Vikings now had a golden opportunity to draw first blood and establish a huge amount of momentum with 5:02 left in the opening stanza.[20]

Who else but Chuck Foreman would the Vikings call on in this situation? He got the call on first down, but was stopped by nose tackle Charles Philyaw after a gain of one. Tarkenton decided to give McClanahan an opportunity to score a Super Bowl six-pointer on the next play, and as the running back looked for a crack of daylight up the middle, he was hit by Phil Villapiano and the ball popped out on the 3-yard line and was recovered by Willie Hall to get the Raiders out of a major jam.

Stabler looked to capitalize on this twist of fate. Pinned deep in his own territory, he decided to play it conservative with two straight runs by Banaszak that gained three yards. On third-and-seven, Stabler stayed on the ground, but this time it paid off with huge dividends. The Raiders were establishing their dominance of Minnesota's right side, consisting of greats Jim Marshall, Alan Page, and Wally Hilgenberg, and Stabler seized the chance to take advantage of this.

Gene Upshaw, Art Shell, and Dave Casper, were such a powerful blocking trio that virtually no one could pierce their wall of flesh. On this day, they played even above their own expectations if at all possible. With Upshaw pushing Page to the inside, Shell shoving Marshall to the outside, Casper taking on whoever got in his path, and van Eeghen wiping out Hilgenberg as he came up to fill the hole, Clarence Davis was able to roam free through eleven purple-clad defenders almost at will. On third down from the Oakland seven, Davis took Stabler's handoff, swept to the left side, and took off on a 35-yard run. On the day, Davis ran for 137 yards, with 105 of those yards coming on different variations of the that play run behind Upshaw, Shell, and Casper, and with van Eeghen leading him out of the backfield. During the season, van Eeghen was the go-to runner in Oakland's attack, but on this day, he was used primarily for his blocking expertise.

With a new set of downs and major breathing room from the Oakland 41, Stabler went to the air. He connected with Carl Garrett for 11 to get the Raiders into Minnesota territory at the 48. A deep pass to Biletnikoff was incomplete, but Stabler followed that with a 25-yard hookup to Casper on the Minnesota 23. Stabler sent van Eeghen off left tackle for a gain of five, and Davis up the middle for four more. On the final play of the first quarter, Banaszak moved the chains with a 6-yard run off left tackle that allowed the Raiders the chance to start the second quarter with a first-and-goal from the Minnesota eight. Banaszak began the next fifteen minutes with a run off left tackle that picked up one. Two incomplete passes from Stabler intended for Casper brought up fourth down. Errol Mann then redeemed himself from an earlier miss by connecting on a 24-yard field goal that completed a 12-play, 90-yard drive that took 5:23 off the clock and gave the Raiders a 3–0 lead.[21]

Ray Guy kicked off to Leonard Willis, who received the ball on the Minnesota eight and advanced it 18 yards before Floyd

Rice brought him down. The Raiders defense once again made quick work of the Vikings. A Tarkenton pass attempt to Sammy White went incomplete, and two runs by Foreman gained a total of six yards before Clabo punted the ball away on fourth down. His 32-yard kick was downed on the Oakland 36 to give possession back to the Silver and Black.

Stabler now looked to open the offense up in an attempt to cool down his always emotional head coach John Madden, who was upset by the fact that the Raiders should have been up by at least a 14–0 count instead of just a mere three points. A pass to Cliff Branch gained eight on first down. Mark van Eeghen quickly gave the Raiders a new set of downs with a gain of three up the middle, and Davis scampered for six more around the right end. Stabler then hit Branch on a 2-yard pass and Casper for 19 and another first down. Stabler returned to the ground attack, with Carl Garrett getting the call on three straight plays. He ran to the left for 13, up the middle for four, and to the right for three. On third-and-three from the Minnesota six, Stabler surprised the Vikings with a perfect sideline pass to Biletnikoff for a gain of five that got the ball to the one. Once again geared up to stop a running surge into the end zone, the Vikings were fooled when Stabler rolled to his left and hit a wide-open Dave Casper in the end zone for the game's first touchdown. Casper's 1-yard scoring grab climaxed a 10-play, 64-yard drive, and following Mann's extra point, the Raiders were up, 10–0, with 7:10 left in the first half.[22]

Guy's ensuing kickoff was received by Willis on the Minnesota five and returned 20 yards before Herb McMath stopped him. Foreman got the call to open the series, and ran for seven yards off right tackle. He picked up six yards on the following play, but fumbled after Monte Johnson hit him. The ball was recovered by teammate Sammy White, but a holding penalty on offensive tackle Ron Yary took the Vikings back 10 yards. Two incomplete pass attempts brought up fourth down, and Clabo punted away to Colzie, who returned the ball 25 yards to give the Oakland offense great field position at the Minnesota 35.

This possession began with Davis gaining five yards up the middle. A 3-yard run by van Eeghen off left tackle was followed by another run from the talented fullback. This time van Eeghen powered his way up the middle for a gain of nine and a first down at the Minnesota 18. When the Raiders came back to the huddle to plan their continued onslaught over the helpless Vikings, Stabler looked to call a pass play. He turned to Biletnikoff, and the crafty old veteran stated that he wanted a pass down the middle. The "Snake" obliged his future Hall of Fame teammate by calling "Far 99 Right, Post, 10 Flat." At the snap, Biletnikoff came off the line, bolted up the middle, and headed toward the end zone. Minnesota safety Nate Wright was right behind Biletnikoff, so Stabler decided to throw the ball where only his man could get to it. Biletnikoff resembled a baseball player sliding into a base as he made a great catch of a perfect pass at the one while defensive back Jeff Wright sailed over the top of him and with Nate Wright right on him. With the Raiders in a power formation, Banaszak took Stabler's handoff and ran behind a George Buehler block off the right side of the line to finish off his 1-yard plunge. The five-play, 35-yard drive took 2:20 off the clock, and despite Mann's miss on the extra point try, the Raiders were in total command of this Super Bowl with a 16–0 lead with 3:33 to go in the half.[23]

Guy's kickoff went to Willis on the Minnesota six, and was returned 19 yards before McMath brought him down. The Vikings were still attempting to get Foreman going despite Oakland completely shutting him down for the most part. On first down, Tarkenton connected with him on a 5-yard pass, and two straight running plays by Foreman gained 10 yards. Another 5-yard connection from Tarkenton to Foreman was nullified when the Raiders were penalized for holding and the Vikings received an automatic first down on their own 45. Tarkenton then connected with Ahmad Rashad for a gain of seven. Tarkenton tried to go to the talented rookie Sammy White on the next two plays, but Jack Tatum and Skip Thomas were right on the receiver to thwart any opportunity of catching the ball. On fourth down, Clabo's punt sailed 42 yards and was downed at the Oakland six with 1:42 remaining in the half.

Mark van Eeghen opening this Oakland possession with a gain of 11 yards up the middle. He then ran for two to the left side, and tried again on another run up the gut, but this time without any success, as Alan Page dropped him for no gain. On third-and-eight, Davis swept the left side for three yards, and Guy came in on fourth down. His punt sailed 41 yards to Willis, who did not a chance to advance the ball due to Floyd Rice beginning right on him when he touched the pigskin. To make matters worse for Minnesota, they were called for a clipping penalty that took them back to their own 22.

With seven seconds left in half, Foreman finally got the opportunity to showcase his talents. He caught a pass from Tarkenton as his back was turned toward the Oakland defense. After turning around, he shifted his feet from side to side and spun around to avoid Willie Hall. He got by Ted Hendricks and Phil Villapiano before Tatum and Monte Johnson finally stopped him after he gained 26 yards.

As the teams went to the locker room for the halftime festivities, the Raiders were totally dominating the Vikings. They took away Minnesota's running game by shutting down Foreman most of the time with a swarming defense, and their most dangerous receiver, Sammy White, was held without a catch thanks to great coverage by Skip "Dr. Death" Thomas. The Oakland offensive line was overpowering the Minnesota defense, Clarence Davis was running at will, and Fred Biletnikoff was able to come up with big catches to help set up his teammates.

The second half got underway with Ray Guy kicking off to Sammy White on the Minnesota 8. The rookie sensation returned the ball 15 yards before Morris Bradshaw tackled him. Starting the new half from the Minnesota 23, Foreman ran for three yards up the middle. Tarkenton was still looking to connect with his top receiver, but a second down pass attempt to White was broken up by Skip Thomas. The Vikings managed to show some signs of life when Tarkenton found running back Robert Miller with a pass that gained 13 yards. After that it was business as usual for the Raiders defense, as they first stopped White after a gain of seven on a reverse, held Miller to one yard, and then ended Minnesota's possession when Villapiano broke up a pass intended for Miller on third-and-two. Clabo's punt on fourth down was downed on the Oakland 16. It was very apparent that the halftime intermission did nothing to slow the Raiders' dominance on their quest for football's grandest prize.

Stabler opened Oakland's first possession of the second half by throwing to Branch, but the pass was broken up by Bobby Bryant. Mark van Eeghen carried up the middle for six yards, and Davis picked up a first down on a draw play up the middle that gained 13. The Vikings held Oakland to eight yards on the next three plays to force a punt. A 7-yard run by van Eeghen was followed by two gains of one yard apiece off left tackle by Davis and Banaszak. Guy came on and got off a 38-yard punt on fourth-and-one that Willis returned eight yards to the Oakland 44.

Three straight runs off right tackle by Foreman generated nine yards, and the Vikings were once again forced to punt. Clabo's 31-yard kick was returned 12 yards by Colzie to the Minnesota 35.

A 7-yard run by van Eeghen off right tackle started Oakland's next series. Davis attacked the Vikings with an 18-yard pickup to give the Raiders a first down on the Minnesota 29. The Raiders hit a few snags when van Eeghen was dropped for a loss of four yards, and a Stabler to Biletnikoff pass in the end zone fell incomplete. Stabler got Oakland 10 yards closer with a pass to Branch before Mann was called upon on fourth-and-four. Mann added three more points to Oakland's total with a 40-yard field goal that capped the five-play, 31-yard drive, and gave the Raiders a 19–0 lead with 5:16 remaining in the third quarter.

Guy's kickoff went to White on the Minnesota six, and was returned 26 yards before Carl Garrett ended the rookie's jaunt on the 32. The only chance Minnesota now had at this juncture was Tarkenton's right arm. With time obviously not on their side, the Vikings needed three touchdowns quickly. With his running game still being stuffed, Tarkenton and the Minnesota offense had to throw on virtually every down. The Raiders knew this and looked to tee off on the veteran signal caller and his receivers. Skip Thomas broke up his first pass attempt intended for Foreman. Dave Rowe swatted away Tarkenton's next throw, and Otis Sistrunk did his part by hitting the quarterback as he threw on third down. The pass fell incomplete and Clabo was back on the field to return possession back over to the Raiders.

Clabo's punt travelled 37 yards and out of bounds. However, Ted Hendricks was penalized for roughing the kicker, and the Vikings were awarded five yards and an automatic first down on their own 37. With a second chance to salvage this drive, Foreman ran for one yard before Tarkenton connected for 15 to tight end Stu Voight. After being sacked for a loss of four by Villapiano, Tarkenton completed a pass to Foreman that gained three yards. The Raiders were called for holding on the play, and the infraction gave Minnesota five yards and an automatic first down on the Oakland 47. Tarkenton and Rashad hooked up on a 21-yard pass and catch, and Foreman ran up the middle for four more. A pass to White in the end zone fell incomplete before Foreman ran for three off left tackle and caught a swing pass for ten more yards. From the Oakland eight, Tarkenton looked to Sammy White in the end zone, and the rookie finally snagged his first reception of the day to complete the 12-play, 68-yard drive with 47 seconds left in the third quarter. Fred Cox added the extra point, and Oakland's lead was cut to 19–7.

Cox kicked off to Carl Garrett, and he advanced the ball 24 yards before being stopped by Miller on the Oakland 38. The Vikings seemed inspired by their recent touchdown, and came to life, as Alan Page broke through Oakland's incredible offensive line and sacked Stabler for a loss of 11. This was the first time all game that Stabler lost yardage. A 3-yard run off left tackle by van Eeghen got the ball to the 30 as the third quarter went into the record books. Davis churned out 16 yards around the left end, but still fell two yards shy of a first down. Guy came on and got off a 32-yard punt that was downed at the Minnesota 22.

Skip Thomas was the main man of the Oakland defense on three of Minnesota's first four plays of their next possession. He broke up a pass intended for Miller across the middle, and after Miller ran for three yards, Thomas tackled White after a 14-yard pickup on a pass from Tarkenton. "Dr. Death" then nailed Miller for a loss of two yards on the following play. Sammy Johnson ran for one yard up the middle, and Tarkenton went looking for White on third-and-11. White went across the middle and caught Tarkenton's pass at the Oakland 44. After the catch, White was destroyed by a Jack Tatum hit. The "Assassin" blasted White with a ferocious blow to the head that knocked the receiver's helmet off and sent him straight to the ground. It was a bone-jarring blast that left White dazed. However, despite the incredible hit, White somehow managed to hold onto the ball. With four linebackers and just as many defensive backs, the Oakland defense brutalized Minnesota receivers throughout the game. Tatum's hit was just the crown jewel of all the punishment dished out by a secondary consisting of "the Assassin," "Hitman," "Dr. Death," and Willie Brown. After the severe blow to White, Tarkenton returned to the air, and found Stu Voight for a gain of nine. Foreman tried to run on second down, but just like throughout this game, he could not get off on a good run from scrimmage. This time he was dropped for a loss of two by Monte Johnson. On third-and-three from the Oakland 37, Tarkenton was pressured out of the pocket by Ted Hendricks. He scrambled to his left to avoid Hendricks' hot pursuit, looking for any receiver in the open. With Hendricks coming in fast from his right, and Dave Pear rushing toward him head on, Tarkenton unleashed the ball in the direction of Foreman at the Oakland 30. Willie Hall read the play, intercepted the pass, and returned it 16 yards to the Oakland 46.

The Raiders were now in a position to play the game one of two ways. They could either play it conservatively and run time off the clock, or they could attack and leave the Vikings totally demoralized. They chose the latter. From their own 46, van Eeghen gained a yard up the middle, and Davis picked up three off the left side. It was now time to go for Minnesota's jugular vein. Stabler called a deep pattern to Biletnikoff, who caught the ball without anyone covering him. The blown coverage allowed the Raiders' legend to run 48 yards down to the 2-yard line before Bryant caught him and dragged him down. On the next play, Banaszak powered over right tackle for his second touchdown of the game. Banaszak's six-pointer was the unofficial end to the game even though there was still 7:39 remaining to be played. Banaszak took the ball he crossed the goal line with and heaved it into the stands in celebration. The quick four-play, 54-yard drive was topped off by Mann's extra point, which gave the Raiders an insurmountable 26–7 advantage.

Guy's kickoff was received by White on the Minnesota 13 and returned 19 yards. Tarkenton went to the air on every play during this drive, and it proved costly. A swing pass to Miller started things off with a pickup of three. A sideline pass intended for Foreman fell incomplete. He then connected with Voight for

"The Assassin" strikes again. Jack Tatum delivers what was a typical bone-jarring hit on receiver Sammy White of the Minnesota Vikings in Oakland's 32–14 victory in Super Bowl XI, January 9, 1977, held at the Rose Bowl in Pasadena, California. Also shown are Skip "Dr. Death" Thomas (#26) and George "Hitman" Atkinson (#43) (AP Photo/Richard Drew).

12 yards before his next pass was batted down by Dave Rowe. Tarkenton's final completion of the game came on the next play and covered 25 yards to Rashad. On first down from the Oakland 28, Tarkenton looked to his left, and fired a pass toward White. Willie Brown read the play perfectly, intercepted the ball on the 25, and then raced untouched to complete a 75-yard touchdown. Mann's extra point attempt went wide, but no one on the Oakland sideline seemed to care, as the Silver and Black were up, 32–7, with 5:43 left. The celebration was beginning to gain serious momentum along the Oakland sideline, and even John Madden was starting to believe that his name was about to be added to the role call of Super Bowl winning head coaches.

Guy's ensuing kickoff was returned 19 yards to the Minnesota 27 by Sammy White. Bob Lee replaced Fran Tarkenton at this stage, and he did not have any luck either against the relentless Oakland defense. His first pass was broken up by George Atkinson, and his second one only went for a gain of five to Miller. On third down, Lee ran for four and then Foreman was stopped on fourth-and-one for no gain by Monte Johnson.

Oakland took over on downs at the Minnesota 36. A pickup of five by van Eeghen around the left end was followed by Ginn wrapping off nine over the left tackle hole. Mike Rae, who replaced Ken Stabler on this possession, was sacked for a loss of

six. A 3-yard run by van Eeghen up the middle, and an 11-yard pickup by Rae brought up fourth-and-two. The Raiders decided not to punt, and Ginn attempted to bolt up the gut, but was stopped for no gain with 1:56 left.

Minnesota had nothing left but pride, and looked to put together one final drive that ended on a positive note. Connecting on five passes, with two going to White, and three to Sammy Johnson, Lee moved the Vikings to the Oakland 13. From there, Lee found his tight end Stu Voight for the touchdown with 25 seconds left to complete the nine-play, 86-yard drive. Cox added the extra point, and the game was now a 32–14 affair. Cox attempted an onside kick that Mike Siani recovered on the Minnesota 48. The final play of Super Bowl XI occurred as Mike Rae knelt down for a loss of two yards as the clock hit 0:00.

Fred Biletnikoff, the old master who suffered through so many heart-breaking playoff losses, was named the Most Valuable Player after catching four passes for 79 yards, which helped put Oakland in excellent scoring position. John Matuszak and Ted Hendricks hoisted John Madden up on their shoulders for the greatest victory ride of the mentor's career. A short time later, Madden was on the podium in the winning locker room sharing the joy with owner Al Davis, who accepted the first Lombardi Trophy in team history. It was a long trek for the Raiders to climb that climaxed with them perched on top of the gridiron summit. There are numerous clichés that can describe Oakland's rise to the top. They rose from the ashes like the Phoenix, and the albatross was finally removed from around their necks. Those plus others can be linked to this great team, but in the end, all that mattered was that they were finally crowned world champions.

Starting Lineup for Super Bowl XI

OFFENSE

QB — Ken Stabler	LT — Art Shell
RB — Clarence Davis	LG — Gene Upshaw
FB — Mark van Eeghen	C — Dave Dalby
WR — Fred Biletnikoff	RG — George Buehler
WR — Cliff Branch	RT — John Vella
TE — Dave Casper	

DEFENSE

DE — John Matuszak	DE — Otis Sistrunk

Willie Brown: Had 1 INT for 75 yards and 1 TD.

Individual Statistics and Roster

Head Coach: John Madden
Assistant Coaches: Tom Dahms, Lew Erber, Tom Flores, Joe Scannella, Don Shinnick, Ollie Spencer, Bob Zeman
1976 Regular Season Record: 13–1
1st Place AFC Western Division
Scored 350 points to rank 4th out of 28 teams
Allowed 237 points to rank 12th
Led the league in touchdown passes (33)

STARTERS — OFFENSE

QB — Ken Stabler: Active for and started in 12 games. Completed 194 of 291 pass attempts for 2,737 yards, 27 TD and 17 INT. Also led the NFL in passer rating (103.4), passing yards per game (228.1), and pass completion percentage (66.7). Had 7 rushes for -2 yards and 1 TD.
HB — Clarence Davis: Active for 12 games. Rushed for 516 yards on 114 carries and 3 TD. Had 21 receptions for 191 yards.

Champions at last. Hall of Fame receiver Fred Biletnikoff, left, and all-time great quarterback Ken "the Snake" Stabler show the world that the Raiders are #1 at the conclusion of Super Bowl XI on January 9, 1977, in Pasadena, California. Biletnikoff's efforts in Oakland's 32–14 win earned him the game's Most Valuable Player award (AP Photo).

NT — Dave Rowe	CB — Skip Thomas
LOLB — Phil Villapiano	CB — Willie Brown
LILB — Monte Johnson	SS — George Atkinson
RILB — Willie Hall	FS — Jack Tatum
ROLB — Ted Hendricks	

KICKING/PUNTING

K — Errol Mann	P — Ray Guy

Individual Statistics from Super Bowl XI

OFFENSE

Ken Stabler: 12 completions out of 19 pass attempts for 180 yards and 1 TD.
Clarence Davis: Rushed for 137 yards on 16 carries.
Mark van Eeghen: Rushed for 73 yards on 18 carries.
Carl Garrett: Rushed for 19 yards on 4 carries, had 1 reception for 11 yards, and returned 2 kickoffs for 47 yards.
Pete Banaszak: Rushed for 19 yards on 10 carries and 2 TD.
Hubert Ginn: Rushed for 9 yards on 2 carries.
Mike Rae: Rushed for 9 yards on 2 carries.
Fred Biletnikoff: Had 4 receptions for 79 yards.
Dave Casper: Had 4 receptions for 70 yards and 1 TD.
Cliff Branch: Had 3 receptions for 20 yards.
Neal Colzie: Returned 4 punts for 43 yards.
Errol Mann: Had 2 field goals and 2 extra point kicks.

DEFENSE

Phil Villapiano: 1 sack.
Willie Hall: Had 1 INT for 16 yards.

FB — Mark van Eeghen: Started in 14 games. Rushed for 1,012 yards on 233 carries and 3 TD. Had 17 receptions for 173 yards.
WR — Fred Biletnikoff: Active for 13 games. Had 43 receptions for 551 yards and 7 TD.
WR — Cliff Branch: Active for 14 games. Had 46 receptions for 1,111 yards and 12 TD. Rushed for 12 yards on 3 carries.
TE — Dave Casper: Active for and started in 13 games. Had 53 receptions for 691 yards and 10 TD. Rush for 5 yards on 1 carry.
LT — Art Shell: Active for 14 games.
LG — Gene Upshaw: Active for 14 games.
C — Dave Dalby: Active for 14 games.
RG — George Buehler: Active for 14 games.
RT — John Vella: Active for 14 games.

RESERVE OFFENSIVE PLAYERS

Pete Banaszak (RB): Active for 14 games, rushed for 370 yards on 114 carries and 5 TD, had 15 receptions for 74 yards, and 2 kickoff returns for 23 yards.
Warren Bankston (RB/TE): Active for 14 games. Rushed for 3 yards on 1 carry, had 5 receptions for 73 yards and 1 TD, and 2 kickoff returns for 27 yards.
Morris Bradshaw (WR): Active for 14 games, had 1 reception for 25 yards and 1 TD. Rushed for 4 yards on 1 carry.
Carl Garrett (RB): Active for 12 games, rushed for 220 yards on 48 carries and 1 TD, had 9 catches for 108 yards, and 18 kickoff returns for 388 yards.
Hubert Ginn (RB): Active for 7 games, rushed for 53 yards on 10 carries, and had 1 kickoff return for 27 yards.
David Humm (QB): Active for 14 games, and completed 3 of 5 pass attempts for 41 yards.
Rick Jennings (RB/WR): Active for 11 games, rushed for 22 yards on 10

carries, had 1 catch for 10 yards, 1 punt return for 20 yards, and 16 kickoff returns for 417 yards.

Terry Kunz (RB): Active for 7 games, and rushed for 33 yards on 4 carries.

Ted Kwalick (TE): Active for 7 games, and had 4 receptions for 15 yards.

Henry Lawrence (T/G): Active for 8 games.

Dan Medlin (G): Active for 13 games.

Manfred Moore (RB): Active for 1 game, returned 6 punts for 78 yards and 1 kickoff for 28 yards.

Mike Rae (QB): Active for 7 games, completed 35 of 65 pass attempts for 417 yards, 6 TD and 1 INT, and rushed for 37 yards on 10 carries and 1 TD.

Mike Siani (WR): Active for 14 games, and had 11 receptions for 173 yards and 2 TD.

Fred Steinfort (K): Active for 7 games, and made 4 of 8 field goal attempts, and 16 of 19 extra point kicks.

Steve Sylvester (C/G/T): Active for 14 games.

STARTERS — DEFENSE

DE — John Matuszak: Active for 13 games.

DE — Otis Sistrunk: Active for 14 games, and had 1 fumble recovery.

NT — Dave Rowe: Active for 14 games, and had 1 fumble recovery.

LOLB — Phil Villapiano: Active for 14 games, and had 1 INT and 1 fumble recovery.

LILB — Willie Hall: Active for 14 games, and had 2 INT.

RILB — Monte Johnson: Active for 14 games, and had 4 INT and 3 fumble recoveries.

ROLB — Ted Hendricks: Active for 14 games, had 1 INT, and recorded 1 safety.

CB — Skip Thomas: Active for 14 games, had 2 INT and 1 fumble recovery.

CB — Willie Brown: Active for 14 games, and had 3 INT.

SS — George Atkinson: Active for 14 games.

FS — Jack Tatum: Active for 14 games, and had 2 INT.

RESERVE DEFENSIVE PLAYERS

Rodrigo Barnes (LB): Active for 5 games.

Greg Blankenship (LB): Active for 4 games.

Rik Bonness (LB): Active for 14 games.

Neal Colzie (DB): Active for 14 games, had 41 punt returns for 448 yards, and 6 kickoff returns for 115 yards.

Herb McMath (T/E): Active for 14 games, and had 1 fumble recovery.

Charlie Phillips (DB): Active for 14 games, had 1 INT and 2 punt returns for 7 yards.

Charles Philyaw (E): Active for 14 games.

Mike Reinfeldt (DB): Active for 2 games.

Floyd Rice (LB/TE): Active for 10 games.

KICKING/PUNTING

K — Errol Mann: Active for 7 games. Made 8 of 21 field goal attempts, and 35 of 37 extra point kicks for 59 points.

P — Ray Guy: Active for 14 games. Punted 67 times for a 41.6 average, attempted 1 extra point kick, and rushed 1 time for no gain.

1977 Season Review

1. Sept. 18: The defending world champs began the new regular season just like they ended the previous one, as 24–0 victors over the San Diego Chargers. In their 14th consecutive win since October 11, 1976, the Raiders appeared to be unstoppable. Ken Stabler threw two touchdown passes, with the first going to Cliff Branch from seven yards out, and the other to Dave Casper from one. Errol Mann added a 20-yard field goal. Old reliable Pete Banaszak added the final six-pointer on a 2-yard run. On top of the skilled veterans performing up to their high standards, the Raiders also received help from three rookies, Lester Hayes, Randy McClanahan, and Jeff Barnes. Hayes blocked a punt that fellow first-year man McClanahan scooped up and returned to the San Diego 13. Moments later Stabler connected with Branch for Oakland's first touchdown. Jeff Barnes provided his heroics by recovering a fumble on the San Diego 10, which resulted in Casper's touchdown reception.[1]

2. Sept. 25: In a rematch of the past AFC Championship Game, the Raiders and Steelers squared off for another vicious battle. However, when the game was over in Pittsburgh, it seemed like just any other football contest. Despite all the hype of a blood bath, both teams played a fairly clean game, and the Raiders once again came out victorious, 16–7, for their 15th straight win, and the 150th regular season victory in team history. Oakland built up a 16–0 lead in the fourth quarter on three Errol Mann field goals (21, 40, and 41 yards), and an 8-yard run by Mark van Eeghen, who led all rushers with 88 yards. The defense played brilliantly, sacking Terry Bradshaw five times and intercepting three passes, with Willie Brown, Charlie Phillips, and Jack Tatum coming up with the thefts.[2]

3. Oct. 3: The last time the Raiders lost was on October 3, 1976, and they made sure that did not happen again on the same date. In front of a national television audience on Monday Night Football, Oakland overcame a 21-point deficit in the second quarter to beat Kansas City, 37–28. The Silver and Black rallied for 21 points of their own in the third quarter and never looked back. Three touchdown runs provided the firepower, with Clarence Davis accounting for two of them (37 and 2 yards), and Pete Banaszak the other (1 yard). The Oakland offense exploded for 539 total yards. On the ground Mark van Eeghen led all rushers with 116 yards, and Clarence Davis was a close second with 102. Through the air, Ken Stabler was at his usual best. He completed 19 out of 28 pass attempts for 297 yards, and opened the scoring with a 21-yard strike to Fred Biletnikoff. Errol Mann did his part by nailing three field goals from 42, 34, and 22 yards.[3]

4. Oct. 9: In a packed Cleveland Stadium, with an overflow crowd of 80,236 on hand, the Raiders rolled to their 17th consecutive victory, 26–10, against the Browns. Mark van Eeghen continued to impress by once again going over the century mark. This time he ran for 114 yards, and scored both of Oakland's touchdowns on a pair of 3-yard runs. Errol Mann added the other points with four field goals from 39, 28, 27, and 39 yards. The defense helped the cause with interceptions by Charles Phillips and Otis Sistrunk.[4]

5. Oct. 16: All good things must end, but the Raiders 17-game winning streak sure climaxed in an ugly way. Oakland started off good in their attempt to tie the NFL record for consecutive wins. In their opening drive against Denver, Ken Stabler took the Raiders 70 yards, with Dave Casper finishing it off with a 9-yard touchdown reception. Things then went downhill for the Silver and Black. Stabler threw seven interceptions, the offense lost a fumble, were stopped on two fourth down plays, and when it ended, the Broncos had brutalized the defending Super Bowl champs, 30–7. For the first time in a long time, the Raiders were forced to look up at someone else

Otis Sistrunk (#60) confers with Ted Hendricks (#83) during a 1977 game against the Los Angeles Rams at the Los Angeles Memorial Coliseum. He proved to be a dominant defensive lineman for Oakland from 1972 to 1979 (AP Photo/NFL Photos).

teamed up with Mike Siani from 24 yards away, and Errol Mann kicked the go-ahead conversion point to give Oakland a nail-biting 28–27 victory. Mark van Eeghen was the workhorse of the offensive attack. He carried the ball 36 times for 143 yards, and opened the scoring in the first quarter with a 3-yard run.[6]

7. Oct. 30: Revenge is sweet, especially when it comes in front of an opponents' home crowd. After two weeks of looking up at the Denver Broncos, the Raiders were once again on even ground thanks to a 24–14 victory in the Mile High City. Focusing on the ground game, Oakland ran the ball down Denver's throat 57 times for 200 yards. Clarence Davis led the way with 105 rushing yards, and Mark van Eeghen added 88 more. With the running attack going so well, Ken Stabler only had to throw 14 times. Despite so few attempts, the "Snake" still found time to throw a 21-yard touchdown pass to Cliff Branch to open the scoring. The Raiders received their other points from Davis (8-yard run), van Eeghen (1-yard run), and Errol Mann (42-yard field goal), which allowed them a very comfortable 24–0 fourth quarter lead. The defense held the powerful Denver offense to a mere 119 total yards, and sacked quarterback Craig Morton eight times for 62 yards in losses. Punter Ray Guy did his part by keeping Denver pinned deep with some terrific kicks.[7]

8. Nov. 6: The Raiders began the second half of the '77 season in fine fashion, clobbering the Seattle Seahawks, 44–7. Seattle was only in their second year of existence, and was still taking a pounding on a regular basis. Oakland took total control early on and never struggled. Ken Stabler threw three touchdown passes, with them going to Fred Biletnikoff (3 yards), Mike Siani (12 yards), and Dave Casper (15 yards). Clarence Davis (2 yards) and Terry Robiskie (1 yard) each ran for a six-pointer, and Errol Mann kicked three field goals (35, 39, and 37 yards). The running tandem of Davis and Mark van Eeghen pounded the ball all afternoon. Davis ran for 100 yards, and van Eeghen 91. The defense clamped down on Seattle's passing game, allowing only 43 yards through the air. Willie Brown got two interceptions and Monte Johnson one.[8]

9. Nov. 13: After two easy wins, the Raiders had to work a little harder against the Houston Oilers. The hard work paid off, as Oakland rallied from five points down to win, 34–29. Clarence Davis scored on a 3-yard run for the go-ahead touchdown in the third quarter. Ken Stabler was exceptional, completing 23 of 31 pass attempts for 255 yards and two touchdowns, with them going to Dave Casper (1 yard) and Fred Biletnikoff (14 yards). Mark van Eeghen scored on a 2-yard run, and Errol Mann kicked two field

on top of the Western Division, as Denver stood at 5–0, and Oakland at 4–1.[5]

6. Oct. 23: Like true champions, the Raiders rebounded from their massacre. However, it was not an easy task, as four Richard Todd touchdown passes had the New York Jets ahead, 27–14, in the fourth quarter. Two New York turnovers, mixed with a couple missed field goals, kept the Raiders alive. Ken Stabler, calm as always, guided the Silver and Black back from the brink. He started the comeback with his second touchdown pass of the day. In the first quarter, he connected with Dave Casper from 19 yards, and then in the fourth, he found Fred Biletnikoff from seven yards out to pull Oakland to within six points. Stabler then took the Raiders 80 yards in seven plays for the winning touchdown. At the 7:01 mark of the fourth quarter, Stabler

goals (42 and 25 yards) to close out Oakland's scoring for the day. Cliff Branch produced another great showing with 115 receiving yards on eight catches. Willie Brown and Jack Tatum each came up with key fourth quarter interceptions to end Houston scoring threats. With both the Raiders and Denver Broncos at 8–1, the AFC Western Division race was shaping up to be the best in football for the '77 season.[9]

10. Nov. 20: In a shocker, the San Diego Chargers beat the Raiders, 12–7, for their first victory over the Silver and Black since 1968. Oakland suffered a huge blow when Ken Stabler was forced to leave the game in the first quarter due to a twisted knee. San Diego's defense stiffened and kept back up Mike Rae under control by allowing him only one completion in six attempts, and intercepting him once. He did manage to escape the clutches long enough to score Oakland's only touchdown on a 7-yard run.[10]

11. Nov. 28: On Monday Night Football, Ken Stabler returned to the lineup against the Buffalo Bills despite a very tender knee. Throughout the week leading up to this game, Stabler was listed as questionable, but with Oakland fighting for a playoff spot, the "Snake" was ready, willing, and able to perform in a 34–13 cakewalk win over the Bills. He played like the champion he was, firing two touchdowns to Cliff Branch (28 and 12 yards), and one to Fred Biletnikoff (44 yards). Mark van Eeghen ran for 143 yards. In doing so, he once again topped the 1,000-yard mark, becoming the first Raider to ever reach that plateau two years in a row. Clarence Davis ran for 72 yards, and Pete Banaszak scored on two 1-yard runs. Oakland improved to 9–2, but still trailed the red hot 10–1 Denver Broncos in the division.[11]

12. Dec. 4: The Western Division was clinched on this date. Unfortunately, it was not by the Oakland Raiders, but by the Los Angeles Rams of the NFC Western Division. With 2:10 remaining in the fourth quarter, Los Angeles quarterback Pat Haden found Harold Jackson from 43 yards out to give the Rams a 20–14 win over the Silver and Black. The Raiders were a banged up team going into this game, and tried to hang on the best they could. Pete Banaszak (1-yard run), and Dave Casper (21-yard pass from Ken Stabler), provided the Raiders with their points. Stabler, who was still nursing a sore knee, fell victim to four sacks and just as many interceptions. In addition to Stabler's injury, the team suffered from the loss of five key defensive players, and end Otis Sistrunk was only able to stay in the game on a part-time basis due to an injury. Missing completely from the defensive unit were Neal Colzie, George Atkinson, Phil Villapiano, Charles Phillips,

The famed left side of Oakland's offensive line seen here on December 4, 1977, against the Los Angeles Rams at the Los Angeles Memorial Coliseum. The greatest wall of protection ever assembled consisted of tight end Dave Casper (#87), tackle Art Shell (#78), and guard Gene Upshaw (#63). Also shown is quarterback Ken "the Snake" Stabler (#12) (AP Photo/NFL Photos).

and Charles Philyaw. This loss knocked the Raiders out of contention for a division title for only the second time in ten years.[12]

13. Dec. 11: In a rematch of the Super Bowl, the Raiders once again defeated the Minnesota Vikings. With a 35–13 win, Oakland managed to clinch a playoff berth for the tenth time in eleven years. This time, however, they would be going to the post season as a wild card team. No matter how they got in, the Raiders showed their grit to overcome adversity that plagued the team with countless injuries, and performed like the defending champions they were. The Raiders jumped out to a 21–0 first quarter lead on a Mark van Eeghen 2-yard run, a 10-yard pass from Ken Stabler to Cliff Branch, and a 2-yard fumble recovery by linebacker Willie Hall. Stabler and Branch teamed up for another touchdown in the third quarter from 32 yards out. The "Snake" added a third scoring toss to his day when he connected with Carl Garrett from two yards away. On top of having a good day through the air, the Raiders also churned out fine running attack led by van Eeghen's 112 yards.[13]

14.   Dec. 18: Oakland wrapped up their '77 regular season with a 21–20 win over Kansas City. They also finished the campaign with a league high 351 points scored. The Chiefs held a slim 20–18 advantage until Errol Mann lifted the Sliver and Black to victory with a 28-yard field goal halfway through the fourth quarter. He also had field goals from 31 and 19 yards in the first half. Carl Garrett provided the Raiders with their other points on a 5-yard run and a 4-yard reception from Mike Rae.[14]

AFC Divisional Playoff Game, December 24, 1977

The Raiders' run to defend their championship began on Christmas Eve in Baltimore against the Colts. Over the course of three seasons, including the '77 campaign, the Colts compiled a 31–11 regular season record that earned them AFC Eastern Division titles each time. However, they failed in their first two post-season appearances, and hoped that the third time could be the charm in getting to the next round.

Baltimore's offense was high octane led by star quarterback Bert Jones, and the defense was capable of turning up the heat on opposing offenses. With flash on offense and a solid defense, they rolled to nine victories in their first ten games before hitting a snag and finishing at 10–4. It was not a good time to go cold, especially when their playoff opener was against the defending world champions.

The Raiders drew first blood in their initial quest to repeat as champions with thirty seconds left in the opening quarter. After being stopped on their first three possessions, the Raiders covered 60 yards of Memorial Stadium turf in four plays with Clarence Davis running 30 yards for a touchdown. An Errol Mann extra point put Oakland up, 7–0.

The Colts came back to tie things up on a huge play. Defensive back Bruce Laird picked off a Ken Stabler pass and raced 61 yards for the score, and Toni Linhart's conversion knotted the game at 7–7. The Colts then took their first lead of the game on a Linhart 36-yard field goal to lead, 10–7, with 1:58 remaining before the half. The Raiders came close to tying or re-taking the lead, but Clarence Davis fumbled on the Baltimore 23 with 52 seconds left before halftime.

The Raiders came out for the second half ready to right the wrong that happened just seconds before the first thirty minutes came to a climax. They went on a five-play, 70-yard drive that ended with Stabler and Dave Casper teaming up for an 8-yard six-pointer. Mann's extra point upped the Oakland advantage to 14–10. The joy was short-lived, as the Colts struck and regained the lead 16 seconds later when Marshall Johnson returned the ensuing kickoff 87 yards to paydirt. Linhart's conversion made it 17–14.

After Johnson's exciting return put Baltimore up by three, Laird gave the hometown faithful something else to cheer about when he intercepted his second Stabler aerial of the game. Unfortunately for the Colts, they were unable to take advantage of Laird's handy work, and they were forced to punt. Ted Hendricks extended his 6'7" frame to block David Lee's punt at midfield, and rookie Jeff Barnes scooped the loose ball up and made it to the Baltimore 16 before being stopped. The Oakland offense then

seized the golden opportunity presented to it by Hendricks and Barnes. With 7:27 to go in the third stanza, the Stabler-Casper combination hooked up for another six points, this time from ten yards out. Mann's conversion then gave the Raiders a 21–17 lead going into the fourth quarter.

Baltimore's field general, Bert Jones, gave Colts' fans reason to smile during his days as quarterback, but throughout the first three stanzas of this affair, he was not doing well. Thanks to a great defensive effort by the Raiders, Jones was only able to pass for 21 yards against a secondary that covered his receivers so well it looked like they were attached to them. Jones was also pressured, and sacked six times for 114 yards in losses.

In the fourth quarter, Jones was finally able to complete two passes that gained 41 yards, and helped the Colts get downfield. An interference penalty against rookie Lester Hayes on receiver Glenn Doughty in the end zone helped even more, as it placed the ball on the one. The Raiders held on three straight downs, but on fourth-and-goal, the effort was in vain when Ron Lee barely broke the plain. Linhart's extra point was true, and the Colts were once again in the lead by a 24–21 count.

The Raiders counted with a touchdown of their own to regain control of the scoreboard. With 9:12 left in regulation, and aided by a pass interference call against cornerback Nelson Munsey, Oakland took a 28–24 lead when Pete Banaszak powered in from the 1-yard line and Mann added the extra point. Baltimore returned volley with a four-play, 73-yard drive. Jones connected on passes of 30 and 16 yards, and then Lee carried twice for 27 yards, with the second one going for a 13-yard touchdown. Linhart's conversion was tacked on, and the Colts were now up, 31–24.

From this stage on, the Colts decided to go into conservative mode with their offensive attack with close to seven minutes still showing on the clock. It did not work, and they failed to convert on third down and had to give the ball back. With 2:55 to go, Stabler took the Raiders from the Oakland 30 down to the Baltimore 14, with the big play coming on a 42-yard pass to Casper. After three plunges into the line prevented Oakland from obtaining a first down just short of the Baltimore 4-yard, they let 23 seconds tick off the clock. Stabler then called a time out, and Mann entered in an attempt to tie the game and force sudden death overtime. Mann left no doubt on the direction the ball took after it left his foot. It split the uprights with 26 seconds to end regulation with the score 31–31.

The Colts won the sudden death coin toss, and elected to receive the ball, but the offense could not do anything. The Raiders then caught a huge break as the first overtime period was coming to a close. Cliff Branch lost control of the ball after making a catch, and naturally, a frenzy occurred as the loose pigskin awaited thousands on pounds of flesh to jump on it in a split second at the Oakland 37. After finally unpiling the mass of humanity, the officials were able to see that offensive tackle Henry Lawrence had possession of the cherished prize. The Raiders were forced to punt, and Ray Guy pinned the Colts deep on their own 15. They once again stalled and had to punt the ball back over to Oakland.

With the ball on his own 42, Stabler looked to end this marathon successfully for his Raiders. He kept the chains moving by making good on two third down conversions. First, Banaszak gained the needed yards on third-and-one. Branch then came up huge with a catch on third-and-19 that set Oakland up in excellent position on the Baltimore 26, making the necessary yardage by the length of the ball. A completion to Fred Biletnikoff gained eight yards, and Banaszak ran for five to end the first quarter of overtime with the ball on the Baltimore 13.

Going into the wind for the second overtime, Oakland head coach John Madden elected to keep pounding away with his offense instead of opting for Mann to attempt a field goal. Banaszak carried for three yards to the 10 to open the sixth quarter of play. With the Colts looking for the run on second down, it seemed like the perfect time to mix things up.

At the snap, Stabler faked a run, the defense took the bait, and Casper faked a run to the inside, and then made his way to the outside. After getting away from a linebacker, Casper was alone in the left corner of the end zone. Stabler threw a high pass that only Casper could get to. If he missed, the ball would sail out of bounds and the Raiders would get another chance on third down. That scenario never had a chance to play out because the sure-handed Casper reached up and brought the ball in for the winning touchdown in what became known in Raiders lore as "the Ghost to the Post." The 37–31 victory gave Oakland the win 43 seconds into the sixth quarter in what was the third longest playoff game, and it sent the defending champions into their fourth straight AFC Championship Game.

Dave "the Ghost" Casper had only four catches on the day, but they might have been the most productive set of quadruple catches ever by a tight end. Three went for touchdowns, with the final one being the game-winner, and the lone one not going for six points got Oakland deep enough for Mann's game-tying field goal at the end of regulation. Stabler hit on 21 of 40 pass attempts for 345 yards and those three scoring strikes to Casper. Altogether, both teams accounted for an incredible 792 yards of total offense and eight lead changes. The Raiders, much like Ebenezer Scrooge, received enlightenment prior to Christmas Day. However, unlike Scrooge getting his from ghosts of Christmas past, present, and future, the Silver and Black received theirs thanks to a 6' 4" 230-pound All-Pro tight end on a play forever etched in time as "the Ghost to the Post."[15]

AFC Championship Game, January 1, 1978

The Denver Broncos were making their first-ever championship game appearance of any kind against their archrival, and the defending Super Bowl champion Raiders, after disposing of the Pittsburgh Steelers, 34–21, in their divisional playoff contest. The 12–2 Broncos ended Oakland's five-season reign as AFC Western Division champs with first-year head coach Robert "Red" Miller leading the way. Miller was able to accomplish success in Denver after merging a tough defense with a safe, but effective offensive attack, designed to move the ball in a conservative manner, and not a wild and free approach like the Raiders. Miller's field general was veteran quarterback Craig Morton, who came into this game with a sore hip that required him to spend two days in the hospital. Denver's defensive unit came to be known as the "Orange Crush" with future Raider Lyle Alzado and linebacker

Tom Jackson leading the way. The city of Denver was swept away in Broncomania, and the ravenous fans hoped the first day of 1978 would end successfully for their championship-game virgin Broncos in Mile High Stadium.

Denver won the coin toss, elected to receive, but could not move the ball and had to punt. Oakland also suffered the same fate on their opening sortie. After three attempts at moving the chains failed, they were forced to punt. The Raiders caught an early break when Denver's John Schultz ran into Ray Guy. The infraction allowed Oakland to advance the ball close enough for Errol Mann to successfully make a 20-yard field goal to give the defending champs a 3–0 first quarter lead.

Craig Morton refused to let Broncomania expire so quickly, and came out looking to take the lead away from the Raiders. He accomplished this with a lightening strike that made Mile High Stadium erupt. Receiver Haven Moses got by Skip Thomas, caught a Morton pass, and went 74 yards untouched to the end zone. Jim Turner kicked the extra point, and Denver went up, 7–3 at the end of the first quarter. The momentum struck quickly for Denver, and after Fred Biletnikoff was lost with a dislocated shoulder in the second quarter, things looked bleak for the Raiders. However, Oakland's defense played hard, and was shutting down the Denver running game. Attempting to use seven different backs to attack the Raiders' defense, the Broncos were only able to muster up 91 yards for the game. Oakland was also having trouble moving the ball. The "Orange Crush" was taking away Oakland's sweeps to the outside with tremendous lateral movement. With both running games stymied, the game turned into a defensive struggle, and the second quarter went into the books with no scoring allowed, and the Raiders now had thirty minutes left after halftime to erase a four-point deficit.

The Broncos began to move the ball well midway through the third quarter. It was then that an incident occurred which was added to the Raiders' collection of woeful playoff moments. On first-and-goal from the Oakland 2-yard line, running back Rob Lytle took a handoff from Morton and pounded into his offensive line's left side.

Jack "the Assassin" Tatum was the focal point in regards to the Raiders five years earlier in the "Immaculate Reception" game. Once again, it was one of Tatum's famed sledgehammer-like hits that should have gone in favor of the Raiders, but instead they suffered another miscarriage of justice. However, the officials did not see things that way. Tatum blasted Lytle and the ball came loose while he was upright. Oakland defensive lineman Mike McCoy reacted quickly and recovered the ball and began to run. The officials ruled that the play had been whistled dead after Lytle's forward progress was stopped, therefore allowing possession to remain with Denver. Years later, it was said that the officials made a huge mistake, and that it truly was a fumble and the Raiders should have assumed possession. They might even have had a touchdown on the play if McCoy took off with the ball and made it all the way to the end zone, or at worst, got Oakland into good field position. The play would have more than likely turned the tide for Oakland on this day. Instead, Denver was able to keep the ball, and Jon Keyworth scored from the one on the next play. With Turner's conversion, the Broncos were up, 14–3 at the end of three quarters.

The Raiders now found themselves in a huge hole against

an inspired team, and had fifteen minutes left to attempt a repeat visit to the Super Bowl. Ken Stabler and Dave Casper pulled Oakland closer when they teamed up on a 7-yard scoring strike. With Mann's conversion, the Raiders only trailed 14–10 with enough time left to pull out another fantastic finish.

The only trouble with a possible comeback on Oakland's part was that the Denver trio of Bob Swenson, Craig Morton, and Haven Moses, refused to have the Raiders spoil their New Year's Day celebration. Swenson came up with a big play when he intercepted a Stabler pass from his linebacker position. He took the ball away from Casper on the Oakland 31 and returned it 14 yards. Three plays later, Morton threw a 12-yard touchdown pass to Moses that put the Broncos in control at 20–10. On the extra point try, a bad snap from center made it hard for holder Norris Weese to get control of the ball, and Turner never had a chance to attempt the kick.

With 3:16 left in the game, Stabler connected with Casper on a touchdown for the fifth time in two playoff games. This time it was on a 17-yarder, and Mann's extra point brought the score to 20–17. That was the way it ended, and as wide-eyed Denver fans joyously engulfed the field, the Raiders made their way toward the locker room with chants of "We're number one" ringing throughout Mile High Stadium. And as the effects of Broncomania faded for the Silver and Black as they headed into their locker room, so too faded their one-year reign as world champions.[16]

Individual Statistics and Roster

Head Coach: John Madden
Assistant Coaches: Tom Dahms, Lew Erber, Tom Flores, Joe Madro, Joe Scannella, Don Shinnick, Ollie Spencer, Bob Zeman
1977 Regular Season Record: 11–3
2nd Place AFC Western Division
Scored 351 points to rank 1st out of 28 teams
Allowed 230 points to rank 14th
Led the league in points (351), first downs (305), rushing attempts (681), and fewest rushing attempts against defense (408)

STARTERS — OFFENSE

QB — Ken Stabler: Active for and started in 13 games. Completed 169 of 294 pass attempts for 2,176 yards, 20 TD and 20 INT. Rushed for -3 yards on 3 carries.
HB — Clarence Davis: Started in 14 games. Rushed for 787 yards on 194 carries and 5 TD. Had 16 receptions for 124 yards, and 3 kickoff returns for 63 yards.
FB — Mark van Eeghen: Started in 14 games. Rushed for 1,273 yards on 324 carries and 7 TD. Had 15 receptions for 135 yards.
WR — Fred Biletnikoff: Started in 14 games. Had 33 receptions for 446 yards and 5 TD.
WR — Cliff Branch: Active for and started in 13 games. Had 33 receptions for 540 yards and 6 TD.
TE — Dave Casper: Started in 14 games. Had 48 receptions for 584 yards and 6 TD.
LT — Art Shell: Started in 14 games.
LG — Gene Upshaw: Started in 14 games.
C — Dave Dalby: Started in 14 games.
RG — George Buehler: Started in 14 games.
RT — Henry Lawrence: Active for 14 games, and started in 11.

RESERVE OFFENSIVE PLAYERS

Pete Banaszak (RB): Active for 14 games, rushed for 214 yards on 67 carries and 5 TD, had 2 receptions for 14 yards, and 7 kickoff returns for 119 yards.
Warren Bankston (RB/TE): Active for 14 games, and returned 1 kickoff for 0 yards.
Morris Bradshaw (WR): Active for 14 games, and started in 1. Had 5 receptions for 90 yards.
Carl Garrett (RB): Active for 14 games, rushed for 175 yards on 53 carries, and 1 TD. Had 8 receptions for 61 yards, and 2 TD, and 21 kickoff returns for 420 yards.
Hubert Ginn (RB): Active for 10 games, rushed for 6 yards on 5 carries, and returned 3 kickoffs 74 yards.
David Humm (QB): Active for 14 games.
Rick Jennings (RB/WR): Active for 2 games, returned 5 punts 39 yards, and 4 kickoffs 93 yards.
Ted Kwalick (TE): Active for 12 games.
Mickey Marvin (G): Active for 8 games.
Mike Rae (QB): Active for 10 games, and started in 1. Completed 15 of 30 pass attempts for 162 yards, 1 TD and 4 INT. Rushed for 75 yards on 13 carries and 1 TD.
Terry Robiskie (RB): Active for 14 games, rushed for 100 yards on 22 carries and 1 TD, and returned 6 kickoffs 83 yards.
Mike Siani (WR): Active for 12 games, and had 24 receptions for 344 yards and 2 TD.
Steve Sylvester (C/G/T): Active for 14 games.
John Vella (T): Active for 5 games, and started in 3.

STARTERS — DEFENSE

DE — John Matuszak: Started in 14 games, and had 2 fumble recoveries.
DE — Otis Sistrunk: Active for and started in 12 games. Had 1 INT and 1 fumble recovery.
NT — Dave Rowe: Started in 14 games.
LOLB — Floyd Rice: Active for 13 games, and started in 11. Had 2 INT and 1 fumble recovery.
LILB — Monte Johnson: Started in 14 games, and had 2 INT and 1 fumble recovery.
RILB — Willie Hall: Started in 14 games, and had 1 INT, 1 fumble recovery, and 1 TD.
ROLB — Ted Hendricks: Started in 14 games, and had 1 fumble recovery.
CB — Skip Thomas: Active for and started in 12 games. Had 1 INT and 1 fumble recovery.
CB — Willie Brown: Started in 14 games, and had 4 INT.
SS — George Atkinson: Active for 12 games, and started in 11. Had 2 INT and 1 fumble recovery.
FS — Jack Tatum: Active for and started in 11 games. Had 6 INT and 1 fumble recovery.

RESERVE DEFENSIVE PLAYERS

Jeff Barnes (LB): Active for 14 games, and started in 1. Had 2 fumble recoveries.
Neal Colzie (DB): Active for 14 games, and started in 3. Had 3 INT and 32 punt returns for 334 yards.
Lester Hayes (DB): Active for 14 games, and started in 2. Had 1 INT, 2 fumble recoveries, and 3 kickoff returns for 57 yards.
Steve Jackson (DB): Active for 6 games, had 1 INT and 1 fumble recovery.
Rod Martin (LB): Active for 1 game.
Randy McClanahan (LB): Active for 14 games.
Mike McCoy (T): Active for 14 games, and had 1 fumble recovery and 1 kickoff return for 0 yards.
Charlie Phillips (DB): Active for 7 games, and started in 3. Had 2 INT and 1 fumble recovery.
Charles Philyaw (E): Active for 3 games.
Pat Toomay (E): Active for 14 games, and started in 2. Had 3 fumble recoveries.

Phil Villapiano (LB): Active for and started in 2 games.

Jimmy Warren (DB): Active for 2 games.

KICKING/PUNTING

K — Errol Mann: Active for 14 games. Made 20 of 28 field goal attempts, and 39 of 42 extra point kicks for **99** points.

P — Ray Guy: Active for 14 games. Punted 59 times for a **43.3** average.

1978 Season Review

1. Sept. 3: In a rematch of the AFC Championship Game, the Raiders once again fell victim to the Denver Broncos. A Craig Morton to Haven Mosses touchdown pass, and a 1-yard run by Otis Armstrong were all the Broncos needed in a 14–6 win. Denver was helped by two interceptions that killed Oakland rallies, and a fumble recovery that led to their first score. Errol Mann gave the Raiders all their points on field goals from 33 and 22 yards. After this game, the Oakland coaching staff decided to bench 35-year-old Raiders legend Fred Biletnikoff due to diminished skills. His replacement was Morris Bradshaw.[1]

2. Sept. 10: It came to be known in NFL history as the Holy Roller, and it led to an exciting 21–20 victory for the Silver and Black on the game's final play against San Diego. With seconds left in the game, the Raiders trailed by six points, and had time for one final play. Ken Stabler managed to pull victory out from the jaws of defeat quite a few times throughout his pro career, and looked to add to his status in team history. The "Snake" dropped back to pass, was quickly under pressure, and on his way to being sacked. While in the act of falling down on the San Diego 24-yard line, Stabler intentionally fumbled with the hope that one of his teammates would pick it up and make something happen. Pete Banaszak saw the loose ball and tried to pick it up. Unable to get his hands firmly on it, Banaszak kicked the ball toward the goal line. Dave Casper swatted it into the end zone and then pounced on it for the tying touchdown with no time showing on the game clock. Errol Mann then kicked the conversion and the Raiders won in remarkable fashion, 21–20. The Chargers protested the touchdown, claiming that Stabler intentionally grounded the ball. The referee did not see it that way, and ruled it a fumble, not a forward pass attempt. Despite throwing three interceptions, Stabler threw for 307 yards and two touchdowns prior to his initial involvement in the Holy Roller play. Dave Casper and Morris Bradshaw were on the receiving ends of Stabler's scoring strikes, and each amassed over 100 yards with their catches. Casper caught five passes for 100 yards, and scored from six yards out. Bradshaw's touchdown covered 44 yards, and on the day, he hauled in four passes for 107 yards.[2]

3. Sept. 17: There was no fantastic finish in week three for the Raiders, as they routed Green Bay, 28–3. Led by Mark van Eeghen's 151 yards on the ground, Oakland continually pounded away at the Packer defense and eventually wore them down. Oakland's running backs smashed into the line behind future Hall of Fame linemen Gene Upshaw and Art Shell. When all was said and done, the backfield ran for a team record 348 yards. Arthur Whittington ran for two touchdowns (7 and 10 yards), and Terry Robiskie had one (11 yards). Ken Stabler had a bad day, throwing four interceptions, but did connect with Dave Casper for Oak-

land's other touchdown from 11 yards out to open the scoring. Linebacker Phil Villapiano led the defense with an interception and a fumble recovery.[3]

4. Sept. 24: Oakland fell to 2–2 when they lost, 21–14, in the final minutes to New England after blowing a 14-point lead. Ken Stabler was intercepted by defensive back Mike Haynes with less than two minutes remaining and the score tied at 14–14. The Patriots then marched downfield with the big play coming on a 28-yard run by quarterback Steve Grogan. Fullback Sam Cunningham finished the drive off with a 1-yard run. The Patriots outclassed the Raiders with over 400 yards of offensive production. Scoring for Oakland were Dave Casper on a 13-yard pass from Ken Stabler, and Arthur Whittington on a 4-yard run.[4]

5. Oct. 1: Defensive back Neal Colzie was the man of the hour for the Raiders in a 25–19, overtime victory against the Chicago Bears. Oakland forced the extra quarter when Errol Mann kicked his fourth field goal of the game with five seconds left in regulation. His other three-pointers came on kicks from 42, 35, and 34 yards. Terry Robiskie added a 5-yard touchdown run for the Raiders. Colzie became the hero when he intercepted a Bob Avellini pass on the Chicago 27-yard line, and returned it to the three. On third down, Arthur Whittington scored on a 2-yard run to end the game. Ken Stabler chipped in with a brilliant performance that saw him complete 25 of 43 pass attempts for 278 yards. Cliff Branch and Morris Bradshaw led Oakland's receiving group, with Branch hauling in eight passes for 89 yards, and Bradshaw eight catches for 83 yards.[5]

6. Oct. 8: It was Dave Casper who once again pulled the Raiders out from the jaws of defeat just like he did in San Diego one month earlier, this time in a 21–17 win over the Houston Oilers. With 42 seconds left to play, Casper grabbed a 4-yard pass from Ken Stabler out of a defender's hands in the end zone for the game winner. The Raiders came back from a ten-point deficit in the third quarter to register their fourth win of the season. Arthur Whittington scored Oakland's first touchdown on a 4-yard run, and defensive back Charles Phillips returned a fumble 96 yards to close the Houston lead to three points late in the third quarter before Casper's end zone heroics.[6]

7. Oct. 15: Ken Stabler returned to his old ways by hitting on 12 of his first 13 pass attempts. With the "Snake" playing so well, the Raiders blew past Kansas City, 28–6. Stabler finished with 15 completions out of 20 attempts for 222 yards and one touchdown, which went to Dave Casper from four yards out. Mark van Eeghen led all ball carriers with 76 yards, and scored on two short yardage runs from one and three yards. Defensive back Charles Phillips once again added his name to the scoring column by returning an interception 41 yards.[7]

8. Oct. 22: After being near perfect the previous week, Ken Stabler was plagued by the interception bug against Seattle, and the end result was a painful first-ever loss to the Seahawks by the score of 27–7. Even though his stats were impressive (19 of 30 for 204 yards and one touchdown), Stabler threw four interceptions that were turned into 13 points. The Seahawks were well in front when the Raiders avoided a shutout on a 22-yard Stabler-to-Cliff Branch touchdown pass in the fourth quarter. The only good news to come out of this loss was the fact that Denver also went down in defeat to keep the 5–3 Raiders in a first place tie with the Broncos.[8]

9. Oct. 29: For the first time since 1975, the Raiders lost two regular season games in a row. After jumping out to a 20–7 halftime lead over San Diego, the Raiders saw their advantage slowly slip away. With 52 seconds left to play, it vanished completely on a 29-yard touchdown pass from Dan Fouts to Greg McCrary. This tied the game, and Rolf Benirschke's conversion kick gave the Chargers a 24–23 lead. Benirschke added a field goal with ten seconds left in the game to make the final score 27–23. The loss denied Oakland head coach John Madden of his 100th career victory, and it also put the Raiders in second place in the AFC West. Scoring for the Oakland in this defeat were Arthur Whittington (26-yard run), Dave Casper (12-yard pass from Ken Stabler), Mark van Eeghen (12-yard run), and Errol Mann (25-yard field goal).[9]

10. Nov. 5: The Raiders went from doom and gloom back to jubilation by way of a 20–10 victory over Kansas City. Denver lost their game to the New York Jets, so the Raiders were once again tied for the lead in the division at 6–4. The Silver and Black also gave their coach John Madden his 100th career win in only his tenth season, making him the first to reach the century mark in the shortest amount of time. Ken Stabler suffered three sacks, and just as many interceptions. However, the "Snake" did not falter. He threw a 4-yard touchdown pass to Raymond Chester, and guided the offense on two scoring drives in the fourth quarter, capped off by Arthur Whittington (25-yard run), and Mark van Eeghen (1-yard run).[10]

11. Nov. 13: The Raiders always seemed to shine on Monday Night Football, and a 34–21 victory over the Cincinnati Bengals kept their prime time mystique alive. Since Monday Night Football began in 1970, the Raiders had an incredible 11-1-1 record. Ken Stabler was getting blasted throughout the '78 season as a quarterback on the downside of his career after throwing a league-leading 23 interceptions up to this game. However, the "Snake" silenced many of his detractors against the Bengals by throwing three touchdown passes. On the receiving end of Stabler's six-point tosses were Raymond Chester (5 yards), Dave Casper (25 yards), and Morris Bradshaw (11 yards). Mark van Eeghen added an 11-yard scoring run. The defense came up big, as Neal Colzie scored Oakland's first touchdown on a 32-yard fumble recovery. A Mike Davis fumble recovery, and a Charles Phillips interception also led to scores. With Stabler's passing, and the defense coming up with turnovers, the Raiders went into the fourth quarter with a commanding 27–7 lead over the 1–10 Bengals. Oakland stood at 7–4, and was still tied for the division lead with Denver.[11]

12. Nov. 19: On a rainy day in Oakland, in a game where 20 penalties were called, Mark van Eeghen came out a hero in a 29–17 win over the Detroit Lions. Van Eeghen led all ball carriers with 98 yards, and got Oakland off to a 13–0 lead with two touchdown runs, each coming from one yard out. The Lions fought their way back, and took a 14–13 lead. Mark van Eeghen once again put Oakland in front, this time for good. Cliff Branch caught a Ken Stabler pass close to the Detroit goal line, but lost control and fumbled. However, van Eeghen was near the area, and he reacted quickly by jumping on the loose ball in the end zone for his third touchdown of the game. Oakland added nine more points to their total on a Stabler to Dave Casper 2-yard pass, and when linebacker Phil Villapiano sacked quarterback Gary Danielson in the end zone for a safety. The Raiders improved to

8–4 with their third straight win, and were still deadlocked with Denver for the division lead.[12]

13. Nov. 26: Even though they were only in their third year of existence, the Seattle Seahawks were quickly becoming a major pain for the Raiders. With three seconds left in the game, Seattle's Efren Herrera kicked a 46-yard field goal to get by Oakland, 17–16. This marked the first time since 1965 that a team beat the Raiders twice in one regular season. A crucial missed extra point attempt by Errol Mann proved to be the difference. With 5:29 remaining in the fourth quarter, Ken Stabler threw a 31-yard touchdown to Dave Casper, which gave Oakland a 16–14 lead. It was then that Mann's conversion attempt went wide. The Seahawks, led by the passing of Jim Zorn, then drove for what turned out to be the winning score. Oakland's other points came by way of Mark van Eeghen (4-yard run), and a 26-yard field goal from Mann. The loss did not disrupt the AFC West leadership, as Denver also lost their Thanksgiving Day encounter with Detroit. Seattle helped their chances at a run for the division as well. They improved to 7–6, and were only one game behind the 8–5 Raiders and Broncos with three games to go.[13]

14. Dec. 3: Denver earned sole possession of first place in the AFC West with a 21–6 win over Oakland. Their defense came up big, and that proved to be the difference in the game. With Oakland driving for an early touchdown, an interception at the goal line by defensive back Bernard Jackson killed a golden opportunity. Later, in the fourth quarter, linebacker Randy Gradishar scored on a 29-yard fumble recovery to end any hopes that the Raiders might have had. Denver also took advantage of some costly penalties called against Oakland. The only scoring that Oakland was able to muster came on two Errol Mann field goals from 27 and 37 yards. The loss dropped the Raiders to 8–6, and into a second place tie with Seattle. At this point of the season, Oakland was facing a serious threat of playoff elimination for the first time since 1971.[14]

15. Dec. 10: Over the course of eleven seasons, Oakland made it into the playoffs in ten of those. It almost became a tradition to see the renegade Raiders make a run at pro football supremacy from 1967 to 1977. Sometimes, however, things do not go as planned, and this was one of those times, as the Raiders were eliminated from the post-season by the Miami Dolphins, 23–6. The Dolphins seized the opportunity when Oakland lost the ball on seven turnovers, five of which came on Ken Stabler interceptions. The "Snake" was ready to complete his worst season since taking over as Oakland's starting quarterback in 1973. He suffered from 30 interceptions due mostly to injuries sustained by his blockers up front. The Dolphins stuffed Oakland's running game, and pounded away at the receiving corps each time a Raider came close to the ball. Oakland's lone points came on a 16-yard pass from Stabler to the reliable Fred Biletnikoff, whose days as a Raider were quickly fading.[15]

16. Dec. 17: In what would prove to be the final game for many Raiders legends, including head coach John Madden, the Raiders won, 27–20, over the NFC Central Division champion Minnesota Vikings. Oakland jumped out to a 21–0 first quarter lead, as Fred Biletnikoff caught his final touchdown pass of an illustrious career with the Silver and Black. It came from Ken Stabler, and covered 13 yards. For his final game in an Oakland uniform, the great Biletnikoff caught three passes for 34 yards. Within

17 seconds after Biletnikoff's six-pointer, defensive back Charles Phillips put Oakland on the board again with a 31-yard fumble recovery. Mark van Eeghen added a third touchdown of the quarter on a 4-yard run. Errol Mann closed out Oakland's scoring for the '78 season with two field goals from 30 and 45 yards. Minnesota quarterback Fran Tarkenton rallied the Vikings with three touchdown passes, but was also intercepted five times. Cornerback Lester Hayes registered Tarkenton's fifth interception deep in Oakland territory with 1:50 left in the game. The win gave the Raiders a 9–7 record, which helped them increase their streak of winning seasons to twelve in a row. The division went to the Denver Broncos for the second year in a row, and the Raiders finished in a three-way tie for second with San Diego and Seattle.[16]

Individual Statistics and Roster

Head Coach: John Madden

Assistant Coaches: Tom Dahms, Lew Erber, Tom Flores, Joe Madro, Myrel Moore, Steve Ortmayer, Ollie Spencer, Jim Sweeney, Ray Willsey

1978 Regular Season Record: 9–7

2nd Place AFC Western Division

Scored 311 points to rank 10th out of 28 teams

Allowed 283 points to rank 10th

STARTERS — OFFENSE

QB — Ken Stabler: Started 16 games. Completed 237 of 406 pass attempts for 2,944 yards, 16 TD and 30 INT. Rushed for 0 yards on 4 carries.

HB — Arthur Whittington: Active for 16 games, and started in 9. Rushed for 661 yards on 172 carries and 7 TD. Had 23 receptions for 106 yards, and 23 kickoff returns for 473 yards.

FB — Mark van Eeghen: Started in 16 games. Rushed for 1,080 yards on 270 carries and 9 TD. Had 27 receptions for 291 yards.

WR — Morris Bradshaw: Active for 16 games, and started in 14. Had 40 receptions for 552 yards and 2 TD, and rushed for 5 yards on 1 carry.

WR — Cliff Branch: Started in 16 games. Had 49 receptions for 709 yards and 1 TD.

TE — Dave Casper: Started in 16 games. Had 62 receptions for 852 yards and 9 TD. Rushed for 5 yards on 1 carry, and attempted 1 pass.

LT — Art Shell: Started in 16 games.

LG — Gene Upshaw: Started in 16 games.

C — Dave Dalby: Started in 16 games.

RG — Mickey Marvin: Active for and started in 14 games.

RT — Henry Lawrence: Started in 16 games.

RESERVE OFFENSIVE PLAYERS

Pete Banaszak (RB): Active for 16 games, rushed for 137 yards on 43 carries, and had 7 receptions for 78 yards.

Warren Bankston (RB/TE): Active for 8 games.

Fred Biletnikoff (WR): Active for 16 games, and started in 2. Had 20 receptions for 285 yards and 2 TD.

Larry Brunson (WR): Active for 2 games, and returned 6 kickoffs 154 yards.

George Buehler (G): Active for 1 game.

Raymond Chester (TE): Active for 16 games. Had 13 receptions for 146 yards and 2 TD. Returned 2 kickoffs 27 yards.

Clarence Davis (RB): Active for and started in 2 games. Rushed for 4 yards on 14 carries, and had 4 receptions for 24 yards.

Hubert Ginn (RB): Active for 1 game.

Harold Hart (RB): Active for 7 games, rushed for 44 yards on 7 carries, had 1 reception for 1 yard, and 11 kickoff returns for 252 yards.

David Humm (QB): Active for 16 games, completed 14 of 26 pass attempts for 151 yards and 1 INT, and rushed for -4 yards on 5 carries.

Lindsey Mason (T): Active for 16 games, and returned 1 kickoff 12 yards.

Derrick Ramsey (TE): Active for 16 games, and had 7 kickoff returns for 125 yards.

Terry Robiskie (RB): Active for 7 games, and started in 5. Rushed for 189 yards on 49 carries and 2 TD. Had 5 receptions for 51 yards, and 3 kickoff returns for 58 yards.

Booker Russell (RB): Active for 16 games, rushed for 65 yards on 11 carries, and had 2 kickoff returns for -3 yards.

Joe Stewart (WR): Active for 16 games, and had 4 kickoff returns for 120 yards.

Steve Sylvester (C/G/T): Active for 16 games, and started in 2.

STARTERS — DEFENSE

DE — John Matuszak: Started in 16 games, and had 1 fumble recovery.

DE — Dave Browning: Active for 12 games, and started in 7.

NT — Otis Sistrunk: Started in 16 games.

LOLB — Ted Hendricks: Started in 16 games, had 3 INT and 2 fumble recoveries.

LILB — Monte Johnson: Active for 14 games, and started in 13. Had 1 INT and 2 fumble recoveries.

RILB — Willie Hall: Active for and started in 11 games. Had 2 INT and 1 fumble recovery.

ROLB — Phil Villapiano: Started in 16 games, had 2 INT, 2 fumble recoveries, and recorded 1 safety.

CB — Lester Hayes: Started in 16 games, and had 4 INT.

CB — Monte Jackson: Active for 16 games, and started in 14. Had 2 INT.

SS — Charlie Phillips: Started in 16 games. Had 6 INT, 1 TD, and 3 fumble recoveries and **2 TD. Led the NFL with 127 yards on fumble recoveries.**

FS — Jack Tatum: Active for and started in 15 games. Had 3 INT.

RESERVE DEFENSIVE PLAYERS

Jeff Barnes (LB): Active for 16 games.

Willie Brown (DB): Active for 13 games, and started in 2. Had 1 INT.

Neal Colzie (DB): Active fore 16 games. Had 3 INT, 1 fumble recovery, 1 TD, returned 47 punts 310 yards, and 1 kickoff 15 yards.

Mike Davis (DB): Active for 16 games, and started in 1. Had 1 INT and 1 fumble recovery.

John Huddleston (LB): Active for 11 games, and had 1 fumble recovery.

Rod Martin (LB): Active for 15 games, and started in 8.

Mike McCoy (T): Active for 15 games, started in 3, and had 1 fumble recovery.

Charles Philyaw (E): Active for 15 games, and started in 3.

Randy Rich (DB): Active for 2 games.

Dave Rowe (T): Active for and started in 1 game.

Pat Toomay (E): Active for 16 games, and started in 2.

Robert Watts (LB): Active for 2 games.

Greg Westbrooks (LB): Active for 1 game.

KICKING/PUNTING

K — Errol Mann: Active for 16 games. Made 12 of 20 field goal attempts, and 33 of 38 extra point kicks for 69 points.

P — Ray Guy: Active for 16 games. Punted 81 times for a 42.7 average.

1979 Season Review

1. Sept. 2: The Tom Flores era began in fine fashion with a 24–17 win over the Los Angeles Rams. After the most dismal season of his career, Ken Stabler came back strong by throwing for three touchdowns. The Rams jumped out to a 14–0 lead in front of their home crowd, and held a 17–10 halftime advantage. The Oakland defense then shut down the Los Angeles offense, and

the "Snake" took over from there. In the third quarter, Stabler teamed up with Raymond Chester for two touchdowns from 27 and 4 yards out. Stabler's first scoring strike, a 1-yarder, went to Derrick Ramsey in the second quarter. Jim Breech added a 38-yard field to complete Oakland's point production. Arthur Whittington led all ball carriers with 67 yards to give the Raiders a well-balanced offensive attack.[1]

2. Sept. 9: The San Diego Chargers were one of the hottest teams down the stretch in 1978, winning seven of their last eight games. In 1979, they picked up right where they left off by winning their opener then smacking the Raiders all over the field in a 30–10 blowout. Quarterback Dan Fouts led the charge for San Diego with three touchdown passes. The defense completely shut down Oakland's deep threats, and tormented Ken Stabler with two sacks and just as many interceptions. The "Snake" did manage to produce one touchdown drive against this tough defensive unit, with that coming in the third quarter on a 22-yard pass to rookie wide receiver Rich Martini. Jim Breech added a 35-yard field goal for the Raiders.[2]

3. Sept. 16: The Seattle Seahawks came out of a two-game slump with a 27–10 win over Oakland. Quarterback Jim Zorn threw for three touchdowns to lead the attack. Ken Stabler tried valiantly to keep Oakland in the game by performing up to his old standards. He completed 25 of 37 passes for 343 yards and threw for a touchdown to Rich Martini from 12 yards out. Jim Breech gave the Raiders their other points on a 37-yard field goal.[3]

4. Sept. 23: Things continued to go bad for the Raiders, as they received a major beat down from long-time rival Kansas City, 35–7. The win was Kansas City's first over the Raiders in eight games, and it dropped Oakland into the AFC West cellar with a 1–3 record. The Chiefs allowed the Oakland running game only 98 yards, and held Ken Stabler to a mere 91 through the air, sacked him six times, and intercepted him twice. With six minutes left in the game, Jim Plunkett replaced Stabler, and got the Raiders on the board with a 1-yard touchdown pass to Derrick Jensen to avoid Oakland's first shutout since 1966.[4]

5. Sept. 30: Just when everyone was writing off the Raiders, they came back with a vengeance, knocking Denver out of first place with a stunning 27–3 upset victory. Oakland's defensive line broke through time after time to smother and dispute Denver's offensive game plan. They held the running game to 81 yards, and only surrendered a field goal in the second quarter. Ken Stabler completed 11 of 18 for 196 yards and one touchdown, which went to Dave Casper from 28 yards out. Mark van Eeghen led all ball carriers with 74 yards, and scored on a 1-yard run. Jim Breech added two field goals (27 and 21 yards), and linebacker Monte Johnson recovered a fumble in the end zone to give the Raiders their points.[5]

6. Oct. 8: The AFC Eastern Division leading Miami Dolphins took their 4–1 record to Oakland for a Monday Night Football matchup. The Raiders Monday magic continued to work, as they improved to 3–3 with a 13–3 win. This marked Oakland's eighth straight Monday Night Football victory, and gave them a staggering 12-1-1 all-time record on the prime time spectacle. The Oakland defense played brilliantly, virtually shutting down the Miami offense, and sacked quarterback Bob Griese six times and allowed him only 57 yards through the air for the entire game. Their dominance was eminent, as they held Miami to just four

first downs and 35 total yards in a scoreless first half. The Dolphins also refused to give in, and they too clamped down in this defensive struggle. Ken Stabler was sacked three times, and Oakland's running game was held to under 100 yards. Miami's Tony Nathan fumbled the second half kickoff, and Oakland's Clarence Hawkins recovered on the Miami 33-yard line. Stabler capitalized on the turnover, and within four plays, the "Snake" had the Silver and Black in the end zone on a 14-yard pass to Raymond Chester. Jim Breech's conversion attempt went wide to keep the score at 6–0. Linebacker Ted Hendricks quickly increased Oakland's lead by intercepting a Griese pass, and went 22 yards for the touchdown. Miami managed to add a field goal in the third quarter to avoid a shutout.[6]

7. Oct. 14: Oakland continued on their winning ways with a 50–19 shellacking over the Atlanta Falcons for their highest point production in ten years. The victory gave the Raiders a 4–3 record, putting them only one game out of the AFC West's top spot. The defense turned in another great performance by recovering a fumble and intercepting three passes. Lester Hayes took one of those thefts 52 yards for a touchdown. The offense accounted for the rest of the scoring, with Mark van Eeghen leading the way with three short yardage runs on a pair of 1-yarders and another from six yards out. Ken Stabler completed 16 of 22 passes for 186 yards, and tossed two touchdown passes to Clarence Hawkins (20 yards) and Larry Brunson (8 yards). Jim Breech kicked three field goals from 40, 30, and 47 yards to round out Oakland's point explosion.[7]

8. Oct. 21: The Raiders faced a New York Jets defense that had five rookies on it. However, it was the young New Yorkers that came up big in a 28–19 win. Ken Stabler was intercepted five times, with each New York defensive back coming up with a theft. The other one was credited to linebacker Greg Buttle. Three of Stabler's interceptions led to touchdowns, which proved to be the difference in the game. Stabler did help his own team score, with two scoring tosses to Raymond Chester from 25 and three yards. Jim Breech added a pair of 25-yard field goals to complete Oakland's scoring. The loss dropped the Raiders to 4–4, and two games behind the AFC West leading 6–2 San Diego Chargers at the halfway mark of the '79 season.[8]

9. Oct. 25: On a Thursday night, San Diego's Dan Fouts became the first quarterback in NFL history to throw for 300 yards in four straight games. However, his milestone was spoiled by the Raiders, who shocked the division leaders, 45–22. Ken Stabler made up for his poor showing the previous week by playing an almost perfect game. He completed 13 of 17 passes for 212 yards, one touchdown, and suffered no interceptions. On the receiving end of Stabler's scoring strike was Raymond Chester from 34 yards out. Mark van Eeghen led the ground attack with 95 yards, and scored on a 4-yard run. Oakland's other points came on three 1-yard runs by Booker Russell, an Ira Matthews 104-yard kickoff return that electrified a national television audience, and a 38-yard field goal from Jim Breech. With this upset, Oakland stood at 5–4, and was within one game of the AFC West lead shared by San Diego and Denver.[9]

10. Nov. 4: In a battle between cross-town rivals, the Raiders won territorial bragging rights by beating the 1–9 San Francisco 49ers, 23–10. Ken Stabler remained hot by hitting on 16 of 24 passes, with two of his passes going to Cliff Branch for

touchdowns (9 and 8 yards). Mark van Eeghen had 88 yards rushing, and scored on a 1-yard run. Jim Breech added an 18-yard field goal for the 6–4 Silver and Black. The Oakland defense recovered two fumbles, and intercepted two passes. The special teams also came up with big plays by recovering two fumbles on kickoff returns.[10]

11. Nov. 11: The Houston Oilers moved to 8–3 with a 31–17 win over the Raiders. Helping the Oilers to victory were two Dan Pastorini touchdown passes to Ken Burrough, and the power running of Earl Campbell. Big Earl rambled for 107 yards, scored a touchdown, and became the first AFC running back to top the 1,000-yard barrier in his first two years in the league. Ken Stabler threw touchdowns to Raymond Chester (23 yards) and Dave Casper (3 yards). Jim Breech added a 32-yard field goal for Oakland. The Raiders were now two games out of the division lead, but still very much alive for a playoff spot with a 6–5 record.[11]

12. Nov. 18: Kansas City ended a five-game slide with a 24–21 win in Oakland. The loss put a definite cramp in Oakland's quest for the playoffs. It was the first time in 13 years that the Chiefs won in Oakland. This also marked the first time since 1964 that Kansas City was able to sweep the season series against the Raiders. Ken Stabler turned in a good performance regardless of the loss. He connected on 27 of 44 passes for 296 yards and two scores. Derrick Ramsey (16 yards), and Cliff Branch (3 yards), caught the "Snake's" scoring tosses. Mark van Eeghen scored Oakland's other touchdown on a 2-yard run.[12]

13. Nov. 25: Booker Russell, who had 44 yards on the season up to this game, exploded for 100 yards on only eight carries in a 14–10 win over Denver. Russell set up a Ken Stabler to Dave Casper 3-yard touchdown pass with a long run to give the Raiders a 7–0 lead at the half. Russell then extended Oakland's lead to 14–0 with a 1-yard run in the third quarter. The win still gave the Raiders hopes of reaching the playoffs, even though they were slim at best.[13]

14. Dec. 3: Once again the Raiders worked their Monday Night Football magic. In this game against the New Orleans Saints, they were getting slaughtered, 28–7, in the second quarter. However, by the end of the game, the Raiders walked out of the New Orleans Superdome on the winning side of a 42–35 final. This incredible come-from-behind victory raised Oakland's record to 8–6, and kept their playoff hopes in sight. Ken Stabler led the charge with 26 completions out of 43 pass attempts for 294 yards and four touchdowns. After a Stabler to Raymond Chester 3-yard pass opened the scoring, New Orleans exploded for four touchdowns in the second quarter. Oakland narrowed the gap to 28–14 on the last play of the first half when Arthur Whittington crossed the goal line from one yard out. The Saints got the touchdown back in the third quarter when Kenny Bordelon picked off a Stabler pass and took it 19 yards into the end zone to make it 35–14. The "Snake" quickly made up for his mistake by taking the Raiders 63 yards for a touchdown. He completed five of eight passes on the drive, and Mark van Eeghen finished it off with a 1-yard run to bring Oakland close at 35–21 as the third quarter came to a close. The Silver and Black then exploded in the final quarter with Stabler throwing three scoring passes. First he went to Derrick Ramsey from 17 yards out. The tying one came with 3:19 left after Stabler hit Cliff Branch at the Oakland 40, and the speedster outran the defenders to complete a 66-yard reception.

The winning score also went to Branch from eight yards away, and was set up when Saints' running back Chuck Muncie fumbled. Safety Mike Davis recovered the ball, and then flipped it to linebacker Ted Hendricks, who advanced it to the New Orleans 12. On third down, Stabler found Branch for the game winner, to give the Raiders a near-perfect 13-1-1 record on Monday Night Football. Oakland was in second place in the AFC West at 8–6, and trailed Denver and San Diego by two games. Going into the final two weeks of the regular season, the Raiders had to win both games, while Denver had to lose both of theirs, and Miami and New England had to lose at least one down the stretch. The odds were slim for the Raiders, but they clung to the hope of a few more miracles like they produced in New Orleans.[14]

15. Dec. 9: The Raiders did their part in helping their quest for the playoffs with a 19–14 win over the Cleveland Browns. Denver lost their game, and New England was eliminated, so Oakland was still alive at 9–6. The Raiders scored on their opening drive, with Ken Stabler throwing to Cliff Branch from 39 yards out. Jim Breech added two field goals from 25 and 38 yards, and Oakland was in front, 13–0, going into the second half. Breech also booted two more three-pointers in the fourth quarter from 23 and 45 yards away to round out Oakland's scoring. Throughout this time, the Cleveland Browns were known as the "Kardiac Kids" due to their knack at making a game close in the final minutes. These heart-stopping finishes gave the Browns their nickname. They lived up to their reputation against the Silver and Black, as they battled back on two Mike Pruitt touchdown runs. With 1:22 left on the clock, and the Browns trailing by five points, quarterback Brian Sipe, who was tormented by the Oakland defense all day, threw four incomplete passes to turn the ball over to Oakland on downs at the Cleveland 24-yard line. The Raiders then ran out the clock to register their ninth win of the season. Ken Stabler added another great day to his already stellar career by completing 23 of 34 passes for 196 yards. He had great blocking up front, which allowed him ample time to throw, and was not sacked.[15]

16. Dec. 16: The Raiders were eliminated from playoff contention for the second straight year following a 29–24 loss to the Seattle Seahawks. The Raiders jumped out to an early lead on a Lester Hayes 30-yard interception return. The score was tied at the half, 17–17, but Seattle held Oakland at bay long enough to preserve the victory. The Raiders received their other points on an Arthur Whittington 2-yard run, a Jim Breech 20-yard field goal, and a Ken Stabler-to-Mark van Eeghen 2-yard pass. The "Snake's" touchdown to van Eeghen proved to be Oakland's final points of the decade, and the last touchdown pass thrown by Stabler as an Oakland Raider.[16]

Individual Statistics and Roster

Head Coach: Tom Flores
Assistant Coaches: Sam Boghosian, Willie Brown, Lew Erber, Earl Leggett, Joe Madro, Bob Mischak, Myrel Moore, Steve Ortmayer, Ollie Spencer, Charlie Sumner, Ray Willsey
1979 Regular Season Record: 9–7
3rd Place in AFC Western Division
Scored 365 points to rank 7th out of 28 teams
Allowed 337 points to rank 17th

STARTERS — OFFENSE

QB — Ken Stabler: Started in 16 games. Completed 304 of 498 pass attempts for 3,615 yards, 26 TD and 22 INT. Rushed for -4 yards on 16 carries.

HB — Arthur Whittington: Active for 9 games, and started in 7. Rushed for 397 yards on 109 carries and 2 TD. Had 19 receptions for 240 yards, and 5 kickoff returns for 46 yards.

FB — Mark van Eeghen: Started in 16 games. Rushed for 818 yards on 223 carries and 7 TD. Had 51 receptions for 474 yards and 2 TD.

WR — Cliff Branch: Active for 14 games, and started in 13. Had 59 receptions for 844 yards and 6 TD. Rushed 1 time for 4 yards.

TE — Dave Casper: Active for 15 games, and started in 12. Had 57 receptions for 771 yards and 3 TD.

TE — Raymond Chester: Active for 14 games, and started in 13. Had 58 receptions for 712 yards and 8 TD.

LT — Art Shell: Active for and started in 11 games.

LG — Gene Upshaw: Started in 16 games.

C — Dave Dalby: Active for 16 games, and started in 15.

RG — Steve Sylvester: Started in 16 games.

RT — Henry Lawrence: Started in 16 games.

RESERVE OFFENSIVE PLAYERS

Morris Bradshaw (WR): Active for and started in 3 games, and had 3 receptions for 28 yards.

Larry Brunson (WR): Active for 11 games, had 5 receptions for 49 yards and 1 TD, returned 2 punts 8 yards, and 17 kickoffs 441 yards. **Led the NFL in yards per kickoff return (25.9).**

Todd Christensen (TE/RB): active for 12 games.

Bruce Davis (T/G): Active for 12 games.

Clarence Hawkins (RB): Active for 7 games, rushed for 72 yards on 21 carries, had 2 receptions for 24 yards and 1 TD, and 1 kickoff return for 25 yards.

David Humm (QB): Active for 16 games.

Derrick Jensen (RB/TE): Active for 16 games, and started in 8. Rushed for 251 yards on 73 carries, had 7 receptions for 23 yards and 1 TD, and returned 1 kickoff for 0 yards.

Rich Martini (WR): Active for 16 games, and started in 4. Had 24 receptions for 259 yards and 2 TD.

Mickey Marvin (G): Active for and started in 2 games.

Ira Matthews (RB/WR): Active for 16 games. Rushed 2 times for 3 yards, returned 32 punts 165 yards, and 35 kickoffs for 873 yards and 1 TD.

Dan Medlin (G): Active for 15 games, and started in 4.

Jim Plunkett (QB): Active for 4 games, completed 7 of 15 passes for 89 yards, 1 TD and 1 INT. Rushed for 18 yards on 3 carries.

Derrick Ramsey (TE): Active for 16 games, and started in 3. Had 13 receptions for 161 yards and 3 TD.

Terry Robiskie (RB): Active for 3 games, and started in 1. Rushed for 14 yards on 10 carries, had 5 receptions for 36 yards, and 1 kickoff return for 6 yards.

Booker Russell (RB): Active for 16 games. Rushed for 190 yards on 33 carries and 4 TD, had 6 receptions for 79 yards, and 3 kickoff returns for 21 yards.

Joe Stewart (WR): Active for 3 games, had 1 reception for 3 yards, and 2 kickoff returns for 63 yards.

John Vella (T): Active for 11 games.

STARTERS — DEFENSE

DE — Pat Toomay: Active for 14 games, and started in 13. Had 1 fumble recovery.

DE — Dave Browning: Started in 16 games, and had 2 fumble recoveries.

NT — Dave Pear: Started in 16 games.

LOLB — Ted Hendricks: Started in 16 games, had 1 INT and 1 TD.

LILB — Monte Johnson: Active for 16 games, and started in 15. Had 1 INT, 1 fumble recovery, and 1 TD.

RILB — Phil Villapiano: Started in 16 games, and had 4 fumble recoveries.

ROLB — Rod Martin: Active for 16 games, and started in 15. Had 1 fumble recovery.

CB — Lester Hayes: Started in 16 games, had 7 INT and **2** TD.

CB — Henry Williams: Active for 16 games, and started in 13. Had 3 INT and 1 fumble recovery.

SS — Mike Davis: Active for 16 games, and started in 13. Had 3 INT and 1 fumble recovery.

FS — Jack Tatum: Started in 16 games, and had 2 INT.

RESERVE DEFENSIVE PLAYERS

Jeff Barnes (LB): Active for 16 games, and had 1 INT.

Joe Bell (E): Active for 1 game.

Rufus Bess (DB): Active for 16 games, and had 1 INT and 1 fumble recovery.

John Huddleston (LB): Active for 16 games.

Monte Jackson (DB): Active for 8 games, and started in 3. Had 2 INT and 2 fumble recoveries.

Willie Jones (E): Active for 16 games, and started in 3.

Reggie Kinlaw (NT): Active for 16 games, and started in 2.

John Matuszak (E): Active for 12 games, and started in 2.

Charlie Phillips (DB): Active for 16 games, and started in 3, had 4 INT and 1 fumble recovery.

Charles Philyaw (E): Active for 12 games.

Greg Westbrooks (LB): Active for 4 games.

KICKING/PUNTING

K — Jim Breech: Active for 16 games. Made 18 of 27 field goal attempts, and 41 of 45 extra point kicks for 95 points.

P — Ray Guy: Active for 16 games. Punted 69 times for a 42.6 average.

1980 Season Review

1. Sept. 7: Dan Pastorini started off his Oakland career on a high note. He completed 17 of 37 passes for 317 yards and two touchdowns in a 27–14 win over Kansas City. Both of Pastorini's scoring passes went to Bob Chandler (16 and 32 yards). Pastorini set up another touchdown with a long completion, and Mark van Eeghen finished the drive off with a 1-yard run. Two Chris Bahr field goals (41 and 39 yards) rounded out Oakland's opening game of the new decade.[1]

2. Sept. 14: The pass-happy San Diego Chargers played host to the Raiders, and quarterback Dan Fouts proved to be unstoppable. The future Hall of Famer completed 29 of 43 passes for 389 yards and three touchdowns. He was also intercepted four times in the third quarter. Despite the incredible San Diego air attack, the Raiders forced the game into overtime when Jim Plunkett threw for an 18-yard touchdown to Raymond Chester with 33 seconds left in regulation. Chris Bahr's conversion then tied the game at 24–24. Other scoring for Oakland came on a Dan Pastorini to Cliff Branch pass (48 yards), a Willie Jones fumble recovery of 11 yards, and a Chris Bahr field goal from 35 yards. Plunkett was the hero of the moment after coming off the bench to replace Pastorini, who suffered a knee injury while being sacked. In the overtime period, Fouts stole Plunkett's thunder by throwing a 25-yard scoring toss to wide receiver John Jefferson in the corner of the end zone to send the Raiders home as 30–24 losers.[2]

3. Sept. 21: Rumors were running rampant that the Raiders

were going to move to Los Angeles. For this reason, many fans in Oakland decided not to show up for the home opener as a form of protest. It was the first time in eleven seasons that the Oakland Coliseum was not sold out. Despite the ill feelings of the fans, the Raiders beat the Washington Redskins, 24–21. Oakland started off their home schedule in fine fashion by scoring on their opening drive. Chris Bahr did the honors with a 21-yard field goal. The Raiders remained in control throughout the game, and added three touchdowns onto their total. Dan Pastorini threw for two scores to Dave Casper (20 yards), and Bob Chandler (5 yards), and Arthur Whittington scored on a 43-yard run. Kenny King had a big day leading the ground attack with 136 yards on 25 carries.[3]

4. Sept. 28: Throughout their first three games, the Raiders averaged 25 points and 400 yards of total offense. A trip to Buffalo, New York, changed all that, as the Bills stymied the Silver and Black, 24–7, to remain undefeated. With a balanced offensive attack, the Bills outgained Oakland 325 yards to 179. On defense, Buffalo pressured Dan Pastorini and the rest of the offense all day long. Defensive end Ben Williams was Pastorini's biggest problem, as he sacked the Oakland signal caller twice. The Raiders also turned the ball over five times. When not rushing Pastorini, Buffalo's defense smothered Oakland's running game, allowing them a mere 70 yards and keeping the Raiders' offense out of the end zone. Lester Hayes prevented a shutout by returning a interception 48 yards for Oakland's lone six-pointer.[4]

5. Oct. 5: Oakland's offense took a severe blow when Dan Pastorini went down with a season ending broken leg in the first quarter against Kansas City. Jim Plunkett replaced Pastorini, but could not save the Raiders on this day. The Chiefs opened up a 31–0 second quarter lead, and went on to win with ease, 31–17. The Raiders rallied somewhat by scoring the last 17 points of the game, but it did nothing to help Oakland's cause. Chris Bahr got the Raiders on the board first with a 39-yard field goal, and Jim Plunkett threw scoring passes to Cliff Branch (10 yards) and Bob Chandler (6 yards). The Raiders were 2–3, and looked like a team on an out of control spiral toward the depths of gridiron despair. To add insult to injury, the fans remained steadfast in their disdain for the team's possible move to Los Angeles by recording the smallest crowd (43,513) at Oakland Coliseum since 1968.[5]

6. Oct. 12: The Raiders were always a resilient band of renegades that refused to give into adversity. With the score tied at 24–24 in the fourth quarter against San Diego, Oakland broke the tie with an electrifying then-team record 89-yard touchdown run by Kenny King. King also scored on a 31-yard run in the first quarter to open the scoring, and finished the game with 138 yards rushing on just 12 carries. On the ensuing kickoff following King's 88-yarder, the Raiders scored again when Todd Christensen recovered a fumble in the end zone. Cliff Branch scored on a 43-yard pass from Jim Plunkett, Mark van Eeghen ran for a 3-yard touchdown, and Chris Bahr kicked a 42-yard field goal to round out Oakland's point production in this exciting affair. With their 38–24 win, the Raiders improved to 3–3, and closed to within one game of the AFC West leadership owned by 4–2 San Diego.[6]

7. Oct. 20: In a wild Monday Night Football shootout, the Silver and Black won on the road, 45–34, over the defending Super Bowl champion Pittsburgh Steelers. Both Jim Plunkett and Pittsburgh's Terry Bradshaw had hot arms. Plunkett hit on 13 of

21 passes for 247 yards and three touchdowns, while Bradshaw completed 18 of 27 for 299 yards and one six-pointer. Cliff Branch was on the receiving end of two Plunkett scoring tosses from 56 and 34 yards, and he led Oakland's pass catching corps with five receptions for 123 yards. The Raiders were down, 17–7, in the second quarter before exploding. Also scoring for Oakland were Kenny King (27-yard run), Mark van Eeghen (1-yard run), Rod Martin (34-yard fumble recovery), Morris Bradshaw (45-yard pass from Plunkett), and a 36-yard field goal by Chris Bahr, who also added six conversions. This win gave the Raiders their second straight over division leaders, and fourth in a row over the Steelers since 1976.[7]

8. Oct. 26: The Seattle Seahawks seemed to have Oakland's number over the previous two seasons, beating them four times in a row. This time it seemed the Raiders had extreme confidence after defeating two Super Bowl contenders back-to-back. With Jim Plunkett now entrenched as the starting quarterback, the Silver and Black rolled to a 33–14 win over Seattle. After being considered washed up a few years earlier, Plunkett showed that his career was far from over. He had another great game, completing 16 of 25 passes for 215 yards and three touchdowns. All of his scoring passes went to Bob Chandler (5, 12, and 23 yards), and Chris Bahr added four field goals (34, 38, 30, and 25 yards) to give the 5–3 Raiders their third straight win. On the defensive side, Lester Hayes came up big with two interceptions. In addition, Oakland now shared leadership of the AFC West with San Diego.[8]

9. Nov. 2: Jim Plunkett was once again on top of his game, and continuing to silence his critics. Against the Miami Dolphins, Plunkett led Oakland to their fourth consecutive victory, 16–10, by throwing for two touchdowns. Raymond Chester opened the scoring with a 13-yard reception, and Bob Chandler sealed the win with a 17-yard touchdown grab. Chris Bahr added a 48-yard field goal to Oakland's total. The Raiders scored all their points in the first half, and then turned things over to the defense. The defensive unit did a tremendous job, allowing only 10 first downs and 166 total yards, and intercepted three passes. The 6–3 Raiders seemed to be hitting on all cylinders at this juncture, and were still tied for first place with San Diego.[9]

10. Nov. 9: Since taking over the quarterback duties, Jim Plunkett did not know what losing was all about in 1980. Against the Cincinnati Bengals, Plunkett continued his good fortune in a 28–17 win. He completed 19 of 26 pass attempts for 245 yards, and ran for a 4-yard score. Mark van Eeghen ran for a 2-yard touchdown, and Kenny King added an 8-yarder. Arthur Whittington sparked the home crowd with a fantastic 90-yard kickoff return to round out the team's scoring. With their fifth straight win, the Raiders were 7–3, and now in sole possession of first place following a loss by San Diego.[10]

11. Nov. 17: Monday Night Football magic continued to work for the Raiders, as they made it six straight wins with a 19–17 victory over Seattle. Things looked bleak for Oakland going into the third quarter. They were unable to move the ball, and trailed, 14–0, midway through the third. Oakland finally got a good drive together, going 81 yards in six plays, and capped off by a 10-yard run from Arthur Whittington. The Raiders scored every which way a team could in the fourth quarter to ring up their eighth win of the season. First, Ted Hendricks blocked a

punt out of the end zone for a safety. Oakland then closed to within one point on a 1-yard run by Mark van Eeghen. Chris Bahr then kicked a 28-yard field goal for the go-ahead points with less than a minute remaining in the game.[11]

12. Nov. 23: The Raiders were hot, but so were the Philadelphia Eagles, winners in 10 out of their previous 11 games. In a defensive struggle in the City of Brotherly Love, the Eagles got by Oakland, 10–7. The Raiders held a 7–3 fourth quarter lead on a Jim Plunkett to Cliff Branch 86-yard pass. Philadelphia got a break when running back Leroy Harris caught a pass and went 42 yards. Harris' catch and run led to a Wilbert Montgomery 3-yard touchdown run with three minutes left to play. The loss put the Raiders back into a first place tie with San Diego.[12]

13. Dec. 1: For the third time during the season, the Raiders played on a Monday Night Football telecast. They hosted a tough Denver team that came into Oakland riding a three game winning streak, and were only one game out of first place behind Oakland and San Diego. A large contingent of Oakland fans gathered prior to the game to protest what was going from rumor to reality regarding the Raiders leaving for Los Angeles in 1981. A huge percentage of the 54,563 in attendance did not enter the Oakland Coliseum until midway through the first quarter to show support to the protesters. Despite the turmoil brewing between owner Al Davis, Oakland city officials, the fans, and the apparent move, the Silver and Black managed to hang on without much offense to prevail, 9–3. Jim Plunkett, who only connected on nine of 19 pass attempts for a mere 78 yards, scored the game's lone touchdown on an 8-yard run that erased a 3–0 Denver advantage in the third quarter. Chris Bahr had an off night by missing a conversion kick and four field goal attempts. However, he was successful on a 44-yarder in the fourth to complete the scoring. The win put Oakland at 9–4, and kept them in a first place tie with San Diego.[13]

14. Dec. 7: An interception by Aaron Mitchell in the end zone with 1:44 remaining in the game clinched a 19–13 win for the Dallas Cowboys. Despite the loss, the Raiders still were in a first place tie with San Diego, who also dropped their game. Once again suffering offensive woes, the Raiders only produced one touchdown in a game for the third consecutive week. Oakland's lone six-pointer in this game came on their opening drive when Jim Plunkett connected with Raymond Chester from six yards out. Chris Bahr added two field goals from 22 and 38 yards for Oakland's other points.[14]

15. Dec. 14: Jim Plunkett ignited the stale offense by completing 13 of 21 pass attempts for 213 yards, and teamed up with Bob Chandler for two touchdowns from 11 and 38 yards in a 24–21 decision over Denver. Defensive back Burgess Owens started the scoring by intercepting a Craig Morton pass and returning it 58 yards for a touchdown. Chris Bahr provided Oakland's other points with a 44-yard field goal. At 10–5, Oakland and San Diego were still deadlocked for the AFC West lead with one week to go.[15]

16. Dec. 21: After a two-year absence, the Silver and Black assumed their rightful place in the post season, this time as a wild card representative. They achieved this with an easy 33–17 victory over the New York Giants. Jim Plunkett threw for touchdowns to Cliff Branch (31 yards) and Raymond Chester (37 yards). Arthur Whittington ran for a 7 yard score, Derrick Jensen re-

turned a kickoff 33 yards, and Chris Bahr nailed field goals from 42 and 38 yards away. Mark van Eeghen did not score, but he supplied the Oakland offense with a game-high 115 rushing yards. The Raiders finished at 11–5 along with San Diego. The teams split their head-to-head meetings, so that could not decide the division champion. It was then determined that the AFC West title would go to the Chargers on the basis that they had a higher point total against division foes. It did not matter, because the Raiders had secured a playoff spot when the so-called experts predicted they would finish last in the division.[16]

AFC Wild Card Game, December 28, 1980

It was playoff time again in Oakland, and Ken Stabler was getting ready to take the field. However, after a decade of greatness as quarterback of the Silver and Black, the "Snake" was now wearing the colors of the Houston Oilers. The old saying that a person can never go home again did not hold true in Stabler's case, as he took to the field in an attempt to advance his new team one step further in the playoffs.

The Houston Oilers made it to the AFC Championship Game following the two previous seasons, but fell short to the Pittsburgh Steelers both times. In 1980, Houston traded for a true winner in Stabler, and felt that with his pinpoint passing and calm demeanor, the Oilers could rise to the top of the football world. Throw in the incredible ground-pounding talents of the NFL's top running back in one Earl Campbell, and head coach Bum Phillips, Houston had the makings of an almost invincible offensive attack. To add extra punch to an already loaded offensive attack, the Oilers acquired ex–Raider Dave Casper for Stabler to throw to. Houston also did some final shopping in the Oakland area by obtaining hard-hitting safety Jack Tatum to add some bone-jarring punch to the defense.

With all the pieces in place, Houston and their fans got through the regular season with an 11–5 record, which was good for a second place finish in the AFC Central Division behind Cleveland. Houston's first step to Super Bowl XV began against the Raiders inside the Oakland-Alameda Coliseum. Before the game, Raiders fans remembered all the great moments Stabler provided, and they gave the "Snake" a fantastic ovation. When the game started, however, the Oakland faithful directed their attention toward the future, with a Raiders victory being the objective.

The Oakland defensive unit knew Stabler very well, and used it to their advantage throughout this game. They applied constant pressure on him, sacking him seven times and intercepting two of his passes, with Lester Hayes coming up with both on a day that saw the Raiders put forth one of their greatest defensive efforts. Despite the pressure, Stabler still managed to put together a good game, hitting on 15 of 26 passes for 243 yards.

In the first quarter, cornerback Mike Davis recovered an Earl Campbell fumble on the game's first offensive play. Chris Bahr turned the mishap into a 47-yard field goal to give the Raiders a 3–0 lead. By the end of the quarter, Campbell redeemed himself by scoring on a 1-yard run to put the Oilers up, 7–3.

That was it for the Oilers on this day, as the Raiders scored the go-ahead touchdown in the second quarter and never looked back. Oakland got down to the Houston one thanks to a key 38-yard pass from Jim Plunkett to Kenny King. After two running plays failed to get the ball across the goal line, Plunkett took to the air, and found Todd Christensen in the end zone for a 1-yard score in what was his first catch of the year.

Two big plays helped the Raiders obtain a 17–7 lead at the beginning of the fourth quarter. On the final play of the third, Plunkett found Cliff Branch for a 33-yard pickup to get the ball to the Houston 44. On the first play of the fourth quarter, Plunkett connected with Arthur Whittington, who caught the ball on the Houston 20 and went into the end zone untouched. Bahr added a 37-yard field goal, and then it was Lester Hayes who dealt the crushing blow to the Oilers with five-and-a-half minutes left by intercepting a Stabler pass and returning it 20 yards for the game's final points in a 27–7 Oakland victory. With this lopsided win, the Raiders completed the first phase of their quest for the Super Bowl. They would now have to go on the road the rest of the way to achieve the impossible dream.[17]

AFC Divisional Playoff,
January 4, 1981

The Raiders left the warm climes of California and headed to Cleveland, Ohio, to face the Browns on a day not suited for outside activities of any type unless you were a penguin. By game time, the temperature at Cleveland Municipal Stadium was -36 degrees with the wind chill, which would have made a freezer seem like a tropical paradise. Despite the bone-chilling conditions, a sellout crowd of 77,655 turned out to see the "Kardiac Kids" and their signal caller, league MVP, Brian Sipe, take on the Raiders.

This game was quickly becoming a punting contest between Ray Guy and Cleveland's Johnny Evans throughout the first half, as neither team could get acclimated to the frigid weather conditions. The Browns finally broke through at the halfway point of the second quarter when defensive back Ron Bolton intercepted a Jim Plunkett pass intended for Bob Chandler and raced untouched down the sideline and into the end zone. On the extra point attempt, the snap was bad and it came in low to holder Paul McDonald. McDonald had no time to set the ball right for Don Cockroft, and the kick was low. Ted Hendricks jumped up and blocked it, and Cleveland led, 6–0. Right after Bolton's interception return, the Raiders proved undaunted, and went on a 14-play, 64-yard drive capped off by a Mark van Eeghen 1-yard touchdown run with 18 seconds remaining in the first half. Chris Bahr added the extra point, and Oakland took to the warm confines of the locker room with a 7–6 halftime lead.

Following the second half kickoff, Cockroft gave the lead back to Cleveland with a 30-yard field goal to make the score 9–7 at the 3:31 mark of the third quarter. Three minutes later, the Browns tried another field goal, but holder Paul McDonald once again had problems receiving the snap. There was no time to attempt to set the ball down for Cockroft so he tried to run for a first down but was stopped. Later in the same quarter, the hold was good and Cockroft sent a 29-yarder through the uprights to extend the Cleveland advantage to 12–7 with 2:40 remaining in the third quarter.

At 5:38 of the fourth quarter, the Raiders got their chance to ring up some more points. Two plays in particular helped Oakland in this drive. On third-and-four from the Oakland 26, Plunkett sent an underhand toss to Mark van Eeghen, who then turned it into a gain of 13, and more importantly, gave the Raiders a new set of downs to work with starting on their 39. Six plays later, from the Cleveland 14, Plunkett was sacked, but the Browns were hit with an offside penalty. Given the opportunity to repeat the down, Plunkett took advantage of the second chance by connecting with Kenny King for a gain of six down to the Cleveland three. Van Eeghen capped the 12-play, 80-yard drive off with his second 1-yard run, and following Bahr's conversion, the Raiders clung to a slim 14–12 lead. They were now ready to brace themselves for the "Kardiac Kids," the moniker given to the Browns of this time due to their penchant for last minute heroics.

Any comeback the Browns had thoughts of took a quick hiatus when Sipe fumbled on his own 25 and Odis McKinney recovered for Oakland at the 24. The Cleveland defense quickly got the ball back for Sipe to work his magic with 2:22 left showing on the clock by stopping Oakland on fourth-and-one at the 15. Sipe came back out with 85 frozen yards in front of him with one final stab at yet another fantastic finish, with this one getting them a ticket to the conference championship game. In eight plays, Sipe took the Browns to the Oakland 14 with 56 ticks left and a brown and orange clad crowd in a complete frenzy. They saw this type of finish before, but never with so much riding on it. Facing a second-and-nine situation from the 13, it looked like a field goal was going to be the answer for the Browns. However, Don Cockroft was suffering from a sore knee, and had already missed two field goal attempts. The coaching staff decided that the Browns rode on Sipe's right arm all season, so why stop believing in it now. Calling for "Red Right 88," a play that worked so many times before, Sipe broke the huddle and set up under center. At the snap, Sipe looked to the end zone for his future Hall of Fame tight end Ozzie Newsome. The pass was right on target and within Newsome's grasp. With the crowd now ready to erupt, Mike Davis cut in front of the ball and intercepted it with 49 seconds left to kill Cleveland's hopes and add yet another chapter to the city's infamous sports disappointments. Cleveland Municipal Stadium fell silent, the Raiders ran out the clock, and were headed back to the warmth of California and a date with the San Diego Chargers for the right to go to Super Bowl XV.[18]

AFC Championship Game,
January 11, 1981

The San Diego Chargers were making their first trip to a conference or league title game since 1965, and they were loaded with one of the most explosive offensive attacks in the history of pro football. The offense was dubbed "Air Coryell" after head coach Don Coryell. Quarterback Dan Fouts threw for a league-high 4,715 yards and 30 touchdowns. The receiving corps of Kellen Winslow, John Jefferson, and Charlie Joiner became the first group from the same team to each gain 1,000 yards on pass receptions in a single season.

Excitement was high, as San Diego hosted their bitter rivals in front of a Jack Murphy Stadium crowd of 55,428. This game quickly became an offensive exhibition to the surprise of no one. The only thing that was a surprise to San Diego fans at least was how fast the Raiders got on the board. On the third play of the game, Jim Plunkett teamed up with Raymond Chester on a 65-yard touchdown. Undaunted, the Chargers high-octane offense responded to Oakland's quick sortie on a 48-yard touchdown from Fouts to Joiner that tied the game at 7–7.

It was now Oakland's turn to answer back, and Plunkett took the ball over himself from five yards out to give the lead back to the Raiders. Two minutes later, Kenny King caught Plunkett's second touchdown toss of the game from 21 yards out to extend the Oakland advantage to 21–7, and it was still in the first quarter.

Midway through the second stanza, the Raiders took a commanding 28–7 lead on a Mark van Eeghen 3-yard run.

Not wanting to be blown out in their own house, the Chargers came roaring back with an offensive barrage of their own. From the closing minute of the first half to midway through the third quarter, San Diego put up 17 points to close the gap to 28–24 on a Fouts to Joiner 8-yard pass, a Rolf Benirschke 26-yard field goal, and a Chuck Muncie 6-yard run.

The Raiders remained focused and tacked on six more points on two Chris Bahr field goals from 27 and 33 yards to make it a 34–24 Oakland advantage with just under ten minutes left in regulation. The Chargers could not get any more than a field goal from the Raiders' defense the rest of the way, and when the clock hit 0:00, the Silver and Black were going to their third Super Bowl, becoming the first team to ever get to the big game in each decade that it was played.

The Raiders were the least likely team at the start of the playoffs to even be considered a Super Bowl contender to many outside the organization. However, from within the Raider Empire, they believed, and this 1980 team had something to prove. With their classic "us against the world" mentality to guide them, the Raiders earned the AFC championship, and looked ahead to the final leg of their race for gridiron supremacy.[19]

Super Bowl XV

Jan. 25, 1981; Played at the Superdome,
New Orleans, Louisiana

The city of New Orleans had hosted four previous Super Bowls prior to the one scheduled for January 25, 1981. In the previous encounters, feel good stories arose that permeate forever in Super Bowl lore. In 1970, future Hall of Fame quarterback Len Dawson helped Kansas City overcome insurmountable odds to beat the heavily favored Minnesota Vikings after being exonerated of links to gamblers. He also won the game's Most Valuable Player Award. The Dallas Cowboys, dubbed "America's Team," won two Super Bowls in New Orleans with a head coach and quarterback both of strong religious convictions. And how could anyone forget when Pittsburgh's much-beloved owner Art Rooney finally got to be declared a champion at age 74 after decades of despair in the Steel City. Then along came the Oakland Raiders in 1981, the Hells Angels of pro football, who brought "the Tooz," bomb threats, and a bitter feud between Al Davis and NFL commissioner Pete Rozelle into the Big Easy. They also had billboards throughout the city designed with a picture of the Raiders' Super

Bowl XI ring and their classic "Commitment to Excellence" and "Pride and Poise" mottos written on them to show anyone in town that the bad boys were around.

About ten days before the Raiders were set to invade New Orleans, Al Davis testified about his concern that many team owners were making a very good profit on scalping Super Bowl tickets. Now, not only was he getting 27 other owners mad at him, but Davis decided to go for the kill and stated that even the league's reigning czar, Rozelle himself, was in on the take. In defense of Davis, he did not come forth with any new evidence, but rather fortified a story regarding a past high-ranking executive of the Los Angeles Rams, who admitted to some wrongdoings in the past. Rozelle strongly denied any charges claimed against him, and added more strain on his tumultuous relationship with the king of Raider Nation. Adding salt to the wound was the fact that Davis continued on his pursuit to relocate his Raiders to Los Angeles despite negative feedback from Rozelle and his fellow owners. The big buzz throughout the media was if Rozelle would present the Lombardi Trophy to Davis if the Raiders won, and if so, how Davis would react.

Next came a bomb threat to the Raiders' hotel that, after an extensive search, turned up nothing. And then there was John "the Tooz" Matuszak, Oakland's resident wild man and inspiration leader of the defense. The "Tooz" liked to go out on the town on Wednesday nights, and with the party town of New Orleans serving as a backdrop, and wilder than ever with the Super Bowl growing closer, the temptation was just too great for Matuszak to pass up. He was a fierce competitor who knew what was at steak come game time, but he had to release some steam on the famed streets of the "Big Easy." After his one night of good times, Matuszak was then ready to let his fury loose on Super Sunday against the Philadelphia Eagles, who were beginning to serve mainly as a sideshow in this silver and black mecca of mayhem.

The Eagles came into this meeting after years of futility. Since winning the pre–Super Bowl NFL championship in 1960, the Eagles slid into many seasons of sub-par performances. Dick Vermeil was hired as head coach in 1976 after a successful tenure in the college ranks at UCLA. His first two seasons in the "City of Brotherly Love" were anything but that. Philadelphia only won nine out of 28 games, but all that changed by 1978, as they finished at 9–7 and earned a spot in the post-season for the first time in 18 years. Another playoff season came in 1979, and by the dawn of the 1980's, Vermeil and company were considered a solid contender for a championship.

Along the way to a 12–4 record, the Eagles were led on offense by quarterback Ron Ja-

Defensive end John Matuszak seen here in 1981. Nobody embodied the outlaw image of the Raiders any better. Whether it was a quarterback, a running back or the wild life, "the Tooz" pursued them all with voracious intensity (AP Photo/NFL Photos).

worski. "Jaws" threw for 3,529 yards, 27 touchdowns, and 12 interceptions. On the receiving end of Jaworski's throws were a talented group led by veteran Harold Carmichael's 48 catches for 815 yards and nine touchdowns. The other wide receiver, Charlie Smith, was one reception behind Carmichael, and amassed 825 yards and three six-pointers. Tight end Keith Krepfle rounded out Jaworski's air troops with 30 receptions for 450 yards and four touchdowns. Helping to give the Eagles a very balanced attack was running back Wilbert Montgomery, who had earned a stellar reputation around the pro circuit as one of its top offensive weapons. Injuries prevented the consistent 1,000-yard rusher from breaking that plateau in 1980, but he still ran for 778 yards and eight touchdowns in 12 starts. He was also a devastating weapon out of the backfield as a receiver. His 50 catches led the team in that category, and he gained 407 yards and two touchdowns on those catches. Montgomery was completely healed for the Eagles' run to the Super Bowl, and proved it by ripping through the Dallas Cowboys for 194 rushing yards in Philadelphia's 20–7 win in the NFC Championship Game.

The Philadelphia defense was a stingy lot when it came to giving up points, and led the league with 222 tallies allowed. Up front, this unit was led by nose tackle Charlie Johnson and end Claude Humphrey, who recorded 14 sacks. Future Raider Jerry Robinson and Bill Bergey patrolled the field from their linebacker positions, both with the ability to help out in running or passing situations. The defensive backfield was looked at as one of the best in the game, with Herman Edwards pacing the attack through his veteran leadership.

Five days prior to this Super Bowl, 53 Americans were released from Iran after 444 days of captivity in what was called the Iran hostage crisis. During this trying and gripping time, yellow ribbons were displayed everywhere throughout the American landscape and pinned onto countless articles of clothing. The yellow ribbon came to symbolize the anticipation of a loved one returning home from conflict. As an honor to those 53 individuals who lost over a year of their lives away from home and loved ones, the Louisiana Superdome was donned with a massive 80-foot long and 30-foot wide yellow ribbon that greeted all those attending the Super Bowl, and for the viewing audience around the world to witness. Both the Eagles and Raiders had yellow ribbon stickers applied to the back of their helmets as well.

The broadcasting team of announcing legend Dick Enberg and Hall of Famer Merlin Olsen had the honor of calling the action for the NBC Television Network. Long-time multi-talented entertainer Helen O'Connell sang the national anthem, and Marie Lombardi, widow of coaching great Vince Lombardi, presided over the coin toss won by the Eagles. The Raiders were not distraught over losing the first level of competition during this grand spectacle. In their ten wins out of their previous twelve games, they lost the coin toss.

With all the hype and controversy now a memory, at least for sixty minutes of play, referee Ben Dreith gave the signal to start the game. With the Superdome crowd of 75,500, and a world wide audience transfixed on the 100-yard piece of New Orleans real estate, Oakland's Chris Bahr ended all the pre-game buildup when his right foot connected with the ball to begin Super Bowl XV.

Bahr's kick came down on the Philadelphia eight into the awaiting hands of Billy Campfield, who returned it 16 yards. Starting from his own 24, Ron Jaworski handed off to Wilbert Montgomery for a gain of eight yards around the left end. Leroy Harris picked up three yards and a first down, and then Jaworski decided to test the passing lanes. Looking for one of his tight ends, John Spagnola near midfield, Jaworski let the ball go. Within three plays, the first turnover happened, as linebacker Rod Martin read the play perfectly, stepped in front of Spagnola and intercepted. He then ran for 17 yards down to the Philadelphia 30 before being dragged down by Montgomery.

With only two minutes expired of the clock, the Raiders saw themselves in an excellent position to make sometime happen thanks to Martin's quick reaction. Plunkett decided to start things off slowly by handing off to Mark van Eeghen on first down, and the bruising fullback picked up three yards off the right side. Plunkett was faced with a third-and-eight situation after Kenny King carried for one yard. Plunkett went back to King, this time on a pass play, but it fell incomplete. However, defensive lineman Carl "Big Daddy" Hairston was called for jumping offside and a five-yard penalty moved the Raiders to the Philadelphia 23 for another chance at a first down. This time, the Silver and Black succeeded when van Eeghen powered his way for four yards over the right side. Plunkett felt the time was now right to look for speed demon Cliff Branch, and he found him for a gain of 14 yards down to the five. Two van Eeghen runs gained three yards, and now, on third-and-goal from the 2-yard line, Plunkett surprised the defense with a pass. At first, it did not look good, as Plunkett could not find anyone open, and he began to run to his right. It was then that he saw Branch with his arms waving in the end zone. Plunkett then tossed the pigskin toward Branch, and the result was the first touchdown of Super Bowl XV. Bahr added the extra point to cap off the seven-play, 30-yard drive with 8:56 remaining in the first quarter.

Bahr kicked off to Campfield on the 4-yard line, and he returned this one 21 yards. Two Montgomery runs produced a mere four yards, and a Jaworski pass attempt to Charlie Smith was broken up by Lester Hayes to force a punting situation. The Raiders were called for being offside, and were penalized five yards before Max Runager sent a 46-yard boot toward Ira Matthews at the Oakland 20. Matthews only made it two yards upfield before being stopped. King swept left for six yards, and van Eeghen hit the right side for three. With a yard to go for a first down, Plunkett called his own number on a quarterback sneak, but was stopped for no gain and Ray Guy came on to punt. He got off a 44-yard kick that John Sciarra returned 12 yards to give the Eagles a good start on their own 37.

Jaworski went right to the air, connecting with tight end Keith Krepfle for eight yards. Montgomery moved the chains with a gain of three up the middle. The star running back attempted another run on first down, by was dropped for a loss of one by Ted Hendricks on a sweep to the left side. Montgomery made up for the loss on the following play by catching a screen pass from Jaworski for 13 yards and another first down. Now in Oakland territory at the 40, Montgomery lost one yard going off left tackle when Dave Browning met him and refused to give ground. Jaworski returned to the air, but was being pressured quickly by the tough Oakland defense. He looked to dump the ball as soon as possible, and managed to get it into Leroy Harris' hands for a gain of only one yard before Rod Martin drilled the Philly running back into the ground. There was no surprise when Jaworski dropped back on third-and-10. Sending wide receiving-great Harold Carmichael in motion to divert attention away from the other wide receiver, Rodney Parker, Jaworski's plan worked to perfection, as Parker extended his arms and came down with a 40-yard touchdown grab to pull the Eagles to within one point. Amidst the celebrating, a yellow penalty flag was on the ground, and the six points were quickly taken away when it was learned that Carmichael was called for illegal motion, and the Eagles lost five yards instead of attempting the extra point. Dejected, but still having to remain focused, the Eagles broken their huddle in an attempt to get those six points back on the board. The Jaworski to Parker combination was tried again, but this time Odis McKinney batted the ball away on a pass attempt across the middle. Runager got off a 31-yard punt that Matthews called for a fair catch on at the Oakland 14.

With 1:06 left in the opening stanza, a Plunkett to Branch pass of four yards stopped the clock when he went out of bounds after the catch. King then ran off right tackle for two more, bringing up a third-and-four from the 20. With the seconds winding down, Plunkett dropped back, and with his deep receiving threats covered, he looked for a safety valve, and found it in Kenny King. While running to his left, Plunkett landed a perfect screen pass into King's hands while still in stride along the left sideline at the Oakland 39. There was nothing but open field in front, and within nine seconds, King rang up an 80-yard touchdown reception that extended the Raiders' advantage to 14–0 following Bahr's extra point.

The three-play, 86-yard drive took a mere 57 seconds, and following it, Bahr kicked off to Campfield, who received the ball on his 14, and advanced it 12 yards before McKinney stopped him to end the first quarter.

The Eagles were hoping to get out of this hole quickly before things got out of hand. Montgomery ran for eight on first down, and after Reggie Kinlaw clamped down on Harris' attempt to run left, Jaworski went to the air, connecting with Spagnola for a pickup of 22 yards before Mike Davis stopped him on the Oakland 44. Now in Oakland territory, Jaworski looked to get even deeper. His first crack at it was denied when Lester Hayes broke up a pass intended for Smith at the goal line. However, on the next play, Jaworski hit his mark on a 25-yard hookup to Montgomery that got the Eagles to the Oakland 19. Montgomery then ran for five, and Harris for one, bringing up a third-and-four situation. The Raiders assumed Jaworski was going to throw, and they were correct in their thinking. They applied fierce pressure that made Jaworski scramble around looking for a receiver. He managed to get off a pass intended for Montgomery, but it fell incomplete to bring up a field goal situation. Tony Franklin came on successfully sent the ball on its way for a 30-yard trek through the uprights to put Philadelphia on the board with 10:28 left in the first half.

The ensuing kickoff was received by Keith Moody on the one, and he brought it back 19 yards. The Philadelphia defense made quick work of the Raiders on their next possession. A Plunkett to Bob Chandler pass attempt missed its mark, and Arthur Whittington was dropped for a loss of two trying to run up the middle, and Plunkett ended the quick series with a gain of five

yards while trying to avoid a pass rush. Ray Guy came on and let loose with a 42-yard punt that Sciarra returned six yards. The Eagles were called for clipping on the return, and penalized 15 yards.

Starting from the Philadelphia 26 after the penalty was marked off, Jaworski and the Eagles' offense also made a quick exit. A three-yard screen pass to Carmichael was followed by two incompletions. On fourth down, Runager punted 33 yards to Matthews, who was dumped by Sciarra for a loss of a yard down at the Oakland 37.

With 7:23 to go in the half, the Raiders worked the right side of the line, with van Eeghen picking up six and then four yards and a first down in the process. Following an incompletion intended for King on a deep route, Plunkett teamed up with Branch on an 18-yarder that moved the Raiders to the Philadelphia 35. Things then went sour for Oakland. After King ran off right tackle for four yards, a pass intended for Branch was broken up by Herman Edwards, and then Plunkett picked up four while trying to avoid a rush. Bahr attempted a 45-yard field goal, but it went wide right and fell short.

The Eagles felt some momentum shifting their way, and looked to seize the opportunity to pull closer before the end of the first half. From the Philadelphia 27, Montgomery was dropped by Matt Millen for no gain. Jaworski avoided disaster when a pass intended for Carmichael went right into the hands of defensive back Burgess Owens, but he dropped it. Jaworski went back to Carmichael for a 29-yard gain at the two-minute warning. Fighting against the Oakland defense and the clock, Harris ran for three yards and the Eagles called a timeout to stop the clock. Jaworski and Carmichael teamed up on a 14-yard pass, which was followed by two incompletions. Carmichael then hauled in a 16-yard pass to get the Eagles to the Oakland 27 with 1:07 left. After calling their second timeout, Philadelphia failed on three straight pass attempts, two of which were intended for the end zone. Franklin came on to attempt a 28-yard field goal with 43 seconds remaining. At the snap, Ted Hendricks used his 6'7" frame to reach up and swat away the ball. It was recovered by Matt Millen for the Raiders on the Oakland 14, and following a van Eeghen run of five yards, the teams retreated to their locker rooms with the Raiders up, 14–3.

During the first half, Oakland was establishing the tempo with solid running from Mark van Eeghen off the right side behind the stellar blocking of guard Mickey Marvin and tackle Henry "Killer" Lawrence. Plunkett looked confident with two touchdown tosses to his credit, and the defense was getting great penetration up front from John "the Tooz" Matuszak, and the defensive backs were knocking down more pass attempts than allowing. With another thirty minutes to go, the Raiders were looking to keep doing what got them an 11-point lead, and if they did, the second diamond-studded Super Bowl ring in team history would be awarded months later.

The second half got underway with Franklin kicking off to Matthews, who took the ball upfield from the three to the Oakland 24. The Raiders started off not too well, as King was dropped for a loss of three yards by linebacker Bill Bergey. They were also penalized 10 yards due to a holding call on Henry Lawrence. Mark van Eeghen gave the Raiders a little breathing room with a gain of eight yards off the left side. Two pass plays followed that took the Raiders from deep in their territory to inside the Philly 40. A Plunkett to King screen pass gained 13, and then Bob Chandler went deep and caught a 32-yarder to put the ball on the Philadelphia 33. A four-yard run by van Eeghen got the Raiders to the 29. On second down, and with a good offensive flow going, Plunkett smelled the end zone, and looked to devour it. At the snap, Cliff Branch headed toward the right corner of the end zone. Plunkett let loose with a pass lacking velocity, and defensive back Roynell Young was blanketing Branch as the weak pass made its way through the Superdome. Young made a move to intercept, but Branch turned back around one yard, and grabbed the ball out of Young's hands and went into the end zone for his second touchdown reception of the game. Bahr added the conversion to finish off the five-play, 76-yard drive, which now gave the Raiders a commanding 21–3 lead with 12:24 left in the third quarter.

Bahr's kickoff went to Perry Harrington on the Philadelphia 10, but no return was attempted. Starting deep in the hole, Montgomery ran off left tackle for a gain of four. Jaworski gave the Eagles some breathing room with an 18-yard strike to Carmichael that got the ball out to the Philly 32. Montgomery added three yards to the left side before a Jaworski pass attempt to Spagnola was incomplete. However, rookie linebacker Matt Millen was called for pass interference, and the Eagles were awarded five yards and an automatic first down. The Eagles then gained 26 yards over the next three plays on a 19-yard pass from Jaworski to Carmichael, a five-yard run from Harris, and a gain of two by Montgomery. With the ball on the Oakland 34, Jaworski looked to throw a screen pass on third-and-three. Looking left for Spagnola, Rod Martin read the play perfectly and came up with his second interception of the game, and returned it two yards to the Oakland 32 with 8:20 left in the quarter.

The Raiders were starting to feel that the game would be theirs, and looked to distance themselves even more from the Eagles. A five-yard run up the middle by van Eeghen was followed by a minor setback when Plunkett was sacked for a loss of one yard. On third-and-six, Plunkett got the Raiders into Philly territory with a 16-yard toss to Raymond Chester at the Eagles' 48. Going right back to Chester, Plunkett connected this time for 17 yards. Derrick Jensen got his first Super Bowl carry on the next play, and ran for a gain of five yards off the left side. A Claude Humphrey tackle on Whittington resulted in a loss of two yards, and a pass to Chester fell incomplete to bring up fourth down. Bahr did not allow Martin's interception to go for nothing, and he extended the Oakland advantage to 24–3 on a 46-yard field goal with 4:35 left in the third to complete the seven-play, 40-yard drive. Martin's two interceptions were now looming large, as they led to ten points for the Silver and Black.

Campfield received Bahr's kickoff on his six, and returned it 33 yards to give the Eagles what appeared to be excellent field position to start a comeback bid. It was not to be, as Ray Phillips was called for clipping back on the Philadelphia 24, and the penalty was half the distance from where the infraction occurred. So instead of starting almost at midfield, the Eagles would have to begin deep in their own territory on the 12. An incompletion intended for Montgomery started the series off, but then Jaworski let loose with a deep pass that found Charlie Smith for a pickup of 43 yards down at the Oakland 45. The Eagles took to the

ground over the course of the next four plays, with Perry Harrington and Montgomery both gaining four yards, followed by three on another Montgomery carry, and finally Harris ran to the left side for three to get Philadelphia to the Oakland 34. Mixing things up, Jaworski went back to the air, but two straight pass attempts to Carmichael fell incomplete. Jaworski made up for the mishaps by hitting Parker for a gain of 19, and then Louie Giammona ended the third quarter with a run off left tackle that picked up seven yards down to the Oakland five.

The final fifteen minutes began with Montgomery being stopped for no gain by Mike Davis on a sweep to the left. An offside penalty on Lester Hayes moved the ball half the distance to the goal line, but Philadelphia was called for a false start on the next play to bring up a third-and-six from the eight. Jaworski then found the end zone on a pass to Keith Krepfle, and Franklin's extra point pulled the Eagles to within 14 points of the lead, with the score now at 24–10 with 13:59 to go in regulation.

Matthews received Franklin's kick on the three and returned it to the Oakland 11. Mark van Eeghen opened the series with a run off the left side for a pickup of eight, and followed that with one for five yards and a first down. King ran for one up the middle, and then Plunkett went to the passing game, connecting with Chester for a gain of eight. Claude Humphrey was penalized 15 yards for roughing the passer, and Oakland moved to their own 48 after the penalty was marked off. After a pass attempt to Branch fell incomplete, Plunkett hit Chandler on two consecutive downs. The first one went for 23 yards, and the second for five, which put the Raiders on the Philadelphia 24. A run by van Eeghen to the right picked up five, and Whittington added two more following an incomplete pass intended for van Eeghen. Plunkett looked to go back to Chandler on third down from the 17, but the pass was incomplete. Bahr came on and kicked his second three-pointer of the game, this time from 35 yards, to end the 11-play, 72-yard drive, and give the Raiders a 27–10 lead with 8:29 left.

Bahr's kickoff was received by Campfield on the two, and he returned it 20 yards to give Philadelphia their final opportunity, although extremely slim, to make a run at winning. Montgomery swept right for two, and then Jaworski connected with Smith for 16 and Montgomery for 19 to get inside Oakland territory at the 41. Rod Martin stopped Harris for a loss of one on the next play, and then Jaworski fumbled the snap. Willie Jones pounced on the loose pigskin at the Oakland 42 to not only end the series for Philly, but their hopes as well.

With this game all but over with 5:30 left on the clock, the Raiders looked to just run time off the clock and collect their second Vince Lombardi Trophy in the process. It must have been going through everyone's minds in pro football circles as how NFL Commissioner Pete Rozelle and his bitter rival Al Davis would act when the Lombardi trophy had to be presented. Many interesting things must have been said in that regard.

With all the excitement of anticipating a Super Bowl title on the field and across Raider Nation, van Eeghen ran up the middle for a gain of two, and King swept the left side for six more. On third down, Whittington dropped a pass to bring Ray Guy in to punt. He got off a 40-yard kick that Wally Henry returned two yards before Jeff Barnes brought him down right at midfield.

Becoming completely predictable now, Jaworski was forced

to pass on every down with 3:51 remaining. His first pass attempt, intended for Smith, was broken up by Dwayne O'Steen. He then connected with Montgomery for 13 yards before having a pass deflected at the line scrimmage. Montgomery caught one for five yards, and then Willie Jones was called for roughing the passer, and the Raiders were penalized 15 yards. From the Philadelphia 45 on first and ten, Jaworski retreated into the pocket, and fired a pass to Campfield over the middle. Rod Martin came up and intercepted his third pass of the game to establish a Super Bowl record. He picked it off at the Oakland 37, and returned it 25 yards to the Philadelphia 38 with 2:50 left before the Raiders could officially be called world champions.

The Raiders just wanted to simply run out the clock and start the celebration as van Eeghen carried three straight times for a total of 10 yards, which brought the game to the two-minute warning. It was then Derrick Jensen's turn to carry three times. A sweep to the left gained six, and two runs up the middle, each for three yards, ended the game.

Jim Plunkett had one the greatest human-interest stories in the history of pro football. He was cast off just a few years earlier as being washed up. Even going into the 1980 campaign, his chances of playing seemed remote at best. And now here he was, after guiding the Raiders from a 2–3 start to the ultimate reward of the professional gridiron circuit. For the game, Plunkett completed 13 of 21 passes for 261 yards and three touchdowns. For his efforts, he was named Super Bowl XV Most Valuable Player.[20]

This proud group of men clad in silver and black beat all the odds, and rose from the ashes like a Phoenix to climax one of the game's greatest championship runs ever. While the players were celebrating in their locker room, the master renegade himself, Al Davis entered to prepare for the Lombardi Trophy presentation. Despite all the talk of what would happen when Davis and Rozelle faced each other was put to rest quickly. After saying a few words of praise about the Raiders, Rozelle handed the trophy to Davis, who thanked him and that was the extent of the much-anticipated event. Davis was too busy enjoying the moment to use it as a pulpit about things not related to what his beloved band of renegades just accomplished.

Starting Lineup for Super Bowl XV

OFFENSE

QB — Jim Plunkett	LT — Art Shell
RB — Kenny King	LG — Gene Upshaw
FB — Mark van Eeghen	C — Dave Dalby
WR — Cliff Branch	RG — Mickey Marvin
WR — Bob Chandler	RT — Henry Lawrence
TE — Raymond Chester	

DEFENSE

DE — John Matuszak	ROLB — Rod Martin
DE — Dave Browning	CB — Lester Hayes
NT — Reggie Kinlaw	CB — Dwayne O' Steen
LOLB — Ted Hendricks	SS — Mike Davis
LILB — Matt Millen	FS — Burgess Owens
RILB — Bob Nelson	

KICKING/PUNTING

K — Chris Bahr	P — Ray Guy

Individual Statistics from Super Bowl XV

OFFENSE

Jim Plunkett: 13 completions out of 21 pass attempts for 261 yards and 3 TD. Rushed for 9 yards on 3 carries.
Kenny King: Rushed for 18 yards on 6 carries. Had 2 receptions for 93 yards and 1 TD.
Mark van Eeghen: Rushed for 80 yards on 19 carries.
Derrick Jensen: Rushed for 12 yards on 3 carries.
Arthur Whittington: Rushed for -2 yards on 3 carries.
Bob Chandler: Had 4 receptions for 77 yards.
Cliff Branch: Had 5 receptions for 67 yards and 2 TD.
Raymond Chester: Had 2 receptions for 24 yards.
Ira Matthews: Returned 2 kickoffs for 29 yards and 2 punts for 1 yard.
Keith Moody: Returned 1 kickoff for 19 yards.
Chris Bahr: Had 2 field goals and 3 extra point kicks.

DEFENSE

Rod Martin: Had 3 INT for 44 yards.

Individual Statistics and Roster

Head Coach: Tom Flores
Assistant Coaches: Sam Boghosian, Willie Brown, Lew Erber, Chet Franklin, Earl Leggett, Joe Madro, Bob Mischak, Steve Ortmayer, Charlie Sumner, Ray Willsey
1980 Regular Season Record: 11–5
2nd Place AFC Western Division
Scored 364 points to rank 7th out of 28 teams
Allowed 306 points to rank 10th
Led the league in defensive interceptions (35), lowest average rush per carry by the defense (3.4), and turnovers caused by a defense (52)

STARTERS — OFFENSE

QB — Jim Plunkett: Active for 13 games, and started in 11. Completed 165 of 320 pass attempts for 2,299 yards, 18 TD and 16 INT. Rushed 28 for 141 yards on 28 carries and 2 TD.
HB — Kenny King: Active for 15 games, and started in 13. Rushed for 761 yards on 172 carries and 4 TD. Had 22 receptions for 145 yards.
FB — Mark van Eeghen: Started in 16 games. Rushed for 838 yards on 222 carries and 5 TD. Had 29 receptions for 259 yards.
WR — Cliff Branch: Active for 16 games, and started in 15. Had 44 receptions for 858 yards, 7 TD and 1 rush for 1 yard.
WR — Bob Chandler: Started in 16 games and had 49 receptions for 786 yards and 10 TD.
TE — Raymond Chester: Active for 16 games, and started in 10. Had 28 receptions for 366 yards and 4 TD.
LT — Art Shell: Started in 16 games.
LG — Gene Upshaw: Started in 16 games.
C — Dave Dalby: Active for 16 games, and started in 14.
RG — Mickey Marvin: Started in 16 games.
RT — Henry Lawrence: Started in 16 games.

RESERVE OFFENSIVE PLAYERS

Morris Bradshaw (WR): Active for 16 games, and had 6 receptions for 132 yards and 1 TD.
Dave Casper (TE): Active for and started in 6 games.
Todd Christensen (RB/TE): Active for 16 games and had 1 kickoff return for 10 yards.
Bruce Davis (T/G): Active for 16 games.
I.M. Hipp (RB): Active for 1 game.
Derrick Jensen (RB/TE): Active for 16 games, and started in 1. Rushed for 30 yards on 14 carries, had 7 receptions for 87 yards, and 1 kickoff return for 33 yards and 1 TD.

Rich Martini (WR): Active for 16 games, and started in1. Had 1 reception for 36 yards.

Lindsey Mason (T): Active for 16 games.

Ira Matthews (RB/WR): Active for 16 games, rushed for 11 yards on 5 carries, had 3 receptions for 33 yards, 48 punt returns for 421 yards, and 29 kickoff returns for 585 yards.

Dan Pastorini (QB): Active for 5 games, and started all of them before a broken leg ended his season. Prior to his injury, Pastorini completed 66 of 130 pass attempts for 932 yards, 5 TD and 8 INT. He also rushed for 24 yards on 4 carries.

Derrick Ramsey (TE): Active for 16 games, had 5 receptions for 117 yards, and 1 kickoff return for 10 yards.

Steve Sylvester (C/G/T): Active for 7 games, started in 2.

Arthur Whittington (RB): Active for 15 games, and started in 3. Rushed for 299 yards on 91 carries and 3 TD's, 19 catches for 205 yards, 21 kickoff returns for 392 yards and 1 TD.

Marc Wilson (QB): Active for 2 games, and completed 3 out of 5 pass attempts for 31 yards, and rushed for 3 yards on 1 carry.

STARTERS — DEFENSE

DE — John Matuszak: Started in 16 games.

DE — Dave Browning: Started in 16 games.

NT — Reggie Kinlaw: Active for 14 games, and started in 13.

LOLB — Ted Hendricks: Started in 16 games, had 3 INT, 4 fumble recoveries, and recorded 1 safety.

LILB — Matt Millen: Started in 16 games and had 2 INT.

RILB — Randy McClanahan: Active for 14 games, and started in 8, and had 1 INT.

ROLB — Rod Martin: Active for 16 games, and started in 10. Had 2 INT and 2 fumble recoveries.

CB — Lester Hayes: Started in 16 games, had **13** INT, 2 fumble recoveries, and 1 kickoff return for 0 yards. **Also led the NFL in yards gained on interception returns (273).**

CB — Monte Jackson: Active for 16 games, and started in 10, and had 1 INT.

SS — Mike Davis: Started in 16 games, had 3 INT and 3 fumble recoveries.

FS — Burgess Owens: Started in16 games and had 3 INT.

RESERVE DEFENSIVE PLAYERS

Jeff Barnes (LB): Active for 16 games, started in 6, and had 1 fumble recovery.

Joe Campbell (E/NT): Active for 10 games.

Mario Celotto (LB): Active for 11 games.

Cedrick Hardman (E): Active for 16 games and had 1 fumble recovery.

Dwight Harrison (DB/WR): Active for 3 games.

Willie Jones (E): Active for 16 games, had 2 fumble recoveries and 1 TD.

Alva Liles (T): Active for 2 games.

Odis McKinney (DB): Active for 16 games, had 3 INT, 1 fumble recovery, and 1 punt return for 0 yards.

Keith Moody (DB): Active for 5 games, had 1 fumble recovery and 8 kickoff returns for 150 yards.

Bob Nelson (LB): Active for 9 games, started in 8, and had 1 INT.

Dwayne O'Steen (DB): Active for 15 games, started in 6, had 3 INT and 1 fumble recovery.

Dave Pear (T): Active for 7 games, started in 3.

Mike Spivey (DB): Active for 9 games.

Greg Westbrooks (LB): Active for 1 game.

KICKING/PUNTING

K — Chris Bahr: Active for 16 games. Made 19 of 37 field goal attempts and 41 of 44 extra points for 98 points.

P — Ray Guy: Active for 16 games. Punted 71 times for a 43.6 average, rushed 3 times for 38 yards, and threw 1 pass for 32 yards.

1981 Season Review

1. Sept. 6: The defending world champions opened their '81 campaign on a sour note, losing to Denver, 9–7. With a strong defensive effort, the Broncos held the champs to a mere 81 yards on the ground and 84 through the air. The Super Bowl MVP, Jim Plunkett, was sacked five times and intercepted twice. He did give Oakland an early lead by passing to Raymond Chester from nine yards out before Denver's defense clamped down on everything Oakland attempted. In addition to the game, the Raiders also lost Bob Chandler, who had to have his spleen removed following a vicious hit, and defensive lineman Reggie Kinlaw suffered a season-ending knee injury. For the present time, the Raiders still remained in Oakland even though a move to Los Angeles was becoming more imminent.[1]

2. Sept. 14: It took their usual Monday Night Football mystique to pull the Raiders back up. Oakland scored on three touchdown receptions, an interception, a fumble recovery, and a field goal, in a 36–10 runaway victory over the Minnesota Vikings. Jim Plunkett threw two scoring passes to Todd Christensen (21 yards) and Morris Bradshaw (12 yards). Second-year quarterback Marc Wilson connected with Malcolm Barnwell from 61 yards out for the game's final touchdown. Chris Bahr started Oakland's night off with a 21-yard field goal, which was followed by a Burgess Owens 30-yard interception return for a touchdown. Cedric Hardman added the other six-points to Oakland's evening when he ran 52 yards after recovering a fumble. This win came with a high price attached to it. Safety Mike Davis fractured a bone in his right ankle, and would be lost for most of the season. With the season only two weeks along, the Raiders lost four key members. Including Davis, Chandler and Kinlaw in the opener, the team also was without linebacker Bob Nelson, who injured his knee in the pre-season.[2]

3. Sept. 20: Injuries continued to mount for the Silver and Black, as fullback Mark van Eeghen went down with a pulled hamstring on Oakland's opening drive against Seattle. Despite another crucial loss, van Eeghen's replacement, Derrick Jensen, did a good job filling in. With Jensen running and Jim Plunkett throwing, the Raiders ran their record to 2–1 with a 20–10 home victory over the Seahawks. Jensen led all ball carriers with 84 yards, and scored on a 1-yard run. Plunkett ran for a 13-yard score, and threw for another, with Morris Bradshaw being on the receiving end of a 29-yarder. Plunkett had a great day throwing, as he connected on 20 of 30 attempts for 262 yards.[3]

4. Sept. 27: The Detroit Lions had the worst pass defense in the league, but they somehow managed to hold Jim Plunkett to only 102 passing yards, intercepted him once, and recorded five sacks. The Lions lost their starting quarterback, Gary Danielson, to a wrist injury, but running back Billy Sims picked up the offensive slack with 136 rushing yards, and scored the game's only touchdown. Kicker Eddie Murray hit on three field goals, and Detroit shocked the Super Bowl champs, 16–0. This was the first time in 217 prior games that Oakland failed to score. The last time the Raiders suffered a shutout was on September 10, 1966, at the hands of the Houston Oilers.[4]

5. Oct. 4: A week earlier, one of the league's worst defenses shut the Raiders out. In this game, Oakland faced one of the best, and the result was the same. The Denver Broncos allowed the

Raiders only 168 total yards, sacked Jim Plunkett three times, and intercepted him once. When it was all over, Denver won, 17–0, to sweep the season series. Four Oakland turnovers helped the Denver cause. Oakland's defensive unit played admirably in a losing effort, holding Denver to 90 yards through the air, and registering seven sacks. It proved to be the Broncos running attack that gave Oakland problems. Fullback Rick Parros gained 73 yards and Dave Preston 70, with each churning out yardage on crucial downs, and both scoring once.[5]

6. Oct. 11: The wheels were coming off the wagon for the Raiders. For the third straight game, the once proud champions were demoralized and shut out, this time by Kansas City, 27–0. The Chiefs were number one in defense against the run, and lived up to that ranking by allowing Oakland 79 yards on the ground. The unit also applied constant pressure on Jim Plunkett and backup Marc Wilson, and intercepted three passes. In recent weeks, the Raiders running attack was virtually non-existent. Opposing defenses knew that Oakland had to pass to compensate for this, and focused on that strategy. Once that happened, Oakland's passing game was also smothered. Meanwhile, the Chiefs produced a well-balanced offensive attack. Quarterback Bill Kenney threw for 287 yards and two touchdowns while rookie running back Joe Delaney ran for 106 yards and caught three passes for another 104. With this loss, the Raiders fell to 2–4, and were in fourth place in the division. With the offense going nowhere fast, head coach Tom Flores decided to switch quarterbacks. Marc Wilson was called upon to fill the signal calling duties while Plunkett watched from the bench.[6]

7. Oct. 18: After failing to score in three previous games, the Raiders rejuvenated themselves by putting points on the board in their first three possessions against the Tampa Bay Buccaneers. Chris Bahr broke Oakland's worst offensive drought in team history by kicking a whopping 51-yard field goal on the opening drive. Todd Christensen then made it 5–0 when he blocked a punt out of the end zone for a safety. Derrick Jensen scored Oakland's first touchdown in what seemed like an eternity on a 12-yard run. Bahr added his second three-pointer (20 yards), and the Raiders had a 15–0 lead at the half. Tampa Bay came back to take a 16–15 lead in the fourth quarter. In his first start of the season, quarterback Marc Wilson rallied the Raiders on their final drive. He connected on four passes that got Oakland within field goal range with 2:21 left. Bahr's kick was good from 44 yards out, and it gave the Raiders an 18–16 advantage. However, the Bucs refused to go down easy. They got inside the Oakland 30 with five seconds remaining, and called on kicker Bill Capece to win the game for them. Ted Hendricks did not want to see his team go down in defeat again, so he used his 6'7" frame to jump up and block what would have been the game winner. The win gave the Oakland a 3–4 record, but they still faced an up hill struggle.[7]

8. Oct. 25: The win over Tampa Bay did nothing to ignite the slumping champions, and they fell to AFC West leader Kansas City, 28–17, to sink to 3–5. Marc Wilson helped the Raiders jump out to a 17–0 lead at the half by throwing a touchdown to Morris Bradshaw (6 yards), and running for a 3-yarder himself. Chris Bahr kicked a 51-yard field goal to finish Oakland's scoring on the day. The second half belonged to Kansas City, as they exploded for four touchdowns. Rookie running back Billy Jackson

only carried the ball nine times in this game, but he scored on three of them. Oakland still had a chance to come back, but linebacker Gary Spani killed a late rally by returning a fumble 91 yards for Kansas City's final touchdown.[8]

9. Nov. 1: Kenny King led all ball carriers with 102 yards, and Marc Wilson completed 22 of 36 pass attempts for 283 yards and a touchdown in a 27–17 win over the New England Patriots. Wilson's 14-yard scoring strike to Cliff Branch in the fourth quarter erased a four point New England advantage. Defensive end Willie Jones gave the Raiders a little more breathing room by returning a fumble recovery nine yards for an insurance touchdown. Chris Bahr kicked two field goals (51 and 26 yards), and Mark van Eeghen scored on a 3-yard run.[9]

10. Nov. 8: Oakland just missed getting to the .500 mark by losing a close one to the Houston Oilers, 17–16. Marc Wilson rallied Oakland in the second half with tremendous passing. His accuracy led to two Chris Bahr field goals (42 and 43 yards), and a 12-yard touchdown run by Arthur Whittington that gave the Raiders a 16–10 fourth quarter lead. Bahr also had a 29-yard field goal in the second quarter. Filling in for an injured Ken Stabler, Houston back up quarterback John Reaves overshadowed Wilson's performance. He connected with tight end Mike Barber from 25 yards out for what proved to be the game winner with 7:20 left in the fourth quarter.[10]

11. Nov. 15: The Raiders might have been kicked around throughout the '81 campaign, but they still managed to do some kicking of their own. A trip to Miami earned Oakland a 33–17 victory over the AFC Eastern Division–leading Dolphins. The Raiders improved to 5–6, while Miami fell to 7–3–1, but still remained atop their division. Marc Wilson continued to be impressive at the controls of the offense. He jumped on Miami's defense early, and took Oakland into the half with a 21–3 lead on three touchdown passes. His targets were Todd Christensen (13 yards), Bob Chandler (37 yards), and Derrick Ramsey (1 yard). Oakland received their second half points on a Chris Bahr 32-yard field goal, a Chester Willis 15-yard run, and on a safety when Johnny Robinson forced Miami quarterback Don Strock out of the end zone. The defense did a fantastic job holding down the Miami offensive machine, allowing them only 70 yards on the ground.[11]

12. Nov. 22: It was back to reality for the '81 Raiders, as they just could not gain momentum after an impressive win. Going against the most-feared air attack of the early 1980's, the Raiders were shellacked by San Diego's passing barrage, 55–21. Quarterback Dan Fouts threw six touchdown passes, with four going to tight end Kellen Winslow, who added a fifth touchdown to his day when he caught a halfback option pass from Chuck Muncie. Oakland's point production came from Derrick Ramsey (66-yard pass from Marc Wilson), Derrick Jensen (2-yard run), and Marc Wilson (12-yard run). This loss officially eliminated the Raiders from playoff contention for the third time in the past four seasons.[12]

13. Nov. 29: In a battle between the AFC West's sub-par teams, the fourth place Raiders squeaked out a 32–31 win over last place Seattle. Marc Wilson led Oakland back from a 24–3 deficit by completing 20 of 33 pass attempts for 218 yards and three touchdown tosses. Derrick Ramsey caught Wilson's first touchdown from five yards out. Bob Chandler followed with an 8-yarder, and Arthur Whittington's 16-yard reception gave Oakland

the lead. Chris Bahr kicked a 20-yard field goal, and Derrick Jensen added a 3-yard insurance touchdown run. The Raiders also received two points on a safety when Seattle punter Jeff West stepped out of the end zone. A David Krieg to Steve Largent touchdown pass closed the Oakland advantage to one point, but the Raiders held on, and got out of Seattle's Kingdome with their sixth win of the year.[13]

14. Dec. 7: The Raiders put together their first back-to-back wins since September with a 30–27 win over Pittsburgh on Monday Night Football. Marc Wilson once again threw for three scores, on 18 of 29 attempts for 275 yards. Wilson's touchdown passes went to Derrick Ramsey (25 yards), Arthur Whittington (17 yards), and Bob Chandler (38 yards). Kenny King gave Oakland a balanced offensive attack by running for a game-high 102 yards. With the game tied at 20–20 in the fourth quarter, rookie Ted Watts put Oakland ahead to stay with a 53-yard punt return. Chris Bahr later kicked a 29-yard field goal, and the Raiders had battled their way back to .500 with a 7–7 record.[14]

15. Dec. 13: In the Raiders final game in front of Oakland fans before moving to Los Angeles, they were beaten soundly, 23–6, by the Chicago Bears. The five win Bears were led by three Vince Evans touchdown passes. Marc Wilson teamed up with Bob Chandler on a 27-yard pass for Oakland's lone points.[15]

16. Dec. 21: The misery that came to be known as the 1981 season finally came to a climax for the Oakland Raiders. In front of a Monday Night Football audience, the Silver and Black suffered their first losing season since 1964 at the hands of San Diego, 23–10. This loss also ended Oakland's 14-game winning streak on Monday Night Football. Oakland's points came on a Chris Bahr 34-yard field goal, and a Mark van Eeghen 1-yard run. In this game, San Diego's Dan Fouts set a then single-season NFL record by passing for 4,802 yards. The win also gave the Chargers their third consecutive AFC Western Division title. The Raiders ended the dismal year at 7–9, and would now be on their way to a new life in Los Angeles.[16]

Individual Statistics and Roster

Head Coach: Tom Flores
Assistant Coaches: Sam Boghosian, Willie Brown, Lew Erber, Chet Franklin, Earl Leggett, Joe Madro, Bob Mischak, Steve Ortmayer, Charlie Sumner, Ray Willsey
1981 Regular Season Record: 7–9
4th Place AFC Western Division
Scored 273 points to rank 25th out of 28 teams
Allowed 343 points to rank 15th

STARTERS — OFFENSE

QB — Marc Wilson: Active for 13 games, and started in 9. Completed 173 of 366 pass attempts for 2,311 yards, 14 TD and 19 INT. Rushed for 147 yards on 30 carries and 2 TD.
HB — Kenny King: Active for and started in 14 games. Rushed for 828 yards on 170 carries, and had 27 receptions for 216 yards.
FB — Derrick Jensen: Active for 16 games, and started in 13. Rushed for 456 yards on 117 carries and 4 TD. Had 28 receptions for 271 yards.
WR — Morris Bradshaw: Active for 15 games, and started in 8. Had 22 receptions for 298 yards and 3 TD.
WR — Cliff Branch: Active for 16 games, and started in 15. Had 41 receptions for 635 yards and 1 TD.

TE — Derrick Ramsey: Active for 16 games, and started in 12. Had 52 receptions for 674 yards and 4 TD.
LT — Art Shell: Active for 16 games, and started in 13.
LG — Curt Marsh: Active for and started in 11 games.
C — Steve Sylvester: Active for 15 games, and started in 9.
RG — Mickey Marvin: Started in 16 games.
RT — Henry Lawrence: Started in 16 games.

RESERVE OFFENSIVE PLAYERS

Malcolm Barnwell (WR): Active for 16 games, and started in 1. Had 9 receptions for 190 yards and 1 TD, and 15 kickoff returns for 265 yards.
Bob Chandler (WR): Active for 11 games, and started in 7. Had 26 receptions for 458 yards and 4 TD.
Raymond Chester (TE): Active for 16 games, and started in 5. Had 13 receptions for 93 yards and 1 TD.
Todd Christensen (RB/TE): Active for 16 games, had 8 receptions for 115 yards and 2 TD, and returned 4 kickoffs for 54 yards.
Dave Dalby (C): Active for 16 games, and started in 7.
Bruce Davis (T/G): Active for 16 games.
Frank Hawkins (RB): Active for 13 games, rushed for 165 yards on 40 carries, had 10 receptions for 109 yards, and 1 kickoff return for 7 yards.
Lindsey Mason (T): Active for 11 games, and started in 3.
Ira Matthews (RB/WR): Active for 5 games, had 15 receptions for 92 yards, and 7 kickoff returns for144 yards.
Cleo Montgomery (WR): Active for 1 game.
Jim Plunkett (QB): Active for 9 games, and started in 7. Completed 94 of 179 pass attempts for 1,045 yards, 4 TD and 9 INT. Rushed for 38 yards on 12 carries and 1 TD.
Gene Upshaw (G): Active for 15 games, and started in 5.
Mark van Eeghen (RB): Active for 8 games, and started in 3. Rushed for 150 yards on 39 carries and 2 TD, and had 7 receptions for 60 yards.
Arthur Whittington (RB): Active for 16 games, and started in 2. Rushed for 220 yards on 69 carries and 1 TD. Had 23 receptions for 213 yards and 2 TD, returned 2 punts for 4 yards, and 25 kickoffs for 563 yards.
Chester Willis (RB): Active for 15 games. Rushed for 54 yards on 16 carries for 1 TD, had 1 reception for 24 yards, and returned 15 kickoffs for 309 yards.

STARTERS — DEFENSE

DE — John Matuszak: Started in16 games and had 1 fumble recovery.
DE — Dave Browning: Started in 16 games and had 1 fumble recovery.
NT — Johnny Robinson: Started in16 games, had 1 fumble recovery, and recorded 1 safety.
LOLB — Ted Hendricks: Started in 16 games and had 1 fumble recovery.
LILB — Matt Millen: Started in 16 games and had 1 fumble recovery.
RILB — Randy McClanahan: Started in 16 games and had 3 fumble recoveries.
ROLB — Rod Martin: Started in 16 games, had 1 INT and 3 fumble recoveries.
CB — Lester Hayes: Started 16 in games and had 3 INT.
CB — Monte Jackson: Active for 16 games, and started in 10. Had 1 fumble recovery.
SS — Odis McKinney: Active for 16 games, and started in 14. Had 1 fumble recovery.
FS — Burgess Owens: Started in 16 games and had 2 fumble recoveries.

RESERVE DEFENSIVE PLAYERS

Jeff Barnes (LB): Active for 15 games.
Greg Bracelin (LB): Active for 15 games.
Joe Campbell (E/NT): Active for 3 games.
Mario Celotto (LB): Active for 7 games.
Mike Davis (DB): Active for 7 games, and started in 2.
Cedrick Hardman (E): Active for 16 games, had 1 fumble recovery and 1 TD.

Kenny Hill (DB): Active for 9 games, and had 1 kickoff return for 21 yards.

Willie Jones (E): Active for 8 games, and had 1 fumble recovery and 1 TD.

Reggie Kinlaw (NT): Active for 1 game.

Howie Long (E/NT): Active for 16 games.

Dwayne O'Steen (DB): Active for 16 games, started in 6, and had 3 fumble recoveries.

Ted Watts (DB): Active for 16 games, had 2 fumble recoveries, and returned 35 punts for 284 yards and 1 TD.

Greg Westbrooks (LB): Active for 4 games.

KICKING/PUNTING

K — Chris Bahr: Active for 16 games. Made 14 of 24 field goal attempts and 27 of 33 extra points for 69 points.

P — Ray Guy: Active for 16 games. Punted 96 times for a 43.7 average.

The Raiders Move to Los Angeles

The cavernous crown jewel of the Los Angeles sports scene fell silent to the pro gridiron circuit at the end of the 1970's after 34 seasons. In July, 1978, the National Football League hierarchy allowed Los Angeles Rams owner Carroll Rosenbloom to move out of the Memorial Coliseum, for the Anaheim area thirty miles south of LA.[1] The void left by the Rams' exodus saw a populous of over seven million Los Angeles residents rendered NFL orphans after a four-decade love affair. Ironically, the team once regarded as orphans themselves, came to the rescue within three years of the Rams' departure.

The infant stages of the Raiders' transfer to Los Angeles began when Al Davis could not come to a mutual agreement with the City of Oakland regarding the Oakland-Alameda Coliseum.

The commission that presided over the Los Angeles Memorial Coliseum expressed their desire of getting an occupant to fill their 92,000 plus seat stadium on Sunday afternoons to NFL Commissioner Pete Rozelle. The NFL czar informed the commission that expansion was not an option at that time, however, if the city of Los Angeles could persuade an existing team not satisfied with their current situation to relocate, then they had the green light to go forward with a sales pitch to come to the land of sunshine, beaches, and the Hollywood dream factories.[2]

If a team wanted to move their operations to a different locale, a unanimous vote of approval by all other team owners was necessary. With the Rams still playing within the general area of Los Angeles, the Coliseum committee knew that Rams ownership would not grant a positive vote that could make it possible for another team to come in and take away from their fan base. For this reason, the Los Angeles Coliseum Committee smacked the NFL with an anti-trust lawsuit in October, 1978.[3]

With the lawsuit hovering over the league like a hangman's noose, it was decided to change the unanimous vote rule to one needing a majority of three quarters (21 out of a then 28 owners) to approve any decisions. However, to pass the new rule, a unanimous vote of all 28 owners was still needed in this case. All but one cast a positive vote, with the lone holdout being none other than the master of non-conformity himself, Mr. Al Davis. Davis decided to restrain from voting, but did agree to change his opinion if his fellow owners gave him the right to move the Raiders in case the prospect arose.[4]

Officials from Los Angeles had already been in contact through written inquiries about the Raiders relocating, but Davis up to this time had not reciprocated. This was not to lay claim that Davis' wheels were not turning throughout his gray matter. The maverick owner was very astute to the fact that Los Angeles was a huge market just waiting to be saved from pro football absenteeism.[5]

Despite sending inquiries to other potential suitors, it became extremely clear that the City of Angels sought pro football's bad boys most of all. One month after the Rams informed the masses that they were bolting to Anaheim starting in 1980, the Los Angeles County Supervisor Ken Hahn made it abundantly clear that the Raiders were the team the city wanted.[6]

Despite the buzz about football's renegades traveling 400 miles south down Pacific Coast Highway, the Raiders seemed content in Oakland. They had 75 straight sellouts at home, and the fans were some of the most loyal throughout the NFL. Regardless of the passion possessed by the northern California chapter of Raider Nation, there loomed discontent about the Oakland-Alameda Coliseum. Davis had requested improvements to the locker room, the public address system, the press box, and the desire to have luxury suites installed. Unfortunately, even though his team was one of the most successful on the field, Davis' pleas fell on deaf ears.[7]

Davis saw the rise in player salaries looming on the horizon, and felt that luxury suites would allow his organization to achieve a substantial monetary boost that could keep the Raiders competitive when obtaining quality players. It was figured that the Oakland-Alameda Coliseum could hold 64 luxury suites, but nothing seemed to be moving forward in regards to constructing them. Also, the facility seated 54,615, which ranked 24th out of a then 28 teams. Any thoughts of expanding on that number were also thwarted. Back in Los Angeles there stood the Memorial Coliseum with a behemoth seating capacity that almost doubled that of the Oakland structure. To add to the vast seating capacity was the fact that officials in Los Angeles were willing to construct 100 luxury suites on top of other provisions necessary to lure in a team.[8]

The Raiders lease on the Oakland-Alameda Coliseum was set to expire following the 1979 season. In January of 1979, Al Davis was in Los Angeles for that city's final hosting of the Pro Bowl. Jim Hardy, the manager of the Memorial Coliseum, and Bill Robertson, who headed the Los Angeles Coliseum Commission, conversed with Al Davis to lay out a proposal for the Raiders to head south to Los Angeles. It was purportedly told to Davis during this presentation that besides his Raiders, the committee was also courting the Baltimore Colts, Minnesota Vikings, and the Miami Dolphins.[9]

At the time, Davis stated that he was not interested in moving. In the first few months of 1979, he still attempted to get his desires across to the Oakland Coliseum Committee, but to no avail. Later that year, Davis started up very intense conversations with the Oakland contingent that included the city's mayor. Unfortunately, the factions still remained worlds apart.

It seemed NFL Commissioner Rozelle might have caught wind that the league's highly adverse owner was considering, even remotely, testing the waters in Los Angeles. Prior to Minnesota being granted a new domed stadium deal, Mr. Rozelle did not appear to have a problem with the Vikings looking for greener pastures outside the North Star State if conditions were not accepted regarding their current facilities. When the Vikings received what they sought in Minnesota, Rozelle informed anyone who came within an earshot that he did not want any team to move.[10]

Even though Rozelle seemed adamant about any transfer, Davis still discussed his situation with the commissioner. Davis expressed his desire to be granted the same opportunity given to the Vikings when they wanted to relocate before getting a new stadium deal. Davis was not looking for a brand new stadium, but only some much needed improvements on an existing one. He also brought up the possibility of his moving the Raiders to Los Angeles.[11] For this action, Rozelle sent Davis a letter in January, 1980, that proved to be a very negative rebuttal that basically informed Davis that moving without following league rules would lead to repercussions that would prove detrimental. Rozelle knew that there was no way the rest of the owners would approve Davis' intentions.[12]

At the time of Rozelle's unflattering letter, the situation in Oakland was stagnant and not appearing to be remotely close to any resolution. It appeared to be at this juncture that the Raiders were now seriously looking toward Los Angeles as a future residence. Meanwhile, in the week leading up to Super Bowl XIV, the Los Angeles Coliseum Committee created quite a stir. The lawsuit they threatened against the NFL 15 months earlier now had a legitimate leg to stand on. When first looking into their legal standings against the pro gridiron circuit, it appeared null and void without a valid occupant for the Memorial Coliseum. However, with the Raiders now getting closer to transferring, the Los Angeles Coliseum had a better case against the league.[13]

Once the power brokers back in Oakland found out that the Raiders were close to sending out change-of-address cards to the other 27 NFL teams, they wanted a meeting with Davis. Unfortunately, the end result was only a ruse, as the Oakland group decided not to go through with any of Davis' requests.[14] To add to his woes was the fact that Davis realized none of the other team owners would vote favorably for his Raiders to move to the mammoth and profitable metropolis that was Los Angeles.

It was at this time that the legal system and the Raiders became a common bond, involved in nine lawsuits. A judge in Los Angeles gave the Raiders a huge break when he prohibited the NFL from standing in the way of Davis' trek down Pacific Coast Highway.[15]

In retaliation, the city of Oakland got a temporary restraining order against the team. Davis' lawyer saw Oakland's action as an illegal ploy, and referred to it as an act of civil disobedience. What that meant was the action could not prohibit the Raiders from moving. The lawyer felt that Davis was correct in his reasons for leaving, and had the proof to prove it.[16] In that regard, the Raiders had every right to relocate and Oakland was left defenseless while watching moving vans head 400 miles south.

Davis and his lawyer went to Los Angeles. After two days of serious discussions, on March 1, 1980, the maverick owner of pro football's bad boys, placed his signature on a contract that officially made the Silver and Black a soon-to-be part of the Los Angeles sports scene.[17] One week prior to the agreement, Oakland tried in vain to hold on to the Raiders by filing an eminent domain

suit that meant the city looked to take control of the team away from Davis and run the organization. This case was resolved in the spring of 1983 in favor of the Raiders.[18]

The Raiders organization continued to create havoc when Rozelle called a meeting two days after Davis agreed to move to Los Angeles. Rozelle confronted him about his plans, and Davis informed the commissioner that he indeed was relocating and did not think that a vote by his fellow owners was needed. Within 24 hours, Rozelle answered Davis' challenge by slapping the team with a breach of contract lawsuit in the Superior Court of Alameda County. Also included in the league's attack was the desire to take over the Raiders and kick Al Davis out of power, but that motion was swiftly dismissed. One week later, the NFL owners voted on the move, with 22 opposed and five restrained from voting. The Raiders decided to get in on the legal free-for-all by teaming up with the Los Angeles Coliseum's anti-trust suit against the NFL fraternity. The only thing now holding the Raiders from moving was when a federal court decision wiped out the Los Angeles judge's previous ruling that allowed the Raiders to move on the grounds that a trial was in the works, and that the Raiders could receive monetary gains if successful over the league. Simply put, the Raiders had to put their Tinsel town reservations on hold for at least the 1980 campaign.[19]

In May, 1981, the anti-trust trial started in Los Angeles. After two months of both sides bashing each other, it equaled out to a no decision by the jury. The Raiders were once again scheduled to play in Oakland for at least one more year. The Raiders finally caught a break in their quest on May 7, 1982, when a unanimous vote by a jury sided with the Silver and Black, ruling that the league's attempted roadblock of the move was in violation of federal anti-trust laws. On June 14, 1982, the Central District Court came to a decision that the NFL could not prevent the Raiders from relocating, and on July 5, 1982, the Silver and Black committed to a 10-year deal with the City of Angels. To add to the Raiders' streak of good fortunes, on April 13, 1983, a jury awarded the Raiders $35 million from damages received in the anti-trust lawsuit.[20]

The marauders of the 100-yard spectacle of controlled violence were now officially The Los Angeles Raiders, and the people of the city were once again represented on Sunday afternoons.

1982 Season Review

1. Sept. 12: The Raiders began their 23rd season in new surroundings. The city of Los Angeles was now their home, and they looked to improve from the dismal '81 season.

In their first regular season game as the Los Angeles Raiders, the Silver and Black made their new city proud by beating the defending Super Bowl champion San Francisco 49ers, 23–17. Rookie sensation Marcus Allen lived up to his Heisman Trophy status by rushing for a game-high 116 yards on 23 carries, and scored on a 5-yard run. Allen became the first rookie in team history to ever run for 100 yards in his first game. If running the ball brilliantly was not enough, Allen also led Los Angeles with four receptions for an additional 64 yards. Chris Bahr hit on three long-range field goals (41, 42, and 43 yards), and tight end Todd Christensen caught a 3-yard pass from Jim Plunkett to complete the scoring. Christensen's touchdown put the Raiders in the lead with 5:46 remaining in the game. The defense gave up almost 200 yards in the first half, but only surrendered 58 after that. San Francisco's Joe Montana was sacked five times, and he threw an interception to Lester Hayes that killed a threat late in the fourth quarter.[1]

2. Sept. 19: For the second straight week, the Raiders went on the road, and came back to Los Angeles as the victors. This time it was by a 38–14 final over the Atlanta Falcons. Marcus Allen added another brilliant performance to his young career, and was showing why he was the top college player the year before. On the Raiders' first scoring drive, Allen set Los Angeles up at the Atlanta 14 by throwing a 47-yard halfback option pass to Cliff Branch. On the next play, Allen caught a Jim Plunkett pass and vaulted into the end zone with a backward flip. He scored again on a 4-yard run, and finished with a game-high 56 yards on 12 carries, and caught four passes for 39 yards. Also putting points on the board for the Silver and Black were Chris Bahr (35-yard field goal), Cliff Branch (30-yard pass from Jim Plunkett), Frank Hawkins (1-yard run), and Archie Reese (75-yard fumble recovery). The Los Angeles Raiders were in a groove, and appeared to be back on track after the dismal '81 season. Unfortunately for the Raiders and the rest of the NFL, a 57-day player's strike began following the September 20th Monday Night Football telecast. The strike lasted until late November, and the league decided to salvage the season by making it a nine-game schedule with the top eight teams from each conference making the playoffs, which would consist of four rounds.[2]

3. Nov. 22: The move to Los Angeles did nothing to damage the Raiders' Monday Night Football karma. In their much-awaited home debut in the City of Angels, the Silver and Black beat San Diego in true Hollywood fashion. The Chargers exploded out to a 24–7 halftime lead, and the game appeared to have the makings of a boring affair. A 1-yard pass from Jim Plunkett to Todd Christensen gave the Raiders their first half six-pointer. However, this game did include the rulers of prime time, and in the second half, the Raiders fought their way back to remain undefeated. They began the amazing comeback right after the second half got underway. Within seven plays, Los Angeles went 63 yards, and Marcus Allen scored from three yards out to cap off the drive. Defensive back Odis McKinney caused San Diego's great tight end Kellen Winslow to fumble on his own 30. Defensive tackle Ruben Vaughan recovered the loose ball, and four plays later, Allen scored on a 6-yard run to bring the Raiders to within three points of the lead. The Raiders then took the lead with 5:54 remaining in the game when fullback Frank Hawkins capped off an 80-yard drive with a 1-yard run to give Los Angeles a 28–24 advantage as the scoreboard clock hit 0:00. This great comeback gave the Raiders a 19-2-1 record on Monday Night Football. For the third straight game, Allen led all ball carriers with 87 yards, and added 37 more on five receptions.[3]

4. Nov. 28: The Raiders entered the loss column for the first time as representatives of Los Angeles. The defeat came at the hands of the defending AFC champions, the Cincinnati Bengals, 31–17. The Bengals stuffed Marcus Allen, causing him to have his worst day ever. He carried the ball eight times, and produced zero yards. As a team, the Raiders only gained 33 yards on the ground. Jim Plunkett managed to play well despite four interceptions. He supplied Los Angeles with an adequate air attack

by throwing for 318 yards and two touchdowns. Cliff Branch was on the receiving end of both scoring strikes from 34 and 28 yards, and Chris Bahr kicked a 31-yard field goal for the Raiders on this day.[4]

5. Dec. 5: The Raiders jumped out to a 28–7 halftime lead, and held on to win, 28–23, over the Seattle Seahawks. Marcus Allen ran away with top ground-gaining honors by rushing for 156 yards on 24 carries, and scored two touchdowns from two and three yards out. Allen picked up the offensive slack when the passing game could only produce 41 total yards. Linebacker Rod Martin added a 39-yard interception return, and Kenny King ran for a 1-yard touchdown to give Los Angeles their points on the day. Besides the heroics of Marcus Allen, defensive back Burgess Owens came up big with a key interception on the Los Angeles 3-yard line to kill a late Seattle rally with 1:54 left to play. This win gave the Raiders a 4–1 record, and had them in a five-way tie for the AFC leadership.[5]

6. Dec. 12: With 32 seconds left, and trailing by two points, Jim Plunkett dropped back to pass on third and 20 from the Kansas City 35-yard line. Plunkett sent the ball toward the end zone, and second-year man Calvin Muhammad came down with the pass for a touchdown that proved to be the game-winner in a 21–16 Los Angeles win. This was the 200th regular season win in team history. Besides the winning touchdown, Plunkett also threw two more, with both going to Todd Christensen (4 and 8 yards). The Chiefs were 1–5 after this game, and had one of the NFL's worst offenses. The Los Angeles defense took full advantage of their easy prey. The defensive line tormented Kansas City's quarterbacks all day long, registering eight sacks, with Howie Long leading the way with three-and-a-half.[6]

7. Dec. 18: The first battle of Los Angeles ended with local hero Marcus Allen running for the winning touchdown with 29 seconds left in the game, to beat the Rams, 37–31. Trailing, 31–30, Allen finished off a five-play, 57-yard drive with an 11-yard run. Allen added a little flamboyance to his winning touchdown jaunt by leaping over a defensive back at the three and going airborne into the end zone. Allen led all ball carriers with 93 yards, and had two additional touchdown runs, both coming from one yard out. Jim Plunkett had a great game even though he threw four interceptions. He completed 22 of 34 pass attempts for 321 yards and two touchdowns. Cliff Branch caught the first one from 18 yards, and Greg Pruitt hauled in the other one from six yards out. Chris Bahr helped in the cause with a 24-yard field goal. This win clinched a playoff spot for the Raiders.[7]

8. Dec. 26: After a few close finishes, the Silver and Black coasted to a 27–10 victory over the Denver Broncos. The name of this game was defense for Los Angeles, as they converted three turnovers into 12 points, and recorded seven quarterback sacks. A Matt Millen interception in the first quarter led to a Chris Bahr 19-yard field goal. In the second quarter, defensive back James Davis intercepted a pass and returned it to the Denver 5-yard line. On the next play, Kenny King ran for a touchdown. Still in the second quarter, safety Mike Davis sacked Steve DeBerg and he fumbled. Howie Long recovered on the Los Angeles 49, and on the following play, Jim Plunkett found Marcus Allen for a 51-yard touchdown. Plunkett and Allen also teamed up on a 4-yard touchdown earlier. Chris Bahr later added a 36-yard field goal to give the Raiders a 27–0 lead at the half.[8]

Ted "Kick 'Em" Hendricks provided solid leadership from his linebacker position for nine seasons in a Raiders uniform. He also provided teammates with many laughs due to his colorful antics. Here he is seen ready to attack on December 18, 1982, in a game at the Los Angeles Coliseum (AP Photo/NFL Photos).

9. Jan. 2: The Raiders finished on top of the AFC with an 8–1 record, and secured home field advantage throughout the playoffs. They achieved this with a 41–34 win over the San Diego Chargers. Jim Plunkett had his best day of the season by completing 17 of 28 pass attempts for 227 yards and one touchdown, with that going to Frank Hawkins from two yards out. Marcus Allen ran for 126 yards and two touchdowns (2 and 22 yards). Mike Davis returned an interception 56 yards for a score, and James Davis ran another one back 52 yards for a touchdown. Chris Bahr kicked two field goals (22 and 32 yards), and the Raiders were now looking to give the city of Los Angeles their first pro football championship since 1951.[9]

First Round Playoff Game, January 8, 1983

The Cleveland Browns were back in the playoffs for the first time since "Red Right-88" ended their dream season with a Mike Davis interception. The Browns made the playoffs this season by clinching the final spot with a 4–5 record.

A crowd of 57,246 came out to the LA Coliseum to see the Raiders in their first-ever post-season contest as residents of the City of Angels. Chris Bahr got Los Angeles on the board first after they took the opening kickoff and drove 79 yards in five plays, with the key play being a 64-yard pass from Jim Plunkett to Cliff Branch that got the Raiders deep into Cleveland territory. Bahr then kicked a 27-yard field to give the Raiders an early 3–0 lead.

Not to be out done by his brother, Cleveland kicker Matt Bahr slammed home a whopping playoff record 52-yard field goal in the second quarter to tie the game at 3–3. The Raiders came right back to regain the lead following the ensuing kickoff. Eight plays resulted in 88 yards of real estate, with Plunkett getting 79 through the air on five passes. From the two, Plunkett went to the run, and rookie sensation Marcus Allen went into the end zone for his first-ever playoff touchdown. Bahr added the extra point, and the Raiders were up, 10–3. Plunkett had an incredible day, completing 24 of 37 passes for 386 yards, with 241 coming in the first half alone.

Despite a sub-par season record-wise, the Browns played a good first half, refusing to bow under to the mighty Raiders. They held the high-powered Raiders in check and forced a punt. After going 33 yards to the Los Angeles 43, quarterback Paul McDonald got off a perfectly thrown ball that wide receiver Ricky Feacher caught at the goal line despite great coverage from Ted Watts. Matt Bahr added the conversion to tie things up at 10–10 with two minutes left in the first half.

Greg Pruitt was traded to the Raiders before the season after nine campaigns with Cleveland, and he came back to haunt his old team by returning the ensuing kickoff 40 yards. He almost broke it for a touchdown, but was stopped by the last defender in his path at the LA 42. Six plays later, Plunkett guided the Raiders to the Cleveland 20 on an 11-yard pickup himself, and two passes to Allen and Todd Christensen. With nine seconds left on the clock, Chris Bahr hit on a 37-yard three-pointer to give the Raiders a slim 13–10 halftime advantage.

The Browns got the second half kickoff and drove confidently from their own 32 to the Los Angeles 14. However, from there the Browns began on a downward spiral that eventually led to their demise. On first down, McDonald handed off to Charles White, and on his way through the line, he was met by Lyle Alzado, another ex–Cleveland player who came back to haunt his old team. Alzado hit White and he fumbled, with the loose ball being recovered by linebacker Jeff Barnes on the LA 11-yard line. Twelve plays later Allen scored his second touchdown of the game on a 3-yard run, and Chris Bahr's extra point made it a 20–10 ballgame.

Early in the fourth quarter, Frank Hawkins ran for a 1-yard score, and Bahr's conversion ended the scoring at 27–10. The Raiders were now two wins away from Super Bowl XVII, and would host the New York Jets in the second round.[10]

Simply put, Marcus Allen is the greatest all-purpose running back in Raiders history. During his tenure with the team, Allen provided the team with incredible displays of athletic prowess. Here he is seen in action in 1983 (AP Photo).

Second Round Playoff Game, January 15, 1983

The media buzz throughout the Big Apple in the winter of 1982-83 focused on the success of the New York Jets, who were in the playoffs for the second straight year after 13 years of futility. The 6–3 Jets advanced to the second round with an easy win over the defending AFC champion Cincinnati Bengals, 44–17.

New York was led on offense by quarterback Richard Todd, running back Freeman McNeil, who topped all league runners in

1982 with 786 yards, and wide receiver Wesley Walker. The defensive unit was the star attraction, however, and the front four earned the moniker, "The New York Sack Exchange." It consisted of Mark Gastineau, Marty Lyons, Abdul Salaam, and Joe Klecko, and they created havoc on opposing offenses, applying pressure on a regular basis.

New York showed its moxie by jumping out to a 10–0 halftime lead on a 20-yard pass from Todd to Walker and a 30-yard field goal by Pat Leahy. Los Angeles came back in the third quarter on a pair of touchdowns to take a 14–10 lead into the final stanza. Marcus Allen ran for a 4-yard score, and Malcolm Barnwell caught a 57-yard pass from Jim Plunkett. Allen's touchdown came after the Raiders took the second half kickoff and drove 77 yards. Barnwell's go-ahead score came with 1:14 left in the third.

An interesting sideshow was occurring throughout this game, and it ended with an eruption that quickly and forever became part of Raiders lore. It also forced the league to add a new rule. Lyle Alzado and New York offensive tackle Chris Ward were engaged in a one-on-one battle throughout the game. It was a tug of war, with each man winning one half apiece. Alzado was getting the best of Ward in the second half, forcing Todd to throw an interception, was responsible for creating a sack, and had one on Todd himself. Near the end of the third quarter, Ward attempted to push Alzado over a pileup after apparently holding him on many plays.

The frustration of being held on a consistent basis caused a slow burn to begin developing inside Alzado. Never known to be the calm type out on the field, Alzado was nearing the point of no return. When Ward tried to shove him over a pileup, that finally unleashed the Alzado fury. He rushed Ward in an uncontrollable rage, grabbed him by the facemask, and yanked at it until the helmet came off. Now with Ward's helmet in his hand, Alzado quickly decided to return it via airmail. He violently threw it at Ward's groin region. The next season, the NFL added the Alzado Rule that prohibited removing a player's helmet. A penalty of ejection from the game and a fine would accompany the infraction.

Back to the main event, the Raiders were on their way to increasing their lead at the beginning of the fourth quarter until Marcus Allen fumbled deep in New York territory and Joe Klecko recovered for the Jets on the 14. Allen did not have a good day at all, as he was held in check throughout the game by the tough New York defense. He was limited to only 36 rushing yards on 15 carries, and caught six passes for 37.

The Jets crossed midfield, and were looking to regain the lead when defensive back Burgess Owens killed the drive with an interception in the LA end zone. However, the Raiders could not capitalize on the turnover and were forced to punt.

The Jets then went 67 yards in six plays to regain the lead. Facing the Raiders' classic bump-and-run coverage, Wesley Walker managed to escape the tough brand of coverage long enough to catch a pass and gain 45 yards across the middle down to the Los Angeles 1-yard line. One play later, Scott Dierking blasted into the end zone. With Leahy's extra point, the Jets were once again on top, 17–14.

It appeared that the Jets sealed the Raiders' fate when linebacker Lance Mehl picked off a Plunkett pass on the LA 35, and returned it to the 27 with only 2:49 remaining in the fourth quarter. The Silver and Black refused to quit. Twenty-three seconds later, Ted Hendricks gave the offense one final shot at either tying things up or winning it outright when he recovered a Freeman McNeil fumble and brought it back to the LA 33. After reaching the New York 42, Plunkett tried to pass with time running out quickly. With 1:37 left, the Raiders' playoff hopes were put to rest when Mehl intercepted Plunkett once again to clinch the victory for New York.[11]

Individual Statistics and Roster

Head Coach: Tom Flores
Assistant Coaches: Sam Boghosian, Willie Brown, Chet Franklin, Larry Kennan, Earl Leggett, Joe Madro, Bob Mischak, Steve Ortmayer, Terry Robiskie, Charlie Sumner, Tom Walsh, Ray Willsey
1982 Regular Season Record: 8–1
1st Place American Football Conference. Due to strike-shortened season, there were no divisional champions.
Scored 260 points to rank 2nd out of 28 teams
Allowed 200 points to rank 22nd
Led the league in turnovers caused by a defense (29)

STARTERS — OFFENSE

QB — Jim Plunkett: Started in 9 games. Completed 152 of 261 pass attempts for 2,035 yards, 14 TD and15 INT. Rushed for 6 yards on 15 carries.
HB — Marcus Allen: Started in 9 games. Rushed for 697 yards on 160 carries and 11 TD. Had 38 receptions for 401 yards and 3 TD. Completed 1 pass in 4 attempts for 47 yards. **Also led the NFL in total TD (14), Points scored (84), and total yards from scrimmage (1,098)**.
FB — Kenny King: Started in 9 games. Rushed for 264 yards on 69 carries and 2 TD. Had 9 receptions for 57 yards.
WR — Malcolm Barnwell: Started in 9 games. Had 23 receptions for 387 yards and rushed for 18 yards on 2 carries.
WR — Cliff Branch: Started in 9 games. Had 30 receptions for 575 yards and 4 TD. Rushed for 10 yards on 2 carries.
TE — Todd Christensen: Started in 9 games. Had 42 receptions for 510 yards and 4 TD, and rushed for -6 yards on 1 carry.
LT — Bruce Davis: Started in 9 games.
LG — Curt Marsh: Started in 9 games.
C — Dave Dalby: Started in 9 games.
RG — Mickey Marvin: Started in 9 games.
RT — Henry Lawrence: Started in 9 games.

RESERVE OFFENSIVE PLAYERS

Rick Berns (RB): Active for 2 games.
Bob Chandler (WR): Active for 2 games.
Frank Hawkins (RB): Active for 9 games, rushed for 54 yards on 27 carries and 2 TD. Had 7 receptions for 35 yards and 1 TD.
Derrick Jensen (RB/TE): Active for 9 games and had 1 kickoff return for 27 yards.
Cleo Montgomery (WR): Active for 9 games and had 17 kickoff returns for 312 yards.
Calvin Muhammad (WR): Active for 8 games, and had 3 receptions for 92 yards and 1 TD.
Ed Muransky (T): Active for 5 games.
Greg Pruitt (RB): Active for 9 games, rushed for 22 yards on 4 carries, had 2 receptions for 29 yards and 1 TD, 27 punt returns for 209 yards, and 14 kickoff returns for 371 yards.
Derrick Ramsey (TE): Active for 9 games.
Jim Romano (C): Active for 5 games.
Art Shell (T): Active for 8 games.
Steve Sylvester (C/G/T): Active for 4 games.
Billy Taylor (RB): Active for 1 game, and rushed for 3 yards on 4 carries.
Chester Willis (RB): Active for 8 games, rushed for 15 yards on 6 carries, and had 1 kickoff return for 11 yards.
Marc Wilson (QB): Active for 8 games.

STARTERS — DEFENSE

DE — Howie Long: Active for 9 games, started in 5, and had 5 sacks.
DE — Lyle Alzado: Started in 9 games, had 7 sacks and 1 fumble recovery.
NT — Reggie Kinlaw: Active for and started in 8 games, had 1 sack and 1 fumble recovery.
LOLB — Ted Hendricks: Started in 9 games, had 7 sacks and 1 fumble recovery.
LILB — Matt Millen: Started in 9 games, had 2 sacks, 3 INT, 2 fumble recoveries, and 1 kickoff return for 13 yards.
RILB — Bob Nelson: Active for 9 games, started in 8, and had 1 sack.
ROLB — Rod Martin: Started in 9 games, had 1 sack and 3 INT.
CB — Lester Hayes: Started in 9 games and had 2 INT.
CB — Ted Watts: Started in 9 games, had 1 sack and 1 INT.
SS — Mike Davis: Started in 9 games, had 2 sacks, 1 INT and1 fumble recovery.
FS — Burgess Owens: Active for and started in 8 games and had 4 INT.

RESERVE DEFENSIVE PLAYERS

Jeff Barnes (LB): Active for 9 games and had 1 sacks.
Dave Browning (E): Active for 5 games, started in 4, had 1 sack and 2 fumble recoveries.
James Davis (DB): Active for 9 games, had 1 sack, 2 INT and 1 fumble recovery. **Led the NFL with 107 yards on his interception returns**.
Mike Hawkins (LB): Active for 3 games.
Kenny Hill (DB): Active for 9 games and had 2 kickoff returns for 20 yards.
Monte Jackson (DB): Active for 9 games and had 1 INT.
Randy McClanahan (LB): Active for 1 game.
Vann McElroy (DB): Active for 7 games, started in 1, and had 1 INT.
Odis McKinney (DB): Active for 9 games and started 1.
Cal Peterson (LB): Active for 4 games.
Archie Reese (E/T/NT): Active for 9 games, had 1 sack and 1 fumble recovery and 1 TD.
Johnny Robinson (NT): Active for 7 games.
Jack Squirek (LB): Active for 9 games and had 1 fumble recovery.
Ruben Vaughan (T/NT/E): Active for 9 games and had 4 sacks.

KICKING/PUNTING

K — Chris Bahr: Active for 9 games. Made 10 out of 16 field goal attempts and **32** out of 33 extra points for 62 points.

P — Ray Guy: Active for 9 games. Punted 47 times for a 39.1 average and rushed for -3 yards on 2 carries.

1983 Season Review

1. Sept. 4: The Raiders got revenge on the only team to beat them during the 1982 regular season. Led by a tremendous defensive effort, and an excellent ball control offensive attack, Los Angeles beat the Cincinnati Bengals with ease, 20–10. The defense kept switching alignments to confuse the Bengals. The strategy worked very well, as they held Cincinnati to 58 yards rushing, and recorded four sacks, with Lyle Alzado and rookie Bill Pickel each getting two. On offense, Los Angeles held possession for 35:37 minutes. Marcus Allen only ran for 47 yards, but he scored two touchdowns, with both coming from one yard away. Chris Bahr added two field goals (36 and 39 yards), and Los Angeles was in complete control at 20–3 before the Bengals scored a touchdown with one minute left in the game on a sweltering day in Cincinnati.[1]

2. Sept. 11: Los Angeles played their home opener in temperatures hovering in the high 90's. Despite the sauna-like conditions, the Raiders prevailed, 20–6, over the hapless Houston Oilers, who won only once the year before and did not look much better in '83. Kenny King opened the scoring midway through the first quarter on a 2-yard run, but Chris Bahr missed on the extra point try. Greg Pruitt ran for a 10-yard score, and Jim Plunkett threw his first touchdown pass of the season to Todd Christensen from two yards out. The defense played superb in containing quarterback Archie Manning, allowing him just six completions, and held the Oilers to only seven first downs.[2]

3. Sept. 19: Two days prior to the Raiders' Monday Night Football matchup with the Miami Dolphins, the last remaining original owner of the team passed away. Ed McGah died at age 84, and was a much-beloved member of the Raiders' organization. The Silver and Black went out against the Dolphins and dominated the defending AFC champs, 27–14, in honor of McGah. Los Angeles led, 27–0, in the fourth quarter before Miami finally got on the board in the closing minutes. The Raiders got touchdowns from Frank Hawkins (2-yard run), Todd Christensen (14-yard pass from Jim Plunkett), Greg Townsend (66-yard fumble recovery), and Greg Pruitt (5-yard run). Marcus Allen went over the 100-yard mark for the first time in 1983, Plunkett hit on 11 of 15 passes, and Christensen caught six passes for 95 yards. Los Angeles remained undefeated, and on top of the AFC Western Division. This win now gave the Raiders an incredible 20-2-1 record on Monday Night Football.[3]

4. Sept. 25: Los Angeles traveled to Denver to battle the Broncos and their rookie quarterback, John Elway. After a tough defensive struggle in the first quarter, defensive back Vann McElroy sparked the Silver and Black when he intercepted an Elway pass and returned it to the Denver 36-yard line. McElroy added another interception later. Jim Plunkett jumped on the opportunity McElroy presented to him, and on second down, he connected with Cliff Branch for a 35-yard touchdown. Los Angeles never looked back from that point on, and sailed to a 22–7 win to remain undefeated. Branch caught a second touchdown pass from Plunkett in the third quarter, this time a 29-

yarder. Chris Bahr kicked two field goals (27 and 29 yards), and Greg Townsend sacked quarterback Steve DeBerg in the end zone for a safety. It was one of six sacks registered by the outstanding defensive unit that allowed Denver to cross midfield only four times throughout the game. The only bad news for the Raiders was that Marcus Allen suffered a bruised hip that would keep him out of the next game.[4]

5. Oct. 2: The Raiders took an undefeated record, a nine-game winning streak on the road, and the league's number one defense into the nation's capital to butt heads with the defending Super Bowl champion Washington Redskins. The Redskins were a dominant force, and proved their might by running up a 20–7 third quarter lead over the Silver and Black. They took advantage of five turnovers, and the Raiders trailed in a game for the first time all season. Los Angeles scored their touchdown with an NFL record 99-yard pass from Jim Plunkett to Cliff Branch. The celebration was short, however, due to the fact that Branch pulled a hamstring muscle, and would miss the next five games. In the third quarter, the Raiders decided to get back into this game, and did so with a vengeance by scoring four touchdowns over the course of nine-and-a-half minutes. Plunkett threw two touchdown passes to Branch's replacement, Calvin Muhammad, covering 35 and 22 yards, and one to Todd Christensen from two yards out. Los Angeles then got a fifth six-pointer when Greg Pruitt returned a punt 97 yards for a team record. Pruitt's electrifying return gave the Raiders a 35–20 lead midway through the fourth quarter. As stated earlier, the Redskins were a force to be reckoned with in their own right, and they came back to take the lead with 28 seconds left to play. Plunkett had one final chance at victory, but he threw his fourth interception of the game on the first play of the drive, and Washington prevailed, 37–35. Despite his interceptions, Plunkett threw for 372 yards and four touchdowns. Another standout in the loss was defensive lineman Howie Long, who recorded five quarterback sacks. The loss dropped Los Angeles from the unbeaten ranks, but they still held a one game lead in the AFC West.[5]

6. Oct. 9: With nine seconds remaining, Nick Lowery, one of the NFL's best kickers, lined up to attempt a 48-yard field goal with his Chiefs trailing, 21–20. As Lowery's foot met the ball, 6'7" Ted Hendricks jumped up and blocked the kick to preserve the win. Thanks to Hendricks, the Raiders were 5–1, and leading the AFC West by two games. Marcus Allen returned to action after resting his bruised hip, and recovered a Frank Hawkins fumble in the end zone for one touchdown, Chris Bahr then added the extra point, which turned out to be the winning point with 8:29 left to play. Allen also accounted for a touchdown in the third quarter when he threw to Dokie Williams on a halfback option pass that covered 21 yards. The Raiders' other six-pointer came on a 3-yard pass from Jim Plunkett to Todd Christensen to get the Silver and Black on the board in the second quarter.[6]

7. Oct. 16: Since coming into the league in 1976, the Seattle Seahawks quickly became one of the Raiders worst nightmares. They continued to give Los Angeles problems by beating them, 38–36, in the Seattle Kingdome. This was the fifth time in eleven previous meetings that Seattle prevailed over the Silver and Black. Even though the defense gave up 38 points, the unit did a good job limiting Seattle to only 153 offensive yards. The Raiders took

a 17–7 lead into the second half on two Todd Christensen touchdown receptions and a 32-yard field goal from Chris Bahr. Christensen's first touchdown came on a 19-yard pass from Marcus Allen, and his second came on a 12-yard pass from Jim Plunkett. It was then that Seattle got back in the game, thanks to two Plunkett fumbles and one from Allen. The Seahawks quickly turned those errors into points. Plunkett also threw three interceptions, and was replaced by Marc Wilson in the fourth quarter. Wilson got Los Angeles close with two late scoring tosses. His first was a 1-yarder to Allen, and Christensen caught his third scoring strike of the game, this time from 22 yards out. The loss overshadowed a great day for Christensen, as he hauled in 11 receptions for 152 yards. The Raiders received their other five points in the third quarter on a 42-yard Bahr field goal and on a safety recorded by Lyle Alzado when he tackled Robert Pratt in the end zone. The loss cut the Raiders' AFC West lead to one game in front of both Denver and Seattle.[7]

8. Oct. 23: In possibly the best regular season game of 1983, the Raiders took their renegade mystique into Dallas in an attempt to conquer the clean cut, undefeated Cowboys. Tom Flores decided to bench a slumping Jim Plunkett in favor of Marc Wilson, and the change worked out very well. Wilson played brilliantly, completing 26 of 49 pass attempts for 318 yards and three touchdowns in a 40–38 shoot out victory for the Silver and Black. The Raiders put up over 500 yards of total offense, and Dallas had over 300. Derrick Jensen (2 yards), Frank Hawkins (17 yards), and Todd Christensen (1 yard), were on the receiving end of Wilson's scoring tosses. Hawkins led all ball carriers with 118 yards, and scored on a 23-yard run. Chris Bahr chipped in with a great performance by hitting on four field goal tries from 37, 24, and a pair of 26-yarders. This game helped Los Angeles gain some much-needed confidence following a few sub-par games. At the halfway mark of the season, the Raiders were 6–2 and held a one game lead over Denver in the division.[8]

9. Oct. 30: Just when Los Angeles was getting back in the groove, the Seattle Seahawks came to town and did their number on the Raiders once again. A 34–21 win gave Seattle a season sweep over Los Angeles. The loss put the Raiders into a first place tie with Denver at 6–3, and Seattle was a close second at 5–4. Los Angeles was never in this game, and Marc Wilson got sacked five times and threw four interceptions. The Raiders got their points on a Marcus Allen 1-yard run, and two Wilson passes to tight end Don Hasselbeck (4 yards) and Dokie Williams (50 yards).[9]

10. Nov. 6: After his brilliant performance two weeks earlier against Dallas, Marc Wilson's season came to an end when he suffered a broken shoulder against Kansas City at the end of the first half. It appeared that history was repeating itself for the Raiders. In 1980, Jim Plunkett was called on from the bench to replace a quarterback who suffered a season ending injury also against Kansas City. He then guided the Silver and Black to a Super Bowl championship. In the contest, the Raiders trailed, 13–7, after three quarters. Before going down, Wilson threw a 15-yard touchdown pass to Frank Hawkins in the first quarter. Plunkett then rallied Los Angeles in the second half, taking them to a 28–20 win, which gave them a 7–3 record. Plunkett hit on five of nine pass attempts for 114 yards, and a 19-yard touchdown pass to Dokie Williams that put Los Angeles in the lead for good. Prior to that, Marcus Allen scored on a 1-yard run. Linebacker Rod Martin

ended the game in fine fashion by returning an interception 40 yards for a touchdown with three seconds left in the game.[10]

11. Nov. 13: After spotting the Denver Broncos an early 10–0 lead, the Raiders battled back to take a 19–10 advantage into the final minute of the game. Los Angeles got their points on two Chris Bahr field goals (28 and 42 yards), and touchdown runs by Marcus Allen (7 yards), and Frank Hawkins (17 yards). Bahr's extra point attempt following Hawkins' touchdown was botched after the ball went through the hands of holder David Humm. Denver's kicker, Rick Karlis, closed the gap to 19–13 on a 22-yard field goal with 6:35 left to play. With four minutes left, Denver linebacker Tom Jackson knocked the ball from Plunkett's hands, and nose tackle Rubin Carter recovered the fumble on the Los Angeles 42 with 3:40 to go. Rookie quarterback John Elway then ran for a 4-yard touchdown with 58 seconds left to give Denver the lead, 20–19. Plunkett had a tough day. Besides the fumble that led to the Broncos going ahead, he was sacked five times. Despite these perils, Plunkett was tough and crafty. He rallied the Silver and Black back from the brink of defeat on a five-play drive that ate up 48 yards in 54 seconds. Four of those plays were pass completions to tight end par excellence Todd Christensen, who was working against a banged up secondary. With four seconds left, Bahr gave Los Angeles its eighth win of the season by splitting the uprights from 39 yards away to make it a 22–20 final.[11]

12. Nov. 20: The Raiders went clear across the country to face the AFC Eastern Division co-leaders, the Buffalo Bills. Frank Hawkins scored on a 2-yard run on the Raiders first possession. They increased their lead to 24–3 by the opening minutes of the fourth quarter on a Marcus Allen 4-yard run, a 15-yard pass from Jim Plunkett to Todd Christensen, and a Chris Bahr field goal from 41 yards. Not to be shown up in their own stadium, the Bills came back to tie the game, 24–24, with four minutes left in regulation. Throughout Raiders history, they have been known to come back and win a game or two. This was one of those times, and Chris Bahr was once again the one to pull it out thanks to a great Plunkett-led drive that got the offense close enough for a field goal attempt. On the game-winning drive, Plunkett was a perfect six of six in pass completions. Bahr then climaxed the drive with a 36-yard field goal that lifted Los Angeles to a 27–24 victory, and a 9–3 record, which tied them with the Pittsburgh Steelers for the best mark in the AFC. With four games remaining, the Raiders were in first place by two games over Denver in the AFC West.[12]

13. Nov. 27: After two straight fantastic finishes, the Raiders hosted the 3-8-1 New York Giants, and recorded an easy 27–12 victory to be the first AFC team to reach ten wins. Jim Plunkett had a tremendous day, completing 19 of 32 pass attempts for 243 yards and two touchdowns. On the receiving end of Plunkett's scoring strikes were Don Hasselbeck (13 yards), and Malcolm Barnwell (36 yards). Other scores for the Raiders came from Marcus Allen (11-yard run), and two Chris Bahr field goals from 47 and 38 yards. This victory allowed the Raiders to clinch a playoff berth, and lead the division by three games.[13]

14. Dec. 1: Los Angeles produced their highest point total of the season in a 42–10 thrashing over the San Diego Chargers. With their fifth consecutive win, and eighth of the last nine, the Raiders clinched the AFC Western Division title for the 13th time

in 17 seasons. Todd Christensen had a career day with eight receptions for 140 yards and three touchdowns. He caught two from Jim Plunkett (25 and 14 yards), and one from Marcus Allen (43 yards). Frank Hawkins led all ball carriers with 56 yards, and scored two touchdowns (20 yards and 1 yard). The Raiders' defense was spectacular, as they recorded six sacks, with Howie Long leading the way with three. Greg Townsend had two and Rod Martin the other. Martin also returned an interception 29 yards for the Raiders' sixth touchdown of the game.[14]

15. Dec. 11: With the division title secured, Tom Flores decided to rest some of his starters. The St. Louis Cardinals came to Los Angeles with a 6-7-1 record, but had won six of their previous eight games. Los Angeles jumped out to a 17-0 first quarter lead on Jim Plunkett touchdown passes to Kenny King (34 yards), and Cliff Branch (5 yards), and a Chris Bahr 22-yard field goal. Plunkett added a third scoring strike, this time a 20-yarder to Marcus Allen, in the second quarter to increase the advantage to 24-7. Things broke down from there for the Silver and Black. The Cardinals shut them out the rest of the way, and put 27 points on the board to win, 34-24. The loss put the Raiders at 11-4, and snapped a five game winning streak in the process.[15]

16. Dec. 18: With the loss to the Cardinals, the Raiders found themselves tied with the Miami Dolphins for the best record in the AFC. Miami won their finale against the New York Jets two days earlier to improve to 12-4. The Raiders needed a win against San Diego to lock up home field advantage throughout the AFC playoffs. Even though a win would tie Los Angeles with the Dolphins, the Raiders would receive the advantage due to their week three win over Miami. The Chargers drew first blood in the opening quarter, and led, 7-0. From there, Los Angeles went out and did what they had to do to wrap up home field advantage for themselves, and tore the Chargers up in the process by a score of 30-14. Marcus Allen ran for two scores (8 and 5 yards), finished the season with 1,014 rushing yards, and set a single-season team record for most passes caught by a running back (68). Jim Plunkett threw a 4-yard touchdown pass to Cliff Branch, and Chris Bahr kicked three field goals (21, 32 and 28 yards). Linebacker Jeff Barnes had 12 tackles to lead the defense in that category. The Raiders were now the top seed in the AFC, and looked to be the best in the entire league.[16]

AFC Divisional Playoff Game, January 1, 1984

The Raiders and the Pittsburgh Steelers had one of the most-hated, hard-fought rivalries in all of football history. From 1972 to 1976, they met five times in the playoffs, with the Steelers winning three times. On New Year's Day in 1984, the Silver and Black made Pittsburgh pay for those three setbacks.

With future Hall of Fame quarterback Terry Bradshaw ailing with an elbow injury, the fate of the Pittsburgh offense rested on the arm of 7-year backup Cliff Stoudt. The Los Angeles defense made Stoudt pay dearly for his efforts. They sacked him five times, with Lyle Alzado leading the way with three, and had an interception that shifted the momentum over to Los Angeles in a big way.

On a beautiful, sunny day in the City of Angels, a crowd of 90,434 filled the Los Angeles Memorial Coliseum to set a playoff attendance record. Pittsburgh opened the scoring on their second offensive series of the game. The Steelers drove 78 yards, but were stopped just short of the end zone. On fourth-and-inches, head coach Chuck Noll decided to go for the field goal. Gary Anderson was called on, and came through with a 17-yard field goal. It was all down hill for the Steelers from this point on, as the Raiders completely punished and dominated them.

On Pittsburgh's next possession, Stoudt went back to pass on first down from his own 14. The pass was intended for Calvin Sweeney, but Lester "the Judge" Hayes quickly laid down the law, and permanently gave Los Angeles momentum. He intercepted the ball and went 18 yards untouched to give the Raiders a 7-3 lead at the end of the first quarter.

On the Raiders' next touchdown drive, it was the Marcus Allen show. After running for 15 yards on the first two plays of the possession, he caught a pass for 17 yards. With the ball on the Pittsburgh four, Allen capped the drive off with an incredible leap over the goal line. After taking the handoff from Jim Plunkett, Allen took a running start and went airborne at the three. When he landed, the Raiders had their second touchdown, and with Chris Bahr's second extra point added, Los Angeles was up, 14-3. On the day, Allen ran for 121 yards, and caught five passes for an additional 38 yards. Bahr added a 43-yard field goal later in the quarter to increase the Los Angeles advantage to 17-3 at the half.

This game had the makings of a rout, and in the third quarter, the Raiders made it a reality. Los Angeles took the second half kickoff and went 72 yards for their third touchdown. Kenny King put his name in the scoring column with a 9-yard run that increased the bulge to 24-3 following Bahr's conversion.

Five minutes later, the Raiders scored again, with two handoffs to Allen doing the damage. After gaining nine yards on his first carry, Allen took the ball once again and outran everyone for a 49-yard touchdown. With Bahr's extra point, the Raiders' lead was now 31-3.

The only highlight for Pittsburgh occurred when John Stallworth caught his tenth playoff touchdown later in the third quarter to tie him with Fred Biletnikoff for the most in playoff history.

Los Angeles was still not done, and went 65 yards for the game's final points in the closing seconds of the third quarter. Todd Christensen caught three passes in the drive, and Frank Hawkins scored on a 1-yard run. Bahr's extra point then completed the 38-10 lambasting.

The Raiders now looked ahead to hosting the AFC Championship Game. Their opponents would be the one team that seemed to find a way to be a thorn in the Raiders' side more often than not.[17]

AFC Championship Game, January 8, 1984

The Seattle Seahawks were coming off a huge 27-20 upset win over the defending AFC champion Miami Dolphins. They came into their championship game matchup against Los Angeles with the distinction of handing the Raiders two of their four losses during the regular season. The Seahawks hoped to continue their streak against the Silver and Black for at least one more game.

The Raiders' faithful of 88,734 set another playoff attendance record for largest crowd in AFC title game history. The Raiders did not want to let the City of Angels down, and looked to represent it in Super Bowl XVIII.

On Seattle's first offensive series, quarterback Dave Krieg was sacked once and then picked off. The Raiders' defense quickly set the tone for the disaster to come. On the strength of a tremendous pass rush to disrupt Seattle's timing, the Raiders intercepted five passes, recorded four sacks, and smothered the running game, allowing star running back Curt Warner only 26 yards on 11 carries. This performance went down as one of the greatest defensive showings in Raiders history.

This onslaught clad in silver and black completely rattled Krieg into having one of the worst title game performances by a quarterback. He completed three of nine passes for 12 yards and three interceptions until he was pulled in the second half and replaced by Jim Zorn.

The Raiders' plan called for prohibiting Curt Warner from getting to the outside. To stop this, Los Angeles spread their ends out and brought the inside linebackers up closer to the line of scrimmage to fill any holes that remained. The scheme worked, and with Warner neutralized, the Seahawks had to go to the air, which made them predictable and vulnerable. All the Raiders had to do next was punish whoever had the ball. For the day, the Raiders only gave up 64 yards on the ground and 102 through the air.

With the defense completely shutting Seattle down, the Los Angeles offense was able to build a 20–0 halftime lead. Jim Plunkett continued to ring up impressive playoff numbers since the 1980 season. This time he completed 17 of 24 passes for 214 yards and one touchdown. His main target on this day was Malcolm Barnwell, who caught five passes for 116 yards. When not passing, Plunkett handed off to Marcus Allen, and he gave the Raiders an incredibly balanced offensive attack by gaining 154 yards on 25 carries and catching seven passes for 62 yards and a touchdown.

The Seahawks did show some form of life early in the first quarter before all hell broke loose on them. They managed to get to the LA 34 thanks to an interference call on Lester Hayes and a roughing the kicker penalty on Odis McKinney after he blasted punter Jeff West. On the next play, Hayes redeemed himself for his infraction by picking off a Krieg pass intended for Steve Largent and returning it to the Seattle 26. This led to a 20-yard field goal by Chris Bahr to give the Raiders a 3–0 lead at the end of the first quarter.

Los Angeles then proceeded to pour it on in the second quarter with two scoring runs by Frank Hawkins (1 and 5 yards), and a 45-yard Bahr field goal. With Seattle's defense focusing a great deal of attention on the ever-dangerous Cliff Branch, Plunkett went to Barnwell, and the third-year pro responded to the challenge very nicely. A 20-yard reception helped set up the Raiders' first touchdown, and a 49-yarder helped on the second.

The Raiders started the second half with a Matt Millen interception off Krieg, and that was all for the Seattle signal caller. Mike Davis also had an interception against Krieg and his replacement, Jim Zorn, as did Vann McElroy. Zorn, however, did manage to get the Seahawks on the board. He completed 14 of 27 passes for 134 yards and threw scoring strikes to Dan Doornink (11 yards) and Charle Young (9 yards).

Tough and aggressive linebacker Matt Millen awaits the snap so he can deliver punishment to anyone in his path during a 1984 game (AP Photo/NFL Photos).

Los Angeles added a 3-yard touchdown pass from Plunkett to Allen in the third, and a 35-yard field goal from Bahr in the fourth to complete a 30–14 pounding that gave the Raiders their third AFC championship in seven years and their fourth trip to the Super Bowl. They were peaking at the best time, and looked to complete their romp through the playoffs two weeks later in Tampa, Florida, against the Washington Redskins.[18]

Super Bowl XVIII

Jan. 22, 1984; Played at
Tampa Stadium, Tampa, Florida

Washington's All-Pro offensive lineman Russ Grimm claimed that his desire was so great to win another Super Bowl that he would run over his own mother to achieve the gridiron's most coveted prize. Upon hearing of his upcoming opponent's statement, Raider par-excellence Matt Millen returned a verbal volley that he would run over Grimm's mother to win the Super Bowl as well. Lyle Alzado did not want to run over anyone's mother, but did add his thoughts of the upcoming clash between the Raiders and Washington Redskins. Alzado eloquently stating that he wanted to rip the head of Washington quarterback Joe Theismann off his shoulders.

Thus, after a three-year absence, the ominous silver and black shroud of the Evil Empire once again blanketed itself over pro football's ultimate spectacle. This was achieved not only by words, but external design as well. In the week building up to Super Bowl XVIII, the city of Tampa was transformed into an east coast satellite of Raider Nation. Reminders that the Silver and Black were about to embark on "the Cigar City" were abundantly clear, as billboards and benches throughout Tampa were etched with the Raiders shield and motto "Commitment to Excellence." It was the organization's way of letting it be known that the Silver and Black were back and looking to conquer.[19]

The Raiders' opponent for the 18th edition of the pro gridiron's ultimate showdown was the Washington Redskins, who took the field on January 22, 1984, with an extremely impressive resume showcasing their work over the past year. After winning their first league title in forty years the previous season, the defending Super Bowl champion Redskins used the '83 campaign as an encore on their way to establishing themselves as one of the greatest teams in NFL history.

This virtually impenetrable juggernaut from the nation's capital steamrolled over 14 of their 16 regular season victims, and missed out on a perfect record by losing two games by a point apiece. Along the way on the road to destruction, Washington amassed a then–NFL record 541 points with a potent offense and one of the best defensive units.

The offense was loaded with an arsenal that conjured envy and fear in opponents. Quarterback Joe Theismann won the NFL Most Valuable Player Award after finishing the 1983 season as the second-rated passer overall. He completed 60 percent of his attempts for 3,714 yards, 29 touchdowns, and a mere 11 interceptions. His receiving corps consisted of dangerous deep threats Charlie Brown (78 receptions for 1,225 yards and eight touchdowns) and Art Monk (47 catches for 746 yards and five touchdowns). When not throwing to talented receivers, Theismann handed off to one of the game's most dominant running backs of

the early 1980's, battering ram fullback John "the Diesel" Riggins. The reigning Super Bowl MVP did not rest on his laurels after landing the coveted award, as he powered his way to 1,347 yards and set a then-single season NFL record with 24 rushing touchdowns. Joe Washington added flash and dash to the Washington offensive machine with 772 yards on the ground and 454 yards and six touchdowns on 47 catches.[20]

Protecting this lethal collection of offensive firepower was one of the greatest assemblies of trench warriors the game has ever witnessed, with the exception of the Raiders' offensive lines throughout the 1970's and early 80's. Mentored by future Raiders head coach Joe Bugel, Washington's wall of protection commonly referred to as "the Hogs," were made up of All-Pro's Joe Jacoby (left tackle) and Russ Grimm (left guard), Pro-Bowl center Jeff Bostic, right guard Mark May, and right tackle George Starke. Rounding out Washington's potent offensive attack was kicker Mark Moseley, who led the NFL in scoring with 161 points. Riggins finished second with 144 points to make this the first time since 1951 that teammates finished the scoring race ranked one and two.[21]

The defensive unit was just as impressive, leading the league in fewest yards given up on the ground (1,289). Up front, this unit was led by tackle Dave Butz and end Dexter Manley, who combined for 22 sacks. The secondary had Mark Murphy, the league leader in interceptions with nine.[22]

On the road to their second consecutive Super Bowl appearance, the Redskins destroyed the city of Los Angeles' other team, the Rams, by a resounding 51–7 tally in a divisional playoff game. The San Francisco 49ers made Washington work a little harder in the NFC Championship Game. It took until the final seconds to decide the winner in this one, as a Moseley field goal with 40 ticks left on the clock allowed the Redskins to prevail, 24–21. Along the way, John Riggins blasted through both defenses for a total of 242 rushing yards and five six-pointers. His solid rushing performances allowed "the Diesel" to continue on his record trek of topping the century mark for six straight playoff games.[23]

As the 4:45 P.M. kickoff approached, the temperature in Tampa was a mild 68 degrees with a mixture of clouds and sun, and a 20-mph wind swirling about. The three-point underdog Raiders took the field running through a gauntlet created by the beautiful Los Angeles Raiderettes cheerleading squad, and were now a short time away from attempting to remove the Redskins from their championship throne.

The CBS Network had the opportunity to broadcast this clash, with Pat Summerall and John Madden calling the action. Months earlier, on October 31, 1983, the NFL lost one of its founding fathers in Chicago Bears' owner George (Papa Bear) Halas, who passed away at age 88. A moment of silence was conducted in honor of this incredible trailblazer before entertaining legend Barry Manilow bellowed out the national anthem. Bronco Nagurski, the bruising hall of fame fullback on some of Halas' legendary teams, was on hand for the coin toss won by the Raiders. They elected to receive, and Super Bowl XVIII was about to get started.[24]

With Tampa Stadium buzzing with anticipation, Washington's Jeff Hayes placed the ball on the kicking tee, and as the crowd was in full frenzy mode, his right foot connected with the ball and it sailed into the end zone past Greg Pruitt for a touchback. The Raiders would begin the first series of Super Bowl XVIII from their own 20.

Jim Plunkett handed the ball off to Marcus Allen on first down, and he picked up five yards off left tackle. Plunkett went back to Allen on second down, this time on a pass for a gain of six and a first down. For the third straight play, Allen was the focal point, and he carried for a gain of two off left tackle. Plunkett then went looking for his All-Pro tight end Todd Christensen on second-and-eight, but a pass to him over the middle was broken up by defensive back Ken Coffey. Plunkett connected with Kenny King on third down, but he was stopped after gaining a yard on a pass in the right flat. On fourth-and-seven from the LA 34, Ray Guy was called upon to perform the first punt of the game.

Guy got off a 47-yard punt that Nick Giaquinto signaled for a fair catch on at the Washington 19. The defending champions then brought their high-powered offense onto the field for the first time with hopes of taking an early advantage. During the season, Washington's famed offensive line of "the Hogs," lined up extremely tight, but in this matchup they decided to create more space between each other. This was done in an attempt to give John Riggins more running room up the middle and between the tackles. The initial success of this scheme stemmed from the thinking that Pro Bowl center Jeff Bostic would control middle guard Reggie Kinlaw throughout the game, thus allowing Riggins to tear up huge chunks of yardage in that area.[25] The Raiders countered this by lining up their linebackers closer to the line of scrimmage to fill in the holes. With the great cornerback tandem of Lester Hayes and Mike Haynes on Washington's receivers, the linebackers had more freedom to focus on Riggins instead of helping out in pass coverage.

Quarterback Joe Theismann broke the huddle and Riggins lined up in Washington's lone back "Ace Formation" looking to begin what he felt might be another big day for him. On first down, Riggins took a handoff, and Kinlaw established the fact that Bostic was not going to have it that easy against him. He broke free and dropped Riggins after a gain of three up the middle with an assist from Howie Long. Riggins gave the Washington faithful reason to be confident by running for six yards off right tackle, and then picked up a first down on his third straight carry with a gain of two also off right tackle.

With his running game moving the chains, Theismann de-

Quarterback Jim Plunkett lets one fly. His career was resurrected with the Raiders and he won the Super Bowl not once but twice. Here he is seen throwing against Washington in the Raiders' Super Bowl XVIII victory on January 22, 1984, in Tampa, Florida (AP Photo).

cided to look to the pass lanes. His first attempt came after faking a handoff to Riggins, and then throwing to the left flat in the direction of Art Monk. The ball fluttered in the wind and Mike Haynes broke it up and almost picked it off. Two more attempts to Monk failed, as Haynes was there to smother him. The Raiders had succeeded in stopping Washington's short passing game, which they used to set up runs by Riggins after gaining five or six yards through the air. The Raiders were also able to apply pressure on Theismann with their front line of Alzado, Long, Pickel, and Townsend. With Haynes and Hayes covering the receivers so well in this first series, the Silver and Black were sending a message to Washington that they were not intimidated by their explosive offensive attack. In fact, it was the Raiders who appeared to be sending a message that the Redskins should be in fear of them.

On fourth-and-10 from the Washington 30, Jeff Hayes came in to punt. At the snap, Greg Pruitt awaited the kick deep in his own territory, but he never got a chance to touch the pigskin. The Raiders were lined up in a nine-man rush formation, and special teams captain Derrick Jensen cut inside of Washington's Otis Wonsley, and when Clint Didier went over to block Lester Hayes, Jensen had a clear path to the punter. He jumped with outstretched arms and blocked the kick. The ball began rolling toward the Washington end zone with Lester Hayes, Kenny Hill, and Jensen all in pursuit. By the time the loose prized possession made its way to the goal line, Jensen beat out his teammates and landed on the ball for a touchdown. With 10:08 left in the first quarter, Chris Bahr added the extra point, and Los Angeles drew first blood with a 7–0 lead.

Bahr sent the ensuing kickoff to the Washington 10, where Alvin Garrett received it and advanced it 11 yards. Once again the Redskins opened a possession with Riggins getting the call. He ran off left tackle for four yards before being stopped by Matt Millen. A pass intended for Charlie Brown fell incomplete on second down. That was followed by Theismann running away from pressure for a gain of five yards. Facing a fourth-and-one situation, the Redskins decided to punt rather than go for it.

Once again punting from his own 30, Hayes hoped that the same result would not occur this time around. It did not, and Hayes got off a short punt covering 28 yards. Ted Watts got underneath the ball, but he dropped it. The ball was recovered by Washington's Greg Williams at the LA 42 to give possession back to the Redskins.

Theismann looked to capitalize on this mishap, and took to the air on first down, but an attempt to Didier fell incomplete. This marked the fourth straight incomplete pass thrown by the reigning league MVP, but on the following play, he connected with Didier for eight yards. Riggins then picked up two yards and a fresh set of downs at the LA 31. The Redskins looked like they were on the verge of gaining momentum. However, the Raiders' defense snapped them back to reality by stopping Riggins and then Joe Washington on the next two plays after both picked up two yards. On third-and-six, Theismann went back to throwing incompletions, this time with a pass intended for Giaquinto. Mark Moseley tried to salvage the drive with a 44-yard field goal attempt, but the kick sailed wide to the left.

The Raiders took over on their own 28, and Kenny King tore off the biggest ground gainer of the game up to this point with a 10-yard run. He then caught a 7-yard pass from Plunkett in the left flat. A gain of two yards by Marcus Allen followed, and then Plunkett connected with Todd Christensen for a pickup of nine yards and a first down inside Washington territory at the 44. Unfortunately, the play was nullified by a holding penalty on Bruce Davis, which brought the ball back to the LA 46. On first-

and-20, Allen ran a sweep to the right side, but fumbled after a loss of four yards. Charley Hannah was there to save the day by recovering the loose ball on the LA 42. Two pass attempts by Plunkett failed to connect with Christensen and Frank Hawkins, and the Raiders were forced to punt after what began as a drive with some promise. Ray Guy got off a 42-yard punt that Giaquinto returned 11 yards. The Redskins were called for holding on the return and penalized nine yards, which was half the distance from where the foul took place.

From the Washington eight, Riggins swept to the right side for a gain of two, and Theismann picked up a first down with a 10-yard pass to Joe Washington across the middle. An incomplete pass to Didier on the sideline was followed by Riggins getting dropped for a loss of three yards by Rod Martin. Facing a third-and-13-situation, the Redskins got a reprieve when Alzado was called for being offside, and this gave Washington five yards, moving them to their 22. Theismann then ended the drive by having a pass intended for Charlie Brown broken up by Vann McElroy. Jeff Hayes punted, and Greg Pruitt returned the ball eight yards to the LA 38.

Marcus Allen ended the opening quarter in fine fashion by running off left tackle for 17 yards, and added three more off the same spot to end the first fifteen minutes with the Raiders on the Washington 45.

The Raiders began the second quarter with Plunkett throwing to Christensen for a gain of three. Allen gave the yardage back to Washington when Perry Brooks dropped him for a three-yard loss on third down. On fourth down, Ray Guy came on to punt the ball back over to the Redskins. Todd Christensen was the snapper on punts, and had some chalk from the yard markers still on his hands from when he caught a pass two plays earlier. The chalk messed up Christensen's snap, and the ball took off on him. It sailed high, and looked to be going over Guy's head, but his incredible athletic ability showed when he jumped high, and with one hand, brought the ball back down and got off a 42-yard punt that sailed into the end zone for a touchback. The play could have been a recipe for disaster if not for Guy's quick reaction.

Riggins was becoming the workhorse of the Washington offensive attack. On this series he carried for five yards on the first two plays, and after a Theismann pass of five yards to Joe Washington picked up a first down, Riggins again carried the ball, this time for only one yard before Kinlaw slammed him down. Riggins might have been carrying the offensive load, but he was not getting the huge gains like he was used to. Theismann was also having his troubles trying to penetrate the LA pass rush and find open receivers where there weren't any. Prime examples of this occurred on the following two plays, as Matt Millen sacked Theismann for a loss of seven, and then a pass attempt to Brown was overthrown, and Washington had to once again give the ball back over to the Raiders. Greg Pruitt called for a fair catch of Hayes' 41-yard punt on the LA 35 to begin another series for the Silver and Black.

Up to this stage, the Raiders had been going with a conservative game plan of short safe passes. It was now time to open the offense up, returning to the free wheeling Raiders' attack of bombs away. With five minutes expired in the second quarter, Plunkett called the pass play 99 Post, East I and cross, K14 flat. In simple terms, it meant a long pass to Cliff Branch down the middle. Plunkett faked a handoff to Allen, and then dropped back looking for one of football's fastest players over the past decade. Branch and the other wideout, Malcolm Barnwell were lined up on the left side, and shot into the Washington secondary. Barnwell cut across the middle, and defensive back Darrell Green hesitated for a split second. This gave Branch the opening he was looking for, and the 35-year-old sprinter took off down the middle of the field and Plunkett's pass was perfect. Branch hauled it in over his right shoulder for a gain of 50 yards before Anthony Washington brought him down on the 15.

To keep the defense honest, Plunkett sent Allen off right tackle for a gain of three. On second-and-seven from the Washington 12, Plunkett looked to go back to Branch. At the snap, Branch made one quick move to the outside on Anthony Washington, ran straight at him, and then cut to the inside. Center Dave Dalby saved the play when he reacted quickly to linebacker Rich Milot's rush on Plunkett. Milot had an open path to drop Plunkett for a sack, but Dalby took him out of the play with a great block. Plunkett released the ball, and a second later it was in Branch's hands for a touchdown as the Raiderettes were celebrating the six-pointer behind him along the back of the end zone. The three-play, 65-yard drive took 1:34 off the clock, and with 9:14 left in the first half, the Raiders were up, 14–0, after Bahr's conversion kick.

Bahr's kickoff was received by Alvin Garrett on the Washington six, and returned 14 yards. On first down, Rod Martin sacked Theismann for a loss of seven yards, which was followed by an incomplete pass intended for Art Monk. Theismann then connected with Garrett on a pickup of 17 yards, and after a holding penalty took away a 12-yard completion to Didier, Theismann went back to him on a screen pass for an 18-yard gain. Riggins then ran for a total of six yards on the next three plays, with Reggie Kinlaw continuing his dominance over Jeff Bostic. On Riggins' first two carries, Kinlaw stopped him before he could get going. An offside penalty on Howie Long moved the Redskins to midfield, and Riggins picked up a first down with a sweep to the right for four yards. After another penalty on the Raiders, this time for pass interference on Lester Hayes, the Redskins advanced 20 yards on a Theismann pass to Didier. With a new set of downs at the LA 14, the Redskins looked poised to finish off a drive successfully. On first down, Theismann picked up five yards running for his life to avoid a sack, and then Riggins ran off left tackle for two yards. On third-and-three, Rod Martin broke up a pass intended for Joe Washington over the middle. With 3:05 left in the half, the high-powered Washington offensive machine was finally on the board with a Mark Moseley 24-yard field goal that completed the 12-play, 73-yard drive, and now made the score 14–3.

Jeff Hayes sent the ensuing kickoff into the end zone for a touchback, and the Raiders looked to get back the points they just gave up. Allen started the drive off with a sweep to the right that gained 11 yards. The two-minute warning came right after Plunkett was sacked by Darryl Grant for a loss of ten. From the LA 21, Allen ran for seven yards on a draw play, then Plunkett filled the skies with three straight passes. Frank Hawkins caught the first for 14 yards, Christensen followed with 14, and Branch hauled in the third for a 7-yard pickup. A holding penalty on Mickey Marvin took Los Angeles back ten yards, and then Allen ran of eight yards, and that was followed by an incomplete pass intended for Christensen on a deep pattern. On fourth down,

Guy pinned the Redskins back on the Washington 12 with 12 seconds remaining in the half.

The Raiders went into a prevent defense, but defensive coordinator Charlie Sumner saw that the Redskins were bringing Joe Washington into the game as the lone running back. Sumner quickly recalled that Washington caught a pass in the same situation during the regular season against the Raiders. The play gained 67 yards and allowed the Redskins to get back into the game, which they eventually won by two points. To avoid this from happening on football's grandest stage, Sumner immediately pulled run stopper Matt Millen out of the game, replacing him with second-year linebacker Jack Squirek.

Squirek was a pass defense specialist with more agility and quickness to cover on passes. Sumner gave Squirek specific instructions to not take his eyes off Washington and stick to him wherever he went. At the snap, Theismann dropped back looking to his right as Howie Long, Lyle Alzado, and linebacker Bob Nelson were shaking themselves free from blockers and in hot pursuit of the quarterback. Knowing that his time was limited before he would be driven into the ground, Theismann sent a short, floating pass to the left toward Washington. Squirek was in man-to-man coverage, and as the pass sailed in his direction, he reacted quickly, stepped in front of Washington, and jumped up to grab the lob pass at the five, and a few steps later, he completed his task by gaining everlasting immortality with his entrance into the end zone with the ball raised high for the touchdown. A split second later he jumped into Howie Long's arms, and was mobbed by the rest of the team after he got to the sideline.

Squirek's once-in-a-lifetime opportunity proved to be the definite turning point of this game. Bahr's extra point was added to take the Raiders into the locker room at halftime in total command with a 21–3 advantage. On this day, the Raiders decided to spread the wealth when it came to dishing out touchdowns, becoming the only team in Super Bowl history to score three first half touchdowns on special teams, offense and defense.

After the halftime show "Salute to Superstars of the Silver Screen," Chris Bahr was ready to get the second half underway. His kickoff sailed five yards into the end zone, and was returned 35 yards by Garrett to the Washington 30. The Redskins showed flashes of the brilliance that got them to this game by going on a nine-play, 70-yard drive in just over four minutes capped off with Riggins going over for a six-pointer from one yard out off right tackle. On the drive, Riggins carried six times for 20 yards, and Theismann connected on three passes for 50 yards. On the extra point attempt, Don Hasselbeck reached up high and blocked Moseley's kick to make the score 21–9. The Redskins showed moxie on the drive, and with a break or two going their way, they still felt that victory was not out of the realm of possibility.

Jeff Hayes' kickoff was received by Greg Pruitt on the LA 13 and returned 17 yards. The Raiders' offense then went to work to stymie any momentum that Washington thought they had. Allen ran for two up the middle. Plunkett then threw deep for Malcolm Barnwell, but a 38-yard pass interference penalty on Darrell Green set Los Angeles up at the Washington 30. Plunkett went back to the air, hitting Branch for seven to the left and Christensen for six across the middle. Plunkett attempted to end the drive right then and there, but a pass intended for Branch fell incomplete. Allen carried for six up the middle, and Plunkett picked up a first

The beginning of the end. Jack Squirek's 5-yard interception return for a touchdown at the end of the first half of Super Bowl XVIII proved to be the turning point for the Raiders in their dominant win over the Redskins on January 22, 1984. It put Los Angeles in control of the game, 21–3, and secured Squirek's place in Raiders lore (AP Photo).

ground, he fumbled and the ball was recovered by Anthony Washington on the LA 35.

With a small glimmer of hope, Theismann tried to ignite the Washington attack. He hit Didier for a gain of six, Riggins ran for two, and a Joe Washington 1-yard gain up the middle failed to get a first down. Facing a fourth-and-one from the LA 26, the Redskins had to go for it instead of trying for a field goal with only 12 seconds left in the quarter. Riggins got the call, and as he heading off left tackle, Rod Martin bulldozed his way through a blocker and defensive back Mike Davis closed in on "the Diesel." Riggins had nowhere to go but down, as both Martin and Davis converged on him, slamming him down for no gain.

Marcus Allen then delivered the absolute deathblow to the Redskins on the following play. On the last play of the third quarter, from the Los Angeles 26 with 12 seconds left, Allen ran left on a play called 17-Bob Trey-O, then reversed his field and shot up the middle. Anthony Washington tried to catch him, but Allen was not going to be denied. He went untouched to complete a 74-yard scoring jaunt, which was the longest up to that time in Super Bowl history. The play was actually meant to go inside, but when Allen saw safety Ken Coffey coming in unblocked, he spun around and ran up the gut of the Washington defense. Following Bahr's extra point kick, the Raiders headed into the final fifteen minutes well aware that victory was theirs with a 35–9 lead.

The three-point underdogs were now totally destroying the defending champs, and where about to take their crown away from them, but not before beating them up some more. After Washington got the ball back, Theismann began the fourth quarter with a 26-yard completion to Art Monk. Another attempt to connect with Monk fell incomplete, which was followed by Theismann getting sacked by Jeff Barnes for a loss of nine, and an incomplete pass to Joe Washington brought up another punting situation for Jeff Hayes, who kicked the ball out of bounds at the LA 31.

Two runs by Allen gained six yards, and Frank Hawkins ran left for three before Ray Guy returned possession back over to Washington. The Redskins ended this drive six plays after getting from their own 16 to the LA eight with the big play coming on a 60-yard pass from Theismann to Charlie Brown. That was all the excitement the Raiders defense would allow, as Mike Davis ended the drive with a sack that Theismann never saw coming. He fumbled and Rod Martin recovered at the Los Angeles 31. Theismann got up from the blast with his jersey hanging over his shoulder pads and a dazed look engulfing his face.

Following the Raiders' next possession, which lasted four

down with a pass to Frank Hawkins that gave Los Angeles a first-and-goal at the Washington five. On the next play, Allen took the handoff, sliced over the middle, saw an opening and side-stepped a linebacker at the two and dove into the end zone for the six-pointer to finish off the eight-play, 70-yard drive. With Bahr's extra point, the Raiders were up, 28–9, with 7:06 to go in the third quarter.

Alvin Garrett returned Bahr's kickoff 30 yards after receiving it at the goal line. A one-yard pass completion from Theismann to Riggins was all the Redskins could muster in the quick drive, and they were forced to punt. Pruitt called for a fair catch on the LA 28.

Allen got the call on first down and ran for a gain of four up the middle, and caught a Plunkett pass for 12 yards and a first down on the next play. Plunkett then failed to connect with Barnwell and Christensen on deep pass attempts, and was sacked for a loss of eight on third down. Guy's punt went 44 yards, and Darrell Green returned it 34 yards to the LA 46.

Despite Green's good return, the Redskins went another three-and-out, as the Los Angeles defense was just dominating and punishing the so-called invincible Washington offense. Riggins swept right but was stopped after a four-yard pickup by Bob Nelson. He tried to run off right tackle but was clamped down after one yard by Kinlaw. Theismann was then sacked by Bill Pickel for a loss of five to bring up fourth down. Hayes' punt was downed after it rolled to the LA 13.

Kenny King tried to run left on first down, but was stopped for no gain. A Plunkett to Branch pass of nine yards, and a leaping four-yard gain by Allen gave Los Angeles a first down on their own 26. Plunkett went back to Branch, and the speedster caught another nine-yarder, but while struggling to gain some extra plays, Guy punted back to a Washington offense that probably wished it did not have to endure any more punishment. Theismann did manage to complete the first two passes of the drive for 15 yards, but then Mike Haynes ended it with an interception at the LA 42 on a pass intended for Art Monk.

Marcus Allen ended his day in superior fashion by taking off on a 39-yard run that got the Raiders down to the Washington 19. He then exited the game with a Super Bowl record of 191 yards rushing. He was easily named the game's Most Valuable Player. As for the former Super Bowl MVP, John Riggins, he was hammered throughout the game, gaining 64 yards on 26 carries, thus ending his six-game playoff streak of 100-plus yards rushing. He had nowhere to run against the devastating onslaught of silver and black-clad renegades. The entire Washington game plan was completely shut down by a fierce pass rush and the incredible play of Lester Hayes and Mike Haynes, who totally denied the Washington receiving corps of any significant gains.

The Raiders added a 21-yard field goal from Chris Bahr with 2:24 remaining to complete the biggest mauling up to that time in Super Bowl history with a 38–9 final score. Tom Flores got his second victory ride in three years while his band of renegades ran the emotional gamut of cheers and tears. It was truly the crowning glory of this franchise's long and proud tradition of success.

In the winning locker room, after receiving the Vince Lombardi Trophy from NFL Commissioner Pete Rozelle, Al Davis proudly stood on the podium and proclaimed that the team's performance on that day not only showed that they were the greatest Raiders team of all time, but ranked among the greatest of any professional sports organization. He also added during this shining moment the phrase "Just win baby," and oh how they did!

Like so many before him, Lyle Alzado was vindicated with the Raiders after being cast off by another organization but emerging as a champion. Seen here in the closing minutes of the Los Angeles Raiders' dominant 38–9 victory over the Washington Redskins in Super Bowl XVIII, January 22, 1984, in Tampa, Florida (AP Photo).

Starting Lineup for Super Bowl XVIII

OFFENSE

QB — Jim Plunkett
RB — Marcus Allen
FB — Kenny King
WR — Malcolm Barnwell
WR — Cliff Branch
TE — Todd Christensen

LT — Bruce Davis
LG — Charley Hannah
C — Dave Dalby
RG — Mickey Marvin
RT — Henry Lawrence

DEFENSE

DE — Howie Long
DE — Lyle Alzado
NT — Reggie Kinlaw

LOLB — Ted Hendricks
LILB — Matt Millen
RILB — Bob Nelson

ROLB — Rod Martin
CB — Lester Hayes
CB — Mike Haynes

SS — Mike Davis
FS — Vann McElroy

KICKING/PUNTING

K — Chris Bahr

P — Ray Guy

Individual Statistics from Super Bowl XVIII

OFFENSE

Jim Plunkett: 16 completions out of 25 pass attempts for 172 yards and 1 TD. Rushed for -2 yards on 1 carry.

Marcus Allen: Rushed for 191 yards on 20 carries and 2 TD, and 2 receptions for 18 yards.

Frank Hawkins: Rushed for 6 yards on 3 carries, and had 2 receptions for 20 yards.

Kenny King: Rushed for 12 yards on 3 carries, and had 2 receptions for 8 yards.

Greg Pruitt: Rushed for 17 yards on 5 carries. Returned 1 kickoff 17 yards and 1 punt for 8 yards.

Chester Willis: Rushed for 7 yards on 1 carry.

Cliff Branch: Had 6 receptions for 94 yards and 1 TD.

Todd Christensen: Had 4 receptions for 32 yards.

Ted Watts: Had 1 punt return for 0 yards.

Chris Bahr: Had 1 field goal and 5 extra point kicks.

DEFENSE

Jeff Barnes: Had 1 sack.

Mike Davis: had 1 sack.

Rod Martin: Had 1 sack.

Matt Millen: Had 1 sack.

Bill Pickel: Had 1 sack.

Greg Townsend: Had 1 sack.

Mike Haynes: Had 1 INT for 0 yards.

Jack Squirek: Had 1 INT for 5 yards and 1 TD.

Individual Statistics and Roster

Head Coach: Tom Flores

Assistant Coaches: Sam Boghosian, Willie Brown, Chet Franklin, Larry Kennan, Earl Leggett, Bob Mischak, Steve Ortmayer, Terry Robiskie, Art Shell, Charlie Sumner, Tom Walsh, Ray Willsey

1983 Regular Season Record: 12–4

1st Place AFC Western Division

Scored 442 points to rank 3rd out of 28 teams

Allowed 338 points to rank 13th

STARTERS — OFFENSE

QB — Jim Plunkett: Active for 14 games, and started in 13 games. Completed 230 out of 379 pass attempts for 2,935 yards, 20 TD and 18 INT. Rushed for 78 yards on 26 carries.

HB — Marcus Allen: Active for 16 games, and started in 15. Rushed for 1,014 yards on 266 carries and 9 TD, had 68 receptions for 590 yards and 2 TD, and threw for 111 yards on 4 out of 7 pass attempts.

FB — Kenny King: Active for and started in 15 games. Rushed for 294 yards on 82 carries and 1 TD. Had 14 receptions for 149 yards and 1 TD.

WR — Malcolm Barnwell: Started in 16 games. Had 35 receptions for 513 yards and 1 TD. Rushed for 12 yards on 1 carry.

WR — Cliff Branch: Active for and started in 12 games. Had 39 receptions for 696 yards and 5 TD, and rushed for 20 yards on 1 carry.

TE — Todd Christensen: Started in 16 games. Had **92** receptions for 1,247 yards and 12 TD.

LT — Bruce Davis: Started in 16 games.

LG — Charley Hannah: Started in 16 games.

C — Dave Dalby: Started 16 games.

RG — Mickey Marvin: Started in 14 games.

RT — Henry Lawrence: Started in 16 games.

RESERVE OFFENSIVE PLAYERS

Rick Berns (RB): Active for 16 games. Rushed for 22 yards on 6 carries.

Don Hasselbeck (TE): Active for 14 games. Had 2 receptions for 17 yards and 2 TD.

Frank Hawkins (RB): Active for 16 games, and started in 2. Rushed for 526 yards on 110 carries and 6 TD. Had 20 receptions for 150 yards and 2 TD.

David Humm (QB): Active for 6 games. Rushed for -1 yard on 1 carry.

Derrick Jensen (RB/TE): Active for 16 games. Rushed for 5 yards on 1 carry, had 1 reception for 2 yards and 1 TD, and received 1 kickoff for 0 yards.

Shelby Jordan (T): Active for 13 games.

Cleo Montgomery (WR): Active for 14 games. Rushed for 7 yards on 2 carries, had 2 receptions for 29 yards, and returned 21 kickoffs for 464 yards.

Don Mosebar (C/T/G): Active for 14 games.

Calvin Muhammad (WR): Active for 15 games, and started in 4. Had 13 receptions for 252 yards and 2 TD.

Ed Muransky (T): Active for 16 games.

Greg Pruitt (RB): Active for 16 games. Had 31 kickoff returns for 604 yards, and **58** punt returns for **666** yards and 1 TD. **Led the NFL in total kickoff/punt returns (89).** Rushed for 154 yards on 26 carries and 2 TD, and had 1 reception for 6 yards.

Derrick Ramsey (TE): Active for 2 games.

Jim Romano (C): Active for 1 game.

Steve Sylvester (C/G/T): Active for 9 games, and started in 2.

Dokie Williams (WR): Active for 16 games. Had 14 receptions for 259 yards and 3 TD. Returned 5 kickoffs for 88 yards.

Chester Willis (RB): Active for 13 games. Rushed for 0 yards on 5 carries.

Marc Wilson (QB): Active for 10 games, and started in 3. Completed 67 out of 117 pass attempts for 864 yards, 8 TD and 6 INT.

STARTERS — DEFENSE

DE — Howie Long: Started in 16 games, had 13 sacks and 2 fumble recoveries.

DE — Lyle Alzado: Active for and started in 15 games. Had 7 sacks, 1 fumble recovery, and recorded 1 safety.

NT — Reggie Kinlaw: Started in 16 games and had 1 sack.

LOLB — Ted Hendricks: Started in 16 games, had 2 sacks and 1 fumble recovery.

LILB — Matt Millen: Active for 16 games, started in 15, had 2 sacks and 1 INT.

RILB — Bob Nelson: Started in 16 games, had 2 sacks and 1 fumble recovery.

ROLB — Rod Martin: Started in16 games, had 6 sacks and 4 INT.

CB — Lester Hayes: Started in 16 games and had 2 INT.

CB — Ted Watts: Active for 16 games, started in 13, and had 1 INT.

SS — Mike Davis: Started in 16 games, had 2 sacks, 1 INT, and 2 fumble recoveries.

FS — Vann McElroy: Started in 16 games, had 8 INT and 3 fumble recoveries.

RESERVE DEFENSIVE PLAYERS

Jeff Barnes (LB): Active for 16 games.

Don Bessillieu (DB): Active for 4 games.

Darryl Byrd (LB): Active for 16 games.

Tony Caldwell (LB): Active for 16 games and had 1 fumble recovery.

James Davis (DB): Active for 16 games, had1 sack and 1 fumble recovery.

Mike Haynes (DB): Active for 5 games, started in 3, and had 1 INT. Came to the Raiders in a late season trade with the New England Patriots.

Kenny Hill (DB): Active for 16 games.

Odis McKinney (DB): Active for 16 games and had 1 INT.

Irvin Phillips (DB): Active for 5 games.

Bill Pickel (NT/T/E): Active for 16 games, started in 1 game, and had 1 fumble recovery.

Archie Reese (E/NT/T): Active for 10 games and had 4 sacks.

Johnny Robinson (NT): Active for 4 games.

Jack Squirek (LB): Active for 16 games, started in 1, and had 1 sack.

Dave Stalls (E/T/NT): Active for 6 games, had sack and 1 fumble recovery.

Greg Townsend (E/LB/T/NT): Active for 16 games, had 10 sacks, 1 fumble recovery, 1 TD, and recorded 1 safety.

KICKING/PUNTING

K — Chris Bahr: Active for 16 games. Made 21 of 27 field goal attempts and 51 of 53 extra points for 114 points.

P — Ray Guy: Active for 16 games. Punted 78 times for a 42.8 average.

1984 Season Review

1. Sept. 2: The Raiders went into their Silver Anniversary season as defending world champions, possessors of the best winning percentage of any pro football team over the previous twenty seasons, and looked to be more solid than they were one year earlier.

Opening Day saw the defending Super Bowl champs going against one of the previous season's worst teams, the Houston Oilers. As in many previous years, the Silver and Black inflicted pain, pounding, and penalties, in this case, on the hapless Oilers. However, through all the punishment thrown at them, the Oilers were able to hold a 7–0 lead at the half. The world champs did finally come around, and by the end of the game, ripped Houston apart to win, 24–11. The entire backfield of Marcus Allen, Frank Hawkins, and Jim Plunkett all scored by way of 1-yard runs. Chris Bahr missed two extra point tries, but hit on a 28-yard field goal, and the defense recorded a safety after Houston was called for holding in the end zone.[1]

2. Sept. 9: The Los Angeles defense terrorized the Green Bay offense in the Raiders home opener, 28–7, in a contest that saw the unit take no prisoners and show no mercy. On the sixth play of the game, defensive end Lyle Alzado and safety Mike Davis each got a piece of quarterback Lynn Dickey, and forced him out of the game with a bruised back. His replacement, rookie Randy Wright, was thrown to the wolves clad in silver and black, and suffered dearly. With the defense on a relentless pursuit, Wright was pressured and mauled throughout the entire game, intercepted twice, sacked two times, and could only muster 67 yards passing. Defensive back Vann McElroy and linebacker Jeff Barnes were credited with the interceptions. Lester Hayes and Mike Haynes were the greatest set of cover men during this time, and showed why that was true by completely shutting down two of the best receivers in NFL history. James Lofton was held to zero yards, while John Jefferson could only get 19. On the other side, the Raiders' offense did very well. A 3-yard pass from Jim Plunkett to Todd Christensen opening the scoring, and Los Angeles followed that up with touchdown runs by Frank Hawkins (1 yard), Marcus Allen (7 yards), and Derrick Jensen (1 yard).[2]

3. Sept. 16: The Raiders most hated rival, the Kansas City Chiefs, had the Silver and Black on the ropes, but could not deliver the knockout blow. The Chiefs intercepted Jim Plunkett four times, returning one for a touchdown, and held a 13–3 halftime lead. Up to this point, Chris Bahr gave the Raiders their only points with a on a 43-yard field goal. The Raiders then came back with 16 points on a 3-yard pass from Plunkett to Todd Christensen, a 1-yard run by Frank Hawkins, and a 24-yard field goal from Chris Bahr, who missed the extra point try after Christensen's catch, and lead, 19–13. Rookie running back Herman Heard ran one in from five yards out, and with the conversion, the Chiefs clung to a one-point advantage, 20–19, with just under five minutes remaining in the game. Despite his four interceptions, Plunkett completed 28 out of 47 pass attempts for 313 yards. His biggest completion came on a 42-yarder to Malcolm Barnwell that got the ball down to the Kansas City 6-yard line with less than two minutes to go. Four plays later, Bahr kicked the game-winning field goal from 19 yards away to secure a 22–20 victory. This proved to be the fourth straight time that Los Angeles beat the Chiefs in the closing seconds.[3]

4. Sept. 24: For the second consecutive week, the Raiders won in the closing seconds, this time, 33–30, over the San Diego Chargers on Monday Night Football. Ex-Heisman Trophy winners, Marcus Allen and Jim Plunkett were the main stars on a night that had many for the Silver and Black. The Chargers held a 30–20 lead with 10:21 left in the game. Up to that point, the Raiders received their points by way of two Chris Bahr field goals (42 and 36 yards), and two touchdowns from Marcus Allen (1 yard run, and a 30-yard pass from Jim Plunkett). Now trailing by ten late in the game, Plunkett provided a clutch performance to rally his team. After Dokie Williams set Los Angeles up with great field position following a 44-yard kickoff return, Plunkett took the Raiders 53 yards in eight plays. From the two, Allen took a handoff, and sailed over the top and into the end zone to make it 30–26. Marc Wilson had trouble getting a grasp for the ball while holding for Bahr's extra point try, so it remained a four-point deficit for Los Angeles. The defense stopped San Diego's powerhouse offense after nine plays, and returned the ball to Plunkett on the Los Angeles 24-yard line with 3:33 left. Within two minutes, Plunkett had the Raiders on the San Diego 24 with 1:47 to go. A pass from the 13 to Todd Christensen got the ball to the two, where the All-Pro tight end stepped out of bounds to stop the clock with 56 seconds left. Two plays later, Allen flew over the defense for his fourth touchdown of the day, and with the extra point splitting the uprights this time, the Raiders won, 33–30. Allen had a record-setting performance, joining Art Powell as the only other player in Raiders history to score four touchdowns in one game. Plunkett had one of the best days of his pro career by completing 24 of 33 pass attempts for 363 yards and one touchdown. Also having a good evening was Todd Christensen, who caught seven passes for 109 yards.[4]

5. Sept. 30: The Raiders traveled to the Mile High City of Denver with a one game division lead over the Broncos. However, when they left, the Silver and Black were tied for the top spot following a 16–13 loss, which ended an eight-game winning streak for the Raiders over two seasons (including the playoffs). The Broncos ran the ball 48 times for 233 yards against a 3-3-5 defensive formation. This alignment was good against the pass, but not so much against the run. Denver capitalized on this, with Sammy Winder (91 yards), and Gerald Willhite (82 yards), doing most of the damage on the ground. The Los Angeles offense when up against one of the best defense's in the league, and Denver hounded Jim Plunkett all day after his protection broke down. The Raiders scored on a 19-yard pass from Plunkett to Todd Christensen, and two Chris Bahr field goals from 27 and 50 yards.[5]

6. Oct. 7: Marc Wilson replaced Jim Plunkett at quarterback after the latter suffered a pulled stomach muscle in the first quarter. Following eleven months of serving as Plunkett's backup, Wilson led Los Angeles to a 28–14 win over the usually troublesome Seattle Seahawks with 12 completions out of 19 pass attempts

for 309 yards and two touchdowns. The Raiders jumped out to a 14–0 lead on a 1-yard Marcus Allen run, and a 24-yard pass from Wilson to Todd Christensen. The Seahawks came back to tie it at 14–14 in the fourth until Wilson and Allen teamed up on a 58-yard reception to put Los Angeles back in front for good. Allen finished the game with four catches for an incredible 173 yards. Linebacker Rod Martin put the final touches on the win by returning an interception 14 yards for a touchdown. This win put the Raiders on top of the division at 5–1, with Seattle and San Diego a close second at 4–2.[6]

7. Oct. 14: The Raiders went to 6–1 with another fantastic finish. This time a young Minnesota Vikings team that was 2–5 and in the process of rebuilding, gave the world champs all they could handle. This was the sixth time in 1984 that Los Angeles was either losing or tied in the second half. The Raiders got on the board first when Marc Wilson threw to Todd Christensen for a 34-yard touchdown. Chris Bahr added two field goals from 22 and 24 yards. The Vikings came back, and during the third quarter, the game was tied, 13–13. Marcus Allen then fumbled, and the Vikings went 31 yards in six plays to take a 20–13 lead into the fourth quarter. On the next Minnesota possession, the Vikings returned the favor when defensive lineman Bill Pickel forced a fumble from rookie running back Alfred Anderson that linebacker Jack Squirek recovered on the Minnesota 20-yard line. The Raiders had trouble moving the ball on the ground during the first half, but had no problems on this drive. With Frank Hawkins pounded the middle for 12 yards on three carries, and an eight-yard gain by Allen got the ball right on the goal line. On third-and-one from there, Allen got the call and answered it with a touchdown. Bahr's conversion then tied the game at 20–20 with 12:52 left in regulation. With 3:15 left, the Raiders were on the Minnesota 36. Once again, a strong ground attack from Hawkins and Allen ate up the clock and got Los Angeles close enough for Bahr to attempt a chip shot, 20-yard field goal, with two seconds remaining. Since the team moved to Los Angeles, Bahr had not missed a field goal attempt that determined a game's outcome. This day was no exception, as Bahr's kick went through the uprights to give the Silver and Black a 23–20 victory.[7]

8. Oct. 21: With a record setting home crowd of 57,442 on hand in San Diego, the Silver and Black sent them home dejected after a 44–37 shootout victory over the Chargers. Marc Wilson led the offensive assault with five touchdown passes while completing 27 of 37 attempts for 332 yards. Malcolm Barnwell caught two of Wilson's scoring tosses (45 and 51 yards), and in the process, became the first Raiders wide receiver to haul in a touchdown pass in 1984. Marcus Allen was on the receiving end of a 10-yard Wilson touchdown pass, and also led all ball carriers with 107 yards rushing. Derrick Jensen (1 yard), and Dokie Williams (20 yards), caught Wilson's other two touchdown passes, and Chris Bahr kicked three field goals (42, 33, and 32 yards), to complete the Los Angeles scoring barrage. The Chargers led, 20–14, at the half, and then broke down. Bahr's 33-yard field goal closed the gap to three points, and after that, the Raiders scored 17 points in just over two minutes to lead, 34–20. Defensive back Ted Watts intercepted a pass in the end zone with 44 seconds left to kill a San Diego comeback. This was the Raiders' fifth straight win over the Chargers and it put them at 7–1.[8]

9. Oct. 28: The Raiders once again played to a nail-biting

climax, this time in front of a record setting regular season crowd of 92,469 at the Los Angeles Coliseum. Unfortunately, the Silver and Black finished on the losing end of a 22–19 overtime decision to the Denver Broncos, who improved to 8–1, and were the only team to beat the Raiders up to this stage of the '84 season. This also proved to be the first time since moving to Los Angeles that the Raiders were not in first place in the division. Los Angeles led in this one, 12–0, after Rod Martin recorded a safety by tackling Gary Kubiak in the end zone, Marcus Allen scored on a 36-yard pass from Marc Wilson, and Chris Bahr kicked a 44-yard field goal. After Denver closed to within six, Allen scored on a 1-yard run to increase the Los Angeles advantage to 19–6. Two touchdown passes from Kubiak tied the game, and Rick Karlis kicked a 35-yard field goal on the final play of the overtime period to pull out the win.[9]

10. Nov. 4: The Raiders remained in a funk, dropping their second straight, this time to NFC Central Division–leading Chicago, 17–6. This loss put the Raiders at 7–3, and in third place behind Denver (9–1), and Seattle (8–2), in the AFC Western Division. Los Angeles never had the lead at any time against the league's number one defense, and could only muster two field goals from Chris Bahr (44 and 40 yards). The Bears recorded nine quarterback sacks, and knocked both Marc Wilson (injured thumb), and backup David Humm (slightly torn knee ligament), out of the game. Wilson was able to come back and finish the game after Humm went down. With two signal callers hurt, the Raiders looked to old reliable, Jim Plunkett, to come and save the slumping renegades yet again. On injured reserve for the last month with a torn stomach muscle, Plunkett was brought back onto the active roster hours before the next game in Seattle.[10]

11. Nov. 12: After being almost invincible over the first eight weeks of the '84 season, the defending Super Bowl champions were going in a different direction as the year progressed. For the first time in three years, the Raiders lost three straight, and were in serious jeopardy of missing the playoffs. Unable to capitalize on their Monday Night Football magic, Los Angeles fell to Seattle, 17–14, in front of a loud, ravenous Kingdome crowd, without a healthy quarterback to guide them. Coach Tom Flores decided to go with Marc Wilson as his starter despite a bruised thumb on his throwing hand. He completed 16 of 34 passes for 191 yards and three interceptions. The Raiders held a 7–0 lead at the half on a Marcus Allen 1-yard run, and a tough defense that allowed Seattle only 11 yards through the air in the half. The Seahawks came back with 17 points in the third quarter, which proved to be all they needed to secure the win. Another 1-yard run by Allen provided Los Angeles with their other points. The loss sent the Raiders to 7–4, three games behind Denver (10–1), and Seattle (9–2).[11]

12. Nov. 18: The defense was outstanding for Los Angeles against rival Kansas City, and that unit carried the load in a 17–7 win. The Kansas City running game was ranked near the bottom in the AFC, and the Raiders completely suffocated it, allowing the Chiefs only 20 yards on the ground. They did not fair much better in the passing department either, as the dominant Los Angeles defense held them to 162 yards, and recorded four sacks. With the Raiders' offense consisting of banged up quarterbacks, and a running game ranked 20th in the league, the defense took it upon itself to clamp down and make things happen

on their own in an attempt to salvage what began as a promising quest to repeat as Super Bowl champs, and had a shutout going until the final two minutes of the game. Linebacker Rod Martin did his part by getting Los Angeles on the board first when he returned a fumble recovery 77 yards for a touchdown. Dokie Williams added a 12-yard pass from Marc Wilson, and Chris Bahr kicked a 22-yard field goal in the win. With the air attack stymied by injuries to Wilson and Jim Plunkett, the offensive load was turned over to a lackluster running game that managed to keep the ball moving enough to win. The Raiders ran the ball 49 times for 219 yards, with Marcus Allen leading the way with 95. This much-needed victory tied the Silver and Black with the New England Patriots for the final playoff spot.[12]

13. Nov. 25: For the second straight game, the Raiders faced a weak offense that allowed them a slight reprieve on the road to a possible playoff berth. The Indianapolis Colts came to Los Angeles with a 4–8 record, and added another loss to their season by the score of 21–7. The smash-mouth Raiders defense once again ate up an inferior opponent, allowing the Colts a mere 77 yards rushing, 81 passing, and recorded six sacks on Art Schlichter. The Indianapolis defense also got six sacks, but Marc Wilson faired better than his counterpart. He ran for a 14-yard touchdown, and threw one to Todd Christensen (7 yards), and Dave Casper (1 yard). Marcus Allen led all ball carriers with 110 yards, and the 9–4 Raiders were now one game up on New England, who lost, for the fifth playoff spot.[13]

14. Dec. 2: After two weeks of facing sub-par offenses, the Raiders traveled to Miami to play the explosive Dolphins. The '84 Dolphins were 12–1 going into their game with Los Angeles, and already had the AFC Eastern Division clinched. Their second-year quarterback, Dan Marino, was well on his way to shattering numerous single-season passing records, and looked virtually unstoppable from doing whatever he wanted against any defense. In the end, Marino ripped the airways for 470 yards and four touchdowns, but the Raiders proved they were still the champs, and did not go down quietly. In one of the greatest moments in Raiders history, the silver and black clad renegades beat this invincible foe, 45–34, to win their third straight game, and move into the double-digit win column with a 10–4 record. This impressive victory not only gave the team a much-needed boost, but it put them two games up on New England for the fifth and final playoff spot. The 45 points was the most given up by the Dolphins under the legendary coach, Don Shula. The Raiders got a large dose of momentum right away in the first quarter when defensive back Mike Haynes took a Marino pass 97 yards for a touchdown, setting a then-team record for longest interception return in the process. Marcus Allen scored on an 11-yard run, and Chris Bahr kicked a 44-yard field goal to give Los Angeles a 17–13 lead at the half. After Dave Casper extended the Raiders' advantage to 24–13 with a 7-yard pass from Marc Wilson, the Dolphins came back on the arm of Marino to lead, 27–24 at the end of three quarters. The Raiders showed the fortitude that made them world champions eleven months earlier by scoring 21 points in the fourth quarter to pull out this incredible win. Touchdowns came on a 75-yard pass from Marc Wilson to Dokie Williams, and two Marcus Allen runs of six and 52 yards. Allen had a tremendous day with 20 carries for 156 yards rushing and three touchdowns.[14]

15. Dec. 10: The Raiders once again had their Monday Night Football mystique working for them in a 24–3 win over the Detroit Lions. With this victory, the Raiders' Monday Night record was an almost spotless 22-3-1 up to this time. The defensive line were the stars of prime time by destroying Detroit quarterbacks, and registered a team record eight sacks. Leading the Silver and Black assault was Bill Pickel with three-and-a-half sacks, followed by two-and-a-half from Lyle Alzado, one by Greg Townsend, and a half sack apiece by Howie Long and Matt Millen. Scoring for the Raiders were Todd Christensen (12-yard pass from Marc Wilson), Cle Montgomery (69-yard punt return), Chris Bahr (37-yard field goal), and Marcus Allen (73-yard pass from Jim Plunkett). Wilson was still hampered by a thumb injury, but was able to have a good game regardless. He completed 11 of 19 pass attempts for 194 yards and the touchdown pass to Christensen. In the second half, Wilson was forced from the game due to back spasms. Jim Plunkett relieved Wilson with ten minutes left to play, and hit on three out of four passes for 102 yards and a touchdown. This was the fourth straight win for the Raiders, who improved to 11–4, and clinched a wild card playoff berth.[15]

16. Dec. 16: The Raiders were playing for the right to host the AFC Wild Card Game in their regular season finale against the Pittsburgh Steelers. In a sluggish performance, played in front of a Los Angeles Coliseum crowd of 87,291, the Raiders lost to a young and inspired Pittsburgh team, 13–7. The Steelers needed this win to clinch the AFC Central Division title. With two banged up quarterbacks in Marc Wilson and Jim Plunkett, the offense was simply pathetic in this game after being so great one week earlier. Wilson could only complete five of 13 passes for 45 yards, was sacked twice and intercepted once. Plunkett faired a touch better, connecting on nine of 20 attempts for 123 yards and one interception. He was also responsible for the team's lone score when he threw a 2-yard touchdown pass to Dokie Williams in the fourth quarter to avoid a shutout in the closing minutes. The passing game was not the only phase to fail on this day, as the running attack gained a lethargic 57 yards on 20 carries. Losing this game meant that the Raiders had to travel to the noisy Seattle Kingdome, where they had not won in three years.[16]

AFC Wild Card Game, December 22, 1984

The world championship belonged to the Raiders, and would remain theirs until someone came along and took it. Winning a championship is hard, but defending it is even more intense, especially when the road to a repeat Super Bowl victory had to go through a hostile environment where problems occurred in the past.

Three days before Christmas, the Silver and Black headed to the great northwest to begin a quest that they hoped would once again end with the raising of another Vince Lombardi Trophy. The Seattle Seahawks would be the first hurdle in the Raiders' drive to a repeat championship. They were looking to settle the score with Los Angeles over the beat down they suffered eleven months earlier in the AFC title game.

With the unfriendly, ear-splitting confines of the Kingdome as a backdrop, the Seahawks drew first blood in the second quarter. Dave Krieg, who suffered an unmerciful beating physically and mentally at the hands of the Raiders in the previous conference championship game, redeemed himself with a 26-yard touchdown pass to Daryl Turner that capped a nine-play, 93-yard drive with 4:19 left in the first half. Krieg's pass was perfect to Turner, who beat Lester Hayes and Odis McKinney on the play. This drive started after punter Ray Guy kicked the ball out of bounds on the Seattle seven. It was kept alive by a 23-yard interference call on Hayes against Steve Largent.

The Seahawks took advantage of a Frank Hawkins fumble by turning it into a Norm Johnson 35-yard field goal in the third quarter to lead, 10–0, going into the final stanza. Seattle added to their lead with another Johnson three-pointer, this time from 44 yards. They then looked to run out the clock with a grinding running attack led by Dan Doornink. He was the workhouse all day, with 29 carries for 126 yards in a game that saw Seattle pound it out on the ground 51 times for 205 yards. With the running game eating time off the clock, and working effectively, Krieg only went to the air 10 times.

The Raiders, who suffered some offensive woes throughout the season, could not get going until there were five minutes left in the game. Up to that time, their deepest penetration of the game was at the Seattle 41 in the second quarter. Jim Plunkett had worked so much playoff magic for the Raiders in the 1980's, but on this day he could not do much. In his first start since the sixth game of the season, he was sacked six times and picked off twice. He did find a way to get the Raiders on the board with a six-play, 78-yard drive that ended with a 46-yard scoring strike to Marcus Allen that cut the Seattle lead to 13–7. Allen had another good playoff game, with 61 yards on the ground and another 90 on five receptions.

The Raiders had time for one final chance with 45 seconds left. With the ball on his own six, Plunkett tried to get the offense some breathing room by heaving a desperation pass that landed in the hands of defensive back Kenny Easley, and thus ended the Raiders' drive for a championship defense.[17]

Individual Statistics and Roster

Head Coach: Tom Flores
Assistant Coaches: Sam Boghosian, Willie Brown, Chet Franklin, Larry Kennan, Earl Leggett, Bob Mischak, Steve Ortmayer, Terry Robiskie, Art Shell, Tom Walsh, Ray Willsey, Bob Zeman
1984 Regular Season Record: 11–5
3rd Place AFC Western Division
Scored 368 points out of 28 teams to rank 9th
Allowed 278 points to rank 4th

STARTERS — OFFENSE

QB — Marc Wilson: Active for 16 games, and started in 10 games. Completed 153 of 282 pass attempts for 2,151 yards, 15 TD and 17 INT. Rushed for 56 yards on 30 carries and 1 TD.
HB — Marcus Allen: Started in 16 games. Rushed for 1,168 yards on 275 carries and 13 TD. Had 64 receptions for 758 yards and 5 TD. Completed 1 out of 4 pass attempts for 38 yards. **Led the NFL in total TD (18).**
FB — Kenny King: Started in 16 games. Rushed for 254 yards on 67 carries, and had 14 receptions for 99 yards.
WR — Malcolm Barnwell: Active for 16 games, and started in 15. Had 45 receptions for 851 yards and 2 TD.

WR — Cliff Branch: Active for and started in 14 games. Had 27 receptions for 401 yards.
TE — Todd Christensen: Started in 16 games. Had 80 receptions for 1,007 yards and 7 TD.
LT — Bruce Davis: Active for 16 games, and started in 15.
LG — Charley Hannah: Active for 15 games, and started in 9.
C — Dave Dalby: Active for 16 games, and started in 14.
RG — Don Mosebar: Active for and started in 10 games.
RT — Henry Lawrence: Started in 16 games.

RESERVE OFFENSIVE PLAYERS

Warren Bryant (T): Active for 5 games.
Dave Casper (TE): Active for 7 games. Had 4 receptions for 29 yards and 2 TD.
Frank Hawkins (RB): Active for 16 games. Rushed for 376 yards on 108 carries and 3 TD, and had 7 receptions for 51 yards.
David Humm (QB): Active for 3 games. Completed 4 out of 7 pass attempts for 56 yards and 1 INT. rushed for 7 yards on 2 carries.
Derrick Jensen (RB/TE): Active for 16 games. Rushed for 3 yards on 3 carries and 1 TD. Had 1 reception for 1 yard and 1 TD, and 1 kickoff return for 11 yards.
Shelby Jordan (T): Active for 11 games, and started in 1.
Curt Marsh (G): Active for 16 games, and started in 7.
Mickey Marvin (G): Active for 9 games, and started in 6.
Joe McCall (RB): Active for 3 games and rushed for 3 yards on 1 carry.
Cleo Montgomery (WR): Active for 16 games. Rushed for 1 yard on 1 carry, had 14 punt returns for 194 yards and 1 TD, and 26 kickoff returns for 555 yards.
Ed Muransky (T): Active for 3 games.
Andy Parker (TE): Active for 9 games.
Jim Plunkett (QB): Active for 8 games, and started in 6. Completed 108 out of 198 pass attempts for 1,473 yards, 6 TD and 10 INT. Rushed for 14 yards on 16 carries and 1 TD.
Greg Pruitt (RB): Active for 15 games. Rushed for 0 yards on 8 carries, had 2 receptions for 12 yards, 53 punt returns for 473 yards, and 3 kickoff returns for 16 yards.
Jim Romano (C): Active for 6 games, and started in 2.
Jimmy Smith (RB): Active for 7 games.
Dwight Wheeler (T/C/G): Active for 4 games.
Dokie Williams (WR): Active for 16 games, and started in 3. Had 22 receptions for 509 yards and 4 TD. Returned 24 kickoffs 621 yards.
Chester Willis (RB): Active for 16 games, rushed for 4 yards on 5 carries, and had 1 kickoff return for 13 yards.

STARTERS — DEFENSE

DE — Howie Long: Started in 16 games and had 12 sacks and 2 fumble recoveries.
DE — Lyle Alzado: Started in 16 games and had 6 sacks and 1 fumble recovery.
NT — Reggie Kinlaw: Active for and started in 13 games.
LOLB — Brad Van Pelt: Active for 9 games, started in 8, and had 1 INT.
LILB — Matt Millen: Active for 16 games, started in 12, and had 2 sacks.
RILB — Bob Nelson: Active for 12 games, started in 11, and had 1 sacks.
ROLB — Rod Martin: Started in 16 games, had 11 sacks, 2 INT, 1 fumble recovery, and recorded 1 safety.
CB — Lester Hayes: Started in 16 games and had 1 INT.
CB — Mike Haynes: Started in16 games, had 6 INT and 2 fumble recoveries. **Led the NFL in INT return yards (220).**
SS — Mike Davis: Started in 16 games, had 5 sacks, 2 INT and 1 fumble recovery.
FS — Vann McElroy: Started in 16 games, had 4 INT and 4 fumble recoveries.

RESERVE DEFENSIVE PLAYERS

Rick Ackerman (NT/T): Active for 6 games, started in 2, and had 1 sack.
Stan Adams (LB): Active for 4 games, and started in 3.

Jeff Barnes (LB): Active for 16 games, started in 5, had 1 INT, 1 fumble recovery, and 1 sack.

Greg Boyd (E): Active for 5 games.

Darryl Byrd (LB): Active for 16 games, and started in 1.

Tony Caldwell (LB): Active for 16 games.

James Davis (DB): Active for 15 games, had 1 INT and 2 fumble recoveries.

Sean Jones (E): Active for 16 games and had 1 sack.

Larry McCoy (LB): Active for 4 games.

Odis McKinney (DB): Active for 16 games, started in 1, had 1 INT, 1 fumble recovery, 1 sack, and 1 kickoff return for 0 yards.

Mark Merrill (LB): Active for 2 games.

Bill Pickel (NT/T/E): Active for 16 games, started in 3, and had 12 sacks.

Sam Seale (DB): Active for 12 games.

Jack Squirek (LB): Active for 12 games, started in 7, had 2 sacks and 1 fumble recovery.

Stacey Toran (DB): Active for 16 games.

Greg Townsend (E/LB/T/NT): Active for 16 games and had 7 sacks.

Ted Watts (DB): Active for 16 games and had 1 INT.

KICKING/PUNTING

K — Chris Bahr: Active for 16 games. Made 20 of 27 field goal attempts and 40 of 42 extra points for 100 points.

P — Ray Guy: Active for 16 games. Punted 91 times for a 41.9 average.

1985 Season Review

1. Sept. 8: After their attempt to repeat as world champs was thwarted in the Seattle Kingdome nine months earlier, the Silver and Black looked to re-establish themselves with a vengeance. In front of 61,009 at the LA Coliseum, the Raiders sent out a message to the rest of the league that they were back from despair, and the poor New York Jets felt their wrath with a 31–0 beat down. This was the Raiders' first shutout since opening day in 1977, and the first for Tom Flores as head coach. The Raiders' defense led the AFC in sacks the previous year, and set out to defend that ranking by sacking New York quarterback Ken O'Brien ten times, with defensive end Sean Jones leading the way with three. The unit also held the Jets to 62 rushing yards and 131 through the air. Meanwhile, the Los Angeles offense pounded out 356 total yards. They were led by 37-year-old Jim Plunkett, who responded well after missing most of the '84 season with an abdominal injury. He completed 14 of 21 passes for 242 yards and a touchdown to Dokie Williams (41 yards). Marcus Allen led all ball carriers with 76 yards, and scored on runs of one and three yards. Chris Bahr added a 20-yard field goal, and rookie defensive back Stacey Toran finished out the scoring by returning an interception 76 yards.[1]

2. Sept. 12: On only four days rest, the Raiders traveled to Kansas City to do battle with their hated rivals on a Thursday night. Los Angeles could not capitalize on their opening day blowout, and suffered a 36–20 setback. The Raiders led for a good portion to the first half, and then the bottom fell out. Kansas City's defensive line stuffed the Raiders backfield, and their secondary sealed off the passing lanes for Plunkett. When these two things occur, no good can come from an offense. The Chiefs took advantage of their defensive unit's effort, and erased a 14–9 deficit to hand the Raiders their worst defeat since 1981. The only real bright moment for the Raiders on this night was when Todd Christensen made a spectacular catch in the end zone from three yards out. He jumped high, tipped the ball with one hand then caught it for six points. The Raiders received their other points on a Frank Hawkins 1-yard run, and a 2-yard pass from Plunkett to Jessie Hester.[2]

3. Sept. 22: Ten days of rest did nothing to help the Raiders, and they saw themselves in the division cellar at 1–2 following a 34–10 beating from the defending Super Bowl champion San Francisco 49ers. The Raiders' offense was almost non-existent, as they were in the second half of the 1984 season. They could only produce 83 rushing yards, suffered nine quarterback sacks, and lost Jim Plunkett for at least six weeks due to a dislocated shoulder after one of those sacks. A Marc Wilson 1-yard run, and a Chris Bahr 24-yard field goal gave the Raiders their points.[3]

4. Sept. 29: With the offense a bit stagnant as of late, the defense decided to carry the load and put points on the board themselves. With that unit scoring three touchdowns, the Raiders beat the New England Patriots, 35–20. The defensive scoring came when Lester Hayes returned an interception 27 yards, Lyle Alzado put the Raiders in the lead for good by recovering a fumble in the end zone, and Sam Seale returned an interception 38 yards. The defense then shut the Patriot offense down in the second half after they were leading, 20–14. They held New England's running game to 97 yards, while Marcus Allen ran for 98. Marc Wilson had to leave the game in the third quarter with a sprained ankle, and was replaced by rookie Rusty Hilger. Before leaving, Wilson connected with Dokie Williams for a 38-yard touchdown. Hilger's first six pass attempts fell incomplete, but he managed to shake off the jitters long enough to find Todd Christensen for a 2-yard touchdown in the fourth quarter to round out the Raiders' scoring.[4]

5. Oct. 6: The Raiders played host to the first place Kansas City Chiefs. However, when this game was over, Los Angeles and Denver were tied with Kansas City for the division lead following a 19–10 Raiders victory. Thanks to a solid defensive effort, four Chris Bahr field goals (37, 25, and two 41-yarders), and a Marc Wilson 6-yard pass to Jim Smith, the Raiders rose above the .500 mark. The offense appeared to be coming around, as Wilson completed 18 out of 29 pass attempts for 241 yards, and Marcus Allen rushed for 126 yards to give the team a well-balanced attack. The defense came up big by holding Kansas City to 81 yards on the ground, and recorded six sacks, with Howie Long leading the way with two.[5]

6. Oct. 13: The Saints came marching in, but left Los Angeles quietly, to the tune of a 23–13 Raiders victory. Marc Wilson continued to get battered, this time having to play with a shoulder separation sustained in the first quarter following a sack. He managed to tough it out by completing 14 of 31 passes for 169 yards and a 15-yard touchdown to Dokie Williams. Marcus Allen was his consistent self, rushing for 107 yards and scoring on runs of 11 and eight yards. The defense was ranked second in the NFL in quarterback sacks, and they added to their total by recording four against the Saints, with Howie Long leading the way with two. Two weeks earlier, Lyle Alzado scored his first touchdown, and in this game he once again put points on the board by sacking quarterback Dave Wilson in the end zone for a safety. This win allowed the Raiders to remain in a three-way tie with Denver and Seattle for the division lead.[6]

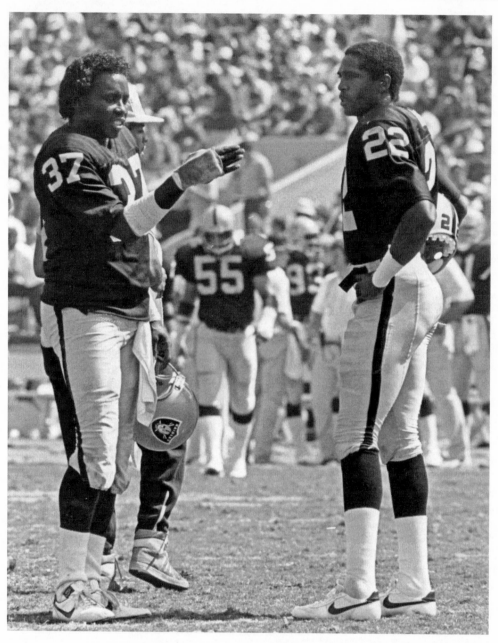

One of the greatest cornerback tandems of all time, Lester Hayes, left, and Mike Haynes discuss how to make life miserable for wide receivers in a game against the San Francisco 49ers on September 22, 1985, at the Los Angeles Memorial Coliseum (AP Photo/NFL Photos).

catches for 71 yards. Chris Bahr added the game-winning conversion to get Los Angeles out of Cleveland Stadium with their fourth straight win. Also scoring for the Raiders in this close game were Frank Hawkins (21-yard run), and Marcus Allen (11-yard pass from Wilson). Punter Ray Guy came through big time for the Raiders by averaging 42 yards on seven punts to keep the Browns out of good field goal position for most of the game. Los Angeles was now 5–2, and along with Denver, on top of the AFC Western Division.[7]

8. Oct. 28: In a game that saw both units play well, the Raiders improved to 6–2 with a 34–21 win over San Diego on Monday Night Football. The defense recorded six sacks to give them 37 on the year, which was one off the league lead in that category. Howie Long had one sack in this game, which gave him a league-leading nine. The unit came in second against the run, and overall, the Raiders were ranked fourth in total defense at the halfway mark of the '85 season. Helping the offense to their best point production up to this stage of the season were Marcus Allen, who ran for 111 yards and three rushing touchdowns (3, 1, and 4 yards), and Todd Christensen (7 receptions for 134 yards). Joining in on the prime time scoring spree were Chris Bahr (20 and 35 yard field goals), and Jessie Hester (13-yard pass from Marc Wilson). This win kept the Raiders in a first place tie with Denver, as the second half of the season was about to get underway.[8]

9. Nov. 3: After five straight wins, the Raiders once again suffered from the curse of the Kingdome. Los Angeles went up to Seattle with everything jelling perfectly, but left the Emerald City demoralized by a 33–3 thrashing, which was their worst defeat in four years. Chris Bahr saved the Raiders from a shutout by hitting on a 30-yard field goal. The only good news out of this disaster was the fact that Denver also lost, so the Raiders still remained shared for the division lead. The amazing thing about this blowout was the fact that the Raiders' offense moved the ball better than the Seahawks did, and controlled time of possession, 27:11 to 12:35, in the third quarter, and were already out of this game by a 26–3 margin. The Seahawks proved that quality beat out quantity, and capitalized on four Marc Wilson interceptions that they returned for 180 yards. They also scored 23 points in two-and-a-half minutes in the second quarter. Even the Los Angeles defense did well statistic wise. They were holding opponents to 281 yards

7. Oct. 20: In a battle of division-leaders, the Raiders beat the Cleveland Browns, 21–20, in a tightly contested game. The Browns were up, 20–14, with 7:53 left in regulation. It was then that Marc Wilson and the offense came alive with 2:53 left to produce an ending worthy of a highlight reel. The Silver and Black drove 60 yards in 13 plays to tie the game with 29 seconds left. Todd Christensen had made many great catches throughout his Raiders career, with this one against Cleveland being near the top of the list. From the Cleveland 8-yard line, Wilson threw to Christensen at the goal line. The All-Pro tight end caught the ball six inches from the end zone while on his knees with a defender glued to him. Christensen led all receivers with six

per game total offense, and they allowed Seattle only 234. Marcus Allen ran for 101 yards to equal the output produced by the entire Seattle backfield. However, despite all the advantages the Raiders had, they still got mauled.[9]

10. Nov. 10: In a wild overtime shootout against San Diego, the Raiders fell for the second straight week, this time by the score of 40–34. San Diego's quarterback, Dan Fouts, led all passers league wide by lighting up the southern California sky for 436 yards and four touchdowns. With this incredible performance, Fouts recorded his sixth career 400-yard passing game to set a pro record. The Chargers rolled up 593 total yards, which was the most ever given up by the Silver and Black. The Raiders also received great effort from many players even in defeat. Marc Wilson completed 18 out of 32 pass attempts for 297 yards and three touchdowns. Jessie Hester caught two passes all game, but they both were for touchdowns covering 35 and 54 yards. Todd Christensen caught seven Wilson passes for 112 yards, one of which went for a 24-yard touchdown that put Los Angeles up, 34–27, in the fourth quarter. Marcus Allen once again topped the century mark with 119 yards, and scored on a 1-yard run. Frank Hawkins added a 1-yard touchdown run, but Chris Bahr had his extra point attempt blocked, which proved crucial in the end. That one point could have given the Raiders the win. The Chargers tied the game up with 1:49 left in regulation on a 14-yard pass from Fouts to Charlie Joiner plus the extra point kick. They emerged victorious when running back Lionel James scampered 17 yards for a touchdown in the overtime period. This loss knocked Los Angeles into second place in the division race behind Denver.[10]

11. Nov. 17: Marcus Allen shined in a tough defensive struggle against the Cincinnati Bengals. With the score knotted at 6–6 with 2:50 remaining in regulation, Allen caught a 7-yard touchdown pass from Marc Wilson to give the Raiders a 13–6 win. Allen pulled off double game-high honors by leading all receivers with six receptions for 54 yards, and all ball carriers with 135 yards. Chris Bahr provided the Raiders with their other points on field goals from 38 and 20 yards. Center Dave Dalby reached a milestone by starting in his 200th consecutive game, and became the 13th player up to this time to achieve that feat. Chris Bahr scored the other Raiders points with two field goals (38 and 20 yards). On the bad side of things, defensive backs Vann McElroy (hamstring), and Mike Davis (arthroscopic knee surgery), left the Los Angeles secondary depleted. Also lost in this game was top renegade Lyle Alzado, who was lost for the remainder of the season with an injury to his Achilles tendon. This win put the Raiders at 7–4, and one game behind Denver.[11]

12. Nov. 24: The Raiders returned to their rightful place on top of the AFC Western Division thanks to a 31–28 overtime showdown with the Denver Broncos. The win gave both teams co-leadership with 8–4 records. Los Angeles produced a well-balanced offensive attack that rang up 201 yards on the ground and 223 through the air. Marcus Allen continued to make headlines with his fifth straight 100-yard rushing game. This time he ran for 173 yards to lead all league runners for the week, and scored on a 61-yard jaunt. Despite throwing three interceptions, Marc Wilson had a good day. He passed for 238 yards, and threw touchdown passes to Todd Christensen (17 yards), and Trey Junkin (3 yards). He also ran for a 1-yard score in the fourth quarter that gave Los Angeles their first lead of the game. Rookie running back

Steve Sewell then scored on a 3-yard run, and Rich Karlis kicked the extra point to tie the game at 28–28. Chris Bahr had a chance to win it in regulation, but missed a 40-yarder with one second left. He redeemed himself in the overtime period by nailing a 32-yarder with 2:42 expired from the clock to send the Raiders back on top in the AFC West. The defense recorded four quarterback sacks, with Sean Jones, who took over Alzado's spot, leading the team with two.[12]

13. Dec. 1: Marcus Allen was establishing himself as the '85 season's running back par-excellence. In a 34–24 win over the Atlanta Falcons, Allen ran for 156 yards to make it six straight games over the century mark. He led the league for the second consecutive week in rushing, and his season total of 1,392 yards set a single-season team record, and he still had three games to add to it. Allen also caught two passes for 42 yards, one of which was a 4-yard touchdown pass from Marc Wilson. Wilson added two more scoring tosses to Jessie Hester (37 yards), and Dokie Williams (7 yards), while throwing for 236 yards. Todd Christensen led all receivers in the game with seven catches for 109 yards. Frank Hawkins scored on a 1-yard run, and Chris Bahr added field goals from 35 and 49 yards to round out the Raiders' scoring. The defense kept pilling on the sacks, this time adding five more to their season total. At 9–4, the Raiders were still tied with Denver atop the division, and set to travel to the Mile High City for their next game.[13]

14. Dec. 8: In a repeat of two weeks earlier, the Raiders once again beat Denver by a field goal in overtime. However, the only thing different this time was that Los Angeles gained sole possession of first place in the division. The Raiders overcame a 14–0 halftime deficit, and tied the game up in the third quarter on a 3-yard pass from Marc Wilson to Todd Christensen, and a 15-yard run by Marcus Allen, plus two Chris Bahr extra point kicks. The score remained at 14–14 until Bahr kicked a 26-yard field goal in overtime to win it, 17–14. Bahr got his chance after Howie Long and Greg Townsend sacked quarterback John Elway. He fumbled deep in his own territory, and Townsend recovered for Los Angeles at the eight. On top of forcing the crucial turnover, the defense stopped Denver's offense cold, allowing only 54 yards in the second half. Marcus Allen ran for 135 yards, and in the process, tied O.J. Simpson and Earl Campbell for second place all-time behind only Walter Payton with his seventh straight 100-yard rushing performance.[14]

15. Dec. 15: The Silver and Black continued to click on all cylinders, and got revenge on Seattle, 13–3, at the LA Coliseum, and clinched their 12th division title since 1967. The Raiders got a great effort from the defense, holding Seattle to 51 yards rushing, recording four sacks, and intercepting two passes. Los Angeles scored on two Chris Bahr field goals of 22 and 27 yards, and a Marcus Allen 7-yard run. Allen closed to within one game of Walter Payton's record of nine straight 100-yard plus games by racking up 109 on the ground.[15]

16. Dec. 23: This was the Battle of Los Angeles, as the Raiders and Rams squared off on Monday Night Football in the NFL's regular season finale for the '85 campaign. Both teams came into the game at 11–4, and already had their perspective divisions clinched. The Silver and Black lived up to their prime time mystique, and looked unstoppable in their sixth straight win, this time a 16–6 affair. Up to this point in their history, the Raiders

held an incredible 24-3-1 record on Monday Night Football since its inception in 1970. Marcus Allen was the man of the hour, as he ran for 123 yards to tie Walter Payton's all-time mark of nine straight 100-yard plus games. For the season, he rushed for 1,759 yards to become the first-ever Raider to lead the NFL in rushing. His combined total of 2,314 yards from scrimmage broke the Rams' Eric Dickerson's record established the previous season. Three Chris Bahr field goals (27, 51, 29 yards), and a 21-yard pass from Marc Wilson to Dokie Williams gave Los Angeles their point production. The defense was stellar once again. This time out, they recorded six sacks against an offensive line consisting of three Pro Bowl performers, and held the Rams to no touchdowns for only the second time all season.[16]

AFC Divisional Playoff Game, January 5, 1986

After a dismal post season showing a year earlier, the Raiders were ready, and considered one of the favorites to win another Super Bowl. Their opponents for this game were the New England Patriots, winners of the AFC Wild Card Game over the New York Jets.

With 87,163 on hand in the Coliseum, the Patriots jumped out to a 7–0 first quarter lead. Their chance came when Fulton Walker fumbled on a punt return and Jim Bowman recovered for the Patriots on the Los Angeles 21. Two plays later, Tony Eason threw a 13-yard pass to Lin Dawson for the opening score.

New England had a chance to extend their lead right after Dawson's touchdown when Ronnie Lippett intercepted Marc Wilson. The Raiders held, and from the LA 41, New England was forced to punt. Greg Townsend then gave the Raiders a huge opportunity by blocking the kick. Jeff Barnes then outraced three Patriots to the ball, and pounced on it at the New England 16. The Patriots were now frazzled by the event, and prevented the Raiders from cashing in on a touchdown. Chris Bahr salvaged the drive with a 29-yard field goal to make it a 7–3 New England lead after one.

Los Angeles came alive in the second quarter, and took the lead with 4:21 expired off the clock on a six-play, 52-yard drive. It started with a 16-yard Walker punt return to the LA 48. Marcus Allen then tore off a gain of 13 that was helped by a facemask penalty moving the ball five yards closer. Marc Wilson then completed his first pass of the day, with it going to Dokie Williams for a 14-yard pickup. The ground forces of Allen and Frank Hawkins then ran off ten yards. A holding penalty ensued, but it did not slow the Raiders' momentum. On the next play, Wilson connected with Jessie Hester from 16 yards out for the go-ahead score. Bahr's extra point made it a 10–7 affair.

On New England's next possession, Mosi Tatupu ran to the left, was hit by Rod Martin and Stacey Toran, fumbled on his own 19, and Howie Long recovered the loose ball for the Raiders. Three runs by Allen followed, with the final one going for 11 yards and a score. On the day, Allen had 121 yards on 22 carries. Bahr added the conversion, and with 8:53 left in the first half, Los Angeles was up, 17–7.

The Patriots looked to stop the Los Angeles momentum, and answered the challenge with a 2-yard run by Craig James to

cut the lead to 17–14 with 3:38 left in the second quarter. They came all the way back after Ronnie Lippett intercepted his second Wilson pass of the game, and Tony Franklin kicked a 45-yard field goal to tie it at 17–17.

With less than two minutes left in the half, Allen ran for 27 yards on two carries, Todd Christensen caught a 31-yard pass from Wilson, and Bahr kicked a 32-yard field goal to complete a 10-play, 67-yard drive, and give the Raiders a 20–17 halftime advantage.

With time almost expired in the third quarter, Franklin once again tied the game with a 32-yard field goal. On the ensuing kickoff, Sam Seale fumbled and Jim Bowman recovered the ball in the end zone for a touchdown with 57 seconds remaining in the third quarter. The Raiders could not muster any other point production, and the Patriots went on to shock Los Angeles, 27–20, and advance to the AFC Championship Game.

The action did not stop when the game ended. New England's general manager Patrick Sullivan, who was also the son of the Patriots' owner, had decided to heckle Boston native Howie Long for a good portion of the game. This was apparently in retaliation for some negative comments that Long expressed about the Patriots' organization that made it into the Boston newspapers during the week leading up to this game. At the end of the game, Sullivan came up to Long and began talking to him by the runway leading to the Coliseum locker rooms. Long decided to play act, and made like he was going to destroy Sullivan. However, Matt Millen thought that a fight was brewing and came in to help out. With a mighty thrust of his helmet, Millen landed a vicious blow to Sullivan that provided him with a cut above the left eye. The Raiders might have lost the game, but they still kept their outlaw image pristine as ever.[17]

Individual Statistics and Roster

Head Coach: Tom Flores
Assistant Coaches: Sam Boghosian, Willie Brown, Chet Franklin, Larry Kennan, Earl Leggett, Bob Mischak, Steve Ortmayer, Terry Robiskie, Art Shell, Tom Walsh, Ray Willsey, Bob Zeman
1985 Regular Season Record: 12–4
1st Place AFC Western Division
Scored 354 points to rank 12th out of 28 teams
Allowed 308 points to rank 9th

STARTERS — OFFENSE

QB — Marc Wilson: Active for 16 games and started in 13. Completed 193 of 388 pass attempts for 2,608 yards, 16 TD and 21 INT. Rushed for 98 yards on 24 carries and 2 TD.
HB — Marcus Allen: Started in 16 games. Rushed for **1,759** yards on 380 carries and 11 TD. Had 67 receptions for 555 yards and 3 TD. Completed 1 of 2 pass attempts for 16 yards. **Also led the NFL in rushing yards per game (109.9) and total yards from scrimmage (2,314).**
FB — Frank Hawkins: Started in 16 games. Rushed for 269 yards on 84 carries and 4 TD. Had 27 receptions for 174 yards. Returned 1 kickoff 14 yards.
WR — Jessie Hester: Started in 16 games. Had 32 receptions for 665 yards and 4 TD. Rushed for 13 yards on 1 carry.
WR — Dokie Williams: Started in 16 games. Had 48 receptions for 925 yards and 5 TD. Returned 1 kickoff 19 yards.
TE — Todd Christensen: Started in 16 games. Had 82 receptions for 987 yards and 6 TD.
LT — Bruce Davis: Started in 16 games.

LG — Charley Hannah: Active for 15 games and started in all of them.

C — Don Mosebar: Active for 16 games and started in 14.

RG — Mickey Marvin: Active for 15 games and started in all of them.

RT — Henry Lawrence: Started in 16 games.

Reserve Offensive Players

Kevin Belcher (T): Active for 4 games.

Cliff Branch (WR): Active for 4 games.

Dave Dalby (C): Active for 16 games.

Rusty Hilger (QB): Active for 4 games. Completed 4 of 13 pass attempts for 54 yards and 1 TD. Rushed 3 times for 8 yards.

Derrick Jensen (RB/TE): Active for 16 games. Rushed 16 times for 35 yards.

Shelby Jordan (T): Active for 16 games and started in 2.

Trey Junkin (TE/LB): Active for 16 games. Had 2 receptions for 8 yards and 1 TD

Kenny King (RB): Active for 16 games. Rushed 16 times for 67 yards and caught 3 passes for 49 yards.

Curt Marsh (G): Active for 7 games.

Tim Moffett (WR): Active for 13 games. Had 5 receptions for 90 yards and 7 kickoff returns for 150 yards.

Cleo Montgomery (WR): Active for 4 games. Returned 8 punts for 84 yards.

Andy Parker (TE): active for 16 games.

Jim Plunkett (QB): Active for 3 games and started in all of them. Completed 71 of 103 passes for 803 yards, 3 TD, and 3 INT. Rushed 5 times for 12 yards.

Jim Smith (WR): Active for 6 games. Had 3 receptions for 28 yards and 1 TD.

Steve Strachan (RB): Active for 4 games and rushed 2 times for 1 yard.

Rickey Williams (RB): Active for 2 games.

Starters — Defense

DE — Howie Long: Started in 16 games and had 10 sacks.

DE — Lyle Alzado: Active for 11 games and started in all of them. Had 3 sacks, 1 fumble recovery, 1 TD, and recorded 1 safety.

NT — Bill Pickel: Started in 16 games and had 12.5 sacks.

LOLB — Brad Van Pelt: Active for 16 games and started in 15. Had 5 sacks and 1 INT

LILB — Matt Millen: Started in 16 games and had 1 sack.

RILB — Reggie McKenzie: Started in 16 games, had 1 sack and 1 fumble recovery.

ROLB — Rod Martin: Started in 16 games, had 7 sacks, 1 INT and 3 fumble recoveries.

CB — Lester Hayes: Active for 16 games and started in 13. Had 4 INT, 1 fumble recovery, and 1 kickoff return for 0 yards.

CB — Mike Haynes: Started in 16 games, had 1 sack, 4 INT, and 1 punt return for 9 yards.

SS — Mike Davis: Active for 11 games and started in 10. Had 1 sack and 1 fumble recovery.

FS — Vann McElroy: Active for 12 games and started in all of them. Had 2 INT and 1 fumble recovery.

Reserve Defensive Players

Jeff Barnes (LB): Active for 16 games and started in 1. Had 2 sacks, 1 INT, and 4 fumble recoveries.

Don Bessillieu (DB): Active for 4 games.

Tony Caldwell (LB): Active for 3 games.

James Davis (DB): Active for 15 games and started in 1.

Elvis Franks (E): active for 3 games and started in 1.

Sean Jones (E): Active for 15 games and started in 4. Had 8.5 sacks and 1 fumble recovery.

Odis McKinney (DB): Active for 10 games and started in 3. Had 1 INT and 1 fumble recovery.

Jerry Robinson (LB): Active for 11 games.

Sam Seale (DB): Active for 16 games. Returned 23 kickoffs for 482 yards, had 1 INT, and 1 TD.

Jack Squirek (LB): Active for 16 games and had 1 INT.

Dave Stalls (E/T/NT): Active for 4 games.

Stacey Toran (DB): Active for 16 games and started in 9. Had 1 sack, 1 INT, and 1 TD.

Greg Townsend (E/LB/T/NT): Active for 16 games, had 10 sacks and 1 fumble recovery.

Fulton Walker (DB): Active for 13 games, had 62 punt returns for 692 yards and 21 kickoff returns for 467 yards.

Mitch Willis (NT/T): Active for 11 games and had 2 sacks.

Kicking/Punting

K — Chris Bahr: Active for 16 games. Made 20 of 32 field goal attempts and 40 of 42 extra point kicks for 100 points.

P — Ray Guy: Active for 16 games. Punted 89 times for a 40.8 average, and rushed 1 time for 0 yards.

1986 Season Review

1. Sept. 7: The Raiders saw one streak end while another continued. Their six-game regular season winning streak came to an end, 38–36, in a shootout against division rivals, the Denver Broncos. Marcus Allen's streak continued, as he gained 102 yards on the ground to establish a new NFL record of ten consecutive games over the century mark. Allen scored on a 2-yard run, and caught a 24-yard pass from Marc Wilson for another touchdown. Wilson was impressive despite the loss, by throwing for 346 yards on 20 completions out of 33 attempts. In addition to his scoring strike to Allen, Wilson also threw touchdown passes to Todd Christensen (16 yards), and Rod Barksdale (57 yards). Chris Bahr kicked two field goals from 43 and 42 yards, and the defense rang up two points when Greg Townsend sacked John Elway for a safety. Los Angeles led in this one, 19–7, and managed to keep Denver in check until the fourth quarter. It was then that the Broncos took advantage of three Raiders turnovers to get back in the game. A Marcus Allen fumble was returned for a touchdown, and another one by Napoleon McCallum on a kickoff return resulted in the go-ahead touchdown.[1]

2. Sept. 14: In a defensive struggle in the nation's capital, the Raiders succumbed to the Washington Redskins, 10–6. The Redskins took away the Raiders' long passing game by plowing through the offensive line and sacking Marc Wilson five times and intercepting him twice. After the game, it was learned that Wilson suffered a separated shoulder and would not be ready for the next game. The game was a battle of place kickers, and into the fourth quarter, Los Angeles was winning the skirmish thanks to two Chris Bahr field goals from 28 and 23 yards. The Redskins finally broke through the tough Los Angeles defense when fifth-year tight end Clint Didier got past defensive back Stacey Toran and caught a Jay Schroeder pass that covered 59 yards. It was the most yardage Didier and Schroeder both gained on one play up to this point in their careers. The catch set Washington up for a game-winning, 3-yard touchdown run by George Rogers. Marcus Allen achieved another individual honor by rushing for 104 yards to extend his streak to eleven straight games over the century mark. This loss dropped the Raiders to 0–2, which was the first time since 1964 that they started the season off with two consecutive defeats.[2]

3. Sept. 21: The Raiders played tough, hard-nosed defensive football for the third straight week, but once again it went for nothing. In front of their largest crowd for a home opener (71,164) since moving to Los Angeles, the Raiders dropped a 14–9 decision to the New York Giants after beating each time in their previous three encounters. Their record of 0–3 was the worst start for the Silver and Black since 1964. Jim Plunkett was named the starting quarterback for the first time in a year due to Marc Wilson nursing his separated shoulder. Plunkett showed he still had something left in his arm, as he completed 21 out of 41 pass attempts for 281 yards with heavy pressure coming at him quite a few times. The amazing thing about Plunkett's completions were that only three went to his wide receivers, which was very rare for a Raiders team. The constant rush applied on Plunkett was greatly responsible for this, because it took away the extra time needed to wait for his receivers to get open. Marcus Allen's NFL record 11-game 100-yard plus streak came to an end after he ran for 40 yards on 15 carries. He did catch five passes for 86 yards before a sprained ankle suffered in the third quarter forced him to the sideline. This was the ninth straight quarter that the Raiders failed to score a touchdown. Despite this, they managed to hold a 6–0 lead at the half on Chris Bahr field goals from 22 and 35 yards out. New York quarterback Phil Simms then got the Giants a go-ahead touchdown in the third quarter with an 18-yard pass to Lionel Manuel, and later the same duo teamed up again for another six-pointer from 11 yards out. Bahr made it closer with a 33-yard field goal to round out the scoring. This loss had the Raiders in a deep hole, as they were already three games behind the 3–0 Seattle Seahawks in the AFC Western Division.[3]

4. Sept. 28: After weeks of trying, the Silver and Black finally got into the win column with a 17–13 victory over San Diego. Marc Wilson was back at the controls, and showed his grit by enduring eight sacks but still passed for 314 yards and two touchdowns on 19 out of 28 attempts. His effort gained him the top spot among his fellow quarterbacks for the week. After spotting the Chargers a 13–0 second quarter lead, the Raiders snapped their ten quarters without a touchdown streak when Wilson threw a 12-yarder to Dokie Williams with 16 seconds left in the first half. Wilson then found Jesse Hester from 40 yards out with only 25 seconds expired from the game clock in the third quarter for the go-ahead touchdown. Chris Bahr added some insurance points for Los Angeles with an 18-yard field goal. The Raiders played without Marcus Allen, who was nursing that sprained ankle suffered the week before. The Los Angeles defense came up big with three interceptions and held the Chargers to a minuscule 56 rushing yards.[4]

5. Oct. 5: The Raiders trailed long-time nemesis Kansas City, 17–0, after the Chiefs scored on their first three possessions. Marc Wilson and Dokie Williams cut the lead the Kansas City lead to ten points when they teamed up for a 12-yard touchdown in the second quarter. An injured hand forced Wilson to leave the game in the third quarter, and Jim Plunkett took over the rest of the way. Napoleon McCallum was filling in for the injured Marcus Allen, and did a fine job. He led all ball carriers with 69 yards, and scored on a 12-yard run to bring the Raiders to within three points of the lead. Plunkett then gave the Silver and Black their first lead of the day with an 18-yard pass to Jesse Hester. In relief, Plunkett hit on eight of 10 passes for 108 yards. Chris Bahr

added a 19-yard field goal, and that was how this edition of the bitter rivalry ended, with the Raiders prevailing, 24–17.[5]

6. Oct. 12: For the fifth time in six games, the Raiders' defense held the opposition to under 100 yards rushing, recorded four sacks, and Los Angeles won their third straight, 14–10, over Seattle, to get even at 3–3. At 38-years of age, Jim Plunkett was the oldest quarterback playing at this time. However, age did not mean anything, as Plunkett delivered a great performance filling in for the injured Marc Wilson. He hit on 15 of 26 pass attempts for 199 yards and was responsible for both Los Angeles touchdowns. Dokie Williams caught a 9-yard scoring pass, and Jessie Hester a 49-yarder. Napoleon McCallum led all ball carriers with 75 yards while once again handling the main running chores for an injured Marcus Allen. Allen did play briefly, but limped off the field in the fourth quarter after aggravating his tender right ankle.[6]

7. Oct. 19: Marcus Allen returned to form against the Dolphins, and his performance helped beat Miami, 30–28, for their fourth straight win. Allen ran for a game-high 96 yards, and two touchdowns, both from two yards out. He also caught a 16-yard pass from Marc Wilson for a third touchdown. Chris Bahr added three field goals from 32, 33, and 40 yards. Miami quarterback Dan Marino lit up the skies for 286 yards and three touchdowns, but his running game was virtually non-existent. For the sixth time this season, the Raiders held an opposing backfield to under 100 yards. In this game they allowed the Dolphins only 53. Meanwhile, the Silver and Black running attack exploded for 214 yards on the ground.[7]

8. Oct. 26: Los Angeles earned top defensive honors for the week in a 28–17 win over the Houston Oilers. Leading the Raiders to their fifth consecutive trip to the win column was a defense that sacked quarterback Warren Moon six times, intercepted four of his passes, and held the Houston running game to 82 yards. Defensive tackle Bill Pickel led the way by blocking three passes, recording one sack, and recovering a fumble. On offense, Marc Wilson threw four touchdown passes, with three going to Todd Christensen (14, 32, and 3 yards). On the day, the All-Pro tight end caught seven passes for 82 yards. Andy Parker caught Wilson's other touchdown pass from seven yards out. Marcus Allen's right ankle flared up again, and Napoleon McCallum picked up the slack by leading all ball carriers with 84 yards. After starting 0–3, the Raiders returned to their days of glory, and stood at 5–3 and tied for second place along with Kansas City behind 7–1 Denver in the division.[8]

9. Nov. 2: The Raiders chances to get within one game of Denver was nullified after the Broncos won, 21–10, in front of a sold out Los Angeles Coliseum crowd of 90,153. Denver quarterback John Elway was nearly perfect, hitting on 11 of 12 pass attempts and one touchdown, while Sammy Winder led the ground attack with 83 yards. The Raiders scored their points on a 38-yard Chris Bahr field goal, and a 20-yard pass from Marc Wilson to Jesse Hester. Los Angeles had a chance to win after regaining possession with 2:21 left in the game and the ball on their own 26. Defensive back Mike Harden thwarted the Raiders' quest for a sixth straight victory by stepping in front of a Wilson pass and taking it back 40 yards for the clinching touchdown. Despite succumbing to four interceptions on the day, Wilson completed 25 out of 47 attempts for a whopping 367 yards. Todd Christensen

helped out with 11 receptions for 158 yards, and Marcus Allen returned full time, and led the Los Angeles ground game with 71 yards.[9]

10. Nov. 9: The Los Angeles defense sacked Dallas quarterback Steve Pelluer six times, and rang up five interceptions in a 17–13 win. Texas native Vann McElroy had two of the five thefts. Marc Wilson was ineffective throughout the first half, completing only four passes out of 14 attempts for 37 yards and three interceptions. At the start of the second half, with the Raiders down, 10–3, head coach Tom Flores decided to relieve Wilson in favor of 38-year-old Jim Plunkett. Shortly there after, Plunkett connected with Dokie Williams on a 20-yard touchdown pass to tie the game. In the fourth quarter, this time trailing, 13–10, Plunkett and Williams team up again from 40 yards for what became the game winner. Williams had one of his best days with five receptions for 107 yards. Chris Bahr provided the other Los Angeles points with a 45-yard field goal in the second quarter.[10]

11. Nov. 16: In a game that featured a soon to be 39-year-old veteran quarterback against a 23-year-old in his second season, age won out over youth. With Jim Plunkett throwing for three touchdowns, the Raiders beat the Cleveland Browns and their rising star signal caller, Bernie Kosar, 27–14. Los Angeles jumped out to a 17–0 lead in the first half on a 40-yard pass from Plunkett to Dokie Williams, a 3-yard pass from Plunkett to Todd Christensen, and a Chris Bahr 40-yard field goal. The Browns closed to within three points on two Kevin Mack short yardage runs, but the Raiders added another Plunkett-to-Williams touchdown, this time from 43 yards, and Bahr finished the scoring off with a 27-yard field goal to give the Silver and Black their seventh win out of the last eight games. Throughout the game, the Los Angeles defense applied constant pressure on Kosar, sacking him six times and intercepting him twice, with Vann McElroy and Stacey Toran getting the honors for the picks. The win gave the Raiders a 7–4 record, and tied them with Kansas City for second place in the division behind 9–2 Denver.[11]

12. Nov. 20: The Raiders moved closer to the division lead by beating San Diego on a Thursday night, 37–31, in overtime. Los Angeles was riding a hot streak, winning eight out of their last nine games, to improve to 8–4. The Broncos lost three days later to see their lead in the AFC West cut to one game. The Raiders made it look like this way going to be a runaway victory early on, as they held a 31–10 advantage in the third quarter. The Chargers then brought their rivals back to reality by exploding for 21 points to tie the game and force overtime. Like so many times throughout his illustrious career, Marcus Allen came through when his team needed it the most. With 6:27 left in the overtime period, Los Angeles drove to the San Diego 28-yard line. On second-and-ten, Allen went off right tackle with a handoff, and within seconds, crossed the goal line to provide Los Angeles with a winning six-pointer. Football is true team effort, and there were others who shined for the Silver and Black on this prime time thriller. Jim Plunkett remained as hot as the team he quarterbacked. His 348 yards in this game earned Plunkett the league's top honor in that category for the week. Since returning to the starting lineup, he threw five touchdown passes, with two coming against the Chargers. On the receiving end of Plunkett's scoring strikes were Dokie Williams (10-yards), and Todd Christensen (11 yards). Christensen led all NFL receivers in week twelve

with 11 receptions for 173 yards. Joining in the Los Angeles scoring barrage were Jerry Robinson (2-yard return of a blocked punt), Lester Hayes (39-yard fumble recovery), and Chris Bahr (52-yard field goal).[12]

13. Nov. 30: The Raiders were forced into another overtime, but this time the results were not as favorable for the Silver and Black. Despite another strong showing by Jim Plunkett (366 yards and two touchdowns), Los Angeles fell victim in an upset, 33–27, to the 4–9 Philadelphia Eagles. The Eagles won the game at the 8:07 mark of overtime when quarterback Randall Cunningham ran for a 1-yard score. The game-winner was set up when Marcus Allen fumbled on the Philadelphia 15. Andre Waters picked up the loose ball and raced 81 yards to the Los Angeles 4-yard line before being stopped by Dokie Williams. Two plays later, Cunningham scored. Even though the team suffered a difficult loss, there were some excellent efforts put forth by the Raiders. Receiver Jesse Hester raked up a whopping 193 yards on just four receptions, with two going for touchdowns (49 and 81 yards). Fulton Walker scored the game's first points on a 70-yard punt return. In addition to Walker's return, Philadelphia's Gregg Garrity also scored on a punt return to mark the first time in NFL history that both teams scored touchdowns in that manner in the same game. The defensive line got a boost when All-Pro Howie Long returned to action after missing two games with a knee injury and recorded a sack. As a unit, the defense sacked Cunningham ten times, with Bill Pickel getting three of them. Chris Bahr added two field goals from 38 and 27 yards, to finish the team's scoring output.[13]

14. Dec. 8: The Monday Night Football magic that the Raiders enjoyed since 1970 did not help this time. A trip to the dreaded Seattle Kingdome provided the ghastly setting for a 37–0 beat down inflicted on the Silver and Black. This was the fifth straight time that the Seahawks sent the Raiders home in defeat from the Emerald City, and the team's worst loss in 24 years. The Seattle defense pounded the Los Angeles offense, allowing them only 40 rushing yards, and 98 through the air. They also registered 11 quarterback sacks. Up to this point of the '86 season, the Raiders allowed 60 sacks, which was the second highest amount in the league. The only bright spot to come out of this debacle was that Todd Christensen became the first NFL player to catch at least 80 passes in four consecutive seasons. This loss hurt Los Angeles' hopes of reaching the playoffs. Both the Raiders and Seahawks were 8–6, and one game behind Cincinnati for the last Wild Card spot.[14]

15. Dec. 14: What looked like another great run at the playoffs during the middle of the season quickly turned into a nightmare for the '86 Raiders. Los Angeles turned the ball over seven times, and the Kansas City Chiefs became the third straight underdog to beat them. The Chiefs jumped out to a 17–0 lead before Jim Plunkett got the Raiders on the board with a 34-yard pass to Rod Barksdale. Chris Bahr added a 19-yard field goal, and Marcus Allen a 2-yard run, but it was not enough in a 20–17 loss. The Raiders had a chance to take a fourth quarter lead, but Napoleon McCallum fumbled on the Kansas City 16 with six minutes to play. The Chiefs went to 9–6, and secured their first winning season in five years. In addition to that, they were on the verge of their first playoff appearance in 15 years. Los Angeles, however, was going in a different direction, as this third consecutive defeat

just about stymied any hopes they had of reaching the play-offs.[15]

16. Dec. 21: Needing a win for even a remote chance at the post season, the Raiders hosted the Indianapolis Colts. When it was all over, so too were the Silver and Black, this time losers by the score of 30–24. This was a huge accomplishment for the Colts, who lost their first 13 games before putting together a three-game winning streak to take into the 1987 season. This fourth straight loss put the Raiders at 8–8, and not gaining a playoff berth for the first time since moving to Los Angeles. Scoring for the Raiders in their finale were Todd Christensen (3-yard pass from Jim Plunkett, and a 14-yard pass from Rusty Hilger), Jerry Robinson (32-yard interception return), and Chris Bahr (20-yard field goal). Rod Barksdale did not score, but his 179 yards on six receptions led all NFL receivers for the final weekend. Even though the Raiders fell short of team goals, on an individual level, Christensen set a single-season NFL record for most receptions by a tight end with 95.[16]

1986 Season Review

Individual Statistics and Roster
Head Coach: Tom Flores
Assistant Coaches: Sam Boghosian, Willie Brown, Chet Franklin, Larry Kennan, Earl Leggett, Bob Mischak, Steve Ortmayer, Terry Robiskie, Art Shell, Tom Walsh, Ray Willsey, Bob Zeman
1986 Regular Season Record: 8–8
4th Place AFC Western Division
Scored 323 points to rank 16th out of 28 teams
Allowed 346 points to rank 19th

STARTERS — OFFENSE

QB — Jim Plunkett: Active for 10 games and started in 8. Completed 133 of 252 pass attempts for 1,986 yards, 14 TD and 9 INT. Rushed 12 times for 47 yards.
HB — Marcus Allen: Active for 13 games and started in 10. Rushed for 759 yards on 208 carries and 5 TD. Had 46 receptions for 453 yards and 2 TD.
FB — Frank Hawkins: Active for 16 games and started in 15. Rushed for 245 yards on 58 carries, had 25 receptions for 166 yards, and 1 kickoff return for 15 yards.
WR — Rod Barksdale: Active for 16 games and started in 15. Had 18 receptions for 434 yards and 2 TD.
WR — Dokie Williams: Active for 15 games and started in all of them. Had 43 receptions for 843 yards, 8 TD, and rushed 3 times for 27 yards.
TE — Todd Christensen: Started in 16 games. Had 95 receptions for 1,153 yards and 8 TD.
LT — Bruce Davis: Started in 16 games.
LG — Charley Hannah: Active in 12 games and started in all of them.
C — Don Mosebar: Started in 16 games.
RG — Mickey Marvin: Started in 16 games.
RT — Henry Lawrence: Active for 16 games and started in 14 of them.

RESERVE OFFENSIVE PLAYERS

Earl Cooper (RB/TE): Active for 5 games.
Jessie Hester (WR): Active for 13 games and started in 1. Had 23 receptions for 632 yards and 6 TD.
Rusty Hilger (QB): active for 2 games. Completed 19 of 38 pass attempts for 266 yards, 1 TD, and 1 INT. Rushed for 48 yards on 6 carries.
Derrick Jensen (RB/TE): active for 1 game.

Shelby Jordan (T): Active for 16 games and started in 2.
Trey Junkin (TE/LB): Active for 3 games and had 2 receptions for 38 yards.
Bill Lewis (C/G): Active for 4 games.
Curt Marsh (G): Active for 2 games and started in both.
Napoleon McCallum (RB): Active for 15 games and started in 5. Rushed for 536 yards on 142 carries and 1 TD. Had 13 receptions for 103 yards, 8 kickoff returns for 183 yards, and 7 punt returns for 44 yards.
Tim Moffett (WR): Active for 16 games, started in 1, and had 6 receptions for 77 yards.
Vance Mueller (RB): Active for 15 games, started in 1, and had 13 rushes for 30 yards, 6 receptions for 54 yards, and 2 kickoff returns for 73 yards.
Andy Parker (TE): Active for 13 games, and had 2 receptions for 8 yards and 1 TD.
Mark Pattison (WR): Active for 2 games, and had 2 receptions for 12 yards.
Chris Riehm (G/T): Active for 12 and started in 2.
Steve Strachan (RB): Active for 16 games, started in 1, and had 18 rushes for 53 yards.
Marc Wilson (QB): Active for 16 and started in 8. Completed 129 of 240 pass attempts for 1,721 yards, 12 TD, and 15 INT. Rushed for 45 yards on 14 carries.

STARTERS — DEFENSE

DE — Howie Long: Active for 13 games and stated in 12. Had 7 sacks and 2 fumble recoveries.
DE — Sean Jones: Started in 16 games and had 15 sacks.
NT — Bill Pickel: Active for 15 games and started in all of them. Had 11 sacks and 2 fumble recoveries.
LOLB — Jerry Robinson: Started in 16 games, had 2 sacks, 4 INT, 1 TD, and 2 fumble recoveries.
LILB — Matt Millen: Started in 16 games, had 1 sack and 3 kickoff returns for 40 yards.
RILB — Reggie McKenzie: Started in 16 games, had 1 sack and 1 INT.
ROLB — Rod Martin: Started in 16 games, had 5 sacks and 1 INT.
CB — Lester Hayes: Active for 14 games and started in all of them. Had 2 INT, 2 fumble recoveries and 1 TD.
CB — Mike Haynes: Active for 13 games, started in all of them, and had 2 INT.
SS — Stacey Toran: Started in 16 games, had 6 sacks, 2 INT, and 1 fumble recovery.
FS — Vann McElroy: Started in 16 games and had 7 INT.

RESERVE DEFENSIVE PLAYERS

Stefon Adams (DB): Active for 16 games, had 1 INT and 27 kickoff returns for 573 yards.
Jeff Barnes (LB): Active for 16 games, and had 2 sacks and 2 INT.
James Davis (DB): Active for 16 games.
Elvis Franks (E): Active for 4 games.
Jamie Kimmel (LB): Active for 16 games.
Linden King (LB): Active for 16 games.
Odis McKinney (DB): Active for 2 games.
Sam Seale (DB): Active for 16 games and started in 5. Had 4 INT and 1 fumble recovery.
Greg Townsend (E/LB/T/NT): Active for 15 games and started in 4. Had 11 sacks and recorded 1 safety.
Fulton Walker (DB): Active for 14 games, had 49 punt returns for 440 yards, and 23 kickoff returns for 368 yards.
Mitch Willis (NT/T): Active for 16 games and started in 1.
Mike Wise (E): Active for 6 games.

KICKING/PUNTING

K — Chris Bahr: Active for 16 games. Made 21 of 28 field goal attempts and 36 of 36 extra points kicks for 99 points.

P — Ray Guy: Active for 16 games. Punted 90 times for a 40.2 average, and rushed 1 time for 0 yards.

1987 Season Review

1. Sept. 13: The Raiders came into the new season trying to forget their collapse at the end of the previous campaign, and hinged their hopes on new starting quarterback Rusty Hilger, even though Marc Wilson relieved him after he jammed his shoulder in the first half. Wilson played well in his back up role, completing 9 of 16 passes for 97 yards, and was awarded the game ball from his teammates. With the Green Bay Packers as their fodder, the Silver and Black snapped a four-game losing streak carried over from '86 with a 20–0 whitewash. Marcus Allen carried the ball 33 times for 136 yards and scored on a 1-yard run. Chris Bahr added two field goals from 40 and 27 yards, and defensive back Vann McElroy brought an interception back 35 yards to complete the scoring. Besides McElroy's contribution, the rest of the defense came up big by recording four sacks, intercepting three passes, limiting Green Bay to 66 rushing yards and 80 passing, and shutting them out for the first time in 122 games. This provided the Raiders with their first shutout victory since the 1985 season opener.[1]

2. Sept. 20: The Silver and Black appeared to be back to their dominant selves by making it two straight with a 27–7 win over the Detroit Lions. This marked the first time since 1984 that the Raiders started off a season 2–0. After trailing, 7–6, at the half, Los Angeles rang up three touchdowns. Quarterback Rusty Hilger led the offense with 20 out of 39 pass completions for 234 yards and threw a 14-yard touchdown pass to Dokie Williams. Marcus Allen led all ball carriers with 79 yards, and scored on a 1-yard run. Running back Vance Mueller scored the Raiders' final touchdown on a 1-yard run. Chris Bahr did his part by hitting on two field goals from 38 and 34 yards out.[2]

Amidst the Raiders' apparent excitement of starting the '87 campaign off on a high note, there loomed a dismal reality that another NFL Player's Strike would cut into the season. Following the September 21st Monday Night telecast between the New York Jets and New England Patriots, the league went on strike. The foremost demand set forth by the Player's Union was to have free agency without any restraints. The players were not happy with the "Rozelle Rule" established in 1976 that allowed compensation to the player's former team when he signed with another organization. The Player's Union and the owners came to no understanding, and negotiations fell through after two weeks of the regular season. The players then agreed to strike on September 22, 1987. The owners had a plan, however, to not have happen what occurred in 1982 when the season was cut to nine games. They decided to cancel games scheduled for September 27th, and then resume the season with replacement players. Each organization quickly put together a roster, many of which had players cut by teams or had some with pro experience prior to this time. A number of regular players crossed the picket lines to rejoin their teams during the strike. After 24 days, the union decided to allow players to go back to work after gaining no ground in the discussions. With some players not supporting the union's actions, coupled with the television networks refusing to stop showing games, and

the public's disgust with the whole thing, it was voted on to return to work. Eventually, the players won after a jury decided in their favor a few years later.[3]

3. Oct. 4: Los Angeles' replacement team was led by ex–NFL quarterback Vince Evans, and he led the team to a 35–17 win over Kansas City in front of only 10,708 in the massive Los Angeles Coliseum. Evans hit on 10 of 18 pass attempts for 248 yards and two touchdowns. He also ran for another score from four yards out. Evans' scoring tosses went to Carl Aikens (27 yards) and Ethan Horton (32 yards). Running back Craig Ellis ran for two 8-yard touchdowns, and Los Angeles remained undefeated.[4]

4. Oct. 12: Despite knowing that replacement players were performing, 61,230 attended the game between the Broncos and Raiders at Denver's Mile High Stadium on a Monday Night. The attendance figure for this game beat out the totals by over 20,000 for the first two weeks of replacement games. With the spotlight of Monday Night Football on him, Joe Dudek ran for 128 yards and two touchdowns in a 30–14 Denver victory. In their first loss of the year, the Raiders scored on a Vince Evans to Mario Perry 3-yard pass and a 55-yard punt return by Rick Calhoun.[5]

5. Oct. 18: The Los Angeles defense did a great job by recording seven sacks, allowing only 97 yards rushing and 147 passing, but it was the San Diego defense that came up big in the end. With 18 seconds left in the game, and the score tied at 17–17, Vince Evans threw a bad pass that defensive back Elvis Patterson stepped in front of at the San Diego 25. He then raced 75 yards for the winning touchdown in a 23–17 win for the Chargers. The Raiders received their points on two Evans to Carl Aikens passes (7 and 32 yards), and a Chris Bahr field goal from 33 yards out.[6]

6. Oct. 25: The strike was over after 24 days, but the Raiders continued on a downward spiral despite having their regular roster back. This time they fell to Seattle at home, 35–13, and were manhandled right from the beginning and were never in the game. This win broke a four-game losing streak for the Seahawks against the Raiders in the Los Angeles Coliseum. Curt Warner ran for 112 yards and two touchdowns. Marc Wilson managed to generate points through the air on a day that saw the Los Angeles ground game produced a scant 44 yards. Wilson threw touchdown passes to Todd Christensen (7 yards), and Dokie Williams (14 yards). Wilson also threw two interceptions, one of which was returned 50 yards for a score. This defeat put the Raiders at 3–3, and in fourth place in the AFC West.[7]

7. Nov. 1: The New England Patriots handed the Raiders their fourth straight loss, 26–23, on the day that Bo Jackson debuted for the Silver and Black at running back after his major league baseball season with the Kansas City Royals ended. There was much anticipation regarding Jackson's arrival after the former Heisman Trophy winner decided to play pro football in addition to his already successful pro baseball career as an outfielder. He came into the game in the second quarter, and carried the ball eight times for 37 yards. The Raiders made a great attempt at coming back in this one, and almost pulled out the win. Down, 23–6, with 12 minutes left in fourth quarter, Todd Christensen caught an 8-yard pass from Rusty Hilger, Marcus Allen ran for a 2-yard score, and Chris Bahr tied the game up with a 39-yard field goal in the closing minute. Bahr also kicked two 31-yard field goals earlier. New England came back in the final 46 seconds

after beginning the drive on their own 20. Tony Franklin attempted a 34-yard field goal with five seconds remaining, but missed. However, he got another chance following an offside penalty called against the Raiders. With one tick left on the clock, Franklin nailed a 29-yarder for the win.[8]

8. Nov. 8: The slide continued for the Silver and Black, as they lost to the Minnesota Vikings, 31–20, in an exact reversal of fortune from the previous season. In 1986, the Raiders lost their first three games then proceeded to win five in a row. The exact opposite was the case in '87. This losing streak equaled the worst during Al Davis' reign, when the '64 team lost their first five games. In fact, Davis must have had a flashback to that mayhem, which caused him to call down to Tom Flores on the sidelines and tell his coach to replace Rusty Hilger with Marc Wilson. This marked the third time in his five starts that Hilger was benched for ineffectiveness. The Vikings also replaced their starting quarterback, Tommy Kramer, with Wade Wilson after Kramer suffered hand cramps. In a battle of quarterbacks who shared the same last name, Wade threw only two passes, but both went for touchdowns, and he also ran for another one. Marc threw two touchdown passes as well, with James Lofton (9 yards), and Dokie Williams (27 yards), on the receiving end of those strikes. Chris Bahr gave the Raiders their other points with field goals from 21 and 35 yards away.[9]

9. Nov. 15: The Raiders' woes went on for another week, as they lost this time to the division-leading San Diego Chargers, 16–14. Los Angeles looked to rally in the fourth quarter after being down by 16 points, and came close by way of two Marc Wilson two touchdown passes to Dokie Williams (5 yards), and James Lofton (47 yards), who caught his scoring toss with 16 seconds left to play. Lofton set a personal milestone by becoming the sixth player in pro football history to gain 10,000 career-receiving yards. The Raiders added to their problems in this game by losing 186 yards on penalties.[10]

10. Nov. 22:Bo Jackson delivered on his expectations by leading all ball carriers with 98 yards, and scored the first touchdowns of his pro career (35 and 1-yard runs). However, it was not enough, as Denver quarterback John Elway outshined Jackson in a 23–17 win. The seven-game losing streak provided the Raiders with the longest during Al Davis' association with the team up to this time in their history. Elway passed for 298 yards and one touchdown, and ran for another one. His great passing arm also helped set up three field goals. Denver's defense played a big part when they sacked Marc Wilson six times, who despite the torment, managed to have a respectable showing with 15 out of 21 attempts for 173 yards and no interceptions. Chris Bahr's 34-yard field goal gave the Raiders their other points in this defeat.[11]

11. Nov. 30: Bo Jackson seemed to just be warming up in the previous game, because he definitely caught fire, blazing at that, with a then team-record 221 rushing yards on 18 carries, and scored on runs of 91 and two yards on a Monday Night Football telecast. He added a third touchdown with a 14-yard catch from Marc Wilson in one of the greatest individual efforts ever witnessed by a member of the Silver and Black. This was also Jackson's 25th birthday, but it was Bo who gave his teammates a present. It came in the way of a 37–14 beat down over the Seattle Seahawks in the dreaded Kingdome, where the Raiders had not won in five previous trips to the great northwest. This was also the 250th regular season win in Raiders' history. On his 2-yard touchdown run, Jackson ran over Seattle's highly toted linebacker Brian Bosworth in what became one of the most famous highlight moments in Raiders history. This spectacular performance also provided fans with one of the greatest film highlights of all-time. Besides Jackson's single-handed demolition of the Seahawks, the Raiders other point-scoring contributors were James Lofton (46-yard pass from Marc Wilson) for the team's first tally of the evening, and two Chris Bahr field goals from 23 yards, and another from 47 yards.[12]

12. Dec. 6: The Buffalo Bills kept a watchful eye on Bo Jackson after witnessing his unbelievable performance one week earlier. However, they failed to stop him completely, as the two-sport superstar ran for game-high 78 yards, and caught four passes for 59 yards and a 14-yard touchdown from Marc Wilson to get the Raiders on the board first, and Los Angeles went on to win their second in a row, this time by the score of 34–21. Marc Wilson provided the team with solid quarterbacking, as he hit on 21 passes out of 32 attempts for 337 yards and three touchdowns. In addition to Jackson's touchdown reception, Wilson connected with James Lofton from 41 yards, and from 23 yards to Dokie Williams. Lofton had a sensational game with six receptions for 132 yards. Chris Bahr kicked two field goals (22 and 33 yards), and Marcus Allen added a scoring run from two yards out.[13]

13. Dec. 13: With their biggest December crowd since 1973 on hand, the Kansas City Chiefs, led by three Nick Lowery field goals, sent 63,834 Arrowhead Stadium spectators home happy by the way of a 16–10 win over the extremely disliked rivals. The big turnout for this game was due to the arrival of Bo Jackson, who played outfield for the Kansas City Royals. All the hoopla was for not, however, as Jackson suffered an ankle injury in the first quarter after carrying the ball three times for one yard. Marcus Allen picked up the slack in the backfield after his fellow Heisman Trophy winning running mate went down. He responded by leading all ball carriers with 60 yards, and scored his team's lone touchdown on a 3-yard run. Chris Bahr added a 23-yard field goal to complete the Raiders' scoring. Even though he fell victim to three interceptions and four sacks, Marc Wilson had another fine performance with 22 completions out of 38 attempts for 339 yards.[14]

14. Dec. 20: The Silver and Black was handed their ninth loss, which ensured them of a losing season for the first time since 1981, and the first since moving to Los Angeles. The Cleveland Browns were responsible for the Raiders' lock on a sub-.500 record with a 24–17 victory. This win snapped a seven-game losing streak to the Raiders dating back to 1974, which included two playoffs encounters. The Raiders opened the scoring in the first quarter on a 39-yard Chris Bahr field goal. The Browns then built a 24–3 lead, but Los Angeles fought back hard, and made Cleveland sweat near the end. In the fourth quarter, defensive back Stacey Toran returned an interception 48 yards for a score, and James Lofton caught a 28-yard pass from Marc Wilson with 1:51 left on the clock to come within seven points. Cleveland's Earnest Byner had a big day with 127 rushing yards, and he sealed the win with a 21-yard gain on third down with 1:24 left in the game.[15]

15. Dec. 27: Los Angeles finished at 5–10 for their worst record since 1962 with the help of a 6–3 loss to the Chicago Bears.

Chicago's legendary running back, Walter Payton, played in his final regular season game, and led all ball carriers with 82 yards. After 13 seasons, Payton retired as the NFL's all-time rushing leader. Despite the presence of two all-time great runners in Payton and Marcus Allen, this game proved to be a battle between kickers. Chris Bahr put the Raiders up with a 48-yard field goal in the first quarter, but it was Chicago's Kevin Butler who won the duel with three-pointers coming from 38 and 30 yards away. Bahr also missed two long-range attempts from over 40 yards. This game also marked the end of Tom Flores' Raiders coaching career after nine seasons at the helm.[16]

Individual Statistics and Roster

Head Coach: Tom Flores
Assistant Coaches: Sam Boghosian, Willie Brown, Sam Gruneisen, Larry Kennan, Earl Leggett, Bob Mischak, Terry Robiskie, Joe Scannella, Art Shell, Charlie Sumner, Tom Walsh, Jimmy Warren, Ray Willsey
1987 Regular Season Record: 5–10
4th Place AFC Western Division
Scored 301 points to rank 17th out of 28 teams
Allowed 289 points to rank 8th

STARTERS — OFFENSE

QB — Marc Wilson: Active for 15 games and started in 7. Completed 152 of 266 pass attempts for 2,070 yards, 12 TD, and 8 INT. Rushed for 91 yards on 17 carries.
HB — Marcus Allen: Active for and started in 12 games. Rushed for 754 yards on 200 carries and 5 TD, had 57 receptions for 410 yards, and completed 1 of 2 pass attempts for 23 yards.
FB — Bo Jackson: Active for 7 games and started in 5. Rushed for 554 yards on 81 carries and 4 TD. Had 16 receptions for 136 yards and 2 TD.
WR — Mervyn Fernandez: Active for and started in 7 games. Had 14 receptions for 236 yards.
WR — James Lofton: Active for and started in12 games. Had 41 receptions for 880 yards and 5 TD, and 1 rush for 1 yard.
TE — Todd Christensen: Active for and started in 12 games. Had 47 receptions for 663 yards and 2 TD.
LT — Brian Holloway: Active for 12 games and started in 8.
LG — Bill Lewis: Active for 8 games and started in 6.
C — Don Mosebar: Active for and started in 12 games.
RG — Dean Miraldi: Active for and started in10 games.
RT — John Clay: Active for and started in 10 games.

RESERVE OFFENSIVE PLAYERS

Carl Aikens (WR): Active for and started in 3 games. Had 8 receptions for 134 yards and 3 TD, and 1 rush for 1 yard.
Barry Black (G): Active for 3 games and started in 2.
Jim Browne (RB): Active for 2 games and started in 1.
Rick Calhoun (RB): Active for 3 games. Rushed for 36 yards on 7 carries, had 1 reception for 17 yards, 8 punt returns for 92 yards, and 9 kickoff returns for 217 yards.
Bruce Davis (T/G): Active for and started in 4 games.
Andy Dickerson (G): Active for 1 game.
Paul Dufault (C): Active for 1 game.
Craig Ellis (RB): Active for 3 games and started in 1. Had 33 rushes for 138 yards and 2 TD, and 5 receptions for 39 yards.
Vince Evans (QB): Active for and started in 3 games. Completed 39 of 83 pass attempts for 630 yards, 5 TD and 4 INT. Rushed for 144 yards on 11 carries and 1 TD.
Vince Gamache (P): Active for 3 games, and had 13 punts for a 39.9 average.

John Gesek (G/C): Active for 3 games and started in 1.
Charley Hannah (G/T): Active for and started in 5 games.
David Hardy (K): Active for 2 games and attempted 1 field goal.
Frank Hawkins (RB): Active for 2 games and started in 1. Rushed for 24 yards on 4 carries, and had 1 reception for 6 yards.
Jessie Hester (WR): Active for 10 games and had 1 reception for 30 yards.
Rusty Hilger (QB): Active for and started in 5 games. Completed 55 of 106 pass attempts for 706 yards, 2 TD, and 6 INT. Rushed for 8 yards on 8 carries.
Ethan Horton (TE/RB): Active for 4 games and started in 2. Rushed for 95 yards on 31 carries, and had 3 receptions for 44 yards and 1 TD.
Trey Junkin (TE/LB): Active for 12 games and started in 1. Had 2 receptions for 15 yards.
Greg Lathan (WR): Active for 3 games and had 5 receptions for 98 yards.
Zeph Lee (RB/DB): Active for 2 games.
Wade Lockett (WR): Active for 2 games.
Mickey Marvin (G): Active for 1 game.
Chris McLemore (RB): Active for 3 games.
Vance Mueller (RB): Active for 12 games. Rushed for 175 yards on 37 carries and 1 TD. Had 11 receptions for 95 yards and 27 kickoff returns for 588 yards.
Andy Parker (TE): Active for 12 games.
Mario Perry (TE): Active for 3 games and started in 2. Had 1 reception for 3 yards and 1 TD.
David Pyles (T): Active for 2 games.
Shawn Regent (C): Active for and started in 3 games.
Chris Riehm (G/T): Active for 1 game.
Steve Smith (RB): Active for 7 games and started in 3. Rushed for 18 yards on 5 carries, and had 3 receptions for 46 yards.
Steve Strachan (RB): Active for 11 games and started in 3. Rushed for 108 yards on 28 carries, and had 4 receptions for 42 yards.
John Tautolo (G): Active for and started in 3 games.
Dwight Wheeler (T/C/G): Active for 4 games and started in 1.
Ron Wheeler (TE): Active for 3 games and started in 1. Had 3 receptions for 61 yards.
Bruce Wilkerson (T/G): Active for 11 games and started in 5.
David Williams (WR): Active for 3 games and started in 2. Had 4 receptions for 104 yards.
Dokie Williams (WR): Active for 11 games and started in 5. Had 21 receptions for 330 yards and 5 TD, and 14 kickoff returns for 221 yards.
Ricky Williams (RB): Active for 1 game.
Chris Woods (WR): Active for 9 games and started in 1. Had 1 reception for 14 yards, 26 punt returns for 189 yards, and 3 kickoff returns for 55 yards.
Scott Woolf (QB): Active for 1 game.
Steve Wright (T/G/TE): Active for 9 games and started in 6.
Jon Zogg (G): Active for 1 game.

STARTERS — DEFENSE

DE — Howie Long: Active for and started in 14 games. Had 4 sacks and 2 fumble recoveries.
DE — Sean Jones: Active for and started in 12 games. Had 6 sacks and 2 fumble recoveries.
NT — Bill Pickel: Active for 12 games and started in 11. Had 1 sack and 2 fumble recoveries.
LOLB — Linden King: Active for 12 games and started in 8. Had 4 sacks, 1 INT, and 1 fumble recovery.
LILB — Matt Millen: Active for and started in 12 games. Had 1 sack, 1 INT, and 1 kickoff return for 0 yards.
RILB — Jerry Robinson: Active for and started in 12 games. Had 4 sacks.
ROLB — Rod Martin: Active for and started in 12 games. Had 3 sacks.
CB — Lionel Washington: Active for 11 games and started in 10.
CB — Mike Haynes: Active for 8 games and started in 7. Had 2 INT.
SS — Stacey Toran: Active for and started in 12 games. Had 3 INT, 1 TD, and 1 fumble recovery.
FS — Vann McElroy: Active for and started in 12 games. Had 4 INT and 1 TD.

RESERVE DEFENSIVE PLAYERS

Rick Ackerman (NT/T): Active for 3 games and started in 2. Had 1 sack and 1 fumble recovery.

Stefon Adams (DB): Active for 9 games, had 1 INT, 5 punt returns for 39 yards, and 3 kickoff returns for 61 yards.

Eddie Anderson (DB): Active for 13 games and started in 3. Had 1 INT and 1 fumble recovery.

Jeff Barnes (LB): Active for 7 games.

Brian Belway (E): Active for 1 game.

Ron Brown (LB): Active for 3 games, had 2 sacks and 1 fumble recovery.

Keith Browner (LB): Active for 1 game.

Bob Buczkowski (E): Active for 2 games and had 1 sack.

Darryl Byrd (LB): Active for 3 games.

Chetti Carr (DB): Active for 2 games.

Ted Chapman (E): Active for 2 games, started in 1, and had 1 fumble recovery.

Joe Cormier (LB): Active for 2 games, started in 1, and had 1 sack.

James Davis (DB): Active for 12 games and started in 1. Had 1 sack, 1 fumble recovery, and 1 punt return for 0 yards.

Jim Ellis (LB): Active for 3 games and started in 2.

Ron Fellows (DB): Active for 12 games and started in 2. Had 2 punt returns for 19 yards.

Ron Foster (DB): Active for 3 games and started in 2. Had 1 kickoff return for 12 yards.

Rick Goltz (E): Active for and started 1 game.

Darryl Goodlow (LB): Active for 2 games.

Phil Grimes (E): Active for 2 games.

Lance Harkey (DB): Active for 2 games, had 2 punt returns for 17 yards and 1 kickoff return for 20 yards.

Rob Harrison (DB): Active for 2 games and started in 1. Had 2 receptions for 18 yards and 9 kickoff returns for 49 yards.

Greg Hill (DB): Active for and started 2 games.

Rod Hill (DB): Active for 4 games and started in 3.

Leonard Jackson (LB): Active for and started 1 game.

Jamie Kimmel (LB): Active for 15 games and had 1 fumble recovery.

Reggie McKenzie (LB): Active for 10 games and started on 5.

Dan McMillen (E): Active for and started 1 game. Had 1 sack.

Mike Noble (LB): Active for and started 1 game. Had 1 fumble recovery.

Mike Rodriguez (LB): Active for 1 game.

Sam Seale (DB): Active for 12 games and started in 5. Had 1 fumble recovery.

Malcolm Taylor (E): Active for 12 games and started in 3. Had 3 sacks.

Willie Teal (DB): Active for 1 game.

Tony Tillmon (DB): Active for 3 games and started in 1.

Greg Townsend (E/LB/T/NT): Active for 13 games and started in 1. Had 8 sacks.

Ronnie Washington (LB): Active for 2 games and started in 1. Had 1 sack and returned 1 kickoff for 0 yards.

Demise Williams (DB): Active for 1 game.

Mitch Willis (NT/T): active for 10 games.

KICKING/PUNTING

K — Chris Bahr: Active for 13 games. Made 19 of 29 field goal attempts and 27 of 28 extra point kicks for 84 points.

P — Stan Talley: Active for 12 games. Punted 56 times for a 40.7 average.

1988 Season Review

1. Sept. 4: With a new head coach, a new offensive scheme, six new starters on offense, and the 1987 Heisman Trophy winner Tim Brown on their roster, the Raiders took the season opener, 24–13, over the San Diego Chargers on a smoldering 108 degree day. Rookie Tim Brown immediately made his presence felt by returning his first kickoff 97 yards for a touchdown. Another former Heisman recipient, Marcus Allen, gave the home crowd some added excitement by leading all ball carriers with 88 yards and two touchdown runs (11 yards and 1 yard). The defense recorded five sacks, and Chris Bahr pitched in with a 25-yard field goal to help the Raiders snap a three-game losing streak carried over from the horrific '87 campaign.[1]

2. Sept. 11: Houston Oilers' running back Allen Pinkett started in place of the injured Mike Rozier, and in the end, he led all ball carriers with 78 yards, and scored the winning touchdown with 31 seconds left in the game. The Raiders jumped out to a 28–14 second quarter advantage on a 1-yard run by Marcus Allen, and three Steve Beuerlein passes to Willie Gault (42 yards), Tim Brown (4 yards), and Steve Smith (9 yards). Houston rallied, taking a 31–28 fourth quarter lead, until Marcus Allen put Los Angeles back on top with his second 1-yard run. Two-and-a-half minutes later, Pinkett crushed the Raiders' hopes by going over the goal line from six yards out to give the Oilers a 37–35 victory to take back to the Lone Star State. The Raiders' defense had to put together a make shift secondary after injuries to Terry McDaniel, Vann McElroy, and Lionel Washington depleted the secondary. Defensive lineman par-excellence Howie Long stepped up to help the battered unit all he could by getting two quarterback sacks, an interception, and forced a fumble.[2]

3. Sept. 18: The battle of Los Angeles put the Raiders at 1–2, while the Rams remained undefeated with a 22–17 win. The game was tied at 10–10 in the third quarter until Rams' linebacker Kevin Greene sacked Steve Beuerlein in the end zone for a safety. Beuerlein was sacked a total of nine times, due partly to playing behind an offensive line depleted by injuries and the trade of tackle Jim Lachey 15 days earlier for quarterback Jay Schroeder. Lachey's replacement, Don Mosebar, was out with a severely sprained ankle, as was center Bill Lewis. Adding to the woes were nine penalties called mostly due to the inexperience of the make shift offensive line. Despite all this, Beuerlein still threw for 375 yards and two touchdowns to Marcus Allen (30 yards) and Tim Brown (49 yards). A 29-yard Chris Bahr field goal rounded out the scoring for the Silver and Black. The Rams wrapped up the win with a 54-yard pass from Jim Everett to Aaron Cox with two minutes remaining in the game.[3]

4. Sept. 26: The Raiders Monday Night Football magic was definitely out in force after they fell behind by 24 points, only to rally in overtime for a 30–27 win against the Denver Broncos. Denver's Mile High Stadium was regarded as one of the toughest place to come into and win, let alone after trailing by 24 points and facing the many skills of quarterback John Elway. The Raiders faced these adversities and fought their way back. The comeback started with Jay Schroeder throwing two touchdown passes to Steve Smith from 40 and 42 yards in the third quarter. Chris Bahr then kicked a 28-yard field goal, which was followed by a Marcus Allen 4-yard run. Bahr's conversion tied it at 24–24. Rich Karlis put the Broncos back on top with a 25-yard field goal, but Bahr matched his kicking counterpart by nailing a 44-yarder with four seconds left in regulation to force overtime. Filling in for the injured Stacey Toran, safety Zeph Lee joined the ranks of Raiders heroes on this night by intercepting an Elway pass and returned it 20 yards to the Denver 31-yard line.

With 2:25 left in overtime, Bahr sealed one of the Silver and Black's greatest comebacks with a 35-yard field goal. This win was the first for quarterback Jay Schroeder in a Raiders uniform, and the first for Mike Shanahan against his old team. The win also placed Los Angeles in a first place tie in the AFC Western Division along with Seattle and San Diego.[4]

5. Oct. 2: The Cincinnati Bengals brought the Raiders back to Earth following an exciting, 45–21, come-from-behind win. The Bengals remained the only unbeaten team as they ripped the Los Angeles defense for 496 total yards. The AFC's top-rated passer, Boomer Esiason, had a field day against a depleted defense missing three starters from the secondary by throwing for 332 yards and three touchdowns. Jay Schroeder threw two scoring strikes for Los Angeles, with the first going to Tim Brown (65 yards), and Mervyn Fernandez (24 yards). Schroeder added a 5-yard touchdown run in the losing effort.[5]

6. Oct. 9: The downward spiral continued for Los Angeles, as the Miami Dolphins beat them, 24–14. Miami became the third consecutive team to jump out to an early lead and held a 24–0 halftime advantage. With this win the Dolphins ended a six-game losing streak to the Raiders dating back to 1979. Los Angeles played a sloppy game. Jay Schroeder was intercepted four times, and there were five turnovers that allowed Miami to get 17 of their points. Schroeder did manage to connect on scoring passes to Mervyn Fernandez (7 yards) and Steve Strachan (13 yards). It seemed like everything was going wrong for the Raiders, whether it was the use of new quarterbacks, an inexperienced offensive line, or injuries. Howie Long hurt his right calf muscle, Marcus Allen was out with a broken bone in his left wrist, and Jerry Robinson, Willie Gault, and center Bill Lewis also sustained injuries.[6]

7. Oct. 16: Bo Jackson hung up his baseball spikes for the season and replaced them with cleats. The Kansas City Royals' outfielder joined the Raiders just in time to play the Chiefs in front 78,516, which was the biggest crowd in Kansas City's Arrowhead Stadium in 16 years. Jackson did not let down the huge throng, as he gained a game-high 70 yards rushing and scored on a 1-yard run in a 27–17 Los Angeles win. Also finding their way into the end zone for the Raiders were Marcus Allen (1-yard run), Steve Smith (1-yard run), and Trey Junkin (4-yard pass from Steve Beuerlein). Beuerlein took over at quarterback when coach Shanahan pulled Jay Schroeder due to lack of production after completing only two of 12 pass attempts. Marcus Allen tried

The pride of the trench warriors, Hall of Fame defensive lineman Howie Long, looks to break free from a blocker to wreak havoc on opposing ball carriers and quarterbacks. Shown here in action on October 2, 1988, against the Cincinnati Bengals at the Los Angeles Memorial Coliseum (AP Photo/NFL Photos).

to play as long as he could with a cast on his wrist, but had to come out when the pain got to bad. The defense chipped in by holding the Kansas City running game to 93 yards, and recorded four sacks. Defensive back Vann McElroy returned from injury and celebrated the occasion by intercepting two passes. The win put the Raiders at 3–4, while the Chiefs fell to 1-5-1.[7]

8. Oct. 23: Massive 260-pound fullback Craig "Iron Head"

Heyward erased a 6–3 lead with a 73-yard touchdown run, and the New Orleans Saints went on to win their seventh game of the season, 20–6. The Raiders' lone points came on an 85-yard pass from Jay Schroeder to Mervyn Fernandez, but Chris Bahr missed on the extra point try. Fernandez finished the game with four receptions for 155 yards. Marcus Allen also did well in the losing cause by rushing for 102 yards. Allen carried the full load of the backfield despite his damaged wrist when Bo Jackson left the game with a pulled hamstring after two plays in which he gained 45 yards on the ground. The team also lost guard Charley Hannah for the season with a broken ankle. At the halfway mark of the '88 campaign, the Silver and Black were 3–5 and remarkably only one game off the AFC West leadership, which was shared by Denver and Seattle.[8]

9. Oct. 30: The Kansas City Chiefs once again provided fodder for the Raiders, as the Silver and Black won, 17–10, to sweep their top rivals in a season series for the first time since 1984. Despites the win, the massive Los Angeles Coliseum looked virtually vacant, as only 36,103 turned out to produce the smallest home crowd the Raiders played in front of since moving to Los Angeles. Jay Schroeder continued to struggle at getting comfortable with the Raiders' scheme of things, and 23-year-old Steve Beuerlein came to the rescue. Playing behind an offensive line that seemed to be jelling, Beuerlein lit up the skies with 18 completions out of 29 attempts for 248 yards. Bo Jackson and Marcus Allen provided a balanced offensive attack with exceptional running. Jackson ran for a game-high 80 yards, and scored on a 22-yard run. Allen rushed for 70 yards, and scored on a 1-yard run. Chris Bahr added a 42-yard field goal to complete the scoring. Allen's touchdown was the 78th of his Raiders career, which gave him the most in team history up to that time, surpassing Fred Biletnikoff. James Lofton also achieved a career milestone by recording his 590th reception to tie him for eighth place on the NFL's all-time list with Harold Carmichael.[9]

10. Nov. 6: The AFC West saw a bottleneck at the top, as Denver, Seattle, and Los Angeles were all tied for the division leadership at 5–5. The Raiders achieved their piece of the summit with a 13–3 win over San Diego. The game was a defensive gridlock, with the score tied at 3–3 in the fourth quarter. Los Angeles finally broke through early in the quarter when Steve Beuerlein connected with Trey Junkin for the game's lone touchdown from seven yards out. Chris Bahr later added field goals from 36 and 29 yards.[10]

11. Nov. 13: The Raiders made it three in a row in another defensive struggle, this time with a 9–3 victory over the San Francisco 49ers. Thanks to a tough defensive effort by the Silver and Black, the 49ers failed to score a touchdown for the first time in two years, and were held to a mere 219 yards of total offense. The top defensive play by the Raiders occurred when they stopped the great wide receiver Jerry Rice on a fourth down reverse with just under two minutes left in the game on the Los Angeles 20 to end San Francisco's chances. The 49ers also did a superb job on the Los Angeles offense, preventing them from crossing the goal line as well. However, thanks to a balanced running attack from Bo Jackson (85 yards), and Marcus Allen (58 yards), the Raiders were able to get close enough for Chris Bahr to connect on three field goals from 45, 50, and 19 yards, to secure the win. The win kept the Raiders in a three-way tie with Denver and Seattle in the AFC Western Division.[11]

12. Nov. 20: The deadlock atop the AFC West continued, as all three leaders lost in week 12. The Raiders lost a golden opportunity to seize control of the division leadership by dropping a 12–6 decision to the Atlanta Falcons. Chris Bahr kicked two field goals from 42 and 31 yards to tie the game at 6–6 in the fourth quarter. Eight minutes later, disaster struck in the form of rookie linebacker, Aundray Bruce. He shot through Steve Beuerlein's protection and blasted the quarterback on the Los Angeles 40-yard line for his second sack of the game. The massive jolt caused Beuerlein to fumble, and Bruce recovered the ball for Atlanta. Atlanta's offense took over after the fumble on the Los Angeles 12-yard line, and four plays later, John Settle sealed the Raiders' fate with a 1-yard touchdown run that proved to be the clincher with 4:07 left in the game. The Falcons played like champions despite a 4–8 record. Their defense clamped down, and held the Raiders to 65 rushing yards on 20 carries, and only 147 through the air.[12]

13. Nov. 28: The Raiders mystique on Monday Night Football was no match for the Kingdome jinx suffered by the Silver and Black on previous trips to the Emerald City of Seattle. The jinx proved once again too powerful, and the Seahawks sent the Raiders home with a 35–27 defeat. The loss dropped the Raiders out of the first place tie now shared by Seattle and Denver. Seattle's quarterback Dave Krieg passed for five touchdowns, each going to a different receiver. When Krieg was not cutting through the defense by air, the running duo of Curt Warner and John L. Williams punished the Raiders on the ground. The Los Angeles defense was stingy against the run all season long, as they allowed a mere 129 yards per game leading into week 13. On this night, however, Warner and Williams both went over the century mark. Despite Seattle's offensive prowess against them, the Raiders did have their chances. Seattle committed five turnovers, with three of them going for touchdowns by Los Angeles. Greg Townsend recovered a fumble in the end zone caused when Bill Pickel sacked Krieg in the end zone. Tim Brown caught a 49-yard pass from Steve Beuerlein, and Steve Smith scored on the 4-yard run. Chris Bahr added two field goals both from 46-yards. Tim Brown showed why he was one of the top draft picks by catching four passes of 114 yards, and had another 189 yards on kickoff and punt returns. On one kickoff return, Brown raced 95 yards to the Seattle three, and Bo Jackson scored from there, but the six-pointer was nullified by a holding penalty. On another occasion, the Raiders were trailing by only one point with 29 seconds left in the half, but a field goal attempt missed its mark.[13]

14. Dec. 4: The Raiders were back in the hunt for a division title thanks to a 21–20 squeaker over Denver. Los Angeles jumped out to a 21–0 third quarter lead and held off a late rally to earn a season sweep over the Broncos for the first time since 1985. Bo Jackson ran for the opening touchdown from four yards out. Steve Smith extended the Los Angeles lead to 14–0 when he caught a 45-yard pass from Jay Schroeder. In what turned out to be the winning touchdown also proved to be the most exciting of the three scored by the Raiders. In the third quarter, Denver had driven deep into Raiders territory. On second down, John Elway attempted a short pass that defensive end Greg Townsend intercepted at the Los Angeles 14. He then took his 6–3, 250 pound frame on an 86-yard trek across the Los Angeles Coliseum turf while 69,201 fans cheered approval for what was his second touch-

down in as many weeks. Chris Bahr added the extra point, which provided the Silver and Black with the slim advantage. With two games remaining, the Raiders, Broncos, and Seahawks were once again tied for first place in the AFC West with 7–7 records.[14]

15. Dec. 11: A trip to Buffalo cost the Raiders a share of the top spot in the division, as the Bills sent Los Angeles back to the west coast as 37–21 losers. With the wind chill knocking the temperature below zero, the Bills rode to victory on the shoulders of their running game. With the offensive line blowing open the running lanes all day, Buffalo's ground attack ate up 255 yards on 48 carries, with Thurman Thomas leading the way with 106 yards. The Raiders were never really in this game, and fell to 7–8, while Buffalo improved to 12–3, which tied them with the Chicago Bears for the best record in the league. The Raiders received their points on two Steve Smith touchdowns (1-yard run, and a 6-yard pass from Jay Schroeder), and a 43-yard pass from Schroeder to Tim Brown. The Seattle Seahawks took over sole possession of first place in the division with Los Angeles and Denver tied for second. A visit by the Seahawks in the regular season finale would decide the fate of the '88 Raiders. A win would earn them the AFC West title due to having a better record against division foes.[15]

16. Dec. 18: The jinx that plagued the Raiders when facing Seattle did not seem to be restricted to the Kingdome. Even in the friendly confines of the Los Angeles Coliseum, the Silver and Black appeared to be cursed by the Seahawks, and due to it, lost out on their bid for a trip to the playoffs for the first time in three years. In a wild offensive shootout, Seattle prevailed, 43–37, with the Seahawks ringing up 490 total yards and Los Angeles 441. Dave Krieg did most of the damage for Seattle, completing 19 of 32 pass attempts for 410 yards and four touchdowns. Norm Johnson added five field goals. Jay Schroeder matched Krieg pass for pass, and finished with just as impressive numbers. He hit on 22 of 49 attempts for 354 yards and three touchdowns. His scoring strikes went to Willie Gault (51 yards), Steve Smith (4 yards), and Mervyn Fernandez (54 yards). Unfortunately, Schroeder's four incomplete pass attempts from the Seattle 45 in the final minute of play proved to be the demise of the Raiders on this day and put an end to the Raiders' quest for a division crown. Tim Brown added a 2-yard run, and Chris Bahr booted field goals from 26, 28, and 24 yards to give Los Angeles their other points in the season finale.[16]

Individual Statistics and Roster

Head Coach: Mike Shanahan
Assistant Coaches: Willie Brown, Alex Gibbs, Sam Gruneisen, Earl Leggett, Nick Nicolau, Terry Robiskie, Pete Rodriguez, Joe Scannella, Art Shell, Charlie Sumner, Tom Walsh, Jimmy Warren
1988 Regular Season Record: 7–9
3rd Place AFC Western Division
Scored 325 points to rank 16th out of 28 teams
Allowed 369 points to rank 23rd

STARTERS — OFFENSE

QB — Jay Schroeder: Active for 9 games and started in 8. Completed 113 of 256 pass attempts for 1,839 yards, 13 TD and 13 INT. **Led the NFL in yards per pass completion (16.3).** Rushed for 109 yards on 29 carries and 1 TD.

HB — Marcus Allen: Active for and started in 15 games. Rushed for 831 yards on 223 carries and 7 TD. Had 34 receptions for 303 yards, 1 TD, and completed 1 of 2 pass attempts for 21 yards.
FB — Bo Jackson: Active for 10 games and started in 9. Rushed for 580 yards on 136 carries and 3 TD. Had 9 receptions for 79 yards.
WR — Tim Brown: Active for 16 games and started in 9. Had 43 receptions for 725 yards and 5 TD, rushed for 50 yards on 14 carries and 1 TD, returned 49 punts for 444 yards, and 41 kickoffs for **1,098** yards and 1 TD. **Also led the NFL in all-purpose yards (2,317), average gain per kickoff return (26.8), combined kickoff/punt returns (90), and combined yards on kickoff/punt returns (1,542).**
WR — James Lofton: Started in 16 games. Had 28 receptions for 549 yards.
TE — Andy Parker: Active for 16 games and started in 11. Had 4 receptions for 33 yards.
LT — Don Mosebar: Active for and started in 13 games.
LG — Charley Hannah: Active for and started in 8 games.
C — Bill Lewis: Active for and started in 14 games.
RG — Bruce Wilkerson: Started in 16 games.
RT — Rory Graves: Active for 16 games and started in 15.

RESERVE OFFENSIVE PLAYERS

Steve Beuerlein (QB): Active for 10 games and started in 8. Completed 105 of 238 pass attempts for 1,643 yards, 8 TD and 7 INT. Rushed for 35 yards on 30 carries and had 1 reception for 21 yards.
Todd Christensen (TE): Active for 7 games and started in 5. Had 15 receptions for 190 yards.
Mervyn Fernandez (WR): Active for 16 games and started in 1. Had 31 receptions for 805 yards and 4 TD, and rushed 1 time for 9 yards. **Led the NFL in yards gained per reception (26.0).**
Mike Freeman (C/G): Active for 2 games.
Willie Gault (WR): Active for 15 games and started in 6. Had 16 receptions for 392 yards and 2 TD, and rushed 1 time for 4 yards.
John Gesek (G/C): Active for 12 games and started in 6.
Brian Holloway (T/G): Active for 2 games.
Trey Junkin (TE/LB): Active for 16 games and started in 1. Had 4 receptions for 25 yards and 2 TD.
Jim Lachey (T): Active for 1 game and started.
Zeph Lee (RB/DB): Active for 8 games, started in 1, and had 1 kickoff return for 0 yards.
Chris McLemore (RB): Active for 7 games.
Vance Mueller (RB): Active for 14 games and started in 1. Rushed for 60 yards on 17 carries, had 5 receptions for 63 yards, and 5 kickoff returns for 97 yards.
Chris Riehm (G/T): Active for 8 games and started in 4.
Steve Smith (RB): Active for 16 games and started in 6. Rushed for 162 yards on 38 carries and 3 TD. Had 26 receptions for 299 yards and 6 TD, and returned 3 kickoffs for 46 yards.
Steve Strachan (RB): Active for 16 games. Rushed for 12 yards on 4 carries, and had 3 receptions for 19 yards and 1 TD.
Dwight Wheeler (T/C/G): Active for 8 games.
Chris Woods (WR): Active for 2 games and returned 1 kickoff 20 yards.
Steve Wright (T/G/TE): Active for 15 games and started in 3.

STARTERS — DEFENSE

DE — Greg Townsend: Active for 16 games and started in 11. Had 11 sacks, 1 INT, 1 TD, 1 fumble recovery and 1 TD.
DE — Mike Wise: Active for 16 games and started in 14. Had 5 sacks and 2 fumble recoveries.
NT — Bill Pickel: Started in 16 games. Had 5 sacks and 1 fumble recovery.
LOLB — Linden King: Active for 14 games and started in 13. Had 1 sack.
LILB — Matt Millen: Active for 16 games and started in 15. Had 1 sack and 1 fumble recovery.
RILB — Jerry Robinson: Active for and started in 15 games. Had 2 sacks and 1 fumble recovery.

ROLB — Rod Martin: Active for 16 games and started in 13.

CB — Ron Fellows: Active for 14 games and started in 10. Had 2 INT and 2 fumble recoveries.

CB — Mike Haynes: Started in 16 games. Had 3 INT and 1 fumble recovery.

SS — Russell Carter: Active for 15 games and started in 12. Had 2 sacks, 1 fumble recovery, and 1 kickoff return for 14 yards.

FS — Vann McElroy: Active for 12 games and started in 11. Had 3 INT and 1 fumble recovery.

RESERVE DEFENSIVE PLAYERS

Stefon Adams (DB): Active for 14 games, had 3 fumble recoveries, 6 punt returns for 45 yards, 8 kickoff returns for 132 yards, and recorded 1 safety.

Eddie Anderson (DB): Active for 16 games, started in 5, and had 2 INT.

Ron Brown (LB): Active of 16 games.

Scott Davis (T/E/LB): Active for 15 games, started in 2, and had 5 sacks.

David Greenwood (DB): Active for 2 games.

Howie Long (E): Active for 7 games and started in 6. Had 3 sacks and 1 INT.

Milt McColl (LB): Active for 15 games.

Terry McDaniel (DB): Active and started in 2 games.

Reggie McKenzie (LB): Active for 16 games and started in 3. Had 1 sack and 1 INT.

Dennis Price (DB): Active for 12 games, started in 4, and had 2 INT.

Malcolm Taylor (E): Active for 15 games, started in 3, and had 1 sack.

Stacey Toran (DB): Active for 12 games, started in 4, had 2 sacks and returned 2 kickoffs for 0 yards.

Norwood Vann (LB): Active for 1 game.

Lionel Washington (DB): Active for 12 games and had 1 INT.

Mitch Willis (NT/T): Active for 1 game.

KICKING/PUNTING

K — Chris Bahr: Active for 16 games. Made 18 of 29 field goal attempts and 37 of 39 extra point kicks for 91 points.

P — Jeff Gossett: Active for 16 games. Punted 91 times for a 41.8 average.

1989 Season Review

1. Sept. 10: The Raiders won their eighth opening day game of the decade with a 40–14 blowout over the San Diego Chargers. Jay Schroeder won the starting quarterback job, but on the very first play, he was body-slammed to the turf by San Diego's Leslie O'Neil and sustained a separated left shoulder. Schroeder continued under center for the inaugural drive, and he drove the Raiders to a touchdown by connecting with running back Vance Mueller on a 26-yard scoring strike. Mueller added a 1-yard touchdown run in the fourth quarter for the Raiders' final tally. Steve Beuerlein relieved Schroeder after that scoring drive, and did an exceptional job. He completed 15 of 22 pass attempts for 206 yards and two touchdowns. On the receiving end of Beuerlein's six-pointers were Mervyn Fernandez from four yards, and Willie Gault from 29. Gault had a great day with four receptions for 131 yards. Marcus Allen ran for a 1-yard touchdown, Jeff Jaeger kicked a 22-yard field goal, and the defense recorded a safety in this overwhelming victory.[1]

2. Sept. 17: The Kansas City Chiefs were on the verge of losing their third straight game to the Raiders, but then the Silver and Black fell apart in this, the 60th meeting between these two fierce rivals. With a 19–17 advantage, Los Angeles was driving for

more points in the fourth quarter when a Jay Schroeder pass was intercepted on the Kansas City 13-yard line. The Chiefs then went 87 yards and scored what turned out to be the winning points on a Christian Okoye 1-yard run halfway through the quarter to give Kansas City a 24–19 victory. The Los Angeles defense gave Kansas City an early Christmas present by committing four penalties worth 60 yards on that winning drive. Before his crucial interception, Schroeder performed well even though his shoulder was still very tender. He completed 14 of 21 passes for 192 yards and two touchdowns. Mervyn Fernandez caught his first one from 25 yards, and Trey Junkin snagged the second from three yards out. Jeff Jaeger added two field goals from 39 and 40 yards. The Chiefs controlled the battle in the trenches, and used the power running of Okoye to wear down a hurting Los Angeles defensive line that had end Scott Davis out of action and perennial All-Pro Howie Long playing on an injured ankle.[2]

3. Sept. 24: The year before, the Raiders went into Denver, and after trailing by 24 points, rallied to win. In this 1989 visit to the Mile High City, it almost looked like history was going to repeat itself. The Broncos had built a 28–0 lead at the half, but with five minutes left in the game, Los Angeles fought back hard to make the score 28–21. Defensive back Lionel Washington got the Raiders started on the comeback trail with a 22-yard interception return for their first touchdown. Within five minutes the Raiders were once again in the end zone after Mervyn Fernandez caught a 75-yard pass from Jay Schroeder. The defense came through five minutes later when linebacker Linden King returned a fumble recovery 15 yards for a score. With time running out, Schroeder attempted a pass, but rookie safety Steve Atwater jumped up and came down with an interception on the Los Angeles 36 with 3:23 left in the fourth. Denver added a field goal for insurance, and the Broncos won, 31–21, to remain undefeated. Even though the Raiders gave a gallant effort, they hurt themselves throughout the game with two fumbled snaps, three interceptions, and 12 penalties that cost them 101 yards.[3]

4. Oct. 1: The Raiders had built a 17–7 lead through three quarters against the Seattle Seahawks. They achieved this by playing great defense, which included a 37-yard fumble recovery for a touchdown by Lionel Washington. On offense, Jay Schroeder was throwing well, and connected with Mervyn Fernandez for a 36-yard touchdown. Jeff Jaeger added a 45-yard field goal to give Los Angeles their ten-point advantage going into the fourth quarter. It was at this time that the Seattle Jinx rose up and put the whammy on the Raiders in their own stadium. The Seahawks stayed focused, and with help from a solid running game and inspired defense, they prevailed, 24–20, to knock Los Angeles into the AFC West basement with a 1–3 record. All Los Angeles could muster up after their ten-point lead was a 28-yard field goal from Jaeger. Curt Warner led all ball carriers with 102 yards, and got Seattle back in the game on a 6-yard run with 14:02 remaining. Brian Blades then gave the Seahawks the lead for good by catching a 19-yard pass from Dave Krieg. This game was costly for Los Angeles, as they lost defensive backs Vann McElroy and Lionel Washington both to pulled hamstrings, and offensive lineman Don Mosebar re-injured an already tender knee. This game also proved costly to head coach Mike Shanahan, who was fired two days after this game and replaced by Raiders great and Hall of Famer Art Shell. On a positive note, Mervyn Fernandez recorded

his second straight 100-yard receiving day with seven receptions for 113 yards, and Greg Townsend had two sacks and forced a fumble.[4]

5. Oct. 19: The Art Shell–era began against the New York Jets on the prime time extravaganza, Monday Night Football, in a matchup between cellar dwellers. Shell's Raiders were in last place in the AFC West, while the Jets resided at the bottom of the AFC East. The Jets suffered from a terrible offense and a poor secondary, and Los Angeles had the worst defense against the run. However, the Raiders' Monday Night magic was working well in Shell's debut, and the team gave their new mentor a 14–7 win. The defense rose up and held the Jets to only 80 yards rushing, which was the first time all season that the unit stopped an opponent from going over the century mark. After a scoreless first half, Los Angeles broke through in fine fashion. Jay Schroeder and Mervyn Fernandez attacked the weak New York secondary, with the end result being a 73-yard touchdown. Fernandez caught the ball near midfield, broke a tackle, and crossed the goal line seconds later for his fifth touchdown reception of the season. With the game tied in the fourth quarter, defensive back Eddie Anderson took it upon himself to give Shell his first win. Anderson intercepted Ken O'Brien on the Los Angeles 13 and raced 87 yards for the winning touchdown.[5]

6. Oct. 15: A 20–14 win over Kansas City helped the Silver and Black climb into a second place tie with Seattle in the AFC Western Division. Despite being ranked last in defense against the run, the Raiders held the ground pounding Christian "the Nigerian Nightmare" Okoye to only 52 yards. Coming into this game, Okoye was averaging close to 100 yards per game. After giving up close to 100 points in their first four games, the defense allowed a mere 21 in their next two under Shell. Bo Jackson was back in his football uniform, and did not waste time establishing himself on the football field. On only 11 carries, Jackson rushed for 85 yards and scored on a 2-yard run. Providing the team's other points were Vance Mueller (6-yard run), and Jeff Jaeger with two field goals from 24 and 50 yards.[6]

7. Oct. 22: Jay Schroeder and Steve Beuerlein each threw an interception, and the Philadelphia Eagles capitalized on them to hand Art Shell his first loss as a head coach by the slight margin of 10–7. Philadelphia quarterback Randall Cunningham turned the first interception into a 1-yard touchdown run, and Luis Zendejas' 34-yard field goal after the second interception proved to be the game winner. Willie Gault prevented the Raiders from being shutout when he caught a 24-yard pass from Beuerlein in the fourth quarter. Gault's touchdown was the first allowed by the Philadelphia defense in three games. Los Angeles had a chance to tie the game with two minutes remaining in regulation, but a field goal attempt by Jaeger went wide.[7]

8. Oct. 29: The Raiders returned to the .500 mark with a 37–24 win over the Washington Redskins. Mervyn Fernandez continued to make his name known among the league's top receivers by catching his sixth and seventh touchdown receptions of the season. Los Angeles' first two touchdowns came on passes from Steve Beuerlein to Fernandez, covering 18 and eight yards. The Raiders kept their offensive assault going, and took total control of the game, winning easily, 37–24. Beuerlein was forced from the game in the third quarter when he suffered a strained right knee. Jeff Jaeger kicked three field goals (26, 29, and 37 yards),

Bo Jackson busted loose on a 73-yard scoring jaunt, and made the Washington defense look clueless by running for 144 yards on just 19 carries. Eddie Anderson returned an interception 45 yards for his second touchdown of the year to complete the team's scoring. The Los Angeles defense did an excellent job by intercepting four passes, recording seven sacks, and holding the running game to 21 yards on 14 carries.[8]

9. Nov. 5: For the first time since opening day, the Raiders climbed above the .500 mark, beating the defending AFC champion Cincinnati Bengals, 28–7, to give Art Shell a 4–1 record since taking over the reins. Bo Jackson turned in a fantastic effort. In just his four game of the season, Jackson led all league runners for the week with 159 yards on 13 carries, which averaged out to 12 yards per carry. Over the course of his four games, Jackson gained 467 yards on 63 carries and scored four touchdowns. In this game against the Bengals, he scored Los Angeles' first two touchdowns. The first one came on a 7-yard run, and the second was from 92 yards, which set a team record for the longest run from scrimmage, surpassing the old record of 91 yards set by Jackson two years earlier against Seattle. Jay Schroeder started in place of the injured Steve Beuerlein at quarterback, and threw for 231 yards and two touchdowns. Vance Mueller (25 yards), and Willie Gault (84 yards) were on the receiving end of Schroeder's touchdown passes. The defense continued to play well, and completely abused the Cincinnati backfield. They sent the entire starting backfield to the sideline in the first half. Running back Eric Ball left with a bruised hip, his running mate James Brooks suffered bruised ribs, and quarterback Boomer Esiason had a bruised lung.[9]

10. Nov. 12: It was back to .500 for the Silver and Black when San Diego rallied for a 14–12 victory. Los Angeles took a 12–0 lead on four Jeff Jaeger field goals from 23, 36, 33, and 32 yards. San Diego's defense proved to be stingy of late when it came to giving up touchdowns. Over their previous eight games, the unit only gave up nine six-pointers, and continued the streak in this game. They also sacked Jay Schroeder three times. It was in the third quarter that the Chargers began their way back against the Raiders when the league's fastest player, Anthony Miller, used his world-class speed to ignite his team. After Jaeger's fourth field goal, Miller took the ensuing kickoff from his nine, and then flew down the field to close the gap to five points after the conversion. Tim Spencer scored the winning touchdown with just under nine minutes left in the game. Bo Jackson had his third 100-yard rushing performance in his fifth game when he ran for 103 yards.[10]

11. Nov. 19: The Houston Oilers were in the hunt for a playoff spot, and helped their chances by dropping the Raiders, 23–7. In the process of winning their third straight game, the Oilers shut down Bo Jackson, allowing him only 54 yards rushing. Steve Beuerlein returned to the starting lineup and did not do any better than Jackson against Houston's defense. Even though he did throw a 22-yard touchdown pass to Mike Dyal, that proved to be his highlight for the game, as he was intercepted three times and sacked four. The Raiders were able to generate a scant 74 yards on the ground and 169 through the air. The lone bright spot on offense came from Mervyn Fernandez, who caught five passes for 102 yards. Houston had no trouble moving the ball, rolling up 419 total yards.[11]

12. Nov. 26: The Raiders improved to 6–6 with a 24–21 win over the New England Patriots to remain in sole possession

of second place in the division. However, any hopes of winning the division where thwarted when the 10–2 Denver Broncos clinched the title. Los Angeles was still in the race for a Wild Card spot thanks to a Jeff Jaeger 32-yard field goal with just under six minutes left in the fourth quarter that broke a 21–21 tie. This was the first time that the second-year kicker booted a game winning three-pointer. Steve Beuerlein had a solid game despite his tender knee. He showed toughness throughout the game, refusing to buckle under even though he was sacked four times and faced constant pressure. He completed 15 out of 26 pass attempts and threw two touchdown passes. Mike Alexander caught a 12-yarder for his first-ever regular season touchdown, and Mervyn Fernandez snagged the other Beuerlein scoring strike from 13 yards out. Steve Smith added an 11-yard run for Los Angeles' final six-pointer. Bo Jackson led all ball carriers with 64 yards on the ground, while the defense only allowed the Patriots 30 yards rushing on 19 carries.[12]

13. Dec. 3: Los Angeles made it two in a row in front a huge home crowd of 87,560 by beating the Denver Broncos, 16–13, but it was not easy. The Broncos came into Los Angeles with an AFC-best 10–2 record, and outperformed the Raiders until the final eight minutes of regulation. Down, 13–6, midway through the fourth quarter, Steve Beuerlein connected with tight end Mike Dyal for a 67-yard touchdown. Dyal had a great game with four receptions for 134 yards. Following Jeff Jaeger's extra point kick, the game was tied at 13–13. Jaeger provided the Raiders with two field goals from 37 and 46 yards that helped them tie this game up. Denver had a chance to pull out a win in regulation. With 52 seconds left, and the ball on the Los Angeles 34-yard line, John Elway attempted a pass to Mark Jackson, but Lionel Washington stepped in front of Jackson for an interception that sent the game into overtime. In overtime, the Raiders moved from their own 29-yard line to the Denver six in six plays. Jaeger then booted the game-winning field goal from 26 yards with seven minutes expired from the clock. The win put Los Angeles at 7–6 and in a three-way tie for the second Wild Card position along with Cincinnati and Miami.[13]

14. Dec. 10: Bo Jackson ran for a game high 114 yards on 22 carries, but it was Marcus Allen who took the Raiders to an 8–6 record, and on the verge of a playoff berth. Jeff Jaeger had the Raiders up, 9–7, on field goals from 25, 30, and 48 yards, but the Phoenix Cardinals came back to take a 14–9 lead with five minutes left in the game. It was then that Allen added another heroic moment to his football resume. With 40 seconds remaining, Allen scored on a 1-yard run to give Los Angeles the win. Steve Beuerlein passed for 255 yards, and Mervyn Fernandez caught five passes for 119 yards. The defense only allowed 126 yards passing, and sacked Phoenix quarterback Gary Hogeboom five times. With two games to go, the Raiders were tied with Miami, and a half-game ahead of 7-6-1 Kansas City and Cleveland in the Wild Card race.[14]

15. Dec. 17: After three straight wins the Raiders fell, 23–17, in the dreaded Seattle Kingdome, where more often than not, the Silver and Black left defeated. Despite the loss, Los Angeles was still alive in the playoff race at 8–7. A win in this game would have clinched a trip to the post-season, and for a while, they were in control of this one on the strength of two Steve Beuerlein touchdown passes to Willie Gault (36 yards) and Trey Junkin (1

yard), plus a 19-yard Jeff Jaeger field goal. In the third quarter, the Raiders led by four points, but then Seattle came back. Quarterback Dave Krieg had a great game, hitting on 25 of 34 passes for 270 yards, and he put the Seahawks in the lead for good with a 13-yard pass to John L. Williams at the end of the third quarter. Norm Johnson added an insurance field goal in the fourth quarter to force the Raiders into a must win situation in their regular season finale against the New York Giants.[15]

16. Dec. 24: The playoffs were on the Raiders' Christmas list, but the New York Giants spoiled their holidays by thumping the Silver and Black, 34–17. Los Angeles held a 17–14 lead in the second quarter on two Steve Beuerlein touchdown passes to Ethan Horton (1 yard) and Mervyn Fernandez (30 yards), and a 42-yard field goal from Jeff Jaeger, which proved to be the last points scored by the Raiders in the 1980's. The Giants clamped down after trailing by three, then ran off twenty points to cruise to an easy win, and clinch the NFC Eastern Division title in the process. Los Angeles finished at 8–8, but made some positive strides under Art Shell's leadership. With the season looking lost at the time of his hiring, Shell posted a 7–5 record and the Raiders just missed the playoffs by one game.[16]

Individual Statistics and Roster

Head Coach: Mike Shanahan (four games), Art Shell (twelve games)
Assistant Coaches: Dave Adolph, Fred Biletnikoff, Alex Gibbs, Sam Gruneisen, Terry Robiskie, Pete Rodriguez, Joe Scannella, Art Shell, Jack Stanton, Bill Urbanik, Tom Walsh
1989 Regular Season Record: 8–8
3rd Place AFC Western Division
Scored 315 points to rank 18th out of 28 teams
Allowed 297 points to rank 10th

STARTERS — OFFENSE

QB — Jay Schroeder: Active for 11 games and started in 9. Completed 91 of 194 pass attempts for 1,550 yards, 8 TD and 13 INT. Rushed for 38 yards on 15 carries.
HB — Bo Jackson: Active for 11 games and started in 9. Rushed for 950 yards on 173 carries and 4 TD. Had 9 receptions for 69 yards.
FB — Steve Smith: Started in 16 games. Rushed for 471 yards on 117 carries and 1 TD. Had 19 receptions for 140 yards and 2 kickoff returns for 19 yards.
WR — Mervyn Fernandez: Active for 16 games and started in 13. Had 57 receptions for 1,069 yards and 9 TD. Rushed for 16 yards on 2 carries.
WR — Willie Gault: Started in 16 games. Had 28 receptions for 690 yards and 4 TD, and returned 1 kickoff 16 yards.
TE — Mike Dyal: Started in 16 games. Had 27 receptions for 499 yards and 2 TD.
LT — Rory Graves: Active for and started in 15 games.
LG — John Gesek: Started in 16 games.
C — Don Mosebar: Active for 12 games and started in 11.
RG — Steve Wisniewski: Active for and started in 15 games.
RT — Bruce Wilkerson: Started in 16 games.

RESERVE OFFENSIVE PLAYERS

Mike Alexander (WR): Active for 16 games, and had 15 receptions for 295 yards and 1 TD.
Marcus Allen (RB): Active for 8 games and started in 5. Rushed for 293 yards on 69 carries and 2 TD, and had 20 receptions for 191 yards.
Steve Beuerlein (QB): Active for 10 games and started in 7. Completed

108 of 217 pass attempts for 1,677 yards, 13 TD and 9 INT. Rushed for 39 yards on 16 carries.

Tim Brown (WR): Active for and started in 1 game. Had 1 reception for 8 yards, 4 punt returns for 43 yards, and 3 kickoff returns for 63 yards.

Bobby Joe Edmonds (RB): Active for 7 games, returned 16 punts for 168 yards and 14 kickoffs for 271 yards.

Vince Evans (QB): Active for 1 game, completed 2 of 2 pass attempts for 50 yards, and rushed for 16 yards on 1 carry.

Ethan Horton (TE/RB): Active for 16 games and started in 1. Had 4 receptions for 44 yards and 1 TD.

Trey Junkin (TE/LB): Active for 16 games, had 3 receptions for 32 yards and 2 TD, and returned 1 kickoff for 0 yards.

Vance Mueller (RB): Active for 16 games and started in 2. Rushed for 161 yards on 48 carries and 2 TD, and had 18 receptions for 240 yards and 2 TD. Returned 5 kickoffs 120 yards.

Kerry Porter (RB): Active for 16 games, and rushed for 54 yards on 13 carries.

Steve Strachan (RB): Active for 16 games.

Dan Turk (C/G): Active for 16 games, started in 4, and returned 1 kickoff 2 yards.

Timmie Ware (WR): Active for 13 games, and returned 4 kickoffs 86 yards.

Steve Wright (T/G/TE): Active for 16 games and started in 3.

STARTERS — DEFENSE

DE — Howie Long: Active for 14 games and started in 11. Had 5 sacks and 1 fumble recovery.

DE — Scott Davis: Active for 14 games and started in 13. Had 5 sacks and 1 fumble recovery.

NT — Bob Golic: Started in 16 games and had 3 sacks.

LOLB — Linden King: Active for 14 games and started in 13. Had 3 fumble recoveries and 1 TD.

LILB — Thomas Benson: Started in 16 games, and had 2 sacks, 2 INT and 2 fumble recoveries.

RILB — Jerry Robinson: Active for and started in 11 games. Had sack and 1 fumble recovery.

ROLB — Greg Townsend: Active for 16 games and started in 12. Had 10 sacks and 1 fumble recovery.

CB — Terry McDaniel: Active for 16 games and started in 15. Had 1 sack and 3 fumble recoveries.

CB — Lionel Washington: Started in 16 games, and had 3 INT, 1 TD, and 3 fumble recoveries.

SS — Mike Harden: Active for 15 games and started in 12. Had 2 INT, 3 fumble recoveries and 1 punt return for 11 yards.

FS — Eddie Anderson: Active for 15 games and started in 10. Had 5 INT and 2 TD.

RESERVE DEFENSIVE PLAYERS

Stefon Adams (DB): Active for 14 games, and had 1 fumble recovery, 1 safety, 19 punt returns for 156 yards, and 22 kickoff returns for 425 yards.

Russell Carter (DB): Active for 9 games.

Joe Costello (E): Active for 2 games.

Derrick Crudup (DB/RB): Active for 4 games.

Mike Haynes (DB): Active for 13 games and started in 1.

Ricky Hunley (LB): Active for 12 games, started in 1, and had 1 fumble recovery.

Emanuel King (LB): Active for 16 games and started in 3.

Pete Koch (NT/E/T): Active for 4 games.

Dan Land (DB/RB): Active for 10 games.

Zeph Lee (DB/RB): Active for 13 games, started in 6, and had 1 kickoff return for 0 yards.

Vann McElroy (DB): Active for 7 games, started in 4, and had 2 INT.

Mark Mraz (E): Active for 11 games and had sack.

Bill Pickel (NT/T/E): Active for 16 games, started in 3, and had 3 sacks.

Dennis Price (DB): Active for 5 games.

Tim Rother (T): Active for 16 games.

Jackie Shipp (LB): Active for and started in 3 games.

Otis Wilson (LB): Active for and started in 1 game.

Mike Wise (E): Active for 16 games, started in 9, and had 3 sacks and 2 fumble recoveries.

KICKING/PUNTING

K — Jeff Jaeger: Active for 16 games. Made 23 of 34 field goal attempts and 34 of 34 extra point kicks for 103 points.

P — Jeff Gossett: Active for 16 games. Punted 67 times for a 40.5 average, and attempted 1 pass.

1990 Season Review

1. Sept. 9: In sweltering 95-degree temperatures, the Raiders kicked off the final decade of the millennium in fine style, beating the defending AFC champion Denver Broncos, 14–9. The defense stole the headlines by scoring both touchdowns. Trailing Denver, 6–0, in the third quarter, linebacker Jerry Robinson intercepted a John Elway pass and returned it five yards for the Raiders' first score of the year. Six minutes later, defensive back Terry McDaniel recovered a fumble and ran it back 42 yards. When not scoring touchdowns, the defense sacked Elway five times, and held Denver's running game to 44 yards on 19 carries.[1]

2. Sept. 16: After shutting down the powerful John Elway–led Broncos, the Raiders travelled to the Seattle Kingdome and exonerated demons of the past. After losing in Seattle on seven out their previous eight encounters, the Silver and Black were able to leave the Emerald City as victors. Jay Schroeder guided the Raiders on a 10-play, 65-yard drive in four-and-a-half minutes to beat the Seahawks, 17–13, and remain undefeated. In the winning drive, Schroeder completed four of six passes, and threw a key 24-yard pass to Mervyn Fernandez, who jumped high to make the catch at the Seattle three. For the game, Schroder hit on 10 of 17 attempts for 236 yards. Greg Bell then took the ball over the goal line two plays later from the one with 1:26 remaining in the game. Los Angeles got their other points on a Schroeder to Fernandez 12-yard pass, and a 47-yard field goal from Jeff Jaeger.[2]

3. Sept. 23: The Raiders and Pittsburgh Steelers resumed their rivalry that dated back to 1972. On this occasion, it was the Silver and Black who prevailed, 20–3, to remain unbeaten in the new decade. Jeff Jaeger kicked two field goals from 40 and 45 yards, and then Marcus Allen and Mervyn Fernandez blew the game open with fourth quarter touchdowns coming two-and-a-half minutes apart from each other. Allen scored on a 1-yard run, and Fernandez teamed up with Jay Schroeder from 60 yards out. In this game, Fernandez ripped through the Pittsburgh secondary for 130 yards on five receptions.[3]

4. Sept. 30: In a clash of two unbeaten teams, the Raiders gave head coach Art Shell his ninth straight home against the Chicago Bears, 24–10. The Raiders were now 4–0, and off to their best start in six years thanks in most part to an incredible defensive effort. The defense held Chicago to 101 yards on the ground, only 128 through the air, recorded six sacks for 66 yards in losses, and defensive end Greg Townsend recovered a fumble for a 1-yard touchdown. Marcus Allen provided the Silver and Black with two short touchdown runs from one and three yards, Jeff Jaeger kicked a 27-yard field goal, and former Chicago Bear

Willie Gault did major damage to his old teammates by catching four passes for 103 yards.[4]

5. Oct. 7: The Buffalo Bills knocked Los Angeles out of the unbeaten ranks thanks to a 24-point barrage that only took six minutes to accomplish. The Raiders were up, 24–14, in the fourth quarter on two Jay Schroeder touchdown passes (11 yards to Willie Gault, and four yards to Steve Smith), a 1-yard run by Marcus Allen, and a Jeff Jaeger 19-yard field goal. Mervyn Fernandez did not score, but he had another excellent game with eight receptions for 134 yards. The Raiders then saw their lead quickly evaporate. Buffalo quarterback Jim Kelly threw a touchdown pass to former Raider James Lofton with 8:37 left in the game to start the comeback. The Bills then took the lead after Steve Tasker blocked a Jeff Gossett punt and James Williams returned it 38 yards for another six points. Scott Norwood added a field goal, and Nate Odomes capped the Buffalo resurgence off by scoring on a 49-yard fumble recovery to make the final score, 38–24. Buffalo's 38 points were the most given up by the Raiders in their first four games combined.[5]

6. Oct. 14: A return to the friendly confines of the Los Angeles Memorial Coliseum was just what the Silver and Black needed following their first defeat. For the tenth straight game, the Raiders prevailed at home, this time beating the Seattle Seahawks, 24–17. In each of their first three possessions, Los Angeles came away with touchdowns, all on the arm of Jay Schroeder. His scoring strikes went to Steve Smith (1 yard), Mervyn Fernandez (3 yards), and Ethan Horton (3 yards). Jeff Jaeger added a 22-yard field goal in the fourth quarter. For the game, Schroeder turned in one of his best showings by completing 19 of 26 passes for 235 yards and no interceptions. The Seahawks fought back hard after being down by 21 points, and closed the gap to four points in the third quarter. The Los Angeles defense clamped down on Seattle from that point on, and the Raiders came away with their fifth win of the season, plus a one game lead over the Kansas City Chiefs in the AFC West.[6]

7. Oct. 21: Things continued to go well for Los Angeles, as Bo Jackson returned after his baseball season concluded. In a 24–9 victory over San Diego, Jackson led the Raiders with 53 yards rushing, and ran for two touchdowns from five and seven yards out. Jay Schroeder threw an 8-yard pass to Willie Gault, and Jeff Jaeger kicked a 24-yard field goal, as Los Angeles improved to 6–1, and headed into the bye week with a two game division lead over Kansas City.[7]

8. Nov. 4: With terrible weather conditions that included rain, sleet, and wind hovering around Arrowhead Stadium, both the Raiders and Kansas City Chiefs had difficulty producing much offense. The Chiefs took a 6–0 first quarter lead on two Nick Lowery field goals, with the second one coming after a Bo Jackson fumble deep in Los Angeles territory. The Raiders gained a one-point advantage in the fourth quarter on a 2-yard run from Steve Smith to make the score 7–6. However, victory was not meant to be for the Silver and Black on this particular Sunday. With 11:58 remaining, the Chiefs climaxed a 42-yard drive with Lowery's third three-pointer of the game, this time from 41 yards, and Kansas City held on from there for a 9–7 win that brought them to within one game of the AFC Western Division lead.[8]

9. Nov. 11: The bye week seemed to be more of hindrance where the Raiders were concerned, as they fell for the second week in a row following their week off. This time it was the Green Bay Packers that did the damage with a 29–16 win. The defeat also ended the Raiders home winning streak at ten. Green Bay quarterback Don Majkowski threw two touchdowns, and Chris Jacke set a team record by kicking five field goals. Marcus Allen ran for two touchdowns from five and two yards, and Jeff Jaeger kicked a 24-yard field goal for Los Angeles.[9]

10. Nov. 19: There was nothing better for the Raiders' karma than to play on Monday night in an attempt to snap their mini losing streak. In front of a sold out crowd in Miami's Joe Robbie Stadium, Los Angeles beat the 8–1 Dolphins, 13–10, with a well-balanced offensive attack, and a tough run defense. Bo Jackson ran for 99 yards, and Marcus Allen added 79, as well as the Raiders' lone touchdown from two yards out. Allen's touchdown was the first rushing one scored against the Miami defense in 26 quarters, and the first offensive touchdown they gave up in 14 quarters. Jeff Jaeger kicked two field goals (23 and 43 yards), and the defense held the Miami running game to a mere 14 yards in 12 attempts while keeping constant pressure on quarterback Dan Marino throughout the game. The Raiders were 7–3, and one game up on Kansas City in the division race.[10]

11. Nov. 25: Los Angeles could not capitalize on their sterling Monday night performance, and lost to long-time rival, Kansas City, 27–24. With the loss, the Raiders fell to 7–4, and found themselves tied with the Chiefs for the division lead. With great blocking in front of him, Kansas City quarterback Steve DeBerg had time to pass for three touchdowns. With this win, the Chiefs swept the season series from the Raiders for the first time since 1981. One bright spot for Los Angeles was the running of Marcus Allen, who ran for a game high 76 yards in 15 carries and scored on runs of three, ten, and five yards. Jeff Jaeger added a 50-yard field goal to complete the Raiders' scoring.[11]

12. Dec. 2: Bo Jackson and defensive end Scott Davis shared the spotlight in a close, 23–20 win over the Denver Broncos that put the Raiders at 8–4 and still in a first place tie in the division along with Kansas City. Jackson carried the offensive load for the Silver and Black with 117 rushing yards on just 13 carries for an incredible nine yards per carry average, and scored on runs of 11 and 62 yards. Steve Smith (4-yard run), and Jeff Jaeger (46-yard field goal), provided Los Angeles with their other points. Jay Schroeder had a good game on a knee he sprained a week earlier. He completed 16 of 23 passes for 164 yards and threw no interceptions. Scott Davis waited until the end of the game to earn his place in the morning papers. With seven seconds left to play, Denver kicker David Treadwell attempted a 41-yard field goal that would have sent the game into overtime if successful. At the snap, the 6'7" Davis jumped up and swatted the ball with his right hand to preserve the victory.[12]

13. Dec. 10: A running shootout between Bo Jackson and Detroit's Barry Sanders provided a national television audience with much of the excitement in a 38–31 Los Angeles win on Monday Night Football. This game was a wild one right from the start, as both teams combined for the second highest first quarter point production in pro football history with 35. The record was 42 set in 1967 in a game between Green Bay and Cleveland. Barry Sanders ran for 176 yards, and went over the 1,000-yard mark for the season, and scored twice. Bo Jackson rushed for 129 yards on 18 carries, and scored on a 55-yard run. After failing to throw a

touchdown pass for 20 straight quarters, Jay Schroder more than made up for it by throwing three in this scoring fest. His first one went to Willie Gault from 68 yards to tie the game. With the Raiders down, 24–21, going in to the third quarter, Schroeder's right arm allowed the Silver and Black to overcome the deficit with scoring strikes to Mervyn Fernandez (10 yards), and Tim Brown (3 yards). On the day, Schroeder hit on 12 of 19 passes for 195 yards. Marcus Allen scored the other Raiders touchdown on a 2-yard run, and Jeff Jaeger booted a 37-yard field goal to complete the scoring. The defense recorded four sacks despite allowing 199 rushing yards and 171 passing. The win put the Raiders at 9–4, and still deadlocked with Kansas City for the division lead.[13]

14. Dec. 16: The Raiders clinched their first playoff berth since 1985 thanks in large part to the brilliant running display of Bo Jackson, who rushed for 117 yards on only eight carries. Jay Schroeder threw two touchdown passes to Time Brown (5 yards and 44 yards), and one to Ethan Horton (1 yard). Jeff Jaeger added a 39-yard field goal in the 24–7 win over Cincinnati. At 10–4, the Silver and Black reclaimed sole possession of first place in the AFC West after Kansas City lost their game with the Houston Oilers.[14]

15. Dec. 22: Los Angeles won for the fourth time in a row, beating Minnesota, 28–24, for the fifth time in their last six encounters with the Vikings. The Raiders came into Minnesota's Metrodome facing tough odds. The Vikings had won 19 of their last 21 home games, but odds against the Raiders never seemed to faze them. Minnesota's defense tried to stop Bo Jackson's hot streak by using an eight-man line, and it worked, as they limited the two-sport superstar to 65 yards on 17 carries. However, the Vikings failed to stop the hot right arm of Jay Schroeder. He completed 10 of 15 passes for 234 yards and four touchdowns, which gave him ten scoring tosses in his last three games. His touchdown strikes went to Mervyn Fernandez (17 yards), Sam Graddy (47 yards), Marcus Allen (19 yards), and Ethan Horton (3 yards). Willie Gault did not score, but made an impression on the Minnesota crowd by catching two passes for a whopping 117 yards. The defense chipped in by pounding away at Minnesota quarterback Wade Wilson, who was forced from the game in third quarter with a separated shoulder after being sacked by Scott Davis. In all, the defense recorded five sacks. This was Minnesota's third straight loss, and it eliminated them from the playoffs for the first time since 1986. On the other side, the Silver and Black were 11–4, and on the verge of clinching their first division title in five years.[15]

16. Dec. 30: The Raiders were playoff bound as newly crowned AFC Western Division champions after beating the San Diego Chargers, 17–12. With their fifth straight win, Los Angeles finished with the second best record in the AFC at 12–4, which earned them a bye in the first round of the playoffs. It also guaranteed them at least one home playoff game. This victory over San Diego was not the team's most impressive of the '90 season, but they got the job done in the end. The Chargers played well above their 6–10 finish, stuffing the run and sacking Jay Schroeder three times. Schroeder was finally able to pierce the San Diego defense when it counted most. Trailing, 12–10, in the fourth quarter, Schroeder hit on five passes in a row for 70 yards, with his last one going to Steve Smith from 17 yards for the winning points. Marcus Allen scored Los Angeles' other touchdown on a 1-yard run, and Jeff Jaeger added a 45-yard field goal for the champs.[16]

AFC Divisional Playoff, January 13, 1991

What price glory, win at all costs, and countless other phrases have been linked to the world of sports since human beings began competing against each other. Such was the case in the Raiders' first playoff game of new decade. The Raiders defeated the Cincinnati Bengals, 20–10, to earn the right to advance to their 12th league or conference championship game. The win was sweet, but an individual loss was bitter, as superstar phenomenon Bo Jackson sustained a career-ending hip injury.

However, in a classic case of something old being new again, the Raiders' offensive attack dusted off the hero of past glories, Marcus Allen, and he led Los Angeles to another playoff victory. With Bo Jackson lost, the 30-year-old Allen turned on the jets, and left the Bengals in the dust. He ran for 140 yards on 21 carries, with the sound of 92,045 cheering Los Angeles Memorial Coliseum patrons ringing in his ears.

Allen usually gave way to Bo Jackson in the second quarter, but this time the roles were reversed. On the second play of the second half, Jackson took a handoff and rambled 34 yards before a tackle cost him his pro football career. It was the last time he ever carried a football. Allen responded to his fallen comrade's departure by rushing for 79 yards on 10 carries in the second half.

The Bengals opened the scoring after a scoreless first quarter with a 27-yard field goal from Jim Breech. The Raiders took the lead on a Jay Schroeder to Mervyn Fernandez 13-yard pass, and Jeff Jaeger's extra point, to lead at the half, 7–3. Jaeger extended the Los Angeles advantage to 10–7 with a 49-yard field goal in the third quarter.

Early in the fourth, Cincinnati evened things up at 10–10 when Boomer Esiason passed to Stanford Jennings from eight yards out on a third down play, and Breech added the conversion. On their next possession, Los Angeles was in a third-and-20 situation on their own 32 after linebacker Carl Zander sacked Schroeder for a loss of ten yards. Schroeder then connected with Tim Brown along the right sideline for a gain of 26 yards. From the Cincinnati 41, Schroeder once again took to the air with what turned out to be his best pass of the game. This time he hooked up with tight end Ethan Horton also along the right sideline, and it went for six points. Jaeger added the extra point, and later a 25-yard field goal to complete the game's scoring, and Los Angeles was on their to the AFC Championship Game.[17]

AFC Championship Game, January 20, 1991

The good news was that the Raiders became the first team in history to play for a league or conference championship in four consecutive decades. The bad news was that the Raiders played in a championship game in January of 1991. With that being said, the Silver and Black travelled clear across the country to face the Buffalo Bills for the right to represent the AFC in Super Bowl XXV.

The Bills were making their first league or championship game appearance in 24 years, which was followed by years of mediocrity, with the occasional glimmer of hope that was quickly dissolved with early playoff losses. The 1990 edition of the Bills were ready to reverse the misfortunes of past seasons, and on a frigid January afternoon inside Rich Stadium, they destroyed Los Angeles, 51–3, to give the Raiders their worst post-season defeat, and one of the all-time classic playoff romps ever recorded.

Buffalo took their no-huddle offensive scheme and drove it down LA's throat, wearing the defense down enroute to their first league or conference title in 25 years. The Bills opened their point barrage with a 13-yard pass from Jim Kelly to James Lofton that capped a nine-play, 75-yard drive. Los Angeles came out fast, with Jay Schroeder throwing a pair of 26-yard passes to Mervyn Fernandez and Willie Gault. The drive stalled after Fernandez dropped a pass at the Buffalo 18. Jeff Jaeger came on to salvage the drive with a 41-yard field goal to cut the Buffalo lead to 7–3.

That was it for the Raiders' offensive highlights on this day. Running back Thurman Thomas ran for a 12-yard touchdown, and linebacker Darryl Talley took a 27-yard interception back for a six-pointer to give the Bills a 21–3 lead at the end of the first quarter. Two Ken Davis touchdown runs from one and three yards, coupled with a Kelly to Lofton 8-yard pass made it 41–3 at the half. In the first half, the Bills rolled up a playoff record 387 offensive yards, with Jim Kelly throwing for 247 of them. After a scoreless third quarter, Davis scored on a 1-yard run for his third touchdown of the afternoon, and Scott Norwood hit on a 39-yard field goal to end the Rich Stadium Armageddon that obliterated the Silver and Black.[18]

Individual Statistics and Roster

Head Coach: Art Shell
Assistant Coaches: Dave Adolph, Fred Biletnikoff, Sam Gruneisen, Kim Helton, Odis McKinney, Steve Ortmayer, Joe Scannella, Jack Stanton, Bill Urbanik, Tom Walsh, Mike White
1990 Regular Season Record: 12–4
1st Place AFC Western Division
Scored 337 points to rank 13th out of 28 teams
Allowed 268 to rank 7th
Led the league in fewest touchdowns allowed by a defense (4)

STARTERS — OFFENSE

QB — Jay Schroeder: Started in 16 games. Completed 182 of 334 pass attempts for 2,849 yards, 19 TD and 9 INT. **Led the NFL in yards gained per pass completion (15.7).** Rushed for 81 yards on 37 carries.
HB — Marcus Allen: Active for 16 games and started in 15. Rushed for 682 yards on 179 carries and 12 TD. Had 15 receptions for 189 yards and 1 TD.
FB — Steve Smith: Active for 16 games and started in 15. Rushed for 327 yards on 81 carries and 2 TD. Had 4 receptions for 30 yards and 3 TD.
WR — Mervyn Fernandez: Active for 16 games and started in 15. Had 52 receptions for 839 yards and 5 TD. Rushed for 10 yards on 3 carries.
WR — Willie Gault: Started in 16 games. Had 50 receptions for 985 yards and 3 TD.
TE — Ethan Horton: Active for 16 games and started in 14. Had 33 receptions for 404 yards and 3 TD.
LT — Rory Graves: Active for and started in 15 games.

LG — Steve Wisniewski: Started in 16 games.
C — Don Mosebar: Started in 16 games.
RG — Max Montoya: Started in 16 games.
RT — Steve Wright: Started in 16 games.

RESERVE OFFENSIVE PLAYERS

Rich Bartlewski (TE): Active for 4 games.
Greg Bell (RB): Active for 6 games, rushed for 164 yards on 47 carries and had 1 reception for 7 yards.
Ron Brown (WR): Active for 16 games, and had 30 kickoff returns for 575 yards.
Tim Brown (WR): Active for 16 games. Had 18 receptions for 265 yards and 3 TD, and 34 punt returns for 295 yards.
Mike Dyal (TE): Active for 3 games and started in 2. Had 3 receptions for 51 yards.
Vince Evans (QB): Active for 5 games, completed 1 pass in as many attempts for 36 yards, and rushed 1 time for -2 yards.
James FitzPatrick (T/G): Active for 11 games and started in 1.
Sam Graddy (WR): active for 16 games, and had 1 reception for 47 yards and 1 TD.
Jamie Holland (WR/RB): Active for 16 games, and had 32 kickoff returns for 655 yards.
Bo Jackson (RB): Active for 10 games. Rushed for 698 yards on 125 carries and 5 TD. Had 6 receptions for 68 yards.
Napoleon McCallum (RB): Active for 16 games, rushed for 25 yards on 10 carries, and had 1 kickoff return for 0 yards.
Vance Mueller (RB): Active for 16 games and started in 1. Rushed for 43 yards on 13 carries.
Andy Parker (TE): Active for 5 games.
Todd Peat (G): Active for 16 games and started in 1.
Dan Turk (C/G): Active for 16 games and had 1 kickoff return for 7 yards.
Bruce Wilkerson (T/G): Active for 8 games and started in 1.

STARTERS — DEFENSE

DE — Howie Long: Active for 12 games and started in 11. Had 6 sacks and 1 fumble recovery.
DE — Greg Townsend: Started in 16 games, had 12.5 sacks, 1 INT and 1 fumble recovery.
DT — Bob Golic: Started in 16 games, had 4 sacks and 2 fumble recoveries.
DT — Scott Davis: Started in 16 games and had 10 sacks.
LLB — Jerry Robinson: Started in 16 games, had 2 sacks and 1 INT.
MLB — Riki Ellison: Active for 16 games and started in 15. Had 1 INT.
RLB — Thomas Benson: Started in 16 games.
CB — Terry McDaniel: Active for 16 games and started in 13. Had 2 sacks, 3 INT, and 2 fumble recoveries.
CB — Lionel Washington: Active for and started in 15 games, and had 1 INT.
SS — Mike Harden: Active for and started in 15 games, and had 3 INT.
FS — Eddie Anderson: Started in 16 games, had 3 INT and 1 fumble recovery.

RESERVE DEFENSIVE PLAYERS

Ron Burton (LB): Active for 5 games.
Mike Charles (NT/E/T): Active for 10 games.
Torin Dorn (DB): Active for 16 games.
Alex Gordon (LB): Active for 10 games.
Ricky Hunley (LB): Active for 11 games.
A.J. Jimerson (LB): Active for 4 games.
Dan Land (DB/RB): Active for 16 games.
Vann McElroy (DB): Active for 3 games.
Elvis Patterson (DB): Active for 16 games and started in 1. Had 1 fumble recovery.
Bill Pickel (NT/T/E): Active for 14 games, started in 3, had 1 sacks and 1 fumble recovery.

Tim Rother (T): Active for 4 games.
Aaron Wallace (LB): Active for 16 games and had 9 sacks.
Mike Wise (E): Active for 12 games, started in 2, and had 1 sack.

KICKING/PUNTING

K&P — Jeff Gossett: Active for 16 games. Made 15 of 20 field goals and 40 of 42 extra points for 85 points. Punted 60 times for a 38.6 average.

1991 Season Review

1. Sept. 1: The Raiders were still suffering the ill effects caused from their thrashing at the hands of the Buffalo Bills in the AFC Championship Game eight-and-a-half-months earlier. Unable to contain an explosive Houston offense, the Raiders suffered their worst opening day defeat, 47–17, since a 55–0 beat down in 1961 to the very same Oilers. On the Raiders first offensive play of the game, Jay Schroeder was sacked. He then threw an interception, and it was all down hill from there for the Silver and Black. Houston quarterback Warren Moon passed for 250 yards and two touchdowns, and ran for another one. When not ripping the Los Angeles defense through the air, Moon handed off to his running back Allen Pinkett, who tore up the ground for 144 yards. Los Angeles received their points on a Schroeder to Willie Gault 59-yard pass, a Vince Evans to Sam Graddy 80-yard toss, and a Jeff Jaeger 39-yard field goal. Graddy started off the '91 campaign in fine fashion even though the Raiders did not. His three receptions for 103 yards led all receivers in the game.[1]

2. Sept. 8: Everything clicked for the Silver and Black in a 16–13 win over the Denver Broncos. Jay Schroeder connected with Willie Gault from 16 yards out for Los Angeles' lone touchdown, and Roger Craig ran for 99 yards. Over on defense, this unit that gave up 51 points in the AFC Championship game, and 47 in their opener, clamped down hard on one of the league's premier quarterbacks in John Elway, sacking him five times. The Raiders received their other points in this game from three Jeff Jaeger field goals (29, 23, and 34 yards).[2]

3. Sept. 15: The Los Angeles defense continued to perform at a high level, and led the way in a 16–0 shutout over the winless Indianapolis Colts. The defense allowed only 80 yards on the ground, 186 through the air, and recorded four sacks. Jeff Jaeger once again kicked three field goals, two from 33 yards and a 41-yarder. Jay Schroeder completed 13 of 22 pass attempts for 181 yards and a touchdown to Mervyn Fernandez, who had a good day with seven receptions for 90 yards. The Raiders' second straight win gave them a 2–1 record, and put them in a first place tie with Denver in the AFC West.[3]

4. Sept. 22: After two fine showings, quarterback Jay Schroeder struggled in a 21–17 loss to the Atlanta Falcons. He connected on only 10 of 32 pass attempts for 116 yards and suffered two interceptions. He was also sacked three times. Despite his meager stats, Schroeder did throw for two scores, with Andrew Glover (4 yards), and Ethan Horton (5 yards) on the receiving ends. Jeff Jaeger added a 49-yard field goal to complete the scoring for the Raiders on this day. Schroeder's counterpart, Chris Miller, also threw for two scores. His first in the third quarter tied the game, and the second one broke the tie at the start of the fourth quarter.[4]

5. Sept. 29: Jeff Jaeger's right foot was responsible for all of the Los Angeles scoring, but it was all the Raiders needed in a 12–6 win over the San Francisco 49ers. Jaeger's fourth field goal kept Los Angeles perfect at home in the infant stages of the '91 season. Jaeger's three pointers came from 44, 20, 49, and 41 yards away. With the offense sputtering throughout the game, the defense came up big for the third time this season. On this occasion, they did it by stopping the 49ers' passing game, and kept the great receiver Jerry Rice from catching a pass until the fourth quarter.[5]

6. Oct. 6: The winless San Diego Chargers came into Los Angeles and handed the Raiders their first home defeat of the year by a 21–13 count. It was only the third home loss for the Raiders in their previous 20 games in the friendly confines of the Los Angeles Memorial Coliseum. Linebacker Henry Rolling did major damage to the Raiders' offense by recovering a Roger Craig fumble and intercepting a Jay Schroeder pass inside San Diego territory. Jeff Jaeger kicked two field goals (39 and 34 yards), and Ethan Horton caught an 11-yard pass from Schroeder for the Raiders on this day. The loss took Los Angeles to 3–3, and one game out of first place in the division race.[6]

7. Oct. 13: Los Angeles travelled to the dreaded Seattle Kingdome to take on the 3–3 Seahawks. Jeff Jaeger's golden right foot once again worked its magic with one second remaining in regulation, as his 49-yard field goal attempt sailed through the uprights to force the game into overtime tied at 20–20. At the 6:37 mark in overtime, Jaeger got his team out of the Kingdome, which was a torture chamber for the Raiders in the past, when he connected on a 37-yard field goal to climax a well-earned 23–20 victory. The Raiders battled back from a 17–0 halftime deficit on two scoring passes from Jay Schroeder to Ethan Horton (8 yards), and Tim Brown (12 yards), and a Jaeger 17-yard field goal. The winning three-pointer in overtime was brought about thanks to a Ronnie Lott interception on the Seattle 19.[7]

8. Oct. 20: The battle of Los Angeles was won by the Raiders, 20–17, with Ronnie Lott once again coming up big. His two interceptions in the fourth quarter led to the tying and winning points for the Silver and Black. Jeff Jaeger continued his dream season by winning his second straight game with a field goal, this time on a 34-yarder with two seconds remaining. Lott's first interception led to a Nick Bell 1-yard touchdown that tied the game with four minutes left. Bell's scoring run was the first on the ground for the Raiders in almost eight games. The team's other point production came on a Jay Schroeder to Willie Gault 9-yard pass, and a 35-yard field goal by Jaeger.[8]

9. Oct. 28: The Raiders were rulers of Monday Night Football since 1970, and were looking to get their 30th victory out of 37 appearances on the prime time stage. On this night, the Raiders and Kansas City Chiefs looked to add to their classic rivalry, as both teams came into this edition at 5–3 and one game out of first place in the division. Los Angeles had won their two previous encounters with late heroics, however, this time they lost by them. Leading, 21–10, in the fourth quarter on a safety, two Jeff Jaeger field goals (18 and 22 yards), a Nick Bell 1-yard run, and a Jay Schroeder to Steve Smith 37-yard pass, the Raiders were driving for what looked like a clinching score. The fortunes

of the Silver and Black then went bad, as Schroeder threw an interception at the goal line, which was returned 83 yards. Christian Okoye scored a few plays later with eight minutes left to close the gap to 21–17. The Chiefs got the ball back following a punt, and then drove 57 yards for the win. With 47 seconds left, quarterback Steve DeBerg threw a 6-yard scoring strike to Tim Barnett to make the final score, 24–21.[9]

10. Nov. 11: Coming off a bye week, the rest did the Raiders some good, as they swept the season series from the Denver Broncos with a 17–16 win. The victory gave Los Angeles a 6–4 record, and put them one game out of first place in the division. This close score marked the 12th time in the previous 16 meetings between these teams that the game was decided by less than a touchdown difference. After trailing by three points at the half, the Raiders came back to take a 17–10 lead in the third quarter on a 23-yard pass from Jay Schroeder to Tim Brown, and a 20-yard field goal from Jeff Jaeger. The Raiders' first score came on an 11-yard pass from Marcus Allen to Andrew Glover in the opening quarter. This game marked the return of Allen to the lineup after a knee injury sidelined him since the opener. Like so many times throughout his illustrious career, Denver quarterback John Elway rallied the Broncos for a score. With 8:37 remaining in the fourth quarter, Elway threw a touchdown pass to Vance Johnson, and David Treadwell then came on to attempt the game-tying extra point kick. What usually proved to be an automatic point turned into anything but that, as Scott Davis shot through a wall of blockers and got his hand on the ball to block it. One year earlier Davis did the same thing to the Broncos to preserve a win. The Broncos had one more chance at victory as the clock was running down. However, James FitzPatrick blasted his 300-pound frame through the line to block a 48-yard field goal attempt with no time left to clinch a win for Los Angeles.[10]

11. Nov. 17: The Raiders scored on all four of their first half possessions to build a 24–7 lead over the Seattle Seahawks. The Silver and Black then added another touchdown to sweep the season series from their division rivals with a 31–7 win. Jay Schroeder was at his best in this one, completing 16 out of 19 pass attempts for 237 yards and three touchdowns, all to a different receiver. On the receiving end of Schroeder's strikes were Willie Gault (4 yards), Andrew Glover (1 yard), and Ethan Horton (51 yards). Horton had a great day with seven receptions for 123 yards. Adding points to the Raiders' easy victory were Jeff Jaeger, who opened the scoring with a career-best 51-yard field goal, and Napoleon McCallum (1-yard run). The defense chipped in with seven sacks, as both units jelled for Los Angeles' best win of the season, and their highest point production up to this time in '91. At 7–4, the Raiders were tied with Kansas City and one game behind the first place Broncos in the division.[11]

12. Nov. 24: The 1–10 Cincinnati Bengals hosted the Raiders, and they paid dearly for the effort. Los Angeles scored over thirty points for the second straight game in a 38–14 romp over the hapless team from the Queen City. This game was over by halftime, as the Raiders rolled up a 28–7 advantage. Steve Smith started things off with a 1-yard run, followed by a Roger Craig 5-yard jaunt. The special teams then got into the act when Tim Brown returned a punt 75 yards, and Elvis Patterson recovered a blocked punt on the Cincinnati three and took it in after Aaron Wallace knocked the ball out of punter Lee Johnson's hand.

Marcus Allen added a 3-yard run and Jeff Jaeger a 28-yard field goal to complete the scoring. Over on defense, Ronnie Lott came up with two interceptions and Anthony Smith's two sacks led the unit's total of four. This third straight win gave the Raiders an 8–4 record, and a share of first place with the Broncos after they lost to Seattle.[12]

13. Dec. 1: Since losing to San Diego in October, the Raiders won five out of their next six, and three in a row. Los Angeles then redeemed themselves against the Chargers with a 9–7 win. At 9–4, the Raiders were still deadlocked in a tie with Denver for the division lead. Jeff Jaeger kicked three field goals from 37, 19 and a career-high 53-yarder. Scott Davis and his 6'7" frame once again provided a magic touch when he blocked a field goal attempt with 1:57 left that could have gave San Diego the win. The defense came up with an incredible effort, as they allowed only 75 rushing yards, 124 through the air, and recorded three sacks.[13]

14. Dec. 8: In January of 1991, the Buffalo Bills destroyed the Raiders in their quest for a Super Bowl berth. Nearly one year later, the Bills once again knocked the Raiders down, but not as hard this time around. Buffalo overcame a 27–14 deficit with two touchdowns in the fourth quarter to force the game into overtime. They could have won it in regulation, but a Scott Norwood extra point attempt after Buffalo's first fourth quarter touchdown went wide. However, Norwood redeemed himself two-and-a-half minutes into the overtime quarter with a 42-yard field goal. The 30–27 win allowed the Bills to clinch the AFC Eastern Division crown. Even though they lost, Los Angeles still clinched a playoff berth when the New York Jets lost. At 9–5, the Raiders were tied with Kansas City for second place in the division. The Raiders received their point production on two Jeff Jaeger field goals (19 and 28 yards), a Jay Schroeder to Tim Brown 78-yard pass, a Nick Bell 12-yard run, and a Marcus Allen 1-yard run.[14]

15. Dec. 16: The New Orleans Saints clinched their first-ever playoff berth with a 27–0 Monday Night Football white-washing of the Raiders to snap a four-game losing streak. The Saints shut Los Angeles down like no one else during the season. Their defense smothered the Silver and Black, allowing them only 71 rushing yards, 46 passing, and registered four sacks. New Orleans quarterback Bobby Hebert completed 28 out of 39 pass attempts for 320 yards. This loss took the Raiders to 9–6, and allowed Denver to clinch the AFC Western Division title.[15]

16. Dec. 22: Rookie quarterback Todd Marinovich started the regular season finale due to Jay Schroeder suffering from an ankle sprain. The left-handed Marinovich reminded Raiders followers of another lefty, Ken Stabler, by playing a near-perfect game in his first NFL start. He hit on 23 of 40 pass attempts for 243 yards and three touchdowns. Tim Brown caught two of Marinovich's scoring tosses from 26 and 23 yards, and Ethan Horton grabbed the other one from seven yards out. Despite the rookie's great debut, it was the Chiefs that walked away with a 27–21 win to improve to 10–6 while Los Angeles finished at 9–7. With the win, Kansas City clinched home field advantage for the AFC Wild Card game against these same Raiders scheduled for the following weekend.[16]

AFC Wild Card Game, December 28, 1991

The Chiefs entered the 1991 playoffs on a four-game winning streak, while the Raiders came into the postseason on a three game slide. The drought continued for the Silver and Black on this day, as Kansas City won a defensive struggle, 10–6, to advance to the next round. After his great debut a week earlier, Todd Marinovich was brought down to Earth by the Kansas City defense, as he suffered four interceptions, with two coming from Deron Cherry. Cherry's first theft was returned to the Los Angeles 11, and on the following play, Steve DeBerg connected with Fred Jones for the game's only touchdown. A pair of Jeff Jaeger field goals from 32 and 26 yards out allowed the Raiders to cut the deficit to one point going into the final quarter. Nick Lowery added an 18-yard field goal to give the Chiefs a little breathing room. The Raiders rallied, and got to the Kansas City 24-yard line with a few minutes remaining. However, four penalties in five plays were followed by a Lonnie Marts interception to end any hopes for the Silver and Black.[17]

Individual Statistics and Roster

Head Coach: Art Shell
Assistant Coaches: Dave Adolph, Fred Biletnikoff, Gunther Cunningham, Kim Helton, Earl Leggett, Odis Mckinney, Steve Ortmayer, Terry Robiskie, Joe Scannella, Jack Stanton, Tom Walsh, Mike White
1991 Regular Season Record: 9–7
3rd Place in AFC Western Division
Scored 298 points to rank 15th out of 28 teams
Allowed 297 to rank 12th

STARTERS — OFFENSE

QB — Jay Schroeder: Active for and started in 15 games. Completed 189 of 357 pass attempts for 2,562 yards, 15 TD and16 INT. Rushed for 76 yards on 28 carries.
HB — Roger Craig: Active for 15 games and started in 13. Rushed for 590 yards on 162 carries and 1 TD. Had 17 receptions for 136 yards.
FB — Steve Smith: Started in 16 games. Rushed for 265 yards on 62 carries and 1 TD. Had 15 receptions for 130 yards and 1 TD.
WR — Mervyn Fernandez: Active for 16 games and started in 13. Had 46 receptions for 694 yards and 1 TD.
WR — Willie Gault: Active for 16 games and started in 15. Had 20 receptions for 346 yards and 4 TD.
TE — Ethan Horton: Started in 16 games. Had 53 receptions for 650 yards and 5 TD.
LT — Bruce Wilkerson: Started in 16 games.
LG — Steve Wisniewski: Active for and started in 15 games.
C — Don Mosebar: Started in 16 games.
RG — Max Montoya: Active for 11 games and started in 10.
RT — Steve Wright: Started in 16 games.

RESERVE OFFENSIVE PLAYERS

Marcus Allen (RB): Active for 8 games and started in 2. Rushed for 287 yards on 63 carries and 2 TD. Had 15 receptions for 131 yards, and completed 1 of 2 passes for 11 yards and 1 TD.
Nick Bell (RB): Active for 9 games and started in 1. Rushed for 307 yards on 78 carries and 3 TD, and had 6 receptions for 62 yards.
Tim Brown (WR): Active for 16 games and started in 1. Rushed for 16 yards on 5 carries, had 36 receptions for 554 yards and 5 TD, 29 punt returns for 330 yards and 1 TD, and 1 kickoff return for 29 yards.

Vince Evans (QB): Active for 4 games. Completed 6 of 14 pass attempts for 127 yards, 1 TD and 2 INT. Rushed for 20 yards on 8 carries.
James FitzPatrick (T/G): Active for 16 games and started in 4.
Andrew Glover (TE): Active for 16 games and started in 1. Had 5 receptions for 45 yards and 3 TD.
Sam Graddy (WR): Active for 12 games. Had 6 receptions for 195 yards and 1 TD, and 22 kickoff returns for 373 yards.
Rory Graves (T): Active for 3 games.
Jamie Holland (WR/RB): Active for 16 games and had 22 kickoff returns for 421 yards.
Doug Lloyd (RB): Active for 1 game.
Todd Marinovich (QB): Active for and started in 1 game. Completed 23 of 40 pas attempts for 243 yards and 3 TD. Rushed for 14 yards on 3 carries.
Napoleon McCallum (RB): Active for 16 games. Rushed for 110 yards on 31 carries and 1 TD. Had 5 kickoff returns for 105 yards.
Reggie McElroy (T/G): Active for 16 games and started in 5.
Joel Patten (T): Active for 1 game.
Dan Turk (C/G): Active for 16 games and had 1 kickoff return for 0 yards.
Marcus Wilson (RB): Active for 1 game and rushed for 21 yards on 6 carries.

STARTERS — DEFENSE

DE — Howie Long: Active for 14 games, started in 13, had 3 sacks and 1 INT.
DE — Greg Townsend: Started in 16 games, had 13 sacks, 1 INT, and 1 fumble recovery.
DT — Bob Golic: Active for 16 games, started in 14, had 1 sack and 1 fumble recovery.
DT — Scott Davis: Started in 16 games and had 6 sacks.
LLB — Winston Moss: Started in 16 games, had 3 sacks and 2 fumble recoveries.
MLB — Riki Ellison: Active for 16 games, started in 15, and had 2 fumble recoveries.
RLB — Thomas Benson: Active for 16 games, started in 14, had 1 sack, and 1 INT.
CB — Terry McDaniel: Started in 16 games and had 1 fumble recovery.
CB — Lionel Washington: Started in 16 games and had 5 INT.
SS — Ronnie Lott: Started in 16 games, had 1 sack, **8** INT, and 1 fumble recovery.
FS — Eddie Anderson: Started in 16 games, had 2 INT and 1 fumble recovery.

RESERVE DEFENSIVE PLAYERS

Derrick Crudup (DB): Active for 16 games.
Torin Dorn (DB): Active for 16 games, started in 1, had 1 fumble recovery and 1 safety.
Nolan Harrison (E/T): Active for 14 games, started in 3, and had 1 sack.
Roy Hart (NT/T): Active for 1 game.
A.J. Jimerson (LB): Active for 13 games.
Mike Jones (LB): Active for 16 games.
Dan Land (DB): Active for 16 games.
Garry Lewis (DB): Active for 16 games and started in 2.
Elvis Patterson (DB): Active for 16 games, had 2 fumble recoveries, 1 TD, and rushed for 34 yards on 1 carry.
Jerry Robinson (LB): Active for 16 games.
Anthony Smith (E): Active for 16 games, started in 2, had 10 sacks and 1 fumble recovery.
Aaron Wallace (LB): Active for 16 games and had 2 sacks.

KICKING/PUNTING

K&P–Jeff Jaeger: Active for 16 games. Made 29 of 34 field goals and 29 of 30 extra points for 116 points. Punted 67 times for a 44.2 average. Completed 1 of 1 pass attempts for 34 yards.

1992 Season Review

1. Sept. 6: Denver quarterback John Elway had earned the reputation of pulling victories out when all seemed lost. On opening day in 1992, Elway added another chapter to his fantastic finishes with a 17–13 win over the Raiders, which snapped Denver's five-game losing streak to Los Angeles. Trailing, 13–10, with three minutes left in the fourth quarter, Elway put together an 85-yard drive, capped off by a Reggie Rivers 1-yard run with 55 seconds remaining. Jay Schroeder fumbled away any hopes of a comeback with his fourth turnover of the game on a day that saw him complete only seven passes out of 24 attempts for 181 yards and two interceptions. Nick Bell (1-yard run), and Jeff Jaeger (two field goals from 41 and 34 yards), provided Los Angeles with their points.[1]

2. Sept. 13: Another close game unfortunately brought the same results, as the Cincinnati Bengals turned back the Raiders in overtime, 24–21, when Jim Breech connected on a 34-yard field goal. The Bengals used their ground game to wear the Raiders down, and received three big mishaps by Los Angeles in the second half to help their cause. Tim Brown fumbled near the goal line in the third quarter, running back Steve Smith let a Jay Schroeder pass go off his fingertips for an interception, and offensive lineman Bruce Wilkerson was called for holding on the Raiders' final drive that took away an important 15-yard gain by Marcus Allen. The Raiders got on the board first when Brown caught a 33-yard pass from Schroeder, and Sam Graddy broke a 7–7 tie with a 37-yard pass from Schroeder. They then fell behind, 21–14, in the third quarter. Los Angeles almost pulled this one out in the end behind Schroeder's passing, as he completed five out of five attempts for 73 yards in a 90-yard drive that tied the game in the closing minutes. Allen finished the drive off with a 1-yard run as the clock showed 1:56 remaining to be played. Schroeder had one of the best days of his career by hitting on 25 of 40 passes for 380 yards, and in the process, dispelled any rumors of a quarterback controversy brewing between him and Todd Marinovich. In overtime, Dan Land received the kickoff, and was hit by Randy Kirk when he slowed down to avoid a would-be tackler. He was accidentally hit by teammate Sam Graddy in the process, and the ball popped loose, bounced once on the ground, and came up right into the awaiting hands of Cincinnati's Antoine Bennett at the Los Angeles 21. Breech then ended the game with his field goal to drop the Raiders to 0–2 for only the second time in the previous 28 years.[2]

3. Sept. 20: It looked like Jay Schroeder silenced his critics with his great performance a week earlier. However, he was benched in favor of Los Angeles native Todd Marinovich for the Raiders' home opener against Cleveland on an extremely hot day. A crowd of 48,102 came out to see two winless teams battle for their first victory of the campaign. What they saw left them and the home team bewildered and still looking for their first win. Eric Metcalf exploded for the Browns, as he caught five passes for 177 yards and three touchdowns, and ran for another, to account for all of Cleveland's six-pointers in a 28–16 win. The Raiders received their points on three Jeff Jaeger field goals (27, 30, and 43 yards), and a 25-yard pass to Willie Gault from Marinovich, who finished the day with 395 yards on 33 completions out of a team record 59 attempts. Sam Graddy also had a solid perform-

ance with six receptions for 114 yards on a day that saw so many things break down for the Silver and Black. The defense did not record a sack for the second straight week, the defensive backfield messed up in coverage on two long pass plays, the offensive line was racked by injuries and dehydration, and the running game was dismal at best, as Eric Dickerson only gained 22 yards on six carries.[3]

4. Sept. 28: Kansas City had their largest home crowd in twenty years present as they hosted the Raiders on a Monday Night Football telecast. Los Angeles was hoping that their Monday night magic could help them secure the team's first victory of the season, but it was not to be, as the Chiefs dropped the Raiders, 27–7. This defeat put the Raiders at 0–4 for the first time since 1964, and gave Kansas City their sixth straight win over Los Angeles. The Silver and Black received their lone touchdown on an Eric Dickerson 40-yard run.[4]

5. Oct. 4: Eight straight losses over ten months were not fitting for the team that reigned over pro football with the most wins over the previous 29 seasons. Jeff Jaeger, like the rest of the Raiders, was in a bad funk, missed eight field goal attempts, and looked to snap out of his slump. He did just that, as he nailed a career-long 54-yard field goal with 7:15 left in the game to give Los Angeles a 13–10 win over the New York Giants. Jaeger had previously missed two earlier field goal attempts with the Giants leading, 10–0. Los Angles then fought back. Jaeger got the Raiders on the board with a 26-yard field goal in the third quarter, and then Todd Marinovich teamed up with Tim Brown on a 68-yard touchdown pass with 4:22 left in the third to tie the game. Los Angeles then went on a seven-play, 44-yard drive capped off by Jaeger's rocket shot. The key play of the winning drive came on a 33-yard pass from Marinovich to Willie Gault. After turning the ball over 15 times in their first four games, the Raiders only had one mishap in this one (a fumble).[5]

6. Oct. 11: Eric Dickerson ran for 52 yards on 16 carries to give him 12,720 career rushing yards, leaving only 19 behind Tony Dorsett as the NFL's number two all-time ground gainer. He also opened the scoring with a 2-yard pass from Todd Marinovich on a day that saw the Raiders win their second game in a row, this time, 20–3, over the two-time defending AFC champion Buffalo Bills. Tim Brown also caught a Marinovich scoring strike from 52 yards, and Jeff Jaeger added field goals from 45 and 36 yards to give the Raiders their points on a day that saw the high powered Bills shocked by a team they were supposed to beat. The Los Angeles defense rose to the occasion with a yeoman's effort, holding a Buffalo team averaging 38 points a game to a mere three.[6]

7. Oct. 18: it was like the good old days for the Silver and Black. They were on a winning streak, and held a second straight opponent from scoring a touchdown. This time it was the Tom Flores–led Seahawks who fell victim to the Raiders by a score of 19–0. Jay Schroeder replaced Todd Marinovich at the 7:30 mark of the game after he suffered a sprained left knee on a sack from Cortez Kennedy. Schroeder made the most of his opportunity by taking Los Angeles on a 10-play, 57-yard drive capped off by Willie Gault catching a 4-yard pass from Schroeder for the game's initial score in the second quarter. Jeff Jaeger added a 53-yard field goal, and Nolan Harrison recorded a safety to give the Raiders a 12–0 lead by scoring in every possible fashion that a team can. Nick Bell added a 66-yard run to finish off the scoring

on a day that saw him rush for a game-high 97 yards on just 10 carries for an amazing 9.7 yards per carry. Anthony Smith led the defense with four of the team's six sacks.[7]

8. Oct. 25: The Dallas Cowboys stood at 5–1 coming into Los Angeles to face the Raiders. Raider Nation came out in droves to the LA Coliseum, producing the largest crowd of the NFL season (91,505), to see if the Silver and Black could make it four in a row. Marcus Allen gave the huge throng something to cheer about, as he got the Raiders on the board first with a 1-yard run, but Jeff Jaeger missed the extra point. After trailing, 7–6, in the third quarter, Los Angeles regained the lead, 13–7, on a Todd Marinovich to Willie Gault 31-yard pass. Things then went downhill for the Raiders, as they failed to cross midfield after taking the lead. Dallas running back Emmitt Smith, meanwhile, ran at will against the LA defense, racking up 152 yards and two touchdowns. Quarterback Troy Aikman added a touchdown run, and the Cowboys left Los Angeles as 28–13 victors.[8]

9. Nov. 8: After a bye week, the Raiders began the second half of the season with a lethargic offensive showing in a 31–10 beat down at the hands of the Philadelphia Eagles. Eric Dickerson led the Raiders backfield with a mere 28 yards rushing, and Todd Marinovich completed three out of 10 pass attempts for 25 yards and three interceptions before Jay Schroeder relieved him midway through the second quarter. Schroeder threw for 127 yards, and teamed up with Tim Brown in the fourth quarter from six yards out for the Raiders only touchdown. Jeff Jaeger gave Los Angeles their other points on a 22-yard field goal in the second quarter. With their second straight loss, the Raiders dropped to 3–6, and fourth place in the AFC West, and three games out of first place.[9]

10. Nov. 15: The Raiders were having a good time playing the Seattle Seahawks in 1992. One month earlier, they recorded a shutout against them, and this time around, they held Seattle scoreless into the fourth quarter. With Jay Schroeder back at quarterback after backing up Todd Marinovich for seven games, the Raiders won, 20–3, and snapped a two-game slide while extending Seattle's to seven straight setbacks. Schroeder did not light up the sky with passes, but his 108 yards on 10 of 23 pass attempts was good enough to get the Raiders 20 points. Following two Jeff Jaeger field goals from 47 and 43 yards in the first quarter, Schroeder threw for a touchdown to Ethan Horton, and Eric Dickerson added a 1-yard run for Los Angeles. The Raiders almost had their second straight against Seattle, but John Kasay kicked a 43-yard field goal with 4:25 remaining in the game to prevent Tom Flores' Seahawks from being blanked in the season series against his old team.[10]

11. Nov. 22: The Raiders just missed out on a shutout in their previous game, but got one this time by shocking the first place Denver Broncos, 24–0, to improve to 5–6. The Broncos were without their elite signal caller John Elway, who was out of action due to a bruised right shoulder. Denver turned to 21-year-old Tommy Maddox in what was his first-ever start. The Los Angeles defense took advantage of the situation, and intercepted Maddox twice, with Terry McDaniel coming up with both, and sacked him three times. When not blasting him into the turf, the Raiders' defensive unit hounded Maddox constantly throughout the game. Meanwhile, the Raiders' offense clicked behind Eric Dickerson's 107 rushing yards, 99 of which he gained in the first half. This was his best day as a Raider, and the 63rd time in his

illustrious ten seasons that he went over the century mark. Jay Schroeder threw three touchdown passes. His first one went to Andrew Glover from one yard out, which gave Schroeder his 100th career touchdown pass and 61st as a member of the Silver and Black. Tim Brown (11 yards), and Marcus Allen (10 Yards), each caught a scoring strike from Schroeder.[11]

12. Nov. 29: A trip to San Diego did not turn out as well for the rejuvenated Raiders, as they lost, 27–3. A Jay Schroeder interception was turned into a touchdown, and so was a Tim Brown fumble. San Diego did not give up 100 yards to an opposing running back in 23 games until Eric Dickerson ran for 103 yards in the first half, and in doing so, he became only the second player in NFL history to exceed 13,000 yards in a career. Jeff Jaeger supplied the Raiders with their only points on a 36-yard field goal in the second quarter.[12]

13. Dec. 6: The Raiders were tired of losing balls on fumbles, interceptions, and just plain old losing, especially to one of their all-time rivals. Six straight losses to the Kansas City Chiefs added to the Raiders' woes, and in front of Los Angeles Coliseum crowd of 45,227, the Silver and Black took out a year's worth of frustration on the Chiefs, dominating them, 28–7, and snapping a four-game losing streak in the process. Jay Schroeder threw for three touchdowns, and Elvis Patterson blocked a punt and recovered it for a score. The Raiders scored on the opening drive when Ethan Horton caught a 6-yard pass that capped a 10-play, 57-yard drive. Patterson's touchdown then gave Los Angeles 14 points in less than ten minutes after only scoring 29 first quarter points in the previous 12 games. Steve Smith caught an 11-yard pass from Schroeder, and Willie Gault a 17-yarder, to give the Raiders the rest of their points.[13]

14. Dec. 14: Any chances the Raiders may have had of making the playoffs came to an abrupt end in a 20–7 loss to the Miami Dolphins on Monday Night Football. This game also brought an end to the Marcus Allen era in a Raiders' uniform. With two meaningless games remaining, the Raiders' all-time leading rusher declared in a post-game interview that his days with the team would be over at the end of the season. His discontent with being reduced to a third string performer, coupled with an ongoing feud with Al Davis, brought the future Hall of Famer to terms with where he would go after the '92 campaign. The Dolphins snapped a skid that saw them lose five of their previous seven games. The Raiders only excitement came with them trailing, 17–0, in the fourth quarter. Miami was going for another touchdown when quarterback Dan Marino looked to tight end Keith Jackson in the end zone. Defensive back Eddie Anderson intercepted the pass in the end zone, and with a great block from Ronnie Lott, he raced 102 yards for a touchdown to set a team record for the longest interception return previously set by Mike Haynes (97 yards) in 1984 against the same Dolphins. An interesting footnote to this game was that it allowed the Raiders to become the only team to have appeared in each of Monday Night Football's 23 seasons.[14]

15. Dec. 20: The Raiders were indeed a part of the playoff race in '92, but not as a participant. They helped the Chargers clinch a trip to the post-season by losing to them, 36–14. San Diego became the first team in NFL history to reach the playoffs after starting the year with four losses. The Chargers scored each time they had possession in the first half, and held a 23–0 lead at

the intermission. Meanwhile, the Raiders were a pathetic case, getting minus four yards in their first nine plays. The offense then failed to score a touchdown in two of their previous three games, and looked to be making it three of four in this one. Jay Schroeder was just terrible, as he completed four of nine passes for 25 yards with an interception. He left the game in the third quarter after experiencing numbness in his shoulder after taking a hit at the end of the first half. Vince Evans replaced him, and managed to get Los Angeles on the board with two touchdown passes to Alexander Wright (21 yards), and Tim Brown (5 yards). Evans completed nine of 20 passes for 115 yards, and also threw two interceptions, but made up for them with his pair of scoring tosses. This game was the last home appearance at the LA Coliseum for Marcus Allen, which held the smallest crowd for a non-strike game (40,152). Soon after the game was over, Allen's locker was empty, which seemed to finalize his departure.[15]

16. Dec. 26: The greatest rushing game of Marcus Allen's pro career came in Super Bowl XVIII against the Washington Redskins in January, 1984. By December of 1992, Allen's fortunes in a Raiders uniform had turned sour, and at 32 years of age, he looked to move on after the final seconds ticked off the game, the season, and his days of donning the Silver and Black, as he watched Los Angeles win a squeaker over the defending Super Bowl champion Redskins, 21–20. Allen rushed for 40 yards in five carries, and caught four passes for 37 more. Vince Evans, the 37-year-old backup signal caller, came on once again in relief of Jay Schroeder after he re-injured his shoulder in the second quarter. Evans then hit on 15 of 22 pass attempts for 214 yards and two touchdowns. Washington led the tightly contested affair, 3–0, at the half. Los Angeles took a 7–3 lead in the third on a 41-yard pass from Evans to Alexander Wright. Art Monk put Washington back on top, 10–7, with a 49-yard catch at the end of the third quarter. With the score at 13–7 early in the fourth, Nick Bell regained the lead for the Raiders with a 5-yard run. Washington came back to go up, 20–14, with two minutes remaining in the game. Los Angeles was allowed one more chance at victory, and with 1:57 left, the Silver and Black put it all on the line. Starting on their own 20, Evans directed the team on an 80-yard drive. The big play was a 50-yard pass to Willie Gault that got the Raiders down go the Washington eight. With 51 seconds left, two runs by Bell, and an incomplete pass, now had Los Angeles facing a fourth-and-goal from the three. At the snap, Washington blitzed, and Evans quickly fired a pass to Tim Brown on a slant pattern across the middle at the goal line. Jeff Jaeger's extra point gave the Raiders their one-point lead with 13 seconds left. In this classic nail-biting drive, Marcus Allen carried two times for 14 yards, and caught a pass for 13. His run of eight yards was the last time he touched the ball as a Raider.[16]

Individual Statistics and Roster

Head Coach: Art Shell
Assistant Coaches: Fred Biletnikoff, Gunther Cunningham, Kim Helton, Ronnie Jones, Earl Leggett, Odis Mckinney, Steve Ortmayer, Terry Robiskie, Joe Scannella, Jack Stanton, Tom Walsh, Mike White
1992 Regular Season Record: 7–9
4th Place in AFC Western Division
Scored 249 points to rank 23rd out of 28 teams

Allowed 281 to rank 11th
Led the league in fewest touchdown passes allowed by a defense (11)

Starters — Offense

QB — Jay Schroeder: Active for 13 games and started in 9. Completed 123 of 253 pass attempts for 1,476 yards, 11 TD and 11 INT. Rushed for 160 yards on 28 carries.
RB — Eric Dickerson: Active for 16 games and started in 15. Rushed for 729 yards on 187 carries and 2 TD. Had 14 receptions for 85 yards and 1 TD.
RB — Steve Smith: Active for 16 games and started in 15. Rushed for 129 yards on 44 carries, and had 28 receptions for 217 yards and 1 TD.
WR — Tim Brown: Active for 15 games and started in 12. Had 49 receptions for 693 yards and 7 TD. Rushed for -4 yards on 3 carries. Returned 37 punts 383 yards and 2 kickoffs 14 yards.
WR — Willie Gault: Started in 16 games. Had 27 receptions for 508 yards and 4 TD. Rushed for 6 yards on 1 carry.
TE — Ethan Horton: Started in 16 games. Had 33 receptions for 409 yards 2 TD.
LT — Bruce Wilkerson: Active for and started in 15 games.
LG — Steve Wisniewski: Started in 16 games.
C — Don Mosebar: Started in 16 games.
RG — Max Montoya: Active for 10 games and started in 9.
RT — Reggie McElroy: Active for 16 games and started in 12.

Reserve Offensive Players

Marcus Allen (RB): Active for 16 games. Rushed for 301 yards on 67 carries and 2 TD. Had 28 receptions for 277 yards and 1 TD.
Nick Bell (RB): Active for 16 games and started in 1. Rushed for 366 yards on 81 carries and 3 TD. Had 4 receptions for 40 yards, and 1 kickoff return for 16 yards.
Vince Evans (QB): Active for 5 games. Completed 29 of 53 pas attempts for 372 yards, 4 TD and 3 INT. Rushed for 79 yards on 11 carries.
Mervyn Fernandez (WR): Active for 15 games and started in 1. Had 9 receptions for 121 yards.
Derrick Gainer (RB): Active for 2 games, and rushed for 10 yards on 2 carries.
Andrew Glover (TE): Active for 16 games, started in 2, and had 15 receptions for 178 yards and 1 TD.
Sam Graddy (WR): Active for 7 games and started in 1. Had 10 receptions for 205 yards and 1 TD, and 5 kickoff returns for 85 yards.
David Jones (TE): Active for 16 games, and had 2 receptions for 29 yards.
Todd Marinovich (QB): Active for and started in 7 games. Split time with Schroeder at quarterback. Completed 81 of 165 pass attempts for 1,102 yards, 5 TD and 9 INT, and rushed for 30 yards on 9 carries.
Napoleon McCallum (RB): Active for 13 games. Had 2 receptions for 13 yards, returned 4 punts 129 yards, and 14 kickoffs 274 yards.
Todd Peat (G): Active for 16 games and started in 8.
Greg Skrepenak (T/G): Active for 10 games.
Kevin Smith (TE): Active for 1 game.
Dan Turk (C/G): Active for 16 games and returned 1 kickoff 3 yards.
Alexander Wright (WR): Active for 10 games and started in 1. Had 12 receptions for 175 yards and 2 TD, and returned 18 kickoffs 325 yards.
Steve Wright (T/G/TE): Active for 7 games and started in 4.

Starters — Defense

DE — Howie Long: Started in 16 games and had 9 sacks.
DE — Greg Townsend: Active for and started in 14 games, had 5 sacks and 1 fumble recovery.
DT — Willie Broughton: Active for 16 games, started in 8 and had 1 sack.
DT — Nolan Harrison: Active for and started in 14 games, had 2 sacks, and recorded 1 safety.
LLB — Aaron Wallace: Started in 16 games, had 4 sacks and 2 fumble recoveries.
MLB — Riki Ellison: Active for and started in 12 games, had 1 sack and 2 fumble recoveries.

RLB — Winston Moss: Active for and started in 15 games and had 2 sacks.

CB — Terry McDaniel: Started in 16 games, had 4 INT and 1 fumble recovery.

CB — Lionel Washington: Started in 16 games and had 2 INT.

SS — Ronnie Lott: Started in 16 games, had 1 INT and 1 fumble recovery.

FS — Eddie Anderson: Started in 16 games, had 1 sack, 3 INT and 1 TD.

Reserve Defensive Players

Anthony Bell (LB): Active for 16 games and started in 5.

Thomas Benson (LB): Active for 1 game.

Aundray Bruce (LB/E): Active for 16 games, started in 4, and had 3 sacks.

Torin Dorn (DB): Active for 15 games and had 1 INT.

Bob Golic (NT/T): Active for 9 games and started in 7.

Derrick Hoskins (DB): Active for 16 games.

Mike Jones (LB): Active for 16 games.

Dan Land (DB): Active for 16 games, had 1 INT and returned 2 kickoffs for 27 yards.

Chester McGlockton (T/E): Active for 10 games and had 3 sacks.

Elvis Patterson (DB): Active for 15 games.

Sam Seale (DB): Active for 5 games.

Anthony Smith (E): Active for 15 games, started in 1, and had 13 sacks.

Dave Waymer (DB): Active for 16 games.

Kicking/Punting

K & P — Jeff Gossett: Active for 16 games. Made 15 of 26 field goals and 28 of 28 extra point kicks for 73 points. Punted 77 times for a 42.3 average. Rushed for -12 yards on 1 carry.

1993 Season Review

1. Sept. 5: The Raiders opened their 34th season with a new starting quarterback. The team had more new signal callers in the four seasons of the 1990's than they had from the mid — 1970's through the 1980's. Looking for someone to rejuvenate the offense, the Silver and Black turned to former Super Bowl–winning quarterback Jeff Hostetler. Unlike his predecessors, Hostetler rocked the LA Coliseum in his debut, beating the Minnesota Vikings, 24–7. He completed 23 of 27 passes for 225 yards and one touchdown to Tim Brown from 17 yards out. Greg Robinson added a 1-yard run, Terry McDaniel a 36-yard interception return, and Jeff Jaeger a 21-yard field goal, to give the Raiders their first opening day win since 1990.[1]

2. Sept. 12: The Hostetler-led Raiders remained perfect, and the Kingdome jinx of the past meant nothing in a 17–13 win over Seattle. This was the seventh straight win for Los Angeles over the Seahawks. Tim Brown had a good day with nine catches for 97 yards that included a 33-yard scoring strike from Jeff Hostetler. Hostetler added a 2-yard run, and Jeff Jaeger a 36-yard field goal to complete the Raiders' point production. On the defensive side, Anthony Smith sacked rookie quarterback Rick Mirer four times to give ex–Raiders coach Tom Flores his sixth straight loss over two seasons.[2]

3. Sept. 19: Cleveland's Eric Metcalf tormented the Raiders a year earlier by scoring four touchdowns. One year later, he did it once again, this time scoring on a 1-yard run with two seconds remaining to pull out a 19–16 win that handed Los Angeles their first loss of the season. The Raiders led throughout this game, and held a 16–3 advantage before Cleveland's comeback. A Jeff Hostetler to Andrew Glover 2-yard pass capped off an eight-play, 80-yard drive, and Jeff Jaeger added three field goals from 24, 27, and 53 yards. Hostetler suffered a sprained left knee on the opening drive, and later a sprained right ankle, but he refused to come out. The Raiders' defense held Cleveland in check during the first half, allowing them only 37 net yards. Things then went south for the Raiders, as Vinny Testaverde replaced Bernie Kosar at quarterback in the fourth quarter. Matt Stover kicked a field goal, and Testaverde connected with Lawyer Tillman on a 12-yard pass to narrow the Los Angeles lead to 16–10. After the ensuing kickoff, the Raiders took over at the own six. Facing a fourth-and-six, and pinned deep in their own territory, the Raiders took a safety, which allowed them some extra kicking room. The Browns then took over on their own 45, trailing, 16–12 with 1:41 left in the game. Two key passes to Mark Carrier got Cleveland to the LA 1-yard line, and that is when Metcalf broke the hearts of all those in Raider Nation.[3]

4. Oct. 3: Vince Evans was called on to lead the Silver and Black with Jeff Hostetler nursing his injuries sustained against Cleveland. Plagued by the lack of a running attack and a fierce pass rush that recorded six sacks, Evans was unable to generate much, and the Raiders were scalped by the Chiefs, 24–9. The Raiders also hurt themselves with 16 penalties for 173 yards in losses. The only positive thing to come out of this game was the performance of Rocket Ismail, who caught four passes for 75 yards that included a 43-yard touchdown from Evans in the fourth quarter. Jeff Jaeger added a 27-yard field goal on this dismal day. The story of this game was Marcus Allen, now wearing a Kansas City uniform. Even though he only rushed for 24 yards against his former teammates, he scored on a 4-yard run in the second quarter to give him his 100th career touchdown, tying him for ninth place on the all-time list with Franco Harris. After the game, Allen met with and embraced many of his old comrades. Despite his change of uniform, Allen was still, and will forever remain, a Raider for all time.[4]

5. Oct. 10: This time around, 38-year-old Vince Evans came off the bench in relief of Jeff Hostetler, and took a last second bite out of the Big Apple, leading Los Angeles to a 24–20 win over the New York Jets to snap a two-game losing streak. After trailing, 17–0, in the second quarter, Evans connected with James Jett from 42 yards out that closed the New York advantage to 17–7 at the half. Los Angeles then tied things up in the third quarter on an Evans to Alexander Wright 68-yard pass, and a Jeff Jaeger 42-yard field goal. For the day, Evans finished with 14 completions out of 22 attempts for 247 yards. Cary Blanchard kicked a field goal to help New York regain the lead at 20–17 with 4:29 left in the game. It was then that Evans rallied the Silver and Black with an 11-play, 72-yard drive capped off when Nick Bell scored on a 1-yard run with four seconds remaining to seal the victory. This was Bell's first game back after missing weeks with a hamstring injury.[5]

6. Oct. 18: The Raiders' Monday Night Football karma was felt by Jeff Jaeger, as his 53-yard field goal lifted Los Angeles to a 23–20 victory over the Denver Broncos. The Raiders took a 13–0 lead on the Broncos on a Jeff Hostetler to Alexander Wright 11-yard pass, and two Jaeger field goals from 32 and 49 yards. The defense was helping the cause in a major way, by registering four sacks, and holding the Denver passing attack to minus six yards

in the first half. Denver did not seem fazed by their opponents, and rallied back to take a 17–13 fourth quarter lead. James Jett then exploded on a 74-yard reception from Hostetler to regain the lead for Los Angeles. Denver refused to fold, and Jason Elam tied the game up at 20–20 with 5:33 remaining. The LA defense then took control, preventing Elway from getting anything going in the closing minutes. Throughout this game, the defense pressured Elway constantly, and sacked him a total of seven times, with Greg Townsend leading the way with three. The Raiders got the ball back with 2:38 left. Tim Brown, who had a great night with six catches for 116 yards, teamed up with Hostetler on a pass that put Los Angeles in field goal range. After failing to get any further than the Denver 35, Jaeger came on to kick the winning three-pointer.[6]

7. Oct. 31: After their second bye week, the 4–2 Raiders were rested and looked to catch the 5–1 division-leading Chiefs as the '93 season neared the halfway mark. On Halloween, the Silver and Black played host to their southern California rivals, the San Diego Chargers, who came into this clash not scoring more than 18 points a game. Jeff Hostetler lit up the Los Angeles sky for 424 yards and two touchdowns, but it was not enough, as the Chargers prevailed, 30–23. The Raiders jumped out to an early lead on their first play from scrimmage when Hostetler connected with Tim Brown from 71 yards out. For the game, Brown caught five passes for 156 yards and another touchdown in the third quarter, this time from 38 yards. The Chargers answered with a touchdown pass from John Friesz to Anthony Miller. The teams then exchanged field goals, with the Raiders getting theirs on a 38-yarder from Jeff Jaeger, and the game was knotted at 10–10 going into the second half. Brown's second touchdown reception of the game regained the lead for Los Angeles, but then Marion Butts countered with a 12-yard run for San Diego. Los Angeles drove down the field, and was looking to regain the lead in this see saw affair. Hostetler threw to Brown on second-and-goal from the three, but cornerback Donald Frank jumped in front of Brown and took off on a 102-yard interception return to give the Chargers their first lead of the game. The teams then matched field goals once again, with Jaeger hitting from 21 and 31 yards. With this loss, the Raiders fell to 4–3, and were tied with Denver for second place in the division behind the 5–2 Chiefs.[7]

8. Nov. 7: Chicago was the Raiders kind of town, as they came away with a close 16–14 victory that was secured when kicker Kevin Butler missed a 30-yard field goal on the final play of the game. The win allowed the Raiders to improve to 5–3, and still one game off the division lead. Los Angeles came into this game ranked 26th in rushing, and looked to get better in that category. They came out running, and rolled up 101 yards on the ground in the first half on the talents of Greg Robinson, Steve Smith, and Napoleon McCallum. The Raiders' defense, meanwhile, led the NFL in pass defense, and showed their talents by limiting quarterback Jim Harbaugh to a mere eight yards through the air in the first half. Eddie Anderson intercepted a pass that set the Raiders up for their only touchdown of the day, scored by McCallum from the one. Jeff Jaeger supplied the Silver and Black with their other points on field goals from 31, and two 21-yarders.[8]

9. Nov. 14: Marcus Allen made his return to the LA Coliseum, and received a very congenial greeting from the sellout

crowd of 66,553. Allen then helped Kansas City rally from a 14–0 deficit by gaining 85 yards on 17 carries, and scored his 105th career touchdown on a 4-yard run in the third quarter, and the Chiefs won, 31–20. With Joe Montana missing his second straight game with a hamstring injury, Dave Krieg was called upon to quarterback the Chiefs. He did a good job in relief by passing for 178 yards and three touchdowns to become the 17th quarterback in NFL history to throw for over 30,000 yards in a career. The Raiders received their points from Napoleon McCallum (4-yard run), Ethan Horton (8-yard pass from Jeff Hostetler), and Jeff Jaeger (35 and 30-yard field goals). This loss gave the Raiders a 5–4 record, and improved Kansas City to 7–2.[9]

10. Nov. 21: This time out, the Raiders did not give up the lead to one of their rivals. Los Angeles had two good drives of 86 and 89 yards in the first half, but stalled and had to settle for a pair of Jeff Jaeger field goals, both from 20 yards, to lead at the half, 6–0. Jaeger added two more three-pointers in the second half from 37 and 27 yards to give the Raiders their 300th all-time regular season victory by a 12–7 count. While Jaeger was adding a field goal per quarter to LA's tally, the Raiders defense clamped down, holding San Diego to 59 rushing yards and 95 passing. Lionel Washington supplied the Raiders with the clincher by intercepting a pass at the Los Angeles 39 with two seconds left in the game.[10]

11. Nov. 28: James Jett caught four passes for 117 yards against the winless Cincinnati Bengals. However, that was all the good that came out of this one, as the Raiders were beaten, 16–10. In a game they should have won, Los Angeles had too many mishaps that allowed the Bengals to prove the old saying correct that on any given Sunday, any team can beat any other team. The Raiders missed four field goals, dropped numerous passes, turned the ball over twice in scoring range, and gave Cincinnati their first win in 11 games on a snow-covered field. The Raiders received their points from Jeff Hostetler (4-yard run), and Jeff Jaeger (34-yard field goal).[11]

12. Dec. 5: The three-time defending AFC champion Buffalo Bills hosted the Raiders. After being turned back by the winless Bengals a week earlier, the Silver and Black went to the other side of the spectrum by beating the Bills, 25–24. Tim Brown provided the offensive punch for the Raiders. Throughout the game, he was open, and Jeff Hostetler took advantage of it. On the day, Brown caught 10 passes for 183 yards to become the first receiver to catch ten passes against the Bills since 1986. His ninth reception of the day provided the winning edge for Los Angeles. Trailing, 24–19, with 4:58 left in the game, Brown got past two defenders at the goal zone, caught a 29-yard pass from Hostetler, and tumbled into the end zone for the game-winner. The Raiders received their other points from Hostetler (11-yard run), and four Jeff Jaeger field goals (37, 34, 26, and 47 yards).[12]

13. Dec. 12: The Raiders made it two in a row with a 27–23 win over Seattle to climb to within one game of first place in the division at 8–5. Tim Brown once again helped lift the Raiders. He returned a punt 74 yards for a touchdown, which helped Los Angeles to an 18-point advantage. Before Brown's return, the Raiders clung to a slim 10–9 lead on a 24-yard Jeff Jaeger field goal and a Jeff Hostetler 4-yard run. Following Brown's return, the Raiders added a Jaeger field goal from 48 yards, and then a 56-yard pass from Hostetler to James Jett that expanded the lead

to 27–9. They then held off a fourth quarter rally to pull out the win.[13]

14. Dec. 19: The Raiders exploded out of the gate, scoring touchdowns on their first two possessions, and beat Tampa Bay, 27–20, to help keep their playoff hopes alive. Alexander Wright caught a 27-yard pass from Jeff Hostetler to cap a no-huddle, six-play drive that covered 72 yards on the game's opening series. Napoleon McCallum followed that up with a 5-yard run. The second quarter belonged to Tampa, as they closed the gap to 17–10 at the half. Los Angeles got a booming 51-yard field goal from Jeff Jaeger in between Tampa's scores. Los Angeles added another Jaeger field goal (33 yards), and a 1-yard run from Hostetler in 1:10 of the fourth quarter, and then held on after a final 10-point surge by the Buccaneers. Hostetler threw for 260 yards, and his touchdown run earned him the distinction of becoming the only Raiders signal caller to run for five scores in a season.[14]

15. Dec. 26: Los Angeles gave the Green Bay Packers a belated Christmas present on a cold, icy day at Lambeau Field. With a 28–0 blanking of the Raiders, the Packers clinched their first playoff berth in 11 years. At kickoff, the temperature was a zero, and the wind chill made it minus 22 degrees in what turned out to be the third coldest game ever played inside legendary Lambeau. The Raiders could only gain 46 yards rushing and 136 through the air. The only bright spot was Tim Brown's seven receptions for 80 yards, which provided the lone offensive excitement on this frigid afternoon. The Raiders were also part of history, as Green Bay's Sterling Sharpe became the first receiver to catch at least 100 passes in two seasons.[15]

16. Jan. 2: The day after New Years ended a lot happier for the Silver and Black than after Christmas a week earlier. Tim Brown led all league receivers with 11 catches for 173 yards, Jeff Hostetler threw for 310 yards, and the Raiders beat Denver, 33–30, to finish at 10–6, and clinch a wild card playoff berth in the process. Brown and Hostetler teamed up on two scoring strikes from four and 24 yards, and Alexander Wright caught another Hostetler touchdown pass from four yards. However, it was Jeff Jaeger who provided the knockout blow to the visiting Broncos. He kicked four field goals from 43, 50, and 37 yards in regulation, and then climaxed a seven-play, 49-yard drive with a 47-yarder to beat Denver for the eighth time in nine previous encounters.[16]

AFC Wild Card Game, January 9, 1994

After wrapping up a playoff spot against the Broncos one week earlier, the Raiders pre-

pared themselves for their first hurdle on the road to the Super Bowl. Once again, their opponents were the Broncos, who returned to Los Angeles for a second week in a row. This time the game did not need an exciting climax to decide the winner. For the Raiders rolled up a 42–24 win to beat Denver for the seventh straight time at the LA Coliseum. Jeff Hostetler threw for three touchdowns in the first half on his way to ringing up 294 yards on 13 out of 19 pass attempts. His scoring strikes went to Ethan Horton from nine yards to open the scoring, Tim Brown (65 yards), and James Jett (54 yards). In the second half, Napoleon McCallum took over by scoring three touchdowns on runs of 26, 2, and 1 yard. McCallum's trio of six-pointers earned him a spot

The passion for the Silver and Black is displayed on this Los Angeles Raiderette's face during the 1993 AFC Wild Card Game against the Denver Broncos at the Los Angeles Memorial Coliseum on January 9, 1994 (AP Photo/NFL Photos).

The end zone was a popular destination for Tim Brown during his illustrious career as a Los Angeles/Oakland Raider. On this occasion, Brown was on the receiving end of a 65-yard touchdown against Denver in the AFC Wild Card Game on January 9, 1994, at the Los Angeles Memorial Coliseum (AP Photo/NFL Photos).

in the record books for most touchdowns in a playoff game that he shared with 13 others. He finished his big day with 81 yards on 13 carries. As a team, the Silver and Black rolled to 427 yards of total offense.[17]

AFC Divisional Playoff, January 15, 1994

The last time the Raiders left Buffalo following a playoff game, they were demoralized, 51–3. Hoping that time could heal all wounds, Los Angeles made another post-season trek across the country and into Orchard Park, New York. With a wind chill of –25 degrees, the Raiders left the frigid conditions behind once again on the losing side, but not as bad this time around. The Raiders led, 17–13, at the half on two 1-yard runs from Napoleon McCallum and a 30-yard field goal by Jeff Jaeger. With Buffalo quarterback Jim Kelly throwing for close to 200 yards in the second half, the Bills took a 22–17 lead in the third quarter. The Raiders came right back on a Jeff Hostetler to Tim Brown 86-yard hook up to lead by the slimmest of margins, 23–22. On the play, Brown caught a short pass, then ran downfield, eluded a defender at the Buffalo 20, and went untouched from there to pay-dirt. The Bills then came right back on Kelly's second touchdown pass to Bill Brooks that proved to be the game winner, and sent the Raiders home on the short end of a 29–23 final.[18]

Individual Statistics and Roster

Head Coach: Art Shell

Assistant Coaches: Fred Biletnikoff, Gunther Cunningham, Ray Hamilton, Jim Haslett, Odis Mckinney, Bill Meyers, Steve Ortmayer, Terry Robiskie, Joe Scannella, Jack Stanton, Tom Walsh, Mike White, Arthur Whittington

1993 Regular Season Record: 10–6

2nd Place in AFC Western Division

Scored 306 points to rank 14th out of 28 teams

Allowed 326 to rank 21st

STARTERS — OFFENSE

QB — Jeff Hostetler: Active for and started in 15 games. Completed 236 of 419 pass attempts for 3,242 yards, 14 TD and 10 INT. Rushed for 202 yards on 55 carries and 5 TD.

RB — Greg Robinson: Active for and started in 12 games. Rushed for 591 yards on 156 carries and 1 TD. Had 15 receptions for 142 yards, and 4 kickoff returns for 57 yards.

FB — Steve Smith: Active for 16 games and started in 13. Rushed for 156 yards on 47 carries, and had 18 receptions for 187 yards.

WR — Tim Brown: Started in 16 games. Had 80 receptions for 1,180 yards and 7 TD. Rushed for 7 yards on 2 carries, and had 40 punt returns for 465 yards and 1 TD.

WR — Alexander Wright: Active for and started in 15 games. Had 27 receptions for 462 yards and 4 TD, and 10 kickoff returns for 167 yards.

TE — Ethan Horton: Started in 16 games. Had 43 receptions for 467 yards and 1 TD.

LT — Gerald Perry: Active for and started in 15 games.

LG — Steve Wisniewski: Started in 16 games.

C — Don Mosebar: Started in 16 games.

RG — Max Montoya: Started in 16 games.

RT — Bruce Wilkerson: Active for and started in 14 games.

RESERVE OFFENSIVE PLAYERS

Nick Bell (RB): Active for 10 games and started in 3. Rushed for 180 yards on 67 carries and 1 TD. Had 11 receptions for 111 yards.

John Duff (TE): Active for 1 game.

Vince Evans (QB): Active for 8 games and started in 1. Completed 45 of 76 pass attempts for 640 yards, 3 TD and 4 INT. Rushed for 51 yards on 14 carries.

Willie Gault (WR): Active for 15 games, had 8 receptions for 64 yards, and returned 7 kickoffs for 187 yards.

Andrew Glover (TE): Active for 15 games, and had 4 receptions for 55 yards and 1 TD.

Daryl Hobbs (WR): Active for 3 games.

Rocket Ismail (WR): Active for 13 games. Had 26 receptions for 353 yards and 1 TD. Rushed for -5 yards on 4 carries, and returned 25 kickoffs for 605 yards.

James Jett (WR): Active for 16 games and started in 1. Had 33 receptions for 771 yards and 3 TD, and rushed for 0 yards on 1 carry. **Led the NFL in yards gained per reception (23.4).**

Randy Jordan (RB): Active for 10 games and started in 2. Rushed for 33 yards on 12 carries, and had 4 receptions for 42 yards.

Ken Lanier (T): Active for and started in 2 games.

Napoleon McCallum (RB): Active for 13 games and started in 1. Rushed for 114 yards on 37 carries and 3 TD. Had 2 receptions for 5 yards, and 1 kickoff return for 12 yards.

Tyrone Montgomery (RB): Active for 12 games. Rushed for 106 yards, and had 10 receptions for 43 yards.

Todd Peat (G): Active for 16 games and had 2 kickoff returns for 18 yards.

Kevin Smith (TE): Active for 10 games and started in 1. Returned 2 kick-offs for 15 yards.

Richard Stephens (G): Active for 16 games and started in 1.

Dan Turk (C/G): Active for 16 games and returned 1 kickoff for 0 yards.

STARTERS — DEFENSE

DE — Howie Long: Started in 16 games and had 6 sacks.

DE — Greg Townsend: Started in 16 games and had 7 sacks.

DT — Chester McGlockton: Started in 16 games, had 7 sacks, 1 INT, and 1 fumble recovery.

DT — Nolan Harrison: Active for 16 games, started in 14, had 3 sacks and 1 fumble recovery.

LLB — Aaron Wallace: Active for 16 games, started in 14, had 2 sacks and 2 fumble recoveries.

MLB — Joe Kelly: Active for 16 games, started in 14, had 1 sack and 1 fumble recovery.

RLB — Winston Moss: Started in 16 games.

CB — Terry McDaniel: Started in 16 games and had 5 INT.

CB — Lionel Washington: Started in 16 games, had 1 sack and 2 INT.

SS — Derrick Hoskins: Started in 16 games, had 2 INT and 1 fumble recovery.

FS — Eddie Anderson: Started in 16 games, had 1 sack, 2 INT, and 1 fumble recovery.

RESERVE DEFENSIVE PLAYERS

Patrick Bates (DB): Active for 13 games and had 1 INT.

Greg Biekert (LB): Active for 16 games.

Willie Broughton (T/NT): Active for 15 games and had 1 sack.

Aundray Bruce (LB/E/TE): Active for 16 games, had 2 sacks and 1 fumble recovery.

Rickey Dixon (DB): Active for 9 games.

Torin Dorn (DB): Active for 15 games.

David Fulcher (DB): Active for 3 games.

Mike Jones (LB): Active for 16 games and started in 2.

Dan Land (DB): Active for 15 games.

Elvis Patterson (DB): Active for 3 games.

Anthony Smith (E): Active for 16 games, started in 2, and had 12 sacks.

James Trapp (DB): Active for 14 games, started in 2, and had 1 INT.

KICKING/PUNTING

K & P — Jeff Jaeger: Active for 16 games. Made 35 of 44 field goals and 27 of 29 extra point kicks for **132** points. Punted 71 times for a 41.8 average. Rushed for -10 yards on 1 carry.

1994 Season Review

1. Sept. 5: The Raiders opened the NFL's 75th season and Monday Night Football's 25th against the dominant San Francisco 49ers. The 49ers were stockpiled with talent, and none were better at their position than wide receiver Jerry Rice. On the national prime time stage, Rice became the NFL's career leader in touchdowns with 127 on a night that saw one of the game's greatest performers, and the rest of his teammates, maul the Raiders, 44–

14. Los Angeles hung around during the first half, and only trailed, 23–14, going into the third quarter. The Raiders got their first points of the new season in the second quarter after linebacker Greg Biekert intercepted a pass and returned it 11 yards to the 49er 30. Seven plays later, Jeff Hostetler connected with a wide-open Tim Brown across the middle for a 7-yard touchdown. Running back Napoleon McCallum scored the team's other touchdown on a 1-yard run. He was later taken off the field in the third quarter on a stretcher after his leg was twisted while being tackled.[1]

2. Sept. 11: Tom Flores won his 100th game as a head coach the week prior to meeting his old team. Thanks to his Seahawks, Flores added another win to his great career with a 38–9 beat down over the Raiders in their home opener. Played in front of 47,319 in the LA Coliseum that sustained major damage following an earthquake eight months earlier, Jeff Hostetler threw three interceptions that were converted into three Seattle touchdowns over the course of nine minutes in the second half. The Raiders lost defensive linemen Chester McGlockton and Aundray Bruce during this game after both were ejected for fighting. The Raiders received their points on a Jeff Jaeger 26-yard field goal and a 41-yard Terry McDaniel fumble recovery. The two-point conversion following the touchdown failed. This win snapped an eight-game winning streak that the Raiders had over Seattle.[2]

3. Sept. 18: Denver has always been known as a tough place to play in for a visiting team due to the thin air that left many sucking wind very quickly. However, the thin air in the Mile High City was just what Los Angeles needed to reverse their fortunes in the early stages of the '94 campaign. In a battle of teams looking for their first win, the Raiders handed the Broncos their worst defeat since 1968 with a 48–16 beating in which they rolled up 424 total offensive yards. Despite a tender elbow, Jeff Hostetler played a great game by completing 21 of 33 passes for 338 yards and four touchdowns. Tim Brown was his usual stellar self with seven receptions for 136 yards that included a 43-yard touchdown catch. Hostetler's other scoring tosses went to Tyrone Montgomery (65 yards), Andrew Glover (7 yards), and Harvey Williams (5 yards), who also ran for a 2-yard touchdown to open the game's scoring. Jeff Jaeger added field goals from 42 and 33 yards, and Terry McDaniel scored his second defensive touchdown in as many weeks with a 15-yard interception return. The rest of the defense did a great job also, sacking quarterback John Elway four times. In their past three games against Denver, the Raiders put 123 points up on the board, and this win gave Art Shell a 10–1 record against the Broncos.[3]

4. Sept. 25: The Raiders played tough against their inner-state rivals, the San Diego Chargers. Unfortunately, the final two seconds provided just enough time for John Carney to kick a winning 33-yard field goal that allowed the Chargers to remain undefeated with a 26–24 victory. Lionel Washington gave Los Angeles a 24–23 lead when he intercepted a Stan Humphries pass and returned it 31 yards with seven minutes left in the game. Washington's touchdown climaxed a Raiders surge that saw them rally from a twenty-point deficit. Down, 23–3, midway through the third quarter, Los Angeles scored on a Jeff Hostetler 1-yard run and a Hostetler to Rocket Ismail 24-yard pass before Washington's theft gave them a one-point lead.[4]

5. Oct. 9: Coming off their bye week, the Raiders faced the New England Patriots. New England quarterback Drew Bledsoe

led all league signal callers for the week with 321 yards through the air against Los Angeles. Despite his top spot among his peers, the Raiders beat Bledsoe and the rest of the Patriots, 21–17, thanks to three Terry McDaniel interceptions. The Los Angeles defensive back was quickly rising up in status with his trio of thefts, and for the third time in five games, McDaniel scored a touchdown. This time he opened the team's scoring with a 15-yard interception return with the Raiders down, 3–0, in the first quarter. One of McDaniel's other picks led to the deciding touchdown. Jeff Hostetler took advantage of his teammate's effort by scoring on a 3-yard run that erased a 17–14 New England lead with 9:34 left in the third quarter. Harvey Williams scored the Raiders' other touchdown on a 27-yard pass from Hostetler.[5]

6. Oct. 16: Miami's Bernie Parmalee was a one-man wrecking crew in a 20–17 overtime win against Los Angeles. The third-year running back ran for 150 yards, made two special team tackles, added another stop on an interception return, and recovered a fumble on a punt return that set up the tying touchdown. For his efforts, Parmalee was awarded two game balls for his offensive work, and the other for his job on special teams. The Raiders had a 10–0 first quarter advantage on a 19-yard field Jeff Jaeger field goal, and an Anthony Smith 25-yard fumble recovery. LA took a 17–10 third quarter lead on a 7-yard pass from Jeff Hostetler to Tim Brown, who had six receptions for 86 yards. The Dolphins forced overtime when Dan Marino teamed up with Keith Byars on an 18-yard pass. This marked the 27th time in Marino's career that he rallied Miami from a fourth quarter deficit. It was in overtime that Parmalee struck yet again by running for 45 yards following the kickoff. His 26-yard run got Miami to the LA 38, and another run put them at the 26. The 10-play 65-yard drive was then capped off on a Pete Stoyanovich 29-yard field goal to win it at the 5:46 mark in overtime.[6]

7. Oct. 23: Tim Brown caught eight passes for 130 yards, and Harvey Williams rushed for 107 yards in a 30–17 win over Atlanta to give the Raiders a 3–4 record. After Atlanta took a 10–0 first quarter lead, the Raiders stormed back in the second stanza on a Harvey Williams 1-yard run, and a Jeff Hostetler to Tim Brown 20-yard pass that put LA up for good. Brown and Hostetler teamed up again in the third quarter from 31 yards out, and Jeff Jaeger hit on field goals from 46, 31, and 24 yards to give the Raiders a much-needed victory.[7]

8. Oct. 30: The Raiders got back to .500 thanks to a 17–14 win over the 1–7 Houston Oilers. However, it was not easy. Jeff Hostetler was having a bad game, with only 92 yards through the air, and he suffered two interceptions. Like the true champion that he was, Hostetler managed to work through his dismal day, and led Los Angeles to the winning score with 1:50 left in the game. Trailing, 14–10, up to that point, Hostetler took the Raiders on a 67-yard drive that was capped off on an 11-yard pass to Tim Brown in the back of the end zone. During this drive, Hostetler hit on four of five passes for 59 yards. The Oilers were undaunted and looked to force overtime by going from their own 15 to the LA 34. With time expired in regulation, Al Del Greco attempted a 52-yard field goal that appeared to be on track, but it bounced off the crossbar and landed on the playing field to send 40,473 of Raider Nation home happy and relieved. Also scoring for the Raiders were Harvey Williams (2-yard run), and Jeff Jaeger (35-yard field goal).[8]

9. Nov. 6: Kansas City's Arrowhead Stadium was quickly becoming a lousy place to play in if someone was clad in silver and black during the late 1980's and early 90's. For the seventh straight time at home, the Chiefs beat their long-time foes, 13–3, to place Los Angeles one game below .500 at 4–5. This game marked the 100th career victory for head coach Marty Schottenheimer on a day that saw the Raiders get hit with 15 penalties for 115 yards, and Jeff Jaeger miss two field goal tries. Jaeger did connect on a 50-yarder to prevent a shutout.[9]

10. Nov. 13: In another chapter of the "Battle of Los Angeles," the Raiders prevailed, 20–17, over their backyard rivals the Rams. A 47-yard Jeff Jaeger field goal proved to be the difference. Jaeger also added a three-pointer from 44 yards earlier in the fourth quarter, and Jeff Hostetler threw two touchdown passes in the first half to Andrew Glover (27 yards), and Rocket Ismail (10 yards). Hostetler was forced from the game in the fourth quarter after spraining the big toe on his left foot. Before giving way to backup Vince Evans, Hostetler completed 17 of 25 passes for 218 yards. This game marked the final matchup between two teams from Los Angeles, as both organizations only had six more games remaining before leaving the City of Angels to other locales.[10]

11. Nov. 20: Los Angeles climbed back into the division race with a 24–19 win over the New Orleans Saints. This victory, coupled with a San Diego loss, moved the Raiders to 6–5, and only two games behind the division-leading Chargers. Los Angeles built a 24–7 lead in the fourth quarter on three Jeff Hostetler touchdown passes, with two going to Tim Brown (12 and 30 yards), and one to Rocket Ismail from 17 yards. Brown finished the day with eight receptions for 132 yards. Despite throwing two interceptions, Hostetler was near perfect with 22 of 28 completions for 310 yards. The Saints made things interesting in the late going on two Jim Everett to Torrance Small scoring tosses.[11]

12. Nov. 27: Los Angeles went back to .500, and now saw themselves three games out of first place after a 21–3 loss to the Pittsburgh Steelers. Pittsburgh had a revival of their famed "Steel Curtain" defense, and added to their league-leading 45 sacks with five against the Raiders. They hit hard, and smothered the Los Angeles offense, allowing only 57 rushing yards and a mere 122 through the air. Jeff Hostetler was forced from the game after a hit by linebacker Chad Brown caused him to suffer blurred vision and a minor concussion. The Raiders managed to avoid the shutout thanks to a 32-yard field goal by Jeff Jaeger.[12]

13. Dec. 5: The Raiders not only improved to 7–6, but they prevented one of their rivals, the San Diego Chargers, from clinching the AFC West with a 24–17 win. Even though he was dinged up over the last few weeks, Jeff Hostetler came out strong in this one. He completed 22 of 29 passes for 319 yards and two touchdowns. Hostetler opened the scoring with a 76-yards throw to Alexander Wright. His other scoring strikes went to Rocket Ismail from six yards away with the game tied at 17–17. Ismail also caught an earlier 6-yard touchdown pass from Vince Evans. Jeff Jaeger rounded out the scoring with a 43-yard field goal. The Raiders had trouble in the fourth quarter throughout the season, as they were outscored 98 to 49. This time, however, they had a 10–3 advantage, and held on as the Chargers attempted a gallant surge in front of their home crowd. With 1:28 left in regulation, San Diego went from their 8-yard line to the LA 48 before a holding

penalty stopped their momentum. Aaron Wallace then ended any hopes of a comeback when he sacked quarterback Stan Humphries. This marked the fourth time in five years that the Raiders came out of San Diego victorious.[13]

14. Dec. 11: Los Angeles made it two in a row against division foes with a 23–13 win over the Denver Broncos. Jeff Jaeger set a team record with five field goals, and the defense took it from there, to help Los Angeles improve to 8–6 and still alive in the playoff race. This win was the Raiders' fifth straight over Denver, 11th out of 12 previous encounters, and eighth consecutive in the LA Coliseum. Denver's great field general John Elway watched this one from the sidelines due to a strained muscle behind his left knee. The Los Angeles defense kept the Broncos out of the end zone on two occasions after they had first downs at the LA 1-yard line. Both times Denver came away with only field goals instead of six-pointers, which proved to be the difference in the game. Jaeger's record-setting day was made possible with three-pointers from 44, 29, 47, 30, and 28 yards. Harvey Williams added a touchdown on a 5-yard pass from Jeff Hostetler.[14]

15. Dec. 18: The Raiders climbed into sole possession of second place in the AFC West with yet another victory over a division rival. A 17–16 squeaker of Seattle allowed Los Angeles to go to 9–6. The Raiders had wanted to strike deep throughout this game, and in the fourth quarter, they did just that after trailing, 16–10. After a false start penalty, Jeff Hostetler saw Tim Brown sprinting down the right sideline. Hostetler knew he had the makings of something big, and he let the pigskin fly. Brown hauled the pass in at the Seattle 40, and then took it all the way to complete a 77-yard touchdown. Jeff Jaeger's extra point kick then gave the Raiders their winning advantage. He also added a 24-yard field goal, and Harvey Williams, who led the game with 93 yards on the ground, ran for a 5-yard score. The Seahawks did manage to add some suspense to the climax when John Kasay missed on a 50-yard field goal attempt with nine seconds left. An interesting footnote to this game did not include a player, but a remote control car. With Seattle leading, 13–10, and on the LA 10 with a first down, it was then that the car took a Sunday drive out across the field during a timeout. It started going around in circles, and eventually it was removed and play resumed. However, the disruption seemed to take the edge off Seattle's offensive surge, as they were hit with a five-yard penalty, were stopped for no gain on a running play, and finally two passes fell incomplete. They had to settle for a field goal instead of what more than likely should have been a touchdown.[15]

16. Dec. 24: In what was the final game of the regular season, the last one for the Los Angeles Raiders, and the final game for Art Shell as head coach of the Raiders, the Silver and Black fell victim to the Kansas City Chiefs, 19–9. A sellout crowd of 64,130 turned out in the LA Coliseum to witness former local hero Marcus Allen destroy his old team with 132 yards on 33 carries, and also become the ninth in NFL history to pass the 10,000-yard career rushing barrier. Both teams finished at 9–7, but the Chiefs got the playoff nod due to their season sweep over Los Angeles. The Raiders could have made the post season if Chicago had beaten New England, but it was not to be for the '94 edition of the Silver and Black. What began as a year in which the Raiders were picked by many to go deep in the playoffs, ended with noth-

ing, and shortly after this game, Art Shell was let go as head coach. They did, however, set a league record with 156 penalties called against them. In the Raiders' final game representing the city of Los Angeles, their points came on a Jeff Jaeger 30-yard field goal, and a Vince Evans to Alexander Wright 65-yard pass for the last score ever rung up as Los Angeles Raiders.[16]

Individual Statistics and Roster

Head Coach: Art Shell
Assistant Coaches: Fred Biletnikoff, Gunther Cunningham, John Fox, Ray Hamilton, Jim Haslett, Odis Mckinney, Bill Meyers, Bob Mischak, Steve Ortmayer, Jack Reilly, Jack Stanton, Tom Walsh, Mike White, Arthur Whittington
1994 Regular Season Record: 9–7
3rd Place in AFC Western Division
Scored 303 points to rank 19th out of 28 teams
Allowed 327 to rank 17th

STARTERS — OFFENSE

QB — Jeff Hostetler: Started in 16 games. Completed 263 of 455 pass attempts for 3,334 yards, 20 TD and 16 INT. Rushed for 159 yards on 46 carries and 2 TD.
RB — Harvey Williams: Active for 16 games and started in 10. Rushed for 983 yards on 282 carries and 4 TD. Had 47 receptions for 391 yards and 3 TD. Returned 8 kickoffs for 153 yards.
RB — Tom Rathman: Started in 16 games. Rushed for 118 yards on 28 carries, and had 26 receptions for 194 yards.
WR — Tim Brown: Started in 16 games. Had 89 receptions for 1,309 yards and 9 TD. Returned 40 punts for 487 yards.
WR — Alexander Wright: Active for 16 games and started in 15. Had 16 receptions for 294 yards and 2 TD. Returned 10 kickoffs for 282 yards.
TE — Andrew Glover: Started in 16 games. Had 33 receptions for 371 yards and 2 TD.
LT — Gerald Perry: Active for and started in 12 games.
LG — Steve Wisniewski: Started in 16 games.
C — Don Mosebar: Started in 16 games.
RG — Kevin Gogan: Started in 16 games.
RT — Greg Skrepenak: Active for 12 games and started in 10.

RESERVE OFFENSE PLAYERS

Wes Binder (RB): Active for 9 games and had 2 receptions for 14 yards.
Jarrod Bunch (RB): Active for 3 games.
John Duff (TE): Active for 4 games.
Vince Evans (QB): Active for 9 games. Completed 18 of 33 pass attempts for 222 yards and 2 TD. Rushed for 24 yards on 6 carries.
Daryl Hobbs (WR): Active for 10 games and had 5 receptions for 52 yards.
Rocket Ismail (WR): Active for 16 games. Had 34 receptions for 513 yards and 5 TD. Rushed for 31 yards on 4 carries, and returned 43 kickoffs for 923 yards.
Robert Jenkins (T): Active for 10 games and started in 4.
James Jett (WR): Active for 16 games and started in 1. Had 15 receptions for 253 yards.
Calvin Jones (RB): Active for 7 games, rushed for 93 yards on 22 carries, and had 2 receptions for 6 yards.
Napoleon McCallum (RB): Active for 1 game and rushed for 5 yards on 3 carries and 1 TD.
Tyrone Montgomery (RB): Active for and started in 6 games. Rushed for 97 yards on 36 carries, and had 8 receptions for 126 yards and 1 TD.
Max Montoya (G): Active for 13 games.
Kevin Smith (TE): Active for 3 games, rushed for 2 yards on 1 carry, and had 1 reception for 8 yards.

Dan Turk (C/G): Active for 16 games.

Bruce Wilkerson (T/G): Active for 11 games and started in 6.

Jamie Williams (TE): Active for 16 games, had 3 receptions for 25 yards, and returned 1 kickoff for 0 yards.

STARTERS — DEFENSE

DE — Nolan Harrison: Started in 16 games, had 5 sacks and 2 fumble recoveries.

DE — Anthony Smith: Started in 16 games, had 6 sacks and 1 fumble recovery.

DT — Jerry Ball: Active for 16 games, started in 13, had 3 sacks and 1 fumble recovery.

DT — Chester McGlockton: Started in 16 games, had 9 sacks and 1 fumble recovery.

LLB — Rob Fredrickson: Active for 16 games, started in 12, and had 3 sacks.

MLB — Greg Biekert: Active for 16 games, started in 14, had 1 sacks and 1 INT.

RLB — Winston Moss: Active for 16 games, started in 14, and had 2 sacks.

CB — Terry McDaniel: Started in 16 games, had 7 INT and 3 fumble recoveries.

CB — Albert Lewis: Active for 14 games, started in 9, and had 1 sack.

SS — Derrick Hoskins: Active for 15 games, started in 9, and had 1 fumble recovery.

FS — Eddie Anderson: Active for and started in 14 games. Had 2 sacks and 1 fumble recovery.

RESERVE DEFENSIVE PLAYERS

Patrick Bates (DB): Active for 16 games, started in 9, and had 2 fumble recoveries.

Cary Brabham (DB): Active for 7 games.

Aundray Bruce (LB/E/TE): Active for 16 games.

Scott Davis (T/E/LB): Active for 16 games and started in 1.

James Folston (LB): Active for 7 games.

Donald Frank (DB): Active for 16 games, had 1 INT and 1 fumble recovery.

Rob Holmberg (LB): Active for 16 games.

Mike Jones (LB): Active for 16 games and started in 2.

Dan Land (DB): Active for 16 games.

Austin Robbins (T): Active for 2 games.

James Trapp (DB/WR): Active for 16 games, started in 2, and had 1 sack.

Aaron Wallace (LB): 2 sacks: Active for 16 games and started in 6.

Lionel Washington (DB): 3 INT: Active for 11 games, started in 7, had 3 INT and 1 TD.

Alberto White (E): Active for 8 games and had 2 sacks.

KICKING/PUNTING

K & P — Jeff Jaeger: Active for 16 games. Made 22 of 28 field goals and 31 of 31 extra points for 97 points. Punted 77 times for a 43.9 average.

Raiders Move Back to Oakland

When the Raiders relocated to Los Angeles in 1982, they were still in the midst of their glory days. The City of Angels embraced the Silver and Black as saviors from pro football–less Sundays. The bad boys of the gridiron were always regarded as a melting pot of personalities much like Los Angeles. This helped to provide the Raiders with a new, vast, fan base that took to the team with unbridled passion. The sale of Raiders merchandise rose to unbelievable heights, and from 1982 through 1985, the Raiders ruled Los Angeles, with massive crowds filing in to the

LA Coliseum to watch the Silver and Black pound out victorie and opponents on a consistent basis.

By the latter portion of the decade, however, the massive Coliseum was virtually barren, as the team's fortunes began to decline. The area adjacent to the Coliseum was not the safest to be in, and fights in the stands were commonplace on game day The team's lack of success coupled with the unsafe environmen meant less people were less willing to come out and support the Raiders.

By 1987, Al Davis realized that the Coliseum would not sui his needs for very much longer, and looked to different locale outside of the Los Angeles city limits.[1] The nearly 70-year-olc Coliseum still did not have the luxury suites or other improvements that Davis was promised at the dawn of the decade wher he was wooed to the City of Angels. The time was right to seek what Davis felt his Raiders deserved. He wanted a modern facility with all the perks necessary to compete in the highly competitive professional sports marketplace.[2]

In August 1987, the city of Irwindale rose to the forefront as the designated new home of the Raiders. Located 18 miles east of Los Angeles, Irwindale officials planned to build the Raiders a new stadium in an old rock quarry. The Raiders were even paid $10 million as an offer of good faith. However, the deal fel through, but the Raiders kept the non-refundable ten mil.[3]

During the summer months of the following year, speculation was high that the Raiders were looking to return to their native Oakland, with Alameda County officials and the NFL both in approval of the trek back to northern California. Over the course of three years, after delays mounted, Davis decided to remain in Los Angeles on September 11, 1991. The new deal caused fans in Oakland to use Raiders merchandise as kindling for numerous bonfires.[4]

The new deal struck by Davis and Los Angeles did not mean that the Emperor of Raider Nation was satisfied with his current dwellings. He sought what seemed to be a great opportunity to build a stadium in Hollywood Park, located 11 miles southwest of downtown Los Angeles in Inglewood. Everything seemed to finally be coming together between the Raiders and the city they called home for a decade. Once again, however, a pitfall loomed. For it appeared that the NFL wanted to bring another team into the area and share the new Hollywood Park facility with the Raiders.[5]

Davis had grown weary of sharing a stadium with another occupant, as he had to co-exist with the USC Trojans at the LA Coliseum. Davis wanted his own gridiron palace dedicated solely to his Raiders and nothing else would appease him. Apparently the league would not budge on their idea of dual existence in Hollywood Park, and things were at a stalemate.

Davis did not want a shoving match with the league that could prove to be nothing more than another delay in getting the best deal possible for his team.

He found resolve to the dilemma in the same geographic location that he left 13 years earlier. On June 23, 1995, Davis signed a 16-year agreement with the city of Oakland to return the team back to its place of origin. One month later, the city and team came to a mutual understanding about improvements that Davis wanted and never received back in the early 1980's.[6] Happy to have the Silver and Black back, city officials gave approval to renovate the Oakland Coliseum with luxury suites plus other amenities that would please Davis. The project got underway in late 1995, and by the '96 season, the work was complete.

The ruse by the NFL involving the Raiders and the proposed Hollywood Park project eventually made its way through the legal system. In 1999 Davis filed a $1.2 billion lawsuit against the league, claiming the pro grid circuit sabotaged the Raiders attempt to build the Hollywood Park stadium by wanting another team to share it. Davis also claimed that the Raiders still owned the Los Angeles market even after being out of the area for four years. Two years later, on May 21, 2001, a jury in Los Angeles ruled against Davis after a trial that lasted six weeks.[7]

There is no telling where the Raiders will be in the future. In their beginning, they were looked upon as orphans, and in some ways they still are. They were the final franchise selected into the original AFL, played in three stadiums in their first seven years, and flip-flopped between two cities throughout their existence. There are some factions that still feel the team belongs to Los Angeles despite their return to Oakland. On a positive note, this incredible team with its illustrious past has two fan bases that care deeply about them, not to mention a global plethora of diehard fanatics.

1995 Season Review

1. Sept. 3: In a classic case of what was once old is now new again, the Raiders opened their 36th season in the city where they started. After 13 seasons in Tinseltown, the team returned to Oakland. With the song "The boys are back in town" blasting throughout a sold out Oakland Coliseum with a crowd donned in a sea silver and black regalia, and many players of the past on hand, the Raiders prevailed in their gallant return to northern California, 17–7, over the San Diego Chargers. Prior to their departure to Los Angeles, the Raiders won close to 80 percent of their home games in Oakland, and looked to keep that incredible dominance going. Jeff Hostetler, guiding a new ball-control offensive attack, found Tim Brown from five yards out for the Raiders first score of the season, and their first in Oakland since 1981. This game provided many firsts to members of this team, as Cole Ford, who came late to the team as a replacement for an injured Jeff Jaeger, kicked his first field goal as a Raider from 46 yards, and rookie Napoleon Kaufman scored his first-ever regular season touchdown on a 16-yard run to give first-year head coach Mike White his first victory as mentor.[1]

2. Sept. 10: Oakland next invaded RFK Stadium on a day that saw the Redskins sell out for the 215th straight time to expand on their NFL record. Jeff Hostetler and the Raiders had a simple plan as this game progressed. It called for them to take what the defense gave them, and it was a far cry from the Raiders creed established by Al Davis back in the 1960's to take what you wanted. Regardless, it worked for Oakland in a 20–8 win in the nation's capital. Jeff Hostetler completed 22 of 29 passes for 205 yards and touchdown tosses to Andrew Glover (1 yard), and Derrick Fenner (8 yards), with only one completion going for more than 20 yards. Harvey Williams ran for a game-high 84 yards, and Cole Ford kicked two field goals from 19 and 34 yards for the undefeated Silver and Black.[2]

3. Sept. 17: Marcus Allen went over 15,000 all-purpose yards to become only the fifth player in history to reach that incredible plateau. It figured that long-time rival Kansas City would be the ones to give the Raiders their first loss since returning to Oakland. In a battle of unbeatens, the Chiefs won, 23–17, on what the papers called a "freak play." Oakland was in control of this game for three quarters, leading, 17–7. The Raiders built their ten-point bulge on two Harvey Williams' 1-yard runs, and a 33-yard field goal from Cole Ford. The Chiefs then fought back to tie, and almost pulled it out with 1:52 remaining in regulation. Facing third down from the Oakland two, Marcus Allen took a handoff and ran into massive Jerry Ball, who dropped the future Hall of Famer for a loss of four yards. Lin Elliott then missed a 24-yard field goal attempt to send the affair into overtime. On the Chiefs first possession in the extra quarter, Allen fumbled on Oakland's 38 after picking up 20 yards on a reception. The Raiders looked to capitalize on their former start's mishap, and were just inside Kansas City territory when the "freak play" transpired. Jeff Hostetler looked for Tim Brown with a pass to the outside, but an umpire blocked the pass route and defensive back James Hasty came in and picked the ball off and went 64 yards to paydirt, providing the Chiefs with their eighth straight win over the Raiders in Arrowhead Stadium.[3]

4. Sept. 24: after giving up the lead against Kansas City, the Raiders decided to win the same way they lost the previous week. After spotting the Philadelphia Eagles a 17–0 advantage in the first quarter, the Silver and Black roared back with 48 points to win big, 48–17. In the rout, the defense was responsible for scoring 14 points on fumble returns by tackle Austin Robbins (6 yards), and linebacker Rob Fredrickson (35 yards). A Terry McDaniel interception was turned into a Harvey Williams 4-yard run. Williams also scored on a 1-yard run in the second quarter. As a unit, the defense recorded seven quarterback sacks with Pat Swilling getting three. Jeff Hostetler threw a 7-yard touchdown to Derrick Fenner, Vince Evans tossed a 54-yarder to Daryl Hobbs, and Cole Ford booted two field goals from 35 and 28 yards to complete the dismantling. This win gave the 3–1 Raiders a piece of the AFC West lead with Kansas City.[4]

5. Oct. 1: This time the Raiders did not have to fight their way back from a deficit. From beginning to end the Silver and Black totally dominated the New York Jets, coming out of Giants Stadium with a 47–10 win, and in doing so, they handed the Jets their worst home defeat in six years. Jeff Hostetler teed off on a New York secondary wracked by injuries, throwing for 261 yards on 14 of 23 attempts for four touchdowns. Tim Brown also had the opportunity to torment the New Yorkers with eight receptions for 156 yards and two touchdowns (18 and 66 yards). Andrew Glover and Daryl Hobbs each had one catch in this game, and both went for touchdowns. Glover's was from two yards and Hobbs from six. Also getting in on the Oakland barrage were Harvey Williams (8-yard run), Mike Jones (47-yard fumble recovery), and Cole Ford (29 and 26 yard field goals). Williams led all ball carriers with 97 yards, and Napoleon Kaufman added 95 more on a day that saw Oakland roll up 457 yards of total offense.[5]

6. Oct. 8: The Oakland Raiders came into week six tied for first place in the division, and left the weekend as AFC West leaders after a 34–14 rout over the Seattle Seahawks. The new

ball-control offensive scheme installed by first-year head coach Mike White allowed the Raiders to be the league's highest-scoring team en route to a 5–1 record. Harvey Williams ran for a career-high 160 yards and a 25-yard touchdown. He also threw for a 13-yard score to Andrew Glover. Jeff Hostetler was simply brilliant throwing the ball. He completed 20 of 33 passes for 333 yards and touchdowns to Tim Brown (80 yards), and Kerry Cash (16 yards). Jeff Jaeger was back to handling the kicking chores, and started off Oakland's day with field goals from 37 and 24 yards.[6]

7. Oct. 16: Oakland's high-powered offensive attack hit a major snag on the prime time stage when a trip to Denver on Monday Night Football ended in a 27–0 rout. John Elway threw for 324 yards and two touchdowns, and the defense held Oakland to 19 yards of offensive production in the second and third quarters.[7]

8. Oct. 22: Oakland shook off their goose egg from the previous week, and beat the Indianapolis Colts, 30–17, to remain one game off the division lead at 6–2. This game was highlighted by Napoleon Kaufman's 84-yard kickoff return for a touchdown. With Jeff Hostetler out due to fractured cartilage near his windpipe, 40-year-old Vince Evans stepped in brilliantly. Getting away from the no-huddle, ball-control offense that the Raiders used up to this point of the '95 season, the team returned to attack mode that suited them so well for most of their existence. Evans completed 23 of 35 passes for 335 yards, and threw for two touchdowns to Rocket Ismail (73 and 46 yards), who caught three passes for 125 yards. Jeff Jaeger added three field goals from 28, 24, and 35 yards. The defense also returned to their old rough and tumble ways, getting penalized nine times, recording four sacks, and recovering two fumbles.[8]

9. Nov. 5: Jeff Hostetler used Oakland's bye week to heal up and returned to action in a 20–17 win over the Cincinnati Bengals that gave the Raiders a record of 7–2 and sole possession of second place in the AFC West. The Raiders did not explode or dominant, but rather maintained a steady flow in this game. Putting aside their passing attack on a cold 32-degree Cincinnati afternoon, the Raiders relied on a churning-it-out type of offensive scheme that saw Harvey Williams rush for 134 yards and included a 2-yard touchdown run. When he did throw, Hostetler connected on 17 of 29 passes for 178 yards and a touchdown pass to Tim Brown (34 yards). Jeff Jaeger added field goals from 37 and 46 yards. The Raiders won the battle in the trenches, and the defense played tough, got into some minor altercations with the Bengals, and recorded four sacks.[9]

10. Nov. 12: Jeff Hostetler returned to the place of his championship glory when the Raiders traveled to Giants Stadium to battle New York. On another bad weather day, with winds blasting through at 35 miles-per-hour, Hostetler rallied the Silver and Black to a 17–13 victory. The win gave the Raiders an 8–2 record, which was the second-best mark in the AFC behind the 9–1 Kansas City Chiefs. With Oakland trailing, 13–10, midway through the fourth quarter, Hostetler led the offense on the winning 71-yard drive that was climaxed by Harvey Williams scoring on a 6-yard run with 6:52 left in the game. Williams finished with a game-high 85 rushing yards. During the winning drive, Williams and Napoleon Kaufman carried the load due to swirling winds that made throwing the ball extremely difficult. When he was able to throw, Hostetler completed 13 of 19 passes for 152

yards and a 40-yard scoring strike to Rocket Ismail. Jeff Jaeger added a 30-yard field goal to complete Oakland's scoring. Chester McGlockton provided the final blow to the Giants when he swatted away a Dave Brown pass attempt on fourth down with New York on the Oakland 28 in the closing minutes.[10]

11. Nov. 19: The Dallas Cowboys of the 1990's relied on the big three of quarterback Troy Aikman, running back Emmitt Smith, and wide receiver Michael Irvin, for virtually all of the offensive firepower during their run at three Super Bowl titles in four seasons. Against the Raiders, this incredible trio of talent once again provided the necessary means for Dallas to win, 34–21. In doing so, the Cowboys handed the Raiders their first home loss since returning to Oakland. Aikman threw for 227 yards, Smith ran for 110 and three touchdowns, and Irvin caught seven passes for 109 yards. With Dallas dominating Oakland by 24 points in the third quarter, backup quarterback Vince Evans rallied the Silver and Black with two touchdown passes to Tim Brown (24 yards), and Kerry Cash (16 yards), which closed the gap to ten points. The Raiders got their other touchdown in the second quarter on a Harvey Williams 7-yard run. Evans came into the game in the second half after Jeff Hostetler reinjured his left shoulder, and the seasoned veteran hit on 20 of 41 passes for 232 yards. With the loss, Oakland fell to 8–3 and two games off the division lead.[11]

12. Nov. 27: With Kansas City losing a day earlier, the Raiders looked to close to within one game of first place on a Monday Night Football telecast against the defending AFC champion San Diego Chargers. Even though the Chargers were bringing up the rear of the division at 4–7, they took great pleasure in ruining any opportunities for the Raiders to enjoy success. On this night, the Chargers did just that by outlasting Oakland in a low-scoring affair, 12–6. It was a kicker's paradise on this night, as John Carney booted four field goals to Jeff Jaeger's two. Jaeger's kicks were from 30 and 26 yards. Vince Evans played the entire game, and suffered three interceptions by defensive back Dwayne Harper, who also saved a sure touchdown by tackling Harvey Williams after he gained 60 yards. For the game, Williams ran for 101 yards on 20 carries. Harper's final theft ended any hopes for a Raiders victory after he cut in front of Tim Brown on the Oakland 28 with 56 seconds left in the game.[12]

13. Dec. 3: The wheels were coming off the wagon so to speak, as Oakland dropped their third straight game, and in doing so, gave Kansas City the AFC West championship with a 29–23 win. This was Kansas City's fifth straight win over the Raiders, and 12th of the previous 13. Marcus Allen ran for a season-high 124 yards, which allowed him the honor of becoming the first player in NFL history to rush for over 10,000 yards and gain 5,000 more receiving. As was the case when these two teams collided, tempers flared, pushing and shoving ensued, and six personal fouls were handed out. In all, the Raiders were flagged on ten occasions for 90 yards of losses. Vince Evans put together a good game with 24 completions in 38 attempts for 227 yards, but suffered two interceptions. Billy Joe Hobert also saw action at quarterback, and hit on five of 11 passes for 118 yards and two touchdowns to James Jett (26 yards), and Tim Brown (1-yard). Oakland's other points came on a Terry McDaniel 42-yard interception return and a 46-yard Jeff Jaeger field goal.[13]

14. Dec. 10: for the first time in Raiders history, the Silver

nd Black dropped three consecutive home games in the Oakland Coliseum. The Pittsburgh Steelers had the honor of giving Oakland the dubious distinction with a 29–10 victory for their seventh straight win, while the Raiders fell for the fourth consecutive week to put a road block in their path to the playoffs. Billy Joe Hobert started the game at quarterback in an attempt to jumpstart an offense that failed to produce a touchdown in three weeks. The Steelers came in with a defensive plan to stop the run and apply pressure on Hobert in his first NFL start. Everything worked according to plan, as Oakland's offensive line could not stop Pittsburgh's onslaught. The Raiders were held to a mere 28 yards on the ground, and Hobert was picked off four times. The Raiders were able to score thanks to an Aundray Bruce 1-yard interception return, and a 39-yard Jeff Jaeger field goal.[14]

15. Dec. 17: This game was a story of two teams going in different directions fast. The Seattle Seahawks were surging toward a playoff berth while the Raiders were getting farther away. With Chris Warren running for 105 yards and three touchdowns, the Seahawks clobbered Oakland, 44–10, in the Kingdome for their third straight win. Jeff Hostetler returned in an attempt to restore the glory of early season success, but he only threw for 127 yards, and failed to get Oakland into the end zone. Billy Joe Hobert relieved him, and managed to get the Raiders an offensive touchdown after being down by 37 points midway through the fourth quarter. Hobert connected with Tim Brown on a whopping 80-yarder, and Jeff Jaeger supplied the team with a 42-yard field goal in the first quarter.[15]

16. Dec. 24: The Raiders received an end to their bleak finish on the day before Christmas, when the Denver Broncos put them out of their misery to the tune of a 31–28 loss. This marked Oakland's sixth straight loss, knocked them out of the playoffs, and placed them in the AFC West cellar at 8–8 in what appeared to be a promising season only weeks earlier. Just a win was all the Raiders needed to secure a playoff spot, and they looked to finally be on the right track after Tim Brown scored on two Billy Joe Hobert passes from four and 48 yards to give Oakland a 28–17 lead going into the fourth quarter. Hobert also threw an earlier touchdown pass to Daryl Hobbs from 11 yards to open the scoring in the first quarter. Vince Evans added another touchdown pass in the second quarter on a 9-yarder to Derrick Fenner. John Elway then did what he did so many times throughout his illustrious career. He led the Broncos back from despair, this time by throwing a touchdown and setting up two Jason Elam field goals, with the final one coming from 37 yards out with 48 seconds left to pull out the win. After Elway's touchdown pass, he ran for a two-point conversion to tie the game. Oakland then looked to counter it, and appeared to be going in the right direction. Unfortunately, James Jett lost the ball after a 19-yard reception, and Denver's Glenn Cadrez recovered the loose ball on the Denver 28 with 3:52 left in regulation. For a great comeback artist like Elway, it was an eternity. However, it did not take that long to end Oakland's season. After a roughing the quarterback penalty, Elway led the Broncos on a 10-play, 53-yard drive that ended with Elam's game winning three-pointer.[16]

Individual Statistics and Roster

Head Coach: Mike White
Assistant Coaches: Fred Biletnikoff, Willie Brown, Joe Bugel, Jim Fassel, John Fox, Garrett Giemont, Fred Guidici, John Guy, Bishop Harris, Bill Meyers, Floyd Peters, Steve Shafer, Kevin Spencer, Fred Whittingham, Mike Wilson
1995 Regular Season Record: 8–8
5th Place in AFC Western Division
Scored 348 points to rank 15th out of 30 teams
Allowed 332 points to rank 10th
Led the league in fewest touchdown passes allowed by a defense (14)

STARTERS — OFFENSE

QB — Jeff Hostetler: Active for and started in 11 games. Completed 172 of 286 pass attempts for 1,998 yards, 12 TD and 9 INT. Rushed for 119 yards on 31 carries.
RB — Harvey Williams: Started in 16 games. Rushed for 1,114 yards on 255 carries and 9 TD. Had 54 receptions for 375 yards.
RB — Derrick Fenner: Active for 16 games and started in 13. Rushed for 110 yards on 39 carries, and had 35 receptions for 252 yards and 3 TD.
WR — Tim Brown: Started in 16 games. Had 89 receptions for 1,342 yards and 10 TD. Returned 36 punts for 364 yards.
WR — Rocket Ismail: Started in 16 games. Had 28 receptions for 491 yards and 3 TD. Rushed for 29 yards on 6 carries. Returned 36 kickoffs for 706 yards.
TE — Kerry Cash: Active for 16 games and started in 10. Had 25 receptions for 254 yards and 2 TD.
LT — Robert Jenkins: Active for 15 games and started in 13.
LG — Steve Wisniewski: Started in 16 games.
C — Dan Turk: Started in 16 games.
RG — Kevin Gogan: Started in 16 games.
RT — Greg Skrepenak: Active for and started in 14 games.

RESERVE OFFENSIVE PLAYERS

Joe Aska (RB): Active for 1 game.
Eric Bell (RB): Active for 16 games, and rushed for 10 yards on 2 carries.
Vince Evans (QB): Active for 9 games and started in 3. Completed 100 of 175 pass attempts for 1,236 yards, 6 TD and 8 INT. Rushed for 36 yards on 14 carries.
Cole Ford (K): Active for 5 games.
Russ Freeman (T): Active for 15 games and started in 1.
Andrew Glover (TE): Active for 16 games and started in 7. Had 26 receptions for 220 yards and 3 TD.
Daryl Hobbs (WR): Active for 16 games and started in 1. Had 38 receptions for 612 yards and 3 TD, 1 punt return for 10 yards, 1 kickoff return for 20 yards, and 1 pass attempt for 0 yards.
Billy Joe Hobert (QB): Active for 4 games and stated in 2. Completed 44 of 80 pass attempts for 540 yards, 6 TD and 4 INT. Rushed for 5 yards on 3 carries.
James Jett (WR): Active for 16 games, and had 13 receptions for 179 yards and 1 TD.
Calvin Jones (RB): Active for 9 games, rushed for 19 yards on 5 carries, and returned 5 kickoffs for 92 yards.
Napoleon Kaufman (RB): Active for 16 games and started in 1. Rushed for 490 yards on 108 carries and 1 TD. Had 9 receptions for 62 yards, and returned 22 kickoffs for 572 yards and 1 TD.
Gerald Perry (T/G): Active for and started in 3 games.
Barret Robbins (C): Active for 16 games.
Richard Stephens (G): Active for 13 games and started in 1.

STARTERS — DEFENSE

DE — Anthony Smith: Active for 16 games, started in 11, had 7 sacks and 3 fumble recoveries.
DE — Pat Swilling: Started in 16 games and had 13 sacks.
DT — Jerry Ball: Active for and started in 15 games. Had 3 sacks and 1 fumble recovery.
DT — Chester McGlockton: Started in 16 games, had 7 sacks and 2 fumble recoveries.

LLB — Rob Fredrickson: Active for 16 games, started in 15, had 1 INT and 4 fumble recoveries.

MLB — Greg Biekert: Active for 16 games, started in 14, and had 1 sack.

RLB — Mike Jones: Started in 16 games, had 1 INT and 2 fumble recoveries.

CB — Terry McDaniel: Started in 16 games and had 6 INT.

CB — Albert Lewis: Active for 16 games, started in 15, had 1 sack and 1 fumble recovery.

SS — Derrick Hoskins: Active for and started in 13 games. Had 1 INT.

FS — Eddie Anderson: Active for and started in 14 games. Had 1 INT and 2 fumble recoveries.

RESERVE DEFENSIVE PLAYERS

Aundray Bruce (LB/E/TE): Active for 14 games, had 5 sacks, 1 INT and 1 TD.

Matt Dyson (LB): Active for 4 games.

James Folston (LB): Active for 15 games.

Keith Franklin (LB): Active for 2 games.

Nolan Harrison (E/T): Active for 7 games and started in 6.

Rob Holmberg (LB): Active for 16 games and had 1 sack.

Carl Kidd (DB): Active for 13 games.

Joe King (DB): Active for 16 games and started in 2.

Dan Land (DB): Active for 15 games and started in 3.

Mike Morton (LB): Active for 12 games and had 1 fumble recovery.

Najee Mustafaa (DB): Active for 15 games and started in 1.

Bruce Pickens (DB): Active for 16 games, started in 1, and had 1 fumble recovery.

Austin Robbins (T): Active for 16 games, had 2 sacks, 2 fumble recoveries, and 1 TD.

James Trapp (DB): Active for 14 games, started in 2, and had 1 fumble recovery.

Aaron Wallace (LB): Active for 13 games, had 2 sacks, and 1 fumble recovery.

KICKING/PUNTING

K & P — Jeff Jaeger: Active for 11 games. Made 13 of 18 field goals and 22 of 22 extra point kicks for 61 points. Punted 75 times for a 41.2 average.

1996 Season Review

1. Sept. 1: The Raiders became a part of history by being the Baltimore Ravens first-ever opponent. They also became the first to lose to the Ravens. With Jeff Hostetler out with an injury, and top receiver Tim Brown suffering from leg cramps for most of the second half, the Raiders fell, 19–14, to extend their losing streak over two seasons to seven games. Before Brown left the game, he was responsible for Oakland touchdowns with receptions covering seven and 10 yards, both thrown by Billy Joe Hobert. After Brown left the game, Oakland was only able to produce 44 yards of total offense in the second half. Hobert was tormented by a blitzing Baltimore defense that sacked him three times and intercepted him twice. Baltimore quarterback Vinny Testaverde led the offensive charge by throwing for 254 yards and ran for the Ravens first-ever regular season score from nine yards out.[1]

2. Sept. 8: Things continued to slide downward for the Silver and Black, as they lost to Kansas City, 19–3, for the 13th time out of the previous 14 meetings with the Chiefs. It also marked their eighth straight loss. Eight of Kansas City's points came after fumble recoveries. A hit by Derrick Thomas on Billy Joe Hobert caused a fumble that James Hasty returned 80 yards

for a score, and another Thomas hit on Hobert made the sign caller lose the ball in the end zone. It was recovered by center Barrett Robbins for a safety. The Raiders managed to escape a shutout when Cole Ford connected on a 38-yard field goal in the fourth quarter.[2]

3. Sept. 15: Oakland hosted the second-year Jacksonville Jaguars with Jeff Hostetler back at the offensive controls, and the Raiders snapped an eight-game losing streak with a 17–3 victory. It was not a pretty game by any means, but a win is a win. Neither team was sharp, and penalties on both sides accounted for 14 yards in losses. The Raiders moved out to a 10–3 lead on Hostetler to Tim Brown 19-yard pass, and a 32-yard Cole Ford field goal. Oakland's final points of the day provided the most entertainment when massive 320-pound defensive tackle Jerry Ball intercepted a pass and rambled 66 yards for a touchdown to possibly set a record for the heaviest Raider to ever score for them. This game marked the Raiders' first home appearance in the newly renovated Oakland Coliseum. Ironically, the Coliseum suffered as badly as its tenants when the game clock on the scoreboard failed to work, and running water in the restrooms and locker rooms were in scarce supply.[3]

4. Sept. 22: Over the course of nine plays in the first quarter, the San Diego Chargers racked up 21 points, and then held on to beat Oakland, 40–34. The Raiders fought back on three touchdown passes from Jeff Hostetler and two from Billy Joe Hobert. Hostetler connected on 26 of 44 passes for 293 yards, and threw for scores to Derrick Fenner (4 yards), Rickey Dudley (6 yards), and Tim Brown (6 yards). Brown also caught an 11-yarder from Hobert, and Kenny Shedd hauled in the game's final touchdown from 28 yards out.[4]

5. Sept. 29: It seemed that in recent times, ex–Raiders came back to torment their former team. Marcus Allen did it in a Kansas City uniform, and in 1996, Jeff Jaeger did it as a Chicago Bear. After being released by Oakland during training camp, Jaeger showed the Raiders that they made a terrible mistake by kicking four field goals to help the Bears win, 19–17. The Raiders built a 17–3 third quarter lead on a Derrick Fenner 1-yard run, a Tim Brown 5-yard pass from Jeff Hostetler, and a Cole Ford 28-yard field goal. With Chicago fans booing their disapproval, the Bears rose to the occasion, intercepting Hostetler twice in the second half, and four times altogether. Jaeger then added three of his four field goals in the fourth quarter after two interceptions to provide the winning points.[5]

6. Oct. 6: The winless New York Jets were just what the sub-par Raiders needed to help get them some what back on track. Running back Joe Aska ran for 136 yards that included a 30-yard touchdown, and Jeff Hostetler threw for three touchdowns, with rookie tight end Rickey Dudley catching two of them from 23 and two yards in a 34–13 win. Daryl Hobbs caught Hostetler's other scoring toss from three yards, and Cole Ford added field goals from 26 and 35 yards. This game provided a piece of history when New York's Nick Lowery kicked his 373rd three-pointer to tie Jan Stenerud's all-time NFL mark for most field goals in a career.[6]

7. Oct. 13: The Raiders were freed from their last place tie in the AFC West with Seattle thanks to a 37–21 beating over the Detroit Lions. Oakland exploded for a 34-point lead on the arm of Jeff Hostetler, who completed 27 of 38 passes for 295 yards

and four touchdowns. James Jett caught seven passes for 112 yards and two of Hostetler's touchdowns from four and 58 yards. Napoleon Kaufman caught one from 10 yards, and Rickey Dudley added one from 62 yards. Cole Ford kicked three field goals (29, 23, and 33 yards), and Oakland won their second straight game for the first time since November of the previous year.[7]

8. Oct. 21: It was a three-peat in the win column for the Raiders, as they worked some old prime time magic on the San Diego Chargers to the tune of a 23–14 final score. It helped the Silver and Black to a 4–4 record at the halfway mark of the season. Cole Ford kicked three field goals (36, 32, and 34 yards), Napoleon Kaufman added a 12-yard run to open the scoring, and Derrick Fenner caught a 17-yard pass from Jeff Hostetler to provide the points needed to win. This was a hard-hitting affair that saw San Diego quarterback Stan Humphries knocked out of the game with a dislocated shoulder. His teammate, All-Pro linebacker Junior Seau, was also forced from the game temporarily after butting helmets with fellow Charger Kurt Gouveia. The Raiders were also penalized 11 times for 97 yards in a contest that was reminiscent of the rough and tumble Raiders teams of previous decades.[8]

9. Nov. 4: It was back to the prime time stage for the Raiders following their bye week. Once again facing a division rival, this time the 7–1 Denver Broncos, Oakland lost a heart breaker, 22–21, on a late John Elway rally. Trailing, 21–16, with 4:14 left in the game, Elway threw a 49-yard touchdown pass to Rod Smith for his 33rd career fourth quarter comeback victory. This was also the first time that the Raiders ever lost a home game on a Monday Night Football telecast after going 12–0 up to this point in their history. Despite the defeat, Oakland got great performances from Jeff Hostetler (22 of 34 for 250 yards and two touchdowns), and Tim Brown (8 receptions for 126 yards). Brown caught one of Hostetler's scoring tosses from 42 yards, and Derrick Fenner hauled in the other one from 15. Hostetler also ran for a 5-yard touchdown.[9]

10. Nov. 10: Tampa Bay came into their game with the Raiders posting a lone victory against eight defeats. Oakland, however, was kind enough to allow the hapless Bucs the opportunity to win in overtime, 20–17. The Raiders were up, 17–10, in the third quarter on a Harvey Williams to James Jett 18-yard halfback option pass, a Jeff Hostetler to Daryl Hobbs 8-yard pass, and a Cole Ford 45-yard field goal. Tampa Bay came back to tie it in the fourth quarter when Trent Dilfer threw a 2-yard pass to powerhouse fullback Mike Alstott. It was then that Oakland gave Tampa a reprieve when Ford missed a 28-yard field goal attempt with five seconds left in regulation to force overtime. The Bucs took advantage of their rare break during this tough season, and with 3:04 remaining in the extra quarter, Michael Husted sent the ball through the uprights for a winning 23-yard field goal to give the Raiders their sixth loss of the '96 campaign.[10]

11. Nov. 17: Another overtime and another game-winning field goal pulled another team out of the doldrums. The Minnesota Vikings got great performances from quarterback Brad Johnson and wide receiver Jake Reed to snap a four-game losing streak with a 16–13 win over Oakland. This game was played in terrible weather conditions, as rain fell over the Oakland area throughout the game. The Raiders received the ball for the opening series of overtime, but were forced to punt. They never

touched the ball again. The Vikings went on a 16-play, 71-yard romp across the soggy turf to set up a 31-yard field goal by Scott Sisson with 3:07 left in the overtime period. Oakland received their points on a Terry McDaniel 56-yard interception return, and two Cole Ford field goals from 41 and 26 yards.[11]

12. Nov. 24: After two straight losses in overtime, the Raiders finally had reason to celebrate when they travelled to Seattle and beat the Seahawks, 27–21, to improve to 5–7. Jeff Hostetler tossed touchdowns to James Jett (17 yards), and Rick Cunningham (3 yards), Napoleon Kaufman rushed for 104 yards, and Derrick Fenner ran for Oakland's final touchdown of the day from one yard out. Cole Ford added two field goals from 47 and 26 yards, and the Raiders clung to a very slim but still very realistic chance of making the playoffs.[12]

13. Dec. 1: The Miami Dolphins came into Oakland, where they never won in eight previous attempts. The Dolphins left the same way they entered the Oakland Coliseum, defeated once again by the silver and black-clad Raiders. This time it was by a 17–7 count, with Derrick Fenner scoring on a 6-yard run, Tim Brown on a 22-yard pass from Jeff Hostetler, and Cole Ford on a 38-yard field goal. In addition to his touchdown reception, Brown also set an NFL career record when he returned his 293rd punt. Oakland's defensive unit did a great job shutting down the Miami running attack for a mere 34 yards. Miami's great quarterback Dan Marino came into this game with a league low four interceptions on the year, however, on this day, despite throwing for 290 yards, he was picked off three times. He did manage to find Randal Hill on a 4-yard touchdown to avoid Miami's first shutout since 1987. This win gave Oakland a 6–7 record, and an outside chance of reaching the post season if they won out the rest of the way.[13]

14. Dec. 9: The first of three hurdles on the way to the playoffs was conquered by the Silver and Black on Monday Night Football. Not only did the Raiders improve to 7–7, but also they ended seven years of total dominance at the hands of their longtime rivals, the Kansas City Chiefs. After losing seven straight, and 13 of the last 14 encounters with the Chiefs, Oakland finally broke free from their tormentors with a 26–7 victory. With rain falling down on Oakland, Jeff Hostetler lit up the scoreboard for three touchdown passes to Andrew Glover (1 yard), Derrick Fenner (23 yards), and Tim Brown (34 yards). The Raiders also recorded a safety when Kansas City quarterback Rich Gannon was called for intentional grounding in the end zone, and Cole Ford added a 43-yard field goal.[14]

15. Dec. 15: Ranking first in penalties was nothing out of the ordinary for the Raiders, and they added to their league-leading status with a team record 20 infractions for 157 yards in a 24–19 loss to the Denver Broncos. The 20 penalties were only two off the NFL record set in 1944. Oakland also had four turnovers that led to 17 of Denver's points. The Broncos finished their home schedule with a spotless 8–0 record, and John Elway threw for a touchdown, Terrell Davis ran for 80 yards, and scored a touchdown that allowed him to tie a single-season team record with 14 six-pointers. Oakland got their points on two Cole Ford field goals (38 and 35 yards), a 1-yard fumble recovery by Lance Johnstone, and a 7-yard pass from Jeff Hostetler to Daryl Hobbs.[15]

16. Dec. 22: Oakland was denied on their quest to end the season at .500 when the Seattle Seahawks beat them, 28–21. In

front of a dismal Oakland Coliseum crowd of only 33,456, the Raiders held a 14–3 lead on four Cole Ford field goals (47, 23, 28, and 24 yards), and on a blocked punt that produced a safety. The Seahawks then came back with 10 points in the last 55 seconds of the first half to close the gap to one point at the intermission. Seattle then scored the go-ahead touchdown in the third quarter on a 32-yard pass from Gino Torretta to Joey Galloway. Lamar Smith ran for the two-point conversion, and then added his second touchdown run of the game to extend Seattle's lead to 28–14 in the third quarter. Derrick Fenner ran for a 1-yard score late in the quarter for Oakland's final touchdown of the season. The Raiders lost six of eight fumbles, and tied their own league record for most penalties in a season set previously two years earlier. With seven in this game, they finished the '96 campaign with 156.[16]

Individual Statistics and Roster

Head Coach: Mike White

Assistant Coaches: Fred Biletnikoff, Willie Brown, Joe Bugel, Garrett Giemont, John Guy, Bishop Harris, Larry Kennan, Bill Meyers, Floyd Peters, Steve Shafer, Kevin Spencer, Rusty Tillman, Fred Whittingham, Mike Wilson

1996 Regular Season Record: 7–9

4th place in AFC Western Division

Scored 340 points to rank 12th of 30 teams

Allowed 293 points to rank 8th

Led the league in yards per rush (4.8)

STARTERS — OFFENSE

QB — Jeff Hostetler: Active for and started in 13 games. Completed 242 of 402 pass attempts for 2,548 yards, 23 TD and 14 INT. Rushed for 179 yards on 37 carries and 1 TD.

RB — Napoleon Kaufman: Active for 16 games and started in 9. Rushed for 874 yards on 150 carries and 1 TD. **Led the NFL in yards per rushing attempts (5.8).** Had 22 receptions for 143 yards and 1 TD, and returned 25 kickoffs for 548 yards.

RB — Derrick Fenner: Active for 16 games and started in 11. Rushed for 245 yards on 67 carries and 4 TD. Had 31 receptions for 252 yards and 4 TD.

WR — Tim Brown: Started in 16 games. Had 90 receptions for 1,104 yards 9 TD. Rushed for 35 yards on 6 carries, returned 32 punts for 272 yards and 1 kickoff for 24 yards.

WR — James Jett: Started in 16 games. Had 43 receptions for 601 yards 4 TD.

TE — Rickey Dudley: Active for 16 games and started in 15. Had 34 receptions for 386 yards 4 TD.

LT — Pat Harlow: Active for 10 games and started in 9.

LG — Steve Wisniewski: Started in 16 games.

C — Barret Robbins: Active for and started in 14 games.

RG — Kevin Gogan: Started in 16 games.

RT — Lincoln Kennedy: Started in 16 games.

RESERVE OFFENSIVE PLAYERS

Joe Aska (RB): Active for 15 games and started in 2. Rushed for 326 yards on 62 carries and 1 TD. Had 8 receptions for 63 yards, and returned 1 kickoff for 17 yards.

Rick Cunningham (T): Active for 13 games, and had 1 reception for 3 yards and 1 TD.

Jerone Davison (RB): Active for 2 games, and had 4 receptions for 21 yards.

Andrew Glover (TE): Active for 14 games, started in 4, and had 9 receptions for 101 yards and 1 TD.

Tim Hall (RB): Active for 2 games, and rushed for 7 yards on 3 carries.

Marcus Hinton (TE): Active for 2 games.

Daryl Hobbs (WR): Active for 16 games and started in 1. Had 44 receptions for 423 yards and 3 TD. Returned 10 punts for 84 yards, 1 kickoff for 14 yards, and completed 1 of 1 pass attempt for 7 yards.

Billy Joe Hobert (QB): Active for 8 games and started in 3. Completed 57 of 104 pass attempts for 667 yards, 4 TD, and 5 INT. Rushed for 13 yards on 2 carries, and punted 9 times for a 41.2 average.

Robert Jenkins (T): Active for 10 games and started in 6.

Trey Junkin (TE/LB): Active for 6 games.

David Klingler (QB): Active for 1 game, completed 10 of 24 pass attempts for 87 yards, and rushed for 36 yards on 4 carries.

Charles McRae (T/G): Active for 12 games and started in 1.

Kenny Shedd (WR): Active for 16 games, started in 1, had 3 receptions for 87 yards and 1 TD, returned 3 kickoffs for 51 yards, and recorded 1 safety.

Olanda Truitt (WR): Active for 10 games.

Dan Turk (C/G): Active for 16 games and started in 2.

Harvey Williams (RB): Active for 13 games and started in 5. Rushed for 431 yards on 121 carries, had 22 receptions for 143 yards, and completed 1 of 2 pass attempts for 18 yards and 1 TD.

STARTERS — DEFENSE

DE — Lance Johnstone: Active for 16 games, started in 10, had 1 sack, 1 fumble recovery, and 1 TD.

DE — Pat Swilling: Started in 16 games, had 6 sacks and 1 fumble recovery.

DT — Russell Maryland: Started in 16 games and had 2 sacks.

DT — Chester McGlockton: Started in 16 games and had 8 sacks.

LLB — Rob Fredrickson: Active for and started in 10 games.

MLB — Greg Biekert: Active for 16 games, started in 15, and had 1 fumble recovery.

RLB — Mike Jones: Active for and started in 15 games and had 1 sack.

CB — Terry McDaniel: Active for 16 games, started in 15 and had 5 INT.

CB — Albert Lewis: Active for 16 games, started in 14, had 3 sacks and 2 INT.

SS — Lorenzo Lynch: Started in 16 games and had 3 INT.

FS — Darren Carrington: Active for 15 games, started in 10 and had 1 INT.

RESERVE DEFENSIVE PLAYERS

Eddie Anderson (DB): Active for 7 games and started in 5.

Leo Araguz (P): Active for 3 games, had 13 punts for 534 yards and a 41.1 average, and rushed for 0 yards on 1 carry.

Jerry Ball (NT): Active for 16 games, had 3 sacks, 1 INT, 1 TD, and 1 fumble recovery.

Larry Brown (DB): Active for 8 games, started in 1 and had 1 INT.

Aundray Bruce (LB/E): Active for 16 games, had 4 sacks and 1 fumble recovery.

Paul Butcher (LB): Active for 16 games and had 1 fumble recovery.

Rich Camarillo (P): Active for 1 game.

Perry Carter (DB): Active for 4 games.

James Folston (LB): Active for 12 games.

La'Roi Glover (T): Active for 2 games.

Nolan Harrison (E/T): Active for 15 games, started in 2 and had 2 sacks.

Rob Holmberg (LB): Active for 13 games, started in 1 and had 1 sack.

Carl Kidd (DB): Active for 16 games, had 1 INT, 1 fumble recovery, and returned 29 kickoffs for 622 yards.

Dan Land (DB/RB): Active for 16 games, started in 2 and had 2 fumble recoveries.

Lamar Lyons (DB): Active for 6 games.

Mike Morton (LB): Active for 16 games, started in 6, had 1 sack and 2 INT.

Anthony Smith (E): Active for 6 games, started in 4, had 2 sacks and 1 fumble recovery.

James Trapp (DB): Active for 12 games, started in 4 and had 1 INT.

KICKING/PUNTING

K — Cole Ford: Active for 16 games. Made 24 of 31 field goals and 36 of
36 extra point kicks for 108 points.

P — Jeff Gossett: Active for 12 games. Punted 57 times for a 39.7 average.
Rushed for 28 yards on 3 carries, and had 1 kickoff return for 0 yards.

1997 Season Review

1. Aug. 31: The Raiders opened a second straight season
against a new franchise. In 1996 it was the Baltimore Ravens after
their move from Cleveland, and kicking off the '97 campaign
would be the Tennessee Oilers, formerly of Houston, and later
to be named the Titans. With 30,171 in the Liberty Bowl in Memphis, Tennessee, Eddie George christened the Titans new locale
in exceptional fashion, running for a team-record 216 yards in a
24–21 overtime win. George scored on a 29-yard run in the fourth
quarter to help the Oilers regain the lead after squandering a 13–
0 advantage. Two touchdown passes from Jeff George to Tim
Brown (59 and 27 yards), put the Raiders out in front by one
point prior to Eddie George's go-ahead jaunt. Eddie George added
a two-point conversion run to give the Oilers a 21–14 lead. Jeff
George and Tim Brown hooked up again one final time to pull
the Raiders to within one point. The Oakland signal caller found
Brown in the back of the end zone, and the great receiver made
an incredible catch of a pass thrown over his head from 16 yards
out. Cole Ford then added the tying point with 22 seconds left
in regulation. Tim Brown's spectacular day of eight receptions for
158 yards earned him top honors among his fellow NFL receivers.
After both teams failed to break the tie on their first possessions
in overtime, the Oilers took the ball from their own 35, and quarterback Steve McNair got them close enough with two
completions to tight end Frank Wycheck. After Eddie George ran
for six yards, kicker Al Del Greco drilled a game-winning 33-
yard field goal.[1]

2. Sept. 8: The Raiders were once again involved in a nail-
biter, but the end result was still the same. This time in their
home opener, Oakland lost to Kansas City, 28–27, with three
seconds left in the game. Napoleon Kaufman opened the Raiders'
home schedule with a 10-yard scoring run in the first quarter.
Cole Ford added a 32-yard field goal, and the Raiders trailed at
the half, 13–10. Jeff George came out in the third quarter and
took Oakland 76 yards in three plays after the second half kickoff.
The quick drive was capped off when Rickey Dudley caught a
37-yard pass from George. After a Marcus Allen fumble, the
Raiders took full advantage of their former teammate's error.
Forty-two seconds after the turnover, George once again found
Dudley for six points, this time from 16 yards out. Ford later
added a 34-yard field goal, and the Raiders appeared to be in control with a 27–13 lead. After capitalizing on two turnovers by
Kansas City, Oakland returned the favor when Darren Anderson
intercepted a Jeff George pass with Oakland up, 27–16. Anderson
then dashed 55 yards for a touchdown to cut the Oakland advantage to 27–22. The Chiefs then scored the game-winner on a
33-yard pass from Elvis Grbac to Andre Rison with three seconds
left in the game. Two exciting clashes resulted in close scores, but
the Raiders had nothing to show for it record-wise, as they were
still looking for that elusive first win.[2]

3. Sept. 14: A trip down south proved successful, as the
Raiders finally nailed down their first victory under head coach
Joe Bugel by defeating the Atlanta Falcons, 36–31. Jeff George
returned to Atlanta after being released by the Falcons, and had
a good homecoming. He threw for 286 yards and one touchdown,
and teamed up with Rickey Dudley on a 76-yard pass that set
the Raiders up for a Cole Ford field goal from 31 yards out. Ford
had an earlier 49-yard three-pointer with no time left in the first
half. Oakland added two more points to their total when Atlanta
quarterback Billy Joe Tolliver was run out of the end zone for a
safety with just over three minutes left in the game. Other scores
for the Raiders in their first win came from Napoleon Kaufman,
who ran for 140 yards on 14 carries, and had scoring jaunts
covering 68 and 58 yards. James Jett caught George's touchdown
pass from 51 yards, and Kenny Shedd returned a fumble 25 yards.[3]

4. Sept. 21: The Raiders were back to their heart-pounding
finishes. Unfortunately, it was also gut wrenching to Raider
Nation, as they suffered another close loss, this time to the New
York Jets, 23–22. Oakland outperformed their old AFL rivals
throughout this game, but a blocked field attempt led to their
demise. With 12:51 left in the fourth quarter, Corwin Brown
blocked Cole Ford's attempt, and Ray Milkens scooped up the
ball and raced 72 yards. John Hall converted on the extra point
try, which provided the Jets with a one-point lead that eventually
sent the Raiders from the Big Apple to heart break city. This was
a tough day for Cole Ford. He missed four field goal attempts
and an extra point kick. He did manage to connect on a 43-yard
three-pointer in the second quarter. Mishaps took away from
great performances by Jeff George, Napoleon Kaufman, Tim
Brown, and James Jett. George threw for 374 yards and three
touchdowns, Kaufman ran for 126 yards, and Brown caught 10
passes for 153 yards and one of George's scoring strikes from 29
yards. James Jett hauled in George's other two touchdown tosses
from 56 and 11 yards on a day that saw him gather in five
receptions for 148 yards.[4]

5. Sept. 28: After falling behind the St. Louis Rams, 14–0,
in the second quarter, the disapproval of Raiders fans rang out
with boos. Just when things were going bad, they somehow got
worse, or so it seemed at first. Jeff George threw an interception,
but defensive tackle Jeff Zgonina was called for roughing the
passer, and the theft was nullified. Oakland's fortunes then turned
around. George ran for 11 yards on the next play, and then got
the Raiders on the board with an 8-yard pass to James Jett. George
then connected with Rickey Dudley on a 34-yard pass to get Oakland to within one point. The extra point was missed, and the
Raiders went into the second half trailing, 14–13. George teamed
up with Jett once again for the go-ahead touchdown in the third
quarter from 14 yards out. Harvey Williams caught a two-point
conversion pass from George to make the score 21–14. It was then
that Oakland's ground forces got into the act. Napoleon Kaufman,
who tore up the St. Louis defense for 162 rushing yards on 26
carries, extended Oakland's lead to 28–14 with a 1-yard run to
close out the third quarter scoring. After a St. Louis field goal,
George countered with his fourth scoring strike of the day, a 5-
yarder to Dudley to make it a 35–17 game, which was how it
ended. Dudley had a good game with five receptions for 106 yards
and two touchdowns. Defensive back Eric Turner helped in the
cause by thwarting two St. Louis drives with interceptions. This

was the first meeting between the Rams and Raiders since both left Los Angeles two years earlier.[5]

6. Oct. 5: Oakland's top-ranked offense got good performances from Jeff George, who passed for 271 yards, and Napoleon Kaufman, who caught a trio of passes for 100 yards. However, it was not enough in a 25–10 loss to the San Diego Chargers. This loss sunk the Raiders to the bottom of the division standings at 2–4. San Diego's Gary Brown rushed for 181 yards and one touchdown, while Greg Davis nailed six field goals in the win. Kaufman's 13 yards accounted for all of Oakland's rushing output for the game. Even though he was held in check running out of the backfield, he did a good job catching it. His 70-yard touchdown reception from George provided Oakland with their lone six-pointer, and Cole Ford added a 24-yard field goal as time expired in the first half.[6]

7. Oct. 19: After a dismal rushing performance against the Chargers two weeks earlier, Napoleon Kaufman came off the bye week in fine fashion. He carried the ball 28 times for a single-game team record 227 yards. He sent a massage to the undefeated Denver Broncos right from the start that he was going to have a big day. On Oakland's first offensive play, Kaufman ran for 51 yards to put the Raiders in good position. That run led to a 14-yard pass from Jeff George to James Jett that put the Raiders up with only two-and-a-half minutes expired in the first quarter. Denver tied it up with one second left in the opening stanza on a Terrell Davis 2-yard run. George countered with a 5-yard touchdown toss to Rickey Dudley to regain the lead for Oakland. Denver's Jason Elam ended the first half with a 44-yard field goal as time expired to cut Oakland's lead to 14–10. Terrell Davis then put the Broncos in the lead for the first time with his second scoring run. Eric Turner put the Raiders back on top with a 65-yard interception return off John Elway to give the Silver and Black a 21–17 advantage. Midway through the fourth quarter, Kaufman put his name on top of the Raiders' all-time single-game rushing list. On third-and-one from the Oakland 17, Kaufman took a handoff, shot through a mass of humanity at the line of scrimmage, headed toward the sideline, and was off on an 83-yard romp that allowed him to surpass Bo Jackson's 1987 record of 221 yards. It also gave the Raiders some extra breathing room with a 28–17 lead. The Broncos came back on an Elway-to-Ed McCaffrey 29-yard pass with 2:15 left. Davis ran for the two-point conversion, and that was all the scoring in this game. The Raiders prevailed, 28–25, to hand Denver their first loss of the '97 campaign.[7]

8. Oct. 26: The Seattle Kingdome was usually never a kind place for the Raiders to visit. This time proved to be no exception, as the Seahawks prevailed in a high-scoring affair, 45–34. Seattle quarterback Warren Moon was already a legend when he began his 20th pro season in 1997, and continued to build on his status by throwing for 409 yards and five touchdowns against Oakland. The Raiders led, 25–18, at the half, and the Seahawks clamped down on the Oakland offensive attack from that point on, allowing it only nine points in the second half. The Raiders received their first tally of the game on a 55-yard run from Napoleon Kaufman, who finished the day with 112 yards on the ground. Jeff George and James Jett teamed up from 13 yards out to put Oakland up, 14–3. Moon then tossed his first two scoring strikes to give Seattle an 18–14 lead. The Raiders came back to reclaim

the lead on a Cole Ford field goal from 53 yards, and a Lionel Washington 44-yard interception return with 39 seconds left in the first half. Tim Brown caught a two-point conversion pass from George to give Oakland their first half point production. The Raiders opened up their advantage to 31–18 early in the third quarter on another George to Jett scoring strike that covered 17 yards. The two-point conversion attempt failed. It was at this time that Moon added three more touchdown passes, with all of them going to Joey Galloway. Todd Peterson chipped in with two field goals to complete Seattle's second half romp. Cole Ford gave the Raiders their final points of the game in between Galloway's first two touchdown receptions with a 22-yard field goal. This loss gave the Raiders a 3–5 record at the halfway mark of the season.[8]

9. Nov. 2: The Raiders had the league's worst defense, and the Carolina Panthers took full advantage of it. In their third season of existence, the Panthers set team records with five rushing touchdowns and 216 yards on the ground in a 38–14 win. Fred Lane paved the way on this record-setting day with 147 yards on 28 carries and three touchdowns. The Raiders were never in this game, and scored their first points on a 23-yard pass from Jeff George to Napoleon Kaufman after Oakland was already down, 21–0, in the second quarter. James Jett caught a 16-yard pass from George for Oakland's other points. This blowout loss overshadowed great performances by Jeff George (24 of 38 for 304 yards passing), and Tim Brown (10 receptions for 163 yards).[9]

10. Nov. 9: The 2–7 New Orleans Saints travelled to Oakland to face the 3–6 Raiders in a contest between two teams with very little chance of reaching the playoffs. Things were not going well for the Raiders, as their low-ranked defense allowed the Saints to score for the first time in two games. The unit only gave up 13 points, but that was enough for New Orleans to win, 13–10. Oakland scored all their points in the second quarter to take a 10–0 lead on a 1-yard run by Harvey Williams, and on a Cole Ford 43-yard field goal. Doug Brien then kicked a 48-yard field goal on the final play of the first half to give the Saints their first points in nine quarters. The game was tied on the first play of the fourth quarter when Ray Zellars ran for a 1-yard score. Brien kicked a 44-yard three-pointer with 2:57 left that proved to be the game-winner. Jeff George attempted to salvage the game, but an interception with 1:09 remaining killed any hopes for the Raiders on this day.[10]

11. Nov. 16: The Raiders did not like being at the bottom of the AFC Western Division, and looked to share it. The San Diego Chargers obliged them by allowing the Silver and Black to romp all over them by a 38–14 count, and improve to 4–7, which tied them with the Lighting Bolts for last place. Napoleon Kaufman ran for 109 yards, and that helped him break the 1,000-yard mark for the season. However, it was reserve running back Harvey Williams that stole the headlines on a day that saw Oakland produce a season-high point total. Williams ran for two 1-yard scores and caught two scoring strikes from Jeff George that covered eight and 32 yards. The Raiders received their other points on a 9-yard pass from George to James Jett, and a 23-yard field goal compliments of Cole Ford. The win ended Oakland's three-game losing streak and extended San Diego's to three.[11]

12. Nov. 24: The Denver Broncos played host to one of only two teams to beat them up to this point of the '97 season

The Broncos did not give Oakland any hopes of sending them down in defeat once again, and destroyed the Raiders, 31–3. John Elway passed for 280 yards, tight end Shannon Sharpe caught 10 passes for 142 yards, and running back Terrell Davis scored three touchdowns. Jeff George's arm took the Raiders to the second-best passing attack in the league, but he was unable to produce any six-pointers in this game, and was sacked four times. The Broncos had the number one offense, and lived up to that stellar billing by romping over and around Oakland's league-worst defense for 370 yards of total offense. Cole Ford provided the Raiders with their only points on a 41-yard field goal with 16 seconds left in the first half.[12]

13. Nov. 30: Miami's legendary quarterback Dan Marino established numerous records throughout his illustrious career, and set one against the Raiders in a 34–16 win. Marino passed for 241 yards, which allowed him to go over the 3,000-yard mark for an NFL 12th time. He threw for two touchdowns, and Karim Abdul-Jabbar ran for 85 yards in Miami's easy win. Oakland got on the board first when Jeff George passed to Tim Brown for a 24-yard touchdown in the first quarter. On the day, Brown was his usual spectacular self, catching eight passes for 125 yards. The Raiders did not score again until they were down, 17–7, in the third quarter. Cole Ford then added a 44-yard field goal midway through the quarter. Miami rang up two more touchdowns after that. James Jett caught three passes for 86 yards, which included a 27-yard touchdown reception from George early in the fourth quarter. George threw for 272 yards and two scoring tosses, but was intercepted once, had a fumble recovered in the end zone for a Miami touchdown, and was sacked six times.[13]

14. Dec. 7: The Kansas City Chiefs hosted the hapless Raiders, and showed no hospitality to their long-standing rivals. The Chiefs rolled up 418 yards of total offense while giving up 93. They compiled 27 first downs to just five for Oakland, and mauled the Silver and Black in Arrowhead Stadium, 30–0. This marked the 15th time in their last 17 matchups that Kansas City defeated the Raiders. The win allowed Kansas City to remain in a first place division tie with Denver at 11–3. The loss dropped Oakland to 4–10, which gave them ten defeats for the first time since 1987.[14]

15. Dec. 14: Following their beat down loss to Kansas City, the Raiders made this one a little closer, but it in end, they still lost. This time, another division foe, the Seattle Seahawks, came into Oakland and got past the Silver and Black by a slim one point, winning, 22–21. The game was the Raiders to win, as they were in control with a 21–3 halftime lead. To make maters worse was the fact that Seattle rallied with a quarterback who never threw a pass in an NFL game before taking the field against Oakland. With Warren Moon out with bruised ribs, and his backup John Friesz out of commission due to a fractured thumb, Jon Kitna was forced into action. It looked like Kitna was a seasoned veteran by the way he guided Seattle back from an 18-point deficit against the worst defense in the league. He completed 23 of 37 passes for 283 yards and one touchdown. Running back Chris Warren gave the Seahawks a solid ground effort by gaining 70 yards on 19 carries that included one touchdown. Todd Peterson provided the knockout blow for Seattle by connecting on a 49-yard field goal with 2:20 left to give Seattle their seventh win. As for the Raiders, they fell to 4–11, which gave them their worst

record since 1962. The Raiders received all their six-pointers off the arm of Jeff George. On the receiving end of George's touchdown tosses were Olanda Truitt (19 yards), James Jett (37 yards), and Rickey Dudley (5 yards).[15]

16. Dec. 21: The Raiders ended their worst season in 35 years, and Joe Bugel's lone season as head coach, with a 20–9 loss to the Jacksonville Jaguars. Despite the dismal season that ended at 4–12, Tim Brown went into the off-season on a positive note. His 14 receptions set a single-game team record, and his 104 catches for 1,390 yards established the greatest individual single-season receiving totals in Raiders history. Jeff George had a good game in the finale, connecting on 24 of 37 pass attempts for 244 yards, and Napoleon Kaufman chipped in with a game-high 94 rushing yards. Oakland got their points on a Cole Ford 33-yard field goal, and a 2-yard pass from George to Rickey Dudley. They attempted a two-point conversion, but like so many other things throughout the '97 season, it failed.[16]

Individual Statistics and Roster

Head Coach: Joe Bugel
Assistant Coaches: Dave Adolph, Fred Biletnikoff, Willie Brown, Garrett Giemont, John Guy, Bishop Harris, Robert Jenkins, Bill Meyers, Ray Perkins, Keith Rowen, Steve Shafer, Kevin Spencer, Rusty Tillman, Bill Urbanik, Fred Whittingham
1997 Regular Season Record: 4–12
4th place in AFC Western Division
Scored 324 points to rank 17th out of 30 teams
Allowed 419 points to rank 28th

STARTERS — OFFENSE

QB — Jeff George: Started in 16 games. Completed 290 of 521 pass attempts for **3,917** yards, 29 TD and 9 INT. Rushed for 44 yards on 17 carries.
RB — Napoleon Kaufman: Started in 16 games. Rushed for 1,294 yards on 272 carries and 6 TD. Had 40 receptions for 403 yards 2 TD, and attempted 1 pass for 0 yards.
RB — Derrick Fenner: Active for 9 games and started in 7. Rushed for 24 yards on 7 carries, and had 14 receptions for 92 yards.
WR — Tim Brown: Started in 16 games. Had **104** receptions for 1,408 yards and 5 TD. Rushed for 19 yards on 5 carries, and returned 1 kickoff for 7 yards.
WR — James Jett: Started in 16 games. Had 46 receptions for 804 yards 12 TD.
TE — Rickey Dudley: Started in 16 games. Had 48 receptions for 787 yards 7 TD.
LT — Pat Harlow: Started in 16 games.
LG — Steve Wisniewski: Started in 16 games.
C — Barret Robbins: Started in 16 games.
RG — Lester Holmes: Active for and started in 15 games.
RT — Lincoln Kennedy: Started in 16 games.

RESERVE OFFENSIVE PLAYERS

Joe Aska (RB): Active for 7 games, rushed for 10 yards on 12 carries, and returned 2 kickoffs for 46 yards.
Rick Cunningham (T): Active for 7 games.
Jerone Davison (RB): Active for 8 games, started in 1, rushed for 4 yards on 2 carries, and had 2 receptions for 34 yards.
Tim Hall (RB): Active for 16 games, rushed for 120 yards on 23 carries, had 1 reception for 9 yards, and returned 9 kickoffs for 182 yards.
Desmond Howard (WR): Active for 15 games, had 4 receptions for 30 yards, returned 27 punts for 210 yards, and **61** kickoffs for 1,318 yards.

David Klingler (QB): Active for 1 game, completed 4 of 7 pass attempts for 27 yards and 1 INT, and rushed for 0 yards on 1 carry.

Chad Levitt (RB): Active for 10 games, started in 2, rushed for 3 yards on 2 carries, had 2 receptions for 24 yards, and returned 1 kickoff for 12 yards.

Bob Rosenstiel (TE): Active for 4 games.

Kenny Shedd (WR): Active for 16 games, had 10 receptions for 115 yards, 2 fumble recoveries and 1 TD, and returned 2 kickoffs for 38 yards.

Adam Treu (C): Active for 16 games.

Olanda Truitt (WR): Active for 14 games, had 7 receptions for 91 yards and 1 TD, and returned 2 kickoffs for 51 yards.

Curtis Whitley (C): Active for 15 games and started in 1.

Harvey Williams (RB): Active for 14 games and started in 6. Rushed for 70 yards on 18 carries and 3 TD. Had 16 receptions for 147 yards and 2 TD.

STARTERS — DEFENSE

DE — Darrell Russell: Active for 16 games, started in 10, and had 3 sacks.

DE — Anthony Smith: Active for and started in 13 games. Had 6 sacks, 1 fumble recovery, and recorded 1 safety.

DT — Russell Maryland: Started in 16 games and had 4 sacks.

DT — Chester McGlockton: Started in 16 games, had 4 sacks and 1 fumble recovery.

LLB — Rob Fredrickson: Active for 16 games, started in 14 and had 2 sacks.

MLB — Greg Biekert: Started in 16 games and had 2 sacks.

RLB — Mike Morton: Active for and started in 11 games, had 1 fumble recovery and returned 1 kickoff for 14 yards.

CB — Terry McDaniel: Active for 13 games, started in 12 and had 1 INT.

CB — Albert Lewis: Active for 14 games, started in 11 and had 2 sacks.

SS — James Trapp: Started in 16 games, had 2 INT and 2 fumble recoveries.

FS — Eric Turner: Active for 16 games, started in 15, had 2 INT, 3 fumble recoveries, and 1 TD.

RESERVE DEFENSIVE PLAYERS

Eddie Anderson (DB): Active for 11 games and started in 1.

Calvin Branch (DB): Active for 6 games.

Larry Brown (DB): Active for 4 games.

Aundray Bruce (LB/DE): Active for 10 games, started in 3 and had 1 sack.

Perry Carter (DB): Active for 16 games and started in 7.

James Folston (LB): Active for 16 games, started in 7 and had 1 fumble recovery.

Rob Holmberg (LB): Active for 16 games, had 1 fumble recovery, and returned 1 kickoff for 15 yards.

Grady Jackson (DT): Active for 5 games.

Kevin L. Johnson (DT): Active for 15 games.

Lance Johnstone (DE): Active for 14 games, started in 6, had 3 sacks and 1 fumble recovery.

Dan Land (DB): Active for 16 games and had 1 INT.

Lorenzo Lynch (DB): Active for 15 games, had 1 sack and 2 INT.

John Henry Mills (LB): Active for 16 games.

Greg Townsend (DE/LB/DT): Active for 4 games.

Aaron Wallace (LB): Active for 5 games.

Lionel Washington (DB): Active for 9 games, started in 3, had 2 INT and 1 TD.

KICKING/PUNTING

K — Cole Ford: Active for 16 games. Made 13 of 22 field goals and 33 of 35 extra point kicks for 72 points.

P — Leo Araguz: Active for 16 games. Punted 93 times for a 45.0 average.

1998 Season Review

1. Sept. 6: The Jon Gruden era began against long-time rival Kansas City. The change of coaching regimes did nothing for Oakland's reversal of fortune over the Chiefs, as Oakland fell 28–8, for the 16th time in the previous 18 encounters with Kansas City. Linebacker Derrick Thomas was a one-man wrecking crew recording six sacks on quarterback Jeff George, falling one short of his own NFL record. In all, the Chiefs had 10 sacks and recovered five Oakland fumbles. When the Raiders did finally get on the scoreboard for their only points, they were even a direct result of a sack. Thomas once again got to George, and as he was being sacked, the ball came loose, and big offensive lineman Lincoln Kennedy scooped the ball up and ran 27 yards to the Kansas City 10. Harvey Williams ran for a 2-yard score soon after, and Rickey Dudley caught a two-point conversion pass for Donald Hollas.

2. Sept. 13: Jeff George threw for 303 yards, Tim Brown caught six passes for 127 yards, Napoleon Kaufman ran for 139 yards, and the Oakland Raiders gave their 35-year-old head coach Jon Gruden his first-ever regular season win with a 20–17 final against the New York Giants. The Raiders came out quick, scoring on an 80-yard run by Kaufman on their first offensive play. After that, Oakland had to fight through 16 penalties for 113 yards in losses, and overcome a see saw affair that had New York take the lead on two occasions before Greg Davis kicked the go-ahead field goal from 26 yards with 1:59 left in the game. Davis also had a 41-yarder earlier. Oakland's other points came on a George to Brown 22-yard pass that gave the Raiders a 17–14 lead in the third quarter. Defensive back Eric Turner then took it upon himself to secure the win on two straight plays. First, Turner sacked quarterback Danny Kannell for an 11-yard loss, and then picked off his pass on fourth down to seal the deal.[2]

3. Sept. 20: James Jett caught five passes for 116 yards, but it was not enough to help Oakland overcome the defending Super Bowl champion Denver Broncos. Playing without John Elway due to a badly strained hamstring muscle for most of the game, the Denver defense took over in a 34–17 win. Bubby Brister replaced Elway in the second quarter, and his first pass was a temporary blessing to Raider Nation, as Eric Turner intercepted it and raced 94 yards to give Oakland a brief 10–7 lead. Greg Davis added a 44-yard field goal earlier for the Raiders. Rickey Dudley provided Oakland with their other points on an 11-yard pass from Jeff George. Things then went bad for the Silver and Black. Linebacker Bill Romanowski and defensive back Ray Crockett led the defensive charge that resulted in three interceptions and four sacks. The interceptions were turned into touchdowns, with Crockett taking his second pick 80 yards to paydirt.[3]

4. Sept. 27: A trip to the Lone Star State gave the Raiders a 13–12 win over the Dallas Cowboys to even their record at 2–2. With the win, Oakland handed Dallas quarterback Jason Garrett, who was filling in for the injured Troy Aikman, his first loss in four career starts. Napoleon Kaufman ran for a game-high 110 yards, and Eric Turner thwarted a final effort by Garrett to rally the Cowboys. Trailing, 13–10, with 1:31 left, Turner intercepted a pass in the end zone intended for Michael Irvin. Charles Woodson also had an end zone interception against Garrett earlier. After Turner's pick, the Raiders utilized clock management, and punter Leo Araguz gave Dallas a safety with two seconds remaining instead

of chancing a punt return. The Raiders got their only touchdown on a lucky bounce after Jeff George let a rocket shot loose that was intended for James Jett. The ball hit cornerback Kevin Smith on his shoulder pads and bounced off right into Jett's awaited hands on the Dallas 30. He then raced into the end zone without any opposition to complete a 75-yard touchdown reception. Greg Davis gave Oakland their other points on field goals from 30 and 38 yards.[4]

5. Oct. 4: Tempe, Arizona was the next destination for the Silver and Black and a meeting with the Cardinals. Both teams came into this game at 2–2, and the Raiders left Sun Devil Stadium with their first winning record of the season thanks to a 23–20 win. Jeff George suffered a groin injury right before the end of the first quarter, and was replaced with Donald Hollas with Oakland on the losing end of a 7–3 score. Also ailing for the Raiders was Napoleon Kaufman with a sprained ankle. Prior to his injury, Kaufman was ranked third in the AFC in rushing yards. Hollas did a good job filling in, connecting on 12 of 22 passes for 104 yards, and he scored Oakland's final touchdown on a 1-yard run in the second quarter to put the Raiders up, 23–14. Oakland's defense took over from that point, and recorded three sacks and three interceptions, one of which was returned by Charles Woodson for a 46-yard touchdown. Greg Davis ended three other drives successfully with field goals from 51, 40, and 34 yards.[5]

6. Oct. 11: The Raiders and Chargers used to engage in some high-scoring affairs over the course of 39 seasons, but not on this day. In a game that saw 27 punts, five interceptions, and bleak offensive firepower (both teams produced a combined 354 yards), the good news was that the Raiders squeezed out a 7–6 win in the final 1:28. Oakland's Leo Araguz earned his pay with 16 punts, which was one shy of an NFL record. Donald Hollas' second game as signal caller was not one for the ages, as he completed 12 out of 35 passes for 101 yards and an interception, and failed to get a first down throughout the second half. Any hopes of victory were then placed on the shoulders of third string quarterback Wade Wilson. He did not fair any better, and could not connect on his first six passes. He did, however, decide to save the dramatics until the end, when he found James Jett all alone for a 68-yard touchdown in the closing minute-and-a-half of the game. Greg Davis then booted his only point of the day through the uprights to get Oakland out of this dismal encounter with a 4–2 record going into the bye week.[6]

7. Oct. 25: The Raiders were looking to keep their home record of 7–0 against the Cincinnati Bengals intact, as they came off their bye week rested and ready to make a run at the playoffs for the first time in five years. Oakland accomplished their goal with a 27–10 win over the Bengals to improve to 5–2 for sole possession of second place in the AFC West behind the 7–0 Denver Broncos. For six years, Donald Hollas waited for his chance to see a pass he threw go for a touchdown. His wait ended on this day when two of his nine completions went for touchdowns. Tim Brown caught Hollas' first-ever touchdown pass from 19 yards to open the scoring, and James Jett followed that up with a 39-yarder in the second quarter to break a 7–7 tie. Lance Johnstone scooped up a fumble and ran 40 yards for Oakland's third touchdown, and Greg Davis closed out the team's scoring with two second half field goals from 22 and 48 yards. Napoleon Kauf-

man aided his team with a steady supply of ground assault by running for 143 yards in 31 carries.[7]

8. Nov. 1: The Raiders took their four-game winning streak and number one ranked defense into the Seattle Kingdome for a Sunday night prime time showdown. The number one status remained intact after the defense recovered four fumbles, had an interceptions, and held the Seattle running game to 80 yards in a 31–18 win to improve to 6–2 and extend their win streak to five games. Donald Hollas threw for 237 yards and two touchdowns to Tim Brown (28 yards) and Rickey Dudley (27 yards). Right after Dudley's score, free safety Albert Lewis, who was 38 years old and filling in for Eric Turner, out due to a foot injury, became the oldest player in league history to return an interception for a touchdown. Lewis covered 74 yards, and helped in giving the Silver and Black 14 points within a span of 2:38 in the third quarter. Darryl Ashmore helped teammate Jon Ritchie out after the latter fumbled, as Ashmore jumped on the ball in the end zone for Oakland's final score with just under eleven minutes left in the game. Greg Davis added a 35-yard field goal for the Raiders.[8]

9. Nov. 8: The Raiders went to Baltimore to face the 2–6 Ravens. Two streaks ended at the conclusion of this game, and Oakland was not the ones celebrating. Baltimore ended a four-game losing streak, while Oakland's five-game winning streak fell by the wayside with a 13–10 defeat. Jeff George returned to action for the first time in a month, but his groin injury acted up, and he was forced to the sideline after the Raiders' first offensive series. Donald Hollas, riding a three-game winning streak as a starter, came in and connected on 17 of 26 passes for 249 yards. Unfortunately, he also threw two interceptions that proved to be the difference makers in this one. His first pick was returned by Rod Woodson for an 18-yard touchdown, and the second one by Duane Starks on the game's final play officially ended Oakland's hopes of a fantastic finish. Rickey Dudley had a good game despite the loss. He caught six passes for 105 yards, and scored the Raiders' lone touchdown on a 5-yard pass from Hollas in the fourth quarter. This touchdown tied the game at 10–10 until Matt Stover kicked a go-ahead 30-yard field goal with 9:14 left. Greg Davis gave the Raiders their other points on a 23-yard field goal in the second quarter.[9]

10. Nov. 15: The matchups between the Raiders and Seahawks as of late were proving to be victorious for the road warriors. In four of their last five meetings, the away team brought home the win. This time, however, there was no place like home for the Raiders. Thanks to a Greg Davis 37-yard field goal with 21 seconds left in the fourth quarter, Oakland improved to 7–3 with a 20–17 win. The first half of this game saw both teams return punts for scores. Seattle's Joey Galloway opened the scoring with a 56-yard return, and then Desmond Howard got Oakland on the board with 1:30 left in the first half with a 63-yard jaunt to send Oakland into the half trailing, 10–7. Davis tied the game at 10–10 with a 26-yard field goal at the 8:17 mark of the fourth quarter. Harvey Williams, who finished the game with 79 yards rushing, gave the Raiders their first lead of the afternoon with a 25-yard touchdown run with 3:50 remaining in the contest. Seattle came right back to tie it, and then Davis kicked the game-winning field goal three-and-a-half minutes later. The defense came up with five sacks and three interceptions. Charles Woodson preserved the win with an interception off Warren Moon on the

game's final play. The price of victory was high for the Silver and Black, as Eric Allen was lost for the season with torn ligaments in his left knee after he picked off a pass. Joining Allen on the injury list was safety Anthony Newman with a damaged toe. The losses of these two seriously depleted a secondary already suffering with the absence of Eric Turner.[10]

11. Nov. 22: The Denver Broncos rolled to an 11–0 record, and John Elway topped the 50,000-yard plateau in career passing yards, in a 40–14 beating over the Raiders. Oakland kept the game close going into the fourth quarter after Donald Hollas threw touchdown passes to Rickey Dudley (29 yards) and James Jett (14 yards) to make it a 17–14 Denver advantage. The Broncos then showed why they were the premier team of the time by breaking away in the fourth quarter with 23 points.[11]

12. Nov. 29: The Raiders looked to rebound following their big loss with a home game against the Washington Redskins. Oakland brought a 3–0 record against NFC teams, and an AFC-high, 27 turnovers into this matchup. None of this mattered to the 2–9 Redskins, and they beat the Raiders, 29–19, to put a major cramp on their playoff quest. Trent Green threw for three touchdowns to help the Redskins win their first road game in six attempts. Jeff George returned to the lineup, but proved very ineffective, completing only seven of 15 attempts for 65 yards and one interception. Donald Hollas replaced George in the second half with Oakland trailing, 17–7. He fared much better with 16 completions in 29 attempts for 134 yards and two touchdowns. He also suffered an interception. His two touchdown passes went to Terry Mickens (12 yards) and Tim Brown (2 yards). Oakland's other touchdown came on a Napoleon Kaufman 23-yard run that tied the game in the first quarter.[12]

13. Dec. 6: The Raiders were reeling, and lost for the third straight week, this time to Miami, 27–17. This was only the second time that Miami defeated the Raiders in Oakland. Miami's defense had four turnovers that produced 24 points in the first half, and they never looked back. Linebackers Zach Thomas and Robert Jones each returned interceptions for scores on a day that saw the Dolphins tie a team record with six interceptions. The unit also sacked Donald Hollas eight times. Oakland got their points on a Greg Davis 40-yard field goal and two Tim Brown receptions. Brown caught a Hollas pass from seven yards, and a 2-yarder from Wade Wilson, who replaced Hollas in the fourth quarter after he completed 12 of 31 passes for 152 yards and those six picks. Brown added another fine performance to his outstanding career with nine catches for 104 yards.[13]

14. Dec. 13: It seemed like history was repeating itself, as this edition of the Raiders resembled the '95 squad that crumbled late in the season after starting out so well. This time, the Buffalo Bills boosted their playoff chances, while diminishing Oakland's, with a 44–21 victory that handed the hapless Raiders their fourth straight loss. Oakland went with 39-year-old, third-string quarterback Wade Wilson, and he had a miserable day that saw him sacked five times, suffer an interception, and had a fumble returned for a touchdown. The Raiders were never even close to competing for the lead in this game, and got their first points after trailing, 17–0, on a Wilson to Rickey Dudley 18-yard pass. Desmond Howard returned a punt 75 yards for Oakland's second tally, and with the game totally out of reach, Wilson connected with Tim Brown from 30 yards out for the game's final points.[14]

15. Dec. 20: A trip to San Diego was just what the Raiders needed to snap a four-game slide. This was Wade Wilson's third start in three seasons, and even though he did not set any records or even play that well, he still guided the 8–7 Raiders to a 17–10 win. This was a bitter sweet victory in the way that even though Oakland won, their playoff hopes were dashed for the fifth straight season. Wilson must have felt like a Hall of Famer by throwing for touchdowns on two consecutive possessions, with them going to James Jett (45 yards) and Tim Brown (12 yards), to give the Raiders a 14–3 lead at the half. Greg Davis chipped in with a 25-yard field goal, and the Oakland defense held off the Chargers long enough to secure the win.[15]

16. Dec. 26: The Kansas City Chiefs continued to have their way with the Raiders, this time winning, 31–24, for the 17th time in the last 19 meetings between these two long-time foes. Oakland looked like they were going to exonerate the Kansas City demons by jumping out to a 14–0 first quarter lead on a 13-yard pass from Wade Wilson to Tim Brown, and a Randy Jordan 10-yard run. The Chiefs came back to tie the game in the third quarter on Bam Morris' second touchdown run of the game. Greg Davis put Oakland back on top, 17–14, with a 44-yard field goal halfway through the third, and that was the last time Oakland led. A Pete Stoyanovich field goal and a Derrick Thomas 44-yard fumble return put the Chiefs up, 24–17, going into the fourth quarter. A 15-yard pass from Jeff George to James Jett tied things back up, and the Chiefs then scored the game-winner on a 20-yard pass from Elvis Grbac to Tony Gonzalez. It seemed that groin injuries were in fashion for the Raiders when Wade Wilson and Donald Hollas both went down in the second half. Napoleon Kaufman also suffered from the same injury. Jeff George was called upon to finish the game, and the season, after not playing a complete game for most of the year. The quarterback situation became so dire that if George went down, Tim Brown was getting ready to fill in by taking snaps on the sideline. Their 8–8 record prevented the Raiders from having a winning season since 1994.[16]

Individual Statistics and Roster

Head Coach: Jon Gruden
Assistant Coaches: Dave Adolph, Fred Biletnikoff, Chuck Bresnahan, Willie Brown, Bill Callahan, Frank Gansz, Jr., Garrett Giemont, Robert Jenkins, Don Martin, John Morton, Skip Peete, Keith Rowen, David Shaw, Willie Shaw, Gary Stevens, Mike Waufle
1998 Regular Season Record: 8–8
2nd place in AFC Western Division
Scored 288 points to rank 22nd out of 30 teams
Allowed 356 points to rank 20th

STARTERS — OFFENSE

QB — Jeff George: Active for 8 games and started in 7. Completed 93 of 169 pass attempts for 1,186 yards, 4 TD and 5 INT. Rushed for 2 yards on 8 carries.
RB — Napoleon Kaufman: Active for and started in 13 games. Rushed for 921 yards on 217 carries and 2 TD. Had 25 receptions for 191 yards.
FB — Jon Ritchie: Active for 15 games and started in 10. Rushed for 23 yards on 9 carries. Had 29 receptions for 225 yards.
WR — Tim Brown: Started in 16 games. Had 81 receptions for 1,012 yards and 9 TD. Rushed for -7 yards on 1 carry, and returned 3 punts for 23 yards.
WR — James Jett: Started in 16 games. Had 45 receptions for 882 yards and 6 TD. Rushed for 3 yards on 1 carry.

TE — Rickey Dudley: Active for 16 games and started in 15. Had 36 receptions for 549 yards and 5 TD. Rushed for -2 yards on 1 carry.
LT — Mo Collins: Active for 16 games and started in 11.
LG — Steve Wisniewski: Started in 16 games.
C — Barret Robbins: Started in 16 games.
RG — Derrick Graham: Active for and started in 12 games.
RT — Lincoln Kennedy: Started in 16 games.

RESERVE OFFENSIVE PLAYERS

Darryl Ashmore (T): Active for 15 games, started in 4, and had 1 fumble recovery and 1 TD.
Jeremy Brigham (TE): Active for 2 games.
Derek V. Brown (TE): Active for 16 games, started in 4, and had 7 receptions for 89 yards.
Rick Cunningham (T): Active for 12 games.
Pat Harlow (T): Active for and started in 5 games.
Donald Hollas (QB): Active for 12 games and started in 6. Completed 135 of 260 pass attempts for 1,754 yards, 10 TD, and 16 INT. Rushed for 120 yards on 29 carries and 1 TD.
Desmond Howard (WR): Active for 15 games and started in 1. Had 2 receptions for 16 yards, returned 45 punts for 541 yards and 2 TD, and 49 kickoffs for 1,040 yards.
Randy Jordan (RB): Active for 16 games, rushed for 159 yards on 47 carries and 1 TD, and had 3 receptions for 2 yards.
Terry Mickens (WR): Active for 16 games, started in 2, and had 24 receptions for 346 yards and 1 TD.
Kenny Shedd (WR): Active for 15 games, had 3 receptions for 50 yards, and returned 2 kickoffs for 32 yards.
Adam Treu (C): Active for 16 games.
Harvey Williams (RB): Active for 16 games and started in 3. Rushed for 496 yards on 128 carries and 2 TD, had 26 receptions for 173 yards, and completed 1 of 1 pass attempt for 27 yards.
Jermaine Williams (RB): Active for 10 games.
Rodney Williams (WR): Active for 1 games, and returned 4 kickoffs for 63 yards.
Wade Wilson (QB): Active for 5 games and started in 3. Completed 52 of 88 pass attempts for 568 yards, 7 TD, and 4 INT. Rushed for 24 yards on 7 carries.

STARTERS — DEFENSE

DE — James Harris: Started in 16 games, had 1 sack and 1 fumble recovery.
DE — Lance Johnstone: Active for 16 games, started in 15, had 11 sacks, 1 fumble recovery and 1 TD.
DT — Darrell Russell: Started in 16 games, had 10 sacks and 1 fumble recovery.
DT — Russell Maryland: Active for and started in 15 games and had 2 sacks.
LLB — Terry Wooden: Active for 16 games, started in 10, had 2 sacks, 1 INT and 1 fumble recovery.
MLB — Greg Biekert: Started in 16 games, had 3 sacks and 1 fumble recovery.
RLB — Richard Harvey: Started in 16 games, had 4 sacks and 1 INT.
CB — Charles Woodson: Started in 16 games, had 5 INT and 1 TD.
CB — Eric Allen: Active for and started in 10 games, and had 5 INT.
SS — Anthony Newman: Active for and started in 11 games, and had 2 INT.
FS — Albert Lewis: Active for 15 games, started in 12, had 1 sack, 2 INT and 1 TD.

RESERVE DEFENSIVE PLAYERS

Vincent Amey (DE): Active for 4 games, started in 1, and had 1 kickoff return for 0 yards.
Calvin Branch (DB): Active for 16 games, had 1 fumble recovery, and returned 5 kickoffs for 70 yards.

Bucky Brooks (DB): Active for 6 games, and had 1 punt return for 0 yards.
Aundray Bruce (LB/DE): Active for 1 game.
Perry Carter (DB): Active for 6 games.
Ernest Dixon (LB): Active for 3 games.
James Folston (LB): Active for 16 games, started in 5, had 1 sack, and 1 reception for 1 yard.
Grady Jackson (DT): Active for 15 games, started in 1, had 3 sacks and 1 fumble recovery
John Henry Mills (LB): Active for 5 games.
Mike Morton (LB): Active for 16 games, had 2 fumble recoveries, and returned 1 kickoff for 3 yards.
Chuck Osborne (DT): Active for 6 games.
Anthony Prior (DB): Active for 4 games, and had 1 punt return for 0 yards.
Louis Riddick (DB): Active for 15 games, started in 3, and had 1 fumble recovery.
Travian Smith (LB): Active for 2 games.
Pat Swilling (LB/DE): Active for 16 games, had 2 sacks and 1 fumble recovery.
James Trapp (DB): Active for 16 games.
Eric Turner (DB): Active for and started in 6 games. Had 1 sack, 3 INT, and 1 TD.
Marquis Walker (DB): Active for 16 games, started in 7, had 2 INT and 1 fumble recovery.
Aaron Wallace (LB): Active for 4 games and had 1 fumble recovery.

KICKING/PUNTING

K — Greg Davis: Active for 16 games. Made 17 of 27 field goals and 31 of 31 extra point kicks for 82 points.
P — Leo Araguz: Active for 16 games. Punted 98 times for a 43.4 average. Threw 1 pass for -1 yard, and rushed for -12 yards on 1 carry.

1999 Season Review

1. Sept. 12: The Raiders opened their 40th season with a matchup against Green Bay and quarterback Brett Favre. Oakland went out to a 24–14 fourth quarter lead on two Randy Jordan 1-yard runs, a Tyrone Wheatley 5-yard run, and a 41-yard field goal by Michael Husted. The only problem was that the Raiders were facing a legend at home. Favre engineered the 11th fourth quarter comeback, and 14th game-winning march of his already illustrious career. He first closed the gap to 24–21 with his third touchdown pass of the game, and then took Green Bay on an 11-play, 82-yard drive with 1:51 remaining. He connected with tight end Jeff Thomason for a 1-yard score with 11 seconds left to hand the Raiders a 28–24 defeat, which was the fourth consecutive year that they lost their regular season opener.[1]

2. Sept. 19: Russell Maryland took the wind out of Minnesota's sails by being a one-man wrecking crew in a 22–17 shocker for Oakland. Maryland recovered a fumble, intercepted a pass, and led the defensive charge that provided a strong pass rush and recorded six sacks as a unit. The previous season, the Vikings were virtually unstoppable, setting an NFL record with 556 points. Someone must not have told the Raiders to be in awe, because they held the Minnesota ground attack to just 34 yards. Oakland was behind at the half, 10–6, with their points coming on two Michael Husted field goals from 36 and 37 yards. Rich Gannon put Oakland on top for the first time at the halfway mark of the third quarter by connecting on a 9-yard pass to James Jett.

Maryland came up with his interception on Minnesota's next possession, and it led to a 42-yard Husted field goal to extend the Oakland advantage to 16–10. With 1:08 remaining in the third, Gannon took one in himself from five yards out to make it 22–10, but the Raiders failed on a two-point conversion pass. It seemed like this was the time that Oakland prepared to collapse after holding a nice lead. Minnesota quarterback Randall Cunningham, who despite getting quite a bit of pressure, still threw for 364 yards. Aided by a roughing the passer foul on Tony Bryant, and another penalty on Eric Turner, the Vikings got to the Oakland 28. From there Cunningham found Jake Reed for a score that narrowed the gap to five points with 14 minutes left in the game. This time, however, Oakland's defense spoiled any hopes of a second straight comeback bid by stopping the Vikings on three possessions, and picked off a pass at the end to get out of the Metrodome with their first win of the '99 season.[2]

3. Sept. 26: Rich Gannon threw for 295 yards, and Tim Brown caught nine passes for 121 yards in a home opening, 24–17 win over Chicago. Gannon threw two touchdown passes, with his 20-yarder going to Brown to open the scoring in the first quarter. He added a 13-yard toss to Rickey Dudley in the second quarter to give Oakland a 14–10 halftime lead. The Bears came back to take a 17–14 advantage into the final stanza. Michael Husted then hit on a 47-yard field goal with two minutes gone in the fourth quarter to tie the game. The Raiders then forged ahead with 6:44 left on an 8-yard run by Tyrone Wheatley. This was Wheatley's first start for the Silver and Black, and he only carried the ball eight times for 41 yards, but most of that came on the crucial drive that he capped off. In the early stages of the '99 season, Oakland stood at 2–1, and in a three-way tie for first place in the AFC West with Kansas City and Seattle.[3]

4. Oct. 3: First place only lasted one week for the Raiders, as they lost a heart-breaker to Seattle, 22–21. With ear-splitting noise omitting from the Seattle faithful, the Raiders jumped out to a 14–3 lead in the second quarter on a Tyrone Wheatley 7-yard run and a 6-yard pass from Rich Gannon to Tim Brown. In the third quarter, Oakland increased their bulge to 21–9 on a 3-yard pass from Gannon to Rickey Dudley, and looked to be in control of the game at this point. Oakland's number one defense against the run stopped Seattle's running game, allowing them only 75 yards on 26 carries, applied constant pressure on quarterback Jon Kitna, and Eric Turner intercepted a pass that set up Dudley's score. Then the bottom fell out for the Silver and Black. Kitna managed to shake loose from a fierce and steady rush to connect with Reggie Brown on a 24-yard touchdown pass. A 68-yard punt return resulted in a field goal, and Seattle was right back in it at 21–19. A Gannon interception then gave the Seahawks their first lead of the game, which Todd Peterson provided with a 45-yard field goal with 10:07 remaining in the fourth quarter. Michael Husted missed a long-range field goal attempt from 61 yards out with four seconds left to give Seattle their slim victory over the Raiders in the dreaded Kingdome. The site of many disappointments for the Raiders over the years, the Kingdome was wrapping up its time as a Seattle residence. The new decade would bring the Seahawks a new home field and the Raiders did not shed one tear knowing that the Kingdome would soon be a memory.[4]

5. Oct. 10: With injuries to key personnel mounting, coupled with the retirement of legendary quarterback John Elway,

the two-time defending Super Bowl champion Denver Broncos were winless as they headed into Oakland. Denver's head coach Mike Shanahan might have been winless coming into this game, but he was 7–1 against the team that fired him ten years earlier. The Broncos got out to a 13–0 lead, but Oakland's fifth-ranked offense fought back in the second half to tie the game on two Michael Husted field goals from 47 and 19 yards, and a 21-yard pass from Rich Gannon to Derrick Walker. On the day, Gannon was a very effective 25 of 36 for 248 yards. Denver's signal caller, Brian Griese, managed to outshine his counterpart by leading the Broncos on an 11-play, 63-yard drive with 10:18 left in the game. Jason Elam then capped the drive off with what proved to be the game-winning field goal from 26 yards away for a 16–13 final.[5]

6. Oct. 17: Tyrone Wheatley ran for 97 yards and two touchdowns from three and 11 yards, and Eric Turner intercepted a last chance pass by Buffalo in the end zone with no time left to secure a 20–14 Oakland victory. The win helped even out Oakland's record at 3–3, and Tim Brown became the 16th player in history to reach the 10,000-yard receiving plateau. It also allowed the Raiders to end a two-game losing streak and stopped Buffalo at four straight victories. Michael Husted gave Oakland their other points on field goals from 25 and 32 yards. The Raiders had the number one rushing team, and added to that status by rolling up 195 yards on the ground. It also helped Oakland take valuable time off the clock, as the offense held onto the ball for close to forty minutes.[6]

7. Oct. 14: Rich Gannon lit up the skies over Oakland with 352 passing yards and two touchdowns. Tim Brown had 11 receptions for 190 yards that included a 45-yard touchdown from Gannon, and the Raiders got by the New York Jets, 24–23, to improve to 4–3. Playing with a sore wrist, Gannon brought Oakland back from a 20–3 third quarter deficit on three touchdowns. Gannon first connected with Brown on his touchdown reception, and then drove Oakland 83 yards in 11 plays to get the Raiders deep into New York territory. Zack Crockett finished it off with a 3-yard run to make it a 20–17 New York advantage. Following a New York field goal, Gannon led the Raiders on another 11-play drive that covered 90 yards and was capped off on a Gannon to James Jett 5-yard touchdown connection with 26 seconds left to tie the game. Michael Husted then kicked the extra point to provide the game-winning margin. He also opened the scoring with a 25-yard field goal in the first quarter.[7]

8. Oct. 31: Miami came into Oakland with a 5–1 record and looked to beat the Raiders for the third straight time in Oakland. Playing without legendary signal caller Dan Marino for the third time due to a neck injury, the Dolphins relied on their fourth-ranked defense to stop the Raiders, 16–9. Rich Gannon played with a broken bone in his non-throwing hand, and had troubles all game long. He reinjured the hand, and had to give way to backup Bobby Hoying. Gannon returned for the second half after being given some pain-killing shots, but he could not do anything against one of the premier defensive units. He finished with only seven completions out of 28 attempts for 130 yards and one interception. Miami allowed only 187 yards of total offense, holding Oakland's well-respected ground attack to a mere 80 yards, and gave up only two first downs in 14 third-down situations. Oakland managed to get close enough for Michael Husted to kick three field goals from 49, 34, and 47 yards. The

Raiders were now 4–4 going into their bye week, and every one of their games up to this stage was decided by seven points or less. If they got a reversal of fortune, they could be a force to be reckoned with throughout the second half of the '99 season.[8]

9. Nov. 14: The well-rested Raiders came off their bye week in fine fashion. Second-year head coach Jon Gruden saw his team hit a football trifecta with solid play from his offense, defense, and special teams, in a 28–9 win over San Diego. On offense, Rich Gannon completed 18 of 24 pass attempts for 254 yards and four touchdowns with his broken left wrist still padded. When not throwing the ball, Gannon ran for 43 yards on seven carries to throw off the Chargers. Tyrone Wheatley gained 59 yards on the ground, and Napoleon Kaufman chipped in with 65 to add balance to the offensive attack. Wheatley also had two receptions go for touchdowns from 26 and seven yards. Rickey Dudley caught Gannon's other scoring strikes from two and 12 yards. Tim Brown was his usual fantastic self by catching seven passes for 117 yards, and moved into 14th place on the all-time receiving yardage list with 10,432. Oakland's defense held San Diego's 28th ranked offense to 33 rushing yards and recorded two sacks. Another milestone occurred when defensive back Charles Woodson made his first appearance on offense and caught a pass for 19 yards.[9]

10. Nov. 22: Oakland and Denver had staged many thrilling encounters against each other. With a national prime time audience glued to this Monday Night Football contest, the teams did not disappoint once again. In a game that saw snow and the temperature hovering at 26 degrees, the Raiders took a 21–15 fourth quarter lead after trailing by fifteen points. Rich Gannon fired touchdown strikes to Jon Ritchie (20 yards) and Rickey Dudley (12 yards), and then added a two-point conversion pass to James Jett. Michael Husted then took over with field goals from 33 and 44 yards. The Broncos came back on two Jason Elam field goals to tie it at 21–21 and force overtime. Elam's game-tying kick came from 53 yards away with seven seconds left in regulation. In the overtime period, Gannon was sacked and fumbled. Trevor Pryce was responsible for the hit, the fumble, and the recovery on the Oakland 24. Denver took advantage of this huge break and ended the game on the following play when Olandis Gary ran 24 yards for the clinching touchdown in a 27–21 win.[10]

11. Nov. 28: Oakland faced their third straight AFC West foe, and for the second week, lost a close one, this time to Kansas City, 37–34. The Raiders built a 34–20 lead going into the fourth quarter on two Michael Husted field goals (33 and 30 yards), two Rich Gannon to Rickey Dudley passes (16 and 3 yards), a 6-yard run by Gannon, and a 15-yard interception return by Charles Woodson. Then the Raiders collapsed, giving up 17 fourth quarter points. A whopping 73-yard pass from Elvis Grbac to Tony Gonzalez started the Kansas City surge. Oakland's reserve tight end Derrick Walker then fumbled a short pass, and it was returned 40 yards for a score by Cris Dishman. Pete Stoyanovich tied the game with his extra point kick with 8:36 expired in the quarter. With 2:56 left, Husted missed a 44-yard field goal attempt, and this gave Kansas City continued momentum. Grbac took the Chiefs on a 9-play, 39-yard drive that Stoyanovich finished off with a 44-yard field goal as time ran out to give the Chiefs a well-earned victory over the floundering 5–6 Raiders.[11]

12. Dec. 5: Oakland completed their four-game trek through the AFC West against the first place Seattle Seahawks. Coming into Oakland with an 8–2 record, Seattle looked to continue the Raiders' downward spiral. However, the Raiders looked to even their record at 6–6, and then went out and did just that in a 30–21 win. Once again, Oakland had a double-digit lead in the fourth quarter, but held off Seattle long enough to get another one in the win column. They also kept their hopes of a playoff appearance alive and well. The Raiders capitalized on fumbles and interceptions to produce twenty of their points. Darrien Gordon set up Oakland's first touchdown in the second quarter by returning a fumble 40 yards. Six plays later, Rich Gannon connected with Tim Brown from 14 yards out to give the Raiders a 10–0 lead. A Michael Husted 18-yard field goal opened the scoring in the first quarter. A 21-yard interception return by Charles Mincy set up another Gannon to Brown scoring strike, this time from five yards for a 17–0 lead. On the day, Brown caught six passes for 75 yards, which enabled him to become the third player in NFL history to top the 1,000-yard receiving mark for the seventh straight season. The Seahawks narrowed the gap to 17–14 in the third quarter until a 1-yard run by Zack Crockett gave Oakland some extra breathing room. Another Seattle fumble was recovered by Anthony Newman and turned into a 41-yard field goal by Husted. Newman struck again with 5:55 left in the game when he intercepted a pass and Husted finished off the scoring with a 23-yard three-pointer.[12]

13. Dec. 9: Eddie George exploded on a Thursday night contest in Nashville. When he was through, the ex–Heisman Trophy winner gained a combined 249 yards in a 21–14 win over Oakland. George ran for 199 yards and two touchdowns, and caught six passes for 50 more yards. After a scoreless first half, Tennessee quarterback Steve McNair broke the deadlock with a 1-yard run. Napoleon Kaufman took the ensuing kickoff 92 yards to the Tennessee seven, but a holding penalty negated his great effort. Undaunted, the Raiders put together a 10-play, 90-yard drive capped off by a Zack Crockett 1-yard run that tied the game. A 2-yard pass from Rich Gannon to Rickey Dudley in the fourth quarter made the game closer, but in the end, it was not enough, and Oakland slipped to 6–7.[13]

14. Dec. 19: Napoleon Kaufman ran for 122 yards on just eight carries, Tyrone Wheatley had 111 on 19 rushes, and the Oakland offense rolled up 400 yards in a 45–0 blowout over Tampa Bay. The defense also did a great job in holding the Buccaneers to only 137 yards. Wheatley ran for two touchdowns (30 and 3 yards), as did Kaufman (17 and 75 yards). Tim Brown opened the scoring barrage with a 20-yard pass from Rich Gannon, Lance Johnstone returned a fumble 13 yards, and Joe Nedney added a 26-yard field goal. Brown's touchdown grab was the 75th of his career, leaving him within one of Fred Biletnikoff's Oakland team record. The defense held Tampa Bay's running game to 17 yards in Oakland's first shutout victory since November 22, 1992. This was also the worst defeat handed to the Bucs since 1976.[14]

15. Dec. 26: The Raiders had their playoff hopes dashed with a 23–20 loss to San Diego and a win by Buffalo over New England. This marked the sixth straight season that Oakland failed to make the post-season. The Raiders knew they were officially eliminated in the first quarter of their game when it was learned that Buffalo had won. To make matters worse, Oakland blew a 20–13 fourth quarter advantage. The Raiders got their

points from Joe Nedney on field goals from 52 and 25 yards, a Zack Crockett 1-yard run, and a 7-yard pass from Rich Gannon to Rickey Dudley. Lance Johnstone had three quarterback sacks. The running game was hampered after losing both starting tackles in Mo Collins and Lincoln Kennedy. Without two key members of their wall of protection on the field, the running attack ran for a season-low 46 yards.[15]

16. Jan. 2: Revenge is sweet, and the Raiders certainly got the most out of that statement against Kansas City. In front of an Arrowhead Stadium crowd of 79,026, the Raiders not only beat the Chiefs, 41–38, but eliminated their hated rivals from playoff contention in front of their own fans as well. Kansas City definitely had the Raiders' number throughout the 1990's, coming into this game with 18 wins out of 20 encounters over the course of the decade. It looked like they were going to extend that dominance after building a 17–0 first quarter lead. All the years of torment by their rivals seemed to boil over from that point, and the Raiders stormed back to take a 28–24 halftime lead on the arm of Rich Gannon. Playing in his first game against his old team, Gannon received a nice welcome from the fans prior to the kickoff. As the game progressed, however, the Kansas City throng became less enamored with their former signal caller. On the day, Gannon hit on 25 of 47 passes for 324 yards and three touchdowns. The Raiders first got on the board in the opening quarter when Kenny Shedd returned a blocked punt 20 yards. Gannon's right arm then led Oakland in the second quarter with scoring strikes to Zack Crockett (12 yards), Napoleon Kaufman (22 yards), and Tyrone Wheatley (23 yards). Wheatley, who led all ball carriers for the game with 86 rushing yards, returned the advantage over to Oakland with a 26-yard run in the third quarter after Kansas City held a 31–28 lead. The Chiefs came back in the opening seconds of the fourth quarter on a Kevin Lockett 39-yard catch to make it 38–35. Oakland was not going to be denied, and with spark from past Raiders glory engulfing them, they went on an 11-play, 40-yard drive in two minutes. Gannon connected on six passes, and Joe Nedney then hit on a 38-yard field goal with 45 seconds left in regulation to put the game into a 38–38 deadlock. The Chiefs had a chance to pull it out before the overtime, but Pete Stoyanovich missed on a 44-yard field goal attempt with only a few ticks left on the clock. It is interesting to note that in their previous meeting with the Raiders, Stoyanovich defeated them in the final seconds with a field goal from the same distance. However, this was a new day, and the Raiders were the ones who would go into the off-season on a high note. Oakland's first win of the new millennium took eight plays and 45 yards to produce. Two key passes from Gannon to Rickey Dudley and Tim Brown got Oakland down to the Kansas City 16. From there, with 3:13 expired in overtime, Nedney sent a 33-yard field goal attempt through the uprights to end the game at 41–38, and end the campaign on a positive note for the 8–8 Silver and Black.[16]

Individual Statistics and Roster

Head Coach: Jon Gruden

Assistant Coaches: Fred Biletnikoff, Chuck Bresnahan, Willie Brown, Bill Callahan, Jim Erkenbeck, Frank Gansz, Jr., Garrett Giemont, Woodrow Lowe, Don Martin, John Morton, Skip Peete, Robin Ross, David Shaw, Willie Shaw, Gary Stevens, Mike Waufle

1999 Regular Season Record: 8–8

3rd place in AFC Western Division

Scored 390 points to rank 8th out of 31 teams

Allowed 329 points to rank 16th

STARTERS — OFFENSE

QB — Rich Gannon: Started in 16 games. Completed 304 of 515 pass attempts for 3,840 yards, 24 TD and 14 INT. Rushed for 298 yards on 46 carries and 2 TD. Had 1 reception for -3 yards.

RB — Tyrone Wheatley: Active for 16 games and started in 9. Rushed for 936 yards on 242 carries and 8 TD. Had 21 receptions for 196 yards and 3 TD.

FB — Jon Ritchie: Active for 16 games and started in 14. Rushed for 12 yards on 5 carries, and had 45 receptions for 408 yards and 1 TD.

WR — Tim Brown: Started in 16 games. Had 90 receptions for 1,344 yards, 6 TD, and rushed for 4 yards on 1 carry.

WR — James Jett: Active for 16 games and started in 11. Had 39 receptions for 552 yards and 2 TD.

TE — Rickey Dudley: Started in 16 games. Had 39 receptions for 555 yards and 9 TD.

LT — Mo Collins: Active for 13 games and started in 12.

LG — Steve Wisniewski: Started in 16 games.

C — Barret Robbins: Started in 16 games.

RG — Gennaro DiNapoli: Active for 11 games and started in 9.

RT — Lincoln Kennedy: Active for and started in 15 games.

RESERVE OFFENSIVE PLAYERS

Darryl Ashmore (T): Active for 16 games and started in 2. Had 1 kickoff return for 0 yards.

Jeremy Brigham (TE): Active for 16 games, started in 2, and had 8 receptions for 108 yards.

Zack Crockett (RB): Active for 13 games and started in 1. Rushed for 91 yards on 45 carries and 4 TD. Had 8 receptions for 56 yards and 1 TD.

Bobby Hoying (QB): Active for 2 games. Completed 2 of 5 pass attempts for 10 yards. Rushed for -3 yards on 2 carries.

Randy Jordan (RB): Active for 16 games. Rushed for 32 yards on 9 carries and 2 TD. Had 8 receptions for 82 yards. Returned 10 kickoffs for 207 yards.

Napoleon Kaufman (RB): Active for 16 games and started in 5. Rushed for 714 yards on 138 carries and 2 TD. Had 18 receptions for 181 yards and 1 TD. Returned 42 kickoffs for 831 yards.

Terry Mickens (WR): Active for 16 games and started in 3. Had 20 receptions for 261 yards.

Joe Nedney (K): Active for 3 games. Made 5 of 7 field goal attempts, and 13 of 13 extra point kicks.

Nathan Parks (T): Active for 2 games.

Kenny Shedd (WR): Active for 12 games.

Barry Sims (T/G): Active for 16 games and started in 10.

Adam Treu (C): Active for 16 games, and returned 1 kickoff for 6 yards.

Derrick Walker (TE): Active for 11 games, started in 3, and had 7 receptions for 71 yards and 1 TD.

Jermaine Williams (RB): Active for 15 games and had 1 reception for 20 yards.

Rodney Williams (WR): Active for 5 games.

STARTERS — DEFENSE

DE — James Harris: Started in 16 games, had 2 sacks, 1 INT, and 1 fumble recovery.

DE — Lance Johnstone: Started in 16 games, had 10 sacks, 1 INT, 1 fumble recovery and 1 TD.

DT — Russell Maryland: Started in 16 games, had 1 sacks, 1 INT, and 1 fumble recovery.

DT — Darrell Russell: Started in 16 games, had 9 sacks and 1 fumble recovery.

LLB — K.D. Williams: Active for 9 games, started in 8, had 1 sack, 1 INT and 1 fumble recovery.

MLB — Greg Biekert: Started in 16 games, had 2 sacks and 2 INT.

RLB — Richard Harvey: Active for and started in 15 games, and had 2 sacks.

CB — Charles Woodson: Started in 16 games, had 1 INT, 1 TD, 1 fumble recovery, and 1 reception for 19 yards.

CB — Eric Allen: Started in 16 games, had 3 INT and 1 fumble recovery.

SS — Anthony Newman: Active for 16 games, started in 13, had 2 INT and 1 fumble recovery.

FS — Eric Turner: Active for and started in 10 games. Had 3 INT and 2 fumble recoveries.

RESERVE DEFENSIVE PLAYERS

Eric Barton (LB): Active for 16 games, started in 3, and had 3 sacks.

Calvin Branch (DB): Active for 16 games, started in 1, and returned 6 kickoffs for 96 yards.

Bobby Brooks (LB): Active for 1 game.

Tony Bryant (DE): Active for 10 games, and had 4 sacks.

Roderick Coleman (DT): Active for 3 games.

Darrien Gordon (DB): Active for 16 games and started in 2. Had 1 sack, 3 INT, 2 fumble recoveries, and returned 42 punts for 397 yards.

Johnnie Harris (DB): Active for 4 games.

Grady Jackson (DT): Active for 15 games, had 4 sacks and 1 fumble recovery.

Charles Mincy (DB): Active for 16 games and started in 1. Had 2 INT, 1 fumble recovery, and 1 kickoff return for 0 yards.

Chuck Osborne (DT): Active for 16 games and had 1 sack.

Marcus Ray (DB): Active for 8 games.

Travian Smith (LB): Active for 16 games, started in 1, and had 1 fumble recovery.

Sam Sword (LB): Active for 10 games, started in 5, and had 1 sack.

Marquis Walker (DB): Active for 16 games, had 1 sack and 1 INT.

KICKING/PUNTING

K — Michael Husted: Active for 13 games. Made 20 of 31 field goals and 30 of 30 extra points for 90 points.

P — Leo Araguz: Active for 16 games. Punted 76 times for a 40.1 average.

2000 Season Review

1. Sept. 3: With the exception of their inaugural season in 1960, the Raiders advanced to the conference championship game in the first year of every decade. Hoping to continue this streak into the new millennium, the 2000 edition of the Silver and Black began their quest against San Diego, who they were 4–0 against in season openers. In a low-scoring affair, the Raiders remained perfect in their openers with the Chargers by a 9–6 count. San Diego quarterback Ryan Leaf played in his first NFL game in 20 months, and Oakland was not very kind to him. The Silver and Black defense beat and bloodied Leaf throughout the game, intercepted him three times, and forced two fumbles. Oakland clung to a 2–0 lead in the fourth quarter on a safety caused when Darrell Russell tackled Robert Chancey in the end zone. Chancey redeemed himself later by scoring on a 3-yard run to give the Chargers a 6–2 lead. The Raiders then went on an eight-play, 53-yard drive that saw Rich Gannon throw for 48 of those yards. He capped the drive, and the game, off with a 10-yard strike to Andre

Rison with 2:53 left for the go-ahead touchdown. The amazing thing was that Rison was not even supposed to be on the field for the play. How and why he got there nobody seemed to care about after he scored the winning points.[1]

2. Sept. 10: The Indianapolis Colts jumped out to a 21–0 lead and led, 24–7, at the half on the power of two Peyton Manning touchdown passes, and an Edgerrin James run. The Raiders were a more polished outfit in 2000 than in recent years, and came back to win a wild one, 38–31. Rich Gannon accounted for three touchdowns, but decided to run for them instead of throw. His three scoring runs were from three, seven, and six yards, and established a single-game team record for most touchdowns scored by a quarterback himself. Gannon's feat also provided the Colts with a team record of most touchdowns scored by an opposing quarterback since 1954. Tyrone Wheatley added two scoring jaunts from six and one yard, Sebastian Janikowski connected on his first-ever regular season field goal (24 yards), and the Raiders remained undefeated. The Colts attempted a rally, but Tory James intercepted a Manning pass intended for Marvin Harrison in the end zone with one minute left in the game to secure the win and give Oakland their first 2–0 start since 1995. This was also the Raiders' 350th regular season win in team history.[2]

3. Sept. 17: Jon Gruden had not beaten the Denver Broncos in four tries as Oakland's head coach. Unfortunately, the streak continued with a 33–24 loss. The Broncos handed Oakland their first defeat of the new millennium thanks in large part to a rookie reserve running back. Mike Anderson was called upon to carry the running duties after superstar Terrell Davis and Olandis Gary were unavailable due to injuries. Anderson rose to the challenge by running for an incredible 187 yards. In front of Oakland's first sellout crowd in 25 games, the Raiders overcame a 17–0 first quarter deficit to tie the game at 24–24. The Raiders achieved this yeoman's effort on two Rich Gannon to Tim Brown passes covering 11 and nine yards, a Sebastian Janikowski 19-yard field goal, and a Randy Jordan 3-yard return of a blocked punt. With Tim Brown's two touchdown catches, he surpassed the great Fred Biletnikoff for the most in Raiders' history with 77. Oakland did manage to keep Denver out of the end zone in the second half, but they got close enough for ex–Raider Joe Nedney to kick three of his four field goals on the day that proved to be the deciding factor.[3]

4. Sept. 24: The Cleveland Browns came into Oakland extremely confident. In only their second season back after the original team moved to Baltimore following the '95 season, the expansion Browns entered Network Associates Coliseum with a 2–1 slate. The Browns confidence was increased when they opened the game with a near-perfect drive that resulted in a 15-yard touchdown pass from Tim Couch to Darrin Chiaverini to give them a 7–0 lead. However, over the course of their remaining time in Oakland, the Browns' bravado was beaten out of them. With heavy metal music blaring out across the Coliseum, and the fans of Raider Nation urging them on, the Silver and Black ran off 28 straight points, and cruised to an easy 36–10 victory. Tyrone Wheatley scored two touchdowns on runs both covering two yards, Zack Crockett added his own 2-yard run, and William Thomas returned an interception 46 yards for all of Oakland's six-pointers on the day. Sebastian Janikowski booted two field goals from 37 and 31 yards, and the team recorded a safety to end

the scoring festivities. The Oakland defense applied pressure on quarterback Tim Couch throughout the game, intercepted him twice, and recorded three sacks.[4]

5. Oct. 8: The Raiders came into this game against neighboring San Francisco looking to begin a season at 4–1 for the first time in five years. Jon Gruden's "Dink and Dunk" offense was clicking very well, as it allowed the Raiders to rank third in the AFC in points per game, and second in scoring. The offensive line was also doing a tremendous job keeping defenders from driving Rich Gannon into the turf by allowing just three sacks, which tied them for the fewest in the league. The Oakland offense continued to excite the football community with a 34–28 overtime win that saw both teams combine for 943 offensive yards. Rich Gannon had one of the best days as a quarterback could. He proved to be a multiple threat by completing 21 of 43 passes for 310 yards and two touchdowns, while also rushing for 85 yards and a score. Tim Brown was on the receiving end of both of Gannon scoring strikes, and caught seven passes for an incredible 172 yards. The Raiders got out to a 6–0 lead in the second quarter on two Sebastian Janikowski field goals from 23 and 35 yards. The 49ers came right back to take a 14–6 halftime lead on two Jeff Garcia touchdown passes. Oakland came alive in the second half, and had a 28–14 advantage in the fourth quarter. Tyrone Wheatley scored the Raiders' first touchdown of the game on a 1-yard run in the third quarter. Gannon ran for the two-point conversion to tie things up at 14–14. Gannon and Brown then put the Raiders in the lead for the first time since the second quarter by hooking up on a 30-yard touchdown toss. Gannon added a 13-yard run to give the Raiders a 14-point lead. Quarterback Jeff Garcia brought the 49ers back to tie by tossing two more touchdown passes. Terrell Owens closed the Oakland advantage to seven points after shaking off three defenders to record a 31-yard reception with 9:51 left in the fourth quarter. When Oakland got the ball back following the ensuing kickoff, Pierson Prioleau intercepted a Gannon pass and returned it to the Oakland 13. With just under nine minutes left in regulation, Garcia fired his fourth scoring toss of the day, this time to Charlie Garner from nine yards away. Janikowski missed a 41-yard field goal with 4:46 left, and Oakland stopped the 49ers on fourth-and one to force the overtime period. Janikowski once again blew an opportunity to win this one with his foot by missing on a 35-yard field goal attempt. The 49ers then tried for a three-pointer to win, but Anthony Dorsett blocked Wade Richey's try from 29 yards with 6:21 left in overtime. Five plays later, aided by a pass interference that gave the Oakland the ball just shy of the San Francisco 30, the Raiders emerged victorious. With 4:45 left in overtime, Gannon and Brown connected for a 31-yard touchdown that allowed the Raiders to improve to 4–1.[5]

6. Oct. 15: The Raiders were dominated by the Kansas City Chiefs throughout the 1990's, but the dawn of a new millennium reversed the curse. For the second time in the calendar year of 2000, Oakland beat the Chiefs, this time by a 20–17 count. Rich Gannon returned to Arrowhead Stadium and made Kansas City wish they never let him go. Making successful plays happen through audibles and scrambling to avoid defenders, Gannon completed 28 of 33 passes for 244 yards and two touchdowns. His first six-point toss went to Napoleon Kaufman (4 yards) in the first quarter to open the scoring. The Chiefs then exploded

for 17 points in the second quarter to take a ten-point advantage into the second half. A 47-yard field goal by Sebastian Janikowski closed the gap to 17–10 in the third quarter. Gannon then fired his second touchdown pass of the game, this time to Tyrone Wheatley from seven yards out, and with Janikowski's extra point, the game was knotted at 17-all in the fourth quarter. With time running out in regulation, the Raiders marched 64 yards in eight plays to produce the win. On the drive, Gannon connected with Wheatley on two passes totaling 29 yards, and ran for a 12-yard pickup himself. With 25 seconds left, Janikowski sealed the victory with a 43-yard field goal to help the Raiders improve to 5–1. This proved to be the third straight Oakland–Kansas City matchup determined by a field goal. Tim Brown reached another milestone in his brilliant career. His five receptions gave him 801 career catches, which allowed him to climb up to number eight all-time in that category.[6]

7. Oct. 22: The Raiders were getting to be known as a third quarter team, dominating opponents by a whopping 44–6 margin. However, on this day, they scored in every quarter but the third. It did not matter, because Oakland took advantage of a weak Seattle defense ranked 29th out of 31 teams, and mauled the Seattle Seahawks, 31–3, to start off a season at 6–1 for the first time in ten years. Tyrone Wheatley ran for a career-high 156 yards that included an 80-yard scoring jaunt. He must have loved playing against the Seahawks due to the fact that he amassed 336 yards in his previous three games against them. After spotting Seattle an early 3–0 lead, the Raiders ran up 31 straight points against a very young and inexperienced team. Rich Gannon completed 15 of 22 passes for 176 yards and three touchdowns. On the receiving end of Gannon's tosses were Tim Brown (16 and 9 yards), and James Jett (23 yards). Sebastian Janikowski added a 32-yard field goal to complete the romp.[7]

8. Oct. 29: On the Sunday night prime time stage, the Raiders continued on their assault through their AFC Western Division foes with a 15–13 victory over the winless San Diego Chargers. However, it was not an easy win. San Diego played hard in an attempt to enter the win column for the first time in the decade, and also put a halt to a long-time foe's winning streak. Sebastian Janikowski was suffering from inconsistency throughout his rookie campaign, but on this day, he more than made up for it with a national television audience watching. "Sea Bass" kicked four field goals in the first half, with two coming from 40 yards, and the others from 54, and 29 yards to give the Raiders a 12–0 halftime advantage. His 54-yarder was a then-team record, which he would break multiple times throughout his career. For the second straight week, the Raiders failed to score in the third quarter after gaining a reputation for being a high-octane offensive machine in that stanza throughout their first six games. San Diego got their first points of the game in the third when Jim Harbaugh connected with Freddie Jones on an 8-yard pass to pull within five points of the lead. With 5:58 remaining in the game, the Harbaugh-Jones tandem struck again, this time from 21 yards, to put the Chargers in the lead by the slimmest of margins, 13–12, after the extra point was missed. Out to show they were a force to be reckoned with, the Silver and Black set out to record their seventh victory. Rich Gannon connected on passes to David Dunn and Andre Rison, and Tyrone Wheatley ran the ball three times to help the Raiders get to the San Diego

5-yard line with 16 seconds left. From there, Janikowski drilled a 24-yard field goal to pull out a hard-fought 15–13 win. This was the rookie's second time in the last three games that one of his field goals provided Oakland with a win. Harbaugh had one final chance at victory, and sent a long pass downfield on the game's last play, but it was intercepted by Marquez Pope to secure the win.[8]

9. Nov. 5: Rich Gannon once again broke the hearts of his old Kansas City teammates, and this time he was assisted by another ex–Chief in a 49–31 Oakland win. Gannon threw for 242 yards on 20 of 31 pass attempts and four touchdowns, with two going to former Kansas City receiver Andre Rison. Rison's only two catches of the game went for scores from ten and six yards out. Rickey Dudley added the other two from 20 and two yards. Tyrone Wheatley led the ground assault with 112 yards on 20 carries that included a 1-yard touchdown run. Also helping out in Oakland's scoring fest were Zack Crockett (1-yard run), and Randy Jordan (43-yard run). The hero of the last two games, Sebastian Janikowski, missed this one due to a bacterial infection in his foot. Filling in for him was punter Shane Lechler, who did a great job connecting on all seven extra point kicks. This win allowed the Raiders to have their best start since 1977, as they were looking more and more like true contenders on the verge of restoring the team's glory that faded since the mid–1980's. This was also the first time since 1988 that the Raiders swept a season series from the Chiefs.[9]

10. Nov. 13: The Raiders came into this Monday Night Football game against Denver riding a six-game winning streak. Their record on Monday night was 33-17-1, and they needed one more win to tie the record for most victories on the prime time spectacle. The Broncos entered this game ranked number one in the AFC with 29.8 points per game, while Oakland was second with 28.4. This also proved to be the final Monday Night Football game ever played in Mile High Stadium. The Raiders looked good in the first half, compiling 216 yards to only 100 for Denver. After spotting Denver a 7–0 lead, the Raiders got on the board in the first quarter on a Brett Conway 19-yard field goal. Rich Gannon then moved the team deep into Denver territory with key passes. A Zack Crockett 1-yard run finished off the march to give the Raiders their first lead of the game with 2:55 left in the opening half. Oakland was unable to stay the course in the final thirty minutes, and never regained the lead. The Broncos started their comeback when Jason Elam tied things up at 10–10 with a 23-yard field goal in the third quarter. Two minutes later, Ian Gold returned a blocked punt 12 yards to put Denver up, 17–10, going into the fourth quarter. Brian Griese lit up the thin Denver air with 177 yards passing in the second half, and an 11-yard scoring toss to Byron Chamberlain extended the Denver advantage to 24–10 in the opening minutes of the final stanza. Just as momentum was apparently swinging toward the home sideline of Mile High Stadium, the Raiders temporarily took it away. With 6:30 remaining in regulation, Gannon drove the team downfield on four passes, and Crockett scored his second 1-yard touchdown run of the game. The Raiders got possession back two minutes later, and Gannon teamed up with Tim Brown on a 22-yard scoring toss, and Conway's extra point tied this wild one at 24–24 with 1:06 left. Following the ensuing kickoff, Griese directed Denver from his own 33 to give Elam an opportunity for a 41-yard

field goal attempt. The ball split the uprights with no time left on the clock to put Oakland at 8–2, and give ex–Raiders' coach and present Denver mentor Mike Shanahan an 11–1 record against his old team.[10]

11. Nov. 19: The Raiders were looking for their first win in New Orleans since Super Bowl XV in January of 1981. Two trips in 1988 and '91 resulted in defeats, and Oakland looked to make the third time the charm. It would not be an easy task down in the "Big Easy," as the Saints were 7–3, riding a six-game winning streak, and led the NFL with 44 sacks, and ranked third best defense overall. However, despite bringing constant pressure on Rich Gannon, and sacking him five times, the Saints could not stop him completely. Gannon was able to dodge the aggressive onslaught on enough occasions to connect on 14 of 21 passes for 168 yards and two touchdowns. He also led the Raiders in rushing with 55 yards on seven carries. Oakland jumped out to a 17–0 lead thanks to a Sebastian Janikowski 49-yard field goal, a 34-yard pass from Gannon to Andre Rison, and a 6-yard run by Zack Crockett. New Orleans came back to cut Oakland's advantage to four points going in to the fourth quarter. After seeing recent seasons collapse down the stretch, the Raiders refused to allow the same dismal climax to occur yet again. Gannon threw for a 21-yard touchdown to Tim Brown, and Crockett recorded his second 6-yard scoring run that allowed the Raiders to get out of New Orleans win a 31–22 victory and improve to 9–2.[11]

12. Nov. 26: The Atlanta Falcons were having a brutal year. Up to this point of the season, they stood at 3–9, and their encounter with the Raiders did nothing to improve team moral. A trip to Oakland resulted in a 41–14 mauling and gave the Falcons their tenth loss of the season. Meanwhile, the Raiders recorded their tenth win. Atlanta got out to a 7–3 lead in the first quarter, and after that, things went bad. The Raiders ran off 35 straight points throughout the second and third quarters, and coasted to an easy victory that gave them their first 10–2 start since 1977, and tied them with Minnesota for the best record in the league. Rich Gannon threw for 231 yards on 15 of 22 attempts and two touchdowns, and Tyrone Wheatley ran for a game-high 85 yards that included a 1-yard touchdown. Gannon's six-point tosses went to Tim Brown from 28 yards, and James Jett from 84. This marked the third straight game in which Brown caught a touchdown pass. Also scoring touchdowns for Oakland were Zack Crockett on an 8-yard run, and Davis Dunn on an 88-yard kickoff return. Sebastian Janikowski's first field goal from 24 yards gave Oakland their initial points, and his 35-yarder in the fourth quarter closed out the scoring.[12]

13. Dec. 3: The Raiders travelled to Three Rivers Stadium for the first time since 1980 to wage a conflict with their longtime hated rivals, the Pittsburgh Steelers. Oakland came into this game against the 6–6 Steelers with the league's top-ranked running game and the AFC's second-best points per game average (29.3). Trailing, 7–0, at the end of the first quarter, the Raiders struck back to lead, 17–7, at the end of the first half. Sebastian Janikowski got Oakland on the board with a 40-yard three-pointer, and that was followed by an Eric Allen 27-yard interception return and a 21-yard pass from Rich Gannon to Randy Jordan. Pittsburgh quarterback Kordell Stewart hurt his knee in the first quarter, but despite the discomfort, he forged ahead. In the opening drive of the second half, Stewart took the Steelers 91

yards and capped it off with a 6-yard touchdown toss to Mark Bruener to make it a 17–14 ball game. The Pittsburgh defense rose up and stopped one of the most potent offenses in the league throughout the second half. Stewart capitalized on the yeoman's effort displayed by his defense, and scored the go-ahead touchdown on a 17-yard run to give the Steelers a 21–17 fourth quarter lead. Janikowski brought Oakland back to within one point with a 42-yard field goal, but missed on a 44-yarder with four minutes left. The Steelers held on from there to preserve a slim 21–20 victory.[13]

14. Dec. 10: The Raiders rebounded from their close defeat a week earlier by trouncing the New York Jets, 31–7, in front of a prime time Sunday night audience. Both teams were on the verge of clinching playoff berths, and this contest was viewed as a classic battle between east coast and west coast. The Raiders quickly dispelled any notions that this was going to be a heart-pounding affair throughout, and clinched their first post-season appearance in seven years. They ran off 31 straight points before the Jets rang up a fourth quarter score. After a scoreless opening quarter, the Raiders exploded for 21 points in the second stanza thanks to Eric Allen's 50-yard interception return, Andre Rison's 7-yard catch from Rich Gannon, and Tyrone Wheatley's 1-yard run. This was Allen's second score in as many weeks off an interception. Gannon threw his second touchdown pass of the game to Tim Brown from four yards out, and Sebastian Janikowski kicked a 32-yard field goal to complete Oakland's scoring in this rout.[14]

15. Dec. 16: The Raiders came into this game with Seattle averaging the second-best point production per game in the AFC at 28.8. Unfortunately, they fell just short of that and lost, 27–24. Played in a mixture of cold, wind, and rain, the Raiders fell to 11–4, and were in a dismal position to lose first place in the AFC Western Division. Fortunately, luck was on Oakland's side, as Kansas City beat Denver the following day to keep the Raiders one game ahead of the Broncos. With 11:48 left in the game, the Raiders looked to be in control, 24–13. Giving them an 11-point lead came compliments of Andre Rison, who caught a 14-yard pass from Rich Gannon, Randy Jordan's two touchdown runs of six and seven yards, and a 25-yard field goal from Sebastian Janikowski. Seattle quarterback Jon Kitna suffered a bruised knee in the third quarter, but came back and proceeded to take the Seahawks on a drive that was finished by Shaun Alexander's 4-yard run. They missed on a two-point conversion pass, and now trailed, 24–19. Then came a controversial call that completely swung momentum over to the Seahawks. Seattle running back Ricky Watters took off for a 53-yard gain, and as he got to the Oakland 25, defensive back Charles Woodson made a great move by knocking the ball out of his hands. The loose pigskin skidded across the damp turf and Oakland's Marquez Pope recovered it on the two. However, the slick conditions forced Pope's momentum to carry him into the end zone. He was then touched by a Seattle player for what was ruled a safety. The Raiders protested that Pope should have been either downed at the point where he recovered the ball at the two, or it ruled a touchback with Oakland getting possession on their own 20. The official call of a safety stood, and now Seattle trailed by three points with 2:24 left in the game and they would get the ball back. Kitna then threw a 9-yard touchdown pass to rookie Darrell Jackson with 28 seconds left. Gannon attempted to pull this one out, but his third inter-

ception of the game with 12 seconds remaining sealed the win for Seattle. The loss overshadowed a great performance by Tyrone Wheatley, who ran for 146 yards. It also meant that the Raiders would have to wait until their regular season finale to possibly clinch their first division title in ten years.[15]

16. Dec. 24: Oakland refused to keep their faithful members of Raider Nation in suspense, and gave them a division title on the day before Christmas. They achieved this with a 52–9 thrashing of the Carolina Panthers for their ninth home win in ten previous games. A crowd of 60,637 was on hand to witness this point barrage that tied a team record first set in 1963. Rich Gannon lit up the Christmas Eve sky for 230 yards and five touchdowns. He apparently liked his tight ends on this day, because he connected with Rickey Dudley and Jeremy Brigham on four of his scoring strikes. Dudley's touchdowns came from one and 21 yards, and Brigham's from four and two yards. Tim Brown was on the receiving end of Gannon's other touchdown toss from nine yards out. The defense got into the scoring act when Eric Allen returned an interception 37 yards, and Darrien Gordon scooped up a fumble and raced 74 yards for Oakland's final regular season touchdown. Sebastian Janikowski chipped in with a 42-yard field goal in the second quarter. It was now on to the playoffs, with two opponents standing in the way of a Super Bowl appearance. It would also be the first time since 1980 that the Raiders would host a playoff game in Oakland.[16]

AFC Divisional Playoff Game, January 6, 2001

The Raiders fell two points shy of their second-place AFC ranking at 29.9 points per game. However, the tough Oakland defense held the Miami Dolphins scoreless, and the Raiders were on their way to their ninth AFC Championship Game berth thanks to a 27–0 blowout win. The 12–6 Dolphins came out to Oakland with the sixth-ranked defense, and on the Raiders' first offensive series, it looked like the Raiders might be in for a tough go of it. The offense made a quick three and out, and then turned the ball over to the Dolphins. Oakland's defense unit decided to get the festivities started by pitching in while their offensive comrades got in sync. Fifth-year defensive back Tory James was in his first season with the Raiders, and immediately added his name to the long list of post-season heroes who wore the silver and black. Miami had reached the Oakland 17, and were on the verge of breaking the scoreless tie in the first quarter. Quarterback Jay Fiedler dropped back and fired a pass intended for Leslie Shepherd at the ten. James snagged the pass instead, and raced 90 yards down the sideline to complete his scoring jaunt with only three-and-a-half minutes expired off the clock. James added another interception to his day's work in the fourth quarter. Sebastian Janikowski added the conversion, and Oakland never looked back. Janikowski extended Oakland's lead to 10–0 with a 36-yard field with 4:52 left in the first quarter. Janikowski increased the Oakland advantage to 13–0 with a 33-yard field goal in the second quarter. By this time, Rich Gannon and the offense were beginning to click. In the first half, Gannon hit on 10 of 13 passes for 117 yards, and was responsible for giving Oakland a 20–0 lead at the half when he teamed up with James Jett from six yards out with 1:53 left before halftime. Janikowski added the extra point. Throughout the second half, Gannon turned the offense over to his top-rated running game, and it responded with 145 yards on 35 carries. Tyrone Wheatley paced the ground attack with 56 yards, and scored Oakland's final touchdown on a 2-yard run with 5:56 left in the game. In addition to James' two thefts, Eric Allen had an interception, Charles Woodson recovered a fumble, and Tony Bryant and Roderick Coleman each recorded a sack in the Raiders' first-ever post-season shutout win.[17]

AFC Championship Game, January 14, 2001

The Oakland Raiders faced some tough defensive opposition during their playoff history. In the 1960's it was the Kansas City Chiefs who ended the Raiders' Super Bowl quest, and in the 70's their dream was stymied one game shy of the epic clash by Pittsburgh's "Steel Curtain," Miami's "No Name Defense," and Denver's "Orange Crush." The changing of the millennium did little to prevent that, as the Baltimore Ravens stood poised, fierce, and ready, to block the Silver and Black from a fifth Super Bowl appearance.

The Ravens came into their first-ever AFC Championship Game in only their fifth season of existence following the Cleveland Browns organization's move to Baltimore in 1996. They posted a 14–4 record leading up to this game, and entered Oakland's Network Associates Coliseum winners of nine straight games.

The 2000 edition of the Baltimore Ravens had one of the greatest single-season defensive units ever assembled. Led by middle linebacker pare-excellence Ray Lewis, this unit was ranked first in the league with 49 turnovers, 26 fumble recoveries, allowed the fewest points in history (165) since the NFL went to a 16-game schedule in 1978, recorded four shutouts, let opposing offenses cross the Baltimore 20-yard line on only 27 occasions, and boasted of holding enemy running backs to a league-low 61 yards per game. Their style of play was to attack quickly and aggressively to throw their opponents out of sync.

The Raiders were no slouches on defense either. They only allowed two six-pointers in the last 15 quarters at home. With both defenses on a roll coming into this matchup, it came as no surprise that the first quarter ended in a scoreless tie. Four minutes into the second quarter, things changed. Baltimore tight end Shannon Sharpe caught a pass from Trent Dilfer on a slant pattern with the Ravens pinned back on their own 4-yard line. Over the course of the next few seconds, Sharpe got his hands on the ball ten yards from the line of scrimmage, and after safety Marquez Pope missed a chance at stopping him there, Sharpe was off on a playoff-record 96-yard sprint to the end zone to complete the drive that took a mere three plays and 1:27 off the clock. Matt Stover added the extra point, and the Ravens were up, 7–0.

Rich Gannon was forced to leave the game on Oakland's next possession following Sharpe's touchdown. Baltimore's massive 360-pound tackle Tony Siragusa sent his girth crashing down on Gannon, and in the process, injured both the quarterback's shoulders. Gannon did return in the second half, but was unable to throw with any velocity. He passed for only 80 yards,

was intercepted twice, and sacked four times. Baltimore's impressive defense also clamped down on Oakland's running game, allowing it just 24 yards.

Three minutes after Sharpe's six-pointer, Baltimore's Duane Starks intercepted a pass on the Oakland 21, and four plays later, Stover kicked a 31-yard field goal to give the Ravens a 10–0 lead at the end of the first half.

The Raiders caught a break early in the third quarter. Johnnie Harris picked off a pass on the Baltimore 42 and returned it two yards to give Oakland good field position. Nine plays later, the Raiders had the ball on the Baltimore 12 thanks to a 15-yard pass from Gannon to Jeremy Brigham. With five minutes expired in the second half, Oakland finally got their first points on the board when Sebastian Janikowski kicked a 24-yard field goal to make it a 10–3 ballgame.

The Ravens got their points back on a nine-play, 51-yard drive. Trent Dilfer got the Ravens to the Oakland 19 on key plays coming on passes to Brandon Stokley and Ben Coates. From there, Oakland's defense stiffened, and Stover came on and nailed a 28-yard three-pointer to give Baltimore a 13–3 lead going into the fourth quarter.

Middle linebacker Ray Lewis was a one-man wrecking machine on the Silver and Black. He caused five turnovers, broke up two passes, and stuffed any Oakland ball carrier that crossed his path. In the fourth quarter, Lewis added to his gridiron masterpiece by recovering a fumble at the Oakland six. Stover then added his third field goal of the game seven plays later, this time from 21 yards. By this juncture, the Ravens were up, 16–3, and on the verge of getting ready to head for the Super Bowl as the clock showed only 7:28 remaining.

As this title game was slowly creeping toward its climax, Oakland looked dazed by the Baltimore defensive vice grip applied to them. However, things did get interesting, if only for a fleeting moment. Oakland's Terry Kirby fumbled, but it was reversed after the Raiders challenged the call, and Oakland regained possession on the Baltimore 15. Three plays later, Bobby Hoying threw a touchdown pass to Andre Rison that would have put the Raiders right back in this game. Unfortunately, Rison was penalized for pushing off defensive back Chris McAlister. Two plays later, Hoying had a pass picked off by linebacker Jamie Sharper on the Baltimore 1-yard line. A short time later, the Ravens were crowned AFC champions with their 16–3 victory, and won the Super Bowl two weeks later over the New York Giants with an extremely convincing 34–7 mauling.[18]

The rebirth of glory during the 2000 campaign, reminiscent of Raiders' teams throughout the late 60's, 70's and early 80's, hit a snag on this January afternoon in Oakland. Their three points tied a team low set in the AFC Championship Game following the 1990 season. However, it was a positive thing to witness the Raiders once again closing in on a Super Bowl after a decade of never even getting that close.

Individual Statistics and Roster

Head Coach: Jon Gruden
Assistant Coaches: Fred Biletnikoff, Chuck Bresnahan, Willie Brown, Bill Callahan, Bob Casullo, Jim Erkenbeck, Garrett Giemont, Woodrow Lowe, Ron Lynn, Don Martin, John Morton, Skip Peete, Robin Ross,

Davis Shaw, Gary Stevens
2000 Regular Season Record: 12–4
1st Place in AFC Western Division
Scored 479 points to rank 3rd out of 31 teams
Allowed 299 points to rank 9th
Led the league in offensive rushing yards (2,470)

STARTERS — OFFENSE

QB – Rich Gannon: Started in 16 games. Completed 284 of 473 pass attempts for 3,430 yards, 28 TD, and 11 INT. Rushed for 529 yards on 89 carries and 4 TD.

RB – Tyrone Wheatley: Active for 14 games and started in 13. Rushed for 1,046 yards on 232 carries and 9 TD. Had 20 receptions for 156 yards and 1 TD.

RB – Jon Ritchie: Active for 13 games and started in 12. Had 26 receptions for 173 yards.

WR – Tim Brown: Started in 16 games. Had 76 receptions for 1,128 yards and 11 TD. Rushed for 12 yards on 3 carries.

WR – James Jett: Active for 16 games and started in 14. Had 20 receptions for 356 yards and 2 TD.

TE – Rickey Dudley: Started in 16 games. Had 29 receptions for 350 yards, 4 TD and 1 rush for -7 yards.

LT – Matt Stinchcomb: Active for 13 games and started in 9.

LG – Steve Wisniewski: Started in 16 games.

C – Barret Robbins: Started in 16 games.

RG – Mo Collins: Started in 16 games.

RT – Lincoln Kennedy: Started in 16 games.

RESERVE OFFENSIVE PLAYERS

Darryl Ashmore (T): Active for 16 games.

Jeremy Brigham (TE): Active for 15 games and started in 3. Had 13 receptions for 107 yards and 2 TD.

Brett Conway (K): Active for 1 game. Made 1 field goal attempt and 3 extra point kicks for 6 points.

Zack Crockett (RB): Active for 16 games and started in 4. Rushed for 130 yards on 43 carries and 7 TD. Had 10 receptions for 62 yards.

David Dunn (WR): Active for 16 games. Had 4 receptions for 33 yards, 8 punt returns for 99 yards, and 44 kickoff returns for 1,073 yards and 1 TD.

Mondriel Fulcher (TE): Active for 10 games.

Bobby Hoying (QB): Active for 4 games. Completed 0 of 2 pass attempts and rushed for -3 yards on 2 carries.

Randy Jordan (RB): Active for 16 games. Rushed for 213 yards on 46 carries and 3 TD. Had 27 receptions for 299 yards and 1 TD.

Napoleon Kaufman (RB): Active for 14 games and started in 2. Rushed for 499 yards on 93 carries, had 13 receptions for 127 yards and 1 TD, and returned 9 kickoffs 198 yards.

Terry Kirby (RB): Active for 2 games. Rushed for 51 yards on 11 carries, and had 3 receptions for 19 yards.

Jerry Porter (WR): Active for 12 games and had 1 reception for 6 yards.

Andre Rison (WR): Active for 16 games and had 41 receptions for 606 yards and 6 TD.

Barry Sims (T/G): Active for 16 games and started in 7.

Adam Treu (C): Active for 16 games.

STARTERS — DEFENSE

DE – Tony Bryant: Started in 16 games, had 5 sacks and 1 fumble recovery.

DE – Lance Johnstone: Active for 14 games, started in 9, and had 3 sacks.

DT – Grady Jackson: Active for 16 games, started in 15, had 8 sacks and 1 fumble recovery.

DT – Darrell Russell: Started in 16 games, had 3 sacks, 1 fumble recovery, and recorded 1 safety.

LLB – William Thomas: Started in 16 games, had 1 sack and 6 INT.

MLB – Greg Biekert: Started in 16 games, had 2 sacks and 2 fumble recoveries.

RLB – Elijah Alexander: Started in 16 games and had 2 sacks.

CB – Charles Woodson: Started in 16 games, had 4 INT, 1 fumble recovery, and 1 reception for 8 yards.

CB – Eric Allen: Active for 16 games, started in 15, had 1 sack, 6 INT and 3 TD. **Led the NFL in non-offensive touchdowns (3).**

SS – Marquez Pope: Active for 15 games, started in 14, had 1 sack, INT, and 5 fumble recoveries.

FS – Anthony Dorsett: Started in 16 games and had 1 sack.

RESERVE DEFENSIVE PLAYERS

Eric Barton (LB): Active for 4 games.

Calvin Branch (DB): Active for 16 games, had 1 fumble recovery and returned 2 kickoffs 48 yards.

Bobby Brooks (LB): Active for 16 games.

Roderick Coleman (T): Active for 13 games, started in 1, had 6 sacks and 1 fumble recovery.

Darrien Gordon (DB): Active for 13 games. Had 1 fumble recovery, TD, 29 punt returns for 258 yards and 1 kickoff return for 17 yards.

Johnnie Harris (DB): Active for 15 games and started in 2.

Tory James (DB): Active for 16 games, started in 1, and had 2 INT.

Brandon Jennings (DB): Active for 2 games.

Eric Johnson (DB/LB): Active for 16 games.

Austin Robbins (T): Active for 3 games.

Travian Smith (LB): Active for 16 games.

Josh Taves (E): Active for 16 games, had 3 sacks and 1 INT.

Regan Upshaw (E): Active for 16 games, started in 7, had 6 sacks and fumble recoveries.

KICKING/PUNTING

K – Sebastian Janikowski: Active for 14 games. Made 22 of 32 field goals and 46 of 46 extra points for 112 points.

P – Shane Lechler: Active for 16 games. Punted 65 times for a 45.9 average.

2001 Season Review

1. Sept. 9: The Raiders added running back Charlie Garner and the greatest receiver in NFL history, Jerry Rice, to their already potent offensive attack. Oakland took their firepower to Arrowhead Stadium in Kansas City to open the '01 campaign against the Chiefs and their new head coach, Dick Vermeil. In another classic matchup between these two long-time foes, the Silver and Black reigned supreme in an exciting 27–24 contest. Despite two fumbles and an interception returned for a touchdown, Rich Gannon still found a way to prevail. He led the entire league on opening week with 341 passing yards on 31 of 46 attempts and two touchdowns. Gannon gave the Chiefs an opportunity to take an early first quarter lead when one of his passes was picked off and returned 51 yards for a touchdown by Eric Warfield. Sebastian Janikowski cut into the Kansas City advantage with two field goals from 43 and 42 yards. The Chiefs then extended their lead to 17–6 in the third quarter before Oakland got their offense humming. Gannon teamed up with Tim Brown on Oakland's first touchdown of the new season. It came from 33 yards out, and Gannon's two-point conversion run cut the Kansas City advantage to 17–14. For the day, Brown had eight receptions for 132 yards to lead the NFL in that category. The Raiders then evened it up at 17–17 with a 36-yard field goal from Sebastian Janikowski

Oakland moved ahead for the first time with 3:19 remaining in the fourth when Gannon threw a 15-yard scoring strike to Jon Ritchie. The Chiefs came back to tie it on a Trent Green to Marvin Minnis touchdown. David Dunn then returned the ensuing kickoff 40 yards, and Gannon quickly threw a 33-yard strike to Brown. This set up Janikowski 31-yard field goal to win it with 15 seconds left. On top of Brown's great receiving day, Jerry Rice's debut in an Oakland uniform also went well, as he caught eight passes for 87 yards.[1]

Two days after the NFL regular season opened, the United States was attacked, with terrorists seizing control of airplanes and crashing them into the World Trade Center in New York City and the Pentagon in Washington, D.C. These actions forced the league to cancel the games scheduled for the weekend of September 16.[2]

2. Sept. 23: In an attempt to create a temporary diversion away from the troubles of the world, the NFL resumed play with the Raiders travelling to Miami. The Dolphins had beaten Oakland in five of their last six encounters, with the exception being in the previous post-season. Miami also owned an NFL–best 27–4 record in home openers since 1970, and managed to extend the impressive mark with an 18–15 victory, but they had to work for it. The Raiders were in control of the lead for a large part of the game. Sebastian Janikowski's two field goals from 42 and 25 yards gave Oakland a 6–0 lead early in the second quarter. Miami managed to squeak ahead with 20 seconds left in the half on a Jay Fiedler 2-yard run and an Olindo Mare extra point kick. The third quarter saw Miami cling to a 10–9 lead, as the teams matched field goals, with Janikowski adding his third of the day, this time from 45 yards. With 12:41 left in the game, Anthony Dorsett returned an interception 26 yards to once again put Oakland in the lead, 15–10. The Raiders tried a two-point conversion run but failed. Oakland held Miami off until the final 1:41. Starting at his own 20, Fiedler drove the Dolphins down the field on five key passes. The final one came on fourth-and-three to Dedric Ward at the Oakland 9-yard line with 27 seconds to go. Fiedler ended the clutch drive himself, running for the game-winner from two yards out with five seconds left. James McKnight ran for the two-point conversion, and Miami moved to 2–0, while Oakland lost their first of the '01 campaign.[3]

3. Sept. 30: Coming into this game, Seattle quarterback Matt Hasselbeck was sacked a league-leading twelve times. The Oakland defense did their part to keep the signal caller in first place by driving him into the turf seven times in a convincing 38–14 win at home. Rich Gannon completed 19 of 28 passes for 217 yards and three touchdowns. He also ran for one himself from five yards. Jerry Rice caught his first touchdown as a Raider on a 33-yard pass from Gannon to open the scoring. He liked the feeling so much that he performed an encore right before the half by catching Gannon's second scoring strike from 14 yards. For the game, Rice had five receptions for 91 yards to allow him the opportunity to extend his streak of games with at least one catch to 228. Tyrone Wheatley caught Gannon's other touchdown toss from three yards. Eric Allen returned a fumble 26 yards, and Sebastian Janikowski added a 20-yard field goal.[4]

4. Oct. 4: Jerry Rice needed one touchdown reception to reach 190 in his career. Rich Gannon wasted little time getting the greatest receiver in NFL history to that plateau. With 6:16 to go in the opening quarter, Rice hauled in a 5-yard pass from Gannon to give Oakland a lead they never relinquished in a 28–21 victory over the Dallas Cowboys. This was the 11th time in 12 tries that the Raiders won at home. Tyrone Wheatley added touchdown runs of four and one yard, and Zack Crockett ran another one in from the three to help Oakland improve to 3–1 while the Cowboys remained winless. Tim Brown liked to play against Dallas, having caught 18 passes for 224 yards in three previous meetings against "America's Team." He added another good performance by catching seven passes for 114 yards. Gannon also had another fine showing by completing 21 of 28 attempts for 209 yards.[5]

5. Oct. 14: The Indianapolis Colts and their number one offense welcomed the Raiders and their top-rated quarterback Rich Gannon to the RCA Dome. With such offensive firepower between these teams, a lot of yardage was expected. They did not disappoint, as the teams combined for 669 yards, and more important was the fact that Oakland came away with a 23–18 victory. Gannon connected on 18 of 32 passes for 243 yards, and Tim Brown smoked the Indy secondary for 145 yards on seven catches to lead the charge. Sebastian Janikowski kicked three field goals (39, 42, and 37 yards), Anthony Dorsett returned an interception 39 yards, and Tyrone Wheatley ran for a 1-yard touchdown to provide Oakland with their points.[6]

6. Oct. 28: In their previous encounter, the Raiders faced the number one offense. This time around, the top-ranked defense awaited them in Philadelphia. Once again, the Raiders showed that they were also one of the best in the league by winning their fifth game of the season, 20–10, over the Eagles. Philadelphia's defense might have been ranked first, but it was the Oakland defensive unit that dominated in this contest. They held the Eagles without a third down conversion until the final five minutes, gave up only 11 first downs, ended quarterback Donovan McNabb's consecutive game with at least one touchdown pass streak at nine, and sacked him four times. Meanwhile, the Raiders had a good time against the Philly defense. Rich Gannon did an excellent job leading a ball-controlled attack that kept possession of the ball for forty minutes and gained 354 yards. He hit on 17 of 26 passes for 158 yards, and Charlie Garner led the ground forces with 77 yards. He also opened the scoring with a 2-yard run in the first quarter. Zack Crockett added a 1-yard run, and Sebastian Janikowski kicked two field goals from 42 and 32 yards.[7]

7. Nov. 5: The Broncos and Raiders squared off for the 12th time on Monday Night Football. Denver had seven straight wins over Oakland on the prime time spectacle, and won 11 of 12 previous meetings dating back to 1995. However, this time the Silver and Black snapped the streak and won, 38–28, to improve to 6–1 and have sole possession of first place in the AFC West. With Network Associates Coliseum rocking with silver and black clad fans engulfing the stands, and head coach Jon Gruden showing off his trademark snarl, Oakland won their ninth straight regular season home game. Rich Gannon led the offense with 242 passing yards on 25 of 34 attempts. He threw three scoring strikes, with two going to Tim Brown (11 and 19 yards), and Jon Ritchie (4 yards). With his two touchdown receptions, Brown moved into fifth place on the all-time career list with 89. For the game, he caught nine passes for 95 yards. Zack Crockett scored on runs of one and three yards, and Sebastian Janikowski added a 31-yard field goal.[8]

8. Nov. 11: The Raiders had their troubles over the years in Seattle's Kingdome. Those days were over, as the Seahawks now called Husky Stadium home in 2001, but the ghosts of the dreaded Kingdome continued to haunt the Silver and Black in a 34–27 loss. Seattle's star running back Shaun Alexander ran over and around the Oakland defense for 266 yards on 35 carries to set a team rushing record, and fell just shy of the NFL single-game rushing mark. Alexander added three touchdowns on the ground. Rich Gannon tried in vain to keep the Raiders in the win column by turning in another great performance. He completed 24 of 38 passes for 257 yards and two touchdowns. The first one went to Tim Brown from four yards, and his other one was hauled in by Roland Williams from five yards out with 3:40 left in the fourth quarter to cut the Seattle lead to only seven points. Other scores for Oakland came on a Terry Kirby 90-yard kickoff return, and two Sebastian Janikowski field goals from 52 and 37 yards.[9]

9. Nov. 18: Jerry Rice showed that despite a uniform change, he was still the greatest receiver in NFL history by catching eight passes for 131 yards and three touchdowns (12, 30, and 20 yards), in a 34–24 win over San Diego. With the win, Oakland extended their league-best streak to ten straight at home. Rich Gannon threw for 311 yards on 25 of 38 attempts and four touchdowns. Besides the three scoring passes to Rice, Gannon teamed up with Tim Brown from 10 yards out for his other one. Sebastian Janikowski rounded out the Raiders' point production with field goals from 24 and 25 yards. Oakland improved their record to 7–2, were leading the conference with a 27.8 points per game average, and held a two-game lead in the division as they prepared for the stretch run of the '01 campaign.[10]

10. Nov. 25: The Raiders took their high-powered offense across the country to face the New York Giants. Oakland left a rain-soaked Giants Stadium as 28–10 winners, which was the fourth straight time they beat the Giants. Rich Gannon was leading the NFL in passing, and added to his status by hitting on 13 of 20 passes for 221 yards and three touchdowns. Tim Brown caught two of Gannon's scoring strikes from 46 and 19 yards on a day that saw him gather in six receptions for 117 yards. Charlie Garner was on the receiving end of Gannon's other touchdown pass from 21 yards, and Zack Crockett ran for a 1-yard six-pointer. The Raiders were at 8–2, winners of seven of their last eight, and now owned a three-game advantage in the AFC West.[11]

11. Dec. 2: Ken "the Snake" Stabler was responsible for many exciting finishes in Raiders history. Twenty-two years after the original "Snake" threw his final pass in an Oakland uniform, another quarterback bearing the same moniker created a fantastic climax of his own. Unfortunately, Jake "the Snake" Plummer wore the colors of the Arizona Cardinals, and he directed them to a 34–31 overtime victory. This was a wild shootout that saw 18 points scored in the final 1:47 of the fourth quarter. The barrage started with Sebastian Janikowski giving Oakland their first lead since the opening quarter with a 24-yard field goal that put the Raiders up, 24–23, with 1:47 left. Plummer answered with a 50-yard pass to David Boston, and then ran for a two-point conversion to give Arizona a 31–24 lead with 1:18 to go. The Raiders struck back to tie it with 12 seconds left on a Rich Gannon to Jerry Rice 12-yard pass and a Janikowski extra point. In overtime, David Dunn fumbled a punt on the Oakland 25. Arizona then

wasted no time securing their fifth win of the season, and handing Oakland their first loss at home after 10 straight wins. Bill Gramatica came on and booted the game-winner from 36 yards away and then celebrated his fourth three-pointer of the day by doing a victory somersault. It was a shame to see this one slip away after Oakland battled back from a 20–7 halftime deficit. Tim Brown got the Raiders on the board first with a 5-yard reception from Gannon, and added another one from 22 yards in the fourth quarter. Zack Crockett scored Oakland's other touchdown on a 1-yard run. Rich Gannon finished the game with 29 completions in 45 attempts for 302 yards. In addition to the loss, the Raiders had to deal with rumors circulating that head coach Jon Gruden would be leaving to fill the vacant Notre Dame position, and that defensive tackle Darrell Russell was getting close to serving a one-year suspension by the league for using the drug Ecstasy.[12]

12. Dec. 9: The Kansas City Chiefs dominated the Raiders during the 1990's, but in the early stages of the new decade, Oakland was reversing their fortunes against their long-standing foes. They achieved this by beating the Chiefs, 28–26, for the fifth straight time. Oakland struggled a bit and had to work for their ninth win of the season after falling behind, 10–0, in the first quarter. Tyrone Wheatley started the Raiders on the road back with a 6-yard run to close the gap to three points. After giving the touchdown back, and trailing, 17–7, Rich Gannon led the Raiders back for good. He first ran for a 5-yard touchdown, and then threw one to Jerry Rice from eight yards to put Oakland up, 21–17. Tim Brown extended the advantage to 28–17 with an 88-yard punt return, which was the first time in three years that he touched the ball in that capacity. Two key moments on defense played a huge part in Oakland pulling this one out. Charles Woodson stymied a fourth down pass attempt by knocking the ball away from an intended receiver in the end zone with the Chiefs on the four and 3:03 left to play. Regan Upshaw then sealed the win by forcing Kansas City quarterback Trent Green to fumble while attempting to tie the game on a two-point conversion try with 1:38 remaining in the game. With a 9–3 record, the Raiders owned a two-game lead in the AFC West with four weeks to go.[13]

13. Dec. 15: The Raiders hit the double-digit win figure for the second straight year, and the good old days were back for the Silver and Black. With a 13–6 win over San Diego, Oakland clinched their second straight AFC Western Division title, and was the first team in 2001 to earn a playoff berth. Tim Brown also clinched a personal milestone by becoming only the second player in NFL history to have nine straight seasons of 1,000-plus yards receiving. His teammate, Jerry Rice, was the other one with 11. The Raiders got points in this low scoring affair from Sebastian Janikowski on field goals from 20 and 31 yards, and Rice snagged a 40-yard pass from Rich Gannon, who completed 20 of 28 attempts for 221 yards. The defense came up huge to halt scoring threats. Linebacker William Thomas came up with two interceptions off Doug Flutie, and Darrell Russell picked off a pass on the Oakland 12 that led to Rice's score.[14]

14. Dec. 22: A Saturday night matchup between the Raiders and Tennessee Titans resulted in another low-scoring contest. Unfortunately, Oakland came out on the losing end this time by a 13–10 count. After a scoreless first half, the Titans went into the fourth quarter leading, 10–0. The Raiders then rallied on a 4-

ard pass from Rich Gannon to Roland Williams, and a 25-yard field goal by Sebastian Janikowski that tied things up at ten apiece. Janikowski's three-pointer was set up by an Eric Allen interception. With 1:48 to go in the fourth, ex–Raider Joe Nedney put the Titans out in front for good with a 21-yard field goal. Oakland had a chance to tie it and force overtime, but Janikowski missed a 42-yard field goal try with 11 seconds left. He was suffering the effects of a groin injury, and missed two other attempts throughout the game.[15]

15. Dec. 30: The Raiders were in a funk after clinching the AFC West crown two weeks earlier. Their slump continued as they travelled to Denver and lost, 23–17, in a city where they had not won since 1994. Rich Gannon looked unstoppable throwing in the first half, completing his first 16 passes and went 20 of 22 throughout the half. He continued his hot streak at the beginning of the second half by hitting on six straight passes, with one going to Jeremy Brigham for a 1-yard score that gave Oakland a 17–13 lead going into the fourth quarter. Beside Gannon's scoring strike to Brigham, he also threw one to Charlie Garner in the second quarter from six yards out, and Sebastian Janikowski kicked a 28-yard field goal for the Raiders. On the day, Gannon completed 35 of 49 passes for 313 yards, but tossed two interceptions, one of which was on fourth down with no time left in the game. Denver went ahead for good with just under ten minutes remaining on a Brian Griese to Rod Smith pass, and Jason Elam extended the lead with a late 42-yard three-pointer to hand Oakland their fifth loss. The Raiders saw a milestone achieved when Jerry Rice recorded his 13th season of at least 1,000 receiving yards. He topped the mark on this day with the help of nine receptions for 108 yards.[16]

16. Jan. 6: The New York Jets exonerated the demons that had a stranglehold on them when facing the Raiders with a close 24–22 victory. This proved to be New York's first win in Oakland since 1962, and only their second over the Silver and Black in eight previous attempts. Kicker John Hall was the toast of the Big Apple when he connected on a 53-yard field goal with 59 seconds remaining to send the 10–6 Jets into the playoffs for the first time in three years. This loss sank the Raiders for the fourth time in their last six games, and cost them a first round bye in the post-season. Oakland's points in this regular season finale came on three Brad Daluiso field goals from 23, 44, and 37 yards, a Tyrone Wheatley 3-yard run, and an 18-yard pass from Rich Gannon to Roland Williams. Daluiso was called upon to handle the kicking duties with Sebastian Janikowski nursing a foot infection.[17]

AFC Wild Card Game, January 12, 2002

It was déjà vu for the Raiders and Jets, as they battled it out once again. This time, however, there would be no tomorrows for the losers. Oakland left their lethargic late season showings behind, and got back on track with a 38–24 win at home to advance to the divisional round of the playoffs. Over his final regular season games, Rich Gannon threw seven interceptions after tossing only two in the first nine. Just like the rest of the Raiders, Gannon got out of his slump by not completing a pass to anyone in a different uniform, but did connect with his own receivers on 23 of

29 attempts for 294 yards and two scores. The Raiders opened up with a 16–3 halftime lead and never looked back. Sebastian Janikowski returned, and kicked three field goals from 21, 41, and 45 yards. Tim Brown scored the game's only first half touchdown on a 2-yard pass from Gannon. The Raiders then added 22 points in the fourth quarter on a Zack Crockett 2-yard run, a 21-yard pass from Gannon to Jerry Rice, and an electrifying 80-yard run by Charlie Garner with 1:27 remaining in the game to ice the win for the Silver and Black. On the day, Garner ran for 158 yards on 15 carries. Rice exploded for 183 yards on nine catches despite being double-teamed, and his touchdown reception gave him 20 in the post-season, putting him one behind Thurman Thomas and Emmitt Smith for the all-time record.[18]

AFC Divisional Playoff, January 19, 2002

The Raiders had been involved in many exciting games over the course of their long and proud history. Some stood out so much that they were given names to remember them by. "The Sea of Hands" and "the Ghost to the Post," conjure up memories that will forever be cherished and bragged about by Raider Nation. However, on the opposite side of the spectrum are gut-wrenching defeats, with the greatest being the "Immaculate Reception" and Rob Lytle's fumble that was not ruled a fumble in the AFC Championship Game in January of 1978. Another vile incident was added to the Raiders' playoff woes in the way of what became known as the "Tuck Rule," and it took away certain victory and allowed the Silver and Black to be devoured by the jaws of defeat on a snowy night in Foxboro, Massachusetts. The Raiders were leading the New England Patriots, 13–10, with 1:43 left in the fourth quarter. All signs pointed to an Oakland victory, and their reservations were all but confirmed for a repeat trip to the AFC Championship Game. With snow making a winter wonderland of the playing surface, New England's rookie quarterback Tom Brady went back to pass. Charles Woodson came in hard on a blitz. He blindsided Brady and slapped the ball out of his hand. Linebacker Greg Biekert jumped on the loose ball at the Oakland 47 and all that was left was for the clock to wind down to zero. It was then that the collective hearts throughout Raider Nation went from exaltation to despair. Instant replay was called in, and after reviewing the play, the referee ruled that Brady was in the act of throwing and pulled the ball down in a forward motion, which constituted an incomplete pass, not a fumble. This drastic turn of events resulted in New England keeping possession, and after moving a little closer, Adam Vinatieri launched a 45-yard field goal with 27 seconds left to tie it and send it into overtime. The Patriots won the coin toss in the overtime period, and drove down the field to give Vinatieri an opportunity to seal Oakland's fate. From 23 yards away, he did just that, as the ball split the uprights with 8:29 expired in overtime to give New England a 16–13 win, and start them on their way to becoming the team of the decade. Oakland received their points on two Sebastian Janikowski field goals (38 and 45 yards), and a 13-yard pass from Rich Gannon to James Jett that opened the scoring in the second quarter.[19]

Individual Statistics and Roster

Head Coach: Jon Gruden

Assistant Coaches: Fred Biletnikoff, Chuck Bresnahan, Willie Brown, Bill Callahan, Bob Casullo, Jim Erkenbeck, Garrett Giemont, Aaron Kromer, Ron Lynn, Don Martin, John Morton, Fred Pagac, Skip Peete, David Shaw, Marc Trestman

2001 Regular Season Record: 10–6

1st Place in AFC Western Division

Scored 399 points to rank 4th out of 31 teams

Allowed 327 points to rank 19th

Led the league with fewest interceptions thrown (9)

STARTERS — OFFENSE

QB — Rich Gannon: Started in 16 games. Completed 361 of 549 pass attempts for 3,828 yards, 27 TD, and 9 INT. Rushed for 231 yards on 63 carries and 2 TD.

RB — Charlie Garner: Active for 16 games and started in 15. Rushed for 839 yards on 211 carries and 1 TD. Had 72 receptions for 578 yards and 2 TD.

RB — Jon Ritchie: Active for 15 games and started in 10. Had 19 receptions for 154 yards and 2 TD.

WR — Tim Brown: Started in 16 games. Had 91 receptions for 1,165 yards and 9 TD. Rushed for 39 yards on 4 carries.

WR — Jerry Rice: Active for 16 games and started in 15. Had 83 receptions for 1,139 yards and 9 TD.

TE — Roland Williams: Active for 16 games and started in 15. Had 33 receptions for 298 yards and 3 TD.

LT — Barry Sims: Active for and started in 15 games.

LG — Steve Wisniewski: Started in 16 games.

C — Adam Treu: Active for 16 games and started in 14.

RG — Frank Middleton: Active for 13 games and started in 11.

RT — Lincoln Kennedy: Active for and started in 15 games.

RESERVE OFFENSIVE PLAYERS

Darryl Ashmore (T): Active for 14 games and started in 1.

Jeremy Brigham (TE): Active for 14 games and started in 3. Had 12 receptions for 85 yards and 1 TD.

Mo Collins (G/T): Active for 6 games and started in 5.

Zack Crockett (RB): Active for 16 games. Rushed for 145 yards on 57 carries and 6 TD. Returned 2 kickoffs 10 yards.

Brad Daluiso (K): Active for 1 game. Made 1 of 2 field goal attempts and 1 of 2 extra point kicks for 4 points.

David Dunn (WR): Active for 10 games. Had 1 reception for 8 yards, returned 19 punts for 169 yards, and 20 kickoffs for 458 yards.

Mondriel Fulcher (TE): Active for 13 games and started in 1.

Aaron Graham (C): Active for 14 games.

James Jett (WR): Active for 11 games and had 2 receptions for 19 yards.

Randy Jordan (RB): Active for 16 games. Rushed for 59 yards on 13 carries and had 9 receptions for 63 yards.

Terry Kirby (RB): Active for 11 games. Rushed for 49 yards on 10 carries, had 9 receptions for 62 yards, and returned 46 kickoffs for 1,066 yards and 1 TD.

Marcus Knight (WR): Active for 5 games and started in 1.

Toby Myles (T): Active for 1 game.

Rodney Peete (QB): Active for 1 game.

Jerry Porter (WR): Active for 15 games and started in 1. Had 19 receptions for 220 yards and rushed for 13 yards on 2 carries.

Barret Robbins (C): Active for and started in 2 games.

Matt Stinchcomb (G/T): Active for 15 games and started in 1.

Marques Tuiasosopo (QB): Active for 1 game. Completed 3 of 4 pass attempts for 34 yards, and rushed for 1 yard on 1 carry.

Tyrone Wheatley (RB): Active for 11 games and started in 3. Rushed for 276 yards on 88 carries and 5 TD. Had 12 receptions for 61 yards and 1 TD.

Jermaine Williams (RB): Active for 1 game.

STARTERS — DEFENSE

DE — Regan Upshaw: Active for 16 games, started in 15, and had 7 sack

DE — Tony Bryant: Started in 16 games and had 5 sacks.

DT — Darrell Russell: Active for 11 games and started in 7. Had 2 sack and 1 INT.

DT — Grady Jackson: Started in 16 games, had 4 sacks and 1 fumble re covery.

LLB — William Thomas: Active for 16 games and started in 15. Had sacks, 3 INT, and 2 fumble recoveries.

MLB — Greg Biekert: Started in 16 games, had 3 sacks and 1 fumble re covery.

RLB — Elijah Alexander: Active for 14 games, started in 13, and had 1 sack

CB — Charles Woodson: Active for 16 games, started in 15, had 2 sack and 1 INT.

CB — Eric Allen: Active for 16 games, started in 15, had 1 INT and 1 fum ble recovery.

SS — Marquez Pope: Active for 16 games, started in 12, and had 1 INT

FS — Anthony Dorsett: Started in 16 games, had 1 sack, 2 INT, and fumble recovery.

RESERVE DEFENSIVE PLAYERS

Trace Armstrong (E): Active for 3 games and had sack.

Eric Barton (LB): Active for 16 games and started in 1.

Bobby Brooks (LB): Active for 16 games.

Roderick Coleman (T): Active for 14 games, started in 6, had 6 sack and 1 fumble recovery.

Chris Cooper (T/E): Active for 12 games, started in 1, and had 1 INT.

Derrick Gibson (DB): Active for 16 games and had 1 INT.

DeLawrence Grant (E/LB): Active for 2 games.

Johnnie Harris (DB): Active for 16 games, started in 5, and had sack.

James Hasty (DB): Active for 1 game.

Junior Ioane (T): Active for 3 games.

Tory James (DB): Active for 16 games, started in 2, and had 5 INT.

Brandon Jennings (DB): Active for 8 games.

Eric Johnson (DB/LB): Active for 7 games.

Darren Mickell (E): Active for 1 game.

Travian Smith (LB): Active for 16 games, started in 2, had 2 sacks, 1 INT and 1 fumble recovery.

Josh Taves (E): Active for 8 games, started in 3, and had 1 sack.

KICKING/PUNTING

K — Sebastian Janikowski: Active for 15 games. Made 23 of 28 field goal and 42 of 42 extra points for 111 points.

P — Shane Lechler: Active for 16 games. Punted 73 times for a 46.2 av erage, and rushed for 2 yards on 1 carry.

2002 Season Review

1. Sept. 8: The two-time defending AFC Western Division champion Raiders looked to move ahead after their disheartening loss to New England in the "Tuck Rule" game. They also had to adjust to a new coaching regime for the first time in four year after the popular Jon Gruden became part of a trade deal between Oakland and the Tampa Bay Buccaneers in February, 2002.

The Raiders were a good team on the verge of a Super Bowl berth as the 2002 regular season began, and along with it came the head coaching debut of Bill Callahan. Oakland began on their quest for the Lombardi Trophy by playing host to the Seattle Seahawks. If the opener was any indication of what kind of season it was going to be, then things were going to be just fine for the Silver and Black.

In a 31–17 win, the Raiders hammered out 423 yards and 27 first downs. Right from the start, Oakland sent a massage that they were ready to achieve greatness in '02. Going with a no huddle offensive scheme, Rich Gannon led the Raiders on an 8-play, 65-yard drive that was capped off when Gannon threw to Tim Brown for an 8-yard score four minutes into the game. The rest of this game showcased the explosive Oakland offense that spread the wealth against Seattle. Gannon hit on 19 of 28 passes for 214 yards and two touchdowns. In addition to his first one to Brown, Gannon connected with Charlie Garner on a 26-yarder. Garner also ran for a 20-yard touchdown on a day that saw the multi-purpose back rush for 127 yards on 15 carries and catch five passes for 64 more yards. Randy Jordan scored on a 12-yard run, and Sebastian Janikowski was true on a 27-yard field goal to complete Oakland's opening day scoring fest.[1]

2. Sept. 15: The Raiders took their offensive juggernaut on the road. Their first away game took them to the place where bitter memories still lingered. The 2002 season marked the 30th anniversary of the "Immaculate Reception," which saw Pittsburgh's Franco Harris pull the ball out of the air on the game's last play and dash 60 yards for the winning touchdown. Obviously, none of the current Raiders were on the '72 roster, or many were not even born yet, but when these two teams met, those that were aware of what occurred were still reminded of that dark moment in Raiders history.

Thirty years later, this edition of the Silver and Black left no doubt who the alpha dog was in a 30–17 romp that increased their all-time record against the Steel City to 11–9. Once again, the Raiders used a no huddle offensive scheme. Rich Gannon threw the ball an incredible 41 times in the first half alone, and ate up the clock by tossing short to medium range passes.

When the game was over, Gannon owned team records with 43 completions in 64 attempts for 403 yards. He connected with Jerry Porter on a 21-yard pass for his only touchdown pass of the game. Charlie Garner ran for a 36-yard score, Terry Kirby returned a kickoff 96 yards, and Sebastian Janikowski hit on long range field goals from 41 and 45 yards, to help the Raiders remain perfect in the infant stages of the season. Jerry Rice led the receiving corps with 11 receptions for 94 yards, Rod Woodson recovered three fumbles again his old team, and Charles Woodson intercepted a pass at the end of the game.[2]

3. Sept. 29: Coming off a bye week, the Raiders resumed play by hosting the Tennessee Titans, and looked forward to adding to their league-leading 443.5 yards per game average. In a game reminiscent of the old high-flying AFL days, the quarterbacks, Rich Gannon and Steve McNair, accounted for 779 yards through the air and six touchdowns. Gannon, who walked off the field on the winning end of a 52–25 shootout, completed 29 of 39 attempts for 381 yards and four touchdowns. On the receiving end of Gannon's scoring strikes were Charlie Garner (17 yards), Jerry Rice (10 yards), Jerry Porter (10 yards), and Tim Brown (41 yards). Rice added another illustrious sixty minutes worth of work to an already amazing career by catching seven passes for 144 yards. He also placed his name yet again in the NFL record books. In the fourth quarter, he caught an 11-yard pass from Gannon to give him the most yards gained from scrimmage. His 21,281 after this game surpassed Walter Payton's mark of 20,649.

Safety Rod Woodson enjoyed witnessing an NFL record so

much that he decided to get in the act himself. He did so by intercepting three passes for 100 yards, which gave him a new record of 1,339 return yards off interceptions.

Tim Brown did not set a record, but he did move up a notch on the all-time reception chart. His six catches gave him 954 and moved him past Andre Reed for third place behind Jerry Rice and Cris Carter. This game was one of the most explosive in Raiders history. On top of Gannon's four scoring tosses, Oakland scored on sensational plays by rookie Phillip Buchanon (83-yard punt return), Terry Kirby (79-yard punt return), and Rod Woodson (82-yard interception return). Sebastian Janikowski's 28-yard field goal was the most dossal means in which Oakland scored on this day. The amazing thing was that the Raiders were penalized 10 times for 117 yards and still found a way to gain 464 offensive yards and boost their points per game average to 37.7.[3]

4. Oct. 6: The Raiders were averaging 37 points a game, with the Buffalo Bills close behind at 33. With all this firepower, the lights on the scoreboard at Buffalo's Ralph Wilson Stadium had a good chance of shorting out before the game was completed. This game lived up to all the hype, as the teams amassed a combined 974 offensive yards. More important was that the Raiders once again prevailed, this time with a 49–31 final score.

Rich Gannon passes for 357 yards on 23 of 38 attempts and three touchdowns. He also ran for a 1-yard score. Jerry Porter, who had seven catches for 117 yards, opened the scoring with a 29-yard grab, Charlie Garner caught a 69-yarder, and the great Jerry Rice hauled in Gannon's other touchdown toss from 20 yards out.

The running game did not want to feel left out of the scoring barrage, and added touchdown runs from Zack Crockett (1 yard), and Garner (36 yards). Garner was brilliant with 94 yards on the ground on only eight carries, and four catches for 83 yards. Oakland's other six-pointer came on an 81-yard interception return by rookie Phillip Buchanon. The Raiders were perfect and dominant in the first quarter of the season, and looked to continue on their path of destruction through the NFL.[4]

5. Oct. 13: The Raiders were burning up the offensive side of football throughout the first quarter of the '02 season. Rich Gannon was the league's top passer, and as a unit, the offense was averaging over 450 yards a game.

Their counterpart in week five was the St. Louis Rams, who had the most explosive offense between 1999 and 2001. Dubbed, "The Greatest Show on Turf," the Rams destroyed defenses, raking up huge numbers and two NFC titles and a Super Bowl win. However, the 2002 season began quite the opposite for them, as the defending NFC champions fell into a deep hole at 0–5. It seemed that the league's new kings of offense clad in silver and black were ready to solidify their status with a trip to St. Louis.

The Rams enjoyed their elite standing in the NFL community over the past three seasons, and did not want to relinquish it just yet. They then set out and proved it by shocking the Raiders, 28–13, despite excellent performances from Rich Gannon and Jerry Rice. Gannon completed 30 of 45 passes for 332 yards, just missing the opportunity to become the first to ever throw for at least 350 yards in four consecutive games. Rice was his usual Hall of Fame caliber self, catching seven passes for 133 yards.

Terry Kirby caught a 2-yard pass from Gannon for Oakland's only six-pointer, and Sebastian Janikowski nailed field goals from

43 and 32 yards. The Rams were without their two-time NFL Most Valuable Player, quarterback Kurt Warner, who was nursing a broken finger. Backup Marc Bulger performed well in relief, throwing for 186 yards and three touchdowns and running one in himself. Star running back Marshall Faulk ran for 158 yards and caught one of Bulger's scoring tosses.[5]

6. Oct. 20: San Diego's head coach Marty Schottenheimer had a .792 winning percentage against the Raiders coming into this game. Oakland had won seven out of their previous eight against the Lightening Bolts. In a clash for sole possession of first place in the AFC West, the Chargers allowed Schottenheimer to increase his personal dominance over the Silver and Black by handing them their second straight loss by a 27–21 count.

Two weeks earlier, the Raiders looked to be a sure pick to run away with their third straight AFC West crown. Now, after two losses, Oakland was in third place and a game-and-a-half behind San Diego.

In their first four games, the Raiders averaged 40.5 points and scored on their opening series in the first three games. In the next two, they failed to score a touchdown in the first half. Looking to turn things around from their first loss a week earlier, the Raiders took the ball down the field in their opening possession, but Sebastian Janikowski missed on a 27-yard field goal attempt, and later on one from 48 yards.

After not scoring in the first half, Oakland quickly found their groove. Within 19 minutes, the Raiders rang up 21 points on three Rich Gannon passes. Down by fourteen, Gannon first connected with Jerry Rice from three yards, and then to Jerry Porter from 17 to tie the game in the first six seconds of the fourth quarter.

San Diego's quarterback Drew Brees broke the tie with a 1-yard sneak. Gannon came right back with an 82-yard drive that included two passes to Charlie Garner covering 30 yards, and one to Tim Brown for 16. Jon Ritchie brought the Raiders to within one point by catching a 7-yard pass from Gannon with 1:21 left. Janikowski's extra point then sent the game into overtime.

With 11:22 left in the extra quarter, LaDainian Tomlinson ended the game with a 19-yard run, and while celebrating with fellow Chargers, the group was pelted with garbage from disgruntled Raiders fans.[6]

7. Oct. 27: After banging heads with the Kansas City Chiefs for 42 previous seasons, only one game separated the teams. The all-time record between these two was 41-40-2, and the Chiefs were able to even things up with a 20–10 win in Arrowhead Stadium.

Running back Priest Holmes amassed 184 yards of offense, and the NFL's worst defensive unit contained the league's most potent. Rich Gannon was able to continue his dominance despite the third straight loss. He threw for 334 yards, and became only the third player to throw for over 300 yards in six consecutive games. The others were Kurt Warner and Steve Young.

Over his great career, Tim Brown compiled close to 1,800 receiving yards against Kansas City. He once again displayed exceptional skills by leading all league receivers for the week with 13 receptions for 144 yards.

Doug Jolley put the Raiders up temporarily on a 1-yard catch from Gannon, and Sebastian Janikowski added a 32-yard field goal in the fourth quarter to cut Kansas City's lead to 13–10. A

Jerry Rice fumble on the Oakland 22 with 4:39 left was turned into the a Kansas City touchdown when Trent Green threw a 4-yard pass to Tony Richardson with just under two minutes remaining. The Raiders were now heading into dire straits with their third straight setback, and were two games out of first place in the division at 4–3.[7]

8. Nov. 3: In a battle of the Bay Area, the Raiders played host to the San Francisco 49ers. This was also the first time that Jerry Rice faced the team that saw him emerge as the most prolific receiver in NFL history.

In this game, Rice caught six passes for 74 yards against his old team, but could not help Oakland in the end. The 49ers sent the Silver and Black down for the fourth straight week, this time by a 23–20 final. San Francisco quarterback Jeff Garcia threw for 282 yards and connected on 17 of 19 second half passes to keep the 49ers moving and eat up valuable time off the clock.

The 49ers did an excellent job holding onto possession, keeping the ball for over 15 consecutive minutes at the end of the game. Receiver Terrell Owens was Garcia's favorite target with 12 catches for 191 yards, which included some on third down to keep the chains moving in the 49ers favor.

Rich Gannon was well below his average, throwing for only 164 yards, and with that total, he saw his NFL record of six straight 300-plus yards per game passing end.

This game was a true battle for Bay Area bragging rights. It was knotted up at 13–13 going into the fourth quarter. The Raiders got their 13 points on two Sebastian Janikowski field goals from 42 and 23 yards, and on a Gannon to Jerry Porter 1-yard pass that opened the game's scoring in the first quarter.

With just under two minutes taken off the clock in the fourth quarter, Garcia put the 49ers back into the lead with a 2-yard pass to Tai Streets. Gannon then connected with Porter on fourth down to keep a drive alive, and Charlie Garner finished it off a short time later with a 10-yard run. Janikowski's extra point kick once again tied the game with 6:28 remaining in regulation.

Jose Cortez tried to lift the 49ers to victory as time expired, but he missed on a chip shot field goal attempt. He earned total redemption with 6:23 left in overtime by hitting on a 23-yard three-pointer to drop the Raiders to 4–4 at the midway point of the season and tied with Kansas City for last place in the AFC West.[8]

9. Nov. 10: Nothing like a little old fashion Monday night magic to give the Silver and Black a reversal of fortune. On the 500th Monday Night Football telecast, the Raiders travelled to Denver and beat the Broncos handily, 34–10.

Rich Gannon completed an incredible 21 passes in a row, and Jerry Rice became the first player in history to score 200 touchdowns. Sebastian Janikowski got Oakland in the board first with a 47-yard field goal in the opening quarter. Safety Rod Woodson then cut in front of a pass intended for Clinton Portis and raced 98 yards for a touchdown with 2:57 left in the first quarter. This was the 12th time in Woodson's career that he took an interception back for a score, which helped him extend his NFL record in that category.

Janikowski gave Oakland a 13–0 lead early in the second quarter with a 32-yard field goal, and then Rice cracked the 200-career touchdown barrier on a 6-yard pass from Gannon with 1:22 left in the first half. Jerry Porter caught a two-point conversion pass from Gannon to give Oakland a solid 21–7 advantage in the first thirty minutes of play.

Porter opened the third quarter by scoring on a 22-yard pass from Gannon to increase the lead to 27–7. Denver had won eight of their previous nine meetings against the Raiders, but that dominance was close to ending. The Gannon to Rice combination teamed up on a 34-yard scoring strike to put the game away with 0:41 left in the game. Gannon finished with one of the best performances ever by a quarterback. He hit on 34 of 38 pass attempts for 352 yards, three touchdowns, and no interceptions. On his big record-setting night, Jerry Rice caught nine passes for 103 yards to go with his two six-pointers.[9]

10. Nov. 17: The defending Super Bowl champion New England Patriots came out to Oakland in a rematch of the "Tuck Rule" game that ended the Raiders' previous season. Both teams had quarterbacks that ranked near the top in league passing categories. Rich Gannon came into this game leading the NFL with 2,898 passing yards, and was tied for second with 19 touchdown tosses. His counterpart, Tom Brady, was the league leader with 21 scoring strikes, and his 2,472 yards through the air placed him third in that category.

In this rematch, neither signal caller threw for a touchdown, but Gannon ran for one from two yards out, and Zack Crockett added two more scoring runs also from the 2-yard line. Sebastian Janikowski added two field goals from 39 and 28 yards to go with his team's three six-pointers, and the Raiders won, 27–20, despite 12 penalties for 115 yards in losses.

Oakland won this game with a well-balanced offensive attack and a good defensive effort that prevented the Patriots entry into the end zone. The unit also sacked Brady four times. The Patriots got their points on a Teddy Bruschi interception return and a Kevin Faulk kickoff return following Janikowski's final three-pointer in the fourth quarter. Oakland was now at 6–4, and only one game off the division lead shared by Denver and San Diego.[10]

11. Nov. 24: Rich Gannon, Charlie Garner, and Jerry Rice all had the offense humming once again. Gannon threw for 340 yards and three touchdowns, Garner rushed for 100 yards, and Rice caught seven passes for 110 yards in a 41–20 win over the Arizona Cardinals. This win allowed the 7–4 Raiders to climb back into a first place tie with San Diego and Denver in the division.

Gannon's eighth game of 300-plus passing yards brought him to within one of the NFL's single-season record. His scoring strikes went to Jerry Porter (7 and 14 yards), and Rice (37 yards). Garner ran for an 8-yard score, and Tyrone Wheatley, who rushed for 82 yards on the day, put his name in the scoring column with a 2-yard run. Sebastian Janikowski added field goals from 37 and 51 yards for the high-powered Raiders.[11]

12. Dec. 2: Another Monday night appearance saw three Raiders rewrite the league record books. Tim Brown became the third player to catch 1,000 career passes, and also placed third all-time with 14,000 yards on those receptions. Jerry Rice extended his NFL record of 192 receiving touchdowns, and Rich Gannon tied the single-season record with his ninth 300-plus yards passing. For the game, he completed 32 of 34 attempts for 351 yards.

All these records were established in a 26–20 Oakland

victory over the New York Jets. Scoring for the Raiders in their fourth straight win were Rice on a 26-yard pass from Gannon, Zack Crockett on a 1-yard run, and Sebastian Janikowski on four field goals from 23, 48, 36, and 29 yards.[12]

13. Dec. 8: What looked to be a wild west showdown with both San Diego and Oakland tied for the division lead at 8–4 turned out to be a one-sided affair. In a 27–7 Oakland win, Rich Gannon was about to turn 37 years old on December 20th, but his teammates decided to give him an early birthday gift of sole possession of an NFL record.

At the halfway mark of the fourth quarter, Gannon completed a 9-yard pass to Jerry Rice that put him over the 300-yard passing mark for the tenth time in a single season. In doing so, he broke free from a four-way tie in the record book with Dan Marino, Warren Moon, and Kurt Warner.

Gannon finished the game with 328 yards on 26 of 41 attempts. Jerry Rice caught seven passes for 113 yards, and Doug Jolley six for 104 yards. Despite all the yards gained through the air, the Raiders got all their touchdowns on the ground. Charlie Garner opened the scoring with a 4-yard run, Zack Crockett added a 1-yarder in the third, and Tyrone Wheatley finished Oakland's scoring with a 4-yard six-pointer. Sebastian Janikowski blasted a 51-yard field goal and a 20-yarder for the first place Raiders. Even though this game was played in San Diego, about half of the crowd was there to cheer the Raiders.[13]

14. Dec. 15: With six defensive backs guarding the secondary, and a tenacious pass rush charging in, the Miami Dolphins held the much-heralded Raiders offensive attack to 218 yards in a 23–17 win. Miami's Jason Taylor led the defensive surge on Rich Gannon with three of the Dolphins five sacks. Gannon only threw for 162 yards. The win allowed Miami to tie Oakland for the best record in the AFC at 9–5. Jerry Porter scored Oakland's only touchdown on a 20-yard pass from Gannon in the fourth quarter. The same combination teamed up on the two-point conversion. Sebastian Janikowski supplied the Raiders with their other points on field goals from 26, 38, and 45 yards.[14]

15. Dec. 22: Oakland's number one ranked offense awaited the Denver Broncos with hopes of wrapping up another division crown. The Raiders quickly established their desire to win a third straight AFC West title by jumping out to a 21–3 halftime lead. They then went on to finish off the Broncos by a 28–16 final score.

Rich Gannon's name once again entered the NFL record book when he set a new single-season mark with 411 completions, and had one more game to add to it. Gannon also accounted for two of Oakland's six-pointers himself on a 3-yard run and on an 8-yard pass to Charlie Garner. Zack Crockett provided Oakland with their other touchdowns on a pair of 1-yard runs. His first one opened the game's scoring, and his other one ended it.[15]

16. Dec. 28: Rich Gannon extended his NFL single-season completion record to 418 in Oakland's regular season finale against the Kansas City Chiefs on a rain-soaked field. The weather in Oakland was perfect for ducks, as rain pelted the area, causing the Network Associates Coliseum to become a mud bath.

This game also turned out to be perfect for the Raiders, who shut out the Chiefs, 24–0, which allowed them to go into the playoffs on a high note. This marked the first time in 88 games against the Chiefs that Oakland shut them out.

Gannon only threw 14 passes, completing seven for 79 yards

and a touchdown. Charlie Garner carried the offensive load on this wet day with 135 yards rushing on 29 carries and one six-pointer. Garner scored on a 1-yard run to open the scoring in the second quarter, and Gannon threw a 15-yard pass to Doug Jolley to give Oakland a 14–0 halftime advantage. The Raiders received their other points on a Sebastian Janikowski 27-yard field goal and a Zack Crockett 8-yard run.[16]

AFC Divisional Playoff Game, January 12, 2003

The Raiders began their third straight playoff run against the New York Jets, a team they had beaten in nine out of their previous 11 meetings. Oakland continued their dominance over the New Yorkers by winning this time in convincing fashion, 30–10. Newly crowned NFL Most Valuable Player Rich Gannon completed 20 of 30 passes for 283 yards and two touchdowns. Jerry Porter was the star of the receiving corps with six catches for 123 yards, and caught one of Gannon's touchdown passes from 29 yards out. Jerry Rice hauled in Gannon's other scoring strike from nine yards, which was the 21st post-season six-pointer of his incredible career. It enabled him to tie the NFL record in that category, and he also set a post-season record that he did not have to share, with that being 2,133 receiving yards. Charlie Garner did his part by leading all ball carriers with 93 yards on 21 carries.

At first, the Jets hung tough. The game was deadlocked at 10–10 going into the second half, with Zack Crockett (1-yard run), and Sebastian Janikowski (29-yard field goal), giving Oakland their points up to that time. Defensive back Tory James then gave the Raiders a great opportunity to pull ahead after he jumped high for an interception on the New York 45. Gannon then marched the Silver and Black downfield, breaking the tie with his scoring toss to Porter. From there, it was all Oakland, as they piled on 13 fourth quarter points to secure their 14th trip to a league or conference championship game. Putting points on the scoreboard for the Raiders in the final stanza were Rice on his catch from Gannon, and Janikowski, with field goals from 34 and 31 yards. The defense clamped down on New York quarterback Chad Pennington with heavy pressure that resulted in four sacks led by two from Roderick Coleman, two fumbles, and two interceptions. Besides James' game-changing theft, Eric Barton added one.[17]

AFC Championship Game, January 19, 2003

The Raiders took their number one playoff seed onto the doorstep of a fifth Super Bowl berth with a team jelling at the right time, winning eight of their last nine games. They also had nine starters in their 30's, and felt that this might be the last opportunity with this group to get a ticket to the big dance. Only one obstacle stood in the way of another silver and black Super Bowl. The Tennessee Titans were coming out to Oakland to see if they could knock off football's offensive juggernaut and return to their second Super Bowl in four seasons.

The last time these two teams met in September, it was a wild, high-scoring affair won easily by Oakland, 52–25. Four months later, the teams staged another scoreboard lighting extravaganza, tallying 65 points between them. Just like in the first encounter, Oakland prevailed, this time, 41–24, and bore the title of 2002 AFC champions. In a classic Raiders' old school performance, passes filled the air, points were rung up, cheap shots and hard hits were aplenty, and penalties dished out, with Oakland getting flagged 14 times for 127 yards in losses.

Rich Gannon completed 29 of 41 passes for 286 yards, and threw for three touchdowns. He also led the team with 41 rushing yards on eight carries and scored a touchdown himself. Gannon teamed up with Jerry Porter in the first quarter to cap a seven-play, 69-yard drive with a 3-yard pass to give the Raiders a 7–0 lead following Sebastian Janikowski's extra point kick. The Titans came right back to tie it on a 33-yard pass from Steve McNair to Drew Bennett. Gannon countered with another drive consisting of seven plays and covering 85 yards. He finished this one off with a 12-yard strike to Charlie Garner, and Janikowski converted on the extra point try to give Oakland a 14–7 lead at the end of the opening fifteen minutes.

Tennessee came out in the second quarter to take a 17–14 lead on a 29-yard field goal from Joe Nedney and a 9-yard run by McNair. The joy of Tennessee faithful everywhere was short-lived, however. Eric Barton jump-started the Oakland attack by ripping the ball away from running back Robert Holcombe on the Tennessee 16. After two plays, the Raiders were back on top and this time for good. Gannon tossed his third six-pointer of the game, this time to Doug Jolley from one yard out. Janikowski provided the Raiders with his third conversion kick to give Oakland a 21–17 advantage. On the ensuing kickoff, Tennessee's John Simon fumbled, Oakland recovered, and five plays later, Janikowski extended Oakland's lead to seven points with a 43-yard field goal. He then upped the Raiders' advantage to 27–17 in the third quarter with a 32-yard three-pointer.

The Titans refused to go down quietly. They went on an eight-play, 67-yard scoring trek that McNair climaxed with a 13-yard run to make it a 27–24 Oakland lead going in to the fourth quarter. Their progress to the Oakland end zone was assisted by a personal foul penalty on cornerback Terrance Shaw after it seemed the Titans were about to be denied. On the following play after the penalty, McNair scored.

Gannon took the Raiders 66 yards on nine plays, and scored on a 2-yard run. Janikowski added the conversion that once again brought the Raiders back up to a ten-point lead. Zack Crockett added a 7-yard run, and Janikowski another extra point, and the Raiders were on their way to the Super Bowl after a 19-year absence.[18]

Super Bowl XXXVII

Jan. 26, 2003; Played at Qualcomm Stadium in San Diego, California

It had been 19 years since the Silver and Black readied themselves for the ultimate clash of the sports world. Jon Gruden had worked tirelessly to return the Raiders to their past glory, and took them to the threshold of a Super Bowl berth twice in his time at the helm. It seemed like a forgone conclusion that Gruden

nd the Raiders would eventually compete for a world champi-
nship. On January 26, 2003, the day did come when Gruden
nd the Raiders were seeking the grand prize of professional foot-
all. Unfortunately, it was as opponents and not comrades in arms.

After the 2001 season, Gruden left Oakland to coach the
ampa Bay Buccaneers. Tampa was on the verge of higher success
anks to an impressive defense that ranked among the top units
or the previous four seasons. The offense was a different story. It
as nestled in the lower depths of league rankings, and team offi-
ials knew that with an offensive attack matching that of their
hampionship-caliber defense, conquest of the professional grid-
on would be theirs for the taking. This was where Gruden's spe-
ialty lied, and when he came to the Sunshine State, the hopes of
scoring juggernaut seemed apparent. With his re-building of
e Raiders' offense into a league power, Gruden looked to work
e same magic in Tampa.

Despite his strong work ethic and knowledge, Gruden was
nable to turn the Tampa offense around as initially hoped. The
uccaneers were still ranked near the bottom of the league at 25th
n total offense, but Gruden was able to steady the ship enough
o keep the team going in the right direction. Quarterback Brad
ohnson had a good season with 3,049 yards passing, 22 touch-
owns, a mere six interceptions, and his efforts earned him a Pro
owl selection. The running tandem of Michael Pittman and
Mike Alstott provided a solid ground attack. Pittman lead the
round game with 718 yards, and snagged 59 catches out of the
ackfield. Battering ram fullback Alstott powered his way for 548
ards and 35 receptions on his way to a Pro Bowl nod. Keyshawn
ohnson look top honors on the receiving end of things with a
eam-high 76 catches for 1,088 yards and five touchdowns, and
Keenan McCardell added 61 catches for 670 yards and six touch-
owns.[19]

The defense came through just like expected. The unit led
he entire league in total defense by allowing 252.8 yards a game,
nd giving up only 12.3 points per game. They also topped the
ro circuit in fewest passing touchdowns allowed (10), intercep-
ions (31), and fewest passing yards allowed (155.6).[20]

Super Bowl XXXVII was the official title of this matchup,
ut unofficially it was being dubbed "the Gruden Bowl," and at
ts climax, which team would be the winner. Would Tampa Bay
fficials walk away with the Lombardi Trophy as a testament to
heir savvy in getting the offensive guru to Florida, or would Al
Davis and his Raiders add a fourth sterling silver statue of
reatness to their bulging trophy case with Gruden's replacement?
Prior to kickoff, those questions were the main focus of the game,
nd would be answered after sixty minutes of controlled violence.

The game was broadcast by ABC, with the great tandem of
Al Michaels and legendary Raiders' coach John Madden calling
he action. After Celine Dion sang "God Bless America," and the
Dixie Chicks belted out the national anthem, the ball was placed
n the tee by Sebastian Janikowski. With flash bulbs going off at
steady pace, "Sea Bass" sent the ball 65 yards to open the fes-
ivities.

Aaron Stecker received the kick on the 5-yard line and re-
urned it 21 yards to the Tampa 26. Brad Johnson opened Tampa's
irst series with a pass to Mike Alstott for four yards. After Michael
Pittman ran for one yard, Johnson looked to return to the air on
hird-and-five. Johnson fired a pass in the direction of Keenan

McCardell near midfield. Charles Woodson came up huge for the
Raiders by intercepting the ball and returned it to the Tampa 36
before being pushed out of bounds.

Given this incredible opportunity, Rich Gannon looked to
capitalize with one of the NFL's most explosive offenses at his
command. He opened up with a pass to Charlie Garner that
gained eight yards, and picked up a first down on the Tampa 19
with a completion to Tim Brown. After successive runs by Garner
and Gannon failed to pick up a first down, Gannon dropped back
to pass on third-and-seven. Tampa's top-rated defense made their
first statement by coming at Gannon hard, and Simeon Rice
sacked him for a loss of six yards. Janikowski came on in an
attempt to salvage something from Woodson's effort, and capped
the seven-play, 14-yard drive with a 40-yard field goal to give the
Silver and Black the game's first points with 10:44 left on the clock
in the opening stanza.

Janikowski kicked off to Stecker, who ran the ball back 27
yards to the Tampa 29 and apparently fumbled. The officials ruled
that Oakland's Eric Johnson recovered, but instant replay reversed
the call, and Tampa retained possession.

Brad Johnson went to work on the Oakland defense by once
again opening a series with a pass. This time he completed an 11-
yard pass to Joe Jurevicius to the Tampa 40. Following two failed
pass attempts to Pittmann and Keyshawn Johnson, Brad Johnson
went back to Jurevicius for a 23-yard pickup to the Oakland 37
before he was pushed out of bounds. Pittman then shot around
the left side, and ran for a gain of 23 yards down to the 14 before
Rod Woodson stopped him. The Raiders stiffened from this point,
allowing only one yard on the next three downs. Martin Gramatica tied the "Gruden Bowl" at 3–3 when he sent a 31-yard
field goal through the uprights to finish off the nine-play, 58-yard
drive with 7:55 left in the first quarter.

The Raiders took over on their own 30 following the ensuing
kickoff. After a six-yard pass from Gannon to Garner, the Raiders'
advance ended with an incomplete pass and a sack by Greg Spires
on Gannon that resulted in a loss of five yards. Shane Lechler got
off a great punt of 53 yards that pinned the Buccaneers back at
their own 16.

The defenses took over for the remainder of the first quarter,
as Tampa punted twice and Oakland once. After getting the ball
at midfield with 1:35 left, Gannon hooked up with Garner on
first down for a gain of eight. Garner tried his hand at running
on second-and-two, but was dropped for no gain by Simeon Rice.
Gannon went looking for Doug Jolley on third down, but safety
Dexter Jackson picked the pass off at the Tampa 40 and returned
it nine yards. Pittman got to midfield with a run that gained one
yard as the opening quarter came to an end with the score knotted
at 3-all.

The second quarter began with Tampa going 26 yards in
nine plays with key plays coming on two Brad Johnson throws
to Keyshawn Johnson totaling 20 yards. After consecutive runs
by Alstott netted only two yards, the Johnson and Johnson team
tried to connect again on third down, but this time the pass fell
incomplete to bring up a fourth-and-eight situation. Gramatica
came on, and with a 43-yard field goal hitting its mark at 11:20,
the Buccaneers were on top for the first time in their Super Bowl
experience, 6–3.

The ensuing kickoff was brought 23 yards to the Oakland

34 by Marcus Knight. Gannon went right to work through the air, connecting with Jerry Rice for nine yards. Garner blasted up the middle for a gain of two yards, which gave the Raiders a fresh set of downs to work with. Gannon took to the friendly skies once again, this time looking for Jerry Porter just across midfield. Unfortunately, Dexter Jackson came up and picked off his second pass and returned it to the Oakland 45-yard line. Jackson placed his name in the record book as the only player to intercept two passes in the first half of a Super Bowl.

Tampa could not take advantage of Jackson's second theft, and after two incomplete passes and a Pittman run of five yards, they had to punt. Tom Tupa got off a punt that pinned the Raiders deep on their own 11-yard line. The Raiders did not fare any better, as Gannon threw two incomplete passes, and was sacked by Rice in between those failed attempts. Lechler returned possession back over to Tampa with a punt that Karl Williams took back to the Oakland 27 to set the offense up in excellent shape. Pittman got the call on the first two plays of this drive, and ran for gains of six and 19 yards to put Tampa on the Oakland two. It was then time for battering ram fullback Mike Alstott to go to work. On his first carry, he was stopped for no gain, but on the next play, he would not be denied. Powering his way up the middle, Alstott hit paydirt for the first six-pointer of Super Bowl XXXVII. Gramatica was true on the extra point attempt, and Tampa led, 13–3 with 6:28 left in the first half.

On their next possession, the Raiders moved the ball from their own 29-yard line to just shy of midfield before running out of downs. Lechler punted the ball back to Tampa with 3:45 remaining in the half. Starting on their own 23, Tampa's Pittman ran three straight times, picking up 17 yards in the process. Johnson then connected with Alstott on a pass for 16 yards that got the Bucs into Oakland territory at the 42. Over the course of the next several plays, Tampa moved to the Oakland five. On first-and-goal from there, Johnson connected with Keenan McCardell for the touchdown with 34 seconds left in the half. Gramatica's conversion extended the Tampa bulge to 20–3 as the teams went to their locker rooms for the intermission.

The second half began with Gramatica kicking off to Marcus Knight, who took the ball from his own five to the Oakland 27. Gannon had trouble locating his dynamic duo of Jerry Rice and Tim Brown in the first half. Thanks to the effort of the top-ranked defense, they were held to only three catches between them. It appeared to be the same in the infant stages of the second half, as Gannon was unable to hook up with them in their opening possession. However, he did connect with Jerry Porter and Doug Jolley for a total of eight yards on the first two plays, but then an incomplete pass intended for Marcus Knight brought up fourth down. On fourth-and-two, Lechler got off a 44-yard punt that allowed the Bucs to begin their first series of the second half deep on their own 11 after an illegal blocking penalty during the punt moved them back ten yards.

It did not seem to matter how deep the Bucs were pinned down on this day. They were on a roll, and over the next eight minutes, Tampa's offense marched 89 yards on 14 plays. The drive was climaxed when Brad Johnson and Keenan McCardell teamed up again for a six-pointer, this time coming on an 8-yard pass. Gramatica's conversion with 5:36 remaining in the third quarter now gave the Buccaneers a commanding 27–3 advantage.

The ensuing kickoff traveled 67 yards off Gramatica's foot and into the hands of the awaiting Marcus Knight on the Oakland three. Knight advanced the ball to the Oakland 32, and Gannon came back out to attempt the greatest comeback in Super Bowl history. If any team had the capability of pulling it off, it was the 2002 Raiders and their explosive offense that could strike quickly from anywhere on the field. However, the main thing for Gannon to do was to get the ball into the hands of his teammates. On first down, he accomplished this with an 8-yard pass to Charlie Garner. On the following play, Gannon threw again, and this one went for six points. Unfortunately, the points were awarded to Tampa when defensive back Dwight Smith picked off a pass intended for Jerry Rice and raced 44 yards for a touchdown. Gramatica added the extra point, and the Bucs were beginning to wonder what their Super Bowl rings were going to look like, as they were up, 34–3.

The Raiders began their next offensive series from their 18-yard line with 4:41 left in the third quarter. After Gannon was sacked on first down, and a pass intended for Tim Brown fell incomplete, Doug Jolley came up with 25-yard reception that moved Oakland close to midfield. Jerry Rice caught a pass for six yards, but the following two Gannon tosses missed their marks. On a rare occasion, the Tampa defense made an error. On Gannon's third down pass attempt, linebacker Shelton Quarles was penalized for pass interference, which gave Oakland a new set of downs after the six-yard infraction was marked off. Gannon went back to work through the air, mostly because he had no other choice but to throw if he wanted to get the Raiders back into contention, even though the odds of that were extremely slim at this juncture. He connected with fullback Jon Ritchie for a gain of seven yards that got Oakland to the Tampa 39. Following an incomplete pass intended for Jerry Porter, Gannon decided to try his luck with him again, and this time Porter caught the ball for Oakland's first touchdown of the game with 2:22 left in the quarter. At first, the officials ruled that Porter was out of bounds when he caught the ball. However, the play was challenged by the Raiders, and the call was reversed, thus giving the Silver and Black a rare break in this affair. It was claimed after review that Porter came down with one foot in the end zone and dragged his other out. Gannon attempted a two-point conversion, but was sacked and the score now stood at 34–9.

The Bucs took over possession following Janikowski's kickoff on their own 31 with 2:06 left in the quarter. This series could have been called "the Michael Pittman Show," as the running back touched the pigskin on every down. On first down, he carried for a gain of one yard, but an offensive holding penalty took the Bucs back ten yards. On first-and-twenty, he tried to get around left end, but was stopped after picking up two yards. Two more Pittman attempts netted the Bucs six yards as the quarter officially went into the books.

The final fifteen minutes of Super Bowl XXXVII began with Pittman running for one yard on third-and-nine. Tom Tupa came in to punt, and linebacker Tim Johnson shot through and blocked the kick. Eric Johnson was there to scoop the loose ball up, and ran 13 yards for another Oakland touchdown. Gannon tried another two-point conversion, this time a pass to Tim Brown, but it fell incomplete to make it a 34–15 ballgame.

The Bucs moved the ball from the Tampa 24 to Oakland's

-yard line following the ensuing kickoff. From there they stalled, and Gramatica came on to attempt a field goal, but holder Tom Tupa fumbled the snap from center. Gramatica picked up the ball and was brought down by Tory James for a loss of four yards at the Oakland 22, which was where the Raiders assumed possession with 9:02 left in the game.

Gannon caught fire on this drive. On the first two plays, he connected on passes to Doug Jolley and Tyrone Wheatley to move the ball out to the Oakland 38. Following an incomplete pass attempt to Garner, he once again hit on consecutive passes, this time to Jerry Rice and Jolley to get into Tampa territory. The drive hit two snags with the ball on the Tampa 45. An incomplete pass and a holding penalty took the Raiders back to their 45. Gannon then threw to Garner for a gain of seven. Facing a third-and-13 from the Tampa 48, Gannon finally found one of his main receivers, connecting with Jerry Rice for a touchdown, which gave the game's greatest receiver another record. This time Rice's name went into the Super Bowl record book as the first to ever catch a touchdown pass in four different Super Bowls. Until this play, Rice was limited to four short receptions. Gannon's two-point conversion pass to Jerry Porter was incomplete, but the Raiders were now back in this one, and making Tampa fans a bit nervous. With 6:06 left, the Silver and Black now only trailed, 34–21, thanks to two quick six-pointers.

Looking to eat up as time off the clock as possible to kill Oakland's new found momentum, Tampa went to their ground game on five of their next six plays. Pittman ran for a total of three yards on the first two plays, and then Brad Johnson threw to Mike Alstott for nine yards and a first down. Three more Michael Pittman runs only netted three yards, but the Bucs achieved what they set out to do, as they got the clock down to 2:44 before turning the ball back over to Oakland after Tupa's punt on fourth down.

Gannon and Rice went back to work on the Tampa defense immediately by teaming up for an 11-yard pickup. Gannon ran for one yard on the next play, and was then sacked for a loss of nine by Warren Sapp on second down. On third-and-18 from his own 29, Gannon let loose with a pass intended for Marcus Knight, but it was intercepted by Derrick Brooks at the Oakland 44. Brooks then applied the death blow to Raider Nation on this day when he made a trek to the end zone with two minutes left. Gramatica's conversion upped the score to 41–21.

Oakland took over on their 27 following the ensuing kickoff, and Gannon still looked to attack the defense. After an incomplete pass on first down, he hit on three straight pass attempts to Jolley, Rice, and Garner, which got the ball to the Tampa 49 with 12 seconds left. He then looked for Marcus Knight, but Dwight Smith was there to intercept a tipped pass on the 50, and took it back for his second six-pointer of the game with two seconds left. Smith's touchdown proved to be the 200th one scored in Super Bowl history. Another bit of history was established with Smith's theft. It marked Gannon's fifth interception of the game, which set a Super Bowl record for one quarterback, and was sacked five times as well. He still managed to throw for 272 yards, with 216 of them coming after being down, 20–3. Gramatica added another conversion kick, and the Tampa Bay Buccaneers were officially crowned Super Bowl champions as the final two seconds ran off their impressive 48–21 mauling. A short time later, Jon

Gruden hoisted the Lombardi Trophy toward the heavens. It was just a shame that Gruden was not wearing silver and black when he clasped firmly on the holy grail of professional football.[21]

Starting Lineup for Super Bowl XXXVII

OFFENSE

QB — Rich Gannon	LT — Barry Sims
RB — Charlie Garner	LG — Frank Middleton
WR — Tim Brown	C — Adam Treu
WR — Jerry Porter	RG — Mo Collins
WR — Jerry Rice	RT — Lincoln Kennedy
TE — Doug Jolley	

DEFENSE

DE — DeLawrence Grant	RLB — Eric Barton
DE — Regan Upshaw	CB — Charles Woodson
DT — Sam Adams	CB — Tory James
DT — John Parrella	SS — Anthony Dorsett
LLB — Bill Romanowski	FS — Rod Woodson
MLB — Napoleon Harris	

KICKING/PUNTING

K — Sebastian Janikowski	P — Shane Lechler

Individual Statistics from Super Bowl XXXVII

OFFENSE

Rich Gannon: 24 completions out of 44 pass attempts for 272 yards, 2 TD and 5 INT. Rushed for 3 yards on 2 carries.
Charlie Garner: Rushed for 10 yards on 7 carries and had 7 receptions for 51 yards.
Zack Crockett: Rushed for 6 yards on 2 carries.
Jerry Rice: Had 5 receptions for 77 yards and 1 TD.
Jerry Porter: Had 4 receptions for 62 yards and 1 TD.
Doug Jolley: Had 5 receptions for 59 yards.
Tim Brown: Had 1 reception for 9 yards, and returned 1 punt for 0 yards.
Jon Ritchie: Had 1 reception for 7 yards.
Tyrone Wheatley: Had 1 reception for 7 yards.
Chris Cooper: Returned 1 kickoff for 6 yards.
Marcus Knight: Returned 8 kickoffs for 143 yards.
Darrien Gordon: Returned 3 punts for 29 yards.
Sebastian Janikowski: Had 1 field goal.

DEFENSE

Charles Woodson: 1 INT for 12 yards.

Individual Statistics and Roster

Head Coach: Bill Callahan
Assistant Coaches: Fred Biletnikoff, Chuck Bresnahan, Willie Brown, Bob Casullo, Garrett Giemont, Chris Griswold, Jim Harbaugh, Aaron Kromer, Ron Lynn, Don Martin, John Morton, Jay Norvell, Fred Pagac, Skip Peete, Marc Trestman, Chris Turner, Mike Waufle
2002 Regular Season Record: 11–5
1st Place AFC Western Division
Scored 450 points to rank 2nd out of 32 teams
Allowed 146 points to rank 3rd
Led the league in total offensive yards (6,237), first downs (366), and passing yards (4,475)

STARTERS — OFFENSE

QB — Rich Gannon: Started in 16 games. Completed **418** of **618** pass attempts for **4,689** yards, 26 TD, and 10 INT. **Also led the NFL in yards passing per game (293.1), pass attempts per game (38.6), and pass completions per game (26.1).** Rushed for 156 yards on 50 carries and 3 TD.

RB — Charlie Garner: Active for 16 games and started in 15. Rushed for 962 yards on 182 carries and 7 TD. Had 91 receptions for 941 yards and 4 TD.

WR — Tim Brown: Started in 16 games. Had 81 receptions for 930 yards and 2 TD. Rushed for 19 yards on 6 carries.

WR — Jerry Porter: Active for 16 games and started in 13. Had 51 receptions for 688 yards and 9 TD. Rushed for 6 yards on 4 carries.

WR — Jerry Rice: Started in 16 games. Had 92 receptions for 1,211 yards and 7 TD. Rushed for 20 yards on 3 carries.

TE — Roland Williams: Active for 16 games and started in 12. Had 27 receptions for 213 yards.

LT — Barry Sims: Active for and started in 15 games.

LG — Mo Collins: Active for and started in 10 games.

C — Barret Robbins: Started in 16 games.

RG — Frank Middleton: Started in 16 games.

RT — Lincoln Kennedy: Active for and started in 15 games.

RESERVE OFFENSIVE PLAYERS

Brad Badger (G/T): Active for 7 games.

Zack Crockett (RB): Active for 16 games, and rushed for 118 yards on 40 carries and 8 TD.

Ronald Curry (WR): Active for 1 game and returned 3 kickoffs 68 yards.

Mondriel Fulcher (TE): Active for 2 games.

Madre Hill (RB): Active for 2 games.

James Jett (WR): Active for and started in 1 game.

Doug Jolley (TE): Active for 16 games, started in 4, and had 32 receptions for 409 yards and 2 TD.

Randy Jordan (RB): Active for 14 games, rushed for 14 yards on 3 carries and 1 TD, and had 2 receptions for 19 yards.

Terry Kirby (RB): Active for 6 games. Rushed for 51 yards on 16 carries, had 17 receptions for 115 yards and 1 TD, 1 pass attempt for 0 yards, and returned 19 kickoffs for 425 yards and 1 TD.

Marcus Knight (WR): Active for 16 games and started in 1. Had 3 receptions for 26 yards and returned 29 kickoffs for 705 yards.

Jon Ritchie (RB): Active for 16 games, started in 2, and had 10 receptions for 66 yards and 1 TD.

Matt Stinchcomb (G/T): Active for 16 games and started in 6.

Adam Treu (C): Active for 16 games.

Marques Tuiasosopo (QB): Active for 3 games and rushed for -3 yards on 2 carries.

Langston Walker (T/G): Active for 12 games and started in 2.

Tyrone Wheatley (RB): Active for 14 games, rushed for 419 yards on 108 carries and 2 TD, and had 12 receptions for 71 yards.

Alvis Whitted (WR): Active for 9 games and returned 4 kickoffs for 50 yards.

Marcus Williams (TE/WR): Active for 14 games.

STARTERS — DEFENSE

DE — DeLawrence Grant: Active for 16 games, started in 14, had 3 sacks and 1 fumble recovery.

DE — Tony Bryant: Active for and started in 8 games. Had 2 sacks and 1 fumble recovery.

DT — Sam Adams: Active for 15 games, started in 14, and had 2 sacks.

DT — John Parrella: Active for 16 games, started in 15, and had 1 sack.

LLB — Bill Romanowski: Started in 16 games, had 4 sacks and 1 INT.

MLB — Napoleon Harris: Active for 15 games, started in 13 and had sack.

RLB — Eric Barton: Started in 16 games, had 6 sacks and 2 INT.

CB — Charles Woodson: Active for 8 games, started in 7, had 1 INT, and 1 fumble recovery.

CB — Tory James: Active for 14 games, started in 13, had 4 INT, and returned 1 kickoff for 0 yards.

SS — Derrick Gibson: Active for 16 games, started in 11, and had 1 fumble recovery.

FS — Rod Woodson: Started in 16 games, had 8 INT and 3 fumble recoveries.

RESERVE DEFENSIVE PLAYERS

Trace Armstrong (E): Active for 15 games, started in 8, had 4 sacks, 1 INT. and 1 fumble recovery.

Phillip Buchanon (DB): Active for 6 games, started in 2, had 2 INT, 1 TD, 2 fumble recoveries, and returned 15 punts for 178 yards and 1 TD.

Kenyon Coleman (E): Active for 1 game.

Roderick Coleman (T): Active for 14 games, started in 2, and had 1 sacks.

Derek Combs (DB): Active for 4 games, and returned 5 kickoffs for 71 yards.

Chris Cooper (T/E): Active for 16 games, started in 1, and had 1 sack.

Anthony Dorsett (DB): Active for 16 games, started in 7, and had 1 fumble recovery.

Junior Ioane (T): Active for 6 games and had 1 sack.

Brandon Jennings (DB): Active for 10 games.

Eric Johnson (DB/LB): Active for 16 games.

Tim Johnson (LB): Active for 6 games.

Mike Jones (LB): Active for 3 games.

Clarence Love (DB): Active for 11 games and started in 3.

Carey Scott (DB): Active for 1 game.

Terrance Shaw (DB): Active for 16 games, started in 7, had 2 INT. and 1 fumble recovery.

Travian Smith (LB): Active for 16 games, started in 2, and had 5 sacks.

Kevin Stemke (P): Active for 2 games and punted 5 times for a 42.4 average.

Regan Upshaw (E): Active for 5 games, started in 1, and had 2 sacks.

KICKING/PUNTING

K — Sebastian Janikowski: Active for 16 games. Made 26 of 33 field goals and 50 of 50 extra points for 128 points.

P — Shane Lechler: Active for 14 games. Punted 53 times for a 42.5 average.

2003 Season Review

1. Sept. 7: The defending AFC champions came into the new campaign as the league's oldest team, with 15 players 30 or older. They did not look at this as a negative, but as an experienced group of leaders set to defend their title, and many prognosticators believed that they had enough gas left in their tanks to make another run at glory.

The AFC's elite opened the season on the prime time stage, as the Tennessee Titans hosted the defending AFC champion Oakland Raiders. The reigning NFL Most Valuable Player, Rich Gannon, completed 24 of 38 passes for 268 yards and two touchdowns. Running back Charlie Garner also had a big night with eight receptions for 112 yards, and caught a 46-yard scoring strike from Gannon. However, it was not enough, as the Titans got revenge from their loss in the conference title game with a 25–20 win. The Raiders took a 10–9 lead with 1:06 left in the first half on Garner's touchdown catch and a Sebastian Janikowski 47-yard field goal. Tennessee came back to take a 12–10 halftime lead on a three-pointer of their own. The teams then traded field goals with Oakland's coming on another 47-yarder from "Sea Bass." The Titans extended their lead to 22–13 with 7:51 remaining in the game. Gannon then threw a perfect pass to Tim Brown from 25 yards out to close the gap to 22–20, but another field goal by Craig Hentrich finished off the scoring and the Raiders as well.[1]

2. Sept. 14: The Raiders had won 18 of their previous 25 meetings with the Cincinnati Bengals, and increased their advantage over them with a 23–20 win. Oakland jumped out to a 10–0 lead on the league's worst team over the last decade thanks to a Sebastian Janikowski 40-yard field goal and a 4-yard run by Tyrone Wheatley that was set up after rookie Justin Fargas tore through the Bengal defense on a run that covered 53 yards. Cincinnati looked to make a game of it, and going into the fourth quarter, the teams were deadlocked at 13–13, as the Raiders added a Janikowski 26-yard field goal. Cornerback Phillip Buchanon broke the stalemate by returning an interception off Jon Kitna 83 yards for the score. Kitna redeemed himself by hitting Peter Warrick for an 8-yard touchdown with 1:18 left in the game to once again tie matters up. Rich Gannon, who suffered from back spasms, and had a dismal game with only 13 completions in 28 attempts for 103 yards, managed to forge ahead when it counted most. He led the Raiders 55 yards downfield, hitting on three of five passes for 38 yards. Helping out was a 15-yard interference penalty that put Oakland even deeper into Cincinnati territory. With nine seconds remaining in regulation, Janikowski drilled a 39-yard field goal attempt to win it. Despite the win, the Raiders were not clicking, and were outgained by a weak team, 416 to 237 yards.[2]

3. Sept. 22: In the fourteenth Monday Night Football matchup between the Raiders and Denver, which was the most between any teams on Monday night, the Broncos smacked Oakland around to the tune of 31–10 beating. The league's number offense of a year earlier was stymied right out of the gate, as Oakland failed to get a first down in the opening quarter, and saw themselves well behind at the half, 24–0, after mustering only a single yard of offensive production. For the game, the Raiders were held to 195 total yards and 11 first downs. Zack Crockett got Oakland on the board in the third quarter on a 4-yard run that capped off an 80-yard drive. Emotions turned sour early in the fourth quarter after Phillip Buchanon ran a punt back 56 yards to the Denver 21. Pumped up from his jaunt, Buchanon got involved in a trash-talking debate with some of the Mile High Stadium throng, which resulted in Buchanon getting showered with beer. The Oakland offense stalled at that point, and Sebastian Janikowski gave the Raiders their tenth point of the evening on a 41-yard field goal.[3]

4. Sept. 28: San Diego head coach Marty Schottenheimer was one of the few sideline generals up to this stage of Raiders history to have a big advantage over them. He brought a 20–6 record against the Silver and Black into this game, but his 0–3 Chargers were in worse shape than the Raiders in the early stages of the '03 campaign. They were allowing almost 30 points a game, and this seemed like the perfect time for Oakland's once-powerful-but-now-stagnant offense to rejuvenate itself. Like a hungry animal pouncing on weaker prey, the Raiders got big performances from Rich Gannon (348 passing yards), Tim Brown (6 receptions for 110 yards), and Jerry Rice (7 catches for 118 yards), and managed to win a scoring fest, 34–31, but it was not easy.

Oakland opened the scoring on a 36-yard touchdown pass from Gannon to Brown. Gannon fired his second six-pointer of the game to tight end Doug Jolley, but the Raiders still trailed at the half, 21–14. Sebastian Janikowski added a 23-yard field goal in the fourth quarter, but Oakland looked to be fading fast, as San Diego responded with a Lorenzo Neal 3-yard run to extend the Lightening Bolts advantage to 31–17. It was then that the Silver and Black showed flashes of their old self. In the final six minutes of regulation, Gannon led the Oakland charge with his arm. First came a 60-yard touchdown pass to Alvis Whitted that brought Oakland to within 31–24 with 4:38 left. The Raiders' defense held, forcing San Diego to punt. Gannon and Rice teamed up on two receptions, and Charlie Garner shot through the Chargers for a 24-yard scoring run, and following Janikowski's conversion, the game was tied at 31–31 with 1:24 to go in regulation. This wild affair between two long-time rivals went into overtime, and Gannon took the team from the Oakland eight to the San Diego 28, with the big play being a 29-yard catch by Rice to get the Raiders out from deep in their own territory on the first play of the drive. With 5:01 left in overtime, Janikowski was true on a 46-yard field goal attempt to pull the defending AFC champs to 2–2.[4]

5. Oct. 5: A trip to the Windy City appeared next on Oakland's schedule, and a date with the winless Chicago Bears. The Raiders got a 92-yard rushing performance from Charlie Garner, two interceptions and a fumble recovery from Charles Woodson, and after a Zack Crockett 1-yard run gave them a 6–0 lead, the Silver and Black looked ready to blow the Bears out of Soldier Field in the second quarter, as they got inside Chicago's 25-yard line four times. However, the Oakland offense stalled, which was quickly becoming the trend of the '03 season for them. Sebastian Janikowski, who missed on the first extra point kick of his career earlier in the game, managed to salvage each drive by connecting on four field goals from 36, 39, 32, and 31 yards out to give the Raiders an 18–3 halftime lead. After hearing boos from the home crowd for much of the game, the Bears got going. On the first play of the fourth quarter, Chicago quarterback Kordell Stewart connected with Marty Booker on a 14-yard touchdown to cut the Raiders lead to 18–13. The Bears then took the lead for the first time in the game when Stanley Pritchett scored on a run from eight yards out. Stewart then ran for the two-point conversion to put the Bears up, 21–18 with 6:58 remaining in the game. Janikowski once again pulled the sputtering Raiders offense out of trouble with a game-tying 49-yard field goal with 3:30 to play. Chicago's offense took over following the ensuing kickoff on their own 27. Stewart kept the drive alive when he vaulted over the Raiders' defense for a first down on a fourth-and-one situation at midfield with 22 seconds left in regulation. After a penalty nullified a Stewart run to the Oakland 31, he attacked through the air, placing the ball into Dez White's hands at the 31. Two plays later, kicker Paul Edinger sent the ball 48 yards with no time left on the clock. His kick was good, and the Bears won their first of the year, while the Raiders slipped to 2–3.[5]

6. Oct. 12: The Silver and Black looked to turn their fortunes around with a trip to Cleveland, a city where the Raiders never lost. Since 1971, they came into Cleveland five times and left victorious each time, with the most recent being a nail-biting one-point victory in 1985. Oakland looked to continue their road

dominance over the Browns by scoring on their first possession. Safety Anthony Dorsett recovered a William Green fumble, and six plays later, Rich Gannon and Teyo Johnson hooked up for a 10-yard touchdown. Following that, the Cleveland defense clamped down on Oakland's "dink and dunk" attack. Racking up 12 penalties also put a damper on Oakland's offensive production, which included five straight in one possession. The Browns took a 13–7 fourth quarter lead, and looked to hold off the Raiders' one final run at victory. The defending AFC champs still had a glimmer of hope to pull this one out, and drove to the Cleveland 24 with 28 seconds to play. On fourth-and-one, Gannon threw a side-arm pass to Jerry Rice, and the most prolific receiver in football history jumped in the air and stretched out to make a catch on the sideline. His right knee appeared to be inbounds when he caught the ball, but the line judge ruled the opposite way, and the Raiders suffered their fourth loss of the season, and their first in Cleveland.[6]

7. Oct. 20: The undefeated Kansas City Chiefs came into Oakland for a Monday Night Football clash off to their best start in the 44 year history of the franchise. A pumped up Chiefs team looked to blast their fiercest rivals in this prime time encounter, and led 10–0 going in to the second half. Rich Gannon suffered a bruised right shoulder right before halftime, and gave way to backup Marques Tuiasosopo, who only threw six passes up to this point throughout the season. Inspired by the chance to showcase his gridiron wares on a national televised stage, Tuiasosopo hit on 16 of 28 pass attempts for 224 yards, and led the Raiders on two scoring drives capped off by a 27-yard Sebastian Janikowski field goal and a Zack Crockett 1-yard run. Unfortunately, it was not enough, as the Silver and Black fell for the fifth time in '03 by a final of 17–10. The Raiders made it a nail-biter until the very end, as Tim Brown was stopped short of the goal line at the one as time ran out.[7]

8. Nov. 2: Coming off their bye week, the Raiders hoped to turn their season around against the 1–6 Detroit Lions, or at least regain some respectability. With Rich Gannon still nursing his shoulder, the Oakland offense was turned over to Marques Tuiasosopo, who like his counterpart, Detroit quarterback Joey Harrington, was a former Pac-10 Offensive Player of the Year. The Lions had not won since opening day, and were losers in 14 out of their previous 15 games. On this day, it was Harrington who received the accolades, as he threw for a touchdown, and Jason Hanson kicked three field goals to help Detroit snap their losing skid with a 23–13 victory. Tuiasosopo suffered a knee injury in his first NFL start, and gave way to Rick Mirer, who had not took a snap in three years. Mirer was able to throw for 125 yards, but suffered two interceptions. The Raiders received their points on a Charlie Garner 7-yard run, and two Sebastian Janikowski field goals from 55 yards, which set a new team record, and 24 yards. With the team quickly falling apart, dissension in the ranks began to engulf the locker room, as coach Bill Callahan was being blamed for being too headstrong and not able to communicate with his players like his predecessor Jon Gruden was capable of doing.[8]

9. Nov. 9: The Raiders entered their next game on a four-game losing streak, and down to their third string quarterback. However, the New York Jets were not much better, as they came into Oakland also with a 2–6 record. Just ten months earlier,

these two teams met in a divisional playoff game, and now they were both looking at the possibility of reached a .500 finish at best. Oakland came into this game with the league's lowest amount of rushing attempts at 168, but with their offense reduced to starting a third string quarterback, suddenly the running game returned. For the game, Tyrone Wheatley carried 23 times for 7 yards, and Justin Fargas 16 times for 62 yards, as the Raiders powered their way to a 21–10 lead at the half. Phillip Buchanon opened the scoring with a 78-yard punt return, followed by a 1-yard run from Zack Crockett, and Rick Mirer connected with Jerry Porter on a 2-yard pass. Sebastian Janikowski added a 22-yard field goal in the fourth quarter to round out Oakland's scoring. All things seemed to be right in Raider Nation up to then, but throughout this season, if something bad could happen, it usually did. On this occasion, New York quarterback Chad Pennington threw a 3-yard scoring strike to Jerald Sowell with 1:09 remaining in regulation, and then forced the game into overtime by throwing to Anthony Becht for the two-point conversion. The Jets then won 27–24 on a 38-yard field goal from Doug O'Brien to send the Raiders to 2–7, which was their worst start since going 1-6-1 in 1964.[9]

10. Nov. 16: The Minnesota Vikings came into this game with a 6–3 record and the league's top offense, which was averaging 376.2 yards per game. In this strange season for the Raiders, they lost to teams they should have beaten, then turned around and defeated the Vikings, 28–18. Phillip Buchanon got the Raiders pumped up by returning an interception 64 yards with just 49 seconds expired in the first quarter. The Raiders never looked back from that point on, and got two touchdowns from Zack Crockett on runs of one and two yards, and Tyrone Wheatley (2 yard run). Rick Mirer steadied the offensive ship with safe passes completing nine of 13 attempts for 195 yards and no interceptions. In the midst of celebration over snapping their losing streak, the Raiders were hit with news that four of their players tested positive for using the steroid THG, and were facing four game suspensions. The players in question were defensive tackles Dana Stubblefield and Chris Cooper, center Barret Robbins, and linebacker Bill Romanowski.[10]

11. Nov. 23: Jerry Rice came into this game needing two receptions to become the first player in history with 1,500 career catches, and he also looked to extend his NFL–record of 266 games with a catch. Rice achieved both goals by catching two passes for 51 yards against the Kansas City Chiefs, but the Raiders fell, 27–24, despite a valiant effort. After losing for the first time all season the previous week, the Chiefs were in danger of losing again, as Oakland came from ten points down in the fourth quarter to tie the game. Quarterback Trent Green then rallied the Chiefs by connecting with Marc Boerigter for 16 yards on fourth-and-16 to keep a late drive alive. This allowed Morten Anderson to kick the game-winning field goal from 35 yards out with four seconds remaining to sweep Oakland for the first time since 1998. The Raiders received their points from Rick Mirer (13-yard run), Tyrone Wheatley (15-yard run), Sebastian Janikowski (41-yard field goal), and Jerry Rice, whose 47-yard touchdown reception in the fourth quarter proved to be the one that got him to the 1,500 catch plateau. Jerry Porter also had a good day receiving, with seven catches for 89 yards.[11]

12. Nov. 30: The Mike Shanahan–led Denver Broncos in

aded Oakland, and the former Raiders coach looked to extend his 13–4 record against his old team. Amidst wet weather conditions, the Broncos did not struggle against the hapless Raiders, and won, 22–8, to sweep Oakland and send them to their ninth loss of the season. Denver's Clinton Portis was the offensive weapon for the men from the Mile High City, as he ran for 170 yards on 34 carries and two touchdowns. A safety and two long-range Sebastian Janikowski field goals from 46 and 48 yards provided Oakland with their point production.[12]

13. Dec. 7: Pittsburgh running back Jerome Bettis ran for 106 yards to move into ninth place on the all-time rushing list, and the Steelers whipped the Raiders, 27–7, to give them their tenth loss for the bleak season. Antwaan Randle El was responsible for setting up three Pittsburgh scores with two catches and a punt return. Rick Mirer had an awful day under center, as he threw for only 68 yards and suffered two interceptions. Oakland's lone touchdown came when Tyrone Wheatley opened the game's scoring with a 22-yard run in the first quarter.[13]

14. Dec. 14: The last time the Baltimore Ravens met the Raiders, it was for the AFC championship in January of 2001. The Ravens were still playing solid football, and came into Oakland with an 8–5 record, a three-game winning streak, and holding a one game lead in the AFC North Division. Once again winning a game they should not have, the Raiders shocked the Ravens, 20–12. A Phillip Buchanon interception sparked the Raiders, and the team capitalized on it when Zack Crockett scored on a 1-yard run on Oakland's opening drive, and the Silver and Black never looked back in a game controlled by tough defense, penalties and numerous errors. Also scoring for the Raiders were Sebastian Janikowski (37 and 23 yard field goals), and Jerry Rice on a 21-yard pass from Rick Mirer.[14]

15. Dec. 22: The Green Bay Packers stood at 8–6 and tied with Minnesota for first place in the NFC North as they came into Oakland for a Monday Night Football matchup. Packer quarterback Brett Favre came into this game with 341 touchdown passes, and needing two to overtake Fran Tarkenton for second place on the all-time list. He also brought a heavy heart with him, as his father passed away the night before. With his father as his inspiration, Favre obliterated the Raiders for 311 yards and four touchdown passes in the first half alone, and finished with 399 yards in a 41–7 blowout win. The closest Oakland got to making a game of it was when they trailed, 14–7, in the first quarter. Their lone score came on a Charlie Garner 25-yard run.[15]

16. Dec. 28: The season of despair finally came to an end for the Silver and Black against the 3–12 San Diego Chargers. Coming into this game, San Diego's great running back La-Dainian Tomlinson ran for 397 yards and two touchdowns in his last three meetings with the Raiders. This time around, Tomlinson continued his brilliance against Oakland, as he ran for a career-high 243 yards on 31 carries and scored twice in a 21–14 victory. The Raiders were without defensive back Charles Woodson and running back Charlie Garner due to each of them violating team policies. The Raiders got their final points of the dismal season thanks to great efforts on special teams from Phillip Buchanon (80-yard punt return) and Doug Gabriel (85-yard kickoff return). The loss tied Oakland with San Diego for last place in the AFC West with the league's worst 4–12 records. Two days following the finale, Bill Callahan was fired.[16]

Individual Statistics and Roster

Head Coach: Bill Callahan

Assistant Coaches: Tim Adams, Fred Biletnikoff, Chuck Bresnahan, Willie Brown, Bob Casullo, Garrett Giemont, Chris Griswold, Jim Harbaugh, Aaron Kromer, Ron Lynn, Don Martin, John Morton, Jay Norvell, Fred Pagac, Skip Peete, Marc Trestman, Chris Turner, Mike Waufle

2003 Regular Season Record: 4–12

3rd Place in AFC Western Division

Scored 270 points to rank 26th out of 32 teams

Allowed 379 points to rank 25th

STARTERS — OFFENSE

QB — Rick Mirer: Active for 9 games and started in 8. Completed 116 of 221 pass attempts for 1,267 yards, 3 TD and 5 INT. Rushed for 83 yards on 20 carries and 1 TD.

RB — Charlie Garner: Active for 14 games and started in 9. Rushed for 553 yards on 1120 carries and 3 TD. Had 48 receptions for 386 yards and 1 TD.

RB — Zack Crockett: Active for 16 games and started in 7. Rushed for 145 yards on 48 carries and 7 TD. Had 7 receptions for 53 yards.

WR — Tim Brown: Active for 16 games and started in 15. Had 52 receptions for 567 yards and 2 TD.

WR — Jerry Rice: Active for 16 games and started in 15. Had 63 receptions for 869 yards and 2 TD, and 1 pass attempt for 0 yards.

TE — Doug Jolley: Active for 15 games and started in 9. Had 31 receptions for 250 yards and 1 TD.

LT — Barry Sims: Started in 16 games.

LG — Brad Badger: Active for 16 games and started in 11.

C — Barret Robbins: Active for and started in 9 games.

RG — Mo Collins: Active for and started in 10 games.

RT — Lincoln Kennedy: Active for 12 games and started in 10.

RESERVE OFFENSIVE PLAYERS

Ronald Curry (WR): Active for 16 games and started in 2. Had 5 receptions for 31 yards and rushed for 0 yards on 1 carry.

Justin Fargas (RB): Active for 10 games and started in 1. Rushed for 203 yards on 40 carries, had 2 receptions for 2 yards, and returned 16 kick-offs for 315 yards.

Doug Gabriel (WR): Active for 12 games. Had 1 reception for 17 yards, and returned 29 kickoffs for 646 yards and 1 TD.

Rich Gannon (QB): Active for and started in 7 games. Completed 125 of 225 pass attempts for 1,274 yards, 6 TD, and 4 INT. Rushed for 18 yards on 6 carries.

Chris Hetherington (RB): Active for 14 games and started in 1. Had 2 receptions for 23 yards.

Corey Hulsey (G/T): Active for 4 games.

Ronney Jenkins (RB): Active for 7 games. Returned 25 kickoffs for 553 yards.

Rob Johnson (QB): Active for 2 games. Completed 6 of 13 pass attempts for 54 yards and 1 INT. Rushed for 15 yards on 2 carries.

Teyo Johnson (TE): Active for 16 games and started in 5. Had 14 receptions for 128 yards and 1 TD.

Tee Martin (QB): Active for 2 games. Completed 6 of 16 pass attempts for 69 yards and 1 INT. Rushed for 28 yards on 5 carries.

Frank Middleton (G): Active for 10 games and started in 8.

Jerry Porter (WR): Active for 10 games and started in 1. Had 28 receptions for 361 yards and 1 TD. Rushed for 10 yards on 1 carry.

J.R. Redmond (RB): Active for 1 game, rushed for 30 yards on 9 carries, and had 1 reception for 6 yards.

O.J. Santiago (TE): Active for 12 games and started in 7. Had 5 receptions for 69 yards, and returned 1 kickoff for 9 yards.

Chad Slaughter (T): Active for 6 games and started in 1.

Matt Stinchcomb (G/T): Active for 6 games and started in 4.

John Stone (WR): Active for 1 game.

Adam Treu (C): Active for 16 games and started in 4.

Marques Tuiasosopo (QB): Active for 4 games and started in 1. Completed 25 of 45 pass attempts for 324 yards and 3 INT. Rushed for 22 yards on 6 carries.

Langston Walker (T/G): Active for 16 games and started in 8.

Tyrone Wheatley (RB): Active for 15 games and started in 5. Rushed for 678 yards on 159 carries and 4 TD. Had 12 receptions for 120 yards.

Alvis Whitted (WR): Active for 16 games and started in 2. Rushed for 37 yards on 6 carries, had 7 receptions for 106 yards and 1 TD, and returned 4 kickoffs for 48 yards.

Joe Wong (G): Active for 2 games.

STARTERS — DEFENSE

DE — Trace Armstrong: Active for 10 games, started in 7, and had 3 sacks.

DE — Tyler Brayton: Started in 16 games, had 2 sacks and 1 fumble recovery.

DT — Chris Cooper: Active for 16 games, started in 9, had 2 sacks and 3 fumble recoveries.

DT — Roderick Coleman: Active for 16 games, started in 12, had 5 sacks and 1 fumble recovery.

LLB — Travian Smith: Active for 10 games, started in 7 and had 1 sack.

MLB — Napoleon Harris: Started in 16 games and had 2 sacks.

RLB — Eric Barton: Started in 16 games and had sack.

CB — Charles Woodson: Active for and started in 15 games. Had 1 sack, 3 INT, and 1 fumble recovery.

CB — Phillip Buchanon: Active for 16 games and started in 10. Had 6 INT, 2 TD, 2 fumble recoveries, returned 36 punts for 491 yards and 2 TD, and had 2 kickoff returns for 25 yards.

SS — Derrick Gibson: Active for 15 games, started in 14, had 1 sack and 2 INT.

FS — Rod Woodson: Active for and started in 10 games. Had 2 INT and 1 fumble recovery.

RESERVE DEFENSIVE PLAYERS

Nnamdi Asomugha (DB): Active for 15 games, started in 1, and had 1 fumble recovery.

Larry Atkins (LB): Active for 3 games.

Lorenzo Bromell (E): Active for 6 games, started in 4, and had 2 sacks.

Anthony Dorsett (DB): Active for 16 games, started in 6, had 1 fumble recovery, and returned 1 punt for 0 yards.

Akbar Gbaja-Biamila (E): Active for 13 games and had 1 sack.

Sean Gilbert (T/E): Active for 6 games.

DeLawrence Grant (E/LB): Active for 13 games, started in 4, and had 1 sack.

Grant Irons (E): Active for 1 game.

Eric Johnson (DB/LB): Active for 16 games, started in 2, had 1 INT and returned 1 punt for 1 yard.

Tim Johnson (LB): Active for 12 games and started in 4.

Clarence Love (DB): Active for 13 games.

John Parrella (T): Active for and started in 5 games.

Shurron Pierson (E/LB): Active for 6 games.

Bill Romanowski (LB): Active for and started in 3 games, and had 2 sacks.

Terdell Sands (T): Active for 3 games and started in 1.

Carey Scott (DB): Active for 5 games.

Siddeeq Shabazz (DB): Active for 4 games.

Terrance Shaw (DB): Active for 16 games and started in 8.

Dana Stubblefield (T): active for 8 games, started in 6, and had 1 fumble recovery.

Sam Williams (E): Active for 1 game.

KICKING/PUNTING

K — Sebastian Janikowski: Active for 16 games. Made 22 of 25 field goals and 28 of 29 extra points for 94 points.

P — Shane Lechler: Active for 16 games. Punted 96 times for a **46.9** average. **Also led the NFL in yards punted (4,503).**

2004 Season Review

1. Sept. 12: The Raiders opened their 45th season with new head coach and a meeting with a nemesis from thirty years earlier, the Pittsburgh Steelers. In a game reminiscent of their 1970's confrontations, the Steelers won by a close 24–21 final. Pittsburgh used a hard-charging running attack, coupled with defense built on pressuring the opposition, to gain a 14–0 lead on Oakland. The Raiders came back to tie the game at 21–21 with 4:51 remaining. Rich Gannon led the charge by passing for 305 yards and two touchdowns to Doug Gabriel (58 yards) and Alvis Whitted (38 yards). The Raiders tied it up with Whitted catching a two-point conversion pass from Gannon. Sebastian Janikowski added two field goals from 28 and 38 yards out. The Raiders great comeback was nullified when Pittsburgh kicker Jeff Reed split the uprights from 42 yards away with seven seconds remaining for a 24–21 victory.[1]

2. Sept. 19: Norv Turner's home debut as head coach ended well team-wise, as the Raiders beat the Buffalo Bills, 13–10. On an individual basis, Jerry Rice saw his NFL–record 274 games with a catch streak come to an end. Instead, it was second-year man Ronald Curry who rose to the forefront over the soon-to-be 42-year-old receiving marvel. The Raiders looked to rely less on Rice and wanted to bring some of the young receivers into the fold more often. Curry responded with a game-high five receptions for 89 yards, and caught a 43-yard touchdown pass from Rich Gannon to opening the scoring. Sebastian Janikowski provided Oakland with their other points on field goals from 21 and 33 yards out.[2]

3. Sept. 26: The Raiders next played host to Tampa Bay and former coach Jon Gruden and receiving legend Tim Brown on a Sunday night prime time matchup. This was the first meeting between these two teams since Tampa Bay's beat down over Oakland in the Super Bowl. This was also a game that saw the two oldest teams take the field. The Bucs were the oldest in the league with an average age of 27.8, while the Raiders had the oldest in the AFC at 27.3. In the end, it was the Raiders who prevailed, 30–20, to improve to 2–1, while the Bucs remained winless at 0–3. Quarterback Rich Gannon suffered a severe injury when he broke a vertebra in his neck, which eventually led to his retirement. Backup Kerry Collins assumed the leadership role, and led the Silver and Black on four scoring drives while completing 16 of 27 pass attempts for 288 yards and one touchdown to Ronald Curry from 19 yards out. Phillip Buchanon scored on a 32-yard interception return, Tyrone Wheatley a 2-yard run, and Sebastian Janikowski added three field goals from 23, 40, and 39 yards, to give Oakland the ten-point advantage in the end. Tim Brown also provided some emotion upon his return to Raider Nation when he caught his 100th career touchdown pass in the fourth quarter.[3]

4. Oct. 3: Houston's Reliant Stadium and a date with the Texans provided the setting for the Oakland debut of Kerry Collins as the team's starting signal caller. By the end of this game, the Raiders earned the dubious honor of being the team that

allowed Houston to put together their first winning streak in franchise history. After 36 games, the Texans won back-to-back games by beating Oakland, 30–17. Despite an impressive day statistics-wise, Collins provided the Texans with 13 of their points on turnovers. He hit on 21 of 38 passes for 237 yards, but threw three interceptions. One bright spot for the Raiders was the running of Amos Zereoue, who ran for 117 yards on 14 carries and two touchdowns (55 and 3-yard runs). A 50-yard field goal by Sebastian Janikowski gave Oakland their other points.[4]

5. Oct. 10: The Raiders looked to attack an Indianapolis secondary depleted by injuries and ranked last in pass defense. The only thing was that the Colts had star quarterback Peyton Manning and running back Edgerrin James. Manning was leading the league with 11 touchdown passes, and ranked number one in the AFC with 1,123 passing yards. The Colts utilized both their offensive assets to compensate for the banged up defensive backfield, and beat the Raiders, 35–14, for the team's first home win against the Silver and Black since the 1970 AFC Championship Game when they were in Baltimore. Manning threw for 198 yards and three touchdowns, while James tore through the Raiders defense for 136 yards and a score. Oakland tried to attack the league's last place secondary, as Kerry Collins threw for 245 yards on 28 of 44 attempts and one touchdown to 6'6" tight end Courtney Anderson from 21 yards out. However, Collins also threw three interceptions, one of which was returned for a score. Ronald Curry caught a game-high 10 passes for 72 yards, and Justin Fargas scored Oakland's other touchdown on a 1-yard run. This was the Colts fourth straight win, and the Raiders sank to 2–3 with the loss.[5]

6. Oct. 17: The Denver Broncos came into Oakland with a 4–1 record and left with another victory, as they dominated the Raiders, 31–3. Quarterback Jake Plummer threw three touchdown passes, and Reuben Droughns ran for 176 yards and a score. The Raiders got on the scoreboard first thanks to a 35-yard field goal from Sebastian Janikowski, but that was all the excitement the Raiders could muster in this miserable defeat that saw the team produce only 145 yards of total offense.[6]

7. Oct. 24: A showdown between two 2–4 teams was what occurred in Oakland, and the New Orleans Saints improved while the Raiders continued to spiral downward after a 31–26 loss. The Saints snapped a three-game losing streak thanks to two touchdown runs from Deuce McAllister, nine receptions for 123 yards from Joe Horn, and the passing of Aaron Brooks, who threw for 282 yards and one touchdown. Kerry Collins managed to have a good day after struggling the past few weeks. He threw for 350 yards and two touchdowns to Doug Jolley (34 yards) and Jerry Porter (13 yards). Sebastian Janikowski also had a big day despite the outcome, as he nailed four field goals from 28, 42, 44, and 40 yards.[7]

8. Oct. 31: LaDainian Tomlinson was the most potent offensive weapon in football at this time, especially when it came to suiting up against the Silver and Black. It was then that he became a human highlight reel, as he exploded for 640 rushing yards in his last four games against Oakland. However, on this day, Tomlinson only gained 71 yards on 19 carries, but the Chargers still won quite easily, 42–14. San Diego quarterback Drew Brees led the Lighting Bolts on this day, playing an almost near-perfect game. He completed 22 of 25 pass attempts for 281 yards and five touchdowns to set a team record for passing efficiency. Kerry

Collins seemed to be improving statistics-wise, as he hit on 24 of 39 passes for 263 yards and a touchdown to Doug Jolley (13 yards), but he also threw two interceptions. Tyrone Wheatley supplied the Raiders with their other six-pointer on a 5-yard run.[8]

9. Nov. 7: The Raiders came into their game with the defending NFC champion Carolina Panthers on a five-game losing streak, and 13 straight losses on the road. The Panthers were having problems of their own getting in the win column after a great '03 season. They were 1–6, and seemed to be the team Oakland needed to face to have a reversal of fortune. The Panthers did indeed provide the perfect fodder for the Silver and Black, who snapped both of their negative streaks to the tune of a 27–24 victory. Tyrone Wheatley ran for two 1-yard touchdowns, and Amos Zereoue chipped in with a 7-yarder to pace the offensive attack. Kerry Collins, who led the Panthers in their early existence, threw for 231 yards on 20 completions out of 32 attempts, and Sebastian Janikowski added two field goals from 26 and 19 yards. His 19-yarder proved to be the game-winner after a 38-yard pass interference penalty placed the ball on the Carolina four. Three plays later, with six seconds remaining in regulation, "Sea Bass" exonerated the demons that seemed to be engulfing the Silver and Black.[9]

10. Nov. 21: Coming off their bye week after a win, the rested Raiders made it close, but still fell short, this time by a 23–17 final against San Diego. The Chargers got offensive jolts from LaDainian Tomlinson's 164 rushing yards, Antonio Gates' eight receptions for 101 yards, and Drew Brees' 226 passing yards. They each scored a touchdown as well. The win helped keep San Diego tied with the Denver Broncos atop the AFC West, while the Raiders sank to last place in the division at 3–7. Oakland got a good performance out of Kerry Collins, who connected on 18 out of 30 passes for 227 yards and two touchdowns. Ronald Curry (22 yards) and Teyo Johnson (8 yards), hauled in the scoring tosses. Sebastian Janikowski added Oakland's other points on a 31-yard field goal.[10]

11. Nov. 28: Things did not get any easier for the Raiders, as they had to face the other team tied for first place in the AFC West. However, it seemed that the mountain air of Denver did the Raiders some good, as they shocked the Broncos in a squeaker, 25–24. With snow providing a winter wonderland, Kerry Collins supplied some early holiday joy for Raider Nation by throwing for 339 yards and four touchdowns. Jerry Porter and Ronald Curry came up with huge days catching Collins' aerials. Porter hauled in six for 135 yards and three touchdowns (42, 14, and 5), while Curry snagged six for 110 and a score from six yards out. Porter's 5-yard score came on fourth-and-goal with the Raiders trailing, 24–19, and only 1:49 left on the clock. The Broncos had a chance at the end, as Jake Plummer took the team 49 yards down to the Oakland 25. Jason Elam came on to attempt what would have been the game-winner, but Langston Walker blocked it to preserve the win.[11]

12. Dec. 5: An Oakland–Kansas City game used to mean a battle for division supremacy, but at this stage of the 2004 season, it meant staying out of the AFC West cellar. In another classic struggle between these two once proud combatants, the Chiefs won for the 46th time in this series, 34–27.

Kansas City quarterback Trent Green played this game with sore ribs, but still found a way to rip the Oakland defense for 340 yards, and connected with Eddie Kennison on a 70-yard touchdown pass with 2:04 left to provide the game-winner. In this heart-breaking loss, Kerry Collins did a great job by throwing for 343 yards and three touchdowns. Ronald Curry caught nine passes for 141 yards and touchdown receptions of 34 and 26 yards. Jerry Porter caught Collins' other touchdown pass from 51 yards, and Sebastian Janikowski kicked two field goals (27 and 36 yards).[12]

13. Dec. 12: The Atlanta Falcons were on the verge of clinching the NFC South Division, and could do it in the Georgia Dome against the Raiders. After spotting Oakland an early 3–0 lead on a Sebastian Janikowski 52-yard field goal, the Falcons exploded for three touchdowns, and never looked back in a 35–10 blow out victory. Warrick Dunn ran for 103 yards, and T.J. Duckett scored four rushing touchdowns to set a single-game team record. Oakland lost two fumbles and had an interception returned for a score by former Raider Rod Coleman. With Atlanta well ahead, Zack Crockett scored Oakland's lone six-pointer on a 1-yard run in the fourth quarter.[13]

14. Dec. 19: Two years earlier, the Raiders and Tennessee Titans were among the NFL's elite. Now, each was looking to get the season over with, as both teams came into this game with 4–9 records. Oakland had one of the worst running games, and a pass rush that ranked last in the league with 17 sacks. Still, they somehow found a way to defeat the Titans for the 26th time in the history of the series. In a high-scoring game reminiscent of the old free wheeling AFL days, the Silver and Black won, 40–35. Kerry Collins threw for 371 yards and equaled a career high five touchdown passes. His counterpart, Billy Volek, passed for 492 yards and four scores. Jerry Porter caught eight passes for 148 yards and three touchdowns from 32, 18 and 3 yards. Teyo Johnson caught a touchdown pass from 18 yards and Doug Gabriel from 45. Oakland added a Sebastian Janikowski 42-yard field goal and a safety to close out their point explosion.[14]

15. Dec. 25: A Christmas Day matchup with Kansas City produced another tight contest that went down to the wire. The Raiders held a 30–28 lead with 1:03 left in the game after Sebastian Janikowski connected on a 46-yard field goal. He also had two other long-distance three-pointers from 40 and 45 yards. On the ensuing kickoff following Oakland's go-ahead field goal, Janikowski sent a squib kick into a sea of Kansas City special teamers. Exciting return man Dante Hall took the kick and ran it back to the Oakland 36 before Janikowski stopped him. With 22 seconds left, Lawrence Tynes kicked a 38-yard field goal to give the Chiefs a big dose of holiday joy with a 31–30 win. Jerry Porter (5 yards), and Alvis Whitted (32 yards), both caught touchdown passes from Kerry Collins, and Zack Crockett scored on a 3-yard run in the heart-breaking loss.[15]

16. Jan. 2: The Raiders hosted the 8–7 Jacksonville Jaguars in the regular season finale. On a muddy field, Jacksonville won, 13–6. The Raiders had an opportunity to send the game into overtime in the closing seconds, but Kerry Collins coughed up the ball on fourth-and-goal from the 2-yard line. He managed to regain possession, but was tackled for a loss of yardage. Collins, who at times looked good throughout the year, finished the '04 campaign on a sour note. He threw three interceptions and fumbled once. Sebastian Janikowski managed to prevent a shutout by hitting on two field goals from 35 and 27 yards. The Raiders

got a great performance from Zack Crockett, who bolted across the muddy turf for 134 rushing yards on 22 carries.[16]

Individual Statistics and Roster

Head Coach: Norv Turner
Assistant Coaches: Joe Avezzano, Martin Bayless, Fred Biletnikoff, Willie Brown, Sam Clancy, Jeff Fish, Chris Griswold, Pat Jones, Aaron Kromer, Clayton Lopez, Don Martindale, John Morton, Fred Pagac, Skip Peete, Jimmy Raye, Rob Ryan, Steve Sarkisian, Chris Turner
2004 Regular Season Record: 5–11
4th Place in AFC Western Division
Scored 320 points to rank 18th out of 32 teams
Allowed 442 points to rank 31st

STARTERS — OFFENSE

QB — Kerry Collins: Active for 14 games and started in 13. Completed 289 of 513 pass attempts for 3,495 yards, 21 TD and 20 INT. **Led the NFL in pass attempts per game (36.6).** Rushed for 36 yards on 16 carries.
RB — Tyrone Wheatley: Active for 8 games and started in 7. Rushed for 327 yards on 85 carries and 4 TD. Had 15 receptions for 78 yards.
RB — Zack Crockett: Active for 16 games and started in 9. Rushed for 232 yards on 48 carries and 2 TD. Had 16 receptions for 87 yards.
WR — Doug Gabriel: Active for 16 games and started in 5. Had 33 receptions for 551 yards and 2 TD. Rushed for 7 yards on 2 carries, returned 2 punts for 7 yards, and returned 53 kickoffs for 1,140 yards.
WR — Jerry Porter: Started in 16 games. Had 64 receptions for 998 yards and 9 TD. Rushed for 4 yards on 1 carry, and returned 1 kickoff for 6 yards.
TE — Doug Jolley: Active for 16 games and started in 13. Had 27 receptions for 313 yards and 2 TD.
LT — Barry Sims: Started in 16 games.
LG — Brad Badger: Active for 16 games and started in 12.
C — Adam Treu: Started in 16 games.
RG — Jake Grove: Active for 9 games and started in 8.
RT — Robert Gallery: Active for 16 games and started in 15.

RESERVE OFFENSIVE PLAYERS

Courtney Anderson (TE): Active for 9 games and started in 4. Had 13 receptions for 175 yards and 1 TD.
Ronald Curry (WR): Active for 12 games and started in 3. Had 50 receptions for 679 yards and 6 TD, 3 yards on 1 rush, 1 pass attempt, and 4 kickoff returns for 63 yards.
Justin Fargas (RB): Active for 12 games. Rushed for 126 yards on 35 carries and 1 TD. Had 11 receptions for 68 yards.
Carlos Francis (WR): Active for 5 games, and had 14 kickoff returns for 259 yards.
Rich Gannon (QB): Active for and started in 3 games. Completed 41 of 68 pass attempts for 524 yards, 3 TD and 2 INT. Rushed for 26 yards on 5 carries.
Chris Hetherington (RB): Active for 5 games and started in 2. Rushed for 4 yards on 1 carry, had 3 receptions for 28 yards, and 1 kickoff return for 23 yards.
Corey Hulsey (G/T): Active for 3 games.
Teyo Johnson (TE): Active for 8 games, started in 1, and had 9 receptions for 131 yards and 2 TD.
Frank Middleton (G): Active for and started in 7 games.
Johnnie Morant (WR): Active for 4 games, and had 1 reception for 20 yards.
J.R. Redmond (RB): Active for 16 games and started in 1. Rushed for 119 yards on 21 carries, had 32 receptions for 233 yards, and 8 kickoff returns for 153 yards.
Jerry Rice (WR): Active for 6 games, started in 5, and had 5 receptions for 67 yards.

Chad Slaughter (T): Active for 10 games.

John Stone (G): Active for 4 games, had 3 receptions for 80 yards, and 1 kickoff return for 20 yards.

Langston Walker (T/G): Active for 16 games and started in 1.

Alvis Whitted (WR): Active for 11 games, started in 5, had 9 receptions for 327 yards and 2 TD, and returned 1 kickoff 36 yards.

Roland Williams (TE): Active for 12 games and started in 3.

Amos Zereoue (RB): Active for 15 games and started in 6. Rushed for 425 yards on 112 carries and 3 TD. Had 39 receptions for 284 yards.

STARTERS — DEFENSE

DE — Tyler Brayton: Active for and started in 15 games, had 2 sacks and 1 INT.

DE — Bobby Hamilton: Active for 16 games, started in 15, and had 1 sack.

DT — Ted Washington: Started in 16 games and had 3 sacks.

DT — Warren Sapp: Started in 16 games, had 2 sacks and 2 fumble recoveries.

LLB — DeLawrence Grant: Active for and started in 9 games, and had 2 sacks.

MLB — Danny Clark: Started in 16 games and had 2 sacks.

RLB — Napoleon Harris: Active for 14 games and started in 9.

CB — Phillip Buchanon: Active for and started in 14 games. Had 3 INT, 1 TD, 2 fumble recoveries, and returned 21 punts for 121 yards.

CB — Charles Woodson: Active for 13 games and started in 12. Had 2 sacks, 1 INT, 1 fumble recovery, and 1 punt return for 4 yards.

SS — Marques Anderson: Active for 14 games, started in 10, had 1 INT and 2 fumble recoveries.

FS — Ray Buchanan: Started in 16 games and had 1 INT.

RESERVE DEFENSIVE PLAYERS

Nnamdi Asomugha (DB): Active for 16 games, started in 7, and had 1 sack.

Jarrod Cooper (DB): Active for 9 games, had 1 sack and 1 fumble recovery.

Akbar Gbaja-Biamila (E): Active for 14 games and had 1 sack.

Grant Irons (E): Active for 8 games, started in 2 and had 1 sack.

Tim Johnson (LB): Active for 16 games, had sack and 1 INT.

Tommy Kelly (E/T): Active for 10 games, started in 3, had 4 sacks and 1 fumble recovery.

Keyon Nash (DB): Active for 2 games.

John Parrella (T): Active for 16 games.

Terdell Sands (T): Active for 15 games.

Stuart Schweigert (DB): Active for 16 games and started in 3.

Travian Smith (LB): Active for 8 games, started in 4 and had 1 fumble recovery.

David Terrell (DB): Active for 16 games.

Maugaula Tuitele (LB): Active for 1 game.

Denard Walker (DB): Active for 16 games, started in 4, had 1 INT and 1 fumble recovery.

Brock Williams (DB): Active for 2 games.

Sam Williams (E): Active for 9 games and started in 4.

KICKING/PUNTING

K — Sebastian Janikowski: Active for 16 games. Made 25 of 28 field goals and 31 of 32 extra points for 106 points.

P — Shane Lechler: Active for 16 games. Punted 73 times for a **46.7** average.

2005 Season Review

1. Sept. 8: The 86th NFL season kicked off with the New England Patriots looking to become the first team to win three

An Oakland Raiderette performs during a game on August 26, 2005, at McAfee Coliseum in Oakland, California (AP Photo/ Paul Spinelli).

straight Super Bowls, and the Oakland Raiders providing the first challenge in their path to a three-peat. The Silver and Black hung tough in the first half, trailing, 17–14. Kerry Collins connected with Courtney Anderson from two yards out to open the scoring on the game's first series, and later wide receiver Randy Moss began the Oakland chapter of his career by hauling in an incredible 73-yarder from Collins. The second half was a different story, as the defending champion Patriots tighten up on defense, and shut the Raiders out until Collins and Anderson teamed up again, this time from five yards out, with 3:04 remaining in the fourth quarter. New England got 306 yards passing and two touchdowns tosses from Tom Brady, and went on to win, 30–20, for the 35th time in their last 39 games.[1]

2. Sept. 18: After a ten-day layoff, the Raiders were ready to play in a second straight prime time affair by hosting rival Kansas City. In another classic matchup in this storied series, the Chiefs stopped the Raiders ten yards short of a touchdown with under a minute to play, and won for the fifth straight time over Oakland, 23–17. A Samie Parker fumble allowed the Raiders one

final chance at victory. Kerry Collins drove Oakland to the Kansas City 10 with 1:58 remaining. Facing a fourth down situation, Collins looked to Jerry Porter in the end zone. It was a high pass that Porter jumped for, and as he got his fingertips on it, defender Benny Sapp swatted the ball away to preserve the victory. The Raiders received their points on a LaMont Jordan 1-yard run, a 64-yard pass from Collins to Randy Moss, and a Sebastian Janikowski 29-yard field goal.[2]

3. Sept. 25: Philadelphia kicker David Akers was in severe pain due to badly strained hamstring muscle, but managed to rise above it and split the uprights with a game-winning 23-yard field goal in the final nine seconds to give the Eagles a 23–20 win and put the Raiders at 0–3 for the first time since 1992. Philadelphia quarterback Donovan McNabb was also in pain due to abdomen, chest, and groin injuries, but he fought through them to pass for 365 yards and two touchdowns. The Raiders gave it everything they had, and hung with the defending NFC champs until the very end. LaMont Jordan opened the scoring with an 8-yard pass from Kerry Collins, and Sebastian Janikowski extended the Raiders lead to 10–6 at the half with a 28-yard field goal in the final minute of the second quarter. Philly battled back on McNabb's two scoring strikes, one in which Terrell Owens caught the 100th touchdown pass of his career. In the fourth quarter, Janikowski added a 26-yard three-pointer, and Collins threw a 27-yard pass to Doug Gabriel that tied the game at 20–20 with 2:17 left in regulation. Collins finished the game with 345 yards through the air, and Randy Moss caught five passes for 86 yards.[3]

4. Oct. 2: Since gong to the Super Bowl three years earlier, the Silver and Black had posted a more-than-dismal 9–26 record, and looked to turn things around at home against "America's Team," the Dallas Cowboys. With LaMont Jordan leading the ground attack with 126 yards, Randy Moss the receiving corps with four catches for 123 yards, and Sebastian Janikowski splitting the uprights four times, the Raiders shook off the demons, and won for the first time in '05 by a 19–13 count going into their bye week. The defense also did their part by holding off a late Dallas surge just shy of the goal line. Jordan scored on a 2-yard run, and Janikowski provided the Raiders with the remainder of their points on field goals from 30, 23, 49, and 43 yards.[4]

5. Oct. 16: San Diego's Marty Schottenheimer had the most wins against the Raiders as a head coach with 23 going into this game. He continued his mastery over the Silver and Black with a 27–14 victory. The Raiders were able to hang tough in all their first four games, but they were totally out of it against the Chargers, who beat them for the fourth straight time for the first time since the early 1960's. Oakland lost Randy Moss early in the game with bruised ribs and a groin injury, Kerry Collins threw his first pick of the year, the defense helped keep San Diego drives going by committing penalties, and the ground game could only muster up 39 yards. Oakland received both their touchdowns from LaMont Jordan (7 and 1-yard runs).[5]

6. Oct. 23: The Raiders rebounded in fine fashion with a 38–17 beat down over the Buffalo Bills to give them their first game scoring more than 20 points up to this stage of the '05 campaign. LaMont Jordan churned out 122 yards on the ground, and had a career-high three scoring runs from 1, 17, and 7-yards out, while Doug Gabriel led all receivers with five receptions for 101 yards. Randy Moss, still nursing his injuries, caught a 22-yard

scoring toss from Kerry Collins, Zach Crockett ran for a 2-yard touchdown, and Sebastian Janikowski added a 25-yard field goal in the impressive win. Kerry Collins also shined on this great day as he hit on 19 of 27 attempts for 261 yards.[6]

7. Oct. 30: Usually a penalty flag thrown in a Raiders game meant some type of infraction against the silver and black-clad renegades. This time, however, it did not hamper the Raiders but helped them overcome the Tennessee Titans, 34–25, for their second straight win, and third in the last four. With the Titans looking to take their first lead of the game in the second quarter, Adam "Pacman" Jones raced 82 yards on a punt return, but Tennessee's Tank Williams was called for unnecessary roughness, and the play was ruled null and void. Three plays later, Warren Sapp shook off blockers and dropped quarterback Steve McNair, who fumbled in the process. The loose pigskin was scooped up by Jarrod Cooper in the end zone to extend the Oakland advantage to 24–12 at that time. Jerry Porter had a huge day catching Kerry Collins passes, as he hauled in six for 123 yards and two scores from 26 and 44 yards. Collins, who completed 17 of 29 attempts for 238 yards, added another touchdown toss to his day's work when he connected with LaMont Jordan from 18 yards out. Sebastian Janikowski gave the Raiders their other scores on two field goals (22 and 32 yards).[7]

8. Nov. 6: The Silver and Black appeared to be back, and getting close to reaching the .500 mark, and looked to climb out of the AFC cellar against their long-time rivals, the Chiefs of Kansas City. With Kerry Collins throwing touchdown passes to Jerry Porter (4 yards) and Randy Moss (7 yards), and Sebastian Janikowski kicking field goals from 32, 49, and 48 yards, the Raiders held a 23–20 lead going into the final seconds of the game. It was at this time that Oakland suffered another heartbreaker. With only five ticks left on the game clock, the Chiefs had the ball on the Oakland 1-yard line. Long-time NFL coach Dick Vermeil took a chance. Instead of going for the tie to force overtime, Vermeil decided to go for broke. He called a running play, and sent Larry Johnson into the line. Johnson dove for the promise land, and crossed over into the Oakland end zone for another classic finish to this long-standing series. This was the Chiefs' sixth straight win over the Raiders, who remained in the AFC West basement with a 3–5 record.[8]

9. Nov. 13: Kerry Collins suffered his worst performance of the '05 season by throwing three interceptions and getting sacked four times despite passing for two scores and 310 yards in a 31–17 loss to Denver. All Oakland's points came in the fourth quarter when Collins threw to Randy Moss (29 yards), and Doug Gabriel (14 yards), and Sebastian Janikowski kicked a 40-yard field goal.[9]

10. Nov. 20: Oakland coach Norv Turner returned to Washington, where he coached the Redskins for seven seasons, and his new team managed to get him a 16–13 win. Kerry Collins threw for 289 yards, and connected with Jerry Porter from 49 yards out for Oakland's lone touchdown. Sebastian Janikowski provided the other points on field goals from 30, 25, and 19 yards. His 19-yarder with 1:08 left in regulation gave the Raiders their fourth win of the season and snapped a two-game slide.[10]

11. Nov. 27: It was time for another losing streak to end, but unfortunately it happened against the Raiders. Jason Taylor and Vonnie Holliday led the defensive charge with three sacks

apiece, and quarterback Gus Frerotte threw for 261 yards and two scores, as the Miami Dolphins won, 33–21. The Dolphins had not given up 300 yards passing in 40 games going into this one with the Raiders, and the streak continued, as they allowed Kerry Collins 226 yards, while sacking him seven times, once for a safety, and picked him off on three occasions. Collins did manage to run for an 18-yard touchdown, and LaMont Jordan added two from one and eight yards out for Oakland's point production on a day that saw them slip to 4–7 and firmly entrenched as AFC West cellar dwellers. On an individual basis, Jordan was standing out for the Raiders, as he was the only NFL player with 700 or more yards rushing and over 400 yards receiving.[11]

12. Dec. 4: It was quickly becoming obvious that San Diego loved playing the Raiders, as they once again pounded them, this time in a 34–10 decision. Drew Brees tossed two touchdown passes in the Chargers' fifth straight win over Oakland. The Raiders put their ten points on the board compliments of a 16-yard pass from Kerry Collins to Courtney Anderson, and a 37-yard field goal from Sebastian Janikowski.[12]

13. Dec. 11: This game featured a rematch between two old AFL powerhouses from the late 1960's. However, nearly forty years had passed since a New York Jets — Oakland Raiders game held a national audience captive. Both teams came into this game firmly resting in last place in their respective divisions, with the Jets at 2–10, and the Raiders at 4–8. Even if they combined their wins, they would still have been three games behind the AFC West–leading Denver Broncos. Regardless, the show had to go on, and someone more than likely had to win. In this case, it was the Jets who won the battle of the basements, 26–10. To make matters worse for the Silver and Black was the fact that New York beat them convincingly with a backup running back (Cedric Houston), and a third-string quarterback (Brooks Bollinger). Houston ran for a game-high 74 yards and one score, while Bollinger threw a touchdown pass to help break a seven-game losing streak. The hapless Raiders managed to get ten points on a 20-yard pass from Marques Tuiasosopo to Jerry Porter, and a 42-yard field goal from Sebastian Janikowski.[13]

14. Dec. 18: On a wet and windy day in Oakland, the football performance of both the Raiders and Cleveland Browns resembled the weather conditions, pure ugliness. The Raiders led throughout the game on a 28-yard pass from Kerry Collins to Randy Moss. However, as time expired, Cleveland kicker Phil Dawson sent a 37-yard field goal attempt into the Black Hole of McAfee Coliseum to pull out a 9–7 win. The only bright spot for the Raiders on this day was the running of LaMont Jordan, who gained 132 yards on 25 carries.[14]

15. Dec. 24: 'Twas the day before Christmas, and all the Raiders could produce was a fourth quarter 43-yard field goal by Sebastian Janikowski to prevent Oakland from getting shut out in a 22–3 loss to Denver. On the other side of the field, the Broncos received a nice holiday gift by being crowned 2005 AFC Western Division champs.[15]

16. Dec. 31: The Raiders were definitely in the holiday spirit of giving, as they gave the New York Giants a division title by losing, 30–21, on New Year's Eve. With Tiki Barber running for a whopping 203 yards, which included a 95-yard jaunt to open the scoring, and Plaxico Burress catching five passes for 128 yards and a touchdown, the Giants won the NFC East and clinched

home field for at least one playoff game. Meanwhile, the Raiders fell for the sixth straight time, but did get a good performance from Kerry Collins against his old teammates. He connected on 26 of 48 pas attempts for 331 yards, and threw for all three of Oakland's touchdowns. Randy Moss, who had seven receptions for 116 yards, caught two of Collins' scoring tosses from 15 and 44 yards, and Doug Gabriel caught the other one from eight yards out. He also had a great day receiving, with eight catches for an even 100 yards. With the conclusion of Oakland's third straight losing season, owner Al Davis decided to part ways with Norv Turner, and the coach was fired a few days after this game.[16]

Individual Statistics and Roster

Head Coach: Norv Turner
Assistant Coaches: Joe Avezzano, Martin Bayless, Fred Biletnikoff, Willie Brown, Sam Clancy, Jim Colletto, Jeff Fish, Chris Griswold, Pat Jones, Clayton Lopez, Don Martindale, Keith Millard, Fred Pagac, Chuck Pagano, Skip Peete, Jimmy Raye, Rob Ryan, John Shoop, Chris Turner
2005 Regular Season Record: 4–12
4th Place in AFC Western Division
Scored 290 points to rank 23rd out of 32 teams
Allowed 383 points to rank 25th

STARTERS — OFFENSE

QB — Kerry Collins: Active for and started in 15 games. Completed 302 of 565 pass attempts for 3,759 yards, 20 TD and 12 INT. Rushed 17 for 39 yards on 17 carries and 1 TD.
RB — LaMont Jordan: Active for and started in 14 games. Rushed for 1,025 yards on 272 carries and 9 TD. Had 70 receptions for 563 yards and 2 TD.
RB — Zack Crockett: Active for 16 games and started in 10. Rushed for 208 yards on 60 carries and 1 TD. Had 13 receptions for 111 yards.
WR — Randy Moss: Active for 16 games and started in 15. Had 60 receptions for 1,005 yards and 8 TD
WR — Jerry Porter: Active for 16 games and started in 14. Had 76 receptions for 942 yards and 5 TD. Rushed for -8 yards on 1 carry.
TE — Courtney Anderson: Active for 14 games and started in 13. Had 24 receptions for 303 yards and 3 TD.
LT — Barry Sims: Started in 16 games.
LG — Brad Badger: Active for 16 games and started in 8.
C — Adam Treu: Active for 16 games and started in 10.
RG — Ron Stone: Started in 16 games.
RT — Robert Gallery: Started in 16 games.

RESERVE OFFENSIVE PLAYERS

Ronald Curry (WR): Active for 2 games and had 2 receptions for 12 yards.
Omar Easy (RB): Active for 16 games.
Justin Fargas (RB): Active for 14 games, rushed for 28 yards on 5 carries, and had 1 reception for 9 yards.
Zeron Flemister (TE): Active for 12 games and started in 3. Returned 2 kickoffs for 16 yards.
John Paul Foschi (RB/TE): Active for 10 games, started in 5, and had 6 receptions for 37 yards.
Doug Gabriel (WR): Active for 14 games and started in 2. Had 37 receptions for 554 yards and 3 TD. Rushed for 5 yards on 1 carry, and returned 4 kickoffs for 64 yards.
Jake Grove (C/G): Active for 10 games and started in 8.
Corey Hulsey (G/T): Active for 11 games and returned 1 kickoff for 0 yards.
Brad Lekkerkerker (T): Active for 1 game.
Johnnie Morant (WR): Active for 1 game.

Chad Slaughter (T): Active for 11 games.

Marques Tuiasosopo (QB): Active for and started in 1 game. Completed 14 of 26 pass attempts for 124 yards, 1 TD and 2 INT. Rushed for 19 yards on 2 carries.

Langston Walker (T/G): Active for and started in 6 games.

Alvis Whitted (WR): Active for 15 games, had 14 receptions for 183 yards, and rushed for 51 yards on 2 carries.

Randal Williams (WR): Active for 16 games, started in 4, and had 13 receptions for 164 yards.

STARTERS — DEFENSE

DE — Bobby Hamilton: Active for 14 games, started in 13, had 2 sacks and 2 fumble recoveries.

DE — Derrick Burgess: Active for 16 games, started in 12, had **16** sacks and 2 fumble recoveries.

DT — Ted Washington: Started in 16 games.

DT — Warren Sapp: Active for and started in 10 games. Had 5 sacks and 1 INT.

LLB — Kirk Morrison: Active for 16 games, started in 15, and had 2 fumble recoveries.

RLB — Danny Clark: Active for 16 games, started in 15, and had 1 sack.

CB — Nnamdi Asomugha: Started in 16 games.

CB — Renaldo Hill: Active for 16 games, started in 13, and had 1 INT.

CB — Fabian Washington: Active for 16 games, started in 11, and had 1 fumble recovery.

SS — Jarrod Cooper: Active for 16 games, started in 10, had sack and 2 fumble recoveries.

FS — Stuart Schweigert: Active for 16 games, started in 13, had 2 INT and 3 fumble recoveries.

RESERVE DEFENSIVE PLAYERS

Calvin Branch (DB): Active for 6 games.

Tyler Brayton (E): Active for 16 games, started in 3 and had 1 sack.

Chris Carr (DB): Active for 16 games, had 3 fumble recoveries, 34 punt returns for 186 yards, and 73 kickoff returns for **1,752** yards. **Also led the NFL in combined kick and punt returns (107) and total yards gained on kick and punt returns (1,938).**

Isaiah Ekejiuba (LB): Active for 10 games.

Derrick Gibson (DB): Active for and started in 6 games. Had 1 sack and 1 fumble recovery.

DeLawrence Grant (E/LB): Active for 9 games and had 1 sack.

Anttaj Hawthorne (T): Active for 2 games.

Grant Irons (E): Active for 15 games and started in 1.

Ed Jasper (T): Active for 15 games, started in 1 and had 2 sacks.

Tim Johnson (LB): Active for 16 games.

Tommy Kelly (E/T): Active for 16 games, started in 12 and had 4 sacks.

Ryan Riddle (E): Active for 12 games.

Stanford Routt (DB): Active for 14 games, started in 2 and had 1 sack.

Terdell Sands (T): Active for 9 games, had 1 sack and 1 fumble recovery.

Reggie Tongue (DB): Active for 4 games and started in 1.

Denard Walker (DB): Active for 9 games.

Charles Woodson (DB): Active for and started in 6 games, had 1 INT and 3 punt returns for 20 yards.

KICKING/PUNTING

K — Sebastian Janikowski: Active for 16 games. Made 20 of 30 field goals and 30 of 30 extra points for 90 points.

P — Shane Lechler: Active for 16 games. Punted 82 times for a 45.7 average, and rushed for 2 yards on 1 carry.

2006 Season Review

1. Sept. 11: The Raiders and San Diego Chargers were the second act of a prime time twin bill that opened the 2006 season, and marked the return of Art Shell as the Raiders' head coach after a 12-year absence. The Oakland Raiders came into this game against a team that had beaten them five straight times. San Diego's head coach, Marty Schottenheimer, owned the Silver and Black over the years with a dominant 25–7 record against them. One of these sterling marks was going to continue. Unfortunately it was Schottenheimer's and his Chargers that extended their reign over the Raiders with a 27–0 shutout. LaDainian Tomlinson ran for 131 yards and one touchdown to lead the assault.

This was the first time since 1961 that the Chargers blanked Oakland, and only the second time in their history that the Raiders were shut out at home. The first was in 1981 against the Denver Broncos.[1]

2. Sept. 17: The Baltimore Ravens had not given up a touchdown in two games, and Oakland did not score one in a 28–0 loss. The tough Baltimore defense pounded Oakland's quarterbacks for six sacks and forced just as many turnovers. Aaron Brooks was taken out of the game in the first quarter with a sprained right rotator cuff and replaced by Andrew Walter, who fumbled three times and threw three interceptions. The Raiders were saved from a second shutout by Sebastian Janikowski's two field goals from 34 and 51 yards.[2]

3. Oct. 1: The Raiders looked good coming off their bye week. They jumped out to a 21–3 lead on touchdowns by Sam Williams (30-yard fumble recovery), Randy Moss (5-yard pass from Andrew Walter), and LaMont Jordan (59-yard run). Nnamdi Asomugha added two interceptions, and the Raiders looked like the dominant team they were just four years earlier. However, reality set in, and the Cleveland Browns came back with three Charlie Frye TD passes to down the Silver and Black, 24–21. The only good thing to come out of this loss was the fact that the Raiders showed they were capable of scoring on offense.[3]

4. Oct. 8: The Raiders came into this game ranked last in total offense and passing. In two previous meetings with the San Francisco 49ers, the Raiders went into overtime, with the teams each winning once. This time, however, an extra quarter was not necessary in a 34–20 San Francisco win. Running back Frank Gore came into this game ranked second in the league in yards from scrimmage, and against Oakland, he helped himself maintain upper echelon status by rushing for a career-high 134 yards. After spotting the Raiders a 13–7 halftime lead, the 49ers exploded for 24 straight points. Sebastian Janikowski hit on field goals from 33 and 36 yards, and Randy Moss scored his 100th career touchdown reception on a 22-yard pass from Andrew Walter to give the Raiders their short-lived lead. Marques Tuiasosopo added an 8-yard scoring toss to Courtney Anderson with the game already out of reach to give Oakland their other points.[4]

5. Oct. 15: No big surprise was the fact that the Raiders had the worst offense in the league, averaging only 225 yards per game. They also ranked last with 106.8 yards passing. Their opponents, the Denver Broncos, were tied with Seattle for the longest active home winning streak with 12, and the defense was ranked second in points allowed with 8.5. On a Sunday Night Football telecast, the Raiders lost, 13–3, to become the only team in 2006 without a win, and were now on an 11-game losing streak going back to the previous season. Failing to score a touchdown for the third time in five games, the Raiders were once again saved from being

shut out by Sebastian Janikowski, who kicked a 47-yard field goal in the third quarter. The Broncos became the first team since the 1934 Detroit Lions to start a season by allowing only one touchdown through five games.[5]

6. Oct. 22: The Arizona Cardinals came into Oakland on a six-game losing streak after winning their opener. The Raiders were hoping to stop their skid as well on a day that saw the franchise's all-time winning head coach John Madden get his Pro Football Hall of Fame ring in a pregame ceremony. Madden's presence must have given the Silver and Black some good karma for a change, and they produced their first win of the season by a 22–9 count.

Throughout their first five games, the Raiders scored a league-low 50 points. They looked to change that by getting out to an early lead on their second possession of the game. After the Cardinal missed on a field goal attempt, the Raiders went on a long drive that ReShard Lee finished off with a 1-yard run. Oakland then added another six-pointer that was helped by a Terdell Sands interception that came off a deflected Matt Leinart pass by Derrick Burgess. Andrew Walter wasted no time with the golden opportunity given him. On the first play following the interception, Walter hooked up with Randy Moss from 32 yards out to give the Raiders a 14–0 lead after the opening fifteen minutes. On the day, Moss caught seven passes for 129 yards in what would be his best game of the season. The teams traded field goals in the second quarter, with Sebastian Janikowski hitting on a 31-yarder for Oakland. The Raiders' defensive unit looked to hold the team's 17–3 lead. They stopped Arizona on an incomplete pass and two sacks before rookie defensive back Michael Huff tackled Marcel Shipp in the end zone for a safety that extended the Oakland advantage to 22–3. The Cardinals added two field goals before it was all over. With this first win of the season, the Raiders snapped an 11-game losing streak that began one day shy of a year since their last win.[6]

7. Oct. 29: This clash with the Steelers was not as anticipated as a typical Oakland-Pittsburgh matchup of thirty years earlier when both teams were kings of pro football. Even though the Steelers were defending Super Bowl champions, they came into McAfee Coliseum against the 1–5 Raiders with only a 2–4 slate. The only thing similar to the glory days of the Raiders was that they put together a winning streak. In a shocker, the Raiders knocked off Pittsburgh, 20–13, to extend their winning streak to two games. Pittsburgh signal caller Ben Roethlisberger had been the talk of the Steel City during his first two seasons, enjoying great success. However, he had troubles against Oakland's defense, getting picked off twice in the first quarter. In a tough, defensive battle, it was Oakland who contained the defending champs throughout the first three quarters. Cornerback Fabian Washington got his first-ever pro interception, and fellow defensive back Nnamdi Asomugha added another pick, returning his 24 yards to give the Raiders a 7–0 advantage after the first quarter. After Pittsburgh added two field goals, the Raiders got a 19-yard three-pointer from Sebastian Janikowski to go into halftime up, 10–6. With the help of two penalties, Oakland got close enough for Janikowski to kick a 41-yard field goal that gave the Raiders a 13–6 lead. Just like Pittsburgh, the Raiders were having their problems moving the ball. They were unable to get first downs, had balls dropped by receivers, and suffered penalties. The Steelers at-

tempted to take advantage of their opponent's woes, and put together a good drive. On third-and-goal, Roethlisberger looked to the end zone in an attempt to tie the game up. Defensive back Chris Carr had other ideas for Big Ben's aerial. Carr intercepted the pass on the goal line, and did not stop running until he registered a 100-yard return for a touchdown. Carr's jaunt produced the second-longest interception return in Raiders history, falling two yards short of the record set by Eddie Anderson in 1992. It also gave the Raiders a convincing 20–6 fourth quarter advantage. Pittsburgh closed the gap to 20–13 on a Roethlisberger to Willie Parker 25-yard pass that produced this game's only lone offensive touchdown. This was an ugly offensive game that truly was offensive to watch. Oakland mustered up a total of 98 yards, which was the lowest amount they ever had in a win.[7]

8. Nov. 6: A trip to Seattle's Qwest Field allowed the Raiders the privilege of playing both representatives from the previous Super Bowl on consecutive weeks. The defending NFC champion Seahawks came into this Monday Night Football matchup with some karma of their own, winning six of their last nine prime time encounters. The Raiders used to be the masters of Monday night, but that seemed like an eternity ago. For the Raiders of 2006 were only like the powerhouse teams of the 70's and 80's in uniform colors and nothing else. On a wet, windy night, Oakland's former AFC West nemesis recorded nine sacks, and had no trouble holding off the NFL's worst offensive unit in a 16–0 Seattle win. They did it without the services of quarterback Matt Hasselbeck and All-Pro running back Shaun Alexander, both out due to injuries. Their replacements did a great job. Seneca Wallace threw for 176 yards and a touchdown, while Maurice Morris ran for a career-high 138 yards. Once the dominant kings of Monday Night Football, the Raiders now became the first team in the history of the prime time spectacle to be held scoreless twice in the same season.[8]

9. Nov. 12: The Raiders came home to host the 6–2 Denver Broncos, and managed to jump out to a 7–0 first quarter lead. LaMont Jordan opened the scoring with a 1-yard run that was set up by an interception from Nnamdi Asomugha. The Broncos played a bad game, with Jake Plummer throwing three interceptions and the running game only gaining 66 yards. However, they were playing the hapless Raiders, and despite having a bad day, they still got out of Oakland with a 17–13 win. After the Raiders added two Sebastian Janikowski field goals from 55 (tied his own team record originally set in 2003 for longest field goal) and 20 yards to take a 13–7 lead, the Broncos came back. After a scoreless third quarter, Denver took their first lead of the game on a Plummer to Kyle Johnson 1-yard pass and Jason Elam's extra point kick. Elam added a 24-yard field goal to complete the scoring. Even though the Raiders were very bad, they had a good defensive showing, with Fabian Washington getting two interceptions.[9]

10. Nov. 19: One thing can be said of the '06 Raiders, with that being they were consist. Not only did they lose again, but by the same 17–13 score from the previous week. This time was another division rival, the Kansas City Chiefs that did them in. Also like in their last game, the Raiders got out to 13–7 halftime lead only to see it vanish. A pair of Sebastian Janikowski field goals (41 and 36 yards), and a 2-yard pass from Aaron Brooks to Courtney Anderson supplied Oakland's point production. After

closing the gap to 13–10 going into the fourth quarter, the Chiefs rallied to victory in the final minute of the game. Quarterback Trent Green returned after missing ten weeks due to a concussion, and drove the Chiefs 80 yards for the winning score. On the drive, Green completed three of five passes for 50 yards. Larry Johnson delivered the final touches with a go-ahead 1-yard run with 1:32 left. On the day, Johnson abused the Oakland defense for 154 rushing yards. This was the seventh straight time the Chiefs beat the Raiders, with all the wins coming by seven points or less.[10]

11. Nov. 26: Even though the Oakland offense was pathetic, the defensive unit was getting attention. Boasting the AFC's best pass defense, the unit also did not allow 20 points to be scored against it in six consecutive games. In their game against San Diego, the defense gave up one point more than in the previous six. Unfortunately, the offense failed to ring up more than what the defense allowed, and the result was a 21–14 loss to the Chargers. LaDainian Tomlinson was one of the league's top running backs at this time, and always seemed to turn it up a notch when playing the Raiders. He ran for a game-high 109 yards and two touchdowns, and also threw for another to have a hand in each of San Diego's six-pointers. After the Raiders took a 7–0 second quarter lead on a ReShard Lee 1-yard run, Tomlinson answered the challenge with a 4-yard run to help tie it at the half. Oakland came back to take a 14–7 lead into the fourth quarter on an Aaron Brooks to John Madsen 2-yard pass. This time out, Tomlinson took to the air, finding tight end Antonio Gates from 19 yards out with a halfback option pass with 9:46 to go in the game. Oakland did not regain the lead, and Tomlinson put the final touches on his day with a 10-yard run for the go-ahead score. The Chargers were 9–2 after the game, while the Raiders fell to 2–9, which guaranteed them of a fourth straight losing season for the first time in team history.[11]

12. Dec. 3: Houston Texans' quarterback David Carr came into this game with an NFL-high 69.9 completion percentage. He then ran into the tough Oakland defense, and had one of the worst days ever for a signal caller. Carr was held to -5 yards passing, was sacked five times, and held without a complete throughout the second half, while his ground attack was held to 129 yards. This type of bleak performance against anyone else would have led Houston out of town with a blowout defeat. However, they played against the Raiders, and despite the dismal showing, the Texans improved to 4–8 with a 23–14 victory. Two long punt returns and two fumbles assisted Houston in getting 16 points on the board in the second half. The Raiders got all their points in the second quarter, and held a 14–7 halftime lead on a Justin Fargas 3-yard run and a Kirk Morrison 35-yard fumble recovery.[12]

13. Dec. 10: Oakland's top-rated pass defense travelled to Cincinnati to face the Bengals. The Raiders came out strong, showing why they had the best pass defense when Nnamdi Asomuhga intercepted a Carson Palmer pass on the third play of the game. Unfortunately, the offense turned it right back over to Cincinnati on the following play thanks to a fumble. Palmer then led the Bengals on two scoring drives that resulted in touchdowns by Chris Henry (8-yard pass from Palmer), and Rudi Johnson (1-yard run). Asomugha tried once again to help with his second interception of the game in the second quarter. This time, it led to a Sebastian Janikowski 33-yard field goal. The Bengals got a

touchdown run by Johnson and Palmer threw for another score and Cincinnati won, 27–10, to improve to 8–5 with their fourth straight win. Oakland received their only touchdown of the game on a 5-yard pass from Aaron Brooks to Ronald Curry in the fourth quarter. This sixth consecutive setback dropped the Raiders to 2–11, and the abysmal '06 campaign could not end quick enough for the Silver and Black.[13]

14. Dec. 17: Two former residents of Los Angeles collided at McAfee Coliseum, as the Raiders hosted the St. Louis Rams. Even with the worst defense against the run, the Rams took advantage of five turnovers and managed to hand Oakland their third shutout loss of the year by a 20–0 final. Running back Steven Jackson led the St. Louis attack with 127 yards rushing and two touchdowns.[14]

15. Dec. 23: The Kansas City Chiefs ended a three-game losing streak with a 20–9 win over Oakland. Meanwhile, the Raiders fell to the Chiefs for the eighth straight time, and this defeat also marked the 14th consecutive time Oakland lost to an AFC West team. Larry Johnson ran for 137 yards and one touchdown for the Chiefs. The Raiders received three field goals from Sebastian Janikowski that came from 25, 37, and 53 yards. Andrew Walter filled in for the injured Aaron Brooks at quarterback, and had 22 turnovers in just eight starts. In this game, the Raiders suffered five turnovers that included two interceptions and three fumbles. This marked the seventh time in '06 that the Raiders failed to score an offensive touchdown. The team was completely frustrated by what was occurring on the field. They worked hard, but still found ways to lose. Defensive lineman Warren Sapp, who was a winner in college and the pros before coming to Oakland, expressed his frustration by going into a fit a rage on the sideline after witnessing yet another horrible offensive showing. Now at 2–13, the Raiders were in the midst of an eight-game losing streak, and tied the 1962 team for the most losses in a season.[15]

16. Dec. 31: The Raiders at least came out of this horrific experience called the 2006 season with a team record. However, it was not one that would be recalled with pride. A trip to Giants Stadium provided the Raiders with a 23–3 loss to the Jets, and with it, they set a team record for most losses in a season with 14, breaking a 44-year-old mark. They finished with a league-worst 2–14 slate, and also became the 11th team since the league began a 16-game schedule in 1978 to score less than 200 points. A shutout was averted thanks to a Sebastian Janikowski 35-yard field goal in the second quarter. The last day of the year brought an end to the worst team in Raiders history. Despite the dismal finish, the Raiders did improve drastically on defense, going from 27th place defensively to a third place ranking. They also went into halftime leading in eight games, so it seemed that the organization had something to build on. Unfortunately, the return of head coach Art Shell was short-lived. One week following the conclusion of the season, he was relieved of his duties.[16]

Individual Statistics and Roster

Head Coach: Art Shell
Assistant Coaches: Fred Biletnikoff, Willie Brown, Ted Daisher, Irv Eatman, Jeff Fish, Robert Ford, Don Martindale, George Martinez, Jim McElwain, Keith Millard, Fred Pagac, Chuck Pagano, Skip Peete, Rob

Ryan, John Shoop, Darryl Sims, Jackie Slater, Tom Walsh, Lorenzo Ward

2006 Regular Season Record: 2–14

4th Place in AFC Western Division

Scored 168 points to rank 32nd out of 32 teams

Allowed 332 points to rank 18th

Led the league in fewest passing yards allowed by a defense (2,413)

STARTERS — OFFENSE

QB — Andrew Walter: Active for and started in 8 games. Completed 147 of 276 pass attempts for 1,677 yards, 3 TD and 13 INT. Rushed for 30 yards on 14 carries.

RB — LaMont Jordan: Active for 9 games and started in 8. Rushed for 434 yards on 114 carries and 2 TD. Had 10 receptions for 74 yards.

RB — Zack Crockett: Active for 16 games and started in 9. Rushed for 163 yards on 39 carries and had 10 receptions for 53 yards.

WR — Randy Moss: Active for and started in 13 games. Had 42 receptions for 553 yards and 3 TD.

WR — Alvis Whitted: Active for 14 games and started in 13. Had 27 receptions for 299 yards, and rushed for 4 yards on 1 carry.

TE — Courtney Anderson: Active for 16 games, started in 12. Had 25 receptions for 285 yards and 2 TD.

LT — Robert Gallery: Active for and started in 10 games.

LG — Barry Sims: Active for 11 games and started in 7.

C — Jake Grove: Started in 16 games.

RG — Kevin Boothe: Active for 16 games and started in 14.

RT — Langston Walker: Started in 16 games.

RESERVE OFFENSIVE PLAYERS

James Adkisson (WR): Active for 2 games and had 1 reception for 9 yards.

Brad Badger (G/T): Active for 7 games.

Aaron Brooks (QB): Active for and started in 8 games. Completed 110 of 192 pass attempts for 1,105 yards, 3 TD and 8 INT. Rushed for 124 yards on 22 carries.

Will Buchanon (WR): Active for 1 game and had 1 reception for 9 yards.

Ronald Curry (WR): Active for 16 games and started in 4. Had 62 receptions for 727 yards and 1 TD. Rushed for 4 yards on 1 carry, completed 0 of 2 pass attempts, and had 1 INT.

Adimchinobe Echemandu (RB): Active for 4 games.

Justin Fargas (RB): Active for 16 games and started in 6. Rushed for 659 yards on 178 carries and 1 TD. Had 13 receptions for 91 yards.

John Paul Foschi (RB/TE): Active for 1 game.

Doug Gabriel (WR): Active for 3 games and had 5 receptions for 84 yards.

Corey Hulsey (G/T): Active for and started in 5 games.

ReShard Lee (RB): Active for 16 games and started in 3. Rushed for 72 yards on 21 carries and 2 TD. Had 20 receptions for 138 yards, and returned 4 kickoffs for 49 yards.

John Madsen (WR): Active for 15 games and started in 1. Had 11 receptions for 146 yards and 1 TD.

Paul McQuistan (T): Active for 14 games and started in 6.

Johnnie Morant (WR): Active for 10 games, started in 2, and had 7 receptions for 70 yards.

Chris Morris (C): Active for 5 games.

Jerry Porter (WR): Active for 4 games and had 1 reception for 19 yards.

Chad Slaughter (T): Active for 15 games and started in 6.

Adam Treu (C): Active for 11 games.

Marques Tuiasosopo (QB): Active for 2 games. Completed 6 of 13 pass attempts for 68 yards, 1 TD and 2 INT. Rushed for 29 yards on 4 carries.

Randal Williams (WR): Active for 16 games, started in 9, and had 28 receptions for 293 yards.

STARTERS — DEFENSE

DE — Tyler Brayton: Active for 16 games and started in 14.

DE — Derrick Burgess: Started in 16 games and had 11 sacks.

DT — Warren Sapp: Started in 16 games and had 10 sacks.

DT — Tommy Kelly: Started in 16 games and had 3 sacks.

LLB — Sam Williams: Active for 15 games, started in 12, had 1 sack and 1 fumble recovery.

MLB — Kirk Morrison: Started in 16 games, had 1 sack, 2 INT and 1 fumble recovery.

RLB — Thomas Howard: Active for 16 games and started in 15.

CB — Nnamdi Asomugha: Active for and started in 15 games. Had 1 sack and 8 INT.

CB — Fabian Washington: Active for and started in 14 games. Had 4 INT.

SS — Michael Huff: Started in 16 games and recorded 1 safety.

FS — Stuart Schweigert: Started in 16 games and had 1 fumble recovery.

RESERVE DEFENSIVE PLAYERS

Ricky Brown (LB): Active for 13 games.

Chris Carr (DB): Active for 16 games and started in 2. Had 1 INT, 1 TD, 1 fumble recovery, 35 punt returns for 216 yards, and 69 kickoff returns for 1,762 yards. **Also led the NFL in combined kick and punt returns (104) and total yards gained on kick and punt returns (1,978).**

Jarrod Cooper (DB): Active for 16 games.

Isaiah Ekejiuba (LB): Active for 12 games.

Derrick Gibson (DB): Active for 16 games and started in 1.

Anttaj Hawthorne (T): Active for 16 games.

Kevin Huntley (T): Active for 6 games, had 2 sacks and 1 fumble recovery.

Grant Irons (E): Active for 2 games and started in 1.

Lance Johnstone (E): Active for 11 games, started in 1, and had 2 sacks.

Tyrone Poole (DB): Active for 12 games, started in 2, had 1 sack and 1 INT.

Stanford Routt (DB): Active for 16 games, started in 2, and had 1 INT.

Terdell Sands (T): Active for 16 games, started in 1, had 1 sack and 1 INT.

Duane Starks (DB): Active for 4 games.

Robert W. Thomas (LB): Active for 16 games and had 1 fumble recovery.

KICKING/PUNTING

K — Sebastian Janikowski: Active for 16 games. Made 18 of 25 field goals and 16 of 16 extra points for 70 points.

P — Shane Lechler: Active for 16 games. Punted 77 times for a 47.5 average.

2007 Season Review

1. Sept. 9: For the third straight year, the Raiders opened a season with a different head coach. This time around, it was Lane Kiffin patrolling the sideline, but the results on the field were the same for the hapless Raiders. In a clash of two of the NFL's worst teams, the Detroit Lions beat Oakland, 36–21. This was the fifth straight season that Oakland lost their opener. The Raiders made it interesting in front of 61,547 home fans by overcoming a 17–0 deficit on three scoring drives engineered by former Detroit quarterback Josh McCown. A 4-yard pass from McCown to Ronald Curry got the Raiders on the board for the first time in '07. LaMont Jordan following that up with a 12-yard run, and Oakland then took a 21–20 lead with 7:23 remaining in the game on a 7-yard pass from McCown to Justin Griffith. The Lions then scored the go-ahead touchdown with 4:15 left, added ten more points, and then stopped Oakland by causing two turnovers. Despite the outcome, McCown had a great day in his Oakland debut with 313 passing yards on 30 of 40 attempts.[1]

2. Sept. 16: Mike Shanahan came into his 21st career matchup against the Raiders needing one more win to become only the second active head coach beside Washington's Joe Gibbs to have 20-plus wins against one team. Shanahan did accomplish the feat, but his Denver Broncos had to work hard for it. The Raiders battled back from a 17–3 deficit to force overtime. Sebastian Janikowski opened Oakland's scoring with a 38-yard field goal in the second quarter. The Raiders then ran off 17 points to take the lead. Jerry Porter caught a 46-yard pass from Josh Mc-Cown, Gerard Warren sacked Denver quarterback Jay Cutler in the end zone for a safety, and Thomas Howard returned an interception 44 yards. Howard's touchdown was followed by Mc-Cown throwing to Ronald Curry for the two-point conversion to make it a 20–17 Oakland advantage with 8:55 left in regulation. The Broncos forced overtime after Jason Elam kicked a 20-yard field goal with 2:18 left, and McCown threw a long pass that was picked off in the closing minutes. Janikowski drilled a 52-yard field goal four minutes into overtime, and he was swarmed by his celebrating teammates while the Denver throng fell silent with dejection. The only ones in the stadium not feeling the agony of defeat were the Broncos themselves. For Shanahan had called a timeout prior to the snap, which meant that Janikowski had to attempt his three-pointer again. On his second kick, the ball hit the uprights and Denver was alive for another possession. From their 42-yard line, the Broncos took the ball down to the Oakland six, and wasting no time, Shanahan sent Elam on for a field goal on first down. He sent the chip shot through from 23 yards for an exciting 23–20 win. This heartbreaker overshadowed a fine running display by LaMont Jordan, who pounded out 159 yards on 25 carries.[2]

3. Sept. 23: Turnabout is fair play, and the Raiders did to the Cleveland Browns what the Broncos did one week earlier to them. In the process, Oakland gave rookie head coach Lane Kiffin his first victory by a 26–24 count. On the final play of the game, Cleveland's Phil Dawson sent a 40-yard apparent game-winning field goal through the uprights. However, Kiffin pulled what Shanahan did to him by calling a timeout just as Dawson awaited the snap. The Browns did not realize that a time out was called, and the celebration was short-lived. After the timeout, Dawson once again attempted a field goal. Just as the ball sailed off Dawson's foot, a loud thud was heard. It was compliments of defensive end Tommy Kelly, who broke loose and got a hand on the ball to swat it away. Kelly's effort gave the Raiders not only their first win, but snapped an 11-game losing streak that carried over from the previous year of disaster. LaMont Jordan ran for 121 yards and scored on a 1-yard run for the go-ahead touchdown in the third quarter to put Oakland up, 23–17. Janikowski added a 48-yard field goal in the fourth quarter to extend the lead to 26–17. Sea Bass also had three earlier field goals from 32, 22, and 23 yards, and Ronald Curry added a six-pointer on a 41-yard pass from Josh McCown to give the winners their points.[3]

4. Sept. 30: The Miami Dolphins came into this game with Oakland as the AFC leader in turnovers, and a defense that could not hold a lead. At 0–3, Miami seemed the perfect fodder for the Silver and Black. This proved to be the case, and the Raiders rolled to a 35–17 win to even their record at 2–2 and equal their win total from the previous season. It was the Daunte Culpepper and Justin Fargas show that hit Miami like a hurricane. Culpepper

threw the ball only 12 times for 75 yards, but connected with Jerry Porter on two touchdowns from seven and 27 yards. He then let his feet do the work, and ran for scores from two, five, and three yards out to account for all of Oakland's touchdowns. Fargas came in to take over for an injured LaMont Jordan right before the half, and destroyed the weak Miami defense for 179 yards on 22 carries.[4]

5. Oct. 14: LaDainian Tomlinson loved playing against the Raiders. The 2006 NFL Most Valuable Player lived up to his award early in the '07 campaign by once again single handedly thwarting the Silver and Black. He ran for 198 yards on 24 carries, and scored four touchdowns in a 28–14 win. His tally of quadruple six-pointers allowed Tomlinson to take over fifth place on the all-time career rushing touchdown list with 106. Meanwhile, in his second start as Oakland's quarterback, Daunte Culpepper was tormented by the San Diego defense for two interceptions and six sacks. The Raiders' league-leading running game was held in check, with the Chargers giving up only 53 yards on the ground. Culpepper did manage to get time enough to find Zach Miller on a 1-yard pass to produce Oakland's lone touchdown. Thomas Howard provided the Raiders with their other six points on a 66-yard interception return.[5]

6. Oct. 21: The Kansas City Chiefs extended their winning streak over the Raiders to nine straight with a 12–10 victory. Oakland also extended a streak of their own, but not one to be proud of. For the 17th consecutive time, they succumbed to teams from the AFC Western Division. The Raiders held a 7–6 lead on a 21-yard pass from Daunte Culpepper to Ronald Curry in the third quarter. Kansas City's Larry Johnson ran for 112 yards and scored the go-ahead touchdown early in the fourth quarter. Sebastian Janikowski added a 37-yard field goal for Oakland to close out the scoring. For the second straight week, the Raiders well-respected running game was contained, this time only gaining 55 yards on 24 carries.[6]

7. Oct. 28: LaMont Jordan came into this game with an 11-yard average on plays from scrimmage. The Tennessee Titans' defense led the league against the run. The Titans lived up to their league status by shutting down Jordan for 16 yards on 12 carries in a 13–9 win. On top of stopping the run, Tennessee also recorded five sacks and two turnovers. Running back LenDale White had no trouble making his way through Oakland's defense for a career-high 133 yards. Sebastian Janikowski prevented the Raiders from being shut out by kicking three long-range field goals from 50, 43, and 54 yards.[7]

8. Nov. 4: The Houston Texans and Oakland Raiders both took the field at McAfee Coliseum on three game losing streaks. Sage Rosenfels got his third career start, and first of the season in place of injured Matt Schaub. He made the most of the opportunity by leading Houston on a fourth quarter surge to get past Oakland, 24–17, and stay unbeaten in three tries against the Silver and Black. It seemed that Rosenfels liked to wait until the fourth quarter to start slinging scoring strikes. All his touchdown passes came in the final stanza, and this time it was one to Andre Davis from 42 yards out that allowed the Texans to pull away from the Raiders after they began creeping back into the game. After trailing, 17–0, at the half, Oakland came back on a Sebastian Janikowski 22-yard field goal, and a 1-yard run by Justin Fargas, who ran for 104 yards on 23 carries. Then came Davis' score to make

t a 24–10 ball game midway through the fourth quarter. Oakland added a 28-yard pass from Josh McCown to Tim Dwight with :30 left to make the final outcome appear closer. Houston's Ron Dayne provided his team with a solid running performance (122 yards on 21 carries), against one of the league's most lethargic rushing defenses.[8]

9. Nov. 11: The defending NFC champion Chicago Bears were having their problems. They were 3–5 at the halfway point of the season, and ranked near the bottom of the league in rushing production and defense against the run. The good news was that the Bears won two of their three games away from the Windy City, and were about to engage the Raiders at McAfee Coliseum with Oakland riding a four game losing streak. In a game that was not pretty to watch, Chicago managed to win in the closing minutes, 17–6. Sebastian Janikowski provided Oakland with field goals from 37 and 52 yards to give them a 6–3 lead with 4:04 left in the game. Rex Grossman, who replaced injured Brian Griese as Chicago's quarterback, threw a 59-yard pass to Bernard Berrian with 3:11 left. Cedric Benson added a 3-yard run with :35 remaining to seal Oakland's fate and drop them to 2–7.[9]

10. Nov. 18: Minnesota's rookie running sensation Adrian Peterson was out of action with a knee injury, but his replacement, Chester Taylor, did a number on the dismal Raiders. In a 29–22 win that sent Oakland down for the fifth straight time, Taylor smoked them for 164 yards on the ground and three touchdowns. Daunte Culpepper tried his best against his former team by completing 23 of 39 pass attempts for 344 yards that included a 10-yard scoring toss to John Madsen. Sebastian Janikowski added five field goals (42, 30, 42, 49, and 52 yards) for Oakland's other points. Oakland had one of the NFL's best running attacks in the early portion of the season, but now they continued to be stagnant, gaining only 61 yards on 27 carries. To add further insult to injury for the 2–8 Raiders was the loss of star defensive back Nnamdi Asomugha to a concussion.[10]

11. Nov. 25: Hell must have frozen over and pigs really did fly. These two little quips are said when things occur that seemed highly unlikely of ever happening. Case in point was the Raiders beating Kansas City. However, after nine straight defeats, the improbable happened when Oakland got past the Chiefs in Kansas City, 20–17. The Raiders also broke free from the shackles of a 7-game losing streak against their fellow AFC West associates. The running game returned in the form of Justin Fargas, who rambled for 139 yards on 22 carries, and scored on a 14-yard jaunt with 9:34 left in the game to lift the Raiders from a 17–13 deficit. LaMont Jordan had a 5-yard run, and Sebastian Janikowski a pair of field goals from 25 and 54 yards. The Raiders now stood at 3–8, and were one victory shy of the team's 400th all-time win.[11]

12. Dec. 2: Justin Fargas became the starting running back in week nine, and was averaging close to 100 yards a game since his promotion. He helped spark a running game that went stagnant, rise to fifth place among NFL backfield's going into their game against Denver. Fargas once again rose to the occasion by running for 146 yards on 33 carries that included a 5-yard touchdown run, in a 34–20 win. This victory gave the Raiders two in a row, snapped a five-game losing streak to the Broncos, and gave the franchise its 400th all-time regular season win. Oakland capitalized on four turnovers, turning them into 24 points. Besides Fargas' scoring run, the Raiders put three other touchdowns on

the board compliments of Josh McCown. Tim Dwight (15 yards), Zach Miller (13 yards), and Jerry Porter (13 yards), had the honors of snagging McCown's six-pointers, and Sebastian Janikowski added two field goals from 38 and 44 yards.[12]

13. Dec. 9: The 11–2 Green Bay Packers won four straight against the Raiders, and looked to clinch the NFC North with a victory at legendary Lambeau Field. The Packers then proceeded to make easy work of the Raiders, thumping them, 38–7. Brett Favre threw for 266 yards and a touchdown, and running back Ryan Grant tore up the turf for 156 yards and a score to pace Green bay's offense. Special team performer Will Blackmon also achieved some headline-grabbing attention by returning a punt 57 yards for a touchdown, and added another six-pointer to his resume when he recovered a fumbled punt by Tim Dwight in the end zone. The Raiders received their only score of the day in the second quarter on a 25-yard pass from Josh McCown to Jerry Porter.[13]

14. Dec. 16: Things did not get any easier for the Raiders when they faced the reigning Super Bowl champion Indianapolis Colts, who entered this game having already clinched a playoff spot with an 11–2 record. This time, the Raiders did not fold like they did the previous week. They still found themselves on the losing end of a 21–14 final score, but at least made a game of it. After spotting the Colts a 10–0 first quarter lead, Oakland came back to grab a 14–13 fourth quarter advantage on a Justin Fargas 2-yard run with 10:29 left. Oakland's other touchdown came on a 3-yard pass from Josh McCown to Ronald Curry. The Colts' legendary quarterback Peyton Manning put an end to Oakland's dreams of an upset. He did that by connecting on all seven passes he threw during a 91-yard drive. The end result was a 20-yard pass to Anthony Gonzalez that put Indy up for good with 4:49 remaining.[14]

15. Dec. 23: The 10–4 Jacksonville Jaguars needed a win to clinch a playoff berth. They then went out and left no doubt that they wanted a post-season invitation after a 49–11 dismantling of the Raiders. Fred Taylor opened the game with a 62-yard touchdown run, and the Jaguars never looked back. Sebastian Janikowski kicked a 41-yard field goal, and Zach Miller caught a 2-yard pass from JaMarcus Russell. Ronald Curry caught a two-point conversion following Miller's score. To make things exciting in such a blowout, Warren Sapp made the ghosts of Raiders past proud by getting ejected after three unsportsmanlike penalties.[15]

16. Dec. 30: Another season of despair ended for the Silver and Black with a 30–17 loss to the San Diego Chargers in the first career start for quarterback JaMarcus Russell. Russell had his first pass as a starter picked off and lost a fumble that was recovered for a touchdown. Despite some rocky moments, Russell threw for 224 yards on 23 of 31 attempts and a touchdown covering 32 yards to Jerry Porter. Dominic Rhodes did a good job running the ball for Oakland, compiling 122 yards on 29 carries and scored on a 1-yard run. Sebastian Janikowski added a 53-yard field goal to Oakland's point total in their season finale. The 11–5 Chargers won the AFC West crown, and LaDainian Tomlinson earned his second straight rushing championship against the 4–12 Raiders.[16]

Individual Statistics and Roster

Head Coach: Lane Kiffin

Assistant Coaches: Willie Brown, Tom Cable, Charles Coe, James Cregg, John DeFilippo, Jeff Fish, Curtis Fuller, Randy Hanson, Adam Henry, Mark Jackson, Don Johnson, Greg Knapp, Sanjay Lal, Don Martindale, George Martinez, Keith Millard, Darren Perry, Tom Rathman, Rob Ryan, Brian Schneider, Kelly Skipper

2007 Regular Season Record: 4–12

4th Place in AFC Western Division

Scored 283 points to rank 23rd out of 32 teams

Allowed 398 points to rank 26th

STARTERS — OFFENSE

QB — Josh McCown: Active for and started in 9 games. Completed 111 of 190 pass attempts for 1,151 yards, 10 TD and 11 INT. Rushed for 143 yards on 29 carries.

RB — Justin Fargas: Active for 14 games and started in 7. Rushed for 1,009 yards on 222 carries and 4 TD. Had 23 receptions for 188 yards.

RB — Justin Griffith: Active for 16 games and started in 11. Rushed for 27 yards on 7 carries, had 26 receptions for 165 yards and 1 TD, and returned 1 kickoff for 11 yards.

WR — Ronald Curry: Active for 16 games and started in 13. Had 55 receptions for 717 yards and 4 TD. Rushed for 1 yard on 1 carry, and attempted 1 pass that was incomplete.

WR — Jerry Porter: Started in 16 games. Had 44 receptions for 705 yards and 6 TD.

TE — Zach Miller: Started in 16 games. Had 44 receptions for 444 yards and 3 TD.

LT — Barry Sims: Started in 16 games.

LG — Robert Gallery: Started in 16 games.

C — Jeremy Newberry: Active for and started in 14 games.

RG — Cooper Carlisle: Started in 16 games.

RT — Cornell Green: Active for and started in 10 games.

RESERVE OFFENSIVE PLAYERS

Daunte Culpepper (QB):Active for 7 games and started in 6. Completed 108 of 186 pass attempts for 1,331 yards, 5 TD and 5 INT. Rushed for 40 yards on 20 carries and 3 TD.

Tim Dwight (WR): Active for 6 games and started in 1. Had 6 receptions for 98 yards and 2 TD. Rushed for 12 yards on 2 carries, returned 9 punts for 54 yards, and 1 kickoff for 30 yards.

Adimchinobe Echemandu (RB): Active for 2 games.

Jake Grove (C/G): Active for 7 games and started in 2.

Johnnie Lee Higgins (WR): Active for 16 games and started in 2. Had 6 receptions for 47 yards, rushed for 3 yards on 2 carries, and returned 20 punts for 103 yards.

LaMont Jordan (RB): Active for 12 games and started in 7. Rushed for 549 yards on 144 carries and 3 TD. Had 28 receptions for 247 yards.

John Madsen (WR): Active for 16 games and started in 3. Had 8 receptions for 102 yards and 1 TD.

Chris McFoy (WR): Active for 3 games and had 1 reception for 19 yards.

Paul McQuistan (T): Active for 16 games and started in 6.

Chris Morris (C): Active for 10 games.

Oren O'Neal (RB): Active for 14 games, started in 1, and had 1 reception for 1 yard.

Dominic Rhodes (RB): Active for 10 games and started in 2. Rushed for 302 yards on 75 carries and 1 TD. Had 11 receptions for 70 yards, and returned 16 kickoffs for 312 yards.

JaMarcus Russell (QB): Active for 4 games and started in 1. Completed 36 of 66 pass attempts for 373 yards, 2 TD and 4 INT. Rushed for 4 yards on 5 carries.

Tony Stewart (TE): Active in 16 games.

Travis Taylor (WR): Active in 1 game.

Andrew Walter (QB): Active in 1 game. Completed 5 of 8 pass attempts for 38 yards.

Mike Williams (WR): Active in 6 games and started in 1. Had 7 receptions for 90 yards.

STARTERS — DEFENSE

DE — Jay Richardson: Active in 16 games, started in 11 and had 1 sack.

DE — Derrick Burgess: Active for and started in 14 games. Had 8 sacks and 1 fumble recovery.

DT — Warren Sapp: Started in 16 games, had 2 sacks and 1 fumble recovery.

DT — Terdell Sands: Active in 16 games and started in 11.

LLB — Thomas Howard: Started in 16 games, had 1 sack, 6 INT, 2 TD and1 fumble recovery.

MLB — Kirk Morrison: Started in 16 games, had 1 sack, 4 INT and fumble recovery.

RLB — Robert W. Thomas: Active in 14 games and started in 10.

CB — Nnamdi Asomugha: Active for and started in 15 games. Had INT, and returned 1 punt for 0 yards.

CB — Stanford Routt: Active for 16 games, started in 14, and had 3 INT.

SS — Michael Huff: Started in 16 games, had 1 sack, 1 INT and 1 fumble recovery.

FS — Stuart Schweigert: Active for 15 games, started in 10, and had INT.

RESERVE DEFENSIVE PLAYERS

Jon Alston (LB): Active for 13 games.

John Bowie (DB): Active for 2 games.

Tyler Brayton (E): Active for 16 games. Returned 1 kickoff for 6 yards and had 1 fumble recovery.

Ricky Brown (LB): Active for 16 games and started in 1.

Chris Carr (DB): Active for 16 games and started in 2. Returned 8 punts for 52 yards and 59 kickoffs for 1,327 yards.

Chris Clemons (LB): Active for 16 games and started in 2.

Jon Condo (LB): Active for 16 games.

Jarrod Cooper (DB): Active for 6 games and had 1 fumble recovery.

Isaiah Ekejiuba (LB): Active for 10 games.

Hiram Eugene (DB): Active for 16 games, started in 5, had 8 sacks and 1 fumble recovery.

Mario Henderson (T): Active for 1 game.

Chris Johnson (DB): Active for 13 games.

Tommy Kelly (E/T): Active for 7 games, started in 6, and had 1 sack.

Josh Shaw (T): Active for 1 game.

B.J. Ward (DB): Active for 4 games.

Gerard Warren (T): Active for 12 games and started in 5. Had 4 sacks and recorded 1 safety.

Fabian Washington (DB): Active for 15 games, started in 3, and had 1 INT.

Sam Williams (E): Active for 11 games and started in 4.

KICKING/PUNTING

K — Sebastian Janikowski: Active for 16 games. Made 23 of 32 field goals and 28 of 28 extra points for 97 points.

P — Shane Lechler: Active for 16 games. Punted 73 times for a **49.1** average, and rushed for -4 yards on 1 carry.

2008 Season Review

1. Sept. 8: The dawn of a new season for Raider Nation used to mean another opportunity to conquer the majority of opponents and contend for playoff berths. Unfortunately, that was then and this was 2008. After five seasons of absolute futility, the start of a new season only meant that a season of breaking even would be considered a success. Regardless of the lethargic

showings of recent years, for better of worse, the '08 campaign got underway. Before the Raiders realized they were in a game, they were down 27–0 going into the fourth quarter. Adding two fourth quarter touchdowns only made the 41–14 mauling appear not as bad. Denver quarterback Jay Cutler passed for 300 yards and two scores, while his counterpart, JaMarcus Russell threw for 180 yards on 17 of 26 attempts and two touchdowns. Ashley Lelie caught Russell's first six-pointer from eight yards out, and Ronald Curry registered a 4-yarder to close out the game's scoring. Justin Fargas led all ball carriers in the losing effort with 97 yards on 18 carries. This win allowed the Broncos to snap a seven-game losing streak on Monday night road games. The hapless Raiders, who once dominated the prime time spectacle, dropped their sixth consecutive Monday night affair, being outscored in those clashes 73 to 41.[1]

2. Sept. 14: Oakland had snapped a nine-game losing streak against Kansas City the previous season, and looked to string together a winning streak of their own against their long-standing rivals. Darren McFadden proved his worth as the team's number one draft pick by running for 164 yards and scored on a 19-yard jaunt to help Oakland even their record at 1–1 with a 23–8 victory. This loss gave Kansas City their 11th in a row. Michael Bush added 90 yards rushing, and included a 32-yard touchdown run. As a team, the Raiders ran for 300 yards, which was the third highest total ever given up by a Kansas City defense. Sebastian Janikowski gave Oakland their other points on three field goals from 25, 40, and a then-team record 56 yards that opened the game's scoring.[2]

3. Sept. 21: Buffalo's Ralph Wilson Stadium was the site of a contest between two teams that produced some of the fewest wins since 2000. The Bills came into this game with 55 victories, and the Raiders 53. Buffalo, however, stood at 2–0 in the early stages of the '08 season, and escaped this clash with Oakland still perfect thanks to a slim 24–23 win. Sebastian Janikowski gave Oakland a 9–7 halftime lead on field goals from 23, 35, and 32 yards. The Raiders extended their advantage to 23–14 in the fourth quarter on a JaMarcus Russell 1-yard run, and on a pass from Russell to Johnnie Lee Higgins that covered 84 yards. The Bills came back to score ten points in the final four minutes, with the game-winner coming on a 38-yard field goal from Rian Lindell with no time left on the clock. This win allowed Buffalo to start off a season at 3–0 for the first time since 1992.[3]

4. Sept. 28: San Diego came into this game tied with Kansas City for the longest win streak against the Raiders at nine. After sixty minutes of slugging it out with the Silver and Black, the Chargers owned the record outright. They achieved their 10th straight win over Oakland with a 28–18 tally. LaDainian Tomlinson had some of his finest moments against the Raiders, and he continued his magic touch by rushing for 106 yards and two touchdowns. Oakland put up a fight throughout the first three quarters, holding a 15–3 lead going in to the final stanza. A pair of Sebastian Janikowski field goals (22 and 28 yards), a safety, and a 63-yard pass from JaMarcus Russell to Zach Miller provided the Raiders with their points up to that time. For the game, Russell completed 22 of 37 passes for 277 yards. The bottom then fell out for Oakland after holding a 12-point lead. San Diego ran off 25 fourth quarter points to pull out the win. The Raiders were only able to get three points in the second half thanks to a 32-yard field goal from Janikowski. The Chargers forged ahead for the

first time in the game on a 47-yard field goal from Nate Kaeding with 1:51 left in the game. Tomlinson then added some insurance with his second six-pointer of the game, with this one coming on a 41-yard run. This loss proved to be the end of the Lane Kiffin coaching reign in Oakland. The much-publicized, turbulent relationship between Kiffin and owner Al Davis came to a climax after Oakland collapsed in this game. Assistant coach Tom Cable was appointed interim head coach upon the dismissal of Kiffin.[4]

5. Oct. 12: The Tom Cable–era began in Oakland with a trip to the Superdome in New Orleans. This game provided the Raiders with their worst beating of the season up to this point. After taking an early 3–0 lead on a 24-yard field goal by Sebastian Janikowski, Oakland was completely shut down. The Saints on the other hand rang up 34 points, primarily on the arm of quarterback Drew Brees, who completed 87 percent of his passes for 320 yards and three touchdowns. Former Heisman Trophy winner Reggie Bush put his mark on this game by catching his 200th career pass, which tied him with Anquan Boldin of the Arizona Cardinals for the fastest to reach that number of career receptions. He also added two touchdowns to his day's work, running for a 3-yarder and hauling in one of Brees' scoring strikes from 15 yards out.[5]

6. Oct. 19: The New York Jets came out to McAfee Coliseum with Brett Favre as their quarterback. Over his long and successful career, Favre was a perfect 4–0 against the Raiders, with all of them coming as a member of the Green Bay Packers. A change of uniform provided Favre with his lone loss to Oakland, as the Silver and Black pulled out a 16–13 overtime win. Like so many times throughout the decade, Sebastian Janikowski supplied the Raiders with another crucial field goal, and this one proved to be a classic. With 2:30 remaining in overtime, Janikowski broke his own team record he set one month earlier by sending a 57-yard three-pointer through the uprights to give Tom Cable his first win as Oakland's head coach. The teams waged a defensive battle in the first half, with the game knotted at 3–3 after the first thirty minutes of play. Janikowski gave Oakland their first half points on a 29-yard field goal near the end of the opening quarter. Javon Walker caught an 8-yard pass from JaMarcus Russell in the third quarter to break the tie, and Janikowski added a 37-yard field goal to give the Raiders a 13–10 lead with just under three minutes left in regulation. The Raiders could have won it without the need for overtime, but Tom Cable called for a timeout just as New York's Jay Feely missed a long field goal attempt. If the timeout was not asked for, the Raiders would have had the game locked up. Instead, Feely got another chance, and this time he was good on a 52-yarder with three seconds left. In overtime, the teams staged a punting exhibition for the first five series. Russell then connected on passes of 16 yards to Javon Walker and 27 to Zach Miller that set Oakland up for Janikowski's winning kick.[6]

7. Oct. 26: In a 29–10 win, Baltimore's Joe Flacco set a season team record for completions by a rookie quarterback. A tough Ravens' defense did their part by extending their streak of 26 straight games of not allowing a 100-yard rushing performance. With different blitz packages thrown at them, the Raiders were held to only 35 yards throughout the first half. During that time, the Ravens jumped out to a 19–0 lead. Oakland scored their ten points in the third quarter on a 22-yard Sebastian Janikowski field goal, and on a 2-yard pass from JaMarcus Russell to Justin Griffith.[7]

8. Nov. 2: The Atlanta Falcons came into Oakland and handed the lethargic Raiders a 24–0 loss in a half filled McAfee Coliseum that rang out with boos early in the game. The disgruntled fans had reason for their nasty attitude, as the Falcons held Oakland to 77 yards, which was their lowest offensive production in 47 years. Atlanta quarterback Matt Ryan teamed up with Michael Jenkins for two touchdowns, running back Michael Turner ran for 139 yards, and the Atlanta defense prevented the Raiders from obtaining a first down in the first half.[8]

9. Nov. 9: Carolina quarterback Jake Delhomme suffered the worst game of his career. He threw four interceptions, and completed only seven passes for 72 yards. However, against the Raiders, such a poor showing still did not mean a loss was a sure thing. The rest of the Carolina Panthers rallied despite their signal caller's performance and won, 17–6, holding Oakland without a touchdown for the second straight week. Sebastian Janikowski gave the Raiders their points on two third quarter field goals from 38 and 45 yards. DeAngelo Williams led the Carolina offensive attack with 140 yards on the ground and scored on a 69-yard run. The Raiders got 89 yards rushing from Justin Fargas on a day that saw Andrew Walter fill in for the injured JaMarcus Russell at quarterback. Walter was also forced to the sideline for a time after suffering an ankle injury in the fourth quarter. Prior to his departure, Walter threw two interceptions.[9]

10. Nov. 16: The Miami Dolphins were ranked at the bottom of the league in special teams performance. Johnnie Lee Higgins capitalized on that misfortune by returning a punt 93 yards to give the Raiders a 15–14 lead with 4:30 left in the game. However, this game did involve the Raiders, who somehow managed to jump into the jaws of defeat when victory was within their grasp. Also not helping was the fact that teams coming from the west coast to play in the eastern portion of the country were winless in 12 attempts up to this point of the '08 season. Whatever the reasoning, Miami quarterback Chad Pennington took the Dolphins 61 yards in 10 plays to allow Dan Carpenter the opportunity to drill a 38-yard field goal through the uprights with 38 ticks left on the clock to secure a 17–15 win. The loss dropped the Raiders to 2–8 while Miami kept their playoff hopes strong by improving to 6–4. Sebastian Janikowski kicked field goals from 21 and 37 yards, and Jay Richardson sacked Pennington in the end zone for a safety to give Oakland their other points.[10]

11. Nov. 23: Running back Justin Fargas had some of his best days as a pro against the Denver Broncos, averaging 121.5 yards per carry on the ground in two previous meetings with Oakland's divisional foe. Fargas continued his century-topping ways in a trip to Denver, rushing for 107 yards in 24 carries, and the Raiders shocked the 6–4 Broncos with a 31–10 win. With this win, the Raiders ended a four-game losing streak, and beat Denver for the second time in eight previous encounters. JaMarcus Russell was near perfect with 10 of 11 pass attempts connecting with his receivers. He passed for 152 yards and one touchdown covering four yards to Ashley Lelie. Rookie Darren McFadden ran for two 1-yard scores. McFadden's first touchdown run of the game was the first time in 206 plays that Oakland produced an offensive touchdown. Johnnie Lee Higgins returned a punt 89 yards, and Sebastian Janikowski kicked a 26-yard field goal for the 3–8 Raiders.[11]

12. Nov. 30: In a battle of teams with four wins between them, the 1–10 Kansas City Chiefs beat the Raiders in Oakland for the sixth straight time thanks to a 20–13 final. Kansas City running back Larry Johnson led all ball carriers in the game with 92 yards rushing, and scored the go-ahead touchdown in the fourth quarter on a 2-yard run. Justin Fargas ran for 82 yards and scored Oakland's lone six-pointer from one yard out. Sebastian Janikowski added field goals from 25 and 51 yards in the team's ninth loss of the year.[12]

13. Dec. 4: Oakland held a perfect 3–0 record against San Diego in previous Thursday night matchups. However, on this occasion, the Raiders had no chance in a 34–7 beat down. In their 11th straight win over the Raiders, San Diego's Philip Rivers threw for three scores, with Darren Sproles catching two of them. Vincent Jackson caught Rivers' other touchdown toss, and hauled in five passes for 148 yards on the day. Justin Miller provided Oakland with their only touchdown on a 92-yard kickoff return. JaMarcus Russell helped San Diego get 17 points off three touchdowns that included two interceptions and a fumble. He suffered an ankle injury following his second interception, and Andrew Walter came on and was picked off once.[13]

14. Dec. 14: The New England Patriots jumped out to a 35–14 first half lead, and coasted to an easy 49–26 win. Matt Cassel threw four touchdown passes, with two going to ex–Raider Randy Moss. Those 35 points were the most allowed by the Raiders in the first half since the AFL-NFL merger in 1970. Oakland fell to 3–11, which made them the first team to ever lose at least 11 games for a sixth straight season. JaMarcus Russell threw for 242 yards and had touchdown passes of 56 yards to Johnnie Lee Higgins and 10 yards to Ronald Curry. Justin Miller returned a kickoff 91 yards and Darren McFadden scored on an 11-yard run.[14]

15. Dec. 21: The Raiders came alive in their home finale to snap the Houston Texans' four-game winning streak with a 27–17 win. Johnnie Lee Higgins stood out with a 29-yard touchdown reception from JaMarcus Russell, and on an 80-yard punt return. Russell added a second scoring strike to Chaz Schilens from 20 yards out to open the scoring. Russell turned in a solid performance by connecting on 18 of 25 pass attempts for 236 yards and no interceptions. Justin Fargas paced the ground attack with 93 yards. Sebastian Janikowski added two field goals from 33 and 30 yards to complete Oakland's scoring in the game.[15]

16. Dec. 28: The Raiders went into the off-season on a high note by recording a 31–24 win over the Tampa Bay Buccaneers for their second straight win. Reserve running back Michael Bush took advantage of the opportunity given him by hammering his way through the Tampa defense for 177 rushing yards and touchdown runs of four and 67 yards. JaMarcus Russell converted on scoring strikes to Chaz Schilens (3 yards) and Johnnie Lee Higgins (12 yards), and Sebastian Janikowski ended Oakland's scoring for the '08 campaign with a 25-yard field goal in the fourth quarter.[16]

Individual Statistics and Roster

Head Coach: Lane Kiffin (four games), and Tom Cable (12 games)
Assistant Coaches: Willie Brown, Tom Cable (four games), James Cregg, John DeFilippo, John Fassel, Randy Hanson, Adam Henry, Mark Jackson, Don Johnson, Greg Knapp, Sanjay Lal, James Lofton, Don Martindale, George Martinez, Keith Millard, Darren Perry, Tom Rathman, Brad Roll, Rob Ryan, Brian Schneider, Kelly Skipper

2008 Regular Season Record: 5–11
3rd Place in AFC Western Division
Scored 263 points to rank 29th out of 32 teams
Allowed 388 points to rank 24th

Starters — Offense

QB — JaMarcus Russell: Active for and started in 15 games. Completed 198 of 368 pass attempts for 2,423 yards, 13 TD and 8 INT. Rushed for 127 yards on 17 carries and 1 TD.

RB — Justin Fargas: Active for and started in 14 games. Rushed for 853 yards on 218 carries and 1 TD. Had 10 receptions for 52 yards.

RB — Luke Lawton: Active for 16 games and started in 7. Had 6 receptions for 30 yards, and returned 2 kickoffs for 29 yards.

WR — Ronald Curry: Active for 13 games and started in 10. Had 19 receptions for 181 yards and 2 TD. Rushed for 1 yard on 1 carry.

WR — Javon Walker: Active for 8 games and started in 7. Had 15 receptions for 196 yards and 1 TD.

TE — Zach Miller: Active for 16 games and started in 15. Had 56 receptions for 778 yards and 1 TD.

LT — Kwame Harris: Active for 14 games and started in 11.

LG — Robert Gallery: Started in 16 games.

C — Jake Grove: Active for and started in 12 games.

RG — Cooper Carlisle: Active for and started in 15 games.

RT — Cornell Green: Started in 16 games.

Reserve Offensive Players

Michael Bush (RB): Active for 15 games. Rushed for 421 yards on 95 carries and 3 TD. Had 19 receptions for 162 yards, completed 1 of 2 pass attempts for 8 yards, and returned 1 kickoff for 14 yards.

Jason Davis (RB): Active for 1 game.

Justin Griffith (RB): Active for 7 games and started in 3. Rushed for 2 yards on 2 carries, and had 9 receptions for 85 yards and 1 TD.

Johnnie Lee Higgins (WR): Active for 16 games and started in 3. Had 22 receptions for 366 yards and 4 TD. Rushed for 34 yards on 3 carries, returned 44 punts for **570** yards and 3 TD, and 36 kickoffs for 842 yards.

Jonathan Holland (WR): Active for 3 games.

Ashley Lelie (WR): Active for 13 games and started in 6. Had 11 receptions for 197 yards and 2 TD.

John Madsen (WR): Active for 4 games.

James Marten (T): Active for 1 game.

Darren McFadden (RB): Active for 13 games and started in 5. Rushed for 499 yards on 113 carries and 4 TD. Had 29 receptions for 285 yards.

Paul McQuistan (T): Active for 1 game.

Chris Morris (C): Active for 16 games and started in 1.

Chaz Schilens (WR): Active for 16 games and started in 6. Had 15 receptions for 226 yards and 2 TD, and rushed for -2 yards on 1 carry.

Tony Stewart (TE): Active for 16 games and started in 4. Had 11 receptions for 81 yards.

Darrell Strong (TE): Active for 1 game.

Marques Tuiasosopo (QB): Active for 2 games, completed 1 of 2 pass attempts for 4 yards, and rushed for 11 yards on 2 carries.

John Wade (C): Active for 5 games and started in 4.

Andrew Walter (QB): Active for 2 games and started in 1. Completed 22 of 49 pass attempts for 204 yards and 3 INT. Rushed for 19 yards on 5 carries.

Seth Wand (T): Active for 1 game.

Todd Watkins (WR): Active for 8 games.

Starters — Defense

DE — Jay Richardson: Active for 16 games, started in 11, had 3 sacks and recorded 1 safety.

DE — Kalimba Edwards: Active for 14 games, started in 11, had 5 sacks and 1 fumble recovery.

DT — Tommy Kelly: Started in 16 games and had 4 sacks.

DT — Gerard Warren: Started in 16 games and had 4 sacks.

LLB — Ricky Brown: Active for 7 games and started in 6.

MLB — Kirk Morrison: Started in 16 games, had 1 sack and 1 INT.

RLB — Thomas Howard: Started in 16 games, had 1 sack and 1 INT.

CB — DeAngelo Hall: Active for and started in 8 games. Had sack, 3 INT and 1 fumble recovery.

CB — Nnamdi Asomugha: Active for and started in 15 games. Had 1 INT.

SS — Gibril Wilson: Active for 16 games and started in 15. Had 1 sacks, 2 INT, 3 fumble recoveries, and recorded 1 safety.

FS — Hiram Eugene: Active for 16 games and started in 10.

Reserve Defensive Players

Jon Alston (LB): Active for 14 games, started in 4, and rushed for 22 yards on 1 carry.

Rashad Baker (DB): Active for 10 games, started in 1, and had 3 INT.

Tyvon Branch (DB): Active for 8 games, had 1 INT, 1 fumble recovery, and returned 6 kickoffs for 89 yards.

Derrick Burgess (E/LB): Active for and started in 10 games. Had 3 sacks.

Jon Condo (LB): Active for 16 games.

Marquis Cooper (LB): Active for 8 games.

Isaiah Ekejiuba (LB): Active for 16 games and had 1 fumble recovery.

Greyson Gunheim (E): Active for 3 games, had 1 sack and 1 kickoff return for 9 yards.

Mario Henderson (T): Active for 11 games and started in 5.

Michael Huff (DB): Active for 16 games and started in 7.

Chris Johnson (DB): Active for 15 games, started in 7, and had 3 INT.

William Joseph (T): Active for 8 games.

Justin Miller (DB): Active for 7 games, and returned 32 kickoffs for 794 yards and 2 TD.

Stanford Routt (DB): Active for 15 games and started in 4.

Terdell Sands (T): Active for 16 games. Had 2 sacks and 1 fumble recovery.

Trevor Scott (E): Active for 16 games and had 5 sacks.

Robert W. Thomas (LB): Active for 2 games and started in 1.

Michael Waddell (DB): Active for 1 game.

Fred Wakefield (E/T): Active for 7 games.

Sam Williams (E): Active for 16 games, started in 2, had 1 INT and 1 fumble recovery.

Kicking/Punting

K — Sebastian Janikowski: Active for 16 games. Made 24 of 30 field goals and 25 of 26 extra points for 96 points.

P — Shane Lechler: Active for 16 games. Punted 90 times for a 48.8 average, and rushed for 0 yards on 1 carry. **Led the NFL in yards punted (4,391).**

2009 Season Review

1. Sept. 14: Oakland opened their golden anniversary season in dire straits. Their opening day opponents were the San Diego Chargers, who had won 11 straight over them coming into this game. Superstar running back LaDainian Tomlinson loved playing against the Raiders, averaging 119 yards rushing against them. Oakland had lost their last ten appearances in prime time games, and had the league's worst record (24–72) over the previous six seasons. They were also the only team in NFL history with at least 11 losses in six consecutive seasons. Despite their dismal resume, the Raiders refused to give up against San Diego on a Thursday night national telecast. Oakland jumped out to a 7–0 lead on a Michael Bush 4-yard run that capped a 10-play, 84-

yard drive in six minutes and ten seconds. Tomlinson, who the Raiders held to 55 yards on the ground, tied it up with a 1-yard run. Sebastian Janikowski put the Raiders back on top, 10–7, with a 37-yard field goal. San Diego's Nate Kaeding booted a long 47-yard three-pointer with 40 seconds left in the first half to send the teams into halftime knotted at ten apiece. After a scoreless third quarter, Janikowski once again lifted Oakland to a three-point advantage with a 35-yard field goal. The Chargers then took their first lead of the game with 7:22 left on a Phillip Rivers 15-yard pass to Vincent Jackson. Oakland's rookie wide receiver Louis Murphy responded well to his first pro start by catching a 57-yard touchdown toss from JaMarcus Russell that finished off a nine-play, 71-yard drive with 2:34 left, and gave the Raiders a 20–17 lead. On the night, Murphy had four receptions for 87 yards. Zach Miller also did well with 96 yards receiving on six catches. The Raiders played tough and refused to quite, but Rivers managed to crush their hopes of an upset. He took the Chargers 89 yards in nine plays, capping the drive on a 5-yard pass to Darren Sproles with 18 seconds left to pull out a 24–20 win. On the winning drive, Rivers completed six of seven passes for 79 yards.[1]

2. Sept. 20: Kansas City came into this game with a 14–5 home field advantage over the Raiders since 1990. Oakland looked to stop that victory total from reaching 15 in what became a kicking battle through the first three quarters. Oakland led, 6–3, on two thunderous Sebastian Janikowski field goals from 48 and 54 yards. The Chiefs then put the first six-pointer up on the board when quarterback Matt Cassel, in his Kansas City debut, connected with Dwayne Bowe from 29 yards to give the Chiefs a 10–6 lead with 2:38 left in the game. Despite the lethargic offensive showings that saw Oakland barely break the 100-yard barrier, they put together a 9-play, 69-yard drive that Darren McFadden finished off with a 5-yard run as the game clock showed a mere 1:07 left on it. On the winning drive, JaMarcus Russell found Louis Murphy for a gain of 19 and Todd Watkins for 28 before McFadden took a pitchout and ran untouched into the end zone for the 13–10 win. The Raiders showed will power by not falling to another long-time rival in the closing minutes or seconds.[2]

3. Sept. 27: The Denver Broncos came into this game as winners of their last nine division openers. The Broncos easily made it ten with a 23–3 win over Oakland to remain undefeated under rookie head coach Josh McDaniel. Quarterback Kyle Orton opened the scoring with a pass to Brandon Marshall, and Correll Buckhalter (108 yards) and rookie Knowshon Moreno (90 yards) provided Denver with a solid running attack. On the opposite side, the Raiders once again showed little signs of offensive life, with JaMarcus Russell throwing for only 61 yards and two interceptions, while Darren McFadden led the team with 45 rushing yards. Sebastian Janikowski's 48-yard field goal in the second quarter prevented a shutout for the 1–2 Raiders.[3]

4. Oct. 4: Sebastian Janikowski saved the Raiders yet again from total embarrassment. He produced two field goals from 46 and 33 yards to avoid a shutout in a 29–6 loss to the Houston Texans. Janikowski was responsible for all of Oakland's point production over the course of the past two games. The Raiders had only one offensive touchdown since opening day, and it did not look like things were even remotely turning around. JaMarcus Russell only threw for 128 yards, and Justin Fargas led the team

in rushing with 24 yards on 10 carries. Darren McFadden tore hi[s] knee cartilage, and would be lost for at least two to four weeks. To add to the team's grief was bad publicity over an investigatio[n] involving head coach Tom Cable's alleged assault on one of hi[s] assistants, Randy Hanson.[4]

5. Oct. 11: Just when things could not possibly get any wors[e] for the Silver and Black they did. A trip to Giants Stadium agains[t] the undefeated New York Giants produced a 44–7 debacle. Th[e] only good news to come out of this mauling for Oakland was th[e] fact that they managed to cross the goal line for the first time i[n] three weeks. Michael Bush scored on a 5-yard run with the gam[e] already out of control, and he led the team in rushing with 3[?] yards. Many of the Giants claimed after this encounter that i[t] seemed the Raiders were not even trying to play. It felt more lik[e] a scrimmage to the New Yorkers than a real game. The win wa[s] that easy. The Giants rolled up 483 yards on their way to thei[r] best start since 1990. Quarterback Eli Manning made the mos[t] of his 83rd consecutive start by throwing for two scores an[d] leading the Giants to four touchdowns on their first four posses[-]sions. For the Raiders, this was their third straight loss by at leas[t] 20 points for the first time in team history. They were also onl[y] the second team in 32 seasons to go four straight games with 20[0] total offensive yards. In this slaughter, the Silver and Black onl[y] produced 124 offensive yards. JaMarcus Russell helped the Raider[s] earn the dubious honor by throwing for 100 yards on eight of 1[3] pass attempts, was sacked six times, and fumbled on three occa[-]sions.[5]

6. Oct. 18: Another opponent from the tough NFC Eas[t] loomed for the Raiders, this time the 3–1 Philadelphia Eagles[.] Sometimes the unexpected happens, and on this day in Oakland[,] it did. With the Raiders' offense establishing negative records, th[e] Philadelphia offense came into this game with a second place league ranking in points per game. However, Oakland found a way to shock the Eagles with in 13–9 upset win. Zach Mille[r] scored on an 86-yard pass from JaMarcus Russell in the first quarter to give Oakland a 7–3 lead that they never relinquished[.] Miller's score was the longest by a Raiders tight end in team history. Sebastian Janikowski added field goals from 29 and 46 yards, and the Oakland defense pounded Philly quarterback Donovan McNabb for six sacks, which was the most by Oakland since 2005. When not driving him into the turf, Oakland tormented McNabb throughout the day with constant pressure. This was the first time in the season that Philadelphia failed to score a touchdown. Despite two interceptions, Russell did well by hitting on 17 of 28 pass attempts for 224 yards. Justin Fargas added 87 yards rushing to Oakland's offensive output. An interesting and humorous event occurred in this game that might have been a first throughout the history of pro football. While the Raiders were lined up for a kickoff, a pigeon flew by and lined up perfectly with the rest of Oakland's special teams unit. It did not move until the ball was kicked, and then flew in unison with the rest of the unit downfield. It was a great sideshow attraction on a day that saw the downtrodden Raiders rise up and put one in the win column.[6]

7. Oct. 25: Mark Sanchez became the first rookie quarterback to start off a season 3–0. The New York Jets then dropped three straight, but got back on track thanks to a 38–0 beat down over the Raiders. Sanchez ran for one score and threw for another.

fellow rookie, running back Shonn Greene, ran for 144 yards and two touchdowns. JaMarcus Russell was benched in the second quarter with Oakland trailing, 21–0, in favor of Bruce Gradkowski, after a fumble and two interceptions led to two touchdowns. This was just the fifth time that the Raiders were shut out at home, with the other four coming over the previous four dismal seasons. This also marked the worst home loss suffered by the Raiders in team history.[7]

8. Nov. 1: The number 13 is considered unlucky, but not when it marked how many times in a row the San Diego Chargers had beaten the Raiders. In this 24–16 win over the hapless Raiders, LaDainian Tomlinson ran for two scores and Phillip Rivers threw for one. Tomlinson's two rushing touchdowns gave him 22 for his career against the Raiders. He also caught three touchdowns and threw for three more when playing Oakland. With JaMarcus Russell back as the starter, the Raiders managed to get close enough for three Sebastian Janikowski field goals from 48, 41, and 28 yards. Justin Fargas added a touchdown run from three yards out. It was another bad day for Russell, who completed 14 of 22 passes for 109 yards and an interception. He was also battered for five sacks. With his team crumbling all around him, head coach Tom Cable had added grief thrust upon him when his ex-wife and current girlfriend claimed he displayed violent behavior against them. These allegations came out just weeks after Cable's apparent assault on one of his assistant coaches.[8]

9. Nov. 15: Kansas City was looking to become the first team to beat the Raiders seven straight times in Oakland. They achieved this with a 16–10 win that saw them score their first rushing touchdown of the season. This loss, which gave the 2–7 Raiders a share of the AFC West basement with the Chiefs, took away from a fine performance by Michael Bush's 119 yards rushing on 14 carries. JaMarcus Russell had another terrible outing with nine completions in 24 attempts for 67 yards. Oakland received their ten points on a Justin Fargas 1-yard run and a 50-yard field goal from Sebastian Janikowski. Both scores came in the first quarter, allowing the Raiders to hold a brief 10–7 lead over their long-time foes.[9]

10. Nov. 22: The Cincinnati Bengals were looking to make some noise in the AFC. With a 7–2 record, the Bengals were one game up on the Super Bowl champion Pittsburgh Steelers in the AFC North, and looked to increase their momentum with a trip out to face the struggling Raiders. However, Cincinnati was winless (0–8) throughout their history when playing the Raiders in Oakland. The Raiders were on the verge of starting their fourth straight season off at 2–8, and hoped to stop that from occurring against the powerful Bengals. Bruce Gradkowski was given the chance to start the game at quarterback over the non-productive JaMarcus Russell. He used the opportunity to shock the football world by guiding the Silver and Black to a 20–17 upset victory, and extend their home winning streak against the Bengals to 9–0. Things looked bleak at first for Oakland, as Cincinnati held a 14–0 second quarter lead. Gradkowski then got the Raiders on the board with a 10-yard pass to Zach Miller with 59 seconds left in the first half. Sebastian Janikowski added a booming 52-yard field goal in the third quarter to cut the deficit to four points. The Bengals increased their lead to 17–10 late in the third, and that was how it remained until the final 33 seconds of the game. Gradkowski once again found his mark, this time it was Louis Murphy

from 29 yards out. Janikowski's extra point kick tied the game at 17–17, and overtime looked like a sure thing. Brandon Myers changed all that by forcing a fumble on the ensuing kickoff. With 15 seconds, Janikowski came through with a game winning 33-yard three-pointer to lift the Raiders to their third win of the '09 season.[10]

11. Nov. 26: The Raiders looked to take the momentum gathered from their big win over the Bengals into the national spotlight on Thanksgiving Day against another strong playoff hopeful, the Dallas Cowboys. This marked only the second time that the Raiders were featured on Thanksgiving Day. The first was a loss to the Detroit Lions in 1970. Oakland's magic from the previous game diminished this time around, as the Cowboys never allowed them the chance to contend in this one, and won easily, 24–7. This proved to be the first time that the Cowboys beat the Raiders in Dallas after three unsuccessful attempts. The Cowboys rolled up 494 offensive yards, with quarterback Tony Romo throwing for 309 of them. They also had two receivers go over the century mark in Miles Austin (145 yards), and Jason Witten (107 yards). The Raiders were shut out through the first half, failing to cross midfield in that time. Oakland's lone points in the Lone Star State were provided by Darrius Heyward-Bey's first-ever touchdown reception, coming on a 4-yard strike from Bruce Gradkowski in the third quarter.[11]

12. Dec. 6: The week began with a public outcry for Al Davis to step down as Oakland's General Manager. In grand fashion, the plea was posted on a billboard close to the stadium that read, "Mr. Davis, do the right thing, please hire a GM."[12] However, the week ended with another incredible upset victory. Once again, the Raiders shocked the football community by knocking off the defending Super Bowl champion Pittsburgh Steelers, 27–24, to improve to 4–8. The Steelers clung to a 10–6 lead through three quarters, with Oakland getting their points on field goals of 48 and 43 yards by Sebastian Janikowski. The Raiders then erupted for 21 points in the final 15 minutes to pull out the game in the final nine seconds. All three touchdowns came on the arm of Bruce Gradkowski. With this great showing, Gradkowski joined team legend Ken Stabler as the only two Raiders quarterbacks to throw for three scores in the fourth quarter of one game. Stabler achieved his piece of team history in 1979, with it also coming against the Steelers. Gradkowski began his quest for the record book by connecting with Chaz Schilens from 17 yards out. Three minutes later it was a 75-yarder to Louis Murphy, and five minutes later it was the same duo that teamed up again, this time from 11 yards out. This marked the second time in three weeks that the Gradkowski-Murphy tandem helped Oakland pull out a win in the closing seconds. On the day, Gradkowski completed 20 of 33 attempts for 308 yards, and Murphy hauled in four of those aerials for 128 yards.[13]

13. Dec. 13: The joy of victory was quickly replaced by defeat in a 34–13 loss to the Washington Redskins. Washington quarterback Jason Campbell threw for two scores, and Quinton Ganther ran for a pair of six-pointers in the fourth quarter to take away any hopes of an Oakland comeback. Bruce Gradkowski injured his knee after completing 10 of 18 pass attempts for 153 yards. Also injured was star defensive back Nnamdi Asomugha, who left in the third quarter with a banged up forearm. JaMarcus Russell assumed the signal caller duties after Gradkowski went

down, and the former starter connected on 10 of 16 passes for 74 yards. Justin Fargas ran for a 1-yard touchdown, and Sebastian Janikowski kicked a pair of field goals from 34 and 54 yards to supply Oakland with their points.[14]

14. Dec. 20: In the past, the Raiders owned the Denver Broncos in December matchups, posting an impressive 18–5 slate against them. This time out, the Raiders made it an exciting, down-to-the-wire affair, and extended their dominance over Denver in December thanks to a 20–19 victory. JaMarcus Russell had been dismal at best during most of his outings as Oakland's signal caller throughout this season, but on this day, he provided the team with some last second heroics. Russell came into this game in the fourth quarter to relive starter Charlie Frye after he received a hard blow to the head. Trailing, 19–13, with 5:54 to go in the game, the Oakland offense got the ball down to the Denver 10 with 35 seconds showing on the clock. Russell then found Chaz Schilens for the game-tying touchdown, and Sebastian Janikowski supplied the extra point kick that elevated the Silver and Black to their fifth win of the year. Janikowski also had two field goals from 54 and 28 yards, and Michael Bush scored on a 23-yard run. Bush had a great day running the ball, with 133 yards on 18 carries.[15]

15. Dec. 27: Quarterback Charlie Frye returned to his native Ohio to face the Cleveland Browns after starting his pro career with them. His homecoming turned into another dismal affair for the Raiders, as they suffered a 23–9 setback. This game saw the Raiders rack up 13 penalties for 126 yards, and they never seemed to get out of the hole they dug for themselves. They also had two players ejected in Stanford Routt (head butting), and Tony Stewart (contact with an official). The Browns jumped out to a 10–0 first quarter lead, and never gave it up. Frye passed for an impressive 333 yard, but was intercepted three times. Even though Frye never got the Raiders into the end zone, he managed to get close for Sebastian Janikowski to provide Oakland with their only points on this cold day in Cleveland. "Sea Bass" connected on a 44-yarder to get the Raiders on the board in the first quarter, and then followed that up with one from 34 yards. Janikowski saved his best effort of the day for last. His sent a whopping 61-yard kick through the uprights with no time left in the first half to establish a new team record for longest field goals in Raiders history.[16]

16. Jan. 3: The Raiders concluded the first decade of the millennium against the Baltimore Ravens in a matchup of two of the league's most penalized teams. With Willis McGahee running for 167 yards and three touchdowns, the Ravens clinched a playoff berth with a 21–13 win over host Oakland. The Raiders looked to JaMarcus Russell once again to possibly rally the team. However, a third quarter interception led to a McGahee six-pointer, and a Russell fumble on the Baltimore 23 killed a solid scoring opportunity for Oakland with 9:23 left in the game. This defeat put the Raiders at 5–11, which made them the only team in NFL history to finish seven straight seasons with at least 11 losses.[17]

Individual Statistics and Roster

Head Coach: Tom Cable
Assistant Coaches: Dwaine Board, Willie Brown, John Fassel, Paul Hackett, Mike Haluchak, Randy Hanson, Adam Henry, Sanjay Lal, Bert

Leone, John Marshall, Jim Michalczik, Chris Morgan, Aaron Pelc, Brad Roll, Rich Scangarello, Kelly Skipper, Ted Tollner, Lionel Washington

2009 Regular Season Record: 5–11
3rd Place in AFC Western Division
Scored 197 points to rank 31st out of 32 teams
Allowed 379 points to rank 23rd

STARTERS — OFFENSE

QB — JaMarcus Russell: Active for 12 games and started in 9. Completed 120 of 246 pass attempts for 1,287 yards, 3 TD and 11 INT. Rushed for 44 yards on 18 carries.
RB — Michael Bush: Active for 16 games and started in 7. Rushed for 589 yards on 123 yards and 3 TD. Had 17 receptions for 105 yards and threw 1 pass that was incomplete.
RB — Darren McFadden: Active for 12 games and started in 7. Rushed for 357 yards on 104 carries and 1 TD. Had 21 receptions for 245 yards.
WR — Darrius Heyward-Bey: Active for and started in 11 games. Had 9 receptions for 124 yards and 1 TD. Rushed for 19 yards on 2 carries.
WR — Louis Murphy: Active for 16 games and started in 9. Had 34 receptions for 521 yards and 4 TD. Rushed for 31 yards on 6 carries.
TE — Zach Miller: Active for and started in 15 games. Had 66 receptions for 805 yards and 3 TD.
LT — Mario Henderson: Started in 16 games.
LG — Chris Morris: Active for 16 games and started in 10.
C — Samson Satele: Active for 15 games and started in 12.
RG — Copper Carlisle: Started in 16 games.
RT — Cornell Green: Active for and started in 12 games.

RESERVE OFFENSIVE PLAYERS

Khalif Barnes (T): Active for 6 games and started in 2.
Justin Fargas (RB): Active for 12 games and started in 4. Rushed for 491 yards on 129 carries and 3 TD. Had 17 receptions for 113 yards.
Charlie Frye (QB): Active for and started in 3 games. Completed 53 of 87 pass attempts for 581 yards, 1 TD and 4 INT. Rushed for 41 yards on 4 carries.
Robert Gallery (T): Active for and started in 6 games.
Bruce Gradkowski (QB): Active for 7 games and started in 4. Completed 82 of 150 pass attempts for 1,007 yards, 6 TD and 3 INT. Rushed for 108 yards on 18 carries.
Johnnie Lee Higgins (WR): Active for 15 games and started in 5. Had 19 receptions for 263 yards, rushed for 21 yards on 2 carries, and returned 34 punts for 177 yards.
Jonathan Holland (WR): Active for 14 games and returned 28 kickoffs for 550 yards.
Luke Lawton (RB): Active for 13 games and started in 3. Had 7 receptions for 31 yards, and returned 1 kickoff for 17 yards.
J.P. Losman (QB): Active for 1 game. Threw 1 pass that was incomplete.
Paul McQuistan (T): Active for 3 games.
Brandon Myers (TE): Active for 11 games and started in 2. Had 4 receptions for 19 yards.
Oren O'Neal (RB): Active for 4 games and rushed for 0 yards on 1 carry.
Erik Pears (T): Active for 12 games and started in 4.
Louis Rankin (RB): Active for 2 games and returned 6 kickoffs for 108 yards.
Marcel Reece (TE): Active for 2 games, had 2 receptions for 20 yards, and returned 3 kickoffs for 58 yards.
Gary Russell (RB): Active for 12 games and started in 4. Rushed for 0 yards on 3 carries. Had 12 receptions for 96 yards, and returned 18 kickoffs for 330 yards.
Chaz Schilens (WR): Active for and started in 8 games. Had 29 receptions for 365 yards and 2 TD.
Tony Stewart (TE): Active for 15 games and started in 4. Had 10 receptions for 78 yards, and returned 2 kickoffs for 19 yards.
Javon Walker (WR): Active for 3 games and returned 1 kickoff for 0 yards.
Langston Walker (T/G): Active for 7 games and started 2.

odd Watkins (WR): Active for 13 games and started in 1. Had 8 receptions for 90 yards.

TARTERS — DEFENSE

E — Richard Seymour: Started in 16 games and had 4 sacks.

E — Greg Ellis: Active for and started in 14 games. Had 7 sacks and 2 fumble recoveries.

T — Tommy Kelly: Started in 16 games and had 1 sack.

T — Gerard Warren: Started in 16 games and had 2 sacks.

LB — Trevor Scott: Active for 16 games, started in 6, and had 7 sacks.

1LB — Kirk Morrison: Started in 16 games, had 2 sacks and 1 fumble recovery.

LB — Thomas Howard: Active for 16 games and started in 15. Had 2 sacks and 1 fumble recovery.

B — Chris Johnson: Active for and started in 15 games and had 3 INT.

B — Nnamdi Asomugha: Started in 16 games and had 1 INT.

S — Tyvon Branch: Started in 16 games and had 1 sack.

S — Michael Huff: Active for 16 games and started in 12. Had sack, 3 INT and 1 fumble recovery.

RESERVE DEFENSIVE PLAYERS

n Alston (LB): Active for 9 games and started in 4.

hn Bowie (DB): Active for 3 games.

rome Boyd (DB): Active for 1 game.

Ricky Brown (LB): Active for and started in 5 games.

Desmond Bryant (T): Active for 16 games and had 1 fumble recovery.

Jon Condo (LB): Active for 16 games.

Isaiah Ekejiuba (LB): Active for 16 games.

Hiram Eugene (DB): Active for 14 games, started in 4, had 1 INT and 1 fumble recovery.

William Joseph: Active for 6 games.

Justin Miller (DB): Active for 1 game. Returned 6 kickoffs for 106 yards.

Michael Mitchell (DB): Active for 16 games, had 1 sacks and 2 fumble recoveries.

David Nixon (LB): Active for 3 games.

Slade Norris (LB): Active for 4 games.

Jay Richardson (E): Active for 16 games and had 3 sacks.

Stanford Routt (DB): Active for 16 games, started in 1, and had 1 sack.

Matt Shaughnessy (E): Active for 16 games, started in 2, had 4 sacks and 1 fumble recovery.

Sam Williams (E): Active for 16 games and started in 2. Returned 1 punt for 0 yards and 2 kickoffs for 11 yards.

KICKING/PUNTING

K — Sebastian Janikowski: Active for 16 games. Made 26 of 29 field goals and 17 of 17 extra points for 95 points.

P — Shane Lechler: Active for 16 games. Punted 96 times for a **51.1** average. **Also led the NFL in yards punted (4,909).**

Part II. The Team

ALL-TIME ROSTER*

This section is dedicated to every player in Raiders history who made the official roster from 1960 to 2009. After each player's name will be the following information: Years with the Raiders; how they were acquired (whenever possible); position; jersey number; height and weight; college attended; dates of birth and death (if applicable).

Rick Ackerman: 1984, 1987; came to the Raiders as a free agent in November 1984; Defensive Tackle; #58 and 97; 6-4, 250 lbs.; Memphis State; June 16, 1959.

Sam Adams: 2002; came to the Raiders as a free agent in 2002; Defensive Tackle; #95; 6-3, 350 lbs.; Texas A&M; June 13, 1973.

Stanley Adams: 1984; came to the Raiders as a free agent in 1982; Linebacker; #59; 6-2, 215 lbs.; Memphis State; May 22,1960.

Stefon Adams: 1986–89; Raiders 3rd round draft selection in 1985 draft; Defensive Back; #44; 5-10, 190 lbs.; East Carolina; August 11,1963.

James Adkisson: 2006; came to the Raiders as a free agent in December 2005; Tight End; #88; 6-5, 230 lbs.; South Carolina; January 11, 1980.

Ben Agajanian: 1962; came to the Raiders as a free agent in 1962; Kicker; #3; 6-0, 220 lbs.; New Mexico; August 28, 1919.

Carl Aikens: 1987; came to the Raiders as a free agent in 1987; Wide Receiver; #83; 6-1, 187 lbs.; Northern Illinois; June 5, 1962.

Elijah Alexander: 2000–01; came to the Raiders as a free agent in March 2000; Linebacker; #58; 6-2, 235 lbs.; Kansas State; August 2, 1970–March 24, 2010.

Mike Alexander: 1989; Raiders 8th round selection in 1988 draft; Wide Receiver; #80; 6-3, 195 lbs.; Penn State: March 19, 1965.

Dalva Allen: 1962–64; came to the Raiders in a trade with the Houston Oilers in 1962 mid-way through the exhibition season; Defensive End; #80; 6-4, 245 lbs.; Houston; January 13, 1935.

Eric Allen: 1998–01; came to the Raiders in a trade with the New Orleans Saints in March 1998; Defensive Back; #21; 5-10, 185 lbs.; Arizona State; November 22, 1965.

Jackie Allen: 1969; Raiders 6th round draft selection in 1969 draft; Defensive Back; #22; 6-1, 187 lbs.; Baylor; September 24, 1947.

Marcus Allen: 1982–92; Raiders 1st round selection in1982 draft; Running Back; #32; 6-2, 210 lbs.; University of Southern Cal-

ifornia (USC); March 26, 1960.

Jon Alston: 2007–09; came to the Raiders as a free agent in September 2007; Linebacker; #55; 6-0, 225 lbs.; Stanford; June 4, 1983.

Lyle Alzado: 1982–85; came to the Raiders in a trade with the Cleveland Browns in April 1982; Defensive End; #77; 6-3, 260 lbs.; Yankton; April 3, 1949–May 14, 1992.

Vince Amey: 1998; Raiders 7th round selection in 1998 draft; Defensive Tackle; #92; 6-3, 300 lbs.; Arizona State; February 9, 1975.

Courtney Anderson: 2004–06; Raiders 7th round selection in 2004 draft; Tight End; #83; 6-6, 270 lbs.; San Jose State; November 19, 1980.

Eddie Anderson: 1987–97; came to the Raiders as a free agent in September 1987; Safety; #33; 6-1, 215 lbs.; Fort Valley State; July 22, 1963.

Marques Anderson: 2004; came to the Raiders in a trade with the Green Bay Packers in September 2004; Safety; #23; 5-11, 212 lbs.; University of California Los Angeles (UCLA); May 26, 1979.

Leo Araguz: 1996–99; came to the Raiders as a free agent in December 1996; Punter; #2; 5-11, 190 lbs.; S. F. Austin; January 18, 1970.

Dan Archer: 1967; Raiders number six Redshirt draft selection in 1966; Offensive Tackle; #78; 6-5, 245 lbs.; Oregon; September 29, 1944.

Ramon Armstrong: 1960; came to the Raiders in the expansion draft from the New York Titans; Offensive Tackle; #66; 6-1, 235 lbs.; Texas Christian; October 6, 1937.

Trace Armstrong: 2001–03; came to the Raiders as a free agent in March 2001; Defensive End; #93; 6-4, 275 lbs.; Florida; October 5, 1965.

Doug Asad: 1960–61; came to Raiders as a free agent in 1960; Tight End; #83; 6-2, 205 lbs.; Northwestern; August 27, 1938.

Darryl Ashmore: 1998–01; came to the Raiders as a free agent in April 1998; Offensive Tackle/Guard; #73 and 77; 6-7, 310 lbs.; Northwestern; November 1, 1969.

Joe Aska: 1995–97; Raiders 3rd round selection in 1995 draft; Running Back; #35; 5-11, 240 lbs.; Central Oklahoma; July 14, 1972.

Nnamdi Asomugha: 2003–09; Raiders 1st round selection in 2003 draft; Cornerback; #21; 6-2, 210 lbs.; California; July 6, 1981.

*All information in this section was taken from Oakland/Los Angeles Raiders Media Guides from 1962 through 2009, www.profootballreference.com, and the book Total Football: The Official Encyclopedia of the National Football League, 1997.

Larry Atkins: 2003; came to Raiders as a free agent in November 2003; Linebacker; #59; 6-3, 240 lbs.; University of California Los Angeles (UCLA); July 21, 1975.

Pervis Atkins: 1965–66; came to the Raiders as a free agent in 1965; Wide Receiver; #39 and 81; 6-1, 195 lbs.; New Mexico State; November 24, 1937.

George Atkinson: 1968–77; Raiders 7th round selection in 1968 draft; Defensive Back; #43; 6-0, 185 lbs.; Morris Brown; January 4, 1947.

Brad Badger: 2002–06; came to the Raiders as a free agent in 2002; Offensive Tackle; #70; 6-4, 320 lbs.; Stanford; January 11, 1975.

Chris Bahr: 1980–88; came to the Raiders as a free agent in July 1980; Kicker; #10; 5-10, 170 lbs.; Penn State; February 3, 1953.

Rashad Baker: 2007–08; Raiders picked him off waivers on December 19, 2007; Defensive Back; #27; 5-10, 200 lbs.; Tennessee; February 22, 1982.

Keith Baldwin: 1988; acquired by Raiders in 1988 off waivers prior to 11th regular season game; Defensive End; #99; 6-4, 265 lbs.; Texas A&M; September 6, 1961.

Eric Ball: 1995; came to the Raiders as a free agent in May 1995; Running Back; #42; 6-2, 225lbs.; University of California Los Angeles (UCLA); July 1, 1966.

Jerry Ball: 1994–96; came to the Raiders as a free agent in July 1994; Defensive Tackle; #93; 6-1, 320lbs.; Southern Methodist; December 15, 1964.

Pete Banaszak: 1966–78; Raiders 5th round selection in 1966 draft; Running Back; #40; 6-0, 210lbs.; Miami (Florida); May 21, 1944.

Estes Banks: 1967; Raiders 8th round selection in 1967 draft; Running Back; #38; 6-3, 215 lbs.; Colorado; December 18, 1945.

Warren Bankston: 1973–78; came to the Raiders in a trade with Pittsburgh Steelers, 1973; Tight End; #46; 6-4, 235 lbs.; Tulane; July 22, 1947.

Al Bansavage: 1961; came to the Raiders in a trade with the San Diego Chargers during off-season, 1961; Linebacker; #53; 6-2, 230 lbs.; University of Southern California (USC); January 9, 1938–August 19, 2003.

Joe Barbee: 1960; came to the Raiders as a free agent in 1960; Offensive Tackle; #77; 6-3, 250 lbs.; Kent State; August 30, 1933–August 12, 1969.

Rod Barksdale: 1986; came to the Raiders as a free agent in April 1985; Wide Receiver; #88; 6-1, 185 lbs.; Arizona; September 8, 1962.

Jeff Barnes: 1977–87; Raiders 5th round selection in 1977 draft; Linebacker; #56; 6-2, 230 lbs.; California; March 1, 1955.

Khalif Barnes: 2009; came to the Raiders as a free agent in March 2009; Offensive Tackle; #70; 6-5, 325 lbs.; Washington; April 21, 1982.

Larry Barnes: 1960; came to the Raiders as a free agent in 1960; Linebacker; #52; 6-1, 228 lbs.; Colorado State; October 6, 1931.

Pat Barnes: 1998; came to the Raiders as a free agent in October 1998; Quarterback; #4; 6-3, 215 lbs.; California; February 23, 1975.

Rodrigo Barnes: 1976; came to the Raiders as a free agent in 1976; Linebacker; #51; 6-1, 215 lbs.; Rice; February 10, 1950.

Malcolm Barnwell: 1981–84; Raiders 7th round selection in 1980 draft; Wide Receiver; #80; 5-11, 185 lbs.; Virginia Union; June 28, 1958.

Jan Barrett: 1963–64; came to the Raiders as a free agent following the fifth game of the 1963 regular season; Tight End; #82; 6-3, 222 lbs.; Fresno State; November 13, 1939–October 7, 1973.

Rich Bartlewski: 1990; came to the Raiders as a free agent in 1990; Tight End; #94; 6-5, 250 lbs.; Fresno State; August 15, 1967.

Eric Barton: 1999–03; Raiders 5th round selection in 1999 draft; Linebacker; #50; 6-2, 240 lbs.; Maryland; September 29, 1977.

Patrick Bates: 1993–94; Raiders 1st round selection in 1993 draft; Defensive Back; #24 and 29; 6-3, 220 lbs.; Texas A&M; November 27, 1970.

Kevin Belcher: 1985; Raiders 7th round selection in 1985 draft; Offensive Tackle; #76; 6-5, 285 lbs.; Wisconsin; November 9, 1961.

Anthony Bell: 1992; came to the Raiders as a free agent in March 1992; Linebacker; #59; 6-3, 245 lbs.; Michigan State; July 2, 1964.

Greg Bell: 1990; came to the Raiders in a trade with the Los Angeles Rams in June 1990; Running Back; #28; 5-10, 210 lbs.; Notre Dame; August 1, 1962.

Joe Bell: 1979; came to the Raiders as a free agent in 1979; Defensive End; #68; 6-3, 250 lbs.; Norfolk State; April 20, 1956.

Nick Bell: 1991–93; Raiders 2nd round selection in 1991 draft; Running Back; #38 and 43; 6-2, 265 lbs.; Iowa; August 19, 1968.

Brian Belway: 1987; came to the Raiders as a free agent in 1987; Defensive End; #79; 6-6, 265 lbs.; Calgary; May 28, 1963.

Wes Bender: 1994; came to the Raiders as a free agent in May 1994; Running Back; #49; 5-10, 235 lbs.; University of Southern California (USC); August 2, 1970.

Duane Benson: 1967–71; Raiders 11th round selection in 1967 draft; Linebacker; #50; 6-2, 215 lbs.; Hamline; August 5, 1945.

Tom Benson: 1989–91; came to the Raiders as a free agent in March 1989; Linebacker; #54; 6-2, 240 lbs.; Oklahoma; September 6, 1961.

Rick Berns: 1982–83; came to the Raiders as a free agent in December 1982; Running Back; #40; 6-2, 215 lbs.; Nebraska; February 5, 1956.

Rufus Bess: 1979; came to the Raiders as a free agent in 1979; Defensive Back; #38; 5-9, 180 lbs.; South Carolina State; September 13, 1956.

Don Bessillieu: 1983, 1985; came to the Raiders in 1983; Defensive Back; #47; 6-1, 200 lbs.; Georgia Tech; May 4, 1956.

Steve Beuerlein: 1988–90; Raiders 4th round selection in 1987 draft; Quarterback; #7; 6-2, 210 lbs.; Notre Dame; March 7, 1965.

Greg Biekert: 1993–01; Raiders 7th round selection in 1993 draft; Linebacker; #54; 6-2, 255 lbs.; Colorado; March 14, 1969.

Fred Biletnikoff: 1965–78; Raiders 2nd round selection in 1965 draft; Wide Receiver; #14 and 25; 6-1, 190 lbs.; Florida State; February 23, 1943.

Darnell Bing: 2006; Raiders 4th round selection in the 2006 draft; Linebacker; #59; 6-2, 220 lbs.; University of Southern California (USC); September 10, 1984.

Rodger Bird: 1966–68; Raiders 1st round selection in 1966 draft; Defensive Back; #21; 5-11, 195 lbs.; Kentucky; July 2, 1943.

Dan Birdwell: 1962–69; Raiders 6th round selection in 1961 draft; Defensive Tackle; #53; 6-4, 250 lbs.; Houston; October 14, 1940–February 14, 1978.

Sonny Bishop: 1963; came to the Raiders in a trade with the Kansas City Chiefs before 1963 pre-season; Offensive Guard; #66; 6-2, 240 lbs.; Fresno State; October 1, 1939.

Barry Black: 1987; came to the Raiders as a free agent in 1987; Offensive Guard; #67; 6-2, 280 lbs.; Boise State; March 7, 1965.

George Blanda: 1967–75; came to the Raiders in a trade with the Houston Oilers in 1967; Quarterback/Kicker; #16; 6-2, 215 lbs.; Kentucky; September 17, 1927–September 27, 2010.

Greg Blankenship: 1976; came to the Raiders as a free agent in 1976; Linebacker; #57; 6-1, 212 lbs.; Cal-State–Hayward; March 24, 1954.

Rik Bonness: 1976; Raiders 3rd round selection in 1976 draft; Linebacker; #54; 6-3, 220 lbs.; Nebraska; March 20, 1954.

Kevin Boothe: 2006; Raiders 6th round selection in 2006 draft; Offensive Guard; #67; 6-5, 315 lbs.; Cornell; July 5, 1983.

John Bowie: 2007–09; Raiders 4th round selection in 2007 draft; Defensive Back; #35; 5-11, 190 lbs.; Cincinnati; May 11, 1984.

Greg Boyd: 1984; came to the Raiders in 1984; Defensive Tackle; #76; 6-6, 274 lbs.; San Diego State; September 15, 1952.

Jerome Boyd: 2009; came to the Raiders as a free agent in December 2009; Defensive Back; #30; 6-2, 225 lbs.; Oregon; May 26, 1986.

Max Boydston: 1962; came to the Raiders in a trade with the Dallas Texans in 1962; Tight end; #84; 6-2, 210 lbs.; Oklahoma; January 22, 1932–December 12, 1998.

George Boynton: 1962; came to the Raiders as a free agent in 1962; Defensive Back; #27; 5-11, 190 lbs.; East Texas State; July 6, 1937.

Cary Brabham: 1994; came to the Raiders as a free agent in May 1994; Defensive Back; #40; 6-0, 195 lbs.; Southern Methodist; August 11, 1970.

Greg Bracelin: 1981; came to the Raiders as a free agent in August 1981; Linebacker; #54; 6-1, 210 lbs.; California; April 16, 1957.

Morris Bradshaw: 1974–81; Raiders 4th round selection in 1974 draft; Wide Receiver; #81; 6-1, 195 lbs.; Ohio State; October 19, 1952.

Calvin Branch: 1997–00, 2005; Raiders 6th round selection in 1997 draft, re-signed with the team as a free agent in 2005; Defensive Back; #27; 5-11, 200 lbs.; Colorado State; May 8, 1974.

Cliff Branch: 1972–85; Raiders 4th round selection in 1972 draft; Wide Receiver; #21; 5-11, 170 lbs.; Colorado; August 1, 1948.

Tyvon Branch: 2008–09; Raiders 4th round selection in 2008 draft; Defensive Back; #33; 5-11, 197 lbs.; Connecticut; December 11, 1986.

Gene Branton: 1987; came to the Raiders as a free agent in June 1986; Tight End; #82; 6-5, 245 lbs.; Texas Southern; November 23, 1960.

Alex Bravo: 1960–61; came to the Raiders as a free agent in 1960; Defensive Back; #47; 6-0, 190 lbs.; Cal Poly, San Luis Obispo; July 27, 1930.

Tyler Brayton: 2003–07; Raiders 1st round selection in 2003 draft; Defensive End; #91; 6-6, 280 lbs.; Colorado; November 20, 1979.

Jim Breech: 1979; came to the Raiders as a free agent in 1978; Kicker; #5; 5-6, 155 lbs.; California; April 11, 1956.

Jim Brewington: 1961; came to the Raiders as a free agent before the final pre-season game in 1961; Offensive Tackle; #73; 6-6, 270 lbs.; North Carolina College; February 25, 1939.

Jeremy Brigham: 1998–01; Raiders 5th round selection in 1998 draft; Tight End; #87; 6-6, 255 lbs.; Washington; March 22, 1975.

Lorenzo Bromell: 2003; came to the Raiders as a free agent in November 2003; Defensive End; #95; 6-6, 260 lbs.; Clemson; September 23, 1975.

Aaron Brooks: 2006; came to the Raiders as a free agent in March 2006; Quarterback; #2; 6-4, 220 lbs.; Virginia; March 24, 1976.

Bobby Brooks: 2000–01; came to the Raiders as a free agent in April 1999; Linebacker; #55; 6-2, 245 lbs.; Fresno State; March 3, 1976.

Bucky Brooks: 1998; came to the Raiders as a free agent in November 1998; Defensive Back; #33; 6-0, 195 lbs.; North Carolina; January 22, 1971.

Willie Broughton: 1992–93; came to the Raiders as a free agent in March 1992; Defensive Tackle; #97; 6-5, 285 lbs.; Miami; September 9, 1964.

Bob Brown: 1971–73; came to the Raiders in a trade with the Los Angeles Rams in 1971; Offensive Tackle; #76; 6-4, 280 lbs.; Nebraska; December 8, 1941.

Charles Brown: 1962; came to the Raiders as a free agent in 1962; Offensive Tackle; #76; 6-4, 245 lbs.; Houston; August 1, 1936.

Darrick Brown: 2008; came to the Raiders as a free agent in 2008; Defensive Back; #39, 6-4, 200 lbs.; McNeese State; February 18, 1984.

Derek Brown: 1998; came to the Raiders as a free agent in May 1998; Tight End; #86; 6-6, 270 lbs.; Notre Dame; March 31, 1970.

Doug Brown: 1964; came to the Raiders in a trade with the Kansas City Chiefs in 1964; Defensive Tackle; #74; 6-4, 250 lbs.; Fresno State; May 31, 1938.

Larry Brown: 1996–97; came to the Raiders as a free agent in February 1996; Defensive Back; #24; 5-11, 185 lbs.; Texas Christian; November 30, 1969.

Ricky Brown: 2006–09; came to the Raiders as a free agent in 2006; Linebacker; #57; 6-2, 235 lbs.; Boston College; December 27, 1983.

Ron Brown: 1987–88; came to the Raiders as a free agent in 1987; Defensive End; #64 and 96; 6-4, 235 lbs.; University of Southern California (USC); April 28, 1964.

Ron Brown: 1990; came to the Raiders as a free agent in March 1990; Defensive Back; #24; 5-11, 185 lbs.; Arizona State; March 3, 1961.

Tim Brown: 1988–03; Raiders 1st round selection in 1988 draft; Wide Receiver; #81; 6-0, 195 lbs.; Notre Dame; July 22, 1966.

Willie Brown: 1967–78; came to the Raiders in a trade with the Denver Broncos in 1967; Defensive Back; #24; 6-1, 210 lbs.; Grambling; December 2, 1940.

Jim Browne: 1987; came to the Raiders as a free agent in 1987; Running Back; #47; 6-1, 215 lbs.; Boston College; March 16, 1962.

Keith Browner: 1987; came to the Raiders as a free agent in 1987; Linebacker; #51; 6-6, 245 lbs.; University of Southern California (USC); January 24, 1962.

Dave Browning: 1978–82; Raiders 2nd round selection in 1978

draft; Defensive End/Tackle; #73; 6-5, 245 lbs.; Washington; August 18, 1956.

Aundray Bruce: 1992–98; came to the Raiders as a free agent in February 1992; Defensive End; #56 and 99; 6-5, 265 lbs.; Auburn; April 30, 1966.

Larry Brunson: 1978–79; came to the Raiders in a trade with the Kansas City Chiefs in 1978; Wide Receiver; #82; 5-11, 180 lbs.; Colorado; August 11, 1949.

Desmond Bryant: 2009; came to the Raiders as a free agent in April 2009; Defensive Tackle; #67 and 90; 6-5, 290 lbs.; Harvard; December 15, 1985.

Tony Bryant: 1999–02; Raiders 2nd round selection in 1999 draft; Defensive End; #94; 6-6, 275 lbs.; Florida State; September 3, 1976.

Warren Bryant: 1984; came to the Raiders as a free agent in November 1984; Offensive Tackle; #66; 6-7, 285 lbs.; Kentucky; November 11, 1955.

Ray Buchanan: 2004; came to the Raiders as a free agent in 2004; Safety; #34; 5-9, 193 lbs.; Louisville; September 29, 1971.

Phillip Buchanon: 2002–04; Raiders 1st round selection in 2002 draft; Cornerback; #31; 5-10, 185 lbs.; Miami (Florida); September 19, 1980.

Will Buchanon: 2006; came to the Raiders as a free agent in December 2006; Wide Receiver; #13; 6-3, 190 lbs.; University of Southern California (USC); April 5, 1983.

Bob Buczkowski: 1987; Raiders 1st round selection in 1986 draft; Defensive End; #95; 6-5, 270 lbs.; Pittsburgh; May 5, 1964.

Bill Budness: 1964–70; Raiders 4th round selection in 1963 draft; Linebacker; #48; 6-2, 215 lbs.; Boston University; January 30, 1943.

George Buehler: 1969–78; Raiders 2nd round selection in 1969 draft; Offensive Guard; #64; 6-2, 270 lbs.; Stanford; August 10, 1947.

Drew Buie: 1969–71; Raiders 9th round selection in 1969 draft; Wide Receiver; #89; 6-0, 178 lbs.; Catawba; July 12, 1947.

Jarrad Bunch: 1994; came to the Raiders in 1994; Running Back; #45; 6-2, 250 lbs.; Michigan; August 9, 1968.

Gerald Burch: 1961; Raiders 13th round selection in 1961 draft; Tight end; #86; 6-1, 195 lbs.; Georgia Tech; December 13, 1939.

Derrick Burgess: 2005–08; came to the Raiders as a free agent in 2005; Defensive End; #56; 6-2, 260 lbs.; Mississippi; August 12, 1978.

Ron Burton: 1990; came to the Raiders as a free agent in February 1990; Linebacker; #59; 6-1, 245 lbs.; North Carolina; May 2, 1964.

Michael Bush: 2008–09; Raiders 4th round selection in 2007 draft; Running Back; #29; 6-2, 243 lbs.; Louisville; June 16, 1984.

Paul Butcher: 1996; came to the Raiders in 1996; Linebacker; #59; 6-0, 230 lbs.; Wayne State; November 8, 1963.

Darryl Byrd: 1983–84,1987; came to the Raiders as a free agent in 1983; Linebacker; #54 and 50; 6-1, 225 lbs.; Illinois; September 3, 1960.

Tony Caldwell: 1983–85; Raiders 3rd round selection in 1983 draft; Linebacker; #57; 6-1, 225 lb.; Washington; April 1, 1961.

Rick Calhoun: 1987; came to the Raiders as a free agent in 1987; Running Back; #21; 5-7, 190 lbs.; Cal State–Fullerton; May 30, 1963.

Rich Camarillo: 1996; came to the Raiders in 1996; Punter; #16; 5-11, 196 lbs.; Washington; November 29, 1959.

Joe Campbell: 1980–81; came to the Raiders in a trade with the New Orleans Saints in 1980; Defensive End; #77; 6-6, 250 lbs.; Maryland; May 8, 1955.

Stan Campbell: 1962; came to the Raiders as a free agent in 1962; Offensive Guard; #67; 6-0, 226 lbs.; Iowa State; August 26, 1930–March 14, 2005.

Joe Cannavino: 1960–61; came to the Raiders in the expansion draft from the Buffalo Bills; Defensive Back; #27; 5-11, 185 lbs.; Ohio State; January 20, 1935.

Billy Cannon: 1964–69; came to the Raiders in a trade with the Houston Oilers in 1964; Tight End; #33; 6-1, 215 lbs.; Louisiana State; August 2, 1937.

Cooper Carlisle: 2007–09; came to the Raiders as a free agent in 2007; Offensive Guard; #66; 6-5, 295 lbs.; Florida; August 11, 1977.

Chetti Carr: 1987; came to the Raiders as a free agent in 1987; Wide Receiver; #20; 5-9, 185 lbs.; Northwest Oklahoma; January 1, 1963.

Chris Carr: 2005–07; came to the Raiders as a free agent in 2005; Defensive Back/Kick Returner; #23; 5-10, 180 lbs.; Boise State; April 30, 1983.

Darren Carrington: 1996; came to the Raiders as a free agent in April 1996; Defensive Back; #21; 6-2, 200 lbs.; Northern Arizona; October 10, 1966.

Joe Carroll: 1972–73; Raiders 11th round selection in 1972 draft; Linebacker; #51; 6-1, 220 lbs.; Pittsburgh; May 29, 1950.

Louis Carter: 1975; Raiders 3rd round selection in 1975 draft; Running Back; #33; 5-11, 200 lbs.; Maryland; February 6, 1953.

Perry Carter: 1996–98; came to the Raiders as a free agent in November 1996; Defensive Back; #20; 6-0, 190 lbs.; Mississippi; August 5, 1971.

Russell Carter: 1988–89; came to the Raiders in a trade with the New York Jets in May 1988; Defensive Back; #29; 6-2, 200 lbs.; Southern Methodist; February 10, 1962.

Kerry Cash: 1995; came to the Raiders as a free agent in May 1995; Tight End; #88; 6-4, 245 lbs.; Texas; August 7, 1969.

Dave Casper: 1974–80, 1984; Raiders 2nd round selection in 1974 draft, re-signed with the team as a free agent in July 1984; Tight End; #87 and 88; 6-4, 230 lbs.; Notre Dame; September 26, 1951.

Carmen Cavalli: 1960; came to the Raiders in the expansion draft from the Buffalo Bills; Defensive End; #85; 6-4, 245 lbs.; Richmond; June 11, 1937.

Mario Celotto: 1980–81; came to the Raiders as a free agent in 1980; Linebacker; #52; 6-3, 225 lbs.; University of Southern California (USC); August 23, 1956.

Bob Chandler: 1980–82; came to the Raiders in a trade with the Buffalo Bills in 1980; Wide Receiver; #85; 6-1, 180 lbs.; University of Southern California (USC); April 24, 1949–January 27, 1995.

Ted Chapman: 1987; came to the Raiders as a free agent in 1987; Defensive End; #77; 6-3, 260 lbs.; Maryland; April 5, 1964.

Mike Charles: 1990; came to the Raiders as a free agent in June 1990; Defensive Tackle; #95; 6-4, 305 lbs.; Syracuse; September 23, 1962.

Raymond Chester: 1970–72, 1978–81; Raiders 1st round selection in 1970 draft; re-joined Raiders in a trade with the Baltimore Colts in 1978; Tight End; #87 and 88; 6-4, 235 lbs.; Morgan State; June 28, 1948.

odd Christensen: 1979–88; came to the Raiders as a free agent in September 1979; Tight End; #46; 6-3, 230 lbs.; Brigham Young; August 3, 1956.

randon Christenson: 2002; came to the Raiders as a free agent in 2002; Tight End; #48; 6-1, 256 lbs.; Northwestern Oklahoma State University; May 10, 1977.

on Churchwell: 1960; came to the Raiders in the expansion draft from the Houston Oilers; Defensive Tackle; #75; 6-1, 253 lbs.; Mississippi; May 11, 1936.

anny Clark: 2004–05; came to the Raiders as a free agent in March 2004; Linebacker; #55; 6-2, 245 lbs.; Illinois; May 9, 1977.

ohn Clay: 1987; Raiders 1st round selection in 1987 draft; Offensive Tackle; #78; 6-5, 300 lbs.; Missouri; May 1, 1964.

hris Clemons: 2007; came to the Raiders as a free agent in 2007; Linebacker/Defensive End; #48; 6-3, 240 lbs.; Georgia; October 30, 1981.

ony Cline: 1970–75; Raiders 4th round selection in 1970 draft; Defensive End; #84; 6-3, 244 lbs.; Miami (Florida); July 25, 1948.

enyon Coleman: 2002; Raiders 5th round selection in the 2002 draft; Defensive End; #90; 6-5, 285 lbs.; University of California Los Angeles (UCLA); April 10, 1979.

od Coleman: 1999–03; Raiders 5th round selection in 1999 draft; Defensive Tackle; #57; 6-2, 285 lbs.; East Carolina; August 16, 1976.

erry Collins: 2004–05; came to the Raiders as a free agent in 2004; Quarterback; #5; 6-5, 240 lbs.; Penn State; December 30, 1972.

o Collins: 1998–03; Raiders 1st round selection in 1998 draft; Offensive Guard/Tackle; #79; 6-4, 325 lbs.; Florida; September 22, 1976.

erric Collons: 1993; came to the Raiders as a free agent in February 1993; Defensive Tackle; #92; 6-6, 295 lbs.; California; December 4, 1969.

eal Colzie: 1975–78; Raiders 1st round selection in 1975 draft; Defensive Back; #20; 6-2, 205 lbs.; Ohio State; February 28, 1953–August 19, 2001.

erek Combs: 2002; came to the Raiders as a free agent in March 2002; Cornerback; #43; 6-0, 195 lbs.; Ohio State; February 28, 1979.

on Condo; 2007–09; came to the Raiders as a free agent in 2006; Linebacker/Safety; #59; 6-3, 250 lbs.; Maryland; August 26, 1981.

an Conners: 1964–74; Raiders 2nd round selection in 1963 draft; Linebacker; #55 and 60; 6-0, 230 lbs.; Miami (Florida); February 6, 1941.

rett Conway: 2000; came to the Raiders in 2000; Kicker; #5; 6-2, 208 lbs.; Penn State; March 8, 1975.

ob Coolbaugh: 1961; Raiders 15th round selection in 1961 AFL draft; Wide Receiver; #43; 6-3, 200 lbs.; Richmond; July 5, 1939.

hris Cooper: 2001–03; Raiders 6th round selection in 2001 draft; Defensive Tackle; #75; 6-5, 275 lbs.; Nebraska–Omaha; December 27, 1977.

Earl Cooper: 1986; came to the Raiders in a trade with the San Francisco 49ers in May 1986; Tight End; #49; 6-2, 230 lbs.; Rice; September 17, 1957.

Jarrod Cooper: 2004–07; came to the Raiders as a free agent in October 2004; Safety; #40; 6-1, 215 lbs.; Kansas State; March 31, 1978.

Marquis Cooper: 2008; came to the Raiders as a free agent in November 2008; Linebacker; #95; 6-3, 215 lbs.; Washington; March 11, 1982–March 6, 2009.

Horace Copeland: 1999; came to the Raiders as a free agent in June 1999; Wide Receiver; #80; 6-3, 200 lbs.; Miami (Florida); January 2, 1971.

Joe Cormier: 1987; came to the Raiders as a free agent in 1987; Linebacker; #95; 6-6, 245 lbs.; University of Southern California (USC); May 3, 1963.

Dave Costa: 1963–65; Raiders 7th round selection in 1962 draft; Defensive Tackle; #46; 6-1, 250 lbs.; Utah; October 27, 1941.

Joe Costello: 1989; came to the Raiders as a free agent in March 1989; Linebacker; #94; 6-3, 240 lbs.; Central Connecticut; June 1, 1960.

Dobie Craig: 1962–63; came to the Raiders as a free agent in 1962; Wide Receiver; #42; 6-4, 210 lbs.; Howard Payne; February 14, 1938.

Roger Craig: 1991; came to the Raiders as a free agent in April 1991; Running Back; #22; 6-0, 225 lbs.; Nebraska; October 26, 1964.

Zack Crockett: 1999–06; came to the Raiders as a free agent in March 1999; Running Back; #32; 6-2, 240 lbs.; Florida State; December 2, 1972.

Wayne Crow: 1960–61; came to the Raiders as a free agent in 1960; Running Back/Defensive Back; #22; 6-0, 205 lbs.; California; May 5, 1938.

Derrick Crudup: 1989, 1991; Raiders 7th round selection in 1988 draft; Defensive Back; #23; 6-2, 215 lbs.; Oklahoma; February 15, 1965.

Daunte Culpepper: 2007; came to the Raiders as a free agent in July 2007; Quarterback; #8; 6-4, 260 lbs.; Central Florida; January 28, 1977.

Rick Cunningham: 1996–98; came to the Raiders as a free agent in July 1996; Offensive Tackle; #68; 6-7, 315 lbs.; Texas A&M; January 4, 1967.

Ronald Curry: 2002–08; Raiders 7th round selection in 2002 draft; Wide Receiver; #1 and 89; 6-2, 220 lbs.; North Carolina; May 28, 1979.

Dave Dalby: 1972–85; Raiders 4th round selection in 1972 draft; Center/Offensive Guard; #50; 6-2, 248 lbs.; University of California Los Angeles (UCLA); October 19, 1950–August 30, 2002.

Brad Daluiso: 2001; came to the Raiders as a free agent in 2001; Kicker; #3; 6-1, 180 lbs.; University of California (UCLA); December 31, 1967.

Clem Daniels: 1961–67; came to the Raiders as a free agent in 1961;Running Back; #36; 6-1, 220 lbs.; Prairie View; July 9, 1937.

David Daniels: 1966; came to the Raiders in a trade with the Houston Oilers in 1966; Defensive Tackle; #75; 6-5, 275 lbs.; Florida A&M; April 5, 1941.

Ben Davidson: 1964–71; came to the Raiders as a free agent in

1964; Defensive End; #83; 6-8, 280 lbs.; Washington; June 14, 1940.

Cotton Davidson: 1962–69; came to the Raiders in a trade with the Dallas Texans in 1962; Quarterback; #19; 6-0, 188 lbs.; Baylor; November 30, 1931.

Bruce Davis: 1979–87; Raiders 11th round selection in 1979 draft; Offensive Tackle; #79; 6-6, 280 lbs.; University of California Los Angeles (UCLA); June 21, 1956.

Clarence Davis: 1971–78; Raiders 4th round selection in 1971 draft; Running Back; #28; 5-10, 195 lbs.; University of Southern California (USC); June 28, 1949.

Greg Davis: 1998; came to the Raiders as a free agent in June 1998; Kicker; #7; 6-0, 200 lbs.; The Citadel; October 29, 1965.

James Davis: 1982–87; Raiders 5th round selection in 1981 draft; Defensive Back; #45; 6-0, 195 lbs.; Southern; June 12, 1957.

Jason Davis: 2008; came to the Raiders in 2008; Running Back; #34; 5-10, 245 lbs.; Illinois; November 2, 1983.

Mike Davis: 1978–85; Raiders 2nd round selection in 1977 draft; Defensive Back; #36; 6-3, 205 lbs.; Colorado; April 15, 1956.

Scott Davis: 1988–91, 1994; Raiders 1st round selection in 1988 draft; Defensive End; #70; 6-7, 280 lbs.; Illinois; July 8, 1965.

Jerone Davison: 1996–97; came to the Raiders as a free agent in July 1996; Running Back; #48; 6-1, 235 lbs.; Arizona State; September 16, 1970.

Mike Dennery: 1974–75; Raiders 13th round selection in 1974 draft; Linebacker; #54; 5-11, 225 lbs.; Southern Mississippi; June 26, 1950.

Jerry DePoyster: 1971–72; came to the Raiders as a free agent in 1971; Kicker; #4; 6-1, 200 lbs.; Wyoming; July 6, 1946.

Don Deskins: 1960; came to the Raiders in the expansion draft from the Los Angeles Chargers; Offensive Guard; #79; 6-3, 240 lbs.; Michigan; May 10, 1932.

Andy Dickerson: 1987; came to Raiders in 1987; Offensive Guard; #64; 6-5, 260 lbs.; California Lutheran; March 10, 1963.

Eric Dickerson: 1992; came to the Raiders in a trade with the Indianapolis Colts in 1992; Running Back; #29; 6-3, 220 lbs.; Southern Methodist; September 2, 1960.

Eldridge Dickey: 1968–71; Raiders 1st round selection in 1968 draft; Wide Receiver; #10; 6-2, 198 lbs.; Tennessee State; December 24, 1945.

Bo Dickinson: 1964; came to the Raiders in a trade with the Houston Oilers in 1964; Running Back; #23, 30, and 33; 6-2, 220 lbs.; Southern Mississippi; July 18, 1935.

John Diehl: 1965; came to the Raiders in 1965; Defensive Tackle; #73; 6-7, 265 lbs.; Virginia; January 27, 1936.

Gennaro DiNapoli: 1998–99; Raiders 4th round selection in 1998 draft; Offensive Guard; #64; 6-3, 300 lbs.; Virginia Tech; May 25, 1975.

John Dittrich: 1960; came to the Raiders as a free agent in 1960; Offensive Guard; #68; 6-1, 236 lbs.; Wisconsin; May 7, 1933–July 5, 1995.

Ernest Dixon: 1998; came to the Raiders in 1998; Linebacker; #58; 6-1, 243 lbs.; South Carolina; October 17, 1971.

Hewritt Dixon: 1966–70; came to Raiders in a trade with the Denver Broncos in 1966; Running Back; #35; 6-1, 230 lbs.; Florida A&M; January 8, 1940–November 24, 1992.

Rickey Dixon: 1993; came to the Raiders in a trade with the Cincinnati Bengals in July 1993; Defensive Back; #31; 5-11, 19 lbs.; Oklahoma; December 26, 1966.

Torin Dorn: 1990–93; Raiders 4th round selection in 1990 draf Defensive Back; #46; 6-0, 190 lbs.; North Carolina; Februar 29, 1968.

Anthony Dorsett: 2000–03; came to the Raiders as a free agen in March 2000; Defensive Back; #33; 5-11, 205 lbs.; Pittsburgl September 14, 1973.

Dick Dorsey: 1962; came to the Raiders in 1962; Wide Receive #21 and 81; 6-3, 200 lbs.; University of Southern Californi (USC); March 11, 1936.

Al Dotson: 1968–70; came to the Raiders in a trade with th Kansas City Chiefs in 1968; Defensive Tackle; #71; 6-4, 26 lbs.; Grambling; February 25, 1943.

Bob Dougherty: 1960–63; came to the Raiders as a free agent i 1960; Linebacker; #47; 6-1, 230 lbs.; Kentucky; April 20, 1932 May 12, 2006.

Scott Dreisbach: 1999–00; came to the Raiders as a free agent i April 1999; Quarterback; #10; 6-3, 210 lbs.; Michigan; De cember 16, 1975.

Rickey Dudley: 1996–00; Raiders 1st round selection in the 199 draft; Tight End; #83; 6-6, 250 lbs.; Ohio State; July 15, 197.

Paul Dufault: 1987; came to the Raiders as a free agent in 1987 Center/Offensive Guard; #54; 6-4, 255 lbs.; New Hampshir February 15, 1964.

John Duff: 1993–94; came to the Raiders as a free agent in Ma 1993; Tight End/Defensive End; #84; 6-7, 250 lbs.; New Mex ico; July 31, 1967.

David Dunn: 2000; came to the Raiders as a free agent in Feb ruary 2000; Wide Receiver/Kick Returner; #88; 6-3, 210 lbs Fresno State; June 10, 1972.

Tim Dwight: 2007; came to the Raiders in 2007; Wide Receive #17; 6-1, 180 lbs.; Iowa; July 13, 1975.

Mike Dyal: 1989–90; came to the Raiders as a free agent in Ma 1988; Tight End; #84; 6-2, 240 lbs.; Texas A&I; May 20, 196(

Matt Dyson: 1995; Raiders 5th round selection in 1995 draft; De fensive Tackle/Linebacker; #59; 6-3, 265 lbs.; Michigar August 1, 1972.

John Eason: 1968; Raiders 8th round selection in 1968 draft; Tigh End; #82; 6-2, 220 lbs.; Florida A&M; July 30, 1945.

Omar Easy: 2005; came to the Raiders as a free agent in 200! Running Back; #33; 6-2, 245 lbs.; Penn State; October 2! 1977.

Adimchinobe Echemandu: 2006–07; came to the Raiders as free agent in 2006; Running Back; #20; 5-10, 225 lbs.; Cali fornia; November 21, 1980.

Bobby Joe Edmonds: 1989; came to the Raiders in 1989; Wid Receiver; #41; 5-11, 186 lbs.; Arkansas; September 26, 1964.

Kalimba Edwards: 2008; came to the Raiders as a free agent i 2008; Defensive End; #58; 6-5, 264 lbs.; South Carolina; De cember 26, 1979.

Lloyd Edwards: 1969; Raiders 3rd round selection in 1969 draf Tight End; #36; 6-3, 248 lbs.; San Diego State; November 2(1946.

Mike Eischeid: 1966–71; came to the Raiders as a free agent i 1966; Kicker; #11; 6-0, 190 lbs.; Upper Iowa; September 2! 1940.

Isaiah Ekejiuba: 2005–09; came to Raiders as a free agent i

October 2005; Linebacker; #50; 6-4, 240 lbs.; Virginia; October 5, 1981

Craig Ellis: 1987; came to the Raiders as a free agent in 1987; Running Back; #33; 5-11, 185 lbs.; San Diego State; January 26, 1961.

Greg Ellis: 2009; came to the Raiders as a free agent in June 2009; Defensive End; #99; 6-6, 262lbs.; North Carolina; August 14, 1975.

Im Ellis: 1987; Raiders 10th round selection in 1987 draft; Linebacker; #58; 6-3, 240 lbs.; Boise State; March 25, 1964.

Glen Ellison: 1971; came to the Raiders in 1971; Running Back; #27; 6-1, 215 lbs.; Arkansas; March 9, 1947.

Riki Ellison: 1990–92; came to the Raiders as a free agent in May 1990; Linebacker; #50; 6-2, 230 lbs.; University of Southern California (USC); August 15, 1960.

Hunter Enis: 1962; came to the Raiders in a trade with the San Diego Chargers in 1962; Quarterback; #14; 6-2, 195 lbs.; Texas Christian; December 10, 1936.

Bill Enyart: 1971; came to the Raiders in a trade with the Buffalo Bills in 1971; Linebacker; #46; 6-4, 235 lbs.; Oregon State; April 28, 1947.

Hiram Eugene: 2006–09; came to the Raiders as a free agent in September 2005; Defensive Back; #31; Louisiana Tech; November 24, 1980

Vince Evans: 1987–95; came to the Raiders as a free agent in 1987; Quarterback; #11; 6-2, 215 lbs.; University of Southern California (USC); June 14, 1955.

Bill Fairband: 1967–68; Raiders 3rd round selection in 1967 draft; Linebacker; #86; 6-4, 225 lbs.; Colorado; June 11, 1941.

Justin Fargas: 2003–09; Raiders 3rd round selection in 2003 draft; Running Back; #20; 6-1, 220 lbs.; University of Southern California (USC); January 25, 1980.

Ron Fellows: 1987–88; came to the Raiders in a trade with the Dallas Cowboys in August 1987; Defensive Back; #21; 6-0, 175 lbs.; Missouri; November 7, 1958.

Derrick Fenner: 1995–97; came to the Raiders as a free agent in April 1995; Running Back; #34; 6-3, 240 lbs.; North Carolina; April 6, 1967.

Mervyn Fernandez: 1987–92; Raiders 10th round selection in 1983 draft, and joined the team in March 1987; Wide Receiver; #86; 6-3, 200 lbs.; San Jose State; December 29, 1959.

Dan Ficca: 1962; came to the Raiders in a trade with the San Diego Chargers in 1962; Offensive Guard; #69; 6-1, 245 lbs.; University of Southern California (USC); February 7, 1939.

George Fields: 1960–61; came to the Raiders as a free agent in 1960; Defensive Tackle; #80; 6-3, 245 lbs.; Bakersfield J.C.; born in 1936.

Garry Finneran: 1961; came to the Raiders as a free agent in 1961; Defensive Tackle; 6-4, 250 lbs.; #76; University of Southern California (USC); February 23, 1934.

James FitzPatrick: 1990–91; came to the Raiders as a free agent in April 1990; Offensive Tackle/Guard; #73; 6-7, 320 lbs.; University of Southern California (USC); February 1, 1964.

George Fleming: 1961; Raiders 2nd round selection in 1961 draft; Running Back; #21; 5-11, 188 lbs.; Washington; June 29, 1938.

Zeron Flemister: 2005; came to the Raiders as a free agent in 2005; Tight End; #88; 6-4, 250 lbs.; Iowa; September 8, 1976.

Tom Flores: 1960–61, 1963–66; came to the Raiders as a free agent in 1960; Quarterback; #15; 6-1, 202 lbs.; Pacific; March 21, 1937.

James Folston: 1994–98; Raiders 2nd round selection in 1994 draft; Linebacker; #55; 6-3, 240 lbs.; Northeast Louisiana; August 14, 1971.

Cole Ford: 1995–97; came to the Raiders as a free agent in September 1995; Kicker; #5; 6-2, 210 lbs.; University of Southern California (USC); December 31, 1972.

John Paul Foschi: 2005; came to the Raiders as a free agent in 2005; Tight End/Running Back; #49; 6-3, 266 lbs.; Georgia Tech; May 19, 1982.

Ron Foster: 1987; came to Raiders as a free agent in 1987; Defensive Back; #41; 6-0, 200 lbs.; Cal State–Northridge; November 25, 1963.

Carlos Francis: 2004–06; Raiders 4th round selection in 2004 draft; Wide Receiver; #10 and 82; 5-10, 190 lbs.; Texas Tech; January 3, 1981.

Donald Frank: 1994; came to the Raiders as a free agent in 1994; Defensive Back; #47; 6-0, 197 lbs.; Winston-Salem; October 24, 1965.

Keith Franklin: 1995; came to the Raiders as a free agent in November 1995; Linebacker; #58; 6-2, 230 lbs.; South Carolina; March 4, 1970.

Elvis Franks: 1985–86; came to the Raiders as a free agent in November 1985; Defensive End; #94; 6-4, 270 lbs.; Morgan State; July 9, 1957.

Rob Fredrickson: 1994–97; Raiders 1st round selection in 1994 draft; Linebacker; #53; 6-4, 240 lbs.; Michigan State; May 13, 1971.

Mike Freeman: 1988; came to the Raiders as a free agent in 1988; Offensive Guard; #61; 6-3, 256 lbs.; Arizona; October 13, 1961.

Russell Freeman: 1995; came to the Raiders as a free agent in July 1995; Offensive Tackle; #70; 6-7, 300 lbs.; Georgia Tech; September 2, 1969.

Charlie Frye: 2009; came to the Raiders as a free agent in June 2009; Quarterback; #3; 6-4, 220 lbs.; Akron; August 28, 1981.

David Fulcher: 1993; came to the Raiders as a free agent in 1993; Linebacker; #45; 6-3, 236 lbs.; Arizona State; September 28, 1964.

Mondriel Fulcher: 2000–01; Raiders 7th round selection in 2000 draft; Tight End; #89; 6-3, 245 lbs.; Miami (Florida); October 15, 1976.

Charles Fuller: 1961–62; Raiders 19th round selection in 1961 AFL draft; Running Back; #20; 5-11, 175 lbs.; San Francisco State; January 22, 1939–August 8, 2001.

Doug Gabriel: 2003–06; Raiders 5th round selection in 2003 draft; Wide Receiver; #85 and 80; 6-2, 215 lbs.; Central Florida; August 27, 1980.

Derrick Gainer: 1992; Raiders 8th round selection in 1989 draft; Running Back; #27; 5-11, 235 lbs.; Florida A&M; August 15, 1966.

Chon Gallegos: 1962; came to the Raiders in 1962; #12; 5-9, 175 lbs.; San Jose State; September 28, 1939.

Robert Gallery: 2004–09; Raiders 1st round selection in 2004 draft; Offensive Tackle; #76; 6-7, 325 lbs.; Iowa; July 26, 1980.

Vince Gamache: 1987; came to the Raiders as a free agent in 1987; Kicker; #3; 5-11, 174 lbs.; Cal State–Northridge; November 18, 1961.

Rich Gannon: 1999–04; came to the Raiders as a free agent in February 1999; Quarterback; #12; 6-3, 210 lbs.; Delaware; December 20, 1965.

Bob Garner: 1961–62; came to the Raiders in 1961; Defensive Back; #28; 5-10, 1899 lbs.; Fresno State; Born in 1935.

Charlie Garner: 2001–03; came to the Raiders as a free agent in April 2001; Running Back; #25; 5-10, 190 lbs.; Tennessee; February 13, 1972.

Carl Garrett: 1976–77; came to the Raiders in a trade with the New York Jets in 1976; Running Back; #31; 5-10, 205 lbs.; New Mexico Highlands; August 31, 1947.

Willie Gault: 1988–93; came to the Raiders in a trade with the Chicago Bears in July 1988; Wide Receiver; #83; 6-1, 180 lbs.; Tennessee; September 5, 1960.

Akbar Gbaja-Biamila: 2003–04; came to the Raiders as a free agent in 2003; Defensive End; #98; 6-5, 260 lbs.; San Diego State; May 6, 1979.

Jeff George: 1997–98; came to the Raiders as a free agent in February 1997; Quarterback; #3; 6-4, 215 lbs.; Illinois; December 8, 1967.

John Gesek: 1987–89; Raiders 10th round selection in 1987 draft; Offensive Guard; #63; 6-5, 275 lbs.; Sacramento State; February 18, 1963.

Claude Gibson: 1963–65; came to the Raiders in a trade with the San Diego Chargers; Defensive Back; #25; 6-1, 190 lbs.; North Carolina State; May 26, 1939.

Derrick Gibson: 2001–06; Raiders 1st round selection in 2001 draft; Defensive Back; #26 and 36; 6-2, 215 lbs.; Florida State; March 22, 1979.

Sean Gilbert: 2003; came to the Raiders as a free agent in October 2003; Defensive Tackle; #90; 6-5, 318 lbs.; Pittsburgh; April 10, 1970.

Fred Gillett: 1964; came to the Raiders in 1964; Tight End; #44; 6-3, 225 lbs.; Los Angeles State; December 16, 1936.

Hubie Ginn: 1976–78; came to the Raiders as a free agent in 1976; Running Back; #29; 5-10, 185 lbs.; Florida A&M; January 4, 1947.

Tom Gipson: 1971; Raiders 14th round selection in 1971 draft; Defensive Tackle; #73; 6-6, 290 lbs.; North Texas State; July 28, 1948.

Andrew Glover: 1991–96; Raiders 10th round selection in 1991 draft; Tight End; #87; 6-6, 250 lbs.; Grambling; August 12, 1967.

La'Roi Glover: 1996; Raiders 5th round selection in 1996 draft; Defensive Tackle; #92; 6-1, 280 lbs.; San Diego State; July 4, 1974.

Kevin Gogan: 1994–96; came to the Raiders as a free agent in April 1994; Offensive Guard; #66; 6-7, 325 lbs.; Washington; November 2, 1964.

Alan Goldstein: 1960; came to the Raiders in the expansion draft from the Buffalo Bills; Wide Receiver; #81; 6-0, 204 lbs.; North Carolina; January 8, 1936–October 14, 1991.

Bob Golic: 1989–92; came to the Raiders as a free agent in March 1989; Defensive Tackle; #79; 6-3, 280 lbs.; Notre Dame; October 26, 1957.

Jerry Golsteyn: 1984; came to the Raiders in a trade with the Tampa Bay Buccaneers in May 1984; Quarterback; #14; 6-4, 210 lbs.; Northern Illinois; August 6, 1954.

Rick Goltz: 1987; came to the Raiders as a free agent in 1987; Defensive End; #94; 6-4, 255 lbs.; Simon Fraser; March 19, 1955.

Darryl Goodlow: 1987; came to the Raiders as a free agent in 1987; Linebacker; #90 and 98; 6-2, 235 lbs.; Oklahoma; November 2, 1960.

Alex Gordon: 1990; came to the Raiders in 1990; Linebacker; #59; 6-5, 246 lbs.; Cincinnati; September 14, 1964.

Darrien Gordon: 1999–00; came to the Raiders as a free agent in May 1999; Cornerback; #23 and 34; 5-11, 190 lbs.; Stanford; November 14, 1970.

Jeff Gossett: 1988–96; came to the Raiders in a trade with the Houston Oilers in August 1988; Punter; #6 and 7; 6-2, 200 lbs.; Eastern Illinois; January 25, 1957.

Sam Graddy: 1990–92; came to the Raiders as a free agent in March 1989; Wide Receiver; #85; 5-10, 180 lbs.; Tennessee; February 10, 1964.

Bruce Gradkowski: 2009; came to the Raiders after being claimed off waivers from the Cleveland Browns, February, 2009; Quarterback; #5; 6-1, 220 lbs.; Toledo; January 27, 1983.

Aaron Graham: 2001; came to the Raiders as a free agent in 2001; Center; #68; 6-4, 301 lbs.; Nebraska; May 22, 1973.

Derrick Graham: 1998; came to the Raiders as a free agent in June 1998; Offensive Guard; #74; 6-4, 315 lbs.; Appalachian State; March 18, 1967.

Jeff Graham: 1995; came to the Raiders as a free agent in March 1995; Quarterback; #8; 6-5, 215 lbs.; Long Beach State; February 5, 1966.

DeLawrence Grant: 2001–05; Raiders 3rd round selection in 2001 draft; Defensive End; #95 and 99; 6-3, 280 lbs.; Oregon State; November 18, 1979.

Rory Graves: 1988–91; came to the Raiders as a free agent in October 1987; Offensive Tackle; #60; 6-6, 295 lbs.; Ohio State; July 21, 1963.

Dave Grayson: 1965–70; came to the Raiders in a trade with the Kansas City Chiefs in 1965; Defensive Back; #45; 5-10, 187 lbs.; Oregon; June 6, 1939.

Charley Green: 1966; came to the Raiders in a trade with the Boston Patriots in 1966; Quarterback; #12; 6-0, 190 lbs.; Wittenberg; March 14, 1943.

Cornell Green: 2007–09; came to the Raiders as a free agent in March 2007; Offensive Tackle; #74; 6-6, 315 lbs.; Central Florida; August 25, 1976.

David Greenwood: 1988; came to the Raiders in 1988; Defensive Back; #41; 6-3, 210 lbs.; Wisconsin; March 25, 1960.

Justin Griffith: 2007–08; came to the Raiders as a free agent in 2007; Running Back; #36; 6-0, 230 lbs.; Mississippi State; April 13, 1981.

Phil Grimes: 1987; came to the Raiders as a free agent in 1988; Defensive End; #97; 6-5, 260 lbs.; Central Missouri; February 26, 1965.

Kyle Grossart: 1980; came to the Raiders as a free agent in 1980; Quarterback; #17; 6-4, 210 lbs.; Oregon State; Birth date not available.

Jake Grove: 2004–08; Raiders 2nd round selection in 2004 draft; Center/Offensive Guard; #64; 6-4, 300 lbs.; Virginia Tech; January 22, 1980.

Greyson Gunheim: 2008–09; came to the Raiders as a free agent in May 2008, and resigned by team in December 2009; Defensive End; #97; 6-5, 265 lbs.; Washington; April 8, 1986.

Louie Guy: 1964; came to the Raiders in a trade with the New York Jets in 1964; Defensive Back; #22; 6-0, 190 lbs.; Mississippi; May 26, 1941.

Ray Guy: 1973–86; Raiders 1st round selection in 1973 draft; Punter; #8; 6-3, 190 lbs.; Southern Mississippi; December 22, 1949.

Roger Hagberg: 1965–69; came to the Raiders as a free agent in 1965; Running Back; #30; 6-1, 215 lbs.; Minnesota; February 28, 1939–April 15, 1970.

DeAngelo Hall: 2008; came to the Raiders in a trade with the Atlanta Falcons in 2008; Defensive Back; #23; 5-10, 197 lbs.; Virginia Tech; November 19, 1983.

Tim Hall: 1996–97; Raiders 6th round selection in 1996 draft; Running Back; #45; 5-11, 220 lbs.; Robert Morris; February 15, 1974–September 30, 1998.

Willie Hall: 1975–78; came to the Raiders as a free agent in 1975; Linebacker; #39 and 83; 6-2, 225 lbs.; University of Southern California (USC); September 29, 1949.

Bobby Hamilton: 2004–05; came to the Raiders as a free agent in 2004; Defensive End; #98; 6-5, 285 lbs.; Southern Mississippi; July 1, 1971.

Charley Hannah: 1983–88; came to the Raiders in a trade with the Tampa Bay Buccaneers in July 1983; Offensive Guard; #73; 6-5, 270 lbs.; Alabama; July 26, 1955.

Mike Harden: 1989–90; came to the Raiders as a free agent in September 1989; Defensive Back; #45; 6-1, 195 lbs.; Michigan; February 16, 1959.

Cedrick Hardman: 1980–81; came to the Raiders in a trade with the San Francisco 49ers in 1980; Defensive End; #86; 6-4, 245 lbs.; North Texas State; October 4, 1948.

Charles Hardy: 1960–62; came to the Raiders as a free agent in 1960; Wide Receiver; #82; 6-0, 185 lbs.; San Jose State; November 7, 1933–May, 2001.

David Hardy: 1987; came to the Raiders as a free agent in 1987; Kicker; #4; 5-7, 180 lbs.; Texas A&M; July 7, 1959.

Lance Harkey: 1987; came to the Raiders as a free agent in 1987; Defensive Back; #24; 5-10, 180 lbs.; Illinois; October 30, 1965.

Pat Harlow: 1996–98; came to the Raiders in a trade with the New England Patriots in April 1996; Offensive Tackle; #75; 6-6, 295 lbs.; University of Southern California (USC); March 16, 1969.

James Harris: 1998–99; came to the Raiders as a free agent in March 1998; Defensive End; #93; 6-6, 285 lbs.; Temple; May 13, 1968.

John Harris: 1960–61; came to the Raiders as a free agent in 1960; Defensive Back; #28 and 29; 6-1, 195 lbs.; Santa Monica J.C.; May 7, 1933.

Johnnie Harris: 1999–01; came to the Raiders as a free agent in February 1999; Defensive Back; #37; 6-2, 210 lbs.; Mississippi State; August 21, 1972.

Kwame Harris: 2008; came to the Raiders as a free agent in 2008; Offensive Tackle; #77; 6-7, 310 lbs.; Stanford; March 15, 1982.

Napoleon Harris: 2002–04; Raiders 1st round selection in 2002 draft; Linebacker; #58; 6-2, 255 lbs.; Northwestern; February 25, 1979.

Dwight Harrison: 1980; came to the Raiders in 1980; Defensive Back; #28; 6-0, 187 lbs.; Texas A&I; October 12, 1948.

Nolan Harrison: 1991–96; Raiders 6th round selection in 1991 draft; Defensive Tackle/Defensive End; #74; 6-5, 280 lbs.; Indiana; January 25, 1969.

Rob Harrison: 1987; Raiders 10th round selection in 1987 draft; Running Back; #25; 6-2, 220 lbs.; Cal State–Sacramento; August 31, 1963.

Harold Hart: 1974–75, 1978; Raiders 11th round selection in 1974 draft, re-signed as a free agent in 1978; Running Back; #23 and 34; Texas Southern; July 13, 1952.

Roy Hart: 1991; came to the Raiders as a free agent in June 1991; Defensive Tackle; #61; 6-0, 280 lbs.; South Carolina; July 10, 1965.

James Harvey: 1966–71; Raiders 2nd round future pick in 1965 AFL draft; Offensive Guard; #70; 6-5, 250 lbs.; Mississippi; August 20, 1943.

Richard Harvey: 1998–99; came to the Raiders as a free agent in August 1998; Linebacker; #52; 6-1, 235 lbs.; Tulane; September 11, 1966.

Don Hasselbeck: 1983; came to the Raiders in a trade with the New England Patriots in September 1983; Tight End; #87; 6-7, 245 lbs.; Colorado; April 1, 1955.

James Hasty: 2001; came to the Raiders in 2001; Defensive Back; #34; 6-0, 203 lbs.; Central Washington, Washington State; May 23, 1965.

Clarence Hawkins: 1979; came to the Raiders in 1979; Running Back; #26; 6-0, 205 lbs.; Florida A&M; July 15, 1956.

Frank Hawkins: 1981–87; Raiders 10th round selection in 1981 draft; Running Back; #27; 5-9, 210 lbs.; Nevada, Reno; July 3, 1959.

Mike Hawkins: 1982; came to the Raiders as a free agent in 1982; Linebacker; #57; 6-3, 240 lbs.; Texas A&I; October 29, 1955.

Wayne Hawkins: 1960–70; came to the Raiders in the expansion draft from the Denver Broncos; Offensive Guard; #65; 6-0, 240 lbs.; Pacific; June 17, 1938.

Anttaj Hawthorne: 2005–06; Raiders 6th round selection in 2005 draft; Defensive Tackle; #77; 6-3, 310 lbs.; Wisconsin; November 15, 1981.

Lester Hayes: 1977–86; Raiders 5th round selection in 1977 draft; Defensive Back; #37; 6-0, 200 lbs.; Texas A&M; January 22, 1955.

Mike Haynes: 1983–89; came to the Raiders in a trade with the New England Patriots in November 1983; Defensive Back; #22; 6-2, 200 lbs.; Arizona State; July 1, 1953.

Don Heinrich: 1962; came to the Raiders as a free agent in 1962; Quarterback; #11; 6-0, 182 lbs.; Washington; September 19, 1930–February 29, 1992.

Mario Henderson: 2007–09; Raiders 3rd round selection in 2007 draft; Offensive Tackle; #75; 6-7, 300 lbs.; Florida State; October 29, 1984.

Ted Hendricks: 1975–83; came to the Raiders as a free agent in August 1975; Linebacker; #83; 6-7, 240 lbs.; Miami (Florida); November 1, 1947.

Dick Hermann: 1965; came to the Raiders in 1965; Linebacker; #46; 6-2, 215 lbs.; Florida State; July 11, 1942.

Ken Herock: 1963–65, 1967; came to the Raiders as a free agent in 1963; Tight End; #84 and 86; 6-2, 230 lbs.; West Virginia; July 16, 1941.

Jessie Hester: 1985–87; Raiders 1st round selection in 1985 draft;

Wide Receiver; #84; 5-11, 170 lbs.; Florida State; January 21, 1963.

Chris Hetherington: 2003–04; came to the Raiders as a free agent in 2003; Running Back; #44; 6-3, 245 lbs.; Yale; November 27, 1972.

Darrius Heyward-Bey: 2009; Raiders 1st round selection in 2009 draft; Wide Receiver; #12; 6-2, 210 lbs.; Maryland; January 26, 1987.

Johnnie Lee Higgins: 2007–09; Raiders 3rd round selection in 2007 draft; Wide Receiver; #15; 6-0, 185 lbs.; UTEP; September 8, 1983.

Don Highsmith: 1970–72; Raiders 13th round selection in 1970 draft; Running Back; #32; 6-0, 210 lbs.; Michigan State; March 12, 1948.

Rusty Hilger: 1985–87; Raiders 6th round selection in 1985 draft; Quarterback; #12; 6-4, 205 lbs.; Oklahoma State; May 9, 1962

Greg Hill: 1987; came to the Raiders in 1987; Defensive Back; #36; 6-1, 194 lbs.; Oklahoma State; February 12, 1961.

Kenny Hill: 1981–83; Raiders 8th round selection in 1980 draft; Defensive Back; #48; 6-0, 195 lbs.; Yale; July 25, 1958.

Madre Hill: 2002; came to Raiders as a free agent in March 2002; Running Back; #23; 6-0, 205 lbs.; Arkansas; January 2, 1976.

Renaldo Hill: 2005; came to the Raiders as a free agent in 2005; Defensive Back; #22; 5-11, 190 lbs.; Michigan State; November 12, 1978.

Rod Hill: 1987; came to the Raiders in 1987; Defensive Back; #38; 6-0, 185 lbs.; Kentucky State; March 14, 1959.

Marcus Hinton: 1995–96; came to the Raiders as a free agent in May 1995; Tight End; #85; 6-4, 260 lbs.; Alcorn State; December 27, 1971.

I.M. Hipp: 1980; came to the Raiders in 1980; Running Back; #20; 5-10, 200 lbs.; Nebraska; February 15, 1956.

Daryl Hobbs: 1993–96; came to the Raiders as a free agent in May 1992; Wide Receiver; #80; 6-2, 175 lbs.; Pacific; May 23, 1968.

Billy Joe Hobert: 1993–96; Raiders 3rd round selection in 1993 draft; Quarterback; #9 and 12; 6-3, 230 lbs.; Washington; January 8, 1971.

Al Hoisington: 1960; came to the Raiders as a free agent in 1960; Wide Receiver; #84; 6-3, 200 lbs.; Pasadena J.C.; November 18, 1933.

Jamie Holland: 1990–91; came to the Raiders in a trade with the San Diego Chargers for a draft selection in May 1990; Wide Receiver; #82; 6-1, 195 lbs.; Ohio State; February 1, 1964.

Jonathan Holland: 2008–09; Raiders 7th round selection in 2007 draft; Wide Receiver; #10 and 23; 6-0, 191 lbs.; Louisiana Tech; February 18, 1985.

Donald Hollas: 1997–98; came to the Raiders as a free agent in May 1997; Quarterback; #12; 6-3, 215 lbs.; Rice; November 22, 1967.

Brian Holloway: 1987–88; came to the Raiders in a trade with the New England Patriots in September 1987; Offensive Guard/ Offensive Tackle; #76; 6-7, 285 lbs.; Stanford; July 25, 1959.

Rob Holmberg: 1994–97; Raiders 7th round selection in 1994 draft; Linebacker; #57; 6-3, 230 lbs.; Penn State; May 6, 1971.

Lester Holmes: 1997; came to the Raiders as a free agent in May 1997; Offensive Guard; #71; 6-4, 315 lbs.; Jackson State; September 27, 1969.

Jerry Hopkins: 1968; came to the Raiders in 1968; Linebacker; #52; 6-2, 235 lbs.; Texas A&M; January 24, 1941.

Ethan Horton: 1987, 1989–93; came to the Raiders in 1987, and then re-joined the team as a free agent in May 1989; Running Back/Tight End; #23 and 88; 6-4, 240 lbs.; North Carolina; December 19, 1962.

Derrick Hoskins: 1992–95; Raiders 5th round selection in 1992 draft; Defensive Back; #20; 6-2, 210 lbs.; Southern Mississippi; November 14, 1970.

Jeff Hostetler: 1993–96; came to the Raiders as a free agent in March 1993; Quarterback; #15; 6-3, 215 lbs.; West Virginia; April 22, 1961.

Desmond Howard: 1997–98; came to the Raiders as a free agent in March 1997; Wide Receiver; #80; 5-10, 180 lbs.; Michigan; May 15, 1970.

Thomas Howard: 2006–09; Raiders 2nd round selection in 2006 draft; Linebacker; #53; 6-3, 240 lbs.; UTEP; July 14, 1983.

Bobby Hoying: 1999–01; came to the Raiders in a trade from the Philadelphia Eagles for a draft pick in August 1999; Quarterback; #14; 6-3, 220 lbs.; Ohio State; September 20, 1972.

Marv Hubbard: 1969–75; Raiders 11th round selection in 1968 draft; Running Back; #39 and 44; 6-1, 235 lbs.; Colgate; May 7, 1946.

John Huddleston: 1978–79; came to the Raiders as a free agent in 1978; Linebacker; #57; 6-3, 230 lbs.; Utah; April 10, 1954.

Bob Hudson: 1973–74; came to the Raiders in a trade with the Green Bay Packers in 1973; Running Back; #36; 5-11, 205 lbs.; Northeast Oklahoma; March 21, 1948.

Michael Huff: 2006–09; Raiders 1st round selection in 2006 draft; Defensive Back; #24; 6-1, 205 lbs.; Texas; March 6, 1983.

Corey Hulsey: 2003–06; came to the Raiders as a free agent in 2003; Offensive Guard; #71; 6-4, 325 lbs.; Clemson; July 26, 1977.

David Humm: 1975–79, 1983–84; Raiders 5th round selection in 1975 draft. Came back to the Raiders as a free agent in November 1983; Quarterback; #11; 6-2, 190 lbs.; Nebraska; April 2, 1952.

Ricky Hunley: 1989–90; came to the Raiders as a free agent in September 1989; Linebacker; #99; 6-2, 250 lbs.; Arizona; November 11, 1961.

Kevin Huntley: 2006; came to the Raiders as a free agent in 2006; Defensive End; #94; 6-7, 270 lbs.; Kansas State; April 8, 1982.

Michael Husted: 1999; came to the Raiders as a free agent in March 1998; Kicker; #5; 6-0, 195 lbs.; Virginia; June 16, 1970.

Junior Ioane: 2000–02; Raiders 4th round selection in 2000 draft; Defensive Tackle; #92; 6-4, 320 lbs.; Arizona State; July 21, 1977.

Gerald Irons: 1970–75; Raiders 3rd round selection in 1970 draft; Linebacker; #86; 6-2, 230 lbs.; Maryland State; May 2, 1947.

Grant Irons: 2003–06; came to the Raiders as a free agent in 2003; Defensive End; #96; 6-6, 285 lbs.; Notre Dame; July 7, 1979.

Raghib Ismail: 1993–95; Raiders 4th round selection in 1991 draft. Joined the team in September 1993 after playing in the Canadian Football League with the Toronto Argonauts; Wide Receiver; #86; 5-11, 175 lbs.; Notre Dame; November 18, 1969.

Bo Jackson: 1987–90; Raiders 7th round selection in 1987 draft; Running Back; #34; 6-1, 230 lbs.; Auburn; November 30, 1962.

Bobby Jackson: 1964; came to the Raiders in a purchase from the San Diego Chargers in 1964; Running Back; #32; 6-3, 238 lbs.; New Mexico State; March 16, 1940.

Grady Jackson: 1997–01; Raiders 6th round selection in 1997 draft; Defensive Tackle; #90; 6-2, 320 lbs.; Knoxville; January 21, 1973.

Leonard Jackson: 1987; came to the Raiders as a free agent in 1987; Linebacker; #91; 6-4, 240 lbs.; Oklahoma State; October 5, 1964.

Monte Jackson: 1978–82; came to the Raiders in a trade with the Los Angeles Rams in 1978; Defensive Back; #42; 5-11, 195 lbs.; San Diego State; July 14, 1953.

Richard Jackson: 1966; came to the Raiders in 1966; Linebacker; #32; 6-3, 255 lbs.; Southern; July 22, 1941.

Steve Jackson: 1977; came to the Raiders in 1977; Defensive Back; #42; 6-0, 192 lbs.; Louisiana State; April 6, 1955.

Victor Jackson: 1987; came to the Raiders as a free agent in 1987; Defensive Back; #49; 6-0, 205 lbs.; Bowie State; August 6, 1959.

Proverb Jacobs: 1963–64; came to the Raiders as a free agent in 1963; Offensive Tackle; #77; 6-4, 260 lbs.; California; May 25, 1935.

Jeff Jaeger: 1989–95; came to the Raiders as a free agent in March 1989; Kicker; #18; 5-11, 195 lbs.; Washington; November 26, 1964.

Harry Jagielski: 1961; came to the Raiders in 1961; Defensive Tackle; #70; 6-0, 257 lbs.; Indiana; December 25, 1931–October 9, 1993.

George Jakowenko: 1974; came to the Raiders as a free agent in 1974; Kicker; #6; 5-9, 170 lbs.; Syracuse; June 26, 1948.

Tory James: 2000–01; came to the Raiders as a free agent in February 2000; Defensive Back; #20; 6-2, 190 lbs.; Louisiana State; May 18, 1973.

Sebastian Janikowski: 2000–09; Raiders 1st round selection in 2000 draft; Kicker; #11; 6-2, 255 lbs.; Florida State; March 3, 1978.

Ed Jasper: 2005; came to the Raiders in 2005; Defensive Tackle; #95; 6-2, 293 lbs.; Texas A&M; January 18, 1973.

Jon Jelacic: 1961–64; came to the Raiders as a free agent in 1961; Defensive End; #88; 6-3, 250 lbs.; Minnesota; December 19, 1936–September 17, 1993.

Robert Jenkins: 1994–96; came to the Raiders as a free agent in June 1994; Offensive Tackle; #64; 6-5, 295 lbs.; University of California Los Angeles (UCLA); December 30, 1963.

Ronney Jenkins: 2003; came to the Raiders as a free agent in 2003; Running Back; #27; 5-11, 188 lbs.; Northern Arizona; May 25, 1977.

Brandon Jennings: 2000–01; came to the Raiders as a free agent in April 2000; Defensive Back; #39; 6-0, 190 lbs.; Texas A&M; July 15, 1978.

Rick Jennings: 1976–77; Raiders 11th round selection in 1976 draft; Wide Receiver; #33; 5-9, 180 lbs.; Maryland; April 17, 1953.

Derrick Jensen: 1979–86; Raiders 3rd round selection in 1978 draft; Running Back/Tight End; #31; 6-1, 225 lbs.; Texas Arlington; April 27, 1956.

Russell Jensen: 1985; came to the Raiders as a free agent in May 1985; Quarterback; #18; 6-2, 215 lbs.; California Lutheran; July 13, 1961.

James Jett: 1993–01; came to the Raiders as a free agent in April 1993; Wide Receiver; #82; 5-10, 170 lbs.; West Virginia; December 28, 1970.

A. J. Jimerson: 1990–91; Raiders 8th round selection in 1990 draft; Linebacker/Defensive End; #58; 6-3, 235 lbs.; Norfolk State; May 12, 1968.

Chris Johnson: 2007–09; came to the Raiders as a free agent in March 2007; Defensive Back; #37; 6-1, 200 lbs.; Louisville; September 25, 1979.

Eric Johnson: 2000–03; came to the Raiders as a free agent in April 2000; Linebacker; #41; 6-0, 210 lbs.; Nebraska; April 30, 1976.

Kevin Johnson: 1997; came to the Raiders as a free agent in April 1997; Defensive Tackle; #98; 6-1, 305 lbs.; Texas Southern; October 30, 1970.

Monte Johnson: 1973–80; Raiders 2nd round selection in 1973 draft; Linebacker; #58; 6-5, 240 lbs.; Nebraska; October 26, 1951.

Rob Johnson: 2003; came to the Raiders in 2003; Quarterback; #7; 6-4, 204 lbs.; University of Southern California (USC); March 18, 1973.

Teyo Johnson: 2003–04; Raiders 2nd round selection in 2003 draft; Tight End; #82; 6-5, 260 lbs.; Stanford; November 29, 1981.

Tim Johnson: 2002–05; came to the Raiders as a free agent in 2002; Linebacker; #51; 5-11, 235 lbs.; Youngstown State; February 7, 1978.

Mark Johnston: 1964; came to the Raiders in 1964; Defensive Back; #0; 6-0, 203 lbs.; Northwestern; March 4, 1938.

Lance Johnstone: 1996–00, 2006; Raiders 2nd round selection in 1996 draft, re-signed as a free agent in 2006; Defensive End; #51; 6-4, 250 lbs.; Temple; June 11, 1973.

Doug Jolley: 2002–04; Raiders 2nd round selection in 2002 draft; Tight End; #88; 6-4, 250 lbs.; Brigham Young; January 2, 1979.

Calvin Jones: 1994–95; Raiders 3rd round selection in 1994 draft; Running Back; #27 and 44; 5-11, 205 lbs.; Nebraska; November 27, 1970.

David Jones: 1992; came to the Raiders as a free agent in April 1992; Tight End; #82; 6-2, 225 lbs.; Delaware State; November 9, 1968.

Horace Jones: 1971–75; Raiders 12th round selection in 1971 draft; Defensive End; #82; 6-3, 255 lbs.; Louisville; July 31, 1949.

Jim Jones: 1961; came to the Raiders in 1961; Defensive Back; #32; 6-1, 204 lbs.; Washington; May 6, 1935–November, 1982.

Mike Jones: 1991–96, 2002; came to the Raiders as a free agent in April 1991, and re-signed by the team as a free agent in June 2002; Linebacker; #52; 6-1, 230 lbs.; Missouri; April 15, 1969.

Sean Jones: 1984–87; Raiders 2nd round selection in 1984 draft; Defensive End; #99; 6-7, 265 lbs.; Northeastern; December 19, 1962.

Willie Jones: 1979–82; Raiders 2nd round selection in 1979 draft; Defensive End; #90; 6-4, 245 lbs.; Florida State; November 22, 1957.

Charles Jordan: 1993; came to the Raiders as a free agent in May 1993; Wide Receiver; #85; 5-10, 175 lbs.; Long Beach-City College; October 9, 1969.

LaMont Jordan: 2005–07; came to the Raiders as a free agent in

2005; Running Back; #34; 5-10, 230 lbs.; Maryland; November 11, 1978.

Randy Jordan: 1993, 1998–02; came to the Raiders as a free agent in October 1993, and re-joined team as a free agent in May 1998; Running Back; #28; 5-11, 220 lbs.; North Carolina; June 6, 1970.

Shelby Jordan: 1983–86; came to the Raiders in a trade with the New England Patriots in September 1983; Offensive Tackle; #74; 6-7, 285 lbs.; Washington (mo.); January 23, 1952.

William Joseph: 2008–09; came to the Raiders as a free agent in March 2008, and then resigned in November 2009; Defensive Tackle; #96; 6-5, 315 lbs.; Miami (Florida); September 3, 1979.

L. C. Joyner: 1960; came to the Raiders as a free agent in 1960; Defensive Back; #46; 6-1, 187 lbs.; Diablo Valley J.C.; August 15, 1930–Died 2006.

Trey Junkin: 1985–89, 1996; came to the Raiders as a free agent in 1985, and re-joined the team as a free agent in June 1996; Tight End; #52 and 87; 6-2, 240 lbs.; Louisiana Tech; January 23, 1961.

Napoleon Kaufman: 1995–00; Raiders 1st round selection in 1995 draft; Running Back; #26; 5-9, 180 lbs.; Washington; June 7, 1973.

Tom Keating: 1966–72; came to the Raiders in a trade with the Buffalo Bills in 1965; Defensive Tackle; #74; 6-2, 247 lbs.; Michigan; September 2, 1942.

Joe Kelly: 1993; came to the Raiders as a free agent in April 1993; Linebacker; #57; 6-2, 235 lbs.; Washington; August 12, 1967.

Tommy Kelly: 2004–09; came to the Raiders as a free agent in May 2004; Defensive Tackle; #93; 6-6, 300 lbs.; Mississippi State; December 27, 1980.

Lincoln Kennedy: 1996–03; came to the Raiders in a trade with the Atlanta Falcons in May 1996; Offensive Tackle; #72; 6-6, 335 lbs.; Washington; February 12, 1971.

Greg Kent: 1966; Raiders 6th round selection in 1965 draft; Offensive Tackle; #73 and 80; 6-6, 275 lbs.; Utah; July 18, 1943.

Bob Keyes: 1960; came to the Raiders in 1960; Running Back; #24; 5-10, 183 lbs.; San Diego; Born in 1936.

Carl Kidd: 1995–96; came to the Raiders as a free agent in June 1995; Defensive Back; #46; 6-1, 200 lbs.; Arkansas; June 14, 1973.

Jamie Kimmel: 1986–88; Raiders 4th round selection in 1985 draft; Linebacker; #59; 6-3, 240 lbs.; Syracuse; March 28, 1962.

Emanuel King: 1989; came to the Raiders as a free agent in March 1989; Linebacker; #92; 6-4, 250 lbs.; Alabama; August 15, 1963.

Joe King: 1995; came to the Raiders as a free agent in May 1995; Defensive Back; #31; 6-2, 195 lbs.; Oklahoma State; May 7, 1968.

Kenny King: 1980–85; came to the Raiders in 1980 draft-day trade with the Houston Oilers; Running Back; #33; 5-11, 205 lbs.; Oklahoma; March 7, 1957.

Linden King: 1986–89; came to the Raiders as a free agent in August 1986; Linebacker; #52; 6-4, 250 lbs.; Colorado State; June 28, 1955.

Reggie Kinlaw: 1979–84; Raiders 12th round selection in 1979 draft; Defensive Tackle; #62; 6-2, 245 lbs.; Oklahoma; January 9, 1957.

Terry Kirby: 2000–01; came to the Raiders as a free agent in November 2000; Running Back; #42; 6-1, 225 lbs.; Virginia; January 20, 1970.

Dick Klein: 1963–64; came to the Raiders in a trade with the Boston Patriots in 1963; Offensive Tackle; #70; 6-4, 260 lbs.; Iowa; February 11, 1934 — December 27, 2005.

David Klinger: 1996–97; came to the Raiders as a free agent in June 1996; Quarterback; #7; 6-3, 215 lbs.; Houston; February 17, 1969.

Marcus Knight: 2001–02; came to the Raiders as a free agent in April 2000; Wide Receiver; #83; 6-1, 180 lbs.; Michigan; June 19, 1978.

Pete Koch: 1989; came to the Raiders as a free agent in March 1989; Defensive End; #74; 6-6, 260 lbs.; Maryland; January 23, 1962.

Dave Kocourek: 1967–68; came to the Raiders in a trade with the Miami Dolphins in 1967; Tight end; #88; 6-5, 240 lbs.; Wisconsin; August 20, 1937.

Warren Koegel: 1971; Raiders 2nd round selection in 1971 draft; Center; #56; 6-3, 260 lbs.; Penn State; November 1, 1949.

Tim Kohn: 1997; Raiders 3rd round selection in 1997 draft; Offensive Guard; #72; 6-5, 310 lbs.; Iowa State; December 6, 1973.

Kelvin Korver: 1973–77; Raiders 2nd round selection in 1973 draft; Defensive Tackle; #71; 6-6, 270 lbs.; Northwestern (Iowa); February 21, 1949.

Walt Kowalczyk: 1961; came to the Raiders in 1961; Running Back; #35; 6-0, 208 lbs.; Michigan State; April 17, 1935.

Ted Koy: 1970; Raiders 2nd round selection in 1970 draft; Tight End; #38; 6-1, 210 lbs.; Texas; September 15, 1947.

Joe Krakoski: 1963–66; came to the Raiders as a free agent in 1963; Defensive Back; #27; 6-2, 195 lbs.; Illinois; December 18, 1937.

Bob Kruse: 1967–68; Raiders 12th round selection in 1967 draft; Offensive Guard; #62; 6-2, 250 lbs.; Wayne State; February 10, 1942.

Terry Kunz: 1976–77; Raiders 8th round selection in 1976 draft; Running Back; #34; 6-1, 215 lbs.; Colorado; October 26, 1952.

Ted Kwalick: 1975–77; came to the Raiders as a free agent in 1975; Tight End; #89; 6-4, 225 lbs.; Penn State; April 15, 1947.

Jeff Kysar: 1995–96; Raiders 5th round selection in 1995 draft; Offensive Tackle; #79; 6-7, 320 lbs.; Arizona State; June 14, 1972.

Jim Lachey: 1988; came to the Raiders in a trade with the San Diego Chargers in 1988; Offensive Tackle; #74; 6-6, 294 lbs.; Ohio State; June 4, 1963.

Daryle Lamonica: 1967–74; came to the Raiders in a trade with the Buffalo Bills in 1967; Quarterback; #3; 6-3, 215 lbs.; Notre Dame; July 17, 1941.

Dan Land: 1989–97; came to the Raiders as a free agent in January 1989; Defensive Back; #25; 6-0, 195 lbs.; Albany State; July 3, 1965.

Ken Lanier: 1993; came to the Raiders as a free agent in July 1993; Offensive Tackle; #79; 6-3, 290 lbs.; Florida State; July 8, 1959.

Jack Larscheid: 1960–61; came to the Raiders as a free agent in 1960; Running Back; #23; 5-6, 162 lbs.; Pacific; May 10, 1933 — February 5, 1970.

Paul Larson: 1960; came to Raiders as a free agent in 1960; Quarterback; #12; 5-11, 185 lbs.; California; March 19, 1932.

Bill Laskey: 1966–70; came to the Raiders in a trade with the Buffalo Bills in 1966; Linebacker; #42; 6-3, 235 lbs.; Michigan; February 10, 1943.

Isaac Lassiter: 1965–69; came to the Raiders as a free agent in 1965; Defensive End; #77; 6-5, 270 lbs.; St. Augustine; November 15, 1940.

Greg Lathan: 1987; came to the Raiders as a free agent in 1987; Wide Receiver; #81; 6-1, 195 lbs.; Cincinnati; September 2, 1964.

Henry Lawrence: 1974–76; Raiders 1st round selection of 1974 draft; Offensive Tackle; #70; 6-4, 270 lbs.; Florida A&M; September 26, 1951.

Larry Lawrence: 1974–75; came to the Raiders as a free agent in 1974; Quarterback; #13; 6-1, 208 lbs.; Iowa; April 11, 1949.

Luke Lawton: 2008–09; came to the Raiders as a free agent in August 2008; Running Back; #44; 5-11, 237 lbs.; McNeese State; August 26, 1980.

Shane Lechler: 2000–09; Raiders 5th round selection of 2000 draft; Punter; #9; 6-2, 225 lbs.; Texas A&M; August 7, 1976.

ReShard Lee: 2006; came to the Raiders as a free agent in 2006; Running Back; #42; 5-10, 220 lbs.; Middle Tennessee State; October 12, 1980.

Zeph Lee: 1987–89; Raiders 9th round selection of 1986 draft, resigned as a free agent in 1987; Running Back/Defensive Back; #40; 6-3, 205 lbs.; University of Southern California (USC); June 17, 1963.

Brad Lekkerkerker: 2005; came to the Raiders as a free agent in 2004; Offensive Tackle; #75; 6-7, 330 lbs.; U.C. Davis; May 8, 1978.

Ashley Lelie: 2008; came to the Raiders as a free agent in 2008; Wide Receiver; #87; 6-3, 200 lbs.; Hawaii; February 16, 1980.

Chad Levitt: 1997; Raiders 4th round selection of 1997 draft; Running Back; #31; 6-1, 230 lbs.; Cornell; November 21, 1975.

Albert Lewis: 1994–98; came to the Raiders as a free agent in March 1994; Defensive Back; #24 and 29; 6-2, 205 lbs.; Grambling; October 6, 1960.

Bill Lewis: 1986–89; Raiders 7th round selection of 1986 draft; Center/Offensive Guard; #51; 6-7, 275 lbs.; Nebraska; July 12, 1963.

Garry Lewis: 1990–91; Raiders 7th round selection of 1990 draft; Defensive Back; #21; 5-11, 185 lbs.; Alcorn State; August 25, 1967.

Harold Lewis: 1962; came to Raiders as a free agent in 1962; Running Back; #21; 6-0, 200 lbs.; Houston; September 22, 1935.

Tahaun Lewis: 1991; Raiders 9th round selection of 1991 draft; Defensive Back; #20; 5-10, 175 lbs.; Nebraska; September 28, 1968.

Alva Liles: 1980; came to the Raiders in 1980; Defensive Tackle; #60; 6-3, 255 lbs.; Boise State; March 6, 1956.

Doug Lloyd: 1991; Raiders 6th round selection of 1989 draft, resigned in March 1991; Running Back; #37; 6-1, 220 lbs.; North Dakota State; August 31, 1965.

Wade Lockett: 1987; came to the Raiders as a free agent in 1987; Wide Receiver; #87; 6-1, 190 lbs.; Cal State–Fullerton; February 13, 1964.

Billy Ray Locklin: 1960; came to the Raiders as a free agent in 1960; Offensive Guard; #73; 6-2, 225 lbs.; New Mexico State; August 13, 1937.

James Lofton: 1987–88; came to the Raiders in a trade with the Green Bay Packers in April 1987; Wide Receiver; #80; 6-3, 190 lbs.; Stanford; July 5, 1956.

Howie Long: 1981–93; Raiders 2nd round selection of 1981 draft; Defensive End/Defensive Tackle; #75; 6-5, 275 lbs.; Villanova; January 6, 1960.

J.P. Losman; 2009; came to the Raiders as a free agent in December 2009; Quarterback; #7; 6-2, 210 lbs.; Tulane; March 12, 1981.

Billy Lott: 1960; came to the Raiders in the expansion draft from the Houston Oilers; Running Back; #31; 6-0, 203 lbs.; Mississippi; November 8, 1934–May 15, 1995.

Ronnie Lott: 1991–92; came to the Raiders as a free agent in March 1991; Defensive Back; #42; 6-0, 200 lbs.; University of Southern California (USC); May 8, 1959.

Tom Louderback: 1960–61; came to the Raiders as a free agent in 1960; Linebacker; #60; 6-2, 235 lbs.; San Jose State; March 5, 1933.

Clarence Love: 2002–03; came to the Raiders as a free agent in March 2002; Defensive Back; #38; 5-10, 180 lbs.; Toledo; June 16, 1976.

Lorenzo Lynch: 1996–97; came to the Raiders as a free agent in March 1996; Defensive Back; #43; 5-11, 210 lbs.; Sacramento State; April 6, 1963.

Lamar Lyons: 1996; came to the Raiders as a free agent in May 1996; Defensive Back; #44; 6-3, 210 lbs.; Washington; March 25, 1973.

Jacque MacKinnon: 1970; came to the Raiders as a free agent in 1970; Tight End; #37; 6-4, 235 lbs.; Colgate; November 10, 1938.

Ed Macon: 1960: came to the Raiders as a free agent in 1960; Defensive Back; #28; 6-0, 177 lbs.; Pacific; March 7, 1927.

John Madsen: 2006–08; came to the Raiders as a free agent in 2006; Tight End; #85; 6-5, 240 lbs.; Utah; May 9, 1983.

Errol Mann: 1976–78; came to the Raiders as a free agent in 1976; Kicker; #14; 6-0, 205 lbs.; North Dakota; June 27, 1941.

Don Manoukian: 1960; came to the Raiders as a free agent in 1960; Offensive Guard; #67; 5-9, 242 lbs.; Stanford; June 9, 1934.

Marv Marinovich: 1965; Raiders 28th round selection in 1962 AFL draft; Offensive Guard; #68; 6-3, 250 lbs.; University of Southern California (USC); August 6, 1939.

Todd Marinovich: 1991–92; Quarterback; Raiders 1st round pick in 1991 draft; #12; 6-4, 220 lbs.; University of Southern California (USC); July 4, 1969.

Curt Marsh: 1981–86; Raiders 1st round selection in 1981 draft; Offensive Guard; #60; 6-5, 275 lbs.; Washington; August 25, 1959.

James Marten: 2008; claimed off waivers from the Dallas Cowboys in September 2008; Offensive Tackle; #69; 6-7, 315 lbs.; Boston College; April 18, 1984.

Rod Martin: 1977–88; Raiders 12th round selection of 1977 draft; Linebacker; #53; 6-2, 225 lbs.; University of Southern California (USC); April 7, 1954.

Tee Martin: 2003; came to the Raiders as a free agent in 2003; Quarterback; #17; 6-2, 225 lbs.; Tennessee; July 25, 1978.

Rich Martini: 1979–80; Raiders 7th round selection in 1977 draft; Wide Receiver; #89; 6-2, 185 lbs.; California–Davis; November 19, 1955.

Mickey Marvin: 1977–87; Raiders 4th round selection of 1977 draft; Offensive Guard; #65; 6-4, 270 lbs.; Tennessee; October 5, 1955.

Russell Maryland: 1996–99; came to the Raiders as a free agent in February 1996; Defensive Tackle; #67 and 97; 6-1, 300 lbs.; Miami (Florida); March 22, 1969.

Lindsey Mason: 1978–81; Raiders 3rd round selection of 1978 draft; Offensive Tackle; #71; 6-5, 270 lbs.; Kansas; August 1, 1955.

Arch Matsos: 1963–65; came to the Raiders in a trade with the Buffalo Bills in 1963; Linebacker; #56; 6-6, 212 lbs.; Michigan State; November 22, 1935.

Ira Matthews: 1979–81; Raiders 6th round selection in 1979 draft; Running Back/Wide Receiver; #43; 5-8, 175 lbs; Wisconsin; August 23, 1957.

John Matuszak: 1976–82; came to the Raiders as a free agent in 1976; Defensive End/Defensive Tackle; #72; 6-8, 290 lbs.; Tampa; October 25, 1950–June 17, 1989.

Tom Maxwell: 1971–73; came to the Raiders in a trade with Baltimore Colts in 1971; Defensive Back; #42; 6-2, 195 lbs.; Texas A&M; May 5, 1947.

Doug Mayberry: 1963; came to the Raiders in 1963; Running Back; #33; 6-1, 220 lbs.; Utah State; March 23, 1937.

Joe McCall: 1984; Raiders 3rd round selection of 1984 draft; Running Back; #43; 6-0, 200 lbs.; Pittsburgh; February 17, 1962.

Napoleon McCallum: 1986, 1990–94; Raiders 4th round selection of 1986 draft — rejoined Raiders in a trade with the San Diego Chargers in April 1990; Running Back; #34; 6-2, 230 lbs.; U.S. Naval Academy; October 6, 1963.

Randy McClanahan: 1977, 1980–82; came to the Raiders as a free agent in 1977 and in 1980; Linebacker; #57; 6-5, 235 lbs.; Southwestern Louisiana; December 12, 1954.

Kent McCloughan: 1965–70; came to the Raiders in a trade with the Houston Oilers in 1965; Defensive Back; #47; 6-1, 190 lbs.; Nebraska; February 12, 1940.

Milt McColl: 1988; came to the Raiders in 1988; Linebacker; #56; 6-6, 248 lbs.; Stanford; August 28, 1959.

Josh McCown: 2007; came to the Raiders in a trade with the Detroit Lions in 2007; Quarterback; #12; 6-4, 213 lbs.; Sam Houston State; July 4, 1979.

Larry McCoy: 1984; came to the Raiders in 1984; Linebacker; #90; 6-2, 240 lbs.; Lamar; August 12, 1961.

Mike McCoy: 1977–78; came to the Raiders in a trade with the Green Bay Packers in 1977; Defensive Tackle; #76; 6-5, 275 lbs.; Notre Dame; September 6, 1948.

Terry McDaniel: 1988–97; Raiders 1st round selection of 1988 draft; Defensive Back; #36; 5-10, 180 lbs.; Tennessee; February 8, 1965.

Reggie McElroy: 1991–92; came to the Raiders as a free agent in May 1991; Offensive Guard/Offensive Tackle; #77; 6-6, 290 lbs.; West Texas State; March 4, 1960.

Vann McElroy: 1982–90; Raiders 3rd round selection of 1982 draft; Defensive Back; #26; 6-2, 195 lbs.; Baylor; January 13, 1960.

Darren McFadden: 2008–09; Raiders 1st round selection in 2008 draft; Running Back; #20; 6-2, 210 lbs.; Arkansas; August 27, 1987.

Nyle McFarlan: 1960; came to the Raiders as a free agent in 1960; Defensive End; #26; 6-2, 205 lbs.; Brigham Young; November 25, 1935.

Chris McFoy: 2007; came to the Raiders as a free agent in 2007; Wide Receiver; #14; 6-1, 200 lbs.; University of Southern California (USC); August 14, 1983.

Chester McGlockton: 1992–97; Raiders 1st round selection in 1992 draft; Defensive Tackle; #91; 6-4, 320 lbs.; Clemson; September 16, 1969.

Reggie McKenzie: 1985–88; Raiders 10th round selection of 1985 draft; Linebacker; #54; 6-1, 235 lbs.; Tennessee; February 8, 1963.

Odis McKinney: 1980–86; came to the Raiders in a trade with the New York Giants in May 1980, rejoined Raiders as a free agent in October 1985; Defensive Back; #23; 6-2, 190 lbs.; Colorado; May 19, 1957.

Chris McLemore: 1987–88; Raiders 11th round selection of 1987 draft; Running Back; #20; 6-1, 230 lbs.; Arizona; December 31, 1963.

Herb McMath: 1976; Raiders 4th round selection of 1976 draft; Defensive Tackle; #61; 6-4, 250 lbs.; Morningside; September 6, 1954.

Dan McMillen: 1987; came to Raiders as a free agent in 1987; Linebacker; #92; 6-4, 240 lbs.; Colorado; February 23, 1964.

Jim McMillin: 1963–64; came to Raiders in a trade with the Denver Broncos in 1963; Defensive Back; #45; 6-0, 190 lbs.; Colorado State; September 18, 1939.

Chuck McMurtry: 1962–63; came to the Raiders in a trade with the Buffalo Bills in 1962; Defensive Tackle; #73; 6-0, 280 lbs.; Whittier; February 15, 1937–February, 1984.

Paul McQuistan: 2006–09; Raiders 3rd round selection in 2006 draft; Offensive Tackle; #79; 6-5, 305 lbs.; Weber State; April 30, 1983.

Charles McRae: 1996; came to the Raiders in 1996; Offensive Tackle; #73; 6-7, 305 lbs.; Tennessee; September 16, 1968.

Dan Medlin: 1974–76, 1979; Raiders 6th round selection of 1972 draft, rejoined team in 1979; Offensive Guard; #79; 6-4, 255 lbs.; North Carolina State; October 12, 1949.

Terry Mendenhall: 1971–72; came to the Raiders as a free agent in 1971; Linebacker; #54; 6-1, 210 lbs.; San Diego State; April 16, 1949.

Mike Mercer: 1963–65; came to the Raiders as a free agent in 1963; Kicker; #10; 6-0, 200 lbs.; Northern Arizona; November 21, 1936.

Mark Merrill: 1984; came to the Raiders as a free agent in November 1984; Linebacker; #52; 6-4, 235 lbs.; Minnesota; May 5, 1955.

Darren Mickell: 2001; came to the Raiders as a free agent in May 2001; Defensive End; #98; 6-4, 280 lbs.; Florida; August 3, 1970.

Terry Mickens: 1998–00; came to the Raiders as a free agent in April 1998; Wide Receiver; #85; 6-1, 200 lbs.; Florida A&M; February 21, 1971.

Frank Middleton: 2001–04; came to the Raiders as a free agent in April 2001; Offensive Guard; #73; 6-4, 330 lbs.; Arizona; October 25, 1974.

Matt Millen: 1980–88; Raiders 2nd round selection in 1980 draft; Linebacker; #55; 6-2, 255 lbs.; Penn State; March 12, 1958.

Alan Miller: 1961–63, 1965; came to the Raiders in a trade with the Boston Patriots in 1961; Running Back; #37; 6-0, 219 lbs.; Boston College; June 19, 1937.

Bill Miller: 1964, 1966–68; came to the Raiders in a trade with the Buffalo Bills in 1964; Wide Receiver; #89; 6-1, 195 lbs.; Miami (Florida); April 17, 1940.

Derek Miller: 2006; came to the Raiders in 2006; Tight End; #46; 6-7, 254 lbs.; Maryland; June 10, 1983.

Justin Miller: 2008–09; came to the Raiders off waivers in November 2008; Defensive Back; #22; 5-10, 202 lbs.; Clemson; February 14, 1984.

Nick Miller: 2009; came to the Raiders as a free agent in April 2009; Wide Receiver; #89; 5-9, 180 lbs.; Southern Utah University; March 29, 1987.

Zach Miller: 2007–09; Raiders 2nd round selection in 2007 draft; Tight End; #80; 6-5, 256 lbs.; Arizona State; December 11, 1985.

John Henry Mills: 1997–98; came to the Raiders as a free agent in June 1997; Linebacker/Tight End; #56; 6-0, 235 lbs.; Wake Forest; October 31, 1969.

Charles Mincy: 1999; came to the Raiders as a free agent in May 1998; Defensive Back; #42; 6-0, 195 lbs.; Washington; December 16, 1969.

Gene Mingo: 1964–65; came to the Raiders in a trade with the Denver Broncos in 1964; Kicker; #21; 6-1, 190 lbs.; No college experience; September 22, 1938.

Dean Miraldi: 1987; came to the Raiders as a free agent in February 1987; Offensive Guard; #64; 6-6, 285 lbs.; Utah; April 8, 1958.

Rick Mirer: 2002–03; came to the Raiders as a free agent in March 2002; Quarterback; #3; 6-3, 210 lbs.; Notre Dame; March 19, 1970.

Rex Mirich: 1964–66; Raiders 20th round future selection in 1963 AFL draft; Defensive Tackle; #87 and 78; 6-4, 250 lbs.; Northern Arizona; March 11, 1941.

Bob Mischak: 1963–65; came to the Raiders in a trade with the New York Jets in 1963; Tight End/Offensive Guard; #87 and 67; 6-0, 230 lbs.; U.S. Military Academy; October 25, 1934.

Mike Mitchell: 2009; Raiders 2nd round selection in 2009 draft; Safety; #34; 6-1, 220 lbs.; Ohio University; June 10, 1987.

Tom Mitchell: 1966; Raiders 3rd round selection of 1966 draft; Tight End; #82; 6-2, 235 lbs.; Bucknell; August 22, 1944.

Ron Mix: 1971; came to the Raiders in a trade with the San Diego Chargers in 1971; Offensive Tackle; #77; 6-4, 250 lbs.; University of Southern California (USC); March 10, 1938.

Tim Moffett: 1985–86; Raiders 3rd round selection of 1985 draft; Wide Receiver; #83; 6-1, 180 lbs.; Mississippi; February 8, 1962.

Mel Montalbo: 1962; came to the Raiders in 1962; Defensive Back; #22; 6-1, 190 lbs.; Utah State; March 29, 1938.

Alfred Montez: 1996; came to the Raiders as a free agent in May 1996; Quarterback; #10; 6-2, 225 lbs.; Western New Mexico; October 18, 1972.

Cle Montgomery: 1981–85; came to the Raiders as a free agent in December 1981; Running Back/Wide Receiver; #28; 5-8, 180 lbs.; Abilene Christian; July 1, 1956.

Tyrone Montgomery: 1993–94; came to the Raiders as a free agent in April 1992; Running Back; #21; 6-0, 190 lbs.; Mississippi; August 3, 1970.

Max Montoya: 1990–94; came to the Raiders as a free agent in 1990; Offensive Guard; #65; 6-5, 295 lbs.; University of California Los Angeles (UCLA); May 12, 1956.

Keith Moody: 1980; came to the Raiders as a free agent in 1980; Defensive Back; #26; 5-11, 175 lbs.; Syracuse; June 13, 1953.

Bob Moore: 1971–75; Raiders 5th round selection of 1971 draft; Tight End; #88; 6-3, 220 lbs.; Stanford; February 12, 1949.

Manfred Moore: 1976; came to the Raiders off waivers from the Tampa Bay Buccaneers in 1976; Running Back; #36; 6-0, 200 lbs.; University of Southern California (USC); December 22, 1950.

Johnnie Morant: 2004–06; Raiders 5th round selection in 2004 draft; Wide Receiver; #19; 6-4, 229 lbs.; Syracuse; December 7, 1981.

Chris Morris: 2006–09; Raiders 7th round selection in 2006 draft; Offensive Guard/Center; #61; 6-3, 299 lbs.; Michigan State; February 22, 1983.

Riley Morris: 1960–62; came to the Raiders as a free agent in 1960; Defensive End; #55 and 92; 6-2, 230 lbs.; Florida A&M; March 22, 1935.

Dave Morrison: 1968; Raiders 16th round selection of 1968 draft; Defensive Back; #49; 5-11, 180 lbs.; Southwest Texas State; Birth date not available.

Kirk Morrison: 2005–09; Raiders 3rd round selection in 2005 draft; Linebacker; #52; 6-1, 238 lbs.; San Diego State; February 19, 1982.

Tom Morrow: 1962–64; came to the Raiders as a free agent in 1962; Defensive Back; #35; 5-11, 180 lbs.; Southern Mississippi; June 3, 1938.

Mike Morton: 1995–98; Raiders 4th round selection of 1995 draft; Linebacker; #50; 6-4, 235 lbs.; North Carolina; March 28, 1972.

Don Mosebar: 1983–94; Raiders 1st round selection of 1983 draft; Center/Offensive Guard/Offensive Tackle; #72; 6-6, 295 lbs.; University of Southern California (USC); September 11, 1961.

Randy Moss: 2005–06; came to the Raiders in a trade with the Minnesota Vikings in March 2005; Wide Receiver; #18; 6-4, 210 lbs.; Marshall; February 13, 1977.

Winston Moss: 1991–94; came to the Raiders in a trade with the Tampa Bay Buccaneers in April 1991; Linebacker; #99; 6-3, 245 lbs.; Miami (Florida); December 24, 1965.

Rich Mostardi: 1962; came to the Raiders in 1962; Defensive Back; #27; 5-11, 188 lbs.; Kent State; July 1, 1938.

Mark Mraz: 1989; came to the Raiders as a free agent in December 1988; Defensive End; #97; 6-4, 260 lbs.; Utah State; February 9, 1965.

Vance Mueller: 1986–91; Raiders 4th round selection of 1986 draft; Running Back; #31 and 42; 6-0, 220 lbs.; Occidental; May 5, 1964.

Calvin Muhammad: 1982–83; Raiders 12th round selection of 1980 draft; Wide Receiver; #82; 5-11, 190 lbs.; Texas Southern; December 10, 1958.

Shay Muirbrook: 1997; came to the Raiders in April 1997; Linebacker; #52; 6-0, 230 lbs.; Brigham Young; November 15, 1973.

Ed Muransky: 1982–84; Raiders 4th round selection of 1982 draft; Offensive Guard/Offensive Tackle; #76; 6-7, 275 lbs.; Michigan; January 20, 1960.

Jesse Murdock: 1963; came to the Raiders as a free agent in 1963; Running Back; #0; 6-2, 203 lbs.; California Western; September 17, 1938–September 25, 1965.

Louis Murphy: 2009; Raiders 4th round selection in 2009 draft; Wide Receiver; #18; 6-2, 200 lbs.; University of Florida; May 11, 1987.

Najee Mustafaa: 1995; came to the Raiders as a free agent in May 1995; Defensive Back; #48; 6-1, 190 lbs.; Georgia Tech; June 20, 1964.

Brandon Myers: 2009; Raiders 6th round selection in 2009 draft; Tight End; #83; 6-4, 250 lbs.; Iowa; September 4, 1985.

Toby Myles: 2000–01; came to the Raiders as a free agent in March 2000; Offensive Guard/Offensive Tackle; #70 and 77; 6-5, 320 lbs.; Jackson State; July 23, 1975.

Keyon Nash: 2002, 2004; Raiders 6th round selection of 2002 draft; Defensive Back; #44; 6-3, 215 lbs.; Albany State; March 11, 1979.

Joe Nedney: 1999; came to the Raiders as a free agent in December 1999; Kicker; #6; 6-5, 220 lbs.; San Jose State; March 22, 1973.

Bob Nelson: 1980–85; came to the Raiders as a free agent in July 1980; Linebacker; #51 and 55; 6-4, 235 lbs.; Nebraska; June 30, 1953.

Jeremy Newberry: 2007; came to the Raiders as a free agent in 2007; Center; #62; 6-5, 313 lbs.; California; March 23, 1976.

Anthony Newman: 1998–99; came to the Raiders as a free agent in March 1998; Defensive Back; #30; 6-0, 215 lbs.; Oregon; November 25, 1965.

Pete Nicklas: 1962; Raiders 30th round selection in 1962 AFL draft; Offensive Tackle; #70; 6-4, 240 lbs.; Baylor; July 24, 1939.

David Nixon: 2009; came to the Raiders as a free agent in November 2009; Linebacker; #56; 6-3, 225 lbs.; Brigham Young; March 16, 1985.

Mike Noble: 1987; came to the Raiders as a free agent in 1987; Linebacker; #53; 6-4, 220 lbs.; Stanford; October 31, 1963.

Jim Norris: 1962–64; Raiders 7th round selection of 1961 AFL draft; Defensive Tackle; #72 and 74; 6-4, 238 lbs.; Houston; October 14, 1939.

Slade Norris: 2009; Raiders 4th round selection of 2009 draft; Linebacker; #58; 6-3, 245 lbs.; Oregon State; October 25, 1985.

Joe Novsek: 1962; Raiders 17th round selection in 1961 AFL draft; Defensive End; #71; 6-4, 237 lbs.; Tulsa; May 29, 1939.

Carleton Oates: 1965–72; Raiders 21st round selection of 1964 AFL draft; Defensive Tackle; #85; 6-3, 260 lbs.; Florida A&M; April 24, 1942.

Dave Ogas: 1968; came to the Raiders in 1968; Linebacker; #61; 6-0, 225 lbs.; San Diego State; July 23, 1946.

Paul Ogleby: 1960; came to the Raiders as a free agent in 1960; Offensive Tackle; #74; 6-4, 235 lbs.; University of California Los Angeles (UCLA); January 9, 1939.

Ralph Oliver: 1968–69; Raiders 11th round selection of 1968 draft; Linebacker; #56; 6-2, 220 lbs.; University of Southern California (USC); April 24, 1944.

Oren O'Neal: 2007, 2009; Raiders 6th round selection in 2007 draft; Running Back; #46; 5-11, 245 lbs.; Arizona State; September 8, 1983.

Chuck Osborne: 1998–99; came to the Raiders as a free agent in June 1998; Defensive Tackle; #98; 6-2, 290 lbs.; Arizona; November 2, 1973.

Clancy Osbourne: 1963–64; came to the Raiders as a free agent in August 1963; Linebacker; #81; 6-3, 220 lbs.; Arizona State; December 23, 1934.

Dwayne O'Steen: 1980–81; came to the Raiders in a trade with the Los Angeles Rams in 1980; Defensive Back; #35; 6-1, 195 lbs.; San Jose State; December 20, 1954–September 15, 2001.

Gus Otto: 1965–72; Raiders 4th round selection of 1965 AFL draft; Linebacker; #34 and 45; 6-1, 220 lbs.; Missouri; December 8, 1943.

Jim Otto: 1960–74: came to Raiders in the AFL expansion draft in 1960 after being selected by the Minneapolis franchise that eventually became the Raiders; Center; #50 and 00; 6-2, 255 lbs.; Miami (Florida); January 5, 1938.

Burgess Owens: 1980–82; came to Raiders in a trade with the New York Jets in 1980; Defensive Back; #44; 6-2, 200 lbs.; Miami (Florida); August 2, 1951.

Jonathan Palmer: 2007; came to the Raiders as a free agent in 2007; Offensive Guard; #78; 6-5, 335 lbs.; Auburn; December 3, 1983.

Nick Papac: 1961; came to the Raiders in 1961; Quarterback; #12; 5-11, 190 lbs.; Fresno State; May 18, 1935.

Babe Parilli: 1960; came to the Raiders as a free agent in 1960; Quarterback; #10; 6-1, 196 lbs.; Kentucky; May 7, 1930.

Andy Parker: 1984–88, 1990; Raiders 5th round selection of 1984 draft, rejoined team in 1990; Tight End; #81; 6-5, 245 lbs.; Utah; September 8, 1961.

Nate Parks: 1999–00; came to the Raiders as a free agent in October 1999; Offensive Guard/Offensive Tackle; #71; 6-5, 305 lbs.; Stanford; October 24, 1974.

John Parrella: 2002–04; came to the Raiders as a free agent in March 2002; Defensive Tackle; #97; 6-3, 300 lbs.; Nebraska; November 22, 1969.

Dan Pastorini: 1980; came to the Raiders in a trade with the Houston Oilers in 1980; Quarterback; #7; 6-3, 205 lbs.; Santa Clara; May 26, 1949.

Joel Patten: 1991; came to the Raiders as a free agent in March 1991; Offensive Tackle; #71; 6-7, 305 lbs.; Duke; February 7, 1958.

Elvis Patterson: 1990–93; came to the Raiders as a free agent in March 1990; Defensive Back; #43; 5-11, 195 lbs.; Kansas; October 21, 1960.

Mark Pattison: 1986; Raiders 7th round selection of 1985 draft; Wide Receiver; #89; 6-2, 190 lbs.; Washington; December 13, 1961.

Dave Pear: 1979–80; came to the Raiders in a trade with the Tampa Bay Buccaneers in 1979; Defensive Tackle; #74; 6-2, 250 lbs.; Washington; June 1, 1953.

Erik Pears: 2009; came to the Raiders as a free agent in March 2009; Offensive Tackle; #72; 6-8, 305 lbs.; Colorado State; June 25, 1982.

Todd Peat: 1990, 1992–93; came to the Raiders as a free agent in March 1990; Offensive Guard; #64 and 74; 6-2, 305 lbs.; Northern Illinois; May 20, 1964.

Rodney Peete: 2000–01; came to the Raiders as a free agent in August 2000; Quarterback; #16; 6-0, 230 lbs.; University of Southern California (USC); March 16, 1966.

Gerald Perry: 1993–95; came to the Raiders as a free agent in March 1993; Offensive Tackle; #71; 6-6, 305 lbs.; Southern; November 12, 1964.

Mario Perry: 1987; Raiders 11th round selection in 1987 draft; Tight End; #84; 6-5, 235 lbs.; Mississippi; December 20, 1963.

Raymond Perryman: 2001; Raiders 5th round selection of 2001 draft; Defensive Back; #31; 5-11, 200 lbs.; Northern Arizona; November 27, 1978.

Volney Peters: 1961; came to Raiders from the San Diego Chargers for cash in 1961; Defensive Tackle; #79; 6-4, 240 lbs.; University of Southern California (USC); January 1, 1928.

Calvin Peterson: 1982; came to the Raiders as a free agent in 1982; Linebacker; #54; 6-3, 225 lbs.; University of California Los Angeles (UCLA); October 16, 1952.

Charles Phillips: 1975–80; Raiders 2nd round selection of 1975 draft; Defensive Back; #47; 6-3, 215 lbs.; University of Southern California (USC); December 22, 1952.

Irvin Phillips: 1983; came to the Raiders off waivers in 1982; Defensive Back; #25; 6-1, 190 lbs.; Arkansas Tech; January 23, 1960.

Jess Phillips: 1975; came to the Raiders in a trade with the New Orleans Saints in 1975; Running Back; #35; 6-1, 208 lbs.; Michigan State; February 28, 1947.

Charles Philyaw: 1976–79; Raiders 2nd round selection of 1976 draft; Defensive End; #77; T6-9, 295 lbs.; Texas Southern; February 25, 1954.

Bill Pickel: 1983–90; Raiders 2nd round selection of 1983 draft; Defensive Tackle/Defensive End; #71; 6-5, 260 lbs.; Rutgers; November 5, 1959.

Bruce Pickens: 1995; came to the Raiders as a free agent in March 1995; Defensive Back; #39; 5-11, 195 lbs.; Nebraska; May 9, 1958.

Shurron Pierson: 2003; Raiders 4th round selection in 2003 draft; Linebacker; #55; 6-0, 250 lbs.; South Florida; May 31, 1982.

Frank Pitts: 1974; came to the Raiders in a trade with the Cleveland Browns in 1974; Wide Receiver; #85; 6-2, 195 lbs.; Southern; November 12, 1943.

Jim Plunkett: 1978–86; came to the Raiders as a free agent in September 1978; Quarterback; #16; 6-2, 220 lbs.; Stanford; December 5, 1947.

Tyrone Poole: 2006; came to the Raiders as a free agent in 2006; Defensive Back; #38; 5-8, 188 lbs.; Fort Valley State; February 3, 1972.

Marquez Pope: 2000–01; came to the Raiders as a free agent in May 2000; Defensive Back; #49; 5-11, 205 lbs.; Fresno State; October 29, 1970.

Jerry Porter: 2000–07; Raiders 2nd round selection of 2000 draft; Wide Receiver; #81, 84, and 86; 6-2, 220 lbs.; West Virginia; July 14, 1978.

Kerry Porter: 1989; came to the Raiders as a free agent in April 1989; Running Back; #31; 6-1, 205 lbs.; Washington State; September 23, 1964.

Art Powell: 1963–66; came to the Raiders as a free agent in 1963; Wide Receiver; #84; 6-2, 212 lbs.; San Jose State; February 25, 1937.

Charlie Powell: 1960–61; came to the Raiders in a trade with the Los Angeles Chargers in 1960; Defensive End; #27; 6-3, 230 lbs.; No college experience; April 4, 1932.

Warren Powers: 1963–68; came to the Raiders as a free agent in 1963; Defensive Back; #20; 6-0, 188 lbs.; Nebraska; February 19, 1941.

Gene Prebola: 1960; came to the Raiders in the expansion draft from the Houston Oilers in 1960; Tight End; #89; 6-3, 225 lbs.; Boston University; June 30, 1938.

Dennis Price: 1988–89; Raiders 5th round selection of 1988 draft; Defensive Back; #20; 6-1, 170 lbs.; University of California Los Angeles (UCLA); June 14, 1965.

Anthony Prior: 1998; came to the Raiders in 1998; Defensive Back; #25; 5-11, 185 lbs.; Washington State; March 27, 1970.

Bob Prout: 1974; came to the Raiders in 1974; Defensive Back; #29; 6-1, 190 lbs.; Knox; May 11, 1951.

Greg Pruitt: 1982–84; came to the Raiders in a trade with the Cleveland Browns in 1982; Running Back/Punt Returner; #34; 5-10, 190 lbs.; Oklahoma; August 18, 1951.

Palmer Pyle: 1966; came to the Raiders as a free agent in 1966; Offensive Guard; #68; 6-2, 240 lbs.; Michigan State; June 12, 1937.

David Pyles: 1987; came to the Raiders as a free agent in 1987; Offensive Tackle; #63; 6-5, 275 lbs.; Miami (Ohio); September 3, 1960.

Jeff Queen: 1972–73; came to the Raiders in a trade with the San Diego Chargers in 1972; Running Back/Tight End; #47; 6-1, 217 lbs.; Morgan State; August 15, 1946.

Mike Rae: 1976–78; Raiders 8th round selection of 1973 draft; Quarterback; #15; 6-0, 190 lbs.; University of Southern California (USC); July 26, 1951.

Derrick Ramsey: 1978–83; Raiders 5th round selection of 1978 draft; Tight End; #84; 6-5, 235 lbs.; Kentucky; December 23, 1956.

Louis Rankin: 2008; came to the Raiders as a free agent in December 2008; Running Back; #40; 6-1, 205 lbs.; Washington; May 4, 1985.

Tom Rathman: 1994; came to the Raiders as a free agent in July 1994; Running Back; #44; 6-1, 230 lbs.; Nebraska; October 7, 1962.

Marcus Ray: 1999; came to the Raiders as a free agent in April 1999; Defensive Back; #42; 5-11, 215 lbs.; Michigan; August 14, 1976.

J.R. Redmond: 2003–04; came to the Raiders as a free agent in 2003; Running Back; #27; 5-11, 215 lbs.; Arizona State; September 28, 1977.

Marcel Reece: 2009; came to the Raiders as a free agent in December 2009; Running Back; #45; 6-3, 240 lbs.; Washington; June 23, 1985.

Archie Reese: 1982–83; came to the Raiders as a free agent in 1982; Defensive Tackle; #74; 6-3, 270 lbs.; Clemson; February 4, 1956.

Shawn Regent: 1987; came to the Raiders as a free agent in 1987; Center; #62; Boston College; April 14, 1963.

Mike Reinfeldt: 1976; came to the Raiders as a free agent in 1975; Defensive Back; #37; 6-2, 195 lbs.; Wisconsin, Milwaukee; May 6, 1953.

Billy Reynolds: 1960; came to the Raiders as a free agent in 1960; Running Back; #46; 5-10, 188 lbs.; Pittsburgh; July 20, 1931–December 2, 2002.

M.C. Reynolds: 1962; came to the Raiders in a trade with the

Buffalo Bills in 1962; Quarterback; #17; 6-0, 193 lbs.; Louisiana State; February 11, 1935–September 8, 1991.

Dominic Rhodes: 2007; came to the Raiders as a free agent in 2007; Running Back; #33; 5-9, 203 lbs.; Midwestern State; January 17, 1979.

Floyd Rice: 1976–77; came to the Raiders as a free agent in 1976; Linebacker; #52; 6-3, 225 lbs.; Alcorn A&M; August 31, 1949.

Jerry Rice: 2001–04; came to the Raiders as a free agent in June 2001; Wide Receiver; #80; 6-2, 200 lbs.; Mississippi Valley State; October 13, 1962.

Harold Rice: 1971; Raiders 11th round selection of 1969 draft; Defensive End; #67; 6-2, 235 lbs.; Tennessee State; June 23, 1945.

Ken Rice: 1964–65; came to the Raiders in a trade with the Buffalo Bills in 1964; Offensive Tackle; #75; 6-2, 240 lbs.; Auburn; September 14, 1939.

Randy Rich: 1978; came to the Raiders in 1978; Defensive Back; #27; 5-10, 178 lbs.; New Mexico; December 28, 1953.

Jay Richardson: 2007–09; Raiders 5th round selection in 2007 draft; Defensive End; #98; 6-5, 276 lbs.; Ohio State; January 27, 1984.

Louis Riddick: 1998; came to the Raiders as a free agent in April 1998; Defensive Back; #41; 6-2, 210 lbs.; Pittsburgh; March 15, 1969.

Ryan Riddle; 2005; Raiders 6th round selection of 2005 draft; Linebacker; #57; 6-2, 255 lbs.; California; July 5, 1981.

Preston Ridlehuber: 1968; came to the Raiders in 1968; Running Back; #37; 6-2, 217 lbs.; Georgia; November 2, 1943.

Chris Riehm: 1986–88; came to the Raiders as a free agent in August 1986; Offensive Guard; #77; 6-6, 280 lbs.; Ohio State; April 14, 1961.

Charles Rieves: 1962–63; came to the Raiders in 1962; Linebacker; #32 and 48; 6-1, 218 lbs.; Houston; January 6, 1939.

Andre Rison: 2000; came to the Raiders as a free agent in 2000; Wide Receiver; #80; 6-1, 188 lbs.; Michigan State; March 18, 1967.

Jon Ritchie: 1998–01; Raiders 3rd round selection of 1998 draft; Running Back; #40; 6-1, 250 lbs.; Stanford; September 4, 1974.

Hank Rivera: 1962; Raiders 10th round selection in 1962 AFL draft; Defensive Back; #23 and 41; 5-11, 180 lbs.; Oregon State; December 25, 1938.

David Rivers: 2004; Quarterback; came to the Raiders as a free agent in 2004; #14; 6-3, 220 lbs.; Western Carolina; September 1, 1977.

Austin Robbins: 1994–95, 2000; Raiders 4th round selection of 1994 draft, then signed again as a free agent in April 2000; Defensive Tackle; #95; 6-6, 290 lbs.; North Carolina; March 1, 1971.

Barret Robbins: 1995–03; Raiders 2nd round selection of 1995 draft; Center; #63; 6-3, 315 lbs.; Texas Christian; August 26, 1973.

Bo Roberson: 1962–65; came to the Raiders in a trade with the San Diego Chargers in 1962; Wide Receiver; #40; 6-1, 190 lbs.; Cornell; July 23, 1936.

Cliff Roberts: 1961; came to the Raiders in 1961; Defensive Tackle; #71; 6-3, 260 lbs.; Illinois; Born in 1938.

Greg Robinson: 1993–94; Raiders 8th round selection of 1993 draft; Running Back; #28; 5-10, 205 lbs.; Northeast Louisiana; August 8, 1969.

Jerry Robinson: 1985–91; came to the Raiders in a trade with the Philadelphia Eagles in October 1985; Linebacker; #57; 6-2, 230 lbs.; University of California Los Angeles (UCLA); December 18, 1956.

Johnny Robinson: 1981–83; Raiders 4th round selection of 198_ draft; Defensive Tackle/Defensive End; #68; 6-2, 255 lbs.; Louisiana Tech; February 14, 1959.

Terry Robiskie: 1977–79; Raiders 8th round selection of 197_ draft; Running Back; #35; 6-1, 210 lbs.; Louisiana State; November 12, 1954.

John Roderick: 1968; came to the Raiders in a trade with the Miami Dolphins in 1968; Wide Receiver; #41; 6-0, 180 lbs.; Southern Methodist; August 21, 1944.

Mike Rodriguez: 1987; came to the Raiders in 1987; Defensive Tackle; #74; 6-1, 275 lbs.; Alabama; December 5, 1961.

Herb Roedel: 1961; came to the Raiders in 1961; Offensive Guard; #61; 6-3, 230 lbs.; Marquette; March 30, 1939.

Jim Romano: 1982–84; Raiders 2nd round selection of 1982 draft; Center; #52; 6-3, 255 lbs.; Penn State; September 7, 1959.

Bill Romanowski: 2002–03; came to the Raiders as a free agent in March 2002; Linebacker; #53; 6-4, 245 lbs.; Boston College; April 2, 1966.

Bob Rosensteil: 1997; came to the Raiders as a free agent in April 1997; Tight End; #89; 6-3, 240 lbs.; Eastern Illinois; February 7, 1974.

Tim Rother: 1989–90; Raiders 4th round selection in 1988 draft; Offensive/Defensive Tackle; #78; 6-7, 275 lbs.; Nebraska; September 28, 1965.

Stanford Routt: 2005–09; Raiders 2nd round selection in 2005 draft; Defensive Back; #26; 6-1, 195 lbs.; Houston; July 23, 1983.

Dave Rowe: 1975–78; came to the Raiders in a trade with the San Diego Chargers in 1975; Defensive Tackle; #74; 6-7, 270 lbs.; Penn State; June 20, 1945.

Karl Rubke: 1968; came to the Raiders in 1968; Defensive End; #54; 6-4, 240 lbs.; University of Southern California (USC); December 6, 1935.

Booker Russell: 1978–79; came to the Raiders as a free agent in 1978; Running Back; #34; 6-2, 230 lbs.; Southwest Texas State; February 28, 1956–March 9, 2000.

Darrell Russell: 1997–01; Raiders 1st round selection in 1997 draft; Defensive Tackle/Defensive End; #96; 6-5, 325 lbs.; University of Southern California (USC); May 27, 1976–December 15, 2005.

Gary Russell: 2009; came to the Raiders as a free agent in May 2009; Running Back; #22; 5-11, 215 lbs., Minnesota; September 6, 1986.

JaMarcus Russell: 2007–09; Raiders 1st round selection in 2007 draft; Quarterback; #2; 6-6, 265 lbs.; Louisiana State; August 9, 1985.

Ron Sabal: 1960–61; came to the Raiders as a free agent in 1960; Offensive Tackle; #64; 6-2, 245 lbs.; Purdue; July 23, 1936.

Terdell Sands: 2003–08; came to the Raiders as a free agent in 2003; Defensive Tackle; #92; 6-7, 337 lbs.; Tennessee–Chattanooga; October 31, 1979.

O.J. Santiago: 2003; came to the Raiders as a free agent in 2003; Tight End; #83; 6-7, 265 lbs.; Kent State; April 4, 1974.

Warren Sapp: 2004–07; came to the Raiders as a free agent in

2004; Defensive End/Defensive Tackle; #99; 6-2, 300 lbs.; Miami (Florida); December 19, 1972.

Samson Satele: 2009; came to the Raiders in a trade with the Miami Dolphins in March 2009; Center; 6-3, 300 lbs.; Hawaii; November 29, 1984.

Chaz Schilens: 2008–09; Raiders 7th round selection in 2008 draft; Wide Receiver; #81; 6-4, 225 lbs.; San Diego State; November 7, 1985.

Ray Schmautz: 1966; came to the Raiders in 1966; Linebacker; #58; 6-1, 225 lbs.; San Diego State; January 26, 1943.

Jay Schroeder: 1988–92; came to the Raiders in a trade with Washington in 1988; Quarterback; #10 and 13; 6-4, 215 lbs.; University of California Los Angeles (UCLA); June 28, 1961.

Roy Schuening: 2009; came to the Raiders as a free agent in December 2009; Guard; #67; 6-3, 315 lbs.; Oregon State; April 8, 1984.

Harry Schuh: 1965–70; Raiders 1st round selection in 1965 draft; Offensive Tackle; #71 and 79;6-3, 260 lbs.; Memphis State; September 25, 1942.

Stuart Schweigert: 2004–07; Raiders 3rd round selection in 2004 draft; Defensive Back; #30; 6-2, 210 lbs.; Purdue; June 21, 1981.

Carey Scott: 2003; came to the Raiders as a free agent in 2003; Defensive Back; #37; 5-11, 214 lbs.; Kentucky State; August 11, 1979.

Trevor Scott: 2008–09; Raiders 6th round selection in 2008 draft; Defensive End; #91; 6-5, 256 lbs.; Buffalo; August 30, 1984.

Sam Seale: 1984–87; Raiders 8th round selection in 1984 draft; Wide Receiver/Defensive Back; #43 and 88; 5-9, 185 lbs.; Western State (CO); October 6, 1962.

Paul Seller: 1971–73; came to the Raiders as a free agent in 1971; Offensive Tackle; #65; 6-4, 260 lbs.; Notre Dame; November 1, 1945.

Richard Seymour: 2009; came to the Raiders in a trade with the New England Patriots in September 2009; Defensive End; #92; 6-6, 310 lbs.; Georgia; October 6, 1979.

Siddeeq Shabazz: 2003; Raiders 7th round selection in 2003 draft; Defensive Back; #28; 5-11, 200 lbs.; New Mexico State; February 5, 1981.

Matt Shaughnessy: 2009; Raiders 3rd round selection in 2009 draft; Defensive End; #77; 6-5, 270 lbs.; Wisconsin; September 23, 1986.

Glenn Shaw: 1963–64; came to the Raiders as a free agent in 1963; Running Back; #32; 6-2, 230 lbs.; Kentucky; July 11, 1938.

Terrance Shaw: 2002–03; came to the Raiders as a free agent in March 2002; Defensive Back; #22; 6-0, 200 lbs.; Stephen F. Austin; January 11, 1973.

Kenny Shedd: 1996–99; came to the Raiders as a free agent in June 1996; Wide Receiver; #84; 5-10, 165 lbs.; Northern Iowa; February 14, 1971.

Art Shell: 1968–82; Raiders 3rd round selection in 1968 draft; Offensive Tackle; #78; 6-5, 285 lbs.; Maryland State; November 26, 1946.

Rod Sherman: 1967, 1969–71; Raiders 1st round future selection in 1966 draft; Wide Receiver; #13 and 23; 6-0, 190 lbs.; University of Southern California (USC); December 25, 1944.

Jackie Shipp: 1989; came to the Raiders as a free agent in March 1989; Linebacker; #58; 6-2, 240 lbs.; Oklahoma; March 19, 1962.

George Shirkey: 1962; purchased from the Houston Oilers in 1962; Defensive Tackle; #77; 6-4, 260 lbs.; Stephen F. Austin; August 20, 1936.

Mike Siani: 1972–77; Raiders 1st round selection in 1972 draft; Wide Receiver; #49; 6-2, 195 lbs.; Villanova; May 27, 1950.

Jack Simpson: 1962–64; came to the Raiders in a trade with the Denver Broncos in 1962; Linebacker; #49 and 50; 6-0, 225 lbs.; Mississippi; August 20, 1936.

Willie Simpson: 1962; came to the Raiders in 1962; Running Back; #20 and 39; 6-0, 218 lbs.; San Francisco State; March 11, 1938.

Barry Sims: 1999–07; came to the Raiders as a free agent in July 1999; Offensive Guard/Offensive Tackle; #65; 6-5, 305 lbs.; Utah; December 1, 1974.

Otis Sistrunk: 1972–79; came to the Raiders in a trade with the Los Angeles Rams in 1972; Defensive End/Defensive Tackle; #60; 6-4, 270 lbs.; No college experience; September 18, 1946

Greg Skrepenak: 1992–95; Raiders 2nd round selection in 1992 draft; Offensive Tackle; #78; 6-6, 315 lbs.; Michigan; January 31, 1970.

Chad Slaughter: 2002–06; came to the Raiders as a free agent in January 2002; Offensive Tackle; #78; 6-8, 340 lbs.; Alcorn State; June 4, 1978.

Richard Sligh: 1967; Raiders 10th round selection in 1967 draft; Defensive Tackle; #73; 7-0, 310 lbs.; North Carolina College; August 18, 1944–December 23, 1998.

Greg Slough: 1971–72; Raiders 6th round selection in 1971 draft; Linebacker; #45 and 58; 6-3, 230 lbs.; University of Southern California (USC); February 26, 1948.

Anthony Smith: 1991–97; Raiders 1st round selection in 1990 draft; Defensive End; #94; 6-3, 270 lbs.; Arizona; June 28, 1967.

Bubba Smith: 1973–74; came to the Raiders in a trade with the Baltimore Colts in 1973; Defensive End; #77; 6-7, 265 lbs.; Michigan State; February 28, 1945.

Charles Smith: 1968–74; Raiders 4th round selection in 1968 draft; Running Back; #23; 6-0, 205 lbs.; Utah; January 18,1946.

Hal Smith: 1961; came to the Raiders in a trade with the Boston Patriots in 1961; Defensive Tackle; #72; 6-5, 250 lbs.; University of California Los Angeles (UCLA); October 3, 1935.

James Smith: 1960; came to the Raiders as a free agent in 1960; Running Back; #38; 6-1, 210 lbs.; Compton J.C.; October 18, 1936.

Jim Smith: 1985; came to the Raiders in a trade with the Pittsburgh in September 1985; Wide Receiver; #86; 6-2, 195 lbs.; Michigan; July 20, 1955.

Jimmy Smith: 1984; came to the Raiders in 1984; Running Back; #29; 6-0, 205 lbs.; Elon and Purdue; September 25, 1960.

Kenny Smith: 2005; came to the Raiders as a free agent in 2005; Defensive Tackle; #54; 6-4, 300 lbs.; Alabama; September 8, 1977.

Kevin Smith: 1992–94; Raiders 7th round selection in 1992 draft; Tight End; #39 and 83; 6-4, 255 lbs.; University of California Los Angeles (UCLA); July 25, 1969.

Ron Smith: 1974; came to the Raiders in a trade with the San Diego Chargers in 1974; Defensive Back; #27; 6-1, 195 lbs.; Wisconsin; May 3, 1943.

Steve Smith: 1987–93; Raiders 3rd round selection in 1987 draft; Running Back; #35; 6-1, 235 lbs.; Penn State; August 30, 1964.

Travian Smith: 1998–04; Raiders 5th round selection in 1998 draft; Linebacker; #53 and 56; 6-4, 240 lbs.; Oklahoma; August 26, 1975.

Willie Smith: 1961; came to the Raiders in a trade with the Denver Broncos in 1961; Running Back; #63; 6-2, 260 lbs.; Michigan; November 1, 1937.

Mike Sommer: 1963; came to the Raiders as a free agent in 1963; Running Back; #29; 5-11, 190 lbs.; George Washington; October 9, 1934.

Ollie Spencer: 1963; came to the Raiders as a free agent in 1963; Offensive Guard; #63 and 67; 6-2, 245 lbs.; Kansas; April 17, 1931–April 28, 1991.

Mike Spivey: 1980; came to the Raiders in 1980; Defensive Back; #45; 6-0, 197 lbs.; Colorado; March 10, 1954.

Jack Squirek: 1982–85; Raiders 2nd round selection in 1982 draft; Linebacker; #58; 6-4, 230 lbs.; Illinois; February 16, 1959.

Ken Stabler: 1970–79; Raiders 2nd round selection in 1968 draft; Quarterback; #12; 6-3, 215 lbs.; Alabama; December 25, 1945.

Dave Stalls: 1983, 1985; came to the Raiders in 1983; Defensive Tackle; #61 and 74; 6-5, 250 lbs.; Northern Colorado; September 19, 1955.

Duane Starks: 2006–07; came to the Raiders as a free agent in 2006; Defensive Back; #22; 5-10, 170 lbs.; Miami (Florida); May 23, 1974.

Fred Steinfort: 1976; Raiders 5th round selection in 1976 draft; Kicker; #4; 5-11, 185 lbs.; Boston College; November 3, 1952.

Kevin Stemke: 2002; came to the Raiders as a free agent in 2002; Punter; #10; 6-2, 194 lbs.; Wisconsin; November 23, 1978.

Rich Stephens: 1992–96; came to the Raiders as a free agent in June 1992; Offensive Guard/Offensive Tackle; #77; 6-7, 315 lbs.; Tulsa; November 1, 1965.

Joe Stewart: 1978–79; Raiders 4th round selection in 1978 draft; Wide Receiver; #80; 5-11, 180 lbs.; Missouri; November 18, 1955.

Tony Stewart: 2007–09; came to the Raiders as a free agent in 2007; Tight End; #86; 6-5, 260 lbs.; Penn State; August 9, 1979.

Matt Stinchcomb: 1999–03; Raiders 1st round selection in 1999 draft; Offensive Tackle; #74; 6-6, 310 lbs.; Georgia; June 3, 1977.

Jack Stone: 1961–62; came to the Raiders in a trade with the Dallas Texans in 1961; Offensive Tackle; #75; 6-2, 245 lbs.; Oregon; July 28, 1936.

John Stone: 2003–04; came to the Raiders as a free agent in 2003; Wide Receiver; #86 and 15; 5-11, 180 lbs.; Wake Forest; July 7, 1979.

Ron Stone: 2004–05; came to the Raiders as a free agent in 2004; Offensive Guard; #67; 6-5, 325 lbs.; Boston College; July 20, 1971.

Steve Strachan: 1985–89; Raiders 11th round selection in 1985 draft; Running Back; #39; 6-1, 220 lbs.; Boston College; March 22, 1963.

Bill Streigel: 1960; came to the Raiders as a free agent in 1960; Linebacker; #75; 6-2, 235 lbs.; Pacific; May 28, 1936.

Darrell Strong: 2008; came to the Raiders as a free agent in 2008; Tight End; #82; 6-5, 265 lbs.; Pittsburgh; May 21, 1986.

Dana Stubblefield: 2003; came to the Raiders as a free agent in 2003; Defensive Tackle; #94; 6-2, 290 lbs.; Kansas; November 14, 1970.

Bob Svihus: 1965–70; Raiders 3rd round selection in 1964 AFL draft; Offensive Tackle; #76; 6-4, 245 lbs.; University of Southern California (USC); June 21, 1943.

Steve Sweeney: 1973; Raiders 9th round selection in 1973 draft; Wide Receiver; #89; 6-3, 205 lbs.; California; September 6, 1950.

Pat Swilling: 1995–96, 1998; came to the Raiders as a free agent in April 1995; Defensive End; #56; 6-3, 250 lbs.; Georgia Tech; October 25, 1964.

Sam Sword: 1999; came to the Raiders as a free agent in April 1999; Linebacker; #56; 6-1, 240 lbs.; Michigan; December 9, 1974.

Steve Sylvester: 1975–83; Raiders 10th round selection in 1975 draft; Offensive Guard/Offensive Tackle/Center; #66; 6-4, 260 lbs.; Notre Dame; March 4, 1953.

Stan Talley: 1987; came to the Raiders as a free agent in March 1987; Kicker; #5; 6-5, 215 lbs.; Texas Christian; September 5, 1958.

Jack Tatum: 1971–79; Raiders 1st round selection in 1971 draft; Defensive Back; #31 and 32; 5-10, 200 lbs.; Ohio State; November 18, 1948–July 27, 2010.

John Tautolo: 1987; came to the Raiders as a free agent in 1987; Offensive Tackle; #61; 6-4, 280 lbs.; University of California, Los Angeles (UCLA); May 29, 1959.

Josh Taves: 2000–01; came to the Raiders as a free agent in February 2000; Defensive End; #99; 6-7, 285 lbs.; Northeastern; May 13, 1972.

Billy Taylor: 1982; came to the Raiders as a free agent in 1982; Running Back; #49; 6-0, 210 lbs.; Texas Tech; July 6, 1956.

Malcolm Taylor: 1987–88; came to the Raiders as a free agent in April 1987; Defensive Tackle; #96; 6-6, 280 lbs.; Tennessee State; June 20, 1960.

Willie Teal: 1987; came to the Raiders as a free agent in 1987; Defensive Back; #20; Louisiana State; December 20, 1957.

Tony Teresa: 1960; came to the Raiders as a free agent in 1960; Running Back; #25; 5-9, 188 lbs.; San Jose State; December 8, 1933–October 16, 1984.

David Terrell: 2004; came to the Raiders in 2004; Defensive Back; #35; 6-0, 190 lbs.; UTEP; July 8, 1975.

Robert Thomas: 2006–08; came to the Raiders as a free agent in 2006; Linebacker; #55 and 94; 6-1, 237 lbs.; University of California Los Angeles (UCLA); July 17, 1980.

Skip Thomas: 1972–78; Raiders 7th round selection in 1972 draft; Defensive Back; #26; 6-1, 205 lbs.; University of Southern California (USC); February 7, 1950.

William Thomas: 2000–01; came to the Raiders as a free agent in August 2000; Linebacker; #59; 6-2, 225 lbs.; Texas A&M; August 13, 1968.

Art Thoms: 1969–76; Raiders 1st round selection in 1969 draft; Defensive Tackle; #80; 6-5, 250 lbs.; Syracuse; October 20, 1946.

Tony Tillmon: 1987; came to the Raiders as a free agent in 1987; Defensive Back; #29; 5-10, 170 lbs.; Texas; September 12, 1963.

Larry Todd: 1965–70; came to the Raiders as a number one future selection in 1964; Running Back; #22; 6-1, 185 lbs.; Arizona State; October 7, 1942–January 17, 1990.

Reggie Tongue: 2005; came to the Raiders in 2005; Defensive Back; #29; 6-0, 204 lbs.; Oregon State; April 11, 1973.

Pat Toomay: 1977–79; came to the Raiders in a trade with the Tampa Bay Buccaneers in 1977; Defensive End; #67; 6-6, 245 lbs.; Vanderbilt; May 17, 1945.

Stacey Toran: 1984–88; Raiders 6th round selection in 1984 draft; Defensive Back; #30; 6-3, 200 lbs.; Notre Dame; November 10, 1961–August 5, 1989.

Greg Townsend: 1983–93; Raiders 4th round selection in 1983 draft; Defensive End/Linebacker; #93; 6-3, 280 lbs.; Texas Christian; November 3, 1961.

James Trapp: 1993–97; Raiders 3rd round selection in 1993 draft; Defensive Back; #27 and 37; 6-0, 190 lbs.; Clemson; December 28, 1969.

Orville Trask: 1962; came to the Raiders in a purchase from the Houston Oilers in 1962; Defensive Tackle; #79; 6-4, 260 lbs.; Rice; December 3, 1934–November 12, 2008.

Adam Treu: 1997–06; Raiders 3rd round selection in 1997 draft; Offensive Guard/Offensive Tackle/Center; #62; 6-5, 300 lbs.; Nebraska; June 24, 1974.

Dalton Truax: 1960; came to the Raiders in a trade with the Dallas Texans in 1960; Defensive Tackle; #72; 6-2, 236 lbs.; Tulane; January 17, 1935.

Olanda Truitt: 1996–97; came to the Raiders as a free agent in May 1996; Wide Receiver; #17 and 88; 6-0, 190 lbs.; Mississippi State; January 4, 1971.

Marques Tuiasosopo: 2001–06, 2008; Raiders 2nd round selection in 2001 draft; Quarterback; #8; 6-1, 220 lbs.; Washington; March 22, 1979.

Dan Turk: 1989–96; came to the Raiders as a free agent in June 1989; Center; #67; 6-4, 290 lbs.; Wisconsin; June 25, 1962–December 23, 2000.

Eric Turner: 1997–99; came to the Raiders as a free agent in May 1997; Defensive Back; #29 and 42; 6-1, 215 lbs.; University of California Los Angeles (UCLA); September 20, 1968–May 28, 2000.

Richard Tyson: 1966; Raiders 4th round selection in 1966 draft; Offensive Guard; #71; 6-2, 245 lbs.; Tulsa; January 5, 1943.

Gene Upshaw: 1967–81; Raiders 1st round selection in 1967 draft; Offensive Guard; #63; 6-5, 255 lbs.; Texas A&I; August 15, 1945–August 20, 2008.

Regan Upshaw: 2000–01; came to the Raiders as a free agent in March 2000; Defensive End; #91; 6-4, 260 lbs.; California; August 12, 1975.

Herman Urenda: 1963; came to the Raiders as a free agent in 1963; Wide Receiver; #39 and 83; 6-0, 182 lbs.; Pacific; April 24, 1938.

Vernon Valdez: 1962; came to the Raiders in a trade with the Buffalo Bills in 1962; Defensive Back; #25; San Diego University; August 12, 1935.

Randy Van Divier: 1982; came to Raiders as a free agent in 1982; Offensive Guard; #67 and 68; 6-5, 270 lbs.; Washington; June 5, 1958.

Mark van Eeghen: 1974–81; Raiders 3rd round selection in1974 draft; Running Back; #30; 6-2, 220 lbs.; Colgate; April 19, 1952.

Norwood Vann: 1988; came to the Raiders in 1988; Linebacker; #50; 6-1, 228 lbs.; East Carolina; February 18, 1962.

Brad Van Pelt: 1984–85; came to the Raiders in a trade with the Minnesota Vikings in October 1984; Linebacker; #91; 6-5, 235 lbs.; Michigan State; April 5, 1951–February 17, 2009.

Ruben Vaughan: 1982; came to the Raiders as a free agent in 1982; Defensive Tackle/Defensive End; #99; 6-2, 240 lbs.; Colorado; August 5, 1956.

John Vella: 1972–79; Raiders 2nd round selection in 1972 draft; Offensive Guard/Offensive Tackle; #75; University of Southern California (USC); April 21, 1950.

Phil Villapiano: 1971–79; Raiders 2nd round selection in 1971 draft; Linebacker; #41; 6-2, 225 lbs.; Bowling Green University; February 26, 1949.

Bob Voight: 1961; came to the Raiders as a free agent in 1961; Defensive End; #78; 6-5, 265 lbs.; Los Angeles State; Born in 1938.

Michael Waddell: 2008; came to the Raiders as a free agent in 2008; Defensive Back; #32; 5-10, 183 lbs.; North Carolina; January 9, 1981.

John Wade: 2008; came to the Raiders as a free agent in March 2008; Center; #71; 6-5, 299 lbs.; Marshall; January 25, 1975.

Fred Wakefield: 2008;came to the Raiders in 2008; Defensive End/Defensive Tackle; #78; 6-7, 288 lbs.; Illinois; September 17, 1978.

Denard Walker: 2004–05; came to the Raiders as a free agent in 2004; Defensive Back; #25; 6-1, 190 lbs.; Louisiana State University; August 9, 1973.

Derrick Walker: 1999; came to the Raiders as a free agent in May 1999; Tight End; #86; 6-0, 250 lbs.; Michigan; June 22, 1967.

Fulton Walker: 1985–86; came to the Raiders as a free agent in September 1985; Defensive Back/Kick Returner; #41; 5-11, 195 lbs.; West Virginia; April 30, 1958.

Javon Walker: 2008–09; came to the Raiders as a free agent in March 2008; Wide Receiver; #84; 6-3, 220 lbs.; Florida State; October 14, 1978.

Langston Walker: 2002–05, 2009; Raiders 2nd round selection in 2002 draft, re-signed as a free agent in October 2009; Offensive Tackle; #66 and 70; 6-8, 345 lbs.; California; September 3, 1979.

Marquis Walker: 1998–99; came to the Raiders as a free agent in April 1998; Defensive Back; #38; 5-10, 175 lbs.; Southern Missouri; July 6, 1972.

Aaron Wallace: 1990–95, 1997–98; Raiders 2nd round selection of 1990 draft, re-signed as a free agent in June 1997; Linebacker/Defensive End; #51 and 59; 6-3, 245 lbs.; Texas A&M; April 17, 1967.

Andrew Walter: 2005–08; Raiders 3rd round selection in 2005 draft; Quarterback; #16; 6-6, 230 lbs.; Arizona State; May 11, 1982.

Seth Wand: 2007–08; came to the Raiders as a free agent in 2007; Offensive Tackle; #72; 6-7, 327 lbs.; N.W. Missouri State; August 6, 1979.

B.J. Ward: 2007; came to the Raiders in 2007; Defensive Back; #28; 6-3, 208 lbs.; Florida State; November 4, 1981.

Tim Ware: 1989; came to the Raiders in 1989; Wide Receiver; #15; 5-10, 171 lbs.; University of Southern California (USC); April 2, 1962.

Gerard Warren: 2007–09; came to the Raiders in a trade with the Denver Broncos in August 2007; Defensive Tackle; #61; 6-4, 325 lbs.; Florida; July 25, 1978.

Jimmy Warren: 1970–74, 1977; came to the Raiders as a free agent in 1970; Defensive Back; #20 and 22; 5-11, 175 lbs.; Illinois; July 20, 1939–August 9, 2006.

Ron Warzeka: 1960; came to the Raiders as a free agent in 1960; Defensive End; #78; 6-4, 250 lbs.; Montana State; December 24, 1935.

Fabian Washington: 2005–06; Raiders 1st round selection in 2005 draft; Defensive Back; #27; 5-11, 185 lbs.; Nebraska; June 9, 1983.

Lionel Washington: 1987–94, 1997; came to the Raiders in a trade with the St. Louis Cardinals in 1987, re-signed as a free agent in June 1997; Defensive Back; #23 and 48; 6-0, 185 lbs.; Tulane; October 21, 1960.

Ronnie Washington: 1987; came to the Raiders as a free agent in March,1987; Linebacker; #91; 6-1, 240 lbs.; Northeast Louisiana; July 29, 1963.

Ted Washington: 2004–05; came to the Raiders as a free agent in 2004; Defensive Tackle; #92; 6-5, 365 lbs.; Louisville; April 13, 1968.

Todd Watkins: 2008–09; came to the Raiders as a free agent in February 2008; Wide Receiver; #19; 6-3, 185 lbs.; Brigham Young University; June 22, 1983.

Robert Watts: 1978; came to the Raiders as a free agent in 1978; Linebacker; #54; 6-3, 225 lbs.; Boston College; June 16, 1954.

Ted Watts: 1981–84; Raiders 1st round selection in 1981 draft; Defensive Back; #20 and 41; 6-0, 195 lbs.; Texas Tech; May 29, 1958.

Dave Waymer: 1992; came to the Raiders as a free agent in April 1992; Defensive Back; #44; 6-1, 200 lbs.; Notre Dame; July 1, 1958–April 30, 1993.

Carl Weathers: 1970–71; came to the Raiders as a free agent in 1970; Linebacker; #49 and 51; 6-2, 220 lbs.; San Diego State; January 14, 1948.

Gary Weaver: 1973–74; Raiders 7th round selection in 1973 draft; Linebacker; #52; 6-1, 224 lbs.; Fresno State; March 13, 1949.

Warren Wells: 1967–70; came to the Raiders as a free agent in 1967; Wide Receiver; #81; 6-1, 190 lbs.; Texas Southern; November 14, 1942.

Greg Westbrooks: 1978–81; came to the Raiders as a free agent in 1978; Linebacker; #52; 6-3, 215 lbs.; Colorado; February 24, 1953.

Tyrone Wheatley: 1999–03; came to the Raiders as a free agent in August 1999; Running Back; #47; 6-0, 235 lbs.; Michigan; January 19, 1972.

Dwight Wheeler: 1984, 1987–88; came to the Raiders as a free agent in 1984, re-signed as a free agent in March 1987; Center/Tackle; #67; 6-3, 280 lbs.; Tennessee State; January 13, 1955.

Ron Wheeler: 1987; came to the Raiders as a free agent in 1987; Tight End; #82; 6-5, 235 lbs.; Washington; September 5, 1958.

Alberto White: 1994; Raiders 10th round selection in1992 draft, re-signed in May 1994; Defensive End; #96; 6-3, 245 lbs.; Texas Southern; April 8, 1971.

Gene White: 1962; Raiders 33rd round selection in 1962 AFL draft; Running Back; #29; 6-1, 197 lbs.; Florida A&M; Born in 1940.

Curtis Whitley: 1997;came to the Raiders as a free agent in 1997; Offensive Guard/Center; #66; 6-1, 290 lbs.; Clemson; May 10, 1969.

Scott Whittaker: 1997; came to the Raiders as a free agent in April 1997; Offensive Tackle/Center; #78; 6-7, 300 lbs.; Kansas; May 7, 1974–December 2, 2003.

Alvis Whitted: 2002–06; came to the Raiders as a free agent in 2002; Wide Receiver; #87; 6-0, 185 lbs.; North Carolina State; September 4, 1974.

Arthur Whittington: 1978–81; Raiders 7th round selection in 1978 draft; Running Back; #22; 5-11, 180 lbs.; Southern Methodist; September 4, 1955.

Bruce Wilkerson: 1987–94, 1998; Raiders 2nd round selection in 1987 draft; Offensive Guard/Offensive Tackle; #68; 6-5, 295 lbs.; Tennessee; July 28, 1964.

Brock Williams: 2003–04; came to the Raiders as a free agent in 2003; Defensive Back; #37 and 29; 5-10, 195 lbs.; Notre Dame; August 11, 1979.

David Williams: 1987; came to the Raiders in 1987; Wide Receiver; #19 and 89; 6-3, 190 lbs.; Illinois; June 10, 1963.

Demise Williams: 1987; came to the Raiders in 1987; Defensive Back; #33; 6-1, 225 lbs.; Oklahoma State; July 9, 1964.

Dokie Williams: 1983–87; Raiders 5th round selection in 1983 draft; Wide Receiver; #85; 5-11, 180 lbs.; University of California Los Angeles (UCLA); August 25, 1960.

Harvey Williams: 1994–98; came to the Raiders as a free agent in April 1994; Running Back/Tight End; #22; 6-2, 225 lbs.; Louisiana State; April 22, 1968.

Henry Williams: 1979; Raiders 6th round selection in 1979 draft; Defensive Back; #45; 5-10, 180 lbs.; San Diego State; December 2, 1956.

Howie Williams: 1964–69; came to the Raiders as a free agent in 1964; Defensive Back; #29; 6-1, 190 lbs.; Howard; December 4, 1936.

Jamie Williams: 1994; came to the Raiders as a free agent in May 1994; Tight End; #88; 6-4, 250 lbs.; Nebraska; February 25, 1960.

Jermaine Williams: 1998–99; came to the Raiders as a free agent in April 1998; Running Back; #34; 6-0, 235 lbs.; Houston; August 14, 1973.

K.D. Williams: 1999; came to the Raiders as a free agent in March 1998; Linebacker; #59; 6-0, 235 lbs.; Henderson State; April 21, 1973.

Marcus Williams: 2002; came to the Raiders as a free agent in 2002; Tight End; #85; 6-6, 230 lbs.; Washington State; December 12, 1977.

Mike Williams: 2007; came to the Raiders in a trade with the Detroit Lions in 2007; Wide Receiver; #17; 6-5, 229 lbs.; University of Southern California (USC); January 4, 1984.

Randal Williams: 2005–06; came to the Raiders as a free agent in 2005; Tight End; #86; 6-3, 220 lbs.; New Hampshire; May 21, 1978.

Ricky Williams: 1985–87; came to the Raiders in 1985; Defensive Back; #25; 6-1, 195 lbs.; Langston; April 27, 1960.

Rodney Williams: 1998–99; came to the Raiders as a free agent in March 1998; Wide Receiver; #89; 6-0, 195 lbs.; Arizona; August 15, 1973.

Roland Williams: 2001–02, 2004; came to the Raiders in a trade with the St. Louis Rams in April 2001; Tight End; #86; 6-5, 265 lbs.; Syracuse; April 27, 1975.

Sam Williams: 2003–09; Raiders 3rd round selection in 2003 draft; Defensive End; #54; 6-5, 265 lbs.; Fresno State; July 28, 1980.

Willie Williams: 1966; came to the Raiders as a free agent in 1966;

Defensive Back; #49; 6-0, 185 lbs.; Grambling; December 29, 1942.

Fred Williamson: 1961–64; came to the Raiders as a free agent in 1961; Defensive Back; #24; 6-3, 215 lbs.; Northwestern; March 5, 1938.

J.R. Williamson: 1964–67; Raiders 9th round selection in 1963 AFL draft; Linebacker; #52; 6-2, 220 lbs.; Louisiana Tech; October 9, 1942.

Chester Willis: 1981–84; Raiders 11th round selection in 1981 draft; Running Back; #38; 5-11, 195 lbs.; Auburn; May 2, 1958.

Mitch Willis: 1985–87; Raiders 7th round selection in 1984 draft; Defensive Tackle; #98; 6-8, 275 lbs.; Southern Methodist; March 16, 1962.

Gibril Wilson: 2008; came to the Raiders as a free agent in 2008; Defensive Back; #28; 6-0, 197 lbs.; Tennessee; November 12, 1981.

Marc Wilson: 1980–87; Raiders 1st round selection in 1980 draft; Quarterback; #6; 6-6, 205 lbs.; Brigham Young; February 15, 1957.

Marcus Wilson: 1991; Raiders 6th round selection in 1990 draft, re-signed as a free agent in April 1991; Running Back; #40; 6-1, 215 lbs.; Virginia; April 16, 1968.

Mark Wilson: 2007; came to the Raiders as a free agent in 2006; Offensive Tackle; #63; 6-7, 320 lbs.; California; November 11, 1980.

Nemiah Wilson: 1968–74; came to the Raiders as a free agent in 1968; Defensive Back; #26 and 48; 6-0, 165 lbs.; Grambling; April 6, 1943.

Otis Wilson: 1989; came to the Raiders as a free agent in April 1989; Linebacker; #50; 6-2, 225 lbs.; Louisville; September 15, 1957.

Wade Wilson: 1998–99; came to the Raiders as a free agent in May 1998; Quarterback; #16; 6-3, 210 lbs.; East Texas State; February 1, 1959.

Jeff Winans: 1976; came to the Raiders as a free agent in 1976; Offensive Guard/Defensive Tackle; #73; 6-5, 265 lbs.; University of Southern California (USC); October 12, 1951.

Mike Wise: 1986–90; Raiders 4th round selection in 1986 draft; Defensive End; #90; 6-7, 270 lbs.; California–Davis; June 5, 1964–August 21, 1992.

Steve Wisniewski: 1989–01; Raiders 2nd round selection in 1989 draft; Offensive Guard; #76; 6-4, 305 lbs.; Penn State; April 7, 1967.

Scott Wolff: 1987; came to the Raiders as a free agent in 1987; Quarterback; #17; 6-1, 190 lbs.; Mount Union; December 26, 1961.

Joe Wong: 2003; came to the Raiders as a free agent in 2003; Offensive Guard/Tackle; #77; 6-6, 315 lbs.; Brigham Young University; February 24, 1976.

Dick Wood: 1965; came to the Raiders in a trade with the New York Jets in 1965; Quarterback; #18; 6-5, 200 lbs.; Auburn; February 29, 1936.

Terry Wooden: 1998; came to the Raiders in 1998; Linebacker; #57; 6-3, 239 lbs.; Syracuse; January 14, 1967.

Chris Woods: 1987–88; Raiders 1st round selection in 1984 supplemental draft, joined team in May 1987; Wide Receiver; #88; 5-11, 185 lbs.; Auburn; July 19, 1962.

Charles Woodson: 1998–05; Raiders 1st round selection in 1998 draft; Defensive Back; #24; 6-1, 200 lbs.; Michigan; October 7, 1976.

Rod Woodson: 2002–03; came to the Raiders as a free agent in April 2002; Defensive Back; #26; 6-0, 205 lbs.; Purdue; March 10, 1965.

Alexander Wright: 1992–94; came to the Raiders in a trade with the Dallas Cowboys in October 1992; Wide Receiver; #89; 6-0, 195 lbs.; Auburn; July 19, 1967.

Steve Wright: 1987–93; came to the Raiders as a free agent in March 1987; Offensive Tackle; #66; 6-6, 290 lbs.; Northern Iowa; April 8, 1959.

Alvin Wyatt: 1970; Raiders 6th round selection in 1970 draft; Defensive Back; #41; 5-10, 185 lbs.; Bethune-Cookman; December 13, 1947.

Frank Youso: 1963–65; came to the Raiders as a free agent in 1963; Offensive Tackle; #78; 6-4, 255 lbs.; Minnesota; July 5, 1936.

Rich Zecher: 1965; Raiders 9th round selection in 1965 AFL draft; Offensive Tackle; #74; 6-2, 240 lbs.; Utah State; October 14, 1943.

Amos Zereoue: 2004; came to the Raiders as a free agent in 2004; Running Back; #28; 5-8, 212 lbs.; West Virginia; October 8, 1976.

John Zogg: 1987; came to the Raiders as a free agent in 1987; Offensive Guard; #69; 6-4, 290 lbs.; Boise State; November 19, 1960.

All-Time Head Coaches

Eddie Erdelatz

Tenure as Head Coach: February 9, 1960–September 18, 1961

Coaching Record with Raiders: 6–10

It is often said that a person can never go home again. Whoever made that claim obviously never knew Eddie Erdelatz. Born

Edward Joseph Erdelatz in San Francisco on April 21, 1913, the man who served as the first head coach in Raiders history fell in love with the sport of football at an early age. The gridiron served as an almost therapeutic remedy for the young man despite its violent nature.[1]

Two weeks after his birth, his mother passed away, thus leaving young Eddie with a huge void. His childhood was not an easy one, but once he discovered football, the emptiness he felt was filled by the joy he received participating in the sport.[2]

Erdelatz's new solace allowed him many things such as fellowship, sportsmanship, competition, and exercise. It also provided the young man from the San Francisco Bay area with a desire to pursue football as a career. Upon graduation from high school, Erdelatz continued his education and football career at California's St. Mary's College.

With the legendary Slip Madigan as his mentor, Eddie proved his grit as a fierce competitor from his end position. He earned the reputation by playing through pain. Whether it was a shoulder separation, mangled knee, or an infection that could have cost him his leg, Erdelatz refused to leave the field.[3]

After three seasons as a starter, Madigan knew very well of the desire Eddie possessed, and looked to give him his first opportunity in the coaching profession. In 1936, Madigan appointed Erdelatz St. Mary's line coach. After two years, he left his alma mater for an assistant job at the University of San Francisco, but returned in 1940. Following another two-year stint at St. Mary's, he entered the Navy during World War II, eventually rising to the rank of Lieutenant Commander by war's end in 1945. With his military commitment complete, Eddie accepted an assistant coaching position at the Naval Academy in Annapolis, Maryland.[4]

After being away from his beloved California for some time, Erdelatz yearned to return to his home state. The opportunity arose in 1948 with his acceptance as defensive coordinator for the San Francisco 49ers. However, the allure of finally becoming a head coach once again sent him clear across the country and back to Annapolis.

By 1950, the Naval Academy's football program was an abomination. Over the previous five seasons, the Midshipmen had won only four games. Rebuilding a program is never an easy task, and Erdelatz soon found that out. The stress quickly began to wreak havoc on his body, and over the course of his first season at the helm, he lost fifty pounds.[5]

Despite many negative repercussions, Erdelatz gained a lasting legacy at Navy by having a winning record against their ultimate rival Army. The legend began in his first season when Army came into the annual slugfest with a spotless 8–0 record and a 28-game unbeaten streak. Navy sported a lethargic 2–6 slate, but when playing a fierce rival, records do not always seem to matter. Such was the case in 1950, as the Midshipmen gave their first-year coach an outstanding effort, and won 14–2 thanks to an incredible defensive effort.[6]

In his first two seasons at Navy, Erdelatz compiled a mediocre 5-12-1 record, but never had another losing season at Annapolis during his watch, which included a 5-3-1 record against Army. His teams also won the 1955 Sugar Bowl and 1958 Cotton Bowl.

His successful resurrection of Navy's program brought much attention to Erdelatz, and he suddenly found himself being courted by other teams. He came very close to accepting the head coaching job at Texas A&M in 1958, but remained at Annapolis. Following the 1958 campaign, his name was coming up quite often as a serious contender for the head coaching position with the San Francisco 49ers. Despite all the talk of him possibly going to the 49ers, Erdelatz focused on the upcoming season at Navy.[7]

The athletic department at Annapolis seemed to be agitated by all the attention their football coach was receiving. They figured that eventually Erdelatz was going to leave Navy for another job. Many disagreements began to occur between the two factions, and on April 8, 1959, Erdelatz had enough and shocked the college football world by announcing his resignation as coach.

The Washington Redskins quickly came calling for his services as an assistant, but he turned the offer down. Erdelatz was also considered for jobs with the New York Giants and the University of Southern California, but neither ever materialized.

After sitting out a year, Erdelatz was offered the head coaching position with the Los Angeles Chargers of the new American Football League. He turned that job down, but on February 9, 1960, he accepted the same role with the Oakland Raiders, and in doing so, managed to return to the part of the country he so loved.

With the Raiders being the last team selected to play in the AFL, the talent pool was not all that great, and the challenge of making something out of nothing fell directly on Erdelatz. This appeared to be close to the situation he found himself in a decade earlier when he inherited a dismal Navy team that he eventually brought back from the dead. He was now ready to attempt the same feat in the pro ranks, and dove right in.

Along with his assistant coaches, Erdelatz milled over countless prospects looking to latch on with the first installment of the Oakland Raiders. In the end, he managed to assemble a respectable squad that fought hard in virtually every game throughout the 1960 season. Erdelatz did not believe in long practice sessions. They only lasted an hour in the mornings and afternoons, but he did believe in running sprints on a regular basis. Everywhere the inaugural Raiders went they had to run at full throttle. In the end, the Raiders might not have had the best players in that first season, but they probably had the best conditioned of any AFL team in 1960.[9]

Throughout the season, Erdelatz suffered from a stomach ulcer that caused him great discomfort. Disagreements with the front office over many issues also added to his stress level. The inability to get ownership to sign any top draft picks prior to the 1961 season seemed to be the beginning of the end for Eddie. After seeing his team get pounded by a combined score of 99–0 in Oakland's first two games, Erdelatz's tenure as mentor came to a conclusion on September 18, 1961, when he was relieved of his position in a quick manner by team officials shortly after noon.

After leaving the Raiders, the congenial man who yearned to make football his career never coached again. He worked as an executive with a California-based financial company until his death at age 53 on November 10, 1966.[11]

Marty Feldman

Tenure as Head Coach: September 18, 1961–October 16, 1962
Coaching Record with Raiders: 2–15

After the Raiders' offensive prowess became non-existent early in the 1961 season, a coaching change was made in an attempt to turn the team's fortunes around. This was no shocking revelation in the world of sports. When a team goes stagnant, one result remains clear, with that being the removal of a head coach. It is the nature of the beast known as the coaching carousel.

The Raiders realized this philosophy early in their existence hen Eddie Erdelatz failed to deliver. The front office, players, nd fans all turned to his replacement, Marty Feldman, for a hange of fortunes. Regarded in the football community as one f the best offensive minds in the business, Feldman was promoted o head coach with 12 games to go in the 1961 season.[1]

Marty Feldman's path to becoming mentor of the Oakland Raiders began with his birth on September 12, 1922, in Los Aneles, California. After graduating from Southgate High School, Feldman left his native state to play freshman football at the University of Oregon in 1940.[2]

Late the following year, the United States found itself enulfed in war with Japan and Germany. Like most young men of is generation, Feldman answered his country's call to duty, thus utting a hold on his college education and football career. He oined the Marine Corps, and during four-and-a-half years of ervice, Feldman earned three Purple Heart medals for injuries ustained in combat.[3]

After World War II ended in 1945, Feldman picked up where e left off prior to the global conflict. He decided not to return o Oregon, electing rather to stay in California and enrolled at tanford University where he continued his football career while ursuing bachelor's and master's degrees in anthropology and conomics. In addition to excelling in the classroom, Feldman chieved status on the gridiron by earning All-Coast honors as a uard in 1947, and also gained acclaim as a rugby player. His performance in rugby was so impressive that he was enshrined into he Stanford Athletic Hall of Fame for his exploits in that sport.[4]

Upon graduation, Feldman decided to go into the coaching rofession, and was granted an opportunity by his alma mater. n 1948 he coached the Stanford freshman football team, and four ears later, he earned a full-time position on Charles Taylor's staff. n 1955 he left Stanford for his first head coaching position at alley Junior College, and then joined Bob Titchenal's staff as an ssistant at San Jose State for the next three years.[5]

In 1960, Eddie Erdelatz brought him into the Raiders' fold y appointing him coach of both the offensive and defensive lines. n 1961, Feldman began the season solely as offensive line coach ntil his elevation to head coach on September 18th. He was ooked at as an excellent offensive strategist, and held in high eseem by his peers. He also believed in listening to his assistants or any advice. One of his fortes was belief in the passing game, nd he wanted to open up the Oakland air attack to its fullest otential.[6] Unfortunately, some of the best-laid plans fall by the vayside. In Feldman's case, it was not having the adequate tools eeded for success. He did get the Raiders to at least produce oints, but not enough to win and allow him to continue coaching he team. Apparently, he never considered his promotion in Oakand as a long-term arrangement. In fact, he was so sure that his lays were numbered as coach that while flying to a game late in he '61 season, Feldman assembled his team around him and inormed them that he was going to lose his job.[7] His premonition vas incorrect that time around. He did return to the sidelines in 962, but after a 0–5 start, and in the midst of an eleven game osing streak, Feldman was fired on October 16th. In addition to is previously mentioned credits, Feldman did recruiting and couting for the Los Angeles Rams, Dallas Cowboys, and the Canadian Football League's Toronto Argonauts. He also enjoyed he acting profession, and in 2006 appeared in the horror film

Bug.[8] He is not to be confused with the late comedian who shared the same name, and appeared in the classic film *Young Frankenstein*.

William "Red" Conkright

Tenure as Head Coach: October 16, 1962–December 16, 1962
Coaching Record with Raiders: 1–8

The old saying that the third time is the charm did not seem to hold true for the Raiders' coaching lineage. On October 16, 1962, William "Red" Conkright became the third head coach in Oakland's brief but tumultuous history.

Conkright was born on April 17, 1914, in Beggs, Oklahoma. He remained in his home state while establishing himself as a football player at the University of Oklahoma from 1934 to 1936, and also excelled in wrestling. Red was a stellar lineman at 6-1 and 200 pounds, which was good size during that time period. He was respected enough by his teammates that they elected him captain of the Sooners. In his senior season he was selected All-Conference, and his abilities caught the attention of those in the professional ranks.[1]

George Halas, the legendary head coach of the Chicago Bears, was impressed with Conkright's talent and made him Chicago's fifth round selection in the 1937 NFL draft. After playing one season in Chicago, Red went to the Cleveland Rams from 1939 to 1942, and then again in 1944 following stays with Detroit and Washington in 1943. In the pros, Conkright played center, offensive and defensive end, and linebacker in a time when a player had to perform on both sides of the ball.[2]

In 1945, Red went into coaching, serving on Adam Walsh's staff with the Cleveland Rams the year they won the NFL championship. Other stints, prior to his coming to Oakland in 1962 as an assistant under Marty Feldman, included assistant at Mississippi State in 1950–51, and as head coach of Stephen F. Austin College from 1959 to 1961.[3]

After Feldman's dismissal as Oakland's coach on October 16, 1962, Conkright was appointed mentor on an interim basis. The team was terrible and showed no signs of improvement under Conkright. The only distinction achieved during his brief tenure was the team's lone win of the year. His one contribution to the lethargic offensive attack was to incorporate the "Statue of Liberty" play, which obviously did little to wow friend and foe alike.[4]

The powers that controlled the Raiders knew after nine games that Conkright was not going to be what they were looking for to reverse the team's downward spiral, and after the '62 season ended, he was released from his duties. Conkright lived until age 66, dying on October 1, 1980, in Houston, Texas.[5]

Al Davis

Tenure as Head Coach: January 15, 1963–April 8, 1966
Coaching Record with Raiders: 23-16-3

In the case of the Oakland Raiders, the third time was not the charm. Prior to 1963, the organization had gone through three head coaches in as many seasons. However, the fourth time proved to be the charm, and it was a gem that shined as bright as the diamonds of the multiple Super Bowl rings the franchise earned throughout Al Davis' watch.

On January 15, 1963, the football world was officially introduced to Oakland's new head coach, Al Davis, who would mold and shape the tattered franchise into one of professional sports most intriguing and dominant organizations.

The climb to gridiron supremacy began for the patriarch of the Silver and Black Empire clear across the United States in Brockton, Massachusetts, on July 4, 1929. His parents decided to move to Brooklyn, New York, when Davis was young. The family resided on tree-lined Presidents Street in Crown Heights, and Davis' father made a good income as the owner of a garment manufacturing company.[1]

Al Davis became enamored with sports by following his hometown Brooklyn Dodgers and New York Yankees baseball teams. The Yankees were the American sports scene's elite, winning World Series at a feverish pace in the late 1930's and 40's. The Dodgers were one of the major league's downtrodden organizations in the 1930's, but by the time Davis became a teenager, they were on their way to becoming a dominant force in the National League, and just beginning their cherished "Boys of Summer" era.

To Davis, the Yankees represented power, striking fear into the opposition, while the Dodgers primarily used speed and power on the base paths to rise to the top. The makeup of these two powerhouse teams left an impact on Davis, and twenty years later he applied these concepts to the Raiders. Power, speed, fear, and taking what they wanted when they wanted it, became the philosophy behind the Silver and Black beginning in 1963, with the roots of their style going back to the Yankees and Dodgers.[2]

The city of Oakland and dominance of the football community was still a world away as Davis progressed on his path toward adulthood and eventual conquest of his chosen profession. Also, for the time being, the influence that the Yankees and Dodgers had on the Brooklyn teen was tucked away temporarily in his gray matter, while he made his way through Erasmus Hall High School where he was a reserve on the basketball team.

Upon graduation, Davis attended Wittenberg University in Ohio. After one semester, he came back east and enrolled at Syracuse University, where he remained throughout the rest of his college days. He played junior varsity football and basketball, waited on tables in the campus cafeteria to help with his finances, and earned a degree in English. It was while at Syracuse that Davis began pursuing information about football with a passion and turned his desire for the sport into a career.[3]

Davis never played varsity football at Syracuse, but attended practice, absorbing the action on the field like a sponge from the bleachers. With a passion and drive to succeed, he took meticulous notes and diagrams. The head coach of the Orangemen noticed the young, intense Davis day after day, but did not know who he was or what his agenda could be. The possibility that he was a spy for an upcoming opponent entered the coach's mind, and apparently for that reason he did not want Davis surveying his domain and had him banned from the area.[4] If only the coach had been congenial enough to get to know Davis, he might have allowed him access to his world. Regardless of the snub, Davis was not deterred. If anything, it sparked his desire even more.

Upon graduation from Syracuse, Davis set out on his quest to secure a coaching position. His first step toward the greatness that he would eventually achieve began with an impromptu visit to Adelphi College in Garden City, New York, close to the western edge of Long Island. At first, Davis was once again met with opposition.

Davis introduced himself to the small college's athletic director, and told him about some articles he wrote pertaining to blocking assignments. Despite the sales pitch, the athletic director informed Davis that the college was not hiring. Davis remained congenial while being turned down and left the office jockeying his next move in his mind.[5]

Instead of seeking other avenues, Davis remained steadfast in his desire at getting a position with Adelphi. He next took his plea to the top of the academic food chain. He met with the college president, and after using his charm, football knowledge, and

"Just win, baby!" Al Davis (center) accepts his third Super Bowl trophy on January 22, 1984, with head coach Tom Flores, left, and NFL Commissioner Pete Rozelle at far right. Legendary sportscaster Brent Musburger interviews the victorious duo after the game in Tampa, Florida (AP Photo).

passion for the game, plus quite possibly a little cunning maneuvering, Davis landed a coaching job within a half hour. The president relayed his interest in the young upstart to the athletic director, and Davis was hired as an assistant in charge of the offensive line from 1950 to 51.[6]

All Al Davis wanted was a chance, and once given the opportunity, he proved himself worthy by exhibiting a great feel for the game, coupled with a keen eye for talent and detail. He also used his football knowledge to command a presence about him that never diminished with the passing of time. Whether he was loved or despised, the aura he cast was a giant one.

While serving in the Army during the Korean Conflict, Davis remained stateside, and became head coach of the Ft. Belvoir football team in Virginia from 1952 to 1953. Following his military service, Davis received his first opportunity in the professional ranks with the Baltimore Colts in the capacity of player personnel man in 1954. In 1955, he returned to the teaching aspect of the game with an appointment as line coach and chief recruiter for The Citadel.[7]

After two seasons at The Citadel, the young assistant on the rise then headed west to California, where destiny would lead him to football immortality. All the accolades bestowed on Davis from this point on occurred in California, with the first coming at the University of Southern California in 1957 as line coach.

In 1960, the American Football League was getting set to begin operations, and opened countless doors for players and coaches, many of whom, including Al Davis, became legends. Sid Gillman was well established as a future legend by the time the Los Angeles Chargers made him their first head coach in 1960. The Chargers relocated to San Diego the following year. Gillman was considered the patriarch of the modern passing game, with his offensive scheme being to attack a defense swiftly and repeatedly. His head coaching tenure in the pros prior to the Chargers was with the Los Angeles Rams from 1955 to 1959.

Gillman had met Al Davis while both were speaking at football clinics in the 1950's. Gillman became very impressed with Davis, as he shared the same desire to attack defenses through the air anytime throughout the game, not just when facing crucial situations.[8]

It was this offensive guru that had the vision to see something special in the 30-year Al Davis, and brought him into the Chargers' fold as offensive end coach in 1960. Under Gillman's guidance, Davis was exposed to one of football's greatest minds, and he absorbed all the knowledge available about the vertical passing game that made use of the entire field for three seasons. During the time with Davis on staff, the Chargers rang up points and victories at a rapid pace, and won two AFL Western Division championships.

While the Chargers were among the upper echelon of AFL teams, several hundred miles north, the Oakland Raiders were the league's downtrodden on the verge of total collapse and despair to put it mildly. First off, the team had no place to call a real home field, having played in three different stadiums in as many years. They had nine wins over the course of their first three seasons, with six of them coming in the inaugural campaign. Three head coaches came and went, and home crowds were sparse at best. People in the area just did not care about the pathetic excuse for a pro football team that the Raiders supplied. In fact, relocation

seemed likely in late 1962, as New Orleans, Cincinnati, and San Antonio were all looking to obtain a pro franchise.[9] The ownership wanted to keep the team in Oakland, but knew that the team's fortunes had to turn around quickly or their gridiron investment would go bust.

Between the AFL's winter meetings in San Diego, Oakland's owners, Wayne Valley and Ed McGah, began looking for any soul alive who could revive the Raiders from the clutches of the Grim Reaper.

At the time, only the Raiders and the NFL's Cleveland Browns were seeking new head coaches. With so many men looking for an opportunity to elevate themselves within the coaching profession, and only two teams looking for a new head coach, Oakland did not have to worry about competing with any of the other AFL teams. For this reason, Valley and McGah were able to be extremely selective in their quest for the right man to perform a miracle with the awful franchise. However, one man stood out above all others in the minds of the powers that be within the Oakland organization. The individual they wanted was San Diego's 33-year-old offensive coach Al Davis, whose incredible football mind earned him a reputation as one of the best in the sport.

Helping in the process was Kansas City's head coach Hank Stram. The future Hall of Fame coach was just coming off an AFL championship with the Dallas Texans, who relocated to Kansas City in 1963, and he gave Davis high praise to Valley and McGah. He knew of the talent Davis possessed while facing Stram's Texans for three seasons, and could not think of anyone better to fill the job in Oakland.[10] Even though the Chiefs and Raiders became hated rivals from the 1960's and beyond, Stram always had the highest regards for Davis, and even wrote forewords for books about the Raiders in the 1980's. The Raiders contacted Davis, who was the only candidate for the job, and after a six-hour interview, the position was his.

Armed with a three-year contract, Davis immediately went to work to make the Raiders at first respectable and then consistent winners. With an incredible supply of physical and mental stamina, Davis began by re-organizing the front office and finding players to fit his coaching philosophies.

He did not want any distractions so he rented a place without windows to serve as the new headquarters, and even banned clocks from being hung.[11] Time of day did not matter to the new headmaster of the Raiders, and if he had to work 24 hours a day to develop a winner, then that is what would be done. He brought in new assistant coaches just as eager and passionate as he was, and changed the team colors from black and gold to silver and black. The colors selected were to represent a new beginning and emulate the powerful Army teams of the 1940's known as the "Black Knights of the Hudson," and the silver of the Detroit Lions, who were one of the most dominant teams in football during the 1950's.[12] He wanted the men who put on those uniforms to be proud that they were Raiders, and wanted the rest of the league to fear them and want to be one of them.

Davis was not only going to have to be a good coach, but a fine salesman as well. He was a very intelligent and aggressive young man, and used the English language in a tranquil but convincing voice to sell his ideas to not only recruits but the public as well. He instilled a "Commitment to Excellence," which became the team's ever-lasting motto, and also "Pride and Poise," that meant having a belief in what you are doing, and doing it with absolute control and confidence.[13]

With his phrases serving as a calling card, Davis set out to mold and shape a team based on his philosophies. With his love of the wide-open attack providing the core of Oakland's new offensive scheme, Davis set out to acquire the players needed to make the vertical game succeed.

Taking the concept he learned from Sid Gillman with the Chargers, Davis wanted to have five receivers going out into the secondary to stretch the defense out, and a strong-armed quarterback that could throw deep to any of them. The wide receivers needed blazing speed, tight ends the ability to catch, running backs had to be capable of going deep for passes, and massive offensive linemen who had to possess quickness and strength to overpower the assault on a quarterback. All these pieces would allow the Raiders to attack on any down from anywhere on the field. An old adage in football was to take what the defense gives you, but Davis refused to comply with it. His attitude was to take what you wanted whenever you wanted it, and strike fear into a defense knowing that the Raiders were going to come at them fast and hard on every play.[14]

On the other side of the ball, Davis wanted a defensive scheme that totally dominated an opponent into submission, leaving them battered and desperately wanting just to get off the field. The Raiders were not going to win every game, but they wanted to win enough games to compete for championships and let opponents know, that they were in a slugfest each and every time they played the Raiders. Attack and fear were added to "Commitment to Excellence" and "Pride and Poise" to serve as calling cards for the Raiders from 1963 on.

When the final roster was set for Davis' first team, there were 19 new players from the previous season. From this time on, the Raiders became a team willing to give an opportunity to players who were regarded as outcasts or problems with other teams. Al Davis did not care about a man's standing on the social register, only his ability to perform on the field. He looked beyond the problems players faced with other organizations, and with a renewed sense of worth, these men played like hell for Davis.[15] He treated them like men, and allowed each of them the freedom of expression that was frowned upon by other teams. In the years that followed, the Raiders' knack at picking up misfits and malcontents earned them a bad boy reputation, but the response was always the same. To hell with the rest of the league became the attitude along with more colorful expressions, and soon the Raiders were feared, hated, respected, and envied. They would also be champions and their winning percentage over the forty-year period from 1963 to 2003 ranks them among the elite of any organization in the world of professional sports.

The 1963 Raiders quickly shocked the football community by finishing with a 10–4 record, and just missing out on a Western Division title by one game to Davis' former team, the San Diego Chargers. The nine-game improvement was one of the greatest single-season turnarounds in pro football history, and earned Al Davis the 1963 AFL Coach of the Year Award. The success also helped the franchise draw interest from the people of Oakland and the surrounding area. Before too long, the once stagnant organization had people clamoring to obtain tickets, and the love

affair with the Silver and Black was off and running. Davis remained Oakland's head coach until the end of the 1965 season compiling a 23-16-3 record.

With the battle going strong to compete with the NFL, Al Davis was asked by the AFL owners to assume the role of commissioner after Joe Foss resigned the post in early 1966. The owners admired his skill at how he saved the Raiders from despair and felt that he could do the same for the AFL. At first Davis wanted to remain the head coach of the Raiders, but eventually took the job, and on April 8, 1966, officially began as the league's top man. After moving to league headquarters in New York City, Davis began a relentless assault on the established NFL by increasing the pursuit of their top players, the most famous being quarterbacks Roman Gabriel and John Brodie. It seemed to him that the NFL was on the ropes, and he looked to deliver the knockout blow any way he could.[16]

Unknown to Davis was the fact that the NFL was secretly meeting with AFL owners even before Davis became commissioner in an attempt to iron out differences and merge into one league. So all the while that Davis was looking for ways to attack the NFL in submission, his fellow AFL comrades were engaged in skullduggery with the enemy, without Davis' knowledge.[17]

On June 8, 1966, a merger was agreed upon between the two leagues to take effect in 1970 with NFL commissioner Pete Rozelle in charge. The sneaking around behind his back left Davis with a great deal of animosity toward the AFL owners. Here he was attempting to add more prominence to the league, and possibly overthrow the same group that laughed at the AFL just seven years earlier, and a merger was being planned without him knowing. Davis was a street smart individual mixed with high intelligence. The combination was a deadly one for a person scorned, and Davis never forgot what transpired. It was even claimed that Oakland's owner Wayne Valley felt that Davis was nothing more than a figurehead as commissioner, and that Valley and the other owners would work out a deal without his input.[18] Instead of remaining a lame duck commissioner until the merger took place four years in the future, Davis resigned the position on July 25, 1966, to pursue other options within the football world.

It did not take Davis long to decide on what his next move would be. He returned to Oakland and bought 10 percent of the Raiders. He was now a part of the general partnership of the Silver and Black along with Valley and Ed McGah, and also named head of football operations. Under his guidance, the Raiders won the 1967 AFL championship, and emerged as one of the most dominant teams in football for the next 18 years. Still collecting castoffs from other teams, Davis molded other team's misfits into winners and created an "us against the world" aura that still permeates today. Possibly, this mentality originated from the way he was treated during his two months as AFL commissioner. Davis basically put up a wall between the Raiders and the rest of the league, daring anyone to knock it down. With their black and silver colors representing evil brutes that no one else wanted, the NFL's orphanage for wayward gridiron performers quickly adopted Davis' philosophies and pounded any opposition in their way to continued success.

Davis and fellow team owner Wayne Valley had a rocky relationship at best, possibly made worse by Valley's apparent comment about Davis just being a mere figurehead in the AFL's battle ith the NFL. Whatever the reasons behind the dislike, they may ever be completely sorted out. However, Davis pulled off a coup f his own, six years after the snub as commissioner against Valley. pparently while Valley was enjoying himself at the 1972 Summer Olympic Games in Munich, Davis had a new partnership contract rawn up that made him managing general partner with almost otal control over the organization. Ed McGah placed his signature n the document, meaning that the majority of the general part- ers agreed to the terms. Valley was not happy to say the least, nd sued to overturn the agreement. Unfortunately for Valley, he ost the case, and in 1976, he sold his interest in the team.[19] Many alled the move ruthless and cunning, but no matter how it is de- cribed, Al Davis was now firmly entrenched as master of Raider Nation. He also assumed the role of general manager, joining erry Jones of Dallas and Cincinnati's Mike Brown as the only ther owners who serve their teams in that capacity. Despite his ise to the forefront of the Raiders' organization as an executive, is coaching roots run deep, and he has been known to advise, vhile some say meddle, in decisions on the field. Some of his oaches through the years embraced his vast knowledge, and thers not so much.

Through the years that followed, Davis continued on his nission to make the Raiders the best organization in football, as hree Super Bowl titles in seven years will attest. His passion and elief in the Raiders is undying, as is his loyalty to those who erved him well. Many legal battles over the team's move to Los Angeles, and then back to Oakland, gained Davis more headlines nd negativity during the 1980's and beyond. Also, heated dis- greements with players and coaches also served as fodder for cribes across the country. His ongoing feuds with fellow NFL wners and the late Pete Rozelle were legendary, only fueling the ires of controversy surrounding the silver and black evil empire.

Despite the negative remarks and feelings centered around his man, Al Davis is also a trailblazer that allowed opportunities o people he felt worthy regardless of skin color, gender, or eth- icity. Under Davis, the Raiders hired the first Latino head coach n Tom Flores, the first African-American one of the modern era n Art Shell, and Amy Trask became the first-ever woman to rise o the presidency of an NFL franchise.

Al Davis has also been bestowed with countless awards given o him over the years for his achievements. In May of 1991, he vas presented with the first-ever NFL Players Association's Retired Players Award of Excellence for his many contributions to the nen who played the game. In March of 1998, Davis was inducted nto the NFL Alumni's "Order of the Leather Helmet," which is presented to individuals who made important contributions to professional football. On December 29, 1999, the *Oakland Tribune* nd the Alameda Newspaper Group named Davis the Bay Area's nost significant sports figure of the 20th century. He also received Letterman of Distinction Award from his alma mater, Syracuse University, and was inducted into the Orange Bowl Hall of Fame.[20]

These sterling honors prove the incredible impact that Davis as had on the game of professional football. However, the crowned jewel of all honors bestowed on this man occurred on August 1, 1992, when he was inducted into the Pro Football Hall of Fame, forever immortalized with the game's greats, many of whom he helped get there, and with many more he influenced on their way to Canton someday.

Mr. Davis remains the only individual whose involvement in professional football included player personnel director, assistant coach, head coach, league commissioner, general manager, and main owner and chief executive of an NFL franchise. This man who took a passion and a dream and rose to legendary status truly is an example of his "Commitment to Ex- cellence."

John Rauch

Tenure as Head Coach: April 8, 1966–January 16, 1969
Coaching Record with Raiders: Regular Season: 33-8-1; Post- season: 2–2

John Rauch refused to give up football at an early age, choos- ing to defy the odds and become a frequent winner regardless of the level of competition. Born on August 20, 1927, in Phila- delphia, Pennsylvania, Rauch was diagnosed with a heart murmur at age 14 and told to give up football. His passion for the gridiron far outweighed the risks presented to him. Ignoring the doctor's warning, Rauch achieved status in three sports while at Yeadon High School.[1]

Rauch's prowess as a scholastic quarterback became well known among college recruiters, and he decided to get away from the cold weather, electing to continue his education and football career south of the Mason-Dixon line in the warm climes of Georgia.

The pigskin fans throughout the Peach State were glad to see the Pennsylvania signal caller clad in a Georgia Bulldogs uni- form. From 1945 through 1948, Rauch quarterbacked Georgia to a 36-8-1 record, which included four post-season bowl appear- ances. He was selected All-Southeastern Conference three times, All-American in 1948, and left the Georgia campus as college football's all-time passing leader with 4,044 yards through the air.[2]

With Rauch's many accolades, his next gridiron endeavor was obvious, with that being professional football, and he was se- lected by the Detroit Lions as the second pick in the 1949 NFL draft. However, instead of going to the Motor City, he was sent to the New York Bulldogs in exchange for the rights to Heisman Trophy winner Doak Walker. In his first season with the Bulldogs, Rauch was used at both quarterback and defensive back. After three seasons of pro football, Rauch ended his playing days in his hometown of Philadelphia with the Eagles in 1951. Upon taking off his shoulder pads for the final time, Rauch decided to stay affiliated with football by getting into the coaching profession.[3]

The following year saw Rauch return to the south as an as- sistant coach with the University of Florida. In 1954, he went to Tulane, and then back to his alma mater in 1955, where he handled both the offensive and defensive backfields for Georgia until 1958.

From 1959 to 1961, Rauch coached the backfields at West Point, and briefly returned to Tulane before entering the pro ranks with his appointment as the first assistant hired by Al Davis after he took over as Oakland's head coach in 1963. Rauch was given responsibility of offensive backfield coach, as well as Davis' top- ranked assistant due to his previous experience as a player and coach.[4]

In 1966 Rauch became the fifth head coach in Raiders history when Al Davis left the team to become AFL commissioner. Despite his vast wealth of football knowledge, Rauch was very uneasy taking over the head coaching reins. He was a master tactician, but found it hard to communicate with the players. He was better suited to work more behind the scenes for a head coach rather than to be one himself.[5]

The Oakland players in turn had a difficult time with Rauch in charge. In spite of the friction, the Raiders won the AFL championship in 1967, posted a sterling 33-8-1 under Rauch, and helped him earn the 1967 AFL Coach of the Year Award.

By the end of the 1968 season, Rauch had enough of the Silver and Black, and resigned as head coach, with one of the reasons apparently being the meddling of Al Davis, who returned to the team as part owner. Rauch felt that Davis was undermining his coaching decisions on a regular basis, and did not want any part of it.[6]

Despite his apparent uneasiness with being a head coach, he decided to continue in that capacity with the Buffalo Bills in 1969. In a true reversal of fortune, Rauch went from the AFL's elite to the worst team in the league. After posting a dismal 7-20-1 record over two seasons, Rauch left the Bills, not over his coaching, but a less-than-friendly verbal confrontation with Buffalo owner Ralph Wilson, Jr., centering around non-congenial comments that Rauch apparently said about some former Buffalo players.[7]

It was then on to scouting for the Green Bay Packers, which was followed by a position with the Philadelphia Eagles as quarterback coach in 1972. After the entire Eagles staff was terminated at season's end, Rauch became head coach of the Canadian Football League's Toronto Argonauts in 1973. He appeared to have the team going in the right direction, as the team made the playoffs in his first season at the helm. By early September of the following year, with Toronto struggling, Rauch was relieved of his duties.[8]

Rauch came back to the NFL in 1975, serving as a backfield coach with the Atlanta Falcons, and as offensive coordinator with the Tampa Bay Buccaneers in 1976, but his stay there only lasted five games into the team's inaugural season. After not getting along with Tampa's head coach John McKay, Rauch resigned his post, and finished out the '76 campaign as an assistant in Atlanta.[9]

By 1977, Rauch went into a semi-retirement, working from a home base in Tampa as a high school coach and writer for the St. Petersburg Independent. He was lured back into the spotlight of professional football as director of operations for the Tampa Bay Bandits of the United States Football League in the early to mid 1980's. His accomplishments as Georgia's quarterback in the 1940's were acknowledged in 2003 with his induction into the College Football Hall of Fame. John Rauch lived to 80 years of age, passing away in his sleep on June 10, 2008, in his Florida home.[10]

John Madden

Tenure as Head Coach: February 4, 1969–January 4, 1979
Coaching Record with Raiders: Regular Season: 103-32-7; Post-season: 9–7

John Madden's appearance and persona conjure up imag of a favorite uncle, always there with a joke or some world advice. His celebrity status, marinated over forty years in th public eye, made Madden comfortable attending a $1,000 pla dinner with power brokers from all facets of high society, or sac dling up to the counter of a roadside diner for meat and potato with the average Joe from small town America.

Madden's name has become synonymous with broadcastin and the most successful football video game ever produced f quite a long time. So long in fact that it is somewhat forgotte that he was a pro football coach, and a great one at that. Withi an organization that had such an incredible winning heritage, be the coach with the most victories is an honor all its own. Ad to all this a Super Bowl championship, a Coach of the Year awar 100 wins in ten seasons, and enshrinement in the Pro Footba Hall of Fame. All this and more is what John Madden meant t the Silver and Black.

Madden's journey to becoming one of football's most pop ularized figures began in Austin, Minnesota on April 10, 193(His parents moved to a suburb of San Francisco called Daly Cit when Madden was six years old. His baptism into the world (football came on an empty lot behind the family home. It wa then on to Jefferson High School where Madden established him self in football, basketball, and baseball.[1]

When not involved in sports, Madden learned about lit hanging around street corners, pool halls, and card games.[2] Th form of education might be considered unorthodox in many cir cles, but it allowed the young man to gain street smarts in additio to what he learned in the classroom. This combination made hir a well-rounded, unpretentious individual who could deal wit people from all walks of life. Unbeknownst to him at the time this also laid the foundation for his ability to be so successful wit the band of outlaws and characters in cleats that he would guid to glory as head master of the Silver and Black Empire.

An interesting tidbit from Madden's formative years was h friendship with John Robinson, who would also go on to make name for himself in the college coaching profession at the Uni versity of Southern California in the late 1970's and early 80's In January of 1977, the two friends who shared so many memories enjoyed mutual success within one week of each other. On Ne Year's Day, Robinson's Trojans capped off an 11–1 season b winning the Rose Bowl, college football's most prestigious post season spectacle of the time. Eight days later, his old pal Joh Madden left the same stadium with a Super Bowl championshi

Upon high school graduation, Madden enrolled at the Col lege of San Mateo, Oregon, and Grays Harbor College before set tling on California Polytechnic State University in San Lui Obispo. While there, Madden helped the football team go 18–2 and earned All-Conference status for himself as a two-way tackle He was also a catcher on the baseball team. In 1959, he receive(a Bachelor's Degree in Education, and a Master's Degree in th same field two years later.[4]

Clear across the country in the City of Brotherly Love, th Philadelphia Eagles made Madden their 21st round selection o the 1958 draft. Any aspirations of a pro playing career were ende(shortly after they began. During the first scrimmage of the 195 training camp in which Madden participated in, a running bac fell across his right leg, tearing ligaments and cartilage in the kne

After surgery, Madden remained in Philadelphia throughout the season while receiving physical therapy.[5]

It was while rehabbing his knee that one door closed for Madden and another one opened. One day, Madden was hobbling down the hall of Philadelphia's training facility when he noticed quarterback Norm Van Brocklin watching game films. Van Brocklin went down in history as one of the greatest signal callers of all time, and was already of legendary status when Madden crossed paths with him.

Van Brocklin saw the big offensive lineman with the damaged limb outside the door and invited him in to watch films. When a legend decides to invite you to sit down and share his knowledge, you accept, without reservations. This proved to be the embryonic stage of Madden's illustrious future. Every morning after that initial contact, Madden listened to Van Brocklin intensely, absorbing every word spoken to him by the great field general.[6]

In 1960, Madden received an offer to play from the Los Angeles Chargers of the newly formed American Football League. However, his knee was still in a brace, which did not allow him any mobility and forbade him from running. With his playing days quickly fading, Madden returned to Cal Poly to earn his Master's Degree in Education. This was also the time when Madden took his first job as a coach, igniting an incredible ride that went on for the next 18 years.[7]

Madden joined the staff at Hancock Junior College in Santa Maria, California, in 1960. After two seasons he was promoted to head coach, and guided the team to a 13–5 record over the next two campaigns.

He then left the junior college ranks after proving his ability to handle the coaching profession. In 1964 Madden accepted an offer from San Diego State to coach the defense. While there, he was a member of a staff that included future coaching legends Don Coryell and Joe Gibbs. With this fantastic array of talent on one staff, the Aztecs enjoyed great success from 1964–'66, compiling a 26–4 record, and were regarded as one of the best small colleges in the country.[8]

A telephone call from John Rauch kicked off Madden's trek to eventual greatness. Rauch told Madden that he was expanding his Raiders staff, and wanted the young Californian to tutor Oakland's linebackers. That was in 1967, and the rest is history. Madden naturally accepted the offer, which would be his final stop in his coaching career. It was also the place that earned him everlasting fame and fortune after his ten-season stay was over.

In 1969, at age 32, Madden approached Al Davis about the vacant head coaching position created when John Rauch departed for Buffalo. Madden felt that he could win every game, and had a confident attitude when interviewed.[9] He was never associated with a losing program in his initial decade of coaching, was intelligent, very congenial, and players under him seemed to respond to his personality, which gave him the opportunity to gain their belief in him.

Al Davis was young himself, and apparently saw the coaching potential and confidence that Madden projected. The Managing General Partner liked what he heard from his young assistant, and on February 4, 1969, a union was formed between Davis and Madden that truly represented the team's belief of "Commitment to Excellence," and created the greatest winning percentage over the course of a decade that the sport had ever witnessed.

The legendary John Madden is given the greatest ride a coach can ever receive. Ted Hendricks, left, helps hoist the jubilant Madden at the end of the Raiders' win over the Minnesota Vikings in Super Bowl XI on January 9, 1977, in Pasadena, California (AP Photo).

Madden set the bar high for all first-year coaches, and almost achieved his prophecy of never losing a game. The '69 Raiders went 12-1-1, earned Madden the 1969 AFL Coach of the Year Award, and advanced to the AFL championship game for the third straight time. Even though he inherited an extremely talented team, this did not mean that success was a certain guarantee. All the talent in the world, without the proper leadership, can self-destruct just as fast as any other.

Thanks to Madden, that did not happen. He stayed the course that Al Davis incorporated in 1963, with attack being the focal point on both sides of the ball. He also allowed Davis to share his unlimited knowledge about the game with him, not looking at Mr. Davis as a distraction, but rather a benefit.[10] This is not to claim that the relationship between these two was always lollypops and moonbeams. Like in any union, a difference of opinion is almost a certainty. However, they developed a dynamic duo that powered the Raiders to continuous glory over the coach's reign.

Madden also had the unique quality of allowing his players to express themselves as individuals. At the time, most teams made it a rule to be clean-shaven and wear suits and ties on road trips.

Other coaches felt these rules helped unify a team, but Madden thought otherwise. On the Raiders, these rules were regarded as petty, and in no way influenced the outcome of a game. He did not care how his men dressed or groomed themselves. He was also there for them on a personal level by getting to know the players on an individual basis. Whether it was listening to problems or going out for dinner and drinks, he was accessible. This did not mean that Madden was a pushover. He was far from that. He worked the Raiders hard, but was fair, having the ability to perfectly mix fire and ice successfully. He only had three simple rules, and made sure that they were burned into his player's craniums. Be on time, pay attention at practice or meetings, and then play like hell on game day.[11]

This band of desperados in turn became a close-knit group that would have battled into the bowels of Dante's Inferno for Madden. Many were problems and castoffs from other organizations, given a fresh start with a team that only cared how they performed on the field, and they loved the freedom of expression that Madden allowed.

Antics were legendary under Madden's regime. From the often-eccentric All-Pro linebacker Ted Hendricks riding onto the practice field on horseback, or a naked female running across the same field, countless sideshows accompanied the Raiders of this time period.[12] He even allowed the Hell's Angels to watch practice. With his team being referred to as the Hell's Angels of pro football, the infamous motorcycle club became fans of the Raiders, and turned out in support of them.[13]

Through it all, Madden knew that regardless how absurd things got, the team followed his three simple rules. He also relied on his veterans to provide leadership and order on the field and in the locker room. They also helped new arrivals get acclimated into the Raiders' fold. Not only were his players on the cutting edge, but so too was Madden prone to occasional slightly-less-than-mellow antics.

John Madden was a big man at 6-4, 260 pounds, and would get worked up into a frenzy over referees calls he deemed unfair by prowling the sideline red-faced, ranting profanities, and waving his arms about wildly.[14] His appearance resembled that of a hungry bear on the lookout for a picnic area filled with endless supplies of caloric delight. His rants were of such grand fashion that they became a sideshow all their own throughout the sixty minutes of mayhem he controlled for a decade.

Even though Madden erupted like a volcano, he had a calming neutralizer in veteran quarterback Ken Stabler. The "Snake" was the complete opposite of his coach, and the ice water that ran through his veins more often than not brought Madden's blood pressure back to a somewhat normal range. Stabler would saunter up next to his ballistic mentor and begin telling him, no matter how dire the situation, that everything was going to be alright.[15]

With Stabler and a cast of others playing their hearts out every week, double digit winning seasons and division crowns became the norm for the Silver and Black. With victories mounting on his coaching record at a steady pace, the only albatross for Madden and his Raiders was an elusive Super Bowl berth. Each year, the Raiders marched into playoffs only to come up short of their ultimate goal that they were usually favored to win. Five times in Madden's first seven seasons, his Raiders suited up for a league or conference championship game only to lose sixty

minutes shy of professional sports greatest spectacle. Another bid to reach a conference title game was thwarted by a demoralizing post-season loss to Pittsburgh in 1972 on the final play in what was forever dubbed "The Immaculate Reception."

In 1976, all the previous years of frustration quickly evaporated in Raider Nation. For it was in America's bicentennial year that the Silver and Black captured the elusive Super Bowl championship. They marched through the regular season, emerging with a near-spotless 13–1 slate, then shook off the demons of the past two conference title games, the Pittsburgh Steelers, to gain entry into Super Bowl XI. The Raiders made the most of the opportunity, handing the Minnesota Vikings a classic beating in an easy 32–14 win. It was the team's crowning glory after years of being labeled as chokers in the big game.

With the win, John Madden officially added his name to the roll call of immortal coaches that enjoyed a victory ride off the field of conquest on the shoulders of their team. When it came time for Madden to take his much awaited and very deserving victory ride, it proved to be one of the toughest tasks his Raiders had to face after the convincing win over Minnesota. Lifting Madden's massive frame might not have been easy, but just like during the game, his players came through with flying colors.

There were more victories that followed the Super Bowl victory, but two years after his most glorious coaching moment, the game began to take its toll. A long-time fear of flying had wreaked havoc on Madden's nerves, and a severe bout with ulcers added to his problems. Madden was informed by a doctor after an exam that the stress his body had been under, aged his body to that of a 70-year-old. He was only 42 at the time, and knew that if he went on at this pace, his future health would be in jeopardy. So citing health reasons, the greatest coach in Raiders history called it quits at a press conference on January 4, 1979.[16]

Even upon his retirement from coaching the Raider renegades, Madden received a gift out of the ordinary, and he would not have wanted or expected anything less. Once again the free spirited Ted Hendricks came through with possibly the most unique retirement present of all time. Deciding to stop over Madden's home shortly after the coach's retirement press conference, Hendricks did not want to arrive empty handed. While driving over, he noticed a yield sign posted along the road. After knocking it down, the linebacker tossed the sign in his vehicle and presented it to his beloved coach as a token of appreciation.[17]

Over the course of his ten seasons at the helm, Madden guided the Raiders in some of the team's greatest games, and came away with numbers unequal to those of any others in the profession. Besides his predecessor, John Rauch, he was the only coach in Raiders history to never experience a losing season. Six times in ten seasons, Oakland recorded 10 or more wins with Madden as coach, and his .759 winning percentage in regular season games ranks as the highest among coaches with 100 or more career victories. His Raiders won 17 straight games between 1976 and 77, coming up one shy of the then record held by the Miami Dolphins, which Oakland stopped in 1973. Madden's teams were also able to string together long winning streaks, with at least five per season over his reign. Only legends George Halas and Curly Lambeau reached the 100-win plateau at an earlier age, and in the modern era, besides Madden, only Don Shula was able to reach 100 victories in ten seasons.[18]

John Madden then moved on to the broadcasting profession and emerged as a legend. Beginning in 1979, Madden provided color commentary and analysis for NFL games, eventually being part of the broadcast team on all four major networks. Starting with CBS, he was teamed with fellow broadcasting legend Pat Summerall in 1981, and would call eight Super Bowls together.[19] The duo then worked for FOX Sports after CBS temporarily cancelled its coverage of professional football.

In 2002, Madden left FOX for ABC's Monday Night Football alongside the great Al Michaels. In 2006, Madden shifted over to NBC along with Michaels to do Sunday Night Football. After thirty years and 476 straight broadcasting assignments, Madden retired on April 16, 2009, as one of the most popular and revered football announcers of all time.[20] During his three decades in the broadcasting booth, he received 16 nominations and won 14 Emmy Awards for Most Outstanding Sports Personality/Analyst. He won two American Sportscaster Association — Sports Personality of the Year Awards in 1985 and 1992, and was the first NFL analyst to receive the Golden Mike Award from the Touchdown Club of America in 1982. He also gained incredible success through the years with a video game bearing his name, which still continues to out sell almost every other game regardless of the genre.[21]

With all the awards filling up Madden's trophy case, one still remained unconquered. For reasons known only to the election committee, the Pro Football Hall of Fame did not recognize his coaching accomplishments for decades. Finally, after coaching his final game 28 years earlier, Madden was honored by being selected to the Hall of Fame on February 4, 2006. It was ironic that his election came on the exact date of his hiring by Al Davis as coach in 1969. On August 5, 2006, John Madden officially took his place among the game's immortals at the Hall of Fame induction ceremonies in Canton, Ohio. For his presenter, Madden chose Al Davis, who proudly stood at the podium to welcome his fellow Hall of Famer into the fold of everlasting gridiron greatness. After all, who better to present Madden into the hallowed halls of immortals than the man who took a chance on a young coach with only two years of pro coaching experience, provided him with countless gifted athletes, and served as a mentor, employer, and most importantly, a friend for over four decades. Together, they formed a legacy that will never be denied the greatness that the Raiders achieved during their time together.

Tom Flores

Tenure as Head Coach: February 8, 1979–January 20, 1988
Coaching Record with Raiders: Regular Season: 83–53, Postseason: 8–3

From being the team's first quarterback to a two-time Super Bowl winning head coach, Tom Flores ran the gamut of every level of competition during his affiliation with the Silver and Black. Through it all, Flores has emerged from the experience a champion and Raiders icon. Along with Hall of Famer Mike Ditka, he remains the only other person throughout the history of professional football to win Super Bowls as a player, assistant and head coach.

Besides brief stops in other locales, the bulk of Flores' personal and professional life was spent in the confines of California. His initiation into the golden state of California came with his birth on March 21, 1937, in Sanger, a town located in the San Joaquin Valley. His parents were farm workers of very limited monetary means, and when Tom was a child, he went to work in the fields along with his parents picking fruit, and earning pennies for each tray he filled. The hard work instilled a solid work ethic in Flores, and he looked to carry that intestinal fortitude into future endeavors.[1]

Athletics quickly proved to be one of his fortes, and Flores became a three-sport star in football, basketball, and baseball. After establishing himself as a prep star at Sanger High School, Flores decided to continue his education and athletic pursuits. He first went to Fresno City College, where he quarterbacked the team in 1954 and 1955. In 1955, he was elected team captain, and earned honorable mention as a Junior College All-American. His quarterback skills were soon put to good use at College of the Pacific for the next two seasons. In 1956, he gained increased status by being the sixth-ranked passer in the country, and fourth in total offensive production. For his efforts, Flores was selected honorable mention All-Pacific Coast and All-American. On top of starring on the gridiron, he also lettered in basketball and baseball, all while earning a Bachelor's degree in Education.[2]

It appeared that landing a spot on an NFL roster was a foregone conclusion for Flores at this point, but a shoulder injury suffered at Pacific stymied the pro scouts pursuit of employing him. Undaunted, he looked to become a teacher, but was offered a contract with the Calgary Stampeders of the Canadian Football League in 1958. However, his damaged shoulder continued to flare up north of the border, and he was unable to show his talents. A tryout with the Washington Redskins the following year also proved futile due to the shoulder. Not long after his trip to the nation's capital, Flores chose to undergo surgery to repair his shoulder and become a teacher.[3]

Just when Flores was set to lead the youth from the classroom, events altered his course. In 1960, the American Football league was set to begin play, and it gave opportunities to many eager to continue their gridiron dreams.

Flores' journey to becoming a life-long legend of the Silver and Black began with a simple recommendation. Ernie George was an assistant on Oakland's first coaching staff and a former coach at Pacific. George received a sterling recommendation in regards to Flores from Pacific graduate and NFL quarterback Eddie LeBaron. George discussed the idea of bringing Flores to camp with head coach Eddie Erdelatz, and the rest is Raiders history.[4]

The 23-year-old signal caller with a shoulder good as new arrived in camp, and after beating out twelve other quarterback candidates, he was given the reins of the Oakland offense. In receiving the starting position, he earned the distinction of becoming the first Hispanic quarterback in pro football history, and the AFL's completion percentage leader in 1960.[5] He also earned the nickname "the Iceman" for his ability to remain calm under pressure while standing up to pass rushes. After a second place finish in the same category the following year, Flores was forced to sit out the 1962 season after contracting non-contagious tuberculosis.

In the Raiders breakout season in 1963, new head coach Al Davis started Flores off slowly, allowing him the time to regain his strength and form. By season's end, he showed his old form by leading the team to eight wins in nine games to finish the campaign at 10–4.

In 1967, with Oakland on the cusp of their first championship, Flores was traded to the Buffalo Bills. After serving as a backup for two seasons, Flores went to Kansas City to perform in the same capacity. Despite missing out on the Raiders rise to power in '67, Flores was able to experience the sweet smell of success when the Chiefs won Super Bowl IV, and he retired as a player following the 1970 season.

In 1971, Flores decided to once again return to teaching, however, instead of a high school curriculum, it was X's and O's that filled his lessons. The Buffalo Bills gave him his first opportunity at coaching by making Flores an assistant in charge of quarterbacks.[6]

Famous playwright Eugene O'Neil reached theater immortality with his successful *The Iceman Cometh*. In February of 1972, the football equivalent to O'Neil's masterpiece could have been called "The Iceman Returneth." For after a five-year absence from the Oakland organization, Flores was welcomed back into the Silver and Black fold with his appointment as the receivers coach, where he had the privilege of working with former teammate, and future Hall of Famer, Fred Biletnikoff and soon-to-be Raiders legend, Cliff Branch. During his time as an assistant under John Madden, the Raiders won five AFC Western Division titles, one AFC championship, and Super Bowl XI. Upon Madden's retirement following the 1978 season, Flores seemed the most likely candidate to replace him as mentor.

Taking over the helm after a legend like Madden seemed to be an intimidating proposal, but Flores was ready for the challenge, and in time, he became just as revered not only in the football community, but in his ethnic community as well, becoming the first Hispanic head coach in the professional ranks.[7]

Tom Flores looked at his new challenge without the slightest bit of apprehension. He had no problem taking over, and truly was the perfect fit for the job. After fourteen years of affiliation with the Raiders, he knew the system, and the players knew and respected the soft-spoken gentleman, who was able to convey his passion and philosophies upon his band of renegades. He had the most knowledge about the Raiders' organization than any other head coach in team history, and it seemed to be his destiny to lead them to great heights. Flores proved very astute at preparing the team, and those that worked and played for him were astonished at just how much football knowledge he possessed.[8]

After nearly missing the playoffs in his first year as head coach, the Raiders began the 1980 season at 2–3, and rumors began to surface that Flores was on the hot seat, and could be fired if the fall from grace continued.[9] From that point on, Flores righted the wrongs, and the team went on to finish at 11–5, and then proceeded to become the first wild card team to win the Super Bowl in one of the greatest Cinderella stories the football world had ever witnessed. Three years later, Flores once again stood on the victory podium to accept yet another Vince Lombardi trophy. In his first five seasons at the helm, Flores posted a 55–27 regular season record, and an 8–1 post-season mark on the way to two Super Bowl championships, which were the only ones that the AFC reigned victorious in, throughout the 1980's. He also was selected as the NFL Coach of the Year in 1982 when he guided the Raiders to an 8–1 record during the strike-shortened season.

The Raiders made playoff appearances following the '84 and '85 campaigns, but made early exits each time. By 1987, Flores saw the team beginning to deteriorate, as age and poor draft picks were slowly draining the team of its luster. After going 5–11 that year, Flores saw a huge re-building project facing him, and decided that he did not want to go through the hassle and stepped away from the sideline and into an executive position in the Raiders' front office.[10]

On January 20, 1988, Tom Flores appeared before the Los Angeles media donned in suit and tie, with his Super Bowl XVIII ring on his finger. He was surrounded by Raiders greats of the past and Al Davis by his side, with the Raiders' emblem directly behind him. It was then that he officially announced his retirement as head coach of the Silver and Black. When asked if he had any advice for his successor, in true Raiders fashion, he said, "Just win, baby."[11]

The following year, Flores traveled to the great northwest to assume the role of president and general manager of the Seattle Seahawks. He eventually returned to the sideline in 1992, but after three unsuccessful seasons coaching the Seahawks, he once again retired from coaching, this time permanently with a lifetime record of 97–87.

Flores realized that silver and black ran through his bloodstream, and once again came back to the organization as a broadcaster. Currently teamed with Greg Papa on KSFO 560 AM, "the Iceman" delivers the radio coverage of all Raiders games. In this capacity, he is able to share with a listening audience, a wealth of experience from every aspect of this great organization. Through it all, Mr. Tom Flores was, and forever will remain, a gentleman and Raiders legend.

Mike Shanahan

Tenure as Head Coach: February 29, 1988–October 2, 1989
Coaching Record with Raiders: 8–12

Mike Shanahan's back-to-back Super Bowl championships with the Denver Broncos in the late 1990's solidified his coaching legacy with many of those enshrined in the Pro Football Hall of Fame. He was also a proven winner as an assistant in both college and the professional ranks, earning multiple championships in that capacity as well. The road to success has many smooth and bumpy avenues. To reach a level of excellence in whatever field one chooses is cherished after learning from mishaps along the way to an ultimate goal. For Mike Shanahan, the bumpy road on his path to elite status among NFL coaches went through the city of Los Angeles in the late 1980's.

The man who became the eighth head coach in Raiders history began his life's journey on August 24, 1952, in Oak Park, Illinois, just outside of Chicago. While at East Leyden High School in Franklin Park, Illinois, Shanahan was a three-sport star and his athletic prowess eventually led to his being elected into the school's hall of fame. In football, he was a record-setting wish-one quarterback, a guard in basketball, and high jumper and quarter-miler in track.[1]

Shanahan decided on Eastern Illinois University to continue his education and football career. He saw some playing time as a freshman, but none in his sophomore year. It was as a junior during an August practice, when his days as a college quarterback ended abruptly, when he sustained a vicious hit that caused one of his kidneys to rupture. The injury caused his heart to stop for half-a-minute and he nearly died. However, the incident did not sway his passion for the game, and Shanahan looked to remain close to the action by entering the coaching profession. He displayed a willingness to learn, and his college coach, Jack Dean, decided to keep him around. One year later, Shanahan served as student coach, and upon graduation with a Bachelor's degree in Physical Education, he remained at Eastern Illinois as a graduate assistant while he worked toward a Master's degree.[2]

His desire and knowledge impressed the athletic director at Eastern Illinois, and he recommended Shanahan to Oklahoma's head coach Barry Switzer.[3] In 1975, Shanahan was off to his first coaching job outside of Illinois, as he joined Switzer's staff as quarterback coach. Switzer and his staff came away very impressed by Shanahan's work ethic, and the Sooners went on to win the national title that season, allowing Shanahan to earn his first championship ring. The following year, Oklahoma went on to win the Fiesta Bowl.

In 1977, Shanahan went to work on Joe Salem's staff at Northern Arizona as the offensive coordinator, and got the offense to be one of the top-ranked in the country. He was a very strict coach who worked his players hard to reach a high level of success. However, when he saw that an individual was giving a yeoman's effort, there was nothing he would not do for him.[4]

After a three-year absence from his native state, Shanahan found himself back at Eastern Illinois University under head coach Darrell Mudra in 1978. Eastern Illinois had only one winning season in the previous 18, so the challenge to turn things around looked highly insurmountable. With his strong desire to succeed, Shanahan took the offense to new heights, and the unit set 25 school records, went 12–2, and won the Division I AA championship with Shanahan calling the plays.[5]

With another championship ring added to his collection, Shanahan reunited with Joe Salem at Minnesota University in 1979. He learned the "run and shoot" offense from its master, Mouse Davis, and incorporated it into Minnesota's offensive attack. In no time at all, Shanahan had the Gophers' offense running on high octane, averaging 373.5 yards-per-game and setting 10 school records.[6]

Mike Shanahan's name was now associated with success and powerhouse offensive attacks, and his talents were next used at the University of Florida starting in 1980 under Charley Pell. With Shanahan running the offense, the Gators went from 0-10-the previous year, to 8-4, 7-5, 8-4, and 9-2-1, over the next four seasons, and with trips to bowl games following each campaign.

With a 77-29-3 record in the college ranks, plus a sterling reputation as one of the top offensive minds in the country, Shanahan was more than qualified to take his wares to the sport's elite level, the National Football League.

The Denver Broncos offered Shanahan his first opportunity in the pros in 1984 on Dan Reeves' staff.[7] He was assigned quarterback coach, and in that capacity, he got to work with second-year pro John Elway, who eventually gained superstar status under Shanahan's guidance. He was then appointed offensive coordinator, and under him, the Broncos were ranked among the league leaders in numerous offensive categories. Denver won three division titles and two AFC championships during Shanahan's stay in the Mile High City.

While Shanahan was earning accolades as a very astute offensive guru, the Los Angeles Raiders were looking for a new mentor, in addition to a new look, after going through their worst season in over twenty years.

Al Davis had an epiphany of sorts when it came to the offensive scheme he incorporated for the Raiders back in 1963. The explosive attack of taking what they wanted worked to their advantage for a quarter of a century. However, after seeing his team fall from grace over the previous two seasons, Davis saw it as a sign that possibly the rest of the league had finally caught up to the Raiders' offensive style of quick attack. It was then that he decided to change his philosophy.[8] Davis had always remained steadfast in his desire to hire from within the organization, therefore keeping the vision of Raiders football confined to those who lived it and understood it. However, adopting a new offensive scheme called for a fresh face not initially draped in silver and black.

Bill Walsh of the San Francisco 49ers was the most successful head coach in the 1980's with a ball-control offense instead of the big play strikes. He had also been a Raiders assistant in 1966. He later took the idea set forth in Oakland to use running backs as receivers, and added that to his game plan with the 49ers. Walsh very rarely went for the long ball strike that was so prevalent in the Raiders' attack, preferring to rely on the short passes. In this system, interceptions are kept to a minimum, and allowed the offense to move the chains on a more consistent basis, and it also gave the defense more time to rest.[9]

Another team following the same philosophy was the Denver Broncos. Their offensive coordinator was Mike Shanahan, who was given credit for developing Denver's offensive game plan and making John Elway rise to superstar status. In 1986 and 87, the Broncos won the AFC championship, and beat the Raiders in all four meeting over the course of the two seasons.

After several interviews from inside and outside the Silver and Black Empire, Al Davis hired Shanahan as the Raiders' eighth head coach on February 29, 1988. Davis felt that hiring Shanahan would accomplish taking the guru of offensive football away from the team that was dominating the division, and restore the Silver and Black to past glory, with the same philosophy that helped all the programs Shanahan was linked to.[10]

Everything seemed perfect on paper, but almost immediately, things started to go sour for the Shanahan/Raiders union. Shanahan was more of a Madison Avenue suit and tie kind of man, where the Raiders were more blue collar, lunch-pail toting kind of guys. Being the first outsider hired as head coach under Al Davis, he had trouble adjusting to the wild, freewheeling persona that was a staple of the renegade Raiders mystique for a quarter century. He attempted to right what he saw or thought was wrong by incorporating nitpicky disciplinary rules that immediately were met with strong disapproval. One of the major rules that had everyone steamed, prohibited players from sitting on their helmets during games, which was a trademark of the team for many years.[11] The congeniality between him and his coaching staff quickly eroded also. He fired long-time assistants Charlie Sumner and Raiders legend Willie Brown. Al Davis was furious with Shanahan over these moves, and rehired Brown in a front office capacity, while Sumner left for a coaching position with the New England Patriots. He also looked to fire assistants Tom Walsh and Joe Spinella, but Davis stepped in to stop it.[12]

On the field, Shanahan did install a short passing offensive scheme, but it did not work in Los Angeles. The one major flaw was that he did not bring John Elway with him. The Raiders at the time had Steve Beuerlein and Jay Schroeder at quarterback, both of whom were very talented, but neither one was of the elite class that Elway was. John Elway was arguably one of the greatest to ever play the position, and possibly the best athlete to ever play quarterback in the NFL. Because Shanahan was missing this piece of the offensive puzzle, he was unable to make his offensive scheme work. Add to this the constant scrutiny from Al Davis questioning his play calling, many disgruntled players and assistants, and it had the makings of a disaster.

Even though the Raiders improved by two games under Shanahan from the previous season, his time appeared limited in Los Angeles. With his first head-coaching job hanging by a very weak thread going into the 1989 season, Shanahan did nothing to help his cause by starting out at 1–4. By that time, Al Davis had seen enough, and on October 2, 1989, he fired a head coach for the first time since taking over the Raiders.[13]

Upon his release, Shanahan returned to the Broncos as an assistant in charge of the quarterbacks. His first year back, Denver captured their third AFC championship in four years. After allegedly getting in the middle of a dispute brewing between head coach Dan Reeves and quarterback John Elway, Shanahan was let go by Reeves in 1991.

Shanahan latched on with the San Francisco 49ers in 1992, and earned a Super Bowl ring as the team's offensive coordinator in 1994. The following year he returned to Denver as the head coach. With Shanahan reunited with Elway, the Broncos won back-to-back Super Bowls in 1997 and '98 to firmly establish the duo's legacies in the Mile High City. From 1996 through '98, the Broncos set a league record with 46 wins against only 10 losses.

After Elway retired following the '98 season, Shanahan never returned to the Super Bowl, and over the next ten seasons, was scrutinized for it. On December 30, 2008, Shanahan was fired when Denver did not make the post-season for the third straight year. He was not out of work that long, however. On January 5, 2010, Shanahan was once again at the helm of a team, this time the Washington Redskins hired him. He was not only given the reins as head coach, but was also named executive vice president of football operations.

Art Shell

Tenure as Head Coach: October 3, 1989–February 2, 1995
Coaching Record with Raiders: Regular Season: 54–38, Post-season: 2–3

John Madden once claimed that Art Shell would be a head coach in the NFL some day.[1] He made that observation in 1984,

and five years later, Madden's prophecy came true. He was a goo judge of talent during his successful tenure as Oakland's all-tim leader in wins. He saw in Shell the characteristics needed to tak on the challenging occupation of mentoring fifty different per sonalities, facing a harsh media, and every other obstacle that th coaching profession was capable of throwing at the special indi viduals who choose it. Art Shell, at least, did not enter the pro fession with rose-colored glasses on. He knew the trials and tribu lations that professional football created for many years, prior t his elevation as the ninth head coach in Raiders history.

Shell's trek to sideline general began in Charleston, Sout Carolina, on November 26, 1946. Like all athletes that reach th professional level of competition, the accolades bestowed upo them began flocking in early. Shell was no exception to this rule While attending Bonds-Wilson High School in North Charleston Shell gained all-state acclaim in not one sport but two. In footbal he was tops in the state at center and defensive tackle. When h took to the hardwood in winter, his exceptional play at cente garnered him his dual all-state honors. In 1990, Shell's high schoc career placed him into the South Carolina Hall of Fame.[2]

After conquering the scholastic level, Shell moved up a run on the competitive ladder by taking his athletic prowess to Mary land State College, where acknowledgments of his football talent continued to mount. He earned All-Conference recognition thre times as a tackle on both sides of the ball from 1965 to 1967, an was selected All-American in 1966 and '67. Basketball still playe a part in Shell's life, and he lettered in round ball two times.[3]

Armed with a Bachelor of Science degree in Industrial Ar in his possession upon graduation in 1968, it was Shell's footba abilities that took him places the South Carolina native could no have possibly prepared for. His talents led him to fame and even tual immortality, as both a Raider and as a member of the Pr Football Hall of Fame.

Art Shell represented class and style. He blended these two sterling traits with power and finesse to become one of the greates offensive tackles the game has ever seen. During his 15-year tenu in the trenches, not only did Shell establish himself as a grea player, but he also became enthralled with what went into th makings of a team, from the X's and O's on the chalk board t the execution on the field. He possessed impeccable knowledg about his job, and studied everyone else's as well.

Two of Shell's former coaches provided him with characte studies that would prove invaluable to him throughout his ow coaching career. From John Madden, he observed how to approac players as individuals. This helped when knowing how and whe to push a player regardless of the situation, whether it was in th classroom, at practice, or during a game. In Madden's successor Tom Flores, Shell received the art of being patient when havoc wa swirling about all around him. This trait allowed the coach to re main focused and concentrate on how to right a wrong quickly

Observing these two Super Bowl winning coaches did no mean that Shell was looking to emulate anyone. He was his ow man, displaying a soft-spoken demeanor, and presented himsel in a gentlemanly fashion. However, when the time came to discus a standard that did not best exemplify the Raiders' creed of "Com mitment to Excellence," Shell made sure his point was heard. H did this by quietly explaining to the player in question on ho to correct any problem. Shell's message might have been delivere a quiet manner, but it came across loud and clear for the player refocus, do the task right, or seek another occupation.

Shell's desire to coach began early in his playing career with e Raiders. Of anyone throughout the history of the organization, ith the exception of Tom Flores, nobody could have been more ited to cross over from shoulder pads and helmet, to clip board d headset, other than Art Shell.

With his playing days nearing the end, Shell discussed his aching ambitions with Al Davis. Shell was the complete package garding knowledge of Raiders football, a tremendous demeanor, d respect at being one of the game's best. Davis held the All- o lineman in his highest regards, and let it be known to Shell at when the time came for him to retire and seek a coaching b, that he would help in the transition.[4]

It is well known that Al Davis' loyalty to his former players ins deep. When Shell retired following the 1982 season, Davis ade sure he found a place for him on Tom Flores' coaching staff. eginning in 1983, Shell entered the coaching profession as the aiders' offensive line coach. His first season as a coach ended the ay anyone in the profession wishes it could. The '83 Raiders n away from their post-season competition, and completed their uest by mauling the Washington Redskins in Super Bowl XVIII reign as world champions and place a third Super Bowl ring n Shell's finger.

The year 1989 was, by far, the culmination of Shell's pro- ssional life. It started out in January with his selection into the ro Football Hall of Fame. Two months after his Hall of Fame ishrinement on August 5, 1989, he received a late night call from l Davis informing him that a coaching change was imminent. Davis was ready to terminate Mike Shanahan and wanted Shell o take over as head coach of the Los Angeles Raiders.[5]

On October 3, 1989, Art Shell officially became the ninth ead coach in Raiders history. The appointment was the ful- llment of his coaching aspirations, and it also allowed Shell to ecome the first African-American head coach of the modern era. ellow Hall of Famer, Fritz Pollard, was the first in the NFL's ormative years of the early 1920's.[6]

The color of Shell's skin never made a difference to Al Davis, nd should not have, to anyone with a brain. The only colors that attered with his hiring were silver and black. In that regard, hell was more than qualified, and was a Raider through and hrough. Like John Madden and Tom Flores before him, Shell nderstood the philosophy and mystique of the Raiders. His iring also helped to restore the Raiders of old, which were lost nder Mike Shanahan's suit and tie approach.

Shell inherited a 1–3 team upon his hiring, and turned things round right from the very beginning of his appointment. Upon is introduction as head coach, Shell stated that the Raiders were bout winning, and he looked to place players in positions that e felt would give the team its best chances at achieving and con- inuing the proud tradition that was Raiders football. He not only alked the talk, but backed it up as well, right out of the gate.[7]

In his first game as head coach on October 9, 1989, Shell's Raiders defeated the New York Jets, 14–7, in front of a sold out os Angeles Memorial Coliseum crowd on a Monday Night Foot- all telecast. From that point on, the Raiders finished the season t 7–5 under Shell, which included a 6–0 mark at home, and just issed out on a playoff spot by one game.

In his first full season at the helm, Shell guided the 1990 Raiders to a 12–4 record, an AFC Western Division title, and came within one game of reaching the Super Bowl. For his yeo- man's effort in turning around the team's fortunes, Shell was se- lected as the 1990 NFL Coach of the Year.

Shell had the Raiders back in the playoff in 1991, and after slipping to 7–9 in 1992, he once again had the Silver and Black back on track. In 1993, the football experts did not give the Raid- ers much of a chance to be successful. However, Shell's team proved them all wrong by posting a 10–6 record, and won their first playoff game. That season also saw the Raiders become the first team to reach the 300-win plateau in the years from 1960 to 1993.

In 1994, the Raiders once again had a winning record at 9– 7, but failed to make the playoffs, and did not reach the expecta- tions that Al Davis felt they should have. In what Davis later claimed to be one of the hardest things he had to do throughout his career, and one he would regret, he terminated Shell on Feb- ruary 2, 1995.[8]

After 27 years as a Raider, Art Shell was out of the loop. However, a man with his vast knowledge was not going to sit on the shelf for long, and in no time, was hired by the Kansas City Chiefs as their defensive line coach. After two seasons, he went to the Atlanta Falcons, and was on their staff when the team won the 1998 NFC championship. It was then on to corporate head- quarters, where Shell became senior vice president for the NFL in charge of football operations and development. His silver and black roots ran deep, and within a few years, the opportunity to return to the scene of his glorious past presented itself once again in 2006.

Mike White

Tenure as Head Coach: February 2, 1995–December 24, 1996
Coaching Record with Raiders: 15–17

Like many in the coaching profession, Mike White had the desire to lead a team at the professional level. Unlike many, White seized his opportunity after nearly forty years in the grueling, often harsh business of coaching, when Al Davis appointed him the Raiders' tenth head coach on February 2, 1995.

Mike White's journey to the helm of the Silver and Black began in Berkeley, California, on January 4, 1936. The native Cal- ifornian established his athletic forte early and often, earning letters in football, basketball, track, baseball, and swimming while attending Acalanes High School.[1]

Establishing one's self in a sport at the collegiate level is chal- lenging enough, let alone in four. However, that was what Mike White accomplished at the University of California, Berkeley. While showcasing his diverse athleticism, he also worked his way to a degree in Business. He played defensive end for Cal from 1955 to 1957, and was so well respected by his teammates that they elected him captain in his senior year. White was also captain of the rugby team, a guard in basketball, and ran hurdles, long- jumped, and participated in the decathlon during track season. Athletics were obviously the hub of White's existence, so it came as no surprise when he decided on the coaching profession to relate his expertise onto future generations.[2]

Cal's football coach, Pete Elliott, knew the type of man he had in Mike White, and gave him his introduction into coaching by making him a graduate assistant in 1958. White's first year in the profession ended with Cal winning the Pacific Coast Conference title and earning a trip to the Rose Bowl.

In 1959, White was elevated to a full-time assistant position, working with the freshman team for future Hall of Fame coach Marv Levy. In 1963, after serving the Cal team as receivers coach and recruiting coordinator, White went to serve as Stanford's offensive coordinator for the next eight years. He found much success with the Cardinals, guiding an offense that won back-to-back PAC-8 championships and Rose Bowl victories in 1970 and '71. Under his tutelage, future Raiders quarterback Jim Plunkett won the Heisman Trophy in 1970. In addition to Plunkett, White molded nine other standout collegiate quarterbacks while at Stanford, Cal, and Illinois, throughout the 1970's and 80's.[3]

His success at Stanford brought attention from his alma mater, and White was given his first head-coaching job by a slumping Cal program badly in need of fixing. The task for a coach to turn around a program can be a monumental effort, especially in his inaugural attempt.

Mike White refused to shy away from the major overhaul needed, and his perseverance paid off, as he built the Cal football program into one of respectability throughout the 1970's. His overall record from 1972 through 1977 was 34-31-1, and included a PAC-8 championship in 1975. That '75 team also had the distinction of leading the nation in total offense with 458.6 yards per game. For his yeoman efforts, White was bestowed many coach of the year awards after that campaign.[4]

In 1978, White received his first opportunity in the pro ranks, serving as offensive line coach for the San Francisco 49ers. One year later, he became administrative assistant to coaching legend and Hall of Famer Bill Walsh, the architect of the San Francisco dynasty of the 1980's.

After a few years, the lure of a college campus, coupled with a challenge to rebuild yet another program in despair, brought White out of his native California in 1980 to mentor the Fighting Illini of Illinois. Within one season, White had the team on the road to respectability by posting a 7-4 record for the program's first winning season in seven years. The following year, White elevated Illinois to another rung up the ladder of success by guiding them to their first bowl game appearance in 18 years when they went to the Liberty Bowl.[5]

In 1983, White took the Fighting Illini to national prominence within three seasons. That season, his team posted a near-perfect 10-1 record, including nine straight wins, a Big-Ten championship, a trip to the coveted Rose Bowl, and once again received numerous coach of the year accolades. That '83 team was also the only Big-Ten member to ever beat a team from each of the other major conferences in one single season. In eight seasons at Illinois, White compiled a 47-41-3 record.[6]

In 1990, White's reputation as a well-respected member of the coaching community earned him an offer from the Los Angeles Raiders. Returning to the state of his birth, White accepted the job of quarterbacks coach under Art Shell, a post he held for three seasons. In 1993 and 94, he mentored the offensive line before being given the opportunity to fulfill a long-time desire to be a head coach on the professional level.

Al Davis knew Mike White throughout the latter's 37 yea in the coaching profession, and the patriarch of the Silver a Black empire had no question that White was more than qualifi to assume the ultimate level of pro coaching.

After reaching the summit of his coaching dreams near forty years into the profession, White dove right in to the task once again turning around a program that was on the verge mediocrity at best. White was very aware of the minor me down between quarterback Jeff Hostetler and Art Shell in game against Miami. Hostetler was getting pounded on we after week and the frustration began to set in. The entire tea basically shut it down in the final regular season game again rival Kansas City.[7]

White knew of Hostetler's value to the team, and rig after assuming the head coaching position, he travelled to t quarterback's West Virginia home to discuss the future directio of the team. He told Hostetler that he needed him to be the lead of the team, and if there was ever a problem, to discuss it imm diately, instead of letting any animosities fester and ruin th rhythm of the team.[8]

This was also the time that the Raiders decided to return t Oakland and White looked to make the team's homecoming success. Just like Mike Shanahan's attempt seven years earlie White revamped the offense with a philosophy geared toward th short passing game much like the 49ers had enjoyed unlimite success with, during the 1980's and early 90's. White's plan calle for a well-balanced, ball-control attack with short passes and no-huddle system. The plan also called for about the first 15 play to be set, and after that, Hostetler would be able to make the cal as he saw fit. The new system pleased the veteran signal calle and the Raiders were ready to show off their new look. It wer away from the Raiders' attack offense once again, but White wa willing to sink or swim with it in Al Davis' pool. If it worke great for him, but if it did not, he would be shown the door in very swift manner.[9]

White's reputation as a savior definitely preceded hir through the first ten weeks of his inaugural season. In that tim span of baptism under fire, White led the Silver and Black to conference-leading 8-2 record while averaging 25 points game. The bottom then fell out on Raider Nation, as injuries t key personnel mounted and destroyed the flow of the team. I the end, the Raiders dropped their final six games to finish at 8 8.

Needless to say, Al Davis was not pleased with the way thing ended in '95, but decided to give White another attempt to salvag what he started. Davis did not like the way the '96 season began with the team starting out of the blocks at 1-4. However, the rallied to get to 4-4 before things collapsed once again. After 7-9 finish, Davis had seen enough and dismissed White o Christmas Eve in 1996. White was in the business a long time and knew the hazards of the fickle profession. Termination wa just a part of the job much like accolades are. He was more upse that he did not achieve success, like so many times before, tha he was in getting released of his duties.

White later took a front office job with the Kansas City Chiefs as Director of Football Administration, and since 2006 h has been involved in a family camp sponsored by the Californi Alumni Association.[10]

Joe Bugel

Tenure as Head Coach: January 30, 1997–January 6, 1998
Coaching Record with Raiders: 4–12

Joe Bugel was born on March 10, 1940, in Pittsburgh, Pennsylvania. After starring as a two-way performer at Munhall High School, Bugel tried out as a walk-on at Western Kentucky. He so impressed the coaching staff that he was eventually awarded a scholarship. During his time at Western Kentucky, Bugel earned All-Conference acclaim as an offensive guard from 1960 through '63, and also saw time at linebacker. He also performed well in the classroom, earning a Bachelor's Degree in Physical Education in 1963, and a Master's Degree in Counseling a year later.[1]

Having degrees in physical education and counseling seemed the perfect combination for someone who was embarking on a career in coaching. Bugel's induction into the profession did not take him far away, as he landed an assistant position with his alma mater from 1964 to 1968. Stops at Navy (1969–72), Iowa State (1973), and Ohio State under Woody Hayes in 1974, eventually gained him enough experience to elevate himself into the professional ranks.[2]

Bugel's initial opportunity in the NFL came courtesy of the Detroit Lions, where he served as offensive line coach in 1975 and 1976. From the Motor City, Bugel headed to the great southwest and a job with the Houston Oilers in the same capacity that he served the Lions. During his tenure as mentor of Houston's wall of protection from 1977 to '80, the unit's superb blocking allowed the offense to set team records in rushing and passing in 1980, and in 1978, Bugel's boys gave up the least amount of sacks in the league.[3]

With his reputation as a solid assistant now finally entrenched, Bugel travelled to the nation's capital to mold and shape the Washington Redskins' wall of protection as offensive coordinator in 1981. It was here that Bugel's legacy was forever embossed in the annals of Redskins' lore. He put together the "Hogs," one of the greatest offensive lines ever assembled. Running behind this famed unit of trench warriors, John "the Diesel" Riggins battered defenders on the way to the Hall of Fame, and quarterback Joe Theismann passed virtually at will, in Washington's quest at capturing their first Super Bowl title in 1982. In 1983, the Redskins were almost unstoppable throughout the regular season, scoring a then NFL record 541 points, on their way to a second straight NFC championship with Bugel promoted to assistant head coach. Washington added another Super Bowl title to Bugel's resume in 1987.

In 17 seasons as an assistant, the teams Bugel was affiliated with, produced a 159–99 for a .616 winning percentage. In that time span, he helped lead teams to 13 winning seasons, eight playoff appearances, six conference title game appearances, and three Super Bowls, coming out victorious twice.

With a few exceptions throughout their history, the Cardinals have predominantly had a reputation as a sub-par franchise. Whether in Chicago, St. Louis, or Arizona, losing seasons always seemed commonplace for the Cardinals. To assume that the task of being the head coach for this organization was challenging would be a drastic understatement. However, Joe Bugel was willing to accept his appointment as sideline general in 1990 with the hopes of turning pro football's sad sacks into winners. Unfortunately, like so many prior to his tenure, Bugel came out of the experience with more losses than wins. He did manage to guide the Cardinals to a level of some respectability in the extremely tough NFC Eastern Division, when they finished at 7–9 in his final campaign at the helm in 1993.

Much like his predecessor, Mike White, Joe Bugel came to the Oakland Raiders after four decades in the coaching profession. While serving as White's assistant head coach, Bugel became very popular and well respected by the players.[4] Upon White's dismissal following the 1996 season, Al Davis began a month long search for a new head coach. On the urging from many of the players, Davis decided to give Bugel a chance at taking over for White. So, at the age of 56, Bugel was given the keys to the Silver and Black Empire by Al Davis on January 30, 1997, with his appointment as the eleventh head coach in Raiders history.[5]

Initially labeled as dynamic by Mr. Davis upon his promotion, Bugel's stock quickly fell with the emperor of the Raiders' kingdom. At first, Bugel's philosophy was reminiscent of what the old Raiders stood for, with that being smash mouth football and always on the attack. In some regards, Bugel did breathe some life into the offense. By season's end, Oakland's 4.8 yards per gain rushing average led the league and broke the team record of 4.63 set in 1968, '72, '73, and '87. The Raiders also finished fifth in the AFC in total offense.[6] All that seemed fine, and in time Bugel might have had the Raiders back in contention for gridiron supremacy. However, time was not on his side with Al Davis hovering impatiently.

Bugel's fate seemed sealed, or at least hanging on by the slightest of hopes, after Oakland lost by one point to long-time rival Kansas City after blowing a 27–13 lead in the second week of the season. Davis might have had reason to be optimistic when his Raiders presented the Denver Broncos with their first loss of the year in October, and were at 3–4 nearing the second half of the season. The Raiders then sank to depths not seen since their early disastrous campaigns. They lost eight of their final nine games to finish at 4–12, which was their worst record since 1962.

Right after the season, Davis and his staff began calling around the league asking for permission to talk with some of the NFL's top assistants about coaching the Raiders in the very near future. This was not a vote of encouragement for Joe Bugel, and the inevitable occurred on January 6, 1998, when he was relieved of his duties by Davis.[7]

After the Raiders, Bugel served the San Diego Chargers as offensive line coach from 1998 to 2001. In 2004, Joe Gibbs returned to coaching the Washington Redskins with hopes of bringing back the glory days that he established in the 1980's and early 90's. Upon his hiring, Gibbs brought Bugel back to the nation's capital as an assistant. He remained with the Redskins through the 2009 season, and retired on January 13, 2010, after 32 years of NFL coaching as one of the greatest offensive line coaches in league history.[8] If the Pro Football Hall of Fame finds it in their collective minds to enshrine position coaches, Joe Bugel will one day be among the immortals.

Jon Gruden

Tenure as Head Coach: January 22, 1998–February 18, 2002
Coaching Record with Raiders: Regular Season: 38–26, Post-season: 2–2

For twenty seasons following the 1979 retirement of the great John Madden, the Raiders faithful had not seen such an animated display of passion that became a sideshow all its own. The red-faced ranting and arms flaying wildly about emotion was returned to the Silver and Black with the arrival of Jon Gruden as the team's 12th head coach in 1998, and Raider Nation loved every minute of it.

In comparison to Madden, Gruden was young at the time of his appointment, and like the franchise's all-time leader in wins, Gruden was a powder keg with a short fuse. His game day face, complete with a trademark scowl, quickly became a classic image that will forever remain part of Raiders lore.

Jon Gruden was born on August 17, 1963, in Sandusky, Ohio, about 75 miles west of Cleveland. With such close proximity to Cleveland, the young Gruden became a Browns fan. He attended training camp sessions open to the public, and like so many pre-teenage boys, had a Cleveland Browns uniform that he romped around in, imagining himself as a hero for his favorite home team.[1] Unlike most youngsters, Gruden had football in his blood, passed down from his father Jim, who served as a long-time scout with the San Francisco 49ers, and assistant coaching stints with Tampa Bay and the University of Notre Dame.[2]

While his father was working as an assistant for Notre Dame under head coach Dan Devine, the Gruden family relocated to South Bend, Indiana. After graduating from Clay High School in South Bend, Gruden elected to return to his native Ohio to continue his education and play the sport he loved so much. His first decision was Muskingum College in New Concord, but he left following one year to attend the University of Dayton.[3]

The Dayton Flyers were two seasons removed from winning the Division III NCAA championship, and were still a force when Gruden arrived in 1982. While working his way toward a degree in Communications, Gruden served the Flyers as a backup quarterback during a run from 1982 to '84 that saw the team compile a 24–7 record. After graduating in 1985, Gruden decided to follow family tradition by embarking on a coaching career that eventually would lead him to the Raiders. It also allowed him the opportunity to become a member of an elite fraternity consisting of sideline generals who guided a team to Super Bowl glory.

Gruden's journey through the coaching ranks began as a graduate assistant at the University of Tennessee in 1986 and '87. He then served as quarterback coach at Southeast Missouri State in 1988, and in 1989, he coached the receivers at the University of Pacific.[4]

In 1990, Gruden's father helped his son get an interview with the San Francisco 49ers. Jon so impressed the 49ers' offensive co-ordinator, Mike Holmgren, with his vast knowledge, that he was hired as offensive quality control coach.[5]

Gruden returned to the college game for a one-year stint as receiver coach at the University of Pittsburgh. After five stops in five years, the young up-and-coming coach put down roots for three seasons working with the receivers for the Mike Holmgren-led Green Bay Packers from 1992 through '94.

When another Holmgren disciple, Ray Rhodes, got the head-coaching job with the Philadelphia Eagles in 1995, he took Gruden with him as his offensive coordinator. With that appointment, Gruden became the youngest at the time to serve in that capacity. His first season in the City of Brotherly Love saw the Eagles make the playoffs and rank fourth in rushing. In 1996 Philadelphia returned to the post-season with a Gruden-controlled offense that led the NFC in passing and total offense while finishing second in rushing.[6] After ranking near the top of the conference again in 1997, Gruden's name was gaining a lot of attention across the NFL landscape.

With seven seasons as an NFL assistant now behind him that saw teams he was affiliated with make five trips to the post-season, Gruden was more than ready and qualified to take over the reins of an organization.

The Oakland Raiders were fading from the ranks of respectability by the end of 1997, and needed to inject new life into the once proud and dominate franchise. At age 34, Gruden was given the opportunity to turn the Raiders around. On January 22, 1998, he was announced as the new head coach, becoming the third youngest in Raiders history, right behind Al Davis and John Madden, to hold that distinction.[7]

Hoping to join two Raiders legends in successful coaching runs, Gruden dove into his new challenge with a passionate work ethic that left most of his peers a distant second in the dedication to task department. One major advantage that allowed Gruden to get a heads up on his competition was the fact that he required very little sleep, and while in a vertical state longer than most human beings could tolerate, he worked diligently to transform the Raiders from cellar dwellers to champions. His passion and dedication truly lived up to the Raiders' creed of "Commitment to Excellence."

Gruden's orders were to pump new life into a franchise both on the field and off. He was allowed to bring in his own staff, and cleaned house with the old while bringing in a new, aggressive coaching regime. Among the newcomers were offensive coordinator Bill Callahan, who was brought over from Philadelphia and Willie Shaw was admitted to the Silver and Black fold to rebuild the defense.

The young workaholic then locked himself in a room with film and a computer for months. Once he had everything set on paper, he took his ideas to the practice field, and immediately made an impression on his team. He installed an offensive scheme along with Bill Callahan called the "dink and dunk," which relied on short passes to all eligible receivers. It was just another name for the west coast offense that made the San Francisco 49ers huge success under Bill Walsh in the 1980's. It also worked wonders for Mike Holmgren in Green Bay. With Gruden's father being affiliated with the 49ers for so many years, coupled with the younger Gruden's close association with Holmgren, it came as no surprise that he would incorporate the same type of scheme into the Raiders.[8]

It was no surprise to anyone that Al Davis was in favor of the attack style offense, and he had seen other coaches he brought in fail with the same type of plan that Gruden wanted. Gruden however, truly believed in his "dink and dunk," and would attempt to prove to Davis that he could make it work. He was a

ery intense individual who wanted things
one his way, and even got out on the field
ght with his charges to show them how it
ould and would be done.

Despite all his mastery of the offensive
de of the ball, Gruden's initial campaign as
entor of the Raiders had a tough go of
ings, especially late in the season. After
arting off 7–3, the Raiders finished at 8–8
ter losing starters for a total of 59 games.
hey ranked 18th in total offense, 21st in
assing, and the wall of protection gave up
whopping 67 sacks. One of the biggest
urdles for the young coach to grasp was
lling plays from the sideline. In his
sistant days, he called them from the press
ox, and it was just something new that he
ould have to adapt to. On the positive side,
Villie Shaw's defense went from 30th the
revious year to fifth in 1998.[9]

The 1999 campaign ended the same
ay as the 1998 season, finishing at 8–8.
Many positives did come out of that season,
owever. Oakland began the season with one
f the league's toughest schedules, and played
ery hard, which was a reflection of their
oach. The offense began to show signs that
was going in the right direction by
nishing fifth in the league in yards gained.
he defense did not fare as well, falling from
fth to 12th, and defensive coordinator
Villie Shaw was terminated because of the
ide.[10]

By the dawn of the new millennium,
on Gruden's plan to revive the Raiders became a reality, and in
doing, the young Turk was beginning to show the old master,
l Davis, that the short passing game was capable of providing
reat things. In 2000, all of Gruden's plans that he put in motion
vo years earlier finally came together. The Raiders posted a 12–
record, captured their first AFC Western Division title in ten
ears, and advanced to the AFC championship game. The "dink
nd dunk" offense with quarterback Rich Gannon at the controls
d the league in rushing (155 yards per game), and finished third
scoring (30 points per game). The defense did their part by
nking near the top in many categories.[11]

In 2001, the 10–6 Raiders added another division crown to
eir glorious lineage, finished second in the conference in passing
231.7 yards per game), and fourth in total offense (335.1 yards
er game). The line did a spectacular job protecting the quarter-
ack, allowing an all-time team low 27 sacks.[12] The Raiders came
close to a repeat trip to the AFC championship game, but a
ontroversial call late in their first round playoff game against
Iew England cost them the chance.

Jon Gruden was definitely getting the Raiders back on track,
nd quickly becoming an icon with the fans. A horror film called
Child's Play featured a possessed doll with a scowl on his face
amed Chucky. During games, Gruden displayed a similar look,
nd before long, he received the nickname Chucky and dolls of

The animated Jon Gruden provided the Raiders with four quality years as head coach
and countless memories of great facial expressions that showcased his unbridled passion
for the game (AP Photo/Jim Barcus).

the movie version quickly found their way into the Oakland Coliseum, some donned in Raiders apparel. There was no doubt that
Gruden had arrived, was part of Raider Nation, and beloved by
it. It seemed that the ride would never end, and someday very
soon, Gruden would lead the Raiders to the top of the football
world, culminated by him hoisting the Lombardi Trophy as their
coach.

Unfortunately, things sometimes do not work out as
planned. With the Raiders on the cusp of returning to glory, and
anticipation high for the future, Gruden was shockingly traded
to the Tampa Bay Buccaneers on February 18, 2002, for two first-
round draft picks, two second-round picks, and $8 million in
cash.[13] The reason behind one of the most controversial moves
the team ever made apparently stemmed from Al Davis' desire
for more vertical passing plays, despite Gruden's success with the
"dink and dunk." Another speculation was that Gruden's contract
only had one more year left on it. With his success and popularity,
it was obvious that he was going to command an extremely large
chunk of change. Maybe Davis did not feel Gruden would be
worth breaking the bank to keep, so the crafty old emperor of
the Silver and Black kingdom orchestrated a very unique and
highly unheard of deal that traded his coach to another team.

Gruden was welcomed in Tampa, and signed a five-year,
$17.5 million contract.[14] Just like he did in Oakland upon his ar-

rival, Gruden went to work hard in an effort to get the Buccaneers to the point of challenging for a championship. He shaped up a weak offense by bringing in free agents, and with the NFL's number one defense already in place, the Bucs finished the season 12–4 and won the NFC championship. In an ending that could have been a Hollywood motion picture, Gruden's Bucs faced his old team in Super Bowl XXXVII. They say revenge is sweet and Gruden showed his old boss that he made a terrible mistake by dealing him away. In front of countless millions watching around the world, Tampa Bay crushed the Raiders, 48–21, and was crowned 2002 world champions. Gruden did get to hoist the Lombardi Trophy, by not while clad in silver and black. It would have only seemed right to see Gruden win a Super Bowl with the Raiders after all the hard work he put in to get the team to the level that they could compete for a world title. It was a crushing blow to the Oakland organization, and the team has never been the same since the day that Gruden's Bucs pounded them into submission.

Gruden remained with Tampa Bay until the end of the 2008 season, where he posted three other winning campaigns. After the '08 Bucs lost four in a row to finish what began as a year that saw them looking like a possible Super Bowl threat, Gruden was released on January 16, 2009. He then signed a contract with ESPN as a Monday Night Football announcer.[15]

Bill Callahan

Tenure as Head Coach: March 12, 2002–December 31, 2003
Coaching Record with Raiders: Regular Season: 15–17, Postseason: 2–1

Being given the good fortune of inheriting the most explosive offensive attack in football at the dawn of the new millennium, Bill Callahan guided the Silver and Black to their fifth Super Bowl appearance in his first year as head coach. This was an incredible feat for someone who never held a head coaching position on any level. One advantage that Callahan had was that he had a major role in making the Oakland offense so dominant as coordinator of this juggernaut.

The man who became the thirteenth head coach of the Raiders began his life on July 31, 1956, in Chicago, Illinois. After high school, Callahan stayed in his native state, choosing Illinois Benedictine in Lisle, Illinois, to further his education and football career. He became one of the best small college quarterbacks of his time, earning NAIA honorable mention All-American following his junior and senior seasons after three years as a starter.[1]

After his stellar showing as a collegiate signal caller, Callahan decided on a career in coaching. His first job after college graduation was at Oaklawn High School in Oaklawn, Illinois, were he taught and coached football and baseball beginning in 1978. The next year, Callahan went to De La Salle High School in Chicago.[2]

With two years of experience behind him, Callahan elevated his coaching aspirations by taking a position in the college ranks with the University of Illinois in 1980 as a graduate assistant. He was then promoted to a full-time assistant in 1981 in charge of tight ends, the offensive line, quarterbacks, and special teams until the end of the 1986 campaign.[3]

After two years at Northern Arizona as the offensive li coach, Callahan returned to his place of birth, accepting the c fensive coordinator position at Southern Illinois in 1989. Duri his one season there, Callahan's impact on the offense allowed unit to rewrite the school's record book on 18 different occasion

With his impressive lone season at Southern Illinois creati such success, Callahan's stock rose in the coaching communi and it was then on to the Big Ten Conference in 1990. The Ur versity of Wisconsin provided Callahan with his next challeng and as offensive line coach, the trench warriors under his tutela produced nine first-team All-Big-Ten performers. Callahan w also on staff when the Badgers put together a 10-1-1 season th included the 1993 Big Ten championship, and a Rose Bowl victo over UCLA.[5]

Following the 1994 season, Callahan departed the "Dai State" for his first exposure into the world of professional footba In 1995, he was appointed offensive line coach of the Philadelph Eagles, and for the next two seasons, his linemen opened alle for running backs to amass enough yards to rank second in t NFC in rushing.[6]

In 1998, Callahan was appointed offensive coordinator ai tight ends coach of the Raiders after joining fellow Philadelph assistant coach Jon Gruden in Oakland when the latter was name head coach in 1998. From 1999 through the 2001 season, Callaha served the Silver and Black as offensive coordinator and offensi line coach.[7] During that stretch, the Raiders saw a revival in the status among the league's elite teams, with Callahan's unit earnir many accolades along the way.

In 1999, the Raiders finished third in the league in rushir yards and fifth in total offense. The following year, Oakland running game captured the top spot in the NFL with a 154.4 yare per game average. The Raiders also gained the number on ranking in first downs by rushing (128), second in rushing touch downs (23), and third in scoring (29.9 points per game), and tot offense (361 yards per game). Callahan's offensive linemen als clamped down on the opposition so well that they set a tea record for fewest sacks allowed in both 2000 and 2001.[8]

On March 12, 2002, nearly one year after Jon Gruden le the Raiders for Tampa Bay, Bill Callahan was announced as th new head coach. The 2002 Raiders under Callahan were one the most explosive offensive juggernauts in history. For the fir time in team history, the Raiders led the league in passing, an also topped the circuit in total offense. Oakland won their thin straight Western Division championship and the AFC titl Besides John Madden in 1969, and Art Shell in 1990, Callaha was the only other Raiders head coach to win a division title an reach a conference title game in his first full season. With th team's fifth trip to the Super Bowl, Callahan became only th fourth head coach to make it all the way to the ultimate show down in his rookie campaign. Unfortunately, the sweet smell success enjoyed throughout this great season, ended with a dis astrous 48–21 blowout loss to Gruden's Buccaneers in Super Bov XXXVII.

Things began to sour in the Callahan-Raiders union through out 2003. After getting mauled in the Super Bowl, Oaklan started the 2003 season at 2–5, and their opportunity to defen their AFC crown was fading quickly. Disdain began to engulf th locker room, as many veterans spoke openly about their feeling ward Callahan. It was claimed by some of the players that he was truly trying to wreck the season, and things got nastier between the sides with the passing of each week.[9] On the other side of the coin, it was said that Callahan saw the team getting older, and new fresh, young talent was needed if the Raiders were going to continue on their successful venture. To achieve this, Callahan had to cut back on salaries, which added more fuel to the already out of control situation. Callahan even referred to his Raiders as the dumbest team in America after the way they performed in a late season lost to Denver.[10] At the conclusion of a horrible 4–12 season, it proved to be just a matter of time before Callahan was trading in his Raiders colors for some new ones. To alleviate any suspense regarding Callahan's future in Oakland, Al Davis fired him on December 31, 2003, three days after a season-ending loss to San Diego.[11]

From Oakland, Callahan returned to the college game, taking over one of the most storied programs in history at the University of Nebraska. After posting a 27–22 record in four seasons with the Cornhuskers, Callahan was let go. Despite winning a Big 12 North title in 2006, Nebraska suffered through their first five-game losing streak in fifty seasons, and Callahan finished his four-season tenure with the worst winning percentage compiled by a Nebraska coach in 46 years.[12]

It did not take Callahan long to land back on his feet. On January 18, 2008, he was appointed Assistant Head Coach of the New York Jets. In his first season there, Callahan helped three of his offensive linemen gain Pro Bowl honors, and the trio of center Nick Mangold, guard Alan Faneca and tackle D'Brickashaw Ferguson once again were selected in 2009. The Jets also set a team record in 2009 with 2,756 rushing yards, and led the league with 4.5 yards per carry average under Callahan's expertise.[13]

Norv Turner

Tenure as Head Coach: January 26, 2004–January 3, 2006
Coaching Record with Raiders: 9–23

Norv Turner came to Oakland at the age of 52 after much success as an offensive mastermind behind grooming future Hall of Famers and Pro Bowl quarterbacks. Al Davis became enamored with his resume, reaping of exceptional offensive schemes that helped the Dallas Cowboys earn two of their three Super Bowl titles in the 1990's, and allowed his status to rise throughout the football community.

Born on May 17, 1952, at Camp Lejeune, North Carolina, Turner proved his athletic talents clear across the country in Martinez, California. While at Alhambra High School, Turner performed as a quarterback and safety. Upon graduation in 1970, he entered the University of Oregon, where he earned three letters as a backup quarterback from 1972 to '74. During two of his seasons, he played behind future Hall of Famer Dan Fouts.[1]

After graduation in 1975, Turner began his coaching career as a graduate assistant with Oregon. The following year he returned to California for the next nine seasons. At the University of Southern California, he first served as receivers coach from 1976 to 1979. He then coached the defensive backfield in 1980, the quarterbacks from 1981 to '83, and finally was given the of-

fensive coordinator's job in 1984. During his stint at one of college football's most prestigious institutions, Turner had the privilege of mentoring one of the greatest defensive backfields the collegiate ranks had ever witnessed, with Ronnie Lott and Dennis Smith as the catalysts. In addition to being a part of a national championship with the Trojans in 1978, Turner was also on staff for four Rose Bowl victories.[2]

After nine seasons of incredible success at USC, Turner decided that the professional level was his next stop. Close to a quarter century later, he is still coaching at the highest level of competition.

Turner's first pro coaching position took him to close proximity of USC's campus when he was appointed receivers coach with the Los Angeles Rams in 1985, and remained there until 1990. In 1991, Turner began a three-season run with the Dallas Cowboys as their offensive coordinator. It was in the Lone Star State that he emerged in the upper echelon of his profession.

With Turner controlling the offense, the Cowboys won two Super Bowls in 1992–93, and made legends out of quarterback Troy Aikman, running back Emmitt Smith, and wide receiver Michael Irvin. Aikman respected Turner so much that he had his mentor serve as his presenter at his Pro Football Hall of Fame induction ceremony in 2006.[3]

Under Turner's watch in Dallas, the offense ranked high in many categories. The passing game called for short to medium passes that could eat up time off the clock. It was a share-the-wealth type of attack in the fact that wide receivers, tight ends, and running backs, were all potential targets. In no time, the big three of Aikman, Smith, and Irvin, became household names across the NFL landscape. Smith led the league in rushing three times, while Aikman and Irvin ranked near the top among peers at their positions.[4]

When teams make coaching changes, they set their focus on personnel from championship teams. With the Dallas offense making headlines around the country on a daily basis, the master of the unit's success quickly became a hot commodity for teams seeking new head coaches.

Ironically, it proved to be the Cowboys' fiercest rivals who lured Turner and his two Super Bowl rings away from "America's Team." The Washington Redskins placed hopes of renewal into the hands of Turner by naming him head coach in 1994. In seven seasons guiding the Redskins, Turner produced four winning campaigns that included an NFC Eastern Division title in 1999. It was the team's first championship of any kind in eight years. Turner also made Pro Bowl quarterbacks out of Gus Frerotte and Brad Johnson, who became only the second signal caller in Washington's long history to throw for over 4,000 yards in a single season.[5]

In 2000, after starting off 6–2, the Redskins slipped to 7–6. After a close loss to division rival, the New York Giants, Turner was relieved of his duties, becoming the first head coach since the AFL-NFL merger in 1970 to be terminated in the midst of a winning season. Turner went back to being an offensive coordinator for the next three seasons with San Diego (2001) and Miami (2002–03).[6]

In 2004, he was once again back as the man in charge when Al Davis made him the Raiders' fourteenth head coach, and third in the past five years. Turner placed his signature on the dotted line of a contract worth a reported 1.75 million in January of 2004. His task was to bring the Raiders offense back to respectability with a power running attack coupled with a vertical passing game that Davis so craved over the decades.[7]

Not long after the ink was dry on his lucrative contract, Turner stated that it did not matter whether a player was an All-Pro or a third-stringer, he would have to work hard and prove himself. There were no exceptions. Turner also took the offense under his control by assuming all the play calling duties.[8]

An immediate turnaround was not imminent as the 2004 season progressed, and the Raiders led the league in penalties, which was nothing new for the marauders of the football world. Their 5–11 finish still placed them in the AFC West cellar, but they did improve by one game over the previous season.

The following year blossomed with high expectations when the Raiders acquired running back LaMont Jordan and wide receiver Randy Moss. The hope was these two marquee players would be Oakland's version of Emmitt Smith and Michael Irvin. Many felt that the Raiders were on their way back to challenge for league dominance.

Unfortunately, things did not go as planned, and the 2005 season proved to be an absolute nightmare for throngs of silver and black worshippers. The Raiders completely fell apart in the second half of the season, losing eight of their last nine games, and ended the year at 4–12, tying the '97 and '03 teams for the worst finish in the organization's history since 1962. The offense was only capable of ringing up 51 points and a half dozen six-pointers in the last five games. The stagnant unit's 18.1 points per game came in ranked 23rd in the league and never seemed to click in unison. Turner's charges did not seem focused throughout the year, and many venomously critiqued his play calling decisions. A major riff was brewing between the coach and Randy Moss when the star receiver began losing interest with each defeat, and was not giving his all during practice and games.[9] Also, the Raiders went winless in six tries against AFC West foes for the first time in Al Davis' reign.

Davis had seen enough. He brought Turner into the Raiders fold due to the coach's offensive expertise and previous success. It appeared that none of it showed while he was in Oakland, and on January 3, 2006, Norv Turner became another coaching casualty in the continuing saga of Raiders football throughout the first decade of the new millennium.[10]

Two weeks after his dismissal, Turner landed an offensive coordinator's job with the San Francisco 49ers for the 2006 season. On February 19, 2007, he became another former Raiders head coach to bolt to a rival AFC West foe. In Turner's case, it was with the Lighting Bolts from San Diego. As the Chargers head coach since the 2007 season, Turner has enjoyed much success, winning three straight AFC West titles during his tenure.[11]

Art Shell

Tenure as Head Coach: February 10, 2006–January 4, 2007
Coaching Record with Raiders: 2–14

The old adage of "what was once old is new again" definitely applied to the Oakland Raiders on February 10, 2006, when Al Davis announced to the football world that Art Shell was back at

the helm of the Silver and Black after a search that saw Davis i terview seven other candidates.[1]

While working as senior vice president for the NFL, Sh received a phone call from Al Davis informing him that he want the former Raider to interview for the vacant head coaching p sition. Shell was intrigued, and got on a plane in Tampa and fl into Oakland immediately. A lengthy meeting the following d with Davis produced Oakland's new head coach. For it was A Shell who was once again back in the Raiders fold after an 11-ye absence.[2]

This time around, Shell started in a hole. Due to a mon lapsing between coaches, Shell had to scurry about trying to a semble a staff before the scouting combine was set to begin days after his appointment.[3] However, that was the least of h problems. Looking back on his second stint as the Raiders' hea coach, Shell might have wondered why he ever came back.

Within one month after his hiring, he got into a very inten disagreement with receiver Jerry Porter, and the repercussions fe tered throughout the season. Shell even suspended him for "co duct detrimental to the team." After the two-game suspensio Porter found himself sitting the bench. Randy Moss, never o to back away from a good conflict, also began attacking the coac In a sullen mood throughout the year, Moss whined on a regul basis about how Shell conducted practice sessions, and the wa he treated veteran players.[4]

Shell decided to hire Tom Walsh as his offensive coordinato They were long-time associates with the Raiders, going back t 1982. Walsh was there in Shell's final season as a player, and a through his coaching days in Los Angeles. Out of pro footba since 1995, Walsh was operating a bed-and-breakfast in Idah before coming back to assist his friend once again. This wa another area in which Shell got lambasted. It seemed that tim had passed Walsh by, and his game plan was not working at al Shell was forced to demote Walsh to tight ends coach after 1 games.[5]

The actual 2006 season was a total abomination. The Raide finished at 2–14, which gave them the most single-season losse in franchise history. They scored a league-low 168 points, onl had 12 offensive touchdowns, and gave up the most sacks in th league with 72. Needless to say, Al Davis claimed at the end c the season that it was a tough year for the Raiders. Also, needles to say, the Art Shell experiment did not work out, and eleve months after being re-hired, the long-time Raider was once agai relieved of his duties on January 4, 2007.[6] It was a sad way to en an incredible career, but the legacy that Art Shell created over 2 seasons with the Raiders will never be tarnished. He was, and al ways will remain, one of the greatest legends to ever don the Silve and Black.

Lane Kiffin

Tenure as Head Coach: January 23, 2007–September 30, 200
Coaching Record with Raiders: 5–15

With the Raiders in full collapse, winning only 15 of thei previous 64 games, this once-proud franchise was in need o someone to guide the team out of absolute despair. They wer ace a team where everyone wanted to go and play. Success was theirs for the taking year after year, and a run at the Super Bowl emed like a foregone conclusion as the playoffs rolled around. hroughout the late 1960's until the mid–80's, death, taxes, and the Raiders in the post-season seemed like the only things that uld be counted on with the passing of time. Unfortunately, all at changed by the late 1980's. With a few exceptions, the aiders' playoff runs were not commonplace, and after the 2002 per Bowl blowout loss to Tampa Bay, the post-season was not en on the radar screen for the Silver and Black.

Oakland became a place where players dreaded going as the st decade of the new millennium neared its end. Who in their ght mind would want to go to the Raiders became the focal int of any football conversation regarding futility. However, ere was one man who did want to come to Oakland, with hopes resurrecting the Raiders from the gridiron Armageddon that ey became, and his name was Lane Kiffin.

With the exception of the Mike Shanahan ordeal in the late 80's, the Raiders organization enjoyed success with men in their 's as head coaches. Beginning with Al Davis, and followed by hn Madden and Jon Gruden, the Raiders turned to these young urks in hopes of righting the wrongs of the organization.

Lane Kiffin appeared groomed for the task of head coaching om both his pedigree and as a branch off one of college football's ost prestigious and highly successful programs. On a personal vel, he is the son of Monte Kiffin, a well-respected defensive ach with years of NFL experience behind him. On a profes-onal level, his resume was boosted due to his association with e University of Southern California under former Trojan coach-g legend Pete Carroll.[1]

This man who appeared destined to make coaching his life's ork was born on May 9, 1975, in Bloomington, Minnesota. fter graduating from Jefferson High School in 1994, Kiffin went a warmer climate to continue his education. At California's resno State, he was a backup quarterback through his junior ar. He also participated in basketball. By his senior year, Kiffin ecided to bypass the remainder of his eligibility to focus on a aching career. He then delved into the profession first as a stu-ent assistant at Fresno State in 1998. The following year found iffin coaching the offensive line as a graduate assistant at Colo-do State University.[2]

Kiffin made a temporary jump to the NFL's Jacksonville guars in 2000 as a quality control assistant. In 2001 it was back the college ranks and to California after accepting an offer from SC at the beginning of Pete Carroll's incredible assault through e collegiate football universe. While with the Trojans, Kiffin as on staff for two national championships in 2003 and '04, layed for another one in 2005, and saw USC ranked near the p of the polls in the other seasons.

After starting as tight end coach in 2001, and receivers coach 2002, Carroll made his young charge responsible for the passing me as well. Under Kiffin's tutelage, quarterback Matt Leinart d the Trojans to an undefeated season, back-to-back national ampionships, plus he brought home the Heisman Trophy for mself in 2004. The following season, Kiffin became offensive ordinator, and once again he helped the Trojans reach the na-onal championship game, and produced another Heisman inner in running back Reggie Bush. Kiffin also assumed the

duties of recruiting coordinator, and still worked with the wide receivers.[3]

While wearing many hats during the early years of Pete Car-roll's Southern Cal dynasty, Kiffin was responsible for sending many players he mentored into the National Football League. It only seemed natural that before too long, Kiffin would join former Trojans into the professional ranks.

That day came on January 23, 2007, when the Raiders or-ganization made Lane Kiffin the sixteenth head coach in team history. With his hiring, the 31-year-old became the youngest head coach in Raiders history, and the youngest in the modern era of the NFL (from 1946 to present).[4]

The union between Al Davis and his new coach began in a mild state of confusion, as the king of Raider Nation called his new coach Lance instead of Lane.[5] However, if that was the only mishap regarding this relationship, then it was extremely minor. Unfortunately, it was just the beginning of another volatile chapter in Raiders history that fermented over the course of twenty months and ended with both parties spewing venomous verbiage.

Things began to go sour when Oakland selected quarterback JaMarcus Russell number one overall in the 2007 draft against Kiffin's wishes. Davis wrote a letter to Kiffin telling him to get over the fact that Russell was selected and just coach the team on the field.[6] During training camp, Kiffin was not happy with lack of depth the team possessed, and lambasted some of Oakland's high-salaried players. Needless to say, Davis was again not pleased by Kiffin's public airing of the team's dirty laundry.[7] One thing that Kiffin apparently had a hand in was getting rid of disgruntled receiver Randy Moss, who was sent to the New England Patriots on April 29, 2007. Amidst all the controversy, the 2007 season came and went, with the Raiders finishing horribly at 4–12.

Right after the final game of the '07 season, controversy reared its ugly head once again, as stories about Kiffin's desire to get rid of defensive coordinator Rob Ryan began to circulate. Kiffin denied the reports while Davis claimed that his head coach wanted Ryan fired and replaced with Kiffin's father Monte. Two days later, Davis allegedly stated in a letter, that Kiffin would have no say so in managing the assistant coaches or deciding on what players the Raiders would take on draft day or any roster moves. Kiffin was supposedly handed a letter of resignation at this same time, which he refused to acknowledge or sign. Both of these sto-ries were quickly denied by the organization.[8]

As training camp opened on July 23, 2008, the Davis-Kiffin feud was not going away and continued to build with constant verbal jabs flying from both individuals. On September 8, Oakland got mauled in their season opener, 41–14, by the Denver Broncos. Two days later, Kiffin refused to deal with the problems on defense, allowing Rob Ryan to handle matters regarding that unit. On September 12, Davis warned Kiffin in a letter that his negative actions are getting him close to being terminated. Finally, two days after giving up a 15 point lead and losing to San Diego on September 28, Kiffin was informed via a phone call that he was fired by Davis.[9]

Two months after his tumultuous tenure in Raider Nation, Kiffin returned to the college ranks, signing on as head coach at the University of Tennessee on November 28, 2008. He led the Volunteers to a 7–6 record in 2009, and left that university after only one season to accept the head job at the USC on January 12,

2010, when Pete Carroll left the Trojans to coach the Seattle Seahawks.

Tom Cable

Tenure as Head Coach: September 30, 2008–Present
(Served as interim coach after Kiffin dismissal. Officially took over as head coach February 3, 2009)
Coaching Record with Raiders: 9–19

The seventeenth head coach in Raiders history began his life on November 26, 1964, in Merced, California. In 1982, Tom Cable graduated from Snohomish High School, located northeast of Seattle, Washington, and accepted a football scholarship to the University of Idaho. While there, from 1982 to 1986, Cable played all four years, three of which were as a starting guard. In 1987, Cable experienced his lone professional season as a player with the Indianapolis Colts. He then decided to go into the coaching profession.[1]

Cable's initial coaching job came at his alma mater as a graduate assistant, and he moved on from there to San Diego State in 1989 to serve in the same capacity. Stints at Cal State Fullerton in 1990 as defensive line coach and at the University of Nevada Las Vegas in 1991 handling the offensive line followed, before Cable laid roots at the University of California. From 1992 to 1997, he served as offensive line coach, and mentored four of his charges to first team All-PAC-10 recognition. The next two years were spent at the University of Colorado, where he was appointed offensive coordinator in addition to coaching the team's wall of protection. In 1999, under Cable's guidance, Colorado's offense finished 14th nationally with a 424.9 yards per game average.[2]

His name was beginning to gain attention, and in 200 Cable accepted his first head coaching position at the Universi of Idaho. In four seasons leading his alma mater, Cable's tean averaged 424.1 yards per game of total offense. He returned on again to his native California in 2004 as offensive coordinat and offensive line coach at UCLA. In two seasons with the Bruin Cable molded an offensive attack that averaged over 400 yards game, and helped the team win 10 games in 2005.[3]

After 19 seasons of college coaching, Cable made the jum to the professional ranks in 2006 with the Atlanta Falcons. Servi in the capacity of offensive line coach, Cable's trench warrio blew open enough holes to allow Atlanta's running backs the op portunity to gain the most yards on the ground in the entire NFL

In 2007, the Oakland Raiders came calling, and Cable trav elled clear across the country to answer. Assigned offensive line coac on Lane Kiffin's staff, Cable's linemen managed to boost tl lethargic 4–12 Raiders to some respectability by helping the ru ning game finish with the sixth ranked rushing attack league wid

On September 30, 2008, Cable was given his first chance head coach in the NFL when Al Davis named him interim coac after Lane Kiffin's departure. He guided the Raiders for the fin 12 games of that season, and was retained as head coach on Fel ruary 3, 2009.[5] Despite allegations of punching assistant coac Randy Hanson and fracturing his jaw during the '09 trainir camp, coupled with accusations from an ex-wife and girlfrien of physical abuse, Tom Cable weathered the storms of controvers and remained Oakland's sideline general throughout the tean 50th season of operations.[6] The organization saw another losir season at 5–11, but Cable, amidst rumors of a possible firing, mar aged to keep his job with hopes of resurrecting the Silver an Black, back to days of glory as the team begins its next fifty season

ALL-TIME SCHEDULES AND RESULTS*

1960

Date	Opponent	Score	Win/Loss	Attendance
(H)† Sept. 11	Houston	22–37	L	12,703
(H) Sept. 16	Dallas	16–34	L	8,021
(A)† Sept. 25	Houston	14–13	W	12,241
(A) Oct. 2	Denver	14–31	L	18,372
(A) Oct. 9	Dallas	20–19	W	21,000
(H) Oct. 16	Boston	27–14	W	11,500
(A) Oct. 23	Buffalo	9–38	L	8,876
(A) Oct. 28	New York	28–27	W	10,000
(A) Nov. 4	Boston	28–34	L	8,446
(H) Nov. 13	Buffalo	20–7	W	8,800
(A) Nov. 27	Los Angeles	28–52	L	15,075

Date	Opponent	Score	Win/Loss	Attendan
(H) Dec. 4	Los Angeles	17–41	L	12,061
(H) Dec. 11	New York	28–31	L	9,037
(H) Dec. 17	Denver	48–10	W	5,159

1961

Date	Opponent	Score	Win/Loss	Attendan
(A) Sept. 9	Houston	0–55	L	16,231
(A) Sept. 17	San Diego	0–44	L	20,216
(H) Sept. 24	Dallas	35–42	L	6,737
(H) Oct. 1	Denver	33–19	W	8,361
(A) Oct. 15	Denver	24–27	L	11,129
(H) Oct. 22	San Diego	10–41	L	12,014
(H) Oct. 29	New York	6–14	L	7,138
(A) Nov. 5	Buffalo	31–22	W	17,027
(A) Nov. 11	New York	12–23	L	16,811
(A) Nov. 17	Boston	17–20	L	18,169

*All information related to this section came from the 2009 Oakland Raiders Media Guide, pp. 203–217.
†(H)— Home; (A)—Away

Date	Opponent	Score	Win/Loss	Attendance
(A) Nov. 26	Dallas	11–43	L	14,500
(H) Dec. 3	Buffalo	21–26	L	6,500
(H) Dec. 10	Boston	21–35	L	6,500
(H) Dec. 17	Houston	16–47	L	4,821

1962

Date	Opponent	Score	Win/Loss	Attendance
(H) Sept. 9	New York	17–28	L	12,893
(H) Sept. 23	Dallas	16–26	L	12,500
(H) Sept. 30	San Diego	33–42	L	13,000
(A) Oct. 5	Denver	7–44	L	22,452
(H) Oct. 14	Denver	6–23	L	7,000
(A) Oct. 20	Buffalo	6–14	L	21,037
(A) Oct. 26	Boston	16–26	L	12,514
(A) Nov. 4	New York	21–31	L	18,247
(H) Nov. 11	Houston	20–28	L	11,000
(H) Nov. 18	Buffalo	6–10	L	12,500
(A) Nov. 25	Dallas	7–35	L	13,557
(A) Dec. 2	San Diego	21–31	L	17,874
(A) Dec. 9	Houston	17–32	L	27,400
(H) Dec. 16	Boston	20–0	W	8,000

1963

Date	Opponent	Score	Win/Loss	Attendance
(A) Sept. 7	Houston	35–13	W	24,749
(H) Sept. 15	Buffalo	35–17	W	17,568
(H) Sept. 22	Boston	14–20	L	17,131
(A) Sept. 28	New York	7–10	L	17,100
(A) Oct. 5	Buffalo	0–12	L	24,846
(A) Oct. 11	Boston	14–20	L	26,494
(H) Oct. 20	New York	49–26	W	15,557
(A) Oct. 27	San Diego	34–33	W	30,182
(H) Nov. 3	Kansas City	10–7	W	18,919
(A) Nov. 8	Kansas City	22–7	W	24,879
(A) Nov. 24	Denver	26–10	W	14,763
(H) Dec. 8	San Diego	41–27	W	20,249
(H) Dec. 15	Denver	35–31	W	15,223
(H) Dec. 22	Houston	52–49	W	17,401

1964

Date	Opponent	Score	Win/Loss	Attendance
(H) Sept. 13	Boston	14–17	L	21,126
(A) Sept. 19	Houston	28–42	L	26,482
(H) Sept. 27	Kansas City	9–21	L	18,163
(A) Oct. 3	Buffalo	20–23	L	36,451
(A) Oct. 10	New York	13–35	L	36,499
(A) Oct. 16	Boston	43–43	T	23,279
(H) Oct. 25	Denver	40–7	W	17,858
(A) Nov. 1	San Diego	17–31	L	25,557
(A) Nov. 8	Kansas City	7–42	L	21,023
(H) Nov. 15	Houston	20–10	W	16,375

Date	Opponent	Score	Win/Loss	Attendance
(H) Nov. 22	New York	35–26	W	15,589
(A) Nov. 29	Denver	20–20	T	15,958
(H) Dec. 6	Buffalo	16–13	W	18,134
(H) Dec. 20	San Diego	21–20	W	20,124

1965

Date	Opponent	Score	Win/Loss	Attendance
(H) Sept. 12	Kansas City	37–10	W	18,569
(H) Sept. 19	San Diego	6–17	L	21,406
(H) Sept. 26	Houston	21–17	W	18,116
(A) Oct. 3	Buffalo	12–17	L	41,246
(A) Oct. 8	Boston	24–10	W	24,824
(A) Oct. 16	New York	24–24	T	54,890
(H) Oct. 24	Boston	30–21	W	20,585
(A) Oct. 31	Kansas City	7–14	L	18,354
(A) Nov. 7	Houston	33–21	W	35,729
(H) Nov. 14	Buffalo	14–17	L	30,369
(A) Nov. 21	Denver	28–20	W	30,369
(H) Dec. 5	Denver	24–13	W	19,023
(H) Dec. 12	New York	24–14	W	19,013
(A) Dec. 19	San Diego	14–24	L	26,056

1966

Date	Opponent	Score	Win/Loss	Attendance
(A) Sept. 2	Miami	23–14	W	26,776
(A) Sept. 10	Houston	0–31	L	31,763
(H) Sept. 18	Kansas City	10–32	L	50,746
(H) Sept. 25	San Diego	20–29	L	37,183
(H) Oct. 9	Miami	21–10	W	30,787
(A) Oct. 16	Kansas City	34–13	W	33,057
(A) Oct. 23	New York	24–21	W	58,135
(A) Oct. 30	Boston	21–24	L	26,941
(H) Nov. 6	Houston	38–23	W	34,102
(A) Nov. 13	San Diego	41–19	W	26,230
(A) Nov. 20	Denver	17–3	W	26,703
(H) Nov. 24	Buffalo	10–31	L	36,781
(H) Dec. 3	New York	28–28	T	32,144
(H) Dec. 11	Denver	28–10	W	31,765

1967

Date	Opponent	Score	Win/Loss	Attendance
(H) Sept. 10	Denver	51–0	W	25,423
(H) Sept. 17	Boston	35–7	W	26,289
(H) Oct. 1	Kansas City	23–21	W	50,268
(A) Oct. 7	New York	14–27	L	63,106
(A) Oct. 15	Buffalo	24–20	W	45,758
(A) Oct. 22	Boston	48–14	W	25,057
(H) Oct. 29	San Diego	51–10	W	53,474
(A) Nov. 5	Denver	21–17	W	29,043
(H) Nov. 19	Miami	31–17	W	37,295
(A) Nov. 23	Kansas City	44–22	W	44,020

Date	Opponent	Score	Win/Loss	Attendance
(A) Dec. 3	San Diego	41–21	W	53,474
(A) Dec. 10	Houston	19–7	W	36,375
(H) Dec. 17	New York	38–29	W	53,011
(H) Dec. 24	Buffalo	28–21	W	30,738

Postseason

Date	Opponent	Score	Win/Loss	Attendance
(H) Dec. 31	Houston (AFL Championship)	40–7	W	53,330
(A) Jan. 14 (at Miami)	Green Bay (Super Bowl II)	14–33	L	75,546

1968

Date	Opponent	Score	Win/Loss	Attendance
(A) Sept. 15	Buffalo	48–6	W	43,057
(A) Sept. 21	Miami	47–21	W	30,021
(A) Sept. 29	Houston	24–15	W	46,098
(H) Oct. 6	Boston	41–10	W	44,253
(H) Oct. 13	San Diego	14–23	L	53,257
(A) Oct. 20	Kansas City	10–24	L	50,015
(H) Oct. 27	Cincinnati	31–10	W	37,083
(H) Nov. 3	Kansas City	38–21	W	53,357
(A) Nov. 10	Denver	43–7	W	50,002
(H) Nov. 17	New York	43–32	W	53,118
(A) Nov. 24	Cincinnati	34–0	W	27,116
(H) Nov. 28	Buffalo	13–10	W	39,883
(H) Dec. 8	Denver	33–27	W	47,754
(A) Dec. 15	San Diego	34–27	W	40,698

Postseason

Date	Opponent	Score	Win/Loss	Attendance
(H) Dec. 22	Kansas City (AFL Playoff)	41–6	W	53,357
(A) Dec. 29	New York (AFL Championship)	23–27	L	62,627

1969

Date	Opponent	Score	Win/Loss	Attendance
(H) Sept. 14	Houston	21–17	W	49,361
(H) Sept. 20	Miami	20–17	W	50,277
(A) Sept. 28	Boston	38–23	W	19,069
(A) Oct. 4	Miami	20–20	T	35,614
(A) Oct. 12	Denver	24–14	W	49,511
(H) Oct. 19	Buffalo	50–21	W	54,418
(A) Oct. 26	San Diego	24–12	W	54,008
(A) Nov. 2	Cincinnati	17–31	L	27,927
(H) Nov. 9	Denver	41–10	W	54,416
(H) Nov. 16	San Diego	21–16	W	54,372
(A) Nov. 23	Kansas City	27–24	W	51,982
(A) Nov. 30	New York	27–14	W	63,865

Date	Opponent	Score	Win/Loss	Attendance
(H) Dec. 7	Cincinnati	37–17	W	54,427
(H) Dec. 13	Kansas City	10–6	W	54,443

Postseason

Date	Opponent	Score	Win/Loss	Attendance
(H) Dec. 21	Houston (AFL Playoff)	56–7	W	53,539
(H) Jan. 4	Kansas City (AFL Championship)	7–17	L	54,544

1970

Date	Opponent	Score	Win/Loss	Attendance
(A) Sept. 20	Cincinnati	21–31	L	56,616
(A) Sept. 27	San Diego	27–27	T	42,109
(A) Oct. 3	Miami	13–20	L	57,540
(H) Oct. 11	Denver	35–23	W	54,436
(H) Oct. 19	Washington	34–20	W	54,471
(H) Oct. 25	Pittsburgh	31–14	W	54,423
(A) Nov. 1	Kansas City	17–17	T	51,334
(H) Nov. 8	Cleveland	23–20	W	54,463
(A) Nov. 15	Denver	24–19	W	50,959
(H) Nov. 22	San Diego	20–17	W	54,594
(A) Nov. 26	Detroit	14–28	L	56,597
(A) Dec. 6	New York Jets	14–13	W	62,905
(H) Dec. 12	Kansas City	20–6	W	54,496
(H) Dec. 20	San Francisco	7–38	L	54,535

Postseason

Date	Opponent	Score	Win/Loss	Attendance
(H) Dec. 27	Miami (AFC Playoff)	21–14	W	54,401
(A) Jan. 3	Baltimore (AFC Championship)	17–27	L	56,368

1971

Date	Opponent	Score	Win/Loss	Attendance
(A) Sept. 19	New England	6–20	L	55,405
(A) Sept. 26	San Diego	34–0	W	54,084
(A) Oct. 4	Cleveland	34–20	W	84,285
(A) Oct. 10	Denver	27–16	W	51,200
(H) Oct. 17	Philadelphia	34–10	W	54,615
(H) Oct. 24	Cincinnati	31–27	W	54,699
(H) Oct. 31	Kansas City	20–20	T	54,715
(A) Nov. 7	New Orleans	21–21	T	83,102
(H) Nov. 14	Houston	41–21	W	54,705
(H) Nov. 21	San Diego	34–33	W	54,681
(H) Nov. 28	Baltimore	14–37	L	54,689
(A) Dec. 5	Atlanta	14–23	L	58,850
(A) Dec. 12	Kansas City	14–16	L	51,215
(H) Dec. 19	Denver	21–13	W	54,651

1972

Date	Opponent	Score	Win/Loss	Attendance
(A) Sept. 17	Pittsburgh	28–34	L	50,141
(A) Sept. 24	Green Bay	20–14	W	56,263
(H) Oct. 1	San Diego	17–17	T	53,455
(A) Oct. 9	Houston	34–0	W	51,378
(H) Oct. 15	Buffalo	28–16	W	53,501
(H) Oct. 22	Denver	23–30	L	53,551
(H) Oct. 29	Los Angeles	45–17	W	54,660
(A) Nov. 5	Kansas City	14–27	L	82,094
(A) Nov. 12	Cincinnati	20–14	W	59,485
(A) Nov. 19	Denver	37–20	W	51,656
(H) Nov. 26	Kansas City	26–3	W	54,801
(A) Dec. 3	San Diego	21–19	W	54,611
(H) Dec. 11	New York Jets	24–16	W	54,843
(H) Dec. 17	Chicago	28–21	W	54,711

Postseason

Date	Opponent	Score	Win/Loss	Attendance
(A) Dec. 23	Pittsburgh (AFC Playoff)	7–13	L	50,350

1973

Date	Opponent	Score	Win/Loss	Attendance
(A) Sept. 16	Minnesota	16–24	L	46,619
(H) Sept. 23	Miami	12–7	W	74,121
(A) Sept. 30	Kansas City	3–16	L	72,621
(A) Oct. 7	St. Louis	17–10	W	49,051
(A) Oct. 14	San Diego	27–17	W	52,630
(A) Oct. 22	Denver	23–23	T	51,270
(A) Oct. 28	Baltimore	34–21	W	59,008
(H) Nov. 4	N.Y. Giants	42–0	W	53,964
(H) Nov. 11	Pittsburgh	9–17	L	53,987
(H) Nov. 18	Cleveland	3–7	L	53,889
(H) Nov. 25	San Diego	31–3	W	53,562
(A) Dec. 2	Houston	17–6	W	25,801
(H) Dec. 8	Kansas City	37–7	W	53,061
(H) Dec. 16	Denver	21–17	W	54,020

Postseason

Date	Opponent	Score	Win/Loss	Attendance
(H) Dec. 22	Pittsburgh (AFC Playoff)	33–14	W	53,662
(A) Dec. 30	Miami (AFC Championship)	10–27	L	75,105

1974

Date	Opponent	Score	Win/Loss	Attendance
(A) Sept. 16	Buffalo	20–21	L	80,020
(H) Sept. 22	Kansas City	27–7	W	52,471
(A) Sept. 29	Pittsburgh	17–0	W	48,304

Date	Opponent	Score	Win/Loss	Attendance
(A) Oct. 6	Cleveland	40–24	W	69,907
(A) Oct. 13	San Diego	14–10	W	40,539
(H) Oct. 20	Cincinnati	30–27	W	54,020
(A) Oct. 27	San Francisco	35–24	W	61,385
(A) Nov. 3	Denver	28–17	W	51,706
(H) Nov. 10	Detroit	35–13	W	54,020
(H) Nov. 17	San Diego	17–10	W	53,880
(H) Nov. 24	Denver	17–20	L	54,020
(H) Dec. 1	New England	41–26	W	54,020
(A) Dec. 8	Kansas City	7–6	W	76,711
(H) Dec. 14	Dallas	27–23	W	54,020

Postseason

Date	Opponent	Score	Win/Loss	Attendance
(H) Dec. 21	Miami (AFC Playoff)	28–26	W	54,020
(H) Dec. 29	Pittsburgh (AFC Championship)	13–24	L	54,004

1975

Date	Opponent	Score	Win/Loss	Attendance
(A) Sept. 22	Miami	31–21	W	78,744
(A) Sept. 28	Baltimore	31–20	W	41,023
(A) Oct. 5	San Diego	6–0	W	34,147
(A) Oct. 12	Kansas City	10–42	L	63,870
(A) Oct. 19	Cincinnati	10–14	L	56,058
(H) Oct. 26	San Diego	25–0	W	53,791
(A) Nov. 2	Denver	42–17	W	52,868
(H) Nov. 9	New Orleans	48–10	W	53,764
(H) Nov. 16	Cleveland	38–17	W	53,944
(A) Nov. 23	Washington (OT)	26–23	W	55,004
(A) Nov. 30	Atlanta (OT)	37–34	W	53,804
(H) Dec. 8	Denver	17–10	W	54,037
(H) Dec. 14	Houston	26–27	L	54,020
(H) Dec. 21	Kansas City	28–20	W	54,020

Postseason

Date	Opponent	Score	Win/Loss	Attendance
(H) Dec. 28	Cincinnati (AFC Playoff)	31–28	W	53,994
(A) Jan. 4	Pittsburgh (AFC Championship)	10–16	L	49,103

1976

Date	Opponent	Score	Win/Loss	Attendance
(H) Sept. 12	Pittsburgh	31–28	W	52,718
(A) Sept. 20	Kansas City	24–21	W	63,225
(A) Sept. 26	Houston	14–13	W	45,426
(A) Oct. 3	New England	17–48	L	59,837

Date	Opponent	Score	Win/Loss	Attendance
(A) Oct. 10	San Diego	27–17	W	52,546
(A) Oct. 17	Denver	17–10	W	63,532
(H) Oct. 24	Green Bay	18–14	W	53,751
(H) Oct. 31	Denver	19–6	W	53,805
(A) Nov. 7	Chicago	28–27	W	57,359
(H) Nov. 14	Kansas City	21–10	W	53,795
(A) Nov. 21	Philadelphia	26–7	W	65,990
(H) Nov. 28	Tampa Bay	49–16	W	53,249
(H) Dec. 6	Cincinnati	35–20	W	54,037
(H) Dec. 12	San Diego	24–0	W	53,658

Postseason

Date	Opponent	Score	Win/Loss	Attendance
(H) Dec. 18	New England (AFC Playoff)	24–21	W	54,037
(H) Dec. 26	Pittsburgh (AFC Championship)	24–7	W	53,821
(A) Jan. 9 Pasadena	Minnesota (Super Bowl XI)	32–14	W	103,424

1977

Date	Opponent	Score	Win/Loss	Attendance
(H) Sept. 18	San Diego	24–0	W	52,960
(A) Sept. 25	Pittsburgh	16–7	W	50,398
(A) Oct. 3	Kansas City	37–28	W	63,393
(A) Oct. 9	Cleveland	26–10	W	81,503
(H) Oct. 16	Denver	7–30	L	54,598
(A) Oct. 23	New York Jets	28–27	W	60,359
(A) Oct. 30	Denver	24–14	W	75,086
(H) Nov. 6	Seattle	44–7	W	54,027
(H) Nov. 13	Houston	34–29	W	54,598
(A) Nov. 20	San Diego	7–12	L	52,127
(H) Nov. 28	Buffalo	34–13	W	54,598
(A) Dec. 4	Los Angeles	14–20	L	71,039
(H) Dec. 11	Minnesota	35–13	W	54,598
(H) Dec. 18	Kansas City	21–20	W	54,499

Postseason

Date	Opponent	Score	Win/Loss	Attendance
(A) Dec. 24	Baltimore (AFC Playoff)	37–31 (OT)	W	60,763
(A) Jan. 1	Denver (AFC Championship)	17–20	L	75,044

1978

Date	Opponent	Score	Win/Loss	Attendance
(A) Sept. 3	Denver	6–14	L	75,092
(A) Sept. 10	San Diego	21–20	W	52,469
(A) Sept. 17	Green Bay	28–3	W	56,212
(H) Sept. 24	New England	14–21	L	53,500

Date	Opponent	Score	Win/Loss	Attendan
(A) Oct. 1	Chicago	25–19 (OT)	W	57,359
(H) Oct. 8	Houston	21–17	W	54,468
(H) Oct. 15	Kansas City	28–6	W	54,422
(A) Oct. 22	Seattle	7–27	L	64,799
(H) Oct. 29	San Diego	23–27	L	54,599
(A) Nov. 5	Kansas City	20–10	W	77,857
(A) Nov. 13	Cincinnati	34–21	W	56,524
(H) Nov. 19	Detroit	29–17	W	54,422
(H) Nov. 26	Seattle	16–17	L	54,599
(H) Dec. 3	Denver	6–21	L	54,616
(A) Dec. 10	Miami	6–23	L	75,419
(H) Dec. 17	Minnesota	27–20	W	54,599

1979

Date	Opponent	Score	Win/Loss	Attendan
(A) Sept. 2	Los Angeles	24–17	W	63,925
(A) Sept. 9	San Diego	10–30	L	52,413
(A) Sept. 16	Seattle	10–27	L	64,761
(A) Sept. 23	Kansas City	7–35	L	69,308
(H) Sept. 30	Denver	27–3	W	54,599
(H) Oct. 8	Miami	13–3	W	54,600
(H) Oct. 14	Atlanta	50–19	W	54,446
(A) Oct. 21	New York Jets	19–28	L	60,372
(H) Oct. 25	San Diego	45–22	W	54,583
(H) Nov. 4	San Francisco	23–10	W	54,583
(A) Nov. 11	Houston	17–31	L	53,383
(H) Nov. 18	Kansas City	21–24	L	54,583
(A) Nov. 25	Denver	14–10	W	75,103
(A) Dec. 3	New Orleans	42–35	W	71,323
(H) Dec. 9	Cleveland	19–14	W	54,583
(H) Dec. 16	Seattle	24–29	L	54,538

1980

Date	Opponent	Score	Win/Loss	Attendan
(A) Sept. 7	Kansas City	27–14	W	57,055
(A) Sept. 14	San Diego	24–30 (OT)	L	52,675
(H) Sept. 21	Washington	24–21	W	47,335
(A) Sept. 28	Buffalo	7–24	L	80,020
(H) Oct. 5	Kansas City	17–31	L	43,513
(H) Oct. 12	San Diego	38–24	W	49,009
(A) Oct. 20	Pittsburgh	45–34	W	53,940
(H) Oct. 26	Seattle	33–14	W	51,141
(H) Nov. 2	Miami	16–10	W	48,473
(H) Nov. 9	Cincinnati	28–17	W	46,070
(A) Nov. 17	Seattle	19–17	W	64,771
(A) Nov. 23	Philadelphia	7–10	L	71,522
(H) Dec. 1	Denver	9–3	W	54,563
(H) Dec. 7	Dallas	13–19	L	54,578
(A) Dec. 14	Denver	24–21	W	75,103
(A) Dec. 21	N.Y. Giants	33–17	W	76,734

Postseason

Date	Opponent	Score	Win/Loss	Attendance
(H) Dec. 28	Houston (AFC Wild Card Game)	27–7	W	54,539
(A) Jan. 4	Cleveland (AFC Playoff)	14–12	W	79,473
(A) Jan. 11	San Diego (AFC Championship)	34–27	W	52,675
(A) Jan. 25 New Orleans	Philadelphia Philadelphia (Super Bowl XV)	27–10	W	75,500

1981

Date	Opponent	Score	Win/Loss	Attendance
(A) Sept. 6	Denver	7–9	L	75,123
(A) Sept. 14	Minnesota	36–10	W	48,446
(H) Sept. 20	Seattle	20–10	W	47,141
(A) Sept. 27	Detroit	0–16	L	80,638
(H) Oct. 4	Denver	0–17	L	52,434
(A) Oct. 11	Kansas City	0–27	L	77,992
(H) Oct. 18	Tampa Bay	18–16	W	44,811
(H) Oct. 25	Kansas City	17–28	L	45,783
(H) Nov. 1	New England	27–17	W	46,796
(A) Nov. 8	Houston	16–17	L	53,465
(A) Nov. 15	Miami	33–17	W	67,531
(H) Nov. 22	San Diego	21–55	L	54,568
(A) Nov. 29	Seattle	32–31	W	64,750
(H) Dec. 7	Pittsburgh	30–27	W	54,555
(H) Dec. 13	Chicago	6–23	L	45,825
(A) Dec. 21	San Diego	10–23	L	52,975

1982

Date	Opponent	Score	Win/Loss	Attendance
(A) Sept. 12	San Francisco	23–17	W	61,125
(A) Sept. 19	Atlanta	38–14	W	59,719
(H) Nov. 22	San Diego	28–24	W	55,060
(A) Nov. 28	Cincinnati	17–31	L	59,446
(H) Dec. 5	Seattle	28–23	W	52,250
(A) Dec. 12	Kansas City	21–16	W	37,043
(H) Dec. 18	L.A. Rams	37–31	W	65,776
(H) Dec. 26	Denver	27–10	W	54,107
(A) Jan. 2	San Diego	41–34	W	52,664

Postseason

Date	Opponent	Score	Win/Loss	Attendance
(H) Jan. 8	Cleveland (AFC Playoff Round 1)	27–10	W	57,246
(H) Jan. 15	New York Jets (AFC Playoff Round 2)	14–17	L	90,688

1983

Date	Opponent	Score	Win/Loss	Attendance
(A) Sept. 4	Cincinnati	20–10	W	55,904
(H) Sept. 11	Houston	20–6	W	43,609
(H) Sept. 19	Miami	27–14	W	60,696
(A) Sept. 25	Denver	22–7	W	75,103
(A) Oct. 2	Washington	35–37	L	55,045
(H) Oct. 9	Kansas City	21–20	W	46,596
(A) Oct. 16	Seattle	36–38	L	64,880
(A) Oct. 23	Dallas	40–38	W	65,070
(H) Oct. 30	Seattle	21–34	L	54,562
(A) Nov. 6	Kansas City	28–20	W	77,865
(H) Nov. 13	Denver	22–20	W	57,562
(A) Nov. 20	Buffalo	27–24	W	73,586
(H) Nov. 27	N.Y. Giants	27–12	W	49,103
(A) Dec. 1	San Diego	42–10	W	49,956
(H) Dec. 11	St. Louis	24–34	L	43,869
(H) Dec. 18	San Diego	30–14	W	64,779

Postseason

Date	Opponent	Score	Win/Loss	Attendance
(H) Jan. 1	Pittsburgh (AFC Playoff)	38–10	W	92,434
(H) Jan. 8	Seattle (AFC Championship)	30–14	W	92,335
(A) Jan. 22 Tampa	Washington (Super Bowl XVIII)	38–98	W	72,920

1984

Date	Opponent	Score	Win/Loss	Attendance
(A) Sept. 2	Houston	24–14	W	52,678
(H) Sept. 9	Green Bay	28–7	W	54,057
(A) Sept. 16	Kansas City	22–20	W	77,260
(H) Sept. 24	San Diego	33–30	W	80,674
(A) Sept. 30	Denver	13–16	L	75,100
(H) Oct. 7	Seattle	28–14	W	80,929
(H) Oct. 14	Minnesota	23–20	W	54,323
(A) Oct. 21	San Diego	44–37	W	60,183
(H) Oct. 28	Denver (OT)	19–22	L	92,469
(A) Nov. 4	Chicago	6–17	L	65,790
(A) Nov. 12	Seattle	14–17	L	64,931
(H) Nov. 18	Kansas City	17–7	W	61,015
(H) Nov. 25	Indianapolis	21–7	W	49,423
(A) Dec. 2	Miami	45–34	W	75,151
(A) Dec. 10	Detroit	24–3	W	70,742
(H) Dec. 16	Pittsburgh	7–13	L	87,291

Postseason

Date	Opponent	Score	Win/Loss	Attendance
(A) Dec. 22	Seattle (AFC Wild Card Game)	7–13	L	64,910

1985

Date	Opponent	Score	Win/Loss	Attendance
(H) Sept. 8	New York Jets	31–0	W	61,009
(A) Sept. 12	Kansas City	20–36	L	74,359
(H) Sept. 22	San Francisco	10–34	L	92,487
(A) Sept. 29	New England	35–20	W	60,793
(H) Oct. 6	Kansas City	19–10	W	61,409
(H) Oct. 13	New Orleans	23–13	W	56,269
(A) Oct. 20	Cleveland	21–20	W	79,833
(H) Oct. 28	San Diego	34–21	W	72,022
(A) Nov. 3	Seattle	3–33	L	64,924
(A) Nov. 10	San Diego	34–40 (OT)	L	60,142
(H) Nov. 17	Cincinnati	13–6	W	59,012
(H) Nov. 24	Denver	31–28 (OT)	W	79,039
(A) Dec. 1	Atlanta	34–24	W	44,712
(A) Dec. 8	Denver	17–14 (OT)	W	75,100
(H) Dec. 15	Seattle	13–3	W	81,201
(A) Dec. 23	L.A. Rams	16–6	W	68,904

Postseason

Date	Opponent	Score	Win/Loss	Attendance
(H) Jan. 5	New England (AFC Playoff)	20–27	L	89,289

1986

Date	Opponent	Score	Win/Loss	Attendance
(A) Sept. 7	Denver	36–38	L	75,898
(A) Sept. 14	Washington	6–10	L	55,622
(H) Sept. 21	N.Y. Giants	9–14	L	73,318
(H) Sept. 28	San Diego	17–13	W	67,147
(A) Oct. 5	Kansas City	24–17	W	78,671
(H) Oct. 12	Seattle	14–10	W	73,055
(A) Oct. 19	Miami	30–28	W	75,284
(A) Oct. 26	Houston	28–17	W	46,459
(H) Nov. 2	Denver	10–21	L	92,496
(A) Nov. 9	Dallas	17–13	W	63,147
(H) Nov. 16	Cleveland	27–14	W	70,030
(A) Nov. 20	San Diego	37–31 (OT)	W	60,692
(H) Nov. 30	Philadelphia	27–33 (OT)	L	60,117
(A) Dec. 8	Seattle	0–37	L	64,944
(H) Dec. 14	Kansas City	17–20	L	68,771
(H) Dec. 21	Indianapolis	24–30	L	55,147

1987

Date	Opponent	Score	Win/Loss	Attendance
(A) Sept. 13	Green Bay	20–0	W	56,999
(H) Sept. 20	Detroit	27–7	W	52,105
(H) Oct. 4	Kansas City	35–17	W	26,645

Date	Opponent	Score	Win/Loss	Attendance
(A) Oct. 12	Denver	14–30	L	63,452
(H) Oct. 18	San Diego	17–23	L	34,807
(H) Oct. 25	Seattle	13–35	L	59,010
(A) Nov. 1	New England	23–26	L	61,000
(A) Nov. 8	Minnesota	20–31	L	63,208
(A) Nov. 15	San Diego	14–16	L	61,970
(H) Nov. 22	Denver	17–23	L	68,116
(A) Nov. 30	Seattle	37–14	W	64,640
(H) Dec. 6	Buffalo	34–21	W	52,100
(A) Dec. 13	Kansas City	10–16	L	70,219
(H) Dec. 20	Cleveland	17–24	L	51,019
(H) Dec. 27	Chicago	3–6	L	86,011

1988

Date	Opponent	Score	Win/Loss	Attendance
(H) Sept. 4	San Diego	24–13	W	45,171
(A) Sept. 11	Houston	35–37	L	47,305
(H) Sept. 18	L.A. Rams	17–22	L	86,027
(A) Sept. 26	Denver	30–27 (OT)	W	76,180
(H) Oct. 2	Cincinnati	21–45	L	45,584
(H) Oct. 9	Miami	14–24	L	55,178
(A) Oct. 16	Kansas City	27–17	W	78,516
(A) Oct. 23	New Orleans	6–20	L	69,134
(H) Oct. 30	Kansas City	17–10	W	44,032
(A) Nov. 6	San Diego	13–3	W	60,786
(A) Nov. 13	San Francisco	9–3	W	64,523
(H) Nov. 20	Atlanta	6–12	L	48,108
(A) Nov. 28	Seattle	27–35	L	64,627
(H) Dec. 4	Denver	21–20	W	69,291
(A) Dec. 11	Buffalo	21–37	L	80,217
(H) Dec. 18	Seattle	37–43	L	66,540

1989

Date	Opponent	Score	Win/Loss	Attendance
(H) Sept. 10	San Diego	40–14	W	43,086
(A) Sept. 17	Kansas City	19–24	L	77,649
(A) Sept. 24	Denver	21–31	L	76,055
(H) Oct. 1	Seattle	20–24	L	48,002
(A) Oct. 9	New York Jets	14–7	W	76,891
(H) Oct. 15	Kansas City	20–14	W	44,131
(H) Oct. 22	Philadelphia	7–10	L	66,883
(H) Oct. 29	Washington	37–24	W	56,763
(H) Nov. 5	Cincinnati	28–7	W	54,241
(A) Nov. 12	San Diego	12–14	L	62,257
(A) Nov. 19	Houston	7–23	L	61,824
(H) Nov. 26	New England	24–21	W	41,349
(H) Dec. 3	Denver	16–13 (OT)	W	90,016
(H) Dec. 10	Phoenix	16–14	W	46,053
(A) Dec. 17	Seattle	17–23	L	64,632
(A) Dec. 24	N.Y. Giants	17–34	L	77,073

1990

Date	Opponent	Score	Win/Loss	Attendance
(H) Sept. 9	Denver	14–9	W	55,684
(A) Sept. 16	Seattle	17–13	W	64,531
(H) Sept. 23	Pittsburgh	20–3	W	51,063
(H) Sept. 30	Chicago	24–10	W	81,237
(A) Oct. 7	Buffalo	24–38	L	80,332
(H) Oct. 14	Seattle	24–17	W	51,101
(A) Oct. 21	San Diego	24–9	W	62,565
(A) Nov. 4	Kansas City	7–9	L	77,937
(H) Nov. 11	Green Bay	16–29	L	52,638
(A) Nov. 19	Miami	13–10	W	72,393
(H) Nov. 25	Kansas City	24–27	L	65,303
(A) Dec. 2	Denver	23–20	W	76,109
(A) Dec. 10	Detroit	38–31	W	80,066
(H) Dec. 16	Cincinnati	24–7	W	55,110
(A) Dec. 22	Minnesota	28–24	W	63,314
(H) Dec. 30	San Diego	17–12	W	64,445

Postseason

Date	Opponent	Score	Win/Loss	Attendance
(H) Jan. 13	Cincinnati (AFC Playoff)	20–10	W	92,488
(A) Jan. 20	Buffalo (AFC Championship)	3–51	L	80,632

1991

Date	Opponent	Score	Win/Loss	Attendance
(A) Sept. 1	Houston	17–47	L	62,425
(H) Sept. 8	Denver	16–13	W	50,812
(H) Sept. 15	Indianapolis	16–0	W	42,008
(A) Sept. 22	Atlanta	17–21	L	59,241
(H) Sept. 29	San Francisco	12–6	W	92,488
(H) Oct. 6	San Diego	13–21	L	46,029
(A) Oct. 13	Seattle	23–20 (OT)	W	64,605
(H) Oct. 20	L.A. Rams	20–17	W	86,203
(A) Oct. 28	Kansas City	21–24	L	77,870
(A) Nov. 10	Denver	17–16	W	76,087
(H) Nov. 17	Seattle	31–7	W	50,302
(A) Nov. 24	Cincinnati	38–14	W	60,046
(A) Dec. 1	San Diego	9–7	W	61,610
(H) Dec. 8	Buffalo	27–30 (OT)	L	86,746
(A) Dec. 16	New Orleans	0–27	L	68,625
(H) Dec. 22	Kansas City	21–27	L	67,012

Postseason

Date	Opponent	Score	Win/Loss	Attendance
(A) Dec. 28	Kansas City (AFC Wild Card Playoff)	6–10	L	77,191

1992

Date	Opponent	Score	Win/Loss	Attendance
(A) Sept. 6	Denver	13–17	L	75,758
(A) Sept. 13	Cincinnati	21–24	L	58,445
(H) Sept. 20	Cleveland	16–28	L	48,537
(A) Sept. 28	Kansas City	7–28	L	77,622
(H) Oct. 4	N.Y. Giants	13–10	W	43,103
(H) Oct. 11	Buffalo	20–3	W	53,017
(A) Oct. 18	Seattle	19–0	W	65,896
(H) Oct. 25	Dallas	13–28	L	92,488
(A) Nov. 8	Philadelphia	10–31	L	66,726
(H) Nov. 15	Seattle	20–3	W	58,564
(H) Nov. 22	Denver	24–0	W	50,129
(A) Nov. 29	San Diego	3–27	L	62,350
(H) Dec. 6	Kansas City	28–7	W	45,227
(A) Dec. 14	Miami	7–20	L	72,220
(H) Dec. 20	San Diego	14–36	L	40,430
(A) Dec. 26	Washington	21–20	W	56,454

1993

Date	Opponent	Score	Win/Loss	Attendance
(H) Sept. 5	Minnesota	24–7	W	45,136
(A) Sept. 12	Seattle	17–13	W	65,639
(H) Sept. 19	Cleveland	16–19	L	49,101
(A) Oct. 3	Kansas City	9–24	L	78,263
(H) Oct. 10	New York Jets	24–20	W	42,156
(A) Oct. 18	Denver	23–20	W	75,937
(H) Oct. 31	San Diego	23–30	L	46,090
(A) Nov. 7	Chicago	16–14	W	66,950
(H) Nov. 14	Kansas City	20–31	L	67,800
(A) Nov. 21	San Diego	12–7	W	63,059
(A) Nov. 28	Cincinnati	10–16	L	59,305
(A) Dec. 5	Buffalo	25–24	W	79,680
(H) Dec. 12	Seattle	27–23	W	38,540
(H) Dec. 19	Tampa Bay	27–20	W	42,453
(A) Dec. 26	Green Bay	0–28	L	59,507
(H) Jan. 2	Denver	33–30 (OT)	W	67,800

Postseason

Date	Opponent	Score	Win/Loss	Attendance
(H) Jan. 9	Denver (AFC Wild Card Playoff)	42–24	W	67,800
(A) Jan. 15	Buffalo (AFC Playoff)	23–29	L	80,290

1994

Date	Opponent	Score	Win/Loss	Attendance
(A) Sept. 5	San Francisco	14–44	L	69,357
(H) Sept. 11	Seattle	9–38	L	48,040
(A) Sept. 18	Denver	48–16	W	75,959
(H) Sept. 25	San Diego	24–26	L	56,037

Date	Opponent	Score	Win/Loss	Attendance
(A) Oct. 9	New England	21–17	W	60,992
(A) Oct. 16	Miami	17–20 (OT)	L	74,207
(H) Oct. 23	Atlanta	30–17	W	43,190
(H) Oct. 30	Houston	17–14	W	43,221
(A) Nov. 6	Kansas City	3–13	L	79,450
(A) Nov. 13	L.A. Rams	20–17	W	68,899
(H) Nov. 20	New Orleans	24–19	W	43,080
(H) Nov. 27	Pittsburgh	3–21	L	60,399
(A) Dec. 5	San Diego	24–17	W	63,604
(H) Dec. 11	Denver	23–13	W	60,146
(A) Dec. 18	Seattle	17–16	W	65,991
(H) Dec. 24	Kansas City	9–19	L	67,642

1995

Date	Opponent	Score	Win/Loss	Attendance
(H) Sept. 3	San Diego	17–7	W	50,323
(A) Sept. 10	Washington	20–8	W	56,454
(A) Sept. 17	Kansas City	17–23 (OT)	L	79,359
(H) Sept. 24	Philadelphia	48–17	W	50,101
(A) Oct. 1	New York Jets	47–10	W	77,716
(H) Oct. 8	Seattle	34–14	W	50,732
(A) Oct. 16	Denver	0–27	L	75,964
(H) Oct. 22	Indianapolis	30–17	W	54,444
(A) Nov. 5	Cincinnati	20–17	W	59,864
(A) Nov. 12	N.Y. Giants	17–13	W	78,005
(H) Nov. 19	Dallas	21–34	L	54,444
(A) Nov. 27	San Diego	6–12	L	63,177
(H) Dec. 3	Kansas City	23–29	L	54,444
(H) Dec. 10	Pittsburgh	10–29	L	54,444
(A) Dec. 17	Seattle	10–44	L	66,127
(H) Dec. 24	Denver	28–31	L	54,444

1996

Date	Opponent	Score	Win/Loss	Attendance
(A) Sept. 1	Baltimore	14–19	L	64,496
(A) Sept. 8	Kansas City	3–19	L	79,523
(H) Sept. 15	Jacksonville	17–3	W	46,433
(H) Sept. 22	San Diego	34–40	L	49,249
(A) Sept. 29	Chicago	17–19	L	66,944
(A) Oct. 6	New York Jets	34–13	W	77,716
(H) Oct. 13	Detroit	37–21	W	50,125
(H) Oct. 21	San Diego	23–14	W	62,583
(H) Nov. 4	Denver	21–22	L	61,656
(A) Nov. 10	Tampa Bay	17–20 (OT)	L	46,300
(H) Nov. 17	Minnesota	13–16 (OT)	L	47,175
(A) Nov. 24	Seattle	27–21	W	55,057
(H) Dec. 1	Miami	17–7	W	61,436
(H) Dec. 9	Kansas City	26–7	W	61,587
(A) Dec. 15	Denver	19–24	L	75,896
(H) Dec. 22	Seattle	21–28	L	47,357

1997

Date	Opponent	Score	Win/Loss	Attendance
(A) Aug. 31	Tennessee	21–24 (OT)	L	30,171
(H) Sept. 8	Kansas City	27–28	L	61,523
(A) Sept. 14	Atlanta	36–31	W	47,922
(A) Sept. 21	New York Jets	22–23	L	77,716
(H) Sept. 28	St. Louis	35–17	W	42,506
(H) Oct. 5	San Diego	10–25	L	43,648
(H) Oct. 19	Denver	28–25	W	57,006
(A) Oct. 26	Seattle	34–45	L	66,624
(A) Nov. 2	Carolina	14–38	L	71,064
(H) Nov. 9	New Orleans	10–13	L	40,091
(A) Nov. 16	San Diego	38–13	W	65,714
(A) Nov. 24	Denver	3–31	L	75,953
(H) Nov. 30	Miami	16–34	L	50,569
(A) Dec. 7	Kansas City	0–30	L	79,818
(H) Dec. 14	Seattle	21–22	L	40,124
(H) Dec. 21	Jacksonville	9–20	L	40,032

1998

Date	Opponent	Score	Win/Loss	Attendance
(A) Sept. 6	Kansas City	8–28	L	79,765
(H) Sept. 13	N.Y. Giants	20–17	W	40,545
(H) Sept. 20	Denver	17–34	L	56,578
(A) Sept. 27	Dallas	13–12	W	63,544
(A) Oct. 4	Arizona	23–20	W	53,240
(H) Oct. 11	San Diego	7–6	W	42,467
(H) Oct. 25	Cincinnati	27–10	W	40,089
(A) Nov. 1	Seattle	31–18	W	66,246
(A) Nov. 8	Baltimore	10–13	L	69,037
(H) Nov. 15	Seattle	20–17	W	51,527
(A) Nov. 22	Denver	14–40	L	75,931
(H) Nov. 29	Washington	19–29	L	41,409
(H) Dec. 6	Miami	17–27	L	61,254
(A) Dec. 13	Buffalo	21–44	L	62,002
(A) Dec. 20	San Diego	17–10	W	60,716
(H) Dec. 26	Kansas City	24–31	L	52,679

1999

Date	Opponent	Score	Win/Loss	Attendance
(A) Sept. 12	Green Bay	24–28	L	59,872
(A) Sept. 19	Minnesota	22–17	W	64,080
(H) Sept. 26	Chicago	24–17	W	50,458
(A) Oct. 3	Seattle	20–21	L	66,400
(H) Oct. 10	Denver	13–16	L	55,704
(A) Oct. 17	Buffalo	20–14	W	71,113
(H) Oct. 24	New York Jets	24–23	W	47,326
(H) Oct. 31	Miami	9–16	L	61,556
(H) Nov. 14	San Diego	28–9	W	43,353
(A) Nov. 22	Denver	21–27 (OT)	L	75,870
(H) Nov. 28	Kansas City	34–37	L	48,632
(H) Dec. 5	Seattle	30–21	W	44,716

ate	Opponent	Score	Win/Loss	Attendance
) Dec. 9	Tennessee	14–21	L	66,357
) Dec. 19	Tampa Bay	45–0	W	46,395
) Dec. 26	San Diego	20–23	L	63,846
) Jan. 2	Kansas City	41–38		
		(OT)	W	79,026

000

ate	Opponent	Score	Win/Loss	Attendance
) Sept. 3	San Diego	9–6	W	56,373
) Sept. 10	Indianapolis	38–31	W	56,769
) Sept. 17	Denver	24–33	L	62,078
) Sept. 24	Cleveland	36–10	W	45,702
) Oct. 8	San Francisco	34–28		
		(OT)	W	68,344
) Oct. 15	Kansas City	20–17	W	79,025
) Oct. 22	Seattle	31–3	W	57,490
) Oct. 29	San Diego	15–13	W	66,659
) Nov. 5	Kansas City	49–31	W	62,428
) Nov. 13	Denver	24–27	L	75,951
) Nov. 19	New Orleans	31–22	W	64,900
) Nov. 26	Atlanta	41–14	W	55,175
) Dec. 3	Pittsburgh	20–21	L	55,811
) Dec. 10	New York Jets	31–7	W	62,632
) Dec. 16	Seattle	24–27	L	68,681
) Dec. 24	Carolina	52–9	W	60,637

Postseason

ate	Opponent	Score	Win/Loss	Attendance
) Jan. 6	Miami	27–0	W	61,998
	(AFC Divisional Playoff)			
) Jan. 14	Baltimore	3–16	L	62,748
	(AFC Championship)			

001

ate	Opponent	Score	Win/Loss	Attendance
) Sept. 9	Kansas City	27–24	W	78,844
) Sept. 23	Miami	15–18	L	73,404
) Sept. 30	Seattle	38–14	W	54,629
) Oct. 7	Dallas	28–21	W	61,535
) Oct. 14	Indianapolis	23–18	W	56,972
) Oct. 28	Philadelphia	20–10	W	65,342
) Nov. 5	Denver	38–28	W	62,637
) Nov. 11	Seattle	27–34	L	67,231
) Nov. 18	San Diego	34–24	W	61,960
) Nov. 25	N.Y. Giants	28–10	W	78,756
) Dec. 2	Arizona	31–34		
		(OT)	L	46,601
) Dec. 9	Kansas City	28–26	W	60,784
) Dec. 15	San Diego	13–6	W	67,349
) Dec. 22	Tennessee	10–13	L	61,934
) Dec. 30	Denver	17–23	L	75,582
) Jan. 6	New York Jets	22–24	L	62,011

Postseason

Date	Opponent	Score	Win/Loss	Attendance
(H) Jan. 12	New York Jets	38–24	W	61,503
	(AFC Wild Card Playoff)			
(A) Jan. 19	New England	13–16		
		(OT)	L	60,292
	(AFC Divisional Playoff)			

2002

Date	Opponent	Score	Win/Loss	Attendance
(H) Sept. 8	Seattle	31–17	W	53,260
(A) Sept. 15	Pittsburgh	30–17	W	62,260
(H) Sept. 29	Tennessee	52–25	W	58,719
(A) Oct. 6	Buffalo	49–31	W	73,038
(A) Oct. 13	St. Louis	13–28	L	66,070
(H) Oct. 20	San Diego	21–27		
		(OT)	L	60,974
(A) Oct. 27	Kansas City	10–20	L	78,685
(H) Nov. 3	San Francisco	20–23		
		(OT)	L	62,660
(A) Nov. 11	Denver	34–10	W	76,643
(H) Nov. 17	New England	27–20	W	62,552
(A) Nov. 24	Arizona	41–20	W	58,814
(H) Dec. 2	New York Jets	26–20	W	62,257
(A) Dec. 8	San Diego	27–7	W	67,968
(A) Dec. 15	Miami	17–23	L	73,572
(H) Dec. 22	Denver	28–16	W	62,592
(H) Dec. 28	Kansas City	24–0	W	62,078

Postseason

Date	Opponent	Score	Win/Loss	Attendance
(H) Jan. 12	New York Jets	30–10	W	62,207
	(AFC Playoff)			
(H) Jan. 19	Tennessee	41–24	W	62,544
	(AFC Championship)			
(A) Jan. 26	San Diego	21–48	L	67,603
Tampa Bay	(SB XXXVII)			

2003

Date	Opponent	Score	Win/Loss	Attendance
(A) Sept. 7	Tennessee	20–25	L	68,809
(H) Sept. 14	Cincinnati	23–20	W	50,135
(A) Sept. 22	Denver	10–31	L	76,753
(H) Sept. 28	San Diego	34–31	W	54,078
(A) Oct. 5	Chicago	21–34	L	61,099
(A) Oct. 12	Cleveland	7–13	L	73,318
(H) Oct. 20	Kansas City	10–17	L	62,391
(A) Nov. 2	Detroit	13–23	L	61,561
(H) Nov. 9	New York Jets	24–27		
		(OT)	L	51,909
(H) Nov. 16	Minnesota	28–18	W	56,653
(A) Nov. 23	Kansas City	24–27	L	78,889
(H) Nov. 30	Denver	8–22	L	57,201

Date	Opponent	Score	Win/Loss	Attendance
(A) Dec. 7	Pittsburgh	7–27	L	53,079
(H) Dec. 14	Baltimore	20–12	W	45,398
(H) Dec. 22	Green Bay	7–41	L	62,298
(A) Dec. 28	San Diego	14–21	L	62,222

2004

Date	Opponent	Score	Win/Loss	Attendance
(A) Sept. 12	Pittsburgh	21–24	L	60,147
(H) Sept. 19	Buffalo	13–10	W	53,610
(H) Sept. 26	Tampa Bay	30–20	W	60,874
(A) Oct. 3	Houston	17–30	L	70,741
(A) Oct. 10	Indianapolis	14–35	L	57,230
(H) Oct. 17	Denver	3–31	L	62,507
(H) Oct. 24	New Orleans	26–31	L	45,337
(A) Oct. 31	San Diego	14–42	L	66,210
(A) Nov. 7	Carolina	27–24	W	73,518
(H) Nov. 21	San Diego	17–23	L	46,905
(A) Nov. 28	Denver	25–24	W	75,936
(H) Dec. 5	Kansas City	27–34	L	51,292
(A) Dec. 12	Atlanta	10–35	L	70,616
(H) Dec. 19	Tennessee	40–35	W	44,299
(A) Dec. 25	Kansas City	30–31	L	77,289
(H) Jan. 2	Jacksonville	6–13	L	41,112

2005

Date	Opponent	Score	Win/Loss	Attendance
(A) Sept. 8	New England	20–30	L	68,756
(H) Sept. 18	Kansas City	17–23	L	62,273
(A) Sept. 25	Philadelphia	20–23	L	67,735
(H) Oct. 2	Dallas	19–13	W	62,400
(H) Oct. 16	San Diego	14–27	L	52,666
(H) Oct. 23	Buffalo	38–17	W	42,779
(A) Oct. 30	Tennessee	34–25	W	69,149
(A) Nov. 6	Kansas City	23–27	L	79,033
(H) Nov. 13	Denver	17–31	L	62,779
(H) Nov. 20	Washington	16–13	W	90,129
(H) Nov. 27	Miami	21–33	L	49,097
(A) Dec. 4	San Diego	10–34	L	66,436
(A) Dec. 11	New York Jets	10–26	L	77,561
(H) Dec. 18	Cleveland	7–9	L	41,862
(A) Dec. 24	Denver	3–22	L	76,212
(H) Dec. 31	N.Y. Giants	21–30	L	44,594

2006

Date	Opponent	Score	Win/Loss	Attendance
(H) Sept. 11	San Diego	0–27	L	62,578
(A) Sept. 17	Baltimore	6–28	L	70,744
(H) Oct. 1	Cleveland	21–24	L	61,426
(A) Oct. 8	San Francisco	20–34	L	68,368
(A) Oct. 15	Denver	3–13	L	76,691
(H) Oct. 22	Arizona	22–9	W	61,595

Date	Opponent	Score	Win/Loss	Attendance
(H) Oct. 29	Pittsburgh	20–13	W	62,385
(A) Nov. 6	Seattle	0–16	L	67,816
(H) Nov. 12	Denver	13–17	L	62,094
(A) Nov. 19	Kansas City	13–17	L	78,097
(A) Nov. 26	San Diego	14–21	L	66,105
(H) Dec. 3	Houston	14–23	L	46,276
(A) Dec. 10	Cincinnati	10–27	L	65,882
(H) Dec. 17	St. Louis	0–20	L	50,164
(H) Dec. 23	Kansas City	9–20	L	61,446
(A) Dec. 31	New York Jets	3–23	L	78,039

2007

Date	Opponent	Score	Win/Loss	Attendance
(H) Sept. 9	Detroit	21–36	L	61,547
(A) Sept. 16	Denver	20–23 (OT)	L	76,784
(H) Sept. 23	Cleveland	26–24	W	51,075
(A) Sept. 30	Miami	35–17	W	70,621
(A) Oct. 14	San Diego	14–28	L	67,523
(H) Oct. 21	Kansas City	10–12	L	62,240
(A) Oct. 28	Tennessee	9–13	L	69,143
(H) Nov. 4	Houston	17–24	L	49,603
(H) Nov. 11	Chicago	6–17	L	62,715
(A) Nov. 18	Minnesota	22–29	L	62,960
(A) Nov. 25	Kansas City	20–17	W	76,210
(H) Dec. 2	Denver	34–20	W	61,990
(A) Dec. 9	Green Bay	7–38	L	70,828
(H) Dec. 16	Indianapolis	14–21	L	62,000
(A) Dec. 23	Jacksonville	11–49	L	66,905
(H) Dec. 30	San Diego	17–30	L	61,906

2008

Date	Opponent	Score	Win/Loss	Attendance
(H) Sept. 8	Denver	14–41	L	62,762
(A) Sept. 14	Kansas City	23–8	W	74,480
(A) Sept. 21	Buffalo	23–24	L	71,297
(H) Sept. 28	San Diego	18–28	L	61,808
(A) Oct. 12	New Orleans	3–34	L	70,068
(H) Oct. 19	New York Jets	16–13 (OT)	W	61,901
(A) Oct. 26	Baltimore	10–29	L	71,254
(H) Nov. 2	Atlanta	0–24	L	61,196
(H) Nov. 9	Carolina	6–17	L	47,888
(A) Nov. 16	Miami	15–17	L	65,113
(A) Nov. 23	Denver	31–10	W	76,067
(H) Nov. 30	Kansas City	13–20	L	61,379
(A) Dec. 4	San Diego	7–34	L	68,097
(H) Dec. 14	New England	26–49	L	62,179
(H) Dec. 21	Houston	27–16	W	43,687
(A) Dec. 28	Tampa Bay	31–24	W	64,847

2009

Date	Opponent	Score	Win/Loss	Attendance
(H) Sep. 14	San Diego	20–24	L	61,940
(A) Sep. 20	Kansas City	13–10	W	69,169
(H) Sep. 27	Denver	3–23	L	45,602
(A) Oct. 4	Houston	6–29	L	70,291
(A) Oct. 11	NY Giants	7–44	L	79,012
(H) Oct. 18	Philadelphia	13–9	W	49,642
(H) Oct. 25	NY Jets	0–38	L	39,354

Date	Opponent	Score	Win/Loss	Attendance
(A) Nov. 1	San Diego	16–24	L	67,016
(H) Nov. 15	Kansas City	10–16	L	40,720
(H) Nov. 22	Cincinnati	20–17	W	34,112
(A) Nov. 25	Dallas	7–24	L	83,489
(A) Dec. 6	Pittsburgh	27–24	W	61,820
(H) Dec. 13	Washington	13–34	L	44,506
(A) Dec. 20	Denver	20–19	W	74,502
(A) Dec. 27	Cleveland	9–23	L	67,964
(H) Jan. 3	Baltimore	13–21	L	38,400

ALL-TIME DRAFT PICKS*

1960

(First Selections — Expansion Draft)

Jim Andreotti, C, Northwestern
Maxie Baughan, C, Georgia Tech
George Blanch, HB, Texas
Cloyd Boyette, T-G, Texas
Willie Boykin, T, Michigan
Carmen Cavalli, E, Richmond
Jim Chastain, T-G, Michigan State
Fran Cursi, QB, Miami
Carroll Dale, E. Virginia Tech
Purcell Daniels, FB, Pepperdine
Don Deskin, T, Michigan
Leon Dumbrowski, T-G, Delaware
Ken Fitch, T, Kansas
Dale Hackbart, QB, Wisconsin
Abner Haynes, HB, No. Texas St.
Vin Hogan, HB, Boston College
Bob Jarus, HB, Purdue
Earl Kohlhaas, G, Penn State
Bobby Lackey, QB, Texas
Neil MacLean, FB, Wake Forest
Larry Muff, E, Benedictine
Don Norton, E, Iowa
Jim O'Brien, T, Boston College
Jim Otto, C, Miami
Chuck Pollard, E, Rice
Billy Roland, G, Georgia
Ray Smith, FB, UCLA
Wade Smith, HB, North Carolina
Jerry Stalcup, G, Wisconsin
John Wilcox, T, Oregon
Al Witcher, E, Baylor
Silas Woods, HB, Marquette
Mike Wright, T, Minnesota

Second Selections

C.J. Alexander, HB, Southeastern
Pervis Atkins, HB, New Mexico St.
Al Bansavage, T-G, USC
Walter Beach, HB, Central Michigan
Johnny Brewer, E, Mississippi
Don Edington, E, Florida
Howard Evans, C, Houston
Fred Hageman, C, Kansas
Bill Herron, E, Georgia
Bob Hogue, T-G, Shepherd
Gerald Lambert, T-G, Texas A&I
Sam McCord, QB, East Texas St.
Rich Mostardo, HB, Kent State
Bob Parker, T-G, East Texas St.
Tony Polychronis, T-G, Utah
Dan Sheehan, T-G, Tenn.–Chattanooga
Howard Turley, E, Louisville
Jim Williams, T-G, North Carolina
Jim Woodward, T-G, Lamar

1961

1. Jim Rutgens, T, Illinois
2. George Fleming, HB, Washington
3. Myron Pottios, G, Notre Dame
4. Elbert Kimbrough, E, Northwestern
5. Dick Norman, QB, Stanford
6. Bobby Crespino, HB, Mississippi
7. Ray Purdin, HB, Northwestern
8. Tom Watkins, HB, Iowa State
9. Lowndes Shingler, QB, Clemson
10. Ken Peterson, T, Utah
11. Dave Mayberry, FB, Utah State
12. Bob Schmitz, G, Montana State
13. Gerald Burch, E, Georgia Tech
14. Clark Miller, T, Utah State
15. Bob Coolbaugh, E, Richmond
16. Chuck Lamson, HB, Wyoming
17. Joe Novsek, T, Tulsa
18. Joe Krakoski, HB, Illinois
19. Charles Fuller, HB, San Francisco St.
20. Preston Fuller, FB, Grambling
21. Mike Jones, QB, San Jose State

22. Blayne Jones, G, Idaho State
23. Roger Fisher, C, Utah State
24. Jack Novak, G, Miami
25. Paul Yanke, E, Northwestern
26. Dean Hinshaw, T, Stanford
27. Clair Appledoom, E, San Jose St.
28. Dave Grosz, QB, Oregon
29. Ed Morris, T, Indiani
30. Bill Face, HB, Stanford

1962

1. Roman Gabriel, QB, No. Carolina St.
3. Ed Pine, C, Utah
4. John Myers, T, Washington
5. Joe Hernandez, HB, Arizona
6. Dan Birdwell, C, Houston
7. Jim Norris, T, Houston
8. Ferrell Yarbrough, E. Northwestern
9. Jim Dillard, HB, Oklahoma State
10. Henry Rivera, HB, Oregon State
12. Jim Skaggs, G, Washington
12. Oscar Donahue, E, San Jose State
13. George Pierovich, FB, California
15. Floyd Dean, E, Florida
16. Pat Russ, T, Purdue
17. Larry Ferguson, HB, Iowa
18. Jim Vollenweider, FB, Miami
19. Dennis Spurlock, QB, Whitworth
20. John Sutro, G, San Jose State
21. Bill Tunnicliff, FB, Michigan
22. Jim Cadile, E, San Jose State
23. Elvin Basham, G, Kansas
24. Mickey Bruce, G, Oregon
25. Tom Cagaanan, HB, Utah State
26. Fred Miller, T, LSU
27. Keith Luhnow, FB, Santa Ana J.C.
28. Marv Marinovich, T, USC
29. Leon Donohue, E, San Jose State
30. Pete Nicklas, T, Baylor
31. Bob Elliot, FB, North Carolina
32. Eugene White, HB, Florida A&M
33. Bill Worrell, T, Georgia

*All information in this section was taken from the Oakland Raiders 2009 Media Guide and www.raiders.com.

1963

6. Butch Wilson, HB, Alabama
7. Dave Costa, T, Utah
8. Roger Locke, E, Arizona State
9. Jerry Logan, HB, West Texas State
10. Ray Schoenke, G, SMU
12. Walt Burdin, LB, McNeese State
12. Doyle Branson, HB, So. Oregon
13. Darnell Haney, E, Utah State
13. Drew Roberts, E, Humboldt State
15. Vern Burke, E, Oregon
16. Jim Moss, HB, West Virginia
17. John Murio, HB, Whitworth
18. Terry Dillon, HB, Montana
19. Tony Fiorentino, G, UCLA
20. Rex Mirich, T, Arizona State
21. Neal Petties, HB, San Diego State
22. Hugh Campbell, E, Washington State
23. Jon Anabo, QB, Fresno State
24. Dick Peters, T, Whittier
25. Bill McFarland, FB, Oklahoma State
26. Dennis Claridge, QB, Nebraska
27. Dick Skelly, HB, Florida
28. Larry Campbell, FB, Utah State
29. Dick Anderson, E, Penn State

1964

1. Tony Lorick, HB, Arizona
2. Dan Conners, T, Miami
3. George Bednar, T, Notre Dame
4. Bill Budness, LB, Boston University
5. Don Green, DB, Susquehanna
7. John Sapinsky, T, William & Mary
8. Vince Petno, DB, Citadel
9. John Williamson, G, Louisiana Tech
9. Herschel Turner, T, Kentucky
10. Mel Renfro, HB, Oregon
11. Larry Rakestraw, QB, Georgia
12. Billy Lothridge, QB, Georgia Tech
13. Mickey Babb, E, Georgia
14. Fred Polser, G, East Texas State
15. Mike Geirs, T, USC
16. Ron Wilkening, HB, No. Dakota St.
17. Fred Lewis, HB, Massachusetts
18. Ran Calcagno, QB, Santa Clara
19. Tom Michel, FB, East Carolina
20. Ed Beard, T, Tennessee
21. Carleton Oats, E, Florida A&M
22. Jim Long, FB, Fresno State
23. Bill Curry, C, Georgia Tech
24. Kent Francisco, T, UCLA
25. Terry Sieg, HB, Virginia
26. Gordon Guest, QB, Arkansas

1965

1. Harry Schuh, T, Memphis State
2. Fred Biletnikoff, WR, Florida State
3. Bob Svihus, T, USC
4. Gus Otto, LB, Missouri

9. Rich Zecher, T, Utah State
10. Craig Morton, QB, California
11. Bill Minor, LB, Illinois
13. Wally Mahle, DB, Syracuse
14. Loren Hawley, DB, California
15. Bill Cronin, DE, Boston College
16. Fred Hill, E, USC
17. Gary Porterfield, E, Tulsa
18. John Dugan, T, Holy Cross
19. Frank McClendon, T, Alabama
20. Bo Scott, HB, Ohio State

1965 Redshirt

1. Larry Todd, HB, Arizona State
2. Jim Harvey, T, Mississippi
3. Stave Mass, T, Detroit
4. Mickey Cox, T, LSU
5. Bob Taylor, G, Cincinnati
6. Gregg Kent, T, Utah
7. John Carroll, T, Texas
8. Henry Pinkett, HB, Baylor
9. Frank Pennie, T, Florida State
10. Brent Barry, T, San Jose State
11. Tom Longo, DB, Notre Dame
12. Dennis Duncan, HB, Louisiana College

1966

1. Rodger Bird, DB, Kentucky
2. Butch Allison, T, Missouri
3. Tom Mitchell, E, Bucknell
4. Richard Tyson, G, Tulsa
5. Pete Banaszak, HB, Miami
7. Franklin McRae, T, Tennessee St.
9. Clifton Kinney, LB, San Diego State
10. Tony Jeter, E, Nebraska
11. Joe Labruzzo, HB, LSU
12. Wayne Foster, T, Washington State
13. John Niland, G, Iowa
14. Mike Johnson, HB, Kansas
15. Steve Renko, FB, Kansas
16. Craig Ritchey, DB, Stanford
17. Ted Holman, DB, Syracuse
18. Art Robinson, E, Florida A&M
19. Jack Shinholser, LB, Florida State
20. Steve Bowman, FB, Alabama

1966 Redshirt

1. Rod Sherman, HB, USC
2. Tom Cichowski, T, Maryland
3. Ron Parson, E, Austin Peay
4. John Crumbacher, T, Tennessee
5. George Patton, T, Georgia
6. Dan Archer, T, Oregon
7. Bill Thomas, HB, Oklahoma
8. Ray Schmautz, LB, San Diego St.
9. Mel Tom, LB, San Jose State
10. Joe O'Brien, FB, Texas–Arlington

1967

1. Gene Upshaw, G, Texas A&I
3. Bill Fairband, LB, Colorado
4. James Roy Jackson, E, Oklahoma
5. Gerald Wakefield, HB, Mississippi
5. Mike Hibler, LB, Stanford
6. Rick Egloff, QB, Wyoming
7. Ron Lewellen, DT, Tennessee–Martin
8. Estes Banks, RB, Colorado
9. Mark Devilling, LB, Muskingum
10. Richard Sligh, T, No. Carolina Central
11. Dwayne Benson, LB, Hamline
12. Bob Kruse, T, Wayne State
13. Len Kleinpete, E, SW Louisiana
14. Casey Boyett, E, BYU
15. Ben Woodson, HB, Utah
16. Don Bruce, G, Virginia Tech
17. Mike Cullin, DE, Slippery Rock

1968

1. Eldridge Dickey, QB, Tennessee State
2. Ken Stabler, QB, Alabama
3. Art Shell, T, Maryland State
4. Charlie Smith, RB, Utah
5. John Naponic, T, Virginia
7. John Harper, C, Adams State
7. George Atkinson, DB, Morris Brown
9. John Eason, TE, Florida A&M
10. Rick Owens, DB, Pennsylvania
11. Marv Hubbard, FB, Colgate
11. Ralph Oliver, LB, San Diego State
12. Larry Plantz, WR, Colorado
13. Larry Blackstone, RB, Fairmont St.
14. Ray Carlson, LB, Hamline
15. Mike Leinert, RB, Texas Tech
16. David Morrison, DB, SW Texas
17. Steve Berry, E, Catawba

1969

1. Art Thomas, DL, Syracuse
2. George Buehler, OL, Stanford
3. Lloyd Edwards, TE, San Diego St.
4. Ruby Jackson, DL, New Mexico St.
6A. Ken Newfield, RB, LSU
6B. Jackie Allen, DB, Baylor
7. Finnis Taylor, DB, Prairie View
9. Drew Buie, WR, Catawba
11. Harold Rice, LB, Tennessee A&I
12. Al Goddard, DB, J.C. Smith
13. Dave Husted, LB, Wabash
14. Harold Busby, WR, UCLA
15. Alvin Presnell, RB, Alabama A&M
16. Junior Davis, LB, Alabama
17. Billy Austin, G, Arkansas AM&N

1970

1. Raymond Chester, TE, Morgan State
2. Ted Koy, RB, Texas
3. Gerald Irons, LB, Maryland State
4. Tony Cline, LB, Miami
5. Art Laster, T, Maryland State
6. Alvin Wyatt, DB, Bethune-Cookman
7. Steve Svitak, LB, Boise State
8. Mike Wynn, DE, Nebraska
9. Ike Hill, DB, Catawba
10. Gordon Bosserman, T, UCLA
11. Emery Hicks, LB, Kansas
12. Jerry DeLoach, G, U.C. Davis
13. Don Highsmith, RB, Michigan St.
14. John Riley, K, Auburn
15. Fred Moore, DB, Washington
16. Tim Roth, C, South Dakota State
17. Eric Stohlberg, WR, Indiana

1971

1. Jack Tatum, DB, Ohio State
2A. Warren Koegel, C, Penn State
2B. Phil Villapiano, LB, Bowling Green
4. Clarence Davis, RB, USC
5. Bob Moore, TE, Stanford
6. Greg Slough, LB, USC
7. Don Martin, DB, Yale
9. Dave Garnett, RB, Pittsburgh
10A. Bill West, DB, Tennessee State
10B. Tim Oesterling, DT, UCLA
11. James Poston, DT, South Carolina
12. Horace Jones, DE, Louisville
13. Mick Natzel, DB, Central Michigan
14. Tom Gipson, DT, North Texas State
15. Andy Giles, LB, William & Mary
16. Tony Stawarz, DB, Miami
17. Chuck Hill, WR, Sam Houston St.

1972

1. Mike Siani, WR, Villanova
2A. Kelvin Korver, DT, NW Iowa
2B. John Vella, T, USC
3. Mel Lunsford, DE, Central St.
4A. Cliff Branch, WR, Colorado
4B. Dave Dalby, C, UCLA
6. Dan Medlin, DT, North Carolina St.
7A. Skip Thomas, DB, USC
7B. Dennis Pete, DB, San Francisco St.
8. Jackie Brown, RB, Stanford
9. Dave Bigler, RB, Morningside
10. Phil Price, DB, Idaho State
11. Joe Carroll, LB, Pittsburgh
12. Kent Gaydos, TE, Florida State
13. Ted Covington, WR, San Fernando St.
14. Dennis Cambal, RB, William & Mary
15A. Charles Hester, RB, Central State

15B. Dave Snesrud, LB, Hamline
16. Willie Wright, WR, No. Carolina A&T

1973

1. Ray Guy, P, Southern Mississippi
2. Monte Johnson, LB, Nebraska
4A. Perry Smith, DB, Colorado State
4B. Joe Wylie, WR, Oklahoma
5A. Louis Neal, WR, Prairie View
5B. Ron Mikalojczyk, T, Tampa
6. Brent Myers, T, Purdue
7. Gary Weaver, LB, Fresno State
8. Mike Rae, QB, USC
9. Steve Sweeney, WR, California
10. Leo Allen, WR, Tuskegee
11. Jerry List, RB, Nebraska
12. James Krapf, LB, Alabama
14. Bruce Polen, DB, William Penn
15. David Leffers, G, Vanderbilt
16. Jerry Gadlin, WR, Wyoming
17. Mike Ryan, C, USC

1974

1. Henry Lawrence, T, Florida A&M
2. Dave Casper, TE, Notre Dame
3. Mark Van Eeghen, RB, Colgate
4. Morris Bradshaw, WR, Ohio State
5. Pete Wessel, DB, Northwestern
6. James McAlister, RB, UCLA
7. Rod Garcia, K, Stanford
9. Kenith Pope, DB, Oklahoma
10. Chris Arnold, DB, Virginia State
11. Harold Hart, RB, Texas Southern
12. Noe Gonzalez, RB, SW Texas St.
13. Mike Dennery, LB, So. Mississippi
14. Don Willingham, RB, Wisc–Milwaukee
15. Greg Mathis, DB, Idaho State
16. Delario Robinson, WR, Kansas
17. James Morris, DT, Missouri Valley

1975

1. Neal Colzie, DB, Ohio State
2. Charles Phillips, DB, USC
3. Louis Carter, RB, Maryland
5. David Humm, QB, Nebraska
7. James Daniels, DB, Texas A&M
9. Harry Knight, QB, Richmond
10. Steve Sylvester, G, Notre Dame
12. Jack Magee, C, Boston College
14. Tom Doyle, DB, Yale
15. Paul Careathers, RB, Tennessee

1976

2A. Charles Philyaw, DE, Texas Southern
2B. Jeb Blount, QB, Tulsa
3. Ric Bonness, LB, Nebraska
4. Herb McMath, DE, Morningside
5. Fred Steinfort, K, Boston College
7. Clarence Chapman, WR, E. Michigan
8A. Jerome Dove, DB, Colorado State
8B. Terry Kunz, RB, Colorado
10. Dwight Lewis, DB, Purdue
11. Rick Jennings, RB, Maryland
12. Cedric Brown, DB, Kent State
13A. Craig Crnick, DE, Idaho
13B. Mark Young, G, Washington State
14. Calvin Young, RB, Fresno State
15. Carl Hargrave, DB, Upper Iowa
16. Doug Hogan, DB, USC
17A. Buddy Tate, DB, Tulsa
17B. Nate Beasley, RB, Delaware

1977

2A. Mike Davis, DB, Colorado
2B. Ted McKnight, RB, Minnesota–Duluth
4. Mickey Marvin, G, Tennessee
5A. Lester Hayes, DB, Texas A&M
5B. Jeff Barnes, LB, California
7. Rich Martini, WR, Cal–Davis
8. Terry Robiskie, RB, LSU
12A. Rod Martin, LB, USC
12B. Rolf Benirschke, K, Cal–Davis

1978

2. Dave Browning, DE, Washington
3A. Derrick Jensen, RB, Texas–Arlington
3B. Lindsey Mason, T, Kansas
4A. Maurice Harvey, DB, Ball State
4B. Joe Stewart, WR, Missouri
5. Derrick Ramsey, TE, Kentucky
6A. Tom Davis, C, Nebraska
6B. Mike Levenseller, WR, Washington St.
7A. Arthur Whittington, RB, SMU
7B. Earl Inmon, LB, Bethune-Cookman
8. Mark Nickols, LB, Colorado State
11A. Dean Jones, WR, Fresno State
11B. Bob Glazebrook, DB, Fresno State
13. Joe Conron, WR, Pacific

1979

2. Willie Jones, DE, Florida State
6A. Ira Matthews, KR, Wisconsin
6B. Henry Williams, DB, San Diego State

7. Jack Matia, T, Drake
8. Robert Hawkins, RB, Kentucky
9. Jim Rourke, T, Boston College
10. Ricky Smith, DB, Tulane
11. Bruce Davis, T, UCLA
12A. Dirk Abernathy, DB, Bowling Green
12B. Reggie Kinlaw, DT, Oklahoma

1980

1. Marc Wilson, QB, BYU
2. Matt Millen, LB, Penn State
5A. Kenny Lewis, RB, Virginia Tech
5B. John Adams, LB, LSU
5C. William Bowens, LB, North Carolina
7. Malcolm Barnwell, WR, Virginia Union
8. Kenny Hill, DB, Yale
10. Walter Carter, DT, Florida State
11. Mike Massey, LB, Arkansas
12. Calvin Muhammad, WR, Tx. Southern

1981

1A. Ted Watts, CB, Texas Tech
1B. Curt Marsh, T, Washington
2. Howie Long, DT, Villanova
4. Johnny Robinson, DT, Louisiana Tech
5. James Davis, DB, Southern
9. Curt Mohl, T, UCLA
10. Frank Hawkins, RB, Nevada–Reno
11. Chester Willis, RB, Auburn
12. Phil Nelson, TE, Delaware

1982

1. Marcus Allen, RB, USC
2A. Jack Squirek, LB, Illinois
2B. Jim Romano, C, Pittsburgh
3. Vann McElroy, S, Baylor
4. Ed Muransky, T, Michigan
5. Ed Jackson, LB, Louisiana Tech
7. Jeff Jackson, DE, Toledo
10. Rich D'Amico, LB, Penn State
11. Willie Turner, WR, LSU
12. Randy Smith, WR, East Texas State

1983

1. Don Mosebar, T, USC
2. Bill Pickel, DT, Rutgers
3. Tony Caldwell, LB, Washington
4. Greg Townsend, DE, TCU
5. Dokie Williams, WR, UCLA
7. Jeff McCall, RB, Clemson

8. Mike Dotterer, RB, Stanford
9. Kent Jordan, TE, St. Mary's
10. Mervyn Fernandez, WR, San Jose St.
11. Scott Lindquist, QB, No. Arizona

1984

2. Sean Jones, DT, Northwestern
3. Joe McCall, RB, Pittsburgh
5. Andy Parker, TE, Utah
6. Stacey Toran, S, Notre Dame
7. Mitch Willis, DE, SMU
8. Sam Seale, WR, Western State
11. Gardner Williams, CB, St. Mary's
12. Randy Essington, QB, Colorado

1985

1. Jessie Hester, WR, Florida State
3A. Tim Moffett, WR, Mississippi
3B. Stefon Adams, DB, East Carolina
4. Jamie Kimmel, LB, Syracuse
5. Dan Reeder, RB, Delaware
6. Rusty Hilger, QB, Oklahoma State
7A. Kevin Belcher, T, Wisconsin
7B. Mark Pattison, WR, Washington
7C. Bret Clark, DB, Nebraska
7D. Nick Haden, C, Penn State
8. Leonard Wingate, DT, So. Carolina State
9. Chris Sydnor, DB, Penn State
10A. Reggie McKenzie, LB, Tennessee
10B. Albert Myres, DB, Tulsa

1986

1. Bob Buczkowski, DE, Pittsburgh
3. Brad Cochran, CB, Michigan
4A. Mike Wise, DE, U.C. Davis
4B. Vance Mueller, RB, Occidental
4C. Napoleon McCallum, RB, Navy
6. Doug Marrone, T, Syracuse
7. Bill Lewis, C, Nebraska
8. Joe Mauntel, LB, Eastern Kentucky
9. Zeph Lee, RB, USC
10. Jeff Reinke, DE, Mankato State
11. Randall Webster, LB, SW Oklahoma St.
12. Larry Shepherd, WR, Houston

1987

1. John Clay, T, Missouri
2. Bruce Wilkerson, T, Tennessee
3. Steve Smith, RB, Penn State
4. Steve Beuerlein, QB, Notre Dame

7. Bo Jackson, RB, Auburn
9. Scott Eccles, TE, E. New Mexico
10A. Rob Harrison, RB, Sacramento St.
10B. John Gesek, G, Sacramento St.
10C. Jim Ellis, LB, Boise State
11A. Chris McLemore, RB, Arizona
11B. Mario Perry, TE, Mississippi

1988

1A. Tim Brown
1B. Terry McDaniel, CB, Tennessee
1C. Scott Davis, DE, Illinois
4. Tim Rother, DT, Nebraska
5. Dennis Price, CB, UCLA
6. Erwin Grabisna, LB, Case W. Reserve
7. Derrick Crudup, DB, Oklahoma
8. Mike Alexander, WR, Penn State
9A. Reggie Ware, RB, Auburn
9B. Scott Tabor, P, California
10. Newt Harrell, G, West Texas State
11. David Weber, QB, Carroll College
12. Greg Kunkel, G, Kentucky

1989

2. Steve Wisnieski, G, Penn State
6A. Jeff Francis, QB, Tennessee
6B. Doug Lloyd, RB, North Dakota St.
8. Derrick Gainer, RB, Florida A&M
9. Gary Gooden, WR, Indiana
10. Charles Jackson, DT, Jackson St.

1990

1. Anthony Smith, DE, Arizona
2. Aaron Wallace, LB, Texas A&M
4. Torin Dorn, CB, North Carolina
6. Marcus Wilson, RB, Virginia
7. Garry Lewis, CB, Alcorn State
8. A.J. Jimerson, LB, Norfolk State
9. Leon Perry, RB, Oklahoma
11A. Ron Lewis, WR, Jackson State
11B. Myron Jones, RB, Fresno State
12A. Major Harris, QB, West Virginia
12B. Demetruis Davis, TE, Nevada–Reno

1991

1. Todd Marinovich, QB, USC
2. Nick Bell, RB, Iowa
4. Raghib Ismail, WR, Notre Dame
6. Nolan Harrison, DT, Indiana
8A. Brian Jones, LB, Texas
8B. Todd Woulard, LB, Alabama A&M
9. Tahaun Lewis, CB, Nebraska

1. Andrew Glover, TE, Grambling
2. Dennis Johnson, CB, Winston-Salem

1992

1. Chester McGlockton, DT, Clemson
2. Greg Skrepenak, T, Michigan
3. Derrick Hoskins, S, So. Mississippi
4. Tony Rowell, C, Florida
7A. Curtis Cotton, S, Nebraska
7B. Kevin Smith, RB, UCLA
8. Alberto White, LB, Texas Southern
9. Tom Roth, G, Southern Illinois

1993

1. Patrick Bates, S, Texas A&M
3A. Billy Joe Hobert, QB, Washington
3B. James Trapp, CB, Clemson
5. Olanda Truitt, WR, Mississippi
7. Greg Biekert, LB, Colorado
8. Greg Robinson, RB, NE Louisiana

1994

1. Rob Fredrickson, LB, Michigan St.
2. James Folston, DE, NE Louisiana
3. Calvin Jones, RB, Nebraska
4. Austin Robbins, DT, North Carolina
5. Roosevelt Patterson, G, Alabama
7. Rob Holmberg, LB, Penn State

1995

1. Napolean Kaufman, RB, Washington
2. Barret Robbins, C, TCU
3. Joe Aska, RB, Central State
4. Mike Morton, LB, North Carolina
5A. Matt Dyson, LB, Michigan
5B. Jeff Kysar, T, Arizona State
6. Eli Herring, T, Brigham Young

1996

1. Rickey Dudley, TE, Ohio State
2. Lance Johnstone, DE, Temple
5. La'Roi Glover, DT, San Diego State
6. Tim Hall, RB, Robert Morris
7A. Sedric Clark, LB, Tulsa
7B. Darius Smith, C, Sam Houston St.
7C. Joey Wylie, G, Stephen F. Austin

1997

1. Darrell Russell, DT, USC
3A. Adam Treu, G, Nebraska
3B. Tim Kohn, G, Iowa State
4. Chad Levitt, RB, Cornell
6A. Calvin Branch, CB, Colorado St.
6B. Grady Jackson, DT, Knoxville

1998

1A. Charles Woodson, CB, Michigan
1B. Mo Collins, T, Florida
2. Leon Bender, DT, Washington St.
3. Jon Ritchie, RB, Stanford
4. Gennaro DiNapoli, G, Virginia Tech
5A. Jeremy Brigham, TE, Washington
5B. Travian Smith, LB, Oklahoma
7A. Vince Amey, DE, Arizona State
7B. David Sanders, DE, Arkansas

1999

1. Matt Stinchcomb, T, Georgia
2. Tony Bryant, DE, Florida State
4. Dameane Doughlas, WR, California
5A. Eric Barton, LB, Maryland
5B. Rod Coleman, LB, East Carolina
6. Daren Yancey, DT, BYU
7. JoJuan Armour, LB, Miami (Ohio)

2000

1. Sebastian Janikowski, K, Florida State
2. Jerry Porter, WR, West Virginia
4. Junior Ioane, DT, Arizona State
5. Shane Lechler, P, Texas A&M
7A. Mondriel Fulcher, TE, Miami
7B. Cliffton Black, S, SW Texas State

2001

1. Derrick Gibson, S, Florida State
2. Marques Tuiasosopo, QB, Washington
3. DeLawrence Grant, DE, Oregon State
5. Raymond Perryman, S, Northern Arizona
6. Chris Cooper, DT, Nebraska–Omaha
7A. Derek Combs, RB, Ohio State
7B. Ken-Yon Rambo, WR, Ohio State

2002

1A. Phillip Buchanon, CB, Miami (Fla.)
1B. Napoleon Harris, LB, Northwestern

2A. Langston Walker, OL, California
2B. Doug Jolley, TE, Brigham Young
5. Kenyon Coleman, DE, UCLA
6A. Keyon Nash, S, Albany State (Ga.)
6B. Larry Ned, RB, San Diego State
7. Ronald Curry, QB, North Carolina

2003

1A. Nnamdi Asomugha, CB, California
1B. **Tyler** Brayton, DE, Colorado
2. Teyo Johnson, TE, Stanford
3A. Sam Williams, DE, Fresno State
3B. Justin Fargas, RB, USC
4. Shurron Pierson, DE, S. Florida
5. Doug Gabriel, WR, Central Florida
6. Dustin Rykert, T, Brigham Young
7A. Siddeeq Shabazz, S, New Mexico State
7B. Ryan Hoag, WR, Gustavus Adolphus

2004

1. Robert Gallery, T, Iowa
2. Jake Grove, C, Virginia Tech
3. Stuart Schweigert, S, Purdue
4. Carlos Francis, WR, Texas Tech
5. Johnnie Morant, WR, Syracuse
6A. Shawn Johnson, DE, Delaware
6B. Cody Spencer, LB, North Texas
7A. Courtney Anderson, TE, San Jose State
7B. Andre Sommersell, LB, Colorado State

2005

1. Fabian Washington, CB, Nebraska
2. Stanford Routt, CB, Houston
3A. Andrew Walter, QB, Arizona State
3B. Kirk Morrison, LB, San Diego State
6A. Anttaj Hawthorne, DT, Wisconsin
6B. Ryan Riddle, LB, California
6C. Pete McMahon, T, Iowa

2006

1. Michael Huff, DB, Texas
2. Thomas Howard, LB, UTEP
3. Paul McQuistan, OL, Weber State
4. Darnell Bing, LB, USC
6. Kevin Boothe, OL, Cornell
7A. Chris Morris, OL, Michigan State
7B. Kevin McMahan, WR, Maine

2007

1. JaMarcus Russell, QB, LSU

2. Zach Miller, TE, Arizona State
3A. Quentin Moses, DE, Georgia
3B. Mario Henderson, T, Florida State
3C. Johnnie Lee Higgins, WR, UTEP
4A. Michael Bush, RB, Louisville
4B. John Bowie, CB, Cincinnati
5A. Jay Richardson, DE, Ohio State
5B. Eric Frampton, S, Washington State
6. Oren O'Neal, RB, Arkansas State
7. Jonathan Holland, WR, Louisiana Tech

2008

1. Darren McFadden, RB, Arkansas

4A. Tyvon Branch, DB, Connecticut
4B. Arman Shields, WR, Richmond
6. Trevor Scott, DE, Buffalo
7. Chaz Schilens, WR, San Diego State

2009

1. Darrius Heyward-Bey, WR, Maryland
2. Mike Mitchell, S, Ohio
3. Matt Shaughnessy, DE, Wisconsin
4A. Louis Murphy, WR, Florida
4B. Slade Norris, LB, Oregon State
6A. Stryker Sulak, DE, Missouri
6B. Brandon Myers, TE, Iowa

2010

1. Rolando McClain, LB, Alabama
2. Lamarr Houston, DT, Texas
3. Jared Veldheer, OT, Hillsdale
4A. Bruce Campbell, DT, Maryland
4B. Jacoby Ford, WR, Clemson
5. Walter McFadden, DB, Auburn
6. Travis Goethel, LB, Arizona State
7A. Jeremy Ware, DB, Michigan State
7B. Stevie Brown, DB, Michigan

INDIVIDUAL RECORDS*

Service: Tim Brown, 16 seasons (1988–2003)
Most Games Played in Oakland/Los Angeles Career: Tim Brown, 240 (1988–2003)
Most Consecutive Seasons: Tim Brown, 16 (1988–2003)
Most Consecutive Games in a Career: Jim Otto, 210 (1960–74)
Most Consecutive Starts: Jim Otto, 210 (1960–74)

Scoring

CAREER

Points: Sebastian Janikowski, 1,000 (2000–09), 313 PAT, 229 FG
Touchdowns: Tim Brown, 104 (1988–2003)
Extra Points: George Blanda, 395 (1967–75)
Most Consecutive Extra Points: George Blanda, 201 (1967–71)
Most Field Goals: Sebastian Janikowski, 229 (2000–09)
Most Field Goals Attempted: Sebastian Janikowski, 292 (2000–09)

SEASON

Most Points: Jeff Jaeger, 132 (1993)
Most Touchdowns: Marcus Allen, 18 (1984)
Most Extra Points: George Blanda, 56 (1967)
Most Field Goals: Jeff Jaeger, 35 (1993)
Most Field Goal Attempts: Jeff Jaeger, 44 (1993)

GAME

Most Points (3 tied)
Art Powell, 24 (Dec. 22, 1963)
Marcus Allen, 24 (Sept. 24, 1984)
Harvey Williams, 24 (Nov. 4, 1997)

Most Touchdowns (3 tied):
Art Powell, 4 (Dec. 22, 1963)
Marcus Allen, 4 (Sept. 24, 1984)
Harvey Williams, 4 (Nov. 4, 1997)

Most Extra Points (5 tied):
Mike Mercer, 7 (Oct. 22, 1963)
Mike Mercer, 7 (Dec. 22, 1963)
Errol Mann, 7 (Nov. 28, 1976)
Sebastian Janikowski, 7 (Oct. 24, 2000)
Sebastian Janikowski, 7 (Sept. 29, 2002)

Most Field Goals:
Jeff Jaeger, 5 (Dec. 11, 1994)
Sebastian Janikowski, 5 (Oct. 29, 2000)
Sebastian Janikowski, 5 (Oct. 5, 2003)
Sebastian Janikowski, 5 (Nov. 18, 2007)

Longest Field Goal: Sebastian Janikowski, 61 yards (Dec. 27, 2009)
Longest Field Goal Attempted: Sebastian Janikowski, 76 yards (Sept. 28, 2008)

Passing

CAREER

Most Passes Attempted: Ken Stabler, 2,481 (1970–79)
Most Touchdown Passes: Ken Stabler, 150 (1970–79)
Most Passes Completed: Rich Gannon, 1,533 (1999–2004)
Most Yards Gained Passing: Ken Stabler, 19,078 (1970–79)

Most Interceptions: Ken Stabler, 143 (1970–79)
Best Percentage (200+Atts.): Rich Gannon, 61.5 (1999–2004)
Most Consecutive Years, 300 or More Yards Passing: Rich Gannon, 6 (1999–2004)

SEASON

Most Passes Attempted: Rich Gannon, 618 (2002)
Most Passes Completed: Rich Gannon, 418 (2002)
Most Yards Passing: Rich Gannon, 4,689 (2002)
Most Touchdown Passes: Daryle Lamonica, 34 (1969)
Most Interceptions: Ken Stabler, 30 (1978)
Best Percentage: Rich Gannon, 67.6 (2002)

GAME

Most Passes Attempted: Rich Gannon, 64 (Sept. 15, 2002)
Most Passes Completed: Rich Gannon, 43 (Sept. 15, 2002)
Most Yards Gained Passing: Jeff Hostetler, 424 (Oct. 18, 1993)
Most Touchdown Passes: Tom Flores, 6 (Dec. 22, 1963); Daryle Lamonica, 6 (Oct. 19, 1969)
Most Consecutive Games Throwing for a Touchdown: Daryle Lamonica, 25 (1968–70)
Most Interceptions: Ken Stabler, 7 (Oct. 16, 1977)
Best Completion Percentage: Ken Stabler, 91.7 —11 out of 12 (Dec. 21, 1975)
Longest Pass Play: Jim Plunkett to Cliff Branch, 99 yards and a touchdown (Oct 2, 1983)

All information related to this section came from Bob Carroll, Michael Gershman, David Neft, John Thorn, Total Football: The Official Encyclopedi of the National Football League, *Awards and Honors Section, pp. 325–329; www.football-almanac.com/football awards; and 2009 Oakland Raide Media Guide, pp. 162–165, 178–192.*

Rushing

CAREER

Most Rushing Attempts: Marcus Allen, 2,090 (1982–92)

Most Yards Rushing: Marcus Allen, 8,545 (1982–92)

Most Touchdowns Rushing: Marcus Allen, 79 (1982–92)

Best Average per Rush (150+Attempts): Bo Jackson, 5.4 (1987–90)

Most Consecutive Games, 100 or More Yards Rushing: Marcus Allen, 11 (1985–86)

SEASON

Most Rushing Attempts: Marcus Allen, 380 (1985)

Most Yards Rushing: Marcus Allen, 1,759 (1985)

Most Touchdowns Rushing: Pete Banaszak, 16 (1975)

Best Average per Rush: Bo Jackson, 6.8 (1987)

GAME

Most Rushing Attempts: Mark van Eeghen, 36 (Oct. 23, 1977)

Most Touchdowns Rushing (8 tied):
Tony Teresa, 3 (Nov. 4, 1960)
Pete Banaszak, 3 (Nov. 23, 1975, Dec. 21, 1975)
Mark van Eeghen, 3 (Oct. 14, 1979)
Booker Russell, 3 (Oct. 25, 1979)
Marcus Allen, 3 (Dec. 18, 1982, Sept. 24, 1984, Dec. 2, 1984, Oct. 28, 1985)
Rich Gannon, 3 (Sept. 10, 2000)
LaMont Jordan, 3 (Oct. 23, 2005)
Daunte Culpepper, 3 (Sept. 30, 2007)

Most Yards Rushing: Napoleon Kaufman, 227 (Oct. 19, 1997)

Best Average per Rush: Napoleon Kaufman, 15.3 (Dec. 19, 1999)

Longest Run from Scrimmage: Bo Jackson, 92 (Nov. 5, 1989)

Receiving

CAREER

Most Pass Receptions: Tim Brown, 1,070 (1988–2003)

Most Yards Gained: Tim Brown, 14,734 (1988–2003)

Most Touchdown Receptions: Tim Brown, 99 (1988–2003)

Best Average Gain per Catch (40 + Receptions): Jessie Hester, 23.7 (1985–87)

Most Consecutive Games with 100 or More Yards Receiving: Art Powell, 3 (1962, 1964)

SEASON

Most Pass Receptions: Tim Brown, 104 (1997)

Most Yards Gained: Tim Brown, 1,408 (1997)

Most Touchdown Receptions: Art Powell, 16 (1963)

Best Average per Catch (16 + Receptions): Warren Wells, 26.8 (1969)

GAME

Most Receptions: Tim Brown, 14 (Dec. 21, 1997)

Most Yards Gained: Art Powell, 247 (Dec. 22, 1963)

Most Touchdown Receptions: Art Powell, 4 (Dec. 2, 1963)

Best Average Gain per Catch (3 + Receptions): Clem Daniels, 57.3 (3 for 172 yards on Sept. 15, 1963)

Punt Returns

CAREER

Most Punt Returns: Tim Brown, 320 (1988–2003)

Best Average per Return (20 + Returns): Claude Gibson, 12.6 (1963–65)

Most Return Yards: Tim Brown, 3,272 (1988–2003)

Most Touchdowns (5 tied):
Claude Gibson, 3 (1963–65)
George Atkinson, 3 (1968–71)
Tim Brown, 3 (1988–2003)
Phillip Buchanon, 3 (2002–03)
Johnnie Lee Higgins, 3 (2007–08)

SEASON

Most Punt Returns: Fulton Walker, 62 (1985)

Most Return Yards: Fulton Walker, 692 (1985)

Most Touchdowns: Johnnie Lee Higgins, 3 (2008)

Best Average per Return (14 + Returns): Claude Gibson, 14.4 (1964)

GAME

Most Punt Returns: Rodger Bird, 9 (Sept. 10, 1967); Cle Montgomery, 9 (Dec. 10, 1984)

Most Return Yards: George Atkinson, 205 (Sept. 15, 1968)

Most Touchdowns (14 players, 6 players multiple games):
Claude Gibson, 1 (Nov. 3, 1963, Dec. 22, 1963, Sept. 12, 1965)
George Atkinson, 1 (Sept. 15, 1968, Oct. 13, 1968, Sept. 20, 1970, Sept. 16, 1970)
Alvin Wyatt, 1 (Sept. 20, 1970)
Ted Watts, 1 (Dec. 7, 1981)

Greg Pruitt, 1 (Oct. 2, 1983)
Cle Montgomery, 1 (Dec. 10, 1984)
Fulton Walker, 1 (Nov. 30, 1986)
Rick Calhoun, 1 (Oct. 12, 1987)
Tim Brown, 1 (Nov. 24, 1991, Dec. 12, 1993, Dec. 9, 2001)
Desmond Howard, 1 (Nov. 15, 1998 and Dec. 13, 1998)
Phillip Buchanon, 1 (Sept. 29, 2002)
Terry Kirby, 1 (Sept. 29, 2002)
Phillip Buchanon, 1 (Nov. 9, 2003 and Dec. 28, 2003)
Johnnie Lee Higgins, 1 (Nov. 16, 2008, Nov. 23, 2008, and Dec. 21, 2008)

Best Average per Return (3 + Returns): Neal Colzie, 42.3 (Nov. 2, 1975)

Longest Punt Return: Greg Pruitt, 97 yards (Oct. 2, 1983)

Kickoff Returns

CAREER

Most Kickoff Returns: Chris Carr, 201 (2005–07)

Most Return Yards: Chris Carr, 4,841 (2005–07)

Most Touchdowns: Justin Miller, 2 (2008); Terry Kirby, 2 (2000–02)

Best Average per Return (20 + Returns): Jack Larscheid, 28.4 (1960–61)

SEASON

Most Kickoff Returns: Chris Carr, 73 (2005)

Most Yards Returned: Chris Carr, 1,762 (2006)

Most Touchdowns: Justin Miller, 2 (2008)

Best Average per Return: Harold Hart, 30.5 (1975)

GAME

Most Kickoff Returns: Desmond Howard, 10 (Oct. 26, 1997)

Most Return Yards: Desmond Howard, 223 (Oct. 26, 1997)

Most Touchdowns (12 players tied, 2 players multiple games):
Jim Smith, 1 (Oct. 9, 1960)
Bo Roberson, 1 (Sept. 30, 1962)
Harold Hart, 1 (Sept. 22, 1975)
Ira Matthews, 1 (Oct. 25, 1979)
Arthur Whittington, 1 (Nov. 9, 1980)
Derrick Jensen, 1 (Dec. 21, 1980)
Tim Brown (Sept. 4, 1988)
Napoleon Kaufman, 1 (Oct. 22, 1995)
David Dunn, 1 (Nov. 26, 2000)
Terry Kirby, 1 (Nov. 11, 2001 and Sept. 15, 2002)
Doug Gabriel, 1 (Dec. 28, 2003)
Justin Miller, 1 (Dec. 4, 2008 and Dec. 14, 2008)

Best Average per Return (3 + Return Attempts): Harold Hart, 53.0 (Oct. 25, 1979)

Longest Kickoff Return: Ira Matthews, 104 yards (Oct. 25, 1979)

Interceptions

CAREER

Most Interceptions: Willie Brown, 39 (1967–78); Lester Hayes, 39 (1977–86)
Most Return Yards: Jack Tatum, 636 (1971–79)
Most Touchdowns: Terry McDaniel, 5 (1988–97)

SEASON

Most Interceptions: Lester Hayes, 13 (1980)
Most Return Yards: Lester Hayes, 273 (1980)
Most Touchdowns: Eric Allen, 3 (2000)

GAME

Most Interceptions (7 players tied):
Tommy Morrow, 3 (Sept. 7, 1963)
Dave Grayson, 3 (Oct. 26, 1969)
Willie Brown, 3 (Oct. 29, 1972)
George Atkinson, 3 (Oct. 6, 1974)
Charles Phillips, 3 (Dec. 8, 1975)
Terry McDaniel, 3 (Oct. 9, 1994)
Rod Woodson, 3 (Sept. 29, 2002)

Most Consecutive Games with an Interception:
Tommy Morrow, 8 (1962–63)
Lester Hayes, 8 (1980)

Most Return Yards: Mike Haynes, 151 (Dec. 2, 1984)
Longest Interception Return: Eddie Anderson, 102 yards (Dec. 14, 1992)

Punting

CAREER

Most Punts: Ray Guy, 1,049 (1973–86)
Most Yards Punting: Ray Guy, 44,493 (1973–86)
Best Average per Punt: Shane Lechler, 46.8 (2000–09)

SEASON

Most Punts: Leo Araguz, 98 (1998)
Most Yards Punting: Shane Lechler, 4,503 (2003)
Best Average per Punt: Shane Lechler, 49.1 (2007)

GAME

Most Punts: Leo Araguz, 16 (Nov. 11, 1998)
Best Average per Punt (3 + Attempts): Shane Lechler, 59.0 (Dec. 24, 2005)

Longest Punt: Wayne Crow, 77 yards (Oct. 29, 1961)

INDIVIDUAL POSTSEASON RECORDS

Most Playoff Game Appearances: Gene Upshaw, 24 (1967–81)
Most Starts: Gene Upshaw, 24 (1967–81)

Scoring

CAREER

Most Points: George Blanda, 99 on 42 extra points and 19 field goals (1967–75)
Most Touchdowns: Fred Biletnikoff, 10 (1965–78); Marcus Allen, 10 (1982–92)
Most Extra Points: George Blanda, 42 (1967–75)
Most Field Goals: George Blanda, 19 (1967–75)
Most Field Goal Attempts: George Blanda, 33 (1967–75)

GAME

Most Points (3 tied):
Fred Biletnikoff, 18 (Dec. 22, 1968)
Dave Casper, 18 (Dec. 24, 1977)
Napoleon McCallum, 18 (Jan. 9, 1994)

Most Extra Points: George Blanda, 8 (Dec. 21, 1969)
Most Field Goals: George Blanda, 4 each (Dec. 31, 1967 and Dec. 22, 1973)
Longest Field Goal: Jeff Jaeger, 49 yards (Jan. 13, 1991)

Passing

CAREER

Most Passes Attempted: Ken Stabler, 325 (1970–79)
Most Passes Completed: Ken Stabler, 188 (1970–79)
Most Touchdown Passes: Ken Stabler, 19 (1970–79)
Most Yards Gained Passing: Ken Stabler, 2,398 (1970–79)
Most Interceptions: Jim Plunkett, 12 (1978–86)
Best Percentage (90 + Attempts): Rich Gannon, 63.6 (1999–2004)

GAME

Most Passes Attempted: Daryle Lamonica, 47 (Dec. 29, 1968)
Most Passes Completed: Rich Gannon, 29: (Jan. 19, 2003)
Most Touchdown Passes: Daryle Lamonica, 6 (Dec. 21, 1969)
Best Passing Percentage: Ken Stabler, 82.4 (Dec. 22, 1973)
Most Interceptions: Rich Gannon, 5 (Jan. 26, 2003)

Most Yards Gained Passing: Daryle Lamonica, 401 (Dec. 29, 1968)
Longest Pass Play: Jeff Hostetler to Tim Brown, 86 yards (Jan. 15, 1994)

Rushing

CAREER

Most Rushing Attempts: Mark van Eeghen, 163 (1974–81)
Most Yards Rushing: Marcus Allen, 933 (1982–92)
Most Touchdowns Rushing: Marcus Allen, 8 (1982–92)
Best Average per Rush (90+ Attempts): Marcus Allen, 5.9 (1982–92)

GAME

Most Rushing Attempts: Marcus Allen, 25 (Jan. 8, 1984)
Most Yards Rushing: Marcus Allen, 191 (Jan. 22, 1984)
Most Touchdowns Rushing: Napoleon McCallum, 3 (Jan. 9, 1994)
Best Average per Rush (Minimum of 6 Rushes): Bo Jackson, 12.8 (Jan. 13, 1991)
Longest Run from Scrimmage: Charlie Garner, 80 yards (Jan. 12, 2002)

Receiving

CAREER

Most Pass Receptions: Cliff Branch, 73 (1972–85)
Most Yards Gained: Cliff Branch, 1,289 (1972–85)
Most Touchdown Receptions: Fred Biletnikoff, 10 (1965–78)
Longest Pass Reception: Tim Brown, 86 yards (Jan. 15, 1994)
Best Average per Catch (15 or More Receptions): Cliff Branch, 17.7 (1974–85)

GAME

Most Pass Receptions (4 tied):
Tim Brown, 9 (Jan. 19, 2003)
Jerry Rice, 9 (Jan. 12, 2002)
Fred Biletnikoff, 9 (Dec. 18, 1976)
Cliff Branch, 9 (Dec. 29, 1974)

Most Yards Gained: Fred Biletnikoff, 190 (Dec. 29, 1968)
Most Touchdown Receptions: Fred Biletnikoff, 3 (Dec. 22, 1968); Dave Casper, 3 (Dec. 24, 1977)
Longest Pass Reception: Tim Brown, 86 yards (Jan. 15, 1994)
Best Average Gain per Catch (3 or More Receptions): James Jett, 37.0 (Jan. 9, 1994)

Punt Returns

CAREER

Most Punt Returns: Neal Colzie, 18 (1975–78)
Most Yards Returned: Neal Colzie, 221 (1975–78)
Best Average per Return (10 or More Returns): Neal Colzie, 12.3 (1975–78)

GAME

Most Punt Returns: Rodger Bird, 5 (Dec. 31, 1967); Neal Colzie, 5 (Dec. 24, 1977); Greg Pruitt, 5 (Jan. 1, 1984)
Most Yards Returned: Neal Colzie, 64 (Dec. 28, 1975)
Best Average per Return (3 or More Returns): Neal Colzie, 17.7 (Dec. 18, 1976)
Longest Punt Return: George Atkinson, 37 yards (Dec. 23, 1972)

Kickoff Returns

CAREER

Most Kickoff Returns: Carl Garrett, 16 (1976–77); Clarence Davis, 16 (1971–78)
Most Yards Gained: Carl Garrett, 481 (1976–77)
Best Average per Return (10 or More Returns): Carl Garrett, 30.0 (1976–77)

GAME

Most Kickoff Returns: Marcus Knight, 8 (Jan. 26, 2003)
Most Yards Gained: Carl Garrett, 169 (Dec. 24, 1977)
Best Average per Return (3 or More Returns): Carl Garrett, 37.0 (Jan. 1, 1978)
Longest Kickoff Return: Carl Garrett, 62 yards (Jan. 1, 1978)

Interceptions

CAREER

Most Interceptions: Lester Hayes, 8 (1977–86)
Most Yards Returned: Willie Brown, 196 (1967–77)
Most Touchdowns: Willie Brown, 3 (1967–77)

GAME

Most Interceptions: Rod Martin, 3 (Jan. 25, 1981)
Most Yards Returned: Tory James, 98 (Jan. 6, 2001)
Most Touchdowns (5 players tied, 2 players multiple games): George Atkinson, 1 (Dec. 21, 1969)

Willie Brown, 1 (Dec. 27, 1970; Dec. 22, 1973; Jan. 9, 1977)
Lester Hayes, 1 (Dec. 28, 1980; Jan. 1, 1984)
Jack Squirek, 1 (Jan. 22, 1984)
Tory James, 1 (Jan. 6, 2001)

Longest Interception Return: Tory James, 90 yards (Jan. 6, 2001)

Punting

CAREER

Most Punts: Ray Guy, 111 (1973–86)
Most Yards Punting: Ray Guy, 4,695 (1973–86)
Best Average per Punt: Mike Eischeid, 42.8 (1966–71)

GAME

Most Punts: Shane Lechler, 9 (Jan. 19, 2002); Ray Guy, 9 (Jan. 4, 1981); Ray Guy, 9 (Dec. 28, 1980)
Most Yards Punting: Ray Guy, 460 (Dec. 28, 1980)
Best Average per Punt (3 + Punts): Ray Guy, 56.0 (Jan. 11, 1981)
Longest Punt: Ray Guy, 71 yards (Jan. 11, 1981)

AWARDS AND HONORS

Most Valuable Player of the Year Award

This award began in 1938.

1963: Clem Daniels (The Sporting News)
1967: Daryle Lamonica (United Press, The Sporting News)
1968: Daryle Lamonica (Washington, D.C. Touchdown Club)
1969: Daryle Lamonica (United Press, The Sporting News, Pro Football Weekly)
1970: George Blanda (The Maxwell Club, The Sporting News)
1974: Ken Stabler (Associated Press, Newspaper Enterprise Association)
1976: Ken Stabler (The Maxwell Club)
1985: Marcus Allen (Professional Football Writers Association, Associated Press, The Sporting News)
2000: Rich Gannon (The Maxwell Club, Washington, D.C. Touchdown Club)

2001: Rich Gannon (Washington, D.C. Touchdown Club)
2002: Rich Gannon (Associated Press, Pro Football Writers Association, Newspaper Enterprise Association, The Sporting News, The Maxwell Club, Miller Lite, Washington, D.C. Touchdown Club)

American Football Conference (AFC) Player of the Year

This award was given out from 1970 to 1984.

1970: George Blanda (United Press, The Sporting News)
1974: Ken Stabler (United Press, The Sporting News)
1976: Ken Stabler (The Sporting News)

American Football Conference (AFC) Defensive Player of the Year

1983: Rod Martin

Offensive Most Valuable Player of the Year

This award began in 1970.

1974: Ken Stabler (Associated Press)
1976: Ken Stabler (Pro Football Weekly)
1985: Marcus Allen (Associated Press, United Press)

Defensive Most Valuable Player of the Year

This award began in 1966.

1980: Lester Hayes (Associated Press, Newspaper Enterprise Association, Pro Football Weekly, United Press)
1984: Mike Haynes (Newspaper Enterprise Association)
1985: Howie Long (Newspaper Enterprise Association)

Rookie of the Year

This award began in 1955.

1970: Raymond Chester (Newspaper Enterprise Association)

1982: Marcus Allen (Professional Football Writers Association, Newspaper Enterprise Association, The Sporting News)
1987: Bo Jackson (Newspaper Enterprise Association)

American Football Conference (AFC) Rookie of the Year

This award began in 1970.

1982: Marcus Allen (United Press)

Offensive Rookie of the Year

This award began in 1967.

1982: Marcus Allen (Associated Press, Pro Football Weekly)

Defensive Rookie of the Year

This award began in 1967.

1998: Charles Woodson (Associated Press)

Football Digest Most Valuable Player Awards

1973: Jack Tatum, NFL Defensive Back of the Year
1974: Cliff Branch, NFL Receiver of the Year
1974: Ken Stabler, NFL Quarterback of the Year
1976: Cliff Branch, NFL Receiver of the Year
1976: Ken Stabler, NFL Quarterback of the Year
1977: Ray Guy, NFL Kicker of the Year
1977: Art Shell, NFL Offensive Lineman of the Year
1978: Ray Guy, NFL Kicker of the Year
1980: Ted Hendricks, NFL Linebacker of the Year
1985: Marcus Allen, NFL Running Back of the Year
1985: Howie Long, NFL Defensive Lineman of the Year

Coach of the Year

This award began in 1947.

1963: Al Davis (United Press)
1967: John Rauch (United Press)
1969: John Madden (Pro Football Weekly)
1990: Art Shell (Professional Football Writers Association, Pro Football Weekly)

American Football Conference (AFC) Coach of the Year

This award began in 1970.

1982: Tom Flores (Professional Football Writers Association, United Press)
1990: Art Shell (United Press)

Comeback Player of the Year Award

This award began in 1972, and was given out by Pro Football Weekly.

1980: Jim Plunkett
1982: Lyle Alzado

NFL Man of the Year Award

This award began in 1970. It was renamed the Walter Payton Award in 1999, and is given to players who excel on the field and for their endeavors in charity work.

1974: George Blanda

The Byron "Whizzer" White NFL Man of the Year Award

This award began in 1966, and is awarded to the player who best serves his team, community, and country.

1979: Gene Upshaw

AFC/NFC Pro Bowl Most Valuable Player of the Game Award

2000: Rich Gannon
2001: Rich Gannon

Oakland/Los Angeles Raiders in the Pro Football Hall of Fame

After each player's name is their position or title followed by date of enshrinement. The players appear in order by the year of their induction.

Jim Otto, Center: August 2, 1980
George Blanda, Quarterback/Kicker: August 1, 1981
Willie Brown, Defensive Back: July 28, 1984
Gene Upshaw, Guard: August 8, 1987
Fred Biletnikoff, Wide Receiver: July 30, 1988
Art Shell, Offensive Tackle: August 5, 1989

Ted Hendricks, Linebacker: August 4, 1990
Al Davis, Owner: August 1, 1992
Mike Haynes, Defensive Back: July 26, 1997
Eric Dickerson, Running Back: August 7, 1999
Howie Long, Defensive Tackle: July 29, 2000
Ronnie Lott, Defensive Back: July 29, 2000
Dave Casper, Tight End: August 3, 2002
Marcus Allen, Running Back: August 3, 2003
James Lofton, Wide Receiver: August 3, 2003
Bob Brown, Offensive Tackle: August 8, 2004
John Madden, Head Coach: August 5, 2006
Rod Woodson, Defensive Back: August 8, 2009
Jerry Rice, Wide Receiver: August 7, 2010

Oakland/Los Angeles Raiders Selected All-Pro

From 1960 to 1969 these were American Football League selections; from 1970 to 2009 they were National Football League selections

1960: Jim Otto (Center)
1961: Jim Otto (Center)
1962: Jim Otto (Center), Fred Williamson (Defensive Back)
1963: Jim Otto (Center), Art Powell (Wide Receiver), Clem Daniels (Running Back), Fred Williamson (Defensive Back)
1964: Jim Otto (Center), Art Powell (Wide Receiver)
1965: Jim Otto (Center), Art Powell (Wide Receiver), Dave Grayson (Defensive Back)
1966: Jim Otto (Center), Wayne Hawkins (Guard), Kent McCloughan (Defensive Back)
1967: Jim Otto (Center), Gene Upshaw (Guard), Harry Schuh (Tackle), Billy Cannon (Tight End), Daryle Lamonica (Quarterback), Hewitt Dixon (Running Back), Ben Davidson (Defensive End), Tom Keating (Defensive Tackle), Dan Conners (Linebacker), Kent McCloughan (Defensive Back)
1968: Jim Otto (Center), Gene Upshaw (Guard), Hewitt Dixon (Running Back), Dan Birdwell (Defensive Tackle), Dan Conners (Linebacker), Willie Brown (Defensive Back), Dave Grayson (Defensive Back)
1969: Jim Otto (Center), Gene Upshaw (Guard), Harry Schuh (Tackle), Fred Biletnikoff (Wide Receiver), Warren Wells (Wide Receiver), Daryle Lamonica (Quarterback), Tom Keating (Defensive Tackle), Dan Conners (Linebacker), Willie Brown (Defensive Back), Dave Grayson (Defensive Back)

1970: Jim Otto (Center), Gene Upshaw (Guard), Fred Biletnikoff (Wide Receiver), Willie Brown (Defensive Back)

1971: Jim Otto (Center), Bob Brown (Tackle), Willie Brown (Defensive Back)

1972: Fred Biletnikoff (Wide Receiver), Gene Upshaw (Guard), Bob Brown (Tackle), Willie Brown (Defensive Back)

1973: Art Shell (Tackle), Willie Brown (Defensive Back), Ray Guy (Punter)

1974: Cliff Branch (Wide Receiver), Gene Upshaw (Guard), Art Shell (Tackle), Ken Stabler (Quarterback), Ray Guy (Punter)

1975: Cliff Branch (Wide Receiver), Ray Guy (Punter)

1976: Cliff Branch (Wide Receiver), Dave Casper (Tight End), Ray Guy (Punter)

1977: Cliff Branch (Wide Receiver), Dave Casper (Tight End), Gene Upshaw (Guard), Art Shell (Tackle), Ray Guy (Punter)

1978: Dave Casper (Tight End), Ray Guy (Punter)

1979: Dave Casper (Tight End), Raymond Chester (Tight End)

1980: Ted Hendricks (Linebacker), Lester Hayes (Defensive Back)

1981: Lester Hayes (Defensive Back)

1982: Marcus Allen (Running Back), Ted Hendricks (Linebacker), Rod Martin (Linebacker), Lester Hayes (Defensive Back)

1983: Todd Christensen (Tight End), Howie Long (Defensive End), Rod Martin (Linebacker)

1984: Todd Christensen (Tight End), Howie Long (Defensive End), Rod Martin (Linebacker), Mike Haynes (Defensive Back), Lester Hayes (Defensive Back)

1985: Marcus Allen (Running Back), Todd Christensen (Tight End), Howie Long (Defensive End), Mike Haynes (Defensive Back)

1986: Todd Christensen (Tight End), Howie Long (Defensive End), Bill Pickel (Middle Guard)

1988: Tim Brown (Kick Returner)

1990: Steve Wisniewski (Guard), Greg Townsend (Defensive End)

1991: Steve Wisniewski (Guard), Don Mosebar (Center), Greg Townsend (Defensive End), Ronnie Lott (Safety), Jeff Gossett (Punter), Jeff Jaeger (Kicker), Tim Brown (Kick Returner)

1992: Steve Wisniewski (Guard), Terry McDaniel (Defensive Back)

1993: Steve Wisniewski (Guard), Anthony Smith (Defensive End), Raghib Ismail (Kick Returner)

1994: Steve Wisniewski (Guard), Chester McGlockton (Defensive Tackle), Terry McDaniel (Defensive Back)

1995: Steve Wisniewski (Guard), Chester McGlockton (Defensive Tackle), Terry McDaniel (Defensive Back)

1996: Steve Wisniewski (Guard), Chester McGlockton (Defensive Tackle), Terry McDaniel (Defensive Back)

1997: Steve Wisniewski (Guard), Tim Brown (Wide Receiver), Chester McGlockton (Defensive Tackle)

1998: Darrell Russell (Defensive Tackle)

1999: Darrell Russell (Defensive Tackle), Charles Woodson (Defensive Back)

2000: Steve Wisniewski (Guard), Lincoln Kennedy (Tackle), Rich Gannon (Quarterback), William Thomas (Linebacker), Charles Woodson (Defensive Back), Shane Lechler (Punter)

2001: Lincoln Kennedy (Tackle), Rich Gannon (Quarterback), Charles Woodson (Defensive Back, Shane Lechler (Punter)

2002: Lincoln Kennedy (Tackle), Barret Robbins (Center), Jerry Rice (Wide Receiver), Rich Gannon (Quarterback), Rod Coleman (Defensive Tackle), John Parrella (Defensive Tackle), Rod Woodson (Safety)

2003: Shane Lechler (Punter)

2004: Shane Lechler (Punter)

2005: Derrick Burgess (Defensive End)

2006: Nnamdi Asomugha (Defensive Back)

2007: Shane Lechler (Punter)

2008: Nnamdi Asomugha (Defensive Back), Shane Lechler (Punter), Johnnie Lee Higgins (Punt Returner)

2009: Nnamdi Asomugha (Defensive Back), Shane Lechler (Punter)

Oakland/Los Angeles Raiders Selected All-American Football Conference (AFC)

1970: Jim Otto (Center), Gene Upshaw (Guard), Willie Brown (Defensive Back), Fred Biletnikoff (Wide Receiver), Daryle Lamonica (Quarterback), Hewritt Dixon (Running Back), Warren Wells (Wide Receiver), Tom Keating (Defensive Tackle), Harry Schuh (Tackle)

1971: Jim Otto (Center), Willie Brown (Defensive Back), Bob Brown (Tackle), Raymond Chester (Tight End), Gene Upshaw (Guard), Clarence Davis (Kick Returner)

1972: Fred Biletnikoff (Wide Receiver), Bob Brown (Tackle), Gene Upshaw (Guard), Willie Brown (Defensive Back), Jim Otto (Center), Raymond Chester (Tight End)

1973: Art Shell (Tackle), Willie Brown (Defensive Back), Ray Guy (Punter), Fred Biletnikoff (Wide Receiver), Ken Stabler (Quarterback)

1974: Cliff Branch (Wide Receiver), Art Shell (Tackle), Gene Upshaw (Guard), Ken Stabler (Quarterback), Ray Guy (Punter), Otis Sistrunk (Defensive Tackle), Phil Villapiano (Linebacker), Jack Tatum (Safety)

1975: Cliff Branch (Wide Receiver), Ray Guy (Punter), Art Shell (Tackle), Phil Villapiano (Linebacker), Jack Tatum (Safety)

1976: Cliff Branch (Wide Receiver), Dave Casper (Tight End), Ray Guy (Punter), Ted Hendricks (Linebacker), Art Shell (Tackle)

1977: Dave Casper (Tight End), Cliff Branch (Wide Receiver), Ray Guy (Punter), Art Shell (Tackle), Gene Upshaw (Guard), Errol Mann, (Kicker) Jack Tatum (Safety)

1978: Dave Casper (Tight End), Ray Guy (Punter), Art Shell (Tackle)

1979: Dave Casper (Tight End), Raymond Chester (Tight End)

1980: Lester Hayes (Defensive Back), Ted Hendricks (Linebacker), Ray Guy (Punter)

1981: Lester Hayes (Defensive Back), Ted Hendricks (Linebacker), Rod Martin (Linebacker)

1982: Marcus Allen (Running Back), Lester Hayes (Defensive Back), Ted Hendricks (Linebacker), Rod Martin (Linebacker)

1983: Todd Christensen (Tight End), Howie Long (Defensive End), Rod Martin (Linebacker), Lester Hayes (Defensive Back)

1984: Howie Long (Defensive End), Rod Martin (Linebacker), Mike Haynes (Defensive Back), Marcus Allen (Running Back), Henry Lawrence (Tackle)

1985: Marcus Allen (Running Back), Todd Christensen (Tight End), Howie Long (Defensive End), Mike Haynes (Defensive Back), Matt Millen (Linebacker)

1986: Todd Christensen (Tight End), Bill Pickel (Middle Guard), Howie Long (Defensive End), Vann McElroy (Safety)

1987: Todd Christensen (Tight End), Vann McElroy (Safety)

1988: Greg Townsend (Defensive End)

1989: Bo Jackson (Running Back), Greg Townsend (Defensive End)

1990: Greg Townsend (Defensive End), Steve Wisniewski (Guard)

1991: Tim Brown (Kick Returner), Jeff Jaeger (Kicker), Ronnie Lott (Safety), Greg Townsend (Defensive End), Steve Wisniewski (Guard)

1992: Terry McDaniel (Defensive Back), Steve Wisniewski (Guard)

1993: Terry McDaniel (Defensive Back), Steve Wisniewski (Guard), Raghib Ismail (Kick Returner), Tim Brown (Wide Receiver), Howie Long (Defensive End)

1994: Tim Brown (Wide Receiver), Terry McDaniel (Defensive Back), Chester McGlockton (Defensive Tackle), Steve Wisniewski (Guard)

1995: Tim Brown (Wide Receiver), Terry McDaniel (Defensive Back), Chester McGlockton (Defensive Tackle), Pat Swilling (Defensive End), Steve Wisniewski (Guard)

1996: Tim Brown (Wide Receiver), Chester McGlockton (Defensive Tackle), Steve Wisniewski (Guard)

1997: Tim Brown (Wide Receiver), Chester McGlockton (Defensive Tackle), Steve Wisniewski (Guard)

1998: Darrell Russell (Defensive Tackle)

1999: Darrell Russell (Defensive Tackle), Charles Woodson (Defensive Back), Barret Robbins (Center), Tim Brown (Wide Receiver), Greg Biekert (Linebacker)

2000: Rich Gannon (Quarterback), Steve Wisniewski (Guard), Charles Woodson (Defensive Back)

2001: Rich Gannon (Quarterback), Shane Lechler (Punter), Charles Woodson (Defensive Back)

2002: Rich Gannon (Quarterback), Lincoln Kennedy (Tackle), Rod Woodson (Safety)

2005: Derrick Burgess (Defensive End)

2007: Shane Lechler (Punter)

2008: Nnamdi Asomugha (Defensive Back), Shane Lechler (Punter), Johnnie Lee Higgins (Punt Returner)

Oakland Raiders Selected to the AFL All-Star Game, 1960–1969

The name of the player is followed by his position and the years he was selected.

George Atkinson, CB: 1968, 1969
Fred Biletnikoff, WR: 1967, 1969
Dan Birdwell, DT: 1968
George Blanda, K: 1967
Willie Brown, CB: 1967, 1968, 1969
Billy Cannon, TE: 1969
Dan Conners, LB: 1966, 1967, 1968
Dave Costa, DT: 1963
Clem Daniels, RB: 1963, 1964, 1965, 1966
Ben Davidson, DE: 1966, 1967, 1968
Cotton Davidson, QB: 1963
Hewritt Dixon, RB: 1966, 1967, 1968
Tom Flores, QB: 1966
Dave Grayson, CB/S: 1965, 1966, 1969
Wayne Hawkins, G: 1963, 1964, 1965, 1966, 1967
Tom Keating, DT: 1966, 1967
Daryle Lamonica, QB: 1967, 1969

Isaac Lassiter, DE: 1966
Archie Matsos, LB: 1963
Kent McCloughan, CB: 1966, 1967
Alan Miller, RB: 1961
Gus Otto, LB: 1969
Jim Otto, C: 1961, 1962, 1963, 1964, 1965, 1966, 1967, 1968, 1969
Art Powell, WR: 1963, 1964, 1965, 1966
Harry Schuh, OT: 1967, 1969
Gene Upshaw, G: 1968
Warren Wells, WR: 1968
Fred Williamson, CB: 1961, 1962, 1963
Nemiah Wilson, CB: 1967

Oakland/Los Angeles Raiders Selections for the AFC–NFC Pro Bowl, 1970–2009

The name of the player is followed by his position and the years he was selected.

Marcus Allen, RB: 1982, 1984, 1985, 1986, 1987
Nnamdi Asomugha, CB: 2006, 2008, 2009
Fred Biletnikoff, WR: 1970, 1971, 1973, 1974
Cliff Branch, WR: 1974, 1975, 1976, 1977
Bob Brown, OT: 1971
Tim Brown, WR/KR: 1988, 1991, 1993, 1994, 1995, 1996, 1997, 1999, 2001
Willie Brown, CB: 1970, 1971, 1972, 1973
Derrick Burgess, DE: 2005, 2006
Dave Casper, TE: 1976, 1977, 1978, 1979
Raymond Chester, TE: 1970, 1971, 1972, 1979
Todd Christensen, TE: 1983, 1984, 1985, 1986, 1987
Jon Condo, Long Snapper: 2009
Dave Dalby, C: 1977
Hewritt Dixon, RB: 1970
Rich Gannon, QB: 1999, 2000, 2001, 2002
Kevin Gogan, G: 1994
Jeff Gossett, P: 1991
Ray Guy, P: 1973, 1974, 1975, 1976, 1977, 1978, 1980
Lester Hayes, CB: 1980, 1981, 1982, 1983, 1984

Mike Haynes, CB: 1984, 1985, 1986
Ted Hendricks, LB: 1980, 1981, 1982, 19
Ethan Horton, TE: 1991
Jeff Hostetler, QB: 1994
Marv Hubbard, RB: 1971, 1972, 1973
Bo Jackson, RB: 1990
Jeff Jaeger, K: 1991
Lincoln Kennedy, OT: 2000, 2001, 200
Kenny King, RB: 1980
Daryle Lamonica, QB: 1970, 1972
Henry Lawrence, OT: 1983, 1984
Shane Lechler, P: 2001, 2004, 2007, 200 2009
Howie Long, DE: 1983, 1984, 1985, 198 1987, 1989, 1992, 1993
Ronnie Lott, S: 1991
Rod Martin, LB: 1983, 1984
Terry McDaniel, CB: 1992, 1993, 199 1995, 1996
Vann McElroy, S: 1983, 1984
Chester McGlockton, DT: 1994, 199 1996, 1997
Matt Millen, LB: 1988
Max Montoya, G: 1993
Don Mosebar, C: 1986, 1990, 1991
Jim Otto, C: 1970, 1971, 1972
Greg Pruitt, KR: 1983
Jerry Rice, WR: 2002
Barret Robbins, C: 2002
Darrell Russell, DT: 1998, 1999
Harry Schuh, OT: 1970
Art Shell, OT: 1972, 1973, 1974, 197 1976, 1977, 1978, 1980
Otis Sistrunk, DT: 1974
Ken Stabler, QB: 1973, 1974, 1976, 197
Jack Tatum, S: 1973, 1974, 1975
Greg Townsend, DE: 1990, 1991
Gene Upshaw, G: 1972, 1973, 1974, 197 1976, 1977
Mark van Eeghen, RB: 1977
Phil Villapiano, LB: 1973, 1974, 1975, 197
Warren Wells, WR: 1970
Steve Wisniewski, G: 1990, 1991, 199 1993, 1994, 1995, 1997, 2000
Charles Woodson, CB: 1998, 1999, 200 2001
Rod Woodson, S: 2002

Part III. Bad Boys, Legends, and Raiders Vignettes

PLAYERS OF YORE

Marcus Allen

The greatest running back in Raiders history without question was Marcus Allen. No stranger to accolades earned on a football field, he came to the Silver and Black after one of the most incredible college seasons in history.

In 1981, Allen became the first collegiate to break the 2,000-yard rushing barrier. On his way to gridiron immortality, Allen tore through defenses for 2,342 yards, a 212.9 per game average, set 12 NCAA records and tied four others. It was no surprise that the 1981 college football awards were dominated by Allen, and rightfully so. On top of being selected consensus All-American, Marcus became USC's fourth Heisman Trophy winner, plus the recipient of the Walter Camp, Maxwell Club, and Football News awards, all in recognition of being the 1981 college football player of the year.[1]

Allen did not rest on his laurels once coming to the Raiders as their number one draft pick in 1982. The awards continued to role in for Marcus during his pro career, as he became the only player in pro football history to be selected Heisman Trophy winner, Rookie of the Year, NFL Player of the Year, Super Bowl Most Valuable Player, and be enshrined in the College and Pro Football Halls of Fame. Along the way, Allen became one of the NFL's premier offensive weapons. He did whatever was asked of him, whether it was running, catching, blocking, or even passing, he did it all to perfection, and became one of the most complete running backs in history.

His versatility as a runner allowed Allen to conform to whatever was needed at the time. From being a fluid, finesse runner, he could then switch to the power back mode. His instincts at reading blocks and getting through small holes allowed him to quickly get into the secondary for solid gains. He was also one of the greatest short-yardage backs, especially near the goal line.[2] His exploits during the 1985 season proved his worth as a complete offensive weapon when he rushed for 1,759 yards and 11 touchdowns, and caught 67 passes for 555 yards and three more six-pointers. It was his greatest season as a professional, and the NFL bestowed its highest honor onto Allen by selecting him Player of the Year. His ability to rise to the occasion on the grandest stage in all of football allowed him to become a Super Bowl immortal. In the Raiders 38–9 mauling over Washington in Super Bowl XVIII, Allen ran for a then–Super Bowl record 191 yards, and scored two touchdowns, one of which being a magnificent 74-yard jaunt through the Washington defense that will forever be replayed in highlight films.

In 11 seasons with the Silver and Black, Allen led the team in rushing seven consecutive years, was All-Pro (1982, 1985), All-AFC (1982, 1984, 1985), and selected to play in five Pro Bowls.

By 1987, the tide turned for Allen as a member of the Los Angeles Raiders. With the arrival of Bo Jackson, Allen's playing time began to diminish. Over the next few years, once Jackson came to the team after his baseball season concluded, Allen became an observer while the two-sport star Jackson got the bulk of playing time. A knee injury forced Allen to miss a good portion of the 1989 season and the next three seasons were as a backup. A nasty contract dispute with Al Davis did not help, and after bitter words were volleyed back and forth between the sides, Allen wanted to be traded.[3]

Getting his wish, Allen became a member of the Kansas City Chiefs in 1993 after becoming the Raiders all-time leading rusher with 8,545 yards. He proved his worth by running for 764 yards and 12 touchdowns while helping the Chiefs advance to the AFC Championship Game. His performance during that season earned him the NFL Comeback Player of the Year Award. He also added a sixth trip to the Pro Bowl in 1994. Allen then finished out his long, illustrious career with the Chiefs in 1997.

When his career was complete, the numbers he compiled were astounding. In 1995, he became the first player to break the 10,000-yard rushing barrier and the 5,000-yard receiving as well. He ran for 12,243 yards and 123 touchdowns on 3,022 carries, and caught 587 passes for 5,411 yards and 21 touchdowns. In 2003, Marcus Allen became the 52nd player to gain entry into the Pro Football Hall of Fame in his first year of eligibility, as if there ever would have been a doubt to the swiftness of his acceptance among the game's immortals.

Lyle Alzado

Lyle Alzado's path to NFL stardom began in Brooklyn, New York, and ended in Los Angeles with the Raiders. From Lawrence High School, where he not only stood out in football but track, he attended Kilgore Junior College for two years before going to Yankton College in South Dakota. Lyle was also a standout boxer, as his Golden Gloves championship will attest. He was also a street fighter and claimed to have been stabbed several times as a teenager.[1]

Yankton College was never looked at as a professional football breeding ground, but Alzado stood out with his aggressive play. A scout from the Denver Broncos happened to notice his dominating play while viewing game film and immediately decided that Alzado had the ability to perform at the next level. He had everything a team looked for in a defender. He was strong, tough, intense, very intimidating, and never let up on those attributes throughout his entire career. On draft day in 1971, the Broncos took their scout's advice and selected Alzado in the fourth round, making him the only player from Yankton College to ever play in the NFL.[2]

Alzado proved the scout right by becoming one of the most furious pass rushers and run defenders in pro football throughout the 1970's and into the 80's, earning the 1977 NFL Defensive Player of the Year Award, as well as the AFC Player of the Year, All-Pro first team, and a trip to the Pro Bowl. The following season he earned second team All-Pro honors, first team All-AFC, and another trip to the Pro Bowl.

In 1979, Alzado got into a contract dispute with Denver, and instead of dealing with the situation, the Broncos traded him to the Cleveland Browns. A change of uniform did not slow Alzado down, and he once again became the driving force for the Browns. In his first year with the Browns, Alzado earned second team All-AFC honors, and in his second season, the Browns won the AFC Central Division title with Alzado leading the way on defense, and he once again earned first team All-AFC and first team All-Pro honors. Alzado's stay in Cleveland ended on bitter terms when the Browns felt he was on the downside of his career following the 1981 season. It was also claimed that personal problems were a factor in Cleveland's decision to part ways with him.[3]

Al Davis always liked Alzado's all-out play, and when he had the opportunity to make the fierce competitor a Raider, he jumped at the chance. For virtually nothing, the Browns traded Alzado to the Raiders in 1982. Out to prove that he was not washed up, Alzado played for the Raiders with reckless abandon.[4] His play was so impressive that he was selected the 1982 NFL Comeback Player of the Year Award and once again found himself on the All-AFC first team for the fourth time. He continued to perform at a high level during the Raiders 1983 championship season, and throughout the following campaign. In 1985 an injury forced him to the sidelines after 11 games, and he retired following that season. In 1990, at the age of 41, Alzado attempted a comeback with the Raiders. However, a knee injury during training camp led to his release. If it were not for that injury, there is no telling what might have happened.

Two years later, Lyle Alzado succumbed to a brain tumor, which many felt was a direct result of his obsessive use of anabolic steroids and human growth hormones, and passed away at 43 years of age. While he was so ill with cancer, Alzado made a plea to everyone who even thought about steroid use to never do it. Throughout his career, Alzado gave much of himself to helping children battling illness, and even as death was closing in on him, he still cared enough to make an example of himself so that he might be able to save others from making the same mistakes he did when it came to using performance enhancing drugs.

Nnamdi Asomugha

Throughout the long history of this incredible team, the have been many great defensive backs who have worn the silv and black and patrolled the secondary with authority. The nam of Nnamdi Asomugha will be among them. He is already regarde as one of the top defensive backs in the highly competitive worl of professional football, and still has much more life in his caree At this point, there is no telling where his abilities will take hin He is considered such a threat to opposing offensives that the try to throw away from his area as much as they can. He has nose for the football, and is capable of making big plays, whic stop opponents in their tracks.[1]

Besides gaining the respect from opponents, Asomugha als has won the admiration of his fellow Raiders. He was elected tea captain in 2007, and has won the team MVP award in 2006 an shared it in 2008. He has been selected to numerous All-Pr teams, as well as the Pro Bowl, and will continue to receive man more awards before his career is complete.[2]

George Atkinson

The "Hit Man" earned a reputation as one of the hardes hitting defensive backs during the 1970's. Atkinson was a soli performer who displayed no fear, but managed to instill it in op ponents who dared come into contact with him by leveling ther with bone-jarring tackles. He would inflict punishment on th opposition with a blow to the head that left receivers dazed an highly intimidated.[1] In the 1976 season opener against the Pitts burgh Steelers, Atkinson applied his famous blast to receiver Lyn Swann, knocking him unconscious. Pittsburgh's head coac Chuck Noll was so enraged by Atkinson's hit that he called it "criminal element" and wanted Atkinson thrown out of th league.[2] Noll's Steelers were not a group of choirboys themselves and maybe his remarks had something to do with the fact tha the Raiders came back to beat Pittsburgh in the game.

On top of his tackling ability, Atkinson was blessed wit blazing speed that enabled him to track down the fastest of re ceivers, and his 30 interceptions ranked second in team histor at the time of his retirement.[3] Along with Jack Tatum, Ski Thomas, and Willie Brown, Atkinson made up the greatest de fensive secondary of their time, and one of the best in the histor of the game.

His speed also provided the Raiders with one of their greates kick returners as well. At the end of his career, he ranked numbe one in team history with 148 punts returns, and third in kicko returns.

Pete Banaszak

The best way to sum up the career of running back Pete Ba naszak is to simply call him a football player.[1] He loved the game and gave it his heart and soul for 13 seasons from 1966 to 1978 The consummate team player, Banaszak did it all. He was a goo blocker and outstanding special teams player. At the time of hi retirement, he held the all-time Raiders record for rushing touch downs with 47, and played in over 100 straight games for th Silver and Black. He was one of the team's all-time, all-aroun ffensive performers, ranked near the top of many team-rushing ecords. He ran for 3,772 career yards, caught 121 passes for 1,022 ards and five touchdowns despite the fact that he was never a ull-time starter. He was an exceptional blocker and loved to play n special teams, going full throttle downfield to make tackles, nd giving it his all when receiving kickoffs and punts.[2]

Plainly stated, Banaszak loved to be around the ball, and he Raiders loved to have him near it. He was one of head coach ohn Madden's favorite players due to his gusto for the gridiron, nd was one of only a few players who served under Madden hroughout his entire reign as Oakland's mentor. Banaszak played n many of the Raiders most memorable games, and earned the ighlight of his solid career in Oakland's 32–14 win over Min-esota in Super Bowl XI when he scored two short-yardage touch-owns.

Fred Biletnikoff

Fred Biletnikoff's career as a wide receiver began in Erie, 'ennsylvania, and ended in Canton, Ohio with his enshrinement nto the Pro Football Hall of Fame. The road from Erie to Canton vas one paved with incredible moments that will never be for-otten by all those who witnessed Biletnikoff's prowess on the ridiron.

Athletic ability was given to him from his father, who was a ational amateur boxing champion. By the time Biletnikoff ompleted his high school days at Tech Memorial, he was a sen-ational four-sport star.[1] Countless colleges came looking to get he Pennsylvania athlete to come to their institutions of higher earning. Biletnikoff decided to head to the sunshine and beaches f Florida, and the fans in Tallahassee were forever grateful for is decision.

While at Florida State, he became the greatest wide receiver n that school's history, setting records for most receptions, re-eiving touchdowns, and points scored. In his senior year of 1964, Biletnikoff became an All-American after ranking fourth in the ation with 57 catches for 987 yards and 11 touchdowns. With our fantastic years now behind him at Florida State, it came as o surprise when Biletnikoff decided on a post-college career.

The Oakland Raiders selected the great collegiate receiver n the second round of the 1965 AFL draft, and 14 seasons later, e left the team as a legend. In his first professional season, he ropped five passes in an exhibition game, but rebounded with n 80-yard touchdown reception later in the same game. This roved to be a prelude of great things for the man who wore num-er 25.

When the 1965 regular season started, Biletnikoff was used nly on kickoff and punt returns. Midway through the season, owever, he was given the opportunity at starting wide receiver nd never relinquished it for 13 years. In his first game as a starter, he rookie sensation electrified the crowd with seven receptions or 118 yards.[2]

From that game on, Biletnikoff never failed to excite the Oakland faithful. Blessed with an exceptional pair of hands, he vas capable of catching any pass thrown in his immediate lirection no matter how difficult it appeared. He was not con-idered very fast by wide receiver standards, but was able to dis-ance himself from quicker defenders by working hard during and

after practice. His fear of failure was so intense that he would chain smoke cigarettes before a game to calm his nerves. He would also work himself up into such a frenzy state that he would vomit prior to kickoff.[3]

At the dawn of each season, when the drudgery of training camp fell upon autumn's warriors, Biletnikoff used this time to retool his classic moves. He meticulously broke down each pattern he ran step by step until his body was like a well-oiled machine. He also honed his hand-eye coordination by hitting a speed bag like boxers.[4] His precise, timed routes became his trademark, and even though defenders knew what to expect from him, he still managed to produce big plays over and over again, leaving op-ponents baffled and in awe. His favorite play was 91-comeback, in which he would come back toward the ball after running a pat-tern along the sideline.[5] He also worked hard off the practice field by studying hours of game film, picking up any weakness that he could use against the man covering him.

His prowess at dazzling defenses became a trademark, but so too did an item referred to as Stickum. It was dubbed flypaper in a can, but officially it was a product used primarily to get a better grip on baseball bats, vaulting poles, and weight bars.[6] It was a sticky yellow goo that Biletnikoff discovered and fell in love with. He would apply a gob of it on his socks and taped forearms, and then dab some onto his fingertips during a game to allow for extra grip when catching a pass. He never used it at practice, and his talents were so great that he did not need it in games. It was more of a mind thing. After each reception that Biletnikoff made, Oakland quarterbacks would ask for another ball from the officials because it would be extremely difficult to throw with that stuff on it. The NFL banned the substance in 1981.

Through the years, Biletnikoff was exceptional in every sit-uation, but when a game hung in the balance, or was one of major importance, he somehow managed to elevate his play to greater heights. In 19 playoff game appearances, he caught 70 passes for 1,167 yards, both of which were playoff records at the time of his retirement, and 10 touchdowns. In the Raiders' Super Bowl XI win over Minnesota, Biletnikoff caught four passes for 79 yards to help set up three scores in a 32–14 rout, and his actions on that day earned him the game's Most Valuable Player Award one month shy of his 34th birthday.

Over the course of his career, the outstanding catching ability displayed by this man helped all those around to be better, especially the quarterbacks. Thanks to Biletnikoff's talents, Daryle Lamonica and Ken Stabler's pass completion ratings were among the top in the league each season they played with him.

During his 14 spectacular campaigns, Biletnikoff compiled accolades that many could only dream of achieving, and when he left the Raiders following the 1978 season, he ranked in the top ten on the all-time reception, yardage, and touchdowns scored lists. His 589 receptions ranked him fourth all-time, while his 8,974 yards gained earned him the fifth spot, and the 76 touch-downs gave him eighth place. He also shared the NFL record of ten consecutive seasons with 40 or more receptions from 1967 to 1976. From 1968 to 1973, Biletnikoff led the team in receptions. His 61 catches in 1971 led the league, and his 58 the following year topped the AFC. He gained All-Pro honors three times (1969, 1970, 1972), All-AFC in 1970, 1972, and 1973, and made six trips to the Pro Bowl. All these were impressive honors, but nothing matched the one bestowed on Fred Biletnikoff on July 30, 1988, when he took his deserved place among pro football's immortals with enshrinement into the Hall of Fame in Canton, Ohio. The year after his induction, he began a long-time tenure as an assistant coach for the Raiders, serving in that capacity from 1989 through 2006. One more chance at immortality was granted him in 1994 when the annual Fred Biletnikoff Award was first presented to the top wide receiver in college football, and serves as a lasting tribute to one of the game's greatest performers.

Dan Birdwell

"Birdie" was one of the most popular players the Raiders employed during the team's rise to prominence in the 1960's. He provided the early Raiders with many comical moments that endure to this day when discussing silver and black-clad court jesters. His massive hands provided entertainment to his fellow renegades due to the ability to take the tops off of soda pop bottles with his thumbs. He once got on the wrong plane for a road game, and a search party finally found him sitting on an empty airplane wondering where everyone else was.[1] However, the ultimate story regarding this man came in a game against the Denver Broncos. After a night on the town in which he allegedly consumed a half gallon of vodka, Birdwell took the field, got into his stance, and then vomited all over the ball and the center's hands.[2]

Birdwell came to the Raiders as their sixth round draft choice in 1962 as a linebacker out of the University of Houston. When Al Davis took over the coaching reins in 1963, he converted Birdwell over to the defensive line. He was blessed with natural strength, and always gave an all-out performance at the snap of the ball. His full throttle mission of search and destroy began with a head slap (legal at that time) to the man blocking him, and then his strength allowed him to bull his way quickly into the backfield. This enabled Birdwell to become one of the most-feared pass rushers in the American Football League. His assault was so fierce that he would come back to the sidelines with a mixture of blood and pieces of an opponent's skin under his fingernails.[3]

Football players are a tough lot, and Birdwell stood out to prove that statement correct. His threshold of pain was so great that after having knee surgery, he soon tired of the large cast that ran from hip to foot. Without getting any approval, Birdwell took it upon himself to free his body from the cast, and removed it himself. The move did not allow the knee to heal the way it should have, and it sped up Birdwell's exit from the game.[4] Following the 1969 season, Birdwell's pro career ended, but he remained close to the game by coaching youth teams while tending to other businesses he was involved in. Birdwell developed heart problems after his playing days, and succumbed to a heart attack on February 14, 1978, at the age of only 37.[5] Taken way too soon from this Earth, Dan Birdwell left behind a lasting legacy in Raiders' lore as a kind-hearted sole off the field, and a force on it.

George Blanda

Longevity in the highly competitive world of professional sports is admirable. Continuous success mixed with longevity is a union of rare occurrence. That is unless one is discussing the pride of Youngwood, Pennsylvania, Mr. George Blanda. This legendary Raider began his pro football career when facemasks were non-existent, and ended it playing alongside men who were either in diapers or not even born yet when Blanda drew his first paycheck from the pro gridiron circuit.

Blanda's assault on pro football's longevity record began in 1949 as a 12th round draft pick of the Chicago Bears after a solid collegiate career at the University of Kentucky. In 1950 he was traded to the Baltimore Colts, but returned to Chicago the following year, and remained in the Windy City until 1958.[1]

It was not until Blanda's fifth season that he earned the full-time starting quarterback job in addition to his kicking chores. The quarterback job was short-lived due to a shoulder separation that sidelined him near the end of the 1954 season. For the next five seasons, the Bears once again reduced Blanda's role to backup quarterback, but he still continued to be a productive kicker. In 1959, the Bears wanted him to be a kicker only and give up quarterbacking, which Blanda stubbornly refused. Instead of going along with the request, he decided to retire.[2] If his career had ended at this stage, it would have been looked at as a good one, but not one that gained him fame and eventual immortality.

It was at the time of Blanda's retirement that the AFL emerged, and it resurrected his career. Thanks to the new league, the nearly forgotten ten-year veteran quarterback blazed a path of greatness that did lead him to ever-lasting fame.

Blanda's rebirth began as the Houston Oilers starting quarterback in 1960. With the AFL's focus on a wide-open offensive attack, the passing game was taken to new heights. Balls flew through the air at a steady pace, and many of the final scores resembled those of basketball games instead of football. Blanda loved the format, and quickly became one of the AFL's first stars after ten years of near obscurity in the NFL. He led the Oilers to three straight AFL championship game appearances, winning the title in 1960 and '61.

The 1961 season proved to be nothing short of explosive for the 34-year-old signal caller. He threw for 3,330 yards, 36 touchdowns, including seven in one game, and was named the AFL Player of the Year. After the 1966 season, Blanda left the Oilers and found his final football residence in Oakland, which was where he truly gained status as a legend.

Starting in 1967 with the Raiders, Blanda found himself as a kicker and backup quarterback once again, but at age forty, accepted his role. When other kickers began using the soccer-style approach, Blanda remained old school with his straight-on delivery, and it worked very well. So well in fact, that it allowed him the opportunity to win the 1967 AFL scoring title with 116 points in Oakland's first championship season. He also started a streak of 201 straight extra point attempts without a miss that lasted until 1971. The following year, Blanda set the Raiders' single-season scoring record with 117 points on 21 field goals and 54 extra points.

Despite all of his accolades while with the Raiders, it was his feats in 1970 that earned the highly competitive Blanda the most recognition at age 43. It all began in week six against the Pittsburgh Steelers. After starting quarterback Daryle Lamonica was injured in the first quarter, Blanda came on and threw three touchdowns, and added four extra points and a field goal. The rst scoring strike on the day was the 225th of his career. The following week, he blasted a 48-yard field goal to tie the game against Kansas City with no time left on the clock to pull out certain defeat. The tie allowed the Raiders to stay on top of the AFC Western Division. This was before the NFL went to an over-time quarter in regular season games. Against the Cleveland Browns, the Raiders were down by seven points with 4:24 left, and Blanda came on for an injured Lamonica. He immediately took the team 63 yards downfield, and capped the drive off with a touchdown pass. His extra point tied the game, and with seven seconds left, he drilled a 52-yard field goal to pull out another win. Victories over the Denver Broncos and San Diego Chargers were also determined by either Blanda's arm or foot, and thanks to both, the Raiders won another division title, and he walked away with the 1970 AFC Player of the Year Award.[3]

Blanda remained a strong force in the Oakland arsenal for five more seasons, still productive at age 47. When he finally retired the following year, Blanda racked up incredible numbers. He was the only player in pro football history to suit up for a quarter of a century plus one year. His longevity helped him become the all-time leading scorer with 2,002 points, which were 553 more than the nearest challenger. He also was the Raiders' all-time leading scorer with 863 points. His 340 total game appearances also set a pro football record. In the passing department, he threw for a career total of 26,920 yards and 236 touchdowns.[4] The dedication and talent of George Blanda was reflected with his selection to the all-time AFL team, the 25-year AFL-NFL team, and on August 1, 1981, with his induction into the Pro Football Hall of Fame in his first year of eligibility. He passed away on September 27, 2010, after a short illness.

Cliff Branch

Speed Kills! The football version of this motto was made famous by wide receiver Clifford (Cliff) Branch, who for over a decade blazed his way across gridirons like a jet plane overhead. His ability to outrun virtually everyone on a football field from the mid–1970's and early 80's allowed Branch to score from anywhere on the field and become a game-breaking threat any time he touched the ball. However, at first, Branch needed some polish to go along with his incredible wheels.

His speed was originally displayed as a scholastic track star at E.E. Worthing High school in Houston, Texas, where he became the first high school sprinter to run the 100-yard dash in under ten seconds. He won the state championship in that event, as well as in the 200-yard dash. He was also a star receiver on the football team, being selected All-District twice.[1]

Branch continued his athletic career at the University of Colorado where his world-class speed was utilized as a split end and kick returner. After football, he dominated during the track season, once running the 100-yard dash in an incredible 9.1 seconds.[2]

The Raiders made Branch their fourth round selection in the 1972 draft, but the team did not know if he was going to report to training camp due to having an opportunity to compete for a spot on the United States Olympic Team during the summer leading up to the Olympics in Munich, Germany.[3] The Raiders won out, but unfortunately, a re-occurring hamstring injury slowed him down at first. The Raiders allowed Branch time to heal before working him out hard, but when he was able to go, the coaching staff actually saw how fast he really was. He was able to turn his speed up a notch and distance himself from anyone covering him. After seeing the rookie do this on a frequent basis, the coaches decided to make Branch a starter.[4]

In the Raiders' regular season opener against Pittsburgh, Branch dropped several passes that he should have caught with ease. This forced head coach John Madden to replace the rookie speedster with another first-year man, Mike Siani. Branch was placed on the special teams for the rest of his initial pro campaign, using his speed to return punts and kickoffs.[5]

He began to work hard on hand-eye coordination, and applied that to extra practice with quarterback Ken Stabler. Branch was also mentored by Fred Biletnikoff, who taught him how to read defensive coverage. By 1974, the speedster had honed his skills with the help of two Raiders greats, and was ready to establish himself as a true professional when he was called into a starting role when Siani suffered a torn Achilles tendon.[6]

With teams using two defensive backs to cover the crafty veteran Biletnikoff, this allowed only one poor soul to guard Branch. This was a perfect situation, as his speed made it easy to separate himself from any defender and get open. With the incredible passing accuracy of Oakland's quarterback Ken Stabler, Branch caught 60 passes for 1,092 yards and 13 touchdowns. His yardage and touchdown totals led the league, and he earned All-Pro honors and a spot on the Pro Bowl team.

Branch continued to perform as one of football's top receivers over the next decade, becoming one of the game's most feared and respected deep threats. He was named to three more All-Pro teams (1975, 1976, 1977), and went to the Pro Bowl in the same years. He was also one of the smallest players in the league, but was extremely durable and never suffered any serious injuries. He played in seven AFC Championship Games, and was one of only a handful of players to earn three Super Bowl rings as a Raider. At the time of his retirement, Branch was the all-time leading receiver in post-season history with 73 catches for 1,289 yards and five touchdowns. He was outstanding in Super Bowl competition, where he had five receptions and two six-pointers in Super Bowl XV against Philadelphia, and six catches for 94 yards and one touchdown against Washington in Super Bowl XVIII.

The speedster from Texas also became only the seventh wide receiver in NFL history to ever play 14 or more seasons.[7] He had 22 games of 100 yards or more receiving, and tied an NFL record by scoring on a 99-yard touchdown against Washington in a 1983 regular season game.

After the 1985 season, Branch retired with 501 career receptions, 8,685 yards, 67 touchdowns, and was near the top of the all-time receiving list. The only time that speed has not helped Branch was when he became eligible for the Pro Football Hall of Fame in 1991. Year after year has passed without Branch getting the opportunity to be among the immortals. Hopefully the election committee will speed their decision up in the near future, and place this gifted receiver among his peers already enshrined.

Bob Brown

Bob Brown opened the Oakland chapter of his career by confidently walking his massive and powerful frame over to a set of wooden goal posts on the Raiders' practice field. He then took his gargantuan, sledgehammer-like arms and gave the goalposts a swift, forearm blast that shattered the wood, causing it to collapse. This was the calling card for the behemoth in cleats known as "the Boomer," who quickly sent the message that he had arrived in Raider Nation, not that he needed any introduction.[1] For the future Hall of Famers' reputation as one of the most dominant offensive linemen in the game's history preceded him.

Big and powerful at 6-4 and 280 pounds, "the Boomer" came into professional football in 1964 after being selected college football's top lineman the previous year. The All-American offensive tackle took his accolades from the University of Nebraska to the Philadelphia Eagles as the second overall draft pick.[2] Anyone opposing this massive wall of flesh and muscle always came away from the experience battered.

Brown's technique was one of reckless abandon, thrusting his powerful frame into oncoming defenders, constantly attacking by using his powerful arms to beat opponents into submission. Brown enjoyed witnessing his handy work, especially by the fourth quarter. After no letting up, the linemen facing him throughout sixty minutes of this abuse were left totally demoralized, exhausted and aching all over.[3]

Before ending his pro career in a silver and black uniform from 1971 to '73, "the Boomer" went from the Eagles to the Los Angeles Rams in 1969 and '70. His incredible talent earned him First Team All-NFL seven times, NFL/NFC Offensive Lineman of the Year three times, All-Decade NFL Team of the 1960's, and six trips to the Pro Bowl, including one with the Raiders in 1971.[4] He received the ultimate individual honor the sport can bestow on its players in 2004 when he was enshrined into the Pro Football Hall of Fame.

Tim Brown

Even though a player must be retired for at least five seasons before being considered for enshrinement in the Hall of Fame, there are some players of elite status whose futures alongside the game's immortals are guaranteed while they are still active. Tim Brown is one of those players who already had a spot reserved for his bust in Canton, Ohio, while he was still catching passes for the Raiders. One of the most prolific offensive weapons in NFL history, he was the only Raider to score on a pass reception, rush, kickoff return and punt return. In 2001, he became the team's all-time scoring leader in touchdowns, reaching 100 to become the first Raider to accomplish this feat.

Brown came to the Raiders as their number one draft pick in 1988, and the sixth overall selection. Despite playing for a high school in Texas that won only four games during his time there, Brown stood out so much that big-time college programs flocked to get him onto their campus.[1] He decided on Notre Dame, and after four years with the Fighting Irish, he established himself as a legend at one of the most storied American universities. He was selected All-American twice, and won the Heisman Trophy in 1987, becoming the first-ever wide receiver to be honored with

college football's highest accolade. He did more than catch passe however. For Tim Brown was the complete offensive packag and was a threat to score any time he touched the ball. So muc so that he was dubbed "Touchdown Timmy." When his days o the historical South Bend campus were over, Brown had amasse 137 receptions, 22 touchdowns, and a school record of 5,024 tot yards.[2]

Trading in his gold helmet for a silver one, Brown entere the NFL with exceptional credentials, and over the course of 1 pro seasons, lived up to all of them. His impact on Raider Natio was swift, as he led the league with 41 kickoff returns for 1,09 yards and one six-pointer for a 26.8-yard average. His 444 yard on 49 punt returns led the AFC in that category. He added 4 receptions for 725 yards and five touchdowns, and his 2,317 yard of total offense produced a record for rookies.

His sophomore campaign ended quickly when he suffere an injury in the opening game, which forced him to miss th entire season. He rebounded in 1990 to rank fourth in the AFC with an 8.7-yard average on 34 punt returns, and chipped in wit 18 receptions for 265 yards and three touchdowns. In 1991, Brow earned All-Pro, All-AFC, and made his second Pro Bowl appear ance after finishing in a tie for first place among AFC punt re turners with an 11.4-yard average. It was during this seasons tha Brown recorded his first punt return for a touchdown. In 1992 Brown began to establish himself as a wide receiver, making 49 catches for 693 yards and seven touchdowns. He still returne punts, and ranked fifth in the AFC with a 10.4-yard average.

It was in 1993 that Brown firmly earned a name as a receiver and began on his path to becoming one of the greatest at that position in the history of the league. He caught 80 passes for a AFC-high 1,180 yards and seven touchdowns, won All-AFC honors, and was selected for his third Pro Bowl, with both accolades coming at wide receiver for the first time in his career.

In 1994, for the second straight year, Brown went to the Pro Bowl as a receiver after once again leading the conference with 1,342 yards on 89 receptions. He scored 10 touchdowns, and received All-AFC recognition and his fifth Pro Bowl selection in a year that saw the Raiders move back to Oakland after playing in Los Angeles for 13 seasons. A sixth Pro Bowl appearance, and a fourth All-AFC selection came Brown's way following the '96 season in which he set an NFL record with 301 career punt returns, and ended the year in fourth place all-time with 3,083 yards on punt returns. He also tied for second place among AFC receivers with 90 receptions for 1,104 yards and nine touchdowns.

Tim Brown's 1997 season could have dubbed "The Year of Fallen Records," as he broke one after another over the course of the regular season. He caught a career-high 104 passes, which tied him for first place among NFL receivers for the year, and established a new single-game team record previously held by Todd Christensen with 95 catches in 1986.[3] Brown then became the team's all-time leading receiver, overthrowing Fred Biletnikoff's 589 career receptions, and set the new total yardage record with 12,803 yards. Other team records that he went on to break were seven 100-yard plus receiving games, five 150-yard plus receiving games (which also tied an NFL record), single-season yardage gained on receptions (1,408), and most catches in one game (14). He was an easy selection to make for the league when it put together the All-Pro and All-AFC teams. He made a seventh Pro

owl appearance, and received the Raiders' "Commitment to Ex-
ellence Award."

The 1998 campaign saw Brown continue on his path to
reatness. It marked the sixth straight year in which he went over
he 1,000-yard barrier on 81 receptions, and also set a team record
rith 9,600 career-receiving yards. He reached yet another mile-
tone in 1999 by catching the 700th pass of his career. His 90 re-
eptions earned him All-AFC honors and his eighth trip to the
'ro Bowl, tying him for the all-time team leadership in that cat-
gory with Art Shell and Howie Long.

The new millennium did nothing to slow Tim Brown down,
s the 2000 campaign produced 76 catches for 1,128 yards and a
ersonal best 11 six-pointers. His final touchdown reception of
he season gave him 77 for his career, which allowed him to move
ast Fred Biletnikoff for the all-time lead in that category.[4] The
ollowing year, Brown became the only player in Raiders' history
o be selected for nine Pro Bowls after catching 91 passes for 1,165
ards and nine touchdowns. This marked the ninth straight season
n which Brown gained over 1,000 yards receiving, and it proved
o be the second longest streak in NFL history, next to Jerry Rice's
1.[5] He also became the Raiders' all-time scoring leader in touch-
lowns with 100, and that total placed him 12th in NFL history
long with Franco Harris of Pittsburgh fame.

Brown helped Oakland win the AFC championship in 2002
y catching 81 passes for 930 yards and two touchdowns. The
ollowing year he had 52 receptions for 567 yards and two six-
ointers. Prior to the 2004 season, Brown went to play for his
ld Oakland coach Jon Gruden in Tampa Bay after turning down
request by the Oakland coaching staff to cut down on his playing
ime. He felt that he could still contribute to the game, and
Gruden gave him the opportunity.[6] Unfortunately, time began
o slow the great receiver down after 16 seasons, and he was
educed to catching a mere 24 passes for 200 yards and one touch-
lown. Despite his low numbers, Brown still managed to hit one
inal milestone, which was when he scored his 100th career touch-
lown receiving.

It became apparent to Brown that it was time to leave the
ame that reaped him so much acclaim. However, he had one
inal request before retiring. He wanted to go out as a member of
he Silver and Black, and the organization was more than willing
o grant their all-time greatest receiver that privilege. In July of
2005, the Raiders signed Brown to a one-day contract, and then
ie announced his retirement.[7] His numbers over 17 seasons are
istonishing. He had 1,094 receptions for 14,934 yards and 100
ouchdowns. His reception and touchdown totals ranked him
hird all-time in those categories at the time of his retirement.

Tim Brown became eligible for enshrinement into the Pro
'ootball Hall of Fame in 2010, and just missed the final cut. How-
ver, the odds are extremely good that his bust is already being
nade due to the fact that it is an absolute guarantee that he will
e among the game's immortals very soon. Throughout his illus-
rious career, Brown displayed class and incredible athletic ability.
He provided the youth of America with a great role model, and
he Silver and Black with one of the greatest to ever wear their
colors.

Willie Brown

The pride of Yazoo City, Mississippi became one of the greatest defensive backs to ever strap on a helmet, and over the course
of sixteen seasons, the name Willie Brown became synonymous
with excellence.

Brown came into professional football after playing under
college coaching legend Eddie Robinson at Grambling as a linebacker. Despite an outstanding collegiate career, he was not selected in the annual draft. Instead, he signed a free agent contract
with the Houston Oilers in 1963, but was released before the regular season began.[1]

Brown then found his way to Denver, and earned a starting
position at defensive back, a position he never played before. To
compensate for his lack of experience at the new position, Brown
looked for any edge he could to secure a place on the team. At
the snap, Brown would hit the receiver he was covering in the
chest with a foreman or hands in an attempt to stymie him and
throw off his timing. This little jolt at the line of scrimmage allowed Brown the opportunity to get an advantage on his man,
and then with outstanding covering skills, he blanketed the
receiver throughout the play. This was the beginning of the bump-
and-run style of defensive coverage, and it helped Brown become
one of the greatest defensive backs in the game's history.[2]

Brown possessed speed, great mobility, and an aggressive
style. He also had exceptional instincts when it came to knowing
where a receiver was going due to lengthy film study, and loved
to cover the best in the game.[3] Those traits, and his reputation as
a stellar defensive back were established with the Broncos starting
in 1964. In that season, he tied a pro football record with four interceptions in one game, and began a streak of picking off at least
one pass per season over the course of 16 years to set an NFL
record. His efforts earned him a spot on the 1964 All-AFL team,
and the following season brought him MVP honors in the AFL
All-Star Game.

In 1967, Brown was brought into the Silver and Black fold
via a trade with Denver. He made an impact on the team right
from the beginning, and was a vital part of Oakland's first championship team in 1967. The next year, his leadership was so respected that his teammates elected him defensive captain, a title
held for the rest of his career.[4]

While with the Raiders, Brown never played on a losing
team, and appeared in three AFL and six AFC Championship
Games. From 1968 through 1975, Brown and the Raiders suffered
five title game losses, but by 1976, the bitter taste of defeat was
obliterated by a convincing 32–14 win over the Minnesota Vikings
in Super Bowl XI. In that game, Brown added the major highlight
of his career by intercepting a pass and returning it 75 yards for
a touchdown. As the leader of possibly the greatest defensive backfield in history, Brown and fellow "Soul Patrol" members Jack
"the Assassin" Tatum, George "Hit Man" Atkinson, and Skip "Dr.
Death" Thomas, terrorized receivers who dared cross their paths.

Following the 1978 season, Brown retired, but could not pry
himself away from the Raiders' organization. The team did not
want all of Brown's knowledge to go to waste, and named him
defensive backfield coach from 1979 to 1988. During his tenure
as coach, he earned two more Super Bowl rings in 1980 and 1983.
He left the team after the 1988 campaign to pursue other coaching

options on the college and high school level before returning to the Raiders in 1995 as Director of Squad Development, and also helped tutor the defensive backs.[5]

Over the course of his 16 pro seasons, Brown played in 205 games and had 54 interceptions. He had 39 interceptions as a Raider, which ties him for first place on the team's all-time list with Lester Hayes. He earned All-Pro honors seven times, was selected to nine Pro Bowls, and was a unanimous pick for the all-time AFL team. Another unanimous decision concerning Willie Brown occurred in 1984 when the Pro Football Hall of Fame enshrined him in his first year of eligibility.

Billy Cannon

By the time Billy Cannon came to the Raiders in 1964, he already had a football career others could have only dreamed of. Even though Cannon left the Louisiana State University campus at the dawn of the 1960's, his name and exploits place him on the upper echelon of LSU gridiron legends.

At 6-1, 210 pounds, Cannon had all the tools necessary for football excellence. He was blazing fast (9.9 100-yard dash), and strong due to a weight lifting regime. He was one of the first to use weight training when it was still considered an unorthodox practice by many so-called experts who felt that bigger muscles would slow a player up. Cannon obviously proved that the myth was just that.[1]

A two-time All-American halfback, Cannon was the main offensive weapon in LSU's drive to the 1958 national championship. He then topped his collegiate career off by bringing the coveted Heisman Trophy to the bayou the following year. The multi-talented performer quickly became the hottest commodity throughout the professional gridiron circuit. He provided the established NFL and the upstart AFL with the first volley in a six-year struggle to obtain high-caliber players.

Cannon signed with both the NFL's Los Angeles Rams and the AFL's Houston Oilers. It took a court ruling to decide that he would go play in Houston.[2] With the most prolific college player from the previous year now brought into the fold, the AFL's status was elevated a few levels with the football-watching masses. His impact on the league and public was immediate, as he helped guide the Oilers to the first two AFL championships and played for a third in 1962. He led the league in rushing in 1961 with 948 yards on his way to earning All-AFL honors. He also racked up 90 receptions in three seasons, twenty of which went for touchdowns.

During the 1964 pre-season, Cannon had a good showing against the Raiders, and Oakland's head coach Al Davis decided that he wanted the offensive weapon in a silver and black uniform. Making it easier to obtain Cannon was the fact that Houston wanted to trade him. Davis jumped at the chance to bring him to Oakland, and Cannon was set to begin on another stellar chapter of his already magnificent career.[3]

Upon his arrival in Oakland, the team already had a tremendous running back, and reigning league Most Valuable Player in Clem Daniels. Davis looked to merge two of the league's top backfield stars, and moved Cannon over to fullback. With his speed and great ability to catch the ball, Davis looked to send Cannon deep on pass routes. These skills got Al Davis to thinking,

and a decision was made to convert the former Heisman winn[into a tight end. His athletic prowess allowed the LSU produ[to perform his new assignment without any problems. He becam[another deep threat in Oakland's arsenal that a defense had [look to contain.[4]

In the Raiders' drive to the 1967 AFL title, Cannon had h[best season with the Silver and Black. His 32 receptions resulte[in 629 yards and 10 touchdowns, and a spot on the All-AFL team[Over his six seasons with the Raiders, Cannon caught 134 pass[for 2,268 yards, and 25 touchdowns in 79 games. In 1970 h[finished out his illustrious pro career with the Kansas City Chief[and became only one of twenty players to compete in the enti[history of the AFL.

During off-seasons, Cannon attended dental school, an[after he retired, he became a highly successful orthodontist i[Baton Rouge. With his popularity so prominent throughou[Louisiana, his income apparently soared upwards well into th[hundreds of thousands of dollars a year. In a shocking turn [events, Cannon was arrested in July of 1983 for his involveme[in a $6 million counterfeiting ring. Cannon pleaded guilty an[served over two-and-a-half years in federal prison. After his releas[in 1986, Cannon got his dental license back, but he had a difficu[time rebuilding his practice. By 1995, he filed for bankruptc[and two years later, he was very strapped financially.[5]

With some connections, Cannon got a job at the dental clini[at Angola State Penitentiary, where he totally revamped the facilit[to a first-class operation. Like everyone, Cannon made a decisio[that was not right. He paid for it and moved on to another chapte[of his life.

Dave Casper

Tight end Dave Casper never seemed to take football ver[seriously. It was claimed that he did not think the game was fu[and he hated training camp and practice.[1] Despite these negativ[feelings, "the Ghost" emerged as one of the greatest tight ends o[his time. The Minnesota native first made his way to storied Notr[Dame before reaching gridiron immortality on the professiona[level with the Silver and Black.

While serving as team captain for the Fighting Irish durin[his senior season, Casper became an All-American and helpe[Notre Dame to a national championship in 1973. The 6-4, 235 [pounder was then ready for the pro ranks, and the Raiders gave hir[the chance by selecting him in the second round of the 1974 draft[

Casper's first two seasons in Oakland were mostly spent as [special team performer. By 1976, after catching only nine passe[in his first two seasons, Casper was not denied any longer, an[earned a starting position during training camp. He proved tha[he belonged among the game's best with a breakout season tha[produced 53 receptions, which was the most by a tight end i[1976. He gained 691 yards, scored 10 touchdowns, earned All-Pr[and Pro Bowl selections, and helped the Raiders reap the ultimat[success that professional football offered. Oakland went 13–1 dur[ing the regular season, and capped off their incredible run with [dominating 32–14 win over the Minnesota Vikings in Super Bow[XI. In that game, Casper caught four passes for 70 yards, an[scored the first touchdown on a 1-yard pass from Ken Stabler. H[also did a tremendous job blocking on running plays.

In 1977, Casper led the team with 48 receptions, and earned ever-lasting fame in a divisional playoff game against the Baltimore Colts when he caught the winning touchdown on a play forever known as "The Ghost to the Post." The following year saw Casper once again partake in Raiders lore by recovering a fumble in the end zone for the winning touchdown after the ball bounced many yards on the final play of a game against San Diego that came to be dubbed "The Holy Roller."

In 1980, after four straight All-Pro and Pro Bowl selections, Casper was traded to the Houston Oilers midway through the season. In Houston, he was once again teamed up with quarterback Ken Stabler, and the pair picked up right where they left off from their Raiders days together. Casper hauled in 56 of "the Snake's" aerials along the way to a fifth Pro Bowl appearance. Casper returned to the Raiders for his final campaign in 1984 before retiring with 378 career receptions for 5,216 yards and 52 touchdowns.

Throughout his great career, Casper was considered the perfect tight end. He possessed good size, a solid built, and was very physical. He had the strength of an offensive lineman, which helped him become a superb blocker, and had a decent amount of speed and quickness off the snap. He could barrel his way through a defense after catching a pass, and then destroy someone on the next play with great run blocking ability. He also had a tremendous pair of hands that allowed him the opportunity to catch any pass thrown in his direction. His best play was cutting across the middle, and then outmuscling a linebacker for the ball. His size and power then made it very difficult to bring him down.[2] Casper's greatness continued to be rewarded after his retirement with selection to the 1970's All-Decade Team, the Silver Anniversary All-Super Bowl Team, and induction in to the Pro Football Hall of Fame in 2002.

Todd Christensen

Articulate, well read, highly cerebral: Todd Christensen possessed the qualities of some of the world's greatest thinkers. He also was a physical threat on a football field, with a mixture of toughness and an incredible pair of hands that made him the premier tight end in pro football throughout the mid–1980's.

Initially, Christensen entered the professional ranks as a 6-3, 230 pound fullback out of Brigham Young University. With good size and speed (4.6 in the 100-yard dash), and the ability to catch the ball, it did not take the powers that be within the NFL to realize the possible worth that Christensen could bring to a team.[1]

At the time of the 1978 draft, the Dallas Cowboys were defending Super Bowl champions, and were regarded by many as the most popular pro football team in the league. It was into this environment that Christensen found himself when "America's Team" selected him in the second round of the draft. The Cowboys drafted him as a running back, but he was placed on injured reserve before having a chance to play in one regular season game.[2]

Prior to the 1979 season, Christensen was approached by legendary Dallas head coach Tom Landry about the possibility of moving over to tight end. Christensen declined Landry's offer, telling the coaching icon that he wanted to remain a running back. His refusal was looked at as not being able to conform to the idea of doing what was best for the team. This was not true, but that was what the Dallas coaching staff perceived it to mean. After that, it did not take the Cowboys long to break their association with Christensen, and by the pre-season, he said goodbye to the Lone Star State.[3]

The New York Giants then acquired him as a free agent, and also wanted him to play tight end, but once again he held strong to his convictions. The Giants also did not take too kindly to the refusal, and released him after he appeared in one game for them.[4]

It was at this point that Christensen's professional career took a dramatic turn for the better when the Oakland Raiders signed him to a free agent contract in October of 1979 before the fifth game of the regular season. Upon his arrival in Raider Nation, Oakland head coach Tom Flores immediately placed him on the special teams unit. In addition to his running and pass catching abilities, Christensen was also an exceptional snapper in punting situations. Flores also asked him to seriously consider moving over to tight end. Even though the Raiders already had three stellar tight ends in Dave Casper, Raymond Chester, and Derrick Ramsey, Christensen felt that this might be his last opportunity, and finally agreed to make the switch.[5]

Christensen began working out with the tight ends, and was listed as number four on the depth chart at that position. Instead of looking at his situation as bleak, he saw it as a challenge, and began working extremely hard to prove that he could make it in the NFL as a tight end. In 1980, Christensen began to make major progress at the new position by continuing to push himself to reach near perfection. He also worked his way up the depth chart when Casper was traded to the Houston Oilers during the season. Following the 1981 season, Raymond Chester retired, which allowed Christensen to yet again climb up to the number two spot. It was also during the '81 campaign that he caught his first passes as a pro, and finished with eight receptions for 115 yards and two touchdowns.

In 1982, Derrick Ramsey began the season as the starter, but he suffered a knee injury before the first regular season game, which gave Christensen the opportunity to take over the tight end chores. He quickly made up for lost time, and led the Raiders in receptions with 42 in a season reduced to nine games due to a player's strike.

It was during the 1983 season that Christensen established himself as a superstar tight end by catching a league-leading 92 passes for 1,247 yards and 12 touchdowns. He earned All-Pro and All-AFC honors, went to the Pro Bowl, and became only the fifth player in team history to surpass 1,000 receiving yards. Up to that time, only three other players in pro football history had more receptions in a single season than Christensen did in 1983.

Over the next three seasons, Christensen became one of the game's greatest tight ends of his time. He earned All-Pro honors every year (1984, 1985, 1986), All-AFC (1985, 1986), and was selected for the Pro Bowl after all three seasons. In 1984, he caught 80 passes for 1,000 yards and seven touchdowns. The following year he ranked second in the AFC and fourth in the league with 82 receptions for 987 yards and six touchdowns. In 1986, Christensen was back on top, leading all receivers with 95 catches for 1,153 yards and eight six-pointers. He set the NFL's all-time single-season record for most receptions by a tight end, and became the only receiver in league history to catch at least 80 passes in four straight seasons.

In another strike-shortened season in 1987 that limited most NFL performers to 12 games, Christensen earned his fourth All-AFC selection and a fifth trip to the Pro Bowl after catching 47 passes for 663 yards to rank second among AFC tight ends. Prior to missing some games due to the strike, Christensen played in 119 consecutive games. The streak ended when replacement players filled in for the regulars while negotiations between the NFL and the Player's Union were worked out.

The 1988 season proved to be the last for Christensen, as he was limited to seven games due to injuries. In his 137 game appearances wearing silver and black, he caught 461 passes for 5,872 yards and 41 touchdowns, which ranked him near the top in many of the Raiders' all-time receiving categories. He was also brilliant in post-season play. In eight playoff games, in which he earned two Super Bowl rings, Christensen had 31 receptions for 358 yards and one touchdown. He will always be remembered as the best tight end in all of football during the mid–1980's, and hopefully the name Todd Christensen will someday appear on the Pro Football Hall of Fame's list of immortals.

Dave Dalby

Replacing a legend such as Jim Otto could not have been an easy task, but after doing so, Dave Dalby went on to make his mentor proud. Drafted in 1972 by the Raiders in the fourth round, Dalby learned the center position from one of the game's all-time greats in Otto. After three seasons of apprenticeship under Otto, Dalby was ready to take the reins. Beginning with the 1975 regular season opener, he never relinquished his starting job until giving way to Don Mosebar two games into the 1985 season, thus making him only the second center in the team's first 25 campaigns. He was also part of one of the greatest offensive lines in history, playing alongside Hall of Famers Gene Upshaw and Art Shell.

Dalby was a tremendous center and snapper on extra points and field goals, and his 14 seasons and 205 consecutive game appearances as a member of the Raiders rank him near the top in team history in those categories. He was the starting center in three Super Bowls (1976, 1980, 1983), and served as offensive captain from 1982 to 1984.[1]

Dalby's long career came to an end during the pre-season in 1986 when he was released. Life after football was extremely unkind to Dalby. His weight skyrocketed to well over 300 pounds, he suffered through a divorce, lost upwards of $700,000 in a real estate investment that crashed after the company was charged with embezzlement, and eventually reduced to living in the back of his van.[2] The only bit of good news that came his way was when he earned a Hall of Fame nomination in 2001.

Life was becoming more and more painful both emotionally and physically for the once stellar anchor of the Raiders' trench warriors. While still a player, Dalby heard about a report claiming that many NFL offensive linemen's life expectancy tops out at 52 years of age. He brought that statistic up on many occasions, possibly transfixed on it.[3] On August 30, 2002, witnesses at Capistrano Beach, north of San Diego, saw a van with Dalby sitting behind the wheel in a parking lot. Suddenly, the van accelerated through the lot and crashed into a tree at a high rate of speed. He was taken to a local hospital where he was pronounced dead at the age of 51, more likely than not the result of an apparent sui-

cide.[4] Despite his post-career woes, the Pro Football Hall of Fame should acknowledge Dalby with not just a nomination, but someday allow his bust to be alongside that of his mentor Jim Otto.

Clem Daniels

Clem Daniels was the first multi-talented offensive weapon that the Raiders had in their formative years. However, it was as a running back under Al Davis where Daniels truly excelled, and he proved to be the standard bearer by which all other Raiders backs sought to measure up to.

Blessed with a good attitude, strong work ethic, and blazing speed (9.8 seconds in the 100-yard dash), Daniels looked to be the type of player that pro football scouts dream about after the McKinney, Texas native made the All-America team as a junior at Prairie View A&M in 1958.[1] However, all the excitement quickly faded when Daniels suffered a knee and ankle injury during his senior year. The same scouts once excited about the running back's talents now stayed away due to the injuries.

With no team in either the NFL or AFL interested in him, Daniels joined the military. The time serving his country allowed him the opportunity to heal up, and within a year, his knee and ankle were both good as new. After his release from the military in 1960, Daniels decided to give football another try.[2]

The only team willing to take a chance on him in 1960 was the AFL's Dallas Texans. He performed well enough in training camp to earn a roster spot, but was never given an opportunity to show off his talents. Throughout the season, Daniels only carried the ball one time for minus two yards. It turned out that the Texans were not interested in him as a running back, and wanted him to switch over to defensive back. Wanting to stay a running back, Daniels and the Texans came to a mutual agreement that allowed him to be released and pursue employment elsewhere.[3]

The Raiders turned out to be the elsewhere where Daniels went. In 1961, Oakland, the worst team in the AFL, signed him to a free agent contract for the season, and granted him his wish to play in the offensive backfield as a fullback.

Throughout the 1961 season, Daniels still remained one of pro football's best-kept secrets. He barely played, carrying the ball for only 154 yards on 31 attempts. The only good thing to come of the experience was that it allowed his body more time to heal, and by 1962, Daniels was not going to be denied any longer.

The 1962 Raiders finished at 1–13, but despite the dismal season, Daniels provided Oakland with a solid running attack, and finished the year with a team-high 766 rushing yards and seven touchdowns. In a game against the Houston Oilers, he ran for 187 yards. He also caught 24 passes for an additional 318 yards and one touchdown. Along with Jim Otto, Daniels was the only other decent player on this terrible team.

The fortunes of the Raiders and Clem Daniels took a major upswing in 1963 when Al Davis became the head coach. After evaluating the team left to him, Davis came away highly impressed with Daniels. He immediately moved him over to halfback to utilize his speed, and wanted the ball in his hands as much as possible. Davis also noticed that Daniels had the ability to catch the ball out of the backfield, and so, thanks to Al Davis' keen eye for talent, a multi-threat offensive weapon was unleashed.[4]

In 1963, with Daniels as the feature back, Oakland finished 10–4. He ran for 1,099 yards to set a then-single season AFL record. He also caught 30 passes for 685 yards and five touchdowns, in addition to the three he scored by rushing. Daniels also added two single-game team records to his dream season by rushing for 200 yards against the New York Jets, and caught three passes for 172 yards for an incredible 57.3 yards-per-catch average against Buffalo. When the league passed out its awards following the season, Daniels earned most of them. He was selected All-Pro and received the 1963 AFL Most Valuable Player Award.

His speed, size, toughness, and ability to catch passes set the standard for all future Oakland running backs to follow. His size enabled Daniels to pound the ball up the middle and block, while his speed allowed him to get around the ends quickly and outrun defenders.

Over the next three seasons, Daniels remained near the top of the AFL rushing charts with 824, 884, and 801 yards. In Oakland's AFL championship season of 1967, he once again led the team's rushing attack with 575 yards despite breaking a leg in the tenth game. The following season, he left Oakland and played one final year with the San Francisco 49ers.

Upon his retirement, Clem Daniels left quite a legacy with the Silver and Black. He was the team's first multi-threat offensive weapon, rushing for 5,109 yards and 30 touchdowns. In the ten-year history of the AFL, no other running back gained more yards. He also caught 201 passes for 3,291 yards and 24 six-pointers. In quiet manner that saw Daniels lead by example, he became a Raiders legend. Not a bad ending for a player nobody seemed to want.

Ben Davidson

A big intimidating lineman sporting a handlebar mustache, Ben Davidson could be considered one of the forefathers of the Raider Renegade mystique. In college he was hit low in the legs on a play that could have injured him severely. Davidson relayed his displeasure with the opposing player by finding his way into the man's helmet, located his eye socket, and then proceeded to gouge it until screaming and a quick exit off the field occurred.[1]

The 6-8, 275 pound Los Angeles, California native played college football at the University of Washington. After a brief stay with the New York Giants, Davidson landed a spot on the Green Bay Packers for their run at an NFL title in 1961. He then went to the Washington Redskins, where hassles about the team's attention to how much a player needed to weight grated on the big man's nerves.[2]

By 1964, he was tired of such petty hassles, and just wanted to play the game. Al Davis came calling, brought him into his home for wayward gridiron hopefuls, and only asked that Davidson destroy anything in his path leading to opposing quarterbacks.[3] The quick and powerful defensive end loved what he heard from his mentor, and then proceeded to deliver with extreme enthusiasm on his seek and destroy mission for a team that prided themselves on hitting the hardest. He had a dislike for signal callers, and felt that they should all wear skirts. He also felt that they should be driven into the turf hard and often. In a game against the New York Jets in 1967, Davidson blasted quarterback legend Joe Namath and knocked his helmet off. A picture of that hit appeared in *Life* Magazine and added to Davidson's rough

and tumble image. A late hit on Kansas City quarterback Len Dawson in 1970 caused a bench-clearing brawl and solidified Davidson's reputation as a Raider renegade.[4] He not only tormented quarterbacks, but anyone not wearing silver and black, and earned selection to play in the AFL All-Star Game for three straight seasons from 1966 to '68. He also was selected to *The Sporting News'* All-AFL team in 1967, the season in which he helped the Raiders claim their first-ever championship. After spending the 1971 season on injured reserve, Davidson retired forever a legend in silver and black.

Clarence Davis

From USC's famed Student Body formations to the skull and crossbones of Raider Nation, Clarence Davis will forever be revered in Silver and Black lore for a pair of classic playoff performances. He made his way from the bright lights of Los Angeles, where he earned second team All-American honors under USC coaching legend John McKay, to the Oakland Raiders as their fourth round selection of the 1971 draft.

The extremely durable and versatile offensive weapon first made a name for himself in the pro ranks as an incredible kickoff return specialist. Davis led the Raiders in that category for the first three years of his career, and his 27.1 average per return ranked him third on the NFL's all-time list at the time of his retirement.[1]

At 5-10, and 205 pounds, Davis was one of the smallest running backs in Raiders' history, but he stood above all others in some of the team's most storied moments. He caught the winning touchdown pass from Ken Stabler in a 1974 playoff game in the closing seconds in what became known as "the Sea of Hands." Two years later, he ran for 137 yards against the Minnesota Vikings to help Oakland win their first Super Bowl.

Davis always provided the Raiders with toughness, and was used on a consistent basis as an offensive threat. A knee injury placed him on injured reserve in 1978, and following that season, he retired, but the name Clarence Davis will never be forgotten due to his yeoman efforts when the team needed them the most. His entire pro career was spent with the Raiders. He played in 88 games, rushing for 3,640 yards and 26 touchdowns. On top of his stellar special teams play in the early stages of his career, Davis also caught 99 passes for 865 yards and two six-pointers.

Hewritt Dixon

After being selected in the eighth round of the 1963 AFL draft by the Denver Broncos, Hewritt Dixon played three seasons in the "Mile High City" as a tight end. In 1966, the Raiders acquired him in a trade, and moved him over to fullback. At 6-2, 235 pounds, Dixon was a combination of incredible speed (9.9 seconds in the 100-yard dash), strength, and possessed a set of great hands. All these tools were applied to Oakland's running game with Dixon as the featured threat out of the backfield.[1] He was like a runaway freight train going downhill, able to obliterate any opposition in his path. With his shoulders lowered and speed and force at his disposal, Dixon brutalized defenders with bone-jarring power. He also had the capability to catch the ball out of the backfield, and was a solid blocker. The triple-threat offensive battering ram's efforts did go unnoticed, as he earned All-AFL honors in 1967 and '68, and four trips to Pro Bowl games (1966, '67, '68, and '70). In 66 games with the Raiders, Dixon rushed for 2,960 yards and 13 touchdowns, and caught 190 passes for an additional 1,750 yards and 10 six-pointers. Dixon passed away at age 52 in Los Angeles, California, after a battle with cancer on November 24, 1992.[2]

Tom Flores

The Iceman always delivered throughout his long affiliation with the Raiders organization. He earned his moniker by being cool under pressure no matter how bad things were going on around him. His initial experience with the team was as its starting quarterback in his, as well as the franchise's first season in 1960. With the exception of the 1962 season, which he missed due to a lung ailment, Flores remained a steady performer with the ability to throw the deep pass, through the team's formative years up to their emergence as a force to be reckoned with. He was traded to the Buffalo Bills in 1967, serving as a backup until his release in 1969. Flores then signed with Kansas City, and once again saw himself in a backup role, this time to future Hall of Famer Len Dawson. The good thing about his stay in Kansas City was that they won the Super Bowl that season, and Flores earned a ring for his efforts. He retired following the 1970 season, and was one of only twenty men who played the entire ten-year run of the American Football League. For his career, "the Iceman" threw for 11,959 yards and 92 touchdowns, and finished as the AFL's fifth ranked all-time passer.[1]

Rich Gannon

Quarterback Rich Gannon was a confident, dedicated team leader who became a fiery field general not afraid to holler at teammates when he felt the need called for such tactics. He was also extremely hard on himself, constantly working to perfect his game. Thanks to these traits, Gannon led the Silver and Black to many victories, and allowed them to build on their "Commitment to Excellence" motto well into the new century.

Pennsylvania has always been a breeding ground for quarterbacking talent, and Rich Gannon helped that state live up to that reputation, while earning All-City honors at Philadelphia's St. Joseph's Prep School. He then became a record-setting signal caller at the University of Delaware. In his time guiding the Blue Hens, he achieved the status of being that school's greatest quarterback. During his four years of college, he compiled 7,432 yards of total offense, and 5,927 passing yards. Both were school records, and 19 more were set by Gannon on his way to earning honorable mention All-America honors following his senior year.[1]

On draft day in 1987, the New England Patriots selected Gannon in the fourth round, and the 98th player picked overall. The only problem was that the Patriots were not convinced his throwing arm was strong enough to be NFL material, and looked to use him in the defensive backfield instead. Gannon immediately objected to the idea, and two weeks after drafting him, the Patriots traded him to the Minnesota Vikings for a pair of future draft picks.[2]

The Vikings were willing to use him at quarterback, and started him off as their third string signal caller. Over the next

three seasons, Gannon only threw 21 passes, and never got into game during the 1989 campaign. Things were different in th post-season, however, as he was forced into action against the de fending Super Bowl champion San Francisco 49ers. Despi losing, 41–13, Gannon turned in an excellent performance, com pleting 13 of 18 passes for 144 yards. His showing proved to Min nesota's coaching staff that he did have the potential, and durin the following season of 1990, he started 12 games.

In 1991, he earned the starting quarterback job by the sixt game, and went on to set a team record by not throwing an in terception in seven consecutive games. After posting an 8–4 recor in 12 starts, the Vikings traded Gannon to the Washington Red skins for a draft pick during the 1993 pre-season. The experienc with the Redskins proved to be very dismal. After playing in eigh games, four as a starter, the team did not want to re-sign him fo the 1994 season after he injured his shoulder and required surger. At this point, Gannon's career seemed destined for failure. He s out the entire season, and his future as a pro quarterback did n look like it was going to get any better.[3]

Despite watching his career go stagnant, Gannon neve stopped believing in his ability, and continued to work hard whil waiting for another opportunity. His wife is the daughter o former NFL running back Bill Brown, so she knew about th game of football, and worked with him in the backyard of the home catching his passes. He had shown that he could play quar terback in the NFL, but it seemed that no team in the leagu cared. He sent out 14 letters asking for a tryout only to be denie each time.

Just when things seemed their bleakest, hope was on th way. In April of 1995, the Kansas City Chiefs signed him to a fre agent contract. Unfortunately, things did not take an immediat upswing for Gannon in Kansas City either. In his first seaso there, he only played in two games, throwing a mere two passe

The 1996 season saw him as a backup in the first 12 game before being named the starter after a fantastic performanc against San Diego, in which he completed 22 of 31 pass attempt for 220 yards and two touchdowns. In 1997 he produced a 6– record as the starter that included a five-game winning streak o Kansas City's way to a 13–3 record. He got the chance to pla when starter Elvis Grbac broke his shoulder. However, when th playoffs came around, Grbac was healed and took over as th starter once again despite Gannon's successful run in his absence Gannon did manage to secure himself the starting job for th complete 1998 season, and threw for 2,305 yards and 10 touch downs, but was not happy with his situation in Kansas City. H then approached team officials about the possibility of becomin a free agent.[4]

Jon Gruden was an assistant coach with Kansas City at th same time Gannon was there. He was able to see the talent tha the quarterback possessed, and quickly became his biggest sup porter. In 1998 Gruden left the Chiefs to become head coach o the Raiders, but he did not forget about what he saw in Gannon

After the 1998 season, Kansas City gave Gannon the oppor tunity to test the free agent market. Once Gruden saw that Gan non was available, he jumped at the chance to put him in an Oak land uniform. In February of 1999, the Raiders signed Gannon t a contract, and another team legend was born. Like so many be fore him, Gannon finally found a home with the Silver and Black

After spending time with four teams since being drafted by the New England Patriots in 1987, Rich Gannon finally achieved status as a top-level quarterback with the Oakland Raiders from '99 until a serious neck injury ended his career in 2004. As the field leader of Jon Gruden's "dink and dunk" offensive scheme, Gannon flourished.[5] With confidence, a strong desire to win, and an accurate passing arm, he led the Silver and Black to three straight AFC Western Division titles from 2000 to 2002, and their first Super Bowl appearance in 19 years after the '02 campaign. He also earned the honor of being the only player to ever win back-to-back MVP awards in the Pro Bowl (2000–01).

In 2002, he was bestowed with being presented with the NFL Most Valuable Player Award, after an incredible season that saw the 37-year signal caller complete 67 percent of his pass attempts, throw for a league-high 4,689 yards and connect on 26 scoring tosses. His 418 completions established a new NFL record, as did his throwing for 300 yards 10 times during a season. He also tied an NFL record with six straight 300-yard passing games, and his yardage total through the air set a team record, and was the seventh highest in league history.

In 2003, Gannon was Oakland's starting quarterback for the first seven regular season games until he hurt his shoulder, and was placed on injured reserve. His 2004 campaign was even shorter, as a helmet-to-helmet collision in the third game forced him to miss the remainder of the year with a neck injury. As the 2005 season approached, the 39-year-old Gannon decided to retire in August, thus ending a career that started off slow, but became one of legendary status over his incredible three-year run from 2000 to 2002 as one of the top signal callers in football. At the time of his retirement, Gannon's 28,743 career passing yards ranked him 30th on the NFL's all-time list. All Gannon ever asked for was chance, and once given the opportunity, he made the most out of it. Upon his retirement, Gannon went on to pursue a career as an NFL game analyst.

Ray Guy

In a move considered unprecedented, the Raiders selected a punter as a first round draft pick in 1973. The decision at the time might have left many shaking their heads in disbelief as to why a team would draft a punter so high. However, over the course of the next fourteen seasons, all doubts were dispelled as to why the Raiders made that decision. From 1973 through 1986, Ray Guy became one of the greatest, if not the greatest to ever play the position. He averaged 42.4 yards per kick over his long career, led the league in punting three times (1974–75, 77), was All-Pro six time (1973–78), and made the Pro Bowl seven times (1973–78, 1980). He was also one of only a handful of Raiders to earn three Super Bowl rings. Guy so impressed the Raiders' coaching staff with his athletic ability that they made him the team's emergency quarterback due to a strong, accurate passing arm.[1] After the 1986 season, Guy began suffering from back problems. He was 38 years old at the time, a veteran of 14 NFL campaigns, and knew that time was not on his side as an athlete. Instead of trying to play on and watch his status as the greatest punter in the game go down, plus hurt the team in the process, he decided to retire.[2] He had nothing left to prove. Like so many other worthy Raiders players, Ray Guy's bust should be in the Hall of Fame. Hopefully soon, the Pro Football Hall of Fame will realize that Ray Guy belongs among the game's immortals.

Wayne Hawkins

Originally drafted by the Denver Broncos, Hawkins joined the Raiders prior to the start of the 1960 season. From that point on, "Hawk" excelled as a powerful blocker from his right guard position until his retirement following the 1970 season.[1] During his tenure, he earned five trips to the AFL All-Star Game (1963–67), All-Pro in 1966, and is a member of the Raiders' all-time team. Hawkins is only one of twenty men to play through the entire ten-year history of the American Football League.

Lester Hayes

During the 1980's, "the Judge" presided over the Raiders' secondary, dishing out his brand of justice on all who tested him. In the mid–1980's, Lester Hayes teamed up with Mike Haynes to become the most dominant set of cornerbacks in the game.

With the legendary Willie Brown's stellar career nearing its end, the Raiders braced themselves for the vacuum created by drafting Lester Hayes in 1977. To replace one of the best cornerbacks in history is obviously a tough mountain to climb. However, the task was made easier once the Raiders saw Hayes make a name for himself by emerging into one of the most respected defensive backs of his time.

At Texas A&M, Hayes played two years at linebacker, and finished out his college career at safety. On the day he was drafted, Hayes was disappointed when 14 other defensive backs were selected ahead of him.[1] The Raiders got Hayes in the fifth round, and it was then that he decided to make all the other teams in the league regret their grave mistake.

At first Hayes was faced with a challenging roadblock. The Raiders wanted him to play cornerback, which he never did before. He worked hard prior to his rookie training camp to familiarize himself with the new position.[2] Helping his confidence once at camp was the fact that Hayes had to cover the great Fred Biletnikoff in practice and did well. By the final game of his rookie season, he captured a starting job and held it for the next decade.[3]

Not only did covering Biletnikoff help Hayes learn to be a cornerback, but the Hall of Fame receiver also introduced him to the world of Stickum, which was a substance that allowed anything it came in contact with to immediately stick to the goo. It was during his rookie year when he went to intercept a pass and it went off his fingertips. He then noticed Biletnikoff's old pal Stickum, put some on his fingers, and then everywhere. The love affair with the flypaper in a can lasted until the NFL banned the substance in 1981.[4]

Hayes became a master at man-to-man coverage and the bump and run. He would line up across from a receiver, crouch down low, and then explode into the opponent at the snap, bumping him for the allowed five yards downfield. The shuck allowed Hayes to disrupt the receiver's timing on pass routes, and then he had the ability to stay right with the receiver throughout the play.[5]

Hayes worked hard on the field to establish himself as a top-rate defender, and off the field, he studied film to find even the most remote tendency that could allow him an edge. He came onto the team with the most intimidating secondary possibly of all-time. A few years later, he established himself as the leader of another group of defensive backs that ruled the early to mid–1980's. Hayes helped the Raiders win two Super Bowls, was selected to five Pro Bowls, four All-Pro teams, and was the 1980 NFL Defensive Player of the Year. Upon his retirement following the 1986 season, his 39 regular season interceptions tied him with Willie Brown for the all-time lead in Raiders history, and he added eight more in the post-season. Lester Hayes has been eligible for induction into the Pro Football Hall of Fame since the early 1990's. Hopefully, the election committee will do the right thing and place this incredible talent in football's shrine of greatness.

Mike Haynes

From historic New England to the glitz and glamour of Los Angeles, Mike Haynes' pro football journey was filled with excellence that eventually led him to everlasting fame in Canton, Ohio. During the late 1970's, and through most of the 80's, Haynes established himself as one of the premier defensive backs in pro football history. Blessed with speed, quickness, and size, he specialized in playing man-to-man coverage to perfection by staying so close to a receiver that it appeared they were in the same jersey. In preparation for an opponent, Haynes studied countless hours of film, and then rearranged his moves according to those of the man he would be facing on game day.[1]

In November of 1983, Haynes became a member of the Raiders, and was teamed up with Lester Hayes at cornerback. Together, these two men gave the Silver and Black the best cornerback tandem in the game, and from that point on, Haynes went on to become a Raiders legend. However, long before he put on a Raiders jersey, Haynes was already a proven star.

Raised in Los Angeles, California, Haynes established himself in high school in both football and track before becoming a star defensive back and punt returner at Arizona State University. After earning All-American honors following his junior and senior seasons, Haynes was ready to take his talents to the pro ranks.[2]

The New England Patriots made him the first defensive back taken in the 1976 draft, and fifth player selected overall. Expectations were high for Haynes when he reported to New England's training camp in the summer of 1976, and he did not let anyone down. He became a starting cornerback and punt return specialist, and was named 1976 AFC Rookie of the Year. From 1976 to 1978, he led the Patriots in interceptions, and was also the team's all-time punt returner with a 10.4-yard average. He earned six trips to the Pro Bowl, and was named All-Pro in 1977, 1978, and 1982.[3]

After seven seasons with New England, Haynes played out his option, and signed with the Los Angeles Raiders in November of 1983. In exchange, the Raiders gave up a first round draft pick in 1984, and a second round pick in 1985.[4] Haynes was well worth losing those draft picks for, as his impact on the Raiders was immediate.

The cornerback dynamic duo of Haynes and Hayes clamped down on any set of receivers who opposed them. This made things extremely miserable for quarterbacks looking to get rid of the ball while being rushed by some of the best linemen (Lyle Alzado, Howie Long) and linebackers (Ted Hendricks, Rod Martin) in

the business. When the Raiders played the Washington Redski in Super Bowl XVIII following the 1983 season, Haynes an Hayes totally shut down a receiving corps regarded as one of t best. Haynes also had an interception in the lopsided 38–9 L Angeles win.

In 1984, he started every game, intercepted six passes, a led the league with 220 yards off those thefts. He also set a tea record with 151 yards returned off two interceptions. He earne All-Pro and All-Conference honors, and another trip to the P Bowl. Two more Pro Bowl selections followed the 1985 and '8 campaigns. Haynes played until the completion of the 198 season, and left the game with 46 career interceptions, plus t distinction of being one of the greatest defensive backs to ev play professional football. He was selected to the 1980's Al Decade Team, the NFL's 75th Anniversary Team, and in 1997 came as surprise to no one when he received the highest hon by becoming a member of the Pro Football Hall of Fame.

Ted Hendricks

Never let it be said that Ted Hendricks did not enjoy havin fun. The free-spirited Hendricks often entertained teammat with antics a bit eccentric, but highly humorous. He once rode horse onto the practice field, and wore a harlequin mask durin a Monday Night Football telecast and a camera picked it up f the whole nation to see. He knocked over a yield sign an delivered to John Madden's home upon hearing of the coach's re tirement from the Raiders because he did not want to arrive empt handed.[1] These were just a few of the prankster's antics out of long list. He also earned two nicknames during his playing day the first being "the Mad Stork," due to his height. The secon came while with the Raiders after accidently kicking a ball carrie in the head with his foot and knocking him out during practice He quickly became "Kick 'Em in the Head Ted," which was short ened to "Kick Em," and it was the one that Hendricks liked ove "the Mad Stork."[2] Besides providing laughs, Hendricks also pro vided amazing talent that took him from a three-time college All American to enshrinement in the Pro Football Hall of Fame. I between these incredible accolades, he put together a 15-yea career beginning in 1969 as a second round draft pick of the Bal timore Colts.

At 6-7, 215 pounds, Hendricks was considered too light t play defensive end in the pros, and too tall to be a linebacke The Colts at first felt the same about Hendricks, and did no know what position he was best suited for. In his rookie yea they used him primarily on special teams for half the season. A the halfway point of the year, head coach Don Shula did not lik the way his team was playing, and looked to make some changes It was then that Hendricks saw action at right linebacker, an from that time on, all the critics were silenced.[3]

In his second season, the Colts won Super Bowl V and Hen dricks received his first All-Pro honor. After five great season with Baltimore, the Colts surprised many by trading Hendrick to the Green Bay Packers while at the top of his game in 1974 What became even more of a shock was when Green Bay let him get away after one season. In his lone season with the Packers Hendricks intercepted five passes, blocked seven kicks, recorded a safety, and made his second All-Pro team.

In 1975, the Packers traded Hendricks to the Raiders for two first round draft picks, but it was Oakland that made out the best in the deal. However, at first it did not appear that way. Once again in his career, for reasons not quite clear, the Raiders used Hendricks only sparingly during the 1975 season. It seemed that they just could not find a regular spot for him. Oakland played a 4–3 defense, which meant four down linemen and three linebackers. When Hendricks arrived, the team had three starting linebackers that they were satisfied with. For this reason, Hendricks was only used in frequent passing situations, or when the opposition was forced to punt. To say the least, the All-Pro linebacker was getting frustrated as each week passed, and he was still standing on the sideline watching the action instead of being a part of it.[4]

An opportunity to start his first game for the Silver and Black rose in a divisional playoff matchup with the Cincinnati Bengals after defensive end Tony Cline went down with an injury prior to the game. The Raiders shifted into a 3–4 defensive alignment, which called for the use of three down linemen and four linebackers. Hendricks set up a few steps back from where the defensive end lined up, and remained in the upright stance of a linebacker. At the snap, it was his job to stop anything run around the end. In passing situations, it was his responsibility to rush the quarterback. He did a fantastic job all afternoon, and sacked Cincinnati quarterback Ken Anderson four times in a 31–28 Oakland win.

By 1976, head coach John Madden realized that Hendricks was going to be a force to be reckoned with, and over the next eight seasons, the All-Pro linebacker did indeed wreck havoc on opposing offenses, helping them win three Super Bowls in the process.

Madden knew that the best place to play Hendricks was everywhere. This might seem impossible, but actually it was quite clear. His assignment became that of a freelance defender, who would go up and down the line of scrimmage behind the defensive linemen while the opposing quarterback was calling the signals prior to the snap. He would then set himself up where he thought the play was going to be run. The job was based on experience and reaction, and he was right almost every time. It was designed to disrupt the flow of the offense, because they never knew where Hendricks was going to be coming from. It was also impossible to create a scheme in practice to defend against him.[5]

Hendricks was strong, solid, powerful, quick, and had great balance. With his long arms, he was able to wrap them around a ball carrier and clamp down like a vice. Once he got those arms around someone, they were not going to get away.[6] The only place the opposition was headed after the grip was applied was down onto the turf with incredible force. His height was also used to disrupt plays by obstructing the quarterback's view, batting down passes, and jumping up to block kicks. Whatever was asked of him he did very well, and his great sense of humor kept teammates loose on the field and in the locker room.

His excellence did not go unnoticed, as he earned eight trips to the Pro Bowl (1971–74, 1980–1983), All-AFC (1976, 1980, 1981, 1982), and in addition to his All-Pro seasons with Baltimore and Green Bay, he was twice honored while with the Raiders in 1980 and 1982.

Other highlights from the outstanding career of Ted Hendricks included playing in 215 consecutive games, which was the most by any linebacker in pro football history, 25 blocked kicks, an NFL record four safeties, 26 interceptions, and a post-season NFL record of four fumble recoveries in a career. He was honored with the 1978 Lineman of the Year Award presented to him by the Raiders' Lineman's Club, selection to the 1970 and 1980 All-Decade NFL Teams, and to the 75th NFL Anniversary All-Time Team.

His football career began in the Sunshine State of Florida on the high school and college level, and reached its climax in magnificent fashion there as well. On January 22, 1984, the Raiders defeated Washington in Super Bowl XVIII in Tampa, Florida, to earn Hendricks his fourth championship ring. At the beginning of his pro career, it appeared that no one knew where to put him in the lineup, but 21 years later, on August 4, 1990, the Pro Football Hall of Fame had no trouble finding a spot for him among the game's immortals in his first year of eligibility.

Marv Hubbard

A battering ram who punished defenders with bone-jarring bursts, Marv Hubbard was one of the toughest offensive weapons of his time. He came to the Raiders out of Colgate University as their 11thh round selection of the 1968 draft, but was cut before he had a chance to play in a regular season game. At the time, Hubbard lacked speed and blocking skills. The team already had Hewritt Dixon at fullback, and Roger Hagberg as his backup.[1]

In an attempt to hone his skills, Hubbard went back east and played minor league football with Hartford of the Continental League. After a solid season, he began receiving offers from the pro ranks. Oakland still owned the rights to him, brought him back into the silver and black fold, moved Roger Hagberg over to tight end to create a spot for him, and Hubbard remained a diehard contributor for the Raiders from 1969 to '75.[2]

Hubbard established himself as a tough, brutal runner who inflicted punishment with his thrusts into an opposing defense. He was especially dangerous pounding the ball between the tackles to wear the defense down. When the plays "68 and 69 Boom Man" were called in the huddle, Hubbard's face was engulfed with a huge smile.[3] For he knew that the ball was going to be placed in his hands, and that within a few seconds, his body was about to slam into one of eleven defenders and inflict more pain on them than on himself.

To absorb as much impact as possible, Hubbard wore a big set of shoulder pads usually designated for linemen. He tested equipment out to see how it would hold up to his punishing thrusts into the heart of the opposition, and padded himself to provide extra protection from jolts. He also broke about a dozen helmets throughout his career due to his bone-jarring jaunts.[4] Hubbard gave his all in every game he played, but always seemed to step it up a notch against the hated Kansas City Chiefs.

His punishing play alone earned him his rightful place in Raiders lore. However, he decided to add to it off the field by displaying a unique brand of celebrating after an Oakland victory. After enjoying some liquid spirits at a local watering hole, Hubbard would leave the establishment, walk next door to a dry cleaning business, and then thrust his fist through the front window. He always prided himself in being able to remove his hand without cutting it on the jagged glass. He accomplished this for some time until Oakland head coach John Madden finally put an end to it after the owner of the business threatened to call the police. It was probably on Madden's mind that his power keg in cleats might have his luck run out, and that his hand could come out of the incident looking like ground meat, which would have put a damper on his availability.[5]

After leading the team in rushing from 1971 through '74, he was hampered by a shoulder separation that never healed and eventually led to his retirement in 1976. He was so proud and smitten to be an integral part of the renegade Raiders that if he did not have to take his uniform off after a game, it would have remained on him at all times. He loved the experience, and all those in Raider Nation who witnessed his performance felt the same way.

Bo Jackson

To be skilled at one sport on a professional level is amazing enough. To have the ability to perform in two is something almost unimaginable, unless the person in question is Bo Jackson, who captivated the sports world in the late 1980's by excelling at baseball and football.

After winning the 1985 Heisman Trophy at Auburn University, and being drafted by Tampa Bay as the first pick in 1986, Jackson decided to play professional baseball for the Kansas City Royals. His decision was made when Tampa Bay officials did not want him to risk injury by playing baseball in the spring before getting a chance to come to training camp. After the Buccaneers told Jackson to make a decision, he chose the diamond over the gridiron.[1] One year of minor league ball followed, and by 1987, he was in the majors as an outfielder, where he blasted out 22 home runs, had 53 RBI, and 10 stolen bases.

Seeing that Jackson never signed with Tampa Bay up to the following draft, he once again became eligible for the 1987 draft. The Raiders took a chance with their seventh round selection and selected the athletic marvel. Al Davis did not want to hinder Jackson by giving him the same ultimatum that Tampa did. The Raiders' owner allowed him the opportunity to play both sports. After baseball season ended, Jackson would then report to the Raiders on a part-time basis.[2]

Jackson's impact on both sports reached legendary heights. He came to the Raiders halfway through the '87 season, and ran for 554 yards on only 81 carries. By 1989, he made the All-Star team in baseball, won the MVP of that contest, and ended the season with 32 home runs and 105 RBI. He then came out to Los Angeles following the end of baseball, replaced his spikes for cleats, and rushed for 950 yards in 11 games for the Raiders.

His status and athletic prowess was unmatched at the dawn of the 1990's. He became a marketing dream, and during his 1990 baseball season, he hit four home runs in four consecutive trips to the plate to tie a Major League record, and ended the year with 28 round trippers. He then joined the Raiders, earning a Pro Bowl selection while helping them on their drive to a 12–4 season and another division title.

During a divisional playoff game against Cincinnati, Jackson suffered a football career-ending hip injury. After surgery and rehab, Jackson played for the Chicago White Sox in 1991 for 23 games. He missed the entire 1992 season after having an artificial

hip replacement, but came back for the '93 campaign, in which he slugged 16 home runs in just 85 games, and helped the White Sox win a division title. His efforts earned him the 1993 A Comeback Player of the Year Award. His hip continued to hampe him, however, and he was forced to retire in 1994.[3]

The athletic prowess displayed by Bo Jackson may never b seen again, but for those who witnessed his incredible talent a the highest levels of competition, it was truly a gift. In his Majo League Baseball career, Jackson collected 657 hits, 96 double 17 triples, and 138 home runs. For the Silver and Black from 198 to 1990, he played in 38 games, rushed for 2,782 yards and 1 touchdowns. He also topped the NFL with the longest runs from scrimmage in three of his four seasons. In 1987 he bolted 91 yard on one carry, 92 in 1989, and 88 in 1990.

Sebastian Janikowski

"The Polish Cannon," "Sea Bass," and "Lightning Feet," ar nicknames given to Sebastian Janikowski. In addition to thes monikers, he was also called All-American and the all-time leading scorer in Raiders' history. Born in Poland, Janikowski came to the United States in the early 1980's. He became an excellen soccer player and football kicker while living in Orlando, Florida His thunderous foot earned him a spot on the USA Today Pre All-American Team in 1996. He was heavily recruited by man of college football's powerhouses, and decided on Florida Stat University.[1]

While with FSU for three seasons, he recorded the highes point total in school history with 324. In 1998 and 1999, he won the Lou Groza Award given to the top kicker in the college ranks It was also the first time that a player won the prestigious hono twice. Besides gaining notoriety on the football field, he also earned negative publicity through involvement in bar fight throughout the Tallahassee, Florida area. He was charged with battery, and on another occasion, for bribing a police officer afte a friend of his got arrested.[2]

While his bribery case was pending, the Oakland Raider selected Janikowski with their first round pick of the 2000 draft making him only the third kicker to be taken so high in the history of the NFL draft. Things looked good for Janikowski, as he wa freed of bribery in June of 2000, but eight days following the acquittal, he was once again in trouble with the law. He was suspected of possessing the drug GHB, and was looking at a prison sentence and possible deportation. In April of 2001, he once again beat the charge with his acquittal. A DUI charge in 2002, and fight in a restaurant added to his legal woes.[3]

Through it all, Janikowski remained a steady performer fo the Raiders. After all, throughout the colorful history of the Silve and Black, there were many who faced legal troubles before, during, and after their time with pro football's renegades. He has se and broken the team record for longest field goal on multiple occasions, with the latest being on December 27, 2009, when he blasted a 61-yarder against Cleveland. On the final day of the 2009 season, against the Baltimore Ravens, Janikowski kicked a 39-yard field goal to give him the 1,000th point of his career. A the conclusion of the team's first fifty seasons, Janikowski also resided on top of the all-time scoring list.

Napoleon Kaufman

On Sundays, Napoleon Kaufman serves his fellow man as a Christian minister. However, over the course of six seasons, Kaufman performed another service in front of a crowd on Sundays as a star running back for the Oakland Raiders.

In high school, Kaufman ran for 5,151 yards and 86 touchdowns for the second-best career rushing marks in the state of California. After earning the reputation as one of the best running backs in the history of California while at Lompoc High School, Kaufman continued his ball handling skills at the University of Washington from 1991 through '94. He became the first player in Huskies' history to rush for over 1,000 yards in three straight seasons, was named All-Pac 10 and second team All-American.[1]

Kaufman was selected in the first round of the 1995 draft by Oakland, and played six seasons with the Silver and Black, serving as their featured back in 1997 and '98. In 1997, he put together one of the best single-season rushing campaigns in team history. On October 19th, he gained 227 yards on the ground against Denver to set a single-game rushing record that still stands over the course of the Raiders' first fifty seasons. He finished the year with 1,294 yards, which places him second on the team's all-time list in that category behind only the great Marcus Allen.[2]

At the end of the 2000 seasons, he retired from the gridiron to answer a greater power, becoming a Christian minister, and going from record-setting running back to the Rev. Napoleon Kaufman.[3]

Daryle Lamonica

Bridging a gap between Tom "the Iceman" Flores and Ken "the Snake" Stabler at the quarterback position in Oakland history was Daryle "the Mad Bomber" Lamonica. On the football field, Lamonica's nickname could only refer to a strong-armed signal caller who threw long passes frequently and with effective results. Many teams throughout history have had such a player running their offense, and the Raiders had one of the best during the late 1960's and early '70's.

The football career of Daryle Lamonica came full circle, beginning in California as a schoolboy athlete in the late 1950's, and ending there nearly twenty years later.[1] In between came stops in South Bend, Indiana, and Buffalo, New York. After a solid four years at Notre Dame University, Lamonica was drafted into the pros by both the NFL's Green Bay Packers and the AFL's Buffalo Bills during the bidding wars going on between the two leagues. The Packers were the NFL's two-time defending champions at the time of selecting Lamonica in 1963.[2] The Packers were a run-oriented team, while the Bills and the rest of the AFL emphasized the pass. With an explosive right arm, Lamonica felt the AFL was more suited to his talents, and he signed with them as a backup to star quarterback Jack Kemp. Rather than refusing Buffalo's offer to play behind Kemp, Lamonica accepted the role with the confidence that one day he would be a starter. He appeared in games quite regularly, performing well over the next three seasons, and helped the Bills to consecutive AFL titles in 1964 and 1965. Just then Lamonica was ready to take over the starting job in 1967, he was traded to the Oakland Raiders in a deal that brought Tom Flores and Art Powell to the Bills in exchange.[3]

In a regular season game against the Raiders in 1964, Lamonica threw a touchdown pass while about to get crushed by onrushing linemen. He stood his ground, and got off a beautiful pass just as he took a vicious hit. Al Davis was Oakland's head coach at the time, and liked Lamonica's spirit and toughness so much that three years later he wanted "the Mad Bomber" running his offensive attack.[4]

Lamonica provided an immediate impact on the Silver and Black. The Raiders followed the AFL's format of pass, pass, and more passes, and it was Lamonica who lit up the skies with long range bombs that helped power Oakland to a 13–1 regular season finish and the 1967 AFL championship. He started every game, passed for 3,228 yards, 30 touchdowns, earned All-AFL honors, selection to the AFL–All-Star Game, and capped off his great season by being named the 1967 AFL Most Valuable Player.

Over the next three seasons, Lamonica was regarded as one of the best quarterbacks in football. He led the Raiders to three straight division titles (1968, 1969, 1970), and helped give the Raiders the opportunity to play for the league or conference championship in each of those seasons. In 1969, "the Mad Bomber" once again brought home the league's MVP award and was named All-AFL and selected to play in the All-Star game. Throughout the '69 campaign, Lamonica began a string of 25 straight games in which he threw at least one touchdown pass. He also set a pro record by throwing six scoring strikes in the first half of a game against his old team, the Buffalo Bills. The following year, in the first year of the merger between the AFL and NFL, Lamonica won the 1970 AFC passing title, earned All-Conference honors, and made another trip to the Pro Bowl. The 1972 season saw Lamonica once again lead the Raiders into the playoffs after they missed out on a post-season berth the year before. He also had enough arm strength left to be selected second team All-Pro, and go to his fourth Pro Bowl.

In the fourth week of the 1973 season, with the Raiders at 1–2, and the offense sputtering, head coach John Madden decided to replace Lamonica with fifth-year pro Ken Stabler. From that point on, Lamonica was reduced to a backup role, playing in a combined 12 games during the 1973 and '74 seasons.[5] After the '74 campaign, Lamonica went to play for the California Sun of the World Football League. The league only lasted one-and-a-half seasons, and in 1975, "the Mad Bomber" decided to retire. Even though he was reduced to a backup role in his final two seasons in Oakland, Daryle Lamonica provided the Raiders with strong field leadership, and earned him everlasting distinction as a true legend of the Silver and Black.

Howie Long

The Dave Casper trade in 1980 gave Oakland a second round draft selection in 1981. The end result of the transaction was one future Hall of Famer for another. With the pick, the Raiders obtained a 6-5, 270 pound force of muscle and mayhem by the name of Howie Long from Villanova University.[1] Over the course of 13 seasons, the Somerville, Massachusetts, native destroyed anyone in his path toward opposing backfields.

Hidden behind movie star good looks lurked a focused, rough and rugged individual once his chinstrap was fastened. Villanova University was never regarded as a football factory, but

Long stood out so much, that his talents did not remain obscure. While watching him on film, then–Raiders head coach Tom Flores came away extremely impressed by his commanding presence all over the field.[2] It did not take the defending Super Bowl champions that much time to ponder over the gem they found, and made Howie Long a Raider.

It almost seemed that he was meant to be a member of football's bad boys long before he travelled across the country to suit up with his silver and black-clad fellow marauders. Long was a native of Boston's south side, where the streets were his playground and fights were just part of the Beantown asphalt jungle. In his early teens, Long would skip school to go unload crates on the docks for twenty dollars a day.[3] When he did attend school, he was expelled for fighting. By this time, his grandmother, who he was living with, decided to send him to live with an uncle in the suburbs.[4] Her hope was that the change to a more docile environment would allow her grandson to change direction and provide a positive impact on his young life. His uncle enrolled the Boston street tough into a private school, and it did not take the football coach long to approach the big teenager, and the rest is history. From that point on, Long's direction was a clear path to gridiron immortality as one of the greatest defensive linemen the game had ever witnessed.

After high school, Long's next stop was Villanova University near Philadelphia, Pennsylvania. On top of excelling as a four-year letterman in football, he also won the Northern Collegiate Heavyweight Boxing Championship. He took incredible hand speed learned from boxing, and applied it to football to get by opposing linemen.[5]

In the 1980 Blue-Gray All-Star Game, Long earned MVP honors, which attracted attention from numerous NFL teams. After being the 48th overall player selected in the 1981 draft, Long began his successful run with the Raiders. In his rookie year, he saw limited action, but still managed to lead Oakland's defensive linemen in sacks. The following year, the team relocated to Los Angeles, and Long became a starter in the strike-shortened season after Dave Browning went down with an injury.[6]

It was at this point that Long's glorious career truly began. He became a master of the rip move, a fast uppercut motion that he used to break free from an opponent's grasp. The rip move combined with quickness, speed, and strength, allowed Long to explode off the ball and obliterate anyone in his way throughout the 1980's and early 90's.[7] He learned all five positions along the defensive line, and used great athletic prowess to move from one to the other on any given play.[8] Those unlucky enough to face him were unable to adjust to the mayhem, and in the end, were left confused and eventually on the losing end of this destructive force wearing number 75. When offensive game plans were being put together by opponents, the main focus when dealing with the Raiders' defensive line was how to stop Long. Many times Long faced double or triple team blocking, but regardless of the man power thrust before him, he still bulldozed his way through to pound running backs and quarterbacks into submission, recording 91½ career sacks along the way.[9]

His performance earned many prestigious accolades including first or second team All-Pro honors in 1983, 1984, 1985, 1986, and 1989. He was named All-AFC four straight times from 1983 to 1986, selected to play in eight Pro Bowls, and was elected to the NFL's All-Decade Team for the 1980's.

Following his retirement after the 1993 campaign, Long went into the acting profession, and appeared in the films *Firestorm, Broken Arrow,* and *3000 Miles to Graceland.* He also did some television appearances and commercial work. Long then landed a spot on the FOX Network's NFL pre-game show, sharing his vast knowledge with the masses every weekend during the season. On July 29, 2000, Howie Long took his place among the game greats with his enshrinement into the Pro Football Hall of Fame.

Todd Marinovich

Todd Marinovich fulfilled every young football player's dreams. He was a highly touted high school quarterback who went to a first-rate university, and then was drafted number one by a pro team that had the best winning percentage over the previous three decades. All this was Marinovich's, and he got to do it all in the near-perfect surroundings of southern California. However, what appeared to be reminiscent of an old Hollywood feel-good story ended with a different scenario.

Marinovich's father Marv was a former team captain at USC and ex–Oakland Raider in the 1960's. He was also one of the first strength and conditioning coaches in the NFL, and also owned research facility dedicated to athletic training.[1] When his son Todd was born, the elder Marinovich decided to apply his knowledge of exercise and nutrition onto the boy while still an infant. He began working on physical conditioning when Todd was one month old, and allowed him to ingest only the healthiest of food and drinks.[2] His taste buds never experienced fast food or snacks so common among American society as a whole. While his father was building his body, his mother nurtured his mind by introducing him to museums, classical music, and jazz.[3]

All the hard work paid off, as Todd Marinovich became an outstanding, well-conditioned athletic machine at the quarterback position. The regimented upbringing brought attention to the young signal caller. Many in the media felt that his father pushed him too hard, and Todd earned the moniker of "Robo QB."[4] Regardless of feelings either way, the younger Marinovich had talent and rang up big numbers first at Mater Dei High School in Santa Ana, and then Capistrano Valley High School in Mission Viejo, California. During his scholastic career, Marinovich set Orange County and national passing records with 9,914 yards. The awards came in at a rapid pace, as did offers from countless colleges and universities.[5]

It was around this time that the young man with the golden arm began experimenting with drugs and alcohol at parties after games. The tight rein that his father had on him appeared to loosen when Marv Marinovich and his wife divorced. Todd went to live with his father, who eased up on his son while trying to reinvent himself as a single man. Todd used this period of new-found freedom to dab into the wilder side of life. Smoking marijuana prior to the beginning of school each day with a group of friends became the norm. The feeling he got was one of a relaxed state that allowed him the chance to deal with all the stress surrounding his fame as a top-rated football player.[6]

After high school, Marinovich followed in his father's footsteps by attending the University of Southern California. In 1989 he became the first freshman to start a season at quarterback since the 1940's. He completed 61.4 percent of his passes, just missing he NCAA record for a freshman signal caller by .1 percent. His performance earned him the 1989 Freshman of the Year Award, presented by *The Sporting News*, as well being named the first freshman quarterback named All-Pac-10. USC went 9-2-1 that season, won the Pac-10, and climaxed the year with a win over Michigan in the Rose Bowl.[7]

Marinovich was proving his talents were the real deal, when, as a sophomore, there was talk of him being a possible Heisman Trophy candidate. Unfortunately, the 1990 season did not unfold as well in reality as it did on paper. Marinovich began not showing up for classes, argued with USC head coach Larry Smith, and played below his expectations frequently. To add to his woes, Marinovich was arrested for possession of cocaine.[8] All the pressures got to him, and he felt the best thing to do was move on.

He decided that he was ready for the next level of competition, and looked ahead to a pro career after only two seasons as a collegiate. He got himself an agent, worked hard under his father's guidance, and now once again in top physical shape, was ready to conquer the NFL. Al Davis came out to watch Marinovich perform in front of a collection of NFL scouts, and the Raiders' owner came away impressed enough in the young man's talent to select him in the first round of the 1991 draft.[9]

After a good showing in his pro debut during an exhibition game, Marinovich was held back during the regular season until the finale against Kansas City. He threw for three scores, and earned the starting job in a playoff game the following week. In a rematch against Kansas City, he did not fare well at all, throwing for 140 yards and four interceptions in a 10–6 loss.

The following year saw Marinovich back on the bench to start the season. However, after the Raiders lost their first two games, he replaced Jay Schroeder. Despite Throwing for an incredible 395 yards in his 1992 debut, the Raiders lost another two games in a row. He rallied and helped lead the team to three wins in the next four games. In the ninth game of the season, a 31–10 loss to Philadelphia, Marinovich completed three of 10 passes for 25 yards, and suffered three interceptions. He was replaced by Jay Schroeder and never entered another game for the Raiders.

Substance abuse took over Marinovich during his brief pro career. While waiting for his chance to play as a rookie, he used the time to party hard. Due to his cocaine possession arrest while at USC, the National Football League made Marinovich subject himself to frequent drug tests. His need for marijuana was so great by this time that he knew there was no way he would stop smoking, which obviously would lead to a failed drug test. To avoid a failure, Marinovich gathered up friends who did not smoke pot and placed their urine samples into bottles that would be used when a random drug test was called for. He kept them in his refrigerator until the time to smuggle it into the Raiders' practice facility. His luck ran out when the urine supply did. He went to another friend after a night of partying, and even though the friend did not smoke pot, he did consume quite a bit of alcohol. Needless to say, the result of Marinovich's next test failed badly, as the urine he used had a blood-alcohol level well past the legal limit. The results made the Raiders send Marinovich into an alcohol detox program.[10]

By his second season, Marinovich attempted to give up pot. That was the good news. However, instead of marijuana, he took up LSD due to the fact that this drug did not show up in tests.

His attention span was obviously altered, and he could not get a handle on the Raiders' offensive plays. Another failed drug test landed him back in a clinic, and after a third one during the 1993 training camp for once again using marijuana, his time in the NFL was officially over. Unfortunately, his demons continued to destroy him with bouts of heroin and cocaine abuse.[11]

By the early 2000's, Marinovich had no money and at times resided on the beach. He had his driver's license suspended and was now hooked on methamphetamines. A 2004 arrest while skateboarding in a prohibited area turned up the drug and syringes in his possession. This was now rock bottom for the young man that almost twenty years earlier had the world at his disposal. Multiple arrests followed, but by 2008, Marinovich was clean and sober for one solid year. He received a job as a lecturer at a Newport Beach drug and alcohol treatment facility, and is helping other athletes overcome the horrors of addiction that took everything away from him.[12]

Rod Martin

Thanks to John Madden's long-time friendship with USC head coach John Robinson, the Raiders landed one of the best linebackers to ever wear the silver and black. Despite being fast and strong, it was said by many NFL scouts that Rod Martin was too light at 195 pounds on a 6'2" frame to play outside linebacker professionally even after earning All-Pac 10 honors while at the University of Southern California.[1]

Unfortunately, it seemed that every team in the NFL agreed with the reports, as round after round passed during the 1977 draft without any team even expressing a remote interest in him. When it came time for the defending Super Bowl champion Oakland Raiders to make their 12th and final pick, they had no idea on who to take. It was at that time when Oakland's head coach John Madden called his long-time friend and USC coach John Robinson. Madden asked Robinson if he could recommend anyone to draft, and it was then that the name of Rod Martin came up. Robinson complimented the linebacker by calling him a tough, hard-working, and dedicated player who was worth taking a chance on. After all, it was the final round of the draft, so Madden decided to take his friend's advice, and that was how Martin's path to greatness as a Raider began.[2]

However, greatness was not on the immediate horizon for Martin when he reported to training camp in July of 1977. When he arrived, Oakland was stocked very well with linebackers. To make matters worse for him was the fact that the Raiders used their fifth round selection on a linebacker named Jeff Barnes, who outweighed Martin by 20 pounds and possessed the same amount of speed. Oakland wanted Barnes as a special teams performer, and Martin did not have any experience on that unit. At that point, he became expendable, and was released during the pre-season. He was then picked up by the San Francisco 49ers, but his time there only lasted two weeks before they released him as well.[3]

Dejected but not discouraged, Martin returned to the Los Angeles area to lift weights in an attempt to add bulk to his frame, and then hopefully find another team willing to give him a tryout. Three teams did give him a look, but none showed an interest in signing him. His real desire was always to return to the Raiders, and that dream came sooner than expected.[4]

By the second half of the 1977 season, Oakland's linebacker corps was depleted by injuries, and they needed someone quick to fill the desperate void. Madden remembered Martin as a hard worker who impressed him, and put in a call to him. Needless to say, Martin jumped at the opportunity to wear the silver and black uniform of the defending champions. In the off-season, Martin trained hard, and came into the 1978 campaign with ten extra pounds of muscle. Now at 205 pounds, he played in nine games, mostly in the second half of the season, and performed well at inside linebacker.[5]

The following year, he moved up to 225 pounds, won a starting job, and never gave it up for almost a decade. Through hard work on the field and in the weight room, Martin proved to everyone who doubted his ability that he not only belonged in the pro ranks, but also at the top of his profession during the 1980's. He quickly earned the respect of his teammates, and they showed him how much he meant to the organization by selecting him the winner of the Oakland Raiders' Lineman of the Year Award in just his first year as a starter.[6]

Martin might have had his teammates' respect, but was still fairly unknown throughout the rest of the league as the 1980's began. However, by the end of January, 1981, his name became mentioned whenever the topic of exceptional linebackers was brought to the forefront.

In the Raiders' dream season of 1980, they became the first-ever wild card entry in the playoffs to win the Super Bowl, and Rod Martin led them to the gridiron Promised Land with an incredible performance. Against the Philadelphia Eagles, Martin anchored a dominant defense by intercepting three passes in a 27–10 win. He set a Super Bowl record for most interceptions by an individual in one game, and his stock of NFL stardom quickly shot up.

Over the next several seasons, honor after honor was bestowed on him, and his place among the best of his time was solidified. Throughout the 1980's, Martin used his speed and strength to hound and pound the opposition into submission. With a huge set of powerful forearms and a vice-like grip, once Martin grabbed a quarterback or ball carrier, they were not going anywhere but down to the ground. He was strong and durable, which his 130 consecutive game streak can attest to.[7]

In 1982, Martin earned All-AFC and All-Pro honors, and in 1983 his teammates elected him defensive captain. On top of that honor, 1983 also saw Martin reach the upper echelon of professional football when he received a trip to the Pro Bowl, his second All-Pro and All-AFC selections, and was named AFC Defensive Player of the Year. Added to his sterling campaign was another Super Bowl ring that he earned thanks to a 38–9 blowout victory over the Washington Redskins. In three playoff games that season, he recorded 21 tackles.

His personal best season came in 1984 when he had 121 tackles and 11 quarterback sacks. For the third straight year, the league recognized his solid play by selecting him to the All-Pro and All-AFC teams in addition to another Pro Bowl. He retired following the 1988 season after playing in 165 games for the Raiders.

There have been many players who excelled in the magnificent colors of the Silver and Black, but Rod Martin is near the top of that list. He never quit even when it appeared that the odds of success were slim. He managed to fulfill his dream of playing for the Raiders by continually working hard at his craft. Rod Martin is a true testament to the Raiders' motto of "Commitment of Excellence."

John Matuszak

The "Tooz" embodied the outlaw image of the Raiders. Whether it was opposing quarterbacks, running backs, or the wild life, Matuszak pursued it all with the same voracious intensity. On the football field this quality allowed him to become a driving force and inspirational leader of a Raiders defense that helped win two Super Bowl titles during his watch. Off the field, this same passion led to altercations with law enforcement, substance abuse, and eventually his demise.

The "Tooz" was a massive, powerful, and extremely imposing figure who could disrupt the flow of an offense with his fierce, reckless abandon style of play. He was also an avid weightlifter, able to bench press well over 400 pounds. He was also a force to be reckoned with in everyday life as well. While in college at Missouri, an altercation resulted in a man needing plastic surgery to repair damage inflicted on his face after he insulted Matuszak's girlfriend.[1]

Matuszak later transferred out of Missouri after not getting along with head coach Dan Devine. His next stop was the University of Tampa. While there, an altercation during a basketball game caused another person's face to be rearranged, and this time it cost Matuszak hundreds of thousands of dollars in an out of court settlement.[2]

On the field he was so impressive that the Houston Oilers made him the number one pick in the entire 1973 draft. After making some All-Rookie teams, his feelings toward Houston's coach, the legendary Sid Gillman, and mentor to Al Davis, turned sour. One day, he was tired of the way he was being treated after an NFL strike in 1974, and went to the Houston Texans of the World Football League. Even though he was signed to a long-term contract with the Oilers, Matuszak decided to play for the Texans. Within five minutes of his first game in a Texans' uniform, twenty sheriffs converged on him with a summons to appear in court. A judge decided that Matuszak was in breach of his contract with the Oilers, and ordered him back to that team.[3]

Needless to say, his time in Houston did not last much longer, and he was traded to the Kansas City Chiefs at midseason. While with the Chiefs, Matuszak's wife at the time tried to run him over with her car, and on another occasion, he overdosed after mixing about four beers with Valium. His heart stopped, but thanks to quick thinking on the part of Kansas City head coach Paul Wiggin, who pounded on his chest until a heartbeat was restored, "the Tooz" lived to play another day. The incident proved to be the end for Matuszak with the Chiefs. He was traded to the Washington Redskins, but was cut right before the regular season opener. Totally dejected, Matuszak returned home to Milwaukee, Wisconsin, where he pondered the idea of going to play in the Canadian Football League.[4]

Over in Oakland, John Madden was faced with a serious dilemma. The Raiders' defensive line was quickly depleted by major injuries to ends, Tony Cline and Horace Jones, and tackle Art Thoms. To counteract the problem, Madden decided to go

ith a 3–4 alignment, and needed a big, physical end. At the
ggestion of Al Davis, The Raiders signed Matuszak.[5]

The Raiders prided themselves in taking in outcasts and hell
isers, and Matuszak fit the mold. They also knew that men like
he Tooz" would play their hearts out for someone who believed
them. In no time, Matuszak proved himself, and became the
rce that many felt he could become. He was still capable of wild
mes off the field, like the occasion when "the Tooz" set a team
cord for getting seven naked young women to join him in a hot
b.[6] However, on the Raiders, he fit in as just another guy letting
ose from time to time. He finished out his career with the team,
tiring in 1982 after back problems hampered his performance.

Already having appeared in the films *North Dallas Forty*
979) and *Caveman* (1981), during his playing days, Matuszak
oked to the acting profession as his next endeavor. He added
he *Ice Pirates* (1984) and *Goonies* (1985) to his film credits, as
ell as appearances in many of the popular television series of the
80's. The man who once boasted that vodka and Valium was
is breakfast of champions, claimed in his popular autobiography,
ruisin' with the Tooz* (1987), that he was clean and looking
rward to getting on with life.[7] Unfortunately, even though the
ook had a happy ending, Matuszak did not. On June 17, 1989,
is girlfriend called for an ambulance after Matuszak suffered
hat was later ruled a heart attack brought on by drugs and al-
hol.[8] Some claim that cocaine also played a part in his demise.[9]
e died en route from his Hollywood home to St. Joseph Medical
enter in Burbank.[10] He was only 38 years old. Despite his walk
n the wild side for many years, Matuszak gave countless hours
f himself to helping charities involving children. Like everyone
n this planet, "the Tooz" was a human being who fought demons,
ut unfortunately, he lost in the end.

Matt Millen

On one occasion in his youth, Matt Millen placed his elbow
a vice to straighten it after calcium deposits formed. When
at did not work, he lifted weights until the elbow was normal
gain.[1] This was a man who represented the epitome of toughness.
Ie was also very strong and extremely passionate about football,
nd gave everything he had to make himself and those around
im better. He was in constant attack mode, going at full throttle
nd slamming into anyone in his path.

Millen loved hitting the weights and opponents with the
ame voracious intensity, and did both very well for nine seasons
n a silver and black uniform. He won two Super Bowl rings with
he Raiders, and added two more with San Francisco in 1989, and
Vashington in 1991, to become the only player in history to earn
uper Bowl victories with three different teams.

Ralph Oliver

Tune in, turn on, and drop out. This was the creed followed
y thousands of the counter culture during the late 1960's.
Virtually every stretch of American society was affected, whether
n a grand scale in big cities, or on a more dossal level in small
owns. Fitting into the fold was the National Football League,
vhich became part of the youth movement that changed a gen-
ration thanks to Oakland linebacker Ralph "Chip" Oliver.

From starting linebacker to commune dweller was the road
taken by Oliver during a tumultuous time in American history
that saw a generation, for the most part, turn away from con-
formity for a more care free lifestyle amidst the ravages of war in
Vietnam and rioting in the streets.

Oliver came out of the University of Southern California as
a member of the Trojans 1967 national championship team. He
was selected by the Raiders in the 11th round of the 1968 draft as
a fast, agile, and nasty linebacker. He fit the perfect mold for a
linebacker, and the Raiders liked what they saw. Al Davis praised
Oliver by calling him one of the best pro prospects in the game,
and by the '69 season, he lived up to that honor by earning a
starting position.[1]

Everything seemed to be going well for the second-year linebacker. He was a starter on a team always in the hunt for a championship, and was earning a good living. Still, it appeared that
Oliver was restless, searching for something else to embrace other
than driving opposing running backs and receivers in to the turf
on Sunday afternoons.[2]

He found what he apparently was looking for after entering
a vegetarian restaurant in Mill Valley, California. People running
the macrobiotic diet eatery were members of a commune called
the One World Family, and consisted of about 75 members.
Oliver was quickly taken in by the tranquil setting. He began fre-
quenting the restaurant and the commune more and more.[3] He
felt a calmer feeling coming over him, and seemed to find what
was missing in his life.

He still remained with the Raiders through the 1969 season,
but his attitude toward the game was changing rapidly. He tried
to convey his findings onto his teammates at a time when most
pro football players still had old school ways. While his teammates
were eating eggs, meat products, and potatoes, which was considered the norm for football players during this time, Oliver
broke out fruit salads, vegetables, and fresh fruit juices. During
pre-game warm ups, Oliver would come out to the field full of
energy, sprint around the stadium, and then hit the ground to
begin yoga moves.[4] Needless to say, his teammates looked at him
like he was some kind of nut, even for the freewheeling Raiders,
who clung to the edge of reality on many occasions. Actually,
Oliver was ahead of his time. Yoga, health foods, and fruit juices
are now embraced by professional athletes, and allow them to
sustain a higher level of performance over both the course of a
season and a career.

Oliver might have been a trailblazer without knowing it,
but when he played, he was looked at as a hippie outcast. By May
of 1970, the commune life completely consumed Oliver. He informed Al Davis and head coach John Madden that the world of
professional football was a silly one, and that he was quitting.[5]
He took off for the simpler life, gave up his worldly possessions,
and started flipping macro burgers.

Jim Otto

For 15 seasons, the "00" on Jim Otto's uniform stood out
like a beacon. Through hard work, dedication, intelligence, a high
threshold for pain, and outstanding leadership skills, he became
a symbol of excellence for all those who ever wore the silver and
black of the Oakland Raiders. Without a doubt, Otto was the great-

est center of all time, and served as the anchor for the best group of trench warriors assembled during the late 1960's and 70's.

No play can start without the center snapping the ball. Once that happens, he is usually lost in a collision of bodies punishing each other for control of the line of scrimmage. Meanwhile, all eyes become focused on the quarterback, running back, or receiver. Otto was different. Through flawless blocking in either running or passing situations, he made the position one of star quality.

The man later referred to as "Mr. Raider" was born in Wausau, Wisconsin. While at Wausau High School, Otto established himself as a gifted athlete in football, hockey, and baseball. He began winning awards for his performance on the football field, earning All-State honors as both a center and linebacker.[1] His All-State selections did not go unnoticed, as scholarship offers came in from all over the country. He decided on the University of Miami in Florida. While in the "Sunshine State," Otto continued to dominate, setting a career school record for most tackles by a linebacker.

Up to this point of his athletic career, things looked great for Otto. After a stellar collegiate career, it seemed apparent that Otto was going to be selected in the National Football League's annual draft for the 1960 season. During the 1959 season, Otto was regarded as a punishing tackler who loved to hit. Along with all the good things being said about the Wisconsin native, there were also negative ones as well. The pro scouts felt that he was too light at 205 pounds to take a chance on him despite his aggressive play. The scouts also found out that Otto had suffered some shoulder injuries, and that finalized their decision to pass on him come draft day.[2]

Otto's spirits were crushed when no team decided to take a chance on a player who performed equally well on both sides of the ball. He refused to give up, and set out to find a team willing to at least give him a tryout. He felt that once he was on the practice field, his talents would prove to any doubters that he belonged among the game's best. Unfortunately, no NFL team even wanted to give him a free agent tryout.

It appeared that good fortune came Otto's way when a new professional football league made up of eight teams called the American Football League was formed in 1959, and he was drafted by the Minnesota franchise. Just when things seemed to be looking up once again, the franchise ownership group decided to join the established NFL instead of taking a chance on a new league, and was not allowed to bring along any of the players they had drafted. However, Otto got another chance when the AFL decided to take all the players drafted by Minnesota and send them to other teams throughout the league. It was then that he became a member of the Houston Oilers, but his journey did not end there.

To fill the void left by Minnesota's departure, the city of Oakland, California, was awarded a franchise to balance out the league at eight teams once again. In an attempt to quickly fill the roster of this last minute entry, Otto was shipped off yet again to another team. This time, however, his traveling days were over.

Otto reported to Oakland's first-ever training camp along with 100 other players that it seemed nobody wanted. It looked like the Oakland team was truly the land of misfits. Now surrounded by other players that nobody else seemed to want, Otto's dreams looked to once again be headed for a crash landing. For

it seemed that the Oakland coaching staff thought he was to light at 205 pounds to play center.[3]

All he ever asked for was a chance, and Oakland head coac Eddie Erdelatz, gave it to him. After all, there was not much tale to choose from in the early days of the Raiders, which was ba for the team, but provided an excellent opportunity for Otto. H began to impress the coaching staff during training camp, ar despite his size, he earned the starting center job in Oakland first season.

The main question regarding Otto was how long could 205-pound center last? It did not take Otto long to answer th question. With the center position firmly his, he immediate began to bulk up his frame. With the help of high-protein mi shakes and a regimented weight lifting program, he became 245-pounder with power and finesse.[4] With a passion seen i only a handful of players, Otto quickly proved that he belonge in the pros. He mixed speed, competitiveness, and technique overpower men much bigger than him, and never stopped work ing even when near perfection was achieved. Otto loved th contact that football provided, and destroyed anyone on the op posing team looking to get past him.

From 1960 until 1971, no other center beside Otto was se lected to the All-Pro first team. Despite the physical wear an tear that a center's body goes through, he managed to remai tough and dedicated to his craft, refusing to give in to the pai and never missed one game during his long career. Counting pr season, regular, and post-season competition, Otto played in 30 straight games. The toll on his body added up to eventually havin 38 major surgeries, with 28 of them coming on his knees. He ha six artificial knee replacements, as well as both shoulders replace After one of those knee operations failed to respond to treatmer during the latter part of his career, his body had finally had enoug punishment, and he was forced to retire prior to the 1975 sea son.[5]

During his illustrious career, the Raiders compiled 115 win against a mere 42 losses and 11 ties. They won seven divisiona titles, one league championship, and played for a league or con ference title six other times.

The man who proudly and deservingly bears the title of M Raider is a lasting symbol to the greatness that is the Oaklan Raiders. He was a charter member of the American Footba League, an original Raider, and on August 2, 1980, he was th first member of the organization to earn his place among pro foot ball's immortals with his enshrinement into the Hall of Fame i his first year of eligibility. He was a true warrior that totally dom inated his position, and his likes will never be seen again. Th Raiders' motto of "Commitment to Excellence" is best exemplifie by the greatness that Jim Otto displayed.

Jim Plunkett

At times throughout Jim Plunkett's career, adversity was constant companion. However, each time it crept up, he refuse to be plagued for very long, and overcame it with the heart of champion. Unfortunately, adversity in one's life can wreak havo on the psyche. It is how an individual deals with it that makes a the difference. In the case of Plunkett, he rose from the ashes eac time with a competitive fire that earned him some of the game' most prestigious accolades, and secured his place among Raiders greats.

Plunkett's position on the football field was quickly cemented at age 14 after winning a throwing contest with a pass covering 70 yards. Four years later it was on to Stanford University where his initial experience on the collegiate level was hampered by a thyroid operation that sapped him of his strength. Unable to show Stanford head coach John Ralston his absolute best, Plunkett was considered for a defensive end position. Plunkett was not willing to go along with the change, holding firm on his desire to stay at quarterback. To work his way back into contention for the job, Plunkett diligently threw an estimated 1,000 passes on a daily basis to strengthen his arm.[1] The hard work paid off, and he went on to establish himself as one of college football's greatest signal callers.

Right from the first opportunity to start at Stanford in 1968, Plunkett threw for 277 yards and four touchdowns. He went on to set numerous passing records in his three seasons as a starter, and earned a solid reputation as a quarterback ready for the next level. His senior year of 1970 was dubbed "the year of the quarterback" in college football due to the outstanding array of talent at the position. When the awards were handed out at season's end, one stood out above all others, with that being Stanford's Jim Plunkett. Through hard work, determination, and a belief in himself and his abilities, Plunkett was presented with college football's ultimate hardware, the Heisman Trophy, plus many others.[2]

Plunkett's status as the top collegiate player in the nation did not go unnoticed by the NFL. The New England Patriots had the number one overall pick in the 1971 draft, and used it to select Plunkett. Regarded by many as the best pro quarterback prospect of the time, Plunkett's impact was immediate, as he helped the Patriots to a 6–8 record for their best finish in five years, and brought home the AFC Rookie of the Year Award for his initial pro effort.

By 1972, adversity began to become Plunkett's best friend. He was sacked close to one hundred times over the next three seasons, and interceptions were being tallied up faster than touchdowns. His confidence was shattered in the process, as was his body. Knee and shoulder injuries began to mount, and by 1975, he was reduced to minimal playing time.[3]

Plunkett asked to be traded, and was granted his wish. He returned to northern California with the San Francisco 49ers hoping to get a fresh start and lead a slumping team back to prominence. Unfortunately, the 49ers and Plunkett did not create a successful venture. After two sub-par seasons, San Francisco released him prior to the 1978 campaign.[4]

Dejected and full of self-doubt, the one-time elite quarterback faced the crossroads of his athletic career. At age 30, retirement seemed like the only answer. However, Plunkett was a classic drop back passer who loved to throw, which was just the type Al Davis enjoyed having in a Raiders uniform. Within two weeks after his release from San Francisco, Davis gave Plunkett another option besides retirement, with that being a three-year contract.[5]

With Ken Stabler still firmly entrenched as the starter in 1978, Plunkett did not once set foot on the field, and only threw 15 passes the following year. In 1980, Stabler was traded to the Houston Oilers for strong-armed quarterback Dan Pastorini, and

they also used their first round selection of the 1980 draft to get Brigham Young's highly touted signal caller, Marc Wilson.

The decade of the 1970's began with Plunkett as a top-rated pro prospect fresh off winning the Heisman Trophy. The following decade dawned with him standing on the sidelines, reduced to third-string. After realizing that he was not going to overthrow team legend Ken Stabler when he first came to Oakland, Plunkett bided his time with the hope that maybe his time would come, and if "the Snake" was traded or decided to retire, then he could compete for the starting job. Upon Stabler's departure, however, Plunkett's hopes sunk low with Pastorini and Wilson now in the equation.

Plunkett asked to be traded, but the Raiders refused. They felt that with his experience, he was the perfect backup in case of emergency.[6] The Raiders' denial to comply with Plunkett's demands proved to be the best rejection he ever had to endure. In the fifth game of the 1980 season, starter Dan Pastorini was lost for the season with a broken leg, and Plunkett was forced into service. The Raiders felt that Wilson was not experienced enough to be thrust into the starter role at the time. So it was Plunkett who came on. He threw for 238 yards and two touchdowns, but also suffered five interceptions in a 31–17 loss to Kansas City. The Oakland coaching staff still felt that Plunkett was the right choice, and was either going to sink or swim with him as the starter of a 2–3 team.

Even though things looked bleak for the Raiders at this stage of the season, it was still early enough that Plunkett might be able to turn things around. After all, Plunkett had faced adversity before and came out a winner. With the opportunity to rejuvenate his stagnant career, Plunkett took the field in a crucial game against the San Diego Chargers, who were considered one of the AFC's elite teams at the time. Undaunted by the apparent titans from San Diego, Plunkett led the Raiders to a 38–24 home win. He hit on 11 of 14 passes and one touchdown. He also did not throw an interception, which helped to instill confidence after the five he tossed a week earlier.

From this point on, Plunkett put on an amazing resurrection, throwing for 2,299 yards and 18 touchdowns while leading Oakland to nine wins in 11 games to finish at 11–5. The once slumping Raiders gained a playoff berth and completed their mission of championship glory by winning Super Bowl XV with Plunkett at the helm. He was honored with selection as the Super Bowl Most Valuable Player, and also brought home the 1980 NFL Comeback Player of the Year Award. His 1980 campaign proved to be one of the greatest stories the sport of football had ever produced.

Three years later, Plunkett once again guided the Raiders to Super Bowl supremacy after losing, and then regaining his starting job during the '83 season. Following his triumph in Super Bowl XVIII, Plunkett's career began to head toward its twilight. Injuries and Father Time slowly began creeping up on the veteran field leader. During a three-season span from 1984 to 86, he only started 17 games, and missed the entire 1987 campaign with a damaged shoulder.[7] By 1988, at age 40, Plunkett's career officially came to an end with his release during the pre-season. His was a career of extreme highs mixed with bouts of lows, but in the end, Jim Plunkett left the game as an example of intestinal fortitude and a Raiders legend.

Art Powell

Art Powell was ruled a troublemaker for speaking his mind about social issues at a time in American history when it was considered taboo. None of that mattered to Al Davis when he was looking for a game-breaking wide receiver to attack defenses in his first year as head coach in 1963.

Powell's career began with the Philadelphia Eagles in 1959, and after three great seasons with the AFL's New York Titans from 1960 through '62, Powell was looking to move on due to the team suffering from financial woes. During his time in the Big Apple, Powell led the Titans in receptions, and earned the reputation as a scoring threat from anywhere on the field.[1]

Powell also earned a reputation as a headstrong, independent thinker, who would not conform to social norms at the time of the turbulent 60's, when race wars were going on. He constantly challenged rules just looking for equality.[2] As always was the case with Al Davis, he did not care about a man's status on the social register. He was willing to give a player the chance at a new beginning, and for that, he usually saw great things result.

Such as the case with Powell, who came to the Raiders as their first truly bona-fide renegade. In four seasons with the Raiders, the gifted receiver found a home after getting a badass reputation elsewhere. He also lived up to his reputation as an offensive powerhouse, quickly establishing himself as the Raiders' first game-breaking deep threat in team history. With a great set of hands, the graceful stride of a sprinter, and size and strength to match, Powell was able to dominate any defensive back in the league.[3] In 1963, he did just that by catching 73 passes for 1,304 yards and 16 touchdowns. He became a team leader, and three out of his four seasons with the Raiders saw Powell top the 1,000-yard receiving mark on his receptions. From 1963 to '66, he caught 254 passes for 4,491 yards and 50 touchdowns in 56 games as a Raider.

Barret Robbins

From being an All-Pro and Pro Bowl center to inmate was the course taken by Barret Robbins. The fall was fast, and fueled by drugs, alcohol, and weapons. These three items provide a recipe for disaster that, unfortunately, drag countless poor souls into the depths of darkness.

Such was the case for Robbins, who went from being at the top of his profession to serving jail time all within the span of three years. He began his pro football career as the second round draft pick of the Raiders in 1995 out of Texas Christian University. Over the next seven years, Robbins established himself as one of the best centers in the league, following the proud lineage of Raider centers set by Jim Otto and Dave Dalby.

Two days before the Raiders were to play the Tampa Bay Buccaneers in Super Bowl XXXVII, Robbins went missing, eventually going to the hospital where it was found out that he suffered from bipolar disorder and depression.[1] He regained his starting job the following season, but was released by the team after testing positive for steroids in 2004. On January 15, 2005, during an altercation with police in Miami, Florida, Robbins was shot three times. He survived, and was charged for attempted murder. In court, Robbins pleaded guilty to five charges, and was sentenced

to five years of probation, and had to stop the use of alcohol, an get treated for his bipolar condition. Things did not work out a planned for the former All-Pro, as his usage of drugs and alcoh did not stop, and the vices landed him in jail and rehab cente from 2005 to 2008, and the money he earned as a profession athlete ran out. Robbins did manage to pull himself up from h despair, and as of 2009, he appeared to be on the road to sobr ety.[2]

Art Shell

Art Shell was the complete package when looking for an o fensive lineman. He was big (6-5, 285 pounds), very strong smart, quick off the snap, and mastered the art of both run block ing and pass protection. He also possessed a quiet, tranquil de meanor, never acted tough even though he was, and let his per formance do the talking for him.[1] All these traits earned him th respect of teammates and opponents alike.

Shell refused to allow an opponent to get him mad. Som tried in an attempt to break his concentration, but all they go out of him was a smile. However, once the ball was snapped, h destroyed any defender in front of him, allowing running back and quarterbacks to do their jobs efficiently. Off the field, She continued to work hard through film study to not only make su of his assignments, but those of all his teammates as well, thu becoming a true student of the game.[2]

The Raiders made Shell their third round draft pick in 1968 and after playing with distinction on special teams for his firs two seasons, won a starting job at left tackle in 1970 along side c guard Gene Upshaw.[3] Once Shell and Upshaw were teamed up they became the greatest pair of offensive linemen in the histor of pro football. This duo of destruction tore up defensive lineme for eleven seasons together, and helped Oakland's offense roll t seven division titles, seven AFC Championship Game appear ances, and two Super Bowl titles in 1976 and 1980.

It was during Oakland's first Super Bowl victory that She and Upshaw showed their total dominance on the game's ultimat stage. On January 9, 1977, in Super Bowl XI, this duo totall dominated the war in the trenches, allowing Oakland's runnin attack to gain 266 yards, and prevented quarterback Ken Stable from getting hassled all day. They controlled the Minnesot Vikings' great All-Pro tandem of Alan Page and Jim Marshall lik they did not even exist. They truly performed the most perfec blocking performance in Super Bowl history, and it showed i the final result, with that being an easy 32–14 win.

Shell was bestowed with many honors throughout his illus trious pro career. He earned eight trips to the Pro Bowl (1972 78, 1980), six All-AFC selections (1973–78), and three All-Pr nods (1973, 1974, 1977). Also coming Shell's way were selection to the 1970's All-Decade Team and the NFL's All-Monday Nigh Football Team; he was also voted the Raiders' Lineman of th Year Award in 1976.

The incredible offensive tackle played in 207 regular seaso games with the Raiders and 23 playoff contests. He had a 15 consecutive game streak snapped in a 1979 pre-season game injur that caused him to miss the first five games of the regular season After retiring following the 1982 season, Shell joined the Raider coaching staff as offensive line coach until 1988. In 1989 h ssumed the head coaching position, and with the promotion, ecame the first African-American of the modern era to hold that itle. That year also provided another milestone in Art Shell's life vhen he received the honor of being enshrined into the Pro Football Hall of Fame.

Otis Sistrunk

Otis Sistrunk's path to professional football was an unconentional journey, but it eventually allowed him the right to be a hampion with the Oakland Raiders. Sistrunk went from high chool to semi-pro football, and became one of the very few to et into the NFL via that route. After serving in the United States Marine Corps, he played in the Continental League's Norfolk Neptunes for three years.[1] At age 22, some scouts from the Los Angeles Rams saw him and brought him into training camp. As ate would have it, Al Davis and Ron Wolf, two of the best talent udges professional football had ever seen, were watching Sistrunk n camp.[2] Within a short time, Sistrunk became a member of the ilver and Black from 1973 to 1978 at defensive tackle. He conidered making the Raiders' squad the highlight of his career after uch an unorthodox beginning. He repaid Oakland by being a olid performer, earning selection to the Pro Bowl in 1974, and elped the defense smother the Minnesota Vikings in Super Bowl XI.

Despite making an impression with his abilities on the field, t was while standing on the sideline that Sistrunk gained everasting fame and his place in Raiders lore. During a Monday Night ootball telecast in 1974, a camera focused on an object that apeared to be the surface of the moon with steam rising up from t. As the camera panned farther away from the object, the pparent moon was really the bald head of Otis Sistrunk emitting team after coming off the field following a defensive series. ormer NFL player turned announcer and actor, Alex Karras, uickly jumped at a golden opportunity to comment on what the iewing audience just witnessed. Karras stated that the image cast efore the camera was Otis Sistrunk from the University of Mars.[3] The short but witty comment immediately stuck, and Sistrunk orever became the lone alumnus from the faraway, yet nonxistent, planetary campus.

Jack Squirek

The play "Rocket Screen" took Jack Squirek on a five-ard trek that transported the second-year linebacker from the uaint surroundings of Cleveland's Cuyahoga Heights High chool to the forefront of the national spotlight in Los Angeles nd beyond.

Squirek possessed size, speed, and an excellent range of moion that made him ideal to play man-to-man coverage from ither the inside or outside linebacker positions.[1] He was used rimarily on special teams and in passing situations for most of is four seasons with the Raiders from 1982 through '85. Iowever, with 12 seconds remaining in the first half of Super Bowl XVIII, and the Raiders up, 14–3, he was inserted in place f Matt Millen to perform his specialty of man-to-man coverge.[2]

Defensive coach Charlie Sumner informed Squirek to stay

focused on running back Joe Washington coming out of the backfield.[3] During the regular season, Washington caught a short pass against the Raiders and turned it into a 67-yard gain that shifted momentum quickly over to the Redskins. Once Sumner saw Washington enter the game, he remembered that play from months earlier, and did not want the Redskins to get another big gainer, plus a huge dose of confidence going into the second half after the Raiders were in control of the Super Bowl up to this stage.

At the snap, Squirek followed his instructions to perfection. The Redskins did indeed call for the same play used against the Raiders during the regular season, but this time, the "Rocket Screen" worked in favor of the opposition. With a rush coming in on him quickly, Redskins' quarterback Joe Theismann lobbed a pass toward Washington, who came out of the backfield heading to the left side of the field. Squirek reacted quickly, cut in front of Washington, and intercepted the pass on the Washington 5-yard line. A few steps later, he was in the end zone with the ball raised high toward the heavens, and gave Los Angeles a 21–3 lead at the half.

Squirek's play completely shifted the game's momentum over to the Raiders, and they never relinquished it in their 38–9 romp to capture the world championship. The image of Squirek crossing the goal line was frozen in time when it appeared on the cover of *Sports Illustrated* the following week, and is continually shown on Super Bowl highlights. The play took all but a few seconds. However, Squirek's actions in the quest for pro football's ultimate team honor will last forever, and solidified his place in Raiders lore.

Ken Stabler

Wine, women, and song: This combination of revelry represented the image of quarterback Ken "the Snake" Stabler off the field, where the light of a honky tonk jukebox served as his beacon. On the football field, however, Stabler displayed the desire of a fierce competitor. His passion was winning games for the Silver and Black, which the Raiders did on a consistent basis under his seven seasons of leadership as starting signal caller for Oakland's band of renegades during the bulk of their glory years.

Stabler earned his moniker, and reputation as a talented left-handed signal caller, at the same time back in his native Foley, Alabama. He was dubbed "the Snake" by his high school coach after running downfield in a slithering motion through an opposing defense.[1] During his tenure under center, Foley High School amassed a near-perfect 29–1 record, and earned Stabler countless accolades. He was also a star on the basketball team, and his talent as a baseball pitcher brought him minor league offers from the New York Yankees and the Houston Astros.[2] His abilities also drew the attention of Alabama's legendary football coach Paul "Bear" Bryant. Stabler decided that the gridiron was in his future, and continued on his winning ways as a collegiate quarterback for the coaching legend by leading Bryant's teams to a 28-3-2 record from 1965 to 67 that included winning the 1965 national championship. As a junior in 1966 he led the Crimson Tide to a spotless 11–0 campaign, and followed that with an 8-2-1 record in his senior year.[3]

The Oakland Raiders made Stabler their second round selection in the 1968 draft. However, at first, the Snake's initial experience in the pro ranks was shaping up to be a bust. He came to the Raiders with a sore knee and lacking the arm strength needed to guide Oakland's long-ball offensive attack.[4] Added to Stabler's woes was the fact that Daryle Lamonica was firmly entrenched as the starter. He was the reigning AFL Most Valuable Player, and led the team to a Super Bowl appearance just months prior to Stabler's arrival.

The Raiders sent Stabler to the semi-pro Spokane Shockers of the Continental League where he played in one game before Oakland brought him back. In an effort to rest up his sore knee, the Raiders placed him on injured reserve.[5] After missing the 1969 season, Stabler came back ready to stick with the team at the dawn of the 1970's and remained in the silver and black colors throughout the entire decade.

He still was not anywhere near the starting job in 1970, but took advantage of his apprenticeship while waiting for the opportunity. He began lifting weights to strengthen his throwing arm and body, and was taken under the tutelage of Raiders great George Blanda. Blanda took a liking to the young man from Alabama, who held for him on extra points and field goal attempts, and began sharing all his vast knowledge, of which Stabler absorbed like a sponge.[6] Stabler also met with Oakland's offensive linemen on a regular basis to discuss what plays would work in different situations. Not only did this help Stabler learn more about the pro game, but it also earned him the respect of the men who protected him.[7] With Blanda and one of the greatest offensive lines in the history of the game teaching him the ropes, Stabler was gaining on an aging Lamonica for the starting role at quarterback.

By 1973, "the Snake" was unleashed on the rest of the NFL, and he made the most of the opportunity given to him. After his knee injuries limited his running skills, Stabler became an accomplished and much revered drop back passer. He was exceptional at locating an open receiver swiftly and efficiently, and within the 10 to 20 yard range, there was no better in regards to accuracy.[8] His cool and calm demeanor allowed "the Snake" to gain the respect and confidence from his teammates, and it also helped to even out the frenzied sideline rants of head coach John Madden.[9] More than anyone else, Stabler was able to bring the emotional Madden down to a somewhat tranquil level. His demeanor and talents also allowed Stabler to pull victory from the jaws of defeat on many occasions, and is still regarded as the team's all-time quarterback. Under his field generalship, the Raiders posted a 71-25-1 regular season record, four division titles, one AFC Championship, and the crown jewel of the gridiron, a victory in Super Bowl XI.

Along the silver and black road to stardom, Stabler earned four Pro Bowl trips (1973, 74, 76, and 77), was voted All-Pro in 1974 and 1976, and bestowed with the honor of beginning selected the NFL Most Valuable Player in 1974 and 1976. In 1976, he also won the league passing championship while leading the team to their first Super Bowl triumph. He also owned most of the team's then-passing records, and reached 100 wins faster than any other quarterback up to that time.

As the 1970's began their descent into the history books, so too did the reign of "the Snake." Team owner Al Davis began to belittle his quarterback after Stabler threw 30 interceptions and only 16 touchdowns in 1978, and the Raiders failed to make the

playoffs for just the second time in the decade. Stabler shot back with many negative remarks about Davis, and the union between the two became broken.[10] After missing the post-season yet again in 1979, it looked like either Davis or Stabler was going to leave town. Seeing that it was Mr. Davis who paid the bills, it was no a good bet to assume that the patriarch of Raider Nation woul be heading to the airport any time soon. This left the "the Snake as the one who was going to be handed a ticket to another desti nation. In March of 1980, Davis traded Stabler to the Housto Oilers for strong-armed quarterback Dan Pastorini. Stabler remaine with the Oilers for two seasons before they released him in 1982 He then signed with the New Orleans Saints before retiring o October 26, 1984, just two months shy of his 39th birthday.

During his illustrious run as field general for the Silver an Black, Stabler threw for 19, 078 yards and 150 touchdowns. Ove the course of his entire career with three teams, he amassed 27 938 yards, 194 touchdowns, and 222 interceptions. He has bee enshrined into many halls of fame, but the biggest snub is th one coming from Canton, Ohio. He has been eligible for the Pr Football Hall of Fame since 1990, and came close on a few occa sions. Why the presence of Ken Stabler's bust does not foreve grace the sport's hallowed halls of immortals is a mystery whos answers lie squarely with those on the election committee. Hope fully, in the very near future, some sense will prevail, and Ke Stabler will get the much-deserved nod from Canton.

Jack Tatum

Legendary Ohio State coach Woody Hayes once said tha safety Jack Tatum hit so hard that his blasts knocked opponent right off their feet.[1] While in high school in Passaic, New Jersey Tatum knocked out two opposing quarterbacks in the sam game.[2] These incidents plus countless others gave this bone-jarring human torpedo the moniker of "the Assassin." Through weigh training, Tatum built his frame into a solid weapon of destruction Along with his physical strength, he had blazing speed, as a 10.(clocking in the 100-yard dash would testify to.

After earning All-American honors twice, and being selecte National Defensive Player of the Year as a senior at Ohio State Tatum was more than ready for the next level of competition. I an attempt to replace a retired David Grayson following the 197(campaign, the Raiders drafted Tatum. Upon his arrival at training camp, the Oakland coaching staff informed Tatum that the safety position was his as long as no one else could beat him out for it For nine seasons in a Raiders uniform, no one ever did.[3] With Ta tum's hitting ability, it was quickly understood that he would no relinquish the opportunity given him. He easily became a starting safety in one of the greatest defensive backfields ever assembled along with Willie Brown, George Atkinson, and Skip Thomas.

Despite the havoc Tatum caused on the opposition, he pos sessed a very laid back personality. He just let his tackling ability do the talking for him. He would just rattle a ball carrier's bones, and then quietly return to the huddle to await another chance at hitting someone.[4] Tatum's impact was felt from the very first game in which he wore the silver and black uniform of the Raiders in 1971. By the end of that first season, the rest of the league respected and feared him. He earned selection onto the All-Rookie team, and was runner up for the NFL's Rookie of the Year Award.

In 1972 Tatum set an NFL record against the Green Bay Packers by returning a fumble recovery 104 yards. He also led the Raiders with four interceptions, and once again in 1977 with six. As the decade of the 1970's rolled along, so did Jack Tatum, as he reaped numerous accolades. All-Pro honors came his way in 1973 through 1975, the Sporting News selected him to their All-Star team from 1975 through 1977, and he was a Pro Bowl selection in 1973, 1974, and 1976. After the 1979 season, Tatum was traded to the Houston Oilers, where he played one season in 1980 before retiring with 37 career interceptions. He left a legacy of hard hits that could fill up many highlight reels, and in the process, earned a spot among the greatest to ever wear a Raiders uniform. Tatum passed away on July 27, 2010, following a heart attack.

Gene Upshaw

Kansas City's Buck Buchanan was a force on the defensive line that terrorized the man in front of him, and opposing running backs and signal callers. Many times he was in the backfield before a handoff or drop back by the quarterback. He was big and powerful, and no offensive lineman could keep him contained for very long.[1]

The Chiefs were one of the top teams in the AFL, and the Raiders knew they were close to being in that position in the mid–1960's. However, the Raiders also knew that league supremacy was going to have to go through Kansas City. Having to play against the dominant Buchanan twice a year was not going to get it done. Oakland needed to neutralize the Kansas City steamroller with someone just as big and powerful.[2]

The Raiders got more than they ever could have dreamed of in one Mr. Eugene Thurman Upshaw, Jr. from Robstown, Texas. Blessed with speed, size, intelligence, desire, and tremendous leadership skills, the 6-5, 255 pound guard par-excellence became one of the most sensational trench warriors in the game's history.

Upshaw was Oakland's first round selection in 1967, locked down the starting left guard job in his rookie campaign, and held it for 15 seasons. He was also big for his time and he helped make Oakland's offensive line the best ever assembled. Upshaw, along with fellow future Hall of Famers Jim Otto and Art Shell, were able to blow open massive holes for running backs, and allowed their quarterbacks enough ample time to survey the field looking for open receivers. With his incredible quickness, Upshaw was a master at leading sweeps.[3] The impact Upshaw had at containing Buchanan was apparent in the fact that in his rookie year, the Raiders were crowned AFL champions. Two more championships were bestowed on the Raiders with Upshaw on the line. With Super Bowl titles following the 1976 and 1980 seasons, Upshaw became the only player in history to perform in three Super Bowls in three different decades. He amassed a streak of 207 consecutive starts, and played in 305 games total for the Silver and Black. He also earned All-League of All-Conference honors 11 straight times, was selected to seven Pro Bowls, placed on the NFL's All-Decade Team for the 1970's and the NFL's 75th Anniversary Team. Needless to say, Gene Upshaw was a slam-dunk for enshrinement into the Pro Football Hall of Fame, and was bestowed that honor in his first year of eligibility in 1987.

Upshaw's leadership abilities earned the respect of his fellow Raiders, and he served them as team captain from 1973 to 1981. Starting in 1970, he also served the team as an NFLPA player representative. In 1980, he was elected NFLPA President, and held that position until June of 1983, when he was appointed Executive Director of the National Football League Players Association.[4] He remained with the NFLPA until his death from pancreatic cancer on August 20, 2008, five days after his 63rd birthday.

Mark Van Eeghen

From Cambridge, Massachusetts to his induction into the Scholar Athlete Hall of Fame, Mark van Eeghen is an excellent example that brains and brawn can go together successfully. Born in Cambridge near prestigious Harvard University, van Eeghen excelled in the classroom and while earning All-State and All-American honors as a high school running back in Rhode Island.[1] He then made his way to Colgate University, regarded as one of the top institutions of higher learning. While pursuing a degree in economics, van Eeghen pursued Colgate rushing records, and upon graduation, was successful at obtaining both.

The Raiders selected van Eeghen in the third round of the 1974 draft much to the surprise of many NFL scouts. The scouting reports on him from around the league claimed that he was not that big or strong to pound the ball between the tackles like a fullback is required to do. It was claimed that Al Davis once took a quick look at van Eeghen during a workout while he was in college, and came away impressed.[2] Davis and the rest of the Raiders knew something about the toughness of Colgate fullbacks, seeing that they had a former one on their roster named Marv Hubbard at the time of van Eeghen being drafted.

When van Eeghen arrived in Oakland, Hubbard was firmly entrenched as the team's bruising fullback, who wore defenses down in battering ram fashion. There was no way van Eeghen was going to overthrow Hubbard in 1974 for his job, so he accepted a backup role for the time being. Hubbard took a liking to the young fullback from his alma mater, and began teaching him things about being a fullback in the NFL. Always an exceptional student, van Eeghen listened and learned throughout his first two campaigns.[3]

When the Raiders opened their 1976 training camp, van Eeghen was still considered the number two fullback on the depth chart. However, during the pre-season, Hubbard changed all that when he suffered his third shoulder separation in one year. The injury put an end to his season, and made him realize that it was probably time to retire. Hubbard's abrupt retirement left Oakland without a starting fullback. This opened the door for van Eeghen to provide the team with solid running between the tackles, blocking, and catching the ball out of the backfield.[4]

There was no doubt that van Eeghen was inexperienced when the season began, but by the end of it, he was the dependable fullback that Oakland had always counted on in the past. With explosive power, quickness of foot, and the blocking up front from the greatest offensive line ever assembled, the former Colgate product bulldozed his way for 1,012 yards in the Raiders' first Super Bowl–winning campaign. Along the way, he proved that he no longer lacked experience, or was too light to take the pounding of such a demanding position.

Mark van Eeghen continued to do an outstanding job over

the next four seasons. Whether it was running, blocking, or catching passes, he excelled and became one of the best examples of what a fullback should be. In 1977, he ran for a team-record 1,273 yards to lead the AFC in rushing, and earned a Pro Bowl spot for himself. In 1978 his 1,050 yards made him the first Raiders running back to top the 1,000-yard rushing barrier for three straight seasons. In 1980, he rushed for 838 yards, added 259 more in four playoff games, and helped Oakland secure another Super Bowl championship. His 107 consecutive game streak ended in 1981 due to missing most of the season with injuries.

By 1982, the Raiders moved to Los Angeles, and were looking to rebuild a team that was getting old after posting their first losing season in 17 years. They took a major step toward injecting youth into their running game by selecting Heisman Trophy winner Marcus Allen with their first pick of the draft. With a running back of Allen's magnitude coming into the Silver and Black fold, and van Eeghen suffering from five seasons of constant beatings, the Raiders felt that their chances were better with Allen leading the running attack.[5]

The Raiders released van Eeghen before the 1982 season. He left the team as their all-time leading rusher with 5,907 yards and scored 35 touchdowns. He added 162 receptions for 1,467 yards and three touchdowns. He did manage to return to the area in which he grew up when the New England Patriots claimed him off waivers before the first game of the '82 campaign. After two seasons with the Patriots, van Eeghen retired after nine seasons of professional football.

Phil Villapiano

The hard-as-nails New Jersey native's road to Al Davis' silver and black kingdom included a four-year stop at Bowling Green University in Ohio, where he established himself as a bona fide NFL prospect. Villapiano was twice named All-Conference at defensive end, and honored with his selection as the 1970 Mid-American Conference Defensive Player of the Year, and Bowling Green's Player of the Year.[1]

The Raiders selected Villapiano in the second round of the 1971 draft, and he spent the next nine seasons making life miserable on opposing offenses from his linebacker position. He also became one of the most popular members of the Raiders, and organized different events as the team's "social director" from training camp through the end of the season.[2]

On the field, Villapiano was a fast, coachable, fierce, and highly-competitive performer, who was capable of playing both inside or outside linebacker. It did not matter where he attacked an opponent from, he loved being a Raider, loved to hit hard and inflict punishment, and became the leader of a linebacker corps that enjoyed much success during Oakland's glory days of the 1970's.[3] He was also tough off the field, getting into a brawl with a motorcycle gang outside a local watering hole with the odds not stacked in his favor.[4] His coach John Madden had an expression of having linebacker eyes, which was a spark that gleamed when the opportunity presented itself to make a vicious hit. Madden saw that in Villapiano, and he delivered for his coach since becoming a starter in his rookie year.[5]

He earned All-AFC honors twice in 1974 and '75, and four trips to the Pro Bowl from 1973 to 1976. His greatest moment

was when he helped the Raiders win Super Bowl XI in Janua of 1977 over the Minnesota Vikings after years of coming up ju shy of the coveted prize. His days as an Oakland Raider ende on April 22, 1980, when he was traded to the Buffalo Bills fc wide receiver Bob Chandler. He played four seasons with the Bil before retiring, but despite his move to Buffalo, he was, and alway will be a Raider through and through.

Carl Weathers

Rocky Balboa and Apollo Creed staged the greatest boxin matches in cinematic history. The roles also catapulted their po trayers, Sylvester Stallone and Carl Weathers, into stardom on th big screen. However, before he was Apollo Creed in four of th six Rocky films, Weathers was a linebacker for the Oaklan Raiders.

The New Orleans native gained his status on the footba field in California, where he played collegiately at Long Beac State and San Diego State. The two-year letterman earned All league honors while playing defensive end and tackle in additio to linebacker.[1] The acting bug already had bitten the solid-buil good-looking Weathers by this time, and he majored in Theatr arts while punishing opposing ball carriers.

In 1970, he signed with the Raiders as a free agent, and saw action in seven games at linebacker and on special teams, earning a reputation as a punishing tackler. After the 1971 season, Weather left the Raiders and played a year in the Canadian Football Leagu with the British Columbia Lions before retiring from football t exclusively pursue his passion for acting.[2] After some minor ap pearances in *Kung Fu, Bucktown, Friday Foster, See, Pop?,* and *Th Four Deuces,* the role of a lifetime was presented to him in 1976 playing opposite Sly Stallone in the Academy Award–winning best picture *Rocky.*[3]

With the huge success from the Rocky films, Weathers wen on to a solid career that saw him in *Predator* (1987), *Action Jackson* (1988), and many more on the big screen and television up to the present time. He also delved into the video game genre, supplying the voice for Colonel Samuel Garrett in *Mercenaries: Journey o Destruction.* He also heads Red Tight Media, a production com pany that specializes in training films for the United States mili tary.[4]

Warren Wells

In four seasons with the Raiders, Warren Wells carried on the tradition first set by Art Powell as a game-breaking threat any time he touched the football. He was blessed with blazing speed and the ability to catch and block. This triple threat quickly proved to be a silver and black-clad menace, striking fear into de fensive backfields around the league. The Raiders great head coach John Madden had many fantastic performers throughout his reign, but claimed that Wells was not only a dangerous receiver but considered the best special teams player he ever employed. With his quickness, he shot down the field weaving at full throttle to get to opposing return men and make the tackle. After starting his pro career with the Detroit Lions in 1964, Wells served in the military for two years and then signed as a free agent with the Raiders in 1967 after being released by Kansas City.[2]

He established himself as the AFL's top deep threat by averaging an incredible 23.3 yards per catch, caught 42 touchdown passes, and twice amassed over 1,000 yards receiving. For his sterling efforts, Wells was honored with selection to the 1968 AFL All-Star Game, 1969 All-AFL Team, and the 1970 All-AFC Team.

In just four seasons, Wells earned his place among the elite receivers in the game. However, his reputation off the field cut into, and eventually ended, what could have been a continued and prosperous career. An alleged charge of attempted rape in 1969 began legal woes that eventually led him out of football and into serving prison time. He also had other altercations with the law on drunken driving charges and carrying a concealed weapon.[3] During three years of probation on the rape charge, part of the arrangement was that Wells could not frequent bars. Unfortunately, he did, and was stabbed by a woman in Texas inside a local watering hole, his presence in which violated his probation.[4] That led to ten months of jail time. He attempted a comeback with the Raiders in 1972, but his skills had faded by then and he was released. In 1976, Wells was again sent to prison after an attempted robbery outside a grocery store in Houston, Texas.[5] It was a sad way to see such a promising career end. Luckily, Wells survived this dark period. He currently resides in Texas, still has an athletic frame, and is a devoted father and grandfather.[6] He proved that people certainly do make mistakes, but can learn from them and grow as a human being.

Fred Williamson

Before the Oakland secondary was patrolled by "the Assassin," "the Hit Man," and "Doctor Death," it was led by Fred "the Hammer" Williamson. After his collegiate career at Northwestern University in the late 1950's, the Gary, Indiana, native was selected by the San Francisco 49ers in the NFL draft. While in training camp, he hit so hard that the coach told him not to hammer on his players with such force. The moniker stuck, and Williamson lived up to it throughout an eight year pro career.[1]

Following the exhibition season in 1960, the 49ers traded Williamson to the Pittsburgh Steelers. After that season, he jumped to the American Football League, signing a free agent contract with the Raiders.[2] Armed with the "Hammer," a karate-type move he used with his forearm to blast the heads of receivers, Williamson created havoc on the opposition that dared enter his area.[3] He played with the Raiders from 1961 through the '64 season, intercepted 25 passes, was selected to the AFL All-Star Game twice (1962–1963), and earned All-AFL honors in the same seasons. The gifted athlete finished off his pro career with the Kansas City Chiefs from 1965 to 1967, helping them win the AFL championship in 1966.

It was then on to a long-standing acting career for Williamson, starting with television roles in 1968, including a role in the 1970 Academy Award–winning film *M*A*S*H*. Many of Williamson's film roles where with fellow football-star-turned-actor Jim Brown. He also became a director and producer in the 1970's, having directed over twenty projects.[4]

Taken Too Soon

Marquis Cooper

Cooper was a linebacker with the Raiders during the 2008 season after spending time with five other teams since 2004. On March 1, 2009, ten days shy of his 27th birthday, Cooper and three friends went on a deep-sea fishing trip 75 miles off the coast of Clearwater, Florida. After attempts to pry a stuck anchor loose by gunning the engine, the boat overturned and all attempts to upright the boat failed. After struggling in cold rough waters overnight, Cooper and two of the others succumbed to the elements after being overcome by hypothermia and drifted away from the boat. Five days later, on March 6, 2009, Marquis Cooper was officially pronounced dead.[1]

Roger Hagberg

Hagberg was a tough backup fullback who was a clutch performer coming off the bench, doing whatever was asked of him as a member of the Oakland Raiders from 1965 through 1969. He possessed talent as a runner, blocker, and receiver out of the backfield. He met an untimely end on April 15, 1970, when his car crashed into a highway guardrail and he was thrown into the path of another car on the way to his home in Oakland.[2]

Tim Hall

Hall earned the distinction of being the first player from Robert Morris College to get drafted into the NFL. After two seasons with the Raiders performing as a backup running back and member of the special teams, Hall was released during the 1998 training camp. Not long after that, on September 30, 1998, he was shot to death in his native Kansas City when a car pulled alongside the one Hall was a passenger in and shots were fired into the vehicle.[3]

Darrell Russell

Defensive tackle Darrell Russell was on the fast track for NFL stardom when the Oakland Raiders made him the number two overall pick in the 1997 draft. At 6-5 and 325 pounds, Russell was a force to be reckoned with, and signed a seven-year, $22 million contract with the Silver and Black. It proved to be the biggest contract ever signed by a rookie. His promising career then became hampered by drug abuse after earning Pro Bowl selections in 1998 and '99. He was eventually suspended three times by the league for violating the substance abuse policy, and released by Oakland following his second suspension. He played briefly with the Washington Redskins in 2003, and the following year, was suspended an unprecedented seventh time. His final experience as a football player ended with his release by Tampa Bay in 2004.[4]

On December 15, 2005, in Los Angeles, Russell was a passenger in a 2004 Pontiac Grand Prix with a former teammate from USC behind the wheel. While traveling at a high rate of speed on La Cienega Boulevard, the car skidded approximately 50 feet, smacked into a curb, two trees, a newsstand, a light pole, obliterated a fire hydrant, and eventually crashed into a passenger-less bus. Russell was taken to Cedars-Sinai Medical Center where he was pronounced dead while the driver died at UCLA Medical Center.[5]

Stacey Toran

Toran came to the Raiders as their sixth round selection of the 1984 draft out of Notre Dame. The defensive back worked extremely hard to establish himself as a professional, and by his second season he earned a starting position. On August 5, 1989, Toran drove out to a restaurant in Marina Del Rey, California. He never had a reputation as a drinker, but on this night, he indulged quite a bit. Less than a block from his home, Toran was killed two months shy of his 28th birthday after his vehicle hit a curb, rolled over and struck a tree. Toxicology reports found that his blood alcohol level was well past the legal limit.[6]

Dan Turk

Turk played 15 seasons of professional football as a center. From 1989 through 1996 Turk was with the Raiders, and in 1995 he served as captain of the special teams. His career ended after two seasons with the Washington Redskins from 1997 to '99. On December 24, 2000, Turk passed away from cancer at age 38.[7]

Eric Turner

After playing for the Cleveland Browns from 1991 through 1996, Eric Turner signed with the Raiders as a free agent in 1997. Turner was truly excited about being a part of the great tradition that engulfed the Raiders organization. He became a starter in his first year and did a fantastic job for the Silver and Black over the course of the next three seasons. During the 1999 season, Turner began to experience intestinal problems, and by the off-season, it was discovered that the talented, hard-hitting defensive back had intestinal cancer. The popular, spiritual, well-respected, and devoted family man, lost his battle with cancer at age 31 on May 28, 2000.[8]

Dave Waymer

The Brooklyn, New York, native entered the NFL as the second round draft pick of the New Orleans Saints in 1980 out of Notre Dame. After ten seasons in New Orleans, the defensive back played two seasons with the San Francisco 49ers before coming to the Los Angeles Raiders in 1992. During the off-season, Waymer died at his ranch in Mooresville, North Carolina, of a heart attack brought on by cocaine use.[9]

Mike Wise

Mike Wise wanted to be a member of the Los Angeles Raiders more than anything. He was granted his wish when the Silver and Black made the 6-8, 280-pound defensive lineman their fourth round selection of the 1986 draft. Now that he was a member of pro football's equivalent to the "Hells Angels," Wise wanted to look the part of a biker bad boy despite truly being a sensitive soul that wrote beautiful poetry. To adapt to the outlaw image, he grew a Fu Manchu mustache, rode a motorcycle, and got a tattoo of the Grim Reaper on his ankle.[10] The image of a badass was solidified, but he still had to prove himself worthy on the field. He even went as far as using hypnotists to generate aggressive thoughts to give him more of an edge. His teammates did not seem to go along with this façade, and did not look at Wise as a force to be reckoned with.

Wise became a loner, but worked his butt off to improve on the field. He did a good job during the 1987 pre-season, and then he landed a starting job for the final 14 games when Howie Long was injured. He gained more and more confidence, and realized that he was now an established veteran, and looked to be compensated for it. The Raiders did renegotiate his contract, but after talking to some other defensive linemen around the league with the same time in the league as his, Wise was still underpaid.[11]

What began as an incredible dream come true for Wise to be a member of the Raiders was now reduced to the harsh reality of the business aspect of the game and all the pitfalls. He became bitter, moody, and fought with teammates over minor things. He had enough, and bolted from Raider Nation to his home in Sacramento, California. He might have felt that the Raiders were going to realize that he was a valuable member of the team, and that they would contact him about coming back with a nice amount of monetary compensation. The thought seemed to have a happy ending, but in reality, it was the farthest thing from the truth. Halfway through the 1991 season, the Raiders released him.[12]

The Cleveland Browns looked to give Wise a chance, and acquired him off waivers. His opportunity with the Browns hit a major snag when a knee injury after three games abruptly put an end to his season. Wise returned to the Browns, but as he was doing a squat press during a spring mini-camp, something in his back popped. He attempted to endure through the discomfort, but was not able to perform up to a level that was required. With his NFL dreams quickly turning into a nightmare, Wise left training camp, and the Browns released him at the beginning of August.[13]

His woes continued, as fears of financial troubles caused him to put his big house up for sale, and the pain in his back made it difficult to even rise out of bed. With everything crashing around him, Mike Wise fell into a deep depression. He took a 9mm Ruger handgun, placed it in front of his right ear and pulled the trigger. His real estate agent found Wise's 28-year-old body on the afternoon of Friday, August 21, 1992, in the bedroom of his home.[14]

EXECUTIVES, STADIUMS, UNIFORMS, CHEERLEADERS, NICKNAMES

The Raiders Founding Fathers

Every moment in Raiders history, whether mediocre, glorious, or infamous, would have never materialized if it were not for the desire of eight Oakland area businessmen. Each accolade or antic achieved by the Raiders stemmed from the willingness of these power brokers to bring the franchise to life at the dawn of the 1960's.

Wayne Valley (1914–1986) — Valley was an outstanding football player at Oregon State, where he started at both fullback and linebacker while working his way toward a business degree in the 1930's. In the 1940's, Valley began a self-employed homebuilding business. His venture eventually was responsible for the construction of thousands of homes throughout the United States, making him one of the biggest contractors in the country. Valley, along with Ed McGah, served in the Raiders' hierarchy longer than any of the other original founders.[1]

Ed McGah (1899–1983) — Like Wayne Valley, Ed McGah was a gifted athlete. His prowess on the semi-professional baseball circuit made him one of the most-remembered players in the Oakland area. His baseball genes were passed on to his son, Ed McGah, Jr., who played at the major league level with the Boston Red Sox organization in 1946 and 1947. Ed McGah, Sr.'s trek to part ownership of the Silver and Black came from humble beginnings. He began and operated a construction company that rose to the top of the field. A big opportunity to work on the Yerba Buena Tunnel during the Bay Bridge project allowed McGah to incorporate revolutionary techniques that brought him high praise and solidified his status among his peers. He also worked in real estate and land development, rising to major prominence over the years leading up to his involvement with the Raiders.[2]

Robert Osborne (1898–1968) — Along with Chet Soda and Charles Harney, city councilman Robert Osborne made up one of three groups with initial interest in bringing a football team to Oakland.[3]

Chet Soda (1908–1989) — Soda was given the task of being the Raiders first spokesman and was also appointed chairman of the board and the team's first general manager. Besides his involvement with the Raiders, Soda earned a lasting legacy in the Oakland area as president of the Board of Port Commissioners of the Port of Oakland. Under his leadership, the port was developed into the second largest in the country. He also oversaw the construction of the Oakland Museum.[4]

Charles Harney (1902–1962) — Harney was the builder of San Francisco's Candlestick Park, which was constructed on a parcel of land that he owned.[5]

Don Blessing (1905–2000) — Blessing joined the ranks of Wayne Valley and Ed McGah as team owners with a stellar athletic background. In the 1928 Summer Olympic Games in Amsterdam, Blessing was the coxswain of a boat that brought home a gold medal for the United States.[6]

Harvey Binns (1914–1982) — Binns was a restaurateur whose involvement with the Raiders ownership group only lasted until the beginning of the 1960 pre-season. He did not approve of the way the team was being run by general manager Chet Soda, and his place among the owners was taken over by industrialist Wallace Marsh.[7]

Art Beckett — Like Binns, Beckett withdrew from the ownership group before the 1960 pre-season, and was replaced by civic leader Roger Lapham, Jr. Lapham (1918–2000), was the son of a former San Francisco mayor and served on boards of directors for some of the largest companies in the Bay Area.[8]

As the team's inaugural campaign entered the record books, the ownership group that began as brothers in arms was quickly disintegrating. With turmoil surrounding the group about management issues, many of the original eight powerbrokers wanted nothing more than to separate themselves from the burden that was quickly hovering around the team.[9]

On January 15, 1961, after a seven-hour meeting, Ed McGah, Wayne Valley, and Robert Osborne emerged as the new ownership of the Oakland Raiders. They bought out the shares belonging to Chet Soda, Don Blessing, Wallace Marsh, Roger Lapham, Jr., and Charles Harney. McGah assumed the role of team president, Valley vice president, and Osborne treasurer.[10] The following year, Osborne left the group due to health problems, thus leaving McGah and Valley as the supreme powers behind the team's future.[11]

On July 25, 1966, Al Davis returned to the organization after serving as AFL Commissioner for two months. He purchased 10 percent of the team for a reported $18,000, and also was appointed general manager and head of football operations.[12] Just like when he miraculously turned the Raiders from losers into winners in 1963, Davis continued on his quest to make the Silver and Black the greatest sports organization in the free world.

It is well documented that Al Davis and Wayne Valley did not have a great relationship, but managed to coexist during the Raiders' rise to supremacy. However, by 1972, Davis looked to seize the majority of control over the team. While Valley was in Munich attending the Summer Olympic Games, Davis had lawyers draw up a new partnership agreement that allowed Davis to reign supreme. Ed McGah was in favor of Davis, and agreed to the new deal. When Valley returned to Oakland, needless to say, he was not happy with the new arrangement. He quickly took the issue to the legal system, but the courts decided in favor of Davis and McGah. Valley hung around for three more years, but by January 1976, he finally sold his share of the team.[13] McGah remained the lone survivor of the original eight founders until his death in 1983.

Other Key Personnel

Ron Wolf — Team Executive

Tireless, meticulous, and a builder of champions can best describe Ron Wolf. For he possessed these traits, and along with Al Davis, Wolf built the juggernaut Raiders teams that dominated pro football for twenty years beginning in 1963.

Born on December 30, 1938, in New Freedom, Pennsylvania near Pittsburgh, Wolf received his baptism under fire as a scout at age 24 when the Raiders were a pathetic lot, to put it mildly. The job at its inception of molding a respectable team in Oakland seemed like an insurmountable task.

Prior to building the Silver and Black wrecking machine, Wolf served in Army intelligence in Europe from 1956 to 1959, and graduated from the University of Oklahoma with a history degree.[14] Much like Al Davis, he was obsessed with football, and learned everything he could about the game. He worked as an editor on the staff of a pro football magazine based in Texas before landing a job with Oakland as a talent scout in 1963.

From that point on, the name Ron Wolf became synonymous with winning. He developed scouting reports for thousands of college seniors, and evaluated hundreds of college programs each year. As director of personnel operations, Wolf tackled the daily task of sitting in a dark room with miles of game films and compiling extensive volumes of data on players from both the professional and collegiate levels.[15] Within no time, all his hard, dedicated work paid off, as the Raiders grew more and more powerful through the 1960's, 70's and early 80's, all in part thanks to Ron Wolf.

When Al Davis became AFL commissioner in 1966, he brought Wolf along to serve as his coordinator of talent. After Davis' brief reign as AFL czar, Wolf returned to Oakland as director of player personnel.[16]

In 1975, Wolf went to serve as vice-president of operations for the expansion Tampa Bay Buccaneers. Under his guidance, Tampa Bay was built into a solid team that advanced to the NFC Championship Game within three years even though he left the team in early 1978 after not having a good working relationship with ownership. It was then back to the Raiders.[17]

Despite building a championship-caliber organization in Oakland, Wolf was not present to reap the rewards when his hard work culminated into the team's first Super Bowl victory following the 1976 season. However, he was on board to collect two Super Bowl rings after the 1980 and '83 campaigns.

On November 27, 1991, after working for the New York Jets in 1990, Wolf joined the Green Bay Packers as executive vice president/general manager with the hopes of helping a once proud franchise back to the top of the pro football world. By hiring Mike Holmgren as head coach, and obtaining Brett Favre as quarterback in 1992, the Packers took off to the top of the NFL. From 1992 to 2000, Green Bay had the NFL's second-best winning record at 131–77. Wolf also earned his third Super Bowl ring in 1996, as the Packers rise back to the summit of pro football was complete. They also won an NFC championship under Wolf the following year. He retired from the Packers in June 2001 with his solid reputation as a builder of champions forever intact.[18]

Al LoCasale — Team Executive

No mention of this team's history could be told without Al LoCasale getting his just due.

Whenever an individual performs numerous tasks on the job, it is said that they wear many hats. In the case of Mr. Al LoCasale, any hat he wore bore the Raiders shield on it, and was worn with great pride for over a third of a century. From Jur 1969 until his retirement in September 2003, LoCasale brough a whole new meaning to the term multi-tasking, and did it wit distinction and dedication.

LoCasale's road to the Raiders began in middle-class Phila delphia, where he learned most of life's lessons on the streets i the 1930's and 40's as the son of a meat-cutter father and a seam stress mother. The allure of football caught him at an early age and he began what turned into a fantastic career in his nativ Philadelphia coaching in high school. He also coached while serv ing in the Navy at Bainbridge Naval Training Center and at h alma mater, the University of Pennsylvania.[19]

He first met Al Davis at eighteen while the 22-year-ol Davis was lecturing at a football coaching clinic in New Jersey The two men with undying passion for the gridiron struck up conversation, and remained in touch through the 1950's.[20]

The duo that would eventually guide the Raiders to greatnes then got to work with each other for the first time in 1959 whe both were employed at the University of Southern California LoCasale was an administrative assistant to USC head coach Do Clark and Davis served on the coaching staff.

The following year, he moved into the pro ranks as an ex ecutive in the newly formed American Football League with th Los Angeles Chargers. After seven years with the Chargers, wher he helped the team win five division and one league champion ship, LoCasale's reputation caught the attention of Paul Brown. The legendary Brown had built the Cleveland Browns into a pow erhouse that ruled football in the 1940's and 50's. He was lookin to do the same thing with a new franchise in 1968, and the firs employee he hired in the "Queen City" was LoCasale. Brown' astute judge of character did not go to waste on LoCasale, as h lived up to his reputation as a football executive. In his only yea with the Bengals, he built up the player personnel departmen that allowed Cincinnati to become the first expansion team t win a division title in just its third campaign.

In May 1969, Al Davis was extremely interested in hirin his old friend, and asked Paul Brown for permission to discus bringing LoCasale to Oakland. The job offer was one that coul not be passed up. Davis wanted LoCasale to reign over the entir organization as executive assistant. A deal was quickly struck, an on June 1, 1969, the dynamic duo of Al's began their silver an black union that saw them oversee the team's glory days that in cluded three Super Bowl Championships.[22]

Over the course of 34 years, LoCasale was involved in ever aspect of running the day-to-day operations of the Raiders Whether setting up public relations events or handling merchan dising, ticket operations, travel schedules, game day operations the Raiderettes cheerleading squad, and looking over the entir front office staff, he did it all with style, intelligence, and a tireles passion.[23] He also had the privilege to work alongside some of th greatest football minds in Hall of Famers Sid Gillman, Pau Brown, and Al Davis.

In addition to doing all of the above, which would mak many other heads spin out of control, LoCasale did work in radi and television broadcasting, wrote books, was a founding membe of the National Football League Working Executives Group served on the Board of Directors for NFL Properties and NFl Films. He also represented the Raiders on the NFL Executiv committee and the National Football League Management Council.[24]

This saga of a dedicated football man is a true testament to the Raiders' creeds of "Commitment to Excellence" and "Pride and Poise." For this man with a passion to succeed should have the final chapter of his stellar gridiron resume end with a place in the Pro Football Hall of Fame. There are other executives on the immortal roll of honor in Canton, Ohio, so why not Mr. Al LoCasale? Whether or not Canton comes calling one day remains to be seen, but nevertheless, all of Raider Nation should give out a collective thank you to him in honor of all the work he did to make the organization's past exploits ones that any fan of the Silver and Black can proudly boast of.

Bill King — Broadcaster

From the first time the human voice was used to relay information across the airways back in the early 1920's, the sports broadcasting profession was an integral part of the medium, known as radio.

The profession began during the golden age of sports, and launched countless careers, many becoming household names. Others rose to elite status and even have statues commemorating their illustrious careers. Their catchphrases and descriptions of the action that unfolded before them were artistically transmitted out to the masses clinging to every word uttered about a team's performance. With the field of play as their canvas, the microphone an easel, eyes and voice as brushes and paints, these individuals created verbal masterpieces over the decades.

Throughout American cities great and small, folks might not remember some of the athletes, but more often than not they can recall the voices that came through their radios calling the event. In Oakland, and for a decade in Los Angeles, when asked to recall the king of pro football broadcasters, without reservation the name Bill King rings out. With his famous catchphrase "Holy Toledo" used to describe sterling moments, King sat on the broadcasting throne for Raiders' games from 1966 to 1992, calling the action during the team's glory days.

King's career began at a time when many of the medium's pioneers were winding down their days calling the action. He then became a bridge that merged the pioneers to the present day collection of broadcasters, earning him a lasting place in the linage of legends.

Born in Bloomington, Illinois, on October 6, 1927, Wilbur "Bill" King began his illustrious broadcasting career while serving in the military near the end of World War II. Stationed on the island of Guam, King worked for the Armed Forces Radio Network, where he relayed the play-by-play of sporting events as they came to him off the wire services. He did such a great job that it seemed like the action on the field was being observed first hand and not thousands of miles away.[25]

After returning home, King went to work in Pekin, Illinois, broadcasting high school sports and minor league baseball games. He elevated himself to doing college basketball games for Bradley University and basketball and football at the University of Nebraska. King moved to California in 1958 at the same time as baseball's New York Giants. The timing was right, and he landed a job announcing for the San Francisco Giants.[26]

Another team that moved west provided King with another opportunity to cover professional sports. The Philadelphia Warriors moved to San Francisco in the early 1960's, and from 1962 to 1983, King served as the team's play-by-play man.[27]

In 1966, King was brought into the silver and black fold as play-by-play man for the Raiders. Perched above the action donning his trademark handlebar mustache and beard, his voice called the greatest moments in Raiders history until the conclusion of the 1992 season.

King became an announcing triple threat when he was wooed by the owners of the Oakland A's to serve their team. He accepted, and from 1981 through 2005, he called the action with his usual rapid-fire delivery. Throughout his legendary career, King called the action for an NBA championship in 1974–75, three Super Bowls (1976, 1980, 1983), and three World Series (1988, 1989, 1990).

The voice of Bill King was silenced on October 18, 2005, with his passing from a pulmonary embolus, but the memories he created will never diminish. In honor of this legendary announcer, the broadcast booth in the Oakland Coliseum was renamed after him on April 2, 2006.[28] "Holy Toledo, Long Live the King!!!"

Stadiums

Kezar Stadium: 1960

A gracious $100,000 donation from the Mary Kezar estate in 1922 allowed the San Francisco Park Commission to start the proceedings of building a stadium to honor Kezar's relatives, who were some of the early founders of the San Francisco area. With an additional $200,000 given by the city and county, ground was broken in 1924, and by May 2, 1925, Kezar Stadium was opened for business. Designed by architect Willis Polk, Kezar Stadium was located at 755 Stanyan Street in San Francisco, and seated 59,942 spectators.[29]

Kezar played host to virtually every type of sporting event imaginable during the 1930's. Professional football made its debut when the San Francisco 49ers began play in the All-America Football Conference in 1946, and remained there through the 1970 NFL season.[30]

In 1960, the Oakland Raiders were given the opportunity to play their first season of operations in either Kezar or Candlestick Park. The Raiders' powers-that-be decided on Kezar due to it being easier to get to from Oakland, and also the fact that it was built for football. The Raiders played their first official game at Kezar on September 11, 1960, against the Houston Oilers, and their final one on November 13, 1960, against the Buffalo Bills. The Raiders had to share the stadium with the NFL's 49ers, and scheduling conflicts between the two teams forced the Oakland team out of the facility. Added to the Raiders' woes at Kezar was the fact that they were averaging attendance of only 10,700 at home games. This prevented the team from establishing solid fan support they had hoped would come from the Oakland area.[31]

The stadium hosted many rock 'n roll venues after professional football left, and it was used in some scenes of the Clint

Eastwood film classic *Dirty Harry* in 1971. In June 1989, the stadium was razed and rebuilt as a smaller facility with 10,000 seats.[32]

Candlestick Park: 1961

Ground was broken for Candlestick in 1958 after the New York Giants baseball team relocated to the Bay Area after the 1957 season, with architect John Bolles in charge of the project, and at a cost of $24.6 million. It went down in history as the first-ever modern baseball facility, and was the first sports structure to be built completely out of reinforced concrete.

Located at 490 Jamestown Avenue in San Francisco, Candlestick Park was opened on April 12, 1960, serving as the home for the Giants for forty years. The 49ers moved into "the Stick" in 1971, and over the years have enjoy much success within its confines. With it being so close to the San Francisco Bay, powerful winds sweep through the stadium, making playing conditions interesting at times.

It was called the "Wind Tunnel," "Cave of the Winds," and "the Stick." It was also called home to the Oakland Raiders during their final three games of the 1960 season, and their entire second campaign. They played their first game at Candlestick on December 4, 1960, against the Los Angeles Chargers, and their final one on December 17, 1961, against the Houston Oilers.

Candlestick was never designed with football in mind, and is still the only pro football stadium that started out exclusively as a baseball park. To accommodate the gridiron-viewing public, the stadium went through major renovations with seating being added around the baseball outfield area. Through the years, the stadium has undergone many name changes. In 1995 it became 3Com Park, then 3Com Park at Candlestick Point from 1996 to 2002. San Francisco Stadium at Candlestick Point became the name in 2002, and by 2004, it was called Monster Park.[33]

Frank Youell Field: 1962–1965

The orphans finally found a home in Oakland, though not a permanent one. While the Oakland Coliseum project was being worked on, the Raiders resided in a foster home of sorts from 1962 through 1965. When Oakland was ready to begin play in their temporary dwellings, their performance was so ghastly that it only seemed fitting that the stadium was named after an undertaker named Frank Youell, who was also a city councilman and supporter of local athletics.

The land used for Frank Youell Field was originally housing built by the federal government for war industry workers that came into the San Francisco area during World War II. The facility came to be after team owners Ed McGah, Robert Osborne, and Wayne Valley were tired of not having a stadium in Oakland to play in. They gave the city a deadline of late November in 1961 to either build a facility or lose the team.

On November 16, 1961, construction began on a 22,000-seat facility to house the Raiders. Impressive it was not. It was a skeletal structure that resembled an erector set, and it seemed that a strong wind might have brought the whole thing down. The aluminum facility at times had no hot running water, and was little more than a glorified high school stadium. Nevertheless, it was home for the Raiders until the permanent stadium was

finished. The Raiders played their first regular season game at Fran Youell Field on September 9, 1962, against the New York Titan and their final one on December 12, 1965, against the New York Je (previously the Titans). The site is now part of Laney College.

Oakland–Alameda County Stadium: 1966–1981, 1995–2009

The Raiders waited six years for a permanent home in Oakland. In 1966, they received it and definitely made the most ou of it. From their first regular season on September 18, 1966, agains the Kansas City Chiefs until December 13, 1981, with the Chicag Bears as opponents, the Silver and Black walked off that turf vic torious eighty percent of the time.

The concept for the Oakland–Alameda Coliseum bega along with the Raiders themselves in 1960. A non-profit grou was established and led by real estate developer Robert Naha. This entourage of East Bay area business magnets watched ove the financial aspects and development of the Coliseum that sav funds privately supplied to get the project through construction This was set in place to free local government officials from bur dening taxpayers with the money required to build it.

The San Francisco–based architect group of Skidmore, Ow ings, and Merrill were awarded the task of bringing the Raiders future home to life. The initial plans for the stadium were pre sented in November 1960, and within one month a site wa chosen. The official home of the Oakland Raiders was to be located on 120 acres west of the Elmhurst district of East Oakland next to the Nimitz Freeway and three miles from Oakland International Airport. The land began to be prepared in 1961, and construction got underway in 1962.

The Raiders were the sole residents of the Oakland–Alameda Coliseum in its first year of existence. The Oakland Clippers o the NASL played soccer there in 1967–68, and Major Leagu Baseball's Kansas City A's relocated to Oakland in 1968 to occupy the Coliseum throughout the spring and summer. Other franchises calling the Coliseum home through the years have been soccer's Oakland Stompers (1978), the Oakland Invaders of the United States Football League (1983–85), and Major League Soccer's San Jose Earthquakes since 2008. The Coliseum has also been the site of many rock concerts and World Series contests over its run as Oakland's most time-honored sports facility.

By the late 1970's, Al Davis was looking to get improvements made to the Coliseum, but to no avail. By 1980, after being denied any considerations regarding luxury suites, seating expansion, and renovations to the locker room, public address system, and the press box, Davis announced he was moving to Los Angeles. The Raiders officially left Oakland in 1982, and the Coliseum fell silent to the NFL for 13 seasons.

As the seasons wore on in Los Angeles, Davis began looking to have a new stadium built there, but when nothing materialized, he returned to Oakland in June 1995. This time around, however, the city of Oakland agreed to terms to improve the Coliseum, and a major facelift began in November 1995, reaching completion by the '96 football season. After remodeling, the Coliseum's capacity was boosted to 63,132, and luxury suites were added. Improvements were also made to the locker rooms, press box, and scoreboard. Like the changes made to the structure itself, the Colseum's name differed through the years as well. In 1966, it was called the Oakland–Alameda County Coliseum. In October, 1998, it became Network Associates Coliseum and McAfee Coliseum in 2005. By 2008, what was once old was new again, as the structure reverted back to its original name.[35]

Los Angeles Memorial Coliseum: 1982–1994

One of America's grandest structures dedicated to athletic competition stands in its glory at 3911 South Figueroa Street in Los Angeles. It served as the Raiders' home from November 22, 1982, against San Diego until the Kansas City Chiefs helped the Silver and Black bring the curtain down on their stay in the City of Angels on December 24, 1994.

The official name of this massive structure is the Los Angeles Memorial Coliseum, standing proudly since 1923 as a shrine to countless great moments in sports history. Legendary performers from around the world have competed in the confines of this hallowed southern California landmark. It is the only American stadium that has played host to Olympic Games (1932 and 1984), pre–Super Bowl NFL Championship Games, a World Series, two Super Bowls, NFC and AFC title clashes, and Pro Bowls. It also serves as the home field for the University of Southern California (USC) and until the 1980's, the University of California, Los Angeles (UCLA). On the collegiate level, the Coliseum provided the site of some of the game's most storied clashes. It also served in countless other venues through the years as well.

The concept behind the building of this magnificent athletic shrine was for it to serve as a memorial to World War I veterans. In 1968, it was re-dedicated to honor veterans of all wars.

With architects John and Donald Parkinson as designers, ground was broken on December 21, 1921, and within 17 months, the gargantuan jewel was completed on May 1, 1923, at a cost of $954,873. When originally opened, the Coliseum seated 76,000, but that number was expanded to 101,574 in time for the 1932 Los Angeles Olympics. This was also when the Olympic torch was constructed above one of the main entrances. The Olympic rings are also still there, right below the torch. This combination of torch and rings serves as the most common photograph when looking at images of this most-famous facility. In addition to those reminders of the Olympics are two life-sized male and female bronze statues added for the 1984 Summer Games.[36]

When the Rams transferred from Cleveland in 1946, the Coliseum became their home, and served as it until 1980. Two years later the Raiders relocated and remained there until moving back to Oakland in 1995. It was then that the Coliseum fell silent to NFL football, but hopefully, in the near future, it will once again provide the setting for professional gridiron confrontations. Until that day, the Los Angeles Memorial Coliseum will stand quietly on Sunday afternoons, but the memories of past glory from inside its confines will never diminish.

Uniforms

1960–62

With the Raiders coming into the AFL as late as they did, the organization had to scramble to find uniforms for the new team. They were able to find a surplus of all they needed at the University of the Pacific, whose colors were black and gold.[37]

Helmet: The helmets were black with no insignia or stripping, but a gold stripe was added down the middle in 1962.

Jerseys: Their black jerseys had white rounded numbers with gold trim around them, and three gold stripes appeared on each arm. Their white jerseys had gold numbers with black trim.

Pants: The pants were white with a gold and black stripe down the legs.

Team Insignia: Drawing of a player's head whose likeness resembled actor Randolph Scott. He is wearing a black helmet with a patch over the right eye. The background is a gold football pointing up with two swords crisscrossed behind the ball. This insignia, though representing the Raiders, never appeared on their helmets from 1960 through 1962.[38]

1963

In 1963, Al Davis took over as head coach and turned a hapless team that won only nine games in three seasons into instant winners, as the Raiders rang up 10 victories in Davis' first season at the helm. One of the things that he changed was what the team wore on the field. The black and gold worn before his arrival represented losing, and Davis was not about that. He kept the black, got rid of the gold, and added silver in its place.[39]

Helmet: The trademark silver helmets arrived on the scene beginning in 1963. The insignia of a Raider appears for the first time on the side of the helmet. The insignia is modified to the one that still represents the team going into their next fifty years. It consists of a shield with a Raider wearing a black helmet, a patch over his right eye, and a pair of swords crisscrossing behind his head with a silver background. On the upper portion of the shield was a black background with silver writing the read "The Oakland Raiders."

Jerseys: Their home jerseys were black with square silver numbers. The away jerseys were white with square silver numbers.

Pants: Were silver with a black stripe down the side of leg.

1964

Insignia: The background was changed on the team insignia to a shield with a black background. The player's helmet became silver with a black stripe down the middle and the word "Raiders" in silver written above his head. The swords and eye patch remained.[40]

Jerseys: The away jerseys remained white, but the numbers were changed to black from silver.

1970

The silver numbers returned on the away jerseys for this one season, and by 1971, they were switched back to black. The only times that the Raiders return to any of the old uniform designs is when they are involved in games with a throw-back theme. They then wear the uniform and helmet design that Al Davis incorporated back in 1963 for special anniversary games.[41]

The Raiderettes: "Football's Fabulous Females"

Cheesecake served with beefcake warriors is the perfect entree for any football fan's Sunday appetite. Some of the professional cheerleading squads have been called incredible, famous, among many other flattering adjectives. However, only one group can be called fabulous, and they reside on the sidelines and in the hearts of Raider Nation the world over. They are the internationally renowned Raiderettes, "Football's Fabulous Females," who are a successful satellite all their own of one of professional sports' corporate giants. Glitz and glamour have been the creed of the Raiderettes for five decades, and they too share a "Commitment to Excellence" that is seen with every move they make. California girls are forever remembered in song on multiple recordings through the years. The aura they omit truly makes these West Coast beauties stand out.

The Raiderettes were formed in 1961, and through the decades, they became one of the most popular squads in pro football.[42] Many young women have graced the sidelines donned in Raiderette outfits, and countless others have tried out. Amidst all the glamour that accompanies "Football's Fabulous Females," there is an incredible amount of hard work and dedication that goes into it. To even get the opportunity of a lifetime and make the squad is challenging enough.

The initial phase on a journey to earning the prestigious honor of becoming a "Fabulous Female" begins with an audition consisting of hundreds of hopefuls from all over the local are. They come from all walks of life, with some cheerleading or dan experience behind them. College students, office workers, an housewives make up some of the women who gather each ye for their shot at cheering for the Silver and Black.

After registering, an interview process is conducted whe the women sit in front of a panel of experienced and highly re spected judges ranging from team officials to ex–Raiderettes wh volunteer their time to help out during auditions.[43]

Each hopeful is required to wear an evening cocktail dre during this part of the proceedings. The judges' questions are de signed to allow them the chance to get to know the participan on a more personal level.[44]

The judges have the difficult task of weeding through th gathering of beauties, looking for a cut above awesome.[45] The look for that certain "It" quality that might be projected with smile or a spark in the eyes to go along with a flashy, clean, an sexy makeup that are required when representing the Silver an Black in the public sector. The players themselves might have a "outlaw" image molded many years ago, but the Raiderettes hav to be the exact opposite. However, looks alone do not solidify spot on this glamorous roster. These women have to be able t perform moves bordering on fluid and athletic.[46]

This is where the second phase of the audition comes int play. Dance routines are performed under the watchful, experi enced eyes of the judges. Those that make it through this segmer come back for a final audition a few weeks later.

The moment of truth arrives for each group of hopeful when dreams are achieved, whil others end, some temporarily, som forever. Regardless of which side young woman winds up on, the all had the moxie to attempt thi quest.

If chosen, all the dividend paid off, but then the hard work re ally begins. Months of tough re hearsals mold and shape the rookie with the veterans until the squa works as one.[47]

Besides cheering at all hom games, these silver and black-cla beauties have to give of themselve for a mandatory 10 events involvin charities or those of local interest Not only are these gridiron glam our girls known throughout thi country, but globally as well, thu solidifying their status as one of th elite pro cheerleading squads of a time in any sport. They also pos for an annual swimsuit calendar which undoubtedly is very popu lar.

More than 1,000 Californi girls have proudly earned the dis tinction of being proclaimed a Oakland or Los Angeles Raiderette

"Football's Fabulous Females," the Oakland Raiderettes, are shown bringing glitz and glamour to the gridiron on December 5, 2004, in a game against the Kansas City Chiefs at Network Associates Coliseum, Oakland, California (AP Photo/David Stluka).

d many have parlayed the experience into careers in modeling d acting. As the Raiderettes head into the next fifty years, their yle and beauty will continue to bring smiles to all who cast their es on pro football's most fabulous collection of the female per-asion.

Player Nicknames

Throughout the centuries, nicknames have been given to individuals. Though some were embraced by the recipients, others rought outrage when the moniker was uttered. The world of ports proved no exception to handing out nicknames at a feverish ace. The Raiders had some of the best, and for that reason, it as worthwhile to compile a list of many that will forever be nked to the renegades of the football world.[48]

en Agajanian — "Bootin"
lijah Alexander — "The Brown Hornet"
ric Allen — "Yoda"
Marcus Allen — "E.T."
yle Alzado — "Three Mile Lyle"
ervis Atkins — "Afterburner"
George Atkinson — "Hitman"
ete Banaszak — "Rooster"
ric Barton — "The Tackling Machine"
red Biletnikoff — "Blinky"
Dan Birdwell — "Birdie"
George Blanda — "The Old Man"
Cliff Branch — "The Money Man"
ob Brown — "Boomer"
Tim Brown — "First Down Brown"
Willie Brown — "Wilbrown"

Tony Bryant — "The Candy Man"
George Buehler — "The Mad Scientist"
Dave Casper — "Ghost"
Don Churchwell — "Bull"
Ben Davidson — "Big Ben"
Anthony Dorsett — "Model Thug"
Rickey Dudley — "Slick Rick"
Tom Flores — "The Iceman"
Claude Gibson — "Hoot"
Lester Hayes — "The Molester" and "The Judge"
Wayne Hawkins — "Hawk"
Ted Hendricks — "The Mad Stork" and "Kick 'Em"
Raghib Ismail — "Rocket"
Sebastian Janikowski — "Sea Bass," "The Polish Cannon" and "The Polish Hammer"
Eric Johnson — "Crazy"
Daryle Lamonica — "The Mad Bomber"
Henry Lawrence — "Killer"
John Matuszak — "The Tooz"
Jim Otto — "Double 00"
Charlie Philyaw — "King Kong"
Jim Plunkett — "Plunk"
Marquez Pope — "The Pounding Pontiff"
Jerry Rice — "World"
Andre Rison — "Bad Moon"
Otis Sistrunk — "The Man From Mars"
Ken Stabler — "The Snake"
Jack Tatum — "The Assassin"
Skip Thomas — "Dr. Death"
Gene Upshaw — "The Governor"
Phil Villapiano — "Foo"
Fred Williamson — "The Hammer"
Steve Wisniewski — "Road House Dog"

NOTES

Introduction

1. *Cleveland Plain Dealer*, Aug. 5, 2009, p. D-1.
2. David S. Neft, with Richard M. Cohen, *The Football Encyclopedia: The Complete History of Professional Football from 1892 to the Present*, p. 318.
3. *www.wikipedia.com*—American Football League page.
4. *Cleveland Plain Dealer*, Aug. 5, 2009, p. D-1.
5. Neft and Cohen, p. 318.
6. Ibid.
7. Jim McCullough, *Pride & Poise: The Oakland Raiders of the American Football League*, p. 2.
8. Ibid., p. 7.
9. Mark Ribowsky, *Slick: The Silver and Black Life of Al Davis*, p. 118–19.
10. McCullough, p. 6.

Part I. The Games

1960

1. *Los Angeles Times*, Sept. 12, 1960, p. C-3.
2. Ibid., Sept. 17, 1960, p. A-5.
3. Ibid., Sept. 26, 1960, p. C-4.
4. Ibid., Oct. 3, 1960, p. C-2.
5. Ibid., Oct. 10, 1960, p. C-8.
6. *Chicago Tribune*, Oct. 17, 1960, p. C-4.
7. *Los Angeles Times*, Oct. 24, 1960, p. C-5.
8. Ibid., Oct. 29, 1960, p. A-3.
9. Jim McCullough, *Pride & Poise: The Oakland Raiders of the American Football League*, p. 21–22
10. *Los Angeles Times*, Nov. 14, 1960, p. C-4.
11. Ibid., Nov. 28, 1960, p. C-1.
12. Ibid., Dec. 5, 1960, p. C-1.
13. Ibid., Dec. 12, 1960, p. C-7.
14. Ibid., Dec. 18, 1960, p. J-4.

1961

1. *Los Angeles Times*, Sept. 10, 1961, p. K-5.
2. Jim McCullough, *Pride & Poise: The Oakland Raiders of the American Football League*, p. 38.
3. *Chicago Tribune*, Sept. 25, 1961, p. C-2.
4. Ibid., Oct. 2, 1961, p. E-3.
5. Ibid., Oct. 16, 1961, p. C-4.
6. Ibid., Oct. 23, 1961, p. C-2.
7. Ibid., Oct. 30, 1961, p. C-2.
8. Ibid., Nov. 6, 1961, p. C-5.
9. *Los Angeles Times*, Nov. 12, 1961, p. L-8.
10. McCullough, p. 45–46.
11. *Chicago Tribune*, Nov. 27, 1961, p. C-4.
12. Ibid., Dec. 4, 1961, p. C-2.
13. McCullough, p. 47–48.
14. *Chicago Tribune*, Dec. 18, 1961, p. C-2.

1962

1. *Chicago Tribune*, Sept. 10, 1962, p. C-3.
2. Ibid., Sept. 24, 1962, p. C-4.
3. Ibid., Oct. 1, 1962, p. C-4.
4. Ibid., Oct. 6, 1962, p. E-2.
5. Ibid., Oct. 15, 1962, p. C-4.
6. Jim McCullough, *Pride & Poise: The Oakland Raiders of the American Football League*, p. 60–61.
7. *Chicago Tribune*, Oct. 27, 1962, p. F-2.
8. McCullough, p. 62.
9. *Chicago Tribune*, Nov. 12, 1962, p. C-5.
10. Ibid., Nov. 19, 1962, p. E-6.
11. Ibid., Nov. 26, 1962, p. C-8.
12. Ibid., Dec. 3, 1962, p. C-4.
13. Ibid., Dec. 10, 1962, p. C-7.
14. Ibid., Dec. 17, 1962, p. C-6.

1963

1. *Los Angeles Times*, Sept. 8, 1963, p. J-5.
2. Ibid., Sept. 16, 1963, p. C-5.
3. Ibid., Sept. 23, 1963, p. B-7.
4. Ibid., Sept. 29, 1963, p. K-2.
5. Ibid., Oct. 6, 1963, p. I-11.
6. Ibid., Oct. 12, 1963, p. A-5.
7. Ibid., Oct. 21, 1963, p. D-7.
8. Ibid., Oct. 28, 1963, p. D-7.
9. *Chicago Tribune*, Nov. 4, 1963, p. C-3.
10. Ibid., Nov. 9, 1963, p. A-2.
11. *Los Angeles Times*, Nov. 29, 1963, p. B-2.
12. Ibid., Dec. 9, 1963, p. B-3.
13. Ibid., Dec. 16, 1963, p. B-4.
14. Ibid., Dec. 23, 1963, p. C-1.

1964

1. *Los Angeles Times*, Sept. 14, 1964, p. B-6.
2. Ibid., Sept. 20, 1964, p. H-7.
3. Ibid., Sept. 28, 1964, p. B-5.
4. Ibid., Oct. 4, 1964, p. B-8.
5. Ibid., Oct. 11, 1964, p. H-5.
6. Ibid., Oct. 17, 1964, p. A-7.
7. Ibid., Oct. 26, 1964, p. B-6.
8. Ibid., Nov. 2, 1964, p. B-5.
9. Ibid., Nov. 9, 1964, p. B-7.
10. Ibid., Nov. 16, 1964, p. B-10.
11. Ibid., Nov. 23, 1964, p. B-6.
12. Ibid., Nov. 30, 1964, p. B-5.
13. Ibid., Dec. 7, 1964, p. B-2.
14. Ibid., Dec. 21, 1964, p. B-4.

1965

1. Jim McCullough, *Price & Poise: The Oakland Raiders of the American Football League*, p. 140–141.
2. *Los Angeles Times*, Sept. 20, 1965, p. B-3.
3. McCullough, p. 141–142.
4. Ibid., p. 142–143.
5. Ibid., p. 143.
6. Ibid., p. 144.
7. Ibid., p. 145.
8. Ibid.
9. Ibid., p. 146.
10. *Los Angeles Times*, Nov. 15, 1965, p. B-4.
11. Ibid., Nov. 22, 1965, p. B-5.
12. Ibid., Dec. 6, 1965, p. B-4.
13. Ibid., Dec. 13, 1965, p. C-8.
14. Ibid., Dec. 20, 1965, p. B-5.

AFL–NFL Merger

1. David S. Neft and Richard M. Cohen, *The Football Encyclopedia: The Complete History of Professional Football from 1892 to the Present*, p. 318–321.
2. Ibid.
3. Ibid.

1966

1. *Los Angeles Times*, Sept. 3, 1966, p. A-2.
2. Ibid., Sept. 11, 1966, p. C-4.
3. Ibid., Sept. 19, 1966, p. B-4.
4. Ibid., Sept. 26, 1966, p. B-5.
5. Ibid., Oct. 10, 1966, p. B-10.
6. Ibid., Oct. 17, 1966, p. B-5.
7. Ibid., Oct. 24, 1966, p. B-5.
8. Ibid., Oct. 31, 1966, p. B-3.
9. Ibid., Nov. 7, 1966, p. B-6.
10. Ibid., Nov. 14, 1966, p. C-7.
11. Jim McCullough, *Pride & Poise: The Oakland Raiders of the American Football League*, p. 171.
12. *Los Angeles Times*, Nov. 25, 1966, p. C-4.
13. Ibid., Dec. 4, 1966, p. H-6.
14. Ibid., Dec. 12, 1966, p. C-4.

1967

1. *Los Angeles Times*, Sept. 11, 1967, p. B-5.
2. Ibid., Sept. 18, 1967, p. C-4.
3. Ibid., Oct. 2, 1967, p. A-6.
4. *Chicago Tribune*, Oct. 8, 1967, p. B-3.
5. *Los Angeles Times*, Oct. 16, 1967, p. B-3.
6. Ibid., Oct. 23, 1967, p. B-6.
7. Ibid., Oct. 30, 1967, p. B-3.
8. Ibid., Nov. 6, 1967, p. B-6.
9. Ibid., Nov. 20, 1967, p. B-5.
10. Ibid., Nov. 24, 1967, p. C-2.
11. Ibid., Dec. 4, 1967, p. B-1.
12. Ibid., Dec. 11, 1967, p. E-8.
13. Ibid., Dec. 18, 1967, p. B-8.
14. Ibid., Dec. 25, 1967, p. C-2.
15. Ibid., Jan. 1, 1968, p. B-1.
16. Ibid., Jan. 15, 1968, p. B-1, Super Bowl play-byplay: www.usato day.com/sports/football/Super Bowl II.
17. John Devaney, *Super Bowl! Exciting Accounts of Pro Football's Championship Games*, p. 57–67; Super Bowl play-by-play: www.usatoday.com/sports/nfl/super/superbowl-II-plays.htm.

1968

1. *Los Angeles Times*, Sept. 16, 1968, p. E-4.
2. Ibid., Sept. 22, 1968, p. G-3.
3. Jim McCullough, *Pride & Poise: The Oakland Raiders of the American Football League*, p. 210–211
4. *Los Angeles Times*, Oct. 7, 1968, p. G-4.
5. Ibid., Oct. 14, 1968, p. E-3.
6. Ibid., Oct. 21, 1968, p. E-5.
7. *Chicago Tribune*, Oct. 28, 1968, p. C-3.
8. *Los Angeles Times*, Nov. 4, 1968, p. E-1.
9. Ibid., Nov. 12, 1968, p. B-2.
10. Ibid., Nov. 18, 1968, p. F-1.
11. Ibid., Nov. 25, 1968, p. B-9.
12. Ibid., Nov. 29, 1968, p. D-2.
13. Ibid., Dec. 9, 1968, p. E-2.
14. Ibid., Dec. 16, 1968, p. F-1.
15. Ibid., Dec. 23, 1968, p. C-1.
16. Ibid., Dec. 30, 1968, p. D-1.

1969

1. *Los Angeles Times*, Sept. 15, 1969, p. D-6.
2. Ibid., Sept. 21, 1969, p. C-17.
3. *Chicago Tribune*, Sept. 29, 1969, p. C-6.
4. *Los Angeles Times*, Oct. 5, 1969, p. C-6.
5. *Chicago Tribune*, Oct. 13, 1969, p. C-5.

6. Ibid., Oct. 20, 1969, p. C-4.
7. *Los Angeles Times*, Oct. 27, 1969, p. D-2.
8. Ibid., Nov. 3, 1969, p. D-1.
9. *Chicago Tribune*, Nov. 10, 1969, p. C-6.
10. *Los Angeles Times*, Nov. 17, 1969, p. D-14.
11. Ibid., Nov. 24, 1969, p. B-1.
12. Ibid., Dec. 1, 1969, p. C-1.
13. Ibid., Dec. 8, 1969, p. F-9.
14. Ibid., Dec. 14, 1969, p. E-1.
15. Ibid., Dec. 22, 1969, p. D-1.
16. Ibid., Jan. 5, 1970, p. B-1.

1970

1. *Los Angeles Times*, Sept. 21, 1970, p. D-1.
2. Ibid., Sept. 28, 1970, p. D-1.
3. Ibid., Oct. 4, 1970, p. C-2.
4. *Chicago Tribune*, Oct. 12, 1970, p. E-5.
5. Ibid., Oct. 20, 1970, p. C-1.
6. *Los Angeles Times*, Oct. 26, 1970, p. D-4.
7. Ibid., Nov. 2, 1970, p. D-7.
8. Ibid., Nov. 9, 1970, p. D-1.
9. Ibid., Nov. 16, 1970, p. E-4.
10. Ibid., Nov. 23, 1970, p. D-1.
11. Ibid., Nov. 27, 1970, p. F-1.
12. Ibid., Dec. 7, 1970, p. G-2.
13. Ibid., Dec. 13, 1970, p. E-1.
14. Ibid., Dec. 21, 1970, p. G-1.
15. Ibid., Dec. 28, 1970, p. F-1.
16. Ibid., Jan. 4, 1971, p. F-1.

1971

1. *Los Angeles Times*, Sept. 20, 1971, p. D-1.
2. Ibid., Sept. 27, 1971, p. D-2.
3. Ibid., Oct. 5, 1971, p. D-1.
4. Ibid., Oct. 11, 1971, p. D-4.
5. *Chicago Tribune*, Oct. 18, 1971, p. C-2.
6. *Los Angeles Times*, Oct. 25, 1971, p. E-4.
7. Ibid., Nov. 1, 1971, p. D-1.
8. Ibid., Nov. 8, 1971, p. D-1.
9. *Chicago Tribune*, Nov. 15, 1971, p. C-2.
10. *Los Angeles Times*, Nov. 22, 1971, p. E-7.
11. Ibid., Nov. 29, 1971, p. F-1.
12. Ibid., Dec. 6, 1971, p. F-4.
13. Ibid., Dec. 13, 1971, p. F-1.
14. Ibid., Dec. 20, 1971, p. D-6.

1972

1. *Los Angeles Times*, Sept. 18, 1972, p. D-3.
2. Ibid., Sept. 25, 1972, p. D-7.
3. *Chicago Tribune*, Oct. 2, 1972, p. C-2.
4. Los Angeles Times, Oct. 10, 1972, p. C-1.
5. Ibid., Oct. 16, 1972, p. C-4.
6. Ibid., Oct. 23, 1972, p. C-6.
7. Ibid., Oct. 30, 1972, p. C-1.
8. Ibid., Nov. 6, 1972, p. C-6.
9. Ibid., Nov. 13, 1972, p. C-6.
10. Ibid., Nov. 20, 1972, p. C-3.
11. Ibid., Nov. 27, 1972, p. D-3.
12. Ibid., Dec. 4, 1972, p. C-3.
13. Ibid., Dec. 12, 1972, p. D-1.
14. Ibid., Dec. 18, 1972, p. D-7.
15. Jack C. Cary, *Pro Football's Great Moments*, pp. 171–175.

1973

1. *Los Angeles Times*, Sept. 17, 1973, p. B-4.
2. Ibid., Sept. 24, 1973, p. B-1.
3. Ibid., Oct. 1, 1973, p. B-5.
4. Ibid., Oct. 8, 1973, p. B-11.
5. Ibid., Oct. 15, 1973, p. C-5.
6. Ibid., Oct. 23, 1973, p. B-2.
7. Ibid., Oct. 29, 1973, p. B-4.
8. Ibid., Nov. 5, 1973, p. C-7.
9. Ibid., Nov. 12, 1973, p. B-4.
10. Ibid., Nov. 19, 1973, p. C-7.
11. Ibid., Nov. 26, 1973, p. B-4.
12. Ibid., Dec. 3, 1973, p. C-4.
13. Ibid., Dec. 9, 1973, p. I-3.
14. Ibid., Dec. 17, 1973, p. C-1.
15. Ibid., Dec. 23, 1973, p. B-1.
16. Ibid., Dec. 31, 1973, p. C-1.

1974

1. *Los Angeles Times*, Sept. 17, 1974, p. D-1.
2. Ibid., Sept. 23, 1974, p. D-5.
3. Ibid., Sept. 30, 1974, p. D-4.
4. Ibid., Oct. 7, 1974, p. D-4.
5. Ibid., Oct. 14, 1974, p. E-5.
6. Ibid., Oct. 21, 1974, p. E-6.
7. Ibid., Oct. 28, 1974, p. D-2.
8. Ibid., Nov. 4, 1974, p. D-3.
9. Ibid., Nov. 11, 1974, p. D-2.
10. Ibid., Nov. 18, 1974, p. D-7.
11. Ibid., Nov. 25, 1974, p. D-2.
12. Ibid., Dec. 2, 1974, p. D-5.
13. Ibid., Dec. 9, 1974, p. E-6.
14. Ibid., Dec. 15, 1974, p. D-1.
15. Ibid., Dec. 22, 1974, p. C-1.
16. Ibid., Dec. 30, 1974, p. D-1.

1975

1. *Los Angeles Times*, Sept. 23, 1975, p. E-1.
2. Ibid., Sept. 29, 1975, p. C-4.
3. Ibid., Oct. 6, 1975, p. D-3.
4. Ibid., Oct. 13, 1975, p. E-1.
5. Ibid., Oct. 20, 1975, p. F-6.
6. Ibid., Oct. 27, 1975, p. D-3.
7. Ibid., Nov. 3, 1975, p. E-6.
8. Ibid., Nov. 10, 1975, p. D-7.
9. Ibid., Nov. 17, 1975, p. D-9.
10. Ibid., Nov. 24, 1975, p. C-1.
11. Ibid., Dec. 1, 1975, p. C-1.
12. Ibid., Dec. 9, 1975, p. E-1.
13. Ibid., Dec. 15, 1975, p. E-2.
14. Ibid., Dec. 22, 1975, p. E-6.
15. Ibid., Dec. 29, 1975, p. D-1.
16. Ibid., Jan. 5, 1976, p. D-1.

1976

1. *Los Angeles Times*, Sept. 13, 1976, p. C-2.
2. Ibid., Sept. 21, 1976, p. D-2.
3. Ibid., Sept. 27, 1976, p. D-2.
4. Ibid., Oct. 4, 1976, p. D-1.
5. Ibid., Oct. 11, 1976, p. C-2.
6. Ibid., Oct. 18, 1976, p. D-6.
7. Ibid., Oct. 25, 1976, p. D-4.
8. Ibid., Nov. 1, 1976, p. E-2.
9. Ibid., Nov. 8, 1976, p. D-1.
10. Ibid., Nov. 15, 1976, p. D-4.
11. Ibid., Nov. 22, 1976, p. D-6.
12. Ibid., Nov. 29, 1976, p. D-5.
13. Ibid., Dec. 7, 1976, p. D-1.
14. Ibid., Dec. 13, 1976, p. E-6.
15. Ibid., Dec. 19, 1976, p. C-1.
16. Ibid., Dec. 27, 1976, p. D-1.
17. Ibid., Jan. 10, 1977, p. D-1; Wikipedia.com, Super Bowl XI page.

18. Wikipedia.com, Super Bowl XI page.
19. Ken Stabler with Dick O'Connor, *Super Bowl Diary: The Autobiography of Ken "the Snake" Stabler*, p. 6–7.
20. *Sports Illustrated*, Jan. 17, 1977, p. 10.
21. *Los Angeles Times*, Jan. 10, 1977, p. D-1.
22. Stabler with O'Connor, p. 10.
23. Ibid., p. 12; Super Bowl play-by-play: www.usatoday.com/sports/nfl/super/superbowl-XI-plays.htm.

1977

1. *Los Angeles Times*, Sept. 19, 1977, p. E-1.
2. Ibid., Sept. 26, 1977, p. E-1.
3. Ibid., Oct. 4, 1977, p. E-1.
4. Ibid., Oct. 10, 1977, p. E-5.
5. Ibid., Oct. 17, 1977, p. D-1.
6. Ibid., Oct. 24, 1977, p. D-1.
7. Ibid., Oct. 31, 1977, p. D-1.
8. Ibid., Nov. 7, 1977, p. D-4.
9. Ibid., Nov. 14, 1977, p. D-2.
10. Ibid., Nov. 21, 1977, p. F-2.
11. Ibid., Nov. 29, 1977, p. E-3.
12. Ibid., Dec. 5, 1977, p. B-1.
13. Ibid., Dec. 12, 1977, p. E-2.
14. Ibid., Dec. 19, 1977, p. E-8.
15. Ibid., Dec. 25, 1977, p. D-1.
16. Ibid., Jan. 2, 1978, p. C-1.

1978

1. *Los Angeles Times*, Sept. 4, 1978, p. C-1.
2. Ibid., Sept. 11, 1978, p. D-1.
3. Ibid., Sept. 18, 1978, p. D-5.
4. Ibid., Sept. 25, 1978, p. D-1.
5. Ibid., Oct. 2, 1978, p. D-6.
6. Ibid., Oct. 9, 1978, p. E-6.
7. Ibid., Oct. 16, 1978, p. C-6.
8. Ibid., Oct. 23, 1978, p. D-1.
9. Ibid., Oct. 30, 1978, p. D-1.
10. Ibid., Nov. 6, 1978, p. D-7.
11. Ibid, Nov. 14, 1978, p. D-1.
12. Ibid, Nov. 20, 1978, p. E-10.
13. Ibid, Nov. 27, 1978, p. D-1.
14. Ibid., Dec. 4, 1978, p. E-1.
15. Ibid., Dec. 11, 1978, p. D-1.
16. Ibid., Dec. 18, 1978, p. E-1.

1979

1. *Los Angeles Times*, Sept. 3, 1979, SD, p. B-1.
2. Ibid., Sept. 10, 1979, p. D-1.
3. Ibid., Sept. 17, 1979, p. D-8.
4. Ibid., Sept. 24, 1979, p. D-4.
5. Ibid., Oct. 1, 1979, p. D-5.
6. Ibid., Oct. 9, 1979, p. D-1.
7. Ibid., Oct. 15, 1979, p. D-5.
8. Ibid., Oct. 22, 1979, p. D-1.
9. Ibid., Oct. 26, 1979, p. E-1.
10. Ibid., Nov. 5, 1979, p. D-6.
11. Ibid., Nov. 12, 1979, p. D-4.
12. Ibid., Nov. 19, 1979, p. D-10.
13. Ibid., Nov. 26, 1979, p. D-7.
14. Ibid., Dec. 4, 1979, p. D-1.
15. Ibid., Dec. 10, 1979, p. D-7.
16. Ibid., Dec. 17, 1979, p. D-8.

1980

1. *Los Angeles Times*, Sept. 8, 1980, p. D-4.
2. Ibid., Sept. 15, 1980, p. D-1.
3. Ibid., Sept. 22, 1980, p. D-2.
4. Ibid., Sept. 29, 1980, p. D-2.

5. Ibid., Oct. 6, 1980, p. D-2.
6. Ibid., Oct. 13, 1980, p. D-2.
7. Ibid., Oct. 21, 1980, p. D-1.
8. Ibid., Oct. 27, 1980, p. D-4.
9. Ibid., Nov. 3, 1980, p. D-4.
10. Ibid., Nov. 10, 1980, p. D-6.
11. Ibid., Nov. 18, 1980, p. D-2.
12. Ibid., Nov. 24, 1980, p. D-1.
13. Ibid., Dec. 2, 1980, p. D-1.
14. Ibid., Dec. 8, 1980, p. D-6.
15. Ibid., Dec. 15, 1980, p. D-2.
16. Ibid., Dec. 22, 1980, p. D-7.
17. Ibid., Dec. 29, 1980, p. B-[?]. Lou Sahadi, *The Raiders: Cinderel Champions of Pro Football*, p. 127–13[?].
18. *Los Angeles Times*, Jan. 5, 198[?], p. D-1; Sahadi, p. 139–144.
19. *Los Angeles Times*, Jan. 12, 198[?], p. D-1; Sahadi, p. 155–162.
20. *Los Angeles Times*, Jan. 26, 198[?], p. B-1; Sahadi, p. 166, 176–182; Super Bowl play-by-play: www.usatoda[?].com/sports/nfl/super/superbowl-XV[?], plays.htm.

1981

1. *Los Angeles Times*, Sept. 7, 198[?], p. C-2.
2. Ibid., Sept. 15, 1981, p. D-3.
3. Ibid., Sept. 21, 1981, p. D-2.
4. Ibid., Sept. 28, 1981, p. D-2.
5. Ibid., Oct. 5, 1981, p. D-2.
6. Ibid., Oct. 12, 1981, p. D-4.
7. Ibid., Oct. 19, 1981, p. D-3.
8. Ibid., Oct. 26, 1981, p. D-6.
9. Ibid., Nov. 2, 1981, p. D-5.
10. Ibid., Nov. 9, 1981, p. D-4.
11. Ibid., Nov. 16, 1981, p. D-3.
12. Ibid., Nov. 23, 1981, p. D-6.
13. Ibid., Nov. 30, 1981, p. D-6.
14. Ibid., Dec. 8, 1981, p. D-1.
15. Ibid., Dec. 14, 1981, p. D-6.
16. Ibid., Dec. 22, 1981, p. D-1.

The Raiders Move to Los Angeles

1. Murray Olderman, *Super: "Jus[?] Win Baby,"* p. 135.
2. Ibid.
3. Ibid., p. 136.
4. Ibid.
5. Ibid.
6. Ibid.
7. Ibid., p. 136–137.
8. Ibid., p. 137.
9. Ibid.
10. Ibid., p. 138–139.
11. Ibid., p. 139.
12. Ibid.
13. Ibid., p. 140.
14. Ibid.
15. Ibid., p. 141.
16. Ibid.
17. Ibid.
18. Ibid., p. 141–142.
19. Ibid.
20. Ibid., p. 142.

1982

1. *Los Angeles Times*, Sept. 13, 1982, p. D-1.
2. Ibid., Sept. 20, 1982, p. D-1.
3. Ibid., Nov. 23, 1982, p. D-1.
4. Ibid., Nov. 29, 1982, p. D-1.
5. Ibid., Dec. 6, 1982, p. D-1.
6. Ibid., Dec. 13, 1982, p. D-1.
7. Ibid., Dec. 19, 1982, p. E-1.
8. Ibid., Dec. 27, 1982, p. D-1.

9. Ibid., Jan. 3, 1983, p. D-1.
10. Ibid., Jan. 9, 1983, p. A-1.
11. Ibid., Jan. 16, 1983, p. C-1.

1983

1. *Los Angeles Times*, Sept. 5, 1983, p. C-1.
2. Ibid., Sept. 12, 1983, p. D-1.
3. Ibid., Sept. 20, 1983, p. D-1.
4. Ibid., Sept. 26, 1983, p. E-1.
5. Ibid., Oct. 3, 1983, p. D-1.
6. Ibid., Oct. 10, 1983, p. D-1.
7. Ibid., Oct. 17, 1983, p. D-1.
8. Ibid., Oct. 24, 1983, p. D-1.
9. Ibid., Oct. 31, 1983, p. D-1.
10. Ibid., Nov. 7, 1983, p. D-1.
11. Ibid., Nov. 14, 1983, p. D-1.
12. Ibid., Nov. 21, 1983, p. D-1.
13. Ibid., Nov. 28, 1983, p. D-1.
14. Ibid., Dec. 2, 1983, p. E-1.
15. Ibid., Dec. 12, 1983, p. D-1.
16. Ibid., Dec. 19, 1983, p. E-1.
17. Ibid., Jan. 2, 1984, p. C-1.
18. Ibid., Jan. 9, 1984, p. D-1.
19. Ibid., Jan. 23, 1984, p. B-1; Super Bowl play-by-play: www.usatoday.com/sports/nfl/super/superbowl-XVIII-plays.htm; Murray Olderman, *Super: "Just Win Baby,"* p. 2.
20. *www.wikipedia.com*— Super Bowl XVIII page.
21. Ibid.
22. Ibid.
23. Ibid.
24. Ibid.
25. Olderman, p. 8.

1984

1. *Los Angeles Times*, Sept. 5, 1984, p. C-1.
2. Ibid., Sept. 10, 1984, p. D-1.
3. Ibid., Sept. 17, 1984, p. D-1.
4. Ibid., Sept. 25, 1984, p. D-1.
5. Ibid., Oct. 1, 1984, p. D-1.
6. Ibid., Oct. 8, 1984, p. D-1.
7. Ibid., Oct. 15, 1984, p. D-1.
8. Ibid., Oct. 22, 1984, p. D-1.
9. Ibid., Oct. 29, 1984, p. D-1.
10. Ibid., Nov. 5, 1984, p. D-1.
11. Ibid., Nov. 13, 1984, p. D-1.
12. Ibid., Nov. 19, 1984, p. D-1.
13. Ibid., Nov. 26, 1984, p. D-1.
14. Ibid., Dec. 3, 1984, p. D-1.
15. Ibid., Dec. 11, 1984, p. D-1.
16. Ibid., Dec. 17, 1984, p. D-1.
17. Ibid., Dec. 23, 1984, p. E-1.

1985

1. *Los Angeles Times*, Sept. 9, 1985, p. 1.
2. Ibid., Sept. 13, 1985, p. 1.
3. Ibid., Sept. 23, 1985, p. 1.
4. Ibid., Sept. 29, 1985, p. 1.
5. Ibid., Oct. 7, 1985, p. 1.
6. Ibid., Oct. 14, 1985, Section 3, p. 1.
7. Ibid., Oct. 21, 1985, Section 3, p. 1.
8. Ibid., Oct. 29, 1985, Section 3, p. 1.
9. Ibid., Nov. 4, 1985, Section 3, p. 1.
10. Ibid., Nov. 11, 1985, Section 3, p. 1.
11. Ibid., Nov. 18, 1985, Section 3, p. 1.
12. Ibid., Nov. 25, 1985, Section 3, p. 1.
13. Ibid., Dec. 2, 1985, Section 3, p. 1.
14. Ibid., Dec. 9, 1985, Section 3, p. 1.
15. Ibid., Dec. 16, 1985, Section 3, p. 1.
16. Ibid., Dec. 24, 1985, Section 3, p. 1.
17. Ibid., Jan. 6, 1986, Section 3, p. 1.

1986

1. *Los Angeles Times*, Sept. 8, 1986, Section 3, p. 1.
2. Ibid., Sept. 15, 1986, Section 3, p. 1.
3. Ibid., Sept. 22, 1986, Section 3, p. 1.
4. Ibid., Sept. 29, 1986, Section 3, p. 1.
5. Ibid., Oct. 6, 1986, Section 3, p. 1.
6. Ibid., Oct. 13, 1986, Section 3, p. 1.
7. Ibid., Oct. 20, 1986, Section 3, p. 1.
8. Ibid., Oct. 27, 1986, Section 3, p. 1.
9. Ibid., Nov. 3, 1986, Section 3, p. 1.
10. Ibid., Nov. 10, 1986, Section 3, p. 1.
11. Ibid., Nov. 17, 1986, Section 3, p. 1.
12. Ibid., Nov. 21, 1986, Section 3, p. 1.
13. Ibid., Dec. 1, 1986, Section 3, p. 1.
14. Ibid., Dec. 9, 1986, Section 3, p. 1.
15. Ibid., Dec. 15, 1986, Section 3, p. 1.
16. Ibid., Dec. 22, 1986, Section 3, p. 1.

1987

1. *Los Angeles Times*, Sept. 14, 1987, Section 3, p. 1.
2. Ibid., Sept. 21, 1987, Section 3, p. 1.
3. Ibid., Sept. 22, 1987, Section 1, p. 1.
4. Ibid., Oct. 5, 1987, Section 3, p. 1.
5. Ibid., Oct. 13, 1987, Section 3, p. 1.
6. Ibid., Oct. 19, 1987, Section 3, p. 1.
7. Ibid., Oct. 26, 1987, Section 3, p. 1.
8. Ibid., Nov. 2, 1987, Section 3, p. 1.
9. Ibid., Nov. 9, 1987, Section 3, p. 1.
10. Ibid., Nov. 16, 1987, Section 3, p. 1.
11. Ibid., Nov. 23, 1987, Section 3, p. 1.
12. Ibid., Dec. 1, 1987, Section 3, p. 1.
13. Ibid., Dec. 7, 1987, Section 3, p. 1.
14. Ibid., Dec. 14, 1987, Section 3, p. 1.
15. Ibid., Dec. 21, 1987, Section 3, p. 1.
16. Ibid., Dec. 28, 1987, Section 3, p. 1.

1988

1. *Los Angeles Times*, Sept. 5, 1988, Section 3, p. 1.
2. Ibid., Sept. 12, 1988, Section 3, p. 1.
3. Ibid., Sept. 19, 1988, Section 3, p. 1.
4. Ibid., Sept. 27, 1988, Section 3, p. 1.
5. Ibid., Oct. 3, 1988, Section 3, p. 1.
6. Ibid., Oct. 10, 1988, Section 3, p. 1.
7. Ibid., Oct. 17, 1988, Section 3, p. 1.
8. Ibid., Oct. 24, 1988, Section 3, p. 1.
9. Ibid., Oct. 31, 1988, Section 3, p. 1.
10. Ibid., Nov. 7, 1988, Section 3, p. 1.
11. Ibid., Nov. 14, 1988, Section 3, p. 1.
12. Ibid., Nov. 21, 1988, Section 3, p. 1.
13. Ibid., Nov. 29, 1988, Section 3, p. 1.
14. Ibid., Dec. 5, 1988, Section 3, p. 1.
15. Ibid., Dec. 12, 1988, Section 3, p. 1.
16. Ibid., Dec. 19, 1988, Section 3, p. 1.

1989

1. *Los Angeles Times*, Sept. 11, 1989, Section 3, p. 1.
2. Ibid., Sept. 18, 1989, Section 3, p. 1.
3. Ibid., Sept. 25, 1989, Section 3, p. 1.
4. Ibid., Oct. 2, 1989, Section 3, p. 1.
5. Ibid., Oct. 10, 1989, Section 3, p. 1.
6. Ibid., Oct. 16, 1989, p. C-1.
7. Ibid., Oct. 23, 1989, p. C-1.
8. Ibid., Oct. 30, 1989, p. C-1.
9. Ibid., Nov. 6, 1989, p. C-1.
10. Ibid., Nov. 13, 1989, p. C-1.
11. Ibid., Nov. 20, 1989, p. C-1.
12. Ibid., Nov. 27, 1989, p. C-1.
13. Ibid., Dec. 4, 1989, p. C-1.
14. Ibid., Dec. 11, 1989, p. C-1.
15. Ibid., Dec. 18, 1989, p. C-1.
16. Ibid., Dec. 25, 1989, p. C-1.

1990

1. *Los Angeles Times*, Sept. 10, 1990, p. C-1.
2. Ibid., Sept. 17, 1990, p. C-1.
3. Ibid., Sept. 24, 1990, p. C-1.
4. Ibid., Oct. 1, 1990, p. C-1.
5. Ibid., Oct. 8, 1990, p. C-1.
6. Ibid., Oct. 15, 1990, p. C-1.
7. Ibid., Oct. 22, 1990, p. C-1.
8. Ibid., Nov. 5, 1990, p. C-1.
9. Ibid., Nov. 12, 1990, p. C-1.
10. Ibid., Nov. 20, 1990, p. C-1.
11. Ibid., Nov. 26, 1990, p. C-1.
12. Ibid., Dec. 3, 1990, p. C-1.
13. Ibid., Dec. 11, 1990, p. C-1.
14. Ibid., Dec. 17, 1990, p. C-1.
15. Ibid., Dec. 23, 1990, p. C-1.
16. Ibid., Dec. 31, 1990, p. C-1.
17. Ibid., Jan. 14, 1991, p. C-1.
18. Ibid., Jan. 21, 1991, p. C-1.

1991

1. *Los Angeles Times*, Sept. 2, 1991, p. C-1.
2. Ibid., Sept. 9, 1991, p. C-1.
3. Ibid., Sept. 16, 1991, p. C-1.
4. Ibid., Sept. 23, 1991, p. C-1.
5. Ibid., Sept. 30, 1991, p. C-1.
6. Ibid., Oct. 7, 1991, p. C-1.
7. Ibid., Oct. 14, 1991, p. C-1.
8. Ibid., Oct. 21, 1991, p. C-1.
9. Ibid., Oct. 29, 1991, p. C-1.
10. Ibid., Nov. 11, 1991, p. C-1.
11. Ibid., Nov. 18, 1991, p. C-1.
12. Ibid., Nov. 25, 1991, p. C-1.
13. Ibid., Dec. 2, 1991, p. C-1.
14. Ibid., Dec. 9, 1991, p. C-1.
15. Ibid., Dec. 17, 1991, p. C-1.
16. Ibid., Dec. 23, 1991, p. C-1.
17. Ibid., Dec. 29, 1991, p. C-1.

1992

1. *Los Angeles Times*, Sept. 7, 1992, p. C-1.
2. Ibid., Sept. 14, 1992, p. C-1.
3. Ibid., Sept. 21, 1992, p. C-1.
4. Ibid., Sept. 29, 1992, p. C-1.
5. Ibid., Oct. 5, 1992, p. C-1.
6. Ibid., Oct. 12, 1992, p. C-1.
7. Ibid., Oct. 19, 1992, p. C-1.
8. Ibid., Oct. 26, 1992, p. C-1.
9. Ibid., Nov. 9, 1992, p. C-1.
10. Ibid., Nov. 16, 1992, p. C-1.
11. Ibid., Nov. 23, 1992, p. C-1.
12. Ibid., Nov. 30, 1992, p. C-1.
13. Ibid., Dec. 7, 1992, p. C-1.
14. Ibid., Dec. 15, 1992, p. C-1.
15. Ibid., Dec. 21, 1992, p. C-1.
16. Ibid., Dec. 27, 1992, p. C-1.

1993

1. *Los Angeles Times*, Sept. 6, 1993, p. C-1.
2. Ibid., Sept. 13, 1993, p. C-1.
3. Ibid., Sept. 20, 1993, p. C-1.
4. Ibid., Oct. 4, 1993, p. C-1.
5. Ibid., Oct. 11, 1993, p. C-1.
6. Ibid., Oct. 19, 1993, p. C-1.
7. Ibid., Nov. 1, 1993, p. C-1.
8. Ibid., Nov. 8, 1993, p. C-1.
9. Ibid., Nov. 15, 1993, p. C-1.
10. Ibid., Nov. 22, 1993, p. C-1.
11. Ibid., Nov. 29, 1993, p. C-1.
12. Ibid., Dec. 6, 1993, p. C-1.
13. Ibid., Dec. 13, 1993, p. C-1.
14. Ibid., Dec. 20, 1993, p. C-1.
15. Ibid., Dec. 27, 1993, p. C-1.
16. Ibid., Jan. 3, 1994, p. C-1.
17. Ibid., Jan. 10, 1994, p. C-1.
18. Ibid., Jan. 17, 1994, p. C-1.

1994

1. *Los Angeles Times*, Sept. 6, 1994, p. C-1.
2. Ibid., Sept. 12, 1994, p. C-1.
3. Ibid., Sept. 19, 1994, p. C-1.
4. Ibid., Sept. 26, 1994, p. C-1.
5. Ibid., Oct. 10, 1994, p. C-1.
6. Ibid., Oct. 17, 1994, p. C-1.
7. Ibid., Oct. 24, 1994, p. C-1.
8. Ibid., Oct. 31, 1994, p. C-1.
9. Ibid., Nov. 7, 1994, p. C-1.
10. Ibid., Nov. 14, 1994, p. C-1.
11. Ibid., Nov. 21, 1994, p. C-1.
12. Ibid., Nov. 28, 1994, p. C-1.
13. Ibid., Dec. 6, 1994, p. C-1.
14. Ibid., Dec. 12, 1994, p. C-1.
15. Ibid., Dec. 19, 1994, p. C-1.
16. Ibid., Dec. 25, 1994, p. C-1.

Raiders Move
Back to Oakland

1. *www.wikipedia.com*— Oakland Raiders page.
2. Ibid.
3. Ibid.
4. Ibid.
5. "Jury rules for NFL." SportsIllustrated.cnn.com/football/nfl/news/2001/05/21/raiders verdict.
6. Ibid.
7. Ibid.

1995

1. *Los Angeles Times*, Sept. 4, 1995, p. C-1.
2. Ibid., Sept. 11, 1995, p. C-8.
3. Ibid., Sept. 18, 1995, p. C-1.
4. Ibid., Sept. 25, 1995, p. C-5.
5. Ibid., Oct. 2, 1995, p. C-7.
6. Ibid., Oct. 9, 1995, p. C-1.
7. Ibid., Oct. 17, 1995, p. C-1.
8. Ibid., Oct. 23, 1995, p. C-1.
9. Ibid., Nov. 6, 1995, p. C-9.
10. Ibid., Nov. 13, 1995, p. C-6.
11. Ibid., Nov. 20, 1995, p. C-1.
12. Ibid., Nov. 28, 1995, p. C-1.
13. Ibid., Dec. 4, 1995, p. C-1.
14. Ibid., Dec. 11, 1995, p. C-1.
15. Ibid., Dec. 18, 1995, p. C-1.
16. Ibid., Dec. 25, 1995, p. C-1.

1996

1. *Los Angeles Times*, Sept. 2, 1996, p. C-1.
2. Ibid., Sept. 9, 1996, p. C-9.
3. Ibid., Sept. 16, 1996, p. C-8.
4. Ibid., Sept. 23, 1996, p. C-8.
5. Ibid., Sept. 30, 1996, p. C-6.
6. *Chicago Tribune*, Oct. 7, 1996, Sports p. 7.
7. *Los Angeles Times*, Oct. 14, 1996, p. C-8.
8. Ibid., Oct. 22, 1996, p. C-1.
9. Ibid., Nov. 5, 1996, p. C-1.
10. Ibid., Nov. 11, 1996, p. C-9.
11. Ibid., Nov. 18, 1996, p. C-5.
12. Ibid., Nov. 25, 1996, p. C-6.
13. Ibid., Dec. 2, 1996, p. C-8.
14. Ibid., Dec. 10, 1996, p. C-1.
15. Ibid., Dec. 16, 1996, p. C-10.
16. Ibid., Dec. 23, 1996, p. C-7.

1997

1. *The Cleveland Plain Dealer*, Sept. 1, 1997, p. 8D.
2. Ibid., Sept. 9, 1997, p. 6D.
3. Ibid., Sept. 15, 1997, p. 11D.
4. Ibid., Sept. 22, 1997, p. 11D.
5. Ibid., Sept. 29, 1997, p. 11D.
6. Ibid., Oct. 6, 1997, p. 13D.
7. Ibid., Oct. 20, 1997, p. 1D.
8. Ibid., Oct. 27, 1997, p. 8D.
9. Ibid., Nov. 3, 1997, p. 7D.
10. Ibid., Nov. 10, 1997, p. 9D.
11. Ibid., Nov. 17, 1997, p. 8D.
12. Ibid., Nov. 25, 1997, p. 3D.
13. Ibid., Dec. 1, 1997, p. 9D.
14. Ibid., Dec. 8, 1997, p. 9D.
15. Ibid., Dec. 15, 1997, p. 7D.
16. Ibid., Dec. 22, 1997, p. 9D.

1998

1. *Los Angeles Times*, Sept. 7, 1998, p. C-10.
2. Ibid., Sept. 14, 1998, p. C-10.
3. Ibid., Sept. 21, 1998, p. C-12.
4. Ibid., Sept. 28, 1998, p. C-1.
5. Ibid., Oct. 5, 1998, p. D-5.
6. Ibid., Oct. 12, 1998, p. D-1.
7. Ibid., Oct. 26, 1998, p. D-8.
8. Ibid., Nov. 2, 1998, p. D-7.
9. Ibid., Nov. 9, 1998, p. D-6.
10. Ibid., Nov. 16, 1998, p. D-8.
11. Ibid., Nov. 23, 1998, p. D-4.
12. Ibid., Nov. 30, 1998, p. D-5.
13. Ibid., Dec. 7, 1998, p. D-7.
14. Ibid., Dec. 14, 1998, p. D-8.
15. Ibid., Dec. 21, 1998, p. D-5.
16. Ibid., Dec. 27, 1998, p. D-5.

1999

1. *Los Angeles Times*, Sept. 13, 1999, p. D-10.
2. Ibid., Sept. 20, 1999, p. D-9.
3. Ibid., Sept. 27, 1999, p. D-9.
4. Ibid., Oct. 4, 1999, p. D-9.
5. Ibid., Oct. 11, 1999, p. D-6.
6. Ibid., Oct. 18, 1999, p. D-9.
7. Ibid., Oct. 25, 1999, p. D-8.
8. Ibid., Nov. 1, 1999, p. D-10.
9. Ibid., Nov. 15, 1999, p. D-1.
10. Ibid., Nov. 23, 1999, p. D-1.
11. Ibid., Nov. 29, 1999, p. D-10.
12. Ibid., Dec. 6, 1999, p. D-6.
13. Ibid., Dec. 10, 1999, p. D-4.
14. Ibid., Dec. 20, 1999, p. D-7.
15. Ibid., Dec. 27, 1999, p. D-8.
16. Ibid., Jan. 3, 2000, p. D-5.

2000

1. *Los Angeles Times*, Sept. 4, 2000, p. D-1.
2. Ibid., Sept. 11, 2000, p. D-1.
3. Ibid., Sept. 18, 2000, p. D-1.
4. Ibid., Sept. 25, 2000, p. D-11.
5. Ibid., Oct. 9, 2000, p. D-9.
6. Ibid., Oct. 16, 2000, p. D-8.
7. Ibid., Oct. 23, 2000, p. D-6.
8. Ibid., Oct. 30, 2000, p. D-1.
9. Ibid., Nov. 6, 2000, p. D-1.
10. Ibid., Nov. 14, 2000, p. D-1.
11. Ibid., Nov. 20, 2000, p. D-13.
12. Ibid., Nov. 27, 2000, p. D-12.
13. Ibid., Dec. 4, 2000, p. D-11.
14. Ibid., Dec. 11, 2000, p. D-1.
15. Ibid., Dec. 17, 2000, p. D-5.
16. Ibid., Dec. 25, 2000, p. D-6.
17. Ibid., Jan. 7, 2001, p. D-1.
18. Ibid., Jan. 15, 2001, p. D-1.

2001

1. *Los Angeles Times*, Sept. 10, 2001, p. D-1.
2. Ibid., Sept. 12, 2001, p. A-1.
3. Ibid., Sept. 24, 2001, p. D-6.
4. Ibid., Oct. 1, 2001, p. D-7.
5. Ibid., Oct. 8, 2001, p. D-8.
6. Ibid., Oct. 15, 2001, p. D-1.
7. Ibid., Oct. 29, 2001, p. D-7.
8. Ibid., Nov. 6, 2001, p. D-1.
9. Ibid., Nov. 12, 2001, p. D-9.
10. *Chicago Tribune*, Nov. 19, 2001, Sports p. 9.
11. *Los Angeles Times*, Nov. 26, 2001, p. D-1.
12. Ibid., Dec. 3, 2001, p. D-1.
13. Ibid., Dec. 10, 2001, p. D-8.
14. Ibid., Dec. 16, 2001, p. D-1.
15. Ibid., Dec. 23, 2001, p. D-13.
16. Ibid., Dec. 31, 2001, p. D-8.
17. Ibid., Jan. 7, 2002, p. D-1.
18. Ibid., Jan. 13, 2002, p. D-1.
19. Ibid., Jan. 20, 2002, p. D-2.

2002

1. *Los Angeles Times*, Sept. 9, 2002, p. D-8.
2. Ibid., Sept. 16, 2002, p. D-1.
3. Ibid., Sept. 30, 2002, p. D-6.
4. Ibid., Oct. 7, 2002, p. D-5.
5. Ibid., Oct. 14, 2002, p. D-8.
6. Ibid., Oct. 21, 2002, p. D-1.
7. Ibid., Oct. 28, 2002, p. D-6.
8. Ibid., Nov. 4, 2002, p. D-7.
9. Ibid., Nov. 12, 2002, p. D-1.
10. Ibid., Nov. 18, 2002, p. D-1.
11. Ibid., Nov. 25, 2002, p. D-7.
12. Ibid., Dec. 3, 2002, p. D-1.
13. Ibid., Dec. 9, 2002, p. D-5.
14. Ibid., Dec. 16, 2002, p. D-1.
15. Ibid., Dec. 23, 2002, p. D-1.
16. Ibid., Dec. 29, 2002, p. D-8.
17. Ibid., Jan. 13, 2003, p. D-1.
18. Ibid., Jan. 20, 2003, p. D-1.
19. Ibid., Jan. 27, 2003, p. A-1.
20. Wikipedia — Super Bowl 37 page.
21. Ibid.; Super Bowl play-by-play: www.usatoday.com/sports/nfl/super/superbowl-XXXVII-plays.htm.

2003

1. *Los Angeles Times*, Sept. 8, 2003, p. D-11.
2. Ibid., Sept. 15, 2003, p. D-11.
3. Ibid., Sept. 23, 2003, p. D-1.
4. Ibid., Sept. 29, 2003, p. D-1.
5. Ibid., Oct. 6, 2003, p. D-7.
6. Ibid., Oct. 13, 2003, p. D-10.
7. Ibid., Oct. 21, 2003, p. D-3.
8. Ibid., Nov. 3, 2003, p. D-10.
9. Ibid., Nov. 10, 2003, p. D-10.
10. Ibid., Nov. 17, 2003, p. D-1.
11. Ibid., Nov. 24, 2003, p. D-9.
12. Ibid., Dec. 1, 2003, p. D-7.
13. Ibid., Dec. 8, 2003, p. D-9.
14. Ibid., Dec. 15, 2003, p. D-8.
15. Ibid., Dec. 23, 2003, p. D-1.
16. Ibid., Dec. 29, 2003, p. D-9.

2004

1. *Los Angeles Times*, Sept. 13, 2004, p. D-5.
2. Ibid., Sept. 20, 2004, p. D-4.
3. Ibid., Sept. 27, 2004, p. D-1.
4. Ibid., Oct. 4, 2004, p. D-11.
5. Ibid., Oct. 11, 2004, p. D-7.
6. Ibid., Oct. 18, 2004, p. D-5.
7. Ibid., Oct. 25, 2004, p. D-8.
8. Ibid., Nov. 1, 2004, p. D-6.
9. Ibid., Nov. 8, 2004, p. D-4.
10. Ibid., Nov. 22, 2004, p. D-5.
11. Ibid., Nov. 29, 2004, p. D-6.
12. Ibid., Dec. 6, 2004, p. D-6.
13. Ibid., Dec. 13, 2004, p. D-8.
14. Ibid., Dec. 20, 2004, p. D-6.
15. Ibid., Dec. 26, 2004, p. D-4.
16. Ibid., Jan. 3, 2005, p. D-6.

2005

1. *Los Angeles Times*, Sept. 9, 2005, p. D-1.
2. Ibid., Sept. 19, 2005, p. D-13.
3. Ibid., Sept. 26, 2005, p. D-13.
4. Ibid., Oct. 3, 2005, p. D-8.
5. Ibid., Oct. 17, 2005, p. D-7.
6. Ibid., Oct. 24, 2005, p. D-8.
7. Ibid., Oct. 31, 2005, p. D-10.
8. Ibid., Nov. 7, 2005, p. D-6.
9. Ibid., Nov. 14, 2005, p. D-1.
10. Ibid., Nov. 21, 2005, p. D-6.
11. Ibid., Nov. 28, 2005, p. D-9.
12. Ibid., Dec. 5, 2005, p. D-9.
13. Ibid., Dec. 12, 2005, p. D-11.
14. Ibid., Dec. 19, 2005, p. D-11.
15. Ibid., Dec. 25, 2005, p. D-9.
16. Ibid., Jan. 2, 2006, p. D-1.

2006

1. *Los Angeles Times*, Sept. 1, 2006, p. D-1.
2. Ibid., Sept. 18, 2006, p. D-10.
3. Ibid., Oct. 2, 2006, p. D-9.
4. Ibid., Oct. 9, 2006, p. D-9.
5. Ibid., Oct. 16, 2006, p. D-11.
6. Ibid., Oct. 23, 2006, p. D-11.
7. Ibid., Oct. 30, 2006, p. D-10.
8. Ibid., Nov. 7, 2006, p. D-5.
9. Ibid., Nov. 13, 2006, p. D-10.
10. Ibid., Nov. 20, 2006, p. D-10.
11. Ibid., Nov. 27, 2006, p. D-7.
12. Ibid., Dec. 4, 2006, p. D-10.
13. Ibid., Dec. 11, 2006, p. D-9.
14. Ibid., Dec. 18, 2006, p. D-9.
15. Ibid., Dec. 24, 2006, p. D-4.
16. Ibid., Jan. 1, 2007, p. D-8.

2007

1. *Los Angeles Times*, Sept. 10, 2007, p. D-9.
2. Ibid., Sept. 17, 2007, p. D-8.
3. Ibid., Sept. 24, 2007, p. D-8.
4. Ibid., Oct. 1, 2007, p. D-9.
5. Ibid., Oct. 15, 2007, p. D-1.
6. Ibid., Oct. 22, 2007, p. D-7.
7. Ibid., Oct. 29, 2007, p. D-8.
8. Ibid., Nov. 5, 2007, p. D-7.
9. Ibid., Nov. 12, 2007, p. D-8.
10. Ibid., Nov. 19, 2007, p. D-8.
11. Ibid., Nov. 26, 2007, p. D-1.
12. Ibid., Dec. 3, 2007, p. D-9.
13. Ibid., Dec. 10, 2007, p. D-7.
14. Ibid., Dec. 17, 2007, p. D-6.
15. Ibid., Dec. 24, 2007, p. D-6.
16. Ibid., Dec. 31, 2007, p. D-13.

2008

1. *Los Angeles Times*, Sept. 9, 2008, p. D-1.
2. *The Cleveland Plain Dealer*, Sept. 15, 2008, p. C-12.
3. Ibid., Sept. 22, 2008, p. C-10.
4. Ibid., Sept. 29, 2008, p. C-10.
5. Ibid., Oct. 13, 2008, p. C-14.
6. Ibid., Oct. 20, 2008, p. C-9.
7. Ibid., Oct. 27, 2008, p. C-9.
8. Ibid., Nov. 3, 2008, p. C-8.
9. Ibid., Nov. 10, 2008, p. C-7.
10. Ibid., Nov. 17, 2008, p. C-10.
11. Ibid., Nov. 24, 2008, p. C-10.
12. Ibid., Dec. 1, 2008, p. C-8.
13. Ibid., Dec. 5, 2008, p. D-7.
14. Ibid., Dec. 15, 2008, p. C-8.
15. Ibid., Dec. 22, 2008, p. C-9.
16. Ibid., Dec. 29, 2008, p. C-8.

2009

1. *Sports Illustrated*, CNN.com, Sept. 15, 2009, p. 1.
2. *The Cleveland Plain Dealer*, Sept. 21, 2009, p. C-10.
3. Ibid., Sept. 28, 2009, p. C-9.
4. Ibid., Oct. 5, 2009, p. C-11.
5. Ibid., Oct. 12, 2009, p. C-6.
6. Ibid., Oct. 19, 2009, p. C-6.
7. Ibid., Oct. 26, 2009, p. C-6.
8. Ibid., Nov. 2, 2009, p. C-6.
9. Ibid., Nov. 16, 2009, p. C-8.
10. Ibid., Nov. 23, 2009, p. C-11.
11. Ibid., Nov. 27, 2009, p. D-8.

12. Ibid., Al Davis Sign, Dec. 3, 009, p. D-10.

13. Ibid., Dec. 7, 2009, p. C-8.

14. Ibid., Dec. 14, 2009, p. C-8.

15. Ibid., Dec. 21, 2009, p. C-8.

16. Ibid., Dec. 28, 2009, p. C-7, C-8.

17. Ibid., Jan. 4, 2010, p. C-9.

Part II. The Team — Head Coaches

Eddie Erdelatz

1. *www.wikipedia.com* — Eddie Erdelatz page.

2. Ibid.

3. Ibid.

4. Ibid.

5. Ibid.

6. *New York Times*, Nov. 12, 1966, Obituary Section.

7. Ibid.

8. Ibid.

9. Tom Flores with Matt Fulks, *Tom Flores' Tales from the Oakland Raiders*, p. 7.

10. Jim McCullough, *Pride & Poise: The Oakland Raiders of the American Football League*, p. 38–39.

11. *New York Times*, Nov. 12, 1966, Obituary Section.

Marty Feldman

1. 1962 Oakland Raiders Media Guide — Marty Feldman entry.

2. Ibid.

3. Ibid.

4. Ibid.

5. Ibid.

6. Ibid.

7. *Oakland Tribune*, Sept. 18, 1961, Sports Section.

8. *www.wikipedia.com* — Marty Feldman page.

William "Red" Conkright

1. *www.wikipedia.com* — William "Red" Conkright page.

2. Ibid.

3. Ibid.

4. Jim McCullough, *Pride & Poise: The Oakland Raiders of the American Football League*, p. 61.

5. *www.wikipedia.com* — William "Red" Conkright page.

Al Davis

1. Mark Ribowsky, *Slick: The Silver and Black Life of Al Davis*, p. 16.

2. *Raiders: The Complete History, Disc 1, East Bay Orphans — The Early Years, Foundations — Vision and Design, and Bombs Away.*

3. Ribowsky, p. 34; *www.raiderzone.com* — Al Davis page.

4. Ribowsky, p. 35.

5. *www.raiderzone.com* — Al Davis page.

6. Ribowsky, p. 36–40, Davis' time at Adelphi.

7. 2009 Oakland Raiders Media Guide — Al Davis entry, p. 7.

8. Ribowsky, p. 93.

9. *Sports Illustrated*, Nov. 4, 1963, p. 27–28.

10. Jim McCullough, *Pride & Poise: The Oakland Raiders of the American Football League*, p. 69.

11. Joseph Hession and Steve Cassady, *Raiders*, p. 151.

12. Murray Olderman, *Super: "Just Win Baby,"* p. vii.

13. *Sports Illustrated*, Nov. 4, 1963, p. 28.

14. *Raiders: The Complete History, Disc 1, Bombs Away.*

15. Olderman, p. 105.

16. Ibid., p. 110.

17. Ribowsky, p. 168.

18. Ibid., p. 163.

19. Ibid., p. 233.

20. 2009 Oakland Raiders Media Guide — Al Davis entry, p. 7.

John Rauch

1. *www.wikipedia.com* — John Rauch page.

2. Ibid.

3. Ibid.

4. Ibid.

5. Mark Ribowsky, *Slick: The Silver and Black Life of Al Davis*, p. 212.

6. Ibid., p. 202–203.

7. *www.wikipedia.com* — John Rauch page.

8. Ibid.

9. Ibid.

10. Ibid.

John Madden

1. John Madden with Dave Anderson, *Hey, Wait a Minute (I Wrote a Book)*, p. 41.

2. Ibid., p. 42.

3. Ibid.

4. 1978 Oakland Raiders Media Guide — John Madden entry.

5. Madden with Anderson, p. 50.

6. Ibid.

7. 1978 Oakland Raiders Media Guide — John Madden entry.

8. Ibid.

9. John Lombardo, *Raiders Forever: Stars of the NFL's Most Colorful Team Recall Their Glory Days*, p. 39.

10. Ibid., p. 40.

11. *Raiders: The Complete History, Disc 1, Bombs Away, One Game Away, and Bonus Features — The Unforgettables — John Madden interview.*

12. Madden with Anderson, p. 104–106; Kevin Cook, "Bad to the Bone." *Playboy Magazine,* Oct. 2009, p. 122–123.

13. Ibid.

14. Lombardo, p. 43.

15. Ibid.

16. Ibid., p. 45.

17. Madden with Anderson, p. 103–104.

18. 1978 Oakland Raiders Media Guide — John Madden entry.

19. *www.wikipedia.com* — John Madden page.

20. Ibid.

21. Ibid.

Tom Flores

1. 1987 Los Angeles Raiders Media Guide — Tom Flores entry; Lou Sahadi, *Domination: The Story of the 1983 World Champion Los Angeles Raiders.*

2. 1987 Los Angeles Raiders Media Guide — Tom Flores entry.

3. Ibid.

4. Joseph Hession and Steve Cassady, *Raiders*, p. 49.

5. Sahadi, p. 13.

6. 1987 Los Angeles Raiders Media Guide — Tom Flores entry.

7. Sahadi, p. 13.

8. Ibid., p. 11.

9. Ibid., p. 10.

10. *Los Angeles Times*, Jan. 21, 1988, p. C-1.

11. Ibid.

Mike Shanahan

1. 1989 Los Angeles Raiders Media Guide — Mike Shanahan entry.

2. *Los Angeles Times*, March 2, 1988, p. 1.

3. Ibid.

4. Ibid.

5. Ibid.

6. Ibid.

7. 1989 Los Angeles Raiders Media Guide — Mike Shanahan entry.

8. Mark Ribowsky, *Slick: The Silver and Black Life of Al Davis*, p. 331.

9. Ron Smith, *Pro Football's Heroes of the Hall*, p. 370–371.

10. Ribowsky, p. 328, and *Los Angeles Times*, March 2, 1988, p. 1.

11. Ribowsky, p. 329.

12. Ibid., p. 334.

13. *Los Angeles Times*, Oct. 4, 1989, p. C-1.

Art Shell

1. John Madden with Dave Anderson, *Hey, Wait a Minute (I Wrote a Book)*, p. 142.

2. 1994 Los Angeles Raiders Media Guide — Art Shell entry.

3. Ibid.

4. John Lombardo, *Raiders Forever: Stars of the NFL's Most Colorful Team Recall Their Glory Days*, p. 32.

5. Ibid.

6. Ibid.

7. 1994 Los Angeles Raiders Media Guide — Art Shell entry.

8. Lombardo, p. 33.

Mike White

1. 1996 Oakland Raiders Media Guide — Mike White entry

2. Ibid.

3. Ibid.

4. Ibid.

5. Ibid.

6. Ibid.

7. *Sports Illustrated*, Sept. 4, 1995

8. Ibid.

9. Ibid.

10. *www.wikipedia.com* — Mike White page

Joe Bugel

1. 1997 Oakland Raiders Media Guide — Joe Bugel entry.

2. Ibid.

3. Ibid.

4. *Kickoff '97 — The Official Magazine of the National Football League* — 1997 NFL preview, p. 156.

5. 1997 Oakland Raiders Media Guide — Joe Bugel entry.

6. Ibid.

7. *www.canoe.ca/stats* fbp/bc-fbp-lgns-bugelout-r.

8. *www.wikipedia.com* — Joe Bugel page.

Jon Gruden

1. *www.wikipedia.com* — Jon Gruden page.

2. Ibid.

3. Ibid.

4. 2001 Oakland Raiders Media Guide — Jon Gruden entry.

5. Ibid.

6. Ibid.

7. Ibid.

8. *www.wikipedia.com* — Jon Gruden page.

9. *Lindy's 1999 Pro Football Preview Magazine*, p. 198.

10. *Lindy's 2000 Pro Football Preview Magazine*, p. 203.

11. *www.wikipedia.com* — Jon Gruden page.

12. 2002 Oakland Raiders Media Guide — Bill Callahan entry.

13. *www.wikipedia.com* — Jon Gruden page.

14. Ibid.

15. Ibid.

Bill Callahan

1. 2002 Oakland Raiders Media Guide — Bill Callahan entry.

2. Ibid.

3. Ibid.

4. Ibid.

5. Ibid.

6. Ibid.

7. Ibid.

8. Ibid.

9. *www.wikipedia.com* — Bill Callahan page.

10. Ibid.

11. Ibid.

12. Ibid.

13. Ibid.

Norv Turner

1. *www.nfl.com/teams/coaches*.

2. Ibid.

3. Ibid.

4. Super Bowl XXVII game program, Jan. 31, 1993, p. 70.

5. *www.nfl.com/teams/coaches*.

6. *www.wikipedia.com* — Norv Turner page.

7. *www.raidersrap.com/turner* 0103.

8. *Lindy's 2004 Pro Football Preview Magazine*, p. 201.

9. *www.raidersrap.com/turner* 0103.

10. Ibid.

11. *www.wikipedia.com* — Norv Turner page.

Art Shell

1. "Shell to Return to Raiders as Head Coach," Feb. 11, 2006, *www.espn.com*.

2. Ibid.

3. Ibid.

4. "Shell Out After One Season as Raiders Coach," Jan. 4, 2007, *www.nfl.com*

5. Ibid.

6. Ibid.

Lane Kiffin

1. *www.wikipedia.com* — Lane Kiffin page.

2. Ibid.

3. Ibid.
4. Ibid.
5. Ibid.
6. David White, "Wrath of Davis: According to Owner, It Wasn't All About Winning," Oct. 1, 2008, *www.sfgate.com.*
7. Ibid.
8. Ibid.
9. Ibid.

Tom Cable

1. 2009 Oakland Raiders Media Guide — Tom Cable entry.
2. Ibid.
3. Ibid.
4. Ibid.
5. Ibid.
6. *www.wikipedia.com* — Tom Cable page.

Part III. Bad Boys... — Players of Yore

Marcus Allen

1. Joseph Hession and Steve Cassady, *Raiders*, p. 145.
2. Tom Flores with Matt Fulks, *Tom Flores' Tales from the Oakland Raiders*, p. 71–75.
3. Marcus Allen with Carlton Stowers, *Marcus: The Autobiography of Marcus Allen*, p. 264.

Lyle Alzado

1. Murray Olderman, *Super: "Just Win Baby,"* p. 62.
2. *www.raidersonline.org*, Lyle Alzado page.
3. Olderman, p. 62.
4. Lou Sahadi, *Domination: The Story of the 1983 World Champion Los Angeles Raiders*, p. 46.

Nnamdi Asomugha

1. 2009 Oakland Raiders Media Guide, p. 35.
2. Ibid.

George Atkinson

1. John Lombardo, *Raiders Forever: Stars of the NFL's Most Colorful Team Recall Their Glory Days*, p. 102.
2. John Madden with Dave Anderson, *Hey, Wait a Minute (I Wrote a Book)*, p. 153.
3. Lombardo, p. 114.

Pete Banaszak

1. John Madden with Dave Anderson, *Hey, Wait a Minute (I Wrote a Book)*, p. 152.
2. John Lombardo, *Raiders Forever: Stars of the NFL's Most Colorful Team Recall Their Glory Days*, p. 113.

Fred Biletnikoff

1. John Lombardo, *Raiders Forever: Stars of the NFL's Most Colorful Team Recall Their Glory Days*, p. 206.
2. *www.raidersonline.org*, Fred Biletnikoff page.
3. John Madden with Dave Anderson, *Hey, Wait a Minute (I Wrote a Book)*, p. 149.

4. Joseph Hession and Steve Cassady, *Raiders*, p. 26.
5. Madden with Anderson, p. 149.
6. *www.wikipedia.com* — stickum page.

Dan Birdwell

1. Murray Olderman, *Super: "Just Win Baby,"* p. 106.
2. Kevin Cook, *Bad to the Bone — Playboy Magazine Oct., 2009*, p. 122.
3. Ibid.
4. Tom Flores with Matt Fulks, *Tom Flores' Tales from the Oakland Raiders*, p. 86.
5. Olderman, p. 106.

George Blanda

1. Herskowitz, Mickey. *The Quarterbacks: The Uncensored Truth About the Men in the Pocket*, p. 105.
2. Ibid.
3. Joseph Hession and Steve Cassady, *Raiders*, p. 34.
4. Ron Smith, *Pro Football's Heroes of the Hall*, p. 44–45.

Cliff Branch

1. John Lombardo, *Raiders Forever: Stars of the NFL's Most Colorful Team Recall Their Glory Days*, p. 179–180.
2. Ibid., p. 180.
3. Tom Flores with Matt Fulks, *Tom Flores' Tales from the Oakland Raiders*, p. 92.
4. Ibid., p. 93.
5. Ibid.
6. Ibid., p. 94.
7. 1986 Los Angeles Raiders Media Guide — Cliff Branch entry.

Bob Brown

1. John Madden with Dave Anderson, *Hey, Wait a Minute (I Wrote a Book)*, p. 181.
2. *www.raidersonline.org*, Bob Brown page.
3. Ibid.
4. Ibid.

Tim Brown

1. *www.wikipedia.com* — Tim Brown page.
2. Ibid.
3. 2001 Oakland Raiders Media Guide — Tim Brown entry.
4. Ibid.
5. 2002 Oakland Raiders Media Guide — Tim Brown entry.
6. *www.wikipedia.com* — Tim Brown page.
7. Ibid.

Willie Brown

1. John Lombardo, *Raiders Forever: Stars of the NFL's Most Colorful Team Recall Their Glory Days*, p. 73.
2. Ibid., p. 73–74.
3. Ron Smith, *Pro Football's Heroes of the Hall*, p. 56.
4. Lombardo, p. 75.
5. Ibid.

Billy Cannon

1. Tom Flores with Matt Fulks, *Tom Flores' Tales from the Oakland Raiders*, p. 97.

2. Ibid., p. 100.
3. Ibid.
4. Ibid., p. 101.
5. "College Football; Never Forgotten, Billy Cannon Is Now Forgiven," Dec. 28, 2003, *www.nytimes.com.*

Dave Casper

1. John Lombardo, *Raiders Forever: Stars of the NFL's Most Colorful Team Recall Their Glory Days*, p. 143.
2. Ron Smith, *Pro Football's Heroes of the Hall*, p. 68.

Todd Christensen

1. Murray Olderman, *Super: "Just Win Baby,"* p. 40.
2. Ibid.
3. Ibid.
4. Ibid.
5. Ibid., p. 40–41.

Dave Dalby

1. 1985 Los Angeles Raiders Media Guide — Dave Dalby entry.
2. Rob Huizenga, M.D., "*You're OK, It's Just a Bruise": A Doctor's Sideline Secrets About Pro Football's Most Outrageous Team*, p. 158.
3. Ibid.
4. "Dalby Dies in Accident," Aug. 31, 2002, *www.latimes.com.*

Clem Daniels

1. *www.raidersonline.org.* — Clem Daniels page
2. Ibid.
3. Tom Flores with Matt Fulks, *Tom Flores' Tales from the Oakland Raiders*, p. 119
4. Ibid.

Ben Davidson

1. Kevin Cook, "Bad to the Bone," *Playboy Magazine,* Oct. 2009, p. 61.
2. John Lombardo, *Raiders Forever: Stars of the NFL's Most Colorful Team Recall Their Glory Days*, p. 157.
3. Ibid.
4. Ibid., p. 158–159.

Clarence Davis

1. John Lombardo, *Raiders Forever: Stars of the NFL's Most Colorful Team Recall Their Glory Days*, p. 137.

Hewritt Dixon

1. Tom Flores with Matt Fulks, *Tom Flores' Tales from the Oakland Raiders*, p. 126–127.
2. *Los Angeles Times*, Nov. 26, 1992, p. 9.

Tom Flores

1. Lou Sahadi, *Domination: The Story of the 1983 World Champion Los Angeles Raiders*, p. 12–13; 1987 Los Angeles Raiders Media Guide — Tom Flores entry.

Rich Gannon

1. 2002 Oakland Raiders Media Guide — Rich Gannon entry.
2. *Cleveland Plain Dealer*, Jan. 26, 2003, p. C-9.
3. Ibid.

4. Ibid.
5. Ibid.

Ray Guy

1. John Lombardo, *Raiders Forever: Stars of the NFL's Most Colorful Team Recall Their Glory Days*, p. 50.
2. Ibid., p. 58.

Wayne Hawkins

1. Tom Flores with Matt Fulks, *Tom Flores' Tales from the Oakland Raiders*, p. 132.

Lester Hayes

1. Murray Olderman, *Super: "Just Win Baby,"* p. 66.
2. Lou Sahadi, *Domination: The Story of the 1983 World Champion Los Angeles Raiders*, p. 59.
3. Ibid.
4. Olderman, p. 66.
5. Sahadi, p. 59.

Mike Haynes

1. Tom Flores with Matt Fulks, *Tom Flores' Tales from the Oakland Raiders*, p. 138–141.
2. *www.raidersonline.org*, Mike Haynes page.
3. Flores with Fulks, p. 138.
4. Ibid., p. 140.

Ted Hendricks

1. John Madden with Dave Anderson, *Hey, Wait a Minute (I Wrote a Book)*, p. 104.
2. Tom Flores with Matt Fulks, *Tom Flores' Tales from the Oakland Raiders*, p. 145.
3. Murray Olderman, *Super: "Just Win Baby,"* p. 50–52.
4. Lou Sahadi, *Domination: The Story of the 1983 World Champion Los Angeles Raiders*, p. 51.
5. Ron Smith, *Pro Football's Heroes of the Hall*, p. 146.
6. Olderman, p. 50.

Marv Hubbard

1. Joseph Hession and Steve Cassady, *Raiders*, p. 76.
2. Ibid.
3. Ibid., p. 75.
4. Ibid.
5. John Madden with Dave Anderson, *Hey, Wait a Minute (I Wrote a Book)*, p. 116–117.

Bo Jackson

1. www.wikipedia.com — Bo Jackson page.
2. Tom Flores with Matt Fulks, *Tom Flores' Tales from the Oakland Raiders*, p. 146.
3. www.wikipedia.com — Bo Jackson page.

Sebastian Janikowski

1. 2009 Oakland Raiders Media Guide — Sebastian Janikowski entry.
2. www.wikipedia.com — Sebastian Janikowski page.
3. Ibid.

Napoleon Kaufman

1. 1999 Oakland Raiders Media Guide — Napoleon Kaufman entry.

2. Ibid.
3. www.wikipedia.com — Napoleon Kaufman page.

Daryle Lamonica

1. www.wikipedia.com — Daryle Lamonica page.
2. Ibid.
3. Mark Ribowsky, *Slick: The Silver and Black Life of Al Davis*, p. 189.
4. *Sports Illustrated*, Jan. 5, 1970, p. 39.
5. John Madden with Dave Anderson, *Hey, Wait a Minute (I Wrote a Book)*, p. 129.

Howie Long

1. Murray Olderman, *Super: "Just Win Baby,"* p. 60.
2. Tom Flores with Matt Fulks, *Tom Flores' Tales from the Oakland Raiders*, p. 156.
3. Lou Sahadi, *Domination: The Story of the 1983 World Champion Los Angeles Raiders*, p. 39.
4. Ibid.
5. Ron Smith, *Pro Football's Heroes of the Hall*, p. 219.
6. Sahadi, p. 42.
7. Smith, p. 218.
8. Ibid.
9. Ibid.
10. www.wikipedia.com — Howie Long page.

Todd Marinovich

1. www.wikipedia.com — Todd Marinovich page.
2. Ibid.
3. Ibid.
4. Ibid.
5. Ibid.
6. Ibid.
7. Ibid.
8. Ibid.
9. Ibid.
10. Ibid.
11. Ibid.
12. Ibid.

Rod Martin

1. Tom Flores with Matt Fulks, *Tom Flores' Tales from the Oakland Raiders*, p. 160.
2. John Madden with Dave Anderson, *Hey, Wait a Minute (I Wrote a Book)*, p. 158.
3. Murray Olderman, *Super: "Just Win Baby,"* p. 53.
4. Ibid.
5. Lou Sahadi, *Domination: The Story of the 1983 World Champion Los Angeles Raiders*, p. 53.
6. Olderman, p. 53.
7. Ibid., p. 54.

John Matuszak

1. Lou Sahadi, *Raiders: Cinderella Champions of Pro Football*, p. 80.
2. Ibid.
3. Ibid., p. 82.
4. Ibid., p. 83.
5. John Madden with Dave Anderson, *Hey, Wait a Minute (I Wrote a Book)*, p. 177.
6. Kevin Cook, "Bad to the Bone," *Playboy Magazine*, Oct. 2009, p. 124.

7. John Matuszak and Steve Delsohn, *Cruisin' with the Tooz*, p. 222.
8. *Los Angeles Times*, June 18, 1989, p. 1.
9. Rob Huizenga, M.D., *"You're OK, It's Just a Bruise": A Doctor's Sideline Secrets About Pro Football's Most Outrageous Team*, p. 221.
10. *Los Angeles Times*, June 18, 1989, p. 1.

Matt Millen

1. Murray Olderman, *Super: "Just Win Baby,"* p. 561.

Ralph Oliver

1. *Sports Illustrated*, Oct. 12, 1970, p. 50.
2. Ibid.
3. Ibid.
4. Ibid.
5. Ibid.

Jim Otto

1. Jim Otto with Dave Newhouse, *The Pain of Glory*, p. 44.
2. Joseph Hession and Steve Cassady, *Raiders*, p. 58.
3. Ibid.
4. Ibid.
5. Ibid.

Jim Plunkett

1. www.raidersonline.org. — Jim Plunkett page.
2. Joseph Hession and Steve Cassady, *Raiders*, p. 157.
3. Lou Sahadi, *The Raiders: Cinderella Champions of Pro Football*, p. 32.
4. Ibid.
5. Ibid.
6. Ibid., p. 33.
7. www.raidersonline.org, Jim Plunkett page.

Art Powell

1. www.raidersonline.org, Art Powell page.
2. Mark Ribowsky, *Slick: The Silver and Black Life of Al Davis*, p. 122.
3. Tom Flores with Matt Fulks, *Tom Flores' Tales from the Oakland Raiders*, p. 183.

Barret Robbins

1. www.wikipedia.com — Barret Robbins page.
2. Ibid.

Art Shell

1. John Lombardo, *Raiders Forever: Stars of the NFL's Most Colorful Team Recall Their Glory Days*, p. 26.
2. Ibid.
3. Ibid., p. 29.
4. Ibid., p. 31.

Otis Sistrunk

1. www.wikipedia.com — Otis Sistrunk page.
2. John Madden with Dave Anderson, *Hey, Wait a Minute (I Wrote a Book)*, p. 180.
3. Ibid.

Jack Squirek

1. Lou Sahadi, *Domination: The Story of the 1983 World Champion Los Angeles Raiders*, p. 57.

2. Murray Olderman, *Super: "Just Win Baby,"* p. 9.
3. Ibid.

Ken Stabler

1. Ken Stabler and Berry Stainback, *Snake*, p. 32.
2. John Lombardo, *Stars of the NFL's Most Colorful Team Recall Their Glory Days*, p. 10.
3. Ibid., p. 13.
4. Ibid., p. 15.
5. Ibid.
6. Ibid.
7. Ibid.
8. Tom Flores with Matt Fulks, *Tom Flores' Tales from the Oakland Raiders*, p. 189.
9. Joseph Hession and Steve Cassady, *Raiders*, p. 110.
10. Lombardo, p. 17–18.

Jack Tatum

1. Joseph Hession and Steve Cassady, *Raiders*, p. 120.
2. Ibid., p. 119.
3. John Lombardo, *Raiders Forever: Stars of the NFL's Most Colorful Team Recall Their Glory Days*, p. 95.
4. Ibid., p. 92.

Gene Upshaw

1. John Madden with Dave Anderson, *Hey, Wait a Minute (I Wrote a Book)*, p. 143.
2. Tom Flores with Matt Fulks, *Tom Flores' Tales from the Oakland Raiders*, p. 196.
3. Ibid.
4. John Lombardo, *Raiders Forever: Stars of the NFL's Most Colorful Team Recall Their Glory Days*, p. 165–166, 173.

Mark van Eeghen

1. John Lombardo, Raiders Forever: Stars of the NFL's Most Colorful Team Recall Their Glory Days, p. 122.
2. Ibid.
3. Ibid., p. 123.
4. Ibid., p. 124.
5. Ibid., p. 125.

Phil Villapiano

1. 1979 Oakland Raiders Media Guide — Phil Villapiano entry.
2. John Lombardo, *Raiders Forever: Stars of the NFL's Most Colorful Team Recall Their Glory Days*, p. 196.
3. Joseph Hession and Steve Cassady, *Raiders*, p. 128.
4. Kevin Cook, "Bad to the Bone," *Playboy Magazine*, Oct. 2009, p. 125.
5. Hession and Cassady, p. 128.

Carl Weathers

1. 1971 Oakland Raiders Media Guide — Carl Weathers entry.
2. www.wikipedia.com — Carl Weathers page.
3. Ibid.
4. Ibid.

Warren Wells

1. John Madden with Dave Anderson, *Hey, Wait a Minute (I Wrote a Book)*, p. 185.

2. Ibid., p. 186.
3. Ibid., p. 187.
4. Ibid.
5. Ibid., p. 189.
6. Damall Binta, "Warren Wells says JaMarcus Russell has a strong arm," www.bleacherreport.com.

Fred Williamson

1. www.wikipedia.com — Fred Williamson page.
2. Ibid.
3. Ibid.
4. Ibid.

Taken Too Soon

1. www.wikipedia.com.
2. *Los Angeles Times*, April 17, 1970, p. E-1.
3. www.nytimes.com —/1998/10/02/sports/nfl — notebook. Oakland — former-player-is-shot-to-death.
4. www.wikipedia.com.
5. *Los Angeles Times*, Dec. 16, 2005, p. B-1.
6. Rob Huizenga, M.D., *"You're OK, It's Just a Bruise." A Doctor's Sideline Secrets About Pro Football's Most Outrageous Team*, p. 217–220.
7. www.bucpower.com/feature — turk.
8. www.raidershack.com — in memoriam — Eric Turner.
9. *Los Angeles Times*, May 1, 1993, p. C-1.
10. Huizenga, p. 275.
11. Ibid., p. 277.
12. Ibid., p. 280.
13. Ibid.
14. Ibid., p. 281.

Part III. Bad Boys...— Executives...

1. www.wikipedia.com — Wayne Valley page; George P. Edmonston, Jr., and Chuck Boice, *"Up Close and Personal": The Valleys*, www.osualum.com.
2. 1969 Oakland Raiders Media Guide — Ed McGah entry.
3. Jim McCullough, *Pride & Poise: The Oakland Raiders of the American Football League*, p. 3.
4. www.sodafoundation.org.
5. http://football.ballparks.com/nfl/San Francisc049ers/oldindex.htm.
6. www.wikipedia.com — Don Blessing page.
7. McCullough, p. 8.
8. Ibid., p. 7–8; Roger Lapham Jr., articles.sfgate.com/2000-01-06/news.
9. McCullough, p. 27–28.
10. *Oakland Tribune*, Jan. 16, 1961, p. 33 E.
11. McCullough, p. 50.
12. www.silverandblackpride.com/2010/5/29/raiders — history.
13. Ibid.
14. Murray Olderman, *Super: "Just Win Baby,"* p. 149.
15. Ibid.
16. Ibid.
17. www.wikipedia.com — Ron Wolf page.
18. Ibid.
19. "He's Come a Long Way Baby," www.raiderdrive.com.

20. Ibid.

21. 2002 Oakland Raiders Media Guide—Al LoCasale entry, p. 28.

22. "He's Come a Long Way Baby," *www.raiderdrive.com*.

23. Ibid.

24. 2002 Oakland Raiders Media Guide—Al LoCasale entry, p. 28.

25. *www.wikipedia.com*—Bill King broadcaster page.

26. Ibid.

27. Ibid.

28. Ibid.

29. *www.wikipedia.com*—Kezar Stadium page; football.ballparks.com/nfl/San Francisco 49ers.

30. *www.wikipedia.com*—Kezar Stadium page.

31. McCullough, p. 23.

32. *www.wikipedia.com*—Kezar Stadium page.

33. *www.wikipedia.com*—Candlestick Park page; football.ballparks.com/nfl/San Francisco 49ers.

34. *www.wikipedia.com*—Frank Youell Field page; football.ballparks.com/nfl/Oakland Raiders.

35. *www.wikipedia.com*—Oakland–Alameda County Coliseum page; 2009 Oakland Raiders Media Guide, Oakland—Alameda County Coliseum entry, p. 286.

36. *www.wikipedia.com*—Los Angeles Memorial Coliseum page; *www.lacoliseum.com*.

37. Mark Ribowsky, *Slick: The Silver and Black Life of Al Davis*, p. 118–119.

38. *www.wikipedia.com*—Oakland Raiders page: "Logos and Uniforms."

39. Ibid.; McCullough, p. 82.

40. *www.wikipedia.com*—Oakland Raiders page: "Logos and Uniforms."

41. Ibid.

42. *www.wikipedia.com*—Oakland Raiderettes page

43. *www.raiders.com/raiderettes*.

44. Ibid.

45. *Raiders: The Complete History Disc 1—Bonus Features: The Raideret*

46. Ibid.

47. Ibid.

48. www.angelfire.com/ca6/raide sbombsquad/raider_nicknames.htm Bob Carroll, Michael Gershma David Neft, and John Thorn, *To Football: The Official Encyclopedia the National Football League*, Play Register.

BIBLIOGRAPHY

This listing includes sources directly consulted as well as books written about or by the Raiders throughout the years.

Books

Allen, Marcus, with Carlton Stowers. *Marcus: The Autobiography of Marcus Allen.* New York: St. Martin's Press, 1997.

Caffrey, Scott. *Story of the Oakland Raiders.* Mankato, MN: Creative Education, 2009.

Carroll, Bob, Michael Gershman, David Neft, and John Thorn. *Total Football: The Official Encyclopedia of the National Football League.* New York: Harper Collins, 1997.

Cassady, Stephen. *Oakland Raiders: The Good Guys.* Mill Valley, CA: Squarebooks, 1975.

Chadwick, Bruce. *John Madden.* Philadelphia, PA: Chelsea House, 1997.

Chandler, Bob, with Norman Chandler Fox. *Violent Sundays.* New York: Simon & Schuster, 1984.

Clary, Jack C. *Pro Football's Great Moments.* New York: Bonanza Books, 1989.

Coelho, Lisa. *Behind the Numbers: Raiders.* S.I.: Lisa Coelho, 2003.

Dandrea, Joe. *If I Were an Oakland Raider.* Akron, Ohio: Playhouse Publishing, 1996.

Devaney, John. *Super Bowl! Exciting Accounts of Pro Football's Championship Games.* New York, Random House, 1971.

Dickey, Glenn. *Just Win Baby: Al Davis and His Raiders.* New York: Harcourt, 1991.

Etkin, Jack, with Joe Hoppel and Steve Zesch. *Bo Stories.* St. Louis, MO: Sporting News, 1990.

Feinberg, William H. *Ken Stabler.* Mankato, MN: Creative Education, 1978.

Flores, Tom, with Matt Fulks. *Tom Flores' Tales from the Oakland Raiders.* Champaign, IL: Sports Publishing, 2003, 2007.

Frisch, Aaron. *History of the Oakland Raiders.* Mankato, MN: Creative Education, 2005.

_____. *Oakland Raiders.* North Mankato, MN: Creative Education, 2006.

Gaines, Traci. *Die Hard Raiders Fans: Go! Oakland Raiders! Cat! (Meow)!* S.I.: Xlibris Corp, 2007.

Goodman, Michael E. *The Story of the Oakland Raiders.* Mankato, MN: Creative Education, 2009.

Hariri, Shahrooz, and Tom Edell. *Raider Fans Trivia Book: The Most Comprehensive Raiders Trivia Book Ever!* Toronto, Ontario: Post Modern Productions, 2001.

Herskowitz, Mickey. *The Quarterbacks: The Uncensored Truth About the Men in the Pocket.* New York: William Morrow, 1990.

Hession, Joseph. *Raiders: Collector's Edition: Raiders Return to Oakland.* San Francisco: Foghorn, 1996.

Hession, Joseph, and Steve Cassady. *Raiders.* San Francisco: Foghorn Press, 1991, 1994.

_____. *Raiders, from Oakland to Los Angeles.* San Francisco: Foghorn, 1987.

Huizenga, Rob, M.D. *"You're OK, It's Just a Bruise": A Doctor's Sideline Secrets About Pro Football's Most Outrageous Team.* New York: St. Martin's Press, 1994.

Italia, Bob. *Oakland Raiders.* Edina, MN: Abdo & Daughters, 1995.

Jackson, Bo, with Dick Schaap. *Bo Knows Bo.* New York: Doubleday, 1991.

Jackson, David Ferrell. *The History of a War, The Raiders in Oakland (1960–1969): The AFL Years.* Oakland, CA: The Bay Area Sports Journal, 1986.

Kelley, K.C. *Oakland Raiders.* Mankato, MN: Childs World, 2009.

Knapp, Ron. *Sports Great Bo Jackson.* Hillside, NJ: Enslow Publishers, 1990.

Kramer, Jon. *Bo Jackson.* Austin, TX: Raintree, Steck—Vaughn, 1996.

LaMarre, Tom. *Stadium Stories: Oakland Raiders.* Guilford, CT: Globe Pequot Press, 2003.

Leder, Jane Mersky. *Marcus Allen.* Mankato, MN: Crestwood House, 1985.

Libby, Bill. *Ken Stabler: Southpaw Passer.* New York: Putnam, 1977.

Lombardo, John. *Raiders Forever: Stars of the NFL's Most Colorful Team Recall Their Glory Days.* Chicago: Contemporary Books, 2001.

Madden, John. *One Knee Equals Two Feet.* New York: Jove Books, 1987.

Madden, John, with Dave Anderson. *Hey, Wait a Minute (I Wrote a Book).* New York: Ballantine Books, 1984.

Matuszak, John, with Steve Delsohn. *Cruisin' with the Tooz.* New York: Charter Books, 1987.

May, Julian. *Oakland Raiders.* Mankato, MN: Creative Education, 1977.

_____. *Oakland Raiders: Super Bowl Champions.* Mankato, MN: Creative Education, 1977.

McCullough, Jim. *Pride & Poise: The Oakland Raiders of the American Football League.* Bloomington, IN: AuthorHouse, 2006.

Miller, Jim, and Kelly Mayhew. *Better to Reign in Hell.* New York: New Press, 2005.

Neft, David F., with Richard M. Cohen. *The Football Encyclopedia: The Complete History of Professional Football from 1892 to the Present.* New York: St. Martin's Press, 1991.

Nelson, Julie. *Oakland Raiders.* Mankato, MN: Creative Education, 2001.

Newhouse, Dave. *The Ultimate Oakland Raiders Trivia Book.* Rochester, NY: American Sports Media, 2001.

_____. *Super: The Raiders in Their Finest Hour.* Oakland, CA: Oakland Raiders, 1981.

Olderman, Murray. *Super: "Just Win Baby."* El Segundo, CA: The Los Angeles Raiders, 1984.

Oliver, Chip. *High for the Game: From Football Gladiator to Hippie. A Former Southern Cal and Oakland Raiders Linebacker Tells All.* New York: Morrow, 1971.

Otto, Jim, with Dave Newhouse. *Jim Otto: The Pain of Glory.* Champaign, IL: Sports Publishing, 1999.

Parker, Craig, and George Kimball. *Football's Blackest Hole: A Fan's Perspective.* Berkeley, CA: Frog, Ltd., 2003.

Peterson, James A., and Gary L. Miller. *Year of the Raiders.* New York: New American Library, 1984.

Plunkett, Jim, and Dave Newhouse. *The Jim Plunkett Story: The Saga of a Man Who Came Back.* New York: Arbor House, 1981.

Potts, Steve. *Oakland Raiders.* Mankato, MN: Creative Education, 1997.

Ribowsky, Mark. *Slick: The Silver and Black Life of Al Davis.* New York: Macmillan, 1991.

Richmond, Peter. *Badasses: The Legend of Snake, Foo, Dr. Death, and John Madden's Oakland Raiders.* New York: Harper Collins, 2010.

Ryan, Pat. *Los Angeles Raiders.* Mankato, MN: Creative Education, 1991.

Sahadi, Lou. *Domination: The Story of the 1983 World Champion Los Angeles Raiders.* New York: Lou Sahadi, 1984.

_____. *Ken Stabler and the Oakland Raiders.* New York: Scholastic Book Services, 1977.

_____. *The Raiders: Cinderella Champions of Pro Football.* New York: The Dial Press, 1981.

San Francisco Chronicle. *Raiders! Oakland's Spectacular Championship Season.* Chicago, IL: Triumph Books, 2003.

San Jose Mercury News. *A Season of Excellence: Oakland Raiders.* San Jose, CA: San Jose Mercury News, 2003.

Simmons, Ira. *Back Knight: Al Davis and His Raiders.* Rocklin, CA: Prima Publishing, 1990.

Smith, Ron. *Pro Football's Heroes of the Hall.* St. Louis, MO: The Sporting News, 2003.

Stabler, Ken, and Berry Stainback. *Snake.* New York: Doubleday, 1986.

Stabler, Ken, and Tom LaMarre. *Winning Offensive Football.* Chicago, IL: Regnery, 1976.

Stabler, Ken, with Dick O'Connor. *Super Bowl Diary: The Autobiography of Ken "the Snake" Stabler.* Los Angeles: Pinnacle Books, 1977.

Stewart, Mark. *Oakland Raiders.* Chicago, IL: Norwood House Press, 2009.

Svihus, Bob. *Raider: How Offensive Can You Be!! 25 Years of Silver and Black Football.* Newport Beach, CA: Peninsula Publishing, 1987.

Tatum, Jack. *They Still Call Me Assassin.* San Diego, CA: Regal Productions & Publishing, 1989.

Tatum, Jack, with Bill Kushner. *Final Confessions of NFL Assassin Jack Tatum.* Coal Valley, IL: Quality Sports Publications, 1996.

_____. *They Call Me Assassin.* New York: Everest House Publishers, 1980.

Travers, Steven. *The Good, the Bad, and the Ugly Oakland Raiders: Heart-Pounding, Jaw-Dropping, and Gut-Wrenching Moments from Oakland Raiders History.* Chicago: Triumph Books, 2008.

Twombly, Wells. *Blanda, Alive & Kicking: The Exclusive Authorized Biography.* Los Angeles: Nash Publishing, 1972.

_____. *Oakland Raiders: Fireworks and Fury.* Englewood Cliffs, NJ: Prentice-Hall, 1973.

Wagaman, Michael. *Unofficial Oakland Raiders Book of Lists.* Rochester, NY: American Sports Media, 2002.

Wagaman, Michael, and Brian Spindler. *Silver & Black Illustrated's Unofficial Oakland Raiders Book of Lists Vol. 2.* London: ASM Publishing, 2009.

Ward, Don. *Super Bowl II: Green Bay Packers vs. Oakland Raiders, January 14, 1968, Miami Orange Bowl.* Mankato, MN: Creative Education, 1983.

_____. *Super Bowl XI: Oakland Raiders vs. Minnesota Vikings, January 9, 1977, Pasadena Rose Bowl.* Mankato, MN: Creative Education, 1983.

_____. *Super Bowl XV: Oakland Raiders vs. Philadelphia Eagles, January 25, 1981, New Orleans Superdome.* Mankato, MN: Creative Education, 1983.

Newspapers and Periodicals

Chicago Tribune

Cleveland Plain Dealer

Kickoff '97: The Official Magazine of the National Football League

Lindy's Pro Football Preview Magazine

Los Angeles Times

New York Times

Oakland Tribune

Playboy

Sports Illustrated

Super Bowl XXVII Game Program

Media Guides

Los Angeles Raiders: 1982–1994

Oakland Raiders: 1962–1981, 1995–2002, 200

DVD

Raiders: The Complete History

Websites

Bleacher Report, www.bleacherreport.com

Buccaneer Resource, www.bucpower.com

ESPN, www.espn.com

Football Almanac, www.football-almanac.com

Los Angeles Memorial Stadium, www.lacoliseum.com

Los Angeles Times, www.latimes.com

National Football League Stadiums, www.football.ballparks.com

New York Times, www.nytimes.com

NFL, www.nfl.com

Oakland Raiders, www.raiders.com

Oakland Raiders Rap, www.raidersrap.com

OSU Alumni Association, www.osualum.com

Pro Football Reference, www.profootballreference.com

Raider Shack, www.raidershack.com

Raiderdrive, www.raiderdrive.com

SFGate, San Francisco Bay Area, www.sfgate.com

Silver & Black Illustrated, www.silverandblack.com

Sports Illustrated, www.sportsillustrated.cnn.com

USA Today, www.usatoday.com

Wikipedia, www.wikipedia.com

INDEX

Numbers in **bold italics** indicate pages with photographs.

ckerman, Rick 205
dams, Sam 205
dams, Stanley 205
dams, Stefon 205
dkisson, James 205
FL–NFL Merger 19
gajanian, Ben ("Bootin") 11, 205
ikens, Carl 119, 205
lexander, Elijah 205
lexander, Mike 128, 205
llen, Dalva 205
llen, Eric 158, 165, 166, 167, 171, 205
llen, Jackie 205
llen, Marcus 91, 92, 93, **94**, 96, 97, 98, 99, 101, 102, 103, 104, 105, 107, 108, 109, 110, 111, 112, 113, 114, 115, 116, 117, 119, 120, 122, 123, 124, 128, 129, 130, 131, 134, 136, 137, 138, 139, 140, 145, 147, 148, 153, 205, 273
lston, Jon 205
lzado, Lyle 93, 94, 96, 97, 100, 102, 103, **105**, 107, 109, 111, 113, 205, 273–274
mey, Vince 205
nderson, Courtney 185, 189, 190, 191, 205
nderson, Eddie 127, 137, 140, 205
nderson, Marques 205
raguz, Leo 156, 157, 205
rcher, Dan 205
rizona Cardinals 128, 157, 170, 175, 191
rmstrong, Ramon 205
rmstrong, Trace 205
sad, Doug 6, 8, 205
shmore, Darryl 157, 205
ska, Joe 150, 205
somugha, Nnamdi 191, 192, 195, 201, 205, 274
tkins, Larry 206
tkins, Pervis 206
tkinson, George ("Hitman") 29, 30, 31, 34, 36, 38, 40, 45, 47, 49, 54, 57, 62, **65**, 69, 206, 274
tlanta Falcons 41, 55, 76, 92, 113, 124, 133, 144, 153, 165, 186, 198

Badger, Brad 206
Bahr, Chris 78, 79, 80, 81, 82, 83, 84, 85, 87, 88, 89, 91, 92, 93, 96, 97, 98, 99, 100, 102, 103, 104, 105, 107, 108, 109, 111, 112, 113, 114, 115, 116, 117, 118, 119, 120, 121, 122, 123, 124, 125, 206
Baker, Rashad 206

Baldwin, Keith 206
Ball, Eric 206
Ball, Jerry 147, 150, 206
Baltimore Colts 38, 39, 41, 46, 54, 70
Baltimore Ravens 150, 157, 167, 183, 190, 197, 202
Banaszak, Pete 22, 23, 25, 29, 31, 33, 36, 38, 40, 41, 43, 46, 47, 49, 50, 54, 55, 56, 58, 59, 60, 62, 64, 67, 69, 70, 71, 73, 206, 274–275
Banks, Estes 206
Bankston, Warren 46, 47, 54, 59, 60, 206
Bansavage, Al 206
Barbee, Joe 206
Barksdale, Rod 115, 117, 118, 206
Barnes, Jeff 67, 70, 93, 98, 104, 107, 114, 206
Barnes, Khalif 206
Barnes, Larry 5, 6, 7, 206
Barnes, Pat 206
Barnes, Rodrigo 206
Barnwell, Malcolm 87, 94, 97, 99, 103, 107, 108, 206
Barrett, Jan 15, 206
Bartlewski, Rich 206
Barton, Eric 176, 206
Bates, Patrick 206
Beckett, Art 303
Belcher, Kevin 206
Bell, Anthony 206
Bell, Greg 129, 206
Bell, Joe 206
Bell, Nick 133, 136, 138, 139, 206
Belway, Brian 206
Bender, Wes 206
Benson, Duane 206
Benson, Tom 206
Berns, Rick 206
Bess, Rufus 206
Bessillieu, Don 206
Beuerlein, Steve 122, 123, 124, 126, 127, 128, 206
Biekert, Greg 143, 171, 206
Biletnikoff, Fred 17, 19, 20, 22, 23, 24, 25, 27, 29, 30, 31, 33, 34, 36, 37, 38, 40, 41, 42, 43, 46, 47, 49, 50, 51, 52, 54, 55, 58, 59, 60, 61, 62, 64, 65, **66**, 67, 68, 69, 71, 73, 74, 75, 206, 275–276, 285
Bing, Darnell 206
Binns, Harvey 303
Bird, Rodger 20, 22, 26, 206
Birdwell, Dan ("Birdie") 25, 27, 206, 276
Bishop, Sonny 207
Black, Barry 207

Blanda, George 21, 22, 23, 25, 29, 30, 31, 33, 34, 35, 36, 37, 38, 39, 40, 41, 42, 43, 44, 45, 46, 47, 48, 49, 50, 51, 52, 54, 55, 56, 207, 276–277
Blankenship, Greg 207
Blessing, Don 303
Bonness, Rik 207
Boothe, Kevin 207
Boston Patriots 6, 8, 9, 10, 11, 12, 14, 15, 17, 20, 22, 29, 33
Bowie, John 207
Boyd, Greg 207
Boyd, Jerome 207
Boydston, Max 207
Boynton, George 207
Brabham, Cary 207
Bracelin, Greg 207
Bradshaw, Morris 54, 55, 59, 63, 73, 74, 79, 87, 88, 207
Branch, Calvin 207
Branch, Cliff 43, 49, 50, 51, 52, 54, 55, 56, 58, 59, 60, 61, 63, 64, 67, 68, 69, 70, 71, 73, 74, 76, 77, 78, 79, 80, 81, 83, 84, 85, 92, 93, 96, 98, 99, 102, 104, 207, 277
Branch, Tyvon 207
Branton, Gene 207
Bravo, Alex 207
Brayton, Tyler 207
Breech, Jim 76, 77, 207
Brewington, Jim 207
Brigham, Jeremy 166, 167, 171, 207
Bromell, Lorenzo 207
Brooks, Aaron 190, 191, 192, 207
Brooks, Bobby 207
Brooks, Bucky 207
Broughton, Willie 207
Brown, Bob ("Boomer") 207, 278
Brown, Charles 207
Brown, Darrick 207
Brown, Derek 207
Brown, Doug 207
Brown, Larry 207
Brown, Ricky 207
Brown, Ron 207
Brown, Tim 122, 124, 125, 131, 133, 134, 136, 137, 138, 139, 140, 141, **142**, 143, 144, 145, 147, 148, 149, 150, 151, 153, 154, 155, 156, 157, 158, 160, 161, 162, 163, 164, 165, 166, 168, 169, 170, 171, 173, 174, 175, 177, 178, 181, 182, 184, 207, 278–279
Brown, Willie 22, 23, 26, 27, 29, 31, 33, 38, 47, 48, 49, **50**, 54, 64, 65, 67, 68, 69, 207, 279–280

Browne, Jim 207
Browner, Keith 207
Browning, Dave 83, 207
Bruce, Aundray 143, 149, 208
Brunson, Larry 76, 208
Bryant, Desmond 208
Bryant, Tony 160, 167, 208
Bryant, Warren 208
Buchanan, Ray 208
Buchanan, Phillip 173, 181, 182, 183, 184, 208
Buchanon, Will 208
Buczowski, Bob 208
Budness, Bill 30, 208
Buehler, George 62, 63, 208
Buffalo Bills 6, 8, 9, 10, 11, 12, 15, 16, 17, 20, 22, 23, 29, 30, 33, 43, 49, 69, 79, 97, 120, 125, 130, 131, 134, 140, 142, 158, 160, 173, 184, 188, 197
Bugel, Joe 153, 155, 243
Buie, Drew 41, 208
Bunch, Jarrad 208
Burch, Gerald 9, 208
Burgess, Derrick 191, 208
Burton, Ron 208
Bush, Michael 197, 198, 199, 200, 201, 202, 208
Butcher, Paul 208
Byrd, Darryl 208

Cable, Tom 197, 200, 201, 250
Caldwell, Tony 208
Calhoun, Rick 119, 208
Callahan, Bill 172, 182, 183, 246–247
Camarillo, Rich 208
Campbell, Joe 208
Campbell, Stan 208
Candlestick Park 306
Cannavino, Joe 208
Cannon, Billy 15, 16, 20, 22, 23, 26, 27, 29, 30, 32, 33, 34, 208, 280
Carlisle, Cooper 208
Carolina Panthers 154, 166, 185, 198
Carr, Chetti 208
Carr, Chris 191, 208
Carrington, Darren 208
Carroll, Joe 208
Carter, Louis 208
Carter, Perry 208
Carter, Russell 208
Cash, Kerry 148, 208
Casper, Dave ("Ghost") 49, 50, 54, 56, 57, 58, 59, 60, 61, 62, 63, 67, 68, **69**, 70, 71, 72, 73, 74, 76, 77, 79, 80, 109, 208, 280–281

Cavalli, Carmen 208
Celotto, Mario 208
Chandler, Bob 78, 79, 80, 81, 84, 85, 87, 88, 89, 208
Chapman, Ted 208
Charles, Mike 208
Cheerleaders see Raiderettes
Chester, Raymond 36, 37, 38, 40, 41, 42, 43, 74, 75, 76, 77, 78, 79, 80, 81, 85, 87, 208–209
Chicago Bears 43, 59, 73, 108, 120, 129, 140, 150, 160, 181, 195
Christensen, Todd 79, 81, 87, 88, 91, 92, 93, 96, 97, 98, 101, 102, 103, 107, 108, 109, 111, 112, 113, 114, 115, 116, 117, 118, 119, 209, 281–282
Christenson, Brandon 209
Churchwell, Don 209
Cincinnati Bengals 29, 30, 33, 34, 36, 40, 43, 49, 54, 55, 59, 74, 79, 92, 96, 113, 123, 127, 131, 134, 136, 140, 148, 157, 181, 192, 201
Clark, Danny 209
Clay, John 209
Clemons, Chris 209
Cleveland Browns 37, 40, 46, 49, 54, 67, 77, 81, 93, 112, 117, 120, 136, 139, 163, 181, 189, 190, 194, 202
Cline, Tony 44, 209
Coleman, Kenyon 209
Coleman, Rod 167, 176, 209
Collins, Kerry 184, 185, 186, 187, 188, 189, 209
Collins, Mo 162, 209
Collons, Ferric 209
Colzie, Neal 54, 55, 62, 63, 69, 73, 74, 209
Combs, Derek 209
Condo, Jon 209
Conkright, William ("Red") 10, 11, 229
Conners, Dan 20, 22, 23, 25, 31, 34, 35, 40, 41, 209
Conway, Brett 165, 209
Coolbaugh, Bob 8, 9, 209
Cooper, Chris 182, 209
Cooper, Earl 209
Cooper, Jarrod 209
Cooper, Marquis 209, 301
Copeland, Horace 209
Cormier, Joe 209
Costa, Dave 209
Costello, Joe 209
Craig, Dobie 10, 11, 13, 209
Craig, Roger 133, 134, 209
Crockett, Zack 160, 161, 162, 163, 165, 169, 170, 171, 173, 175, 176, 181, 182, 183, 186, 188, 209
Crow, Wayne 8, 11, 209
Crudup, Derrick 209
Culpepper, Daunte 194, 195, 209
Cunningham, Rick 151, 209
Curry, Ronald 184, 185, 186, 192, 193, 194, 195, 197, 209

Dalby, Dave 103, 113, 209, 282
Dallas Cowboys 50, 80, 97, 117, 137, 148, 156, 169, 188, 201
Dallas Texans 5, 6, 8, 9, 10, 11
Daluiso, Brad 171, 209
Daniels, Clem 9, 10, 11, 12, 13, 14, 15, 16, 17, 18, 19, 20, 21, 22, 209, 282–283
Daniels, David 209
Davidson, Ben 34, 37, 40, 209–210, 283
Davidson, Cotton 10, 11, 12, 13, 14, 15, 16, 19, 20, 210

Davis, Al 12, 17, 18, 65, 80, 82, 85, 86, 105, 120, 137, 147, 189, 197, 201, 229–233, 230, 235–237, 239, 240, 241, 242, 243, 244, 245, 247, 248, 249, 250, 273, 282, 283, 288, 293, 296, 298, 303, 304, 306, 307
Davis, Bruce 102, 210
Davis, Clarence 40, 42, 43, 45, 46, 47, 49, 51, 52, 54, 55, 56, 59, 60, 61, 62, 63, 64, 67, 68, 69, 70, 210, 283
Davis, Greg 156, 157, 158, 210
Davis, James 92, 210
Davis, Jason 210
Davis, Mike 74, 77, 80, 81, 84, 85, 87, 92, 93, 99, 104, 107, 113, 210
Davis, Scott 126, 130, 131, 134, 210
Davison, Jerone 210
Dennery, Mike 210
Denver Broncos 5, 7, 8, 10, 13, 15, 18, 20, 21, 29, 30, 31, 33, 34, 36, 37, 40, 41, 43, 46, 47, 50, 54, 55, 58, 67, 68, 71, 73, 74, 76, 77, 80, 87, 88, 92, 96, 97, 107, 108, 113, 115, 116, 119, 120, 122, 124, 126, 128, 129, 130, 133, 134, 136, 137, 139, 141, 143, 145, 148, 149, 151, 154, 156, 158, 160, 161, 163, 165, 169, 171, 174, 175, 181, 182, 185, 188, 189, 190, 191, 192, 194, 195, 197, 198, 200, 202
DePoyster, Jerry 210
Deskins, Don 210
Detroit Lions 37, 50, 74, 87, 109, 119, 130, 182, 193
Dickerson, Andy 210
Dickerson, Eric 136, 137, 210
Dickey, Eldridge 40, 210
Dickinson, Bo 210
Diehl, John 210
DiNapoli, Gennaro 210
Dittrich, John 210
Dixon, Ernest 210
Dixon, Hewritt 19, 20, 21, 22, 23, 24, 25, 26, 27, 29, 31, 32, 33, 34, 36, 37, 210, 283–284
Dixon, John 210
Dixon, Rickey 210
Dorn, Torin 210
Dorsett, Anthony 164, 169, 182, 210
Dorsey, Dick 11, 210
Dotson, Al 210
Dougherty, Bob 210
Dreisbach, Scott 210
Dudley, Rickey 150, 151, 153, 154, 155, 156, 157, 158, 160, 161, 162, 165, 166, 210
Dufault, Paul 210
Duff, John 210
Dunn, David 164, 169, 170, 210
Dwight, Tim 195, 210
Dyal, Mike 127, 128, 210
Dyson, Matt 210

Eason, John 210
Easy, Omar 210
Echemandu, Adimchinobe 210
Edmonds, Bobby Joe 210
Edwards, Kalimba 210
Edwards, Lloyd 210
Eischeid, Mike 19, 20, 25, 26, 27, 38, 210
Ekejiuba, Isaiah 210–211
Ellis, Craig 119, 211
Ellis, Greg 211
Ellis, Jim 211
Ellison, Glen 211

Ellison, Riki 211
Enis, Hunter 11
Enyart, Bill 211
Erdelatz, Eddie 5, 8, 227–228
Eugene, Hiram 211
Evans, Vince 119, 133, 138, 139, 144, 145, 147, 148, 149, 211

Fairband, Bill 211
Fargas, Justin 181, 182, 185, 192, 194, 195, 197, 198, 200, 201, 202, 211
Feldman, Marty 8, 10, 228–229
Fellows, Ron 211
Fenner, Derrick 147, 149, 150, 151, 152, 211
Fernandez, Mervyn 123, 124, 125, 126, 127, 128, 129, 130, 131, 132, 133, 211
Ficca, Dan 211
Fields, George 211
Finneran, Garry 211
FitzPatrick, James 134, 211
Fleming, George 8, 9, 211
Flemister, Zeron 211
Flores, Tom ("Iceman") 5, 6, 7, 8, 9, 12, 13, 14, 15, 16, 17, 18, 19, 20, 21, 75, 88, 97, 98, 105, 108, 111, 117, 120, 121, 136, 137, 139, 143, 211, 230, 237–238, 284
Folston, James 211
Ford, Cole 147, 150, 151, 152, 153, 154, 155, 211
Foschi, John Paul 211
Foster, Ron 211
Francis, Carlos 211
Frank, Donald 211
Frank Youell Field 306
Franklin, Keith 211
Franks, Elvis 211
Fredrickson, Rob 147, 211
Freeman, Mike 211
Freeman, Russell 211
Frye, Charlie 202, 211
Fulcher, David 211
Fulcher, Mondriel 211
Fuller, Charles 8, 211

Gabriel, Doug 183, 184, 186, 188, 189, 211
Gainer, Derrick 211
Gallegos, Chon 10, 211
Gallery, Robert 211
Gamache, Vince 211
Gannon, Rich 159, 160, 161, 162, 163, 164, 165, 166, 167, 168, 169, 170, 171, 173, 174, 175, 176, 177, 178, 179, 180, 181, 182, 184, 212, 284–285
Garner, Bob 8, 11, 212
Garner, Charlie 168, 169, 170, 171, 173, 174, 175, 176, 177, 178, 179, 180, 181, 182, 183, 212
Garrett, Carl 59, 61, 62, 63, 64, 69, 70, 212
Gault, Willie 122, 123, 125, 126, 127, 128, 130, 131, 132, 133, 134, 136, 137, 138, 212
Gbaja-Biamila, Akbar 212
George, Jeff 153, 154, 155, 156, 157, 158, 212
Gesek, John 212
Ghost to the Post 71
Gibson, Claude 13, 17, 212
Gibson, Derrick 212
Gilbert, Sean 212
Gillett, Fred 212
Gillman, Sid 231
Ginn, Hubie 60, 62, 65, 212

Gipson, Tom 212
Glover, Andrew 133, 134, 137, 139, 143, 144, 147, 151, 212
Glover, La'Roi 212
Gogan, Kevin 212
Goldstein, Alan 6, 212
Golic, Bob 212
Golsteyn, Jerry 212
Goltz, Rick 212
Goodlow, Darryl 212
Gordon, Alex 212
Gordon, Darrien 161, 166, 212
Gossett, Jeff 130, 212
Graddy, Sam 131, 133, 136, 212
Gradkowski, Bruce 201, 212
Graham, Aaron 212
Graham, Derrick 212
Graham, Jeff 212
Grant, DeLawrence 212
Graves, Rory 212
Grayson, Dave 17, 18, 19, 20, 22, 27, 29, 31, 33, 34, 37, 212
Green, Charley 212
Green, Cornell 212
Green Bay Packers 24, 42, 58, 73, 107, 119, 130, 141, 159, 183, 195
Greenwood, David 212
Griffith, Justin 193, 197, 212
Grimes, Phil 212
Grossart, Kyle 212
Grove, Jake 212
Gruden, Jon 156, 161, 163, 164, 169, 170, 172, 176, 177, 179, 184, 244–246, 245, 284
Gunheim, Greyson 212–213
Guy, Louie 213
Guy, Ray 48, 56, 62, 63, 64, 65, 68, 70, 71, 81, 83, 84, 85, 101, 102, 103, 104, 105, 110, 112, 213, 285

Hagberg, Roger 17, 19, 22, 23, 29, 33, 213, 301
Hall, DeAngelo 213
Hall, Tim 213, 301
Hall, Willie 58, 60, 62, 63, 64, 69, 213
Hamilton, Bobby 213
Hannah, Charley 102, 124, 213
Harden, Mike 116, 213
Hardman, Cedrick 87, 213
Hardy, Charles 6, 7, 8, 213
Hardy, David 213
Harkey, Lance 213
Harlow, Pat 213
Harney, Charles 303
Harris, James 213
Harris, John 213
Harris, Johnnie 167, 213
Harris, Kwame 213
Harris, Napoleon 213
Harrison, Dwight 213
Harrison, Nolan 136, 213
Harrison, Rob 213
Hart, Harold 50, 52, 54, 55, 213
Hart, Roy 213
Harvey, James 213
Harvey, Richard 213
Hasselbeck, Don 97, 103, 213
Hasty, James 213
Hawkins, Clarence 76, 213
Hawkins, Frank 92, 93, 96, 97, 98, 99, 102, 103, 104, 107, 108, 111, 112, 113, 114, 213
Hawkins, Mike 213
Hawkins, Wayne 213, 285
Hawthorne, Anttaj 213
Hayes, Lester 67, 70, 75, 76, 77, 79, 80, 81, 83, 84, 85, 92, 98, 99, 101,

102, 103, 105, 107, 110, 111, *112*, 117, 213, 285–286
Haynes, Mike 101, 102, 105, 107, 109, *112*, 137, 213, 286
Heidi Game 30
Heinrich, Don 10, 213
Henderson, Mario 213
Hendricks, Ted ("the Mad Stork"; "Kick 'em") 54, 55, 56, 59, 63, 64, 65, *68*, 70, 76, 77, 79, 81, 83, 84, 88, *93*, 95, 96, 213, 236, 286–287
Hermann, Dick 213
Herock, Ken 12, 13, 15, 213
Hester, Jessie 112, 113, 114, 116, 117, 213–214
Hetherington, Chris 214
Heyward-Bey, Darrius 201, 214
Higgins, Johnnie Lee 197, 198, 214
Highsmith, Don 40, 42, 214
Hilger, Rusty 111, 118, 119, 120, 214
Hill, Greg 214
Hill, Kenny 102, 214
Hill, Madre 214
Hill, Renaldo 214
Hill, Rod 214
Hinton, Marcus 214
Hipp, I.M. 214
Hobbs, Daryl 147, 149, 150, 151, 214
Hobert, Billy Joe 148, 149, 150, 214
Hoisington, Al 6, 214
Holland, Jamie 214
Holland, Jonathan 214
Hollas, Donald 156, 157, 158, 214
Holloway, Brian 214
Holmberg, Rob 214
Holmes, Lester 214
Holy Roller Game 73
Hopkins, Jerry 31, 214
Horton, Ethan 119, 128, 130, 131, 133, 134, 137, 140, 141, 214
Hoskins, Derrick 214
Hostetler, Jeff 139, 140, 141, 142, 143, 144, 145, 147, 148, 149, 150, 151, 214
Houston Oilers 5, 7, 8, 9, 10, 11, 12, 13, 14, 15, 17, 19, 20, 23, 29, 33, 34, 41, 42, 47, 55, 58, 68, 73, 77, 80, 88, 96, 107, 116, 122, 127, 133, 144
Houston Texans 184, 192, 194, 198, 200
Howard, Desmond 157, 158, 214
Howard, Thomas 194, 214
Hoying, Bobby 160, 167, 214
Hubbard, Marv 34, 37, 40, 41, 42, 43, 45, 46, 47, 48, 49, 50, 51, 52, 54, 55, 56, 214, 287–288
Huddleston, John 214
Hudson, Bob 214
Huff, Michael 191, 214
Hulsey, Corey 214
Humm, David 54, 55, 97, 108, 214
Hunley, Ricky 214
Huntley, Kevin 214
Husted, Michael 151, 159, 160, 161, 214

Immaculate Reception Game 44
Indianapolis Colts 109, 118, 133, 148, 163, 169, 185, 195
Ioane, Junior 214
Irons, Gerald 214
Irons, Grant 214
Ismail, Raghib ("Rocket") 139, 143, 144, 148, 214

Jackson, Bo 119, 120, 123, 124, 127, 128, 130, 131, 154, 214, 288

Jackson, Bobby 215
Jackson, Grady 215
Jackson, Leonard 215
Jackson, Monte 215
Jackson, Richard 215
Jackson, Steve 215
Jackson, Victor 215
Jacksonville Jaguars 150, 155, 186, 195
Jacobs, Proverb 215
Jaeger, Jeff 126, 127, 128, 129, 130, 131, 132, 133, 134, 136, 137, 138, 139, 140, 141, 142, 143, 144, 145, 147, 148, 149, 150, 215
Jagielski, Harry 215
Jakowenko, George 215
James, Tory 163, 166, 176, 179, 215
Janikowski, Sebastian ("Sea Bass") 163, 164, 165, 166, 167, 168, 169, 170, 171, 173, 174, 175, 176, 177, 180, 181, 182, 183, 184, 185, 186, 188, 189, 190, 191, 192, 194, 195, 197, 198, 200, 201, 202, 215, 288
Jasper, Ed 215
Jelacic, Jon 12, 13, 215
Jenkins, Robert 215
Jenkins, Ronney 215
Jennings, Brandon 215
Jennings, Rick 215
Jensen, Derrick 76, 80, 85, 86, 87, 88, 89, 97, 102, 107, 108, 215
Jensen, Russell 215
Jett, James 139, 140, 141, 148, 149, 151, 153, 154, 155, 156, 157, 158, 159, 164, 165, 166, 171, 215
Jimerson, A.J. 215
Johnson, Chris 215
Johnson, Eric 177, 178, 215
Johnson, Kevin 215
Johnson, Monte 57, 63, 64, 65, 68, 76, 215
Johnson, Rob 215
Johnson, Teyo 182, 185, 186, 215
Johnson, Tim 178, 215
Johnston, Mark 215
Johnstone, Lance 151, 157, 161, 162, 215
Jolley, Doug 174, 175, 176, 177, 178, 179, 181, 185, 215
Jones, Calvin 215
Jones, David 215
Jones, Horace 44, 215
Jones, Jim 215
Jones, Mike 147, 215
Jones, Sean 113, 215
Jones, Willie 78, 85, 86, 88, 215
Jordan, Charles 215
Jordan, LaMont 188, 189, 190, 191, 193, 194, 195, 215–216
Jordan, Randy 158, 159, 163, 165, 166, 173, 216
Jordan, Shelby 216
Joseph, William 216
Joyner, L.C. 216
Junkin, Trey 113, 123, 124, 126, 128, 216

Kansas City Chiefs 13, 14, 15, 17, 19, 22, 23, 29, 31, 34, 35, 37, 40, 43, 45, 47, 49, 50, 54, 55, 58, 59, 67, 70, 73, 74, 76, 77, 78, 79, 88, 92, 96, 97, 107, 108, 111, 116, 117, 119, 120, 123, 124, 126, 127, 130, 133, 134, 136, 137, 139, 140, 144, 145, 147, 148, 150, 151, 153, 155, 156, 158, 161, 162, 164, 165, 168, 170, 174, 175, 182, 185, 186, 187, 188, 191, 194, 195, 197, 198, 200, 201
Kaufman, Napoleon 147, 148, 151,

153, 154, 155, 156, 157, 158, 161, 162, 164, 216, 289
Keating, Tom 20, 25, 27, 34, 216
Kelly, Joe 216
Kelly, Tommy 194, 216
Kennedy, Lincoln 156, 162, 216
Kent, Greg 216
Keyes, Bob 216
Kezar Stadium 305–306
Kidd, Carl 216
Kiffin, Lane 193, 194, 197, 248–250
Kimmel, Jamie 216
King, Emanuel 216
King, Joe 216
King, Kenny 79, 81, 82, 83, 84, 85, 88, 89, 92, 96, 98, 101, 103, 216
King, Linden 126, 216
King, Wilbur ("Bill") 305
Kinlaw, Reggie 84, 87, 101, 102, 103, 216
Kirby, Terry 167, 170, 173, 216
Klein, Dick 216
Klinger, David 216
Knight, Marcus 178, 179, 216
Koch, Pete 216
Kocourek, Dave 23, 25, 29, 216
Koegel, Warren 216
Kohn, Tim 216
Korver, Kelvin 216
Kowalczyk, Walt 216
Koy, Ted 216
Krakoski, Joe 13, 216
Kruse, Bob 216
Kunz, Terry 216
Kwalick, Ted 216
Kysar, Jeff 216

Lachey, Jim 216
Lamonica, Daryle ("the Mad Bomber") 21, 22, 23, *24*, 25, 26, 27, 29, 30, 31, 32, 33, 34, 35, 36, 37, 38, 40, 41, 42, 43, 44, 45, 46, 50, 216, 289
Land, Dan 136, 216
Lanier, Ken 216
Larschied, Jack 6, 216
Larson, Paul 216
Laskey, Bill 37, 217
Lassiter, Isaac 17, 34, 217
Lathan, Greg 217
Lawrence, Henry ("Killer") 70, 84, 217
Lawrence, Larry 50, 217
Lawton, Luke 217
Lechler, Shane 165, 177, 178, 217
Lee, ReShard 191, 192, 217
Lee, Zeph 122, 217
Lekkerkerker, Brad 217
Lelie, Ashley 197, 198, 217
Levitt, Chad 217
Lewis, Albert 157, 217
Lewis, Bill 122, 123, 217
Lewis, Garry 217
Lewis, Harold 217
Lewis, Tahaun 217
Liles, Alva 217
Lloyd, Doug 217
LoCasale, Al 304–305
Lockett, Wade 217
Locklin, Billy Ray 217
Lofton, James 120, 124, 217
Long, Howie 92, 96, 98, 101, 102, 103, 109, 113, 114, 117, 122, *123*, 126, 217, 289–290
Los Angeles Chargers 6
Los Angeles Memorial Coliseum 307
Los Angeles Rams 43, 69, 75, 92, 113, 122, 133, 144

Losman, J.P. 217
Lott, Billy 5, 6, 7, 9, 217
Lott, Ronnie 134, 137, 217
Louderback, Tom 7, 9, 217
Love, Clarence 217
Lynch, Lorenzo 217
Lyons, Lamar 217

MacKinnon, Jacque 217
Macon, Ed 5, 6, 217
Madden, John 33, 34, 50, 51, 59, 63, 65, 71, 74, 191, 234–237, *235*, 275, 288, 291, 293, 298
Madsen, John 192, 195, 217
Mann, Errol 58, 59, 60, 62, 63, 64, 65, 67, 68, 70, 71, 72, 73, 74, 75, 217
Manoukian, Don 217
Marinovich, Marv 217
Marinovich, Todd 134, 136, 137, 217, 290–291
Marsh, Curt 217
Marten, James 217
Martin, Rod 79, 83, 84, 85, 86, 92, 97, 98, 102, 103, 104, 108, 109, 114, 217, 291–292
Martin, Tee 217
Martini, Rich 76, 217
Marvin, Mickey 84, 103, 218
Maryland, Russell 159, 160, 218
Mason, Lindsey 218
Matsos, Arch 13, 15, 218
Matthews, Ira 76, 83, 84, 85, 218
Matuszak, John ("the Tooz") 65, *82*, 84, 218, 292–293
Maxwell, Tom 218
Mayberry, Doug 218
McCall, Joe 218
McCallum, Napoleon 115, 116, 117, 134, 140, 141, 142, 143, 218
McClanahan, Randy 67, 218
McCloughan, Kent 20, 25, 218
McColl, Milt 218
McCown, Josh 193, 194, 195, 218
McCoy, Larry 218
McCoy, Mike 71, 218
McDaniel, Terry 122, 129, 137, 139, 143, 144, 147, 148, 151, 218
McElroy, Reggie 218
McElroy, Vann 96, 99, 102, 107, 113, 117, 119, 122, 123, 126, 218
McFadden, Darren 197, 198, 200, 218
McFarlan, Nyle 7, 218
McFoy, Chris 218
McGah, Ed 96, 231, 232, 233, 303
McGlockton, Chester 143, 148, 218
McKenzie, Reggie 218
McKinney, Odis 81, 84, 92, 99, 110, 218
McLemore, Chris 218
McMath, Herb 218
McMillen, Dan 218
McMillin, Jim 12, 218
McMurtry, Chuck 218
McQuistan, Paul 218
McRae, Charles 218
Medlin, Dan 218
Mendenhall, Terry 218
Mercer, Mike 12, 13, 14, 15, 16, 17, 18, 19, 218
Merrill, Mark 218
Miami Dolphins 19, 29, 33, 36, 38, 45, 47, 48, 51, 53, 54, 74, 76, 79, 88, 96, 109, 116, 123, 130, 137, 144, 151, 155, 158, 160, 166, 169, 175, 189, 194, 198
Mickell, Darren 218

Mickens, Terry 158, 218
Middleton, Frank 218
Millen, Matt 84, 85, 92, *99*, 100, 102, 103, 109, 114, 218, 293
Miller, Alan 8, 9, 10, 12, 13, 17, 18, 218–219
Miller, Bill 22, 23, 25, 26, 29, 219
Miller, Derek 219
Miller, Justin 198, 219
Miller, Nick 219
Miller, Zach 194, 195, 197, 200, 201, 219
Mills, John Henry 219
Mincy, Charles 161, 219
Mingo, Gene 16, 17, 219
Minnesota Vikings 45, 61, 69, 74, 87, 108, 120, 131, 139, 151, 159, 182, 195
Miraldi, Dean 219
Mirer, Rick 182, 183, 219
Mirich, Rex 219
Mischak, Bob 219
Mitchell, Mike 219
Mitchell, Tom 19, 219
Mix, Ron 219
Moffett, Tim 219
Montalbo, Mel 219
Montez, Alfred 219
Montgomery, Cle 109, 219
Montgomery, Tyrone 219
Montoya, Max 219
Moody, Keith 219
Moore, Bob 42, 46, 47, 49, 50, 51, 55, 56, 219
Moore, Manfred 219
Morant, Johnnie 219
Morris, Chris 219
Morris, Riley 7, 9, 219
Morrison, Dave 219
Morrison, Kirk 192, 219
Morrow, Tom 12, 219
Morton, Mike 219
Mosebar, Don 122, 126, 219
Moss, Randy 187, 188, 189, 190, 191, 219
Moss, Winston 219
Mostardi, Rich 219
Move to Los Angeles (1982–1995) 90–91
Move to Oakland (1995) 146–147
Mraz, Mark 219
Mueller, Vance 119, 126, 127, 219
Muhammad, Calvin 92, 96, 219
Muirbrook, Shay 219
Muransky, Ed 219
Murdock, Jesse 220
Murphy, Louis 200, 201, 220
Mustafaa, Najee 220
Myers, Brandon 201, 220
Myles, Toby 220

Nash, Keyon 220
Nedney, Joe 161, 162, 220
Nelson, Bob 87, 103, 104, 220
New England Patriots 40, 50, 58, 59, 73, 88, 111, 114, 119, 127, 143, 175, 187, 198
New Orleans Saints 41, 54, 77, 111, 123, 134, 144, 154, 165, 185, 197
New York Giants 46, 80, 97, 116, 128, 136, 148, 156, 170, 189, 200
New York Jets 12, 13, 15, 17, 18, 20, 22, 23, 30, 31, 32, 34, 37, 43, 68, 76, 94, 111, 127, 139, 147, 150, 153, 160, 166, 171, 175, 176, 182, 189, 192, 197, 200
New York Titans 6, 8, 10
Newberry, Jeremy 220

Newman, Anthony 158, 161, 220
Nicklas, Pete 220
Nixon, David 220
Noble, Mike 220
Norris, Jim 220
Norris, Slade 220
Novsek, Joe 220

Oakland-Alameda County Stadium 306–307
Oates, Carleton 23, 34, 35, 220
Ogas, Dave 220
Ogleby, Paul 220
Oliver, Ralph ("Chip") 34, 220, 293
O'Neal, Oren 220
Osborne, Chuck 220
Osborne, Robert 303
Osbourne, Clancy 220
O'Steen, Dwayne 86, 220
Otto, Gus 17, 18, 34, 220
Otto, Jim *46*, 220, 293–294
Owens, Burgess 80, 84, 87, 92, 95, 220

Palmer, Jonathon 220
Papac, Nick 9, 220
Parilli, Babe 5, 6, 7, 9, 10, 12, 220
Parker, Andy 220
Parks, Nate 220
Parrella, John 220
Pastorini, Dan 78, 79, 220
Patten, Joel 220
Patterson, Elvis 119, 134, 137, 220
Pattison, Mark 220
Pear, Dave 220
Pears, Erik 220
Peat, Todd 220
Peete, Rodney 220
Perry, Gerald 221
Perry, Mario 119, 221
Perryman, Raymond 221
Peters, Volney 221
Peterson, Calvin 221
Philadelphia Eagles 40, 59, 80, 82, 83, 117, 127, 137, 147, 169, 188, 200
Phillips, Charles 55, 67, 69, 73, 74, 75, 221
Phillips, Irvin 221
Phillips, Jess 54, 221
Philyaw, Charles 62, 69, 221
Pickel, Bill 96, 102, 104, 108, 109, 116, 117, 124, 221
Pickens, Bruce 221
Pierson, Shurron 221
Pitts, Frank 52, 221
Pittsburgh Steelers 36, 42, 43, 46, 47, 49, 52, 56, 57, 58, 60, 67, 79, 89, 98, 109, 129, 144, 149, 165, 173, 183, 184, 191, 201
Playoff appearances (Raiders) 23–28, 31–32, 34–35, 38–39, 43–44, 47–48, 51–53, 55–56, 59–66, 70–71, 80–86, 93–95, 98–106, 109–110, 114, 131–132, 135, 141–142, 166–167, 171, 176–179
Plunkett, Jim ("Plunk") 76, 78, 79, 80, 81, 82, 83, 84, 85, 86, 87, 88, 91, 92, 93, 94, 95, 96, 97, 98, 99, 100, *101*, 102, 103, 104, 107, 108, 109, 110, 111, 116, 117, 118, 221, 294–295
Poole, Tyrone 221
Pope, Marquez 165, 166, 167, 221
Porter, Jerry 173, 174, 175, 176, 178, 182, 185, 186, 188, 189, 194, 195, 221
Porter, Kerry 221
Powell, Art 12, 13, 14, 15, 16, 17, 18, 19, 20, 21, 107, 221, 296

Powell, Charlie 221
Powers, Warren 16, 20, 22, 23, 25, 221
Prebola, Gene 5, 6, 221
Price, Dennis 221
Prior, Anthony 221
Prout, Bob 221
Pruitt, Greg 92, 93, 96, 100, 102, 103, 221
Pyle, Palmer 221
Pyles, David 221

Queen, Jeff 221

Rae, Mike 58, 59, 61, 65, 69, 70, 221
Raiderettes ("Football's Fabulous Females") *141*, *187*, 308–309, *308*
Ramsey, Derrick 76, 77, 88, 89, 221
Rankin, Louis 221
Rathman, Tom 221
Rauch, John 19, 233–234
Ray, Marcus 221
Redmond, J.R. 221
Reece, Marcel 221
Reese, Archie 92, 221
Regent, Shawn 221
Reinfeldt, Mike 221
Reynolds, Billy 221
Reynolds, M.C. 221–222
Rhodes, Dominic 195, 222
Rice, Floyd 63, 222
Rice, Harold 222
Rice, Jerry 143, 168, 169, 170, 171, 173, 174, 175, 176, 178, 179, 181, 182, 183, 184, 222
Rice, Ken 222
Rich, Randy 222
Richardson, Jay 198, 222
Riddick, Louis 222
Riddle, Ryan 222
Ridlehuber, Preston 30, 222
Riehm, Chris 222
Rieves, Charles 222
Rison, Andre ("Bad Moon") 163, 164, 165, 166, 167, 222
Ritchie, Jon 157, 161, 169, 174, 178, 222
Rivera, Hank 222
Rivers, David 222
Robbins, Austin 147, 222
Robbins, Barret 150, 182, 222, 296
Roberson, Bo 10, 12, 13, 15, 222
Roberts, Cliff 222
Robinson, Greg 139, 140, 222
Robinson, Jerry 117, 118, 123, 129, 222
Robinson, Johnny 222
Robiskie, Terry 68, 73, 222
Roderick, John 222
Rodriguez, Mike 222
Roedel, Herb 222
Romano, Jim 222
Romanowski, Bill 182, 222
Rosensteil, Bob 222
Rother, Tim 222
Routt, Stanford 202, 222
Rowe, Dave 58, 64, 65, 222
Rozelle, Pete 82, 85, 86, *230*
Rubke, Karl 222
Russell, Booker 76, 77, 222
Russell, Darrell 163, 222, 301–302
Russell, Gary 222
Russell, JaMarcus 195, 197, 198, 200, 201, 202, 222

Sabal, Ron 222
St. Louis Cardinals 45, 98

St. Louis Rams 153, 173, 192
San Diego Chargers 8, 10, 11, 13, 15, 16, 17, 18, 19, 20, 21, 22, 23, 29, 31, 33, 34, 36, 37, 40, 41, 42, 43, 46, 47, 49, 50, 54, 58, 59, 67, 69, 73, 74, 76, 78, 79, 81, 88, 89, 92, 93, 97, 98, 107, 108, 112, 113, 116, 117, 119, 120, 122, 124, 126, 127, 130, 131, 133, 134, 137, 140, 143, 144, 147, 148, 150, 151, 154, 157, 158, 161, 163, 164, 170, 174, 175, 181, 183, 185, 188, 189, 190, 192, 194, 195, 197, 198, 199, 201
Sands, Terdell 222
San Francisco 49ers 37, 49, 76, 91, 111, 124, 133, 143, 164, 174, 190
Santiago, O.J. 222
Sapp, Warren 192, 195, 222–223
Satele, Samson 223
Schilens, Chaz 198, 201, 202, 223
Schmautz, Ray 223
Schroeder, Jay 122, 123, 124, 125, 126, 127, 129, 130, 131, 132, 133, 134, 136, 137, 138, 223
Schuening, Roy 223
Schuh, Harry 38, 223
Schweigert, Stuart 223
Scott, Carey 223
Scott, Trevor 223
Sea of Hands Game 52
Seale, Sam 111, 114, 223
Seattle Seahawks 68, 73, 74, 76, 77, 79, 87, 88, 92, 96, 97, 98, 99, 107, 108, 109, 112, 113, 116, 117, 119, 120, 124, 125, 126, 128, 129, 130, 133, 134, 136, 137, 139, 140, 143, 145, 147, 149, 150, 151, 154, 155, 157, 160, 161, 164, 167, 169, 170, 172, 191
Seller, Paul 223
Seymour, Richard 223
Shabazz, Siddeeq 223
Shanahan, Mike 123, 126, 160, 182, 194, 238–240
Shaughnessy, Matt 223
Shaw, Glenn 13, 14, 223
Shaw, Terrance 223
Shedd, Kenny 150, 153, 162, 223
Shell, Art 62, *69*, 73, 126, 127, 128, 143, 145, 190, 192, 223, 240–241, 248, 296–297
Sherman, Rod 22, 34, 35, 38, 41, 223
Shipp, Jackie 223
Shirkey, George 223
Siani, Mike 42, 43, 44, 46, 47, 48, 49, 55, 56, 58, 59, 65, 68, 223
Simpson, Jack 10, 223
Simpson, Willie 223
Sims, Barry 223
Sistrunk, Otis ("the Man from Mars") 42, 49, 64, 67, *68*, 223, 297
Skrepenak, Greg 223
Slaughter, Chad 223
Sligh, Richard 223
Slough, Greg 223
Smith, Anthony 134, 137, 139, 144, 223
Smith, Bubba 51, 223
Smith, Charles 30, 31, 32, 33, 34, 35, 36, 37, 38, 41, 42, 43, 44, 45, 46, 47, 49, 51, 52, 223
Smith, Hal 223
Smith, James 5, 6, 223
Smith, Jim 223
Smith, Jimmy 223
Smith, Kenny 223

mith, Kevin 223
mith, Ron 49, 51, 223
mith, Steve 122, 123, 124, 125, 128, 130, 131, 134, 136, 137, 140, 223
mith, Travian 224
mith, Willie 224
oda, Chet 303
ommer, Mike 224
pencer, Ollie 224
pivey, Mike 224
quirek, Jack 103, *104*, 108, 224, 297
abler, Ken ("the Snake") 40, 42, 43, 44, 45, 46, 47, 48, 49, 50, 51, 52, 53, 54, 55, 56, 57, 58, 59, 60, 61, 62, 63, 64, 65, *66*, 67, 68, *69*, 70, 71, 72, 73, 74, 75, 76, 77, 80, 134, 224, 236, 297–298
talls, Dave 224
tarks, Duane 224
teinfort, Fred 58, 224
temke, Kevin 224
tephens, Rich 224
tewart, Joe 224
tewart, Tony 202, 224
tinchcomb, Matt 224
tone, Jack 224
tone, John 224
tone, Ron 224
trachan, Steve 123, 224
tram, Hank 231
treigel, Bill 224
trong, Darrell 224
tubblefield, Dana 182, 224
umner, Charlie 103
Super Bowl: II vs. Green Bay 24–28; XI vs. Minnesota 61–66; XV vs. Philadelphia 82–86; XVIII vs. Washington 100–106; XXXVII vs. Tampa Bay 176–179
svihus, Bob 224
Sweeney, Steve 46, 224
Swilling, Pat 147, 224
Sword, Sam 224
Sylvester, Steve 224

Talley, Stan 224
Tampa Bay Buccaneers 59, 88, 141, 151, 161, 177, 184, 198
Tatum, Jack ("the Assassin") 42, 43, 49, 63, 64, *65*, 67, 69, 71, 80, 224, 298–299
Tautolo, John 224
Taves, Josh 224
Taylor, Billy 224

Taylor, Malcolm 224
Teal, Willie 224
Tennessee Titans 153, 161, 170, 173, 176, 180, 186, 188, 194
Teresa, Tony 5, 6, 7, 224
Terrell, David 224
Thomas, Robert 224
Thomas, Skip ("Dr. Death") 47, 50, 54, 55, 58, 63, 64, *65*, 71, 224
Thomas, William 163, 170, 224
Thoms, Art 49, 224
Tillmon, Tony 224
Todd, Larry 20, 23, 24, 25, 27, 29, 33, 224
Tongue, Reggie 224
Toomay, Pat 225
Toran, Stacey 111, 114, 115, 117, 120, 122, 225, 302
Townsend, Greg 96, 98, 113, 114, 115, 124, 127, 129, 140, 225
Trapp, James 225
Trask, Orville 225
Treu, Adam 225
Truax, Dalton 225
Truitt, Olanda 155, 225
Tuck Rule Game 171–172
Tuiasosopo, Marques 182, 189, 190, 225
Turk, Dan 225, 302
Turner, Eric 153, 154, 156, 157, 158, 160, 225, 302
Turner, Norv 184, 188, 189, 247–248
Tyson, Richard 225

Uniforms (Raiders) 307
Upshaw, Gene 62, *69*, 73, 225, 299
Upshaw, Regan 170, 225
Urenda, Herman 225

Valdez, Vernon 225
Valley, Wayne 231, 232, 233, 303
Van Divier, Randy 225
Van Eeghen, Mark 54, 55, 59, 60, 61, 62, 63, 64, 65, 67, 68, 69, 73, 74, 75, 76, 77, 78, 79, 80, 81, 82, 83, 84, 85, 86, 88, 89, 225, 299–300
Vann, Norwood 225
Van Pelt, Brad 225
Vaughan, Ruben 92, 225
Vella, John 225
Villapiano, Phil 42, 43, 44, 47, 52, 54, 60, 62, 63, 69, 73, 74, 225, 300
Voight, Bob 225

Waddell, Michael 225
Wade, John 225
Wakefield, Fred 225
Walker, Denard 225
Walker, Derrick 160, 161, 225
Walker, Fulton 114, 117, 225
Walker, Javon 197, 225
Walker, Langston 185, 225
Walker, Marquis 225
Wallace, Aaron 134, 145, 225
Walter, Andrew 190, 191, 192, 198, 225
Wand, Seth 225
Ward, B.J. 225
Ware, Tim 225
Warren, Gerard 194, 225
Warren, Jimmy 40, 41, 225
Warzeka, Ron 226
Washington, Fabian 191, 226
Washington, Lionel 122, 126, 140, 143, 154, 226
Washington, Ronnie 226
Washington, Ted 226
Washington Redskins 36, 54, 79, 96, 100, 115, 127, 138, 147, 158, 188, 201
Watkins, Todd 200, 226
Watts, Robert 226
Watts, Ted 89, 93, 102, 108, 226
Waymer, Dave 226, 302
Weathers, Carl 226, 300
Weaver, Gary 226
Wells, Warren 22, 23, 26, 27, 29, 30, 31, 32, 33, 34, 35, 36, 37, 39, 226, 300–301
Westbrooks, Greg 226
Wheatley, Tyrone 159, 160, 161, 162, 163, 164, 165, 166, 167, 169, 170, 171, 175, 179, 181, 182, 183, 184, 185, 226
Wheeler, Dwight 226
Wheeler, Ron 226
White, Alberto 226
White, Gene 10, 226
White, Mike 147, 148, 241–242
Whitley, Curtis 226
Whittaker, Scott 226
Whitted, Alvis 181, 184, 186, 226
Whittington, Arthur 73, 74, 76, 77, 79, 80, 81, 84, 85, 88, 89, 226
Wilkerson, Bruce 136, 226
Williams, Brock 226
Williams, David 226
Williams, Demise 226
Williams, Dokie 96, 97, 107, 108,

109, 111, 113, 114, 116, 117, 119, 120, 226
Williams, Harvey 143, 144, 145, 147, 148, 151, 153, 154, 156, 157, 226
Williams, Henry 226
Williams, Howie 19, 226
Williams, Jamie 226
Williams, Jermaine 226
Williams, K.D. 226
Williams, Marcus 226
Williams, Mike 226
Williams, Randal 226
Williams, Ricky 226
Williams, Rodney 226
Williams, Roland 170, 171, 226
Williams, Sam 226
Williams, Willie 226–227
Williamson, Fred ("the Hammer") 10, 227, 301
Williamson, J.R. 227
Willis, Chester 88, 227
Willis, Mitch 227
Wilson, Gibril 227
Wilson, Marc 87, 88, 89, 97, 107, 108, 109, 111, 112, 113, 114, 115, 116, 117, 119, 120, 227
Wilson, Marcus 227
Wilson, Mark 227
Wilson, Nemiah 31, 34, 35, 42, 48, 227
Wilson, Otis 227
Wilson, Wade 157, 158, 227
Winans, Jeff 227
Wise, Mike 227, 302
Wisniewski, Steve 227
Wolf, Ron 303–304
Wolff, Scott 227
Wong, Joe 227
Wood, Dick 17, 227
Wooden, Terry 227
Woods, Chris 227
Woodson, Charles 156, 157, 161, 166, 167, 170, 171, 173, 177, 181, 183, 227
Woodson, Rod 173, 174, 177, 227
Wright, Alexander 138, 139, 141, 144, 145, 227
Wright, Steve 227
Wyatt, Alvin 36, 227

Youso, Frank 227

Zecher, Rich 227
Zereoue, Amos 185, 227
Zogg, John 227